DIVERSIONS

A selective guide to more than 15 active and/or cerebral theme vacations, including the best places in Mexico to pursue them.

DIRECTIONS

Mexico's 11 major driving routes, covering the major north-south and east-west highways that lead from border crossings and major cities to the country's farthest jungles and beaches.

A Word from the Editor

The last couple of years have been especially confusing for travelers heading for Mexico. The recent roller-coaster ride that has characterized Mexico's political, personal, financial, and industrial relationships with other North American countries — and the rest of the world, for that matter — has been mirrored by severe swings in currency relationships, and there has never been a time when an up-to-date guide to Mexico was a more useful travel tool.

What's more, the broadening sophistication of contemporary travelers has made it essential that guidebooks evolve in very fundamental ways in order to keep pace with their readers. That's why we've tried to create a guide to Mexico that's specifically organized, written, and edited for this more demanding, modern traveler headed to this increasingly complex country. This is a traveler for whom qualitative information is infinitely more desirable than mere quantities of unappraised data. We think that this book, along with the other guides in our series, represents a new generation of travel guides — one that is especially responsive to modern needs and interests.

For years, dating back as far as Herr Baedeker, travel guides have tended to be encyclopedic, seemingly much more concerned with demonstrating expertise in geography and history than with any real analysis of the sorts of things that genuinely concern a typical tourist. But today, when it is hardly necessary to tell a traveler where Mexico is (in many cases, the traveler has been to that country nearly as often as the guidebook editors), it becomes the responsibility of those editors to provide new perceptions and to suggest new directions to make a guide genuinely valuable.

That's exactly what we've tried to do in this series. I think you'll notice a different, more contemporary tone to the text, as well as an organization and focus that are distinctive and more functional. And even a random reading of what follows will demonstrate a substantial departure from the standard guidebook orientation, for we've not only attempted to provide information of a different sort, but we also have tried to present it in a format that makes it particularly accessible.

Needless to say, it's difficult to decide what to include in a guidebook of this size — and what to omit. Early on, we realized that giving up the encyclopedic approach precluded the inclusion of every single route and restaurant, a realization that helped define our overall editorial focus. Similarly, when we discussed the possibility of presenting certain information in other than strict geographical order, we found that the new format enabled us to arrange data in a way that we feel best answers the questions travelers typically ask.

Large numbers of specific questions have provided the real editorial skeleton for this book. The volume of mail I regularly receive seems to emphasize that modern travelers want very precise information, so we've tried to organize our material in the most responsive way possible. Readers who want to know the best restaurant in Mexico City or the most facinating archaeological area in which to view Maya artifacts will have no trouble whatever extracting that data from this guide.

Travel guides are, above all, reflections of personal taste, and putting one's name on a title page obviously puts one's preferences on the line. But I think I ought to amplify just exactly what "personal" means. I don't believe in the sort of personal guidebook that's a palpable misrepresentation on its face. It is, for example, hardly possible for any single writer to visit thousands of restaurants (and nearly as many hotels) in any given year and provide accurate appraisals of each one. And even if it *were* possible for one human being to survive such an itinerary, it would of necessity have to be done at a dead sprint and the perceptions derived therefrom would probably be less valid than those of any other intelligent individual visiting the same establishments. It is, therefore, impossible (especially in an annually revised and updated guidebook *series* such as we offer) to have only one person provide all the data on the entire world.

I also happen to think that such individual orientation is of substantially less value to readers. Visiting a single hotel for just one night or eating one hasty meal in a random restaurant hardly equips anyone to provide appraisals that are of more than passing interest. No amount of doggedly alliterative or oppressively onomatopoeic text can camouflage a technique that is essentially specious. We have, therefore, chosen what I like to describe as the "thee and me" approach to restaurant and hotel evaluation and, to a somewhat more limited degree, to the sites and sights we have included in the other sections of our text. What this really reflects is personal sampling tempered by intelligent counsel from informed local sources, and these additional friends-of-the-editors are almost always residents of the city and/or area about which they have been consulted.

Despite the presence of several editors, writers, researchers, and local correspondents, very precise editing and tailoring keep our text fiercely subjective. So what follows is the gospel according to the Birnbaums and represents as much of our own taste and instinct as we can manage. It is probable, therefore, that if you prefer chili peppers that leave the roof of your mouth largely intact, can't stand canned fruit juices, and won't tolerate fresh fish that is relentlessly overcooked, then we're likely to have a long and meaningful relationship. Readers with dissimilar tastes may be less enraptured.

I should also point out something about the person to whom this guidebook is directed. Above all, he or she is a "visitor." This means that such elements as restaurants have been specifically picked to provide the visitor with a representative, enlightening, stimulating and, above all, pleasant experience. Since so many extraneous considerations can affect the reception and service accorded a regular restaurant patron, our choices can in no way be construed as an exhaustive guide to resident dining. We think we've listed all the best places in various price ranges, but they were chosen with a visitor's enjoyment in mind.

Other evidence of how we've tried to tailor our text to reflect modern travel habits is most apparent in the section we call DIVERSIONS. Where once it was common for travelers to spend a Mexican visit simply lying beside some pool or beachfront, the emphasis today is more likely to be directed toward pursuing some favorite activity while visiting foreign turf. So we've selected every activity we could reasonably evaluate and organized the material in a way that is especially accessible to activists of either athletic or cerebral bent. It is no longer necessary, therefore, to wade through a pound or two of superfluous prose just to find the most challenging golf course or Aztec pyramid within a reasonable distance of your hotel.

If there is one single thing that best characterizes the revolution in and evolution of current holiday habits, it is that most travelers now consider travel a right rather than a privilege. Travel today translates as the enthusiastic desire to sample all of the world's opportunities, to find that elusive quality of experience that is not only enriching, but comfortable. For that reason, we've tried to make what follows not only helpful and enlightening, but the sort of welcome companion of which every traveler dreams.

Finally, I should point out that every good travel guide is a living enterprise; that is, no part of this text is carved in stone. In our annual revisions, we refine, expand, and further hone all our material to serve your travel needs even better. To this end, no contribution is of greater value to us than your personal reaction to what we have written, as well as information reflecting your own experiences while using the book. We earnestly and enthusiastically solicit your comments about this book *and* your opinions and perceptions about places you have recently visited. In this way, we will be able to provide the most current information — including the actual experiences of real travelers — and to make those experiences more readily available to others. So please write to us at 60 E. 42nd St., New York, NY 10165.

We sincerely hope to hear from you.

STEVE BIRNBAUM

How to Use This Guide

A great deal of care has gone into the organization of this guide-book, and we believe it represents a real breakthrough in the presentation of travel material. Our aim has been to create a new, more modern generation of travel books, and to make this guide the most useful and practical travel tool available today.

Our text is divided into five basic sections in order to present information in the best way on every possible aspect of a Mexican vacation. This organization itself should alert you to the vast and varied opportunities available in this fascinating country, as well as indicating all the specific data necessary to plan a successful trip in Mexico. You won't find much of the conventional "swaying palms and shimmering sands" text here; we've chosen instead to deliver more useful and practical information. Prospective Mexican itineraries tend to speak for themselves, and with so many diverse travel opportunities, we feel our main job is to explain them and to provide the basic information — how, when, where, how much, and what's best — to assist you to make the most intelligent choices possible.

Here is a brief summary of our five basic sections — and what you can expect to find in each one. We believe that you will find both your travel planning and en route enjoyment enhanced by having this book at your side.

GETTING READY TO GO

This mini-encyclopedia of practical travel facts is meant to be a sort of know-it-all companion, with all the precise information necessary to create a journey to and through Mexico. There are more than 3 dozen separate entries, including how to travel, what preparations to make before you leave, how to deal with possible emergencies while traveling, what to expect in the different regions of Mexico, what your trip is likely to cost, and how to avoid prospective problems. The individual entries are specific, realistic, and, where appropriate, cost-oriented.

We expect you to use this section most in the course of planning your trip, for its ideas and suggestions are intended to simplify this often confusing period. Entries are intentionally concise, in an effort to get to the meat of the matter with the least extraneous prose. These entries are augmented by extensive lists of specific sources from which to obtain even more specialized information, plus some suggestions for obtaining travel information on your own.

PERSPECTIVES

Any visit to an unfamiliar destination is enhanced and enriched by an understanding of the cultural and historical heritage of that area. We have, therefore, provided just such an introduction to Mexico, its history, people, food and drink, music, religion, folk life, and other subjects.

THE CITIES

Individual reports on the Mexican cities most visited by tourists and business-people have been prepared with the aid of researchers, contributors, professional journalists, and other experts on the spot. Useful at the planning stage, THE CITIES is really designed to be used during your trip. Each report offers a short-stay guide to its city within a consistent format: An essay introduces the city as a historic entity and a functioning, contemporary place in which to live and work; *At-a-Glance,* a site-by-site survey of the most important (and sometimes most eclectic) sights to see and things to do; *Sources and Resources,* a concise listing of pertinent tourist information meant to answer myriad, potentially pressing questions as they arise, such as where to find the local tourist office, how to get around, which sightseeing tours to take, when Mexico's special events and holidays occur, where to find the brightest nightspots, which are the shops that have the finest merchandise and/or the most irresistible bargains, and where the best golf, tennis, fishing, and swimming are to be found; and *Best in Town,* our cost-and-quality choices of the best places to eat and sleep on a variety of budgets.

DIVERSIONS

This very selective guide is designed to help travelers find the very best places in which to pursue a wide range of physical and cerebral activities, without having to wade through endless pages of unrelated text. With a list of more than 15 specific activities and theme vacations, DIVERSIONS provides a guide to the special places where the quality of experience is likely to be highest. Whether you opt for golf or tennis, scuba or surfing, bullfights or ancient ruins, each category is the equivalent of a comprehensive checklist of the absolute best in Mexico.

DIRECTIONS

Here are 11 Mexican driving itineraries, from Baja's hidden beaches to the jungle ruins of the Maya. DIRECTIONS is the only section of this book that is organized geographically, to cover the major north-south and east-west routes that lead from border crossings and major cities to the farthest reaches of the country.

Each entry includes a guide to sightseeing highlights; a cost-and-quality guide to accommodations along the road (small inns, clean and comfortable motels, country hotels, campgrounds, and detours to off-the-main-road discoveries); hints and suggestions for activities; and a simple one-page line drawing of the route, noting points of interest described in the text.

Although each of the book's sections has a distinct format and a special function, they have been designed to be used together to provide a complete package of travel information. To use this book to full advantage, take a few minutes to read the table of contents and random entries in each section to get a firsthand feel of how it all fits together.

Pick and choose needed information from different sections. Assume, for example, that you have always wanted to survey the most exciting historic Indian ruins in Mexico, but never really knew how to put such a trip together. Start by reading the short, informative section on traveling by car in GETTING READY TO GO. This will provide all the factual information needed to organize and prepare a road trip. It will alert you to insurance needs (and direct you to the insurance chapter in the same section of the book) and other equally detailed potential problems and pleasures of a driving vacation. But where to go and what to see? Turn to DIVERSIONS, *Mexico's Magnificent Archaeological Heritage,* for descriptions of the most compelling archaeological sites and sights in the country. These concise, enticing entries describe what is where and how to get there, allowing you to make intelligent choices among Mexico's scattered Indian ruins. Assume that you have narrowed your choice to the major ruins on the Yucatán Peninsula — Chichén Itzá, Uxmal, and Tulum. Turn to DIRECTIONS for an explicit guide to the Yucatán to enhance your trip (why not a couple of days scuba diving at Cozumel before heading from Tulum to Chichén Itzá?); and peek into THE CITIES for detailed guides to the major towns and resorts of the area, Mérida and Cancún.

In other words, the sections of this book are building blocks to help you put together the best possible trip. Use them selectively as a tool, a source of ideas, a reference work for accurate facts, and a guide to the best buys, the most exciting sights, the most pleasant accommodations, and the tastiest food — *the best travel experience* that you can have.

UNITED STATES

Mexicali

Sonora
Desert

B
A
J
A

C
A
L
I
F
O
R
N
I
A

P
L
A
I
N
S

O
F

S
O
N
O
R
A

S
I
E
R
R
A

M
A
D
R
E

O
C
C
I
D
E
N
T
A
L

A
L
T
I
P
L
A
N
O

GULF OF CALIFORNIA
(Sea of Cortés)

Hermosillo

Ciudad
Juárez

Río Grande
(Río Bravo del Norte)

Chihuahua

SIER

Torreón

Salt

Culiacán

Durango

MEXICO

Mazatlán

Zacatecas

La
Paz

PACIFIC   OCEAN

Tepic

Guanajua

Guadalajara   L. Chapala

CENTRA

Puerto
Vallarta

VOLCANI

Mo

Manzanillo

SIERR

Zihuatane

MEXICO

0	km	500
0	miles	300

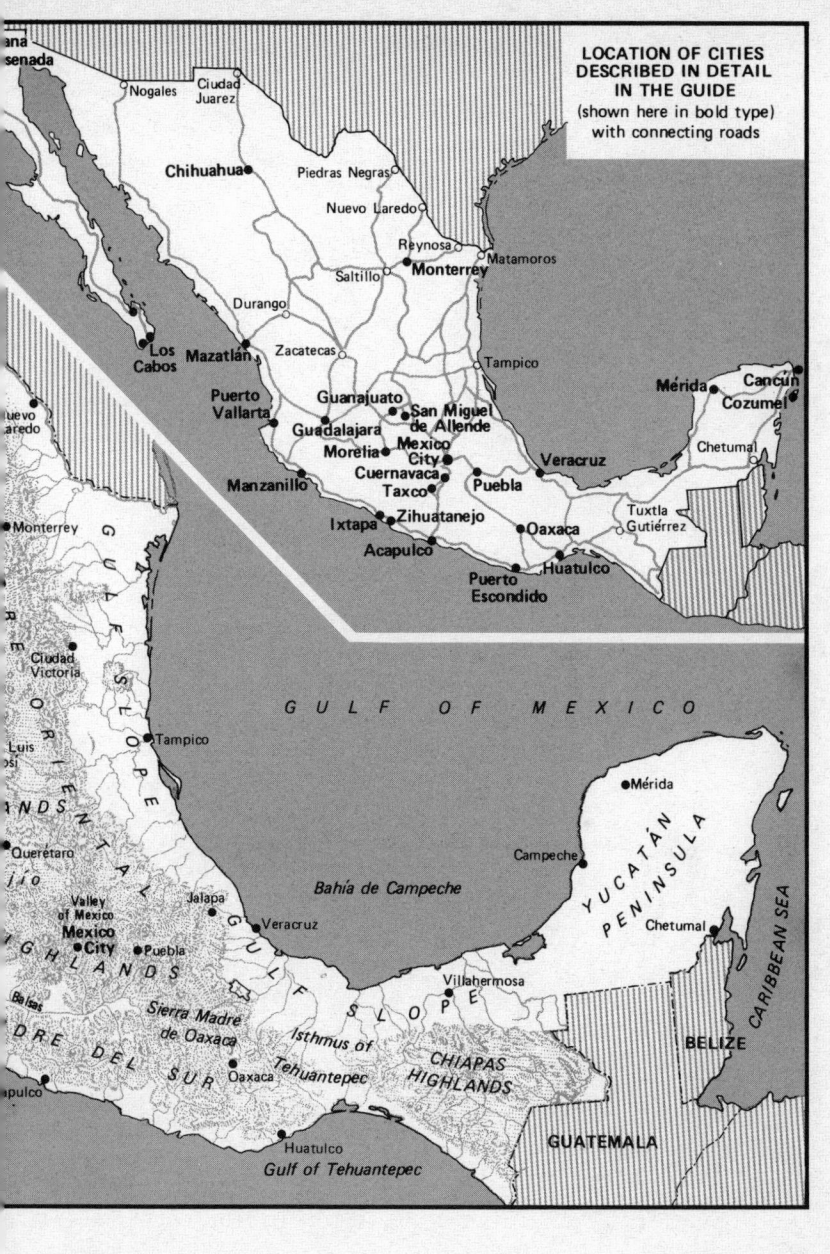

LOCATION OF CITIES
DESCRIBED IN DETAIL
IN THE GUIDE
(shown here in bold type)
with connecting roads

GETTING READY TO GO

When and How to Go

What's Where:
Mexico North to South

 About one-fourth the size of the continental United States, Mexico covers 760,373 square miles, most of which are pretty rugged. The main body of land forms a long, irregularly shaped funnel with a hook (the Yucatán Peninsula) at the end.

TERRAIN: Mexico has 8,300 miles of borders. The United States borders the country on the north, the Pacific Ocean and Gulf of California on the west and south, Guatemala and Belize on the southeast, and the Gulf of Mexico and the Caribbean Sea on the east. Mexico has 4,438 miles of Pacific coastline and 1,774 miles of Gulf of Mexico and Caribbean coastline.

Northeast – Starting from the north, an aerial survey of Mexico's terrain reveals the central plateau, a large stretch of dry highlands in between the **Sierra Madre Oriental** (Sierra Madre East) and **Sierra Madre Occidental** (Sierra Madre West) chain. The plateau encompasses 60% of Mexico's landmass, though a mere 20% of the population lives here. Only 11% of the land is naturally suited for agriculture.

Northwest – The arid northwest sweeps from the foothills of the mineral-rich Sierra Madre Occidental to the sea, extending along the coasts of the **Pacific Ocean** and the **Gulf of California**, called the **Sea of Cortés** by most Mexicans. Relatively uninhabited, the northwest was long considered too dry for agriculture, but in recent years dams have been built, especially in the area around the city of Hermosillo, Sonora.

Central Highlands – The central volcanic highlands seal off the southern end of the central plateau. An intriguing combination of forested mountains and fertile valleys, these highlands are really the heart of Mexico. They were first farmed 3,500 years ago. During the 9th century, the Toltec Indians inhabited this area. Around the 12th century, the Aztec moved in. Both groups spoke dialects of the Nahuatl language, which is related to the language their descendants in the area still speak today. The central highlands have rich soil and contain many mountains veined with silver, gold, and other valuable minerals. In fact, this wealth of natural resources is what attracted the Spaniards to Mexico in the 16th century. In the centuries following the conquest, the mountains were skillfully mined, and colonial towns prospered. The section of the volcanic highlands called the **Bajío** is known as the **Historic Lowlands** because it is lower in altitude than Mexico City and because many strategic revolutionary events took place here during the first quarter of the 19th century. The volcanic highlands are filled with lakes and thermal springs. **Lake Chapala**, the largest in Mexico, is now a summer resort area. Here, too, **Juanacatlán Falls**, the second-largest waterfall in North America, plunges 70 feet in a 500-foot-wide horseshoe-shaped torrent. In the area of the volcanic highlands known as the **Valley of Mexico** (elevation, 7,350 feet) stands the capital, **Mexico City**. Approximately 18 million people live in the metropolitan area, but, in total, the central volcanic highlands contain almost 50% of Mexico's 86.7 million people. The famous twin snow-capped volcanoes, **Popocatépetl** (Smoking Mountain), at 17,887 feet, and **Ixtaccíhuatl** (Sleeping Lady), at 17,343 feet, rise 30 miles from the center of Mexico City, and can be seen from the capital on a clear day (a very rare event lately because of severe air pollution problems).

South – Southern Mexico stretches from the **Sierra Madre de Oaxaca** (the eastern range of the Sierra Madre) to the **Sierra Madre del Sur** (the Pacific coastal mountains). This region encompasses the states of **Guerrero** (where Acapulco is located) and **Oaxaca**. The city of Oaxaca, at an elevation of 5,068 feet, has a population of 169,000; it is the center for regional crafts (particularly ceramics and textiles), as well as the site of the ruins of Monte Albán and Mitla. The state of Oaxaca is inhabited by the Zapotec and Mixtec Indians and is famous for its red soil, which yields a variety of agricultural produce, as well as clay for pottery.

The **Isthmus of Tehuantepec** forms the southern geographic boundary of North America. This was one of the first sites in Mexico (along with the states of Veracruz and Tamaulipas) to yield petroleum in 1901. The town of Salina Cruz on the Pacific coast, a terminal of the trans-isthmus highway and railroad, has many oil storage tanks containing petroleum shipped from as far as the Gulf coast, 130 miles to the northeast. The isthmus cuts through the mountains south of Oaxaca near the narrowest point of the neck of the mainland "funnel."

The corner of Mexico known as the **Chiapas Highlands** is on the southeastern side of the isthmus. Still the most isolated pocket of the country, Chiapas consists of *montaña* (mountain) jungle, extending south to the Guatemala frontier. Since oil was discovered in the Chiapas interior, the days of its relative isolation are numbered. (Oil has also been found in nearby Tabasco and offshore Campeche.) Not as flat as *plano* (level) jungle, *montaña* jungle terrain consists of hills that seem to ripple in thousands of shades of green. Lagoons, lakes, and rivers appear in the middle of forests. Brightly colored birds and butterflies fly overhead. The temperature tends to be moderately warm. There is just one drawback: rain. It rains almost constantly in the *montaña* jungle, and because of its remoteness there is nothing to do when it rains, except wait for the rain to stop. (People in this part of the world learn to be patient.) However, the climate is ideal for raising bananas, mangoes, coffee, and cacaos (used for making cocoa and cocoa butter).

A 50-mile stretch of road from Tuxtla Gutiérrez, the capital of Chiapas, to the 16th-century colonial mission town San Cristóbal de las Casas climbs through a 7,000-foot-high mountain pass. Another road goes through Chiapas to Guatemala. Although Chiapas is one of the most stunning parts of the country, very few foreigners visit it because it is remote and undeveloped.

Yucatán – The southeastern hook of the Mexican mainland embraces the Yucatán Peninsula, which actually consists of three states: **Campeche**, **Yucatán**, and **Quintana Roo**. The Yucatán is *plano* jungle, steamy and very hot throughout most of the year. Yucatán is the province of the contemporary Maya, whose forebears left incredibly intricate fortresses, temples, and cities dotting the jungles of the peninsula. The most famous, **Chichén Itzá**, contains sacrificial wells and altars which the Toltec built after they invaded the Maya city.

In the Caribbean, off the northeastern tip of the Yucatán Peninsula, there are three resort islands. The best known of these is **Cancún**, which was developed into a resort after a series of computerized feasibility studies were conducted by the Mexican government. Less posh, but very popular with scuba divers and snorkelers, is **Cozumel**, a few miles south of Cancún. Nearby, at **Isla Mujeres**, it's great fun to swim among huge schools of rainbow-colored fish and ride giant sea turtles. The capital of Yucatán state, Mérida, is 33 miles inland from the port of Progreso.

Gulf Slope – The Gulf Slope takes in the stretch of coast that curves from the **Isthmus of Tehuantepec** to the **Gulf of Mexico**, including the shoreline of the **Bay of Campeche**. The climate generally is humid and hot. This is one of Mexico's most important oil-producing regions. At one time, Mexico's petroleum exports exceeded all others. However, in recent year's the country's oil exports have decreased substantially and currently account for about 40% of total exports. Much of Mexico's oil leaves from Tampico and Coatzacoalcos, north and south of the port of Veracruz.

When Hernán Cortés landed in Veracruz in 1519, the town was one of the most developed sections of the country. Today, Veracruz is the site of Mexico's first nuclear power plant, which began partial operation in 1986 at Laguna Verde. The development this region has undergone makes it hard to imagine what it was like 3,000 years ago during the civilization of the Olmec, which was based on the Gulf Slope.

Baja – Until relatively recently, **Baja California** was known to many US citizens only because of **Tijuana**, the once-notorious border town. Baja California's ribbons of beach provide shelter for hundreds of species of rare wildlife. Botanists and naturalists from all over the world come to study the more than 740 species of flora that grow here and to observe the interrelationships between the communities of wild birds and mammals that have continued to live without much disturbance by humans, until now. Oil has been discovered off the Baja coast, however, making it more likely that all living patterns on the peninsular strip will change dramatically and irrevocably.

Baja California is a popular winter vacation area. Just 70 miles south of Tijuana is **Ensenada**, a fishing town on Todos Santos Bay known for its splendid water sports facilities and deep-sea fishing. Nearly 700 miles farther south, near the tip of Baja California, a number of new mountainside and oceanfront resorts are under ongoing development. Ferryboats carrying passengers, automobiles, and truck-trailer rigs are operated on three routes, in order of importance: Mazatlán–La Paz; Topolobampo–La Paz; and Guaymas–Santa Rosalía.

The northern and central sections of the mainland's Pacific coast are known for their pretty fishing villages and resorts, the most famous of which are **Mazatlán**, **Puerto Vallarta**, and more recently, **Manzanillo**. According to experts, Baja California and the mainland coast offer some of the best surfing beaches in the world. The Baja peninsula still is comparatively unspoiled by commercial development, despite the opening of a transpeninsular highway in 1973.

When to Go

Most people associate Mexico with winter suntans and beautiful seaside resorts. They aren't wrong. Mexico's Pacific and Caribbean coasts are just about the all-time favorite escapes for North Americans trapped in snow and icy slush. (The winter season begins on December 15, when Mexicans traditionally take their annual 2-week, year-end vacation. It ends around the middle of April, after *Easter.*) But that is only half the story. Mexico is a country blessed with at least two distinct and appealing tourism seasons: winter in its coastal resorts and summer inland. And note the qualifying "at least"; for, in fact, there is always some part of Mexico where the climate is agreeable at any given time in the year.

Mexico is much warmer than the US in winter, with a rainy season from May to October that drops a couple of hours of rain on city and country in afternoons, cooling and clearing the evening air. In summer, when the seaside and lower-altitude spots sometimes get steamy, the highlands are balmy. Towns like Guanajuato and

San Miguel de Allende have as near to perfect climates as it is reasonable to expect on earth.

So there really isn't a "best" time to visit Mexico. It is important to emphasize that more and more vacationers to Mexico who have a choice are enjoying the substantial advantages of off-season travel; that is summer (at most of the coastal resorts), winter (inland), and — to some degree — spring and fall (throughout the country). Getting there and staying there is less expensive during the off-season as airfares, hotel rooms, and car rental rates go down, and less expensive package tours become available; the independent traveler can go farther on less, too.

Seasonal rate variations generally are negligible in the interior cities, but in Baja California; Cozumel, Isla Mujeres, and Cancún on the Caribbean; and Guaymas, Manzanillo, Puerto Vallarta, Mazatlán, Zihuatanejo-Ixtapa, Huatulco, and Acapulco on the Pacific coast, it's easy to save 30% or more off high-season accommodation costs during the late spring, summer, and early fall. In addition, many resorts offer special off-season promotional packages. The very same activities and amenities — from water sports equipment to greens fees for a round of golf — that can add a not so small fortune in extra charges to your bill during the height of the season often are included in the daily room rates during the rest of the year.

Hotel rates and recreation costs are not the only prices to decrease during the off-season. Airfares also generally are less expensive at these times. What's more, the passing of the high season usually spawns a host of package offerings that can include accommodations, car rentals, and other money-saving extras (see *Package Tours*, in this section).

But financial considerations are only part of the allure of off-season travel. Major tourist attractions, beaches, and other facilities tend to be less crowded during the off-season, and — throughout Mexico — life proceeds at a more leisurely pace. The destinations themselves actually take on a different, friendlier cast with the passing of the high-season hordes.

An additional bonus from visiting resort areas during the off-season is that even the most basic services are performed more efficiently. In theory, off-season service is identical to that offered during high season, but the fact is that the absence of demanding crowds inevitably begets much more thoughtful and personal attention. The very same staff that barely can manage to get fresh towels onto the racks at beach resorts during January and February has the time to chat pleasantly during June and July.

It is not only hotel service that benefits from the absence of the high-season mobs. Fine restaurants, absolutely unbreachable when the professional high rollers are passing out tips large enough to pay off the maître d's mortgage, pay rapt attention to mere mortals during the off-season. And the food preparation and service also are likely to be best when the chef is required to create only a reasonable number of meals.

It also should be noted that the months immediately before and after the peak months — what the travel industry refers to as shoulder seasons — often are sought out because they offer fair weather and somewhat smaller crowds. But be aware that very near high-season prices can prevail, most often in the most popular resort areas — such as Acapulco and Cozumel.

CLIMATE: The most common concerns about travel have to do with weather and most of Mexico boasts a warm, temperate climate year round. Although the temperature can drop below 50F, pleasant temperatures in the 70s and 80s (to rather stifling heat in the upper 90s in some parts of the country) are more common. The western highlands and some other mountainous sections tend to have a cooler, temperate climate. More than half of the country has an altitude exceeding 3,000 feet; any region below 3,000 feet is known as *tierra caliente* (hot land) because of the tropical temperatures. (*Please note that although temperatures usually are recorded on the Celsius scale in Mexico, for purposes of clarity we use the more familiar Fahrenheit scale throughout this guide.*)

Within Mexico, climate is more commonly described in terms of the rate of precipitation than in variations in temperature. Most of the country is exceptionally dry, especially Baja California, the 700-mile-long, icicle-shaped peninsula west of the mainland. The north and northwestern reaches of the country also are hot and arid, constantly in need of irrigation for agricultural production. The mountains and the central volcanic highlands experience more frequent rain throughout the year. (During the summer rainy season, there are heavy showers every afternoon for at least a few hours in this area.) The lowlands along the Gulf Coast and sections of the southeast get a lot of rain all year, with consistently formidable humidity. Some parts of the state of Chiapas have as much as 200 inches of rain annually.

Below is a general description of the climate in various Mexican regions and a climate chart to help plan your own visit. For a brief, city-by-city review of weather, see the *Climate and Clothes* entry in the individual city reports in THE CITIES.

North and Northwest: Chihuahua, Coahuila, Durango, Sonora – Generally sunny and dry, daytime highs in this area tend to average in the 70s throughout most of the year. Temperatures reach into the mid-80s from July through September, when this arid region gets its few annual drops of rain.

Baja California: Baja California Norte, Baja California Sur – Temperatures here are in the 80s throughout most of the year. Between November and February it does sometimes drop into the 60s or high 50s during the day. On rare days between April and October the mercury climbs into the 100s. There is very little rain.

Pacific Coast: Colima, Guerrero, Jalisco, Michoacán, Nayarit, Sinaloa – One of the most popular winter vacation areas in North America. Year-round temperatures are in the 70s and 80s in Acapulco, slightly cooler in Mazatlán. The winds blowing in from the ocean keep the coast cool and comfortable, especially during winter and early spring. Sailors be warned: The coastal waters have frequent gales and are subject to hurricanes in summer and fall.

Central Plateau and Central Volcanic Highlands: Aguascalientes, Guanajuato, Hidalgo, Mexico, Morelos, Nuevo León, Puebla, Querétaro, San Luis Potosí, Tlaxcala, Zacatecas – Inland, Mexico's climate is temperate and dry most of the year. In Monterrey, in the northern central plateau, the average daytime temperature is in the low 80s, although from May through August, it often is in the 90s. From November through February, the daytime temperatures are in the 60s and 70s. Mexico City, the capital, at an elevation of 7,350 feet, has temperatures in the 70s most of the year. The mercury sometimes hits the 80s and 90s between May and September. Very rarely, it gets as hot as the low 100s, but the afternoon rains usually cool things pretty quickly.

Southern Mexico: Chiapas, Oaxaca – The area around Oaxaca is semitropical highlands, with daytime temperatures in the 70s and 80s, dropping into the 60s at night. It rains for a few hours in the morning between May and September. The state of Chiapas, near the Guatemalan border, is moist all year with temperatures slightly hotter than in Oaxaca. Chiapas's topography is *montaña* (mountain) jungle.

Yucatán Peninsula: Campeche, Quintana Roo, Yucatán – Hot and humid all year, the Yucatán is *plano* (level) jungle. Temperatures usually are in the 90s between May and November and in the mid-80s from October through March. It is not much cooler after dark than during the day. It rains heavily between May and September.

Gulf Slope and Gulf Coast: Tabasco, Tamaulipas, Veracruz – The weather is sticky and hot along this stretch of coast, too, with temperatures in the muggy 80s for most of the year. The cooler season falls between December and March, when it is in the 70s.

A MEXICAN CLIMATE CHART (Temperature in °F)

City	Jan.–March	April–June	July–Sept.	Oct.–Dec.
Acapulco	78	82	83	81
Aguascalientes	60	70	68	59
Chihuahua	50	70	74	57
Córdoba	64	72	70	66
Cuernavaca	68	72	68	67
Culiacán	69	79	82	70
Durango	57	69	68	59
Guadalajara	62	71	68	62
Guanajuato	61	69	67	61
Guaymas	67	78	87	73
Hermosillo	64	81	89	70
Manzanillo	74	79	82	79
Mazatlán	67	75	81	74
Mérida	76	81	81	76
Mexico City	57	64	81	57
Monterrey	63	78	80	65
Morelia	60	67	64	60
Oaxaca	66	71	69	65
Puebla	59	65	62	58
Querétaro	61	69	67	61
Saltillo	56	69	71	59
San Luis Potosí	59	69	67	60
Tampico	68	80	82	70
Taxco	70	74	70	68
Veracruz	72	79	81	75
Zacatecas	51	60	57	53

Travelers can get current readings and 3-day Accu-Weather forecasts through *American Express Travel Related Services'* Worldwide Weather Report number. By dialing 900-WEATHER and punching in either the area code for any city in the US or an access code for numerous travel destinations worldwide, an up-to-date recording will provide current temperature, sky conditions, wind speed and direction, heat index, relative humidity, local time, highway reports, and beach and boating reports (year-round for Mexico). For cities in Mexico, punch in the first three letters of the city. For instance, by entering ACA, you will hear the weather report for Acapulco. (Service also includes Cancún, Ensenada, Guadalajara, Ixtapa, Mexico City, Puerta Vallarta, and Tijuana.) This 24-hour service can be accessed from any Touch-Tone phone in the US and costs 75¢ per minute. The charge will show up on your phone bill. For a free list of the areas covered, send a self-addressed, stamped envelope to *1-900-WEATHER*, 261 Central Ave., Farmingdale, NY 11735.

 SPECIAL EVENTS: Travelers may want to schedule a trip to Mexico to coincide with some special event and Mexico's benevolent climate and the Mexican's exuberant love of celebration ensures a full calendar of festivities that will enhance any vacation. Octavio Paz, the Nobel Prize–winning Mexican author, once described Mexican festivals (called "fiestas") as a "time when friends who have not exchanged more than the most formal courtesies throughout the year get drunk together, trade confidences, weep together, laugh together, discover they are brothers, and sometimes, to prove it, kill each other."

Many of the original "pagan" holidays still are celebrated, despite centuries of effort by the early Spanish rulers to eradicate them and establish Christian holidays. As a result, a fiesta is held somewhere in Mexico almost every day of the year. Fiestas can last as long as a week and usually take place near the church in the town's main square, or zocalo. Folk dances, unusual costumes, and music far into the night are only part of the celebration. During the day, people flock to the open-air markets, where candy, fruit, toys, and local handicrafts are sold.

Following are some fiestas, religious holidays, and and other special events celebrate throughout the country:

January 6: On the *Day of the Three Kings* (or Wise Men), Mexican children receive *Christmas* presents. In Malinalco (in the state of Mexico), there are native dances.

January 17: On *St. Anthony's Day,* children all over Mexico take their animals to church to be blessed.

February 2: *Día de la Candelaria* (Candelmas) is celebrated all over Mexico with processions, bullfights, dancing, and blessing of seeds and candles. In Tlacotalpan, Veracruz, the fiesta is particularly lively, with dances, horse racing, and watersports competition. In Santa Maria del Tule (just outside the city of Oaxaca), the day is celebrated with colorful dances and fireworks.

March–April (variable): During *Holy Week,* Passion plays are performed all over Mexico, and are especially interesting in Taxco (in the state of Guerrero), Malinalco (in the state of Mexico), and in Ixtapalapa (a borough of Mexico City).

May 3: The feast of the *Holy Cross* is celebrated throughout the country (especially by construction workers), with fireworks and picnics at the building site. There are native dances in Valle de Bravo (in the state of Mexico).

May 15: The *Day of San Isidro,* patron saint of rain and livestock, is celebrated all over Mexico. Animals are adorned with flowers and then blessed.

August 15: *Assumption Day* is celebrated throughout the country. In the Tlaxcala region, carpets of flowers are placed on church floors and the streets of town.

September 15: The ceremony of *El Grito* takes place simultaneously throughout Mexico at 11 PM, Mexico City time. In an internationally televised live broadcast, the President of Mexico appears on the central balcony of the National Palace in Mexico City and repeats the 1810 rallying cry of Father Hidalgo. A replica of the bell at the Dolores church is then rung, followed by the ringing of the Metropolitan Cathedral bells. The zocalo below is filled with celebrating Mexicans, in the same manner as Times Square in New York City on *New Year's Eve.* If you attend, beware of being doused by flour or eggshells filled with confetti, at the least, and be prepared for a jostling. (The best way to see the ceremony is to take a table in the open-air *Terraza Colonial* restaurant atop the *Majestic* hotel or get a room facing the zocalo at the *Gran Hotel de la Ciudad de México.*)

In every municipality in Mexico the same ceremony takes place, with the mayor coming out on the central balcony of City Hall, reciting the Grito, and ringing a replica of the bell of Dolores. In Mexico City and the provinces, magnificent fireworks follow. (Note that *El Grito* also is celebrated in US cities with large communities of Mexican-Americans.)

December 28: *All Fools' Day* is the Mexican equivalent of *April Fools' Day.*

Other national holidays, when banks and other business are closed, are listed in *Time Zones, Business Hours, and Bank Holidays,* in this section. Detailed information on regional festivities can be found in the individual city chapters in THE CITIES, as well as in *Best Festivals,* in DIVERSIONS.

When you are in the mood for a lively mixture of pageantry, history, religion, and pure ethnic spirit, check with the tourist bureau or look at a religious calendar for the dates of feast days that might intersect your path. For specific dates (and to guard against inevitable scheduling changes), it's best to check with the Mexican Ministry of Tourism, which regularly issues a comprehensive list. (For a list of the offices, see *Mexican Consulates and Tourist Offices in the US,* in this section.) More specific information also can be found in the chapters on the individual cities. It's always wise to call and reconfirm dates for the most current information.

Traveling by Plane

Flying is the quickest, most efficient way to get to Mexico and to travel from one part of the country to another once you are there. Touring by car, bus, or train certainly is the most scenic way to travel, but is practical only if you will be covering just one area. Cruise ships may dock at one port for several days, but generally they function more as hotels for passengers cruising Mexico's coastal waters, rather than as especially efficient transportation between single destinations. Air travel is far faster and more direct — the less time spent in transit, the more time spent at your destination. And that is even truer as an increasing number of nonstop and direct flights to Mexican destinations become available from US gateways.

Among the airlines offering flights to and between destinations in Mexico, almost all sell seats at a variety of prices under a vast spectrum of requirements and restrictions. Unless you live close to the border, you probably will spend more for your airfare than for any other single item in your travel budget, so try to take advantage of the lowest fares offered by either scheduled airlines or charter companies. You should know what kinds of flights are available, the rules under which air travel operates, and all the special package options.

SCHEDULED FLIGHTS: Leading airlines offering regularly scheduled flights to Mexico from the US, many on a daily basis, include: *Aeroméxico, Aerocancun, Air France, American, Continental, Delta, Lufthansa, Mexicana, Northwest, Pan American,* and *United.* In addition, new discount carriers frequently enter the market for a brief period, then disappear.

Regional airlines serve specialized domestic routes. For information, consult *Aerocaribe, Aeroméxico, Aeromar, Aero California, Aviacsa, Litoral,* or *Mexicana.*

GATEWAYS: As of this writing, direct flights — with no change of plane between the originating and terminating cities — to Mexico City (and an increasing number of other Mexican destinations) depart from the following US gateways (easy connections are available from most others):

Atlanta	Los Angeles	San Diego
Baltimore	Miami	San Francisco
Chicago	New York (and Newark)	Seattle/Tacoma
Dallas/Fort Worth	Orlando	Tampa/St. Petersburg
Denver	Philadelphia/	Tucson
Detroit	Wilmington	Washington, DC
Houston	San Antonio	

Tickets – When traveling on one of the many regularly scheduled flights, a full-fare ticket provides maximum travel flexibility (although at considerable expense) because there are no advance booking requirements. A prospective passenger can buy a ticket for a flight right up to the minute of takeoff — if a seat is available. If your ticket is for a round trip, you can make the return reservation any time you wish — months before you leave or the day before you return. Assuming foreign immigration requirements are met, you can stay at your destination as long as you like. (Tickets generally are good for a year, and can be renewed if not used.) You also can cancel your flight at any time without penalty. However, while it is true that this category of ticket can be purchased at the last minute, it is advisable to reserve well in advance during popular vacation periods and around holiday times.

Fares – Airfares continue to change so rapidly that even experts find it difficult to keep up with them. This ever-changing situation is due to a number of factors, including airline deregulation, volatile labor relations, increasing fuel costs, and vastly increased competition.

Perhaps the most common misconception about fares on scheduled airlines is that the cost of the ticket determines how much service will be provided on the flight. This is true only to a certain extent. A far more realistic rule of thumb is that the less you pay for your ticket, the more restrictions and qualifications are likely to come into play before you board the plane (as well as after you get off). These qualifying aspects relate to the months (and the days of the week) during which you must travel, how far in advance you must purchase your ticket, the minimum and maximum amount of time you may or must remain abroad, your willingness to decide on a return date at the time of booking — and your ability to stick to that decision. It is not uncommon for passengers sitting side by side on the same wide-body jet to have paid fares varying by hundreds of dollars, and all too often the traveler paying more would have been equally willing (and able) to accept the terms of the far less expensive ticket.

In general, the great variety of airfares to Mexico can be reduced to four basic categories, including first class, coach (also called economy or tourist class), and excursion or discount fares. A fourth category, called business class, has been added by many airlines in recent years. In addition, Advance Purchase Excursion (APEX) fares offer savings under certain conditions.

A **first class** ticket is your admission to the special section of the aircraft — larger seats, more legroom, sleeperette seating on some wide-body aircraft, better (or more elaborately served) food, free drinks and headsets for movies and music channels, and above all, personal attention. First class fares are about twice those of full-fare economy, although both first class passengers and those paying full-fare economy fares are entitled to reserve seats and are sold tickets on an open reservation system. An additional advantage of a first class ticket is the flexibility to include stops in any number of cities en route to or from your final destination in Mexico provided that certain set, but generous, maximum permitted mileage limits are respected. (Note that it is more likely that you will be able to schedule such stopovers at US rather than other Mexican destinations en route.)

Not too long ago, there were only two classes of air travel, first class and all the rest, usually called economy or tourist. Then **business class** came into being. At first, business class passengers were merely curtained off from the other economy passengers. Now a separate cabin or cabins — usually toward the front of the plane — is the norm. While standards of comfort and service are not as high as in first class, they represent a considerable improvement over conditions in the rear of the plane, with roomier seats, more leg and shoulder space between passengers, and fewer seats abreast. Free liquor and headsets, a choice of meal entrées, and a separate counter for speedier check-in are other inducements. As in first class, a business class passenger may travel on any scheduled flight he or she wishes, may buy a one-way or round-trip ticket, and have the ticket remain valid for a year. There are no minimum or maximum stay requirements, no advance booking requirements, and no cancellation penalties, and the fare allows the same free stopover privileges as first class. Note that airlines often have their own names for their business class service — such as Clipper Class on *Pan American* and Medallion Class on *Delta*.

The terms of the **coach** or **economy** fare may vary slightly from airline to airline, and in fact from time to time airlines may be selling more than one type of economy fare. Coach or economy passengers sit more snugly, as many as 10 in a single row on a wide-body jet, behind the first class and business class sections. Normally, alcoholic drinks are not free, nor are the headsets. If there are two economy fares on the books, one (often called "regular economy") still may include a number of free stopovers. The other, less expensive fare (often called "special economy") may limit stopovers to one or two, with a charge (typically $25) for each one. Like first class passengers, however, passengers paying the full coach fare are subject to none of the restrictions that usually are attached to less expensive excursion and discount fares. There are no advance booking requirements, no minimum stay requirements, and no cancellation penalties. Tickets are sold on an open reservation system: They can be bought for a flight right up to the minute of takeoff (if seats are available), and if the ticket is round-trip, the return reservation can be made any time you wish — months before you leave or the day before you return. Both first class and coach tickets generally are good for a year, after which they can be renewed if not used, and if you ultimately decide not to fly at all, your money will be refunded. On some routes between the US and Mexico the cost of economy and business class tickets may vary from a basic (low-season) price in effect most of the year to a peak (high-season) price in winter. Note that these price fluctuations are more likely to apply to flights to coastal resort areas than to inland destinations.

Excursions and other **discount** fares are the airlines' equivalent of a special sale and usually apply to round-trip bookings only. These fares generally differ according to the season and the number of travel days permitted. They are only a bit less flexible than full-fare economy tickets, and are, therefore, often useful for both business and holiday travelers. Most round-trip excursion tickets include strict minimum and maximum stay requirements and can be changed only within prescribed time limits. So don't count on extending a ticket beyond the prescribed time of return or staying less time than required. Different airlines may have different regulations concerning the number of stopovers permitted, and sometimes excursion fares are less expensive during midweek. The availability of these reduced-rate seats is most limited at busy times, such as holidays. Discount or excursion fare ticket holders sit with the coach passengers and, for all intents and purposes, are indistinguishable from them. They receive all the same basic services, even though they may have paid anywhere between 30% and 55% less for the trip. Obviously, it's wise to plan early enough to qualify for this less expensive transportation if possible.

These discount or excursion fares may masquerade under a variety of names, they may vary from city to city (from the East Coast to the West Coast, especially), but they invariably have strings attached. A common requirement is that the ticket be purchased a certain number of days — usually no fewer than 7 or 14 days — in advance of departure, though it may be booked weeks or months in advance (it has to be "ticketed," or paid for, shortly after booking, however). The return reservation usually has to be made at the time of the original ticketing and cannot be changed later than a certain number of days (again, usually 7 or 14 days) before the return flight. If events force a passenger to change the return reservation after the date allowed, the difference between the round-trip excursion rate and the round-trip coach rate probably will have to be paid, though most airlines allow passengers to use their discounted fares by standing by for an empty seat, even if they don't otherwise have standby fares. Another common condition is a minimum and maximum stay requirement; for example, 6 to 14 days, or 1 to 6 days but including at least a Saturday night. Last, cancellation penalties of up to 50% of the full price of the ticket have been assessed — check the specific penalty in effect when you purchase your discount/excursion ticket — so careful planning is imperative.

Of even greater risk — and bearing the lowest price of all the current discount fares — is the ticket where no change at all in departure and/or return flights is permitted, and where the ticket price is totally nonrefundable. If you do buy a nonrefundable ticket, you should be aware of a new policy followed by many airlines that may make it easier to change your plans if necessary. For a fee — set by each airline and payable at the airport when checking in — you *may* be able to change the time or date of a return flight on a nonrefundable ticket. However, if the nonrefundable ticket price for the replacement flight is higher than that of the original (as often is the case when trading in a weekday for a weekend flight), you will have to pay the difference. Any such change must be made a certain number of days in advance — in some cases as little as 2 days — of either the original or the replacement flight, whichever is earlier; restrictions are set by the individual carrier. (Travelers holding a nonrefundable or other restricted ticket who must change their plans due to a family emergency should know that some carriers may make special allowances in such situations; for further information, see *Medical and Legal Aid and Consular Services,* in this section.)

There also is a newer, often less expensive, type of excursion fare, the **APEX**, or **Advanced Purchase Excursion**. As with traditional excursion fares, passengers paying an APEX fare sit with and receive the same basic services as any other coach or economy passengers, even though they may have paid up to 50% less for their seats. In return, they are subject to certain restrictions. The ticket usually is good for a minimum of 7 days in Mexico and a maximum, currently, of 3 months (although this may vary, depending on the airline and the destination); and as its name implies, it must be "ticketed," or paid for in its entirety, a certain period of time before departure — usually somewhere between 7 and 21 days.

The drawback to an APEX fare is that it penalizes travelers who change their minds — and travel plans. The return reservation must be made at the time of the original ticketing, and if for some reason you change your schedule, you will have to pay a penalty of $100 or 10% of the ticket value, whichever is greater, as long as you travel within the validity period of your ticket. But if you change your return to a date less than the minimum stay or more than the maximum stay, the difference between the round-trip APEX fare and the full round-trip coach rate will have to be paid. There also is a penalty of anywhere from $75 to $125 or more for canceling or changing a reservation *before* travel begins — check the specific penalty in effect when you purchase your ticket. No stopovers are allowed on an APEX ticket, but it is possible to create an open-jaw effect by buying an APEX on a split ticket basis; for example, flying to Mexico City and returning from Cancún. The total price would be half the price of a round-trip APEX fare to Mexico City plus half the price of an APEX to Cancún. APEX tickets to Mexico are sold at basic and peak rates (for most Mexican destinations, peak season is from May through September) and may include surcharges for weekend flights.

Standby fares, at one time the rock-bottom price at which a traveler could fly to Mexico, have become elusive. At the time of this writing, most major scheduled airlines did not regularly offer standby fares on direct flights to Mexico. Because airline fares and their conditions constantly change, bargain hunters should not hesitate to ask if such a fare exists at the time they plan to travel.

While the definition of standby varies somewhat from airline to airline, it generally means that you make yourself available to buy a ticket for a flight (usually no sooner than the day of departure), then literally stand by on the chance that a seat will be empty. Once aboard, however, a standby passenger has the same meal service and frills (or lack of them) enjoyed by others in the economy class compartment.

Something else to check is the possibility of qualifying for a **GIT** (Group Inclusive Travel) fare, which requires that a specified dollar amount of ground arrangements be purchased, in advance, along with the ticket. The requirements vary as to the number of travel days and stopovers permitted, and the minimum number of passengers required for a group. The actual fares also vary, but the cost will be spelled out in brochures distributed by the tour operators handling the ground arrangements. In the past, GIT fares were among the least expensive available from the established carriers, but the prevalence of discount fares has caused group fares to all but disappear from some air routes. Travelers reading brochures on group package tours to Mexico will find that, in almost all cases, the applicable airfare given as a sample (to be added to the price of the land package to obtain the total tour price) is the same discount fare available to the independent traveler.

The major airlines serving Mexico from the US also may offer individual fare excursion rates similar to GIT fares, which are sold in conjunction with ground accommodation packages. Previously called ITX and sometimes referred to as individual tour-basing fares, these fares generally are offered as part of "air/hotel/car transfer packages," and can reduce the cost of an economy fare by more than a third. The packages are booked for a specific amount of time, with return dates specified; rescheduling and cancellation restrictions and penalties vary from carrier to carrier. These fares are offered by most major airlines flying between the US and Mexico and usually are offered to the most popular resort destinations in the country — among them Acapulco, Cancún, Cozumel, Guadalajara, Ixtapa, and Puerto Vallarta — and sometimes include a day or more stopover in Mexico City. (For further information on packages, see *Package Tours,* in this section.)

Travelers looking for the least expensive possible airfares should, finally, scan the pages of their hometown newspapers (especially the Sunday travel section) for announcements of special promotional fares. Most airlines traditionally have offered their most attractive special fares to encourage travel in slow seasons and to inaugurate and publicize new routes. Even if none of these factors apply, prospective passengers can be fairly sure that the number of discount seats per flight at the lowest price is strictly limited, or that the fare offering includes a set expiration date — which means it's absolutely necessary to move fast to enjoy the lowest possible price.

Among other special airline promotional deals for which you should be on the lookout are discount or upgrade coupons sometimes offered by the major carriers and found in mail order merchandise catalogues. For instance, airlines sometimes issue coupons that typically cost around $25 and are good for a percentage discount or an upgrade on an international airline ticket — including flights to Mexico. The only requirement beyond the fee generally is that a coupon purchaser must buy at least one item from the catalogue. There usually are some minimum airfare restrictions before the coupon is redeemable, but in general these are worthwhile offers. Restrictions often include certain blackout days (when the coupon cannot be used at all), usually imposed during peak travel periods. These coupons are particularly valuable to business travelers who tend to buy full-fare tickets, and while the coupons are issued in the buyer's name, they can be used by others who are traveling on the same itinerary.

It's always wise to ask about discount or promotional fares and about any conditions that might restrict booking, payment, cancellation, and changes in plans. Check the prices from other neighboring cities. A special rate may be offered in a nearby city but not in yours, and it may be enough of a bargain to warrant your leaving from that city. Ask if there is a difference in price for midweek versus weekend travel, or if there is a further discount for traveling early in the morning or late at night. Also be sure to investigate package deals, which are offered by virtually every airline. These may include car rental, accommodations, and dining and/or sightseeing features in addition to the basic airfare, and the combined cost of packaged elements usually is considerably less than the cost of the exact same elements when purchased separately.

If in the course of your research you come across a deal that seems too good to be true, keep in mind that logic may not be a component of deeply discounted airfares —

there's not always any sane relationship between miles to be flown and the price to get there. More often than not, the level of competition on a given route dictates the degree of discount, so don't be dissuaded from accepting an offer that sounds irresistible just because it also sounds illogical. Better to buy that inexpensive fare while it's being offered and worry about the sense — or absence thereof — while you're flying to your desired destination.

When you're satisfied that you've found the lowest possible price for which you can conveniently qualify (you may have to call the airline more than once, because different airline reservations clerks have been known to quote different prices), make your booking. Then, to protect yourself against fare increases, purchase and pay for your ticket as soon as possible after you've received a confirmed reservation. Airlines generally will honor their tickets, even if the operative price at the time of your flight is higher than the price you paid; if fares go up between the time you *reserve* a flight and the time you *pay* for it, you likely will be out of luck. Finally, with excursion or discount fares, it is important to remember that when a reservation clerk says that you must purchase a ticket by a specific date, this is an absolute deadline. Miss it and the airline may automatically cancel your reservation without telling you.

■ **Note:** Another wrinkle in the airfare scene is that if the fares go *down* after you purchase your ticket, you *may* be entitled to a refund of the difference. However, this is possible only in certain situations — availability and advance purchase restrictions pertaining to the lower rate are set by the airline. If you suspect that you may be able to qualify for such a refund, check with your travel agent or the airline.

Frequent Flyers – Most of the leading carriers serving Mexico offer a bonus system to frequent travelers. After the first 10,000 miles, for example, a passenger might be eligible for a first class seat for the coach fare; after another 10,000 miles he or she might receive a discount on his or her next ticket purchase. The value of the bonuses continues to increase as more miles are logged.

Bonus miles also may be earned by patronizing affiliated car rental companies or hotel chains, or by using one of the credit cards that now offers this reward. In deciding whether to accept such a credit card from one of the issuing organizations who tempt you with frequent flyer mileage bonuses on a specific airline, first determine whether the interest rate charged on the unpaid balance is the same as (or less than) possible alternate credit cards, and whether the annual "membership" fee also is equal or lower. If these charges are slightly higher than those of competing cards, weigh the difference against the potential value in airfare savings. Also ask about any bonus miles awarded just for signing up — 1,000 is common, 5,000 generally the maximum.

For the most up-to-date information on frequent flyer bonus options, you may want to send for the monthly *Frequent* newsletter. Issued by Frequent Publications, it provides current information about frequent flyer plans in general, as well as specific data about promotions, awards, and combination deals to help you keep track of the profusion — and confusion — of current and upcoming availabilities. For a year's subscription, send $33 to Frequent Publications, 4715-C Town Center Dr., Colorado Springs, CO 80916 (phone: 800-333-5937).

There also is a monthly magazine called *Frequent Flyer,* but unlike the newsletter mentioned above, its focus is primarily on newsy articles of interest to business travelers and other frequent flyers. Published by Official Airline Guides (PO Box 58543, Boulder, CO 80322-8543; phone: 800-323-3537), *Frequent Flyer* is available for $24 for a 1-year subscription.

Low-Fare Airlines – Increasingly, the stimulus for special fares is the appearance of airlines associated with bargain rates. On these airlines, all seats on any given flight generally sell for the same price, which is somewhat below the lowest discount fare offered by the larger, more established airlines. It is important to note that tickets offered by the smaller airlines specializing in low-cost travel frequently are not subject to the same restrictions as the lowest-priced ticket offered by the more established carriers. They may not require advance purchase or minimum and maximum stays, may involve no cancellation penalties, and may be available one way or round trip. A disadvantage to low-fare airlines, however, is that when something goes wrong, such as delayed baggage or a flight cancellation due to equipment breakdown, their smaller fleets and fewer flights mean that passengers may have to wait longer for a solution than they would on one of the equipment-rich major carriers.

Taxes and Other Fees – Travelers who have shopped for the best possible flight at the lowest possible price should be warned that a number of extras will be added to that price and collected by the airline or travel agent who issues the ticket. For instance, the $6 International Air Transportation Tax is a departure tax paid by all passengers flying from the US to a foreign destination.

Still another fee is charged by some airlines to cover more stringent security procedures, prompted by recent terrorist incidents. The 8% US Transportation Tax applies to travel within the US or US territories. It does not apply to passengers flying between US cities or territories en route to a foreign destination, unless the trip includes a stopover of more than 12 hours at a US point. Someone flying from Chicago to Los Angeles and stopping in Los Angeles for more than 12 hours before boarding a flight to Mexico City, for instance, would pay the 8% tax on the domestic portion of the trip. Note that these taxes *usually* are included in advertised fares and in the prices quoted by airlines reservations clerks.

Reservations – For those who don't have the time or patience to investigate personally all possible air departures and connections for a proposed trip, a travel agent can be of inestimable help. A good agent should have all the information on which flights go where and when, and which categories of tickets are available on each. Most have computerized reservation links with the major carriers, so that a seat can be reserved and confirmed in minutes. An increasing number of agents also possess fare-comparison computer programs, so they often are very reliable sources of detailed competitive price data. (For more information, see *How to Use a Travel Agent,* in this section.)

When making plane reservations through a travel agent, ask the agent to give the airline your home phone number, as well as your daytime business phone number. All too often the agent uses the agency number as the official contact for changes in flight plans. Especially during the winter — prime time for an escape to Mexico's sunny shores — weather conditions hundreds or even thousands of miles away can wreak havoc with flight schedules. Aircraft are constantly in use, and a plane delayed in the Orient or on the West Coast can miss its scheduled flight from the East Coast the next morning. The airlines are fairly reliable about getting this sort of information to passengers if they can reach them; diligence does little good at 10 PM if the airline has only the agency's or an office number.

Reconfirmation is strongly recommended for all international flights (though it is not generally required on domestic flights) and in the case of flights to Mexico, it is important that you confirm your round-trip reservations — especially the return leg — as well as any point-to-point flights within the country. Some (though increasingly few) reservations to and from international destinations are automatically canceled after a required reconfirmation period (typically 72 hours) has passed — even if you have a confirmed, fully paid ticket in hand. It always is a good idea to call ahead to make sure that the airline did not slip up in entering your original reservations, or in registering any changes you may have made since, and that it has your seat reservation and/or special meal request in the computer. If you look at the printed information on the ticket, you'll see the airline's reconfirmation policy stated explicitly. Don't be lulled into a false sense of security by the "OK" on your ticket next to the number and time of the return flight. This only means that a reservation has been entered; a reconfirmation still may be necessary. If in doubt — call.

If you plan not to take a flight on which you hold a confirmed reservation, by all means inform the airline. Because the problem of "no-shows" is a constant expense for airlines, they are allowed to overbook flights, a practice that often contributes to the threat of denied boarding for a certain number of passengers (see "Getting Bumped," below).

Seating – For most types of tickets, airline seats usually are assigned on a first-come, first-served basis at check-in, although some airlines make it possible to reserve a seat at the time of ticket purchase. Always check in early for your flight, even with advance seat assignments. A good rule of thumb for international flights is to arrive at the airport *at least* 2 hours before the scheduled departure to give yourself plenty of time in case there are long lines.

Most airlines furnish seating charts, which make choosing a seat much easier, but there are only a few basics to consider. You must decide whether you prefer a window, aisle, or middle seat. On flights where smoking is permitted, you also should indicate if you prefer the smoking or nonsmoking section.

The amount of legroom provided (as well as chest room, especially when the seat in front of you is in a reclining position) is determined by pitch, a measure of the distance between the back of the seat in front of you and the front of the back of your seat. The amount of pitch is a matter of airline policy, not the type of plane you fly. First class and business class seats have the greatest pitch, a fact that figures prominently in airline advertising. In economy class or coach, the standard pitch ranges from 33 to as little as 31 inches — downright cramped.

The number of seats abreast, another factor determining comfort, depends on a combination of airline policy and airplane dimensions. First and business classes have the fewest seats per row. Economy generally has 9 seats per row on a DC-10 or an L-1011, making either one slightly more comfortable than a 747, on which there normally are 10 seats per row. Charter flights on DC-10s and L-1011s, however, often have 10 seats per row and can be noticeably more cramped than 747 charters, on which the seating normally remains at 10 per row.

Airline representatives claim that most aircraft are more stable toward the front and midsection, while seats farthest away from the engines are quietest. Passengers who have long legs and are traveling on a wide-body aircraft might request a seat directly behind a door or emergency exit, since these seats often have greater than average pitch, or a seat in the first row of a given section, which offer extra legroom — although these seats are increasingly being reserved for passengers who are willing (and able) to perform certain tasks in the event of emergency evacuation. It often is impossible, however, to see the movie from these seats, which are directly behind the plane's exits. Be aware that the first row of the economy section (called a "bulkhead" seat) on a conventional aircraft (not a widebody) does *not* offer extra legroom, since the fixed partition will not permit passengers to slide their feet under it, and that watching a movie from this first-row seat can be difficult and uncomfortable. These bulkhead seats do, however, provide ample room to use a bassinet or safety seat and often are reserved for families traveling with children.

A window seat protects you from aisle traffic and clumsy serving carts, and also provides a view, while an aisle seat enables you to get up and stretch your legs without disturbing your fellow travelers. Middle seats are the least desirable, and seats in the last row are the worst of all, since they seldom recline fully. If you wish to avoid children on your flight or if you find that you are sitting in an especially noisy section, you usually are free to move to any unoccupied seat — if there is one.

If you are overweight, you may face the prospect of a long flight with special trepidation. Center seats in the alignments of wide-body 747s, L-1011s, and DC-10s are about 1½ inches wider than those on either side, so larger travelers tend to be more comfortable there.

Despite all these rules of thumb, finding out which specific rows are near emergency exits or at the front of a wide-body cabin can be difficult because seating arrangements on two otherwise identical planes vary from airline to airline. There is, however, a quarterly publication called *Airline Seating Guide* that publishes seating charts for most major US airlines and many foreign carriers as well. Your travel agent should have copies, or you can buy the US edition for $39.95 per year and the international edition for $44.95. Order from Carlson Publishing Co., Box 888, Los Alamitos, CA 90720 (phone: 800-728-4877 or 213-493-4877).

Simply reserving an airline seat in advance, however, actually may guarantee very little. Most airlines require that passengers arrive at the departure gate at least 45 minutes (sometimes more) ahead of time to hold a seat reservation. *Pan American,* for example, may cancel seat assignments and may not honor reservations of passengers who have not checked in some period of time — usually around 30 minutes, depending on the airport — before the scheduled departure time, and they *ask* travelers to check in at least 1 hour before all domestic flights and 2 hours before international flights. It pays to read the fine print on your ticket carefully and plan ahead.

A far better strategy is to visit an airline ticket office (or one of a select group of travel agents) to secure an actual boarding pass for your specific flight. Once this has been issued, airline computers show you as checked in, and you effectively own the seat you have selected (although some carriers may not honor boarding passes of passengers arriving at the gate less than 10 minutes before departure). This also is good — but not foolproof — insurance against getting bumped from an overbooked flight and is, therefore, an especially valuable tactic at peak travel times.

Smoking – One decision regarding choosing a seat has been taken out of the hands of many travelers who smoke. Effective February 25, 1990, the US government imposed a smoking ban that prohibits smoking on all flights scheduled for 6 hours or less within the US and its territories. The new regulation applies to both domestic and international carriers serving these routes.

In the case of flights to Mexico, these rules do not apply to nonstop flights flying directly from the US to destinations in Mexico or those flying with a *continuous* flight time of over 6 hours between stops in the US or its territories. Smoking is not permitted on segments of international flights where the time between US landings is under 6 hours — for instance those that include a stopover (even with no change of plane) or connecting flights. To further complicate the situation, individual carriers are starting to ban smoking altogether on certain routes. For instance, *Northwest* offers only non-smoking flights to Mexico.

On those flights that do permit smoking, the US Department of Transportation has determined that nonsmoking sections must be enlarged to accommodate all passengers who wish to sit in one. The airline does not, however, have to shift seating to accommodate nonsmokers who arrive late for a flight or travelers flying standby, and not all airlines can guarantee a seat in the nonsmoking section on international flights. Cigar and pipe smoking are prohibited on all flights, even in the smoking sections.

For a wallet-size guide, which notes in detail the rights of nonsmokers according to these regulations, send a self-addressed, stamped envelope to ASH (Action on Smoking and Health), Airline Card, 2013 H St. NW, Washington, DC 20006 (phone: 202-659-4310).

Meals – If you have specific diet requirements, be sure to let the airlines know well before departure time. The available meals include vegetarian, seafood, kosher, Muslim, Hindu, high-protein, low-calorie, low-cholesterol, low-fat, low-sodium, diabetic, bland, and children's menus. There is no extra charge for this option. It usually is necessary to request special meals when you make your reservations — check-in time is too late. It's also wise to reconfirm that your request for a special meal has made its way into the airline's computer — the time to do this is 24 hours before departure. (Note that special meals usually are not available on flights within Mexico — particularly on the smaller domestic carriers. If this poses a problem, eat before you board, or bring a snack with you.)

Baggage – Travelers from the US face two different kinds of rules. When you fly on a US airline or on a major international carrier, US baggage regulations will be in effect. Though airline baggage allowances vary slightly, in general, all passengers are allowed to carry on board, without charge, one piece of luggage that will fit easily under a seat of the plane or in an overhead bin and whose combined dimensions (length, width, and depth) do not exceed 45 inches. A reasonable amount of reading material, camera equipment, and a handbag also are allowed. In addition, all passengers are allowed to check two bags in the cargo hold: one usually not to exceed 62 inches when length, width, and depth are combined, the other not to exceed 55 inches in combined dimensions. Generally no single bag may weigh more than 70 pounds.

On domestic Mexican flights (aboard such carriers as *Aeroméxico* and *Mexicana*), baggage allowances may be subject to a different weight determination, under which each economy cabin passenger is allowed only a total of 55 pounds (or less) of luggage without additional charge. First class or business passengers may be allowed a total of 66 pounds. (If you are flying from the US to Mexico and connecting to a domestic flight, you generally will be allowed the same amount of baggage as on the international flight. If you break your trip and then take a domestic flight, the local carrier's weight restrictions apply.)

Charges for additional, oversize, or overweight bags usually are made at a flat rate; the actual dollar amount varies from carrier to carrier. If you plan to travel with any special equipment or sporting gear, be sure to check with the airline beforehand. Most have specific procedures for handling such baggage, and you may have to pay for transport regardless of how much other baggage you have checked. Golf clubs may be checked through as luggage (most airlines are accustomed to handling them), but tennis rackets should be carried onto the plane. Aqua-lung tanks, depressurized and appropriately packed with padding, and surfboards (minus the fin and padded) also may go as baggage. Snorkeling gear should be packed in a suitcase, duffel, or tote bag. Some airlines require that bicycles be partially dismantled and packaged (see *Camping and RVs, Hiking and Biking,* in this section).

Airline policies regarding baggage allowances for children vary and usually are based on the percentage of full adult fare paid. Although on many flights children who are ticket holders are entitled to the same baggage allowance as a full-fare passenger, some carriers allow only one bag per child, which sometimes must be smaller than an adult's bag (around 39 to 45 inches in combined dimensions). Often there is no luggage allowance for a child traveling on an adult's lap or in a bassinet. Particularly for international carriers, it's always wise to check ahead. (For more information, see *Hints for Traveling with Children,* in this section.)

To reduce the chances of your luggage going astray, remove all airline tags from previous trips, label each bag inside and out — with your business address rather than your home address on the outside, to prevent thieves from knowing whose house might be unguarded. Lock everything and double-check the tag that the airline attaches to make sure that it is coded correctly for your destination: MEX for Mexico City, or ACA for Acapulco, for instance.

If your bags are not in the baggage claim area after your flight, or if they're damaged, report the problem to airline personnel immediately. Keep in mind that policies regarding the specific time limit within which you have to make your claim vary from carrier to carrier. Fill out a report form on your lost or damaged luggage and keep a copy of it and your original baggage claim check. If you must surrender the check to claim a damaged bag, get a receipt for it to prove that you did, indeed, check your baggage on the flight. If luggage is missing, be sure to give the airline your destination and/or a telephone number where you can be reached. Also, take the name and number of the person in charge of recovering lost luggage.

Most airlines have emergency funds for passengers stranded away from home without their luggage, but if it turns out that your bags are truly lost and not simply delayed, do not then and there sign any paper indicating you'll accept an offered settlement. Since the airline is responsible for the value of your bags within certain statutory limits ($1,250 per passenger for lost baggage on a US domestic flight; $9.07 per pound or $20 per kilo for checked baggage, and up to $400 per passenger for unchecked baggage on an international flight), you should take some time to assess the extent of your loss (see *Insurance,* in this section). It's a good idea to keep records indicating the value of the contents of your luggage. A wise alternative is to take a Polaroid picture of the most valuable of your packed items just after putting them in your suitcase.

Considering the increased incidence of damage to baggage, it's now more than ever a good idea to keep the sales slips that confirm how much you paid for your bags. These are invaluable in establishing the value of damaged luggage and eliminate any arguments. A better way to protect your gear from the luggage-eating conveyers is to try to carry it on board whenever possible.

Be aware that airport security increasingly is an issue worldwide, and in Mexico is taken very seriously. Heavily armed police patrol the airports, and unattended luggage of any description may be confiscated and quickly destroyed. Passengers checking in at a foreign airport may undergo at least two separate inspections of their tickets, passports, and luggage by courteous, but nonetheless serious, airline personnel — who ask passengers if their baggage has been out of their possession between packing and the airport, or if they have been given gifts or other items to transport — before checked items are accepted.

Airline Clubs – US carriers often have clubs for travelers who pay for membership. These clubs are not solely for first class passengers, although a first class ticket *may* entitle a passenger to lounge privileges. Membership (which, by law, requires a fee) entitles the traveler to use the private lounges at airports along their route, to refreshments served in these lounges, and to check-cashing privileges at most of their counters. Extras include special telephone numbers for individual reservations, embossed luggage tags, and a membership card for identification. Airlines serving Mexico that offer membership in such clubs include the following:

> *American:* The *Admiral's Club.* Single yearly membership $175 for the first year; $125 yearly thereafter; spouse an additional $70 per year.
>
> *Continental:* The *President's Club.* Single yearly membership $140 for the first year; $90 yearly thereafter; spouse an additional $25 per year.
>
> *Delta:* The *Crown Club.* Single yearly membership $150; spouse an additional $50 per year.
>
> *Northwest:* The *World Club.* Single yearly membership $190 for the first year; $140 yearly thereafter; spouse an additional $50 per year.
>
> *Pan American:* The *Clipper Club.* Single yearly membership $150 (plus a one-time $25 initiation fee); spouse an additional $45 per year; 3-year and lifetime memberships also available.
>
> *United:* The *Red Carpet Club.* Single yearly membership $200 for the first year; $100 yearly therafter; spouse an additional $50 per year; 3-year and lifetime memberships also available.

Note that such companies do not have club facilities in all airports; other airlines also offer a variety of special services in many airports.

Getting Bumped – A special air travel problem is the possibility that an airline will accept more reservations (and sell more tickets) than there are seats on a given flight.

This is entirely legal and is done to make up for "no-shows," passengers who don't show up for a flight for which they have made reservations and bought tickets. If the airline has oversold the flight and everyone does show up, there simply aren't enough seats. When this happens, the airline is subject to stringent rules designed to protect travelers.

In such cases, the airline first seeks ticket holders willing to give up their seats voluntarily in return for a negotiable sum of money or some other inducement, such as an offer of upgraded seating on the next flight or a voucher for a free trip at some other time. If there are not enough volunteers, the airline may bump passengers against their wishes.

Anyone inconvenienced in this way, however, is entitled to an explanation of the criteria used to determine who does and does not get on the flight, as well as compensation if the resulting delay exceeds certain limits. If the airline can put the bumped passengers on an alternate flight that is *scheduled to arrive* at their original destination within 1 hour of their originally scheduled arrival time, no compensation is owed. If the delay is more than an hour but less than 2 hours on a domestic US flight, they must be paid denied-boarding compensation equivalent to the one-way fare to their destination (but not more than $200). If the delay is more than 2 hours after the original arrival time on a domestic flight or more than 4 hours on an international flight, the compensation must be doubled (but not more than $400). The airline also may offer bumped travelers a voucher for a free flight instead of the denied-boarding compensation. The passenger may be given the choice of either money or the voucher, the dollar value of which may be no less than the monetary compensation to which the passenger would be entitled. The voucher is not a substitute for the bumped passenger's original ticket; the airline continues to honor that as well.

Keep in mind that the above regulations and policies are for flights leaving the US only, and do *not* apply to charters or to inbound flights originating abroad, even on US carriers. Airlines carrying passengers between foreign destinations are free to determine what compensation they will pay to passengers who are bumped because of overbooking. They generally spell out their policies on airline tickets. Some foreign airline policies are similar to the US policy; however, don't assume all carriers will be as generous.

To protect yourself as best you can against getting bumped, arrive at the airport early, allowing plenty of time to check in and get to the gate. If the flight is oversold, ask immediately for the written statement explaining the airline's policy on denied-boarding compensation and its boarding priorities. If the airline refuses to give you this information, or if you feel it has not handled the situation properly, file a complaint with both the airline and the appropriate government agency (see "Consumer Protection," below).

Delays and Cancellations – The above compensation rules also do not apply if the flight is canceled or delayed, or if a smaller aircraft is substituted because of mechanical problems. Each airline has its own policy for assisting passengers whose flights are delayed or canceled or who must wait for another flight because their original one was overbooked. Most airline personnel will make new travel arrangements if necessary. If the delay is longer than 4 hours, the airline may pay for a phone call or telegram, a meal, and, in some cases, a hotel room and transportation to it.

 ■ **Caution:** If you are bumped or miss a flight, be sure to ask the airline to notify other airlines on which you have reservations or connecting flights. When your name is taken off the passenger list of your initial flight, the computer usually cancels all of your reservations automatically, unless *you* take steps to preserve them.

CHARTER FLIGHTS: By booking a block of seats on a specially arranged flight, charter operators offer travelers air transportation for a substantial reduction over the full coach or economy fare. These operators may offer air-only charters (selling transportation alone) or charter packages (the flight plus a combination of land arrangements such as accommodations, meals, tours, or car rentals). Charters are especially attractive to people living in smaller cities or out-of-the-way places, because they frequently leave from nearby airports, saving travelers the inconvenience and expense of getting to a major gateway.

From the consumer's standpoint, charters differ from scheduled airlines in two main respects: You generally need to book and pay in advance, and you can't change the itinerary or the departure and return dates once you've booked the flight. In practice, however, these restrictions don't always apply. Today, most of the charter flights to Mexico have the more popular resort areas as their prime destinations, and although most still require advance reservations, some permit last-minute bookings (when there are unsold seats available), and some even offer seats on a standby basis.

Though charters almost always are round-trip, and it is unlikely that you would be sold a one-way seat on a round-trip flight, on rare occasions, one-way tickets on charters are offered. Although it may be possible to book a one-way charter in the US, giving you more flexibility in scheduling your return, note that US regulations pertaining to charters may be more permissive than the charter laws of other countries. For example, if you want to book a one-way charter back to the US, you may find advance booking rules in force.

Some things to keep in mind about the charter game:

1. It cannot be repeated often enough that if you are forced to cancel your trip, you can lose much (and possibly all) of your money unless you have cancellation insurance, which is a must (see *Insurance,* in this section). Frequently, if the cancellation occurs far enough in advance (often 6 weeks or more), you may forfeit only a $25 or $50 penalty. If you cancel only 2 or 3 weeks before the flight, there may be no refund at all unless you or the operator can provide a substitute passenger.
2. Charter flights may be canceled by the operator up to 10 days before departure for any reason, usually underbooking. Your money is returned in this event, but there may be too little time to make new arrangements.
3. Most charters have little of the flexibility of regularly scheduled flights regarding refunds and the changing of flight dates; if you book a return flight, you must be on it or lose your money.
4. Charter operators are permitted to assess a surcharge, if fuel or other costs warrant it, of up to 10% of the airfare up to 10 days before departure.
5. Because of the economics of charter flights, your plane almost always will be full, so you will be crowded, though not necessarily uncomfortable. (There is, however, a new movement among charter airlines to provide flight accommodations that are more comfort-oriented, so this situation may change in the near future.)

To avoid problems, *always* choose charter flights with care. When you consider a charter, ask your travel agent who runs it and carefully check the company. The Better Business Bureau in the company's home city can report on how many complaints, if any, have been lodged against it in the past. Protect yourself with trip cancellation and interruption insurance, which can help safeguard your investment if you or a traveling companion is unable to make the trip and must cancel too late to receive a full refund from the company providing your travel services. (This is advisable whether you're buying a charter flight alone or a tour package for which the airfare is provided by charter or scheduled flight.)

Bookings – If you do fly on a charter, read the contract's fine print carefully and pay particular attention to the following:

Instructions concerning the payment of the deposit and its balance and to whom the check is to be made payable. Ordinarily, checks are made out to an escrow account, which means the charter company can't spend your money until your flight has safely returned. This provides some protection for you. To ensure the safe handling of your money, make out your check to the escrow account, the number of which must appear by law on the brochure, though all too often it is on the back in fine print. Write the details of the charter, including the destination and dates, on the face of the check; on the back, print "For Deposit Only." Your travel agent may prefer that you make out your check to the agency, saying that it will then pay the tour operator the fee minus commission. It is perfectly legal to write the check as we suggest, however, and if your agent objects too vociferously (he or she should trust the tour operator to send the proper commission), consider taking your business elsewhere. If you don't make your check out to the escrow account, you lose the protection of that escrow should the trip be canceled. Furthermore, recent bankruptcies in the travel industry have served to point out that even the protection of escrow may not be enough to safeguard a traveler's investment. More and more, insurance is becoming a necessity. The charter company should be bonded (usually by an insurance company), and if you want to file a claim against it, the claim should be sent to the bonding agent. The contract will set a time limit within which a claim must be filed.

Specific stipulations and penalties for cancellations. Most charters allow you to cancel up to 45 days in advance without major penalty, but some cancellation dates are 50 to 60 days before departure.

Stipulations regarding cancellation and major changes made by the charterer. US rules say that charter flights may not be canceled within 10 days of departure except when circumstances — such as natural disasters or political upheavals — make it physically impossible to fly. Charterers may make "major changes," however, such as in the date or place of departure or return, but you are entitled to cancel and receive a full refund if you don't wish to accept these changes. A price increase of more than 10% at any time up to 10 days before departure is considered a major change; no price increase at all is allowed during the last 10 days immediately before departure.

At the time of this writing, the following companies regularly offered charter flights to Mexico. As indicated, some of these companies sell charter flights directly to clients, while others are wholesalers and must be contacted through a travel agent.

Amber Tours (7337 W. Washington St., Indianapolis, IN 46251; phone: 800-225-9920). Retails to the general public.

Apple Vacations East (7 Campus Blvd., Newtown Sq., PA 19073; phone: 800-727-3400). This agency is a wholesaler, so use a travel agent.

Apple Vacations West (25 NW Point Blvd., Elk Grove Village, IL 60007; phone: 800-365-2775). This agency is a wholesaler, so use a travel agent.

Club America Vacations (3379 Peachtree Rd., Suite 625, Atlanta, GA 30326; phone: 800-221-2931). This agency is a wholesaler, so use a travel agent.

Club de Vacaciones (775 Park Ave., Suite 200, Huntington, NY 11743; phone: 516-424-9600 in New York State; 800-648-0404 elsewhere in the US). This agency is a wholesaler, so use a travel agent.

Ferien Service (3900 NW 79th Ave., Suite 431, Miami, FL 33166; phone: 305-591-1566). Retails to the general public.

Funway Holidays (PO Box 1460, Milwaukee, WI 53201-1460; phone: 800-558-3050). This agency is a wholesaler, so use a travel agent.

GWV International (300 First Ave., Needham, MA 02194; phone: 800-225-5498). This agency is a wholesaler, so use a travel agent.

Martinair Holland (1165 Northern Blvd., Manhasset, NY 11030; phone: 800-366-4655). Retails to the general public.

MLT Vacations (5130 Hwy. 101, Minnetonka, MN 55345; phone: 800-328-0025). This agency is a wholesaler, so use a travel agent.

Morris Air Service (260 E. Morris Ave., Salt Lake City, UT 84115-3200; phone: 800-444-5660). Retails to the general public.

MTI Vacations (1220 Kensington, Oak Brook, IL 60521; phone: 800-323-7285). Retails to the general public.

Suntrips (2350 Paragon Dr., San Jose, CA 95131; phone: 800-444-7866 in California; 800-937-0747 elsewhere in the US). Retails to the general public.

Tourlite International (1 E. 42nd St., New York, NY 10017; phone: 212-599-2727 in New York; 800-272-7600 elsewhere in the US). Retails to the general public.

Travel Charter (1120 E. Longlake Rd., Detroit, MI 48098; phone: 313-528-3570). This agency is a wholesaler, so use a travel agent.

In addition, *TAESA,* a Mexican charter company, also offers regular flights from Houston and Miami to destinations throughout Mexico. For some destinations, this may involve taking one of their connecting domestic flights.

You also may want to subscribe to the travel newsletter *Jax Fax,* which regularly features a list of charter companies and packagers offering seats on charter flights and may be a source for other charter flights to Mexico. For a year's subscription send a check or money order for $12 to *Jax Fax,* 397 Post Rd., Darien, CT 06820 (phone: 203-655-8746).

DISCOUNTS ON SCHEDULED FLIGHTS: Promotional fares often are called discount fares because they cost less than what used to be the standard airline fare — full-fare economy. Nevertheless, they cost the traveler the same whether they are bought through a travel agent or directly from the airline. Tickets that cost less if bought from some outlet other than the airline do exist, however. While it is likely that the vast majority of travelers flying to Mexico in the near future will be doing so on a promotional fare or charter rather than on a "discount" air ticket of this sort, it still is a good idea for cost-conscious consumers to be aware of the latest developments in the budget airfare scene. Note that the following discussion makes clear-cut distinctions among the types of discounts available based on how they reach the consumer; in actual practice, the distinctions are not nearly so precise.

Courier Travel – There was a time when traveling as a courier was a sort of underground way to save money and visit otherwise unaffordable destinations, but more and more this once exotic idea of traveling as a courier is becoming a very "establishment" exercise. Courier means no more than a traveler who accompanies freight of one sort or another, and typically that freight replaces what otherwise would be the traveler's checked baggage. Be prepared, therefore, to carry all your own travel gear in a bag that fits under the seat in front of you. In addition, the so-called courier usually pays a portion of the total airfare — the freight company pays the remainder — and the courier also may be assessed a small registration fee.

There are over 4 dozen courier companies operating actively around the globe, and several publications provide information on courier opportunities:

A Simple Guide to Courier Travel, by Jesse L. Riddle, is a particularly good reference guide to courier travel. Published by the Carriage Group (PO Box 2394, Lake Oswego, OR 97035; phone: 800-344-9375), it's available for $14.95, including postage and handling.

Travel Secrets (PO Box 2325, New York, NY 10108; phone: 212-245-8703). Provides information useful to those considering traveling as a courier and often lists specific US and Canadian courier companies. Monthly; a year's subscription costs $33.

Travel Unlimited (PO Box 1058, Allston, MA 02134-1058; no phone). Lists 30 to 40 courier companies and agents worldwide. Monthly; for a year's subscription send $25.

World Courier News (PO Box 77471, San Francisco, CA 94107; no phone). Provides information on courier opportunities, as well as useful tips. Each issue highlights a different destination. Monthly; for a year's subscription send $20.

In addition, the courier company *Now Voyager* (74 Varick St., Suite 307, New York, NY 10013; phone: 212-431-1616) regularly sends couriers between the US and Mexico.

Net Fare Sources – The newest notion for reducing the costs of travel services comes from travel agents who offer individual travelers "net" fares. Defined simply, a net fare is the bare minimum amount at which an airline or tour operator will carry a prospective traveler. It doesn't include the amount that normally would be paid to the travel agent as a commission. Traditionally, such commissions amount to about 10% on domestic fares and 10% to 20% on international fares — not counting significant additions to these commission levels that are payable retroactively when agents sell more than a specific volume of tickets or trips for a single supplier. At press time, at least one travel agency in the US was offering travelers the opportunity to purchase tickets and/or tours for a net price. Instead of making its income from individual commissions, this agency assesses a fixed fee that may or may not provide a bargain for travelers; it requires a little arithmetic to determine whether to use the services of a net travel agent or those of one who accepts conventional commissions. One of the potential drawbacks of buying from agencies selling travel services at net fares is that some airlines refuse to do business with them, thus possibly limiting your flight options.

Travel Avenue is a fee-based agency that rebates its ordinary agency commission to the customer. They will find the lowest retail fare, then rebate 5% to 16% (depending on the airline) of that price, minus a ticket-writing charge of $10 for domestic flights or $25 for international flights. The ticket-writing charge is imposed per ticket; if the ticket includes more than eight separate flights, an additional $10 or $25 fee is charged. Customers using free flight coupons pay the ticket-writing charge, plus an additional $5 coupon-processing fee.

Travel Avenue will rebate its commissions on all tickets, including heavily discounted fares and senior citizen passes. Available 7 days a week, reservations should be made far enough in advance to allow the tickets to be sent by first class mail, since extra charges accrue for special handling. It's possible to economize further by making your own airline reservation, then asking *Travel Avenue* only to write/issue your ticket. For travelers outside the Chicago area, business may be transacted by phone and purchases charged to a credit card. For information, contact *Travel Avenue* at 641 W. Lake, Suite 201, Chicago, IL 60606-1012 (phone: 312-876-1116 in Illinois; 800-333-3335 elsewhere in the US).

Consolidators and Bucket Shops – Other vendors of travel services can afford to sell tickets to their customers at an even greater discount because the airline has sold the tickets to them at a substantial discount (usually accomplished by sharply increasing commissions to that vendor), a practice in which many airlines indulge, albeit discreetly, preferring that the general public not know they are undercutting their own "list" prices. Airlines anticipating a slow period on a particular route sometimes sell off a certain portion of their capacity to a wholesaler, or consolidator. The wholesaler sometimes is a charter operator who resells the seats to the public as though they were charter seats, which is why prospective travelers perusing the brochures of charter operators with large programs frequently see a number of flights designated as "scheduled service." As often as not, however, the consolidator, in turn, sells the seats to a travel agency specializing in discounting. Airlines also can sell seats directly to such an agency, which thus acts as its own consolidator. The airline offers the seats either at a net wholesale price, but without the volume-purchase requirement that would be difficult for a modest retail travel agency to fulfill, or at the standard price, but with a commission override large enough (as high as 50%) to allow both a profit and a price reduction to the public.

Travel agencies specializing in discounting sometimes are called "bucket shops," a term once fraught with connotations of unreliability in this country. But in today's highly competitive travel marketplace, more and more conventional travel agencies are selling consolidator-supplied tickets, and the old bucket shops' image is becoming respectable. Agencies that specialize in discounted tickets exist in most large cities, and usually can be found by studying the smaller ads in the travel sections of Sunday newspapers.

Before buying a discounted ticket, whether from a bucket shop or a conventional, full-service travel agency, keep the following considerations in mind: To be in a position to judge how much you'll be saving, first find out the "list" prices of tickets to your destination. Then do some comparison shopping among agencies. Also bear in mind that a ticket that may not differ much in price from one available directly from the airline may, however, allow the circumvention of such things as the advance purchase requirement. If your plans are less than final, be sure to find out about any other restrictions, such as penalties for canceling a flight or changing a reservation. Most discount tickets are non-endorsable, meaning that they can be used only on the airline that issued them, and they usually are marked "nonrefundable" to prevent their being cashed for a list-price refund.

A great many bucket shops are small businesses operating on a thin margin, so it's a good idea to check the local Better Business Bureau for any complaints registered against the one with which you're dealing — before parting with any money. If you still do not feel reassured, consider buying discounted tickets only through a conventional travel agency, which can be expected to have found its own reliable source of consolidator tickets — some of the largest consolidators, in fact, sell only to travel agencies.

A few bucket shops require payment in cash or by certified check or money order, but if credit cards are accepted, use that option. Note, however, if buying from a charter operator selling seats for both scheduled and charter flights, that the scheduled seats are not protected by the regulations — including use of escrow accounts — governing the charter seats. Well-established charter operators, nevertheless, may extend the same protections to their scheduled flights, and, when this is the case, consumers should be sure that the payment option selected directs their money into the escrow account.

Listed below are some of the consolidators frequently offering discount fares to Mexico:

Maharaja Consumer Wholesale (393 5th Ave., New York, NY 10016; phone: 212-213-2020 in New York; 800-223-6862 elsewhere in the US).

TFI Tours International (34 W. 37th St., 12th Floor, New York, NY 10001; phone: 212-736-1140).

25 West Tours (2490 Coral Way, Miami, FL 33145; phone: 305-856-0810; 800-423-6954 in Florida; 800-252-5025 elsewhere in the US).

Check with your travel agent for other sources of consolidator-supplied tickets to Mexico.

■ **Note:** Although rebating and discounting are becoming increasingly common, there is some legal ambiguity concerning them. Strictly speaking, it is legal to discount domestic tickets but not international tickets. On the other hand, the law that prohibits discounting, the Federal Aviation Act of 1958, is consistently ignored these days, in part because consumers benefit from the practice and in part because many illegal arrangements are indistinguishable from legal ones. Since the line separating the two is so fine that even the authorities can't always tell the difference, it is unlikely that most consumers would be able to do so, and in fact it is not illegal to *buy* a discounted ticket. If the issue of legality bothers you, ask the agency whether any ticket you're about to buy would be permissible under the above-mentioned act.

OTHER DISCOUNT TRAVEL SOURCES: An excellent source of information on economical travel opportunities is the *Consumer Reports Travel Letter,* published monthly by Consumers Union. It keeps abreast of the scene on a wide variety of fronts, including package tours, rental cars, insurance, and more, but it is especially helpful for its comprehensive coverage of airfares, offering guidance on all the options from scheduled flights on major or low-fare airlines to charters and discount sources. For a year's subscription, send $37 ($57 for 2 years) to *Consumer Reports Travel Letter* (PO Box 53629, Boulder, CO 80322-3629; phone: 800-999-7959). For information on other travel newsletters, see *Sources and Resources,* in this section.

Last-Minute Travel Clubs – Still another way to take advantage of bargain airfares is open to those who have a flexible schedule. A number of organizations, usually set up as last-minute travel clubs and functioning on a membership basis, routinely keep in touch with travel suppliers to help them dispose of unsold inventory at discounts of between 15% and 60%. A great deal of the inventory consists of complete tour packages and cruises, but some clubs offer air-only charter seats and, occasionally, seats on scheduled flights.

Members pay an annual fee and receive a toll-free hotline number to call for information on imminent trips. In some cases, they also receive periodic mailings with information on bargain travel opportunities for which there is more advance notice. Despite the suggestive names of the clubs providing these services, last-minute travel does not necessarily mean that you cannot make plans until literally the last minute. Trips can be announced as little as a few days or as much as 2 months before departure, but the average is from 1 to 4 weeks' notice.

Among organizations regularly offering such discounted travel opportunities to Mexico are the following:

Discount Club of America (61-33 Woodhaven Blvd., Rego Park, NY 11374; phone: 800-321-9587 or 718-335-9612). Annual fee: $39 per family.

Discount Travel International (Ives Building, 114 Forrest Ave., Suite 205, Narberth, PA 19072; phone: 800-543-0110 or 215-668-7184). Annual fee: $45 per household.

Encore Short Notice (4501 Forbes Blvd., Lanham, MD 20706; phone: 301-459-8020; 800-638-0930 for customer service). Annual fee: $48 per family.

Last Minute Travel (1249 Boylston St., Boston MA 02215; phone: 800-LAST-MIN or 617-267-9800). No fee.

Moment's Notice (425 Madison Ave., New York, NY 10017; phone: 212-486-0503). Annual fee: $19.95 per family.

Spur-of-the-Moment Tours and Cruises (10780 Jefferson Blvd., Culver City, CA 90230; phone: 213-839-2418 in California; 800-343-1991 elsewhere in the US). No fee.

Traveler's Advantage (3033 S. Parker Rd., Suite 1000, Aurora, CO 80014; phone: 800-548-1116). Annual fee: $49 per family.

Vacations to Go (2411 Fountain View, Suite 201, Houston, TX 77057; phone: 800-338-4962). Annual fee: $19.95 per family.

Worldwide Discount Travel Club (1674 Meridian Ave., Miami Beach, FL 33139; phone: 305-534-2082). Annual fee: $40 per person; $50 per family.

Generic Air Travel – Organizations that apply the same flexible-schedule idea to air travel only and sell tickets at literally the last minute also exist. The service they provide sometimes is known as "generic" air travel, and it operates somewhat like an ordinary airline standby service, except that the organizations running it offer seats on not one but several scheduled and charter airlines.

One pioneer of generic flights is *Airhitch* (2790 Broadway, Suite 100, New York, NY 10025; phone: 212-864-2000). Prospective travelers register by paying a fee (applicable toward the fare) and stipulate a range of acceptable departure dates and their desired destination, along with alternate choices. The week before the date range begins, they are notified of at least two flights that will be available during the time period, agree on one and remit the balance of the fare to the company. If they do not accept any of the suggested flights, they lose their deposit; if, through no fault of their own, they do not ultimately get on any agreed-on flight, all of their money is refunded. Return flights are arranged the same way. The company's Sunhitch program includes flights to Mexico.

BARTERED TRAVEL SOURCES: Suppose a hotel buys advertising space in a newspaper. As payment, the hotel gives the publishing company a number of hotel rooms in lieu of cash. This is barter, a common means of exchange among hotels, airlines, car rental companies, cruise lines, tour operators, restaurants, and other travel-service companies. When a bartering company finds itself with empty airline seats (or excess hotel rooms, or cruise ship cabin space, and so on) and offers them to the public, considerable savings can be enjoyed.

Bartered travel clubs often offer discounts of up to 50% to members who pay an annual fee (approximately $50 at press time) which entitles them to select the flights, cruises, hotel rooms, or other travel services that the club obtained by barter. Members usually present a voucher, club credit card, or scrip (a dollar-denomination voucher negotiable only for the bartered product) to the hotel, which in turn subtracts the dollar amount from the bartering company's account.

Selling bartered travel is a perfectly legitimate means of retailing. One advantage to club members is that they don't have to wait until the last minute to obtain flight or room reservations.

Among the companies specializing in bartered travel, several that frequently offer members travel services to and in Mexico include the following:

IGT (In Good Taste) Services (1111 Lincoln Rd., 4th Floor, Miami Beach, FL 33139; phone: 800-444-8872 or 305-534-7900). Annual fee: $48 per family.

Travel Guide (18210 Redmond Way, Redmond, WA 98052; phone: 206-885-1213). Annual fee: $48 per family.

Travel World Leisure Club (225 W. 34th St., Suite 2203, New York, NY 10122; phone: 800-444-TWLC or 212-239-4855). Annual fee: $50 per family.

CONSUMER PROTECTION: Consumers who feel that they have not been dealt with fairly by an airline should make their complaints known. Begin with the customer service representative at the airport where the problem occurs. If he or she cannot resolve your complaint to your satisfaction, write to the airline's consumer office. In a businesslike, typed letter, explain what reservations you held, what happened, the names of the employees involved, and what you expect the airline to do to remedy the situation. Send copies (never the originals) of the tickets, receipts, and other documents that back your claims. Ideally, all correspondence should be sent via certified mail, return receipt requested. This provides proof that your complaint was received.

Passengers with consumer complaints — lost baggage, compensation for getting bumped, smoking and nonsmoking rules, deceptive practices by an airline, charter regulations — who are not satisfied with the airline's response should contact the Department of Transportation (DOT), Consumer Affairs Division (400 Seventh St. SW, Room 10405, Washington, DC 20590; phone: 202-366-2220). DOT personnel stress, however, that consumers initially should direct their complaints to the airline that provoked them.

Travelers with an unresolved complaint involving a foreign carrier also can contact the US Department of Transportation. DOT personnel will do what they can to help resolve all such complaints, although their influence may be limited. Consumers with complaints against Mexican airlines or other travel-related services should instead try contacting either the local tourist authority in the area where the problem occurred or a US representative of the Mexican Ministry of Tourism (see *Sources and Resources,* in this section, for addresses). The agency usually will try to resolve the complaint or, if it is out of their jurisdiction, will refer the matter to the proper authorities.

Remember, too, that the federal Fair Credit Billing Act permits purchasers to refuse to pay charges if they do not receive the travel services for which they've been billed, so the onus of dealing with the receiver for a bankrupt airline falls on the credit card company. Do not rely on another airline to honor the ticket you're holding, since the days when virtually all major carriers subscribed to a default protection program that bound them to do so are long gone. Some airlines may voluntarily step forward to accommodate the stranded passengers of a fellow carrier, but this is now an entirely altruistic act.

The deregulation of US airlines has meant that the traveler must find out for himself or herself what he or she is entitled to receive. The Department of Transportation's informative consumer booklet *Fly Rights* is a good place to start. To receive a copy, send $1 to the Superintendent of Documents (US Government Printing Office, Washington, DC 20402-9325; phone: 202-783-3238). Specify its stock number, 050-000-00513-5, and allow 3 to 4 weeks for delivery.

■ **Note:** Those who tend to experience discomfort due to the change in air pressure while flying may be interested in the free pamphlet *Ears, Altitude and Airplane Travel;* for a copy send a self-addressed, stamped, business-size envelope to the *American Academy of Otolaryngology* (One Prince St., Alexandria, VA 22314; phone: 703-836-4444). And for when you land, *Overcoming Jet Lag* offers some helpful tips on minimizing post-flight stress; it is available from Berkeley Publishing Group (PO Box 506, Mail Order Dept., East Rutherford, NJ 07073; phone: 800-631-8571) for $6.95, plus shipping and handling.

Traveling by Ship

 There was a time when traveling by ship was extraordinarily expensive, time-consuming, utterly elegant, and was utilized almost exclusively for getting from one point to another. No longer primarily pure transportation, cruising is currently riding a wave of popularity as a leisure activity in its own right and the host of new ships (and dozens of rebuilt old ones) testifies dramatically to the attraction of vacationing on the high seas. Cruise lines are flocking to Mexico, as repeat passengers seek new, more unusual itineraries, and first-time visitors choose sea-borne transportation to explore south of the border.

Among the destinations favored by cruise ship passengers, Mexico ranks extremely high. Cruise travel also is the most leisurely way to get to Mexico. From eastern US ports, cruises to Mexico most often head for Cozumel and Playa del Carmen (on the Yucatán Peninsula), or sail through the Panama Canal and call at popular resorts along Mexico's west coast. Sailings from west coast docks reverse the transcanal route, but by far the best known cruise course to Mexico runs from Los Angeles down the west coast of Mexico to such legendary ports of call as Acapulco, Puerto Vallarta, and Mazatlán — a real cruise itinerary, but one that was made famous on TV by that oceanic icon, the "Love Boat."

Many modern-day cruise ships seem much more like motels-at-sea than the classic liners of a couple of generations ago, but they are consistently comfortable and passengers often are pampered. Cruise prices are quite reasonable, and since the single cruise price covers all the major items in a typical vacation — transportation, accommodations, all meals, and entertainment, and a full range of social activities, sports, and recreation — a traveler need not fear any unexpected assaults on the family travel budget.

When selecting a cruise, your basic criteria should be where you want to go, the time you have available, how much you want to spend, and the kind of environment that best suits your style and taste (in which case price is an important determinant). Rely on the suggestions of a travel agent — preferably one specializing in cruises (see "A final note on picking a cruise," below) — but be honest with the agent (and with yourself) in describing the type of atmosphere you're seeking. Ask for suggestions from friends who have been on cruises; if you trust their judgment, they should be able to suggest a ship on which you'll feel comfortable.

There are a number of moments in the cruise-planning process when discounts are available from the major cruise lines, so it may be possible to enjoy some diminution of the list price almost anytime you book passage on a cruise ship. For those willing to commit early — say 4 to 6 months before sailing — most of the major cruise lines routinely offer a 10% reduction off posted prices, in addition to the widest selection of cabins. For those who decide to sail rather late in the game — say 4 to 6 weeks before departure — savings often are even greater — an average of 20% — as steamship lines try to fill up their ships. The only negative aspect is that the choice of cabins tends to be limited, although it is possible that a fare upgrade will be offered to make this limited cabin selection more palatable. In addition, there's the option of buying from a discount travel club or a travel agency that specializes in last-minute bargains; these discounters and other discount travel sources are discussed at the end of *Traveling by Plane,* above.

Most of the time, the inclusion of air transportation in the cruise package costs significantly less than if you were to buy the cruise separately and arrange your own air transportation to the port. If you do decide on one of these economical air/sea packages, be forewarned that it is not unusual for the prearranged flight arrangements to be less than convenient. The problems often arrive with the receipt of your cruise ticket, which also includes the airline ticket on the flight to get you to and from the ship dock. This is normally the first time you see the flights on which you have been booked and can appraise the convenience of the departure and arrival times. The cruise ship lines generally are not very forthcoming about altering flight schedules, and your own travel agent also may have difficulty in rearranging flight times or carriers. That means that the only remaining alternative is to ask the line to forget about making your flight arrangements and to pay for them separately by yourself. This may be more costly, but it's more likely to give you an arrival and departure schedule that will best conform to the sailing and docking times of the ship on which you will be cruising.

Generally, people take a cruise ship to Mexico for the sheer pleasure of being at sea, because it's part of a far broader itinerary, or because of a special interest in a particular area that is best visited by ship. Cruise lines promote sailings to Mexico as "get away from it all" vacations. But the prospective cruise ship passenger will find that the variety of cruises is tremendous, and the quality, while generally high, varies depending on shipboard services, the tone of shipboard life, the cost of the cruise, and operative itineraries.

Although there are less expensive ways to see Mexico, the romance and enjoyment of a sea voyage remain irresistible for many, so a few points should be considered by such sojourners before they sign on for a seagoing vacation (after all, it's hard to get off in mid-ocean). Herewith, a rundown on what to expect from a cruise, a few suggestions on what to look for and arrange when purchasing passage on one, and some representative sailings to and around Mexico.

CABINS: The most important factor in determining the price of a cruise is the cabin. Cabin prices are set according to size and location. The size can vary considerably on older ships, less so on newer or more recently modernized ones, and may be entirely uniform on the very newest vessels.

Shipboard accommodations utilize the same pricing pattern as hotels. Suites, which consist of a sitting room–bedroom combination and occasionally a small private deck that could be compared to a patio, cost the most. Prices for other cabins (interchangeably called staterooms) usually are more expensive on the upper passenger decks, less expensive on lower decks; if the cabin has a bathtub instead of a shower, the price probably will be higher. The outside cabins with portholes cost more than inside cabins without views and generally are preferred — although many experienced cruise passengers eschew the more expensive accommodations for they know they will spend very few waking hours in their cabins. As in all forms of travel, accommodations are more expensive for single travelers. If you are traveling on your own but want to share a double cabin to reduce the cost, some ship lines will attempt to find someone of the same sex willing to share quarters (also see *Hints for Single Travelers,* in this section).

FACILITIES AND ACTIVITIES: You may not use your cabin very much — organized shipboard activities are geared to keep you busy. A standard schedule might consist of swimming, sunbathing, and numerous other outdoor recreations. Evenings are devoted to leisurely dining, lounge shows or movies, bingo and other organized games, gambling, dancing, and a midnight buffet. Your cruise fare normally includes all of these activities — except the cost of drinks.

Most cruise ships have at least one major social lounge, a main dining room, several bars, an entertainment room that may double as a discotheque for late dancing, an exercise room, indoor games facilities, at least one pool, and shopping facilities, which can range from a single boutique to an arcade. Still others have gambling casinos and/or slot machines, card rooms, libraries, children's recreation centers, indoor pools (as well as one or more on open decks), separate movie theaters, and private meeting rooms. Open deck space should be ample, because this is where most passengers spend their days at sea.

Usually there is a social director and staff to organize and coordinate activities. Evening entertainment is provided by professionals. Movies are mostly first-run and drinks are moderate in price (or should be) because a ship is exempt from local taxes when at sea.

■**Note:** To be prepared for possible illnesses at sea, travelers should get a prescription from their doctor for medicine to counteract motion sickness. All ships with more than 12 passengers have a doctor on board, plus facilities for handling sickness or medical emergencies.

Shore Excursions – These side trips almost always are optional and available at extra cost. Before you leave, do a little basic research about the Mexican ports you'll be visiting and decide what sights will interest you. If several of the most compelling of these are some distance from the pier where your ship docks, the chances are that paying for a shore excursion will be worth the money.

Shore excursions usually can be booked through your travel agent at the same time you make your cruise booking, but this is worthwhile only if you can get complete details on the nature of each excursion being offered. If you can't get these details, better opt to purchase your shore arrangements after you're on board. Your enthusiasm for an excursion may be higher once you are on board because you will have met other passengers with whom to share the excitement of "shore leave." And depending on your time in port, you may decide to eschew the guided tour and venture out on your own.

Meals – All meals on board almost always are included in the basic price of a cruise, and the food generally is abundant and quite palatable. Evening meals are taken in the main dining room, where tables are assigned according to the passengers' preferences. Tables usually accommodate from 2 to 10; specify your preference when you book your cruise. If there are two sittings, you also can specify which one you want at the time you book or, at the latest, when you first board the ship. Later sittings usually are more leisurely. Breakfast frequently is available in your cabin, as well as in the main dining room. For lunch, many passengers prefer the buffet offered on deck, usually at or near the pool, but again, the main dining room is available.

DRESS: Most people pack too much for a cruise on the assumption that their daily attire should be chic and every night is a big event. Comfort is a more realistic criterion. Daytime wear on most ships is decidedly casual. Evening wear for most cruises is dressy-casual. Formal attire probably is not necessary for 1-week cruises, optional for longer ones. For information on choosing and packing a basic wardrobe, see *How to Pack,* in this section.

TIPS: Tips are a strictly personal expense, and you *are* expected to tip — in particular your cabin and dining room stewards. The general rule of thumb (or palm) is to expect to pay from 10% to 20% of your total cruise budget for gratuities — the actual amount within this range is based on the length of the cruise and the extent of personalized services provided. Allow $2 to $5 a day for each cabin and dining room steward (more if you wish) and additional sums for very good service. (*Note:* Tips should be paid by and for each individual in a cabin, whether there are one, two, or more.) Others who may merit tips are the deck steward who sets up your chair at the pool or elsewhere, the wine steward in the dining room, porters who handle your luggage (tip them individually at the time they assist you), and any others who provide personal service. On some ships you can charge your bar tab to your cabin; throw in the tip when you pay it at the end of the cruise. Smart travelers tip twice during the trip: about midway through the cruise and at the end; even wiser travelers tip a bit at the start of the trip to ensure better service throughout.

Although some cruise lines do have a no-tipping policy and you are not penalized by the crew for not tipping, naturally, you aren't penalized for tipping, either. If you can restrain yourself, it is better not to tip on those few ships that discourage it. However, never make the mistake of not tipping on the majority of ships, where it is a common, expected practice. (For further information on calculating gratuities, see *Tipping* in this section.)

SHIP SANITATION: The US Public Health Service (PHS) currently inspects all passenger vessels calling at US ports, so very precise information is available on which ships meet its requirements and which do not. The further requirement that ships immediately report illness that occurs on board adds to the available data.

The problem for a prospective cruise passenger is to determine whether the ship on which he or she plans to sail has met the official sanitary standard. US regulations require the PHS to publish actual grades for the ships inspected (rather than the old pass or fail designation), so it's now easy to determine any cruise ship's status. Nearly 4,000 travel agents, public health organizations, and doctors receive a copy of each monthly ship sanitation summary, but be aware that not all travel agents fully understand what this ship inspection program is all about. The best advice is to deal with a travel agent who specializes in cruise bookings, for he or she is most likely to have the latest information on the sanitary conditions of all cruise ships (see "A final note on picking a cruise," below). To receive a copy of the most recent summary or a particular inspection report, contact Chief, Vessel Sanitation Program, Center for Environmental Health and Injury Control, 1015 N. America Way, Room 107, Miami, FL 33132 (phone: 305-536-4307).

CRUISES TO AND AROUND MEXICO: These are several cruise lines that include Mexican ports as part of their itineraries. These lines either sail directly to Mexico or offer passengers the option of joining a leg of longer cruises or positioning cruises with stopovers in Mexico. Among these cruise lines are the following:

Carnival Cruise Lines: The *Holiday* makes 7-day cruises from Miami every Saturday. Ports of call include Playa del Carmen, Cozumel, and other ports in the Caribbean. *Carnival's Jubilee* also makes 7-day cruises every Sunday; leaving from Los Angeles, it sails to Cabo San Lucas, Mazatlán, and Puerto Vallarta. Although information is available from *Carnival Cruise Lines,* at 3655 NW 87th Ave., Miami, FL 33178-2428 (phone: 800-327-9501), reservations must be made through a travel agent.

Chandris Fantasy Cruises: The SS *Britanis* makes 5-day sailings from Miami to Cozumel and Playa del Carmel. Contact *Chandris Fantasy Cruises,* 900 Third Ave., New York, NY 10022 (phone: 800-621-3446) or 200 Blue Lagoon Dr., Miami, FL 33126 (same phone number).

Clipper Cruises: The *Yorktown Clipper* makes 15-day sailings between San Diego and Acapulco. Ports of call include the major resorts along the Mexican Riviera. For information, contact *Clipper Cruises,* 7711 Bonhomme Ave., St. Louis, MO 63105 (phone: 800-325-0010).

Commodore Cruise Line: The *Caribe* and *Enchanted Seas* both offer 7-day sailings from Miami and New Orleans, respectively. These itineraries call at various Caribbean ports in addition to Cozumel and Playa del Carmen. Contact *Commodore Cruise Line,* 800 Douglas Rd., Suite 700, Coral Gables, FL 33134 (phone: 800-237-5361).

Costa Cruises: The *Costa Riviera* and *Costa Marina* sail from Ft. Lauderdale to Cancún, Cozumel, and Playa del Carmen. The new *Costa Classica* will offer the same itineraries this year. For information, contact *Costa Cruises,* 80 SW 8th St., Miami, FL 33130 (phone: 800-462-6782 or 800-322-8263).

Crystal Cruises: The *Crystal Harmony* makes 10- to 14-day Panama Canal sailings between San Juan and Acapulco. Another itinerary offered aboard this ship is a 17-day cruise along the Mexican Riviera. Contact *Crystal Cruises,* 2121 Ave. of the Stars, Los Angeles, CA 90067 (phone: 800-446-6645).

Cunard: The *Queen Elizabeth 2* is one of the largest and most comfortable vessels afloat and each year the *QE2* offers a cruise that includes Mexico among its ports of call. *Cunard's Sagafjord, Sea Goddess I,* and *Vistafjord* all also make several trans-canal cruises stopping at Mexican ports. For information, contact *Cunard,* 555 Fifth Ave., New York, NY 10017 (phone: 800-221-4770 throughout the US).

Dolphin Cruise Line: The *Sea Breeze* makes 7-day sailings from Miami. Ports of call include Cozumel and Playa del Carmen, as well as a number of Caribbean ports. For information, contact *Dolphin Cruise Line,* 901 S. America Way, Miami, FL 33132 (phone: 800-222-1003).

Princess Cruises: This is it folks, the "Love Boat" — or perhaps we should say the Love Boats — in person. Last year, a 7-day cruise aboard the *Fair Princess* brought its passengers from Los Angeles to San Pedro, stopping in Acapulco, Cabo San Lucas, Ixtapa, Mazatlán, Puerto Vallarta, and Zihuatanejo. A 10-day cruise with the same itinerary was featured aboard the *Dawn Princess.* A 7-day cruise was also offered aboard the *Crown Princess,* calling at Cozumel as well as other Caribbean ports. For information, contact *Princess Cruises,* 10100 Santa Monica Blvd., Santa Monica, CA 90067 (phone: 800-421-0522).

Royal Caribbean Admiral Cruise Lines: Features winter-month cruises aboard the *Sun Viking* from Los Angeles to the Mexican Riviera. Last year, the 7-day cruise stopped in Cabo San Lucas, Mazatlán, and Puerto Vallarta. The *Viking Serenade* makes 3- and 4-day cruises between Los Angeles and Ensenada. For more information, contact *Royal Caribbean Admiral Cruise Lines,* 1050 Caribbean Way, Miami, FL 33132 (phone: 800-327-2055).

Royal Cruise Line: Offers a variety of cruises to and from Mexico. Among its offerings last year were Panama Canal cruises aboard the *Crown Odyssey.* These 14-day cruises began in Barbados, sailed through the Panama Canal to Acapulco, Puerto Vallarta, and Zihuatanejo, and then continued on to Los Angeles. This line also offered a 9-day Mexican Riviera cruise and an 11-day *Christmas Riviera* cruise — both of which stopped in several Mexican ports. For information contact *Royal Cruise Line,* One Maritime Plaza, San Francisco, CA 94111 (phone: 800-227-5628 or 415-956-7200).

Royal Viking Lines: The *Royal Viking Sun* makes 21-day cruises from San Francisco to Ft. Lauderdale, stopping in Acapulco, Cabo San Lucas, Puerto Vallarta, and Zihuatanejo. This ship also makes 13-day sailings between Ft. Lauderdale and Acapulco, stopping at various Mexican ports. For information, contact *Royal Viking Lines,* 95 Merrick Way, Coral Gables, FL 33134 (phone: 800-422-8000).

Special Expeditions: The M.S. *Seabird* and M.V. *Sea Lion* make 12-day and 9-day sailings, respectively. The *Seabird* sails from San Diego around the Baja Peninsula to Manzanillo, Cabo San Lucas, San Pedro Mártir, and other Mexican ports, before docking at Loreto. The *Sea Lion* travels from Baja, through Cabo San Lucas and on to Loreto. These cruises specialize in whale watching, natural history, and education. For information, contact *Special Expeditions,* 720 Fifth Ave., New York, NY 10019 (phone: 212-765-7740 in New York State; 800-762-0003 elsewhere in the US).

Note that a number of the larger cruise lines above offer special programs or facilities for handicapped, single, or older travelers. (See the targeted sections of GETTING READY TO GO for organizations that provide information on such special sailings.) Cruise lines also are becoming more sensitive to the special dietary needs and preferences of their passengers. For instance, some lines feature special low-sugar meals and drinks for people with diabetes. Many cruise lines also will provide — if given sufficient advance notice — prepackaged frozen kosher meals year-round for passengers requiring such food preparation. (For information, contact the specific cruise lines listed above.)

FREIGHTERS: An alternative to conventional cruise ships is travel by freighter. These are cargo ships that also take a limited number of passengers (usually about 12) in reasonably comfortable accommodations. The idea of traveling by freighter has long appealed to romantic souls, but there are a number of drawbacks to keep in mind before casting off. Once upon a time, a major advantage of freighter travel was its low cost, but this is no longer the case. Though freighters usually are less expensive than cruise ships, the difference is not as great as it once was. Accommodations and recreational facilities vary, but freighters were not designed to amuse passengers, so it is important to appreciate the idea of freighter travel itself. Schedules are erratic, and the traveler must fit his or her timetable to that of the ship. Passengers have found themselves waiting as long as a month for a promised sailing, and because freighters follow their cargo commitments, it is possible that a scheduled port could be omitted at the last minute or a new one added.

Anyone contemplating taking a freighter from a US port to Mexico, should be aware that at press time, only one freighter line carried passengers on regular sailings to Mexican ports.

Ivaran Lines (One Exchange Plaza, 55 Broadway, 19th Floor, New York, NY 10006; phone: 800-451-1639 or 212-809-1220) has a freighter that can carry 88 passengers in exceptional comfort, with all of the usual cruise ship amenities and a full range of shore excursions. This ship sails regularly from Houston to Tampico, Mexico, as part of a round-trip sailing to South America, before returning to New Orleans. The trip to Tampico takes about 1 day; the full round-trip cruise takes 48 days.

Specialists dealing only (or largely) in freighter travel can help to arrange trips. They provide information, schedules, and when you're ready to sail, booking services. Among these agencies are the following:

> *Freighter World Cruises, Inc.* (180 S. Lake Ave., Suite 335, Pasadena, CA 91101; phone: 818-449-3106). A freighter travel agency that acts as general agent for several freighter lines. Publishes the twice-monthly *Freighter Space Advisory,* listing space available on sailings worldwide. A subscription costs $27 a year, $25 of which can be credited toward the cost of a cruise.

> *Pearl's Travel Tips* (9903 Oaks Lane, Seminole, FL 34642; phone: 813-393-2919). Run by Ilse Hoffman, who finds sailings for her customers and sends them off with all kinds of valuable information and advice.

> *TravLtips Cruise and Freighter Travel Association* (PO Box 188, Flushing, NY 11358; phone: 718-939-2400 in New York; 800-872-8584 elsewhere in the US). A freighter travel agency and club ($15 per year or $25 for 2 years) whose members receive the bimonthly *TravLtips* magazine of cruise and freighter travel.

Those interested in freighter travel also may want to subscribe to *Freighter Travel News,* a publication of the *Freighter Travel Club of America.* A year's subscription to this monthly newsletter costs $18. To subscribe, write to the club at 3524 Harts Lake Rd., Roy, WA 98580.

Another monthly newsletter that may be of interest to those planning to cruise Mexican waters is *Ocean and Cruise News,* which offers comprehensive coverage of the latest on the cruise ship scene. A year's subscription costs $24. Contact *Ocean and Cruise News,* PO Box 92, Stamford, CT 06904 (phone: 203-329-2787).

■**A final note on picking a cruise:** A "cruise-only" travel agency can best help you choose a cruise ship and itinerary. Cruise-only agents are best equipped to tell you about a particular ship's "personality," the kind of person with whom you'll likely be traveling on a particular ship, what dress is appropriate (it varies from ship to ship), and much more. Travel agencies that specialize in booking cruises usually are members of the *National Association of Cruise Only Agencies (NACOA).* For a listing of the agencies in your area (requests are limited to three states), send a self-addressed, stamped envelope to *NACOA,* PO Box 7209, Freeport, NY 11520, or call 516-378-8006.

Traveling by Train

Perhaps the most economical, and often the most satisfying, way to see a lot of a foreign country in a relatively short time is by rail. It certainly is the quickest way to travel between two cities up to 300 miles apart (beyond that, a flight normally would be quicker, even counting the time it takes to get to and from the airport). But time isn't always the only consideration. Traveling by train is a way to keep moving and to keep seeing at the same time, and the fares usually are reasonable. You only need to get to a station on time; after that, put your watch in your pocket and relax. You may not get to your destination exactly at the appointed hour, but you'll have a marvelous time looking out the window and enjoying the ride.

If you are a real train buff, or simply prefer to see more of the countryside through which you are traveling than the center line of a highway, Mexico is the place for you. Mexico has 15,000 miles of railroad lines connecting its mountains, coasts, and jungles. You can take a train from the US-Mexico border or fly to Mexico City and take some fascinating railroad trips from the capital. Among those especially recommended are rail trips to the Gulf Coast and the ancient port city of Veracruz, and to Mérida, the starting point for exploratory journeys to the Maya ruins. (See "Special Routes," below.)

Train travel in Mexico, however, is not for everyone. Travelers accustomed to the high standards of facilities and service found on long-distance trains in the US and Europe will have to adjust their expectations — even the newly upgraded trains are hardly luxurious. Schedules can be erratic, trips tend to take longer than expected, toilets may not always flush, and although porters do their best, English-speaking personnel is limited. If you can shrug in the face of minor inconveniences and postponements, and sustain an accepting and flexible attitude, you'll find that trains are a wonderful way to get to know the Mexican people and see the countryside.

Mexico's railroad network is government-owned, the main lines having been expropriated from British and US concessionaires in 1937, with other lines bought up by the government as late as 1966. The *Mexican National Railways* (*Ferrocarriles Nacionales de México*) issues timetables that are revised yearly or whenever fares change. For information and timetables you can contact the railway's main office in Mexico City (Estación Buenavista, Depto. de Tráfico de Pasajeros, Av. Insurgentes Nte. and Av. Mosqueta, México, DF 06358; phone: 5-547-1097, 5-547-6593, or 5-547-1084). The best way to get information on train numbers, times, and ticket costs, however, is to go personally to one of the railroad's offices and take notes. In the larger cities, however, ticket-window personnel may or may not speak English — or even a reasonable facsimile thereof.

ACCOMMODATIONS AND FARES: Like US fares, the cost of a ticket on a Mexican train is based on the length of the journey and the quality of accommodation the passenger enjoys. The bonus of train travel in Mexico, however, is that it costs a fraction of US prices.

Several kinds of first class tickets are sold and first class accommodations (the means of rail transportation we suggest) include a range of facilities, depending on the route and train. *Regular* first class tickets are for a reserved seat; on longer routes *especial* tickets entitles the passenger to some sort of sleeping compartment. A *general* ticket is good for a seat in first class *if* there is one; if first class is overbooked, you will have to travel in second class. Some trains may provide rooms (*camerín*), bedrooms with two beds (*alcoba*), and suites. Second class accommodations consist of coach seats only. For any long trip it is recommended that you go first class; you will find even first class rail fares suprisingly reasonable. Another advantage of a first class rail ticket is that two stopovers en route are allowed, at an additional charge of 15% of the price of the ticket per stop.

BOOKING: Tickets can be bought directly at individual train stations in Mexico. Advance reservations also can be made from the US through some travel agents or by calling the following foreign passenger services numbers in Mexico City: 5-547-1084 or 5-547-1097.

SERVICES: Mexican passenger trains are a mixture of rolling stock purchased in the US and passenger cars manufactured in Mexico in recent decades by the government-owned *National Railcar Construction Company.*

The quality and type of passenger service cars vary widely — from relatively comfortable to downright rickety. The finest service usually is to be found aboard Pullman cars — some old, but all relatively well maintained. The dining cars, which are a delight, serve inexpensive meals at scheduled times. The menu, with American and Mexican fare, usually offers at least three complete meal options, plus à la carte items. Beer is available.

Passenger service on main routes (such as Monterrey–Mexico City, Mexico City–Morelia, Veracruz–Mexico City, Oaxaca–Mexico City, and Guadalajara–Mexico City) has been upgraded, and the trains usually have a club or smoking car where beer, tequila, and other hard liquor is available at low prices. On a night run, these can become pretty lively places, with domino and card games cropping up.

Passengers paying full fare (anyone over the age of 12) are entitled to carry 50 kilos (about 111 pounds) of baggage. There are porters in each station who will carry luggage. There is no standard fee, but porters expect a tip of about 500 to 1,000 pesos per bag.

SPECIAL ROUTES: Mexico City is served by trains from Mexican towns across the border from El Paso, Presidio, Laredo, and Brownsville, Texas; Nogales, Arizona; and Calexico, California (across from Mexicali). From Mexico City there are connections to most parts of the country. In addition, there are rail connections within specific areas, such as along the developed sections of the Pacific coast.

Several sections of the country are best seen by rail; a visitor could make a very satisfactory tour of Mexico's most spectacular scenery simply by selecting choice rail tours from Mexico City (tickets for most routes can be bought at the *Mexican National Railways* main office; see above). Among the best itineraries are the following:

Copper Canyon – The *El Nuevo Chihuahua–Pacifico* line runs from Chihuahua to Los Mochis. (Actually, traveling the reverse itinerary, west to east offers the most scenic views during daylight hours.) Even if you are not a fanatic rail fancier, you're bound to be impressed with what is one of the most spectacular train rides in the Western Hemisphere. This stretch of railroad cost $104 million to build, and American engineers said it was impossible. Mexican engineers did it. The train climbs 400 miles of rugged Sierra Madre Occidental peaks, goes through 86 tunnels, and crosses 36 bridges (some a mile high), passing over canyons that make the Grand Canyon look like a pothole. It crosses the Continental Divide three times and reaches a height of 7,500 feet. The trains stop at Divisadero to give passengers a view of the canyon, carved by the Urique River and actually four times larger than the Grand Canyon. Note that tickets for this journey can be bought only in Chihuahua or Nuevo Laredo, or from selected US travel agents, such as *Trains Unlimited* (see below).

Mexico City to Veracruz – A 10-hour day trip over the mountains surrounding the Valley of Mexico and into the tropics to the Gulf of Mexico city of Veracruz. Along the way, the rails run through tropical forests and provide views of waterfalls, orange groves, wild orchids, mango trees, and other exotic flora and fauna.

Mexico City to Mérida – A wonderful way to get to Mérida for further tours of the Yucatán Peninsula, the Caribbean coast, and the ruins at Tulum and Chichén Itzá. The rail trail gets to Mérida from Mexico City via the ruins and Palenque and the city of Campeche. (Be forewarned: This trip takes about 36 hours and only second class cars are available.)

Mexico City to the Lake District – The train goes through Morelia, Pátzcuaro, and Uruapan (in the state of Michoacán), one of the richest areas in the country for a variety of activities, including shopping.

A number of other scenic routes are worth a detour. For instance, rail buffs and those interested in a particularly scenic day excursion won't want to miss the ride from Saltillo aboard the *Zacatecas and Coahuila Railroad* to the gold- and silver-mining town of Concepción del Oro. The round trip covers 164 miles and winds along narrow mountain ridges. This trip is well worth taking if only for the wood-burning, stove-heated coaches that date back to 1895. Note that newer trains also serve this route, so check in advance that this treasure of a train is running. (For further information, see the *Nuevo Laredo to Mexico City* and *Reynosa to Mazatlán* routes in DIRECTIONS.

■ **Note:** Although many travel agents can assist you in making arrangements to tour Mexico by rail, you may want to consult a train travel specialist, such as *Accent on Travel* (1030 Curtis St., Suite 201, Menlo Park, CA 94025; phone: 415-326-7330 in California; 800-347-0645 elsewhere in the US), which books rail tours throughout Mexico. *Trains, Unlimited, Tours,* PO Box 1997, Portola, CA 96122; phone: 916-836-1745) also books rail adventures in Mexico, including the Copper Canyon route mentioned above.

Traveling by Bus

 Going from place to place by bus may not be the fastest way to get from here to there, but that (and a little less comfort) is the primary drawback to bus travel. A persuasive argument in its favor is its cost: Short of walking, traveling by bus is the least expensive way to cover a long distance. On average, a bus ticket between two cities in Mexico costs about two-thirds of the corresponding train fare. For this amount, it is *possible* to travel comfortably (the degree of comfort varies widely among routes and buses), if not always speedily, and at the same time enjoy the scenic view.

Unless you are addicted to buses and/or live close to the border, you probably will not choose to travel from the US to Mexico by bus. It is a long haul (at least 3½ days from New York City to Mexico City) and, while inexpensive, usually not worth the expenditure of time. Once in Mexico, however, buses become an extremely cost-efficient and usually convenient means of getting around the country. A map of Mexican bus routes is not much different from a road map: If the way is paved, it's likely that a bus — some bus — is assigned to travel it. The network of express buses — those traveling long distances with few stops en route — is only slightly less extensive. Different companies serve different sections of the country, but all have central offices in Mexico City (see below).

If you should decide to travel to Mexico by bus, *Greyhound* serves the Mexico-US border at Laredo, Texas, where you can pick up a Mexican bus for the journey to Mexico City (or other points south). Round-trip tickets to Laredo are available at the traveler's point of departure in the US. For information on departures from the US, contact the nearest *Greyhound* office or call *Greyhound*'s Laredo office at 512-723-4324.

At US border towns, it is necessary to cross through customs, get Mexican tourist cards, and make connections onto Mexican buses for your destination. Note that it pays to do some checking in advance so that you don't end up waiting too long for the next bus. It is relatively easy to get to Mexico City from the major entry points along the Arizona, California, and Texas borders. For further information, see "Tickets and Connections with US Bus Lines," below.

FOR COMFORTABLE TRAVEL: Dress casually in loose-fitting clothes. Be sure you have a sweater or jacket (even in the summer) and, for when you disembark, a raincoat or umbrella is recommended in areas of high precipitation and during the rainy season (see "Climate," in *When and How to Go,* in this section). Passengers are allowed to listen to radios or cassette players, but must use earphones. Choose a seat in the front near the driver for the best view or in the middle between the front and rear wheels for the smoothest ride — athough, depending on the route and kind of bus, the term "smooth" may be relative.

MEXICAN BUS SERVICES: Mexico has a two-tiered bus system, based on first and second class buses. For the most part, tourists will want to travel only on first class (or deluxe) buses, which are inexpensive but nonetheless provide the indispensable luxury of air conditioning. On second class buses — which are even less expensive and less comfortable — air conditioning is the exception rather than the rule, particularly along rural routes.

The newer, first class buses making long-distance trips also often are furnished with in-bus toilets. (The availability of an in-bus toilet can be quite important; in buses without toilets, it is necessary to ask drivers to stop along the road. They will always be accommodating, but it can be extremely awkward if you are driving through the northwestern deserts, with no trees or cover.) Buses generally are not equipped for food service, but on long trips, as in the US, they do stop at roadside cafés for food (although US travelers may be better off providing their own sustenance). Passengers are allowed to smoke on Mexican buses.

BOOKING: Reservations usually are not necessary on most local bus routes, which run on established and published schedules. In rural areas, the bus often is the main form of transport, and the ticket may be purchased on the bus (only for that ride on that day). However, particularly for long journeys, tickets usually are bought at the bus station before leaving.

Unless you speak fluent Spanish, you will not get much useful information over the telephone. During the busiest rush seasons, such as *Easter Week* or the *Christmas* holidays, purchase your bus tickets well in advance to avoid standing in line for several hours. The same advice applies for 3-day weekends in Mexico. Tickets are sold on a cash only, first-come, first-served basis.

Fares are extremely low. Still, it never hurts to ask about current passes and any discounts available. If you do not speak Spanish, however, in some areas you may find it difficult to ask about discounts or even buy a ticket.

Tickets and Connections with US Bus Lines – In Mexico City, travelers can secure tickets on Mexican bus lines for the return trip north through Mexican territory, and make reservations and purchase tickets for bus lines operating on the US side of the border, all through one main office: *Greyhound de México* (27 Paseo de la Reforma; phone: 535-4200, 535-2618). Tickets are sold for connections by the following Mexican lines: *Autobuses del Oriente, Transportes del Norte, Transportes Chihuahuenses,* and *Tres Estrellas de Oro,* as well for as the Estrella de Oro and Cristóbal Colón routes. *Viajes Mexicorama,* (Plaza del Angel, 161 Calle Londres, Suite 48, Mexico City, Mexico; phone: 5-525-2050) also sells tickets for these connections. Also at this office is a travel agency, *Central de Autobuses* (phone: 5-533-2047 through -2049), which will make reservations and even deliver tickets to your hotel. This can be a great timesaver, since the big bus terminals are near the outskirts of the city.

Bus lines cover every part of Mexico through an interconnecting system of routes. Access to almost any Mexican destination is possible from Mexico City, which is the center of a vast spider web of crisscrossing routes. Bus lines in Mexico are federal concessions awarded to private operators, and each serves certain areas.

Most of the main bus lines converge at one of four super-terminals, according to the region of Mexico through which they travel. The main bus terminals in Mexico City are the following:

Terminal Central del Norte (Northern Terminal; 4907 Av. de los 100 Metros).
Terminal Central del Sur (Southern Terminal; 1320 Taxqueña).

Terminal Observatorio (Western Terminal; 122 Av. Sur).
Terminal Tapo (Eastern Terminal; 200 Calz. Ignacio Zaragoza).

Following is a list of the major bus lines serving Mexico, arranged by geographical region — or an approximation thereof:

Northwest, North Central

Mexico City–Querétaro–Guadalajara–Mazatlán–Tijuana

Tres Estrellas de Oro (Northern Bus Terminal; phone: 5-587-5333). A ticket office is at 203 Dr. Lucio (phone: 5-578-8742). Other main points served: Celaya, Ciudad Obregón, Ciudad Victoria, Colima, Culiacán, Dolores Hidalgo, Ensenada, Guanajuato, Hermosillo, Irapuato, León, Loreto, Manzanillo, Matamoros, Mexicali, Monterrey, Morelia, Puerto Vallarta, Reynosa, San Juan de los Lagos, San Luis Potosí, San Miguel de Allende, Uruapan, and Zamora.

Mexico City–Guadalajara–Nogales–Mexicali–Tijuana

Autobuses Estrella Blanca (Northern Bus Terminal; phone: 5-587-5219). Main points: Acapulco, Aguascalientes, Ciudad Juárez, Ciudad Reynosa, Ciudad Victoria, Chihuahua, Durango, Guadalajara, Guanajuato, León, Matamoros, Matehuala, Mazatlán, Monterrey, Morelia, Nuevo Laredo, Poza Rica, Puerto Vallarta, San Juan de los Lagos, San Luis Potosí, Tampico, and Torreón.

Omnibus de México (Northern Bus Terminal; phone: 5-567-7287 or 5-567-5858). Main points: Aguascalientes, Celaya, Ciudad Juárez, Ciudad Mante, Ciudad Reynosa, Ciudad Valles, Chihuahua, Colima, Durango, Guadalajara, Guanajuato, Irapuato, León, Matamoros, Ojinaga, Poza Rica, Parral, Querétaro, San Luis Potosí, San Miguel de Allende, Tampico, Tepic, Torreón, Tuxpan, and Zacatecas.

Transportes Chihuahuenses TCH (Northern Bus Terminal; phone: 5-587-5355 or 5-587-5377). Main points: Aguascalientes, Chihuahua, Ciudad Juárez, Guadalajara, León, Parral, Querétaro, San Luis Potosí, Torreón, and Zacatecas.

Transportes del Norte (Northern Bus Terminal; phone: 5-587-5511 or 5-587-5400). Downtown ticket office: 137 Insurgentes Centro (phone: 5-546-0032 or 5-566-5515). Main points: Ciudad Valles, Ciudad Victoria, Matamoros, Mexico City, Monterrey, Nuevo Laredo, Querétaro, Reynosa, Saltillo, San Luis Potosí, and Torreón.

Transportes Norte de Sonora (Northern Bus Terminal; phone: 5-587-5633 or 5-567-9221). Other main points served: Agua Prieta, Cananea, Ciudad Obregón, Ensenada, Hermosillo, Mazatlán, Morelia, and Uruapan.

Southeast

ADO Autobuses del Oriente (Eastern Bus Terminal; phone: 5-542-3435; 5-542-7192 through -7198). Main points: Agua Dulce, Campeche, Cancún, Ciudad del Carmen, Ciudad Chetumal, Ciudad Pemex, Coatepec, Coatzacoalcos, Córdoba, Cosamaloapan, Jalapa, Loma Bonita, Mérida, Minatitlán, Nautla, Oaxaca, Palenque, Puebla, Puerto Ceiba, Tehuacán, Teziutlán, Veracruz, Villahermosa, and Villa Isla.

Northeast

ADO Autobuses del Oriente (Northern Bus Terminal; phone: 5-567-8455 or 5-567-8364). Main points: Alamo, Cerro Azul, Gutiérrez Zamora, Huachinango, Huejutla, Naranjos, Oaxaca, Pachuca, Pánuco, Papantla, Potrero, Poza Rica, Puebla, Tampico, Tantoyuca, Tecolutla, Tempoal, Tuxpan, Villa Juárez.

Southwest

Estrella de Oro (Southern Bus Terminal; phone: 5-549-8520 through -8529). Main points: Acapulco, Chilpancingo, Ciudad Lázaro Cárdenas, Cuernavaca, Iguala, Taxco, and Zihuatanejo.

Omnibus Cristóbal Colón (Eastern Bus Terminal; phone: 5-542-7263 through -7266). Main points: Acatlán, Ciudad Ixtepec, Cuautla, Oaxaca, Salina Cruz, San Cristóbal de las Casas, Talismán, Tapachula, Tehuantepec, and Tuxtla Gutiérrez.

Other Routes – Limited service to points of interest for vacationers include routes of these companies:

Línea de Autobuses México-Teotihuacán (Northern Bus Terminal; phone: 5-567-1494).

Líneas Unidas del Sur Flecha Roja (Southern Bus Terminal; phone: 5-689-8000 or 5-549-3846). Main points: Acapulco, Chilpancingo, Ciudad Lázaro Cárdenas, Cuernavaca, Grutas de Cacahuamilpa, Iguala, Puerto Escondido, Taxco, Tehuixtla, Zihuatanejo. This line has first class express service to all points.

Turismos y Autobuses México-Toluca (Western Bus Terminal; Triangulo Flecha; phone: 5-271-1433 or 5-277-2746).

Traveling by Car

DRIVING: Driving certainly is the best way to explore out-of-the-way regions of Mexico. The privacy, comfort, and convenience of touring by car can't be matched by any other form of transport. Trains often whiz much too fast past too many enticing landscapes, tunnel through or pass between hills and mountains rather than climb up and around them for a better view, and frequently deposit passengers in an unappealing part of town. Buses have a greater range, but they still don't permit many spur-of-the-moment stops and starts. A car, on the other hand, provides maximum flexibility, allowing visitors to cover large amounts of territory, to visit major cities and sites, or to move from one small town to the next while exploring the countryside. You go where you want when you want, and can stop along the way as often as you like for a meal, a nap, or a spectacular view.

Mexico's highways and roads are renowned for their scenery. Sudden, unexpected glimpses of tropical flowers, desert plants, pine trees, mountains, and aquamarine waters form the moving backdrop of the road as you drive. The distances between cities and towns usually are reasonable, and a visitor can use a car's flexibility to maximum advantage. When planning your driving route, however, be *very* conservative in estimating driving time — *driving or stopping by the roadside after dark can be very dangerous.* Drivers should be aware of latter-day bandits who have been known to stop, assault, and rob tourists (see "Road Safety and Highway Conditions," below). In DIRECTIONS you will find our choices of the most interesting driving itineraries, as well as approximate distances to help in your calculations.

Before setting out, make certain that everything you need is in order. If possible, discuss your intended trip with someone who has already driven the route to find out about road conditions and available services. If you can't speak to someone personally, try to read about others' experiences. Automobile clubs (see below) can be a good source of driving information, although when requesting brochures and maps, be sure to specify the areas you are planning to visit. (Also see "Roads and Maps," below.) Mexican government tourism offices both in the US and in Mexico also can supply useful information. See *Mexican Consulates and Tourist Offices in the US* in this section for addresses of US offices and the individual city reports in THE CITIES for locations in Mexico.

License – Any valid US driver's license is acceptable in Mexico. (You do not need an International Driving Permit.) Your US license also will be required for renting a car, and in most cases, you will need to present a major credit card. If you are driving across the border from the US, however, remember that a driver's license cannot be used as proof of citizenship. For information on valid proof of citizenship, see *Entry Requirements and Documents,* in this section.

Car Permits – You must have a car permit to drive in Mexico, but getting it is a routine matter at the border. The guards at the border will provide a free permit and a tourist card entitling you to either a specific amount of time in Mexico (30 days to 6 months) or for multiple exits and entries. (A 6-month car permit also may be acquired at one of the Mexican consulates in the US.) It is essential that you show the guards at the border the car's registration and proof of ownership. If you are driving into Mexico in a car rented in the US or in a vehicle belonging to someone else, carry a notarized affidavit stating that you have the right to drive the car in Mexico (in the case of rental firms, the appropriate paperwork will be provided on request). The same applies for a trailer.

Note that it is illegal to sell your car in Mexico. If you wish to leave the country without your car, you can leave it in bond at the airport for a period of no longer than the validity of your tourist card or visa.

Car Insurance – American or Canadian automobile insurance is not valid in Mexico, so you must have Mexican insurance. This can be arranged through major American companies and/or brokers before you go (first ask your own insurer if it handles Mexican insurance) or in towns near the border, where numerous insurance agents can be found. It is best to purchase the most comprehensive policy, to insure that your car is fully covered, and to have it remain in effect for a few days beyond the time you expect to need it. If you don't stay in Mexico for the duration of your policy, you are entitled to a refund.

It is especially important to have a strong policy backed by a reputable Mexican firm — as are those policies available from *Sanborn's Mexican Insurance Service* and other major US insurance companies — because it is common for the police to hold those involved in a car accident until they have established responsibility (and proof of ability to pay damages). US and Canadian visitors have ended up waiting in jail while this proof was being established. An insurance policy is accepted by police as proof of solvency and ability to pay damages, and an adjuster from a good company will act as an ombudsman for a policyholder in the hands of the law. (For more details on car insurance and other forms of travel insurance, see *Insurance,* in this section.)

Maps – Consult road maps. A number of the automobile clubs listed below offer their members (and members of affiliated clubs) free or inexpensive maps. Maps also are available at service stations on both sides of the border.

A company with more than half a century of experience in publishing maps of Mexico City and other areas of Mexico is *Guía Roji,* (31 J. Moran, México, DF 11850; phone: 5-702-0931). For a street guide of Mexico City (very similar to familiar US city street guides), their *Guía Completa de la Ciudad de México Area Metropolitana y Alrededores* is unexcelled. *Guía Roji* also sells road maps of all Mexican states and wall maps of Acapulco, Guadalajara, Mexico City, Monterrey, Puebla, Toluca, and Veracruz. The company's newest publication is a road atlas called *Atlas de Carreteras;* it costs about $2.65 and is extremely useful for the motorist. The street guide and road atlas are both available at sidewalk news kiosks and supermarkets in Mexico City, and from several *Sanborn's Mexican Insurance Service* US offices (2009 S. 10th St., McAllen, TX 78502; phone: 512-686-7011; and 2212 Santa Ursula, Laredo, TX 78040-3122; phone: 512-722-0931).

Another wall map, the *Rand McNally Cosmopolitan Map of Mexico* ($2.95), indicates each Mexican state in a different color. While its size and scale are not practical for touring use, it can be helpful before leaving for Mexico. All major highways are indicated, and there is no problem figuring out what is near what. For use on the road, the *Rand McNally Road Atlas: US, Canada and Mexico* ($7.95 paperback; $11.95 hardcover) is excellent. Both of these books may be found in bookstores or can be ordered directly from *Rand McNally* (150 E. 52nd St., New York, NY 10022; phone: 212-758-7488); call for information on charges for postage and handling.

An up-to-date road map of Mexico, published by the Mexican Ministry of Tourism, is available free from its offices (see *Mexican Consulates and Tourist Offices in the US,* in this section). Perhaps the most detailed series of maps available from the Mexican government are those published by Mexico's *Dirección General de Geografía* (a department similar to the US National Ocean Service). Section maps of Mexico are available in the following types: topographical, geological, soil uses, soil types, potential use, urban, current urban use, urban soil aptitude, urban mosaic, topographical, aeronautical, climatological, and touristical. The selection of maps is so wide-ranging you have to see it to believe it. The Mexico City sales office is at 71 Calle Balderas (phone: 709-2866). Other sales points are in Guadalajara, Mexicali, León, Monterrey, Guanajuato, Chihuahua, Puebla, and San Luis Potosí. Numerous bookstores in other cities also carry the maps. A variety of Mexican maps also are available by writing to the *Servicio Meteorológico Nacional* (192 Av. Observatorio, Tacubaya, México, DF 11860).

A good source for most of the maps listed above, and just about any other kind of map of just about anywhere in the world, including Mexico, is *Map Link* (25 E. Mason St., Suite 201, Santa Barbara, CA 93101; phone: 805-965-4402). They also carry the particularly useful *International Travel Maps (ITM)* series, which covers much of Mexico. If they don't stock a map of the area in which you are interested, they will do their best to get it for you.

Automobile Clubs – To protect yourself in case of on-the-road breakdowns while driving to and through Mexico, you should consider joining a reputable automobile club. Any club should offer three basic services:

1. On-the-road insurance covering accidents, personal injury, arrest and bail bond, and lawyer's fees for defense of contested traffic cases. (For example, *AAA* offers a $100,000 travel-insurance package for auto accidents and personal injury; this coverage includes traveling in Mexico.) Check with your auto club before you go.
2. Around-the-clock (24-hour) emergency breakdown service, including reduced rates on towing to nearest garage in the US. (For instance, *AAA* has a toll-free number for emergency road service: 800-222-4357 throughout the US.) While traveling in Mexico, members may be able to call upon affiliated Mexican clubs for service (see below), otherwise they will be reimbursed at a later date for expenses incurred.
3. Vacation planning and routing services, including advice and maps. The *AAA* and most of the other clubs listed below offer these services for itineraries in both the US and Mexico.

These are the basic types of services; specific policies and programs vary widely from club to club. Before joining any one, get information and brochures from several national clubs and compare benefits and costs to find the services that best match your travel needs.

The largest automobile club in North America is the *American Automobile Association (AAA)* with over 31 million members in chapters throughout the US and Canada. *AAA* affiliates throughout the US provide a variety of travel services to members, including a travel agency, trip planning, fee-free traveler's checks, and roadside assistance. They will help plan an itinerary, send a map with clear routing directions, and will even make hotel reservations. These services apply to traveling in both the US and Mexico. Although *AAA* members receive maps and other brochures at no charge or at a discount (depending on the publication and branch), non-members also can order from an extensive selection of highway and topographical maps. You can join the *AAA* through local chapters (listed in the telephone book under *AAA*) or contact the national office, 1000 AAA Dr., Heathrow, FL 32746-5063 (phone: 407-444-8544).

Travelers to Mexico should note that although *AAA* will not cross the border to aid in emergency service, they will reimburse members (with a receipt to confirm payment) for road service provided in Mexico. Call your local chapter to determine exactly what type of coverage is available to you before you make your trip.

The *American Automobile Association* also is affiliated with a Mexican automobile association, the *Asociación Mexicana Automovilística (AMA)*. With branches in the metropolitan Mexico City area, Cuernavaca, and Puebla, *AMA*'s main office in Mexico City is at 7 Calle Orizaba, Mexico, DF 06700 (phone: 5-207-5616 or 5-525-5615). The association provides a variety of maps in English at no charge. *AAA* members can call the *AMA* for emergency service while traveling in the vicinity of Mexico City; this service may not apply elsewhere in Mexico.

The *Asociación Nacional Automovilística (ANA)* perhaps the most widely based in Mexico, can be helpful to *AAA* members, as well as members of other automobile associations belonging to the *International Federation of Automobile Associations* (ask if a club is a member before joining). The association also sells a useful road map for about 50¢. The main office is in Mexico City at 140 Calle Miguel E. Schultz, Mexico, DF 06470 (phone: 5-705-0258).

There are several large American automobile clubs that also offer maps and touring information for Mexico, as well as various kinds of protection against breakdown on US roads (a few on Mexican highways as well). Before joining one, however, check that it has reciprocity with Mexican clubs or that it at least offers reimbursement for on-the-road repair expenses in Mexico. Listed below are several of the largest:

Allstate Motor Club: A member of the Sears family, run by Allstate Insurance. Join through any Allstate agency or contact Customer Service, PO Box 3096, Arlington Heights, IL 60006 (phone: 800-323-6282).

Amoco Motor Club: Join through any Amoco dealer or contact the national office, PO Box 9043, Des Moines, IA 50369-0001 (phone: 800-334-3300).

Exxon Travel Club: Provides a wide range of services including trip routing, maps and atlases, reimbursement for towing, discounts on car rentals and accommodations, and a variety of insurance packages. Ask for information from the national office, PO Box 3633, Houston, TX 77253 (phone: 713-680-5723).

Ford Auto Club: Contact the Membership Services Division, PO Box 224688, Dallas, TX 75222 (phone: 800-348-5220).

Mexico West Travel Club: PO Box 1646, Bonita CA 92022 (phone: 619-585-3033).

Montgomery Ward Auto Club: Open to (but not limited to) people with a *Montgomery Ward* charge account. Join through the credit manager at any *Montgomery Ward* store, or contact the national office, 200 N. Martingale Rd., Schaumburg, IL 60173 (phone: 708-605-3000 in Illinois; 800-621-5151 elsewhere in the US).

Motor Club of America: National office, 484 Central Ave., Newark, NJ 07107 (phone: 201-733-1234 or 800-227-6459).

United States Auto Club Motoring Division: Ask for information from the national office, PO Box 660460, Dallas, TX 75266-0460 (phone: 214-541-4246 or 800-348-5058).

Preparing Your Car – Before heading off on the road, always make certain that your car is in the best possible mechanical condition. Have it inspected very carefully, paying special attention to brakes and tires, and be sure that your spare tire is in good shape. If you have room, a full-size spare is preferable to the small spares provided with many new cars.

Remember that your tires will be getting the kind of workout they probably don't get at home. Mexican roads are notorious for potholes during the rainy season, and while cobblestone streets are picturesque, there is nothing picturesque about what they do to tires. In Mexico, it can be a long way between tire repair shops when you're on the open highway. For on-the-road repairs, therefore, it's a good idea to take along a tire repair kit including a tire pump, a pressure gauge, and a couple of aerosol inflators. If driving on either one of the small lightweight spares or a tire you've repaired, *drive slowly and carefully.* When you reach the next large town, have any temporary tire repairs attended to by a mechanic — ask the desk clerk at your hotel or the local tourist authority to refer you to a reputable service station that provides this service. (Also see "Mechanics and Car Care," below.)

Other suggestions include the following:

1. In addition to the spare tire, bring the following equipment: an extra set of keys; a flashlight with an extra set of batteries; a white towel (useful for signaling for help, as well as for wiping the car windows); jack and wrench; jumper cables; flares and/or reflectors; a container of water or coolant for the radiator; extra motor oil and transmission fluid; and a steel container of gasoline (see "Gasoline," below). Also make sure you have a couple of extra fan belts, distributor points, a fuel pump replacement kit, condensers, and spark plugs. It is essential that you carry a basic selection of spare parts, as service stations in the smaller Mexican towns are not likely to stock them. It's not uncommon to spend as much as a week waiting for parts to arrive from a foreign-parts distributor in a distant metropolitan area.

2. Make the first days of your trip the shortest, and plan to drive no more than 300 to 400 miles per day (about 6 to 7 hours of driving time) — if that much. When traveling with children, plan on 200 to 250 miles a day (4 to 5 hours) at the most. Stop to rest when you are tired.

3. Before you leave, check the current weather and road conditions. The *AAA* can provide this information for the US. For information on both US and Mexican weather and roads conditions, you can call *American Express Travel Related Services'* 900-WEATHER. CB radios may be used in Mexico, where two channels are designated for tourism: 9 (emergencies) and 11 (aid and rescue); all others are for intercommunication.

Breakdowns – If you break down on the road, immediate emergency procedure is to get the car off the road. Some roads have narrower shoulders than you're used to, so make sure you get all the way off, even if you have to hang off the shoulder a bit. The universal signal for help is raising the hood, and tying a white handkerchief or rag to the door handle or radio antenna. Don't leave the car unattended, and don't try any major repairs on the road.

The major Mexican highways are patrolled by the Mexican Secretary of Tourism's **Green Angel** fleet of emergency service trucks. They are manned by English-speaking crews and carry equipment for a modest range of on-the-road repairs. (Don't expect miracles, just an adequate, average repair job for a common emergency.) The Green Angels (called *Angeles Verdes*) know how to change tires, give first aid, and take care of minor problems. They also carry gasoline and oil and provide information on road conditions. Except for parts and fuel, the service is free. That's why they're called "angels" — they literally cruise the main highways looking for motorists to rescue. Sooner or later, if you break down on a main road, one of the Green Angels will get to you, as crews patrol every day (from 8 AM to 8 PM). Supplementing their efforts are the following hotline emergency numbers for tourists needing guidance or help: 915-250-4817 (24 hours), 915-250-0123, 915-250-8601, 915-250-8419, or 915-250-8221. (When calling within the Mexico City area, do *not* dial 915.)

Mechanics and Car Care – For any but the most simple malfunctions, you probably will need a mechanic. You'll find that Mexican mechanics are for the most part comparable in skills to those at home and the cost of a repair often is considerably less than in the US. (The most common problem is that they may not stock the necessary parts for foreign-made cars.) As mentioned above, tourist authorites and hotel personnel, as well as Green Angels and *Pemex* filling stations (see "Gasoline," below) can help you find honest, reliable mechanics.

It helps to have some idea of what might be wrong with your car and to know something about standard maintenance. An excellent series of booklets on car care, mileage, and mechanical problems and their sources is published by *Shell Oil Company* in its *Answer Book* series, available from some *Shell* dealers or directly from the company at 3484 W. 11th St., Houston, TX 77008 (phone: 713-241-6161).

Other suggestions for breakdowns and on-the-road car care include the following:

1. Have some idea of what needs to be done. Oil needs to be changed approximately every 3,000 miles; a tune-up is needed every 12,000 miles (every 24,000 miles for transistorized ignition cars); spark plugs need to be changed every 25,000 miles; fan and air conditioning belts every 5,000 miles. Learn to recognize warning signals that indicate potentially serious malfunctions.
2. If your car needs to be towed, agree in advance on the price and on the station to which it will be towed. If possible, get an estimate on major repairs before agreeing to any work. Even better, ask for the preliminary estimate in writing.
3. Be aware of dishonest practices. Some mechanics will cheat you. While checking oil they can "short-stick" the dipper so the full amount of oil in your engine doesn't register; so be sure to watch while oil is being checked. When buying gas, make sure the attendant resets the pump, moving the counter back to zero. The best way to avoid being cheated is to know your car's oil and gas consumption.

Gasoline – *Pemex* (an acronym for *Petróleos Mexicanos*) is the only brand of gasoline and oil sold in Mexico since the petroleum industry was nationalized. Gasoline is sold in liters (approximately 3.7 liters equal 1 gallon) and two grades of gas are available: Nova (or regular) from the blue pump, and higher-priced Extra (or premium) from the silver pump (though Extra often is difficult if not impossible to find). Both grades come in leaded and unleaded varieties; ask the gas station attendant for "*con plomo*"if you want *leaded* gas or "*sin plomo*" for *unleaded.*

Gas prices everywhere rise and fall, depending on the world supply of oil. US visitors generally will find gasoline to be slightly less expensive than they are accustomed to paying in the US. Be prepared to pay for gas in cash (American oil company credit cards are not accepted by *Pemex*). And, if you request the attendants to check your oil and water or coolant in your radiator, or wipe your windshield, be sure to tip them between 500 and 1,000 pesos. We recommend tipping gas station attendants even if you are only filling up. They usually are hard working and underpaid, and you'd be amazed at how many pesos it takes to make up the differences between their wages and those of gas station attendants in the US.

Particularly when traveling in rural areas, fill up whenever you come to a gas station. It may be a long way to the next station. You *don't* want to get stranded on an isolated stretch — so it is a good idea to bring along an extra few gallons in a steel container. (Plastic containers tend to break when the car is bouncing over rocky roads. This, in turn, creates the danger of fire should the gasoline ignite from a static electricity spark. Plastic containers also tend to burst at high altitudes.) Also note that in rural areas, gasoline may be diluted with water or kerosene. So if the car stops after you have just filled up, it could be due to impure gasoline.

The prudent traveler should plan an itinerary and make as many reservations as possible in advance in order not to waste gas figuring out where to go, stay, or eat. Drive early in the day, when there is less traffic. Then leave your car at the hotel and use local transportation whenever possible after you arrive at your destination.

Make sure that your tires are properly inflated and your engine is tuned correctly to cut gas consumption. Although it may be equally dangerous to drive at a speed much below the posted limit as it is to drive above it — particularly on major highways where the speed limit is 110 kph (68 mph) — at 88 kph (55 mph) a car gets 25% better mileage than at 112 kph (70 mph). The number of miles per liter or gallon also is increased by driving smoothly. Accelerate gently, anticipate stops, get into high gear quickly, and maintain a steady speed.

Road Safety and Highway Conditions – Travelers who wish to cover the country-side from end to end can count on an increasingly good system of highways to help them make time as the Mexican highway system continues to grow rapidly. Most roads generally are well surfaced, but there are few of the four-lane superhighways found in the US, except around the larger cities. Those choosing to explore only one region will find that the secondary and even lesser roads also are kept in reasonably good condition, although farther off the beaten track, particularly during the rainy season, this may not be the case. Either way, there is plenty to see en route.

Be particularly careful about the following:

1. Be aware of recent road incidents involving assaults and robberies of tourists. These are increasingly frequent and usually befall ill-advised travelers who have underestimated the distances between towns — or the time it takes to cover these distances. Stopping to spend the night in the car or on some deserted stretch of beachfront is the ultimate no-no. Be realistic in calculating the amount of ground you can cover, and make plans on the side of conservatism when you have any doubts. (For a complete description of the major Mexican driving itineraries, see DIRECTIONS.)

2. Try not to drive after dark. The Green Angels (see above) only patrol the roads until 8 PM, and being stranded on a lonely stretch is dangerous at any time — after dark it is downright foolhardy. In addition, the adjacent fields normally are not fenced and you never know when a cow, deer, or other animals will decide to see what's on the other side of the road. (Even in the daytime, cows may stand in the middle of the road and stare you down.) Bicycles and other vehicles without lights are other common nighttime road hazards, as are pedestrians.

3. You occasionally will encounter one-lane bridges on two-lane highways. The driver who flashes his or her lights first is supposed to be the one permitted to cross the bridge first. This is standard procedure both day and night. Make sure you slow down as you approach bridges, and go slowly as you cross. And watch out for *topes* (concrete or steel domes, about 3 inches high, set in the street). They look innocent, but running over one at about 20 miles an hour can give you a severe jolt.

3. Obey speed limits and traffic regulations, especially when driving through towns and cities. As there are very few bypass roads, you will have to slow down as you pass through populated centers. The speed limit on the best highways is 110 kilometers per hour (approximately 68 miles per hour). Speeds always are given in kilometers (a kilometer is equal to approximately .62 miles) and major highway signs use international symbols that are quite easy to understand.

If you do get a traffic ticket, follow police instructions and don't argue. You can report any unfair treatment later, but don't expect any quick resolutions of problems that arise far from major cities. (For information on what to do in the event of a serious accident, see *Medical and Legal Aid and Consular Services,* in this section.)

RENTING A CAR: This is ideal for people who don't have enough time to drive from home but who want to explore the countryside. Most visitors who want to drive in

Mexico rent a car through a travel agent or international rental firm before leaving home or from a local company once they are in Mexico. Another possibility, also arranged before departure, is to rent the car as part of a larger package of travel services.

Renting a car in Mexico is not inexpensive, but it is possible to economize by determining your own needs and then shopping around among the car rental companies until you find the best deal. As you comparison-shop, keep in mind that rates vary considerably, not only from city to city, but also from location to location within the same city. For instance, it might be less expensive to rent a car in the center of a city rather than at the airport. Ask about special rates or promotional deals, such as weekend or weekly rates, bonus coupons for airline tickets, or 24-hour rates that include gas and unlimited mileage.

Rental car companies operating in Mexico can be divided into three basic categories: large national or international companies; regional companies; and local companies. Because of aggressive local competition, the cost of renting a car can be less expensive once a traveler arrives in in Mexico, compared to the prices quoted in advance from the US. Local companies usually are less expensive than the international giants (although travelers who do not speak fluent Spanish may have to rule out smaller local companies that rent primarily to natives).

Given this situation, it's tempting to wait until arriving to scout out the lowest-priced rental from the company located the farthest from the airport high-rent district and offering no pick-up services. But if your arrival coincides with a holiday or peak travel period, you may be disappointed to find that even the most expensive car in town was spoken for months ago. Whenever possible, it is best to reserve in advance, anywhere from a few days in slack periods to a month or more during the busier seasons.

If you can read and speak Spanish, and decide to wait until after you arrive and let your fingers do the walking through the local phone books, you'll often find a suprising number of small companies listed — particularly in the larger metropolitan areas. Often the best guide to sorting through the options is the local tourist board, which usually can provide recommendations and a list of reputable firms.

Even if you do rent in advance, be aware that many Mexican car rental experiences bear little resemblance to the normally efficient process found almost everywhere in the US. It is not at all uncommon, for example, to arrive at an airport rental counter — even that of a giant international company — and have your confirmed reservation greeted with a shrug: No cars available. (If you use a car rental firm's toll-free number to reserve a vehicle, it *may* make a difference if you arrive with written confirmation of your reservations in hand — leave enough time for the rental company to mail it to you before you leave home. Also be sure you get a receipt for any deposit.) It is similarly common that the class and make of car you ordered will be notable by its absence. More shrugs. And even when you do get a car, and even when it is precisely the model you want, chances are that its physical appearance and mechanical condition will be substantially inferior to similar rental cars you are used to driving in the US. Caveat renter.

Travel agents can arrange rentals for clients, but it is just as easy to call and rent a car yourself. Listed below are several national Mexican rental companies, as well as the major international rental companies represented in Mexico that have information and reservations numbers that can be dialed toll-free from the US (note that these numbers are all for the companies' international divisions that handle Mexican rentals):

Alpri Rent a Car (phone: 5-564-2543 or 5-564-5076 for the main office in Mexico City). Rents cars in Cancún, Chihuahua, Cozumel, Mexicali, Mexico City, Monterrey, Reynosa, Tijuana, Villahermosa.

Auto Europe (phone: 800-223-5555). Has over 50 locations throughout Mexico in major cities and resort areas.

Avis Rent-A-Car: (phone: 800-331-1212). Rents cars in most Mexican cities.

Budget Rent-A-Car: (phone: 800-472-3325). Car rentals offered at over 75 locations throughout Mexico.

Dollar Rent-A-Car: (phone: 800-800-4000). Rentals offered at over 25 locations throughout Mexico.

Economovil Rent: (phone: 5-604-5960 or 5-604-2118 for the main office in Mexico City). Rents cars in Acapulco, Cancún, Los Cabos, and Mexico City.

Hertz: (phone: 800-654-3001). Rents cars at over 60 locations throughout Mexico.

National Car Rental: (phone: 800-CAR-EUROPE). Rents cars at over 100 locations throughout Mexico.

Rentacar Monroy: (phone: 5-564-7182 for the main office in Mexico City). Rents cars in Cuernavaca, Mexico City, and Morelos. (As we went to press, they were adding an office in Bahía de Huatulco, Oaxaca.)

Thrifty Rent-A-Car: (phone: 800-367-2277). Rents cars in Cancún, Cozumel, and Mérida.

For further information on local car rental companies, see the *Sources and Resources* sections of the individual city chapters in THE CITIES.

Requirements – Whether you decide to rent a car in advance from a large international rental company with Mexican branches or wait to rent from a local company, you should know that renting a car is rarely as simple as signing on the dotted line and roaring off into the night. If you are renting for personal use, you must have a valid driver's license and will have to convince the renting agency that (1) you are personally credit-worthy; and (2) you will bring the car back at the stated time. This will be easy if you have a major credit card; most rental companies accept credit cards in lieu of a cash deposit, as well as for payment of your final bill. If you prefer to pay in cash, leave your credit card imprint as a "deposit," then pay your bill in cash when you return the car.

If you are planning to rent a car once in Mexico, *Avis, Budget, Hertz,* and other US rental companies usually *will* rent to travelers paying in cash and leaving either a credit card imprint or a substantial amount of cash as a deposit. This is not necessarily standard policy, however, as some of the other international chains, and a number of regional and local Mexican companies will *not* rent to an individual who doesn't have a valid credit card. In this case, you may have to call around to find a company that accepts cash.

Also keep in mind that although the minimum age to drive a car in Mexico is 18 years, the minimum age to rent a car is set by the rental company. Many firms have a minimum age requirement of 21 years, some raise that to 23 or 25 years, and for some models of cars it rises to 30 years. The upper age limit at many companies is between 69 and 75; others have no upper age limit or may make drivers above a certain age subject to special conditions.

Costs – Finding the most economical car rental will require some telephone shopping on your part. As a *general* rule, expect to hear lower prices quoted by the smaller, strictly local companies than by the well-known international names, with those of the national Mexican companies falling somewhere between the two.

Comparison shopping always is advisable, however, because the company that has the least expensive rentals in one city may not have the least expensive cars in another, and even the international giants offer discount plans whose conditions are easy for most travelers to fulfill. For instance, *Budget* and *National* offer discounts of anywhere from 10% to 30% off their usual rates (according to the size of the car and the duration of the rental), provided that the car is reserved a certain number of days before departure (usually 7 to 14 days, but it can be less), is rented for a minimum period (5 days or, more often, a week), is paid for at the time of booking, and in most cases, is returned to the same location that supplied it or to another in the same area. Similar discount plans include *Hertz*'s Leisure Rates and *Avis*'s Supervalue Rates.

If driving short distances for only a day or two, the best deal may be a per-day, per-mile (or per-kilometer) rate: You pay a flat fee for each day you keep the car, plus a per-mile (or per-kilometer) charge. An increasingly common alternative is to be granted a certain number of free miles or kilometers each day and then be charged on a per-mile or per-kilometer basis over that number.

A better alternative for Mexican touring is a flat per-day rate with unlimited free mileage; this certainly is the most economical rate if you plan to drive over 100 miles. (Note: When renting a car in Mexico, the term "mileage" may refer to either miles or kilometers.) Make sure that the low, flat daily rate that catches your eye, however, is indeed a per-day rate: Often the lowest price advertised by a company turns out to be available only with a minimum 3-day rental — fine if you want the car that long, but not the bargain it appears if you really intend to use it no more than 24 hours for in-city driving. Flat weekly rates also are available, as are some flat monthly rates that represent a further savings over the daily rate.

Another factor influencing cost is the type of car you rent. Rentals generally are based on a tiered price system, with different sizes of cars — variations of budget, economy, regular, and luxury — often listed as A (the smallest and least expensive) through F, G, or H, and sometimes even higher. Charges may increase by only a few dollars a day through several classes of subcompact and compact cars — where most of the competition is — then increase by great leaps through the remaining classes of full-size and luxury cars and passenger vans. The larger the car, the more it costs to rent and the more gas it consumes, but for some people the greater comfort and extra luggage space of a larger car (in which bags and sporting gear can be safely locked out of sight) may make it worth the additional expense. In some areas, models with standard stick-shifts are more common and those with automatic transmissions are, therefore, more expensive.

Electing to pay for collision damage waiver (CDW) protection will add considerably to the cost of renting a car. You may be responsible for the *full value* of the vehicle being rented, but you can dispense with the possible obligation by buying the offered waiver at a cost of around $11 to $13 a day for rentals in Mexico. Before making any decisions about optional collision damage waivers, check with your own insurance agent and determine whether your personal automobile insurance policy covers rented vehicles; if it does, you probably won't need to pay for the waiver. Be aware, too, that increasing numbers of credit cards automatically provide CDW coverage if the car rental is charged to the appropriate credit card. However, the specific terms of such coverage differ sharply among individual credit card companies, so check with the credit card company for information on the nature and amount of coverage provided. Business travelers also should be aware that, at the time of this writing, *American Express* had withdrawn its automatic CDW coverage from some corporate *Green* card accounts — watch for similar cutbacks by other credit card companies.

When inquiring about CDW coverage and costs, you should be aware that a number of the major international car rental companies now automatically are including the cost of this waiver in their quoted prices. This does not mean that they are absorbing this cost and you are receiving free coverage — total rental prices have increased to include the former CDW charge. The disadvantage of this inclusion is that you probably will not have the option to refuse this coverage, and will end up paying the added charge — even if you already are adequately covered by your own insurance policy or through a credit card company.

Additional costs to be added to the price tag include drop-off charges or one-way service fees. The lowest price quoted by any given company may apply only to a car that is returned to the same location from which it was rented. A slightly higher rate may be charged if the car is to be returned to a different location (even within the same city).

Also, don't forget to factor in the price of gas. Rental cars usually are delivered with a full tank of gas. (this is not always the case, however, so check the gas gauge when picking up the car, and have the amount of gas noted on your rental agreement if the tank is not full). Remember to fill the tank before you return the car or you will have to pay to have the rental company refill it, and gasoline at the car rental company's pump always is much more expensive than at a service station. This policy may vary for smaller local and regional companies; ask when picking up the vehicle. Before you leave the lot, also check to be sure the rental car has a spare tire and jack in the trunk.

Fly/Drive – Airlines, charter companies, car rental companies, and tour operators have been offering fly/drive packages for years, and even though the basic components of the package have changed somewhat — return airfare, a car waiting at the airport, and perhaps a night's lodging all for one inclusive price used to be the rule — the idea remains the same. You rent a car *here* for use *there* by booking it along with other arrangements for the trip. These days, the very minimum arrangement possible is the result of a tie-in between a car rental company and an airline, which entitles customers to a rental car for less than the company's usual rates, provided they show proof of having booked a flight on that airline. For information on available packages, check with the airline or your travel agent.

■ **Note:** When reserving and picking up your rental car, always ask for any available maps and information on the areas in which you will be driving. For instance, *National Car Rental* offers a full-color brochure outlining 3 scenic driving routes in Mexico as part of its Self-Drive Tours program. For further information and a copy of the brochure, contact *National Car Rental,* Corporate Communications Department, PO Box 35187, 7700 France Ave. S., Minneapolis, MN 55435. (phone: 800-CAR-EUROPE)

Package Tours

If the mere thought of buying a package for travel to and around Mexico conjures up visions of a trip spent marching in lockstep with a horde of frazzled fellow travelers, remember that packages have come a long way. For one thing, not all packages necessarily are escorted tours, and the one you buy does not have to include any organized touring at all — nor will it necessarily include traveling companions. If it does, however, you'll find that people of all sorts — many just like yourself — are taking advantage of packages today because they are economical and convenient, save you an immense amount of planning time, and exist in such variety that it's virtually impossible not to find one that fits at least the majority of your travel preferences. Given the high cost of travel these days, packages have emerged as a particularly wise buy.

In essence, a package is just an amalgam of travel services that can be purchased in a single transaction. A package (tour or otherwise) to and through Mexico may include any or all of the following: round-trip transportation from your home to Mexico, local transportation (and/or car rentals), accommodations, some or all meals, sightseeing, entertainment, transfers to and from the hotel at each destination, taxes, tips, escort service, and a variety of incidental features that might be offered as options at additional cost. In other words, a package can be any combination of travel elements, from a fully escorted tour offered at an all-inclusive price to a simple fly/drive booking allowing you to move about totally on your own. Its principal advantage is that it saves money: The cost of the combined arrangements invariably is well below the price of all of the same elements if bought separately, and particularly if transportation is provided by charter or discount flight, the whole package could cost less than just a round-trip economy airline ticket on a regularly scheduled flight. A package provides more than economy and convenience: It releases the traveler from having to make individual arrangements for each separate element of a trip.

Tour programs generally can be divided into two categories — "escorted" (or locally hosted) and "independent." An escorted tour means that a guide will accompany the group from the beginning of the tour through to the return flight; a locally hosted tour means that the group will be met upon arrival at each location by a different local host. On independent tours, there generally is a choice of hotels, meal plans, and sightseeing trips, as well as a variety of special excursions. The independent plan is for travelers who do not want a totally set itinerary, but who do prefer confirmed hotel reservations. Whether choosing an escorted or independent tour, always bring along complete contact information for your tour operator in case a problem arises, although tour operators often have local affiliates who can give additional assistance or make other arrangements on the spot.

To determine whether a package — or, more specifically, *which* package — fits your travel plans, start by evaluating your interests and needs, deciding how much and what you want to spend, see, and do. Gather whatever package tour information is available for your schedule. Be sure that you take the time to read the brochure *carefully* to determine precisely what is included. Keep in mind that travel brochures are written to entice you into signing up for a package tour. Often the language is deceptive and devious. For example, a brochure may quote the lowest prices for a package tour based on facilities that are unavailable during the off-season, undesirable at any season, or just plain nonexistent. Information such as "breakfast included" or "plus tax" (which can add up) should be taken into account. Note, too, that prices quoted in brochures almost always are based on double occupancy: The rate listed is for each of two people sharing a double room, and if you travel alone the supplement for single accommodations can raise the price considerably (see *Hints for Single Travelers,* in this section).

In this age of erratic airfares, the brochure most often will *not* include the price of an airline ticket in the price of the package, though sample fares from various gateway cities usually will be listed separately, to be added to the price of the ground arrangements. Before figuring your actual cost, check the latest fares with the airlines, because the samples invariably are out of date by the time you read them. If the brochure gives more than one category of sample fares per gateway city — such as an individual tour-basing fare, a group fare, an excursion, or other discount ticket — your travel agent or airline tour desk will be able to tell you which one applies to the package you choose, depending on when you travel, how far in advance you book, and other factors. (An individual tour-basing fare is a fare computed as part of a package that includes land arrangements, thereby entitling a carrier to reduce the air portion almost to the absolute minimum. Though it always represents a savings over full-fare coach or economy, lately the individual tour-basing fare has not been as inexpensive as the excursion and other discount fares that also are available to individuals. The group fare usually is the least expensive fare, and it is the tour operator, not you, who makes up the group.) When the brochure does include round-trip transportation in the package price, don't forget to add the cost of round-trip transportation from your home to the departure city to come up with the total cost of the package.

Finally, read the general information regarding terms and conditions and the responsibility clause (usually in fine print at the end of the descriptive literature) to determine the precise elements for which the tour operator is — and is not — liable. Here the tour operator frequently expresses the right to change services or schedules as long as equivalent arrangements are offered. This clause also absolves the operator of responsibility for circumstances beyond human control, such as avalanches, earthquakes, or floods, or injury to you or your property. While reading, ask the following questions:

1. Does the tour include airfare or other transportation, sightseeing, meals, transfers, taxes, baggage handling, tips, or any other services? Do you want all these services?
2. If the brochure indicates that "some meals" are included, does this mean a welcoming and farewell dinner, two breakfasts, or every evening meal?
3. What classes of hotels are offered? If you will be traveling alone, what is the single supplement?
4. Does the tour itinerary or price vary according to the season?
5. Are the prices guaranteed; that is, if costs increase between the time you book and the time you depart, can surcharges unilaterally be added?
6. Do you get a full refund if you cancel? If not, be sure to obtain cancellation insurance.
7. Can the operator cancel if too few people join? At what point?

One of the consumer's biggest problems is finding enough information to judge the reliability of a tour packager, since individual travelers seldom have direct contact with the firm putting the package together. Usually, a retail travel agent is interposed between customer and tour operator, and much depends on his or her candor and cooperation. So ask a number of questions about the tour you are considering. For example:

- Has the travel agent ever used a package provided by this tour operator?
- How long has the tour operator been in business? Check the Better Business Bureau in the area where the tour operator is based to see if any complaints have been filed against it.
- Is the tour operator a member of the *United States Tour Operators Association* (*USTOA;* 211 E. 51st St., Suite 12B, New York, NY 10022; phone: 212-944-5727)? The *USTOA* will provide a list of its members upon request; it also offers a useful brochure, *How to Select a Package Tour.*
- How many and which companies are involved in the package?
- If air travel is by charter flight, is there an escrow account in which deposits will be held; if so, what is the name of the bank?

This last question is very important. US law requires that tour operators place every charter passenger's deposit and subsequent payment in a proper escrow account. Money paid into such an account cannot legally be used except to pay for the costs of a particular package or as a refund if the trip is canceled. To ensure the safe handling of your money, make your check payable to the escrow account — by law, the name of the depository bank must appear in the operator-participant contract, and usually is found in that mass of minuscule type on the back of the brochure. Write the details of the charter, including the destination and dates, on the face of the check; on the back, print "For Deposit Only." Your travel agent may prefer that you make your check out to the agency, saying that it will then pay the tour operator the fee minus commission. But it is perfectly legal to write your check as we suggest, and if your agent objects too strongly (the agent should have sufficient faith in the tour operator to trust him to send the proper commission), consider taking your business elsewhere. If you don't make your check out to the escrow account, you lose the protection of that escrow should the trip be canceled or the tour operator or travel agent fail. Furthermore, recent bankruptcies in the travel industry have served to point out that even the protection of escrow may not be enough to safeguard your investment. Increasingly, insurance is becoming a necessity (see *Insurance,* in this section), and payment by credit card has become popular since it offers some additional safeguards if the tour operator defaults.

■ **A word of advice:** Purchasers of vacation packages who feel they're not getting their money's worth are more likely to get a refund if they complain in writing to the operator — and bail out of the whole package immediately. Alert the tour operator or resort manager to the fact that you are dissatisfied, that you will be leaving for home as soon as can be arranged, and that you expect a refund. They may have forms to fill out detailing your complaint; otherwise, state your case in a letter. Even if the availability of transportation home detains you, your dated, written complaint should help in procuring a refund from the operator.

SAMPLE PACKAGES TO MEXICO: As discussed above, a typical package tour in Mexico might include transportation to and from Mexico, accommodations for the duration of a stay, a sightseeing tour of the area, and several meals. Although some packages just cover arrangements at a specific hotel, others offer more extensive arrangements and may be built around activities such as fishing or hunting, or special interests such as history, native culture, archaeology, or nature exploration. Simple fly/drive packages including only air transportation and a rental car also are offered to Mexico. (For information on independent car rental options see *Traveling by Car,* in this section, as well as the individual city reports in THE CITIES.)

It is possible to join a Mexican package tour from Mexico City; there is such a wide variety of these offered to different parts of the country for various durations that it usually is easy to find one that fits your schedule. Although this won't save you anything in plane fare to Mexico, it will give you the benefit of native advice and knowledge. To explore the possibility, visit any of the Mexican travel agents listed in *How to Use a Travel Agent.*

Following is a list of many of the major US operators who provide escorted or independent tours to Mexico. Some offer AP ("American Plan" — including all meals), others MAP ("Modified American Plan" — breakfast and one main meal included daily), a few include only breakfast, and others leave you to make your own arrangements for meals. Most tour operators offer several departure dates, depending on the length of the tour and areas visited. As indicated, some operators are wholesalers only, and will deal only with a travel agent.

American Express Travel Related Services (300 Pinnacle Way, Norcross, GA 30071; phone: 800-327-7737 or 404-368-5100). Offers a full range of escorted regional and around-Mexico tours, as well as "free-lance" programs for independent travelers. The tour operator is a wholesaler, so use a travel agent.

Far Horizons (16 Fern Lane, San Anselmo, CA 94960; phone: 415-457-4575). Special-interest archaeological and cultural trips to the Chiapas highlands and the Yucatán Peninsula.

Fishing International (4010 Montecito Ave., PO Box 2132, Santa Rosa, CA 95405; phone: 800-950-4242). Specializes in fishing and hunting packages. Offers fishing in Baja California, Cancún/Cozumel, Matzatlán, and along the Yucatán Peninsula, as well as bird shooting inland. Also books customized packages.

Fling Vacations (999 Postal Rd., Allentown, PA 18103; phone: 800-523-9624). Offers several 7-day packages to Cancún. The tour operator is a wholesaler, so use a travel agent.

Four Winds Travel (PO Box 693, Old Greenwich, CT 06870; phone: 203-698-

0944). Packages 7- to 14-day tours of Copper Canyon and the Yucatán Peninsula.

Frontiers International (PO Box 959, 100 Logan Rd., Wexford, PA 15090; phone: 412-935-1577 in Pennsylvania; 800-245-1950 elsewhere in the US). These experts in top-drawer fishing and hunting trips arrange packages all along Mexico's coasts.

High Country Passage (943 Emerson St., Palo Alto, CA 94301; phone: 415-328-3636). Arranges group tours with an educational bent, studying such wonders as the Maya ruins.

Liberty Travel (contact the central office for the nearest location: 69 Spring St., Ramsey, NJ 07446; phone: 201-934-3500). Offers 3- to 21-day packages throughout Mexico, which include airfare and accommodations.

Marnella Tours (33 Walt Whitman Rd., Huntington Station, NY 11746; phone: 516-271-6969 in New York; 800-645-6999 elsewhere in the US). Offers a wide range of tour programs throughout Mexico.

Maupintour (PO Box 807, Lawrence, KS 66047; phone: 913-843-1211 in Kansas; 800-255-4266 elsewhere in the US). Offers a deluxe, escorted package including a tour of Copper Canyon.

Mountain Travel (6420 Fairmount Ave., El Cerrito, CA 94530; phone: 415-527-8100 in the Bay Area; 800-227-2384 elsewhere in the US and Canada). This adventure specialist offers tours throughout Mexico, with a focus on travel into remote areas (on foot whenever possible), mountaineering, and natural history.

MTA International (1717 N. Highland Ave., Los Angeles, CA 90028; phone: 213-462-6444 in California; 800-876-6824 elsewhere in the US). Offers packages throughout Mexico, particularly in resort areas. The tour operator is a wholesaler, so use a travel agent.

Nature Expeditions International (PO Box 11496, Eugene, OR 97440; phone: 800-869-0639 or 503-484-6529). Their programs in the Gulf of California and along the Yucatán Peninsula emphasize wildlife, natural history, and cultural experiences.

Olson-Travelworld (100 N. Sepulveda Blvd., Suite 1010, El Segundo, CA 90245; phone: 800-421-5785 or 213-605-0711 in California; 800-421-2255 elsewhere in the US). Specializes in deluxe, all-inclusive, and fully escorted tours throughout Mexico. The tour operator is a wholesaler, so use a travel agent.

Questers Tours & Travel (257 Park Ave. S., New York, NY 10010; phone: 800-468-8668 or 212-673-3120). Offers tours of central Mexico and the Yucatán Peninsula.

Trans National Travel (2 Charlesgate W., Boston, MA 02215; phone: 800-262-0123). Offers 3- to 7-day packages the resort areas of Cancún and Cozumel.

Travcoa (PO Box 2630, Newport Beach, CA 92658; phone: 714-476-2800 or 800-992-2004 in California; 800-992-2003 elsewhere in the US). Their deluxe tours in Mexico include destinations such as Copper Canyon, Oaxaca, and the Yucatán Peninsula. The tour operator is a wholesaler, so use a travel agent.

Travel Impressions (465 Smith St., Farmingdale, NY 11735; phone: 800-284-0077 in the Southeast, Midwest, and Western US; 800-284-0044 or 800-284-0055 in the Northeast and elsewhere in the US). Offers a wide range of packages throughout Mexico. The tour operator is a wholesaler, so use a travel agent.

Traveluxe (11 Broadway, Rm. 1168, New York, NY 10004; phone: 212-269-1409 or 800-627-7780 in the continental US). Offers independent packages to Mexico's resort areas.

Camping and RVs, Hiking and Biking

 **CAMPING:** Those interested in trying to escape the hectic pace of metropolitan Mexican life will find camping a gratifying way to enjoy the countryside. The balmy climate and splendid scenery found throughout Mexico can make for delightful adventures. With some planning beforehand, you can live well under the stars and enjoy the often spellbinding environment.

If you can speak some Spanish, or if you're lucky and the camp director speaks some English, you may discover that he or she is a great source of information about the region, and may even be able to arrange tours or recommend the best restaurants, shops, beaches, or attractions in the immediate area. Campgrounds also provide the atmosphere and opportunity to meet other travelers and exchange useful information.

Where to Camp – Formerly, campgrounds and trailer parks were found primarily in northwestern Mexico and the upper Baja California peninsula. Now there are camping facilities along every major highway in Mexico, from the northern border to the Yucatán Peninsula. Some national parks (see *Camping and Hiking in Mexico's National Parks,* DIVERSIONS) have areas set aside for camping, but these do not have hookups for recreational vehicles.

Note: Before pitching your tent, you should know where designated campgrounds are available and where camping is considered *safe* for visitors. *Never* camp along the ocean, on an empty beach, or in any other isolated area not designated for camping.

Although outdoor camping is not as organized in Mexico as it is in the US, there is plenty of information on camping facilities. Maps, brochures, and other information useful for campers are distributed by the Mexican government tourism offices (see *Mexican Consulates and Tourism Offices in the US,* in this section, for locations). A variety of useful publications also are available from American and Mexican automobile clubs (see *Traveling by Car*) and other special-interest associations (see below).

Whenever possible, it's best to consult one of the following camping guides, which list sites across the country:

> *Directorio de Paradores y Campamentos,* available in Mexico City at sporting goods stores for 4,500 pesos (under $2 at press time) or by mail from Grupo Editorial Publicaciones (779 Av. Legaria, Suite 301, Col. Irrigación, México, DF 01150). A very complete, accurate guide to campsites and spas, with maps showing the location of each.
>
> *KOA Handbook and Directory for Campers,* $3 from *Kampgrounds of America* (*KOA;* PO Box 30558, Billings, MT 59114; phone: 406-248-7444).
>
> *The People's Guide to Mexico* by Carl Franz and Lorena Havens ($17.95; John Muir Publications, PO Box 613, Santa Fe, NM 87504-0613; phone: 505-982-4078). Information on everything from finding a campsite to understanding Mexican customs.
>
> *The People's Guide to RV Camping in Mexico* by Carl Franz ($13.95; John Muir Publications; address above). Includes a complete directory of Mexican RV campgrounds and a wealth of other useful information for RV and tent campers alike.
>
> *Rand McNally RV and Park Campground Directory* ($9.95; Randy McNally, 150 E. 52nd St., New York, NY 10022; phone: 212-758-7488). Includes listings identifying facilities at over 350 campgrounds in Mexico.

Campgrounds with adequate recreational-vehicle hookups, which generally (but not always) means they are large enough to offer a good choice of tent sites as well, are located in the following Mexican states and areas:

Aguascalientes: Aguascalientes.

Baja California: Ensenada, Guerrero Negro, La Paz, Mexicali, San José del Cabo.

Baja California Norte: Colonet, Playa Catamar, Santa Inés, San Quintín, Santo Tomás, Tijuana.

Baja California Sur: Bahía Concepción, Cabo San Lucas, Ciudad Constitución, Loreto, Los Barriles, Mulegé, San Felipe, Rosarito.

Campeche: Campeche.

Chiapas: Palenque, San Cristóbal las Casas, Tuxtla Gutiérrez.

Chihuahua: Chihuahua, Ciudad Camargo, Nuevo Casas Grandes.

Coahuila: Saltillo, Torreón.

Colima: Colima, Manzanillo.

Durango: Durango.

Guanajuato: Celaya, Guanajuato, Irapuato, Salamanca, San Miguel de Allende.

Guerrero: Acapulco, Ixtapa-Zihuatanejo.

Hildalgo: Pachuca, Taxquillo.

Jalisco: Ajijic, Chamela, Chapala, Guadalajara (this is a popular camping area), Puerto Vallarta, Tenacatita, Villa Corona.

Michoacán: La Piedad, Los Azufres, Pátzcuaro, Uruapan.

Morelos: Cuernavaca, Tepoztlán.

Nayarit: La Peñita de Jaltemba, Los de Marcos, Montemorelos, Rincón de Guayabitos, San Blas, Tepic.

Nuevo León: Linares, Monterrey.

Oaxaca: Oaxaca, Puerto Escondido.

Puebla: Cholula, Puebla.

Querétaro: Querétaro, Tequisquiapan.

Quintana Roo: Chetumal, Playa del Carmen, Puerto Juárez, Puerto Morelos, Punta Bete, Punta Pumul, Tulum.

Sonora: Santa Ana, Sonoita.

San Luis Potosí: Ciudad Mante, Ciudad Valles, Matehuala, San Luis Potosí, Tamazunchale.

Sinaloa: Culiacán, Los Mochis, Mazatlán

Sonora: Alamos, Bahía Kino, Guaymas, Hermosillo, Navojoa, Puerto Peñasco, San Carlos.

México: Atizapán, Cuautitlán, Teotihuacán, Temascalzingo, Valle de Bravo.

Tamaulipas: Ciudad Victoria, Lake Vicente Guerrero, Lake Padilla, Tampico.

Tlaxcala: Apizaco, Atlihuetzia, Santa Cruz.

Veracruz: Agua Dulce, La Antigua, Orizaba, Tuxpan, Veracruz.

Yucatán: Chichén Itzá, Mérida, Uxmal.

Zacatecas: Morelos, Zacatecas.

For specific information, on these and other campgrounds, see *Directorio de Paradores y Campamentos,* and other publications listed above.

Although it's best to bring your own, you should be able to find camping equipment for sale in Mexican sporting goods stores. The above-mentioned guides, park authorities, and the local tourist offices all are good sources for information on reliable dealers.

■**Note:** Even if you are told that the campground where you are staying provides purified water, to be safe you should use it only for washing (don't even brush your teeth with it). Use only bottled, purified, or boiled water for drinking. To purify tap water, either use a water purification kit (available at most camping supply stores) or bring the water to a full, *rolling,* boil over a campstove. It is inadvisable to use water from streams, rivers, or lakes — even purified. (For further information on health cautions in Mexico, see *Staying Healthy,* in this section.)

RECREATIONAL VEHICLES: The term *recreational vehicles* — RVs — is applied to all manner of camping vehicles, whether towed or self-propelled. RVs will appeal most to the kind of person who prefers the flexibilty in accommodation — there are countless campgrounds throughout Mexico which provide RV hookups — and enjoys camping with a little extra comfort.

The level of comfort in an RV is limited only by the amount of money you choose to spend. They range from simple fold-down campers, which provide no more than shelter, to luxurious, fully equipped homes on wheels, requiring electrical hookups at night to run the TV set, kitchen appliances, and air conditioning. An RV undoubtedly saves a traveler a great deal of money on accommodations; in-camp cooking saves money on food as well. However, it is important to remember that buying or renting an RV is a major expense; charges for sewage disposal, propane gas, and electricity used at campground hookups will add to the basic campsite fees; and either driving a motorized model or towing a camper will reduce your gas mileage considerably.

The basic types of RVs are:

Towable RVs: Hitched to cars or trucks and pulled, at their simplest, these are **fold-down campers**, tents on wheels that unfold into sleeping spaces. More elaborate are **travel trailers** (anywhere from 10 to 30 feet long) and **fifth-wheel models** (built to be towed by a pickup truck). The trailer should be equipped with brakes unless you expect that the combined weight of the trailer and its load will never exceed 3,000 pounds.

Motorized RVs: These come in three basic styles:

1. The **motor home** is a recreational vehicle built on or as part of a motorized vehicle chassis. It usually has kitchen, dining, bathroom, and sleeping facilities, all accessible from the driver's area. Other common features include electricity, heat, air conditioning, and water and propane-gas tanks.

2. **Van conversions** are vans manufactured by auto makers and modified for recreation by customization specialists. Among the custom features are side windows, carpeting, paneling, and sofas.

3. Also in this category are **truck-campers** — camping units that are loaded onto the bed of a pickup. The more elaborate models include kitchens and other facilities. Metal or fiberglass camper shells, which enclose the bed of the truck are less expensive, but leave the interior furnishing up to you.

Gas Consumption – Although an RV undoubtedly saves the traveler a great deal of money on food and accommodations, the major expense in operating any RV is its high gas consumption. It is most expensive to tow a large trailer camper, which decreases auto mileage by 50%. More economical, because it's smaller, is the fold-down tow camper, which will reduce normal car mileage by only about 10% to 15%. Self-propelled RVs have no better mileage records. A truck-camper gets about 20% less mileage than the same truck without a camper, and an average Class A motor home gets only 7 to 12 miles per gallon of gas. Only in a converted van or a pickup truck with a lightweight cover (with minimal interior furnishings) will you find that your gas consumption does not change too drastically.

To reduce gas consumption, travel lightly (for every 100 pounds of weight, you use 1% more gas). Carry only the water you need on the road. Put everything inside your RV to reduce wind resistance, and thereby save on gas. (For more information on gasoline economy, see *Traveling by Car,* in this section.)

Renting – RVs are a poor choice for people who do not like to drive. They also are not for people who want to leave housekeeping chores behind when they set off on vacation. They are sure to sour a person who cannot stand to do any maintenance or simple handyman chores, nor are they for people who want lots of privacy. The best way to introduce yourself to traveling by RV is to rent one.

RV rental rates vary depending on the size and complexity of the RV and the number of days rented and often include customer pick-up and drop-off services at the airport. Some dealers will apply rental fees to the eventual price of purchase. A common source of vans and towable campers (as well as the larger types of RVs) are the car rental companies listed in *Traveling By Car,* in this section. The tourist board offices also may be able to provide recommendations on RV rental sources, as well as where they are permitted.

Useful information on RVs is available from the following sources:

Living on Wheels by Richard A. Wolters. Provides useful information on how to choose and operate a recreational vehicle. As it's currently out of print, check your library.

Recreational Vehicle Industry Association (RVIA; Dept. RK, PO Box 2999, Reston, VA 22090). Issues a useful complimentary package of information on RVs, including a catalogue of RV sources and consumer information. Write to the association for these and other publiciations.

Recreational Vehicle Rental Association (RVRA; 3251 Old Lee Hwy., Suite 500, Fairfax, VA 22030; phone: 800-336-0355 or 703-591-7130). This RV dealers group publishes an annual rental directory, *Who's Who in RV Rentals* ($7.50).

TL Enterprises (29901 Agoura Rd., Agoura, CA 91301; phone: 818-991-4980) publishes two monthly magazines for RV enthusiasts: *Motorhome* and *Trailer Life.* A year's subscription to either costs $22; a combined subscription to both costs $44. Members of the *TL Enterprises' Good Sam Club* can subscribe for half price and also receive discounts on a variety of other RV services; membership costs $19 per year.

Trailblazer (1000 124th Ave. NE, Bellevue, WA 98005; phone: 206-455-8585). A recreational-vehicle and motor-home magazine. A year's subscription costs $24.

Organized Camping Trips – A package camping tour in Mexico is a good way to have your cake and eat it, too. The problems of advance planning and day-to-day organizing are left to someone else, yet you still reap the benefits that shoestring travel affords and can enjoy the insights of experienced guides and the company of other campers. Be aware, however, that these packages usually are geared to the young, with ages 18 to 35 as common limits. Transfer from place to place often is by bus or van (as on other sightseeing tours); overnights are in tents, and meal arrangements vary. Often there is a food kitty that covers meals in restaurants or in the camps; sometimes there is a chef, and sometimes the cooking is done by the participants themselves. When considering a package tour to the wilderness, be sure to find out if equipment is included and what individual participants are required to bring.

A number of associations and general and specialty tour operators offer organized camping tours. Among these organizations are the following:

Baja Expeditions (2625 Garnet Ave., San Diego, CA 92109; phone: 800-843-6967). Offers 9-day camping/rafting trips in Baja.

Caiman Expeditions (3449 E. River Rd., Tucson, AZ 85718; phone: 800-365-ADVE or 602-299-1047). Packages 10-day camping/rafting trips on the Yucatán Peninsula.

Dvorak's Kayak and Rafting Expeditions (17921-B US Highway 285, Nathrop, CO 81236; phone: 800-824-3795 or 719-539-6851). Offers several 8- to 14-day camping/rafting trips in the Chiapas highlands.

Force 10 Expeditions (PO Box 30506, Flagstaff, AZ 86003; phone: 800-922-1491). Takes the adventurous on a 23-day camping trip through the Yucatán Peninsula, and also visits Belize and Guatemala.

National Outdoor Leadership School (PO Box AA, Lander, WY 82520-0579; phone: 307-332-6973). Offers a 21-day Baja camping/sea kayaking trip. Their more intensive 78-day tour includes camping, kayaking, climbing, and hiking.

Trek America (PO Box 1138, Gardena, CA 90249; phone: 800-221-0596). Their camping trips throughout Mexico range from 14 to 46 days.

■**Note:** The *Specialty Travel Index* (305 San Anselmo Ave., Suite 217, San Anselmo, CA 94960; phone: 415-459-4900 in California; 800-442-4942 elsewhere in the US) is a directory to special-interest travel and an invaluable resource. Listings include tour operators specializing in camping, as well as myriad other interests that combine nicely with a camping trip, such as biking, motorcycling, horseback riding, canoeing, kayaking, river rafting, and scuba diving. It costs $5 per copy, $8 for a year's subscription of two issues.

HIKING: If you would rather eliminate all the gear and planning and take to the outdoors unencumbered, park the car and go for a day's hike. It can break up long journeys by car and, more than just giving riders a chance to stretch their legs, is a great way to get to know the country.

Although there are any number of out-of-the-way areas in Mexico where you can hike, the national parks in the central area of the country have some marked hiking trails. These are recommended because they are safer than striking out for the wilds on your own, unless you happen to know the area or the terrain particularly well. For information on major national parks in Mexico, see *Camping and Hiking in Mexico's National Parks,* in DIVERSIONS.

For those who are hiking on their own, without benefit of a guide or group, a map of the trail is a must. (Also, *never* head out for a jaunt in the Mexican wilderness unless you first check on the safety conditions in the area.) Most areas of Mexico are covered by maps issued by the Mexican government, as well as the *International Travel Maps (ITM)* map series. These and other maps of use to hikers (and other outdoor adventurers) are available from *Map Link* (25 E. Mason St., Suite 201, Santa Barbara, CA 93101; phone: 805-965-4402), which carries a wide range of detailed topographical maps and just about any other type of map (of just about anywhere in the world). Their comprehensive guide *The World Map Directory* ($29.95) includes a wealth of sources for travelers afoot, and if they don't stock a map of the area in which you are interested (or the type of map best suited to your outdoor exploration), they will do their best to get it for you.

Organized Hiking Trips – Those who prefer to travel as part of an organized group should contact the following:

American Wilderness Experience (PO Box 1486, Boulder, CO 80306; phone: 800-444-0099). Their Baja Expeditions division offers 9- to 11-day hiking excursions among a variety of adventure packages to Mexico.

American Youth Hostels (PO Box 37613, Washington, DC 20013-7613; phone: 202-783-6161). Often sponsors foreign hiking trips, including tours of Mexico. Contact them for information on current or forthcoming offerings.

Mountain Travel (6420 Fairmont Ave., El Cerrito, CA 94530 (phone: 800-227-2384 or 415-527-8100). This adventure package specialist offers a variety of trips in Mexico, ranging from easy walks that can be undertaken by anyone in good health to those that require basic or advanced mountaineering experience. Recent itineraries included a 12-day camping/hiking/climbing trip in central Mexico.

Nature Expeditions International (PO Box 11496, Eugene, OR 97440; phone: 503-484-6529). Coordinates cultural and historical study tours throughout Mexico which involve hiking the sites.

Outback Expeditions (Box 16343, Seattle, WA 98116; phone: 206-932-7012). Offers kayaking and/or land tour adventure packages that include hiking expeditions.

Outdoor Woman's School–CALL OF THE WILD (2519 Cedar St., Berkeley, CA 94708; phone: 415-849-9292). Offers a wilderness Fit-Trip in Mexico for women only, which includes fitness-related activites, including hiking, and a special diet.

Sierra Club (Outing Dept., 730 Polk St., San Francisco, CA 94109; phone: 415-776-2211). Offers a selection of trips each year. Their Mexican itineraries usually include both walking tours and trips which combine hiking and kayaking.

Wilderness: Alaska/Mexico (1231 Sundance Loop, Fairbanks, AK 99709; phone: 907-457-8907 or 907-452-1821). Has a variety of hiking and kayaking trips throughout Mexico.

In addition to the wilderness specialists listed above, if you are interested in braving the more mountainous regions of Mexico, you also may want to contact the *American Alpine Institute* (1212 24th St., Bellingham, WA 98225; phone: 206-671-1505), a specialist in mountain climbing expeditions. The institute offers 3- to 4-week organized climbing trips in Baja California Sur and south central Mexico. For further information on climbing the highest peaks, see *Mountains and Mountain Climbing* in DIVERSIONS.

An alternative to dealing directly with the above companies is to contact *All Adventure Travel,* a specialist in hiking and biking trips worldwide. This company, which acts as a representative for numerous special tour packagers offering such outdoor adventures, can provide a wealth of detailed information about each packager and programs offered. They also will help you design and arrange all aspects of a personalized itinerary. This company operates much like a travel agency, collecting commissions from the packagers. Therefore, there is no additional charge for these services. For information, contact *All Adventure Travel,* PO Box 4307, Boulder, CO 80306 (phone: 800-537-4025 or 303-939-8885.)

BIKING: For young and/or fit travelers, a bicycle offers a marvelous tool for exploring. Biking does have its drawbacks: Little baggage can be carried, travel is slow, and cyclists are exposed to the elements — in Mexico, the combined effects of wind and sun can be enervating. And unless you are in exceptionally good shape and are an avid bike rider at home, you probably will find the rugged geography and long distances between settlements a deterrent to biking across Mexico. Nevertheless, a lot of people in Mexico do use bicycles for transportation, and it is not uncommon to join a local cyclist pedaling away, calmly, on desert and mountain highways.

Good maps infinitely improve a biking trip, especially those that provide detailed and clear road references. Good sources of maps, recommendations on popular scenic routes, and other information useful to cyclists are the tourist authorities (for addresses, see *Mexican Consulates and Tourist Offices in the US,* in this section) and cycling associations listed below. *Map Link* (see "Hiking," above) also is a good source for maps suitable for cyclists planning Mexican routes. For general biking information, consult *The Complete Book of Bicycling* by Eugene A. Sloane (Simon & Schuster; $24.95) and *Anybody's Bike Book* by Tom Cuthberson (Ten Speed Press; $7.95).

■ **Note:** When biking, wear bright clothes and use lights or wear reflective material to increase your visibility at dusk. Mexican bike riders often do not use lights at night, and they are one of the reasons why driving after dark in Mexico is so hazardous. Visiting bicyclists be forewarned: even if you do have reflectors or lights, stop before dark. Above all, even though many cyclists don't, always wear a helmet.

Choosing, Renting, and Buying a Bike – If you can read Spanish, consult local phone directories for bicycle shops; the local tourist authorities also may be able to point you to sources of bicycle rentals. Except in metropolitan areas, you are not likely to find as wide a selection as in the US. The available models *may* include basic (one-gear), 10-speed, and the increasingly popular mountain bikes. As there is no guarantee, however, of the availability or condition of rentals, serious cyclists may prefer to bring their own bikes.

Airlines generally allow bicycles to be checked as baggage and require that the pedals be removed, handlebars be turned sideways, and the bike be in a shipping carton (which some airlines provide, subject to availability — call ahead to make sure). If buying a shipping carton from a bicycle shop, check the airline's specifications and also ask about storing the carton at the destination airport so that you can use it again for the return flight. Although some airlines charge only a nominal fee, if the traveler already has checked two pieces of baggage there may be an additional excess baggage charge of $70 to $80 for the bicycle. Since regulations vary from carrier to carrier, be sure to call well before departure to find out your airline's specific regulations. If you plan to transport your bike on flights within Mexico, it is particularly important to check in advance as the smaller planes used may have limited baggage facilities. As with other baggage, make sure that the bike is thoroughly labeled with your name, a business address and phone number, and the correct airport destination code.

Organized Biking Trips – A number of organizations offer bike tours in Mexico. Linking up with a bike tour is more expensive than traveling alone, but with experienced leaders an organized tour often becomes an educational, as well as a very social, experience. In addition, traveling with a group is *safer*.

One of the attractions of a bike tour is that shipment of equipment — the bike — is handled by the organizers, and the shipping fee is included in the total tour package. Travelers simply deliver the bike to the airport, already disassembled and boxed; shipping cartons can be obtained from most bicycle shops with little difficulty. Bikers not with a tour must make their own arrangements with the airline, and there are no standard procedures for this (see above). Although some tour organizers will rent bikes, most prefer that participants show up with a bike with which they are already familiar. Another attraction of *some* tours is the existence of a "sag wagon" to carry extra luggage, fatigued cyclists, and their bikes, too, when pedaling another mile is impossible.

Tours vary considerably in style and ambience, so request brochures from several operators in order to make the best decision. When contacting groups, be sure to ask about the maximum number of people on the trip, the maximum number of miles to be traveled each day, and the degree of difficulty of the biking; these details should determine which tour you join and can greatly affect your enjoyment of the experience. Planning ahead is essential because trips often fill up 6 months or more in advance.

Among the companies offering biking trips in Mexico are the following:

Arrow to the Sun Bicycle Touring (PO Box 115 Taylorsville, CA 95983; phone: 800-634-0492 or 916-284-6263). Offers a 12-day biking trip in December from Cancún to Mérida. Also offers 10-day biking tours of Baja California year-round.

Backroads Bicycle Touring (1516 5th St., Berkeley, CA 94710-1713; phone: 415-527-1555). Offers a 7-day tour of the Baja region among its numerous biking trips; accommodations tend toward the deluxe, and bicycle rental is available.

Baja Expeditions (2625 Garnet Ave., San Diego, CA 92109; phone: 800-843-6967). Offers 5- and 8-day biking tours of the Baja region.

Outback Expeditions (Box 16343, Seattle, WA 98116; phone: 206-932-7012). Offers several biking tours of Baja California and Manzanillo.

Other useful sources of information on bicyling in Mexico include the following:

American Youth Hostels (PO Box 37613, Washington, DC 20013-7613; phone: 202-783-6161). A number of biking tours are sponsored annually by this nonprofit organization and its local chapters. Membership is open to all ages and departures are geared to various age groups and levels of skill and frequently feature accommodations in hostels — along with hotels for adults and campgrounds for younger participants.

International Bicycle Touring Society (*IBTS;* PO Box 6979, San Diego, CA 92106-0979; phone: 619-226-TOUR). This nonprofit organization regularly sponsors low-cost bicycle tours led by member volunteers. Participants must be over 21. For information, send them $2 plus a self-addressed, stamped envelope.

League of American Wheelmen (6707 Whitestone Rd., Suite 209, Baltimore, MD 21207; phone: 301-944-3399). This organziation publishes *Tourfinder,* a list of organizations that sponsor bicycle tours in the US and abroad. The list is free with membership ($25 individual, $30 family) and can be obtained by nonmembers who send $5. The *League* also can put you in touch with biking groups in your area.

Preparing

Calculating Costs

$ A realistic appraisal of travel expenses is the most crucial bit of planning required before any trip. It also is, unfortunately, one for which it is most difficult to give precise, practical advice.

Although most travelers still have to plan carefully and manage their travel funds prudently, Mexico remains a significant bargain for Americans. Even with the staggering inflation that the country has experienced in recent years (but which stringent economic policies are desperately trying to alleviate) most travel services seem reasonably priced. Mexico always has been one of the most popular destinations for both the first-time and the seasoned traveler, and the competition for American visitors often works to inspire surprisingly affordable travel opportunities.

In Mexico, estimating travel expenses depends on the mode of transportation you choose, the part or parts of the country you plan to visit, how long you will stay, and in some cases, what time of year you plan to travel. In addition to the basics of transportation, hotels, meals, and sightseeing, you have to take into account seasonal price changes that apply on certain air routings and in popular resort areas, as well as the vagaries of currency exchange.

In general, it's usually also a good idea to organize your trip so that you pay for as much of it as you can in Mexico, using pesos purchased from Mexican banks (which, barring interim variations, generally offer a more advantageous rate of exchange than US sources). That means minimizing the amount of advance deposits paid in US greenbacks and deferring as many bills as possible until you arrive in Mexico, although the economies possible through prepaid package tours and other special deals may offset the savings in currency exchange. (For further information on managing money abroad, see *Credit and Currency,* in this section.)

When calculating costs, start with the basics, the major expenses being transportation, accommodations, and food. However, don't forget such extras as local transportation, shopping, and such miscellaneous items as laundry and tips. The reasonable cost of these items usually is a positive suprise to your budget. Ask about special discount passes that provide unlimited or cut-rate travel by the day or the week on regular city or local transportation. Entries in the individual city reports in THE CITIES give helpful information on local transportation options.

Other expenses, such as the cost of local sightseeing tours and other excursions, will vary from city to city. Tourist information offices are plentiful throughout Mexico, and most of the better hotels will have someone at the front desk to provide a rundown on the costs of local tours and full-day excursions in and out of the city. Travel agents or railway booking offices (see *Traveling by Train,* in this section) can provide information on rail tours.

Budget-minded families can take advantage of some of the more economical accommodations options to be found in Mexico (see our discussion of accommodations in *On the Road,* in this section). Campgrounds are particularly inexpensive and they are located throughout the country (see *Camping and RVs, Hiking and Biking*). Picnicking is another excellent way to cut costs, and Mexico abounds with well-groomed parks, beaches, and other idyllic settings. A stop at a local market can provide a feast of regional specialties at a surprisingly economical price compared to the cost of a restaurant lunch. (Do, however, read our warnings about fresh produce in *Staying Healthy*, in this section.)

In planning a travel budget, it also is wise to allow a realistic amount for both entertainment and recreation. Are you planning to spend time sightseeing and visiting local tourist attractions? Do you intend to rent a catamaran or take parasailing lessons? Is daily golf or tennis a part of your plan? Will your children be disappointed if they don't take a tour of the pyramids or see the pandas at Chapultepec Park? Finally, don't forget that if haunting discotheques, nightclubs, or other nightspots is an essential part of your vacation or you feel that one performance at Mexico City's *Ballet Folkórica* may not be enough, allow for the extra cost of nightlife.

If at any point in the planning process it appears impossible to estimate expenses, consider this suggestion: The easiest way to put a ceiling on the price of all these elements is to buy a package tour. A totally planned and escorted tour, with almost all transportation, rooms, meals, sightseeing, local travel, tips, and a dinner show or two included and prepaid, provides a pretty exact total of what the trip will cost beforehand, and the only surprise will be the one you spring on yourself by succumbing to some irresistible, expensive souvenir.

■ **Note:** The combination of rapid peso devaluation and Mexico's inflation rate has led the government to authorize increases in hotel rates of as much as 35% from time to time. Between the time you originally make your hotel reservations and your arrival, the price in US dollars may vary substantially from the price originally quoted. To avoid avoid paying more than you expected, it's wise to confirm rates by writing directly to hotels or by calling their representatives in the US.

Planning a Trip

123 Travelers fall into two categories: those who make lists and those who do not. Some people prefer to plot the course of their trip to the finest detail, with contingency plans and alternatives at the ready. For others, the joy of a voyage is its spontaneity; exhaustive planning only lessens the thrill of anticipation and the sense of freedom.

However, for most travelers, any week-plus trip to Mexico can be too expensive for an "I'll take my chances" type of attitude. Even perennial gypsies and anarchistic wanderers have to take into account the time-consuming logistics of getting around, and even with minimal baggage, they need to think about packing. Hence at least some planning is crucial.

This is not to suggest that you work out your itinerary in minute detail before you go, but it's still wise to decide certain basics at the very start: where to go, what to do, and how much to spend. These decisions require a certain amount of consideration. So before rigorously planning specific details, you might want to establish your general travel objectives:

1. How much time will you have for the entire trip, and how much of it are you willing to spend getting where you're going?
2. What interests and/or activities do you want to pursue while on vacation? Do you want to visit one, a few, or several different places?
3. At what time of year do you want to go?

4. What kind of geography or climate would you prefer?
5. Do you want peace and privacy or lots of activity and company?
6. How much money can you afford to spend for the entire vacation?

There is an abundance of travel information on Mexico. You can seek the assistance of travel agents, turn to travel clubs such as *AAA* and other motoring organizations, or use general travel sources such as guidebooks, brochures, and maps. Mexican tourist offices in the US and Mexico have brochures and extensive material on all parts of Mexico, and there's a 24-hour information hotline (phone: 5-250-0123, -0493, -0151, or -0589 in Mexico City). The US Department of State's brochure *Travel to Mexico* is another source of useful information. It can be obtained free from the Washington Passport Agency, 1425 K St. NW, Washington, DC 20524 (phone: 202-647-0518).

You now can make almost all of your own travel arrangements if you have time to follow through with hotels, airlines, tour operators, and so on. But you'll probably save considerable time and energy if you have a travel agent make arrangements for you. The agent also should be able to advise you of alternate arrangements of which you may not be aware. Only rarely will a travel agent's services cost a traveler any money, and they may even save you some (see *How to Use a Travel Agent,* below).

Pay particular attention to the dates when off-season rates go into effect. In major resort areas, accommodations may cost less during the off-season (and the weather often is perfectly acceptable at this time). Off-season rates frequently are lower for car rentals and other facilities, too. In general, it is a good idea to beware of holiday weeks, as rates at hotels generally are higher during these periods and rooms normally are heavily booked.

Make plans early. In the high season, hotel reservations are required months in advance for popular destinations such as Acapulco, Mazatlán, Puerto Vallarta, resorts in Baja Sur, and along Mexico's Caribbean coast. If you are flying at peak times and want to benefit from the savings of discount fares or charter programs, purchase tickets as far ahead as possible. (Charter flights to certain popular destinations may be completely sold out months in advance.) Most Mexican hotels require deposits before they will guarantee reservations, and this most often is the case during peak travel periods. (Be sure to request a receipt for any deposit or use a credit card.) Travel during *Easter Week,* the *Christmas/New Year* period, and local festival and national holiday times also require reservations well in advance in Mexico.

Before your departure, find out what the weather will be like at your destination. Consult *When to Go,* in this section, for information on climatic variations, a chart of average temperatures, and some examples of holidays celebrated throughout the country. See *How to Pack,* also in this section, for some suggestions on how to decide what clothes to take. This information, details regarding special regional events that may occur during your stay, and essential information on local transportation and other services and resources, also may be found in the individual city reports of THE CITIES.

Make a list of any valuable items you are carrying with you, including credit card numbers and the serial numbers of your traveler's checks. Put copies in your purse or pocket and leave other copies at home. Put a label with your name and home address on the inside of your luggage for identification in case of loss. Put your name and business address — *never your home address* — on a label on the outside of your luggage. (Those who run businesses from home should use the office address of a friend or relative.)

Review your travel documents. If you are traveling by air, check to see that your ticket has been filled in correctly. The left side of the ticket should have a list of each stop you will make (even if you are only stopping to change planes), beginning with your departure point. Be sure that the list is correct, and count the number of copies to see that you have one for each plane you will take. If you have confirmed reservations, be sure that the column marked "status" says "OK" beside each flight. Have in hand vouchers or proof of payment for any reservation for which you've paid in advance; this includes hotels, transfers to and from the airport, sightseeing tours, car rentals, and tickets to special events.

Although policies vary from carrier to carrier, it's still smart to reconfirm your flight 48 to 72 hours before departure, both going and returning. Reconfirmation is recommended for all international flights; however, it is a *must* for point-to-point flights within Mexico. If you will be driving in Mexico, bring your driver's license, car registration, and any other necessary documentation — such as proof of insurance.

Before traveling to Mexico, you should consider learning some basic Spanish. Although you can get by in Mexico without speaking Spanish — particularly if you stick to the major resort areas and other popular tourist destinations — your trip will be much more rewarding and enjoyable (and, in some instances, safer) if you can communicate with the people who live in the areas you will be visiting. Mexicans will not make you feel silly or stupid if you don't pronounce words properly — in fact they will openly appreciate your efforts if you do try to converse.

Most adult education programs and community colleges offer courses in Spanish. Berlitz, among others, has a series of teach-yourself language courses on records or audiocassette tapes, which are available for $14.95 (plus postage and handling) from Macmillan Publishing Co. (100 Front St., Riverside, NJ 08075; phone: 800-257-5755). For information on pronunciation and a list of common travel terms, see *Useful Words and Phrases,* in this section; an introduction to a number of native drinks and dishes that you may encounter can be found in *Food and Drink,* PERSPECTIVES.

Finally, you always should bear in mind that despite the most careful plans, things do not always occur on schedule — especially in Mexico, where *ahora* ("now") means anytime between today and tomorrow, and *ahorita* ("right now") means anytime within the next few hours. If you maintain a flexible attitude and try to accept minor disruptions as less than cataclysmic, you will enjoy yourself a lot more.

How to Use a Travel Agent

 A reliable travel agent remains the best source of service and information for planning a trip, whether you have a specific itinerary and require an agent only to make reservations or you need extensive help in sorting through the maze of airfares, tour offerings, hotel packages, and the scores of other arrangements that may be involved in a trip to Mexico.

Know what you want from a travel agent so that you can evaluate what you are getting. It is perfectly reasonable to expect your agent to be a thoroughly knowledgeable travel specialist, with information about your destination and, even more crucial, a command of current airfares, ground arrangements, and other wrinkles in the travel scene.

Most travel agents work through computer reservations systems (CRS). These are used to assess the availability and cost of flights, hotels, and car rental firms, and through them they can book reservations. Despite reports of "computer bias," in which a computer may favor one airline over another, the CRS should provide agents with the entire spectrum of flights available to a given destination, as well as the complete range of fares, in considerably less time than it takes to telephone the airlines individually — and at no extra charge to the client.

Make the most intelligent use of a travel agent's time and expertise; understand the economics of the industry. As a client, traditionally you pay nothing for the agent's services; with few exceptions, it's all free, from hotel bookings to advice on package tours. Any money the travel agent makes on the time spent arranging your itinerary — booking hotels, resorts, or flights, or suggesting activities — comes from commissions paid by the suppliers of these services — the airlines, hotels, and so on. These commissions generally run from 10% to 15% of the total cost of the service, although suppliers often reward agencies that sell their services in volume with an increased commission, called an override. In most instances, you'll find that travel agents make their time and experience available to you at no charge, and you do not pay more for an airline ticket, package tour, or other product bought from a travel agent than you would for the same product bought directly from the supplier.

Exceptions to the general rule of free service by a travel agency are the agencies that practice net pricing. In essence, such agencies return their commissions and overrides to their customers and make their income by charging a flat fee per transaction instead (thus adding a charge after a reduction for the commission has been made). Net fares and fees are a growing practice, though hardly widespread.

Even a conventional travel agent sometimes may charge a fee for special services. These chargeable items may include long-distance telephone or cable costs incurred in making a booking, for reserving a room in a place that does not pay a commission (such as a small, out-of-the way hotel), or for special attention such as planning a highly personalized itinerary. A fee also may be assessed in instances of deeply discounted airfares.

Choose a travel agent with the same care with which you would choose a doctor or lawyer. You will be spending a good deal of money on the basis of the agent's judgment, so you have a right to expect that judgment to be mature, informed, and interested. At the moment, unfortunately, there aren't many standards within the travel agent industry to help you gauge competence, and the quality of individual agents varies enormously.

At present, only nine states have registration, licensing, or some other form of travel agent–related legislation on their books. Rhode Island licenses travel agents; Florida, Hawaii, Iowa, and Ohio register them; and California, Illinois, Oregon, and Washington have laws governing the sale of transportation or related services. While state licensing of agents cannot absolutely guarantee competence, it can at least ensure that an agent has met some minimum requirements.

Perhaps the best-prepared agents are those who have completed the CTC Travel Management program offered by the *Institute of Certified Travel Agents* and carry the initials CTC (Certified Travel Counselor) after their names. This indicates a relatively high level of expertise. For a free list of CTCs in your area, send a self-addressed, stamped, #10 envelope to *ICTA*, 148 Linden St., Box 82-56, Wellesley, MA 02181 (phone: 617-237-0280 in Massachusetts; 800-542-4282 elsewhere in the US).

An agent's membership in the *American Society of Travel Agents (ASTA)* can be a useful guideline in making a selection. But keep in mind that *ASTA* is an industry organization, requiring only that its members be licensed in those states where required; be accredited to represent the suppliers whose products they sell, including airline and cruise tickets; and adhere to its Principles of Professional Conduct and Ethics code. *ASTA* does not guarantee the competence, ethics, or financial soundness of its members, but it does offer some recourse if you feel you have been dealt with unfairly. Complaints may be registered with *ASTA* (Consumer Affairs Dept., PO Box 23992, Washington, DC 20026-3992; phone: 703-739-2782). First try to resolve the complaint directly with the supplier. For a list of *ASTA* members in your area, send a self-addressed, stamped, #10 envelope to *ASTA*, Public Relations Dept., at the address above.

There also is the *Association of Retail Travel Agents (ARTA)*, a smaller but highly respected trade organization similar to *ASTA*. Its member agencies and agents similarly agree to abide by a code of ethics, and complaints about a member can be made to

ARTA's Grievance Committee, 1745 Jeff Davis Hwy., Arlington, VA 22202-3402 (phone: 800-969-6069 or 703-553-7777).

Perhaps the best way to find a travel agent is by word of mouth. If the agent (or agency) has done a good job for your friends over a period of time, it probably indicates a certain level of commitment and competence. Always ask not only for the name of the company, but for the name of the specific agent with whom your friends dealt, for it is that individual who will serve you, and quality can vary widely within a single agency. There are some superb travel agents in the business, and they can facilitate vacation or business arrangements.

You may decide to use a travel agent within Mexico to set up tours for the duration or for portions of your stay. Among the leading travel agencies are the following:

American Express Travel Related Services (Main Mexico City office: 635 Patriotismo, Mexico, DF 03710; phone: 5-598-7966). Has three additional Mexico City offices (the most convenient one for tourists is at 234 Reforma, Mexico, DF 06600; phone: 5-533-0380), as well as locations in Acapulco, Cancún, Guadalajara, Ixtapa-Zihuatanejo, Mazatlán, Monterrey, and Puerto Vallarta.

Aviamex Tours de México (Mexico City office: in the *Hotel Fontan*, Paseo de la Reforma and Colón, Mexico, DF 06040; phone: 5-512-9097, 5-512-9239, or 5-512-9032). Also has offices in Acapulco, Cancún, Cozumel, Guadalajara, Mérida, Oaxaca, Puerto Vallarta, and Villahermosa.

Garza Travel (Mexico City office: 69 Marsella, Mexico, DF 06600; phone: 5-533-1168). Also has offices in Cancún and Cozumel.

Turismo Caleta (Mexico City office: 156 Río Lerma, Mexico, DF 06500; phone: 5-207-0217, 5-207-0204, or 5-207-0201). Also has offices in in Acapulco, Cancún, Ixtapa, and Puerto Vallarta.

Viajes Mundomex (Mexico City office: 737 Ciceron, Mexico, DF 11510; phone: 5-202-8199). Also has offices in in Acapulco, Cuernavaca, and Guadalajara.

Viajes Parmac (Mexico City office: 46 Río Duero, Mexico, DF 06500; phone: 5-533-6154 or -6156). Also has offices in Acapulco, Cancún, and Puerto Vallarta.

Wagons-lits Mexicana (Mexico City main phone: 5-518-1180 through -1188). This is the largest travel agency in Mexico, with 14 offices in Mexico City as well as branches in Acapulco, Aguascalientes, Cancún, Chihuahua, Ciudad Juárez, Cuernavaca, Durango, Guadalajara, Hermosillo, León, Mazatlán, Mérida, Monterrey, Morelia, Puebla, Puerto Vallarta, Querétaro, Saltillo, San Luis Potosí, Tijuana, Toluca, Torreón, Tuxtla Gutiérrez, Veracruz, and Villahermosa

Entry Requirements and Documents

Regardless of the transportation you use, you will need a tourist card to enter Mexico. The only exception to this rule is if you intend to visit border towns (those within approximately 12½ miles or 20 km of the Mexican border) and not to travel any farther into Mexico, you can do so without a tourist card for a stay of up to 72 hours.

In order to obtain a tourist card, you must have proof of your US citizenship. This proof may consist of an original or certified copy of a birth certificate, a voter's registration certificate, or a valid passport. A driver's license, credit card, or military papers will not suffice. A naturalized citizen must present at least one of the following documents: naturalization papers, a US passport, or an affidavit of citizenship.

A tourist card can be obtained from a number of sources, including any Mexican

Ministry of Tourism office or Mexican consulate in the US; the Mexican government border offices at any port of entry; and some travel agencies. Regardless of where you obtain the card, when you cross the border you must sign it in the presence of the Mexican immigration official, who also may ask to see proof of your citizenship. For those arriving by plane, the card can be obtained from any airline ticket office and it must be presented along with proof of citizenship when you land in Mexico.

To obtain a tourist card, minors under 18 traveling alone must have a passport and a copy of a letter (indicating permission) signed by both parents or legal guardians. If the minor is traveling with only one parent or guardian, a passport and a letter signed by the other (or proof that this person is the sole legal guardian) is needed.

The tourist card allows you to stay in Mexico for a specified number of days; if you request one for 90 days — the maximum is 6 months — you don't have to stay that long but you are covered for that period of time. If you are entering Mexico by car (or other motorized vehicle) you also can request a tourist card and car permit entitling you to stay in Mexico for up to 6 months. (Car permits are issued at the border after you go through immigration and you will have to provide proof of vehicle registration to be issued the permit.)

During your stay in Mexico, you always should carry your tourist card with you, although you aren't likely to be asked for it after the border crossing. If you happen to lose your card, you should report it immediately to the nearest office of the Secretaría de Gobernación. They should be able to replace it for you.

US citizens will not need any vaccination certificates in order to enter Mexico for a short period of time. There are, however, a number of vaccinations that travelers to Mexico would be well-advised to have before leaving and medicines that should be brought along, particularly if traveling in jungle areas. (See *Staying Healthy,* in this section, for our recommendations and other information on health concerns and precautions.)

PASSPORTS: A valid passport is the best proof of US citizenship to carry when traveling through Mexico. You should carry your passport with you at all times, and if you lose it while abroad, immediately report the loss to the nearest US consulate or embassy (see *Medical and Legal Aid and Consular Services,* in this section, for locations in Mexico). You can get a 3-month temporary passport directly from the consulate, but you must fill out a "loss of passport" form and follow the same application procedure — and pay the same fees — as you did for the original (see below). It's likely to speed things up if you have a record of your passport number and the place and date of its issue (a photocopy of the first page of your passport is perfect). Keep this information separate from your passport — you might want to give it to a traveling companion to hold or put it in the bottom of your suitcase.

US passports are now valid for 10 years from the date of issue (5 years for those under age 18). The expired passport itself is not renewable, but must be turned in along with your application for a new and valid one (you will get it back, voided, when you receive the new one). Normal passports contain 24 pages, but frequent travelers can request a 48-page passport at no extra cost. Every individual, regardless of age, must have his or her own passport. Family passports no longer are issued.

Passports can be renewed by mail with forms obtained at designated locations only if the expired passport was issued no more than 12 years before the date of application for renewal and if it was not issued before the applicant's 16th birthday. The rules regarding teens under 16 and younger applicants vary depending on age and when their previous passport was issued. Those who are eligible to apply by mail must send the completed form with the expired passport, two photos (see description below), and $35 (no execution fee required) to the nearest passport agency office. Delivery can take as little as 2 weeks or as long as 6 weeks during the busiest season — from approximately mid-March to mid-September.

Adults applying for the first time and younger applicants who must apply for a passport in person (as well as those who cannot wait for mail application turnaround) can do so at one of the following places:

1. The State Department has passport agencies in Boston, Chicago, Honolulu, Houston, Los Angeles, Miami, New Orleans, New York City, Philadelphia, San Francisco, Seattle, Stamford, CT, and Washington, DC.
2. A federal or state courthouse.
3. Any of the 1,000 post offices across the country with designated acceptance facilities.

Application blanks are available at all these offices and must be presented with the following:

1. Proof of US citizenship. This can be a previous passport or one in which you were included. If you are applying for your first passport and were born in the United States, an original or certified birth certificate is the required proof. If you were born abroad, a Certificate of Naturalization, a Certificate of Citizenship, a Report of Birth Abroad of a Citizen of the United States, or a Certification of Birth is necessary.
2. Two 2-by-2-inch, front-view photographs in color or black and white, with a light, plain background, taken within the previous 6 months. These must be taken by a photographer rather than a machine.
3. A $42 passport fee ($27 for travelers under 18), which includes a $7 execution fee. *Note:* Your best bet is to bring the exact amount in cash (no change is given), or a separate check or money order for each passport. (Families usually can combine several passport fees on one check or money order.)
4. Proof of identity. Again, this can be a previous passport, a Certificate of Naturalization or of Citizenship, a driver's license, or a government ID card with a physical description or a photograph. Failing any of these, you should be accompanied by a blood relative or a friend of at least 2 years' standing who will testify to your identity. Credit cards or social security cards do not suffice as proof of identity — but note that since 1988, US citizens *must* supply their social security numbers.

As getting a passport — or international visa — through the mail can mean waiting as much as 6 weeks or more, a new mini-industry has cropped up in those cities where there is a US passport office. The yellow pages currently list quite a few organizations willing to wait on line to expedite obtaining a visa or passport renewal; there's even one alternative for those who live nowhere near the cities mentioned above. In the nation's capital there's an organization called the *Washington Passport and Visa Service*. It may be the answer for folks in need of special rapid action, since this organization can get a passport application or renewal turned around in a single day. What's more, their proximity to many foreign embassies and consulates helps to speed the processing of visa applications as well. The fee for a 3- to 5-day turnaround is $30; for next-day service the charge is $50; for same-day service they charge $90. For information, application forms, and other prices, contact *Washington Passport and Visa Service,* 2318 18th St. NW, Washington, DC 20009 (phone: 800-272-7776).

If you need an emergency passport, it also is possible to be issued a passport in a matter of hours by going directly to your nearest passport office (there is no way, however, to avoid waiting in line). Explain the nature of the emergency, usually as serious as a death in the family; a ticket in hand for a flight the following day also will suffice. Should the emergency occur outside of business hours, all is not lost. There's a 24-hour telephone number in Washington, DC (phone: 202-634-3600), that can put you in touch with a State Department duty officer who may be able to expedite your application.

DUTY AND CUSTOMS: As a general rule, the requirements for bringing the majority of items *into Mexico* is that they must be in quantities small enough not to imply commercial import.

If you are accustomed to certain American brands of bourbon or whiskey (although imported brands are increasingly available in Mexico, they are very costly), you are allowed to bring 3 liters of liquor into Mexico duty-free — any amount over this will be taxed. And if you prefer American cigarettes, be advised that the limit is 1 carton (20 packs). Each person also may bring in one still and one video camera, plus 12 rolls of film and 3 video cartridge tapes. For further information on Mexican customs regulations, contact the Mexican Ministry of Tourism offices or Mexican consulates in the US (see *Sources and Resources,* in this section, for addresses).

If you are bringing along a computer, camera, or other electronic equipment for your own use that you will be taking back to the US, you should register it with the US Customs Service to avoid being asked to pay duty both entering and returning from Mexico. (Also see *Customs and Returning to the US,* in this section.) For information on this procedure, as well as for a variety of informative pamphlets on US Customs regulations, contact the local office of the US Customs Service or the central office, PO Box 7407, Washington, DC 20044 (phone: 202-566-8195).

■**One rule to follow:** When passing through customs, it is illegal not to declare dutiable items; penalties range from stiff fines and seizure of the goods to prison terms. So don't try to sneak anything through — it just isn't worth it.

Insurance

It is unfortunate that most decisions to buy travel insurance are impulsive and usually made without any real consideration of the traveler's existing policies. Therefore, the first person with whom you should discuss travel insurance is your own insurance broker, not a travel agent or the clerk behind the airport insurance counter. You may discover that the insurance you already carry — homeowner's policies and/or accident, health, and life insurance — protects you adequately while you travel and that your real needs are in the more mundane areas of excess value insurance for baggage or trip cancellation insurance.

TYPES OF INSURANCE: To make insurance decisions intelligently, however, you first should understand the basic categories of travel insurance and what they cover. Then you can decide what you should have in the broader context of your personal insurance needs, and you can choose the most economical way of getting the desired protection: through riders on existing policies; with onetime short-term policies; through a special program put together for the frequent traveler; through coverage that's part of a travel club's benefits; or with a combination policy sold by insurance companies through brokers, automobile clubs, tour operators, and travel agents.

There are seven basic categories of travel insurance:

1. Baggage and personal effects insurance
2. Personal accident and sickness insurance
3. Trip cancellation and interruption insurance
4. Default and/or bankruptcy insurance
5. Flight insurance (to cover injury or death)
6. Automobile insurance (for driving your own or a rented car)
7. Combination policies

Baggage and Personal Effects Insurance – Ask your insurance agent if baggage and personal effects are included in your current homeowner's policy, or if you will need a special floater to cover you for the duration of a trip. The object is to protect your bags and their contents in case of damage or theft anytime during your travels, not just while you're in flight and covered by the airline's policy. Furthermore, only limited protection is provided by the airline. Baggage liability varies from carrier to carrier, but generally speaking, on domestic flights luggage usually is insured to $1,250 — that's per passenger, not per bag. For most international flights, including domestic portions of international flights, the airline's liability limit is approximately $9.07 per pound or $20 per kilo (which comes to about $360 per 40-pound suitcase) for checked baggage and up to $400 per passenger for unchecked baggage. These limits should be specified on your airline ticket, but to be awarded any amount, you'll have to provide an itemized list of lost property, and if you're including new and/or expensive items, be prepared for a request that you back up your claim with sales receipts or other proof of purchase.

If you are carrying goods worth more than the maximum protection offered by the airline, bus, or train company, consider excess value insurance. Additional coverage is available from airlines at an average, currently, of $1 to $2 per $100's worth of coverage, up to a maximum of $5,000. This insurance can be purchased at the airline counter when you check in, though you should arrive early to fill out the necessary forms and to avoid holding up other passengers.

Major credit card companies also provide coverage for lost or delayed baggage — and this coverage often also is over and above what the airline will pay. The basic coverage usually is automatic for all cardholders who use the credit card to purchase tickets, but to qualify for additional coverage, cardholders generally must enroll.

American Express: Provides $500 coverage for checked baggage; $1,250 for carry-on baggage; and $250 for valuables, such as cameras and jewelry.

Carte Blanche and Diners Club: Provide $1,250 free insurance for checked or carry-on baggage that's lost or damaged.

Discover Card: Offers $500 insurance for checked baggage and $1,250 for carry-on baggage — but to qualify for this coverage cardholders first must purchase additional flight insurance (see "Flight Insurance," below).

MasterCard and Visa: Baggage insurance coverage set by the issuing institution.

Additional baggage and personal effects insurance also is included in certain of the combination travel insurance policies discussed below.

■ **A note of warning:** Be sure to read the fine print of any excess value insurance policy; there often are specific exclusions, such as cash, tickets, furs, gold and silver objects, art, and antiques. And remember that insurance companies ordinarily will pay only the depreciated value of the goods rather than their replacement value. The best way to protect the items you're carrying in your luggage is to take photos of your valuables and keep a record of the serial numbers of such items as cameras, typewriters, laptop computers, radios, and so on. This will establish that you do, indeed, own the objects. If your luggage disappears or is damaged en route, deal with the situation immediately. If an airline loses your luggage, you will be asked to fill out a Property Irregularity Report before you leave the airport. If your property disappears at other transportation centers, tell the local company, but also report it to the police (since the insurance company will check with the police when processing your claim). When traveling by train, if you are sending excess luggage as registered baggage, remember that some trains may not have provisions for extra cargo; if your baggage does not arrive when you do, it may not be lost, just on the next train!

Personal Accident and Sickness Insurance – This covers you in case of illness during your trip or death in an accident. Most policies insure you for hospital and doctor's expenses, lost income, and so on. In most cases it is a standard part of existing health insurance policies, though you should check with your insurance broker to be sure that your policy will pay for any medical expenses incurred abroad. If not, take out a separate vacation accident policy or an entire vacation insurance policy that includes health and life coverage.

Two examples of such comprehensive health and life insurance coverage are the travel insurance packages offered by *Wallach & Co:*

> *HealthCare Global:* This insurance package, which can be purchased for periods of 10 to 180 days, is offered for two age groups: Men and women up to age 75 receive $25,000 medical insurance and $50,000 accidental injury or death benefit; those from ages 76 to 84 are eligible for $12,500 medical insurance and $25,000 injury or death benefit. For either policy, the cost for a 10-day period is $25.

> *HealthCare Abroad:* This program is available to individuals up to age 75. For $3 per day (minimum 10 days, maximum 90 days), policy holders receive $100,000 medical insurance and $25,000 accidental injury or death benefit.

Both of these basic programs also may be bought in combination with trip cancellation and baggage insurance at extra cost. For further information, write to *Wallach & Co.,* 243 Church St. NW, Suite 100-D, Vienna, VA 22180 (phone: 703-281-9500 in Virginia; 800-237-6615 elsewhere in the US).

Trip Cancellation and Interruption Insurance – Most charter and package tour passengers pay for their travel well before departure. The disappointment of having to miss a vacation because of illness or any other reason pales before the awful prospect that not all (and sometimes none) of the money paid in advance might be returned. So cancellation insurance for any package tour is a must.

Although cancellation penalties vary (they are listed in the fine print in every tour brochure, and before you purchase a package tour you should know exactly what they are), rarely will a passenger get more than 50% of this money back if forced to cancel within a few weeks of scheduled departure. Therefore, if you book a package tour or charter flight, you should have trip cancellation insurance to guarantee full reimbursement or refund should you, a traveling companion, or a member of your immediate family get sick, forcing you to cancel your trip or *return home early.*

The key here is *not* to buy just enough insurance to guarantee full reimbursement for the cost of the package or charter in case of cancellation. The proper amount of coverage should be sufficient to reimburse you for the cost of having to catch up with a tour after its departure or having to travel home at the full economy airfare if you have to forgo the return flight of your charter. There usually is quite a discrepancy between a charter fare and the amount charged to travel the same distance on a regularly scheduled flight at full economy fare.

Trip cancellation insurance is available from travel agents and tour operators in two forms: as part of a short-term, all-purpose travel insurance package (sold by the travel agent); or as specific cancellation insurance designed by the tour operator for a specific charter tour. Generally, tour operators' policies are less expensive, but also less inclusive. Cancellation insurance also is available directly from insurance companies or their agents as part of a short-term, all-inclusive travel insurance policy.

Before you decide on a policy, read each one carefully. (Either type can be purchased from a travel agent when you book the charter or package tour.) Be certain that your policy includes enough coverage to pay your fare from the farthest destination on your itinerary should you have to miss the charter flight. Also, be sure to check the fine print for stipulations concerning "family members" and "pre-existing medical conditions," as well as allowances for living expenses if you must delay your return due to bodily injury or illness.

Default and/or Bankruptcy Insurance – Although trip cancellation insurance usually protects you if *you* are unable to complete — or begin — your trip, a fairly recent innovation is coverage in the event of default and/or bankruptcy on the part of the tour operator, airline, or other travel supplier. In some travel insurance packages, this contingency is included in the trip cancellation portion of the coverage; in others, it is a separate feature. Either way, it is becoming increasingly important. Whereas sophisticated travelers have long known to beware of the possibility of default or bankruptcy when buying a charter flight or tour package, in recent years more than a few respected airlines have unexpectedly revealed their shaky financial condition, sometimes leaving hordes of stranded ticket holders in their wake. Moreover, the value of escrow protection of a charter passenger's funds lately has been unreliable. While default/bankruptcy insurance will not ordinarily result in reimbursement in time to pay for new arrangements, it can ensure that you will get your money back, and even independent travelers buying no more than an airplane ticket may want to consider it.

Flight Insurance – Airlines have carefully established limits of liability for injury to or the death of passengers on international flights. For all international flights to, from, or with a stopover in the US, all carriers are liable for up to $75,000 per passenger. For all other international flights, the liability is based on where you purchase the ticket: If booked in advance in the US, the maximum liability is $75,000; if arrangements are made abroad, the liability is $10,000. But remember, these liabilities are not the same thing as insurance policies; every penny that an airline eventually pays in the case of death or injury will likely be subject to a legal battle.

But before you buy last-minute flight insurance from an airport vending machine, consider the purchase in light of your total existing insurance coverage. A careful review of your current policies may reveal that you already are amply covered for accidental death, sometimes up to three times the amount provided for by the flight insurance you're buying at the airport.

Be aware that airport insurance, the kind typically bought at a counter or from a vending machine, is among the most expensive forms of life insurance coverage, and that even within a single airport, rates for approximately the same coverage vary widely. Often policies sold in vending machines are more expensive than those sold over the counter, even when they are with the same national company.

If you buy your plane ticket with a major credit card, you generally receive automatic insurance coverage at no extra cost. Additional coverage usually can be obtained at extremely reasonable prices, but a cardholder must sign up for it in advance. (Note that rates vary slightly for residents of some states.) As we went to press, the travel accident and life insurance policies of the major credit cards were as follows:

American Express: Automatically provides $100,000 in insurance to its *Green, Gold,* and *Optima* cardholders, and $500,000 to *Platinum* cardholders. With *American Express,* $4 per ticket buys an additional $250,000 worth of flight insurance; $6.50 buys $500,000 worth; and $13 provides an added $1 million worth of coverage.

Carte Blanche: Automatically provides $150,000 flight insurance. An additional $250,000 worth of insurance is available for $4; $500,000 costs $6.50.

Diners Club: Provides $350,000 free flight insurance. An additional $250,000 worth of insurance is available for $4; $500,000 costs $6.50.

Discover Card: Provides $500,000 free flight insurance. An additional $250,000 worth of insurance is available for $4; $500,000 costs $6.50.

MasterCard and Visa: Insurance coverage set by the issuing institution.

Automobile Insurance – When you rent a car, the rental company is required to offer you collision protection. In your car rental contract, you'll see that for about $11 to $13 a day, you may buy optional collision damage waiver (CDW) protection.

If you do not accept the CDW coverage, you may be liable for as much as the full retail cost of the rental car, and by paying for the CDW you are relieved of all responsibility for any damage to the car. Before agreeing to this coverage, however, check with your own broker about your existing personal auto insurance policy. It very well may cover your entire liability exposure without any additonal cost, or you automatically may be covered by the credit card company to which you are charging the cost of your rental. To find out the amount of rental car insurance provided by major credit cards, contact the issuing institutions.

You also should know that an increasing number of the major international car rental companies automatically are including the cost of the CDW in their basic rates. Car rental prices have increased to include this coverage, although rental company ad campaigns may promote this as a new, improved rental package feature. The disadvantage of this inclusion is that you may not have the option to turn down the CDW — even if you already are adequately covered by your own insurance policy or through a credit card company.

Your American auto insurance is *not* recognized in Mexico; if you are driving your own car you'll have to arrange for separate Mexican auto insurance. Your insurance agent probably can have the policy written for you through a responsible Mexican company, or you can obtain coverage in any border town. *Sanborn's Mexico Insurance Service* and other major US insurance companies offer special Mexican auto insurance policies that include collision and upset; fire and theft (of your entire car, not parts of or items within it); property damage; bodily injury and medical payments for its occupants. Incidentally, *Sanborn's Mexico Insurance Service* has offices at many border crossings, and if you have purchased your policy from them, those offices capable of issuing refunds will do so on the spot. (For further information, contact *Sanborn's* main office, 2009 S. 10th St., McAllen, TX 78502; phone: 512-686-0711.)

You can obtain auto insurance policies to cover your car (or recreational vehicle) for a certain number of days. Some agents offer multiple-entry insurance if you make more than one trip to Mexico per year in your car. You can buy insurance for 6 months or a year at a less expensive rate, suspend coverage when you cross back into the US, and then reinstate coverage as you cross into Mexico on another trip, all by notifying your agent in writing. People who make frequent regularly scheduled trips to Mexico do this with Mexican insurance companies and save money. If you plan to tow a trailer into Mexico, it also must be insured for identical risks. (This will cost you an additional sum.) Before leaving home, you also should obtain a personal property policy if you hope to recover the value of any goods stolen from your car in Mexico.

Mexican insurance companies have adopted a policy of paying for their own insured party's damages, no matter who is at fault. Be sure you contact the nearest adjuster in Mexico as soon as possible after an accident. (Don't forget to obtain a list of adjusters with addresses and phone numbers throughout Mexico — this is provided by your insurance company when you buy the policy.) Since the police could detain you, it is better not to involve them, unless your policy requires a police report of some kind (which it will, if the accident is at all serious). Discuss this with your agent when you purchase the policy and make certain what verification your policy does require. Obviously, report a car theft to the police at once.

Another type of driving insurance in Mexico is seldom examined by motorists until it's too late. While the standard PL&PD — public liability or property damage policy — covers the policy holder for damages to people or property, you'll need a second type of insurance, sold by private companies in Mexico, to cover legal services and speed your case through the authorities. This is juridical insurance. Basically it works this way: If your car knocks down a traffic signal, lamp post, street sign, or other federal property, you have violated — voluntarily or involuntarily — the communications law and will be accused of *ataques a las vías federales de comunicación* (literally, "attacks on federal communication routes").

If a driver has juridical insurance and knocks down a traffic signal (and it happens very frequently in Mexico City), the adjuster or claims representative will be able to spring the motorist from jail without posting bond in a matter of hours, and will pay all expenses involved. The same holds true if the motorist hits a person. Drivers who remain in Mexican territory for any length of time or who make regular trips there are advised to carry juridical insurance from a nationwide company with representatives in leading cities. The oldest and largest such organization is *Asociación Jurídica Automovilística (AJA).* Their main office is in Mexico City (39 Montecito, Colonia Nápoles, Mexico, DF 03810; phone: 5-687-3999) and a branch office is located in Cuernavaca. Others can be found by looking under "Servicios Jurídicos de Emergencia" in the yellow pages of the phone directory.

Combination Policies – Short-term insurance policies, which may include any combination or all of the types of insurance discussed above, are available through retail insurance agencies, automobile clubs, and many travel agents. These combination policies are designed to cover you for the duration of a single trip.

Policies of this type include the following:

Access America International: A subsidiary of the Blue Cross/Blue Shield plans of New York and Washington, DC, now available nationwide. Contact *Access America,* 600 Third Ave., PO Box 807, New York, NY 10163 (phone: 800-284-8300 or 212-490-5345).

Carefree: Underwritten by The Hartford. Contact *Carefree Travel Insurance,* Arm Coverage, PO Box 310, Mineola, NY 11501 (phone: 516-294-0220).

NEAR Services: In addition to a full range of travel services, this organization offers a comprehensive travel insurance package. An added feature is coverage for lost or stolen airline tickets. Contact *NEAR Services,* 450 Prairie Ave., Suite 101, Calumet City, IL 60409 (phone: 708-868-6700 in the Chicago area; 800-654-6700 elsewhere in the US and Canada).

Tele-Trip: Underwritten by the Mutual of Omaha Companies. Contact *Tele-Trip Co.,* PO Box 31685, 3201 Farnam St., Omaha, NE 68131 (phone: 402-345-2400 in Nebraska; 800-228-9792 elsewhere in the US).

Travel Assistance International: Provided by Europ Assistance Worldwide Services, and underwritten by Transamerica Occidental Life Insurance Company. Contact *Travel Assistance International,* 1133 15th St. NW, Suite 400, Washington, DC 20005 (phone: 202-331-1609 in Washington, DC; 800-821-2828 elsewhere in the US).

Travel Guard International: Underwritten by the Insurance Company of North America, it is available through authorized travel agents, or contact *Travel Guard International,* 1145 Clark St., Stevens Point, WI 54481 (phone: 715-345-0505 in Wisconsin; 800-826-1300 elsewhere in the US).

Travel Insurance PAK: Underwritten by The Travelers. Contact *The Travelers Companies,* Ticket and Travel Plans, One Tower Sq., Hartford, CT 06183-5040 (phone: 203-277-2319 in Connecticut; 800-243-3174 elsewhere in the US).

WorldCare Travel Assistance Association: This organization offers insurance packages underwritten by Transamerica Occidental Life Insurance Company and Transamerica Premier Insurance Company. Contact *WorldCare Travel Assistance Association,* 605 Market St., Suite 1300, San Francisco, CA 94105 (phone: 800-666-4993 or 415-541-4991).

How to Pack

No one can provide a completely foolproof list of precisely what to pack, so it's best to let common sense, space, and comfort guide you. Keep one maxim in mind: Less is more. You simply won't need as much clothing as you think, and you are far more likely to need a forgotten accessory — or a needle and thread or scissors — than a particular piece of clothing.

As with almost anything relating to travel, a little planning can go a long way.

1. Where are you going — city, country, or both?
2. How many total days will you be gone?
3. What's the average temperature likely to be during your stay?

The goal is to remain perfectly comfortable, neat, clean, and fashionable, but to pack as little as possible. Learn to travel light by following two firm packing principles:

1. Organize your travel wardrobe around a single color — blue or beige, for example — that allows you to mix, match, and layer clothes. Holding firm to one color scheme will make it easy to eliminate items of clothing that don't harmonize.
2. Never overpack to ensure a supply of fresh clothing — shirts, blouses, underwear — for each day of a long trip. Use hotel laundries to wash and dry clean clothes. If these are too expensive, there are self-service laundries, called *las lavanderías* in Spanish, in most towns of any size.

CLIMATE AND CLOTHES: Exactly what you pack for your trip will be a function of where you are going and when, and the kinds of things you intend to do. A few degrees can make all the difference between being comfortably attired and very real suffering, so your initial step should be to find out what the general weather conditions are likely to be in the areas you will visit. Airlines and travel agents will provide specific information on weather conditions throughout Mexico. A general rule for touring in Mexico is to pack an umbrella if you plan to visit any time during the rainy season (between May and October) or will be in areas of year-round precipitation.

Throughout most of Mexico, lightweight, casual sportswear is all you will need. In beach resorts, such as Acapulco or Mazatlán, swimsuits, shorts, lightweight dresses, or pants are what women usually wear, while men never wear anything more formal than slacks and a sport shirt. Ties are absent from any beach resort. Mexico City, on the other hand, has a more cosmopolitan atmosphere, and dress tends to be more stylish. You do not have to follow suit, but the elegant restaurants do require dressy clothes. Although shorts are acceptable in beach resorts, they are not recommended in Mexico City.

Keeping temperature and climate in mind, consider the problem of luggage. Plan on one suitcase per person (and, in a pinch, remember it's always easier to carry two small suitcases than to schlepp one that is roughly the size of downtown Detroit). Standard 26- to 28-inch suitcases can be made to work for 1 week or 1 month, and unless you are going for no more than a weekend, never cram wardrobes for two people into one suitcase. Hanging bags are best for dresses, suits, and jackets.

Before packing, lay out every piece of clothing you think you might want to take. Select clothing on the basis of what can serve several functions (whenever possible, clothes should be chosen that can be used for both daytime and evening wear.) Pack clothes that have a lot of pockets for traveler's checks, documents, and tickets. Eliminate items that don't mix, match, or interchange within your color scheme. If you can't wear it in at least two distinct incarnations, leave it at home. Accessorize everything beforehand so you know exactly what you will be wearing with what.

Layering is a good way to prepare for atypical temperatures or changes in the weather. No matter where you are traveling, for unexpectedly cool days or for outings in the mountains, a recommended basic is a lightweight wool or heavy cotton turtleneck which can be worn under a shirt, and perhaps a third layer, such as a wool sweater, jacket, or windbreaker. In warmer weather, substitute a T-shirt and lightweight cotton shirts or sweaters for the turtleneck and wool layers. As the weather changes, you can add or remove clothes as required.

Travelers to Mexico's jungle regions should include long cotton pants, lightweight long-sleeve shirts, and high socks for protection against insects. In the rainy season, torrential downpours are common, and even in the dryer seasons, rain always is a possibility, so keep an umbrella or waterproof poncho (available from camping supplies stores) with you at all times.

Since you are likely to do more walking than usual in Mexico — and since in small towns and in some large cities streets often are cobbled — it is essential to bring comfortable shoes (often this means an old pair, already broken in). Sneakers or other rubber-soled shoes are good for climbing pyramids and other ancient ruins.

Your carry-on luggage should contain a survival kit with the basic things you will need in case your luggage gets lost or stolen: a toothbrush, toothpaste, all medications, a sweater, nightclothes, and a change of underwear. With these essential items at hand, you will be prepared for any sudden, unexpected occurrence that separates you from your suitcase. Also, if you have many 1- or 2-night stops, you can live out of your survival case without having to unpack completely at each hotel.

Sundries – If you are traveling in the heat of summer and will be spending a lot of time outdoors, pack special items so that you won't spend your entire vacation horizontal in a hotel room (or hospital) because of sunburn. Be sure to take a sun hat (to protect hair as well as skin), sunscreen, and tanning lotion. Also, remember that in higher altitudes your face and neck are particularly susceptible to a painful burn.

Other items you might consider packing are a small bottle in which to carry purified water (if you're driving), a pocket-size flashlight with extra batteries, a small sewing kit, a first-aid kit (see *Staying Healthy,* in this section, for recommended components), binoculars, and a camera or camcorder (see *Cameras and Equipment,* in this section).

PACKING: The basic idea of packing is to get everything into the suitcase and out again with as few wrinkles as possible. Simple, casual clothes — shirts, jeans and slacks, permanent press skirts — can be rolled into neat, tight sausages that keep other packed items in place and leave the clothes themselves amazingly unwrinkled. However, for items that are too bulky or delicate for even careful rolling, a suitcase can be packed with the heaviest items on the bottom, toward the hinges, so that they will not wrinkle more perishable clothes. Candidates for the bottom layer include shoes (stuff them with small items to save space), a toilet kit, handbags (stuff them to help keep their shape), and an alarm clock. Fill out this layer with articles that will not wrinkle or will not matter if they do, such as sweaters, socks, a bathing suit, and underwear.

If you get this first, heavy layer as smooth as possible with the fill-ins, you will have a shelf for the next layer — the most easily wrinkled items, like slacks, jackets, shirts, dresses, and skirts. These should be buttoned and zipped and laid along the whole length of the suitcase with as little folding as possible. When you do need to make a fold, do it on a crease (as with pants), along a seam in the fabric, or where it will not show (such as shirttails). Alternate each piece of clothing, using one side of the suitcase, then the other, to make the layers as flat as possible. Make the layers even and the total contents of your bag as full and firm as possible to keep things from shifting around during transit. On the top layer put the things you will want at once: nightclothes, a bathing suit, an umbrella or raincoat, a sweater.

With men's two-suiter suitcases, follow the same procedure. Then place jackets on hangers, straighten them out, and leave them unbuttoned. If they are too wide for the suitcase, fold them lengthwise down the middle, straighten the shoulders, and fold the sleeves in along the seam.

While packing, it is a good idea to separate each layer of clothes with plastic cleaning bags, which will help preserve pressed clothes while they are in the suitcase. Unpack your bags as soon as you get to your hotel. Nothing so thoroughly destroys freshly cleaned and pressed clothes as sitting for days in a suitcase. Finally, if something is badly wrinkled and can't be professionally pressed before you must wear it, hang it for several hours in a bathroom where the bathtub has been filled with very hot water; keep the door closed so the room becomes something of a steamroom. It really works miracles.

SOME FINAL PACKING HINTS: Apart from the items you pack as carry-on luggage, always keep all necessary medicines, valuable jewelry, and travel or business documents in your purse, briefcase, or carry-on bag — *not in the luggage you will check.* Tuck a bathing suit into your handbag or briefcase, too; in the event of lost baggage, it's frustrating to be without one. And whether in your overnight bag or checked luggage, cosmetics and any liquids should be packed in plastic bottles or at least wrapped in plastic bags and tied.

Golf clubs may be checked through as luggage (most airlines are accustomed to handling them), but tennis rackets should be carried onto the plane. Aqua-lung tanks, depressurized and appropriately packed with padding, and surfboards (minus the fin and padded) also may go as baggage. Snorkeling gear should be packed in a suitcase, duffel, or tote bag. Some airlines require that bicycles be partially dismantled and packaged (see *Camping and RVs, Hiking and Biking,* in this section). Check with the airline before departure to see if there is a specific regulation concerning any special equipment or sporting gear you plan to take.

Hints for Handicapped Travelers

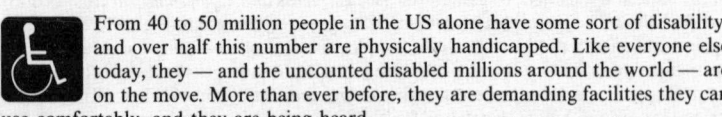 From 40 to 50 million people in the US alone have some sort of disability, and over half this number are physically handicapped. Like everyone else today, they — and the uncounted disabled millions around the world — are on the move. More than ever before, they are demanding facilities they can use comfortably, and they are being heard.

Those who have chosen to visit Mexico are in luck, because more and more disabled travelers are returning from this most luscious of destinations bearing tales of ramped sidewalks, a style of warm-weather architecture that erects fewer barriers between the indoors and the outdoors, and of sightseeing tours designed especially for them. Also, in recent years, a series of imaginative, pan-American programs aimed at improving facilities and services for the handicapped in Mexico and Latin America have been initiated. Chief among these is *Partners of the Americas,* with chapters in 45 states, which coordinates joint projects with these states in various Mexican and Latin American areas. *Partners of the Americas* also maintains an extensive library with information on programs for the handicapped throughout Mexico, as well as Central and South America, and they often can put disabled travelers in touch with self-help organizations of disabled persons in these locations. For more information, contact the central office of *Partners of the Americas,* 1424 K St. NW, Suite 700, Washington, DC 20005 (phone: 800-322-7844 or 202-628-3300).

Despite this effort to develop special facilities for the disabled, however, handicapped travelers face pretty much the same problems in Mexico as in most other parts of the world. Rural areas have no facilities. Cities have some, but there is no consistency.

PLANNING: Good planning is essential: Collect as much information as you can about your specific disability and about facilities for the disabled in Mexico; make your travel arrangements well in advance, and specify to all services involved the exact nature of your condition or restricted mobility, as your trip will be much more comfortable if you know that there are accommodations and facilities to suit your needs. The best way to find out if your intended destination can accommodate a handicapped traveler is to write or call the local tourist authority or hotel and ask specific questions. If you require a corridor of a certain width to maneuver a wheelchair or if you need handles on the bathroom wall for support, ask the hotel manager (some large hotels have rooms designed for the handicapped). A travel agent or the local chapter or national office of the organization that deals with your particular disability — for example, the *American Foundation for the Blind* or the *American Heart Association* — will supply the most up-to-date information on the subject. The following organizations offer general information on access:

ACCENT on Living (PO Box 700, Bloomington, IL 61702; phone: 309-378-2961). This information service for persons with disabilities provides a free list of travel agencies specializing in arranging trips for the disabled; for a copy send a self-addressed, stamped envelope. Also offers a wide range of publications, including a quarterly magazine ($8 per year; $14 for 2 years).

Information Center for Individuals with Disabilities (Fort Point Pl., 1st Floor, 27-43 Wormwood St., Boston, MA 02210; phone: 800-462-5015 in Massachusetts; 617-727-5540 or 617-727-5541 elsewhere in the US; both numbers provide voice and TDD — telecommunications device for the deaf). The center offers information and referral services on disability-related issues, publishes fact sheets on travel agents, tour operators, and other travel resources, and can help you research your trip.

Mobility International USA (*MIUSA;* PO Box 3551, Eugene, OR 97403; phone: 503-343-1284; both voice and TDD). This US branch of *Mobility International,* a nonprofit British organization with affiliates worldwide, offers members advice and assistance — including information on accommodations and other travel services, and publications applicable to the traveler's disability. It also offers a quarterly newsletter and a comprehensive sourcebook, *A World of Options for the 90s: A Guide to International Education Exchange, Community Service and Travel for Persons with Disabilities* ($14 for members; $16 for non-members). Membership includes the newsletter and is $20 a year; subscription to the newsletter alone is $10 annually.

National Rehabilitation Information Center (8455 Colesville Rd., Suite 935, Silver Spring, MD 20910; phone: 301-588-9284). A general information, resource, research, and referral service.

Paralyzed Veterans of America (*PVA;* PVA/ATTS Program, 801 18th St. NW, Washington, DC 20006; phone: 202-416-7708 in Washington, DC; 800-424-8200 elsewhere in the US). The members of this national service organization all are veterans who have suffered spinal cord injuries, but it offers advocacy services and information to all persons with a disability. *PVA* also sponsors *Access to the Skies,* a program that coordinates the efforts of the national and international air travel industry in providing airport and airplane access for the disabled. Members receive several helpful publications, as well as regular notification of conferences on subjects of interest to the disabled traveler.

Royal Association for Disability and Rehabilitation (*RADAR;* 25 Mortimer St., London W1N 8AB, England; phone: 44-71-637-5400). Offers a number of publications for the handicapped. Their comprehensive guide, *Holidays and Travel Abroad 1991/92 — A Guide for Disabled People,* focuses on international travel. This publication can be ordered by sending payment in British pounds to *RADAR.* As we went to press, it cost just over £6; call for current pricing before ordering.

Society for the Advancement of Travel for the Handicapped (*SATH;* 26 Court St., Penthouse, Brooklyn, NY 11242; phone: 718-858-5483). To keep abreast of developments in travel for the handicapped, you may want to join *SATH,* a nonprofit organization whose members include consumers, as well as travel service professionals who have experience (or an interest) in travel for the handicapped. For an annual fee of $45 ($25 for students and travelers who are 65 and older) members receive a quarterly newsletter and have access to extensive information and referral services. *SATH* also offers two useful publications: *Travel Tips for the Handicapped* (a series of informative fact sheets) and *The United States Welcomes Handicapped Visitors* (a 48-page guide covering domestic transportation and accommodations, as well as useful hints for disabled travelers abroad); to order, send a self-addressed, #10 envelope and $1 per title for postage.

Travel Information Service (Moss Rehabilitation Hospital, 1200 W. Tabor Rd., Philadelphia, PA 19141-3099; phone: 215-456-9600 for voice; 215-456-9602 for TDD). This service assists physically handicapped people in planning trips and supplies detailed information on accessibility for a nominal fee.

Blind travelers should contact the *American Foundation for the Blind* (15 W. 16th St., New York, NY 10011; phone: 212-620-2147 in New York State; 800-232-5463 elsewhere in the US) and *The Seeing Eye* (Box 375, Morristown, NJ 07963-0375; phone: 201-539-4425); both provide useful information on resources for the visually impaired. *Note:* Although requirements may vary in Mexico, generally, Seeing Eye dogs must be accompanied by a certificate of inoculation against rabies, hepatitis and/or distemper issued within the previous 3 months and certified by the United States Department of Agriculture. These certificates must be authorized by a Mexican consul (for a fee of about $20 at press time). *The American Society for the Prevention of Cruelty to Animals (ASPCA,* Education Dept., 441 E. 92 St., New York, NY 10128; phone: 212-876-7700) offers a useful booklet, *Traveling With Your Pet,* which lists inoculation and other requirements by country. It is available for $5 (including postage and handling).

In addition, there are a number of publications — from travel guides to magazines — of interest to handicapped travelers. Among these are the following:

Access to the World, by Louise Weiss, offers sound tips for the disabled traveler. Published by Facts on File (460 Park Ave. S., New York, NY 10016; phone: 212-683-2244 in New York State; 800-322-8755 elsewhere in the US; 800-443-8323 in Canada), it costs $16.95. Check with your local bookstore; it also can be ordered by phone with a credit card.

The Diabetic Traveler (PO Box 8223 RW, Stamford, CT 06905; phone: 203-327-5832) is a useful quarterly newsletter for travelers with diabetes. Each issue highlights a single destination or type of travel and includes information on general resources and hints for diabetics. A 1-year subscription costs $19.95. When subscribing, ask for the free fact sheet including an index of special articles; back issues are available for $4 each.

Guide to Traveling with Arthritis, a free brochure available by writing to the Upjohn Company (PO Box 307-B, Coventry, CT 06238), provides lots of good, commonsense tips on planning your trip and how to be as comfortable as possible when traveling by car, bus, cruise ship, plane, or train.

Handicapped Travel Newsletter is regarded as one of the best sources of information for the disabled traveler. It is edited by wheelchair-bound Vietnam veteran Michael Quigley, who has traveled to 93 countries around the world. Issued every 2 months (plus special issues), a subscription is $10 per year. Write to *Handicapped Travel Newsletter,* PO Box 269, Athens, TX 75751 (phone: 214-677-1260).

Handi-Travel: A Resource Book for Disabled and Elderly Travellers, by Cinnie Noble, is a comprehensive travel guide full of practical tips for those with disabilities affecting mobility, hearing, or sight. To order this book, send $12.95, plus shipping and handling, to the *Canadian Rehabilitation Council for the*

Disabled, 45 Sheppard Ave. E., Suite 801, Toronto, Ontario M2N 5W9, Canada (phone: 416-250-7490; both voice and TDD).

The Itinerary (PO Box 2012, Bayonne, NJ 07002-2012; phone: 201-858-3400). This bimonthly travel magazine for people with disabilities includes information on accessibility, listings of tours, news of adaptive devices, travel aids, and special services, as well as numerous general travel hints. A subscription costs $10 a year.

The Physically Disabled Traveler's Guide, by Rod W. Durgin and Norene Lindsay, rates accessibility of a number of travel services and includes a list of organizations specializing in travel for the disabled. It is available for $9.95, plus shipping and handling, from Resource Directories, 3361 Executive Pkwy., Suite 302, Toledo, OH 43606 (phone: 419-536-5353 in the Toledo area; 800-274-8515 elsewhere in the US).

Ticket to Safe Travel offers useful information for travelers with diabetes. A reprint of this article is available free from local chapters of the *American Diabetes Association.* For the nearest branch, contact the central office at 505 Eighth Ave., 21st Floor, New York, NY 10018 (phone: 212-947-9707 in New York state; 800-232-3472 elsewhere in the US).

Travel for the Patient with Chronic Obstructive Pulmonary Disease, a publication of the George Washington University Medical Center, provides some sound practical suggestions for those with emphysema, chronic bronchitis, asthma, or other lung ailments. To order, send $2 to Dr. Harold Silver, 1601 18th St. NW, Washington, DC 20009 (phone: 202-667-0134).

Traveling Like Everybody Else: A Practical Guide for Disabled Travelers by Jacqueline Freedman and Susan Gersten, offers the disabled tips on transportation, as well as lists of accessible accommodations, tour operators specializing in tours for disabled travelers, and other resources. It is available for $11.95, plus shipping and handling, from Modan Publishing, PO Box 1202, Bellmore, NY 11710 (phone: 516-679-1380).

Travel Tips for Hearing-Impaired People, a free pamphlet for deaf and hearing-impaired travelers, is available from the *American Academy of Otolaryngology* (One Prince St., Alexandria, VA 22314; phone: 703-836-4444). For a copy, send a self-addressed, stamped, business-size envelope to the academy.

Travel Tips for People with Arthritis, a free 31-page booklet published by the *Arthritis Foundation,* provides helpful information regarding travel by plane, train, bus, car, and cruise ship, planning your trip, medical considerations, and ways to conserve your energy while traveling. It also includes listings of helpful resources, such as associations and travel agencies that operate tours for disabled travelers. For a copy, contact your local *Arthritis Foundation* chapter, or write to the national office, PO Box 19000, Atlanta, GA 30326 (phone: 404-872-7100).

The Wheelchair Traveler, by Douglass R. Annand, lists accessible hotels, motels, restaurants, and other sites, including establishments throughout Mexico. This valuable resource is available directly from the author. For the price of the most recent edition, contact Douglass R. Annand, 123 Ball Hill Rd., Milford, NH 03055 (phone: 603-673-4539).

A few more basic resources to look for are *Travel for the Disabled,* by Helen Hecker ($9.95), and by the same author, *Directory of Travel Agencies for the Disabled* ($19.95). *Wheelchair Vagabond,* by John G. Nelson, is another useful guide for travelers confined to a wheelchair (hardcover, $14.95; paperback, $9.95). All three are published by Twin Peaks Press, PO Box 129, Vancouver, WA 98666 (phone: 800-637-CALM or 206-694-2462).

PLANE: The US Department of Transportation (DOT) has ruled that US airlines must accept all passengers with disabilities. As a matter of course, US airlines were pretty good about accommodating handicapped passengers even before the ruling, although each airline has somewhat different procedures. Mexican airlines also are generally good about accommodating disabled travelers, but again, policies vary from carrier to carrier. Ask for specifics when you book your flight.

Disabled passengers always should make reservations well in advance and should provide the airline with all relevant details of their condition. These details include information on mobility and equipment that you will need the airline to supply — such as a wheelchair for boarding or portable oxygen for in-flight use. Be sure that the person to whom you speak fully understands the degree of your disability — the more details provided, the more effective help the airline can give you.

On the day before the flight, call back to make sure that all arrangements have been prepared, and arrive early on the day of the flight so that you can board before the rest of the passengers. It's a good idea to bring a medical certificate with you, stating your specific disability or the need to carry particular medicine.

Because most airports have jetways (corridors connecting the terminal with the door of the plane), a disabled passenger usually can be taken as far as the plane, and sometimes right onto it, in a wheelchair. If not, a narrow boarding chair may be used to take you to your seat. Your own wheelchair, which will be folded and put in the baggage compartment, should be tagged as escort luggage to assure that it's available at planeside upon landing rather than in the baggage claim area. Travel is not quite as simple if your wheelchair is battery-operated: Unless it has non-spillable batteries, it might not be accepted on board, and you will have to check with the airline ahead of time to find out how the batteries and the chair should be packaged for the flight. Usually people in wheelchairs are asked to wait until other passengers have disembarked. If you are making a tight connection, be sure to tell the attendant.

Passengers who use oxygen may not use their personal supply in the cabin, though it may be carried on the plane as cargo when properly packed and labeled. If you will need oxygen during the flight, the airline will supply it to you (there is a charge) provided you have given advance notice — 24 hours to a few days, depending on the carrier.

Among the major carriers serving Mexico, the following airlines have TDD toll-free lines in the US for the hearing-impaired:

American (phone: 800-582-1573 in Ohio; 800-543-1586 elsewhere in the US).
Continental: (phone: 800-343-9195).
Delta: (phone: 800-831-4488).
Northwest: (phone: 800-328-2298).
Pan American: (phone: 800-722-3323).
United: (phone: 800-942-8819 in Illinois; 800-323-0170 elsewhere in the US).

Useful information on every stage of air travel, from planning to arrival, is provided in the booklet *Incapacitated Passengers Air Travel Guide.* To receive a free copy, write to the International Air Transport Association (Publications Sales Department, 2000 Peel St., Montreal, Quebec H3A 2R4, Canada; phone: 514-844-6311). Another helpful publication is *Air Transportation of Handicapped Persons,* which explains the general guidelines that govern air carrier policies. For a copy of this free booklet, write to the US Department of Transportation (Distribution Unit, Publications Section, M-443-2, Washington, DC 20590) and ask for "Free Advisory Circular #AC-120-32."

SHIP: Among the ships calling at Mexican ports, *Carnival Cruise Lines' Holiday* and *Jubilee; Crystal Cruises' Crystal Harmony; Holland America's Rotterdam, Noordam, Westerdam,* and *Nieuw Amsterdam;* and *Royal Cruise Line's Crown Odyssey* are considered the best-equipped vessels for the handicapped. Disabled travelers are advised to book reservations at least 90 days in advance to reserve specially equipped cabins.

For those in wheelchairs or with limited mobility, one of the best sources for evaluating a ship's accessibility is the free chart issued by the *Cruise Lines International Association* (500 Fifth Ave., Suite 1407, New York, NY 10110; phone: 212-921-0066). The chart lists accessible ships and indicates whether they accommodate standard-size or only narrow wheelchairs, have ramps, wide doors, low or no doorsills, handrails in the rooms, and so on. (For further information on ships cruising Mexican waters, see *Traveling by Ship,* in this section.)

GROUND TRANSPORTATION: Perhaps the simplest solution to getting around is to travel with an able-bodied companion who can drive. Another alternative in Mexico is to hire a driver/translator with a car — be sure to get a recommendation from a reputable source. The organizations listed above may be able to help you make arrangements — another source is your hotel concierge.

If you are accustomed to driving your own hand-controlled car and determined to rent one, you may have to do some extensive research, as it is difficult in Mexico to find rental cars fitted with hand controls. If agencies do provide hand-controlled cars, they are apt to be offered only on a limited basis in major metropolitan areas and usually are in high demand. The best course is to contact the major car rental agencies listed in *Traveling by Car,* in this section, well before your departure, but be forewarned: You still may be out of luck. Other sources for information on vehicles adapted for the handicapped are the organizations discussed above.

The *American Automobile Association (AAA)* publishes a useful booklet, *The Handicapped Driver's Mobility Guide.* Contact the central office or your local *AAA* club for availability and pricing, which may vary at different branch offices.

In some parts of Mexico, taxis and public transportation also are available, but accessibility for the disabled varies and may be limited in rural areas, as well as in some cities. Check with a travel agent or the Mexican government tourist authorities for information.

TRAIN: For those traveling by train en route to Mexico, some *Amtrak* trains in the US have special seats and bathrooms for the handicapped. Most stations provide wheelchairs, and some have wheelchair lifts. When you book your ticket, notify the *Amtrak* reservations clerk that you are handicapped, and *Amtrak* personnel will assist you. Handicapped passengers are eligible for a 25% discount on round trips (except during some "blackout" periods). Guide dogs for the blind and deaf ride at no additional cost.

If you plan to tour Mexico by train, for information about facilities for the handicapped write to the main office of the *Mexican National Railways* in Mexico City (Estación Buenavista, Depto. de Tráfico de Pasajeros, Av. Insurgentes Nte. and Av. Mosqueta, México, DF 06358; phone: 5-547-1097, 5-547-6593, or 5-547-1084). Blind passengers whose handicap is certified in writing can travel in Mexico by train with a companion at half-fare for each. There are no special services for people with other handicaps, although railway employees are available to assist those with disabilities in boarding trains.

BUS: For those traveling to Mexico by bus, *Greyhound* has special rates for US travel which allow a traveling companion to accompany a handicapped passenger with medical certification of the disability for the price of one fare. However, in general, bus travel — either above or below the border — is not recommended for travelers who are totally wheelchair-bound, unless they have someone along who can lift them on and off or if they are members of a group tour designed for the handicapped and are using a specially outfitted bus. If you have some mobility, however, you'll find local personnel usually quite happy to help you board and exit.

TOURS: Programs designed for the physically impaired are run by specialists who have researched hotels, restaurants, and sites to be sure they present no insurmountable obstacles. The following travel agencies and tour operators specialize in making group and individual arrangements for travelers with physical or other disabilities.

Access: The Foundation for Accessibility by the Disabled (PO Box 356, Malverne, NY 11565; phone: 516-887-5798). A travelers' referral service that acts as an intermediary with tour operators and agents worldwide, and provides information on accessibility at various locations.

Accessible Tours/Directions Unlimited (720 N. Bedford Rd., Bedford Hills, NY 10507; phone: 914-241-1700 in New York State; 800-533-5343 elsewhere in the continental US). Arranges group or individual tours for disabled persons traveling in the company of able-bodied friends or family members. Accepts the unaccompanied traveler if completely self-sufficient.

Dialysis at Sea Cruises (611 Barry Place, Indian Rocks Beach, FL 34635; phone: 813-596-7604 or 800-544-7604 throughout the US and Canada). Offers cruises for dialysis patients that include the medical services of a nephrologist (a specialist in kidney disease) and a staff of dialysis nurses. Family, friends, and companions are welcome to travel on these cruises, but the number of dialysis patients usually is limited to roughly ten travelers per trip.

Evergreen Travel Service (4114-198th St. SW, Suite 13, Lynnwood, WA 98036-6742; phone: 206-776-1184 or 800-435-2288 throughout the continental US and Canada). Offers worldwide tours and cruises for the disabled (Wings on Wheels Tours), sight-impaired/blind (White Cane Tours), and hearing-impaired/deaf (Flying Fingers Tours). Most programs are first class or deluxe, and include a trained escort.

Flying Wheels Travel (143 W. Bridge St., Box 382, Owatonna, MN 55060; phone: 507-451-5005 or 800-535-6790 throughout the US and Canada). Handles both tours and individual arrangements.

The Guided Tour (555 Ashbourne Rd., Elkins Park, PA 19117; phone: 215-782-1370). Arranges tours for people with developmental and learning disabilities and sponsors separate tours for members of the same population who also are physically disabled or who simply need a slower pace.

Handi-Travel (First National Travel Ltd., Thornhill Sq., 300 John St., Suite 405, Thornhill, Ontario L3T 5W4, Canada; phone: 416-731-4714). Handles tours and individual arrangements.

Sprout (893 Amsterdam Ave., New York, NY 10025; phone: 212-222-9575). Arranges travel programs for mildly and moderately disabled teens and adults.

USTS Travel Horizons (11 E. 44th St., New York, NY 10017; phone: 800-487-8787 or 212-687-5121). Travel agent and registered nurse Mary Ann Hamm designs trips for individual travelers requiring all types of kidney dialysis and handles arrangements for the dialysis.

Whole Person Tours (PO Box 1084, Bayonne, NJ 07002-1084; phone: 201-858-3400). Handicapped owner Bob Zywicki travels the world with his wheelchair and offers a lineup of escorted tours (many conducted by himself) for the disabled. *Whole Person Tours* also publishes *The Itinerary,* a bimonthly newsletter for disabled travelers (see the publication source list above).

Travelers who would benefit from being accompanied by a nurse or physical therapist also can hire a companion through *Traveling Nurses' Network,* a service provided by Twin Peaks Press (PO Box 129, Vancouver, WA 98666; phone: 800-637-CALM or 206-694-2462). For a $10 fee, the client receives the names of three nurses, whom he or she can then contact directly; for a $125 fee, the agency will make all the hiring arrangements for the client. Travel arrangements also may be made in some cases — the fee for this further service is determined on an individual basis.

A similar service is offered by *MedEscort International* (ABE International Airport, PO Box 8766, Allentown, PA 18105; phone: 800-255-7182 in the continental US; elsewhere, call 215-791-3111). Clients can arrange to be accompanied by a nurse, paramedic, respiratory therapist, or physician through *MedEscort*. The fees are based on the disabled traveler's needs. *MedEscort* also can assist in making travel arrangements.

Hints for Single Travelers

Just about the last trip in human history on which the participants were neatly paired was the voyage of Noah's Ark. Ever since, passenger lists and tour groups have reflected the same kind of asymmetry that occurs in real life, as countless individuals set forth to see the world unaccompanied (or unencumbered, depending on your outlook) by spouse, lover, friend, or relative. Unfortunately, traveling alone also can turn a traveler into a second class citizen.

The truth is that the travel industry is not very fair to people who vacation by themselves. People traveling alone almost invariably end up paying more than individuals traveling in pairs. Most travel bargains, including package tours, accommodations, resort packages, and cruises, are based on *double occupancy* rates. This means that the per-person price is offered on the basis of two people traveling together and sharing a double room (which means they each will spend a good deal more on meals and extras). The single traveler will have to pay a surcharge, called a single supplement, for exactly the same package. In extreme cases, this can add as much as 30% to 55% to the basic per-person rate.

Don't despair, however. Throughout Mexico, there are scores of smaller hotels and other hostelries where, in addition to a cozier atmosphere, prices still are quite reasonable for the single traveler. Some ship lines have begun to offer special cruises for singles, and some resorts cater to the single traveler.

The obvious, most effective alternative is to find a traveling companion. Even special "singles' tours" that promise no supplements usually are based on people sharing double rooms. Perhaps the most recent innovation along these lines is the creation of organizations that "introduce" the single traveler to other single travelers, somewhat like a dating service. Some charge fees, others are free, but the basic service offered is the same: to match an unattached person with a compatible travel mate. Among such organizations are the following:

Jane's International (2603 Bath Ave., Brooklyn, NY 11214; phone: 718-266-2045). This service puts potential traveling companions in touch with one another. No age limit, no fee.

Partners-in-Travel (PO Box 491145, Los Angeles, CA 90049; phone: 213-476-4869). Members receive a list of singles seeking traveling companions; prospective companions make contact through the agency. The membership fee is $40 per year and includes a chatty newsletter (6 issues per year).

Singleworld (401 Theodore Fremd Ave., Rye, NY 10580; phone: 914-967-3334 or 800-223-6490 in the continental US). For a yearly fee of $25, this club books members on tours and cruises and arranges shared accommodations, allowing individual travelers to avoid the single supplement charge; members also receive a quarterly newsletter. *Singleworld* also offers its own package tours for singles with departures categorized by age group: 35 or younger and all ages.

Travel Companion Exchange (PO Box 833, Amityville, NY 11701; phone: 516-454-0880). This group publishes a newsletter for singles and a directory of individuals looking for travel companions. On joining, members fill out a lengthy questionnaire and write a small listing (much like an ad in a personal column). Based on these listings, members can request copies of profiles and contact prospective traveling companions. It is wise to join well in advance of your planned vacation so that there's enough time to determine compatibility and plan a joint trip. Membership fees, including the newsletter, are $6 a month for a single-sex directory and $11 a month for a complete directory; the minimum enrollment period is 6 months. Subscription to the newsletter alone costs $24 for 6 months or $36 per year.

In addition, a number of tour packagers cater to single travelers. These companies offer packages designed for individuals interested in vacationing with a group of single travelers or in being matched with a traveling companion. Among the better established of these agencies are the following:

Grand Circle Travel (347 Congress St., Boston, MA 02210; phone: 617-350-7500 or 800-221-2610). Arranges extended vacations, escorted tours and cruises for the over-50 traveler, including singles. Membership, which is automatic when you book a trip through *Grand Circle,* includes travel discounts and other extras, such as a pen-pals service for singles seeking traveling companions.

Marion Smith Singles (611 Prescott Place, North Woodmere, NY 11581; phone: 516-791-4852, 516-791-4865, or 212-944-2112). Specializes in tours for singles ages 20 to 50, who can choose to share accommodations to avoid paying single supplement charges. Recent offerings in Mexico included Club Med resorts at Ixtapa, Playa Blanca, and Sonora Bay.

Saga International Holidays (120 Boylston St., Boston MA 02116; phone: 617-451-6808 or 800-343-0273). A subsidiary of a British company specializing in older travelers, many of them single, *Saga* offers a broad selection of packages for people age 60 and over or those 50 to 59 traveling with someone 60 or older. Recent offerings included the 14-night Silver Cities of Mexico tour, with stops in Acapulco, Cuernavaca, Guadalajara, Guanajuato, Mexico City, Morelia, Taxco, and Teotihuacán. Although anyone can book a *Saga* trip, a $15 club membership includes a subscription to their newsletter, as well as other publications and travel services — such as a matching service for single travelers.

Singles in Motion (545 W. 236th St., Suite 1D, Riverdale, NY 10463; phone: 212-884-4464). Offers a number of packages for single travelers, including tours, cruises, and excursions focusing on outdoor activities such as hiking and biking.

Solo Flights (127 S. Compo Rd., Westport, CT 06880; phone: 203-226-9993). Represents a number of packagers and cruise lines and books singles on individual and group tours.

STI (8619 Reseda Blvd., Suite 103, Northridge, CA 91324; phone: 800-525-0525). Specializes in travel for 18- to 30-year-olds. Offers multi-country escorted tours ranging from 2 weeks to 2 months, including itineraries to Mexico.

Travel in Two's (239 N. Broadway, Suite 3, N. Tarrytown, NY 10591; phone: 914-631-8409). This company books solo travelers on packages offered by a number of companies (at no extra cost to clients), offers its own tours, and matches singles with traveling companions. Many offerings are listed in their quarterly *Singles Vacation Newsletter,* which costs $7.50 per issue or $20 per year.

A good book for single travelers is *Traveling On Your Own* by Eleanor Berman, which offers tips on traveling solo and includes information on trips for singles, ranging from outdoor adventures to educational programs. Available in bookstores, it also can be ordered by sending $12.95, plus postage and handling, to Random House, Order Dept., 400 Hahn Rd., Westminster, MD 21157 (phone: 800-733-3000).

Single travelers also may want to subscribe to *Going Solo,* a newsletter that offers helpful information on going on your own. Issued eight times a year, a subscription costs $36; contact Doerfer Communications, PO Box 1035, Cambridge, MA 02238 (phone: 617-876-2764).

An attractive alternative for the single traveler is *Club Med,* which operates scores of resorts in more than 37 countries worldwide and caters to the single traveler, as well as couples and families. Though the clientele often is under 30, there is a considerable age mix; the average age is 37. *Club Med* has five Mexican resorts — in Cancún, Huatulco, Ixtapa, Playa Blanca, and Sonora Bay — and offers single travelers package-rate vacations including airfare, food, wine, lodging, entertainment, and athletic facilities. The atmosphere is relaxed, the dress informal, and the price reasonable. For information, contact *Club Med* (3 E. 54th St., New York, NY 10022; phone: 800-CLUB-MED). For further information on *Club Med* and other resorts geared for singles, see our discussions in *On the Road,* in this section.

Another possibility is the *United States Servas Committee* (11 John St., Room 706, New York, NY 10038; phone: 212-267-0252), which maintains a list of hosts around the world who are willing to take visitors into their homes as guests. Many private houses and farms throughout the countryside make a pleasant home base and offer a chance to meet local people. *Servas* will send an application form and a list of interviewers at the nearest locations for you to contact. After the interview, if you are accepted as a *Servas* traveler, you'll receive a membership certificate. The membership fee is $45 per year for an individual, with a $15 deposit to receive the host list, refunded upon its return.

And there's always camping. Many areas along the coast in Mexico, as well as some sites around the countryside, have a place to pitch a tent and enjoy the scenery. However, it is *not* advisable to camp in any isolated area where it could be unsafe. So check — before you pitch your tent. (For more information, see *Camping and RVs, Hiking and Biking,* in this section.)

WOMEN AND STUDENTS: Two specific groups of single travelers deserve special mention: women and students. Countless women travel by themselves in Mexico, and such an adventure need not be feared. One lingering inhibition many female travelers still harbor is that of eating alone in public places. The trick here is to relax and enjoy your meal and surroundings; while you may run across the occasional unenlightened waiter, dining solo is no longer that uncommon.

A woman traveling alone in Mexico is bound to arouse more than the usual share of attention (by North American standards). This, more than any other single factor, can demoralize a woman on her own. However, exploring Mexico can be terrifically exciting, and people will go out of their way to be helpful. Once the sense of being foreign wears off, a woman traveler can feel at home in most out-of-the-way places, desert and jungle included. A single woman traveler is such a rarity that in many villages people consider it a privilege to meet one and will invite her to visit their families.

Still, a first-time visitor who speaks no Spanish is advised to join a tour of some kind; and even well-prepared or seasoned women travelers in Mexico invariably describe the experience with ambivalent feelings. Although there is little danger of physical harm if you apply commonsense guidelines (as you would if you were traveling in the US or Europe), any woman considering a trip to Mexico on her own must be prepared to encounter psychological discomfort if she minds being whistled at occasionally or if she is self-conscious about traveling alone in a male-dominated, family-oriented society.

Women travelers in Mexico also may be taken aback by the machismo of Mexican men. Women should be forewarned that this male perspective — akin to antediluvian chauvinism in the US — generally is accepted among Mexicans. It is unwise to think that an American woman traveler is going to change the national tide single-handedly.

Defense is the best offense in this case — don't let it spoil your vacation. For more insight, see *The Mexican People,* in PERSPECTIVES.

STUDYING ABROAD: A large number of single travelers are students. Travel *is* education. Travel broadens a person's knowledge and deepens his or her perception of the world in a way no media or "armchair" experience ever could. In addition, to study a country's language, art, culture, or history in one of its own schools is to enjoy the most productive method of learning.

By "student" we do not necessarily mean a person who wishes to matriculate at a foreign university to earn a degree. Nor do we necessarily mean a younger person. A student is anyone who wishes to include some sort of educational program in a trip to Mexico.

There are many benefits for students abroad, and the way to begin to discover them is to consult the *Council on International Educational Exchange* (*CIEE*). This organization, which runs a variety of well-known work, study, and travel programs for students, is the US sponsor of the International Student Identity Card (ISIC). Reductions on airfare, other transportation, and entry fees to most museums and other exhibitions are only some of the advantages of the card. To apply for it, write to *CIEE* at one of the following addresses: 205 E. 42nd St., New York, NY 10017 (phone: 212-661-1414); 312 Sutter St., Suite 407, San Francisco, CA 94108 (phone: 415-421-3473); or 919 Irving St., Suite 102, San Francisco, CA 94122 (phone: 415-566-6222). Mark the letter "Attn. Student ID." Application requires a $14 fee, a passport-size photograph, and proof that you are a matriculating student (this means either a transcript or a letter or bill from your school registrar with the school's official seal; high school and junior high school students can use their report cards). There is no maximum age limit, but participants must be at least 12 years old. The *ID Discount Guide,* which gives details of the discounts country by country, is free with membership. Another free publication of *CIEE* is the informative, annual, 64-page *Student Travel Catalog,* which covers all aspects of youth travel abroad for vacation trips, jobs, or study programs, and also includes a list of other helpful publications. You can order the catalogue from the Information and Student Services Department at the New York address given above.

Another card of value in Mexico, also available through *CIEE,* is the Federation of International Youth Travel Organizations (FIYTO) card, which provides many of the benefits of the ISIC card. In this case, cardholders need not be students, merely under age 26. To apply, send $14 with a passport-size photo and proof of birth date to *CIEE* at one of the addresses above.

Students and singles in general should keep in mind that youth hostels exist in many cities throughout Mexico. They always are inexpensive, generally clean and well situated, and they are a sure place to meet other people traveling alone. Hostels are run by the hosteling associations of 68 countries that make up the *International Youth Hostel Federation* (*IYHF*); membership in one of the national associations affords access to the hostels of the rest. To join the American affiliate, *American Youth Hostels (AYH),* contact the national office (PO Box 37613, Washington, DC 20013-7613; phone: 202-783-6161), or the local *AYH* council nearest you. As we went to press, the following annual membership rates were in effect: $25 for adults (between 18 and 54), $10 for youths (17 and under), $15 for seniors (55 and up), and $35 for families. The *AYH Handbook,* which lists hostels in the US, comes with your *AYH* card (nonmembers can purchase the handbook for $5, plus postage and handling); the *International Youth Hostels Handbooks,* which list hostels worldwide, must be purchased ($10.95 each, plus postage and handling).

Those who go abroad without an *AYH* card may purchase a youth hostel International Guest Card (for the equivalent of about $18) and obtain information on local youth hostels by contacting the *Mexico Youth Hostel Association* (40 Oxtopulco Norte,

Col. Oxtopulco Universidad, CP 04310, Mexico DF; phone 5-535-9341 or 5-535-9928). In addition, the tourist boards provide information sheets on hostels in their areas (see the individual city reports in THE CITIES for locations) and on hosteling package holidays.

Opportunities for study range from summer or academic-year courses in the language and civilization of Mexico designed specifically for foreigners (including those whose school days are well behind them) to long-term university attendance by those intending to take a degree.

Ever since the University of Mexico opened its doors in 1533, students in Mexico have been embarking upon courses of higher education in a variety of subjects. Today, the University of Mexico, located in Mexico City, is only one of 153 public and private universities and 160 other institutions of higher education in the country. Students from the US wishing to study in Mexico have a variety of options. A number of universities in the US sponsor programs at Mexican universities, and it also is possible to register for courses and programs designed specifically for foreign students under the auspices of a Mexican institution. Many US universities accept credits from Mexico, but students are advised to make sure that credits are reciprocal before enrolling. It also is advisable to begin researching and planning a study trip to Mexico about a year before you go. Documentation and application forms should be submitted more than 2 months before the semester in which a student wants to enter the university. The academic year runs from September through June, and most courses are given in Spanish. In addition, there are numerous summer courses and short programs for Americans interested in studying Spanish, Mexican archaeology, history, or literature, or painting or crafts, which are offered informally, in English, without credit, and for very reasonable fees.

Complete details on more than 3,000 available courses at schools abroad (including Mexican universities) and suggestions on how to apply are contained in two books published by the *Institute of International Education* (IIE Books, 809 UN Plaza, New York, NY 10017; phone 212-883-8200): *Vacation Study Abroad* ($24.95, plus shipping and handling) and *Academic Year Abroad* ($31.95, plus shipping and handling). A third book, *Teaching Abroad,* costs $21.95, plus shipping and handling. IIE Books also offers a free pamphlet called *Basic Facts on Study Abroad.*

The National Registration Center for Study Abroad (NRCSA, PO Box 1393, Milwaukee, WI 53201; phone: 414-278-0631) also offers a publication called *The Worldwide Classroom: Study Abroad & Learning Vacations in 40 Countries: 1991-1992,* available for $8, which includes information on over 160 schools and cultural centers that offer courses for Americans with the primary focus on foreign language and culture.

Those who are interested in a "learning vacation" also may be interested in *Travel and Learn* by Evelyn Kaye. This guide to educational travel discusses a wide range of opportunities — everything from archaeology to whale watching — and provides information on organizations that offer programs in these areas of interest. The book is available in bookstores for $23.95, or you can send $26 (which includes shipping charges) to Blue Penguin Publications (147 Sylvan Ave., Leonia, NJ 07605; phone: 800-800-8147 or 201-461-6918). *Learning Vacations* by Gerson G. Eisenberg also provides extensive information on seminars, workshops, courses, and so on — in a variety of subjects. Available in bookstores, it also can be ordered from Peterson's Guides (PO Box 2123, Princeton, NJ 08543-2123; phone: 609-243-9111) for $11.95, plus shipping and handling.

Work, Study, Travel Abroad: The Whole World Handbook, issued by the *Council on International Educational Exchange (CIEE),* is an informative, chatty guide on study programs, work opportunities, and travel hints, with a particularly good section on Mexico and Latin America. It is available for $10.95, plus shipping and handling, from *CIEE* (address above).

AFS Intercultural Programs (313 E. 43rd St., New York, NY 10017; phone: 212-949-4242 or 800-AFS-INFO) sets up exchanges between US and foreign high school students on an individual basis for a whole academic year or a semester.

National Association of Secondary School Principals (*NASSP,* 1904 Association Dr., Reston, VA 22091; phone: 703-860-0200), an association of administrators, teachers, and state education officials, sponsors *School Partnership International,* a program in which secondary schools in the US are linked with partner schools abroad for an annual short-term exchange of students and faculty.

If you are interested in a home-stay travel program, in which you learn about Mexican culture by living with a family, contact the *Experiment in International Living* (PO Box 676, Brattleboro, VT 05302-0676; phone: 802-257-7751 in Vermont; 800-345-2929 elsewhere in the continental US), which sponsors home-stay educational travel in more than 40 countries, including Mexican locations in Guanajuato and Oaxaca. The organization aims its programs at high school or college students.

WORKING ABROAD: Mexican labor laws make it hard for foreign nationals to work in the country. Unemployment is so severe in Mexico that legislation tries to ensure that all available jobs go to Mexicans. However, one US organization sponsors a 7-week voluntary summer program for 18- to 26-year-olds. Projects are in rural villages, where participants work with local organizations on such tasks as school repair or digging ditches for water systems. Spanish language knowledge is required. The cost is about $700 plus travel expenses. For information, write to *American Friends Service Committee,* 1501 Cherry St., Philadelphia, PA 19102 (phone: 215-241-7000).

Hints for Older Travelers

Special discounts and more free time are just two factors that have given Americans over age 65 a chance to see the world at affordable prices. Senior citizens make up an ever-growing segment of the travel population, and the trend among them is to travel more frequently and for longer periods of time.

PLANNING: When planning a vacation, prepare your itinerary with one eye on your own physical condition and the other on a topographical map. The greatest obstacles to travel in Mexico are the climate, terrain, and altitudes involved. An average tour may include sudden changes from high mountain country to jungle-like regions. These pose some danger for anyone with heart or breathing problems. In cities like Mexico City, Oaxaca, and Puebla everyone has trouble breathing, even the most fit.

Older travelers may find the following publications of interest:

The Discount Guide for Travelers Over 55, by Caroline and Walter Weintz, is an excellent book for budget-conscious older travelers. It is available by sending $7.95, plus shipping and handling, to Penguin USA (Att. Cash Sales, 120 Woodbine St., Bergenfield, NJ 07621); when ordering, specify the ISBN number: 0-525-48358-6.

Going Abroad: 101 Tips for the Mature Traveler offers tips on preparing for your trip, commonsense precautions en route, and some basic travel terminology. This concise free booklet is available from *Grand Circle Travel,* 347 Congress St., Boston, MA 02210 (phone: 800-221-2610 or 617-350-7500).

The International Health Guide for Senior Citizen Travelers, by Dr. W. Robert Lange, covers such topics as trip preparations, food and water precautions, adjusting to weather and climate conditions, finding a doctor, motion sickness, jet lag, and so on. Also includes a list of resource organizations that provide medical assistance for travelers. It is available for $4.95 postpaid from Pilot Books, 103 Cooper St., Babylon, NY 11702 (phone: 516-422-2225).

The Mature Traveler is a monthly newsletter that provides information on travel discounts, places of interest, useful tips, and other topics of interest for travelers 49 and up. To subscribe, send $21.95 to GEM Publishing Group, PO Box 50820, Reno, NV 89513 (phone: 702-786-7419).

Travel Easy: The Practical Guide for People Over 50, by Rosalind Massow, discusses a wide range of subjects — from trip planning, transportation options, and preparing for departure to avoiding and handling medical problems en route. It's available for $6.50 to members of the *American Association of Retired Persons (AARP)*, and for $8.95 to non-members (call about current charges for postage and handling). Order from AARP Books, c/o Customer Service, Scott, Foresman & Company, 1900 E. Lake Ave., Glenview, IL 60025 (phone: 708-729-3000).

Travel Tips for Older Americans is a useful booklet with general advice. This US State Department publication (stock number: 044-000-02270-2) can be ordered by sending a check or money order for $1 to the Superintendent of Documents (US Government Printing Office, Washington, DC 20402) or by calling 202-783-3238 and charging the order to a credit card.

Unbelievably Good Deals & Great Adventures That You Absolutely Can't Get Unless You're Over 50, by Joan Rattner Heilman, offers travel tips for older travelers, including discounts on accommodations and transportation, as well as a list of organizations for seniors. It is available for $7.95, plus shipping and handling, from Contemporary Books, 180 N. Michigan Ave., Chicago, IL 60601 (phone: 312-782-9181).

HEALTH: Health facilities in Mexico generally are good; however, an inability to speak the language can pose a serious problem, not in receiving treatment at large hospitals, where many doctors and other staff members will speak English, but in getting help elsewhere or in getting to the place where help is available. A number of organizations help travelers avoid or deal with a medical emergency while traveling. For information on these services, see *Medical and Legal Aid and Consular Services,* in this section.

Pre-trip medical and dental checkups are strongly recommended, particularly for older travelers. In addition, be sure to take along any prescription medication you need, enough to last *without a new prescription* for the duration of your trip; pack all medications with a note from your doctor for the benefit of airport authorities. If you have specific medical problems, bring prescriptions and a "medical file" composed of the following:

1. A summary of your medical history and current diagnosis.
2. A list of drugs to which you are allergic.
3. Your most recent electrocardiogram, if you have heart problems.
4. Your doctor's name, address, and telephone number.

DISCOUNTS AND PACKAGES: Since guidelines change from place to place, older travelers should inquire in advance about discounts on accommodations, transportation, theater and concert performances, movies, museums, and other activities.

Many hotel chains, airlines, bus companies, car rental companies, and other travel suppliers offer discounts to older travelers. Some of these discounts, however, are extended only to bona fide members of certain senior citizens organizations. Because the same organizations frequently offer package tours to both domestic and international destinations, the benefits of membership are twofold: Those who join can take advantage of discounts as individual travelers and also reap the savings that group travel affords. In addition, because the age requirements for some of these organizations are quite low (or nonexistent), the benefits can begin to accrue early. To take advantage of these discounts, you should carry proof of your age (or eligibility). A driver's license, membership card in a recognized senior citizens organization, or a Medicare card should be adequate. Among the organizations dedicated to helping older travelers see the world are the following:

American Association of Retired Persons (AARP; 1909 K St. NW, Washington, DC 20049; phone: 202-872-4700). The largest and best known of these organizations. Membership is open to anyone 50 or over, whether retired or not; dues are $5 a year, $12.50 for 3 years, or $35 for 10 years, and include spouse. The *AARP* Travel Experience program, available through *American Express Travel Related Services* offers members tours, cruises, and other travel programs worldwide designed exclusively for older travelers, including tours and resort packages with accommodations in apartments in Mexico. Members can book these services by calling *American Express* at 800-927-0111 for land and air travel, or 800-745-4567 for cruises.

Mature Outlook (Customer Service Center, 6001 N. Clark St., Chicago, IL 60660; phone: 800-336-6330). Through its *TravelAlert,* tours, cruises, and other vacation packages are available to members at special savings. Hotel and car rental discounts and travel accident insurance also are available. Membership is open to anyone 50 years of age or older, costs $9.95 a year, and includes a bimonthly newsletter and magazine, as well as information on package tours.

National Council of Senior Citizens (1331 F St., Washington, DC 20005; phone: 202-347-8800). Here, too, the emphasis is on keeping costs low. This nonprofit organization offers members a different roster of package tours each year, as well as individual arrangements through its affiliated travel agency *(Vantage Travel Service).* Although most members are over 50, membership is open to anyone (regardless of age) for an annual fee of $12 per person or couple. Lifetime membership costs $150.

Certain travel agencies and tour operators offer special trips geared to older travelers. Among them are the following:

Evergreen Travel Service (4114-198th St. SW, Suite 13, Lynnwood, WA 98036-6742; phone: 206-776-1184 or 800-435-2288 throughout the continental US and Canada). This specialist in trips for persons with disabilities recently introduced Lazybones tours, a program offering leisurely tours for older travelers. Most programs are first class or deluxe, and include an escort.

Gadabout Tours (700 E. Tahquitz, Palm Springs, CA 92262; phone: 619-325-5556 or 800-521-7309 in California; 800-952-5068 elsewhere in the US). Offers escorted tours and cruises to a number of Mexican destinations, including the Baja region, Copper Canyon, and the Yucatán Peninsula.

Grand Circle Travel (347 Congress St., Boston, MA 02210; phone: 800-221-2610 or 617-350-7500). Caters exclusively to the over-50 traveler and packages a large variety of escorted tours, cruises, and extended vacations, including trips to Guadalajara, Mérida, and Oaxaca in Mexico. Membership, which is automatic when you book a trip through *Grand Circle,* includes discount certificates on future trips and other travel services, such as a matching service for single travelers and a helpful free booklet, *Going Abroad: 101 Tips for Mature Travelers* (see the source list above).

Saga International Holidays (120 Boylston St., Boston MA 02116; phone: 617-451-6808 or 800-343-0273). A subsidiary of a British company specializing in the older traveler, *Saga* offers a broad selection of packages for people age 60 and over or those 50 to 59 traveling with someone 60 or older. Recent offerings included a 14-night Silver Cities of Mexico tour, with stops in Acapulco, Cuernavaca, Guadalajara, Guanajuato, Mexico City, Morelia, Taxco, and Teotihuacán. Although anyone can book a *Saga* trip, a $15 club membership includes a subscription to their newsletter, as well as other publications and travel services.

Many travel agencies, particularly the larger ones, are delighted to make presentations to help a group of senior citizens select destinations. A local chamber of commerce should be able to provide the names of such agencies. Once a time and place are determined, an organization member or travel agent can obtain group quotations for transportation, accommodations, meal plans, and sightseeing. Larger groups usually get the best breaks.

Another choice open to older travelers is a trip that includes an educational element. *Elderhostel,* a nonprofit organization, offers programs at educational institutions worldwide, including Cuernavaca, Oaxaca, and Puebla in Mexico. The foreign programs generally last about 2 weeks, and include double occupancy accommodations in hotels or student residence halls and all meals. Travel to the programs usually is by designated scheduled flights, and participants can arrange to extend their stay at the end of the program. Elderhostelers must be at least 60 years old (younger if a spouse or companion qualifies), in good health, and not in need of special diets. For a free catalogue describing the program and current offerings, write to *Elderhostel* (75 Federal St., Boston, MA 02110; phone: 617-426-7788). Those interested in the program also can borrow slides at no charge or purchase an informational videotape for $5.

Interhostel, a program sponsored by the Division of Continuing Education of the University of New Hampshire, sends travelers back to school at cooperating institutions in 25 countries on 4 continents. In Mexico, programs include studies in Cuernavaca, Mexico City, Oaxaca, and San Cristóbal. Participants attend lectures on the history, economy, politics, and cultural life of the country they are visiting, go on field trips to pertinent points of interest, and take part in activities meant to introduce them to their foreign contemporaries. Trips are for 2 weeks; accommodations are on campus in university residence halls or off campus in modest hotels (double occupancy). Groups are limited to 35 to 40 participants who are at least 50 years old (or at least 40 if a participating spouse is at least 50), physically active, and not in need of special diets. For information or to receive three free seasonal catalogues, write to *Interhostel* (UNH Division of Continuing Education, 6 Garrison Ave., Durham, NH 03824; phone: 800-733-9753 or 603-862-1147).

Hints for Traveling with Children

What better way to encounter the world's variety than in the company of the young, wide-eyed members of your family? Their presence does not have to be a burden or an excessive expense. The current generation of discounts for children and family package deals can make a trip together quite reasonable.

A family trip will be an investment in your children's future, making geography and history come alive to them, and leaving a sure memory that will be among the fondest you will share with them someday. Their insights will be refreshing to you; their impulses may take you to unexpected places with unexpected dividends. The experience will be invaluable to them at any age.

PLANNING: Here are several hints for making a trip with children easy and fun:

1. Children, like everyone else, will derive more pleasure from a trip if they know something about their destination before they arrive. Begin their education about a month before you leave. Using maps, travel magazines, and books, give children a clear idea of where you are going and how far away it is.

2. Children should help to plan the itinerary, and where you go and what you do should reflect some of their ideas. If they already know something about the sites they'll visit, they will have the excitement of recognition when they arrive.

3. Children also will enjoy learning some Spanish phrases — a few basics like *hola!* (hello), *adiós* (good-bye), and *gracias* (thanks).

4. Familiarize your children with pesos. Give them an allowance for the trip and be sure they understand just how far it will or won't go.

5. Give children specific responsibilities: The job of carrying their own flight bags and looking after their personal things, along with some other light travel chores, will give them a stake in the journey.

6. Give each child a travel diary or scrapbook to take along.

One useful resource to which you may want to refer is the *Berlitz Jr. Spanish* instructional series for children. The series combines an illustrated storybook with a lively 60-minute audiocassette. Each book features a character, Teddy, who goes to school and learns to count and spell and speak Spanish phrases. The book/cassette package is available for $19.95, plus shipping and handling, from Macmillan Publishing Company, Front and Brown Sts., Riverside, NJ 08075 (phone: 800-257-5755).

Children's books about Mexico provide an excellent introduction to the country and culture and can be found at many general bookstores and in libraries. Bookstores specializing in children's books include the following:

> *Books of Wonder* (132 7th Ave., New York, NY 10011; phone: 212-989-3270; or 464 Hudson St., New York, NY 10014; phone: 212-645-8006). Carries both new and used children's books.
>
> *Cheshire Cat Book Store* (5512 Connecticut Ave. NW, Washington, DC 20015; phone: 202-244-3956). Specializes in books for children of all ages.
>
> *Eeyore's Books for Children* (2212 Broadway, New York, NY 10024; phone: 212-362-0634; or 25 E. 83rd St., New York, NY 10028; phone: 212-988-3404). Carries an extensive selection of children's books; features a special travel section.
>
> *Reading Reptile, Books and Toys for Young Mammals* (4120 Pennsylvania, Kansas City, MO 64111; phone: 816-753-0441). Carries books for children and teens to age 15.
>
> *Red Balloon Bookshop* (891 Grand Ave., St. Paul, MN 55105; phone: 612-224-8320). Carries both new and used books for children.
>
> *White Rabbit Children's Books* (7755 Girard Ave., La Jolla, CA 92037; phone: 619-454-3518). Carries books and music for children (and parents).

Another source of children's books perfect to take on the road is *The Family Travel Guides Catalogue.* This detailed booklet describes a number of informative and fun titles and is available from Carousel Press (PO Box 6061, Albany, CA 94706; phone: 415-527-5849), which also is the mail-order supplier of all titles listed.

And for parents, *Travel With Your Children (TWYCH;* 80 Eighth Ave., New York, NY 10011; phone: 212-206-0688) publishes a newsletter, *Family Travel Times,* that focuses on families with young travelers and offers helpful hints. An annual subscription (10 issues) is $35 and includes a copy of the "Airline Guide" issue (updated every other year), which focuses on the subject of flying with children. This special issue is available separately for $10.

Another newsletter devoted to family travel is *Getaways.* This quarterly publication provides reviews of family-oriented literature, activities, and useful travel tips. To subscribe, send $25 to *Getaways,* Att. Ms. Brooke Kane, PO Box 11511, Washington, DC 20008 (phone: 703-534-8747).

Also of interest to parents traveling with their children is *How to Take Great Trips With Your Kids,* by psychologist Sanford Portnoy and his wife, Joan Flynn Portnoy.

The book includes helpful tips from fellow family travelers, a chapter on child development relating to travel, tips on economical accommodations and touring by car, recreational vehicle, and train, as well as over 50 games to play with your children en route. It is available for $8.95, plus shipping and handling, from Harvard Common Press, 535 Albany St., Boston, MA 02118 (phone: 617-423-5803).

Another book on family travel, *Travel with Children* by Maureen Wheeler, offers a wide range of practical tips on traveling with children, and includes accounts of the author's family travel experiences. It is available for $10.95, plus shipping and handling, from Lonely Planet Publications, Embarcadero West, 112 Linden St., Oakland, CA 94607 (phone: 415-893-8555).

Finally, parents arranging a trip with their children may want to deal with an agency specializing in family travel such as *Let's Take the Kids* (1268 Devon Ave., Los Angeles, CA 90024; phone: 800-726-4349 or 213-274-7088). In addition to arranging and booking trips for individual families, this group occasionally organizes trips for single-parent families traveling together. They also offer a "parent travel network," whereby parents who have been to a particular destination can evaluate it for others.

GETTING THERE AND GETTING AROUND: Begin early to investigate all available family discount and charter flights, as well as any package deals and special rates offered by the major airlines.

PLANE: When you make your reservations, tell the airline that you are traveling with a child. Children ages 2 through 12 generally travel at about half to two-thirds of the adult fare on most international flights. On many international flights, children under 2 travel at about 10% of the adult fare if they sit on an adult's lap. A second infant without a second adult would pay the fare applicable to children ages 2 through 11.

Although some airlines will, on request, supply bassinets for infants, most carriers encourage parents to bring their own safety seat on board, which then is strapped into the airline seat with a regular seat belt. This is much safer — and certainly more comfortable — than holding the child in your lap. If you do not purchase a seat for your baby, you have the option of bringing the infant restraint along on the off-chance that there might be an empty seat next to yours — in which case some airlines will let you use that seat at no charge for your baby and infant seat. However, if there is no empty seat available, the infant seat no doubt will have to be checked as baggage (and you may have to pay an additional charge), since it generally does not fit under the seat or in the overhead racks.

The safest bet is to pay for a seat — this usually will be the same as fares applicable to children ages 2 through 11. You might have to do some number-juggling to determine the cheapest fare for the infant. Airlines are more likely to offer discounts for children when the adult is flying on a more expensive fare rather than an excursion or other discount fare.

Be forewarned: Some safety seats designed primarily for use in cars do not fit into plane seats properly. Although nearly all seats manufactured since 1985 carry labels indicating whether they meet federal standards for use aboard planes, actual seat sizes may vary from carrier to carrier. At the time of this writing, the FAA was in the process of reviewing and revising the federal regulations regarding infant travel and safety devices — it was still to be determined if children should be *required* to sit in safety seats and whether the airlines will have to provide them.

If using one of these infant restraints, you should try to get bulkhead seats which will provide extra room to care for your child during the flight. You also should request a bulkhead seat when using a bassinet (some airlines do provide bassinets) — again, this is not as safe as strapping the child in. On some planes bassinets hook into a bulkhead wall; on others it is placed on the floor in front of you. (Note that bulkhead seats often are reserved for families traveling with children.) As a general rule, babies should be held during takeoff and landing.

Request seats on the aisle if you have a toddler or if you think you will need to use the bathroom frequently. Carry onto the plane all you will need to care for and occupy your children during the flight — formula, diapers, a sweater, books, favorite stuffed animals, and so on. Dress your baby simply, with a minimum of buttons and snaps, because the only place you may have to change a diaper is at your seat or in a small lavatory. The flight attendant can warm a bottle for you.

You also can ask for a hot dog or hamburger instead of the airline's regular dinner, if you give at least 24 hours' notice. Some, but not all, airlines have baby food aboard. While you should bring along toys from home, also ask about children's diversions. Some carriers have terrific free packages of games, coloring books, and puzzles.

When the plane takes off and lands, make sure your baby is nursing or has a bottle, pacifier, or thumb in his or her mouth. This sucking will make the child swallow and help to clear stopped ears. A piece of hard candy will do the same thing for an older child.

Parents traveling by plane with toddlers, children, or teenagers may want to consult *When Kids Fly,* a free booklet published by Massport (Public Affairs Department, 10 Park Plaza, Boston, MA 02116-3971; phone: 617-973-5600), which includes helpful information on airfares for children, infant seats, what to do in the event of overbooked or cancelled flights, and so on.

■**Note:** Newborn babies, whose lungs may not be able to adjust to the altitude, should not be taken aboard an airplane. And some airlines may refuse to allow a pregnant woman in her 8th or 9th month aboard, for fear that something could go wrong with an in-flight birth. Check with the airline ahead of time, and carry a letter from your doctor stating that you are fit to travel — and indicating the estimated date of birth.

SHIP, TRAIN, AND BUS: Some shipping lines offer cruises that feature special activities for children, particularly during periods that coincide with major school holidays like *Christmas, Easter,* and the summer months. On such cruises, children may be charged special cut-rate fares, and there are youth counselors to organize activities. Occasionally, a shipping line even offers free passage during the summer months for children under age 16 occupying a stateroom with two (full-fare) adult passengers. Your travel agent should know which cruise lines offer such programs.

If you plan to travel by train when in Mexico, note that children under 12 usually travel at a reduced rate, and there may be no charge for toddlers, provided they do not occupy a seat. Some regional bus lines also may have lower fares for children or family rates. For more information, see *Traveling by Ship, Traveling by Train,* and *Traveling by Bus,* all in this section.

CAR: Traveling by car allows greater flexibility in traveling and packing. You may want to stock the car with a variety of favorite snacks and if you pack an ice chest and a grill, you can stop for picnics (most beaches are public and free in Mexico). You may want to bring dry ice since ice isn't so easy to come by in rural areas. Near the larger cities, ice cubes are sold at gasoline service stations and ice blocks are available from the local beer distributors. Whether from your hotel kitchen or a local store, only use ice for keeping food chilled in coolers — *never* put it in drinks, as you can't count on the quality of the water from which it was made. If your accommodations include a refrigerator, a good alternative is to make some ice cubes the night before from purified water. (For more information, see *Staying Healthy,* in this section.)

ACCOMMODATIONS AND MEALS: Often a cot will be placed in a hotel room at little or no extra charge. If you wish to sleep in separate rooms, special rates sometimes are available for families; some places do not charge for children under a certain age. In many of the larger chain hotels, the staffs are more used to children. These hotels also are likely to have swimming pools or gamerooms — both popular with most youngsters. Many large resorts also have recreation centers for children. Cabins, bunga-lows, condominiums, and other rental options offer families privacy, flexibility, some kitchen facilities, and often lower costs.

A number of hotel chains with properties in Mexico do not charge for children who occupy the same room as their parents. In addition, a few hotels offer special youth activities programs, particularly during summer months. Detailed information can be obtained from a travel agent.

There are some resort condominium apartments available for rent in Mexico. These provide excellent accommodations for families. The apartment becomes a "home away from home" and a considerable sum can be saved by preparing meals yourself rather than taking the entire crew out to restaurants three times a day. In addition, many complexes do not charge for children under 12 years old, and a few permit anyone under 18 to stay with their families without charge. (Some condos don't allow children, so before you set your heart on a particular one, find out all the details of its rental policy.) Some of the condominium vacation packages include a rental car, which can be quite economical. (For more information on package options, see *Package Tours,* in this section.)

Among the least expensive options is a camping facility; many are situated in beauti-ful, out-of-the-way spots, and generally are good and well-equipped. For further infor-mation on accommodations options for the whole family, see our discussions in *On the Road,* and for information on camping facilities, see *Camping and RVs, Hiking and Biking,* both in this section.

Although it is difficult to find adequate baby-sitting services in most Mexican cities, most better hotels will try to arrange for a sitter for the times you will want to be without children — for an evening's entertainment or a particularly rigorous stint of sightseeing. Whether the sitter is hired directly or through an agency, ask for and check references and keep in mind that the candidates may not speak much, if any, English. In many small villages there are Mexican women who are glad to tend a child for a couple of hours, but this is usually a situation that arises after child and parents have been in the town a few days, long enough to establish a relationship with villagers.

At mealtime, don't deny yourself or your children the delights of a new style of cooking. Children like to know what kind of food to expect, so it will be interesting to look up Mexican dishes before leaving. Encourage your children to try new things, however, even though simple tacos, burritos, and cheese-filled tortillas are similar to hamburgers and grilled cheese sandwiches, they may not fill the bill for some children. In metropolitan and resort areas, you should be able to find American-style food, but you probably will have to settle for local fare everywhere else.

Things to Remember
1. If you are spending your vacation touring Mexico, rather than visiting one spot or engaging in one activity, pace the days with children in mind. Break the trip into half-day segments, with running around or "doing" time built in. Keep travel time on the road to a maximum of 4 to 5 hours a day.
2. Don't forget that a child's attention span is far shorter than an adult's. Children don't have to see every sight or all of any sight to learn something from their trip; watching, playing with, and talking to other children can be equally enlightening.
3. Let your children lead the way sometimes; their perspective is different from yours, and they may lead you to things you would never have noticed on your own.
4. Remember the places that children love to visit: aquariums, zoos, beaches, nature trails, small amusement parks, and so on. Among activities that may pique their interest are bicycling, snorkeling, boat trips, visiting planetariums and children's museums, exploring pyramids and ruins, and viewing natural habitat exhibits.

Throughout Mexico you will find splendid activities that involve no language barrier, which children will love. An especially rewarding and colorful experience for kids is the *Day of the Dead* celebration (November 1–2). In Mexico City, there are plenty of entertaining and educational activities to keep your children busy. Chapultepec Park has an amusement park, a zoo with several giant pandas, and *Atlantis,* a marine park with a wonderful dolphin and seal show. The *Anthropological Museum,* the *Technological Museum of the Federal Electricity Commission,* and the *Museum of Natural History,* all in Chapultepec Park, are filled with exhibits that would capture any child's imagination and interest. The *Ballet Folklórico,* which holds performances on Wednesdays and Sundays in the *Palace of Fine Arts,* is a lively, colorful presentation with music that children and adults love. Xochimilco has the floating gardens, where you cruise along flower-festooned lagoons in your own boat, and is a place children find memorable. *Reino Aventura* (Adventure Kingdom), south of Mexico City, is a 110-acre park with a children's section that includes a marine park, rides, and special movies. The Zacango Zoo near Toluca, with probably the largest aviary in Latin America, is patterned on the no-fences concept. *Plaza Show,* a children's educational park north of Mexico City, has models of prehistoric animals, a walk-through brontosaurus, a feeding zoo of baby animals, and a Galápagos turtle that will take children for a ride.

Other areas also offer ample amusement for children. Near Puebla is *Africam,* a park filled with African animals, through which you can drive in your car. Acapulco's *Cici* marineland and park has an artificial wave pool, water slide, pirate ship, and dolphin seal show. In Monterrey, there is a large amusement park and an excellent new zoo. There also are outstanding zoos in Guadalajara and Morelia. Mexico also has a number of traveling circuses — some three-ring and some one-ring. You can find out from the local tourist office when a circus is coming to any town. They also advertise in the entertainment sections of local Spanish-language newspapers. In northern and central Mexico there are mining towns, ghost towns, and subterranean caves open for exploration by adults and children, and in Mexico's many archaeological zones there are pyramids which house intricate networks of staircases and passageways leading to secret rooms and chambers. There also are several resort areas on both coasts with a variety of recreational facilities and even dude ranches.

Hints for Traveling with Pets

You may wish to bring your pet along on your vacation in Mexico. The rules vary, depending on the type of animal; those governing the movement of dogs and cats are more lenient than those regarding birds.

DOGS AND CATS: Tourists must have a veterinarian's certificate in duplicate that has been stamped by the US Department of Agriculture, and that states that the animal is in good health. Dogs must be accompanied by a certificate of inoculation against rabies, hepatitis, and distemper given within the previous 3 months. These certificates must be made legal by a Mexican consul (for a fee of $20 at press time). It's a simple procedure: The consul stamps the dog's certificates from the vet and these become the animal's permit to travel. A consul will validate only certificates issued in his own area. Certificates should be provided in duplicate so that the consul can retain a copy.

It is equally easy to bring your dog or cat back into the US from Mexico. US Customs will require that a dog has been inoculated against rabies at least 30 days prior to entry (the notarized form required for entry into Mexico will suffice to prove this). If a puppy is under 3 months old (and, therefore, not vaccinated), it must be confined by the owner until the dog has reached 3 months, then vaccinated, and then confined once again for a period of 30 days. Cats need only appear healthy.

The American Society for the Prevention of Cruelty to Animals (ASPCA) offers a very useful booklet, *Traveling With Your Pet,* which lists inoculation and other requirements by state and country, and also includes a number of helpful hints. It is available for $5 (which includes postage and handling). Send check or money order to the *ASPCA* (Education Dept., 441 E. 92 St., New York, NY 10128; phone: 212-876-7700). For further information on pet transportation contact the US Department of Agriculture Veterinary Services (Animal and Plant Health Inspection Service, Veterinary Services, Federal Center Building, 6505 Belcrest Rd., Room 764, Hyattsville, MD 20782; phone: 301-436-8490).

Other publications of interest to those traveling with pets include *Touring With Towser,* which includes tips to follow when traveling with your dog. For a copy send $1.50 to Quaker Professional Services (585 Hawthorne Court, Galesburg, IL 61401). *The Portable Pet,* by Barbara Nicholas, covers such topics as traveling by car, plane, bus, and ship; first aid for your pet; travel supplies that you'll need; quarantine regulations; and airport kennel facilities. It is available for $5.95, plus shipping and handling, from Harvard Common Press, 535 Albany St., Boston, MA 02118 (phone: 617-423-5803).

■**Note:** Don't consider taking your pet to Mexico by either train or bus. The trip is too long and contact with the animal too infrequent. And before considering taking any wild animal home as a "pet," check with the local branch of the US Department of Agriculture for state regulations, as well as health and safety considerations. The best advice is: Don't.

PLANE AND CAR: Many airlines require a health certificate for your pet. *Northwest, Pan American, TWA,* and *United,* for example, all require submission of an Interstate Health Certificate signed by an accredited veterinarian and dated no more than 30 days before travel. Check with your air carrier well before your departure. Mexican domestic airlines post the same requirements as the Mexican government in transporting pets.

It's a good idea to buy a traveling kennel. Most pet stores sell them, as do some airlines. Any animal must be boxed for the plane trip; a kennel also is a good safety measure on a car trip.

If your pet is traveling by plane, label the kennel with your name, address, destination, pet's name, and special handling instructions. Remove the animal's collar before putting it in the kennel. Dogs should not be muzzled. Put a few toys and familiar objects in the kennel to acquaint the animal with its box before the start of the trip.

Some airlines (such as *Pan American* and *TWA*) allow kenneled pets to fly in the passenger compartment — if there is room and the kennel falls within the dimension restrictions of carry-on baggage. A common restriction is that the pet must be kept in the kennel during takeoff and landing and when food is being served. On most airlines, however, the animal must fly in a special area reserved for live cargo. Whether the pet travels in the passenger or cargo compartment, the airline will charge a fee for transport.

■**Note:** For the majority of travelers to Mexico who choose to leave their pets at home, the *American Boarding Kennels Association* (4575 Galley Rd., Suite 400A, Colorado Springs, CO 80915; phone: 719-591-1113) publishes a roster of member boarding kennels throughout the US, as well as an informative pamphlet, *How to Select a Boarding Kennel.*

Staying Healthy

The surest way to return home in good health is to be prepared for medical problems that might occur on vacation. Below, we've outlined some things you need to think about before you go.

Older travelers or anyone suffering from a chronic medical condition, such as diabetes, high blood pressure, cardiopulmonary disease, asthma, or ear, eye, or sinus trouble should consult a physician before leaving home. Those with conditions requiring special consideration when traveling should consider seeing, in addition to their regular physician, a specialist in travel medicine. For a referral in a particular community, contact the nearest medical school or ask a local doctor to recommend such a specialist. Dr. Leonard Marcus, a member of the *American Committee on Clinical Tropical Medicine and Travelers' Health,* provides a directory of more than 100 travel doctors across the country. For a copy, send a 9-by-12-inch, self-addressed, stamped envelope, to Dr. Marcus at 148 Highland Ave., Newton, MA 02165 (phone: 617-527-4003).

FIRST AID: Put together a compact, personal medical kit including Band-Aids, first-aid cream, antiseptic, nose drops, insect repellent, aspirin or non-aspirin tablets, an extra pair of prescription glasses or contact lenses (and a copy of your prescription for glasses or contact lenses), sunglasses, over-the-counter remedies for diarrhea, indigestion, and motion sickness, a thermometer, and a supply of those prescription medicines you take regularly.

In a corner of your kit, keep a list of all the drugs you have brought and their purpose , as well as duplicate copies of your doctor's prescriptions (or a note from your doctor). As brand names may vary in different countries, it's a good idea to ask your doctor for the generic name of any drugs you use so that you can ask for their equivalent should you need a refill. Unless it is an emergency, however, some prescriptions may require the signature of a Mexican physician. (In recent years the Mexican Health Ministry has developed a list of restricted drugs and medicines, which includes certain seasickness tablets, that require a written prescription from a local doctor.)

It also is a good idea to ask your doctor to prepare a medical identification card that includes such information as your blood type, your social security number, any allergies or chronic health problems you have, and your medical insurance information. Considering the essential contents of your medical kit, keep it with you, rather than in your checked luggage.

Typically, tourists suffer two kinds of health problems in Mexico, but neither is inevitable. The first is the stomach upset known the world over as the scourge of travelers: Cairo Crud, Delhi Belly, *la turista,* and, in Mexico, Montezuma's Revenge. The second is more familiar: simple sunburn. And, as a number of diseases are contracted through bug bites (see below), some precaution against biting insects is strongly advised.

DIARRHEA AND STOMACH UPSETS: Without a doubt, a traveler's most serious complaint traveling in Mexico is dysentery or diarrhea, accompanied by severe intestinal pain and a foul taste in the mouth.

It is very important to take the first few days easy, especially if you land in Mexico City, where the high altitude will be tiring and exacerbate the effect of any alcohol on your system. Because Mexicans eat at very different times than Americans (they normally have a light breakfast; a heavy meal in the mid- to late afternoon; and a late dinner, starting any time after 9 PM), your system will have a doubly hard time acclimating to the new regime — so drink and eat lightly on arrival.

Fortunately, the vast majority of intestinal disorders encountered during travel represent only a temporary inconvenience, which will go away with rest and time. Serious intestinal trouble almost invariably is the product of drinking water contaminated by a particular strain of *E. coli* bacteria. These bacteria inhabit the human intestinal tract and are transmitted through fecal matter, and from there into plumbing and any unpurified water system. The result most often is called Montezuma's Revenge.

There is a very simple way to avoid it: Don't drink the water. Brush your teeth with bottled carbonated water (be sure you're not getting a used bottle refilled with tap water). Wash fruit with purified water, and don't drink iced drinks where the ice has been made from tap water. If you are staying in a first class hotel in a major tourist area, you will be in no danger. Elsewhere, and as a matter of course, it is wise to stick to bottled water (ask for *agua purificada* or *agua mineral*) or substitute wine or beer at meals. You also might carry standard GI water purification tablets (tetraglycine hydroperiodide). Just drop one of these tablets in a carafe of water and let it stand for half an hour.

We also recommend that you eat only those fruits that have been peeled (oranges, bananas, and so on), and cooked vegetables. Garnishes of fresh vegetables (even a small amount of shredded lettuce and tomatoes) and salads (especially those with creamy or mayonnaise-based dressings that have been out on serving tables for any period of time) can wreak havoc with your gastrointestinal system the morning after. Stay away from unfamiliar dishes that are hard to identify, and those tempting alcoholic concoctions served in coconuts or pineapples, as well as fruit juices; even in the better hotels, these may be diluted with tap water. Do not drink or eat raw milk, unpasteurized or uncooked dairy products, and above all, stay away from food vendors on streets and beaches.

Be sure to carry along an anti-diarrhea medication and recommended antibiotic in case you do develop symptoms. Before you go, pick up a mild over-the-counter preparation, such as Kaopectate, which if used according to directions, should have you back on your feet within 12 to 14 hours (although this comes in a bulky bottle). Many find Pepto-Bismol equally effective, and it comes in a handier tablet form. An old, favored Mexican remedy is *manzanilla* (chamomile) tea. You also may want to ask your doctor to recommend one of the stronger medications containing an antibiotic. If you are stricken with diarrhea and have no medication with you, have your hotel call a doctor or visit the nearest pharmacy.

It is advisable to bring a small medical kit with you. (See "First Aid," above.) It would be a good idea, especially if you plan on traveling to some out-of-the-way places, to bring disposable syringes (in some US states they are legal only with a prescription — if this is the case, contact your doctor). In Mexico, especially off the main tourist routes, reusable needles may be the norm, and these can be less than sanitary. Improperly disinfected needles can be a source of AIDS (Acquired Immune Deficiency Syndrome) and hepatitis, so insist that the doctor or pharmacist use disposable syringes whenever possible. Also be aware that some over-the-counter remedies sold in Mexico contain drugs such as chloramphenicol, an antibiotic sold only by prescription in the US, which may cause allergic reactions or other side effects.

ATMOSPHERIC PRESSURES: Mexico City lies at an altitude of 7,349 feet above sea level. Those unaccustomed to the city's "thin" air often are advised to take it easy until they become acclimated to their new surroundings. That means no pyramid climbing or other strenuous activities for the first few days.

Another, more serious, problem is that of pollution. Unfortunately, the Mexican capital has some of the worst air on earth; it often is considered a health risk, especially to the young, the sick, and the elderly. Such pollutants as carbon monoxide, sulfur dioxide, mercury, and ozone often exceed the acceptable levels set by the World Health

Organization. Thermal inversion — when a layer of cold air beneath a layer of warmer air holds the polluted air near the surface — compounds the problem during the winter. Such inversions can last for days.

When pollution levels are high, the best course of action is to stay indoors as much as possible, to avoid exercising when you must be outdoors, and to keep car windows closed, especially when traveling through underpasses or when stopping at a gas station. Many doctors advise those with respiratory or cardiovascular problems — especially the elderly — to avoid Mexico City altogether during December, January, and February. Air quality generally is best from May to September.

Back in 1989, when the health threat in Mexico City became critical, the Mexican government took formal action. They imposed emission standards on vehicles and factories, and restricted the use of private automobiles to 6 days a week. (This rule applies both to local residents who are issued a sticker specifying the non-driving day and to nonresidents driving either their own or rented cars. The non-driving day, which occurs only during the Monday–Friday workweek, is determined by the last digit or character on the license plate of the vehicle; charts indicating non-driving days are posted throughout Mexico City.) However, the "clean" gasoline long promised by *Pemex,* Mexico's government-owned oil monopoly, was not yet available as we went to press.

INFECTIOUS HEPATITIS OR JAUNDICE: The most serious potential threat to a good vacation, hepatitis (nicknamed the Big H by gringos) frequently is caused by dirty hypodermic needles, a risk even in hospitals. If you are a diabetic or require regular injections for any other condition, carry disposable plastic hypodermic syringes (available in pharmacies). The unwary traveler also can contract it from improperly prepared food, contaminated drinking water, or unsanitary toilet conditions. Care in all these matters is the best prevention, but an additional measure of protection also can be secured with an immune globulin injection from your family doctor before your departure.

CHAGAS' DISEASE: Travelers who intend to spend time in the forested areas of Mexico also should be aware of the threat from the vinchuca. This insect lives in palm trees and is apt to carry a parasite that causes Chagas' disease, which can lead to a number of serious health problems (most usually, chronic heart disease) that may be asymptomatic for years. Although there is no known cure for Chagas' disease, measures can be taken to avoid contact with the insect carrying it: Do not sleep in natives' huts; when camping at night, stay away from palm trees and stone piles, both of which are homes to the vinchuca. Before going to sleep, apply an insecticide that contains DEET (see below).

Should you require medical or surgical treatment involving blood transfusion, go to a university-affiliated hospital in the capital or other major city. Try to avoid private hospitals (*clínicas*) where donors may not have been adequately screened for Chagas' disease.

MALARIA: If you intend to travel into the jungle, where malaria is prevalent, pick up some antimalarial tablets in a pharmacy in a city before you fly into the bush. These very inexpensive tablets are available everywhere. (Malaria is called *paludismo* in Spanish; ask for *medicina contra paludismo* in Mexico.) Presently, a yellow fever inoculation and prophylactic medication against malaria are recommended and, in many cases, mandatory for travel in many of the tropic and subtropic regions of Mexico, particularly for visitors making extensive trips to the Yucatán Peninsula. As malaria usually is contracted through mosquito bites, precautions against these irritating and potentially harmful bites should be taken (see "Insects and Other Pests," below).

■ **Note:** Before you leave for Mexico, check specifically with your local county or state health department, or call the US State Department's *Citizens' Emergency Center* at 202-647-5225 for the most up-to-date information on health conditions and other vital information.

INSECTS AND OTHER PESTS: Insects in parts of Mexico can be not only a nuisance but also a real threat. To avoid contact in areas of infestation, do not sleep on the ground and, if possible, sleep under mosquito netting.

It is a good idea to use some form of topical insect repellent — those containing DEET (N,N-diethyl-m-toluamide) are among the most common and effective. The US Environmental Protection Agency (EPA) stresses that you should not use any pesticide that has not been approved by the EPA (check the label) and that all such preparations should be used in moderation. If picnicking or camping, burn mosquito coils or candles containing allethrin, pyrethrin, or citronella, or use a pyrethrum-containing flying insect spray. For information about active ingredients in repellents, call the National Pesticide Telecommunications Network's 24-hour hotline number: 800-858-7378.

If you do get bitten — by mosquitoes or other bugs — the itching can be relieved with baking soda, topical first-aid creams, or antihistamine tablets. Should a bite become infected, treat it with a disinfectant or antibiotic cream.

Though rarer, bites from scorpions, snakes, or spiders can be serious. If possible, always try to catch the villain for identification purposes. If bitten, the best course of action may be to head directly to the nearest emergency ward or outpatient clinic of a hospital. Cockroaches and termites thrive in warm climates, but pose no serious health threat.

WATER SAFETY: Mexico is famous for its beaches, but it's important to remember that oceans — both the Atlantic and the Pacific — can be treacherous. A few precautions are necessary. Beware of the undertow, that current of water running back down the beach after a wave has washed ashore; it can knock you off your feet and into the surf. Even more dangerous is the riptide, a strong current of water running against the tide, which can pull you out to sea. If you get caught offshore, don't panic or try to fight the current, because it only will exhaust you; instead, ride it out while waiting for it to subside, which usually happens not too far from shore, or try swimming away parallel to the beach.

Sharks are sometimes sighted, but they usually don't come in close to shore, and they are well-fed on fish. Should you meet up with one, just swim away as quietly and smoothly as you can, without shouting or splashing. Although not aggressive, eels can be dangerous when threatened. If snorkeling or diving, beware of crevices where these creatures may be lurking.

The tentacled Portuguese man-of-war and other jellyfish drift in quiet salt waters and often wash up onto the beach; the long tentacles of these creatures sting whatever they touch. Specialists recommend carrying a small bottle of household vinegar and a container of unseasoned meat tenderizer in your beach bag. If stung, do not wash the area or rub with sand. Instead, pour vinegar over the irritation to neutralize the effect of the sting and then apply a paste made of vinegar and meat tenderizer to break down the residual venom.

Mexico's coral reefs are limited but still razor-sharp. Treat all coral cuts with an antiseptic, and then watch carefully since coral is a living organism with bacteria on its surface which may cause an infection. If you step on a sea urchin, you'll find that the spines are very sharp, pierce the skin, and break off easily. Like splinters, the tips left embedded in the skin are difficult to remove, but they will dissolve in a week or two; rinsing with vinegar may help to dissolve them more quickly. To avoid these hazards, keep your feet covered whenever possible. You also should avoid swimming in (or drinking) water from freshwater streams, rivers, or pools, as they may be contaminated with leptospires, which cause a bacterial disease called leptospirosis (the symptoms resemble influenza).

If complications, allergic reactions (such as breathlessness, fever, or cramps), or signs of serious infection result from any of the above circumstances, *see a doctor.*

SUNBURN: The burning power of the sun can quickly cause severe sunburn or sunstroke. To protect yourself against these ills, wear sunglasses, take along a broad-brimmed hat and cover-up, and use a sunscreen lotion.

PREVENTION AND IMMUNIZATION: Specific information on the health status of any area in Mexico can be secured from its consular services in the US. The Centers for Disease Control publishes a comprehensive booklet, *Health Information for International Travel,* which lists vaccination requirements and other health information for Mexico. To order, send a check or money order for $5 to the Superintendent of Documents (US Government Printing Office, Washington, DC 20402), or charge it to your credit card by calling 202-783-3238. For information on vaccination requirements, disease outbreaks, and other health information pertaining to traveling abroad, you also can call the Centers for Disease Control's 24-hour International Health Requirements and Recommendations Information Hotline: 404-332-4559.

Another useful publication, *Health Hints for the Tropics,* offers tips on preventing illnesses and staying healthy in Mexico, including practical information on immunizations and trip preparation, as well as a list of resources. It is available for $4 by writing to Dr. Karl A. Western, *American Society of Tropical Medicine and Hygiene,* 6436 31st St. NW, Washington, DC 20015-2342.

If you live in or near New York City, you can take advantage of the *International Health Care Service* set up by New York Hospital–Cornell Medical Center (440 E. 69th St., New York, NY 10021; phone: 212-746-1601) "to encourage and facilitate proper preventive health measures." In addition to individual pre-trip counseling and post-trip consultations based on your specific itinerary, it offers a complete range of immunizations at moderate per-shot rates. By appointment only, from 4 to 8 PM Mondays through Thursdays (24-hour coverage for urgent travel-related problems). In addition, sending $4.50 (with a self-addressed envelope) to the address above will procure the service's publication, *International Health Care Travelers Guide.*

A conservative approach to inoculation is especially recommended for multiple-destination travelers, as entry requirements and areas of infection are changeable. Travelers who will be extending their trip with a visit to Central America should find out about additional required or recommended innoculations. The US Public Health Service advises diphtheria and tetanus shots for people traveling in many of these areas and additional inoculations may be recommended for children. Inquire at the appropriate government tourist offices about the immunization requirements for the areas you will be visiting. Where certificates are required, authorities may demand both the origin and batch number of the serum used.

Following all these precautions will not guarantee an illness-free trip, but should minimize the risk. As a final hedge against economic if not physical problems, make sure your health insurance will cover all eventualities while you are away. If not, there are policies designed specifically for travel. Many are worth investigating. As with all insurance, they seem like a waste of money until you need them. For more information, also see *Insurance* and *Medical and Legal Aid and Consular Services,* both in this section.

HELPFUL PUBLICATIONS: Practically every phase of health care — before, during, and after a trip — is covered in *The New Traveler's Health Guide,* by Drs. Patrick J. Doyle and James E. Banta. It is available for $4.95, plus postage and handling, from Acropolis Books Ltd., 13950 Park Center Rd., Herndon, VA 22071 (phone: 800-451-7771 or 703-709-0006).

The *Traveling Healthy Newsletter,* which is published six times a year, also is brimming with health-related travel tips. For an annual subscription, which costs $24, contact Dr. Karl Neumann (108-48 70th Rd., Forest Hills, NY 11375; phone: 718-268-7290). Dr. Neumann also is the editor of the useful free booklet, *Traveling Healthy,* which is available by writing to the *Travel Healthy Program* (PO Box 10208, New Brunswick, NJ 08906-9910; phone: 215-732-4100).

For more information regarding preventive health care for travelers, contact the *International Association for Medical Assistance to Travelers (IAMAT;* 417 Center St., Lewiston, NY 14092; phone: 716-754-4883). The Centers for Disease Control also publish an interesting booklet, *Health Information for International Travel.* To order send a check or money order for $5 to the Superintendent of Documents (US Government Printing Office, Washington, DC 20402), or charge it to your credit card by calling 202-783-3238.

On the Road

Credit and Currency

It may seem hard to believe, but one of the greatest (and least understood) costs of travel is money itself. If that sounds simplistic, consider the fact that you can lose as much as 30% of your dollar's value simply by changing money at the wrong place or in the wrong form. So your one single objective in relation to the care and retention of your travel funds is to make them stretch as far as possible. When you do spend money, it should be on things that expand and enhance your travel experience, with no buying power lost due to carelessness or lack of knowledge. This requires more than merely ferreting out the best airfare or the most charming budget hotel. It means being canny about the management of money itself. Herewith, a primer on making money go as far as possible while traveling.

CURRENCY: The basic medium of exchange in Mexico is the peso, which, like the dollar, is based on a decimal system and sub-divides into 100 units called centavos. Used only as a basis for translating dollars into pesos, the centavo has been taken out of circulation. Paper bills (*billetes*) are found in denominations of 1,000, 2,000, 5,000, 10,000, 20,000, and 50,000 pesos. Coins (*monedas*) are found in 1-peso, 5-peso, 10-peso, 20-peso, 50-peso, 100-peso, 200-peso, 500-peso, 1,000-peso, and 5,000-peso denominations.

Although US dollars may be accepted in Mexico (particularly at points of entry), you certainly will lose a percentage of your dollar's buying power if you do not take the time to convert it into the local legal tender. By paying for goods and services in the local currency, you save money by not negotiating invariably unfavorable exchange rates for every small purchases, and avoid difficulty where US currency is not readily — or happily — accepted. *Throughout this book, unless specifically stated otherwise, prices are given in US dollars.*

There is no limit to the amount of US currency that can be brought into Mexico. To avoid problems anywhere along the line, it's advisable to fill out any customs forms provided when leaving the US on which you can declare all money you are taking with you — cash, traveler's checks, and so on. US law requires that anyone taking more than $10,000 into or out of the US must report this fact on customs form No. 4790, which is available at all international airports. If taking over $10,000 out of the US, you must report this *before* leaving the US; if returning with such an amount, you should include this information on your customs declaration. Although travelers usually are not questioned by customs officials about currency entering or leaving, the sensible course is to observe all regulations just to be on the safe side.

FOREIGN EXCHANGE: Because of the volatility of exchange rates, be sure to check the current value of the peso before finalizing any travel budget. And before you actually depart on your trip, shop around carefully for the most advantageous exchange rate offered by various financial institutions — US banks, currency exchange firms (at home or abroad), or foreign banks.

For the best sense of current trends, follow the rates posted in the financial section of your local newspaper or in such international newspapers as the *International Herald Tribune.* It also is possible to check with your own bank. *Harold Reuter and Company,* a currency exchange service in New York City (200 Park Ave., Suite 332 E., New York, NY 10166; phone: 212-661-0826), also is particularly helpful in determining current trends in exchange rates; or check with *Thomas Cook Foreign Exchange* (for the nearest location, call 800-972-2192 in Illinois; 800-621-0666 elsewhere in the US). *Ruesch International* also offers up-to-date foreign currency information and currency-related services (such as converting foreign currency checks into US dollars). *Ruesch* also offers a pocket-size *Foreign Currency Guide* (good for estimating equivalents while planning) and a helpful brochure, *6 Foreign Exchange Tips for the Traveler.* Contact *Ruesch International* at one of the following addresses: 3 First National Plaza, Suite 2020, Chicago, IL 60602 (phone: 312-332-5900); 1925 Century Park E., Suite 240, Los Angeles, CA 90067 (phone: 213-277-7800); 608 Fifth Ave., Swiss Center, New York, NY 10020 (phone: 212-977-2700); or 1350 Eye St. NW, 10th Floor, Washington, DC 20005 (phone: 800-424-2923 or 202-408-1200).

In Mexico, you will find the official rate of exchange posted in banks, airports, money exchange houses, hotels, and some shops. As a general rule, expect to get more pesos for your US dollar at banks than at any other commercial establishment. Exchange rates do change from day to day, and most banks offer the same (or very similar) exchange rates. (In a pinch, the convenience of cashing money in your hotel — sometimes on a 24-hour basis — *may* make up for the difference in the exchange rate.) Don't try to bargain in banks (or hotels) — no one will alter the rates for you.

If banks are closed, you may want to try the money exchanges *(casas de cambio)* at the major airports (Acapulco, Cancún, Guadalajara, Mazatlán, Mérida, Mexico City, Monterrey, Puerto Vallarta, Tijuana, and Zihuatanejo). Money exchanges are financial institutions that charge a fee for the service of exchanging dollars into pesos. When considering alternatives, be aware that although the rate varies among these establishments, the rates of exchange offered are bound to be less favorable than the terms offered at nearby banks — again, don't be surprised if you get fewer pesos for your dollar than the rate published in the papers.

That said, however, the following rules of thumb are worth remembering.

Rule number one: Never (repeat: *never*) exchange dollars for foreign currency at hotels, restaurants, or retail shops. If you do, you are sure to lose a significant amount of your dollar's buying power. If you do come across a storefront exchange counter offering what appears to be an incredible bargain, there's too much counterfeit specie in circulation to take the chance (see Rule number three, below).

Rule number two: Estimate your needs carefully; if you overbuy, you lose twice — buying and selling back. Every time you exchange money, someone is making a profit, and rest assured it isn't you. Use up foreign notes before leaving, saving just enough for airport departure taxes (which often must be paid in local currency), other last-minute incidentals, and tips.

Rule number three: Don't buy money on the black market. The exchange rate may be better, but it is a common practice to pass off counterfeit bills to unsuspecting foreigners who aren't familiar with the local currency. It's usually a sucker's game, and you almost always are the sucker; it also can land you in jail.

Rule number four: Learn the local currency quickly and keep abreast of daily fluctuations in the exchange rate. These are listed in the English-language *International Herald Tribune* daily for the preceding day, as well as in other major international newspapers. Rates change to some degree every day. For rough calculations, it is quick and safe to use round figures, but for purchases and actual currency exchanges, carry a small pocket calculator to help you compute the exact rate. Inexpensive calculators specifically designed to convert currency amounts quickly for travelers are widely available.

When changing money, don't be afraid to ask how much commission you're being charged, and the exact amount of the prevailing exchange rate. In fact, in any exchange of money for goods or services, you should work out the rate before making any payment.

TIP PACKS: It's not a bad idea to buy a *small* amount of foreign coins and banknotes before your departure. But note the emphasis on "small," because, for the most part, you are better off carrying the bulk of your travel funds abroad in US dollar traveler's checks (see below). Still the advantage of tip packs are threefold:

1. You become familiar with the currency (really the only way to guard against making mistakes or being cheated during your first few hours in a new country).
2. You are guaranteed some money should you arrive when a bank or exchange counter isn't open or available.
3. You don't have to depend on hotel desks, porters, or taxi drivers to change your money.

A "tip pack" is the only foreign currency you should buy before you leave. If you do run short upon arrival, dollars often are accepted at points of entry. In other areas, they either *may* be accepted, or someone may accommodate you by changing a small amount — though invariably at a less than advantageous rate.

TRAVELER'S CHECKS: It's wise to carry traveler's checks on the road instead of (or in addition to) cash, since it's possible to replace traveler's checks if they are stolen or lost; you usually can receive partial or full replacement funds the same day if you have your purchase receipt and proper identification. Issued in various denominations and available in both US and foreign currencies, with adequate proof of identification (credit cards, driver's license, passport), traveler's checks are as good as cash in most hotels, restaurants, stores, and banks.

You will be able to cash traveler's checks fairly easily throughout Mexico, but don't expect to meander into a one-burro town and be able to get instant cash. Also, even in metropolitan areas, don't assume that restaurants, small shops, and other establishments are going to be able to change checks of large denominations. Worldwide, more and more establishments are beginning to restrict the amount of traveler's checks they will accept or cash, so it is wise to purchase at least some of your checks in small denominations — say, $10 and $20.

Although traveler's checks often are available in foreign currencies such as pesos, the exchange rates offered by the issuing companies in the US generally are far less favorable than those available from banks both in the US and abroad. Therefore, it usually is better to carry the bulk of your travel funds abroad in US dollar denomination traveler's checks.

Every type of traveler's check is legal tender in banks around the world, and each company guarantees full replacement if checks are lost or stolen. After that the similarity ends. Some charge a fee for purchase, others are free; you can buy traveler's checks at almost any bank, and some are available by mail. Most important, each traveler's check issuer differs slightly in its refund policy — the amount refunded immediately, the accessibility of refund locations, the availability of a 24-hour refund service, and the time it will take for you to receive replacement checks. For instance, *American Express* guarantees replacement of lost or stolen traveler's checks in under 3 hours at any *American Express* office — other companies may not be as prompt. (Note that *American Express*'s 3-hour policy is based on a traveler's being able to provide the serial numbers of the lost checks. Without these numbers, refunds can take much longer.)

We cannot overemphasize the importance of knowing how to replace lost or stolen checks. All of the traveler's check companies have agents around the world, both in their own name and at associated agencies (usually, but not necessarily, banks), where refunds can be obtained during business hours. Most of them also have 24-hour toll-free telephone lines, and some will even provide emergency funds to tide you over on a Sunday.

Be sure to make a photocopy of the refund instructions that will be given to you by the issuing institution at the time of purchase. To avoid complications should you need to redeem lost checks (and to speed up the replacement process), keep the purchase receipt and an accurate list, by serial number, of the checks that have been spent or cashed. You may want to incorporate this information in an "emergency packet," also including the numbers of the credit cards you are carrying and any other bits of information you shouldn't be without. Always keep these records separate from the checks and the original records themselves (you may want to give them to a traveling companion to hold).

Although most people understand the necessity of carrying funds in the form of traveler's checks as protection against loss or theft, an equally good reason is that traveler's checks may get a better rate of exchange than cash does — usually by at least 1%. The reasons for this are technical and less prevalent in Mexico than elsewhere — the official rate of exchange posted by Mexican banks usually is the rate used to exchange *any* form of US currency — but potential savings still exist and it's a fact of travel life that should not be ignored.

That 1% bonus won't do you much good, however, if you already have spent it *buying* your traveler's checks. Several of the major traveler's check companies charge 1% for the acquisition of their checks; others don't. To receive fee-free traveler's checks you may have to meet certain qualifications — for instance, *Thomas Cook* checks issued in US currency are free if you make your travel arrangements through its travel agency; *American Express* traveler's checks are available without charge to members of the *American Automobile Association (AAA).* Holders of some credit cards (such as the *American Express Platinum* card) also may be entitled to free traveler's checks. The issuing institution (e.g., the particular bank at which you purchase them) may itself charge a fee. If you purchase traveler's checks at a bank in which you or your company maintains significant accounts (especially commercial accounts of some size), the bank may absorb the 1% fee as a courtesy.

American Express, Bank of America, Citicorp, Thomas Cook, MasterCard, and *Visa* all offer traveler's checks. Here is a list of the major companies issuing traveler's checks and the numbers to call in the event that loss or theft makes replacement necessary:

> *American Express:* To report lost or stolen checks throughout the US, call 800-221-7282. In Mexico, call the nearest *American Express* office, or call the Mexican regional center at 905-661-3266 during business hours; 905-598-8133, collect, after 5 PM (Central Standard Time).
>
> *Bank of America:* To report lost or stolen checks throughout the US, call 800-227-3460. In Mexico, call 415-624-5400, collect.
>
> *Citicorp:* To report lost or stolen checks throughout the US, call 800-645-6556. In Mexico, call 813-623-1709, collect.
>
> *MasterCard:* To report lost or stolen checks throughout the US, call 800-223-9920. In Mexico, call 212-974-5696, collect.
>
> *Thomas Cook MasterCard:* To report lost or stolen checks throughout the US, call 800-223-9920. In Mexico, call 609-987-7300, collect.
>
> *Visa:* To report lost or stolen checks throughout the US, call 800-227-6811. In Mexico, call 415-574-7111, collect.

CREDIT CARDS: Some establishments you may encounter during the course of your travels may not honor any credit cards and some may not honor all cards, so there is a practical reason to carry more than one. The following is a list of credit cards that enjoy wide domestic and international acceptance:

American Express: Cardholders can cash personal checks for traveler's checks and cash at *American Express* or its representatives' offices in the US up to the following limits (within any 21-day period): up to $1,000 for *Green* and *Optima* cardholders; $5,000 for *Gold* cardholders; and $10,000 for *Platinum* cardholders. Check cashing also is available to cardholders who are guests at participating hotels in the US and Canada (up to $250) and at participating hotels abroad (up to $100), and for holders of airline tickets, at participating airlines (up to $50). Free travel accident, baggage, and car rental insurance if ticket or rental is charged to card; additional insurance also is available for additional cost. For further information or to report a lost or stolen *American Express* card, call 800-528-4800 throughout the continental US; elsewhere in the US and in Mexico, call 212-477-5700, collect.

Carte Blanche: Free travel accident, baggage, and car rental insurance if ticket or rental is charged to card; additional insurance also is available at additional cost. For medical, legal, and travel assistance worldwide, call 800-356-3448 throughout the US; in Mexico, call 214-680-6480, collect. For further information or to report a lost or stolen *Carte Blanche* card, call 800-525-9135 throughout the US; in Mexico, call 303-790-2433, collect.

Diners Club: Emergency personal check cashing for cardholders staying at participating hotels and motels in the US and abroad (up to $250 per stay). Free travel accident, baggage, and car rental insurance if ticket or rental is charged to card; additional insurance also is available for an additional fee. For medical, legal, and travel assistance worldwide, call 800-356-3448 throughout the US; in Mexico, call 214-680-6480, collect. For further information or to report a lost or stolen *Diners Club* card, call 800-525-9135 throughout the US; 303-790-2433, collect, in Mexico.

Discover Card: Offered by a subsidiary of Sears, Roebuck & Co., it provides cardholders with cash advances at numerous automatic teller machines and Sears stores throughout the US. For further information and to report lost or stolen *Discover* card, call 800-DISCOVER.

MasterCard: Cash advances are available at participating banks worldwide. Check with your issuing bank for information. *MasterCard* also offers a 24-hour emergency lost card service; call 800-826-2181 throughout the US; in Mexico, call 314-275-6690, collect.

Visa: Cash advances are available at participating banks worldwide. Check with your issuing bank for information. *Visa* also offers a 24-hour emergency lost card service; call 800-336-8472 throughout the US; in Mexico, call 415-574-7700, collect.

One of the thorniest problems relating to the use of credit cards abroad concerns the rate of exchange at which a purchase is charged. Be aware that the exchange rate in effect on the date that you make a foreign purchase or pay for a foreign service has nothing at all to do with the rate of exchange at which your purchase is billed to you when you get the invoice (sometimes months later) in the US. The amount which the credit card company charges is either a function of the exchange rate at which the establishment's bank processed it or the rate in effect on the day your charge is received at the credit card service center. (There is a 1-year limit on the time a business can take to forward its charge slips.)

The principle at work in this credit card–exchange rate roulette is simple, but very hard to predict. You make a purchase at a particular dollar versus local currency exchange rate. If the dollar gets stronger in the time between purchase and billing, your purchase actually costs you less than you anticipated. If the dollar drops in value during the interim, you pay more than you thought you would. There isn't much you can do about these vagaries except to follow one very broad, very clumsy rule of thumb: If the dollar is doing well at the time of purchase, its value increasing against the local currency, use your credit card on the assumption that it still will be doing well when billing takes place. If the dollar is doing badly, assume it will continue to do badly and pay with traveler's checks or cash. If you get too badly stuck, the best recourse is to complain, loudly. Be aware, too, that most credit card companies charge an unannounced, un-itemized 1% fee for converting foreign currency charges to US dollars.

SENDING MONEY ABROAD: If you have used up your traveler's checks, cashed as many emergency personal checks as your credit card allows, drawn on your cash advance line to the fullest extent, and still need money, have it sent to you via one of the following services:

American Express (phone: 800-543-4080). Offers a service in the Mexico called "Moneygram," completing money transfers in anywhere from 15 minutes to 5 days. The sender can go to any *American Express* office in the US and transfer money by presenting cash, a personal check, money order, or credit card — *Mastercard, Visa,* or *American Express Optima Card* (no other *American Express* or other credit cards are are accepted). *American Express Optima* cardholders also can arrange for this transfer over the phone. The minimum transfer charge is $25, which rises with the amount of the transaction; the sender can forward funds of up to $10,000 per transaction (credit card users are limited to the amount of pre-established credit line). To collect at the other end, the receiver must show identification (passport, driver's license, or other picture ID) at an *American Express* branch office or at a branch of an affiliated bank in Mexico.

Western Union Telegraph Company (phone: 800-325-4176 throughout the US). A friend or relative can go, cash in hand, to any *Western Union* office in the US, where, for a *minimum* charge of $14 (it rises with the amount of the transaction), the funds will be transferred to a centralized *Western Union* account. When the transaction is fully processed — in the case of most destinations in Mexico, from 1 to 3 business days — you can go to any *Western Union* branch office or correspondent bank to pick up the transferred funds. For a higher fee, the US party to this transaction may call *Western Union* with a *MasterCard* or *Visa* number to send up to $2,000, although larger transfers will be sent to a predesignated location.

If you are literally down to your last cent and have no other way to obtain cash, the nearest US consulate (see *Medical and Legal Aid and Consular Services,* in this section) will let you call home to set these matters in motion.

CASH MACHINES: Automatic teller machines (ATMs) are increasingly common worldwide. If your bank participates in one of the international ATM networks (most do), the bank will issue you a "cash card" along with a personal identification code or number (also called a PIC or PIN). You can use this card at any ATM in the same electronic network to check your account balances, transfer monies between checking and savings accounts, and — most important for a traveler — withdraw cash instantly. Network ATMs generally are located in banks, commercial and transportation centers, and near major tourist attractions.

Some financial institutions offer exclusive automatic teller machines for their own customers only at bank branches. At the time of this writing, ATMs which *are* connected generally belong to one of the following two international networks:

Cirrus: Has over 55,000 ATMs in more than 22 countries worldwide, including nearly 400 locations in Mexico. *MasterCard* holders also may use their cards to draw cash against their credit lines. For a free booklet listing the locations of these machines and further information on the *Cirrus* network, call 800-4-CIRRUS.

Plus System: Has over 30,000 automatic teller machines worldwide, including over 200 locations in Mexico. *MasterCard* and *Visa* cardholders also may use their cards to draw cash against their credit lines. For a free directory listing the locations of these machines and further information on the *Plus System* network, call 800-THE-PLUS.

Information about these networks also may be available at member bank branches. Note that as we went to press, there was an agreement pending between these two companies to join their networks. When finalized, this will allow users of either system to withdraw funds from any *Cirrus* or *Plus System* ATM.

Accommodations

The best Mexican hotels combine the modern, standardized style of American chains with the continental elegance of European service and a lush, tropical charm unique to Mexico. The enormous growth of tourism in Mexico in recent years has been marked by a corresponding growth in accommodations of all kinds and styles. The popular beach resort areas — Acapulco, Mazatlán, Puerto Vallarta, Baja Sur, Cozumel, and Cancún — offer some of the world's most luxurious hotels in splendid settings. But major cities, including Mexico City, Guadalajara, and Monterrey, as well as smaller ones (San Luis Potosí, Saltillo, and Cuernavaca, and so on) also have spacious luxury accommodations that have all the possible amenities and advantages of ideal weather conditions.

There are a variety of chain hotels throughout Mexico, as well as dude ranches, thermal spas, and resorts that feature specific facilities (see *Best in Town* in THE CITIES; *Best en Route* in DIRECTIONS; and sections throughout DIVERSIONS). Since room prices in all Mexican hotels are controlled and regulated by the Mexican Ministry of Tourism, they remain stable within basic categories — reflected in this book in the categories expensive, moderate, and inexpensive.

Westin properties (phone: 800-228-3000) — usually represented by the *Camino Real* hotels — offer luxury accommodations in most major cities in Mexico, including Acapulco, Cancún, Guadalajara, Ixtapa, Manzanillo, Mazatlán, Mexico City, Puerto Vallarta, and Saltillo. The *Stouffer Presidente* group (phone: 800-HOTELS-1 or 800-GRACIAS in the US; 5-255-4222 for the Mexico City office) includes five-star establishments in Cancún, Cozumel, Ixtapa, Loreto, Mexico City, Oaxaca, and San José Del Cabo. You can depend on lovely grounds and excellent service in any one of these, as well as a variety of extra facilities from indoor gardens, manmade lagoons, and massive landscaped grounds to golf courses, swimming pools, tennis courts, discotheques, restaurants, and cocktail lounges.

Other major international hotel chains represented in Mexico (along with toll-free numbers to call in the US) include the following:

> **Best Western** (phone: 800-528-1234). Has over 25 properties throughout Mexico.
> **Club Med** (phone: 800-CLUB-MED). Has 1 property each in Cancún, Huatulco, Ixtapa, Playa Blanca, and Sonora Bay.
> **Hilton** (phone: 800-445-8667). Has 1 property each in Cancún and Puerto Vallarta.
> **Holiday Inn** (phone: 800-465-4329). Has 15 properties located throughout Mexico.

Hyatt (phone: 800-233-1234). Has 2 properties each in Acapulco and Cancún, and 1 each in Guadalajara, Puerto Vallarta, and Villahermosa.

Inter-Continental (phone: 800-327-0200). Has 1 property each in Cancún, Manzanillo, and Monterrey.

Loews (phone: 800-223-0888). Has 3 properties in Mexico City, and 1 each in Cancún, Ixtapa, Puebla, San Miguel de Allende, and Zacatecas.

Marriott (phone: 800-223-6388). Has 1 property each in Cancún and Puerto Vallarta.

Meliá (phone: 800-336-3542). Has 2 properties each in Cabo San Lucas, Cancún, and Cozumel, and 1 in Puerto Vallarta.

Sheraton (phone: 800-325-3535). Has 1 property each in Acapulco, Cancún, Huatulco, Ixtapa, Mexico City, and Puerto Vallarta.

The following leading Mexican groups have properties in Mexico City, most resorts, and/or other popular destinations:

Aristos: (phone: 5-211-0112 for the Mexico City office). Has 1 property each in Cancún, Puebla, San Miguel de Allende, Zacatecas, and Zihuatanejo.

Castel: (phone: 800-678-7244). Has 1 property each in Chihuahua and Toluca.

Fiesta Americana: (phone: 212-949-7250 in New York City; 800-223-2332 elsewhere in the US; or 5-570-8122 for the Mexico City office). Has 25 properties throughout Mexico.

Krystal: (phone: 5-211-0092 for the Mexico City office). Has 1 property each in Cancún, Ixtapa, Mexico City, and Puerto Vallarta.

Misión: (phone: 800-752-3596 throughout the US; 5-525-0393 through -0399 for the Mexico City office). Has 17 properties throughout Mexico.

Real de Minas: (phone: 5-514-2360 or 5-511-1931 for the Mexico City office). Has 6 properties throughout Mexico.

Independent, modern establishments — particularly in resort areas — often are even more elegant than the chains. Medium-size hotels can be equally modern, or at least modernized, but are more likely to offer local ambience and charm. In general, they're also more reasonably priced. Some establishments offer the added allure of cabins or spas where you can bathe in natural mineral springs. In many hotels in Mexico you can enjoy a life of luxury and leisure, sipping exotic drinks beneath a bougainvillea on your own terrace, at a relatively low cost. Services and facilities are plentiful and prices low (compared to the equivalent services in the US).

At the other end of the spectrum, *Best Western* hotels and *Quality Inns* (usually known as *Calinda* hotels in Mexico) offer moderately priced accommodations in Mexico, and there are numerous clean and inexpensive hostelries of every type — modern or colonial, secluded, centrally located, or on the road — that offer basic amenities. Although some of these may provide showers, air conditioning, TV sets, bar service, and swimming pools, establishments in more rustic, out-of-the-way places may offer only the basics. Here the charm consists of a genuine welcome, personal hospitality, often striking scenery, and privacy.

Relais & Châteaux: Although most members of this association are in France, the group has grown to include dozens of establishments in many other countries. Although at the time of this writing, there was only one member property in Mexico (*Las Mañanitas* in Cuernavaca), other Mexican properties may be part of this group by the time you are traveling. Members of this group are of particular interest to travelers who wish lodgings reflecting the ambience, style, and frequently the history of the places they are visiting. Accommodations and service from one *relais* or château to another can range from simple but comfortable to elegantly deluxe, but they all maintain very high standards to retain their memberships, as they are appraised annually.

An illustrated catalogue of all the *Relais & Châteaux* properties is published annually and is available for $5 from *Relais & Châteaux* (2400 Lazy Hollow, Suite 152D, Houston, TX 77063) or from *David B. Mitchell & Company* (200 Madison Ave., New York, NY 10016; phone: 800-372-1323 or 212-696-1323). The association also can provide information on member properties. Reservations can be made directly with the establishments, through *David B. Mitchell & Company,* or through a travel agency.

RENTAL OPTIONS: An attractive accommodations alternative for the visitor content to stay in one spot for a week or more is to rent one of numerous properties available throughout Mexico. These offer a wide range of luxury and convenience, depending on the price you want to pay. One of the charms in staying in an apartment, condominium, cottage, villa, or other rented vacation home is that you will feel much more like a visitor than a tourist.

A vacation in a furnished rental has both the advantages and disadvantages of living "at home" abroad. It can be less expensive than staying in a first class hotel, although very luxurious and expensive rentals are available, too. It has the comforts of home, including a kitchen, which means saving on food. Furthermore, it gives a sense of the country that a large hotel often cannot. On the other hand, a certain amount of housework is involved because if you don't eat out, you have to cook, and though some rentals, especially the luxury ones, come with maid service, most don't. (Although if the rental doesn't include domestic help, arrangements often can be made with a nearby service for far less than in the US.)

For a family, two or more couples, or a group of friends, the per-person cost — even for a luxurious rental — can be quite reasonable. Weekly and monthly rates are available to reduce costs still more. But best of all is the amount of space that no conventional hotel room can equal. As with hotels, the rates for properties in some areas are seasonal, rising during the peak travel season, while for others they remain the same year-round. To have your pick of the properties available, you should begin to make arrangements for a rental at least 6 months in advance.

Rental Property Agents and Discounts – There are several ways of finding a suitable rental property. They are listed along with other accommodations in publications of local tourist boards, and it also is possible to find them through a travel agent. Many tour wholesalers regularly include rental packages among their offerings. In addition, a number of companies specialize in rental vacations. Their plans typically include rental of the property (or several properties, but usually for a minimum 2- or 3-day stay per location), a rental car, and airfare.

The companies listed below rent a variety of properties in Mexico. They handle the booking and confirmation paperwork and can be expected to provide more information about the properties than that which might ordinarily be gleaned from a short listing in an accommodations guide.

> *At Home Abroad* (405 E. 56th St., Suite 6H, New York, NY 10022 (phone: 212-421-9165). Rents modest to luxurious houses (some with pools) and a few apartments. At the time of this writing, their Mexican listings included properties in Acapulco and Puerto Vallarta. The minimum rental period usually is 2 weeks. Photographs of properties can be requested by mail for a $50 registration fee.
>
> *Creative Leisure* (951 Transport Way, Petaluma, CA 94954; phone: 800-4-CONDOS in the US and Canada). Rents moderate to deluxe condominiums in Cancún and other major resort areas. Some rentals include a cook, maid service, transfers to and from the airport, and a car.
>
> *La Cure Villas* (11661 San Vicente Blvd., Suite 1010, Los Angeles, CA 90049; phone: 800-387-2726 or 416-968-2374). Rents private villas in Acapulco, Puerto

Vallarta, and Zihuatanejo. Rentals include local transportation and a full staff, including a cook.

Hideaways International (PO Box 1270, Littleton, MA 01460; phone: 800-843-4433 or 508-486-8955). Rents properties in most major resort areas throughout Mexico. Weekly villa rentals are available for four to ten people. Many come with maid service, although this may be optional. For $75 subscribers receive two issues per year of their guide to current listings, as well as a quarterly newsletter and discounts on a variety of travel services.

Rent a Home International (7200 34th Ave. NW, Seattle, WA 98117; phone: 206-789-9377). Rents private villas in Cabo San Lucas, Cancún, Cozumel, Cuernavaca, Mazatlán, and Puerto Vallarta. Most rentals include a full housekeeping staff.

Rent a Vacation Everywhere (*RAVE;* 328 Main St. E., Suite 526, Rochester, NY 14604; phone: 716-454-6440). Handles moderate to luxurious houses and apartments throughout Mexico, particularly in major resort areas. Minimum rental usually is 1 week or, occasionally, 2 weeks or 1 month.

Travel Resources (PO Box 935, Coconut Grove, FL 33133; phone: 800-327-5039 or 305-444-8583). Rents condominiums and villas in Cancún, Ixtapa, Mazatlán, and elsewhere on Mexico's Caribbean coast. Some villas come with a maid, cook, and gardener; condos have maid service. Daily, as well as weekly, rates can be arranged.

VHR, Worldwide (235 Kensington Ave., Norwood, NJ 07648; phone: 800-NEED-A-VILLA or 201-767-9393). Handles estates, condominiums, and villas in Cozumel and Puerto Vallarta. Most rentals include maid service; some come with a cook.

Villa Leisure (PO Box 209, Westport, CT 06881; phone: 800-526-4244 or 203-222-9611). Rents condominiums, private homes, and villas in Acapulco, Manzanillo, and Puerto Vallarta. Minimum stay is 1 week during the high season, and 4 days during summer. Villa rentals include car, transfers, staff, and private pool or beach; condo rentals include maid service and car. The well-informed staff personally inspects the properties and is a good source of information.

Villas International (71 W. 23rd St., New York, NY 10010; phone: 212-929-7585 in New York State; 800-221-2260 elsewhere in the US). Their offerings range from simple to luxurious houses, as well as apartments. Rentals are offered in a number of locations throughout Mexico, including Acapulco, Cancún, Cozumel, Ixtapa, and Puerto Vallarta. Minimum rental period usually is a week.

In addition, a useful publication, the *Worldwide Home Rental Guide,* lists private villas and cottages throughout Mexico, as well as the managing agencies. Issued twice annually, single copies may be available at newsstands for $10 an issue. For a year's subscription, send $18 to *Worldwide Home Rental Guide,* PO Box 2842, Sante Fe, NM 87504 (phone: 505-988-5188).

When considering a particular vacation rental property, look for answers to the following questions:

- How do you get from the airport to the condominium?
- If the property is on the shore, how far is the nearest beach? Is it sandy or rocky and is it safe for swimming?
- What size and number of beds are provided?
- How far is the property from whatever else is important to you, such as a golf course or nightlife?
- If there is no grocery store on the premises (which may be comparatively expensive, anyway), how far is the nearest market?

- Are baby-sitters, cribs, bicycles, or anything else you may need for your children available?
- Is maid service provided daily?
- Is air conditioning and/or a phone provided?
- Is a car rental part of the package? Is a car necessary?

Before deciding which rental is for you, make sure you have satisfactory answers to all your questions. Ask your travel agent to find out or call the company involved directly.

Accommodation Discounts – Several discount travel organizations provide a substantial savings — up to 50% off list prices — on rental accommodations (and some hotels) throughout Mexico. Reservations are handled by the central office of the organization or members may deal directly with the rental agencies or individual property owners. To take advantage of the full selection of properties, these organizations often require that reservations be made as much as 6 months in advance — particularly for stays during the holidays or peak travel periods.

Concierge (1600 Wynkoop St., Suite 102, Denver, CO 80202; phone: 303-623-6775 in Colorado; 800-346-1022 elsewhere in the US). Offers up to 50% discounts on week-long rentals in Acapulco, the Baja region, Cancún, Mazatlán, Nuevo Vallarta, and Puerto Vallarta. Annual membership fee is $69.95 per couple.

Entry Unlimited (6404 Nancy Ridge Rd., San Diego, CA 92121; phone: 800-843-0265 or 619-558-5838). Up to 50% discounts offered on rentals from 1 night to 1 week (depending on availability) in Acapulco, the Baja region, Cancún, Ixtapa, Mazatlán, and Puerto Vallarta. Annual membership fee $39.95 is per family.

Hotel Express (3052 El Cajon Blvd., San Diego, CA 92104; phone: 800-634-6526 or 619-284-1135). Offers up to 50% off on condominium rentals and hotel accommodations in Acapulco, Cabo San Lucas, Cancún, Ixtapa, Laguna Mar, and Manzanillo. One week is the standard minimum stay; shorter rentals also may be available during the off season. Annual membership fee of $49.95 per family provides discounts on other travel services, but membership is not required for bargains on rental accommodations.

IntlTravel Card (6001 N. Clark St., Chicago, IL 60660; phone: 800-342-0558 or 312-465-8891). Provides discounts on rental and hotel accommodations throughout Mexico. The $36 annual membership fee includes a spouse.

Privilege Card (3473 Satellite Blvd., Suite 200, Duluth, GA 30136; phone: 800-359-0066 or 404-623-0066). Up to 50% discounts available on condominium and apartment rentals in Acapulco, the Baja region, Cancún, and Puerto Vallarta; minimum length of stay depends on availability. Annual membership fee is $49.95 per family.

BED AND BREAKFAST ESTABLISHMENTS: Travelers who have become devotees of this homey accommodation alternative will be happy to hear that bed and breakfast establishments (commonly known as B&Bs) are just beginning to appear among the alternatives offered to travelers in Mexico. Although they are not by any means prevalent in Mexico at this time, their worldwide popularity is spreading.

Bed and breakfast accommodations provide exactly what their name implies. It is unusual for a bed and breakfast establishment to offer the extra services found in conventional hostelries, so the bed and breakfast route often is the least expensive way to go.

Beyond the obvious fundamentals, nothing else is predictable about bed and breakfast establishments. The bed may be in an extra room in a family home, in an apartment with a separate entrance, or in a free-standing cottage elsewhere on the host's property. A private bath isn't always offered, so check before you reserve. Some homes have only one room to let, whereas others may be large enough to have another party or two in residence at the same time.

Breakfast probably will be a Mexican version of the continental variety (fruit plus juice, tortillas or homemade bread, and strong coffee or tea), or perhaps something heartier (such as *huevos rancheros* and spicy *chorizos*). And as often as not, breakfast will be served along with some family history and local lore. If you're in a studio with a kitchenette, you may be furnished with the makings and have to prepare it for yourself. Despite their name, some B&Bs offer an evening meal as well — by prior arrangement and at extra cost.

Some hosts enjoy helping guests with tips on what to see and do and even serve as informal tour guides, while in other places your privacy won't be disturbed. Whichever the case, the beauty of bed and breakfast establishments is that you'll always have a warm reception and the opportunity to meet many more inhabitants of the region than you otherwise would, which means you'll experience their hospitality in a special fashion.

At the time of this writing, unfortunately, there are no US reservations services booking stays at B&Bs in Mexico. If you are interested in this particularly homey form of hospitality, on arrival check with the local tourist authorities who may be able to point you toward local homeowners offering bed and breakfast accommodations to travelers. A useful source of information on bed and breakfast reservations services and establishments is the *Bed & Breakfast Reservations Services Worldwide* (PO Box 39000, Washington, DC 20016; phone: 800-842-1486), a trade association of B&B reservations services, which provides a list of its members for $3.

HOME EXCHANGES: Still another alternative for travelers who are content to stay in one place during their Mexican vacation is a home exchange. The Wright family from St. Louis moves into the home of the Garcia family in Guadalajara, while the Garcias enjoy a stay in the Wright's home. The home exchange is an exceptionally inexpensive way to ensure comfortable, reasonable living quarters with amenities that no hotel could possibly offer; often the trade includes a car. Moreover, it allows you to live in a new community in a way that few tourists ever do: For a little while, at least, you will become something of a resident.

Several companies publish directories of individuals and families willing to trade homes with others for a specific period of time. In some cases, you must be willing to list your own home in the directory; in others, you can subscribe without appearing in it. Most listings are for straight exchanges only, but each directory also has a number of listings placed by people interested in either exchanging or renting (for instance, if they own a second home). Other arrangements include exchanges of hospitality while owners are in residence, or youth exchanges, where your teenager is received as a guest in return for your welcoming their teenager at a later date. A few house-sitting opportunities also are available. In most cases, arrangements for the actual exchange take place directly between you and the foreign host. There is no guarantee that you will find a listing in the area in which you are interested, but each of the organizations noted below includes Mexican homes among its hundreds or even thousands of foreign and domestic listings:

Intervac US/International Home Exchange Service (Box 190070, San Francisco, CA 94119; phone: 415-435-3497). For $45 (plus postage) subscribers receive copies of the three directories published yearly, and are entitled to list their home in one of them; a black-and-white photo may be included with the listing for an additional $10. A $5 discount is given to travelers over age 62.

Loan-A-Home (2 Park Lane, Apt. 6E, Mt. Vernon, NY 10552; phone: 914-664-7640). Specializes in long-term (4 months or more — excluding July and August) housing arrangements worldwide for students, professors, businesspeople, and retirees, although its two annual directories (with supplements) carry a small list of short-term rentals and/or exchanges. $35 for a copy of one directory and one supplement; $45 for two directories and two supplements.

Vacation Exchange Club (PO Box 820, Haleiwa, HI 96712; phone: 800-638-3841). Some 10,000 listings. For $50, the subscriber receives two directories — one in late winter, one in the spring — and is listed in one. For $35, the subscriber receives both directories but no listing.

World Wide Exchange (1344 Pacific Ave., Suite 103, Santa Cruz, CA 95060; phone: 408-476-4206). The $45 annual membership fee includes one listing (for house, yacht, or motor home) and three guides.

Worldwide Home Exchange Club (45 Hans Place, London SW1X OJZ, England; phone: 44-71-589-6055; or 806 Brantford Ave., Silver Spring, MD 20904; no phone). Handles over 1,500 listings a year worldwide, including homes in the Caribbean. For $20 a year, you will receive two listings yearly, as well as supplements.

Better Homes and Travel (formerly *Home Exchange International*), with offices in New York, Los Angeles, London, Paris, and Milan, functions differently in that it publishes no directory and shepherds the exchange process most of the way. Interested parties supply the firm with photographs of themselves and their homes, information on the type of home they want and where, and a registration fee of $50. The company then works with its other offices to propose a few possibilities, and only when a match is made do the parties exchange names, addresses, and phone numbers. For this service, *Better Homes and Travel* charges a closing fee, which ranges from $150 to $450 for switches from 2 weeks to 3 months long, and from $275 to $625 for longer switches. Contact *Better Homes and Travel,* Box 268, 185 Park Row, New York, NY 10038-0272 (phone: 212-349-5340).

HOME STAYS: If the idea of actually staying in a private home as the guest of a foreign family appeals to you, check with the *United States Servas Committee,* which maintains a list of hosts throughout the world willing to throw open their doors to visitors entirely free of charge. At the time of this writing, there were participating hosts throughout Mexico.

The aim of this nonprofit cultural program is to promote international understanding and peace, and every effort is made to discourage freeloaders. *Servas* will send you an application form and the name of the nearest of some 200 interviewers around the US for you to contact. After the interview, if you're approved, you'll receive documentation certifying you as a *Servas* traveler. There is a membership fee of $45 per person, and there also is a deposit of $15 to receive the host list, refunded on its return. The list gives the name, address, age, occupation, and other particulars of the hosts, including languages spoken. From then on, it is up to you to write to the prospective hosts directly, and *Servas* makes no guarantee that you will be accommodated.

Servas stresses that you should choose only people you really want to meet and that during your stay (which normally lasts between 2 nights and 2 weeks) you should be interested mainly in your hosts, not in sightseeing. It also suggests that one way to show your appreciation once you've returned home is to become a host yourself. The minimum age of a *Servas* traveler is 18 (however, children under 18 may accompany their parents), and though quite a few are young people who have just finished college, there are travelers (and hosts) in all age ranges and occupations. Contact *Servas* at 11 John St., Room 706, New York, NY 10038-4009 (phone: 212-267-0252).

Time Zones, Business Hours, and Bank Holidays

 TIME ZONES: Most areas in Mexico operate on Central Standard Time and do not observe Daylight Saving Time. There are a few exceptions. Mountain Standard Time is used in the western coastal states of Sonora, Sinaloa, and Nayarit, as well as in Baja California Sur, directly across the Gulf of California. Pacific Standard Time is used in Baja California Norte from late October to late April, and Mountain Standard Time from late April.

In winter, if it is 9 AM in Mexico City (Central Standard Time), it is 7 AM in Los Angeles (Pacific Standard Time), 8 AM in Denver (Mountain Standard Time), and 10 AM in New York City (Eastern Standard Time). In the summer, when Daylight Saving is in effect in the US, add 1 hour to each of the equivalent US times — except when you're in Baja California Norte.

Mexican timetables use a 24-hour clock to denote arrival and departure times, which means that hours are expressed sequentially from 1 AM. By this method, 9 AM is recorded as 0900, noon as 1200, 1 PM as 1300, 6 PM as 1800, midnight as 2400, and so on. For example, the departure of a train at 7 AM will be announced as "0700"; one leaving at 7 PM will be noted as "1900."

One further confusion may arise when you're keeping an appointment with a Mexican acquaintance. Although you may be certain that you already have adjusted your watch and that it is working correctly, your companion may not show up until an hour or more after the agreed time. This is neither unusual nor considered impolite. It is simply a different regard for time than is common in the US. And your trip to Mexico may be even more delightful if you relax and adopt this south-of-the-border attitude.

BUSINESS HOURS: While Mexicans' working hours number about the same as those kept in the US, the times differ considerably. Executives usually begin working at 10 AM and stop for a leisurely, two-hour lunch around 2 or 3 PM. The afternoon shift runs from about 4 to 7 PM. Mexican stores generally are open from 10 AM to 7 PM.

Most banks are open from 9AM to 1:30 PM Mondays through Fridays. Key branches of some major banks also may offer additional hours, opening from 4 to 6 PM on weekdays. A few banks may keep more familiar hours — staying open from 8:30 AM through 5 PM. Some even may have weekend hours — staying open from 10 AM to 1:30 PM and from 4 to 6 PM on Saturdays, and 10 AM to 1:30 PM on Sundays.

If you are unable to get to the bank, you usually can cash your traveler's checks at money exchanges which are open Mondays through Fridays until 5 PM and Saturdays until 2 PM. The airport money exchanges are open Sundays as well. (For further information, see *Credit and Currency,* in this section.)

BANK HOLIDAYS: Government offices, banks, and stores are closed on national holidays and often on the days just before and after as well. Many offices (but not banks) close between *Christmas* and *New Year's.* Following are the Mexican national holidays and the dates they will be held this year:

January 1: *New Year's Day (Año Nuevo).*

February 5: *Constitution Day* marks the signing of the constitutions of 1857 and 1915.

March 21: *Birthday of Benito Juárez* honors the man often called the "Abraham Lincoln of Mexico."

April 16: *Holy Thursday.*

April 17: *Good Friday.*

May 1: *Labor Day* celebrated with parades.

May 5: Anniversary of Mexico's victory over the French at Puebla in 1862.
September 1: The president's state of the union report *(Informe)* and the opening of Congress.
September 16: *Independence Day.*
October 12: *Columbus Day (Día de la Raza).*
November 2: *All Souls' Day* (known in Mexico as the *Day of the Dead*).
November 20: Anniversary of the Mexican Revolution of 1910.
December 12: *Feast of Our Lady of Guadalupe.*
December 25: *Christmas.*
December 31: Banks closed for annual balance.

Mail, Telephone, and Electricity

 MAIL: Almost every town throughout the country has a post office, and while there are not many public mailboxes *(buzónes)* on street corners, there are drops in most large hotels, office buildings, and in front of and/or in every post office.

All foreign postal service is now airmail. The real problem is how long it takes your letter to get from the post office to the plane: Service in Mexico is notoriously slow. Whether you are sending mail from the US to Mexico, from Mexico to the US, or from one part of the country to another, the mail service is known as "Burro Express," and can take up to several weeks. The good news, however, is that due to the efforts of the Mexican postal authorities, this system is gradually improving.

If you are planning to send packages to destinations either within or outside the country, be sure to have them registered. The procedure is the same as in the US. If your correspondence is important, you may want to send it via one of the special courier services; *Federal Express, DHL,* and other international services are widely availble in Mexico. The cost is considerably higher than sending something via the postal service — but the assurance of its timely arrival is worth it.

There are several places that will receive and hold mail for travelers in Mexico. Mail sent to you at a hotel and clearly marked "Guest Mail, Hold for Arrival" is one safe approach. If you do not know what your address will be, have your mail addressed to the nearest post office in care of the local equivalent of General Delivery: *a/c Lista de Correos.* Note that you are expected to specify the branch, district, zip code *(codigo postal)* and city — and, under the best conditions, this is very risky. Most foreign post offices have a time limit for holding such mail — 30 days is a common limit. To claim this mail, you must go in person to the post office, ask for the local equivalent of General Delivery, and present identification (driver's license, credit cards, birth certificate, or passport).

In sending mail to Mexico, avoid using middle names. Mexicans use the paternal and maternal surnames — the paternal is in the middle — and using a middle name could lead to confusion. When inquiring about mail addressed to you, should there be nothing under the first letter of your last name, ask the post office clerk to look for it under the first letter of your first or middle name. If you plan to remain in one place for more than a month, consider renting a post office box *(apartado postal)* in the central post office to eliminate the chance of mail getting lost in local delivery.

If you are an *American Express* customer (a cardholder, a carrier of *American Express* traveler's checks, or traveling on an *American Express Travel Related Services* tour), you can have mail sent to an *American Express* branch office in cities on your route (this service is offered in cities throughout Mexico). Letters are held free of charge — registered mail and packages are not accepted. You must be able to show an

American Express card, traveler's checks, or a voucher proving you are on one of the company's tours to avoid paying for mail privileges. Those who aren't clients must pay a nominal charge each time they inquire if they have received mail, whether or not they actually have a letter. There also is a forwarding fee, for clients and non-clients alike. Mail should be addressed to you, care of *American Express,* and should be marked "Client Mail Service." Additional information on its mail service and the addresses of *American Express* offices in Mexico are listed in the pamphlet *Services and Offices,* available from any US branch of *American Express.*

While US embassies and consulates abroad usually do not accept mail for tourists, in some metropolitan areas — such as Mexico City — the American embassy *will* hold mail for US citizens. Unless the papers sent are particularly important, it is better not to burden the embassy with the responsibility. It is best to inform them either by separate letter or cable, or by phone (particularly if you are in the country already), that you will be using their address for this purpose.

TELEPHONE: Most large Mexican cities have direct dialing to the US. Telephones from which this is not possible require the assistance of the international operator, who can connect you. Mexico City and several other large metropolitan areas have telephone offices from which long-distance phone calls can be made. If you are staying in a small town or in a hotel with no phone, use the phones in local stores or larger hotels.

The procedure for calling Mexico from the US is as follows: dial 011 (the international access code) + 52 (the country code) + the city code + the local number. (If you don't know the city code, check the front of a telephone book or ask an international operator.) For example, to place a call from anywhere in the US to Mexico City, dial 011 + 52 + 5 + the local number.

To call the US from anywhere in Mexico, dial 95 + the US area code + the local number. For instance, to call a number in New York City, dial 95 + 212 + the local number.

To make a call from one city in Mexico to another, dial 91 + the city code + the local number. To call a number within the same city code coverage area, just dial the local number.

Note that the number of digits in phone numbers is not standardized throughout Mexico. The phone number for a capital may have more digits than numbers in outlying areas. As making connections in Mexico for either local or international calls sometimes can be hit-or-miss, those who have to make an important call — to make a hotel reservation in another city, for instance — should start to do so as far in advance as possible.

Some important phone numbers throughout Mexico include the following:

> **Emergency assistance:** 915-250-0123 and 915-250-0151 (within Mexico City, don't dial 915)
> **Long-distance operator:** 02 (within Mexico)
> **International operator:** 09 (English-speaking)
> **Local information:** 04
> **Countrywide information:** 01

Hotel Surcharges – Avoiding operator-assisted calls can cut international calling costs considerably and bring rates into a somewhat more reasonable range — except for calls made through hotel switchboards. One of the most unpleasant surprises travelers encounter in many foreign countries is the amount they find tacked onto their hotel bill for telephone calls, because foreign hotels routinely add on astronomical surcharges. (It's not at all uncommon to find 300% to 400% added to the actual telephone charges.) A practice initially begun to cover the expense of installing phone equipment and maintaining multilingual personnel to run it around the clock, it now is firmly entrenched as a profit-making operation for many hotels.

Until recently, the only recourse against this unconscionable overcharging was to call collect when phoning from abroad or to use a telephone credit card — available through a simple procedure from any local US phone company. (Note, however, that even if you use a telephone credit card, some hotels still may charge a fee for line usage). Now, *American Telephone and Telegraph (AT&T)* offers *USA Direct*, a service that connects users, via a toll-free number, with an *AT&T* operator in the US, who then will put a call through at the standard international rate. A new feature of this service is that travelers abroad can reach US toll-free (800) numbers by calling a *USA Direct* operator who will connect them. Charges for all calls made through *USA Direct* appear on the caller's regular US phone bill. Note, however, that as we went to press, this service was offered only in the following areas of Mexico: Acapulco, Cancún, Ixtapa, and Puerto Vallarta. For a brochure and wallet card listing the toll-free numbers by country, contact International Information Service, *AT&T Communications*, 635 Grant St., Pittsburgh, PA 15219 (phone: 800-874-4000).

Until such services become universal, it's wise to ask about surcharges *before* calling from a hotel. If the rate is high, it's best to use a telephone credit card; make a collect call; or place the call and ask the party to call right back. If none of these choices is possible, make international calls from the local post office or special telephone center to avoid surcharges. Another way to keep down the cost of calling from Mexico is to leave a copy of your itinerary and telephone numbers with people in the US so that they can call you instead.

Frequent business travelers to non-English-speaking destinations such as Mexico may want to look into corporate membership in *AT&T*'s Language Line Service. By calling a US toll-free number, employees of member companies will be connected with an interpreter in any one of 143 languages and dialects, who will provide on-line interpretive services for $3.50 a minute. From the US, this service is particularly useful for booking travel services in foreign countries where English is not spoken or not fluently spoken. Once abroad, this number can be reached by using the *USA Direct* toll-free number connection feature described above. As we went to press, *AT&T* had no plans to open membership to individual travelers; however, if you require such a service, it may be worth contacting them when you plan to travel. For further information, contact *AT&T* at the address above.

■ **Note:** For quick reference, you might want to get a copy of the helpful pamphlet, *The Phone Booklet,* which lists the nationwide, toll-free (800) numbers of travel information sources and suppliers — such as major airlines, hotel and motel chains, car rental companies, and tourist information offices. Send $2 for postage and handling to *Scott American Corporation,* Box 88, West Redding, CT 06896.

ELECTRICITY: Mexico's electrical current is the same as that used in the US, so American tourists can bring their own electrical appliances from home. Electric shavers, travel irons, and small electric water heaters used for brewing tea or morning coffee can be used in almost all hotels throughout the country, but you are supposed to request permission from the management to use them. And if you want to be fully prepared, bring along an extension cord (the electrical outlet may be farther from the sink than the cord on your razor or hair dryer can reach), and a wall socket adapter with a full selection of plugs to ensure that you'll be able to plug in anywhere.

If you are traveling to remote areas, do not be surprised to find the current weak. Your electrical equipment still should work, but not up to maximum capacity. So if you use an electric razor, it is wise to pack a manual safety razor, too, just in case.

One good source for sets of plugs and adapters for use worldwide is the *Franzus Company* (PO Box 142, Beacon Falls, CT 06403; phone: 203-723-6664). *Franzus* also publishes a useful brochure, *Foreign Electricity is No Deep Dark Secret,* which provides information about converters and adapter plugs for electrical appliances to be used abroad but manufactured for use in the US. To obtain a free copy, send a self-addressed, stamped envelope to *Franzus;* a catalogue of other travel accessories is available on request.

Radio and Television

RADIO: There are hundreds of AM and FM radio stations throughout Mexico. It is possible to listen to almost any kind of music, but you will seldom hear English. There is one English-language radio station in Mexico City. Radio VIP (88 on the FM dial) is a CBS news affiliate that features syndicated news on the hour. In addition, it has morning and evening newscasts direct from the US with political reportage, sports, editorial commentary, stock market reports, and a few recorded international on-the-spot pieces sent from around the world. Besides these and an occasional local item, the station is devoted to nostalgic canned music and is pre-recorded by disc jockeys in the US.

Other radio stations in the country play mostly Mexican country music, known as *ranchero* music. There also are a number of ballad stations, numerous rock stations featuring both imported and domestic recordings, and several AM and FM stations that play classical music.

TELEVISION: Mexico is a nation well initiated in the rites of the tube. Almost all of its broadcasts are in Spanish, with the exception of movies imported from the US. And more and more hotels have cable or satellite TV broadcasting programs direct from the US. The news network, CNN Headline Service, is available on cable channels throughout Mexico. Important US football and baseball games also are telecast in Mexico; local newspapers give times and channels. While the local commentator gives his account in Spanish, the American sportscaster can be heard in the background. US pro football games are increasingly carried live by Mexico City television.

The other American contributions to Mexican TV are the numerous series — police, medical, western, situation comedy, and so on — that are dubbed into Spanish. If you can't understand the language, you can try reading the lips — not terribly amusing, but at least a chance for the television addict to watch his favorite actors be magically transformed into fluent Spanish-speaking stars. Pro football games, soccer, tennis, and all other televised sports, including an occasional jai alai game or bullfight, can be enjoyed with or without the sound. Otherwise, Mexican TV is only for the Spanish speaking, and then only for those who can think of nothing better to do while visiting a country so full of more immediate and active diversions.

Medical and Legal Aid
and Consular Services

MEDICAL AID: Nothing ruins a vacation or business trip more effectively than sudden injury or illness. You can have an accident anytime, but travelers to Mexico are especially vulnerable to certain illnesses. The change in climate, altitude, eating habits; the tension of finding yourself in strange places; and the presence of new, unfamiliar bacteria contribute to lowering your resistance to disease. As always is the case with both diseases and accidents, prevention is the best cure. And in Mexico this adage applies not only to diarrhea or dysentery, but to more serious diseases like hepatitis and typhoid fever.

Before you go, be sure to check with your insurance company about the applicability of your hospitalization and major medical policies while you're away (see *Insurance,* in this section). Also make sure you get the most up-to-date information available about health conditions in Mexico. Consult your personal physician or contact your county or state health departments, which generally also can administer necessary or recommended inoculations. (For information on specific health problems, recommended immunizations, and other precautions, see *Staying Healthy,* in this section.)

If you fall victim to any accident or malady that seems serious, do not hesitate to go to a doctor. The medical care available in Mexico is not very different from that offered in the US. There are private doctors, every kind of specialist, clinics, both private and government hospitals, dentists, optometrists, pharmacies, drugstores, and most drugs found in the US, some of which are available without prescription and at a lower price than in the US. The quality of health care and the sophistication of medical facilities is less certain in rural and remote areas, and for specialized treatment it often is best to arrange for transportation to the nearest metropolitan center.

If a bona fide emergency occurs, the fastest way to get attention may be to go to the emergency room of the nearest hospital. An alternative is to dial one of the following numbers for emergency assistance: 915-250-0123 or 915-250-0151 (within Mexico City, do not dial 915). When calling these numbers, state immediately that you are a foreign tourist and then the nature of your problem and your location. Note that ambulance dispatchers may not be bilingual, so travelers with little or no Spanish language ability should try to get someone else to make the call. You also can dial for the operator and ask for someone who speaks English. In some areas, you may need an international operator to place a call to the local emergency service and stay on the line as an interpreter. Most emergency services send out well-equipped and well-staffed ambulances, although ambulances in some areas of Mexico may not be equipped with the advanced EMS technology found in the US and may provide only basic medical attention and be used mainly for transportation.

If you find it necessary to go to a hospital, either for emergency treatment or for admission as a regular patient, it is advisable to find one that is affiliated with a university in a major city — this is particularly critical should you need a blood transfusion, as such facilities generally have properly screened blood donors for hepatitis, AIDS, and other infectious diseases. (No matter what type of facility you go to, always ask about blood screening.) The next best alternative is to seek treatment at a private, rather than government-owned, hospital. The only exception is if you need highly specialized medical treatment, in which case public hospitals *may* have superior medical equipment. For example, if there is only one kidney dialysis facility, it will be in a public hospital.

In a foreign country, where you may not be fluent in the language, a private facility is more likely to give you the kind of assurance you need to feel comfortable. US and British private hospitals (if you can find one) offer the distinct advantage of being staffed with English-speaking doctors who were trained in the US or the United Kingdom. The emergency rooms of most private hospitals also have staff members who speak English, and your hotel, consulate, tourist office, pharmacy, or local police can direct you to the nearest facilities. Remember that if you are hospitalized, you probably will have to pay, even in an emergency.

If a doctor is needed for something less than an emergency, there are several ways to find one. If you are staying in a hotel or resort, ask for help in reaching a doctor or other emergency services, or for the house physician, who may visit you in your room or ask you to visit an office. Travelers staying at a hotel of any size probably will find that the doctor on call speaks at least a modicum of English — if not, request one who does. When you register at a hotel, it's not a bad idea to include your home address and telephone number; this will facilitate the process of notifying friends, relatives, or your own doctor in case of an emergency.

Any US consul also can provide a list of English-speaking doctors and dentists in the area the consulate serves. (For a list of US consuls in Mexico, see "Legal Aid and Consular Services," below.) Dialing the emergency numbers (see above) also may be of help.

Pharmacies (*farmacias*) are a slight variation on the theme to which you are accustomed. While they're owned and operated by licensed pharmacists, diagnoses, prescription filling, and even drug administration often are done by pharmacists or their assistants. In some areas, pharmacies may take turns staying open for 24 hours. In small towns, where none may be open after normal business hours, you may be able to have one open in an emergency situation — such as for a diabetic needing insulin — for a fee. Contact a local hospital or medical clinic for information on on-call pharmacists.

If your complaint is not serious and you wish to avoid the hassle or expense of consulting a physician, the local *farmacia* will be happy to recommend a drug, administer it either in bulk or single doses, and even give or recommend a doctor to give injections. However, a word of warning is necessary about injections, as the needles often are used more than once and sterilization is not as dependable as it is in the US. If you have a condition that may need occasional injections, bring a supply of syringes with you or buy the disposable syringes available without a prescription at most pharmacies in Mexico.

Emergency assistance also is available from various medical programs designed for travelers who have chronic ailments or whose illness requires them to return home:

International Association of Medical Assistance to Travelers (*IAMAT;* 417 Center St., Lewiston, NY 14092; phone: 716-754-4883). Entitles members to the services of participating English-speaking doctors around the world, as well as clinics and hospitals in various locations in Mexico. Participating physicians agree to adhere to a basic charge of around $40 to see a patient referred by *IAMAT.* To join, simply write to *IAMAT;* in about 3 weeks you will receive a membership card, the booklet of members, and an inoculation chart. A nonprofit organization, *IAMAT* appreciates donations; with a donation of $25 or more, you will receive a set of worldwide climate charts detailing weather and sanitary conditions. (Delivery can take up to 5 weeks, so plan ahead.)

International Health Care Service (New York Hospital–Cornell Medical Center, 525 E. 68th St., Box 210, New York, NY 10021; phone: 212-746-1601). This service provides a variety of travel-related health services, including information on health conditions and English-speaking physicians in Mexico. A pre-travel counseling and immunization package costs $255 for the first family member and $195 for each additional member; a post-travel consultation is $175 to $275, plus lab work. Appointments are required for all services. The *International Health Care Traveler's Guide,* a compendium of facts and advice on health care and diseases around the world, can be obtained by sending $4.50 and a self-addressed, stamped envelope to the service.

International SOS Assistance (PO Box 11568, Philadelphia, PA 19116; phone: 800-523-8930 or 215-244-1500). Subscribers are provided with telephone access — 24 hours a day, 365 days a year — to a worldwide, monitored, multilingual network of medical centers. A phone call brings assistance ranging from a telephone consultation to transportation home by ambulance or aircraft, or, in some cases, transportation of a family member to wherever you are hospitalized. Individual rates are $35 for 2 weeks of coverage ($3.50 for each additional day), $70 for 1 month, or $240 for 1 year; couple and family rates also are available.

Medic Alert Foundation (2323 N. Colorado, Turlock, CA 95380; phone: 800-ID-ALERT or 209-668-3333). If you have a health condition that may not be readily available to the casual observer — one that might result in a tragic error in an emergency situation — this organization offers identification emblems specifying such conditions. The foundation also maintains a computerized central file from which your complete medical history is available 24 hours a day by phone (the telephone number is clearly inscribed on the emblem). The onetime membership fee (between $25 and $45) is based on the type of metal from which the emblem is made — the choices range from stainless steel to 10K gold-filled.

TravMed (PO Box 10623, Baltimore, MD 21204; phone: 800-732-5309 or 301-296-5225). For $3 per day, subscribers receive comprehensive medical assistance while abroad. Major medical expenses are covered up to $100,000, and special transportation home or of a family member to wherever you are hospitalized is provided at no additional cost.

■ **Note:** Those who are unable to take a reserved flight due to personal illness or who must fly home unexpectedly due to a family emergency should be aware that airlines may offer a discounted airfare (or arrange a partial refund) if the traveler can demonstrate that his or her situation is indeed a legitimate emergency. Your inability to fly or the illness or death of an immediate family member usually must be substantiated by a doctor's note or the name, relationship, and funeral home where the deceased will be buried. In such cases, airlines often will waive certain advance purchase restrictions or you may receive a refund check or voucher for future travel at a later date. Be aware, however, that this bereavement fare may not necessarily be the least expensive fare available and, if possible, it is best to have a travel agent check all possible flights through a computer reservations system (CRS).

LEGAL AID AND CONSULAR SERVICES: There is one crucial place to keep in mind when outside the US, namely, the American Services section of the US consulate. If you are injured or become seriously ill, the consulate will direct you to medical assistance and notify your relatives. If, while abroad, you become involved in a dispute that could lead to legal action, the consulate, once again, is the place to turn.

It usually is far more alarming to be arrested abroad than at home. Not only are you alone among strangers, but the punishment can be worse. Granted, the US consulate can advise you of your rights and provide a list of English-speaking lawyers, but it cannot interfere with local legal process. Except for minor infractions of the local traffic code, there is no reason for any law-abiding traveler to run afoul of immigration, customs, or any other law enforcement authority.

The best advice is to be honest and law-abiding. If you get a traffic ticket, pay it. If you are approached by drug hawkers, ignore them. The penalties for possession of marijuana, cocaine, and other narcotics are even more severe abroad than in the US. (If you are picked up for any drug-related offense, do not expect US foreign service officials to be sympathetic. Chances are, they will notify a lawyer and your family and that's about all. See "Drugs," below.)

In the case of minor traffic accidents (such as a fender-bender), it often is most expedient to settle the matter before the police get involved. If the police do get involved in minor accidents or violations, the usual procedure is for the police officer to say that you must pay a fine. If you explain that you are a tourist, the officer usually will offer to settle the fine on the spot. If you speak the language and feel competent, try to bargain the fine — an experienced hand in Mexico would offer half the amount stated — but wisdom decrees that you do what is necessary to get the matter settled on the spot. Otherwise you fill have to pay the fine at the police station.

If, however, you are involved in a serious accident, where an injury or fatality results, the first step is to contact the US consulate (for addresses, see below) and ask the consul to locate an attorney to assist you. If you have a traveling companion, ask him or her to call the consulate (unless either of you has a local contact who can help you quickly). Competent English-speaking lawyers reside in most parts of Mexico and it is possible to obtain good legal counsel on short notice. Also note that you may have to post a substantial bond in order to be released during the legal proceedings — your attorney will be able to advise you on this matter.

The US Department of State in Washington, DC, insists that any US citizen who is arrested abroad has the right to contact the US embassy or consulate "immediately," but it may be a while before you are given permission to use a phone. Do not labor under the illusion, however, that in a scrape with foreign officialdom the consulate can act as an arbitrator or ombudsman on an American citizen's behalf. Nothing could be farther from the truth. Consuls have no power, authorized or otherwise, to subvert, alter, or contravene the legal processes, however unfair, of the foreign country in which they serve. Nor can a consul oil the machinery of a foreign bureaucracy or provide legal advice. The consul's responsibilities do encompass "welfare duties," including providing a list of lawyers and information on local sources of legal aid, assigning an interpreter if the police have none, informing relatives in the US, and organizing and administrating any defense monies sent from home. If a case is tried unfairly or the punishment seems unusually severe, the consul can make a formal complaint to the authorities. For questions about Americans arrested abroad, how to get money to them, and other useful information, call the *Citizens' Emergency Center* of the Office of Special Consular Services in Washington, DC, at 202-647-5225. (For further information about this invaluable hotline, see below.)

Other welfare duties, not involving legal hassles, cover cases of both illness and destitution. If you should get sick, the US consul can provide names of English-speaking doctors and dentists, as well as the names of all local hospitals and clinics; the consul also will contact family members in the US and help arrange special ambulance service for a flight home. In a situation involving "legitimate and proven poverty" of an American stranded abroad without funds, the consul will contact sources of money (such as friends or family in the US), apply for aid to agencies in foreign countries, and in a last resort — which is *rarely* — arrange for repatriation at government expense, although this is a loan that must be repaid. And in case of natural disasters or civil unrest, consulates around the world handle the evacuation of US citizens if it becomes necessary.

The consulate is not occupied solely with emergencies and is certainly not there to aid in trivial situations, such as canceled reservations or lost baggage, no matter how important these matters may seem to the victimized tourist. The main duties of any consulate are administrating statutory services, such as the issuance of passports and visas; providing notarial services; distributing VA, social security, and civil service benefits to resident Americans; taking depositions; handling extradition cases; and reporting to Washington the births, deaths, and marriages of US citizens living within the consulate's domain.

We hope that none of the information in this section will be necessary during your travels through Mexico. If you can avoid legal hassles altogether, you will have a much more pleasant trip. If you run into a confrontation that might lead to legal complications developing with a Mexican citizen or with local authorities, the best tactic is to apologize and try to leave as gracefully as possible. If you do become involved in an imbroglio, the local authorities may spare you legal complications if you make clear your tourist status. Do not get into fights with residents, no matter how belligerent or provocative they are in a given situation. In a foreign country where machismo is part of the national character, some things are best left unsettled.

US EMBASSY AND CONSULATES IN MEXICO: The US Embassy is located in

Mexico City (305 Paseo de la Reforma, México, DF 06500; phone: 5-211-0042). The US government also maintains consulates general in nine other cities of Mexico; consular agents operate in ten additional cities.

Below is a list of all the American consulates in Mexico. If you are not in any of the towns mentioned when a problem arises, contact the nearest office. If you are not a US citizen, contact the consulate of your own nation.

The locations of the US consulates general in Mexico are as follows:

Ciudad Juárez: 924 Av. López Mateos Nte., Ciudad Juárez, Chihuahua 32000 (phone: 16-134048).
Guadalajara: 175 Progreso, Guadalajara, Jalisco 44100 (phone: 36-252700).
Hermosillo: 141 Monterrey, Hermosillo, Sonora 83260 (phone: 62-172375).
Matamoros: 2002 Av. Primera, Matamoros, Tamaulipas 87330 (phone: 891-25250).
Mazatlán: 6 Calle Circunvalación at Venustiano Carranza, Mazatlán, Sinaloa 82000 (phone: 698-52205).
Mérida: 453 Paseo Montejo, Apdo. 130, Mérida, Yucatán 97000 (phone: 99-255011).
Monterrey: 411 Av. Constitución Pte., Monterrey, Nuevo León 64000 (phone: 83-452120).
Nuevo Laredo: 3330 Calle Allende Col. Jardín, Nuevo Laredo, Tamaulipas 88260 (phone: 871-40696).
Tijuana: 96 Calle Tapachula, Tijuana, Baja California Norte 22420 (phone: 66-817400).

Consular agents can be reached in the following cities by calling the numbers listed:

Acapulco: Hotel Club del Sol, Acapulco, Guerrero (phone: 748-57207).
Cancún: 30 Av. Cobá, Cancún, Quintana Roo (phone: 988-42411).
Durango: 204 Juárez Nte., Durango, Durango (phone: 181-12217).
Mulegé: Hotel Serenidad, Mulegé, Baja California Sur (phone: 685-30111).
Oaxaca: 213 Crespo, Oaxaca, Oaxaca (phone: 951-60654).
Puerto Vallarta: 12-A Parian del Puente Local, Puerto Vallarta (phone: 322-20069).
San Luis Potosí: 1430 Venustiano Carranza, San Luis Potosí (phone: 481-72501).
San Miguel de Allende: 72 Dr. Hernández Macias, San Miguel de Allende (phone: 465-22357).
Tampico: 2000 Av. Hidalgo Local 4, Tampico (phone: 121-32217).
Veracruz: 110 Juárez, Veracruz, Veracruz (phone: 29-310142).

You also can obtain a booklet with addresses of most US embassies and consulates around the world by writing to the Superintendent of Documents (US Government Printing Office, Washington, DC 20402) and asking for publication #78-77, *Key Offices of Foreign Service Posts.*

As mentioned above, the US State Department operates a *Citizens' Emergency Center,* which offers a number of services to US citizens traveling abroad and their families at home. In addition to giving callers up-to-date information on trouble spots, the center will contact authorities abroad in an attempt to locate a traveler or deliver an urgent message. In case of illness, death, arrest, destitution, or repatriation of an American citizen on foreign soil, it will relay information to relatives at home if the consulate is unable to do so. Travel advisory information is available 24 hours a day to people with Touch-Tone phones (phone: 202-647-5225). Callers with rotary phones can get information at this number from 8:15 AM to 10 PM (Eastern Standard Time) on weekdays; 9 AM to 3 PM Saturdays. In the event of an emergency, this number also may be called during these hours. For emergency calls only, at all other times, call 202-634-3600 and ask for the Duty Officer.

Drinking and Drugs

DRINKING: There are no laws restricting drinking in Mexico — there is not even a minimum drinking age. In fact, the manufacture of alcoholic beverages, from beer to brandy, is one of Mexico's most important industries. For information on native brews of Mexico, see *Food and Drink,* PERSPECTIVES.

As in the US, national taxes on alcohol affect the prices of liquor in Mexico, and as a general rule, mixed drinks made from imported liquors (such as whiskey and gin) are more expensive than at home. If you like a toddy before dinner, a good way to save money is to buy a bottle of your favorite brand at the airport before leaving the US and enjoy it in your hotel before setting forth. Or stick to locally produced beverages. If you are buying any quantity of alcohol (such as a case of tequila) in Mexico, be aware that whether you are bringing it with you or having it shipped, you will have to pay US import duties on any quantity over the allowed 1 liter (see *Customs and Returning to the US,* in this section.)

DRUGS: Another way to avoid legal trouble in Mexico is to avoid the drug scene — completely. Illegal narcotics are as prevalent in Mexico as in the US, but the moderate legal penalties and vague social acceptance that marijuana has gained in the US have no equivalents in Mexico. Due to the international war on drugs, enforcement of drug laws is becoming increasingly strict throughout the world. Local Mexican narcotics officers and customs officials are renowned for their absence of understanding and lack of a sense of humor — especially where Americans are involved.

Despite the government's campaign against it, marijuana still is grown in abundance throughout Mexico and is widely available. It is, however, just as illegal in Mexico as it is in the US, and penalties for selling, growing, and smoking it are just as severe. Opiates and barbiturates, and other increasingly popular drugs — "white powder" substances like heroin and cocaine, and "crack" (the cocaine derivative) — also are a problem in Mexico, as elsewhere.

The concerted effort by Mexican and other foreign authorities to stamp out drug traffic, with the support and encouragement of the United States, has now become a real war on buyers and sellers in the country — a war that has been — and continues to be — deadly.

Penalties for possession of even small quantities of marijuana range from deportation with stiff fines to jail terms of 2 to 7 years, without bail or appeal. The penalties for other drugs may be even more stringent, and smuggling is dealt with even more severely. It is important to bear in mind that the quantity of drugs involved is of very minor importance.

Do not, under any circumstances, take drugs into, out of, or through Mexico. Persons arrested are subject to the laws of the country they are visiting, and in Mexico these laws and their procedures often are very harsh. Most of the Americans repatriated through the prisoner-exchange agreements between the United States and Mexico were incarcerated for drug offenses. Once you are in jail, the best lawyers in the country won't be able to get you out — and neither will the US government. Eventually, at the whim of the authorities, you will be tried and, upon conviction, given a stiff sentence. The best advice we can offer is: Don't carry, use, buy, or sell illegal drugs.

Those who carry medicines that contain a controlled drug should be sure to have a current doctor's prescription with them. Ironically, travelers can get into almost as much trouble coming through US customs with over-the-counter drugs picked up abroad that contain substances that are controlled in the US. Cold medicines, pain relievers, and the like often have codeine or codeine derivatives that are illegal, except by prescription, in the US. Throw them out before leaving for home.

■ **Be forewarned:** US narcotics agents warn travelers of the increasingly common ploy of drug dealers asking travelers to transport a "gift" or other package back to the US. Don't be fooled into thinking that the protection of US law applies abroad — accused of illegal drug trafficking you will be considered guilty until you prove your innocence. In other words, do not, under any circumstances agree to take anything across the border for a stranger.

Tipping

 TIPPING: Many waiters, waitresses, porters, and bellboys in Mexico depend upon tips for their livelihood. The salaries they receive, if they do receive salaries, are far below the equivalent paid in the US (even with the lower Mexican standards of living taken into consideration). There also are situations in which you wouldn't tip in the US but should in Mexico.

In restaurants, tip between 10% and 20% of the bill. For average service in an average restaurant, a 15% tip to the waiter is reasonable, although one should never hesitate to penalize poor service or reward excellent and efficient attention by leaving less or more. (If you notice a 6% or 15% addition to your bill, this usually is a standard tax, called IVA, not a service charge, and a tip still is in order; if you suspect that a gratuity might already be included, ask.)

Although it's not necessary to tip the maître d' of most restaurants — unless he or she has been especially helpful in arranging a special party or providing a table (a few extra bills *may*, however, get you seated sooner or procure a preferred table) — when tipping is appropriate, the least amount should be the current equivalent of $5 in pesos. In the finest restaurants, where a multiplicity of servers are present, plan to tip 5% to the captain. The sommelier (wine waiter) is entitled to a gratuity of approximately 10% of the price of the bottle of wine.

In allocating gratuities at a restaurant, pay particular attention to what has become the standard credit card charge form, which now includes separate places for gratuities for waiters and/or captains. If these separate boxes are not on the charge slip, simply ask the waiter or captain how these separate tips should be indicated. In some establishments, tips indicated on credit card receipts may not be given to the help, so you may want to leave tips in cash.

If you arrive by air, you probably will find a porter with a cart ready to roll your baggage from customs to the cab stand. He should be paid the current equivalent of about $1 to $2 in pesos, depending on how much luggage you have. If you are traveling by train, porters *expect* a tip of about 25¢ to 35¢ per bag — you might want to go higher. Bellhops, doormen, and porters at hotels generally are tipped at the rate of 50¢ to $1 per piece of luggage, along with a small additional amount if a doorman helps with a cab. If you arrive without the right denominations in pesos, tip in US money. (When in doubt, it is preferable to tip — in any denomination or currency — than not to tip.)

In a large hotel or resort, where it is difficult to determine just who out of a horde of attendants actually performed particular services, it is perfectly proper for guests to ask to have an extra 10% to 15% added to their bill. If you prefer to distribute tips yourself, leave the hotel maid at least $1 per day. Tip the concierge and hall porter for specific services only, with the amount of such gratuities dependent on the level of service provided. For any special service you receive in a hotel, a tip is expected — $1 being the minimum for a small service.

Authorized taxi rates are set either by kilometers traveled or by zone, depending on the city or town; in metered cabs current fares often are posted (especially if there has been an increase in fares and the meter has not yet been adjusted). Many cab drivers set their own unofficial fares, and it is a good idea to ask what it will cost to get to a destination before entering the cab and letting the driver take over. Like so many fees in Mexico, this fare is likely to be negotiable. Cab drivers do not expect tips unless they perform some special service. Cabs that you call by phone are slightly more expensive than those that have meters and you hail in the streets.

In Mexico, tourists often are offered special services by young children in the street. These might include watching your car while you shop and sightsee or cleaning your windshield while you stop at a light. In some instances these services come more as assaults than offers — you will find someone suddenly propped on the hood of your car wiping your windows with a dirty rag. Often the only way to save your window is to pay the washer a few pesos and tell him to go. In the case of children who want to guard your car, you must be firm with them immediately if you don't want their services. They often approach you by opening the door of your car to help you get out. If you don't tell them no and send them away immediately, you will find them standing beside your car, allegedly guarding it, when you return. At this point, the wisest recourse is to give them a couple of hundred pesos. But first check that everything in the car is as you left it. Arriving and departing from airline terminals also can turn into a battle royal with youngsters over carrying your luggage.

In resort areas and smaller cities, you may come across uniformed adult car watchers who earn their livelihoods this way. If you find one near your car, give him the current equivalent of $1 in pesos when you return — once you've unlocked the car and made sure everything is still there. If you park your car in a garage or lot, the parking attendant who returns it to you will expect a comparable tip. Unlike in the US, gas station attendants in Mexico expect a tip, even if they don't clean your windshield or check your oil (you should request these services if you want them); 500 to 1,000 pesos is an adequate tip.

Miscellaneous tips: Ushers in theaters should be given about 50¢ after leading you to a seat and giving you a program. Sightseeing tour guides should be tipped. If you are traveling in a group, decide together what you want to give the guide and present it from the group at the end of the tour. If you have been indvidually escorted, the percentage of the tour price should depend on the degree of your satisfaction, but it should not be less than 10%. Museum and monument guides also are usually tipped a few dollars. Coat checks are worth about 50¢ to $1 a coat, and washroom attendants are tipped — there usually is a little plate with a coin already in it suggesting the expected amount. In barbershops and beauty parlors, tips also are expected, but the percentages vary according to the type of establishment — 10% in the most expensive salons; 15% to 20% in less expensive establishments. (As a general rule, the person who washes your hair should get a small additional tip.) For information on tipping aboard ships, see *Traveling by Ship,* in this section.

At the border, although the Mexican Ministry of Tourism does not approve of the practice, officials who sign your tourist card, check your car, and issue your car permit are not averse to a tip; about $1 to $2 will do.

Tipping always is a matter of personal preference. In the situations covered above, as well as in any others that arise where you feel a tip is expected or due, feel free to express your pleasure or displeasure. Again, never hesitate to reward excellent and efficient attention and to penalize poor service. Give an extra gratuity and a word of thanks when someone has gone out of his or her way for you. Either way, the more personal the act of tipping, the more appropriate it seems. And if you didn't like the service — or the attitude — don't tip.

Duty-Free Shopping

Duty-free shops are located in all the major international airports throughout Mexico. If common sense says that it is always less expensive to buy goods in an airport duty-free shop than to buy them at home or in the streets of a foreign city, travelers should best be aware of some basic facts. Duty-free, first of all, does not mean that the goods travelers buy will be free of duty when they return to the US. Rather, it means that the shop has paid no import tax acquiring goods of foreign make because the goods are not to be used in the country where the shop is located. This is why duty-free goods are available only in the restricted, passengers-only area of international airports or are delivered to departing passengers on the plane. In a duty-free store, travelers save money only on goods of foreign make because they are the only items on which an import tax would be charged in any other store.

There is little reason to delay buying locally made merchandise and/or souvenirs until reaching the airport (for information on local specialties, see the individual city chapters in THE CITIES, and *Shopping at the Source,* in DIVERSIONS). In fact, because airport duty-free shops usually pay high rents, the locally made goods sold in them may well be more expensive than they would be in downtown stores. The real bargains are foreign goods, but — let the buyer beware — not all foreign goods are automatically less expensive in an airport duty-free shop. You can get a good deal on even small amounts of perfume, costing less than the usually required minimum purchase, tax-free. Other fairly standard bargains include spirits, smoking materials, cameras, clothing, watches, chocolates, and other food and luxury items — but first be sure to know what these items cost elsewhere. Terrific savings do exist (they are the reason for such shops, after all), but so do overpriced items that an unwary shopper might find equally tempting. In addition, if you wait to do your shopping at airport duty-free shops, you will be taking the chance that the desired item is out of stock or unavailable.

Religion on the Road

Mexico is a Catholic country, and every town, right down to the most isolated village, has its own church. In some more remote villages you will find an interesting combination of Catholicism and pre-Christian ritual, as reflected in the common sight of a family leaving Sunday morning mass only to walk across the plaza and set up an idol of some warrior god dating back to Maya times. And in larger, more heavily populated areas, some amount of religious variety is reflected in the numerous Protestant churches and Jewish synagogues.

The surest source of information on English-language religious services in an unfamiliar country is the desk clerk of the hotel or resort in which you are staying; the local tourist information office, a US consul, or a church of another religious affiliation also may be able to provide this information. Services in English are available at various churches and other places of worship in Mexico, particularly in metropolitan areas and other in communities with large English-speaking populations. If you aren't in an area with such services, you might find it interesting to attend a Spanish service — even if you don't understand all the words. There are many beautiful churches throughout Mexico, and whether in a stately cathedral or a small village chapel, visitors are welcome.

Customs and Returning to the US

 Whether you return to the United States by air, land, or sea, you must declare to the US Customs official at the point of entry everything you have bought or acquired while in Mexico. The customs check can go smoothly, lasting only a few minutes, or can take hours, depending on the officer's instinct. To speed up the process, keep all your receipts handy and try to pack your purchases together in an accessible part of your suitcase. It might save you from unpacking all your belongings or even from dismantling your entire car.

DUTY-FREE ARTICLES: In general the duty-free allowance for US citizens returning from abroad is $400. This duty-free limit is based on the provision that your purchases accompany you and are for personal use. This limit includes items used or worn while abroad, souvenirs for friends, and gifts received during the trip. A flat 10% duty based on the "fair retail value in country of acquisition" is assessed on the next $1,000 worth of merchandise brought in for personal use or gifts. Amounts over the basic allotment and the 10% dutiable amount are dutiable at a variety of rates. The average rate for typical tourist purchases is about 12%, but you can find out rates on specific items by consulting *Tariff Schedules of the United States* in a library or at any US Customs Service office.

Families traveling together may make a joint declaration to customs, which permits one member to exceed his or her duty-free exemption to the extent that another falls short. Families also may pool purchases dutiable under the flat rate. A family of three, for example, would be eligible for up to a total of $3,000 at the 10% flat duty rate (after each member had used up his or her $400 duty-free exemption) rather than three separate $1,000 allowances. This grouping of purchases is extremely useful when considering the duty on a high-tariff item, such as jewelry or a fur coat.

There are certain articles, however, that are duty-free only up to certain limits. Individuals are allowed 1 carton of cigarettes (200), 100 cigars, and 1 liter of liquor or wine if over 21. Alcohol above this allowance is liable for both duty and an Internal Revenue tax. Antiques, if they are 100 or more years old and you have proof from the seller of that fact, are duty-free, as are paintings and drawings if done entirely by hand.

To avoid paying duty twice, register the serial numbers of computers, watches, and expensive electronic equipment with the nearest US Customs bureau before departure; receipts of insurance policies also should be carried for other foreign-made items. (Also see the note at the end of *Entry Requirements and Documents,* in this section.)

Gold, gold medals, bullion, and up to $10,000 in currency or negotiable instruments may be brought into the US without being declared. Sums over $10,000 must be declared in writing.

Personal exemptions can be used once every 30 days; in order to be eligible, an individual must have been out of the country for more than 48 hours. If any portion of the exemption has been used once within any 30-day period or if your trip is less than 48 hours long, the duty-free allowance is cut to $25.

The allotment for individual "unsolicited" gifts mailed from abroad (no more than one per day per recipient) is $50 retail value per gift. These gifts do not have to be declared and are not included in your duty-free exemption (see below). Although you should include a receipt for purchases with each package, the examiner is empowered to impose a duty based on his or her assessment of the value of the goods. The duty owed is collected by the US Postal Service when the package is delivered. More information on mailing packages home from abroad is contained in the US Customs Service pamphlet *Buyer Beware, International Mail Imports* (see below for where to write for this and other useful brochures).

DUTY-FREE CRAFT ITEMS: In January 1976, the United States passed a Generalized System of Preferences (GSP) to help developing nations improve their economies through exports. The GSP, which recognizes dozens of developing nations — including Mexico — allows Americans to bring certain kinds of goods into the US duty-free, and has designated some 2,800 items as eligible for duty-free treatment.

This system entitles you to exceed your $400 duty-free exemption as long as the purchases are eligible for GSP status. The list of eligible goods includes the following categories: baskets and woven bags; cameras and other photographic equipment; candy; china and silverware; cigarette lighters; earthenware; some furniture; games and toys; golf and ski equipment; some jewelry, unset precious or semi-precious stones, and pearls; jewelry and music boxes; musical instruments, radios, tape recorders, records, and tapes; paper goods and printed matter; perfume and toilet preparations; electric shavers; items made of cork, jade, or shell (other than tortoiseshell); wigs; and wood carvings. Note that, depending on the country of origin, some items may not always be included, and other items not in these categories also may be eligible.

If you have any questions about the GSP status of a particular item, check with the nearest customs office or at the nearest US embassy or consulate (see "Legal Aid and Consular Services," above, for addresses). A useful pamphlet identifying GSP beneficiary nations is the *GSP and the Traveler;* to order ask for "US Customs Publication No. 515" from the US Customs Service, Customs Information, 6 World Trade Ctr., Rm. 201, New York, NY 10048 (phone: 212-466-5550).

CLEARING CUSTOMS: This is a simple procedure. Forms are distributed by airline or ship personnel before arrival. (Note that a $5 per-person service charge — called a user fee — is collected by airlines and cruise lines to help cover the cost of customs' checks, but this is included in the ticket price.) If your purchases total no more than the $400 duty-free limit, you need only fill out the identification part of the form and make an oral declaration to the customs inspector. If entering with more than $400 worth of goods, you must submit a written declaration.

Customs agents are businesslike, efficient, and not unkind. During the peak season, clearance can take time, but this generally is because of the strain imposed by a number of jumbo jets simultaneously discharging their passengers, not because of unwarranted zealousness on the part of the customs people.

Efforts to streamline procedures used to include the so-called Citizens' Bypass Program, which allowed US citizens whose purchases were within their duty-free allowance to go to the "green line," where they simply showed their passports to the customs inspector. Although at the time of this writing this procedure still is being followed at some international airports in the US, most airports have returned to an earlier system. Americans arriving from abroad now have to go through a passport check by the Immigration & Naturalization Service (INS) prior to recovering their baggage and proceeding to customs. (US citizens will not be on the same line as foreign visitors, however, though this additional wait does delay clearance on re-entry into the US.) Although all passengers have to go through this passport inspection, those entering with purchases within the duty-free limit may be spared a thorough customs inspection, although inspectors still retain the right to search any luggage they choose — so don't do anything foolish.

It is illegal not to declare dutiable items; not to do so, in fact, constitutes smuggling, and the penalty can be anything from stiff fines and seizure of the goods to prison sentences. It simply isn't worth doing. Nor should you go along with the suggestions of foreign merchants who offer to help you secure a bargain by deceiving customs officials in any way. Such transactions frequently are a setup, using the foreign merchant as an agent of US Customs. Another agent of US Customs is TECS, the Treasury Enforcement Communications System, a computer that stores all kinds of pertinent information on returning citizens. There is a basic rule to buying goods abroad, and it should never be broken: *If you can't afford the duty on something, don't buy it.* Your list or verbal declaration should include all items purchased abroad, as well as gifts received abroad, purchases made at the behest of others, the value of repairs, and anything brought in for resale in the US.

Do not include in the list items that do not accompany you, i.e., purchases that you have mailed or had shipped home. As mentioned above, these are dutiable in any case, even if for your own use and even if the items that accompany your return from the same trip do not exhaust your duty-free exemption. It is a good idea, if you have accumulated too much while abroad, to mail home any personal effects (made and bought in the US) that you no longer need rather than your foreign purchases. These personal effects pass through US Customs as "American goods returned" and are not subject to duty.

If you cannot avoid shipping home your foreign purchases, however, the US Customs Service suggests that the package be clearly marked "Not for Sale" and that a copy of the bill of sale be included. The US Customs examiner usually will accept this as indicative of the article's fair retail value, but if he or she believes it to be falsified or feels the goods have been seriously undervalued, a higher retail value may be assigned.

FORBIDDEN IMPORTS: Narcotics, plants, and many types of food are not allowed into the US. Drugs are totally illegal, with the exception of medication prescribed by a physician. It's a good idea not to travel with too large a quantity of any given prescription drug (although, in the event that a pharmacy is not open when you need it, bring along several extra doses) and to have the prescription on hand in case any question arises either abroad or when re-entering the US.

Any authentic archaeological find, colonial art, and other original artifacts cannot be exported from Mexico. They will be confiscated upon departure, and the violator runs the risk of being fined or imprisoned. Mexico also restricts export of gold and silver coins; those interested in such items should check with Mexican Customs.

Tourists have long been forbidden to bring into the US foreign-made US trademarked articles purchased abroad (if the trademark is recorded with US Customs) without written permission. It is now possible to enter with one such item in your possession as long as it's for personal use.

The US Customs Service implements the rigorous Department of Agriculture regulations concerning the importation of vegetable matter, seeds, bulbs, and the like. Living vegetable matter may not be imported without a permit, and everything must be inspected, permit or not. Approved items (which do not require a permit) include dried bamboo; beads made of most seeds (but not jequirity beans — the poisonous scarlet and black seed of the rosary pea), Mexican jumping beans, and some viable seeds; coconut shells (unhusked and empty); cones of pine and other trees; roasted coffee beans; most flower bulbs; flowers (without roots); dried or canned fruits, jellies, or jams; polished rice, dried beans and teas; herb plants (not witchweed); nuts (but not acorns, chestnuts, or nuts with outer husks); dried lichens, mushrooms, and seaweed; most dried spices; and woven items made of straw.

Other processed foods and baked goods usually are okay. Regulations on meat products generally depend on the country of origin and manner of processing. As a rule, commercially canned meat, hermetically sealed and cooked in the can so that it can be stored without refrigeration, is permitted, but not all canned meat fulfills this requirement. Be careful in buying canned chili, for instance. Chili made with peppers, beans, and meat in itself is acceptable, but the pork fat that often is part of it, may not be. (The imported brands you see in US stores have been prepared and packaged according to US regulations.) So before stocking up on a newfound favorite, it pays to check in advance — otherwise you might have to leave it behind.

The US Customs Service also enforces federal laws that prohibit the entry of articles made from the furs or hides of animals on the endangered species list. Don't be tempted by sweaters and other garments made from the fine hair of the vicuña (a relative of the domestic llama and alpaca), which is an endangered species. Also beware of shoes, bags, and belts made of crocodile and certain kinds of lizard, and anything made from tortoiseshell; this also applies to preserved crocodiles, lizards, and turtles sometimes sold in gift shops. Some protected species of coral — particularly large chunks of fresh coral and black coral in any form — are restricted (although most jewelry and other items made of coral usually are permitted). And if you're shopping for big-ticket items, beware of fur coats made from the skins of spotted cats. They are sold abroad, but they will be confiscated upon your return to the US, and there will be no refund. For information about other animals on the endangered species list, contact the Department of the Interior, US Fish and Wildlife Service (Publications Unit, 4401 N. Fairfax Dr., Room 130, Arlington, VA 22203; phone: 703-358-1711), and ask for the free publication *Facts About Federal Wildlife Laws.*

Also note that some foreign governments prohibit the export of items made from certain species of wildlife, and the US honors any such restrictions. Before you go shopping in any foreign country, check with the US Department of Agriculture (G110 Federal Bldg., Hyattsville, MD 20782; phone: 301-436-8413) and find out what items are prohibited from the country you will be visiting.

The US Customs Service publishes a series of free pamphlets with customs information. It includes *Know Before You Go,* a basic discussion of customs requirements pertaining to all travelers; *Buyer Beware, International Mail Imports; Travelers' Tips on Bringing Food, Plant, and Animal Products into the United States; Importing a Car; GSP and the Traveler; Pocket Hints; Currency Reporting; Pets, Wildlife, US Customs; Customs Hints for Visitors (Nonresidents);* and *Trademark Information for Travelers.* For the entire series or individual pamphlets, write to the US Customs Service (PO Box 7407, Washington, DC 20044) or contact any of the seven regional offices — in Boston, Chicago, Houston, Long Beach (California), Miami, New Orleans, and New York. The US Customs Service has a taped message whereby callers using Touch-Tone phones can get more information on various topics; the number is 202-566-8195. These pamphlets provide great briefing material, but if you still have questions when you're in Mexico you can contact the US Customs representative at the US Embassy in Mexico City or the nearest US consulate.

Sources and Resources

Mexican Consulates and Tourist Offices in the US

The Mexican government tourist offices and consulates in the US all are sources of general travel information and provide free maps and useful travel literature. For the best results, request information on specific areas, as well as publications relating to your particular areas of interest: accommodations, restaurants, special events, guided tours, and facilities for specific sports. There is no need to send a self-adddressed, stamped envelope with your request, unless specified.

Where required, the consulates also issue tourist cards. They also are empowered to sign other official documents — such as commercial and residence visas — and to notarize copies or translations of American documents, which often is necessary for those papers to be considered legal in Mexico.

The Mexican Embassy is located in Washington, DC (1019 19th St. NW, Suite 810, Washington, DC 20036; phone: 202-293-1710). In most cases, however, visitors to Mexico should direct their inquiries and requests to one of the consulates or tourist offices listed below.

The best places for tourist information within Mexico are listed in the individual reports in THE CITIES. Below is a complete list of Mexican consulates general, consuls, and Mexican government tourist offices in the US.

Consuls

Albuquerque: (Consulate General) Western Bank Bldg., 401 Fifth St. NW, Albuquerque, NM 87102 (phone: 505-247-2139).

Atlanta: (Consulate General) 410 S. Tower, CNN Center, Atlanta, GA 30303-2705 (phone: 404-688-3258).

Austin: (Consulate General) 200 E. Sixth St., Suite 200, Austin, TX 78701 (phone: 512-478-2866).

Boston: (Consulate General) Statler Bldg., 20 Park Plaza, Suite 1212, Boston, MA 02116 (phone: 617-426-4942).

Brownsville: (Consulate General) 724 E. Elizabeth St., PO Box 1711, Brownsville, TX 78520 (phone: 512-542-4431).

Buffalo: (Consul) 1875 Harlem Rd., Buffalo, NY 14212 (phone: 716-895-9800).

Calexico: (Consul) 231 W. 2nd St., Calexico, CA 92231 (phone: 619-357-3863).

Chicago: (Consulate General) 300 N. Michigan Ave., 2nd fl., Chicago, IL 60601 (phone: 312-855-1380).

Corpus Christi: (Consulate General) 800 N. Shoreline Blvd., N. Tower, 4th Floor, Corpus Christi, TX 78410 (phone: 512-882-3375).

Dallas: (Consulate General) 1349 Empire Center, Suite 100, Dallas, TX 75347 (phone: 214-630-7341).

Del Rio: (Consulate General) 1010 S. Main St., Del Rio, TX 78840 (phone: 512-774-5031).

Denver: (Consulate General) 707 Washington St., Suite A, Denver, CO 80203 (phone: 303-830-0523).

Detroit: (Consulate General) 1515 Book Bldg., Washington Blvd., Detroit, MI 48226 (phone: 313-965-1868).

Eagle Pass: (Consulate General) 140 Adams St., Eagle Pass, TX 78852 (phone: 512-773-9255).

El Paso: (Consulate General) 910 E. San Antonio St., PO Box 812, El Paso, TX 79901 (phone: 915-533-3645).

Fresno: (Consulate General) 905 N. Fulton St., Fresno, CA 93728 (phone: 209-233-3065).

Green Bay: (Consul) 901 Howard St., Green Bay, WI 54303 (phone: 414-435-0710).

Honolulu: (Consul) Control Data Bldg., 2828 Paa St., Suite 2115, Honolulu, HI 96819 (phone: 808-833-6331).

Houston: (Consulate General) 3015 Richmond Ave., Suite 100, Houston, TX 77098 (phone: 713-524-2300).

Laredo: (Consulate General) 1612 Farragut St., PO Box 659, Laredo, TX 78040 (phone: 512-723-6360).

Los Angeles: (Consulate General) 2401 W. Sixth St., Los Angeles, CA 90057 (phone: 213-351-6800).

Madison: (Consul) 312 Newcastle Way, Madison, WI 53704 (phone: 608-249-5201).

McAllen: (Consulate General) 1418 Beech St., Suite 102, McAllen, TX 78501 (phone: 512-686-0243).

Miami: (Consulate General) 780 W. 42nd Ave., Suite 525, Miami, FL 33126 (phone: 305-441-8780).

Nashville: (Consul) 226 Capitol Blvd., Suite 212, Nashville, TN 37219 (phone: 615-244-7430).

New Orleans: (Consulate General) World Trade Center, 2 Canal St., Suite 1140, New Orleans, LA 70130 (phone: 504-522-3596).

New York: (Consulate General) 8 E. 41st St., New York, NY 10017 (phone: 212-689-0456).

Nogales: (Consulate General) 137 Terrace Ave., Nogales, AZ 85621 (phone: 602-287-4850

Norfolk: (Consul) 5121 E. Virginia Beach Blvd., Suite EZ, Norfolk, VA 23502 (phone: 804-461-4553).

Philadelphia: (Consulate General) Bourse Bldg., 215 Fifth St., Suite 575, Philadelphia, PA 19106 (phone: 215-922-4262).

Phoenix: (Consulate General) 1190 W. Camelback, Suite 110, Phoenix, AZ 85015 (phone: 602-242-7398).

Portland: (Consul) 545 NE 47th Ave., Portland, OR 97213 (phone: 503-233-5662).

Richmond: (Consul) 2420 Pemberton Rd., Richmond, VA 23233 (phone: 804-747-1961).

Rochester: (Consul) World Travel Bureau, 3 First Ave. SW, Rochester, MN 55901 (phone: 507-288-3130).

Sacramento: (Consul) 9845 Horn Rd., Sacramento, CA 95827 (phone: 916-363-3885).

St. Louis: (Consulate General) 1015 Locust St., St. Louis, MO 63101 (phone: 314-436-3233).

Salt Lake City: (Consulate General) 182 S. 600 East, Suite 202, Salt Lake City, UT 84102 (phone: 801-521-8502).

San Antonio: (Consulate General) 127 Navarro St., San Antonio, TX 78205 (phone: 512-227-9145).

San Bernardino: (Consulate General) 588 W. 6th St., San Bernardino, CA 92401 (phone: 714-889-9836).

San Diego: (Consulate General) 610 A St., Suite 200, San Diego, CA 92101 (phone: 619-231-8414).

San Francisco: (Consulate General) 870 Market St., Suite 528, San Francisco, CA 94102 (phone: 415-392-5554).

San Jose: (Consulate General) 380 N. First St., Suite 100, San Jose, CA 95112 (phone: 408-294-3413).

Seattle: (Consulate General) 2132 Third Ave., Seattle, WA 98121 (phone: 206-448-3526).

Spokane: (Consul) 12005 E. Sprague Ave., Spokane, WA 99214 (phone: 509-926-9531).

Tampa: (Consul) General Shipping Co., 315 Madison St., Tampa, FL 33602 (phone: 813-223-1481).

Tucson: (Consulate General) 553 South Stone Ave., Tucson, AZ 85701 (phone: 602-882-5595).

Ministry of Tourism Offices
Chicago: 70 E. Lake St., Suite 1413, Chicago, IL 60601 (phone: 312-565-2786).

Houston: 2707 N. Loop W, Suite 450, Houston, TX 77008 (phone: 713-880-5153).

Los Angeles: 10100 Santa Monica Blvd., Suite 224, Los Angeles, CA 90067 (phone: 213-203-8191).

New York: 405 Park Ave., Suite 1002, New York, NY 10022 (phone: 212-838-2949).

Washington, DC: 1615 L St. NW, Suite 430, Washington, DC 20036 (phone: 202-293-1710).

Theater and Special Event Tickets

In more than one section of this book there are notations about events that may spark your interest — everything from theater performances to sporting championships — along with telephone numbers and addresses to which to write for descriptive brochures, reservations, or tickets. The Mexican Ministry of Tourism also may be able to supply information on these special events, though they cannot in all cases provide the actual program or detailed information on ticket prices.

Since many of these occasions often are fully booked well in advance, think about having your reservation in hand before you go. Tickets often can be reserved over the phone and charged to a credit card, or you can send an international money order or foreign draft. If you write, remember that any request from the US should be accompanied by an International Reply Coupon to ensure a response. These international coupons, money orders, and drafts are available at US post offices.

Books, Magazines, Newspapers, and Newsletters

BOOKS: Throughout GETTING READY TO GO, numerous books and brochures have been recommended as good sources of further information on a variety of topics.

The following is a list of books recommended for travelers headed for

Mexico. It includes reading material intended to provide background information about Mexico's past, a foundation for understanding what is found in Mexico today, and some perspectives about what is happening around you that you may not personally witness. There are some solid fictional tales set in Mexico, and a few books that call your attention to things you might otherwise not notice — such as exotic flora and local birdlife.

Aura (Bilingual Edition) by Carlos Fuentes (1971, Farrar, Straus & Giroux; $9.95).

Aztec by Gary Jennings (1982, Avon; $5.95).

Burnt Water by Carlos Fuentes (1986, Farrar, Straus & Giroux; $9.95).

A Change of Skin by Carlos Fuentes (1971, Farrar, Straus & Giroux; $9.95).

The Children of Sánchez by Oscar Lewis (1966, Random House; $15.95).

The Conquest of New Spain by Bernal Diaz del Castillo (1963, Penguin; $5.95).

The Cuisines of Mexico by Diana Kennedy (1986, HarperCollins; $24.95).

The Daily Life of the Aztecs on the Eve of the Spanish Conquest by Jacques Soustelle (1961, Stanford University Press; $9.95).

The Death Ship by B. Traven (1973, Lawrence Hill; $9.95).

Distant Neighbors: A Portrait of the Mexicans by Alan Riding (1984, Knopf; $18.95).

Distant Relations by Carlos Fuentes (1982, Farrar, Straus & Giroux; $11.95, hardcover; $8.95, paperback).

Edge of the Storm by Augustín Yañez (1963, University of Texas Press; $12.95).

A Guide to Mexican Witchcraft by William and Claudia Madsen (1977, Ocelot Press; $4.50).

A History of Mexico by Henry B. Parkes (1969, Houghton Mifflin; $11.95).

The Hydra Head by Carlos Fuentes (1978, Farrar, Straus & Giroux; $8.95).

The Labyrinth of Solitude: Life and Thought in Mexico by Octavio Paz (1962, Grove; $11.95).

Many Mexicos by Lesley Byrd Simpson (1966, University of California Press; $42.50, hardcover; $12.95, paperback).

The Maya by Michael D. Coe (1991, Thames and Hudson; $12.95).

Mexico by Michael D. Coe (1984, Thames and Hudson; $11.95).

Mexico in Crisis by Judith Hellman (1983, Holmes and Meier; $32.50, hardcover; $19.95, paperback).

Mexico: Places and Pleasures by Kate Simon (1979, Crowell; $9.95).

The Old Gringo by Carlos Fuentes (1986, HarperCollins; $7.95).

Pedro Páramo by Juan Rulfo (1959, Grove; $7.95).

The Plumed Serpent by D. H. Lawrence (1955, Vintage; $6.95).

The Power and the Glory by Graham Greene (1990, Viking; $4.95).

A Separate Reality by Carlos Castañeda (1991, Pocket Books; $4.95).

So Far from God: A Journey to Central America by Patrick Marnhoum (1985, Viking; $6.95).

Sons of the Shaking Earth by Eric Wolf (1959, University of Chicago Press; $12.95).

Stones for Ibarra by Harriet Doerr (1984, Penguin; $8.95).

The Treasure of the Sierra Madre by B. Traven (1979, University of Wisconsin Press; $18.95, hardcover; $8.95, paperback).

The Underdogs by Mariano Azuela (1963, New American Library; $3.95).

Where the Air Is Clear by Carlos Fuentes (1971, Farrar, Straus & Giroux; $11.95).

The books listed above may be ordered directly from the publishers or found in the travel section of any good general bookstore or any sizable public library. If you still can't find something, the following stores and/or mail-order houses also specialize in travel literature. They offer books on Mexico along with guides to the rest of the world, and in some cases, even an old Baedeker or two.

Book Passage (51 Tamal Vista Blvd., Corte Madera, CA 94925; phone: 415-927-0960 in California; 800-321-9785 elsewhere in the US). Travel guides and maps to all areas of the world. A free catalogue is available.

The Complete Traveller (199 Madison Ave., New York, NY 10016; phone: 212-685-9007). Travel guides and maps. A catalogue is available for $2.

Forsyth Travel Library (PO Box 2975, Shawnee Mission, KS 66201-1375; phone: 800-367-7984 or 913-384-3440). Travel guides and maps, old and new, to all parts of the world, including Mexico. Ask for the "Worldwide Travel Books and Maps" catalogue.

Gourmet Guides (2801 Leavenworth Ave., San Francisco, CA 94133; phone: 415-771-3671). Travel guides and maps, along with cookbooks. Mail-order lists available on request.

Phileas Fogg's Books and Maps (87 *Stanford Shopping Center,* Palo Alto, CA 94304; phone: 800-533-FOGG or 415-327-1754). Travel guides, maps, and language aids.

Tattered Cover (2955 E. First Ave., Denver, CO 80206; phone: 800-833-9327 or 303-322-7727). The travel department alone of this enormous bookstore carries over 7,000 books, as well as maps and atlases. No catalogue is offered (the list is too extensive), but a newsletter, issued three times a year, is available on request.

Thomas Brothers Maps & Travel Books (603 W. Seventh St., Los Angeles, CA 90017; phone: 213-627-4018). Maps (including road atlases, street guides, and wall maps), guidebooks, and travel accessories.

Traveller's Bookstore (22 W. 52nd St., New York, NY 10019; phone: 212-664-0995). Travel guides, maps, literature, and accessories. A catalogue is available for $2.

In addition, *Culturgrams* is a handy series of pamphlets that provides a good sampling of information on the people, cultures, sights, and bargains to be found in over 90 countries around the world. Each four-page, newsletter-size leaflet covers one country, and Mexico is included in the series. The topics included range from customs and courtesies to lifestyles and demographics. These fact-filled pamphlets are published by the David M. Kennedy Center for International Studies at Brigham Young University; for an order form contact the group c/o Publication Services (280 HRCB, Provo, UT 84602; phone: 801-378-6528). When ordering from 1 to 5 *Culturgrams,* the price is $1 each; 6 to 49 pamphlets cost 50¢ each; and for larger quantities, the price per copy goes down proportionally.

Another source of cultural information, is *Do's and Taboos Around the World,* compiled by the Parker Pen Company and edited by Roger E. Axtell. It focuses on protocol, customs, etiquette, hand gestures and body language, gift giving, the dangers of using US jargon, and so on, and can be fun to read even if you're not going anyplace. It's available for $10.95 in bookstores or through John Wiley & Sons, 1 Wiley Dr., Somerset, NJ 08875 (phone: 212-850-6418).

NEWSPAPERS AND MAGAZINES: The most useful local publication the US tourist will find in Mexico is the daily English-language newspaper, the *News.* It is published in Mexico City, and is distributed throughout the country, especially in the areas most often visited by tourists. International news, sports, stock market reports, and at least three of America's top columnists — William Safire, Russell Baker, and Art Buchwald — keep readers connected to what is happening in the rest of the world. The "What's On Today" column of the arts section, written by Irene Sayago, reports on what's happening in the capital in the way of cinema, art exhibits, music, dance, theater, and lectures. The *News'* Sunday magazine, *Vistas,* carries detailed reports on activities in every major resort, written by reporters in the areas.

Mexico City has one other daily English-language publication, the *Daily Bulletin,* which is distributed to hotels, newsstands, and some restaurants. It offers short world news bulletins, some tourist information, and innumerable ads encouraging tourists to buy goods in Mexico before returning home.

Among the major US publications that can be bought (generally a day or two after distribution in the US) in many of the larger cities and resort areas, at hotels, airports, and newsstands, and at *Sanborn* stores are the *Los Angeles Times, Miami Herald, The New York Times, USA Today,* and the *Wall Street Journal.* As with other imports, expect these and other US publications to cost considerably more in Mexico than in the US.

A subscription to the *International Herald Tribune* is a good idea for dedicated travelers. This English-language newspaper is written and edited mostly in Paris, and is *the* newspaper read regularly and avidly by Americans abroad to keep up with world news, US news, sports, the stock market (US and foreign), fluctuations in exchange rates, and an assortment of help-wanted ads, real estate listings, and personals, worldwide in scope. Published 6 days a week (no Sunday paper), it is available at newsstands throughout the US and in cities worldwide. Although you may have some difficulty finding it on newsstands in Mexico, larger hotels may have copies in the lobby for guests — if you don't see a copy, ask the hotel concierge if it is available. A 1-year's subscription in the US costs $349. To subscribe, write or call the Subscription Manager, *International Herald Tribune,* 850 Third Ave., 10th Floor, New York, NY 10022 (phone: 800-882-2884 or 212-752-3890).

MAGAZINES: Sampling the regional fare is likely to be one of the highlights of any visit. You will find reading about local edibles worthwhile either before you go or after you return. *Gourmet,* a magazine specializing in food, frequently carries articles on Mexican food and restaurants (although its scope is much broader). It is available at newsstands throughout the US for $2.50 an issue or for $18 a year from *Gourmet,* PO Box 2886, Boulder, CO 80322-2886 (phone: 800-365-2454).

There are two English-language monthly magazines, *Amistad* and *AmCham Review. Amistad* is published by the American Society of Mexico, located in Mexico City. It has travel articles, gives advice to American citizens about Mexican law, and lists various happenings within the American community in Mexico. *Amistad* is distributed to subscribers only, but you can buy it directly from the editorial offices at 15 Río Pánuco, México, DF 06500 (phone: 5-535-5919).

AmCham Review is the magazine of the Mexican-American Chamber of Commerce. Its articles focus on business in Mexico that is of particular interest to American companies there. You can get a copy by dropping by the chamber offices at 78 Calle Lucerna, México, DF 06600 (phone: 5-705-0995).

Mexico Desconocido, a monthly that is devoted to exploring little-known places in Mexico, is published with an English-language translation of the text. It is available on newsstands in Mexico City for 6,000 pesos (between $2 and $3) or by subscription for 187,500 pesos (about $75) a year from Editorial Jilguero, 110 Monte Pelvoux, #104, Lomas Chapultepec, México, DF 11000 (phone: 5-540-4040).

NEWSLETTERS: Throughout GETTING READY TO GO we have mentioned specific newsletters which our readers may be interested in consulting for further information. One of the very best sources of detailed travel information is *Consumer Reports Travel Letter.* Published monthly by Consumers Union (PO Box 53629, Boulder, CO 80322-3629; phone: 800-999-7959), it offers comprehensive coverage of the travel scene on a wide variety of fronts. A year's subscription costs $37; 2 years, $57.

In addition, the following travel newsletters provide useful up-to-date information on travel services and bargains:

Adventures in Mexico (3170 Apdo. Postal, Guadalajara, Jalisco, 45050, Mexico; no phone). This newsletter offers detailed information for those vacationing (or retiring) in Mexico. A year's subscription (6 issues) costs $16.

Hideaway Report (PO Box 50, Sun Valley, ID 83353; phone: 208-622-3183). This monthly source highlights retreats — including Mexican idylls — for sophisticated travelers. A year's subscription costs $90.

La Vista de Mexico (5289 Aurora Ct., Lilburn, GA 30247; phone: 404-923-1926). This newsletter offers first-hand information on current travel trends in Mexico. A year's subscription (6 issues) costs $24.

Mexico West! (PO Box 1646, Bonita, CA 91902; phone: 619-585-3033). This monthly newsletter features articles on special areas and activities throughout Mexico. A year's subscription costs $35.

Weights and Measures

When traveling in Mexico, you'll find that just about every quantity, whether it is length, weight, or capacity, will be expressed in unfamiliar terms. In fact, this is true for travel almost everywhere in the world, since the US is one of the last countries to make its way to the metric system. Your trip to Mexico may serve to familiarize you with what may one day be the weights and measures used at your grocery store.

There are some specific things to bear in mind during your trip. Fruits and vegetables at a market are weighed in *kilos* (kilograms), as are your luggage at the airport and your body weight. (This latter is particularly pleasing to people of significant size, who, instead of weighing 220 pounds, hit the scales at a mere 100 kilos.) A kilo equals 2.2 pounds and 1 pound is .45 kilo. Body temperature usually is measured in Centigrade or Celsius rather than Fahrenheit, so that a normal body temperature reading is 37C, not 98.6F, and freezing is 0 degrees C rather than 32F.

APPROXIMATE EQUIVALENTS		
Metric Unit	**Abbreviation**	**US Equivalent**
LENGTH		
millimeter	mm	.04 inch
meter	m	39.37 inches
kilometer	km	.62 mile
AREA		
square centimeter	sq cm	.155 square inch
square meter	sq m	10.7 square feet
hectare	ha	2.47 acres
square kilometer	sq km	.3861 square mile
CAPACITY		
liter	l	1.057 quarts
WEIGHT		
gram	g	.035 ounce
kilogram	kg	2.2 pounds
metric ton	MT	1.1 tons
ENERGY		
kilowatt	kw	1.34 horsepower

CONVERSION TABLES: METRIC TO US MEASUREMENTS

Multiply	by	to convert to
LENGTH		
millimeters	.04	inches
meters	3.3	feet
meters	1.1	yards
kilometers	.6	miles
CAPACITY		
liters	2.11	pints (liquid)
liters	1.06	quarts (liquid)
liters	.26	gallons (liquid)
WEIGHT		
grams	.04	ounces (avoir)
kilograms	2.2	pounds (avoir)

US TO METRIC MEASUREMENTS

Multiply	by	to convert to
LENGTH		
inches	25.	millimeters
feet	.3	meters
yards	.9	meters
miles	1.6	kilometers
CAPACITY		
pints	.47	liters
quarts	.95	liters
gallons	3.8	liters
WEIGHT		
ounces	28.	grams
pounds	.45	kilograms

TEMPERATURE

$$°F = (°C \times 9/5) + 32 \qquad °C = (°F - 32) \times 5/9$$

Gasoline is sold by the liter (3.8 to a gallon), but machines measuring air for tires are in pounds, just as in the United States, so no conversion is necessary. Highway signs are written in kilometers rather than miles (1 mile equals approximately 1.6 km; 1 km equals approximately .62 miles). And speed limits are in kilometers per hour, so think twice before hitting the gas when you see a speed limit of 100. That means 62 miles per hour.

The tables and conversion factors listed below should give you all the information you will need to understand any transaction, road sign, or map you encounter during your travels.

Cameras and Equipment

 Vacations are everybody's favorite time for taking pictures and home movies. After all, most of us want to remember the places we visit — and show them off to others. Here are a few suggestions to help you get the best results from your travel photography or videography.

BEFORE THE TRIP

If you're taking your camera or camcorder out after a long period in mothballs or have just bought a new one, check it thoroughly before you leave to prevent unexpected breakdowns or disappointing pictures.

1. Still cameras should be cleaned carefully and thoroughly, inside and out. If using a camcorder, run a head cleaner through it. You also may want to have your camcorder professionally serviced (opening the casing yourself will violate the manufacturer's warranty). Always use filters to protect your lens while traveling.
2. Check the batteries for your camera's light meter and flash, and take along extras just in case yours wear out during the trip. For camcorders, bring along extra Nickel-Cadmium (Ni-Cad) batteries; if you use rechargeable batteries, a recharger will cut down on the extras.
3. Using all the settings and features, shoot at least one test roll of film or one videocassette, using the type you plan to take along with you.

EQUIPMENT TO TAKE ALONG

Keep your gear light and compact. Items that are too heavy or bulky to be carried comfortably on a full-day excursion will likely stay in your hotel room.

1. Invest in a broad camera or camcorder strap if you now have a thin one. It will make carrying the equipment much more comfortable.
2. A sturdy canvas, vinyl, or leather camera or camcorder bag, preferably with padded pockets (not an airline bag), will keep your equipment organized and easy to find. If you will be doing much shooting around the water, a waterproof case is best.
3. For cleaning, bring along a camel's hair brush that retracts into a rubber squeeze bulb. Also take plenty of lens tissue, soft cloths, and plastic bags to protect equipment from dust and moisture.

FILM AND TAPES: If you are concerned about airport security X-rays damaging rolls of undeveloped still film (X-rays do not affect processed film) or tapes, store them in one of the lead-lined bags sold in camera shops. This possibility is not as much of a threat as it used to be, however. In the US, incidents of X-ray damage to unprocessed film (exposed or unexposed) are few because low-dosage X-ray equipment is used virtually everywhere. While the international trend also is toward equipment that delivers less and less radiation, equipment in Mexico tends to be less up-to-date than in some other foreign countries, and is, therefore, less predictable.

If you're traveling without a protective bag, you may want to ask to have your photo equipment inspected by hand. One type of film that should never be subjected to X-rays is the new, very high speed ASA 1000 film. The walk-through metal detector devices at airports do not affect film, though the film cartridges may set them off.

You should have no problem finding film or tapes throughout Mexico, particularly in metropolitan and major resort areas. When buying film, tapes, or photo accessories abroad the best rule of thumb is to stick to name brands with which you are familiar. The availability of film processing labs and equipment repair shops will vary from area to area.

■*A note about courtesy and caution*: When photographing in Mexico (and anywhere else in the world), ask first. In many of the smaller towns, and even some of the cities, the Indians have superstitions or religious beliefs that photographing them is an insult at best and, at worst, a violation. Furthermore, some governments have security regulations regarding the use of cameras and will not permit the photographing of certain subjects. When in doubt, look for an official who can tell you if your chosen subject is on the restricted list.

Useful Words and Phrases

Unlike the French, who tend to be a bit brusque if you don't speak their language perfectly, the Mexicans do not expect you to speak Spanish — but are very flattered when you try. In many circumstances, you won't have to, because the staffs at most hotels, museums, and tourist attractions, as well as at a fair number of restaurants, speak serviceable English, or at least a version of it, which they usually are eager to try — and that means practicing with you. Particularly when you get off the beaten path, however, you will find at least a rudimentary knowledge of Spanish very helpful. Don't be afraid of misplaced accents or misconjugated verbs. Mexicans appreciate your efforts to speak their language and will do their best to understand you. They also will make an effort to be understood.

Mexican Spanish has a number of regional dialects, but the dialect of educated people in Mexico City is regarded as standard, is used on national television, and is understood by almost everybody, even though their local speech may be quite different. Most people can communicate in what is considered "standard" Spanish, and the spelling of standard Mexican Spanish is a very reliable guide to pronunciation.

The list below is a selection of commonly used words and phrases to speed you on your way. Note that in Spanish all nouns are either masculine or feminine, as well as singular and plural, and that the adjectives that modify them must agree in both gender and number. Most nouns ending in *o* are masculine (the corresponding articles are *el* and *uno*); most nouns ending in *a* are feminine (the feminine articles are *la* and *una*). Plurals are formed by adding *s* (the articles are *los, unos, las,* and *unas*). Adjectives almost always follow nouns in Spanish. Otherwise word order is very much as in English.

The following pronunciation rules may also be helpful:

The vowel before the last consonant in a word (except *n* or *s*) is accented, unless there is an accent mark on another vowel. When the last consonant is *n* or *s,* the vowel before the preceding consonant is accented. In addition:

> *a* is pronounced as in *father*
> *e* is pronounced as in *red*
> *i* is pronounced as in *machine*
> *o* is pronounced as in *note*
> *u* is pronounced as in *rude*
> *ei/ey* are pronounced as in *vein*
> *oi/oy* are pronounced as in *joy*
> *ai/ay* are pronounced like *y* in *by*
> *au* is pronounced like *ou* in *house*

In general, in vowel letter sequences (*ae, ie, ue, ia,* etc.), each letter is pronounced. Mexican Spanish consonants are pronounced as in English with these exceptions:

The consonants *b, d,* and *g* are pronounced with the air passage slightly open, producing a softer sound. The consonants *p, t,* and *c/k* are pronounced without the aspiration (the strong puff of breath) which characterizes them in English.
b within words is pronounced like the English *v*
d within words is pronounced like *th* in *other*
g before *e* or *i* is pronounced like a strongly aspirated English *h* or German *ch;* otherwise, as above
h is silent
j is pronounced like a strongly aspirated *h*
ll is pronounced like *y* in *youth*
ñ is pronounced like *ny* in *canyon*
qu is pronounced *k* before *e* or *i: quilo* is pronouced as the English *kilo*
r is pronounced like casual English *d* in *pedal*
rr is trilled, as in Scottish *farm*
s and *z* are pronounced *z* within words preceding a voiced consonant (*b, d, g, m, n, r, l*); otherwise they are pronounced as the English *s*

Greetings and Everyday Expressions

Good morning (also, Good day)	*Buenos días*
Good afternoon/evening	*Buenas tardes*
Good night	*Buenas noches*
Hello	*Hola!*
How are you?	*Cómo está usted?*
Pleased to meet you	*Mucho gusto en conocerle*
Good-bye!	*Adiós!*
So long!	*Hasta luego!*
Yes	*Sí*
No	*No*
Please	*Por favor*
Thank you	*Gracias*
You're welcome	*De nada*
I beg your pardon (Excuse me)	*Perdón*
I'm sorry	*Lo siento*
It doesn't matter	*No importa*
I don't speak Spanish.	*No hablo Español.*
Do you speak English?	*Habla usted inglés?*
I don't understand.	*No comprendo.*
Do you understand?	*Comprende?/Entiende?*
My name is . . .	*Me llamo . . .*
What is your name?	*Cómo se llama?*
miss	*señorita*
madame	*señora* (married)
	doña (unmarried)
mister	*señor*
open	*abierto/a*
closed	*cerrado/a*
entrance	*entrada*
exit	*salida*

push	*empujar*
pull	*tirar*
today	*hoy*
tomorrow	*mañana*
yesterday	*ayer*

Checking In

I have a reservation.	*He hecho una reserva.*
I would like . . .	*Quisiera . . .*
a single room	*una habitación sencilla*
a double room	*una habitación doble*
a quiet room	*una habitación tranquila*
with bath	*con baño*
with shower	*con ducha*
with a sea view	*con vista asi el mar*
with air conditioning	*con aire acondicionado*
with balcony	*con balcón*
overnight only	*sólo una noche*
a few days	*unos cuantos días*
a week (at least)	*una semana (por lo menos)*
with full board	*con pensión completa*
with half board	*con media pensión*
Does that price include . . .	*Esta incluído en el precio . . .*
breakfast?	*el desayuno?*
taxes?	*los impuestos?*
Do you accept traveler's checks?	*Acepta usted cheques de Viajero?*
Do you accept credit cards?	*Acepta tarjetas de credito?*
It doesn't work.	*No funcióna.*

Eating Out

ashtray	*un cenicero*
(extra) chair	*una silla (adicional)*
table	*una mesa*
bottle	*una botella*
cup	*una taza*
plate	*un plato*
fork	*un tenedor*
knife	*un cuchillo*
spoon	*una cuchara*
napkin	*una servilleta*
hot chocolate (cocoa)	*un chocolate caliente*
black coffee	*un café negro*
coffee with milk	*café con leche*
cream	*crema*
milk	*leche*
tea	*un té*

fruit juice	*un jugo de fruta*
lemonade	*una limonada*
water	*agua*
mineral water	*agua mineral*
carbonated	*con gas*
noncarbonated	*sin gas*
orangeade	*una naranjada*
beer	*una cerveza*
port	*oporto*
sherry	*jerez*
red wine	*vino tinto*
white wine	*vino blanco*
cold	*frio/a*
hot	*caliente*
sweet	*dulce*
(very) dry	*(muy) seco/a*
(very) dry	*(muy) seco/a*
bread	*pan*
butter	*mantequilla*
bacon	*tocino*
eggs	*huevos*
hard-boiled	*un huevo cocido*
	por agua
fried	*huevos fritos*
omelette	*torta de huevos*
soft-boiled	*un huevo cocido*
	pasado por agua
scrambled	*huevos revueltos*
honey	*miel*
jam, marmalade	*mermelada*
orange juice	*jugo de naranja*
pepper	*pimienta*
salt	*sal*
sugar	*azúcar*
Waiter!	*Camarero!/Mesero!*
I would like	*Quisiera*
a glass of	*un vaso de*
a bottle of	*una botella de*
a half bottle of	*una media botella de*
a carafe of	*una garrafa de*
a liter of	*un litro de*
The check, please.	*La cuenta, por favor.*
Is a service charge included?	*Está el servicio incluído?*
I think there is a mistake in the bill.	*Creo que hay un error en la cuenta.*

Shopping

bakery	*la panadería*
bookstore	*la librería*
butcher shop	*la carnicería*
camera shop	*la tienda de fotografía*
delicatessen	*la tienda de comestibles preparados*
department store	*el almacén grande*
grocery	*la tienda de comestibles*
jewelry store	*la joyería*
newsstand	*el puesto de periódicos*
pastry shop	*la pastelería*
perfume (and cosmetics) store	*perfumería*
pharmacy/drugstore	*las farmacia*
shoestore	*la zapatería*
supermarket	*el supermercado*
tobacconist	*el estanquero*

inexpensive	*barato/a*
expensive	*caro/a*
large	*grande*
larger	*más grande*
too large	*demasiado grande*
small	*pequeño/a*
smaller	*más pequeño/a*
too small	*demasiado pequeño/a*
long	*largo/a*
short	*corto/a*
old	*viejo/a*
new	*nuevo/a*
used	*usado/a*
handmade	*hecho/a a mano*

Is it machine washable?	*Es lavable a máquina?*
How much does it cost?	*Cuánto cuesta esto?*
What is it made of?	*De qué está hecho?*
camel's hair	*pelo de camello*
cotton	*algodón*
corduroy	*pana*
filigree	*filigrana*
lace	*encaje*
leather	*cuero*
linen	*lino*
suede	*ante*
synthetic	*sintético/a*
tile	*baldosa*
wood	*madera*
wool	*lana*
brass	*latón*
copper	*cobre*
gold	*oro*

gold plated	*dorado*
silver	*plata*
silver plated	*plateado*
stainless steel	*acero inoxidable*

Colors

beige	*beige*
black	*negro/a*
blue	*azul*
brown	*café*
green	*verde*
gray	*gris*
orange	*anaranjado/a*
pink	*rosa*
purple	*morado/a*
red	*rojo/a*
white	*blanco/a*
yellow	*amarillo/a*
dark	*obscuro/a*
light	*claro/a*

Getting Around

north	*norte*
south	*sur*
east	*este*
west	*oeste*
right	*derecho/a*
left	*izquierdo/a*
Go straight ahead.	*Siga todo derecho.*
far	*lejos*
near	*cerca*
gas station	*la gasolinería*
train station	*la estación de ferrocarril*
bus stop	*la parada de autobuses*
subway station	*estación de metro*
airport	*el aeropuerto*
tourist information	*información turística*
map	*el mapa*
one-way ticket	*un billete de ida*
round-trip ticket	*un billete de ida y vuelta*
track	*el andén*
first class	*primera clase*
second class	*segunda clase*
smoking	*fumar*
no smoking	*no fumar*
gasoline	*gasolina*
regular	*nova*
premium	*extra*
leaded	*con plomo*

unleaded	*sin plomo*
diesel	*diesel*
Fill it up, please.	*Llénelo, por favor.*
oil	*el aceite*
tires	*las llantas*
Where is . . . ?	*Dónde está . . . ?*
Where are . . . ?	*Dónde estan . . . ?*
How far is it from here to . . . ?	*Qué distancia hay desdeaquí hasta . . . ?*
Does this train go to . . . ?	*Va este ferrocarril a . . . ?*
Does this bus go to . . . ?	*Va este autobús a . . . ?*
What time does it leave?	*A qué hora sale?*

Danger	*Peligro*
Caution	*Precaución*
Detour	*Desvio*
Do Not Enter	*Paso Prohibido*
No Parking	*Estacionamiento Prohibido*
No Passing	*Prohibido Pasar*
One Way	*Dirección Unica*
Pay Toll	*Peaje*
Pedestrian Zone	*Zona Peatonal*
Reduce Speed	*Despacio*
Steep Incline	*Fuerte Declive*
Stop	*Alto*
Use Headlights	*Encender los faros*
Yield	*Ceda el Paso*

Personal Items and Services

aspirins	*aspirinas*
Band-Aids	*curitas*
barbershop	*la barbería*
beauty shop	*el salón de belleza*
condom	*condón*
dry cleaner	*la tintorería*
hairdresser's	*la peluquería*
laundromat	*la lavandería*
laundry	*la lavandería*
post office	*el correo*
postage stamps	*estampillas*

sanitary napkins	*unos paños higiénicos*
shampoo	*un champú*
shaving cream	*espuma de afeitar*
soap	*el jabón*
tampons	*unos tampones higiénicos*
tissues	*Kleenex*
toilet paper	*papel higiénico*
toothpaste	*pasta de dientes*

Where is the Bathroom?	*Dónde está el baño?*
toilet?	*excusado?*
MEN	*Caballeros*
WOMEN	*Señoras*

Days of the Week

Monday	*Lunes*
Tuesday	*Martes*
Wednesday	*Miércoles*
Thursday	*Jueves*
Friday	*Viernes*
Saturday	*Sábado*
Sunday	*Domingo*

Months

January	*Enero*
February	*Febrero*
March	*Marzo*
April	*Abril*
May	*Mayo*
June	*Junio*
July	*Julio*
August	*Agosto*
September	*Septiembre*
October	*Octubre*
November	*Noviembre*
December	*Diciembre*

Numbers

zero	*cero*
one	*uno*
two	*dos*
three	*tres*
four	*cuatro*
five	*cinco*
six	*seis*
seven	*siete*
eight	*ocho*
nine	*nueve*
ten	*diez*
eleven	*once*
twelve	*doce*
thirteen	*trece*
fourteen	*catorce*
fifteen	*quince*
sixteen	*dieciséis*
seventeen	*diecisiete*
eighteen	*dieciocho*
nineteen	*diecinueve*
twenty	*veinte*
thirty	*treinta*
forty	*cuarenta*

fifty	*cincuenta*
sixty	*sesenta*
seventy	*setenta*
eighty	*ochenta*
ninety	*noventa*
one hundred	*cien*
one thousand	*mil*

PERSPECTIVES

History

Some 30,000 years ago, early man crossed the Bering Strait and entered the western hemisphere. These Paleolithic nomads were hunter-gatherers who followed the seasonal supply of wild food. In their struggle for survival, they wandered south and eastward and scattered over the entire continent. Their dependence on wild grains eventually led to a domestication of certain plants, such as maize, chili peppers, pumpkins, and beans. As their food supply became more stable, the settlers became more sedentary, and the beginnings of civilization arose. Descendants of these Paleolithic wanderers, particularly in the more verdant areas of southern Mexico and Guatemala, attained high levels of civilization. They developed intricate systems of religion, mathematics, and astronomy (the latter two more advanced than those in contemporaneous European cultures), whose principles they used to construct great cities and magnificent pyramids.

About 20,000 years after the first Indians settled in Mexico, Europeans excited by adventure and lusting after riches came upon these civilizations and claimed that they had discovered a New World. But this New World was, in fact, a very old world; its story was one of the great achievements of mankind. With the coming of the white invaders that story became one of the great tragedies of human history. The history of Mexico's estimated 86 million people, then, is the story of the struggle of three peoples — the Indian, the Spanish, and their children, the *mestizos* — to live together.

INDIAN MEXICO

Historians and archaeologists divide the cultural history of Indian Mexico into several major periods: the formative or pre-classic (2300–1 BC), which is characterized by the beginning of sedentary village life with subsistence farming; the classic (AD 1–900), noted for the development of urban centers with genuine political and mercantile functions; the post-classic (900–1521), heralded by the fall of Teotihuacán, one of the great Indian cities; and the modern period, which commenced with the invasion of the Spaniards.

The Olmec was the first highly developed civilization in Mesoamerica (the entire Central American subcontinent where Indian cultures flourished) and, in fact, the first to attain a high level of culture in the western hemisphere. It thrived from 500 BC to AD 1150 in the lowland jungles of Veracruz and Tabasco and is widely regarded as the common ancestor of many of the empires that followed. The Olmec worshiped a jaguar deity, and their monumental art, sculptures, bas-reliefs (known as stelae), and altars reveal the iconography of this cult, which revolved around a fertility god. The art is renowned for its massive proportions, simple and naturalistic style, and materials, some of which, like the basalt boulders, are not native to the area and were probably dragged some 60 miles overland or transported by water. The works suggest some indication of warfare, but the Olmec exerted their power primarily through commercial ties with other regions of Mexico. The Olmec sites that can be visited today served as the residences and ceremonial grounds of the priests, who ruled Olmec society; the common people lived in the surrounding area and worked as farmers, artisans, and soldiers.

The Olmec heritage, including their fertility god, sculptural style, language, and possibly the prototype of the calendar, were transmitted to succeeding Mexican civilizations by traders and warriors. Among these civilizations was Teotihuacán, the foremost city of the classic period. Teotihuacán was built around 200 to 150 BC in the Valley of Mexico (near the present Mexico City), and flourished between AD 200 and 600. Though the tribal identity of the residents of Teotihuacán has never been established, they controlled a network of trade that extended from the central highlands to the coastal lowlands, through the Yucatán Peninsula all the way to Guatemala. Distinct social classes existed in Teotihuacán society, the highest of which was an elite class of priests. Government was theocratic, and the religion was pacific, based on the worship of nature gods — the sun god, the moon goddess, Tlaloc the rain god, and Quetzalcóatl, the plumed serpent who brought civilization to humanity and to whom the people of Teotihuacán built a grand temple. The staple food was maize, and in order to support the large population of the city — over 100,000 — irrigation was developed and used extensively.

Other large sites (Monte Albán, Cholula, El Tajín) existed during the classic period; none, however, reached the level of civilization and sophistication of Teotihuacán, which dominated the area until its mysterious decline and fall around AD 700, for reasons still not known. (For a survey of Mexico's finest archaeological sites, see *Mexico's Magnificent Archaeological Heritage*, DIVERSIONS.)

While urbanization was under way in the central highlands at Teotihuacán, the Maya culture flourished in Chiapas, Tabasco, the Yucatán Peninsula, the Petén area of Guatemala, and the Guatemalan highlands. Having established their civilization in the humid jungles centuries earlier, the Maya lived by farming — a system of shifting cultivation called slash-and-burn agriculture. In the tropics, the soil was thin, and early farmers were forced to rotate the use of their fields in a cycle of planting and fallowing.

Despite the hardships of their environment, the Maya created a grand civilization with high achievements in the arts and sciences. Maya sites were primarily ceremonial centers composed of temples, palaces, and public buildings. Most of the people lived on the outskirts of these centers.

Maya art is typically elaborate, characterized by a great deal of ornamentation and spaces filled with intricate detail. The subject matter is usually commemorative — sculptures represent gods and former rulers. The people are frequently depicted with large noses and sloping foreheads (which the Maya considered a highly desirable cosmetic trait and encouraged by binding their children's heads during early childhood).

The Maya culture declined around AD 900. No one knows exactly why, but it is thought that the civilization was — within a fairly short period of time —

struck by a series of calamities such as hurricanes, earthquakes, and a failure of the agriculture system, as well as by invasions and conquests by marauding tribes.

With the fall of the Maya, the entire Indian civilization was thrown into a period of growing militarism and militancy. Topiltzín Quetzalcóatl, ruler of the Toltec of Tula and revered by later tribes as a benign god, was forced to flee Tula because of an internal power struggle. Tezcatlipoca, the court magician, and his followers gained control of the tribe and initiated campaigns of conquest and invasion. Their influence reached as far as the Yucatán Peninsula, where the site of Chichén Itzá shows notable Toltec characteristics. Throughout Mesoamerica at this time, there was increasing concern for the defense of sites. Hilltops were preferred building locations, and a few sites were built with protective massive walls.

The reign of the Toltec was brief, violent, and innovative. They were the first Mexicans to do metalwork, a skill they transmitted to other tribes. Their dominance waned around AD 1156, when attacks by northern barbarians initiated a great migration from Tula. Along with a variety of northern groups, these refugees settled in different parts of the Valley of Mexico. Within this conglomeration of different groups there was a continual jockeying for power. The last of the nomadic groups to enter the Valley of Mexico, during the 13th century, was the Aztec people (also called Mexicas). During the late post-classic period they rose to rule a vast empire.

A wandering tribe of Aztec Indians passed through the Valley of Mexico in approximately 1345 and fulfilled an ancient prophecy when they saw an eagle perched on a cactus eating a snake. On the spot — an island in Lake Texcoco — they built their capital city, Tenochtitlán. The symbol of the eagle on a cactus with a serpent in its mouth is the national symbol of Mexico and can be seen today on the flag, currency, and government seals.

The Aztec, always led by their god of war, Huitzilopochtli ("Hummingbird on the Left"), were an aggressive people and conquered many neighboring tribes, taking captives for slaves and sacrificial purposes. The Aztec deities were worshiped with offerings of beating human hearts torn from the victims' chests with obsidian knives. Other forms of human sacrifice included the decapitation of women, the drowning of children, and the flaying of victims. Through these acts, the Aztec believed that they would ensure the continuance of their world.

The day-to-day continuity of the empire was based on taxes and payments from their tributary provinces in the form of goods and products, including maize, beans, and cotton cloaks. By the time the Spanish arrived in 1519, the Aztec were the richest tribe in Mexico, collecting tribute from all the peoples between the Gulf of Mexico coast and the Pacific and as far south as Guatemala.

The Aztec were remarkable engineers. They built their city in the swampy lake area of the Valley of Mexico and constructed three causeways to connect it to the rest of the valley. They invented a unique system of floating islands, called *chinampas,* which increased their agricultural land. The islands were made of earth dug from the borders of the lake and held in place by reeds. Trees were planted around the edges, and the roots held the earth together and eventually fixed the islands to the lake bottom. More earth was added until the islands became an almost solid landmass, penetrated by a series of canals. In addition, stone aqueducts were built to bring drinking water from the nearby hills.

Tenochtitlán covered an area of 2,500 acres. At the center of town stood a huge plaza surrounded by 40 temples built to honor the Aztec gods. The pyramid of Huitzilopochtli, the god of war, dominated the area. A wide staircase led up the western side of the largest pyramid. It was this location that reflected the place of religion in the life of the Aztec. It was the essence of their existence, and like other Indian governments, theirs was a theocracy. The gods ruled, the priests interpreted, and the people obeyed. Religious sentiment turned on fear, and the people constantly tried to appease and placate their gods through the sacrifice of humans and animals and offerings of food and flowers. They believed that the gods fed on human blood and would grow weak if not supplied with victims. Once sacrificed, these victims were regarded as embodiments of the deity; portions of their bodies were sometimes ritualistically eaten by priests and warriors to gain strength. In addition to the god of war, the Aztec worshiped a host of other gods, including a rain god, a sun god, a moon god, an earth mother, a god of corn, and a god of plantings. Bloody as the religious celebrations were, they were joyous occasions.

Though the religion might seem gruesome to modern sensibilities, the Aztec lifestyle was comfortable and civilized, and that of the rulers, extravagant. Tenochtitlán was kept remarkably clean; the streets were watered and swept daily, and the people bathed often. The palace of Montezuma, ruler of the Aztec at the time of the Spanish conquest, sprawled on one side of the main plaza. The kitchen facilities and dining halls were large enough to feed Montezuma's court, 300 guests, and 1,000 guards and attendants every day. Montezuma had two wives and a large harem; his staff included artists and craftsmen, jewelers, mummers, jugglers, dancers, and musicians. He had a huge aviary, a zoo, and a freak house on the grounds. Montezuma bathed daily and changed his clothes as many as four times a day, giving away the garments to his attendants after one wearing.

A broad street ran north from the main plaza to another large plaza called Tlaltelolco, the city's marketplace. Surrounded by colonnaded buildings, merchants spread their wares — a vast array of products from as far away as Honduras, Guatemala, and the Yucatán Peninsula. Among the goods available were fruits, vegetables, meats, fish and fowl, cooking utensils, mats, chairs, copper axes, knives and razors of obsidian, pipes and tobacco, jewelry of gold and silver, precious stones such as amethysts, pearls, coral, jade, and turquoise, feather cloaks, mats and shields, clothing, and even slaves.

Aztec traders and merchants who traveled throughout the empire doubled as messengers and spies. They recorded anything of interest on cloth or bark paper and immediately sent it back to Tenochtitlán by relay runners. By means of this system, Montezuma was informed that a band of men who traveled on "houses that float" had landed on a barren beach on the Gulf of Mexico coast on April 21, 1519.

THE SPANISH CONQUEST

The fierce Aztec warriors could have wiped out the band of 555 Spaniards in a single battle, but a strange ambivalence in Montezuma's character kept him from commanding them to do so. Montezuma was a moody, sensitive, highly superstitious man, and a set of coincidental events prevented him from acting.

He was aware of the legend of Quetzalcóatl. (*Quetzal* means "feathers" and *cóatl* translates as "snake"; thus Quetzalcóatl is known as the plumed serpent.) The stories of his origin are as numerous as his plumes. Quetzalcóatl was revered by the Toltec, and legends describe him as bearded and having fair skin and light hair — all qualities very rare among the Indians. He was more enlightened than his contemporaries and in his opposition to sacrifice and slavery brought a humanizing influence to the tribe. These ideas clashed with the accepted dogma of the established priests, and Quetzalcóatl was forced to flee. Heading in a southeasterly direction, he promised to return. What was significant about the legend for the Aztec people was that the year predicted for his return was 1519. Montezuma gave considerable credence, therefore, to the possibility that the leader of these light-skinned men who came from the east might be Quetzalcóatl.

Montezuma's apprehensions were also aroused by the many omens that appeared that year, including comets and earth tremors. The ruler sent emissaries to meet Hernán Cortés (the strangers' leader) and offer him gifts, among which were a few gold items — which only whetted Cortés's appetite, making him more determined than ever to conquer this rich land. In case any of his followers were less stouthearted than he, Cortés burned all his ships, cutting off any chance of retreat.

Luck was on the Spanish side. To begin with, the Indians had never before seen horses, and the sight of men on horseback only reinforced their suspicion that the Spaniards were gods. The resentment of many of the Indian tribes toward the Aztec, who had exploited them for the preceding 200 years, was even more significant. Cortés formed alliances with several such tribes, and by the time he arrived at the gates of Tenochtitlán, his army had increased to some 7,000 Spanish and Indian followers.

A young Indian girl named Malinche, given to Cortés as tribute by a Tabasco chief, served as his interpreter and enabled him to communicate with the Indians. She became Cortés's mistress, and the word *malinchista* is still used to describe a Mexican who prefers foreign ways and customs.

Cortés entered Tenochtitlán on November 12, 1519, and was received as a guest of Montezuma. As long as the Aztec continued thinking that Cortés was Quetzalcóatl, all was well; but the Spaniards knew that the Indians would soon discover the truth. Soon after their arrival, Cortés and six of his officers placed Montezuma under house arrest on the charge that the ruler had ordered an attack on the small colony of Veracruz. Montezuma declared his innocence, but Cortés threatened to kill him if Montezuma did not order his men to surrender. Had Montezuma chosen death, the Spaniards would have been wiped out in a few hours by the Aztec's soldiers, but Montezuma chose to live, thereby surrendering his troops, and Cortés became the ruler of Mexico.

In April of 1520, Cortés received word that the Governor of Cuba, Diego Velásquez, had sent another expeditionary force to Mexico, under the command of Pánfilo de Narváez, with orders to arrest Cortés and take over Mexico. Narváez hesitated just north of Veracruz, trying to decide whether to march inland in pursuit of Cortés. Cortés suffered no such indecision. He set off immediately with 70 men, surprised his rival late at night, disarmed the guards, killed Narváez, and took command of the party. Cortés was occupied with dismantling and sinking the ships of the Cuban expedition when he received news of a revolt in Tenochtitlán. He returned with an augmented force of nearly 1,000 men and managed to enter the castle of Axayacatl, where the Spaniards were holding out against the Aztec. The Aztec initiated a siege; after a month, the Spanish ran out of food and water. They escaped one night during a rainstorm, but lost 400 Spaniards and 2,000 of their Tlaxcala allies in the process.

They retreated to Tlaxcala to regroup. Meanwhile, the city of Tenochtitlán was struck by a plague of smallpox carried to Mexico by a Spanish soldier. Cortés returned in January of 1521 with three divisions and conquered Tenochtitlán after 3 months of fighting. For the next 300 years, Mexico was a Spanish colony.

Many tribes accepted Spanish rule and the Catholic religion. Captured tribes submitted according to custom, because they believed that the conquerors had a stronger god than their own. They also thought that any rule would be an improvement over domination by the Aztec. Little did they know that they were trading relative freedom for serfdom.

The Spanish in Mexico were crueler than most European colonial powers in the countries they controlled. In part this was due to the immense area under Spanish control: By 1535, Spanish colonies were scattered from Mexico through Central America, down the western coast of South America to Chile, and in ensuing years further expeditions extended north beyond the borders of Nueva España to the area that is now part of Texas, New Mexico, Arizona, and California. It is remarkable that the Spanish were able to govern these vast holdings at all.

During the 300 years of Spanish rule, 61 viceroys governed. These men — all natives of Spain and personal representatives of the reigning Spanish king — lived in regal splendor. Land was granted by the king to every soldier who had served under Cortés and as favors to prominent Spaniards. People who desired to colonize the land were also given tracts. Hacendados, hacienda owners, built enormous houses on estates that covered hundreds of square miles. When visitors came they were lavishly entertained with cockfights, bullfights, banquets, and dances. Living graciously was an art; Indian servants provided all the labor for nothing more than their room and board.

The colonial lifestyle reached its peak of refinement in Mexico City. At 5 PM the aristocratic ladies, dressed in gowns made of Chinese silk, would drive in their carriages escorted by mounted cavaliers. Later in the evening they would attend theater and balls. The men spent their afternoons gambling and watching cockfights, and their evenings at balls.

No middle class existed — only a few rich and the masses of poor. Spain was not interested in providing the Indians with an independent means of support; in fact, the colony was completely dependent on Spain economically. Mexico was restricted from exporting to countries other than Spain and could import only from the mother country.

Spain was primarily interested in Mexico's silver. Prior to the 19th century, two-thirds of all the silver in the world came from Mexico. Taxco, Guanajuato, Querétaro, and Zacatecas were built because they were in the mountainous central regions where the richest veins of silver were found. Many of the beautiful homes, public buildings, and lavish churches constructed then still stand today, a heritage recognized when Taxco and Guanajuato were declared national monuments because of the quality of their impressive colonial architecture.

The Indians labored in the mines and on the estates and were fed enough for subsistence. Only a small proportion of them had a chance at any education, and that only due to the efforts of the Spanish friars who taught reading, writing, and Christian doctrine. These crusading priests were unpopular among Spanish landowners, who did not want their servants educated. The first friars who came to Mexico were genuinely interested in establishing missions to educate and serve the masses, but as the Spanish population increased, many priests focused their concern on the spiritual welfare of their rich countrymen, who were inclined to give the church (and its servants) gifts of property and money in the hope of prying the gates of heaven open just a bit. By the end of the 18th century the Catholic church owned about half the land in Mexico and controlled more than half the wealth.

INDEPENDENCE

The domestic situation and the political unrest of Europe in the early 19th century had a terrific impact on Mexico. At the time, the population of Mexico was approximately 6 million: about 3.5 million Indians, 2.5 million Creoles (people of Spanish blood born in Mexico) and mestizos, and 40,000 Spaniards, who had all the power. The other groups greatly resented this ruling minority. Though Spaniards filled the ranks of the aristocracy, many Creoles had been educated in Europe and were highly cultured. The mestizos worked as shopkeepers and ranchers and constituted the first seeds of a middle class. A wide gulf separated Creoles and mestizos from the Indians, but the ideal of independence united them all — independence from their common enemy, known by the native-born as *gachupines,* which translates as "wearers of spurs" and expresses the feeling common to Creoles, mestizos, and Indians of being constantly goaded by the Spaniards sent to govern them.

The decisive factor was the abdication of the Spanish monarch Charles IV in 1808 and the subsequent imprisonment of his son, Ferdinand VII, by Napoleon. Native Latin Americans neither recognized nor wanted to pay tribute to the Bonaparte regime. In 1810, revolutions sprang up throughout the Spanish Empire in Argentina, Chile, Venezuela, Bolivia, Peru, and Colombia. By 1824 every country on the continent had won its freedom from Spain.

During the French Revolution, in 1793, groups of cultured Creoles started discussing the works of authors forbidden by the church — Rousseau, Voltaire, and Descartes, all of whose books had been smuggled into the country. Secretly but inevitably, these literary societies became political cabals. One such group in Querétaro was under the leadership of Captain Ignacio Allende, who led the local garrison, and Father Miguel Hidalgo y Costilla, who served at a church in the nearby village of Dolores.

Father Hidalgo's case was typical of the plight of the Creole. Of pure Spanish blood, he had been born in Mexico and would forever be excluded from the church hierarchy. He was an idealist who cared most about helping the Indians. He defied Spanish law by planting mulberry trees and vineyards (prohibited because it conflicted with Spain's native silk and wine industries) and used the profits to help his parishioners.

Hidalgo and Allende decided to lead a revolt in December of 1810. Their plans leaked out and orders were given to arrest them as conspirators against Spain. The wife of the governor of the state of Querétaro sympathized with the revolutionaries and warned the leaders. Hidalgo acted on September 16 by forcing the jailer of the city of Dolores to liberate the prisoners and jail all the rich Spaniards. The townspeople were summoned to the church, and Hidalgo addressed them from the pulpit, voicing the catchwords of the independence movement, *el grito de* (the cry of) *Dolores*, "*Mexicanos, viva México!*"

Hidalgo rounded up a crew of 300 armed with machetes, knives, axes, sticks, and stones. This force marched on San Miguel (later called San Miguel de Allende in honor of Captain Allende), where the Spanish barricaded themselves in City Hall. Allende promised that no harm would come to them. The Spanish surrendered, but Allende could not control the mob and they sacked the homes of the Spanish. Allende finally subdued the mob, but Hidalgo remonstrated with him for his harsh methods. The two men had envisioned a military coup but had sparked a social revolution — a class war of the poor versus the rich. In spite of their aversion to Spanish rule, the Creole officers did not want to be involved with this ragtag mob and believed that Hidalgo was too sympathetic to the Indians and granted them too many concessions. This was the basis of an eventual split between Allende and Hidalgo.

For the next 6 months, Hidalgo's army ranged around central Mexico, capturing and looting the towns of Guanajuato, Guadalajara, Celaya, Morelia, and Toluca. By spring the force had grown to 80,000, and Hidalgo felt the time was ripe for an attempt on Mexico City. In a mountain pass between Toluca and the capital, however, the army was confronted by organized Spanish troops of 7,000 men armed with rifles and cannon. The battle lasted all day with no decisive victory. Under cover of nightfall, Hidalgo, feeling vastly outmaneuvered, returned to Toluca, but he was captured.

Meanwhile, Allende had abandoned central Mexico and headed north to the Mississippi Valley. On his return to Mexico, he was betrayed by a Creole officer whom he had failed to promote, and was captured by the Spanish. Allende and Hidalgo were shot by Spanish authorities in July 1811.

The revolution had actually lasted only 6 months, but this uprising had shaken the whole structure of Mexico. Ten years elapsed before independence was finally achieved. Another Catholic priest, José María Morelos, continued to fight for independence and the abolition of slavery, but he was captured and shot in December of 1815. In 1820, Agustín de Iturbide, a young mestizo promoted to the rank of brigadier general by Viceroy Apodaca, was sent to combat the forces of a rebel leader named Guerrero. Iturbide was educated, intelligent, politically conscious, and ambitious. Instead of fighting Guerrero he formed an alliance with him. On February 24, 1821, Iturbide proposed a workable peace plan to the Spanish authorities with something in it for everyone: Mexico was to become an independent constitutional monarchy; Spanish, Creoles, Indians, and mestizos were to become citizens with equal rights and opportunities; Catholicism was to be the official religion of Mexico. In addition, Iturbide guaranteed that any Spaniards who wished could return to Spain with their wealth (in cash), and that Mexico would pay for the evacuation of Spanish troops. The war-weary country could have peace with the strength of Iturbide's army supporting it, the church was assured of supremacy, the Creoles and mestizos saw the end of Spanish domination, and the conservatives gained security from the constant threat of rebellion.

Iturbide was declared the Emperor of Mexico by popular demand, and on July 21, 1822, he was crowned Agustín I. But the new ruler was faced with almost insurmountable problems. Those who knew how to govern had returned to Spain. The church and the army were independent and not responsible to the government. The caste system was as strong as ever, though now the Creoles were dominant. Members of the army which had put Iturbide in power hadn't been paid, and to meet this debt, Iturbide printed paper money, which triggered inflation.

Conditions went from bad to worse. Iturbide's former ally, Guerrero, turned against him, as did Antonio López de Santa Anna, an extremely ambitious general who would have a role in Mexico's history for the next half century. With his power thus undermined, Iturbide abdicated in March of 1823. A year later he was shot as a traitor, although historians today consider him a well-intentioned man who was simply overwhelmed by the magnitude of Mexico's problems. His remains are buried in the Cathedral of Mexico City, where he is honored as a hero and remembered as the "author of Mexican independence."

In November 1823 a new congress convened, proposing and ratifying a constitution based on the United States document: The government powers were allocated to three separate branches — legislative, judicial, and executive; the country was divided into 13 autonomous states and was supported by a 20% tax on all imported goods. However, freedom of religion was withheld, and Catholicism was made the official state religion. In 1824, Guadalupe Victoria, a general who had fought against Spain, was elected the first president of the Mexican republic.

The next 53 years proved to be a hard time for the young republic. The Mexicans were not prepared for the kind of government that had been instituted. The territory was huge, encompassing all of current Mexico as well as Texas, New Mexico, Arizona, and California, and it was filled with opposing interest groups. Few roads had been constructed, and each section of the country was isolated; practically anyone who wanted could round up a few dissatisfied followers, overthrow the government in Mexico City, and assume command until the next coup.

During this period many different people grasped power for brief periods, leaving the country in chaos. The most notorious of these was Santa Anna, who was in and out of office 11 times for a total of 30 years as president. In all this time, he did nothing to improve conditions for the Mexican people and, in fact, lost all of Mexico's northern territory to the US. In 1835 two-thirds of the inhabitants of the northern state of Coahuila were Americans who opposed Mexican rule. They protested in riots and military skirmishes, and in 1836 Santa Anna led an army into the area to subdue the rebels. When he killed the 180 men defending the Alamo in a stand for Texas independence, Santa Anna set off a chain of events that led to the loss of almost half of Mexico's territory. Sam Houston and a force of Americans avenged the Alamo incident (going into battle with the cry "Remember the Alamo!") at San Jacinto, where they killed 600 Mexicans and wounded another 200. Santa Anna was taken alive; Houston offered him a choice: Sign over Texas as an independent state, or die. Santa Anna didn't hesitate for the blinking of an eye, and, on paper at least, Mexico was reduced to its present size, almost half of its original territory.

However, the government in Mexico City refused to honor the document signed by Santa Anna. In 1845, the United States annexed Texas and General Zachary Taylor was then sent to patrol the border. The Mexicans clashed with an American cavalry patrol in May 1846, allowing President Polk to ask Congress to declare war on Mexico.

What followed was the Mexican-American War. Ten thousand soldiers under the command of General Winfield Scott entered Veracruz, having bombarded the city thoroughly before landing. Scott penetrated the country as far as Mexico City, waging the first battle in Contreras, a small village outside of the capital. Scott succeeded in routing Santa Anna and then marched on to Churubusco (the site of Mexico's current movie industry). Here, Scott opposed an American-Irish battalion that had changed sides under the mistaken impression that they were engaged in a religious war against the Protestant general. Fifty Irishmen were captured and hanged as traitors, but they are still considered heroes by the Mexicans. The last battle was fought at Chapultepec Castle in Mexico City, a military academy at the time. Though vastly outnumbered, the young cadets fought valiantly without the aid of Santa Anna's army. Inevitably Scott won, and consequently, Mexico conceded most of its northern territory to the US.

By the terms of the Treaty of Guadalupe Hidalgo, the United States paid $15 million for what is today California, northern Arizona, New Mexico, and Texas. In 1854, Santa Anna, who had finagled his way back into power, sold what is now part of southern Arizona and a small strip of lower New Mexico to the United States for an additional $10 million in order to raise money to pay his army. He also sold Indians from the Yucatán as slaves to Cuban plantation owners for 25 pesos a head.

By 1855, a generation had grown up whose lives were free of Spanish domination. These people were divided into two groups — wealthy conservatives supporting the church and liberals who were poor but, in many cases, well educated. A major personality in the latter group was Benito Juárez, an Indian lawyer who, exiled by Santa Anna, had been in New Orleans earning a living by rolling cigars.

There was a great deal of unrest with Santa Anna at the head of the government. The president was old and tired and not capable of fighting another revolution. He departed rather suddenly for Venezuela on a boat ironically named *Iturbide* (the man he had deposed almost 32 years earlier), claiming that to avoid national conflict and trauma he was returning to the nation the powers it had entrusted to him.

But conflict erupted anyway in the form of a civil war that ended in December 1860 with a liberal victory. Benito Juárez became Mexico's first Indian president, and also the first president to be really concerned with the plight of Mexico's people. The country's financial condition was so critical that no one would take the job of secretary of the treasury. Mexico owed 80 million pesos in legitimate claims to foreign powers. Juárez, with no other recourse, announced a 2-year suspension of foreign payments. The governments of England, France, and Spain called a conference to decide on some way of collecting their long-standing debts. France, ruled by Napoleon III, used the situation as an excuse for an attempt to annex Mexico.

In January 1862, a contingent of troops from the three European nations landed in Veracruz with instructions to respect the sovereignty of Mexico but ensure payment of debts. The English and Spanish soon realized that France was acting in bad faith. They withdrew their troops, and Napoleon took advantage of the opportunity to order the occupation of Mexico City. However, the French were soundly defeated en route to the capital in Puebla on May 5, 1862, a date that is celebrated as a national holiday in Mexico.

Napoleon, furious, was not ready to concede the opportunity. He sent reinforcements of 28,000 men, and the French soon took Puebla. The best Mexican generals were captured or killed, and Juárez was forced to retreat from Mexico City north to San Luis Potosí. The French army entered Mexico City and was welcomed by the church dignitaries and the wealthy. The stage was properly set for the entrance of Napoleon's puppet, Maximilian.

Archduke Maximilian was the younger brother of Franz Josef, Emperor of Austria. He was handsome, charming, and popular with the Austrians. Franz Josef was jealous of him and so got him out of the country by making him Governor-General of Venice and Lombardy, then under Hapsburg rule. In 1856, Maximilian married Carlota, daughter of King Leopold I of Belgium. The couple lived a rather frivolous life, especially frustrating for the ambitious Carlota. They were ripe for a big change. Napoleon and a group of Mexican conservatives who had been living in Europe during the brief tenure of Juárez had an easy time convincing them to become Emperor and Empress of Mexico. In May 1864, Maximilian docked at Veracruz, firmly resolved to restore tranquillity to the country — and utterly unequal to the task. He did not have the slightest idea of the troubles facing him or the huge country he had so happily adopted. An idealist with essentially democratic ideas, Maximilian quickly alienated his only supporters — the church and the rich — first by refusing to return church properties that Juárez had confiscated, and then by announcing his intention of taking more church land to help finance his government.

Maximilian never really had a chance to succeed in Mexico. Besides losing the support of the conservatives, he was betrayed by Napoleon. Napoleon had originally intended to seize control of what is today Mexico and Central America and extract as much money as possible from these territories. In order to do this successfully, he had counted on the South winning the Civil War raging in the United States. But with the Battle of Gettysburg in July of 1863, Napoleon realized that the Union would win and that he would have to withdraw his forces supporting the Confederacy. Maximilian was never consulted; he was Napoleon's dupe. The real power behind the throne was the commander of the French army, a man named Bazaine. Napoleon communicated his orders to Bazaine while Maximilian, unaware of the situation, was busy redecorating Chapultepec Castle and entertaining the social elite of Mexico City.

At the conclusion of the Civil War in 1865, the United States started pouring arms into Mexico to aid Juárez, and General Grant ordered General Sheridan to assemble an army along the US-Mexican border to act should the French invade.

With arms and the moral support of the United States, guerrillas were active throughout the country. Bazaine panicked and ordered Maximilian to sign a bill that all Juárist soldiers would be shot upon capture. Maximilian, a kindly, peaceful man, was reluctant, but was no match for the strong-willed commander. In signing the bill, Maximilian unwittingly signed his own death warrant.

By 1866 Napoleon realized his gamble was not going to pay off. He was leery of Bismarck, who was making Prussia the major power in European politics; Napoleon felt he might need his entire army with him in France. He sent orders to Bazaine to begin withdrawal of the army from Mexico. Bazaine did have the decency to warn Maximilian that the army would be leaving, and with it, whatever remained of Maximilian's support.

Maximilian knew that his empire could not survive without the French force, but Carlota, who loved being an empress, persuaded him that it would dishonor the Hapsburg name to withdraw. She felt that she could convince Napoleon to change his orders and sailed to Europe on her dismal, ill-fated mission. She appealed to the Vatican but was turned away, understandably enough, considering her husband's espousal of freedom of religion and his confiscation of church property. In her absolute frustration, she went mad and lived in seclusion in Belgium until 1927 without ever regaining her sanity.

Maximilian, always an irresolute man, wanted to go to Carlota, but he also hated to abandon Mexico. Napoleon urged abdication, but the conservatives in Mexico still hoped to make use of the former archduke. As far as they were concerned, anyone was an improvement over Juárez. If Maximilian left, there would be no opposition to Juárez; if he remained, some compromise might be worked out.

In the end, it was probably his Hapsburg pride that convinced Maximilian to stay. Commanding an army of about 9,000, he made a last stand against a Juárist army of 40,000 at Querétaro. He was given several opportunities to save himself, but he refused, preferring to be with his men. He was captured on May 15, 1867. Requests for clemency poured into Mexico from the heads of the European governments and from William Henry Seward, the US Secretary of State. But Juárez despised mercy as a form of weakness. Maximilian and two of his generals, Miramón and Mejía, were shot on June 19. Maximilian showed great courage and goodwill up to the end, and a famous photograph taken 3 days before the execution shows Maximilian comforting the priest who had come to comfort him and to administer last rites. It was typical of the strange combination of humanity, courage, and naïveté of the emperor. He died with great dignity.

Once again Juárez was in control of a country with an empty treasury and a huge debt. He convinced the British to resume construction of the Veracruz–Mexico City railroad, which they had abandoned 19 years before. He also set up a public education system and encouraged industrial development. In 1871 he was reelected, but he died of a heart attack in July 1872, and Vice President Lerdo de Tejada assumed power.

De Tejada was unpopular with both the Mexicans and the US government. He fulfilled some of Juárez's plans by having the railroad completed and 8,000 schools opened, but he initiated nothing, thus facilitating the election of Porfirio Díaz in 1877. Díaz had been a popular general with Juárez, and initially he seemed to embody Juárez's high principles. The people believed he would institute true democracy. Instead he amended the constitution and governed as a dictator for 35 years.

In his eagerness to restore solvency to the impoverished country, Díaz handed over Mexico's natural resources to foreign developers. He created a new mining code, granting subsoil rights to anyone owning the surface. Foreign investments flowed into the country. Foreigners built the railroads (9,000 miles by the end of the century), developed the mines, introduced new industrial techniques, and owned one-fourth of the land. American investors — US Steel, the Anaconda Corporation, Standard Oil, Cyrus McCormick, J. P. Morgan, William Randolph Hearst, John D. Rockefeller, and the Guggenheims — owned about three-quarters of the mines, more than half the oil fields, and large sugar, rubber, and coffee plantations, plus cotton farms and cattle ranches. The English, French, and Spanish also invested heavily. Mexico's national income increased enormously.

Díaz made peace with the Catholic church by agreeing not to enforce the anti-clerical laws passed during the Juárez regime. He also permitted the Church to buy back much of the land that had been confiscated. Díaz created the first rural police force, finally freeing Mexico's highways of bandits. He also censored the press, controlled the schools and government, and allowed bureaucratic graft to escalate.

The Creoles and mestizos were content, for they constituted the prosperous middle and upper classes. Yet as they grew richer, the Indians got poorer. Díaz accomplished a great deal for commerce and industry but almost completely neglected agriculture; no dams were built, nothing was done about soil erosion, and no new farming methods were introduced in the country.

Despite their situation, the Indians never initiated a revolution. They had served as docile slaves under the Spanish, and though they fought to overthrow Spanish rule, the Creoles organized and led the revolution. When it was all over, they had done nothing more than change masters. The Creoles and mestizos were on top and the plight of the Indians was remarkably unchanged. Even today the Indians hold the menial jobs — if they are employed at all.

By 1904, Mexico had a population of about 10 million, but all the land and wealth were concentrated in the hands of about 500,000 people. Díaz was 74 years old and his advisers urged him to pick a successor. But he intended to stay on until he died. In 1907, Díaz carelessly mentioned to an American journalist that he was planning to retire. The news spread quickly across Mexico and caused a furor. An opposing political party sprang up almost instantly. The anti-*reeleccionistas* were financed largely by an unknown idealist, Francisco Indalecio Madero, who came from a wealthy Creole family in Coahuila. He was 5-foot-2 and had a falsetto voice and a nervous tic. He was a teetotaler, a vegetarian, and a spiritualist — an unlikely revolutionist. Díaz refused to take him seriously, but a great many other people did. The seeds of dissent were germinating.

In 1910, Díaz engineered his reelection simply by not having the votes counted. His 80th birthday almost coincided with the 100th anniversary of Hidalgo's *grito,* so he threw an extravagant celebration and entertained representatives from many nations with parades, pageants, and a ball at the National Palace. To the rest of the world, Mexico seemed at the peak of peace and prosperity. Few imagined that the national situation would blow up within a few months.

Madero found a strange ally in Doroteo Arango, better known as Pancho Villa. A cattle rustler by profession, Villa considered revolution something of a lark — a chance to plunder with the support of an organized band of cowboys of similar moral standards.

In the south, the winds of dissent inspired Emiliano Zapata — long unhappy about the landless condition of most Mexicans — to organize an army of Indians and poor mestizos. They immediately began burning and looting the large haciendas and sugar plantations in the area. On May 12, 1911, Zapata took control of Cuautla. Eight days later Villa captured Ciudad Juárez, and shortly after various state capitals fell into the hands of guerrillas or mobs. Díaz was forced to resign and was permitted to leave Mexico for Europe, where he died.

The people regarded Madero as a savior. He instituted a system for an honest election and was easily elected. In his first reforms, he granted freedom of the press and encouraged workers to organize unions. Sincere as he was, he overlooked one essential problem: He failed to restore the land to the poor Indians.

This sent Zapata on the march once again. But Madero had an even more formidable enemy in the United States, because he opposed foreign investment and would do nothing to protect foreign property. Henry Lane Wilson, the US Ambassador to Mexico and an associate of the Guggenheim interests, convinced President Taft that Mexico was "seething with discontent." One hundred thousand American soldiers were stationed at the border, ready to move in to protect American holdings.

What's more, Madero allowed many of the corrupt politicians and generals from the Díaz regime to remain. Even when a general was found to be plotting against him, Madero — who despised killing — had the man confined to prison, where he could continue to plot. Two generals, Felix Díaz (a nephew of Porfirio Díaz) and Victoriano Huerta, decided they could do a better job than Madero. With the consent of Ambassador Wilson, they staged a coup, seizing Madero and forcing Mexican congressmen to accept Madero's resignation at gunpoint. Huerta then asked Wilson what he should do with Madero, and Wilson told him to do what was best for the country. Huerta interpreted this as carte blanche to do what he had wanted to do all along. While being transferred from one prison to another, Madero was mysteriously "shot by a fanatic," according to Huerta.

Few people supported Huerta, who was more often drunk than sober. Three governors of northern states — Alvaro Obregón of Sonora, Pancho Villa, who ruled a military dictatorship in Chihuahua, and Venustiano Carranza in Coahuila — began a movement to avenge the death of Madero. These three, with the help of Zapata in the south, were the men who would win the final Mexican revolution.

When Woodrow Wilson took office in 1913, he was horrified that US policy supported Huerta. He instituted an arms embargo but ignored the fact that cattle being driven across the border into the US were being sold to buy arms for Carranza.

Carranza and Pancho Villa each thought of himself as the head of the revolutionary armies called the constitutionalists and were suspicious of each other. To Villa, revolution was an opportunity to loot haciendas and sack towns. Carranza, a well-educated, conscientious landowner, abhorred these tactics. In March of 1913 he called for a national uprising to overthrow Huerta and named himself first chief of the Constitutionalist Army.

President Wilson was pressuring Huerta to resign; upon Huerta's refusal, the United States openly began to send arms to Carranza and Pancho Villa. Well equipped with firearms, the two leaders raced each other to Mexico City. Huerta meanwhile took flight for Europe with the entire contents of Mexico's treasury.

Ironically, Obregón arrived in Mexico City first and awaited the arrival of Carranza. Carranza, whose distrust of Villa was almost paranoid, held up coal necessary for the trains to transport Villa's troops to the capital. Upon learning of this, Villa returned to Chihuahua to plot. Carranza entered Mexico City and declared himself president. Zapata, the only one of the four who wanted nothing for himself, steered clear of the whole thing.

General disillusionment set in upon the war-weary country amidst an uneasy truce. Zapatistas and Villistas still had skirmishes with Carranza's forces. Carranza sent his army out under the leadership of Obregón to confront Villa near the town of Celaya, in an all-out battle that lasted 3 days and cost the lives of 12,000 Mexicans, but marked the end of Villa as a threat to the government. Two years later Zapata was shot.

MODERN MEXICO

In 1917 Carranza organized a convention to set up a new constitution, which is still in effect today. Carranza was not genuinely interested in a constitution; his ulterior motive was to fortify his own position, but some radical reforms were instituted because they were supported by Alvaro Obregón, Mexico's strongest general. Rights for workers that had never before existed — including an 8-hour day, yearly vacations, a minimum wage, the right to strike, and abolishment of child labor — were instituted. An article was passed allowing the confiscation of foreign-owned and church property, but Carranza promised that this would not be put into effect while he was president.

Although Carranza did not want to step down in the election of 1920, he opposed a formidable foe in Obregón. Carranza abdicated as Huerta had before him, taking all the gold and silver in the treasury and fleeing to Veracruz to board passage to Europe. He was waylaid and shot before reaching the Mexican port.

The American government was not in favor of Obregón because it thought he was too left-wing. In order to keep the US from backing anyone else, Obregón signed an agreement that no lands acquired before 1917 would be expropriated; if they were, the Mexican government would pay cash for them.

Obregón supported Plutarco Elías Calles as his successor, and Calles was duly elected in 1924. A country schoolteacher, Calles had risen in the ranks of the revolutionaries. In some ways Calles's administration was progressive. He encouraged modern road construction, initiated campaigns of sanitation and hygiene, proposed irrigation schemes, advanced the educational program, and even implemented agrarian reform, distributing 8 million acres of land among 1,500 villages — an average of about 535 acres per village.

Calles was an enemy of the Catholic religion. In 1924 he closed all of the churches, and those priests and nuns who didn't leave the country had to go underground. Calles also ordered the owners of the oilfields to relinquish their titles and sign 50-year leases.

Once again, the US became involved in Mexican politics since most of the oilfields were owned by American companies. This time the American government employed intelligence rather than belligerence. Dwight Morrow was appointed ambassador and he wooed the Mexicans instead of threatening them; he invited Charles Lindbergh (who became Morrow's son-in-law after meeting Anne Morrow during the visit) and Will Rogers to make goodwill visits. Morrow won the confidence of Calles by evincing interest in his educational and irrigation programs. Within 2 months of Morrow's arrival, the Mexican government decreed that foreign companies that had acquired subsoil rights prior to 1917 were entitled to full ownership.

Calles was determined to restore the presidency to Obregón, who was reelected in 1928, but 3 weeks after his election Obregón was assassinated while dining in a restaurant in San Angel, a suburb of Mexico City. This was the last political assassination in recent Mexican history.

Emilio Portes Gil was chosen by the congress to assume the presidency, and in the next election Pascual Ortiz Rubio was elected. Both men had the support of Calles, and during their term the hard line against the church continued.

In 1934, Calles supported a young liberal, Lázaro Cárdenas, as the next presidential candidate, hoping to appease a vociferous group of young idealists who wanted an honest government. Cárdenas was not grateful to Calles and had no compunction about dismissing all pro-Calles senators and cabinet members. To secure his own position, Cárdenas established a single official political party that was based on an elite of trade unionists, communal agriculturalists, military men, and politicians and was responsible for selecting candidates. Even today, any candidate nominated by the party is assured of election. To avoid a coup d'état, Cárdenas rounded up Calles and his coterie and sent them to Texas with orders not to return to the country.

That same year Franklin Roosevelt instituted his "Good Neighbor Policy" to secure good relations with Mexico; he pledged non-interference in Mexican affairs. This policy was strained a few months later when Cárdenas expropriated all the foreign-owned oilfields. The United States and Britain boycotted oil from Mexico and caused the failure of the nationalized oil company, but in 1939 the wartime need for oil put an end to the embargo.

World War II also stimulated other Mexican industrial developments. American, British, and European capital flowed into the country for safe speculation. In 1942 Mexico declared war on the Axis powers. In 1946, Miguel Alemán was elected president and inaugurated a period of vast expansion; a great deal was accomplished for the country and its people. Roads were built, dams constructed, schools and education extended to the remotest areas, and industry was encouraged. Among today's industries are branches of General Motors, Ford, Chrysler, Colgate, Del Monte, Campbell, and General Electric. There are also German, Japanese, French, British, and Swiss plants, most of which are 51% or more owned by Mexican investors and employ a largely Mexican labor force.

Despite recent industrial progress, Mexico is still beset with very severe economic dilemmas. During the mid-1970s, the country was initially swept by an economic crisis triggered by heavy government spending for rapid commercial development and the expansion of social services. The Mexican financial quandaries were further aggravated by widespread international inflation, which took its toll all around the globe. Though Mexico was hardly unique in the source and scope of its economic problems, it certainly suffered more than its fair share.

Even now, many Mexican citizens live in great poverty in urban slums or on small plots of land that provide barely enough for their daily sustenance. The country's birthrate is among the highest in the world, which means many more mouths to feed by the year 2000 — a disturbing prospect for Mexico's leaders.

Almost every recent Mexican president has, out of necessity, tried to deal more effectively with social and economic questions, but for the most part, success has been limited, owing in great part to the entrenched bureaucracy and pervasive corruption in the Mexican political system. President José López Portillo (1976–82) began trying to impose a degree of fiscal responsibility by cutting government spending, restricting imports, freezing wages, and launching an investment program designed to allow the controlled growth of Pemex, Mexico's state-owned oil company. At the start of 1981, major oil finds had placed Mexico in fifth place globally in the extent of its oil reserves and seventh in gas reserves, which in turn brought a great boost to Mexico's economy.

During this boom period, spending by Pemex, along with that in other public and private sectors, knew no bounds. Borrowing capital was quite easy, since foreign bankers were literally lined up, eager to invest. Unfortunately, the economic bonanza was short-lived. By the spring of 1981, an oil glut caused prices to drop more than $10 a barrel. Having accomplished relatively little to cure Mexico's economic ills, Portillo's presidency ended largely in disgrace, marred by uncurbed spending and pervasive corruption. His legacy to his successor, Miguel de la Madrid, was a nationalized banking system in a state of chaos, a peso devalued by almost 500% within a single year, more than 100% annual inflation, and a staggering foreign debt.

During Miguel de la Madrid's administration (1982–88), the country's problems were compounded by other economic woes. De la Madrid's austerity program, carried out under the urging of the International Monetary Fund, proved a failure; attempts to slow inflation by cutting wages and imports made the standard of living for the average Mexican even lower. Among the most pervasive economic problems during the 1980s was the decline in purchasing power of the peso by 50%, along with continued widespread unemployment. The peso was further devalued twice during 1987, amid a growing climate of uncertainty. In 1988, inflation soared to 157%. Labor became increasingly militant, and millions of dollars were being taken out of the country in a panic-stricken flight of capital; despite the government's efforts to repatriate these funds, almost $20 billion remained deposited in foreign banks at the end of 1988. The ongoing oil glut and the continuing uncertainty of oil prices continued to hinder much-needed revenues from crude-oil sales, further exacerbating the country's debt burden, which exceeded $104 billion at the end of de la Madrid's term in office.

The presidential election of 1988 was the most bitterly contested in modern Mexican history. While past presidential elections had been won easily by the candidate of the ruling Partido Revolucionario Institucional (PRI), the 1988 election was preceded by an unusually heated contest among three strong candidates: Cuauhtémoc Cárdenas (son of former President Lázaro Cárdenas), representing the Partido de Renovacion Democrática (PRD); Manuel Clouthier of Partido de Acción Nacional (PAN); and Carlos Salinas de Gortari, representing the PRI. Although the PRI won the presidential office once again, Salinas was elected with a widely questioned 50.7% majority. He took office amidst the normal chorus of public declarations of confidence, accompanied by widespread misgivings and accusations that the elections were a fraud. In spite of this, the new president took decisive action to improve the nation's faltering economy.

President Salinas has continued with de la Madrid's plan to open up the Mexican economy. Mexico began a trade-liberalization program by joining GATT — General Agreement on Trade and Tariffs — in 1986, and at press time, they had begun negotiating with the US on a landmark free-trade agreement that would encourage further foreign investment in Mexico. Also, revised regulations have allowed foreign investors access to many areas formerly excluded from foreign control: Whereas foreign investors could invest only up to 49% of the capital in the past, now they can invest 100% — the result being more jobs for Mexican citizens. In addition to opening up the economy to foreign investment, President Salinas has negotiated the reduction of Mexico's foreign debt through more manageable, longer-term repayments. He also has attempted to reduce spending in a variety of governmental programs and industries, and he's tried to privatize the "parastate sector" (state-owned organizations operating for a profit). Through the implementation of a "Solidarity Pact" (basically, a wage and price freeze), the official inflation rate had fallen to about 30% by the end of Salinas's second year in office (and the economy was fueled by the recent war in the Persian Gulf). What's more, an innovative plan allowing construction companies to build and mangage public works projects at a profit has been designed to provide the broad infrastructure needed for the country's urgent expansion requirements, without burdening the federal budget.

Almost anyone living in Mexico, however, will tell you that the country is in a state far from financial bliss. Critics have argued that Salinas's plan of economic recovery has forced Mexicans to sacrifice too much too quickly. By 1990, purchasing power in Mexico had declined 60% since 1982.

In addition to coping with his nation's pressing financial crisis, President Salinas and his team of young technocrats also have had to confront criticism from the US, regarding matters of drug trafficking and illegal aliens. Even at home, Salinas and his aides have had to face political pressure from the old guard within his party. His opponents also have accused him of being overly autocratic, ignoring previous promises to foster a more legitimate multi-party democracy.

As demonstrated in the last presidential election, the ruling PRI has lost significant segments of the support it once received from Mexican citizens. The 1989 gubernatorial races again demonstrated this eroding position when the PRI — which had never lost a gubernatorial contest in its 60-year history — lost the governorship of the state of Baja California to Ernesto Ruffo of the Partido de Acción Nacional. Skeptics, who believe the PRI did not win the 1988 presidential elections fairly, wonder if the dominant party hasn't reached its full quota of "democratic presidential elections," and accusations of fraud occurring in other PRI-won elections persist. Following landslide victories proclaimed by the PRI in the November 1990 local elections in the state of Mexico, PRI opponents made strong pleas for the government to to adopt an international outside observer to monitor future elections. Others, who are less skeptical, believe that Mexican voters are finally voicing criticism, mainly at the polls, and questioning the ability of the PRI to improve Mexico's economy. Salinas seems clearly committed to an aggressive plan of economic improvement. What seems less clear is whether his methods will soon appease or outrage Mexicans. The hope is that the political posture of the people will sharpen the current president's awareness of his responsibilities to his people, and encourage farsighted, humane solutions to Mexico's thorny dilemmas.

The Mexican People

Although the people of Mexico are of Indian, Spanish, and mestizo (mixed) stock, they share a sense of national identity perhaps best summed up by the expression *"Yo soy puro mexicano"* ("I am pure Mexican"). Ask anyone about his or her background, and you're more than likely to get this response. Mexicans are also quick to assert that their country of 86 million people is part of North America, although more Latin than gringo in consciousness. In addition to sharing the Spanish language with all but one of its southern neighbors (Portuguese is spoken in Brazil), Mexican lifestyles and beliefs are more in harmony with the majority of the western hemisphere nations than with its two influential northern neighbors.

The Mexicans' assertion that they are as North American as people from the United States and Canada frequently accompanies a sigh, as they philosophically observe that this is seldom taken into account by residents of the United States. Many Mexicans share the impression that US foreign policy makers somehow do not consider them as important as Canada in the continental scheme of things. Although the first book to be printed in the Western Hemisphere was published in Mexico in 1539 and the first university in North America, the Royal and Pontifical University of Mexico, was founded in 1551, Mexicans sometimes feel their country's cultural contribution to the hemisphere has not been recognized by the people next door. These attitudes appear to be changing, however, as the two countries have tried to enhance their relations within recent years. A free-trade agreement between the US and Mexico, which was under negotiation at press time, indicates that Mexico is gaining in both political and economic stature. Mexico made headlines, too, when Octavio Paz, the poet and essayist, was awarded the 1990 Nobel Prize for Literature (a first for Mexico), bestowing on Paz and his country the long-overdue respect of the international literary community.

Despite gringo misconceptions about Mexico, the country has a relatively high level of education for a still-developing nation — about 85% of the population is literate. Most of Mexico's 10 million Indians live in villages and speak one of the 90 Indian dialects rather than Spanish, although some speak both the local and national idiom. Dispersed throughout Mexico's northern and northwestern states are the Tarahumara, Apache, Mayo, Yuma, and Seri peoples. Along the Pacific coast stand settlements of the Tarasco descendants, the Purapecha and Huichol tribes. The largest group of Indians, who speak Nahuatl, cluster primarily in the central highlands, with small tribes stretching as far south as Guatemala. (The Aztec and the Toltec peoples were members of the Nahuatl linguistic group.) The Otomí live in the central highlands, too; around Oaxaca, the Mixtec and Zapotec. The Huave, Chamula, Chontal, and Zoque live in the south. Yucatán is the province of the Maya. Near Veracruz, the Huasteca live and the Totonac Indians perform the traditional flying pole dance.

Throughout the countryside, ever since the Revolution of 1910, huge *latifundios* (private estates) have been expropriated to "give the land to those who work it." However, much of the best land remains in the hands of the *latifundistas,* and for the most part, the peasants have tiny plots on *ejidos* (cooperative farms) without the necessary means to work them efficiently. Consequently, production is insufficient for the growing population, and in recent years Mexico has had to import most of its most basic foodstuffs. The minimum salary in Mexico is about $3.50 a day (just about the cost of a fair-size chicken), and the unemployment rate in 1989 was about 20%; another 40% of the work force — tradespeople such as carpenters, bricklayers, and craftsmen — are underemployed, often working only 2 or 3 months and then being laid off for a month or more. To aggravate the situation, Mexico has no unemployment insurance or public welfare funds; the lack of work is so severe that thousands of people cross the border into the United States every year looking for jobs. Although both Mexican and US authorities have been trying to stop the flow of illegal aliens, the paucity of employment opportunities is so extreme that poor Mexicans are willing to run the risk of getting caught. In spite of both governments' joint official stand to the contrary, a number of authorities privately regard the flow of workers into the United States as an effective method of helping to deal with some of Mexico's immediate economic problems.

Though Mexican workers — even in unionized industries — often tend to work the same number of hours as their American counterparts, their work hours are spread longer throughout each day and production per man-hour is lower. In the cities, the working day begins around 10 or 11 AM. Even though most of the stores in Mexico City do not close at midday for a 3-hour siesta, many office workers are given a 2- to 3-hour break so they may enjoy a leisurely lunch with their families. When they return to work they often stay as late as 9 PM. People who work outdoors tend to start sometime around daybreak and work until dusk. Like many other developing nations, Mexico has a dualistic economy. While most people barely make a living, a small segment of the population enjoys the full benefits of 20th-century industrial society. As part of the effort to integrate its economy, Mexico's government has been developing new industries, tourism being one of the largest.

Tourism, Mexico's industry without smokestacks, recorded a 10% growth in 1987, and even though the growth rate declined the following year, dollar earnings from tourism in 1988 were around $2.5 billion, and in 1990 the figure rose to $3.1 billion. In 1989, the Mexican government set a goal of attracting 10 million tourists a year and $5 billion in revenues by 1994; the plan also includes adding 50,000 hotel rooms to the existing 310,000 rooms by the same year. In addition to providing modern accommodations for guests, the surge in tourism is helping more than 2 million Mexican families who make their living producing folk art, particularly silver, ceramics, and woven textiles. These people, too, have been organizing cooperatives, selling their wares at special government stores as well as in regional markets (see the *Shopping* section of each city report in THE CITIES).

Known as *el día de tianguis,* traditional market days are held throughout Mexico, with each village specializing in its local produce and crafts. The most popular market day is Sunday, although markets are held on other days of the week in many towns and villages.

People from the United States who visit Mexico for the first time are generally struck by three basic areas in which Mexican attitudes are startlingly different from theirs: class consciousness, time values, and human relationships. If these seem sweeping generalities, the differences are nonetheless manifested in simple small ways.

The vast disparity between rich and poor is no doubt the first aspect of Mexican life to impress itself upon the visitor's mind as being different from life north of the border. Poverty is widespread, yet there are pockets of incredible wealth and splendor. The Indians still make up most of the lowest socioeconomic bracket. Although many mestizos insist that they are not prejudiced against Indians, they will admit to a certain condescension toward those who are poor and illiterate, and members of the "lower class" are expected to know their place and act suitably servile. This stems from attitudes dating from the Spanish conquest, which was followed by centuries of oppression in which the Indians were virtually slaves of the landowners. After the Revolution of 1810, which culminated in independence from Spain, the new ruling class emerged from the ranks of the Creoles (native Mexicans of European blood) and the mestizos (Creoles with Indian blood). Although in 1810 there were about 2.5 million Creoles and mestizos and 3.5 million Indians, independence did nothing to guarantee Indian equality; it simply vouchsafed national independence from Spanish rule. It wasn't until after the Revolution of 1910 that the Indians were granted some degree of independence. But despite countless political promises and campaign slogans, the Indians still remain trapped in the colonial system of the *patrón* (the local boss who is their intermediary with the rest of the country). They continue to be victims of incredible poverty, pervasive prejudice, and discrimination. Although quick to deny the existence of racial discrimination today, many wealthier Mexicans do acknowledge the presence of barriers to full communication between people from different strata of their society. It becomes quickly apparent to a first-time visitor that in Mexico you either have a servant or you are a servant. In a sense, these are the only two classes.

Even at first glance there is no question that in this respect Mexico is strikingly different from the United States. On the way into Mexico City from the airport, delineations between rich and poor become immediately apparent. Around the ultramodern, artistically dazzling sections of the capital huddle those vast areas of ramshackle cardboard and tar paper shelters that the United Nations calls "spontaneous settlements." In Mexico they are known as *ciudades perdidas* (lost cities). Scarcely more comfortable, if somewhat more sturdy, are the *barrios* — tenements where families of as many as 12 sleep in one or two rooms, sharing a toilet with a few dozen other people. For most Mexicans, *"vivir es sobrevivir"* ("to live is to survive"). People who are driven to seek alternatives to subsistence farming in arid rural sections of Mexico crowd into these marginal settlements. Thousands arrive every day, carrying everything they own on their backs, never seeming to lose their faith that *Diós proverá* (God will provide).

The Mexican government, which shares this migration problem with most of the other nations of the Third World, has instituted a number of programs to provide health and education services to people living in these poorer urban areas and has initiated a series of public finance systems to provide economic assistance for building programs so that people can improve their simple shelters and make them more habitable, hygienic, and safe. Another branch of the government deals with resettlement projects. A number of studies that compile geographic information into the form of computerized data enable this agency to determine the feasibility of establishing new industrial, agricultural, or resort communities in any part of the country. (The Bays of Huatulco, Ixtapa, and the resort island Cancún, were the result of one of these survey projects.) By encouraging people to migrate to planned settlements in relatively uninhabited regions, the government is trying to alleviate the problems of mushrooming spontaneous settlements, which strain already overloaded services and facilities in the cities.

For many Mexicans, the shift from the fields to an urban environment is drastically abrupt and uncomfortable. For one thing, the pace of life in Mexico City is much faster than in any of the villages of 300 or less in which more than 50% of the entire Mexican population lives. People in Mexico City are usually in a hurry. They push and shove and are rarely polite to a stranger unless that person has been introduced by a friend, in which case they are utterly charming. Traffic is a nightmare. (The streets are free-for-all zones that terrify even the most hardened US motorist.) The problems of pollution and traffic jams have led authorities to impose driving restrictions (see "Getting Around" in *Mexico City,* THE CITIES), and in 1991 the government announced plans to relocate the city's largest government-run oil refinery to a less polluted and populated area outside the capital.

Unfortunately, families from all social classes who leave the capital city in search of a better life for their families have not been easily accepted in the provinces (*la provincia,* in Mexico, is considered anywhere outside Mexico City). Mexico City and its residents, who are referred to disparagingly as *chilangos,* are resented by most of the rest of the country for absorbing what they feel is more than a fair share of tax revenues, as well as supplies of food and precious water resources. Signs and bumper stickers actually proclaim, "Do a Good Deed; Kill a Chilango!"

Although Mexicans are generally effervescent, warm, and enthusiastic toward foreigners, they have one pervasive habit that drives time-conscious, punctual gringos to distraction. That is the Mexican tendency to be anywhere from a half hour to 2 hours late — always. Sometimes they don't show up at all. Mexicans know this and willingly admit it, but they can't understand why people from the north get upset. As a tourist, you probably won't be affected too much by problems of punctuality. After many years of experience, guides have learned that they may lose their jobs (and certainly their tips) if they are consistently late. Cab drivers understand that you have to catch a plane, and will generally do their best to show up on time when notified in advance. Mexicans who deal with foreigners have come to understand that people from northern countries have this idiosyncrasy of always being in a hurry, and they cater to what they regard as the northerner's perennial quirk. However, bear in mind that if you buy an item of clothing that has to be altered, or a piece of jewelry that needs to be fixed, it is requisite to tell the tailor or jeweler that you are leaving the city forever at least 2 days before you are actually planning to leave. Nine times out of ten, it still won't be ready when promised. Often work won't have started when the completed job has been promised.

If you make an appointment with a Mexican, be prepared to wait. Allow yourself an extra hour. And don't be surprised — or insulted — if you get stood up. It's nothing personal. Part of the trouble is that Mexicans are almost incapable of saying no. They will accept invitations or make appointments — even when they know they can't keep them — because it seemed like a great idea at the time. Someone who never shows up for appointments — who would be considered completely irresponsible in the US — is fondly regarded as *muy informal* in Mexico. Bear that in mind, and you will avoid a lot of the panic and frustration that first-timers in Mexico often experience.

A curious and in many ways admirable trait of Mexicans is that by and large they like to tell a person what they think that person wants to hear. An unfortunate by-product of this otherwise amiable quality is that strangers stopping to ask directions in a Mexican city will often get completely cock-eyed directions, simply because the person they have consulted doesn't wish to appear rude, but hasn't the vaguest idea of the correct directions himself.

Mexicans regard family relationships and friendships as the most important thing in life. *"Tener amistad vale más que todo"* ("To have friendship is more valuable than everything else") is a phrase that occurs frequently in conversations, and Mexicans are not afraid to show their emotions, especially affection. If you become friends with a person, you probably will find yourself part of a family of grandparents, parents, uncles, aunts, cousins, nephews and nieces, brothers and sisters. Somehow a large Mexican family that would be considered poor by US standards always seems to find room for one more. Even if you can't speak Spanish, you will find people willing to go out of their way to help you. You can be sure that at least one family member will reassure you by saying *"Mi casa es su casa"* ("My house is your house"). Mexicans don't have to "fit you into their busy schedule." They always find time to spend with visitors, making guests feel that nothing is as important as being with them. In the work world, employers understand when an employee has to stay home to care for a sick relative, and taking time off for a funeral — even when it's not that of a member of one's immediate family — is never questioned.

Being accepted into a Mexican family, even for a brief visit, is the best way to understand how the Mexican people live. While most travelers tend to stay in resort areas where they are surrounded by tourists and tourist facilities, those who venture off the traditional paths very often find themselves taken into the homes of new friends and welcomed. With an expansiveness that is in itself foreign to most people from the United States, Mexicans will insist that you let them take care of you.

Family closeness in Mexico has become so claustrophobic that it has given rise to a curious social custom. Since many people continue to live with their families during the years of courtship, engagement, and sometimes even early marriage, finding the privacy needed for intimacy is usually a problem. This is why Mexican couples frequently retire to motels and hotels specifically meant for lovemaking. For a few pesos, rooms with beds and showers can be rented by the hour. Some places even sell male contraceptives.

Sexual attitudes in Mexico seem to be a curious mixture of good-natured acceptance of sexual needs and old-fashioned double standards. While young women living in Mexico City and other larger cities may have more liberal sexual mores, most of their parents continue to subscribe to the traditional values, as do most women living in smaller Mexican towns. It's considered quite acceptable for a man to go to bed with whomever he wants, and the *casa chica* (literally, "little house") in which a married man keeps a mistress is fairly common. Often a man's mistress, as well as his wife, will bear his children. Unless a woman decides to become a married man's mistress, she is expected to remain a virgin until she marries, and is certainly not allowed extramarital relationships once she is married. The influence of the Catholic church is perhaps still felt most strongly in bed, where many Mexicans continue to obey the injunction against contraception.

Birth control and family planning, however, are beginning to gain acceptance, particularly among women. Progressive government campaigns proclaiming *"la familiar pequeña vive mejor"* ("the small family lives better") have been successful in reducing the birthrate from 3.5 per thousand people in 1980 to 2.2 in 1989. Still, while contraceptives are more readily available these days and the birthrate has fallen, one report showed that as many as 60% of the women who obtain contraceptives from government-funded organizations do so without their spouses' knowledge. Most Mexican men are still adamantly opposed to birth control, believing that it could compromise their masculinity and allow their wives to be unfaithful.

Arrogant Mexican misconceptions of male superiority are known as *machismo*. Ask a Mexican man what it means and he will probably tell you it is his pride in his masculinity. A hard-nosed gringo might conclude that it is subconscious insecurity that requires him to continually prove to himself and everyone around him that he is the most gutsy, virile, self-reliant, sexy man in town. This attitude has probably done more to ruin Mexican marriages than any other single cultural trait. Because of machismo, a man is not supposed to help with the housework or spend time on what are considered "women's chores." The idea of women working out of the home has become more prevalent, though, and more and more men are swallowing their masculine pride, "allowing" their wives to "help out" in these difficult times.

Machismo glorifies the image of the so-called man's man. Although more men are beginning to participate in family chores and even child rearing, children are still usually raised by their mother, and young boys grow up almost totally under her influence, learning to worship her. It is very hard, if not impossible, for any other woman to ever live up to a Mexican man's image of his mother. Therefore, married men can treat their wives quite harshly, and young boys often despise their fathers for what they see them doing to their mothers. And yet they tend to follow the same behavior pattern when they get older. Very often, adolescent boys are engaged in silent, undeclared contests to prove that they are as macho as their fathers. Today, machismo is discussed at psychological seminars, and some young men are gradually accepting the idea that sexual conquest and bravado are not terms in which to define masculinity. But these attitudes have existed since the Spanish conquest, and it will be a long time before they are transformed.

Until such time, Mexican men will continue to regard all women outside their immediate family as fair game. (This even applies to their best friend's sister.) Women from the United States who visit Mexico often find that Mexican men are fun to be with for a short time, in spite of the considerable debate over whether or not Latins are lousy lovers. As in any other part of the world, the answer depends on the individual. However, Mexican men are known to go out of their way to compliment, flirt, flatter, and extravagantly praise a woman they want to impress. They very often seem to be able to carry off a performance that would have the average US male in fits of laughter were he to attempt it. It can be a very enjoyable game, as long as the woman understands what is really going on and is prepared to state her terms.

A *macho* in pursuit of a foreign woman will listen to her requests to show up on time much more readily than he will to those of a Mexican woman. The prestige of being seen with a foreigner is worth almost any inconvenience, even the inconvenience of being on time. It helps for a woman to let a Mexican man know that if he is more than half an hour late she won't be there. Once a man sleeps with a woman he regards her as his personal property. He is likely to become very possessive, resenting any social outings that do not include him. He will often object to "his" woman going shopping or to a movie by herself. The ultimate insult for a Mexican man is for "his" woman to go out with another man. Many people seem to think that it's not true that Mexican men are lousy lovers, but it is generally agreed that they make poor husbands, especially for women who have a sense of their own independence.

Foreign men in Mexico find it hard to meet women anywhere outside larger cities. In the small towns, young women are closely watched and no "nice" girl would be allowed to go out alone with a man, especially a foreigner. Even in the cities, it is often difficult for women who work in offices during the day to extricate themselves from their family commitments, although it is quite acceptable to bring a man home to visit. Because of the double standard that expects them to be virgins when they marry, single Mexican women are understandably cautious about sacrificing their future status by sleeping with someone who will be in town for only a week or two.

Whether or not sexual companionship enters into it, a visitor from the United States meeting Mexican people for the first time almost invariably comes away impressed with their general ebullience and *alegría* (joy). A Mexican saying states quite correctly that there is a party going on somewhere in Mexico all the time. Even a funeral brings people together to share food, drink, and above all, one another's company. Mexicans are fond of describing their country with the expression *"Como México no hay dos,"* which translates, "Like Mexico, there aren't two" or "There is no place like Mexico!"

Food and Drink

 Many people have the mistaken idea that all Mexican food is hot and that Mexicans use chili in everything. This ranks in absurdity with the European idea that Americans eat only hamburgers and hot dogs.

Actually, many foods taken for granted around the world today originated in Mexico and were introduced to the rest of the world by returning Spanish conquistadores in the 16th century. Corn is probably Mexico's greatest contribution to world cuisine, but the country has also furnished tomatoes, potatoes (both the sweet and what are called the Irish varieties), chocolate, vanilla, various squashes (including pumpkins), peanuts, assorted beans, avocados, chilies, guava, coconuts, pineapples, papayas — and turkeys!

For 1,000 years before Cortés landed in Mexico, corn was the staple of the native diet, and it remains so today. Besides being used in the popular tortilla, it is the basis of a variety of dishes including tamales, which are prepared very much as they are in the United States (a cornmeal dough is filled with shredded chicken or meat and chili sauce, wrapped in cornhusks, and steamed). Cornmeal is also used in *gorditas* (cornmeal patties filled with cheese, pork rinds, lima beans or potatoes, and then fried), and it's even used in a sweet hot drink, called *atole*.

Just as some form of bread or roll is served with most meals in the United States, the ubiquitous cornmeal tortilla is served with every meal in a Mexican household. It is the basis of hundreds of dishes, not just tacos and enchiladas, but quesadillas (grilled or fried turnovers filled with meat, cheese, potatoes, squash blossoms, or chilies), *tostadas* (toasted tortillas piled high with a variety of ingredients, including refried beans, chicken, *chorizo* — sausage — cheese, lettuce, onions, diced tomatoes, and avocado), and *chalupas* (tortillas with upturned edges fried and topped with meat or chicken and beans, chilies, tomatoes, and onions).

Enchiladas and tacos are Mexico's most popular tortilla-based dishes. The basic difference between the two — both of which are tortillas rolled around a filling — is that the enchilada is baked in a sauce, while the taco is either left as is (*suaves*) or fried with the sauce (*dorado*); the taco is also often accompanied with guacamole (mashed avocado with onions, garlic, chili, and cilantro) — usually served on the side. (Cilantro is a form of parsley used frequently in Mexican food. More pungent than its US counterpart, it is a strong herb that can easily dominate all other spices if not used sparingly.) When it comes to choosing tacos, the unqualifed favorites of most Mexicans are *tacos de carnitas* (heated tortillas wrapped around fried pork, cilantro, and onion) and *tacos a la parrilla* (tortillas filled with thinly sliced charcoal-broiled beef or pork). *Flautas* are extra long tacos.

Enchiladas are a favorite of budget-conscious Mexican cooks, since a small chicken or a few leftovers can provide enough food to feed a family of eight. Enchiladas are usually filled with chicken, but ground or shredded beef, fried pork, sausage, cheese, beans, potatoes, eggs, or any combination of these can be used. Top them with a spicy sauce and grated cheese, and heat through for a delicious main dish. There are a few classic enchiladas: *Enchiladas suizas* are filled with chicken and topped with a green chili sauce, grated cheese, and cream. The term *suiza* (Swiss) is used because of the cream. *Enchiladas de mole* are also made of chicken, with a *mole* sauce rather than chili on top.

If you have been a fan of Mexican food in any other part of the world, you will soon find there is a big difference at the source. In the US, for instance, tacos are crisp tortillas, folded in half, not rolled, with a lot of lettuce and tomato wedged into the shell above the meat or chicken. Visitors also won't find what is known in the US as "chili" — ground meat, beans, onions, garlic, tomato, and so on — except in restaurants catering to Americans. Chili con carne simply is not a part of the Mexican menu, and is really a Texas or Tex-Mex dish. But the major difference between native cuisine at the source and that prepared elsewhere lies in the variety of dishes available in Mexico that never appear on menus in the US, partly because the ingredients are not available.

Another dish that should certainly be tried during a visit to Mexico is *chiles rellenos* (stuffed chilies). This dish uses not the sweet bell peppers popular in the US, but a variety of dark green chili pepper, about 4 to 8 inches long, which has a tangy, delicious flavor. These peppers are stuffed with either cheese or ground meat, dipped in egg batter, fried, and then simmered in a bland tomato sauce. For a 2-month period beginning in mid-August, there is a special way of serving this chili called *chile en nogada*. The stuffing for this is usually ground pork and beef. Along with the ever-present onion and garlic, cooks add piñon nuts, citron, almonds, raisins, seasonal fruits including apples and pears, and diced tomatoes. And instead of simmering the chili in a tomato sauce after it is dipped in batter and fried, it is served with a purée of ground fresh walnuts and a purée of white cheese that is similar to cream cheese. The nuts account for the short time during which the dish is available, since purists will use only fresh walnuts, claiming the flavor changes once the nut has dried. The chili is placed in the center of a plate, covered with sauce, sprinkled with pomegranate seeds, and garnished with a sprig of parsley stuck upright in the center. The seeds, sauce, and parsley together make the red, white, and green colors of the Mexican flag, and coincidentally, the walnut season falls at the same time as Mexico's independence celebration. Every year on September 16, the National Palace in Mexico City offers an elaborate buffet featuring *chile en nogada*. And throughout the country the dish is served to mark independence festivities.

Just as there is regional cooking in the US, with New England clam chowder, southern fried chicken, creole gumbo, and the like, so different Mexican states have regional dishes. Veracruz is famous for its fish dishes, and red snapper Veracruz-style (*huachinango à la Veracruzana*) should definitely be sampled even if you can't get it in Veracruz. It's broiled red snapper in a tomato sauce, with capers, onions, green olives, a sweet yellow pepper, and no chili. Like all regional cooking, what is really reflected is not so much the taste or style of a people but the early cooks' ingenuity in the face of a limited variety of local products. In Baja California and the northwestern port cities, where shellfish is plentiful, lobster is scrambled with eggs, and tamales often are filled with shrimp. Most seaside towns offer a *sopa de mariscos,* or shellfish soup, which is frequently as good as any bouillabaisse in the Mediterranean. And in Oaxaca, where bananas grow in abundance, tamales are flat and rectangular, cooked in banana leaves, and consequently much moister than in other parts of Mexico. Acapulco is famous for its ceviche, or "fish cocktail." Although ceviche is available almost everyplace within shipping distance of the ocean, this seaside resort in the state of Guerrero is unsurpassed in preparing it. Ceviche is a white fish, usually sea bass or snapper, that has been marinated in lime juice for several hours. The citric acid of the lime cooks the fish, so do not be misled or discouraged by people who tell you it is raw. After this it is diced into small pieces and mixed with chopped tomatoes, onion, cilantro, green serrano chili, and sometimes diced avocado.

In northern (*norteño*) cooking, wheat flour rather than cornmeal is used in making tortillas, and almost all the meat is broiled. Goats are one of the few animals that can live in the barren deserts of this region, and logically enough, broiled goat is popular.

Food in the Yucatán Peninsula has been influenced by the cuisines of Cuba, Europe, and Asia, and is distinctively different from that of the rest of the country. There, tacos, called *papazul,* are made with regular tortillas but filled with diced hard-boiled eggs and covered with a sauce made from puréed squash seeds, tomato, and mild chili. A lot of pickling is done in this region, including everything from pigs' feet, beef, and chicken to pork. This pickled meat is then used as filling for tacos and enchiladas. In several rural areas meats are wrapped in banana leaves to conserve the moisture and baked in outdoor ovens. Very little chili is used in preparing Yucatán dishes, but meals are almost always accompanied by a sauce made from the *habanero* chili, the hottest in all of Mexico.

If you happen to be in Mexico City, Mexico's largest city and most cosmopolitan urban center, you will have an opportunity to sample all these regional dishes at restaurants specializing in each cuisine. In most restaurants throughout the country that serve "typical" Mexican food, there are always a number of regional dishes included in the menu. Regional identification can often be made from the name of a dish. For instance, *chile poblano* is a dish from the state of Puebla, as *poblano* is both a noun and an adjective for people and things originating there.

A word about chilies in Mexico. There are over 60 varieties available throughout the country, though the average tourist will encounter only about a dozen of them, and most of those in sauces. Other than the *chile poblano,* the variety commonly eaten whole is the *jalapeño* — an inch or so long, olive green, and very hot. Chili sauces are either red or green, depending on the colors of the chili and tomatoes used in making them. Both kinds will usually have garlic and onion purée mixed in along with a few other spices that vary from cook to cook. All chili sauces are hot, but some are classified in the "watch out" category, and it is a good practice to sample before dousing.

Beyond the regional variations, Mexican cooking is a combination of the indigenous Indian dishes, Spanish cuisine, which also incorporates some Arabic dishes, and French cooking, introduced during the reign of Maximilian. Rice, which is served in some form with most Mexican meals, is Spanish; and paella is a dish common throughout Mexico. Flan, an egg custard with caramelized sugar, is certainly French, and appears on the menu of almost every Mexican restaurant as a dessert.

Barbacoa (barbecue) sounds like another imported idea, but it is not the familiar American method of broiling meat. In Mexico, the only meat prepared this way is lamb. Cut into large pieces and wrapped in the leaves of the maguey or agave plant, the lamb is placed on a rack over hot coals and buried deep in a brick-lined pit in the ground for 24 hours. The juice from the maguey keeps the meat moist, and by the time it is removed from the heat, it literally falls from the bone. It is served with "drunk sauce" (*salsa borracha*), so called because one of the ingredients is pulque, the highly potent fermented juice of the maguey plant. This liquor is blended with a dark red chili known as *pasilla,* lots of garlic, and olive oil. Actually, you can hardly taste the pulque, for the alcohol is burned off in the cooking.

A very popular dish all over Mexico is *carne asada à la Tampiqueño,* a long, fairly thin strip of grilled steak served with refried beans topped with melted cheese, an enchilada of some sort, guacamole, and *rajas,* or strips of *chile poblano* fried with onion.

One very famous specialty in Mexican cooking is *mole* sauce. Although many foreigners turn up their noses at what they imagine to be a hot fudge turkey sundae, it is actually an extremely complicated sauce made of more than 30 ingredients, all of which must be ground or puréed. Unsweetened chocolate is only one of these, and can barely be distinguished as a distinct taste. In 2½ quarts of sauce there are only 2 ounces of chocolate, which must compete with several different chilies, garlic, onion, nuts, anise seeds, and a host of other powerful flavors. If a Mexican hostess goes to the trouble of preparing this elaborate dish for you, know that you are being honored.

Mexican cooks excel in the preparation of soup. You just can't get a bad soup in Mexico, even at the most humble roadside stand. Bean soup, either black or brown, is a thick purée seasoned with *epazote,* an aromatic herb, sometimes called stinkweed in the US. Mixed along with these are *chile chipotle* (a rust-colored spicy chili), cheese, and an occasional strip of fried tortilla added for texture. Bone marrow soup, known as *sopa de medula,* can be extremely hot, and is widely touted as a cure for a hangover; ask, *"Es muy picante?"* ("Is it very hot?") when ordering. Almost every restaurant offers chicken consommé, noodle soup, and *caldo Azteca* (or *caldo Xochitl*), which is chicken soup that is usually served with big chunks of chicken, a little rice, some vegetables, sliced avocado, and the very spicy *chili chipotle,* which can be removed. Other good choices are the *cremas* (cream soups), which are prepared with every conceivable vegetable, as swell as from squash blossoms, cheese, avocados, and even nuts.

A great soup, too hearty to eat as a first course but an excellent lunch or dinner dish, is *pozole,* native to the state of Jalisco. Made with hominy and either chicken or pork in a rich broth, it is served with a side dish of shredded lettuce, diced onion, pieces of crisply fried tortilla, sliced radish, and *chile pequín* powder. All these ingredients are added to taste, but discretion is advised with the *chile pequín* — it is fiery. If you see the words *sopa* and *caldo* on a menu, seeming to refer to the same thing, don't be confused. *Sopa* is soup and *caldo* is broth, and either is likely to make a good appetizer or light meal. *Sopa seca* (dry soup) refers to rice or pasta and is usually served as a separate course before the entrée.

Except in fairly posh establishments that cater to a sophisticated clientele, ordering beef in Mexico can be a chancy proposition. It is cut differently from the way beef is cut in the US, and is not aged. So unless you are eating in a place that brags about its steaks, good policy is to pass on the beef and stay with chicken, pork, or fish. The same is true of lamb, with the exception of *barbacoa.*

Adventurous gourmands may want to try *huitlacoche* (also spelled "guit-lacoche"), a rich and subtle, black corn fungus that has been cultivated as a delicacy since pre-Hispanic times; it is used to fill quesadillas and crêpes, as well as chicken and veal cutlets. Insects — grasshoppers and ants, fried or fresh — are popular dishes in Oaxaca, and *gusanos de maguey* (crisply fried maguey worms) and *escamoles* (ant eggs), both commonly found in the state of Hidalgo, are prized dishes offered in the finest restaurants around the country.

With all the ways in which tortillas are used, one might get the idea that Mexico has no bread, but in fact Mexicans are very fond of bread and pastry, and no town is so small it doesn't have a *panadería* (bakery). The big shops in the cities are a delight to visit, and few visitors have the willpower to leave empty-handed. Mexico's hard rolls, *bolillos* (pronounced bow-LEE-yos), are served in almost every restaurant. They are crunchy on the outside and soft inside, much like Italian or French bread. You almost always will see Mexican diners remove the doughy inner part, which they consider bad for the digestion, and eat only the crusty outer portion. There is also a large assortment of sweet rolls, more commonly found at dinner than breakfast. But it is not unusual for a Mexican to start the day with a sweet roll and large cup of *café con leche,* coffee with hot milk, and then a few hours later sit down to a heartier breakfast. Mexicans are not accustomed to eating bacon, although it is available in most restaurants that cater to a foreign clientele. They do, however, eat a lot of eggs, and the two most popular breakfasts are *huevos à la mexicana* and *huevos rancheros.* (When ordering the former avoid asking for *huevos mexicanos;* the term is *à la mexicana,* and remembering the difference will save you some embarrassment — *huevos* is slang for testicles.) What you're trying to get are eggs scrambled with finely minced onion, tomato, and green chili. *Huevos rancheros* are fried eggs, sunny-side up, that are served on top of a tortilla and covered with red chili sauce. Both of these dishes usually come with cooked or refried beans on the side.

Even if you are not accustomed to eating breakfast, you should eat something, because Mexican mornings are long. Lunch does not really begin until around 2 PM, and many businesses close from 2 to 4 or 5 PM so employees can enjoy a leisurely lunch with their families. If you truly cannot face an egg, hotcakes, French toast, and sometimes waffles are on the menu, as is *avena* (oatmeal), and some of the familiar packaged cereals. Many fruits are also served at breakfast. Mexican papayas, especially the red variety, are bigger and sweeter than you have probably known, and there is also the luxury — especially for US citizens — of freshly squeezed orange juice, available almost anywhere you go. *Molletes* — split *bolillos* (hard rolls) covered with refried beans, topped with cheese, and broiled — are popular for breakfast or late supper, as are tamales.

It may take your stomach a day or two to adjust to Mexico's dining schedule. From 12:30 to 4 PM most restaurants serve what is known as *comida corrida,* a special of the day that includes an appetizer, entrée, and dessert and is usually much cheaper than lunch à la carte choices. The big meal of the day is eaten from 2 to 4 PM; the cocktail hour starts around 7:30 PM; and *cena* (supper) is from 9 PM to midnight.

Desserts in Mexico are probably the least interesting item on the menu. They tend to lean heavily on stewed fruits and various combinations of milk and eggs. Flan, mentioned earlier, is probably the best of these, but another favorite is *leche quemada,* translated literally and quite accurately as burnt milk — milk boiled with sugar and vanilla flavoring until it has been thickened to the consistency of a thick gravy. *Chongos,* a curdled egg, milk, and sugar mixture served in a sweet cinnamon flavored syrup; *natillas,* a type of vanilla pudding; *arroz con leche,* rice pudding; and *capirotada,* a Mexican version of bread pudding, are some other good choices. For lovers of coconut there is *cocada,* coconut cooked with egg yolks, sugar, and sherry.

Mexicans are great coffee drinkers, and coffee is always served as a matter of course at the end of the meal. In better restaurants and coffeehouses it's usually delicious, but in some places it's either very weak (known in Mexico as *agua de calzetín:* literally, water that a sock has been soaked in!), or it's strong enough to keep you up and moving for several days. There is usually sugar on the table, but you'll have to ask for cream, which, in fact, is usually milk or evaporated milk; it's a good idea to ask for the "cream" when placing your order or it's likely to arrive when the coffee is already cold. Most restaurants have espresso and cappuccino, but the local favorite for breakfast or a late supper is *café con leche,* a blend of strong black coffee (or instant coffee) and hot milk that's frequently served in a tall, thick glass. Authentic Mexican coffeehouses, commonly known as *cafés de chinos* (not because the food is Chinese, but because the owners are usually of Chinese descent), use a coffee infusion, coffee steeped in water, made thicker than American coffee. Restaurants that specialize in typical Mexican food may serve only *café de olla* (*olla* means pot); the coffee is boiled in an earthenware pot with *piloncillo,* something between brown sugar and molasses, and cinnamon. Mexicans are tolerant of people dawdling for an hour or more over one cup of coffee. No one will make you feel rushed by giving you dirty looks or presenting you the check, for that matter, unless you ask for it. In fact, it is an institution throughout Mexico to sit around the zocalo at a café drinking hot coffee. Even in incredible heat, this practice is observed on the theory that hot coffee will make you perspire and, therefore, cool you off.

A better way to cool off is with limeade or orangeade, which is always made from fresh juice or any of Mexico's pervasive non-alcoholic fruit drinks. Most popular are *tamarindo, horchata, jamaica,* and *chía,* all sweet and very refreshing. *Tamarindo* is made from the pulp of the tamarind pod, and *jamaica* is a flowering plant that is dried and seeped in hot water; *horchata* is made from rice; and *chía,* made from tiny seeds, tastes something like limeade.

Hot chocolate is a great favorite in Mexico for both breakfast and supper. It is made with a touch of cinnamon, a holdover from Aztec days when, since there was no sugar, honey and cinnamon were mixed with the chocolate and cold water added. Mexicans still don't like their chocolate too sweet, but today milk is used instead of water. If you want chocolate as Europeans and Americans like it, ask for *estilo francés* (French-style). *Atole,* a cornmeal- or cornstarch-based hot drink flavored with chocolate, vanilla, strawberries, or some other fruit, is the favorite accompaniment for tamales.

An amazing variety of teas is sold in the markets — each said to have special curative properties — but choices on restaurant menus are usually limited to *té negro* (black tea) and *té de manzanilla* (chamomile tea), which is the traditional remedy for a queasy stomach.

As for alcohol, Mexico is reputed to have the best beer in the world, though Germans and Britons might take exception. It is made all over the country, from Monterrey in the north to Yucatán in the south, and ranges from a light ale to a very dark, rich bock. The light beers are called *clara* and the dark *obscura.* Some good brands of light beer are Kloster, Carta Blanca, Bohemia, and Superior. The best dark beers are Negro Modelo, Tecate, XX (Dos Equis), and XXX (Tres Equis), the triple X being a little darker and heavier than the double. During December and January, an even darker beer, Noche Buena, is available. It is made in a limited amount and sold only during the holiday season.

Wine in Mexico, however, can be an adventure. Until a few years ago there was little in the way of quality control, and not too many Mexicans drank wine. But the market has increased enormously during the past 10 years, and with it the quality has improved vastly. If you want to try a local wine, it's a good idea to let your waiter suggest a brand, but be sure to specify *del país,* which means "of the country." Now that Mexico's borders are open to imports, wines from other countries are readily available and are sometimes even less expensive than domestic brands in liquor stores and supermarkets. Many restaurants, however, continue to charge exorbitant prices for the imported varieties, so we suggest that you check the right side of the wine list before ordering. Brandy is also one of Mexico's most popular drinks, and, strangely enough, it is often mixed with Coca-Cola, 7-Up, or mineral water. Some institutional receptions only serve a choice of brandy and Coke or brandy and soda.

When in Mexico, try the national drink tequila. Serious drinkers like it straight, with a little salt and lime or lemon, but if your drinking habits sway more toward daiquiris than martinis, ask for a tequila cocktail or a margarita. In ordering straight tequila, specify *añejo.* This means only that it has been aged longer, and is, therefore, much smoother and only slightly more expensive. Tequila is made from the fermented juices of the maguey (agave) plant, and is the most highly refined product. But other alcoholic beverages come from this same juice. Mescal is a sort of amber liquor that's also made from the maguey but aged less than tequila — which means a different flavor and a lower price tag. Often the bottle contains a dead worm from the original plant, and aficionados (of the macho variety) nibble bits of it for an additional bit of flavor while they're drinking. Least expensive of all the maguey liquors is pulque, a milk-colored, thickish fluid with an alcohol content similar to that of beer. Generally, it is preferred in its natural flavor, but it is sometimes mixed with various fruit juices, such as orange, lime, or strawberry. It has a strong, yeasty smell, and is said to be good for the system.

Rum is also made in Mexico. Bacardi has a large plant just north of Mexico City, and several other distillers have plants around the country. All producers make both light and dark rums, and there is also Castillo rum, which is quite dry and often called the poor man's Scotch.

Just one word of warning: Easily half the stomach problems suffered by visitors are due to overindulgence in both food and drink, especially in Mexico City and other mountainous areas, where the altitude creates additional problems. But if you eat in clean places and don't consume twice as much as you normally do, you shouldn't have any trouble. Especially if you remember: Don't drink tap water! Instead, order *una botella de agua purificada* (a bottle of purified water), *agua mineral* (mineral water), *con gas* (carbonated), or *sin gas* (plain).

Music and Dance

No people love music and dance more than the Mexicans. Music is a pervasive presence everywhere in Mexico — street bands, mariachis, organ-grinders, and strolling singers fill the streets. There are probably more fiestas and celebrations in Mexico than anywhere else in the world — almost one every day somewhere in the country. Every village has its patron saint, and every saint's day is celebrated with music, dancing, and fireworks.

Little is known about the nature of early Indian music, except that it was highly religious and pervaded the culture. The Aztec wooed their gods with song and dance, and their children learned the two arts in *cuicacuilli* — houses of song — built near temples. Attendance was compulsory for both boys and girls from the age of 12. The children learned rhythmic and dramatic music — ceremonial cadences used by the Aztec to charm the gods and put fear into men.

The Spanish conquest put an end to much of the Indian music. The Spanish found the music primitive and offensive and, knowing it was an integral part of Indian worship and world view, destroyed it as best they could. As ruthlessly as they pursued the policy of cultural genocide, they were not entirely successful. A number of Indian tribes have retained their early music and dance rituals, and archaeological diggings reveal that the Spanish weren't able to destroy all their instruments. The Aztec played whistles, flutes, drums and other percussion instruments, gourd rattles, and bells made of deer bones and shells. Whistles and flutes were made of baked clay, drums and bells of wood and hides. Today, replicas can be purchased in markets and handicraft shops around the country (especially in areas where Indian groups still play traditional music), or in Mexico City at the *Bazar Sábado* (Saturday Marketplace) and San Jacinto Plaza. Of the Indian tribes that still use traditional music, perhaps the Seri of Sonora are the most prominent. Seri medicine men play the primary role in creating songs (in earlier times priests and warriors would have predominated), but hunters and fishermen sing for luck, and men, women, and children sing about all their daily activities. In addition, some people sing their own personal songs, which they have invented themselves and no one else sings.

If the Spanish failed in their goal to completely destroy Indian culture, it was in good part because the Spanish priests and monks recognized that conversions would be easier if the Indians were allowed to transfer their ceremonial use of music from Indian deities to Christian ones. The result was one of the most startling compromises in religious history, evident today in any town with a fair Indian population. It is not unusual to see brilliantly clad Indian dancers, accompanied by flute and drum players, performing in front of — and sometimes inside — Catholic churches. While this does not take place during the Mass, it is a well-established practice that in no way is disrespectful. A little gaiety has been injected into religion, but the intent is no less serious.

The guitar is one Spanish innovation that the Mexicans adopted whole-heartedly. It is the single most popular instrument in Mexico, and most men fancy themselves at least modest troubadours. Sometimes a group of young men get together to serenade their girlfriends. Such a serenade is called the *gallo,* Spanish for rooster, since the serenade takes place at the hour the roosters begin to crow. Tradition dictates that a young woman so honored cannot turn on a light or let herself be seen.

Amorous young men who lack good singing voices can hire professionals to croon to their loves. A rich man in Guadalajara caused a sensation once when he hired the entire *Russian Cossack Chorus* (which happened to be in town) to sing to his woman. Most folks, however, are content to hire a group of musicians called mariachis. These performers wear costumes similar to those of the *charro* (gentleman cowboy): bolero-style jackets, tight pants, and wide-brimmed hats — all trimmed with silver buttons and embroidery; they also wear pointy-toed boots and a pistol in a fancy holster, usually hanging at the hip. The group normally features a vocalist accompanied by at least one guitar, one or two trumpets, some violins, a *guitarrón* (a large guitar-like instrument), a bass, and a *güiro,* which is similar to a banjo. There was a time when mariachis were hired not only for serenading lovers, but for almost any special occasion — weddings, anniversaries, and *quinceaños* (a girl's 15th birthday in Mexico, which is celebrated much like a 16-year-old girl's in the US). Today, its repertoire is predictable, including such sentimental love songs as the popular "Si Estás Dormida," which begins: "If you are asleep, my love, awake and listen to the voice of one who loves you." If a husband or boyfriend arranges a serenade for a woman's birthday, the favored time for the serenade is the wee hours of the morning, from 2 to 4 AM. There is even a special love song, "Las Mañanitas," for the occasion. No one in Mexico would think of complaining about being awakened by a mariachi.

Nowadays, unfortunately, hiring mariachis has become prohibitively expensive for most Mexicans; so they content themselves with requesting a special song or two at a local bar or restaurant, where a mariachi band is performing. Two of the best places to hear and to hire mariachis is Garibaldi Plaza in Mexico City, where they collect by the hundreds, or in the Plaza de Mariachis, in Guadalajara. On the zocalo of most Mexican cities, you'll usually find a few wandering mariachi groups for hire.

There are almost as many different kinds of songs as there are singers in Mexico. There are primitive songs, which are much richer in imagery and content than many written now, and religious songs, which range from traditional hymns to *pastorelas,* a form of religious opera particularly popular during the *Christmas* season. *Rancheras,* a kind of Mexican country-and-western music, are favorites, as are the songs of the early revolutions, like "La Cucaracha." One of the most beloved of all revolutionary songs, "Adelita," is named after a woman who followed her lover into war. When women of good families became *soldaderas* of their own accord or were carried off by officers, they came to be known as Adelitas.

The Mexican ballads, or *corridos,* are a great deal of fun. In the days before newspapers and radio, *corridos* were often the only source of information for country people. In the tradition of oral storytelling, they imparted all the latest gossip and news of disaster or revolution, heroic exploits, and bandits' raids. The *corrido* singer would learn the items of general interest and relate them to an eager audience at the marketplace. The more sophisticated singers had printers make up leaflets of the songs and would then sell them for a few centavos each. The *corridos,* which reflect the character of the people in their stoicism, pathos, humor, and mockery, were especially popular during the 1910 revolution. At that time one of the favorite subjects was the colorful adventures of Pancho Villa. It is a pity that, with improved communications, only a few of the classic *corridos* are still sung.

In the mid-19th century, the accordion, polka, and waltz were brought to northern Mexico by thousands of Eastern Europeans and Germans, whom the Mexican government, anxious to stave off an increasing American presence and influence, had encouraged to immigrate. As the Eastern European and German folk traditions began to blend with the native Indian culture, a new lively style of music was created. Called *norteña* or Tex-Mex music (due to its origin along the Texas border), it is mostly played with a *bajo sexto* (12-string guitar, not to be confused with the American 12-string, which has lighter strings) and the button accordion. This new style integrated the sound of the traditional *corrido* with the lively, repetitive rhythmic patterns of the waltz and polka. Today it is a major form of music in the border area. When a *norteña* tune has words, they are sung by two male voices, a practice that protects each singer from any humiliation if he happens to sing off-key.

During the initial stages of popularity, *norteña* was considered lewd and risqué. It was heard only in red-light districts, where roving bands played for what few pesos they could solicit. Over the years, however, Tex-Mex has gained recognition as reputable, get-down dance music. Now it can be heard at family barbecues and community dances in border towns where the tradition has managed to survive from generation to generation.

Mexico also has all the modern music from all over the world. Many of the top songs in the US also become favorites in Mexico; sometimes translations can be mildly hilarious. Hard rock is played in discotheques throughout Mexico, but there are also many symphony orchestras, chamber music groups, opera companies, and concerts of all types. Mexicans love music of all kinds.

There is another typical Mexican musical custom that one hears all day long — the street musicians. They range from bands with a *tambora* (drum) that come in from the surrounding pueblos to play a concert on the corner and pick up a few pesos, to a soloist playing a violin or other stringed instrument on the streets in hope of picking up money. Strolling marimba groups stop under the windows of promising-looking apartment buildings, and organ-grinders and guitar players walk into restaurants or onto buses to serenade prospective clients. Street salesmen toot whistles (sometimes conch shells) or just sing out the wares they are selling. There is indeed music in the air in Mexico.

Mexican dance is as diversified as Mexican music. The Aztec shared the

Chinese belief that song and dance kept the world in motion and nature predisposed in favor of man. They danced a lot — to woo their gods and to earn luck in hunting, marriage, war, harvest, and just about every human activity under the sun. The most beautiful and powerful of dances performed today are pre–Spanish conquest in origin, perhaps because the Aztec and Maya never danced frivolously, but only to communicate with their gods. An example of early dance that has survived well — if undoubtedly changed — is the *voladores,* the flying pole dance, one of the most spectacular sights a visitor can see in Mexico. There is a certain mysticism about the *voladores* that is semireligious in nature and dates back to pre-Aztec times. Although in recent years a metal pole has been used, the festivities traditionally begin with a search for a very tall, straight, and strong tree. When it is found, the men of the village offer a prayer to Pulic-Minlab, the god of trees, sprinkle some brandy or other spirits at the base of the tree to deaden its pain, and cut it down; it is then carried carefully back to the village, where a hole is dug and food for the tree placed in the hole to give it strength to support the fliers. The tree is placed upright, and a small revolving platform, large enough to hold five men, is put around the top. Four ropes, fastened to the top, are wound around the pole, and a ladder of strong vines is attached so the men can climb to the top.

Five men take part in the ceremony; one is a musician and the other four are fliers. They all climb to the top of the pole and the musician plays and dances, while the four fliers crouch on the edge of the platform. Then each of the four men ties the end of one of the ropes around his body, and all four leap out into space. The pole must be high enough for the fliers to make 13 revolutions before they reach the ground. This represents the cycle of 52 years, divided into 4 epochs of 13 each; 52 years is the ancient equivalent of the century — the period of time after which the world is born anew. Some of the fliers dress as birds; others wear a crest of feathers. The flying pole dance can be seen on Sundays at El Tajín archaeological site near Papantla, Veracruz; at Papantla, during the feast of *Corpus Christi;* in Mexico City on the esplanade of the *Museum of Anthropology;* and in Acapulco and Taxco.

Like the *voladores,* which is a religious ritual and dance (though its specific significance has been lost for more than a century), most traditional Mexican dances were religious in origin and purpose; now, however, almost all are secular and are performed at fiestas or for the sheer delight of dancing. As in many other folk dance traditions, men dominate, though women participate.

The deer dance of the Yaqui Indians is a favorite all over Mexico. Originally performed to court luck in hunting, it is now featured at many religious fiestas and ceremonies in northern Yaqui country and elsewhere. This exciting dance pantomimes the chase and killing of a deer, with all the dancers portraying animals with amazing realism. Another favorite is the Sandunga dance from Tehuantepec, which is known for its beautiful music.

One of the few very colorful dances introduced after the conquest is the Moors and the Christians, often called *los moros.* The Spaniards lost no time in introducing this dance in the form of sham battles on horseback and even took part in them at bullfights and other celebrations. Half the dancers dress as Moors, wearing black masks, and half as Christians. *Los moros* has been performed in heroic proportions, with 1,000 men on each side, but since 1910 the drama has been reduced to a dozen protagonists on each side. It remains one of the most widespread of ritual dances today, especially popular around the Federal District and central states.

The *jarabe tapatío,* or Mexican hat dance, is typical of music written especially for certain dances, although many of them have words. This popular heel-toe national folk dance is recognized by many people who have never been to Mexico. Other dance rhythms are the *sones,* a mixture of Indian, black, and Spanish tempos; and the *huapangos,* which have a more languorous rhythm and are often hauntingly sad.

While many a traveler would delight in seeing these dances performed as they always have been, in the simple village setting, this is usually not possible. Various folklore groups perform the dances throughout the country, the most famous and most accessible one being the *Ballet Folklórico* in Mexico City. One doesn't have to be a dance buff to be enthralled by their performance every Wednesday and Sunday at the *Bellas Artes* in Mexico City (see "Nightclubs and Nightlife" in *Mexico City,* THE CITIES).

The Bullfight

 Hemingway said there are two kinds of spectators at a bullfight: those who identify with the bull and those who identify with the matador. The first group cannot hope to enjoy a bullfight and never will. People who endow animals with human qualities should avoid this spectacle. While bullfighting is certainly a part of the culture of Mexico — almost every young boy in Mexico wants to grow up to be either a soccer player or a matador — don't go if you feel an aversion to the whole thing. There are plenty of other activities to fill Sunday afternoons.

However, some people who find the idea of bullfighting anathema actually enjoy the reality. They are seduced by the pageantry and drama, the bravery and artistry of the bullfight. They have even been known to cheer in spite of themselves.

In deciding to see a bullfight, remember that the fighting bulls, *toros bravos,* are a special breed. They bear as much resemblance to domestic bulls as a timber wolf does to a collie. They are bred for battle, and they fight because it is their nature, not out of fear or hapless panic. They are tested at the age of 2 to determine their willingness to charge without being annoyed. Bulls that don't pass the test don't get into the ring of an experienced matador. And that is another aspect to consider; the better and bigger the fight, the less gratuitous gore and carnage. The best matadors fight only the best bulls, and the excitement, challenge, and contest are at a maximum. Fighting bulls are mammoth animals, with immense power and strength, and an unflagging will that makes them dangerous opponents right up to the moment of the kill. They are reared carefully and destined only for the battle in the bullring and inevitable death.

Historically, the bullfight has a nobler beginning than another Mexican favorite, soccer, which derives from tossing about the head of a conquered foe. The earliest bullfights were celebrated on the island of Crete in the Mediterranean long before the golden age of Greece or the birth of Christ. They were introduced into Spain by the Moors around the 12th century, and with the conquest of Mexico the Spaniards in turn lost no time in bringing bullfighting to Mexico. Eight years after the conquest, on August 13, 1529, the first bullfight was held in Mexico.

In the beginning, bullfighting was the prerogative of the aristocracy. Noblemen armed with short lances fought the bull from horseback. Accidents were so common that in 1567 Pope Pius V threatened to excommunicate all princes who permitted bullfighting. In the early 18th century bullfighting was taken over by the professionals — where, happily, it remains today.

If you decide to go to a bullfight, be punctual. Half the beauty of the bullfight is the preliminary pageantry. In Mexico City and the larger cities throughout the country, the bullfights begin promptly at 4 PM; the best fights are held during the winter season, from November through February. A complete bullfight will have six bulls and three men. The matador with the most seniority will have the first and fourth bulls, the next man the second and fifth, and the man with the least experience the third bull and the last bull. Sometimes, if a matador has had a particularly bad afternoon, he will fight a gift bull, which he pays for himself, as the seventh bull of the day.

The elaborate ceremony of the bullfight has not altered much through the centuries. It opens with the *desfile,* or starting parade. Then a rider on horseback, the alguacil, emerges from a gate, rides across the ring, salutes the authorities, and asks permission to begin the spectacle. This rider, dressed in black, returns to the portal from which he came and the parade begins. The alguacil leads off, followed closely by the three matadors, walking side by side. Their costumes, or "suits of light," are tight fitting and beautifully embroidered with silver or gold thread. Their assistants, called banderilleros, walk behind them in similar but less costly uniforms. By comparison, the picadors, the mounted lancers, appear most businesslike in yellow breeches, velvet jackets, and frilled shirts. The picadors are followed by lesser ring attendants. The team of mules that eventually drags away the dead bull concludes the parade.

The ring is cleared, the crowd hushed, the *presidente* waves a handkerchief, and a trumpet announces the first bull. As the bull rushes into the ring a barb is dropped into the hide of the animal.

Bullfights have three *tercios* (thirds), like acts in a play. Each one has its own particular character, action, and a tension that builds from *tercio* to *tercio,* culminating in the end of the third act. The bullfight begins playfully. During the first act the banderilleros run the bull to test his behavior. He is least dangerous at this time, charging quickly but wildly. The matador stands behind a wooden barrier and observes the bull, watching how it uses its horns, how it moves, and its peculiarities. He then handles the bull himself. If the animal is lively, he may indulge in a series of veronicas, a two-handed pass, with the heavy cerise-and-gold fighting cape.

Following these preliminaries, the horses come in, the bull is poked with a long pointed pole by the man on horseback called the picador; the matador then lures the bull away from the horse and does more capework (called *quite,* from the Spanish verb *quitar,* which means to take away or remove, which is exactly what he is doing — taking the bull away from the horse). During this phase of the drama the matador uses a heavy gold silk cape. The pass he almost always uses at the very beginning, when he is first facing the bull, is the veronica. The matador profiles himself to the bull holding one end of the cape in front of himself and extending the other end with either his right or left arm. A good pass is smooth and flowing, with the bull passing by and the matador moving nothing but his arms. If the matador is jumpy, or the pass jerky, the pass is considered poor work.

The second *tercio* begins with the clearing of the ring, leaving the bull alone with an assistant to the matador who must place banderillas in the bull's skin. These are 26-inch wooden poles that end in vicious, harpoon-like barbs that are thrust as accurately as possible into the bull's hump — the purpose being to weaken that huge tangle of muscles that controls the bull's head, forcing the bull to keep its head lowered, facilitating the kill in the final *tercio*.

The final act of the fight is the most important, the one in which the matador does his bravest and most artistic work and the bull dies. The matador exchanges the large cape of earlier *tercios* for a small muleta, a piece of red flannel (the color red does not inflame bulls; it is the movement of the cape that excites the animal — bulls are color-blind). The matador by now is familiar with the bull and its charges, and will have decided exactly what kinds of passes to use in the last flourish. If he feels the bull has been weakened too much by the pic and barbs, he will fight it *"por arriba,"* passing the muleta over the bull's horns to keep its head up. If the bull is still strong, he will fight it *"por abajo,"* dragging the cape along the ground to lower the animal's head. The work done with the muleta is called the matador's faena, and usually, if the bull is at all suitable, will be done *por abajo*. It is not unusual for an artistic fighter confronted with a good bull to lead the animal in a complete circle with one fluid, beautiful movement. The matador will do a series of passes — from three to a dozen — that end with a concluding *paso de pecho,* the chest pass, when the bull's horns seem almost to scrape the chest of the matador. When the matador decides the bull is slowing down, he goes in for the killing pass.

Don't be disappointed if you don't see a great variety of showy passes — this is not the sign of a bad matador. Sometimes a poor matador uses fancy passes to cover up his lack of skill. The intelligent matador may use only two or three different passes in his entire faena, if these are the only passes suitable to the bull's style. Watch how the matador works the bull. If he stands close to the bull, doesn't jump back when the horns almost graze his body, passes the bull smoothly, dominates it while staying out of trouble, you are seeing a good fight.

At the end of a good fight, the matador will be called to the center of the ring to take a bow. If he has done a very good job, the audience will wave white handkerchiefs, which is a petition to the judge to award an ear to the matador. Depending on the quality of the fight, the judge will award one or two ears. If the fight has been truly extraordinary, the matador will be given both ears and the tail. When the triumphant matador takes his tour of the ring, it is customary to throw hats, jackets, flowers, and wine flasks to him. Never throw a cushion. It is an insult and it is also against the law.

Spanish writers fondly refer to "His Majesty, the Bull," and the importance of the beast to the success of the bullfight cannot be overemphasized. Bulls that are too small, too weak, or too difficult in style ruin a fight, no matter how gifted the matador. More often than not, when you see a bad fight, it is because the bulls have been poor.

Bullfighting, like all sports, is appreciated more fully as the spectator becomes more knowledgeable. The nuances of style and artistry cannot be immediately discerned. And as Hemingway observed in *Death in the Afternoon:* "Bullfighting is the only art . . . in which the degree of brilliance in the performance is left to the fighter's honor."

There are two seasons in bullfighting: the big or formal season (*corridas formales*), with full matadors; and the little season (*novilladas*), when the novices fight. In the northern border towns of Mexico the big season is in the summer, but in the rest of the country, it is in the winter months. During the formal season, there are usually some Spanish matadors in Mexico, for there are no bullfights in Spain between October and *Easter.*

Several top young matadors in Mexico, who are in their 20s and 30s, are Miguel Espinoza, Jr. ("Armillita"), and the Capetillo brothers — Manuel and Guillermo. These men can look forward to many more years in the ring, for the average bullfighter retires in his 40s. Some of the old guard, though, including Manolo Martínez, Eloy Cabazos, and Curro Rivera, are still going strong. Together with soccer players, bullfighters are the heroes of Mexico. While some Mexican women have been know to test their skills in the bullring, there are, alas, no women matadors of note, for bullfighting remains a truly macho preserve.

Although there are usually some covered seats (called *palcos*) in bullrings in larger cities, most seats are out in the open, and it is important to ask for seats on the shady side of the ring (*la sombra*) to avoid being uncomfortably exposed.

THE CITIES

ACAPULCO

(pronounced Ah-ca-*pul*-co)

The mere mention of Acapulco usually causes a string of extravagant images to come to mind. Whether or not you consider these superlatives justified, Acapulco's reputation as an international beach resort borders on legendary. Throughout the year, and especially in the winter, tourists from all over the world descend on this hotel-lined gem of a bay facing the Pacific Ocean, generating a momentum that is in itself a kind of homage to this resort's reputation.

How you personally feel about Acapulco will depend, in large part, on your reaction to the sheer number of tourists around you — almost 5 million people visited Acapulco last year. It is definitely not a place for "getting away from it all," if by that you mean getting away from all the other people who are also trying to get away from it all. It is not, in fact, a place where you can get away from much of anything, except the rest of the world's rotten weather and your own daily routine. But if you don't mind sharing the pleasures of the sun — and the flesh — with lots of other similarly inclined folk, the beaches and pools in and around Acapulco can be among the most compelling tourist destinations in the Western Hemisphere.

The prime reason anyone comes to Acapulco is the weather — that perfect weather that simply can't be duplicated in any sun-drenched spot within the same distance of the United States. When a winter-paled body makes its hegira to Acapulco, it knows it's going to return home beautifully browned, sporting an even tan devoid of imperfections.

It is possible to enjoy Acapulco without getting into a hectic round of nightclubs, discos, and parties. You can get up early in the morning and have the eastern beaches all to yourself, although it's common to joke that the only people in Acapulco who get up early in the morning are those who go deep-sea fishing. (*A sun warning:* Be very careful if you have sensitive skin. Two hours on an Acapulco beach in the morning can roast you; to say nothing of the afternoon, when the sun is even stronger.)

In the afternoon, it's far better to take a siesta between 1 and 4 PM. Even Acapulco residents stay out of the sun in the middle of the afternoon. In late afternoon, watch the sunset while sipping tequila concoctions. Places like Pie de la Cuesta beach, just outside town, are traditional dusk headquarters, though in recent years they've become inundated by native peddlers so you'll now have to venture farther off to escape the harassment of vendors and beggars. After dusk, return to your hotel and get ready for a quiet, leisurely dinner. Acapulco doesn't have to be frenetic.

But for most of the people who come here, Acapulco means party. A lot of people, Mexican as well as foreign, wouldn't be caught anywhere near a beach until one or two in the afternoon, after they've had a chance to sleep off the night before. The afternoon beach used to be Los Hornos, and the morning beach, Caleta, but times have changed. Caleta is not as classy (or as clean) as it used to be, and the action has moved farther east, from Los Hornos to La Condesa, which is the stretch of beach between the *El Presidente* and the *Hyatt Continental* hotels.

The are two things to heed on this stretch of beach: the Pacific Ocean, which can easily toss you upside down, and the swarm of vendors of all ages who work the strip. The surf, however, never discriminates. At Condesa, things don't get going until noon and don't really start swinging until after one in the afternoon. Lunch is served around 2 PM. Take your time. People don't start drifting back to the beach until late afternoon. Dinner in Acapulco is served around 9 or 10 PM.

More than any other Mexican city, Acapulco reeks of sensuality. This, too, accounts for its popularity. Acapulco's sexiness is part of its legend, and one of the first things you're almost bound to notice is that no one ever wears more than bathing trunks or a bikini during the day. People are constantly flaunting their bodies, even on the city's buses or in supermarkets.

At night, the sounds of tropical guitar and rock music drift through the air, mingling with the sounds of the ocean, the leaves blowing in the soft, humid wind, and the murmur of gentle conversations. There is something languorous in the air, and it can prove disastrous to one's inhibitions. In addition to mellowing people, the sexual atmosphere serves to level differences in social class. There's no way to tell the difference between a genuine jet setter and an Oklahoma secretary or Omaha insurance salesman when everything is pared down to the bare essentials. You can get down to basics very quickly in Acapulco.

The spectacular beauty of Acapulco's bay has been appreciated for centuries, but for years the isolation of the area kept the city from participating in much of Mexico's history. It was founded in 1530 by the Spanish, who cut a sort of horse path through the rugged mountains to it from Mexico City. Today, the drive takes 5½ hours on a road that was blasted through the mountains in 1955. It used to take weeks.

A few years after Acapulco was settled, the Spanish built two boats and began sailing up and down the coast making charts of the shoreline. By 1565, they learned (thanks to Magellan) that it was possible to sail east from Spain and reach Mexico. Trade routes from the Orient to Mexico were opened, and Acapulco's beautiful harbor came into its own. Luxury items such as silk, porcelain, and ivory were transported by boat from China and Japan to Acapulco, then transported by mule train to Mexico City. From the capital, they were sent on to Veracruz for trans-shipment to Spain. Acapulco soon grew to about 10,000 people (it has more than 1.7 million residents today), but this profitable trade did not go unnoticed by the English pirates. The infamous Sir Francis Drake, among others, began to prey on the Spanish galleons. Acapulco's Fort of San Diego was constructed to defend the port city against pirate raids. Destroyed in 1776 by an earthquake, it was rebuilt and still stands today.

After Mexico's War of Independence in 1810, trade with the Orient ceased. Acapulco was a forgotten fishing village until a paved road was finally built from Mexico City in 1922, but even then it took another 10 years for it to get its first tentative start as a beach resort. An international port city since 1945, it really came into its own toward the end of the 1950s, when it began to be known as "The Riviera of the West."

Since then, Acapulco's reputation as a resort has dipped and soared like the water-skiers-cum-parachutists who take off from Condesa beach. At the moment, it is on a plateau after several years of decline — decline due in part, at least, to the studied opinion of the world's well-heeled travelers that Acapulco was no longer a prime choice among the world's most stylish tropical destinations. The rich and famous still go to Acapulco — they go religiously every winter to soak up sun in their villas in the surrounding hills — but they just don't talk about it the way they used to. More important, the stress of coping with such huge numbers of visitors (and the concomitant growth of the resident population, making Acapulco one of the fastest-growing cities in the world) overtaxed the city's resources.

Several years ago, the Mexican government invested $300 million in restoring and revitalizing Acapulco and the surrounding area. A superhighway, scheduled to be completed by this year, joins Cuernavaca and Acapulco, cutting driving time from Mexico City to 3½ hours. Acapulco's main street, Costera Miguel Alemán, is now a well-maintained seaside avenue, and beaches are better than they've been. The government has made a real effort, literally and figuratively, to clean up its act and to solve the problem of constant harassment by street and beach vendors. At press time, the beach around the bay was being cleaned each morning — as were the streets — and the peddlers were being kept away; the hope is these efforts will continue. The state and municipal governments have set up open-air markets on vacant lots around the city; though the markets aren't attractive, they have helped get many vendors off the streets and beaches — for a time at least. Uniformed "tourist police" also have begun to patrol the Costera and to provide visitors with information. There is still room for improvement, especially in town and up in the mountains, where the majority of people live in substandard conditions. Still, there is too much about Acapulco to be prized and protected for the city to lose its luster entirely. You have only to look down on the city at dusk from the heights of a casita in the luxurious *Las Brisas* hotel complex to appreciate that you are in a unique place. The lights flicker like pearls on an endless necklace, and the dark water provides a muted reflection of the blinking brightness. Outside town, only the most blasé can turn down a ride on an Indian pony down the Revolcadero Beach and beyond.

It may be that Acapulco can regain its former place at the top of the pedestal of resorts that appeal to determined hedonists. Surely if money alone could cure overdevelopment, the city would already be all the way back to its former preeminence. The physical surroundings remain awesomely appealing: Just look at those green mountains rising from the white, sandy beaches surrounding the blue bay on three sides, and listen to the palm trees rustling in the Pacific wind. Add to this more than 300 hotels of every description, dozens of restaurants, nightclubs, discotheques, and beaches with skin diving, snorkeling, water skiing, parasailing, and swimming, and you have Acapulco — a very tempting tropical resort.

ACAPULCO AT-A-GLANCE

 SEEING THE CITY: The setting is magnificent, for Acapulco is built where the mountains meet the sea. The first breathtaking view for most people appears at the high point of the hill above the southern border of the city (at the entrance to *Las Brisas* hotel), while driving in from the airport. (The road is known, for good reason, as the Scenic Highway.) And almost every hotel balcony offers an unforgettable view. For a special look, try dining at one of the high-rise, roof-garden restaurants, or go parasailing. The nicest time to soak in the scenery is at sunset, when the sky turns bright pink and gold, the city lights begin to twinkle, and the first stars come out.

 SPECIAL PLACES: These days the action in Acapulco centers along the Costera Miguel Alemán, the broad avenue that runs along the bay. To the left (as you face the ocean) beyond the southwestern headland is Puerto Marqués and then the open sea and the fashionable *Acapulco Princess* and *Pierre Marqués* hotels. To the right is Caleta, where many of the first hotels were built, and still operate, albeit many in rather run-down fashion now. Since the sea is Acapulco's prime attraction, look first at the beaches. Remember that there are no private beaches in Mexico. All are federal property, and the hotels have no jurisdiction over them. Itinerant vendors are everywhere on the popular beaches, and their petitions can be wearisome, but for safety's sake it's best to avoid completely isolated beaches.

Barra Vieja – A long stretch of beach about 24 miles (38 km) southeast of Acapulco, where the Tres Palos lagoon meets the Pacific. The water on the Pacific side is too treacherous for swimming, but small boats are available for exploring the lagoon, which is fringed with palm and banana trees and populated by tropical birds. *Pescado a la talla* (whole fish charbroiled on a spit) is said to have originated here, and is available at any one of the small restaurants along the beach.

Caleta – Back in the days before air conditioning, when the best hotels were built on the adjacent hillside to catch the breeze, this is where everyone began his day. Caleta was the morning beach. It's not so elegant now, and some segments are polluted, although it does attract the traditionalists and those who like their ocean as calm as a pond. Here the thing to do is rent an inner tube and just paddle around. Popular with children is the small aquarium here, which was opened in 1990 to attract more visitors to this end of town.

La Condesa – Running from the *Hyatt Continental* to *El Presidente* hotels, this is the most tourist-infested stretch of sand these days. It's also where the scantiest bikinis are found. One section of the beach is reserved for gays. La Condesa has the most pounding surf on the bay, and up by the Costera are a number of nice luncheon spots with music for dancing.

Los Hornos – Near the docks, this was once the fashionable spot for late-afternoon sunbathers. The water here is calmer, though not very clean; *palapa*-topped eateries line the beach.

Icacos – The first stretch of true Acapulco Bay beach as you drive in from the airport. Here the sheltered waters are calm and quiet and the beach less hectic. *La Palapa* and the *Hyatt Regency* hotels share the sands.

Laguna de Coyuca – A little way beyond Pie de la Cuesta, this primitive freshwater lagoon is a bird sanctuary bordered by coconut palms and full of water hyacinths. The waters teem with catfish, mullet, and snook. The *Maebba Beach Club* offers a tour including transportation to and from Acapulco proper; a visit to a coconut, pineapple, or banana plantation; a half-hour boat trip on the Coyuca Lagoon; lunch; and a few hours at the club — all for about $22 (phone: 858515).

Pie de la Cuesta – More and more foreign tourists are coming to know about it, so it's no longer the private turf of Acapulco regulars. Swimming is dangerous at this beach 5 miles (8 km) west of the city proper, but it's a wonderful place to order a *coco loco* (perhaps at *Steve's Hideaway*), cuddle up in a hammock, and cement friendships as the sun goes down. Continue to *Club de Playa Maebba,* where visitors can enjoy a buffet and use the pool, tennis court and hammocks for a small fee. There's also *Cadenas Ski Club* which offers water skiing, jungle boat rides with delicious meals.

Revolcadero – Out in front of the *Acapulco Princess* and *Pierre Marqués* hotels, and off to either side as well. A favorite of the rich and pampered. Revolcadero is on the open Pacific and is great for body surfing. Indian ponies are available for those who enjoy a canter on the sand. Head even farther south to Barra Vieja, where the Tres Palos Lagoon meets the ocean, to find genuine peace and quiet and to enjoy *pescado a la talla* (whole fish charbroiled on a spit) at *Beto's.* Beware of the sometimes vicious undertow.

Roqueta – The uninhabited island across from Caleta has a beach populated by beer-drinking donkeys; it has a certain vague Robinson Crusoe charm. Boats ferry bathers over from and to Caleta throughout the day. There is a direct route as well as a more scenic one, which takes 45 minutes; buy tickets from the kiosk on the beach. Snorkeling and windsurfing are good, and there are boards for rent.

Calandrias – These little horse-drawn carriages, decorated with brightly colored balloons, run up and down the Costera Miguel Alemán, the avenue that skirts the bay. The standard ride is a tour of the town, but *calandrias* also can be hired as taxis. If you're not in a hurry (and who is in Mexico?), they are more fun, albeit more expensive.

Centro Internacional Acapulco – What was formerly the convention center has been completely remodeled and renamed, and is once again a center of urban activity. For evening, entertainment there are folkloric performances in the plaza Mondays through Saturdays ($35 includes dinner and open bar), along with the *Disco Laser* restaurant (no cover charge), a movie theater, and occasional special productions in the *Juan Ruiz Alarcón* theater. 4455 Costera Miguel Alemán (phone: 847050).

Cici Park – On the beach, across the street from the *Embassy* hotel, this small, well-maintained amusement park has trained dolphins and seals, a pool with manmade waves, two water toboggans, three dolphin shows daily, several bars and restaurants (including a gigantic seafood restaurant), a beach club (accessible from the beach), and seagoing motorcycles. There is also a day-care center where infants and young children will be entertained and cared for by experts while parents play (phone: 841970).

Diego Rivera Mural – A spectacular and little-known mural by one of Mexico's most famous artists surrounds a private home up in the hills of Acapulco. The house is not open to the public, but the mural may be seen by taking the road that leads up to the *Casablanca* hotel (at the gas station about 4 blocks past the zocalo). Bear left at the fork and keep going up; it shouldn't be missed.

Divers – The Acapulco divers, or *clavadistas,* perform mainly at night. They plunge from a 150-foot cliff into a shallow inlet, and each dive must be perfectly timed to coincide with a wave coming in or the diver risks being crushed on the jagged rocks. There is no trick to it, nor are they in any way faking. The exhibition takes place on the cliffs of La Quebrada, adjoining the *Playa las Glorias El Mirador* hotel. Viewers can sit on the terrace or in the hotel's *La Perla* nightclub and have a drink while watching, or pay a small admission to get closer, but it is a spectacle worth seeing at least once. Shows (one dive per show) at 1, 7:15, 8:15, and 10, and 10:30 PM with torch processions. La Quebrada (phone: 831155).

Flea Market – That's what the locals call it (try saying it with authentic Spanish pronunciation) and it's where handicrafts and Mexican curios are sold. The Flea

Market is about 5 blocks from the zocalo and the way is well marked with signs. It's a a good place to browse and bargain. Open daily.

El Fuerte de San Diego (Fort San Diego) – The most historic spot in Acapulco, it was built centuries ago to protect what was then a major port from pirate attacks. Here the insurgents defeated the royalists in the early 1800s. It has been converted into an interesting museum dedicated to the history of Acapulco from pre-Hispanic times through the conquest of the southern seas, trade with the Orient, piracy, and the war of independence from Spain. Closed Mondays. Admission charge. The fort is a few blocks to the left of the zocalo, just across from the piers and customs house (phone: 823828).

Papagayo Park – On the grounds of the old *Papagayo* hotel, this delightful 60-acre park straddling Costera Miguel Alemán has cable cars, bumper cars, a Ferris wheel, carousel, artificial lake, boats, small zoo, and lakeside restaurant.

Plaza Juan Alvarez (The Zocalo) – Getting away from the beaches, this is the heart of Acapulco proper, the main plaza near the piers and docks for deep-sea fishing boats. The zocalo is dominated by the Acapulco Cathedral, an oddity built in 1930 with Byzantine towers and a mosque-like dome. Opposite, at the waterfront, stands a monument to national heroes Guerrero, Morelos, Hidalgo, Juárez, and Cuauhtémoc.

Puerto Marqués Village – About 8 miles (13 km) east of the center of the city, along the Carretera Escénica (the Scenic Highway), past *Las Brisas,* where the jet setters sequester themselves in villas with private swimming pools and descend only for an occasional jaunt into town in *Las Brisas*' famous pink jeeps. At the traffic circle just past *Las Brisas* (in the direction of the airport), turn right and you'll find yourself in the fishing village of Puerto Marqués, where the bay is so calm it hardly shows a ripple. You can rent paddle, sail, and water-ski boats. There are also many seafood restaurants lining the beach and the opposite side of the road. *Pipo's,* one of the best (see *Eating Out*), has a small marina with fishing boats for hire. Punta Diamante, the adjacent headland, is slated to be the next major resort and condominium complex in the area (though at press time, work had barely begun).

Yacht Cruises – One of the best ways to go sightseeing in Acapulco is on the water. Several motor yachts and a catamaran make the 3½-hour cruise around Acapulco Bay, Puerto Marqués, and the La Quebrada cliffs, with a running commentary on the way, for about $35, including lunch or dinner, disco dancing, open bar (local drinks only), and a show in the evening. There are moonlight cruises, even when there's no moon, which include an open bar and performances by Argentine dancers for about $12. The *Bonanza* and *Fiesta Cabaret* offer morning and afternoon trips, as well as starlight cruises (the stars are almost always out) that include an open bar, music, and dancing; evening departure time is 10:30 PM and return is at 1 AM (phone: 822055). *Divers de Mexico* runs a 3-hour champagne sunset cruise with a show provided by the divers at La Quebrada, as well as a daytime *Buccaneer* cruise with the crew dressed up as pirates, each for about $25 (phone: 821397/98). No-frills cruises leave at 11 AM and 4:30 PM and cost about $10. A shorter ride can be taken in the glass-bottom boats that leave Caleta all day long and pass over the underwater Shrine of Our Lady of Guadalupe. Tickets for yacht cruises are available at hotel tour desks.

■**EXTRA SPECIAL:** Costa Chica, the 136-mile stretch of coast southeast of Aca-
pulco, is lined by a paved road that is passable most of the year. (During the rainy months, sections occasionally get washed out.) The road runs through dramatic, uninhabited terrain of lagoons and rocky cliffs. Along this route, in the shadow of the Sierra Madre, several rivers run into the sea. South of the small mining village of Ometepec, Cuajinicuilapa (about 140 miles — 224 km — from Acapulco) is inhabited by the descendants of Bantu tribespeople who were brought to the New World as slaves. The road continues all the way to Guatemala.

SOURCES AND RESOURCES

 TOURIST INFORMATION: Contact the State Tourist Office (Centro Internacional Acapulco; phone: 847050). It's large and the staff is extremely helpful. The consumer protection bureau, in the same building, can aid in ironing out disputes (phone: 846136). They're open from 9 AM to 10 PM daily. A smaller, but much more helpful, Federal Tourist Office is at Hornos Beach (187 Costera Miguel Alemán; phone: 851041); and several information kiosks line the Costera. There is also an Acapulco Tourist Office (10 Privada Roca Sola; phone: 847621 or 847630).

Local Coverage – The tobacco shop in the *Acapulco Plaza* and most of the other classier hotels sell the *International Herald Tribune,* the *Los Angeles Times, The New York Times, USA Today,* and the English-language *News,* published in Mexico City. They're also available at *Sanborn's* (Costera Miguel Alemán) for considerably less than the hotels normally charge. *Acapulco News* and *Adventure in Acapulco,* local weekly and monthly publications respectively, give tips in English on local happenings.

 TELEPHONE: The area code for Acapulco is 74. When calling calling from one city to another within Mexico, dial 9l before the area code.

 CLIMATE AND CLOTHES: Expect beach weather all year with temperatures generally in the 80s or 90s during the day and in the 70s or 80s at night. Expect some rain, mostly in the form of afternoon showers, from June through September. Whenever you come, bring lots of sunscreen. Dress is casual during the day, and upscale resortwear is worn in most restaurants and nightclubs in the evening.

 GETTING AROUND: Airport Limousine – Limos take five passengers to a car. You can pick one up when you get off the plane and have one pick you up at your hotel. They run about half the price of a private cab (phone: 852227 or 852332).

Bus – Buses run up and down the Costera all the way from Puerto Marqués to La Caleta Beach and are inexpensive. With newer vehicles in operation, service is much improved — but do watch out for pickpockets when it's crowded.

Taxi – Acapulco cabs don't have meters, which means that you have to give the driver your destination and agree on a price before getting in. There are cabstands in front of most of the hotels, and you can ask the doorman about reasonable prices. If you flag down a cab in the street, you'll have to do your own haggling. The going rate should be no more than $2.50 from the Costera area near the *El Presidente* hotel to the zocalo, in the center of downtown. The ride from the *Hyatt Regency,* at the far east end of the Costera, to La Caleta Beach should cost about $5. No trip within Acapulco proper should cost more than $7, although the fare will be higher when the destination is Revolcadero Beach or Pie de la Cuesta, both a ways out of town.

Car Rental – Many agencies, most visibly *Avis* (phone: 842581), *Hertz* (phone: 856889), and *Dollar* (phone: 843066), rent cars in Acapulco. All have offices at the airport; otherwise just stroll along the Costera. Air conditioned, automatic-transmission cars also are available, but should be reserved well in advance. Jeeps and Volkswagen Beetles can be rented as well. *Sands* (phone: 841031) rents only jeeps. Be aware, however, that even the costliest cars are likely to be in far worse condition than the exact same make and model routinely rented from companies in the US, and often have just enough gas to get from the airport to town. Be certain to buy insurance when renting an auto; without it, even a small accident can turn into a nightmare.

Motorcycles – Honda Elites may be rented at *Cici* (phone: 841970) for $15 to $20 for up to 4 hours; daily rates are also available. On the beach across the street from the *Embassy* hotel.

SPECIAL EVENTS: *Carnaval* (Mardi Gras), just before *Lent,* is Acapulco's biggest fiesta. The *International Billfish Tournament* is held in late November or early December. *Guadalupe Day,* December 12, something of a national holiday, is celebrated with special fervor in Acapulco. December 12 is also the date of the *International Diving Championship,* which is held at Las Quebradas, the cliff at *Playa las Glorias El Mirador* hotel (74 Quebrada). An inter-club tournament is held in February. Also, there are fiestas throughout the year in the many villages near Acapulco. The government tourist office has data about what's in the offing.

SHOPPING: One of the most popular activities in Acapulco is buying things. Frequent visitors arrive with little more than a toothbrush in their luggage, since resortwear and sports clothes are an Acapulco specialty. Stores also offer a wide selection of Mexico's best handicrafts. For a productive shopping outing, or just some enjoyable browsing, simply stroll Costera Miguel Alemán from the *Condesa* hotel to the *Malibu.* One of the newest shopping complexes, completely enclosed and air conditioned, is the *Plaza Bahia Mall,* next to the *Acapulco Plaza.* The *Marbella Shopping Center,* done in white marble, is on the Diana Circle. For some of Acapulco's more elegant shops, visit *La Vista Shopping Center* (on Carr. Escénica, 2 miles/3 km before the *Princess,* heading toward the airport). Observing the siesta tradition, many shops close in the early afternoon, reopening at 4 or 5 PM. Here are some of the better places to make a purchase:

Aca Joe – Now making fashion waves in the US, it carries stylish casual togs for teens. 1999 Costera Miguel Alemán and the *Galería Plaza* (phone: 848645).

Artesanías Finas Acapulco – A vast selection of handicrafts, jewelry, leather goods, and clothing from all over Mexico. Open daily. Horacio Nelson and James Cook (phone: 848049).

Benny – At last, a fashionable shop devoted to men. On Costera Miguel Alemán, 15 Horacio Nelson (phone: 841547), and at *La Vista Shopping Center.*

Casa Aries – Luggage and leather goods ranging from wallets to skirts and jackets. *Las Brisas Hotel* (phone: 841580).

La Colección de Sergio Bustamante – The world-renowned artist's fantastical eggs, animals, and people in ceramics, papier-mâché and brass are displayed here. The *Princess* arcade and 711-B Costera Miguel Alemán (phone: 844992).

Galería Rudic – Paintings and other works of art by the finest Mexican artists. Costera Miguel Alemán and Yañez Pinzon (phone: 841104).

Gucci – Decent knock-offs of the real Gucci shoes and accessories of Italy, at fairly reasonable prices. On the Costera across from the *Galería Plaza* and at *El Patio Shopping Center* (phone: 840969).

Marietta – Eye-catching fashions and accessories for women. In *Torre de Acapulco* on Costera Miguel Alemán and at the *Princess* (phone: 843100).

El Mundo de Esteban – Very high-fashion, New York–style clothing for men and women, chic Acapulco wear, lovely hats and tunics, and glamorous evening dress. 2010 Costera Miguel Alemán (phone: 843084).

Polo Ralph Lauren – Men's and women's sportswear and accessories by the famed designer. In the *Princess Hotel,* Costera Miguel Alemán across the street from the American Express office (phone: 843325).

Ronay – If silver jewelry is your delight, this is the place. Costera Miguel Alemán, beneath *Carlos 'n' Charlie's* restaurant (phone: 843343).

Rubén Torres – Stunning sportswear for men and women. 1999 Costera Miguel Alemán (phone: 840786).

Suzett's – Striking gold designs, especially in rings with precious stones. At the *Hyatt Regency* (phone: 842888).

Tane – Silver jewelry, flatware, and objets d'art of impeccable design and quality. At the *Hyatt Regency* (phone: 859648).

Taxco el Viejo – A most imaginative silver shop that also sell items in gold, leather, wool, wood, and ceramic. A block from the cliffs from which the famous divers leap, at 830 Quebrada (phone: 837300).

SPORTS: Acapulco is mostly a town for participating, not spectating, but there is something here for virtually every taste.

Boating – Catamarans and other boats of varying size are available for rent on all the bay beaches. The best places to go are Caleta and Puerto Marqués. *Divers de Mexico* (phone: 821398 or 836020) rents private, chartered yachts for about $60 per hour.

Bullfighting – Not a sport, aficionados will tell you, but a spectacle. Established matadors perform Sunday afternoons starting at 5:30 PM during December and *Easter Week.* Hotel travel desks have the details and the tickets. The bullring is near Caleta Beach. Tickets cost from $10 to $25.

Fishing – Deep-sea charter boats leave around 8 AM and return around lunchtime. The Pacific waters yield pompano, bonito, barracuda, yellowtail, red snapper, and shark. A few miles southeast of the city in the Tres Palos Lagoon, and at Coyuca Lagoon near Pie de la Cuesta, you can rent small boats with awnings, and fish for freshwater catfish. *Divers de México* (phone: 821398 or 836020) has nine American yachts, some air conditioned, all Coast Guard–approved and with uniformed crews, costing $220 to $500 per day for 4 to 30 passengers, or $50 per chair. *Club de Esquies Beto* has speedboats from which five can fish that rent for $25 per hour, with a minimum of 3 hours, and fishing boats for four for $150 (phone: 822034). Freshwater fishing costs about $35 an hour with a 3-hour minimum; including equipment.

Golf – There are three courses worth knowing about: the 9-hole public course in front of the *Elcano* hotel (on Costera Miguel Alemán); an 18-hole course at the *Acapulco Princess* (Revolcadero Beach); and an 18-hole course at the *Pierre Marqués Club de Golf* at the hotel adjoining the *Princess,* also on Revolcadero Beach. All three courses have resident pros and charge greens fees. Reservations for starting times are advised during the winter season. The *Pierre Marqués Club de Golf* is the longest and most challenging; the *Acapulco Princess* layout usually is in the best condition.

Horseback Riding – Revolcadero Beach is the place to go for a canter astride a smallish Indian pony. Some horses are also available at Pie de la Cuesta.

Parasailing – The next best thing to sky diving is going aloft in a parachute pulled by a speedboat. There's no trouble finding the boatmen — they are on every beach. The cost is about $20 for 6 to 7 minutes. Be warned: It can be dangerous.

Scuba Diving – Lessons and equipment are available at all the major hotels. The Arnold brothers run a school (205 Costera Miguel Alemán), in front of the *Las Hamacas* hotel (phone: 820788). *Divers de Mexico,* which is owned by a very helpful American woman, has dive packages that include pool instruction and lunch (phone: 821398 or 836020). Most dives are made in the waters off Roquetta Island.

Surfing – Surfing, though limited in Acapulco, is possible at the *Copacabana* and *Princess* hotels' beaches. Although surfing is not allowed in the bay area, inner tubes may be rented at Caleta for paddling around the bay.

Tennis – Acapulco has a number of tennis clubs, some with indoor, air conditioned courts as well as outdoor courts; others have lighted courts for night play. Altogether, there are about 30 courts in town. In addition to those at the *Acapulco Princess* and the *Acapulco Plaza* hotels, there is a tennis club at *Villa Vera* (Av. del Prado), and at the golf club in town, *Club de Golf Acapulco* (next to the Centro Internacional).

Water Skiing – Acapulco is the ideal place to learn or to perfect skills. Boats are available at all the major hotels. Caleta Beach and Puerto Marqués are especially good places to start since the water is calmer here. Prices run about $25 to $40 per hour. At Coyuca Lagoon visitors can watch demonstrations of barefoot skiing.

Wrestling – Matches are held Wednesday and Sunday nights at the *Coliseo Arena,* which draws a rough crowd. There often is more fighting in the stands than in the ring.

 **NIGHTCLUBS AND NIGHTLIFE:** If traditional Mexican entertainment is what you're after, Acapulco has its share of Mexican fiestas. Slightly corny, but great fun, the fiestas usually feature mariachi music, folkloric dancing, a Mexican buffet, and an open bar. Each place offers some variation on the same Mexican theme. Fiestas at the Centro Internacional Acapulco and the *Marbella Shopping Center* feature the spectacular *Flying Indians of Papantla.* Javier de León's excellent folkloric ballet performs at the *Calinda* hotel. At *Las Brisas*'s *El Mexicano* restaurant, the festivities begin with a *tianguis* (marketplace) of handicrafts and end with a spectacular fireworks display. The fiestas cost $25 to $30 per person, and reservations can be made through most hotel travel desks.

Acapulco really gets going after dark — well after dark. The discos don't get crowded until after 11 PM, so one way to get a table is to arrive around 10:30. The big hotels usually have several places to fill the evening hours, depending on your mood, and they often feature live entertainment. *A fashion note:* As casual as Acapulco is both day and night, its nightspots do not look kindly on shorts, old jeans, or bare feet.

Aca Tiki – The floating dinner party aboard this huge trimaran begins with cocktails on the top deck and a cruise around the bay, followed by a formal dinner, a Latin American floor show, and disco music for dancing — a very enjoyable experience. The trimaran leaves from the pier across from the San Diego Fort at 7:30 PM and gets back around 10:30 PM (phone: 846140 or 846786, for reservations).

Atrium – The old *Bocaccio* club has been renamed and redecorated: no tables, no chairs — just bars, a dance floor, and a DJ spinning disco recordings. $25 covers all drinks (except champagne and cognac) and snacks. Closed Mondays and Tuesdays. 5040 Costera Miguel Alemán (phone: 841900).

Baby 'O – One of Acapulco's top discos, imaginative and fashionable, it looks like a stylized mud hut from the outside. A pajama party is held annually. Opens at 10:30 PM, and the beat goes on until 5 or 6 AM. Costera Miguel Alemán, out where the Costera begins (phone: 847474).

Cat's – A laser show in the early hours of the morning is the main attraction. Open Thursdays through Saturdays. 32 Juan de la Cosa, across the street from the *Acapulco Plaza* (phone: 847235).

Le Dome – One of the port's original discos, its interior is the most compelling attraction. 402 Costera Miguel Alemán (phone: 841190).

Eve – It's practically on the water and one of the prettiest discos in town. 115 Costera Miguel Alemán (phone: 844777).

Extasis – Built on the water's edge, it offers a great view of the ski show at the *Colonial* next door. 200 Costera Miguel Alemán (phone: 833090).

Extravaganzza – Aptly named, the club is huge, modern, and posh, with an immense glass wall providing an awesome view of the entire bay. Truly spectacular, it shouldn't be missed, even by non-discophiles. Next door to *Los Rancheros* on the Carr. Escénica headed to *Las Brisas* (phone: 847165).

Fantasy – The façade is alight with a cascade of tiny lights; the interior is like a glass ship. *La Vista Shopping Center* (phone: 846764).

El Fuerte – This Spanish-style nightclub claims to have the best flamenco show this side of Seville. Shows at 10 and 11:30 PM, except Sundays. In the *Las Hamacas Hotel*, 239 Costera Miguel Alemán (phone: 826161).

Gallery – A disco and show bar where the 11 PM and 1 AM shows star female impersonators. The entertainment is surprisingly good. 11 Av. Deportes, across the street from the *Holiday Inn* (phone: 843497).

Hard Rock Café – At this south-of-the-border branch, dancing is in air conditioned comfort, day and night, but the live music — and real fun — begins at 11 PM when everyone — waiters and customers alike — gets into the act. Good food too. 37 Costera Miguel Alemán (phone: 846680).

Jackie 'O – No longer the new, chic disco in town, it still attracts a young and energetic clientele. Costera Miguel Alemán, at *El Patio Shopping Center* across from the *Hyatt Continental* (phone: 840843).

Magic – A selective door policy has made this one disco everybody wants to get into. People come here to be seen as much as to dance. Costera Miguel Alemán at Fragata Yucatán (phone: 848815).

News – One of Acapulco's largest and most popular dance spots, it seats 1,200 people in booths and love seats (no chairs). On the Costera across the street from the *Hyatt Regency* (phone: 845904).

La Perla – On the cliffs overlooking the sea, this is a supper club where the floor show is provided by the famed Acapulco divers. There are two orchestras for dancing. The first evening show is at 7:15 PM (phone: 821111).

Poseidon – Some of Mexico's best nightclub performers appear here. At the *Torres Gemelas Hotel* on the Costera (phone: 844828).

Tiffany's – Victorian decor, with plush upholstery and all that. The sound system allows guests seated at tables to actually carry on a conversation. At the *Princess* (phone: 843100).

BEST IN TOWN

 **CHECKING IN:** It's best to arrive in Acapulco with a prepaid reservation directly from your hotel, including a written confirmation stating the price. Overbooking is a frequent risk, so if there's trouble, make a scene, demand to talk to the reservations manager, and/or threaten to call the Tourism Ministry (5-250-0123 in Mexico City, day or night). The loudest squeaking wheel usually gets the oil, and noisy, demanding guests usually get service. Winter rates are often more than double summer rates. In winter expect to pay up to $250 for a double room in very expensive hotels, $145 to $175 for expensive, about $100 for moderate, and $70 or less for inexpensive. All telephone numbers are in the 74 area code unless otherwise indicated. When calling from one city to another within Mexico, dial 91 before the area code.

Acapulco Princess – Designed to evoke the most dramatic elements of Mexico's Aztec and Maya heritage, the shape of its main building is pyramidal, with exterior balconies hung with exotic tropical blossoms. Try to arrange for accommodations in this building if you want to be near the action. A fine 18-hole course serves as a prime lure for golfers. There are also 5 swimming pools (one with a bar under a waterfall), a beach, a sauna, 11 tennis courts, jeeps, parachute rides, 7 restaurants (of which *Hacienda* is best), a lobby bar, and a disco. 1,019 rooms. Rate includes breakfast and dinner. Airport Rd., 12 miles (19 km) south of Acapulco (phone: 843100; 800-223-1818 in the US; FAX: 843664). Very expensive.

Las Brisas – One of the truly unique resort hotels of the world and still our favorite in Acapulco, this striking amalgam of lovely casitas, built in 1957, has been carved into the side of the tallest of the hilltops surrounding Acapulco Harbor, offering a superb view as well as superb accommodations. Privacy is paramount here, and the service is mostly splendid, with a private beach club (at the foot of the steep hill) that satisfies the desire for swimming in the Pacific. There are 300 rooms — including some 1-, 2-, and 3-bedroom suites, as well as 4- to 6-bedroom homes — most with private or semi-private swimming pools strewn with fresh blossoms each day. Try to arrange a room with your own pool. There are 2 saltwater pools (at the beach club), 5 lighted tennis courts, water sports, nearby golf and fishing, and private restaurants open to hotel guests only. Rate includes continental breakfast and membership in the hotel's private *La Concha* beach club, which serves some of the best ceviche in Mexico. The *Bella Vista* restaurant serves good seafood (see *Eating Out*). Airport Rd., 8 miles (13 km) south of Acapulco (phone: 841580; 800-228-3000 in the US; FAX: 841580). Very expensive.

Hyatt Regency – The sight of towering ceiba trees and graceful fountains welcomes guests as they approach. It offers large, comfortable, recently remodeled rooms, a good-size pool framed by palms, water sports at the beach, 4 lighted tennis courts, a pro shop for guests only, 2 restaurants, coffee shop, 3 bars, exercise classes, 700 rooms. Costera Miguel Alemán (phone: 842888; FAX: 843087). Very expensive.

Pierre Marqués – Sharing the Revolcadero beachfront (and ownership) with the next-door *Princess,* this place was constructed by billionaire J. Paul Getty and retains its authentic luxurious mien. A shuttle now runs between the two hotels. Probably the most underrated of Acapulco's accommodations, its facilities include 3 swimming pools, a pleasant, uncrowded stretch of beach, a true championship golf course (the best around), fishing, tennis, 2 restaurants, and a cocktail lounge. The only drawback: very little shade. There are 344 rooms, including junior and master suites. Rate includes breakfast. Airport Rd., about 11 miles (18 km) south of Acapulco (phone: 842000; 800-223-1818 in the US; FAX: 848554). Very expensive.

Continental Acapulco – An Acapulco landmark, it has a large pool surrounding an island, and its beach is enormous. It also has 433 rooms, 3 restaurants, a coffee shop, lobby bar with live music, 2 pool bars, and 2 lighted tennis courts. Costera Miguel Alemán (phone: 840909; FAX: 842081). Expensive.

Fiesta Americana Condesa Acapulco – Next to *El Presidente* on the beach, this large hotel — the best on the Costera — has 2 swimming pools, a social program for kids, a lobby bar where live music attracts nighttime crowds, and a restaurant with more tranquil music. 500 rooms. Costera Miguel Alemán (phone: 842828; 800-FIESTA-1 in the US; FAX: 830575). Expensive.

Sheraton Acapulco – Set on a hillside on secluded Guitarrón Beach on the east end of Acapulco Bay, it has 17 villas comprised of 226 rooms and 8 suites. Facilities include 2 pools (one with a swim-up bar), 2 restaurants, and a lobby bar with live music. 110 Costera Guitarrón (phone: 843737; 800-325-3535 in the US). Expensive.

Villa Vera – A glamorous jet set favorite, the place where the movie stars go and starlets follow. There are 80 spacious rooms, suites, and villas (many of which have private pools), an excellent restaurant, a large hotel pool, Jacuzzi, and 3 clay tennis courts. There's no beach, but guests may use the beach at the *Maralisa.* No children under 16. In town, at 35 Lomas del Mar (phone: 840333; 800-223-6510 in the US; FAX: 847449). Expensive.

Acapulco Malibu – This smaller, circular hostelry, with its own tropical garden, offers water skiing as well as its beach and swimming pool. Though the 80 rooms are somewhat on the glitzy side, they're almost always full. 20 Costera Miguel Alemán (phone: 841070; FAX: 840475). Moderate.

Acapulco Plaza – Its exterior resembles a funnel-shaped parking garage, but it's more luxurious inside. The *La Jaula* bar hangs in the lobby gardens, seemingly suspended in midair. About half of the 1,008 rooms are small; the other half are very comfortable suites. The *Oasis Club* has a pleasant and quiet private Jacuzzi on the third floor, and *Club Mirage,* on the second floor, offers more of the same, and also allows children. A tennis club (4 courts on the roof of the shopping center), 2 pools , a fine beach, 50 shops in its shopping center, a health club, 4 restaurants, and a coffee shop. Service at the front desk is not always friendly. Affiliated with Holiday Inns. 123 Costera Miguel Alemán (phone: 858050; 800-HOLIDAY in the US; FAX: 855493). Moderate.

Boca Chica – One of Acapulco's older, smaller places, right on the water, with 2 restaurants (one a sushi and oyster bar) and 2 pools (one is a natural saltwater cove). Snorkeling is at its best here. Rate includes breakfast and dinner. Caletilla Beach (phone: 836601 or 836741; FAX: 839513). Moderate.

La Palapa – The 30 floors beneath a scalloped gold crown contain nothing but suites (335) with balconies, indoor bars, and plenty of closet space. Plants give the place an airy feel. The hotel also has a large pool with swim-up bar, water sports center, social program, live music nightly, and an electronic-gameroom. 210 Fragata Yucatán (phone: 845363; 800-334-7234 in the US; FAX: 848399). Moderate.

Paraíso Radisson – Right on Hornos Beach, it has 422 newly redecorated rooms with balconies and satellite TV. There's a pool, cafeteria, a restaurant on the beach, and a rooftop restaurant with a breathtaking view of Acapulco Bay. 163 Costera Miguel Alemán (phone: 855050; 800-228-9822 in the US; FAX: 855543). Moderate.

El Presidente – This rather sterile giant on the beach has 2 swimming pools, a sauna, nightclub, restaurant, 2 bars, and a social program in case you can't find enough to do. 407 rooms. Costera Miguel Alemán (phone: 841700; 800-777-1700 in the US; FAX: 841376). Moderate.

Ritz – A modern high-rise, it has a pleasant lobby with wicker furniture, pool, restaurant, and video games. Costera Miguel Alemán on Hornos Beach (phone: 857336; FAX: 857076). Moderate.

Tortuga – This peach-colored property, with an atrium from which plants dangle impressively, has 250 large rooms, a swimming pool, sauna, 2 bars, and 2 restaurants, including *La Fonda.* Close to, but not on, the beach. 132 Costera Miguel Alemán (phone: 848889; FAX: 847385). Moderate.

Autotel Ritz – With 103 rooms, a restaurant, and pool. MAP available. Costera Miguel Alemán and Wilfrido Massieu (phone: 858023; FAX: 855647). Inexpensive.

Bali-Hai – One of the advantages of this motel is that guests can enjoy a quiet room in the back and still be right on the main strip. Restaurant; swimming pool. Room service is available. Near the *Acapulco Plaza.* 186 Costera Miguel Alemán (phone: 856336; FAX: 857972). Inexpensive.

Etel – Spotlessly clean rooms and 1- to 4-bedroom apartments equipped with air conditioning, fans, and a marvelous view. There is also a pool set in a pretty garden. Up a steep street at 92 Pinzona (phone: 822240). Inexpensive.

Los Flamingos – This is where the film stars of the 1940s came to frolic, and the place is alive with memories. There is a pool, restaurant, and bar. The panoramic view is a constant spectacle. Rate includes breakfast. On a hillside at López Mateos and Flamingos (phone: 820690; FAX: 839806). Inexpensive.

Las Hamacas – Across from the beach on the strip, this hostelry offers a pool with bar, garden dining room, and flamenco shows in its nightclub. Of the 160 rooms, those off the pool are nicer and quieter, though they have no view. 239 Costera Miguel Alemán (phone: 837746; 800-421-0767 in the US). Inexpensive.

Majestic – Up in the hills overlooking the bay, it offers 195 rooms, a pool, parking, and transportation to the Costera. 73 Av. Pozo del Rey (phone: 834710; FAX: 821614). Inexpensive.

Playa las Glorias El Mirador – People generally come here to sip cocktails at *La Perla* and watch the cliff divers, but besides the dramatic view, the hotel offers 3 pools, a nightclub, and 133 pleasant rooms with large bathrooms. It's best for those who don't need a beach at hand. 74 Quebrada (phone: 831155; 800-342-AMIGO in the US; FAX: 820638). Inexpensive.

Posada del Sol – Near *CiCi Park,* this is an efficient place with an oddly American flavor. It has 232 rooms and bungalows, a restaurant, bar, and pool. 1390 Costera Miguel Alemán (phone: 841010; 800-445-9008 in the US; FAX: 840305). Inexpensive.

Sands – In the center of things, yet tranquil, it has a restaurant, 2 pools, a bar, 2 squash courts, and 59 modest but good-size rooms and 34 bungalows. The staff is pleasant. 178 Costera Miguel Alemán and Juan de la Cosa (phone: 842260; 800-422-6078 in the US; FAX: 841053). Inexpensive.

El Tropicano – Just 2 blocks from the beach, it has 127 rooms and 12 suites, cable TV, 2 pools, restaurants, a garden, and a disco. Part of the Best Western group. 510 Costera Miguel Alemán (phone: 841100; 800-528-1234 in the US; FAX: 841308). Inexpensive.

Del Mar – Almost hidden from view and tiny, with only 2 floors and 14 small rooms, this quaint lodging is surely the least expensive in Acapulco. While it's short on conveniences, there is air conditioning in some rooms and a small open-air restaurant and bar. This is one of the few budget places where you have to book ahead. 254 Costera Miguel Alemán, at Hornos Beach (phone: 851723). Very inexpensive.

 EATING OUT: Acapulco has more restaurants than you'll be able to test even during a 2-week stay. Many of the finest are in the best hotels (including the *Hyatt Regency* and the *Acapulco Plaza*). Dining out here is relatively costly. Expect to pay $80 for two at those places we've listed as very expensive; $50 to $60, expensive; up to $40, moderate; under $30, inexpensive. Prices do not include drinks, wine, or tips. Most restaurants below accept MasterCard and Visa; a few also accept American Express and Diners Club. All telephone numbers are in the 74 area code unless otherwise indicated. When calling from one city to another within Mexico, dial 91 before the area code.

Casa Nova – With modern decor and a wonderful view of Acapulco Bay, this spot serves pasta, antipasto, and Italian treatments of shrimp, and fish. Open daily. Reservations necessary. 5256 Carr. Escénica, across the street from *Las Brisas Hotel* (phone: 846819). Very expensive.

Coyuca 22 – A great place for a pre-dinner drink and conversation, it looks like the set of a romantic Hollywood musical extravaganza of the 1940s. You almost expect to see Fred Astaire and Ginger Rogers come dancing around the pool. The menu includes lobster thermidor; a highlight of the decor is a handsome unicorn sculpture by Victor Salmones. Open daily for dinner only. Closed May through October. Reservations necessary. 22 Coyuca (phone: 835030). Very expensive.

Bella Vista – Set atop a hill overlooking the entire city and bay, the prime eating place at the *Las Brisas* hotel provides a wonderful view. Menu items include lobster thermidor, fresh fish, and shrimp served with coconut and rice. Open daily for breakfast and dinner. Reservations necessary. Airport Rd., 8 miles south of Acapulco (phone: 841580 or 800-228-3000). Expensive.

Black Beard's (also known as Barbas Negras) – Not surprisingly, the decor is early pirates' den. The menu concentrates on steaks, lobster, chicken, baked potato with sour cream, and a salad bar. It's next to Condesa Beach, and you usually have to wait for a table. Open daily for dinner only. No reservations. Costera Miguel Alemán (phone: 842549). Expensive.

El Campanario – A beautiful bell-tower dining room with colonial decor atop a mountain, with a panoramic view of Acapulco and very well-prepared international dishes and seafood. Open daily. Reservations advised. Calle Paraíso (phone: 848830). Expensive.

Dino's – Homemade Italian bread is what makes this place special, and dining on the terrace makes things even more pleasant. You can get some continental dishes but standard Italian-American fare characterizes most of the menu. Open daily. No reservations. 137 Costera Miguel Alemán (phone: 840037). Expensive.

D Joint – Also known as "DJ's," it's the best joint in town for roast beef. An excellent place for sandwiches and chili, too. Open daily. Reservations advised. 79 Costera Miguel Alemán (phone: 843709). Expensive.

Embarcadero – A showplace with a South Seas motif, it offers such temptations as charcoal-broiled mahimahi with rice and bananas. Open daily. Reservations advised. Costera Miguel Alemán near *Cici Park* (phone: 848787). Expensive.

Hard Times – Trendy and fun, it's a place where you can select your meal from an international menu — or just order tacos and beer. The salad is marvelous, with artichoke leaves, avocado, beets, cauliflower, red cabbage, and much more. As you may have guessed, the motif is Depression era. Dinner only. Closed Sundays. Reservations advised. 400 Costera Miguel Alemán (phone: 840064). Expensive.

Kookaburra – With romantic dining under the stars and a stunning view of the bay, this spot specializes in seafood, steaks, and barbecue. There is also a wonderful ceviche bar (Mexico's answer to sushi). Dinner only. Reservations advised. Carr. Las Brisas (phone: 844418). Expensive.

Madeiras – A pretty place with terrace dining and a view of the bay, it drips ferns and sophistication. The prix fixe menu includes baby lamb chops, sea bass, red snapper baked in sea salt, Cornish hen, and frogs' legs in white wine or garlic sauce. Dinner only. Closed Sundays. Reservations advised. Carr. Escénica, in the *La Vista Shopping Center* (phone: 846921). Expensive.

Miramar – Elegant, yet cozy, it too offers a spectacular view. Diners sit on multi-level terraces, and enjoy fine French fare. The *pato à la naranja* (duck with orange sauce) is crisp and beautifully presented. Closed Sundays during the summer. Reservations necessary. In *La Vista Shopping Center* (phone: 847874). Expensive.

Normandie – Easily the best French restaurant in Acapulco and perhaps in all of Mexico, it is run by Nicole Lepine, a Gallic lady, and her daughter. Open daily. Dinner only. Closed May through October. Reservations advised. In town at Costera Miguel Alemán and Malespina (phone: 851916). Expensive.

Suntory – Operated by a leading distiller of Japanese whiskey, this fasionable place offers authentic Japanese food. Open daily. Reservations advised. 36 Costera Miguel Alemán (phone: 848088). Expensive.

Beto's – Right on Condesa Beach, it's very popular for lunch, live music, and good seafood. Open daily. Reservations advised. Costera Miguel Alemán, at Condesa Beach (phone: 840473). Moderate.

Carlos 'n' Charlie – The atmosphere is lively, but expect to wait in line half an hour or more. House specialties include charcoal-broiled spareribs and stuffed shrimp, and good sangria. Open daily for dinner only. No reservations. 999 Costera Miguel Alemán (phone: 840039). Moderate.

Chez Guillaume – Quiet and elegant, it serves well-prepared continental dishes including seafood crêpes, soufflés, and scampi. The bar attracts an international crowd. Open daily for dinner only. Reservations advised. 110 Av. del Prado (phone: 841231). Moderate.

Hard Rock Café – A combination rock 'n' roll hall of fame, bar, restaurant, dance hall, and boutique. The food, everything from shrimp fajitas to filet mignon, is tasty, and portions are generous. Live rock music is played from 11 PM to 2 AM. Service is friendly. There's always a line at the boutique, which sells sportswear bearing the familiar *Hard Rock* logo. Reservations advised. 37 Costera Miguel Alemán, next to *Cici* (phone: 846680). Moderate.

Huachinango Charlie's – *Huachinango* means red snapper, one of the best dishes served at this relaxed, informal seafood house. Open daily. Reservations advised. 115 Costera Miguel Alemán (phone: 840029). Moderate.

Mimi's Chili Saloon – Behind a bird's-egg-blue façade, it offers hamburgers, burritos, fried chicken, frozen margaritas, and a lovely view of the ocean. Closed Mondays. Reservations advised. Costera Miguel Alemán (phone: 842549; in *Black Beard's*). Moderate.

Paraíso – Serving delicious red snapper right on Condesa Beach, this spot is similar to, but wackier than, its neighbor *Beto's* (see above). Open daily. Reservations advised. Costera Miguel Alemán, at Condesa Beach (phone: 845988). Moderate.

Shangri-La – An Oriental garden with lily pond and bridge is the setting and, as you might expect, the fare is standard Cantonese. If you can't live without egg foo yong and fried rice, this is your best bet in Acapulco. Open daily for dinner only. Reservations advised. Just off the Costera at 5 Calle Piedra Picuda (phone: 841300). Moderate.

Villa Demos – A beautiful garden restaurant specializing in homemade fettuccine and other Italian dishes. We recommend the veal *piccata.* There is a terrace for outdoor dining, as well as indoor service. Closed Mondays in the off-season. Reservations advised. 6 Av. del Prado, off Costera Miguel Alemán (phone: 842040). Moderate.

Pipo's – There are three of them; each one looks raunchy, but regulars insist that they serve the best seafood on the Mexican Pacific. Open daily. Reservations unnecessary. Across from the sportfishing docks, at 3 Almirante Bretón (phone: 822237); Puerto Marqués (phone: 846343); 105 Costera Miguel Alemán (phone: 840165). Branch on the Costera, moderate; all others, inexpensive.

Acapulco Fat Farm – Also known as "La Granja del Pingüe," this cozy little eatery is run by high school and college students who formerly lived at the Acapulco Children's Center, an orphanage. The name points to the ice cream, pastries, and pies that are the specialties here, but there's less fattening fare, too — good soups, sandwiches, and Mexican food. There's a book exchange, and live music is played Thursdays through Tuesdays. No reservations. No credit cards accepted. 10 Juárez, 2 blocks west of the zocalo (phone: 835339). Inexpensive.

El Fiaco – An informal place where barbecued meats are done to a turn. The menu has some other interesting touches — fondue, for example. Lots of people come here to relax and drink beer and enjoy a snack. Open daily. Reservations unnecessary. No credit cards accepted. 235 Hornitos (phone: 830557). Inexpensive.

Los Rancheros – Easy to overlook for its hilltop location, this is a good place to sample authentic Mexican food while gazing out at the Pacific. Open daily. Reservations unnecessary. On Carr. Escénica en route to *Las Brisas* (phone: 841908). Inexpensive.

CANCÚN AND COZUMEL

(pronounced Cahn-*koon* and Co-zoo-*mehl*)

For many years, small groups of divers and determined sun worshipers had the lagoons, beaches, and islands of Mexico's Caribbean coast along the Yucatán Peninsula almost to themselves. People planning a trip to the Yucatán had to choose among the Maya ruins at Chichén Itzá, Uxmal, and Tulum; sun and sea sports along the coast of Quintana Roo, including Xel-Ha (pronounced Shell-*ha*) and Akumal; or the islands of Isla Mujeres, Cancún, or Cozumel. Transportation was too difficult to make all sides of the vacation coin easily accessible. About the only visitors who had enough time to do it all were the wealthy divers who belonged to private clubs tucked away in silent lagoons along the coast and who flew private planes into the Yucatán for stays of 3 weeks or more.

In those days, Mexico's largest island, Cozumel, was the preferred Caribbean destination of less well-heeled travelers. They flew into Mérida, grabbed a plane to Cozumel, and flopped there on the sand for several days of swimming, diving, fishing, and lots and lots of lazing. Cancún was an undeveloped spit of land off the coast to the north.

No more. All that changed when FONATUR, the government agency charged with improving Mexico's tourist facilities, chose Cancún as its first multimillion-dollar experiment in resort development. It was discovered that Cancún had all the natural attributes of a resort area — beautiful sea and some of the best diving in the world, adequate space and facilities, proximity to the ruins — and FONATUR proceeded without hesitation. So new it wasn't even marked on road maps in 1970, Cancún has blossomed into one of the world's most bustling — and some feel overdeveloped — young resorts.

In reality Cancún is a Caribbean island — more a sandbar shaped like an emaciated sea horse — 14 miles long and ¼ mile wide, connected by a causeway at its nosepoint to Cancún City, the support city on the mainland where over 200,000 people now live. For most of the island's length, island and peninsula are separated by unruffled Nichupte Lagoon. Most of the island's resort hotels are scattered along the skinny east-west sand spit that forms the seahorse's head. Along its back, the Caribbean surf rolls in along a 12-mile length of shore with intermittent stretches of powdery white beach. There are a couple of commercial hotels in Cancún City, catering mostly to business travelers, but good for budget travelers as well, and there are some pleasant hotels with pools that offer free transportation to and from the beach.

One of the major dividends of the development at Cancún is that travelers no longer have to choose between culture and carousal. Part of the Cancún master plan — a 15-year program of development — is a system of roads, transportation, and communications that connects the resort area to the major ruins and Mérida. Both Cancún and Cozumel benefit from a beeline road from the sea to Chichén Itzá, along which tour buses roll daily. And both are helped by the improvement of the shoreline road to Xel-Ha and the small but interesting ruins at Tulum and Cobá.

But the sea is still the major attraction. The crystalline Caribbean offers visibility to 100 feet, and the stretch of sea along the peninsula and into Belize is world-famous as an area rich in fish, wrecks, and coral. Nichupte Lagoon is protected from the open sea. But the government poured some $80 million into the area to assure a complete resort infrastructure — recreational facilities like the 18-hole Robert Trent Jones, Sr. golf course, a panoply of hotels, ships for touring and boats for sailing — to augment the area's Caribbean attributes.

Although Cancún's neighbor, Cozumel, was the first island to be developed in the area, it has grown at a much slower pace than Cancún and tends to attract visitors who are more interested in the fabulous skin diving and fishing than the nightlife and "glamour" of Cancún. Plans for several new hotels were dropped because of potential threats to the island's ecological system — not to mention its tranquility. Even more secluded is Isla Mujeres. With its few charming, but fairly simple, hotels and the wide expanses of beach, the island has a small, but loyal following of snorkelers, divers, and loafers.

What the people of Cancún, Cozumel, or Isla Mujeres never imagined, however, was Hurricane Gilbert, which, in September 1988, sent huge waves and torrential winds over the three islands, seemingly determined to destroy everything in its path. However, "Gilberto" was no match for the resiliency of the Mexican people. With an outpouring of assistance from the rest of the country — and indeed the world — palms were replanted, windows replaced, and rubbish removed. Within a few months, it was just a question of waiting for the sea to return the beach sand and for the new palm trees to take root. Many of the beaches on Cancún's Caribbean side, however, are still not as wide as they once were, while others on the Bahia Mujeres side are wider than before Gilbert hit.

Paseo Kukulcán, the boulevard running from one end of Cancún to the other, has been expanded from two lanes to four to accommodate the anticipated crowds descending to see the "new Cancún." For in addition to the construction attendant to the hurricane-related repairs, many new hotels and support facilities are also being built. Cancún's weather and facilities are an authentic lure, but this is not the place for those who prize peace and privacy.

CANCÚN–COZUMEL AT-A-GLANCE

SEEING THE CITY: The best way to get a bird's-eye view of Cancún is from *Pelican Pier Avioturismo's* ultra-light seaplane that takes off from the lagoon for a 15-minute flight over the hotel zone (phone: 30315 or 31935). Kukulcán Boulevard is the only street on the island. In mainland Cancún City,

Avenida Tulum is the main drag, but Avenida Yaxchilan is shaping up as the address of the more fashionable shops and restaurants. The village of San Miguel on Cozumel is about 10 blocks long and a few blocks wide; with many shops, restaurants, and boutiques, it offers much to see and savor.

SPECIAL PLACES: Cancún is spread out, but there are lots of ways to get around. Taxis are plentiful, city bus service is good, and cars, motor scooters, and bicycles are available for rent. There are regular bus and boat tours to several areas along with scheduled air service to more distant points and charters from *Pelican Pier Avioturismo* (phone: 30315 or 31935). On Cozumel, you can easily tour the little village of San Miguel on foot or drive around the rest of the island.

CANCÚN

Beaches – Many of the hotels on the island are on the beach; the beaches themselves, however, are federal property, so anyone can use them. The most popular public beach on the island is called Chac-Mool, and it is lovely. The "back side" of the island faces out on calm, lovely lagoons, favorite spots for divers and novice swimmers.

Cruises – Any number of voyages may be made from Cancún or nearby points. Ferries (without car capacity) leave Punta Sam and Puerto Juárez several times each day for Isla Mujeres. If you wish to take your car, take the ferry from Puerto Morelos. There are also daily ferries (one with car capacity) from Playa del Carmen for Cozumel. The *Fiesta Maya,* with continental breakfast, lunch, an open bar, a show, orchestra on board, and glass bottom, sails to Isla Mujeres every morning, and costs about $30. Many hotel travel desks offer day cruises to Isla Mujeres that include lunch and snorkeling equipment for about $30. Catamarans sail from the *Cancún Yacht Club* through the Lagoon of Love to the ruins at El Rey, said to have been the harem of Maya kings. The *Corsario,* a 50-foot replica of an 18th-century pirate ship, sails daily to Isla Mujeres for snorkeling at El Garrafón, with a seafood lunch included. The *México,* billed as the world's largest water jet, makes the round trip daily to Cozumel. *Aviomar* offers the Escape to Cozumel tour, which leaves the Playa Linda Pier daily at 9 AM via bus and waterjet to Cozumel; the day includes sightseeing, swimming, refreshments, and lunch on the beach — all for $76 (phone: 46433 or 46935). There are also 7 daily round trips from Cozumel to Playa del Carmen (phone: 20847 in Cozumel; 46656 in Cancún).

Dr. Alfredo Barrera Marín Botanical Gardens

Close to Cancún City, in the direction of Tulum, is this nature preserve covering 150 acres. Trails wind through the semi-evergreen tropical forests that border a mangrove swamp. Closed Mondays. Admission charge (no phone).

El Castillo

A small reproduction of El Castillo pyramid (the original is in Chichén Itzá) has been erected in front of *Plaza Caracol.* Every night, except Tuesdays, the phenomenon of the spring and fall equinox is reproduced, when the movement of the sun across El Castillo produces the illusion of a serpent creeping down the staircase. The show — in Spanish — begins at 7 PM; in English, at 8 and 9 PM. Admission charge.

COZUMEL

Cozumel Museum – Impressive 3-D models of underwater caves in the offshore reefs, historical and ethnographical exhibits. There's also a library, temporary exhibits, a restaurant, and crafts shop. Closed Saturdays. Admission charge (no phone).

Plaza – The heart of Cozumel is a wide plaza near where the ferry docks, a spot everyone manages to find. Most of the shops and restaurants are here. Motor scooter renters must be careful not to park on the plaza; parking is forbidden and "motos" may be hauled off to scooter prison — and you'll be inconvenienced by having to pay the fine and arranging for their release.

Chankanab Lagoon and Botanical Gardens – About 5 miles (8 km) south of town, it's something of a natural aquarium filled with multicolored tropical fish. Since suntan lotion collects in the water and harms the fish, swimming and snorkeling are not permitted in the lagoon, but are permitted at the nearby beach.

San Francisco Beach – On the southern tip of Cozumel, the island's best beach now can be reached by paved road, but it's also fun getting there aboard one of the vessels making the *Del Zorro* cruise (phone: 20831). If you're not on a cruise providing lunch, either of the two seafood restaurants here is a good choice.

Punta Morena – At this beach on the open Caribbean side of the island the surf is rougher and swimming can be dangerous. *Mezcalito's,* a thatch-hut restaurant out this way, is a good place to try grilled fish and a beer (see *Eating Out*).

EXCURSIONS

Isla Mujeres – The name means Isle of Women, but that's not quite accurate. The Spanish so dubbed it because they found many sculptures of females there. A dot 5 miles long and ½ mile wide, it is 6 miles north of Cancún and 6 miles off Puerto Juárez on the Yucatán Peninsula. Most places have phones, and there are a few paved roads, but its tiny town, wide and beautiful beaches, lagoons, reefs, and transparent waters make it a pleasant retreat for snorkelers, skin divers, and sun worshippers. The island's few fairly simple and charming hotels and restaurants are moderate to inexpensive; try *Maria's Kan Kin,* the hotel/restaurant that serves delicious but fairly pricey fresh seafood and bathtub-size pink piña coladas). Ferries run regularly from Puerto Juárez and Punta Sam on the mainland coast, just north of Cancún. By day, try the *Fiesta Maya* or *Carnaval,* which include an open-air bar and lunch; by night, the *Noche Pirata.*

The trimaran *Aqua Quinn* (phone: 31883 or 30100) sails daily to Isla Mujeres from Cancún for snorkeling at El Garrafón, with lunch and open bar included. It leaves at 11 AM and returns around 5 PM. The *El Corsario,* a motorized galleon for snorkeling, provides guests with a visit to the giant sea turtle pen, and a buffet lunch (phone: 30200). At El Garrafón, there's a sea museum with an aquarium and pieces of wrecked historic galleons.

Contoy Island – A national park, completely undeveloped, Contoy is a coral island populated by sea gulls, pelicans, petrels, cormorants, herons, and other sea birds whose numbers are, unfortunately, diminishing. It is especially popular with divers, picnickers, and bird watchers. Boats make daily excursions, which include a fresh fish lunch.

Akumal – Once a private club run by undersea explorers in search of treasure from the Spanish Main, it now has a hotel, *Club Akumal,* with grounds that contain cannons recovered from the ancient wrecks. If you would like some adventure right out of *The Deep,* minus the hazards, Akumal has an underwater museum where anchors and guns encrusted in coral lie among the rocks, much the way they originally were discovered. There's a dive shop and restaurant. The hotel is a great spot for lunch. Although Akumal stands by itself (about 70 miles — 112 km — from Cancún), it is also the beginning of a string of resorts along the coast.

One of the newest of these resorts is Puerto Aventuras, about 6 miles (10 km) north of Akumal. Still in the early stages of development, it's likely to become one of Mexico's most exclusive enclaves on the Caribbean coast. It's nestled in the natural beauty of the region and enhanced with transplanted Asian palms and orchids brought in from the Brazilian Amazon. The resort's 240-slip marina is set in a crystal-clear cove fed by underground springs. The *Puerto Aventuras Golf Club* (phone: 987-22233) has been built around several pre-Columbian structures and incorporates ancient cenotes (sinkholes); at press time 9 holes were open. The golf club also has 3 public outdoor tennis courts ($10 an hour). A glimpse of the area's maritime history can be seen at the *Pablo Bush Romero CEDAM* (Center of Exploration of Marine Archaeology); its collection includes 18th-century silver goblets, gold coins, medallions, cannon, and other relics salvaged from the *Mantanceros,* a Spanish merchant ship that sank off the coast of Akumal in 1741 (no admission charge; no phone). The *Puerta del Mar* (no local phone; 5-208-1628, 5-208-7156, 5-208-6517 for reservations in Mexico City) is a luxury complex with 68 villa-like suites, a pool, and a restaurant. Though the resort's restaurants are still limited, there are a few good casual spots, including *Carlos 'n' Charlie's* (between the *Puerta del Mar* and *Club de Playa* hotels; no phone) and *Papaya Republic* (in the south part of town; no phone).

Chemuyil – A few miles down the road from Akumal, a sign welcomes you to Chemuyil, "the most beautiful beach in the world," where there's a charming hotel (it had no name at press time; for details, see "Best en Route" in *The Yucatán Peninsula,* DIRECTIONS).

Xel-Ha – A lagoon not far from Akumal that is a natural aquarium. The water is clear, even for the Caribbean, and the many species of tropical fish can be seen quite easily from the shore. Even better is putting on a swim mask and fins to join them for a while. Equipment can be rented. Admission charge.

Sian Ka'an – Extending south of Tulum to Punta Alticub is a 1.2-million-acre biosphere reserve, containing tropical forests, mangrove swamps, salt marshes, palm-rimmed beaches, archaeological ruins, and coral reefs, which combines the protection of wildlife with the balanced use of its resources. It's a paradise for bird watchers and crocodile and butterfly lovers. If you venture far enough into the jungle (not recommended as a solo journey), you're likely to come across a jaguar or some other member of the large cat species. There are two fine hotels on the reserve, where you also are likely to run into some millionaire yachtsman cruising the Caribbean: the pricey *Club de Pesca Boca Paila* (represented by *Carltony Tours,* A.P. 59, Cozumel, Q.R.; phone: 21176; in the US, 800-245-1950) and the *Pez Maya* (phone: 20072 in Cozumel; 800-327-2880 in the US). Considerably more rustic accommodations are available at *El Retiro* at Punta Xamach (clean cabins, but no private baths), or at *Posada Cuzam* at Punta Allen (thatch palm tepees). In Punta Allen, Candy Guzmán will provide a good meal, but only if you ask nicely, and arrangements can be made with one of the fishermen to visit *los cayos* (the keys). For guided visits, contact the *Association of Friends of Sian Ka'an* (Plaza Américas, Suite 48, Cancún, Q. R.; phone: 42201).

■**EXTRA SPECIAL:** A once thriving Maya center — built on a cliff above the sea and thought to be a major trading post — Tulum remains a place of mystery. Apparently inhabited at the time of the Spanish conquest, when other ceremonial cities had been abandoned, it was fortified and surrounded by a great wall. Tulum reached its apogee between AD 1000 and 1600, during the decline of the Maya civilization, and lacks the magnitude of such earlier cities as Chichén Itzá and Uxmal. The buildings found at Tulum are comparatively small in scale. However, the setting of Tulum — overlooking the fine white beaches and crystalline blue waters of the Caribbean — is magnificent and the trip should not be missed. The ruins are about 80 miles (120 km) from Cancún, with which it is connected by daily bus service. Admission charge.

Discovered only in 1972, Cobá was one of the largest cities in the Yucatán, covering about 80 square miles. Like Tulum, it is thought to have been a trade center with a population of 50,000 and was connected by a network of highways with other major Maya cities such as Chichén Itzá and Uxmal. About a half mile south of Tulum is a road that heads 30 miles (48 km) inland to this fascinating jungle-bound site on the banks of an island lagoon.

SOURCES AND RESOURCES

TOURIST INFORMATION: The Cancún Tourist Office is in the FONATUR building (at Cobá and Nader; phone: 43238), and there's an information booth (on Av. Tulum and Tulipanes, near the *Ki-Huic Market*). Hotel personnel are also very helpful. On Cozumel, the tourist office (phone: 20972) is in the Plaza del Sol building, and there is an information booth on the main square and at the tourist dock. Isla Mujeres also has a tourist office (18 Fco. I. Madero; phone: 20164). The best sources of information on Cancún are a pocket-size, biannual magazine, *Cancún Tips,* and the monthly periodical *Cancún Scene,* both available in many hotel rooms or on sale around town. Two similar publications, *Cozumel: What to Do and Where to Go* and *Cozumel Today,* provide up-to-date information. On Isla Mujeres *The Islander* tells you what's going on. Hotel travel desks are other good sources.

Local Coverage – The *News,* an English-language daily, is flown in from Mexico City; its Sunday travel supplement, *Vistas,* usually carries reports on Cancún and Cozumel.

TELEPHONE: The area code for Cancún and Isla Mujeres is 988; for Cozumel, 987. When calling from one city to another within Mexico, dial 91 before the area code.

CLIMATE AND CLOTHES: Chamber of Commerce types claim that Cancún has some of the best weather on the Caribbean, with 200 rain-free days each year and an average temperature of 80F. Still, it can be cool and windy at times and actually chilly at night. Rain is most likely during the last half of May, the first half of June, and September. Dress is elegant but informal; jackets are seldom worn and there's never a need for a tie. Cozumel and Isla Mujeres are scruffier than Cancún.

GETTING AROUND: Bus – Cancún probably has the best municipal bus service in Mexico. Routes follow a straight line, and the vehicles are seldom crowded. Transfers between the airport and hotels are handled by a fleet of minibuses that depart promptly, handle all luggage, and charge about $3 per person. From 6 AM until midnight, another bus flock covers the distance between Cancún City and the Tourist Zone's hotels and shopping area; fare is about 25¢, and it's a popular way to get around. Buses run along the island, passing all the hotels, and go on into the city. Buses also go out to Puerto Juárez, where the ferries leave for Isla Mujeres. Intercity buses, *Aerotransportes del Caribe* (*ADC;* phone: 41365) and *Autotransportes del Oriente* (*ADO;* phone: 43301) offer four departures daily for Akumal, Tulum, and Chetumal. There are ten departures each day for Chichén Itzá and Mérida.

Taxi – Small green and white cabs are available at reasonable fares, according to zone, in the Cancún area (fare from the farthest hotel to the city is about $6). Usually taxis are available at all the hotels on the island. If not, a doorman or bellman will call one quickly. In Cancún City there is a taxi stand on Avenida Tulum.

Car Rental – On Cancún, several agencies offer rental cars and jeeps for about $35 to $165 a day, including mileage: *Avis* (phone: 42147, 42328), *Dollar* (phone: 41709), *Econo-Rent* (phone: 48482), *Thrifty* (phone: 30373), and *Rent-autos Kankun* (phone: 41175). On Cozumel, *Rentadora Cozumel* (phone: 21120) has jeeps — the best bet for local roads — for about $60 a day, including insurance, tax, and mileage.

Mopeds – Small motorbikes are an easy way to get around and are available at many Cancún hotels. The *Casa Maya* (phone: 30138 or 30354) and *Frankie's* at the *Krystal* (phone: 32033) rent mopeds for about $35 a day. On Cozumel, *Rentadora Cozumel* (phone: 21120 or 21530) charges $25 for a 24-hour rental. They also rent bicycles for $3 a day. On Isla Mujeres, motorbikes — available about 50 paces from the ferry dock, also for about $20 a day — are the only way to go.

Tours – There are dozens of tour operators in Cancún, all of them with offices in hotels on the island. Guests at smaller hotels can arrange for tours with any of these operators. Both bus and automobile tours are available.

 SPECIAL EVENTS: The annual *Regata del Sol al Sol,* hosted in April or May by the *Isla Mujeres Yacht Club,* begins in St. Petersburg, Florida and finishes on Isla Mujeres. The annual billfish tourney held on Cozumel each May brings in sportsmen from all over, especially Florida, which sends a virtual fleet. Very much worth seeing on the first day of spring or fall is the Chichén Itzá phenomenon, when light and shadow strike the Castillo Pyramid in such a manner that the snake god Kukulkán (also known as "Quetzalcoatl") appears to be crawling down the side of the monument. The annual *Cancún Fair* takes place in November, with bullfights, cockfights, dances, and shows.

 **SHOPPING:** In addition to such regional items as *guayabera* shirts (dressy-casual with tucked fronts, sometimes embroidered), *huipil* dresses, and Panama hats, goods and handicrafts from all over Mexico (and the world) are sold in Cancún. The big and bustling *Ki-Huic* (Av. Tulum near Cobá) is the city-sponsored crafts market featuring some 44 stalls with an occasional find but generally not the best prices in town. In the Hotel Zone, or Zona Turística, some of the most elegant shops can be found at the *El Parián, Plaza Caracol, Mayfair, La Mansión-Costa Blanca, Flamingo Plaza, Plaza Nautilus,* and *Plaza Terramar* shopping centers.

On Cozumel, the work of some 200 first-rate Mexican artists is displayed at *Bazar Cozumel* (Av. Juárez), which features silver tapestries with modern art motifs, weavings, pottery, and much more at fair prices. Also worth visiting is *Plaza del Sol,* a nest of nearly a dozen arts, crafts, jewelry, and import boutiques, including *Los Cinco Soles,* a good shop for papier-mâché, carved wood, and onyx.

Shops on all three islands generally are open from 10 AM to 2 PM and from 4 to 7 PM; even stores that post their hours as such, though, may not open consistently on time.

CANCÚN

Artland – Rubbings, batiks, paintings, and jewelry, all inspired by Maya designs. Hotel Zone, *Flamingo Plaza* (phone: 32663).

Caroli – Jewelry and art objects crafted from sterling silver and semi-precious stones. Hotel Zone, *Flamingo Plaza* (phone: 50985).

La Casita – Arts, crafts, decorative items, leather, jewelry, and Mexican-inspired clothing displayed in a delightful setting. Downtown, 114 Tulum (no phone).

Los Castillo and Lily Castillo – Both stores are branches of one of Taxco's finest silversmith's, and both carry the beautifully designed and crafted jewelry and art objects that have made the Castillo name famous for generations. *Los Castillo* is known for its "wedded" metals, a union of silver, copper, and brass, and they now they are doing some exceptional work in stoneware with silver inlays. Hotel Zone, both in *Plaza Caracol* (phone: 31084, *Los Castillo*).

Dominique Imports – French perfume, jewelry, and fashions. Downtown at 33 and 45 Tulum, and *Plaza Caracol* on the island (no phone).

Don Cotton – Wonderful T-shirts in vivid colors with rain forest, Caribbean, and

Cancún motifs. The owners also run *Tango* (see below). Hotel Zone, *Plaza Caracol* (no phone).

Enea – One-of-a-kind designs for women and a unique selection of handicrafts that use unusual combinations of materials, such as pottery and straw. Downtown, 79 Tulum (phone: 41729).

Galerías Colonial – Tableware with beautifully painted patterns, carved marble knickknacks, and chess sets. Hotel Zone, *Plaza Caracol* (no phone).

Galería Maty Roca – Paintings, sculptures, and lighographs by some of Mexico's best contemporary artists. Señora Roca is a friendly woman who is a good source of information, not only on art but Cancún, as well. Hotel Zone, *Mayfair Shopping Center* (no phone).

Georgia – Women's fashions by Georgia Charukas whose romantic designs were inspired by the traditional Mexican wedding dress. Hotel Zone, *Mayfair Shopping Center* (no phone).

Gucci – The same name but *not* the real thing. Leather shoes and accessories are knock-offs of the traditional Gucci designs for men and women, but manufactured in Mexico at considerable savings. Hotel Zone, *Plaza Caracol* (no phone).

Las Mariposas – Super Mexican clothes — muslin caftans, batik shirts, tunics, tops, and shirts — all at reasonable prices. Ask if they don't have your size; they often can fulfill your request in a day or two. Silver and coral jewelry is sold here, too. *Plaza America* (no phone).

Pali – An unusual and varied selection of some of the very best of Mexico's handicrafts — ceramics, textiles, papier-mâché — at reasonable prices. Hotel Zone, *Flamingo Plaza* (phone: 33256).

Ronay – One of Mexico's most prestigious jewelers, specializing in gold designs. Hotel Zone, *Plaza Caracol* (phone: 31261).

Tane – Silver and vermeil jewelry, tableware, and art objects — many with traditional pre-Hispanic designs. Others are antique replicas. In the *Camino Real* (phone: 30100) and *Hyatt Regency* (phone: 30966) hotels.

Tango – More colorful T-shirts from the same owners of *Don Cotton* (see above). *Plaza Caracol* (phone: 30114).

COZUMEL

La Casita – The parent of the Cancún store and the source of more smashing Mexican resort clothes, as well as Sergio Bustamante's imaginative sculptures of animals and birds. Av. Rafael E. Melgar (phone: 20198).

Orbi – Imported perfume, jewelry, and specialty foods. Av. Rafael E. Melgar (phone: 20685).

ISLA MUJERES

La Bahía – Near the ferry dock, this shop carries an upscale selection of beachwear and also sells and rents diving gear (no phone).

Rachat and Romé – Outstanding jewelry designed and crafted by a friendly Cuban who owns this wonderful place. In the flamingo-colored building just a few steps from the ferry dock (no phone).

SPORTS: In Cancún, sports tend to be for participants, not spectators. The most convenient place to get the latest information is in the lobbies of most hotels.

Boating – Craft large and small, power and sail, crewed and uncrewed, are available in Cancún. Make arrangements at any hotel travel desk, and at *Marina Stouffer Presidente* (phone: 30330), *Club Lagoon* (phone: 31111), *Aqua-Quinn* (phone: 31883), *Marina Camino Real* (phone: 30100), and *Royal Yacht Club* (phone: 50391).

The *Regata del Sol al Sol,* from St. Petersburg, Florida, ends at Isla Mujeres. It's held yearly in April or May, and is followed by the *Amigos* regatta around the island.

Bullfights – Cancún has its own small bullring, which occasionally attracts major matadors. *Corridas* are held on Wednesdays.

Fishing – White marlin, bluefin tuna, and sailfish lure strong men and women to do battle on the deep sea. Sailfish are in season from March to mid-July; bonitos and dolphin, May to early July; wahoo and kingfish, May to September; and plenty of barracuda, red snapper, bluefin, grouper, mackerel, and white marlin year-round. Closer to shore, light tackle anglers attempt to hook the elusive permit. Boats, both large and small, are available at *Club Lagoon, Wild Goat Marina* (phone: 31111), *Avioturismo* (phone: 30315), *Royal Yacht Club* (phone: 50391), and *Aqua Tours* (phone: 30227 or 31883). Here again, hotels can make all the arrangements. Firms charge about $65 per person per day or $240 to $310 for a half day for groups. On Isla Mujeres *Cooperativa Isla Mujeres* (Av. Rueda Medina; phone: 20274) and *Mexico Divers* (near the dock; phone: 20131) arrange trips for 4 for about $350 a day.

Golf – On the island, the Robert Trent Jones, Sr., golf course, *Pok-Ta-Pok* (phone: 30871), offers gently rolling fairways bordered by palms, with the Caribbean breeze making play comfortable throughout the day. Clubs and carts may be rented; open daily. The greens fee is $30; carts, $20 per round. There is also a restaurant.

Horseback Riding – *Hacienda San José de las Vegas* has escorted horseback tours through the jungle, four times a day, Mondays through Saturdays. On Sundays, they rent horses by the hour. At Km 11.5 on the road to Tulum (phone: 40373).

Jet Skiing – The lagoon is great for this water sport, which requires a minimum of learning time. The skis slow down and stay with you should you fall off. Available at the *Royal Yacht Club* (phone: 50391) and *Marina Jet Ski* (phone: 30766).

Scuba and Snorkeling – Cancún's best scuba diving and snorkeling place is in the reef-filled waters off its southern point. Dive trips and equipment rental can be arranged through your hotel. A 5-hour dive trip including pool checkout and an ocean dive costs about $40, including equipment. Snorkel gear rents for about $5 per person for the day. Guided scuba trips by boat cost about $50 including equipment. The variety of the reefs and the clarity of the water (average undersea visibility, year-round, is 100 feet, but you can often see much farther) make Mexico's Caribbean a top area for underwater exploring. Cozumel takes the diving honors. Its prime attractions are the reefs 500 yards off the island's leeward shore, along El Cantil (The Drop-Off), the edge of the shelf that borders the Yucatán Channel to the south. Famous 6-mile-long Palancar Reef has — in addition to forests of black, staghorn, and other species of live coral and friendly swarms of Day-Glo-colored fish — a number of antique wrecks in which to poke around. Besides diving to look and take pictures, you can try your skill at capturing (by hand) giant lobsters, crab, and conch. Spearfishing is forbidden in the waters around Cozumel and Cancún.

Several dive shops on Cozumel — including *Del Mar Aquatics* (in *La Ceiba;* phone: 20816), *Casa del Mar* (phone: 21944), *Aqua Safari* (phone: 20101), *Viajes y Deportes de Cozumel* (in the *Stouffer Presidente;* phone: 20923), *Neptuno Divers* (phone: 20999), and *Discover Cozumel* (phone: 20280) — offer rental equipment, instruction, and dive trips. Most hotels also offer diving facilities at somewhat higher rates, but the convenience is worth it. Scuba pool instruction (about 3 hours) costs about $50 per person. A 4- to 5-day seminar with a certified instructor that includes theory, shallow shore dives, a boat dive to a shallow reef, and a full boat dive to Palancar Reef is about $300 per person (less in the off-season). A full day's guided diving tour from Cozumel to Palancar, including equipment and lunch, is about $40. Equipment rentals run about $6 for a tank and weights; $6 to $12 for a regulator; $5 for fins, mask, and snorkel. Underwater camera rental is about $30 per day at *Cozumel Images* at the *Casa del Mar* hotel (phone: 21900).

For an area that offers scuba divers so much, Cozumel seems short on good snorkeling spots; best are the shallow reefs to the south, where depths range from 5 to 35 feet. Chankanab Lagoon, midway down the leeward coast, with its underwater grottoes and fairly large fish population, is a good place for beginners to get their fins wet. The snorkeling on Isla Mujeres is excellent. Scuba equipment and dive trips are available through *Cooperativa Gustavo Orozco* (phone: 20274) and *Buzos de México* (no phone).

Swimming and Sunning – Although Cancún's beaches on its surf-pounded Caribbean side still are not as wide as they were before Hurricane Gilbert, they are much improved since the 1988 storm, and its more serene Bahía de Mujeres and lagoon shores are even wider in some areas. The texture and whiteness of the sand is so distinctive they inspired special studies by geologists, who found that many of the sand's individual grains contain microscopic, star-shaped fossils of an organism called Discoaster, extinct for 70 million years. Through the ages, the sea has ground and polished these grains till they've become brilliant and powder soft. What's more, their limestone composition has an air conditioning effect that makes the island's sand — even under the noonday sun — feel comfortable to bare feet or bodies in bikinis. Except right in Cancún City, chances are your hotel will have its own beach as well as a pool, but the master plan has provided several public strands — Playa Tortugas and Playa Chac-Mool are just two examples.

Cozumel's beaches — mostly on the island's leeward side, north and south of San Miguel — are shaped into distinctive coves. The majority of hotels are there, too, and you'll probably spend most of your sun and sea time beside your own hotel or on nearby sands. You can visit others, including the lengthy one about 10 miles (16 km) south of San Miguel at San Francisco (a bit crowded these days, particularly on weekends); the more secluded shore of Passion Island, cupped in its north coast bay; and Punta Moreno, on the rough side with a sheltered lagoon nearby. Because the undertow can be tricky, it's a good idea to observe the currents before you take the plunge (plan to enter the water at one point, exit at another), and never swim alone.

On Isla Mujeres, the lazy, unspoiled beaches and El Garrafón, with its undersea formations and colorful fish, are why most visitors come.

Tennis – On Cancún there are courts at the *Calinda Cancún Beach* (phone: 31600), *Camino Real* (phone: 30100), *Casa Maya, Aristos* (phone: 30555), *Fiesta Americano Condesa* (phone: 51000), *Fiesta Americana Coral Beach* (phone: 32200), *Hyatt Cancún. Caribe* (phone: 30044), *Krystal* (phone: 31133), *Marriott Casa Magna* (phone: 52000), *Pok-Ta-Pok Golf Club* (phone: 30871), *Meliá Cancún* (phone: 51160), and the *Sheraton* (phone: 31988). On Cozumel there are tennis courts at *La Ceiba* (phone: 20379), the *Cozumel Caribe* (phone: 20100), the *Fiesta Americana Sol Caribe* (phone: 20700), the *Fiesta Inn* (phone: 22900), the *Melia Mayan Cozumel* (phone: 20072), the *Stouffer Presidente* (phone: 20322), and the *Villablanca* (phone: 20730).

Water Skiing – The lagoon behind the island of Cancún is the ideal place to learn or perfect this exhilarating sport. Make arrangements at any island hotel, at *Las Velitas Marina* on the beach at *Club Caribe* (phone: 30311), *Marina Jet Ski* (phone: 30766), or at the *Club Lagoon* (phone: 30222). Boat time costs about $50 an hour.

Windsurfing – Once you've learned to stand on a surfboard, 2 or 3 hours of instruction are all you need. In Cancún lessons are available at several hotels, including the *Club Lagoon.* Boards rent for about $10 an hour. Lessons cost $25, and several places offer weekly rates that include lessons. There are regattas Sundays at *Club Cancún.*

 NIGHTCLUBS AND NIGHTLIFE: After-dark activity in Cancún has picked up considerably in the past few years. Reigning disco favorites are easily discernible by the crowds gathering outside before opening time (around 10 PM). Current hot spots are *Christine's* at the *Krystal, Risky Business* (downtown on Av. Tulum), *La Boom* (Kukulcán Blvd.; phone: 31458 or 31641), the chic *Aquarius* (at the *Camino Real*), *Dady 'O* (near the *Convention Center*), the lively *Daphny's* (at the *Sheraton*), and the *Hard Rock Café* (at *Plaza Lagunas*). *Carlos 'n' Charlie's Cancún* on the marina is a good place for food, drink, dancing, and meeting people; it's open until midnight. *Sixties* in the *Marriott* plays dance music from the 1950s, '60s, and '70s.

For lots of silly fun, there's the Pirate's Night Adventure cruise, available in both Cancún and Cozumel; for more information call the Cancún Visitor's Bureau (phone: 31021). Not to be missed is the *Folkloric Ballet* at the Cancún *Convention Center*, performed daily except Sundays. A buffet dinner is served at 7 PM, and the show begins at 8:30 PM (phone: 30199). A torchlit beach, a delicious buffet, and exotic drinks make for a romantic evening at the *Hyatt Cancún Caribe's* Mexican Night, Mondays, Wednesdays, Fridays, and Saturdays at 7:00 PM. The *Sheraton* hosts a similar event on Wednesdays at 7:30 PM, and *Plaza las Glorias* hosts one on Tuesdays.

On Cozumel, *Scaramouche*, downtown, is lively and attempts sophistication. *Neptuno*, next to *El Acuario* restaurant on the *malecón*, is popular also. No matter where you go, the crowds tend to be young.

On Isla Mujeres, there's *Buho's Disco Bar, Calypso, Tequila Video Disco*, and *Casablanca*, as well as beach parties and night cruises.

BEST IN TOWN

CHECKING IN: All the hotels on Cancún are relatively new (or brand new), aspire to be lavish, and boast some of the highest prices in Mexico. Travelers on a budget, however, can find less costly accommodations away from the major beaches. During high season (December to May), expect to pay $180 to $270 per day for a double room in those places we call very expensive (the highest price would be for a two-bedroom villa); about $175 in expensive; $75 to $100 in moderate, and $60 or less in inexpensive. Prices drop as much as 50% during the summer months. Even with close to 6,000 hotel rooms (and more added every month), Cancún really does not have enough hotel space to meet the demand during the winter months, so it is best to go only with a confirmed reservation.

The more luxurious Cozumel hotels are either in the North Zone or South Zone, above and below the town. The in-town hotels (which have neither beach nor pool) appeal most to budget travelers. Hotel prices on Cozumel are similar to those on Cancún, and it is also best to arrive here with a prepaid reservation. Hotel rates on Isla Mujeres tend to be moderate to inexpensive. All telephone numbers on Cancún and Isla Mujeres are in the 988 area code; on Cozumel, 987 unless otherwise indicated. When calling from one city to another within Mexico, dial 91 before the area code.

■**Note:** Parking can be a problem at some hotels.

CANCÚN

Camino Real – Virtually surrounded by water, Westin Hotels' magnificent 381-room pleasure palace has an enclosed saltwater swimming lagoon, a bar in the pool, 3 tennis courts, 3 restaurants, *Aquarius* disco — the works. On the island (phone: 30100; in the US, 800-228-3000; FAX: 31730). Very expensive.

Fiesta Americana – Its appearance is unique, with a Mexican pink façade and a fountain-filled lobby. Each of the 280 rooms has rattan furnishings and a balcony overlooking the water. The pool area is very nicely laid out with thatch-roofed, open-air restaurant and bars, beyond which is the aqua blue bay. Snorkeling gear is available poolside. The lobby is a pretty place for before-dinner cocktails, with a strolling mariachi band. On the island (phone: 31400; in the US, 800-FIESTA-1; FAX: 31495). Very expensive.

Fiesta Americana Condesa – A Grand Tourism hotel (Mexico's 5-star rating), it has three towers, each with its own atrium lounge covered by a glass, *palapa*-shaped roof. The decor is mostly rattan complemented by fresh, vivid colors. There are 500 rooms — including 27 suites with Jacuzzis on private terraces — a split-level pool with a 66-foot waterfall, 5 restaurants, 5 lighted tennis courts, a jogging track, spa, and a lobby bar where live music is played in the evenings. The beach, most of which was swept away by Hurricane Gilbert, had still only partially returned as we went to press. Blvd. Kukulkán (phone: 51000; in the US, 800-FIESTA-1; FAX: 51650). Very expensive.

Fiesta Americana Coral Beach – With two rather overwhelming, modern, peach-colored towers, it offers all-suite accommodations, 3 restaurants, 3 bars, a night-club, a coffee shop, huge pool, 5 lighted artificial grass tennis courts, and a gym. Hotel Zone (phone: 32900; in the US, 800-FIESTA-1; FAX: 32905). Very expensive.

Hyatt Cancún Caribe – A graceful white arc a short walk from the *Convention Center*, this 200-room resort has 60 villas, 4 restaurants, 3 lighted tennis courts, 3 pools, a Jacuzzi, water sports, and an art gallery in the lobby. On the island, Km 8.5 of Blvd. Kukulcán (phone: 30044; in the US, 800-233-1234; FAX: 31514). Very expensive.

Hyatt Regency – Beautifully housed under a glass atrium, all 300 rooms have ocean views. It has a pool, 3 bars, and 3 restaurants (phone: 30966; in the US, 800-233-1234; FAX: 73369). Very expensive.

Krystal Cancún – Lush and thick, with greenery outside and in, it offers 318 rooms, tennis, and 5 fine restaurants, including a good breakfast buffet. On the island (phone: 31133; in the US, 619-792-1443; FAX: 31205). Very expensive.

Marriott Casa Magna – A 6-story hostelry of contemporary design, it is stunningly decorated with Mexican textures and colors. All rooms have balconies providing a view of either the Caribbean or the lagoon. Four restaurants — including a Japanese steakhouse — nightclub, pool, Jacuzzi, and 2 lighted tennis courts. Hotel Zone (phone: 52000; in the US, 800-228-9290). Very expensive.

Meliá Cancún – With a waterfall that cascades over part of the entrance, this marble and glass complex has a huge, central atrium that looks and, unfortunately, feels like a tropical jungle. It's all beautifully decorated with bright tiles, bentwood, and wicker. Four restaurants, 5 bars, 3 lighted artificial grass tennis courts, and 18 holes of golf. Hotel Zone (phone: 51160; in the US, 800-336-3542; FAX: 51085). Very expensive.

Meliá Turquesa – A giant white pyramid that slopes down to the beach, it offers 446 rooms decorated in tranquil colors and equipped with satellite TV and mini-bars. There also are 2 restaurants, 3 bars, a coffee shop, pool, and 2 lighted artificial grass tennis courts. Hotel Zone (phone: 32544; in the US, 800-336-3542; FAX: 51029). Very expensive.

Stouffer Presidente – On the golf links and boasting 1 tennis court, fishing, and water skiing, this stately, 295-room hostelry is a favorite of sports enthusiasts. Its beach and location are among the best on Cancún. On the island (phone: 30200, 30414, or 30202; in the US, 800-HOTELS-1; FAX 21360). Very expensive.

Villas Tacul – A colony of 23 Spanish-style villas with gardens, patios, and kitchens, where guests can set up luxurious housekeeping, eat out at the *palapa*, cook for themselves or arrange for someone to come in — or all of the above. With 2 to 5 bedrooms per house, on a narrow but pleasant beach. Good for families and congenial 2- or 3-couple groups. Km 5.5 on the Blvd. Kukulcán (phone: 30000; in the US, 800-842-0193; FAX: 30349). Very expensive.

Calinda Cancún Beach – Situated on the best beach on the island, between the Nichupté Lagoon and Bahía Mujeres, this hostelry isn't as lavish as many others on the island, but it's very popular — the kind of place people return to year after year for the especially friendly atmosphere. Restaurant, bars, pool, tennis, and gym (phone: 31600; in the US, 800-228-5151; FAX: 31857). Expensive.

Cancún Sheraton – This 748-room gem — self-contained and as big as a village — is set apart on its own beach, which it shares with a small Maya temple. Facilities include 6 tennis courts, 6 pools, and *Daphny's* video bar with live music; there are also aerobics classes and scuba lessons. On the island (phone: 31988). Expensive.

Casa Maya – Originally built as condominiums, the 350 rooms and suites here are large, to say the least, with immense walk-in closets, sinks the size of bathtubs, and tubs the size of swimming pools. Among the amenities are moped rental, 3 lighted tennis courts, a swimming pool, restaurant, and cordial service. The place seems to be especially popular with families. On the island (phone: 30555; in the US, 713-931-6283; FAX: 31188). Expensive.

Club Med – Completely rebuilt after Hurricane Gilbert and boasting one of the widest beaches on the island, it's now one of the prime places to stay in Cancún. The 410 rooms, each with 2 European single beds and traditional Mexican decor, are set in 3-story bungalows facing either the ocean or the lagoon. Windsurfing, sailing, snorkeling, scuba diving (including scuba instruction) are included in the basic rate, as are all meals. Lunch and dinner include complimentary wine. There's entertainment nightly. At Punta Nizuc (phone: 42409 or 800-CLUB-MED). Expensive.

Conrad – Opened in early spring last year, this new complex features 385 rooms, including 92 in the deluxe concierge tower, which offers special facilities for guests: a private pool and cocktail lounge, and complimentary continental breakfast. The decor is typically tropical, and all rooms provide a view of either the ocean or lagoon. Facilities include 5 outdoor swimming pools, 2 lighted tennis courts, a health club and recreation center, 6 whirlpool baths, a water sports center, and a boat dock for access to scuba diving, snorkeling, small boating in the large bay, water skiing, board sailing, and evening cruises. There are 2 restaurants and 2 lounges. Paseo Kukulcán, at Punta Nizuc on the southern end of the island (phone: 50086 or 50537; 800-HILTONS in the US; FAX: 50074). Expensive.

Miramar Misión – This 189-room hostelry has several bars, 3 restaurants, and nightly entertainment. On the island (phone: 31755; FAX: 31136). Expensive.

Omni – Each of the 285 rooms has a large terrace, and there are 35 suites and 27 villas as well. Facilities include 2 lighted tennis courts, 8 restaurants, bars, a gameroom, and a health center. Their beautiful beach was all but washed away by Hurricane Gilbert, but hammocks have been strung up on the grounds for lounging and sipping tropical drinks by the sea. Four of the rooms are especially equipped for handicapped guests, and there are access ramps to all public areas. Km 16.5 Blvd. Kukulcán (phone: 50714; 212-517-7998 in the US; FAX: 50184). Expensive.

Royal Solaris Super Club – A Maya pyramid-like structure, it has 223 rooms (including 3 suites), an Olympic-size pool, health club, and social programs. The beach, narrower since Hurricane Gilbert hit, is in fairly good shape. Km 23 Blvd. Kukulcán (phone: 50100; FAX: 50354). Expensive.

America – There are 180 large rooms, each with its own terrace, at this pleasant place. It is not right on the beach, but does provide free shuttle service to its own beach club. Pool, restaurant, bar, coffee shop. Av. Tulum (phone: 41500; in the US, 800-899-6283; FAX: 41953). Moderate.

Aristos Cancún – The friendly scale and Mexican hospitality make for easy comfort here. Smallish but pleasant 244 rooms. Inviting pool area, beach, 2 lighted tennis courts, and restaurant. Km 9.5 on the Blvd. Kukulcán (phone: 30011; FAX: 30078). Moderate.

Club Lagoon – This secluded collection of adobe-type dwellings, on quiet Laguna Nichupté, including rooms and 2-level suites, is a real find. One picturesque courtyard opens onto another, with flowers playing colorfully against the white cottages; the best face the lagoon. It also has 2 restaurants, 2 bars, and a nautical center. On the island (phone: 31111; FAX: 31326). Moderate.

Fiesta Inn Golf and Beach Club – Decorated in shades of soft pastels, the 120 rooms here are set right at the edge of the *Pok-Ta-Pok* golf course. Guests receive a 50% discount on greens fees, and they are allowed use of the facilities and services of other Fiesta Americana hotels on the island (charges are automatically billed to rooms). There is no beach, but free transportation is provided to the hotel's beach club. On the island (phone: 32200; 800-FIESTA-1 in the US; FAX: 32532). Moderate.

Playa Blanca – A pioneer among the Cancún hotels, it opened in 1974 on a small beachfront and is now part of the Best Western chain. It has 161 rooms, a pool, and every water sport imaginable. Since it's next door to the marina, the boating facilities are excellent. On the island (phone: 30344; in the US, 212-517-7770; FAX: 30904). Moderate.

La Posada del Capitan Lafitte – In Punta Bete, this delightful beachfront bungalow complex is set in an area especially good for lounging in a hammock or exploring one of the patch reefs that lie just a few yards offshore. There is a restaurant. Twenty miles (32 km) south of the Cancún airport. For information and reservations, contact *Turquoise Reef Resorts,* Box 2664, Evergreen, CO 80439 (no local phone; 800-538-6802 in the US). Moderate.

Antillano – Amid the bustle of Tulum Avenue, this 48-room, modern white structure is a pleasant, economical place to stay. Cancún City (phone: 41532; FAX: 41878). Inexpensive.

Kailuum – Next door to the *La Posada del Capitan Lafitte* bungalows, it shares the same tranquil surroundings. The 40 tents here have comfortable mattresses and maid service but no electricity or telephones. Two centrally located bathhouses have flush toilets and running hot and cold water. No children allowed. For reservations and information, contact *Turquoise Reef Resorts,* Box 2664, Evergreen, CO 80439 (no local phone; 800-538-6802 in the US). Inexpensive.

Plaza Caribe – A good bet downtown, across from the bus station. The air conditioned rooms fill up fast. Cancún City (phone: 41377; in the US, 800-334-7234; FAX: 46352). Inexpensive.

Plaza del Sol – Half-moon-shaped, with two stylized canoes over its portals, it has 87 rooms, a pool, restaurant, bar, and free transportation to the beach. Cancún City (phone: 43888; FAX: 44393). Inexpensive.

COZUMEL

Club Cozumel Caribe – A twisting, palm-canopied drive leads to this expansive 280-room property with attractive grounds. It offers tennis, a small pool, and a restaurant. Rate includes all meals, drinks, water sports, sightseeing, and a moonlight cruise. San Juan Beach (phone: 20100; in the US, 800-327-2254; FAX: 20288). Very expensive.

Fiesta Americana Sol-Caribe – A beautiful 322-room resort (102 of the rooms are in a new tower) 'twixt beach and jungle, it has 3 tennis courts, good diving facilities, and a fine dining room. South Zone (phone: 20700; in the US, 800-FIESTA-1; FAX: 21301). Expensive.

Stouffer Presidente Cozumel – The original luxury establishment on the island and still one of the best. Pleasant beach, nice pool, tennis, excellent dining room. South Zone (phone: 20322; in the US, 800-HOTELS-1; FAX: 21360). Expensive.

Meliá Mayan Cozumel – Set on the isolated north end of the coast, this 12-story high-rise on the beach has 188 rooms and suites, an abundance of terraces, 2 tennis courts, a *Fiesta Mexicana* on Thursdays, and a *Caribbean Fiesta* on Fridays. Playa Santa Pilar (phone: 20072; in the US, 800-336-3542; FAX: 21599). Expensive to moderate.

Barracuda – Near the shopping area, this small place has in-room bars. Breakfast is served on the beach. No pool. Rate includes continental breakfast. Av. Rafael Melgar, south of town (phone: 20002; FAX: 20884). Moderate.

Cabañas del Caribe – A semi-tropical hideaway on one of the island's best beaches, it has a small pool, 39 rooms, and 9 cabañas. Informal, friendly. North Zone (phone: 20017; in the US, 800-336-3542; FAX: 21599). Moderate.

La Ceiba – The best equipped and located for scuba divers, this 115-room hostelry has satellite TV, spa, tennis, a restaurant, and cocktail lounge. Paradise Point (phone: 20379 or 20844; in the US, 800-621-6830; FAX: 20065). Moderate.

El Cozumeleño – This property has 104 large rooms, 3 restaurants, a bar, tennis court, and a free-form pool. Santa Pilar (phone: 20050; FAX: 20381). Moderate.

Fiesta Inn – Another member of the Fiesta group, this one is a 3-story, colonial-style hostelry surrounded by beautiful gardens and connected to the beach by a tunnel. The 178 rooms and 2 suites have satellite TV. Facilities include a large pool, tennis court, motorcycle rental, dive shop, restaurant, bar, and coffee shop. Km 1.7 Costera Sur (phone: 22900; in the US, 800-FIESTA-1; FAX: 22154). Moderate.

Mara – Most of the 48 rooms face the lovely beach. Pleasant pool, restaurant, and dive shop. North Zone (phone: 20300; in the US, 800-221-6509; FAX: 239290). Moderate.

La Perla – Right on the beach, this 4-story hotel has its own swimming cove and a pier with diesel, light, and water connections for private yachts. Also a pool, deli-bar, dive packages, and a quiet, comfortable, unpretentious atmosphere. 2 Av. Francisco y Madero, PO Box 309 (phone: 20188). Moderate.

Playa Azul – A family favorite, it has 60 rooms and suites, a restaurant, bar, and water sports. North of San Miguel, at Km 4 on Carr. San Juan (phone: 20033; FAX: 21793). Moderate.

Aguilar – It has a pool (but no beach), gardens, glass-bottom boat rides, and motor-cycle rentals. In town (phone: 20307). Inexpensive.

Villablanca – Though its facilities resemble those of a resort hotel — tennis court, pool, dive shop, boat for up to 60 divers, classes in all water sports — this property has only 30 rooms and suites, some with Roman baths and all with air conditioning and fans. Across the street, on the water's edge, is its restaurant-bar-beach club, *Amadeus.* Km 2.9 Playa Paraíso (phone: 20730; in the US, 306-891-3949). Inexpensive.

ISLA MUJERES

Cabañas María del Mar – At the north end of the island, it has 35 units (including 10 cabañas), a restaurant, and a full-service 20-slip marina. The proprietors, the Limas, make everyone feel at home. Av. Carlos Lazo (phone: 20179). Moderate.

Perlas del Caribe – Formerly the *Rocas del Caribe,* it's been expanded and remodeled into a 3-story hotel with 97 rooms, all with balconies; there is a restaurant and pool. 2 Av. Madero (phone: 20444; FAX: 20011). Moderate.

Berny – A downtown hostelry, with 37 rooms, pool, and restaurant. Av. Juarez (phone: 20025; FAX: 20026). Inexpensive.

Kan Kin – It's also known as *Maria's,* after the popular restaurant (see *Eating Out*) that now has expanded to include several colorful, air conditioned rooms. The setting is gorgeous, and El Garrafón Beach is a short walk away. Five miles (8 km) south of town, at Km 5 (phone: 20015; FAX: 20395). Inexpensive.

Posada del Mar – This pleasant 42-room hostelry is one of the best on the island, with palm-shaded grounds, a restaurant, bar, pool, Laundromat, and air conditioning. Across from the beach, 15 Av. Rueda Medina (phone: 20300). Inexpensive.

Rocamar – Thirty-four basic but pleasant rooms, all with a view. Av. Nicolas Bravo y Garero (phone: 20101). Inexpensive.

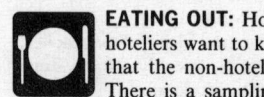 **EATING OUT:** Hotel food on Cancún is better than average because the hoteliers want to keep the money spent on food in the house, which means that the non-hotel restaurants must work extra hard to lure customers. There is a sampling of ethnic cooking, and by all means try Yucatecan specialties, which are quite different from standard Mexican fare. Start the day with eggs *moltuleños* — fried eggs on a tortilla — black beans, and a spicy sauce. And don't miss delicious and filling Yucatán lime soup, which also contains chicken, vegetables, and tortillas. Expect to pay $40 to $60 for two in restaurants we list as expensive, about $30 at moderate places, and $20 in inexpensive. Prices do not include wine, tips, or drinks.

Almost all the restaurants on Cozumel are in town, although a few, open only for lunch, are out on the beaches. Restaurant prices on Cozumel and Isla Mujeres are somewhat more moderate than those on Cancún. All restaurants accept MasterCard and Visa; a few also accept American Express and Diners Club. Unless noted otherwise, restaurants are open daily. All telephone numbers on Cancun and Isla Mujeres are in the 988 area code; on Cozumel, 987 unless otherwised indicated. When calling from one city to another within Mexico, dial 91 before the area code.

CANCÚN

Blue Bayou – Cajun and creole fare and specialty drinks are served in a multilevel dining area suspended among waterfalls and lush tropical greenery. Live jazz. Dinner only. Reservations necessary. *Hyatt Cancún Caribe* (phone: 30044, ext. 54). Expensive.

Bogart's – International dishes served with quiet elegance in exotic Moroccan surroundings. No shorts or T-shirts. Seatings at 7 and 9:30 PM. Reservations advised. At the *Krystal* (phone: 31333). Expensive.

Carlos 'n' Charlie's – Fun 'n' games are the strong points at this branch of Mexico's well-known restaurant chain, where good spareribs and shrimp are served. There's also a small dockside disco where diners can dance the night away. Open daily. No reservations. On the island (phone: 31304). Expensive.

Chac-Mool – The menu is continental, sprinkled with seafood specialties and homemade pasta. Classical music adds to the atmosphere. Reservations advised. Km 10 Blvd. Kukulcán, next to the *Aristos Hotel* (phone: 31107). Expensive.

La Dolce Vita – Modern decor is the backdrop to intimate dining, where the sweet life is manifested in tasty pasta and seafood dishes. Open daily. Reservations advised. 87 Cobá in Cancún City (phone: 41384). Expensive.

La Habichuela – The place local folk go for a night out and for *mar y tierra,* alias surf and turf. Open daily. Reservations advised. 25 Margaritas in Cancún City (phone: 43158). Expensive.

Hacienda el Mortero – An authentic copy of a Mexican hacienda in Súchil, Durango, it specializes in steaks and Mexican haute cuisine. Open daily. Reservations advised. In the *Krystal Hotel,* Km 9 on the Blvd. Kukulcán (phone: 31133). Expensive.

Maxime – Formerly the mayor's home, this elegant dining place has European furniture, Oriental rugs, English china, and French crystal — not to mention 4 sitting rooms, 1 dining room, and an upstairs piano bar. The French chef recommends the breast of chicken in red wine or the shrimp in puff pastry. Jackets are not required, nor are shorts and sandals permitted. Open daily. Reservations advised. On the island (phone: 30438). Expensive.

El Pescador – Perhaps the best seafood eatery in Cancún, it serves fresh lobster, shrimp, and red snapper on Mexican pottery. Don't miss the Yucatecan lime soup or the hot rolls, and try for a table outside, on the fan-cooled terrace. Closed Mondays. Reservations unnecessary. 5 Tulipanes, Cancún City (phone: 42673). Expensive.

Scampi – Superb Northern Italian fare — delicious pasta, meat, and seafood — is served in a beautiful setting. The service is impeccable. Reservations advised. *Hyatt Regency* (phone: 30966). Expensive.

Señor Frog's – Under the same ownership as *Carlos 'n' Charlie's,* it offers a similar menu (see above). Open for breakfast, lunch, and dinner. Reservations unnecessary. At Km 5.5 Blvd. Kukulcán (phone: 32931). Expensive.

Seryna – Japanese specialties such as sushi, teppanyaki, sukiyaki, yosenabe, shabu-shabu, tempura, and other traditional dishes are served in a pretty setting. Open daily. Reservations advised. Plaza Flamingo (phone: 51155 or 32995). Expensive.

Augustus Caesar – Seafood and traditional Italian dishes are served with flair in pretty surroundings. Live music is featured from 8:30 PM to midnight. No shorts or T-shirts. Open daily. Reservations advised. At *La Mansión-Costa Blanca Shopping Center* (phone: 33384). Expensive to moderate.

Bombay Bicycle Club – Casual and comfortable, this spot offers fare from the States — good hamburgers, barbecued ribs, and calorie-filled desserts. Excellent, friendly service. Open 7 AM to midnight. No reservations. Blvd. Kukulcán, across from Playa Tortuga (no phone). Moderate.

La Mamá de Tarzan – Another link in the ubiquitous Anderson's chain, this one is a cafeteria-style eatery with good salads, a lively bar, nightly fiesta, and dancing on the pier. Open daily. Reservations advised. Opposite Chac-Mool Beach (31092). Moderate.

Pop – Gringo-style breakfast, lunch, and dinner, and cheerful service. Open daily. No reservations. 26 Tulum (phone: 41991). Moderate.

Torremolinos – Paella, crayfish, and crab done the Spanish way. Closed Tuesdays. No reservations. Tulum and X'caret (phone: 43639). Moderate.

Pizza Rolandi – All kinds of Italian dishes are served in an informal, outdoor setting. Open daily. Reservations unnecessary. 12 Av. Cobá, Cancún City (phone: 44047). Moderate to inexpensive.

Los Alemendros – Authentic Yucatecan food and the same management as its famous Mérida namesake. Open daily. Reservations unnecessary. Av. Bonampak and Sayíl in Cancún City (phone: 40807). Inexpensive.

Augustus Pizza – Popular with kids, it's an Italian pizza parlor in the great US tradition. Open daily. Reservations unnecessary. *Convention Center,* on the island (phone: 30530). Inexpensive.

Café Amsterdam – Reasonably priced European dishes are served in this intimate bistro. The delicious bread is baked on the premises, and there is a huge salad and fresh fruit bar. Open from 7 AM to 11 PM; closed Mondays. Reservations unnecessary. 70 Av. Yaxchilan (phone: 44098). Inexpensive.

100% Natural – The place to go for fresh fruit drinks, salads, sandwiches, and fruit and vegetable platters. Live jazz nightly. No reservations. 6 Sunyaxchen (no phone). Inexpensive.

COZUMEL

El Acuario – Once a real aquarium, it's now an elegant seafood restaurant, with entertainment provided by an immense tankful of exotic tropical fish in the middle of the room. Open daily. Reservations advised. On the *malecón* (phone: 21097). Expensive.

Carlos 'n' Charlie's and Jimmy – The Cozumel branch of Mexico's favorite restaurant chain, where people come for ribs and good times. Open daily. Reservations advised. On the *malecón.* (phone: 20191). Expensive.

Morgan's – Lobster thermidor and special coffees are favorites at this very comfortable, popular wood cabin serving good steaks and seafood on the main plaza. Open daily. Reservations advised (phone: 20584). Expensive.

Pepe's Grill – This romantic spot by the waterfront has excellent seafood and steaks. A variety of live music is featured nightly. Open daily. Reservations advised. Av. Rafael Melgar (phone: 20213). Expensive.

Casa Denis – The menu varies at this cozy spot where Yucatecan dishes are served under a tropical fruit tree. Reservations advised. Just off the south side of the main square in San Miguel (phone: 20067). Moderate.

Mezcalito's – Set on the surf-pounded Caribbean side of Cozumel, this large open-air *palapa* serves up some of the tastiest grilled shrimp and fish on the island. The atmosphere — white sand, ocean breezes, and friendly chatter — is unbeatable. A good spot, too, just to stop for a cold beer or a piña colada. No reservations. Punta Morena (no phone). Moderate.

Plaza Leza – A sidewalk café serving good Mexican snacks, charcoal-broiled steaks, and seafood. Open daily. Reservations advised. On the main plaza (phone: 21041). Moderate.

Las Palmeras – Just opposite the ferry dock, it's a great meeting place offering a varied menu for every meal. The homemade biscuits and French toast are a treat for breakfast. Open daily. Reservations unnecessary. On the *malecón* (phone: 20532). Moderate.

La Laguna – A big *palapa* at Chankanab where nachos, hamburgers, and the like are served from 10 AM to 4 PM. Open daily. No reservations (no phone). Inexpensive.

El Portal – This is a favorite for breakfast. Open daily. Reservations unnecessary. On the *malecón* (no phone). Inexpensive.

San Francisco – The fare — what else? — is seafood, and a band plays in the afternoons. Open daily for lunch only. Reservations unnecessary. A quarter-mile from San Francisco Beach and about 9 miles (14 km) from town (no phone). Inexpensive.

Las Tortugas – Simple but good Mexican fare is served here along with good, cold beer. Don't be put off by the nondescript surroundings. Open daily. Reservations unnecessary. 82 Av. 10 Norte, in the heart of town. (no phone) Inexpensive.

ISLA MUJERES

Ciro's Lobster House – A wide selection of Mexican wines accompanies the lobster and red snapper served here. Open daily. Reservations advised. 11 Matamoros, in town (phone: 20102). Expensive.

Gomar – Lobster and fresh fish are best enjoyed on the romantic terrace, where tables sport bright, striped Mexican cloths during the day; white at night. You can also dine indoors. Open daily. Reservations unnecessary. Hidalgo and Madero (phone: 20142). Moderate.

Hacienda Gomar – In addition to a good seafood buffet and exotic drinks, there is a natural aquarium where one can swim among giant, hundred-year-old turtles —

and even ride them. Open daily. No reservations. On the west side of the island on the road to El Garrafón Beach (no phone). Moderate.

María's Kan Kin – Travel the 2 miles (3 km) out of town to this delightful villa with its unassuming façade and a knockout view. As if open-air dining on fresh seafood, generous, tasty tropical cocktails, and the seductive surroundings weren't enough, the menu itself is a work of art: hand-done in colors on woven straw. A meal that's less than leisurely is unthinkable here. Open daily. Reservations advised. Near El Garrafón Beach (phone: 20015). Moderate.

Los Pájaros – Facing the beach on the north end of town, this *palapa*-style eatery serves good Mexican fare. Reservations unnecessary. *Posada del Mar Hotel* (phone: 20044). Moderate.

Buho's Paradise – Great for late snacks. Open daily. Reservations unnecessary. Next to *Cabañas María del Mar* (phone: 20179). Inexpensive.

Pizza Rolandi – Pizza cooked in a wood-burning oven, plus other Italian dishes. Open daily. Reservations unnecessary. Hidalgo between Madero and Abasolo (phone: 20429). Inexpensive.

CHIHUAHUA

(pronounced Chee-*wah*-wah)

Chihuahua, the capital of Mexico's largest state (also called Chihuahua), sits on a plain almost 5,000 feet high, with the Sierra Madre to the west. The broad boulevards and convivial squares of this metropolis provide a welcome contrast to the arid, desolate plateau that stretches 232 miles from here to the US border at El Paso, a 5-hour drive away. Though founded in 1709, more than a century after the town of Ciudad Juárez at the border, Chihuahua has retained much more evidence of its colonial past and frontier existence. Like Juárez, however, it has gone through a series of name changes. The city was first built by a decree from the governor of Nueva Vizcaya, Don Antonio Deza, and was known as San Francisco de Cuellar. In 1718 the name was changed to San Felipe de Real de Chihuahua when the settlement achieved the status of a town. But this mouthful was later shortened to Chihuahua when Mexico won its independence from Spain.

Chihuahua originally derived its wealth from surrounding silver mines and cattle ranches. Silver was discovered in this region by the Spanish as early as 1679. For centuries there have been rumors that many of the older houses in the city have enough silver in their walls to make demolition profitable; they are only rumors. Chihuahua is still one of the nation's leading producers of silver, though it is not made into jewelry here as in Taxco, but agriculture, lumber, and in-bond factories (assembly plants for US products) have also become major sources of income. The city has prospered as an economic center of the area and today claims almost 1 million inhabitants.

Chihuahua has a violent history, and two of the most famous figures in Mexico's revolutionary wars are closely linked with it. It was here that the father of Mexican independence, the priest Miguel Hidalgo, and his patriot conspirators were executed by the Spaniards in 1811. Chihuahua was also the home of General Pancho Villa, whose revolutionary army, the División del Norte (Army of the North), was decisive in overthrowing Porfirio Díaz in 1910 and securing victory in the civil war that followed. Chihuahua was briefly the capital of Mexico, in 1864 and 1865, when President Benito Juárez, "the Abraham Lincoln of Mexico," made the city his base during the French invasion of Mexico. On a lighter note, the state of Chihuahua is also the home of the actor Anthony Quinn, who was born in the town of Cusihuiriachic.

But Chihuahua is most famous for the tiny, hairless dogs, *perros chihuahue-ños,* first raised in the area. Breeders claim, however, that they are now very scarce, and if you want to buy one of these creatures, you may be charged several hundred dollars. (Natives of Chihuahua are called *chihuahuenses,* and confusing the similar words would constitute a grave offense.)

The state of Chihuahua has some of the most beautiful scenery in Mexico. There is the Cascada de Basaseachi (Basaseachi Falls) a waterfall more than 1,000 feet high set in a lush pine forest; and the awesome Sierra de la

Tarahumara, including the Copper Canyon, a network of about 20 vast canyons 3,000 to 4,000 feet deep and a mile across. The canyons, lying 150 miles (240 km) west of the city, are best reached from Chihuahua. The *Chihuahua-Pacífico* railway, running along the rim of Copper Canyon, is spectacularly scenic, and the opportunity to ride it is what brings many travelers to Chihuahua.

A surprise for many visitors is the presence of a substantial Mennonite population in the state of Chihuahua. In the 1920s, Mennonite farmers settled in a fertile valley about 80 miles (128 km) northwest of the city, just outside Cuauhtémoc. At that time, they numbered some 2,000; the colony has since grown to more than 55,000, some of whom have begun to search for new farmland in South America. The hardworking Mennonites are accomplished farmers, and their produce, especially their cheese, is prized throughout Mexico. The Mennonites do not vote in Mexican elections or serve in the military, but they have had to pay taxes on their 123,500 acres of land since 1972.

The indigenous Tarahumara Indians, by contrast, are dwindling in number. They live a very rugged — perhaps primitive — life: ingesting peyote; roaming from the cool plateaus of the Sierra del la Tarahumara in the summer to the semitropical canyon floor in the winter; fishing and hunting for survival. (It is said that they are able to run so swiftly that they can catch deer.) The Tarahumara are also weavers and potters and can be easily recognized on the streets of Chihuahua by their roughly woven, red and white serapes and long, flowing hair tied with narrow headbands.

Some may view Chihuahua primarily as a stopover on the long drive from Ciudad Juárez to Mexico City. But the time has come to consider it on its own merits: a historical spot with unique attractions, as well as the jump-off or, better yet, end point for the spectacular Copper Canyon tour through Tarahumara country.

CHIHUAHUA AT-A-GLANCE

SEEING THE CITY: The best view over the town is from the *Mirador* (lookout) on Santa Rosa hill. Just follow Venustiano Carranza.

SPECIAL PLACES: Because of its historic importance to Mexico and its own natural beauty, Chihuahua provides the wherewithal to fill hours of exploring colonial and revolutionary landmarks as well as museums within the city limits, or afternoon or daylong treks into the countryside.

DOWNTOWN

Cathedral – This magnificent edifice was built in an ornate baroque style. Work on the cathedral was begun by the Jesuits in 1726 after Bishop Benito Crespo visited the town and commented that the small church built there originally did not adequately reflect the wealth of such a prosperous community. The bishop's words had the intended effect. But the cathedral was not finished until 1825, by the Franciscans, due to frequent Indian uprisings in the area. Dedicated to St. Francis of Assisi, patron saint of the city, the façade is elaborately adorned with statues of St. Francis (below the clock) and the Twelve Apostles. The *Museum of Sacred Art,* housed in the cathedral and opened in 1985, contains 18th-century art; its entry is at the west side of the cathedral, and visiting hours are 10 AM to 2 PM and 4 to 6 PM, Mondays through Fridays. Admission charge. Plaza de la Constitución (phone: 1205577).

Palacio del Gobierno (Government Capitol) – Father Miguel Hidalgo and Ignacio Allende, leaders of the 1810 uprising against Spain, were brought here after their capture in Acatita de Baján. They were imprisoned and eventually executed here by the Spanish in 1811. The original building was a Jesuit college, built in 1717 for the education of the sons of leading Spanish families and of Indian *caciques* (chiefs). The building was largely destroyed by fire in 1941, but has been reconstructed on the original plans. The murals around the patio depict famous episodes in the history of Chihuahua and are the work of artist Pina Mora. A plaque commemorates the spot on which Padre Miguel Hidalgo was killed on the morning of July 30, 1811. Open daily. No admission charge. On the north side of Plaza Hidalgo (phone: 129754).

Palacio Federal (Federal Palace) – This reconstructed colonial building contains the tower in which Hidalgo and his cohorts were confined during their trial. And it was from this building that they were taken to be killed. It now houses postal and telegraph offices, as well as a small museum. Museum open daily. Admission charge. Plaza Hidalgo across from the capitol (phone: 151526, ext. 390).

Iglesia de San Francisco (San Francisco Church) – The oldest church in Chihuahua was built by the Franciscan monks in 1721. Adjoining it and connected by underground passageways is the Chapel of San Antonio. It was here, in 1811, that Miguel Hidalgo's decapitated body was interred by the Franciscan fathers. They protected it until 1823, when independence was finally won, and then exhumed it and sent it on to Mexico City. There is a tablet in the chapel telling this gory tale but omitting the fact that directly after the execution, the head was sent to Guanajuato, where it was publicly displayed for the next 10 years. Plaza Zaragoza.

Statue of Hidalgo – The 45-foot monument of marble and bronze is dedicated to the heroes of the War of Independence. It features a life-size replica of Father Miguel Hidalgo and smaller figures of his co-conspirators. All of the figures were cast in Brussels and sent back to Chihuahua to stand in the center of the modest Plaza de Hidalgo.

Quinta Gameros (Regional Museum) – In a resplendent turn-of-the-century Art Nouveau mansion (designed by a Colombian architect who trained in Brussels and built for a bride who changed her mind and married another), this regional museum is filled with blown-glass Italian chandeliers, carved-wood furniture, and gold leaf paintings on walls and woodwork. Upstairs is a replica of the ruins at Paquimé, photos of old Chihuahua, and rooms devoted to the lifestyle of the area's Mennonite community. Closed Mondays. Admission charge. 401 Bolívar (phone: 123834).

Museo de Arte Popular (Museum of Popular Art) – Small but extensive, it displays a typical Tarahumara Indian home, along with artifacts, textiles, pottery, toys, colorful clothing, musical instruments, masks, baskets, and cooking utensils. The shop sells crafts from the region. Closed Sundays and Mondays. Admission charge. Near the *Palacio del Sol Hotel* at 5 Reforma and Independencia.

Quinta Luz (Museum of the Revolution) – Once the home of Pancho Villa, a hero of the Mexican Revolution of 1910. One of his wives, Doña Luz Corral, lived here until her death in 1981. The museum is full of Villa memorabilia, including the bullet-riddled car in which the general was assassinated in 1923. Open daily. Admission charge. 3014 Calle 10 (phone: 152882).

Pancho Villa's Mausoleum – An architectural extravaganza incorporating more than half a dozen styles, it was built by Villa in 1913 as his final resting place. In fact, Villa was buried 200 miles to the south, where he was assassinated, and a couple of years later his body (minus his head, which had mysteriously been removed) was moved to Mexico City. The cemetery in which the empty mausoleum stands has metamorphosed into Revolution Park.

Colonial Aqueduct – This impressive feat of engineering was begun in 1751, and is still responsible for supplying 20% of the city's water. The aqueduct is especially pretty at night by lamplight. A short section of it can easily be seen at Av. Zarco and Calle 34. (Av. Zarco is also the place to view some of the city's finest homes.)

State Penitentiary – Smack in the middle of town and built in 1908, it still offers the cheapest rooms in town. Pancho Villa contributed a few of the bullet holes visible in the façade. 2200 Av. 20 de Noviembre (phone: 127632 or 120673).

Teatro de los Héroes (Heroes Theater) – This impressive modern structure replaces the landmark theater that burned. It offers theatrical performances, concerts, and expositions. División del Norte and Calle 23 (phone: 139794).

ENVIRONS

Cascada de Basaseachi (Basaseachi Falls) – One of the world's highest waterfalls, its icy mountain water spills down almost 1,000 feet into a rapidly moving tributary of the Mayo River. The canyon below is covered with beautiful jade-green pools, and there is a steep, narrow path through pine-covered forest leading from the rim of the canyon to the pools below. The trip used to take a hard 4 days of wilderness travel, with the last part of the journey on foot or burro. Now the route follows a paved road to La Junta and then, at the gas station, turns onto the road to Tomochi. From Tomochi to the falls is a 45-minute drive over a well-maintained dirt road. The walk down to the falls takes about 15 minutes. If you want to stay overnight in Tomochi, *Cabañas Alanrosa* (phone: 152049) offers modest cabins. Ocampo, the nearest town, also has lodging. Frank Peters (see Campos Menonitas below) runs day trips to Basaseachi for $75 per couple (phone: 23087).

Campos Menonitas (Mennonite Farming Community) – Eight miles (13 km) north of the small town of Cuauhtémoc (via Hwy. 28) and a scenic 1½-hour drive west from Chihuahua, some 55,000 Mennonites live on and farm 123,500 acres of fertile land in the area that produces 90% of Mexico's apples. Though traditionally a people who keep to themselves, these Mennonites have opened up a home, their cheese cooperative, and their hardware store (which sells handmade rolltop desks, wooden washing machines, and kerosene stoves, among other things) to visitors. The 2½-hour tours, which include the opportunity to buy handicrafts and sample the local cheese and are led by English-speaking Frank Peters, and cost $25 for one or two people. Peters' father runs an RV park with 40 hook-ups, for now the only lodging available in the Mennonite community; otherwise, stay at *Posada del Sol* (phone: 158-23333), a little more than a mile (1.6 km) outside Cuauhtémoc en route to the Mennonite community. For more information about the tours and the trailer park, write to R. V. Peters, Apdo. 401, Cd. Cuauhtémoc, Chihuahua (phone: 158-23087).

■ **EXTRA SPECIAL: Copper Canyon** – One of the most extraordinary sights in all Mexico and actually a network of 20 canyons, it could easily swallow four Grand Canyons. Reached via the *Chihuahua-Pacífico Railway*, this "they said it couldn't be done" project was completed in November 1961, 90 years after its inception. The magnificent route traverses 86 tunnels and 37 bridges. The trip takes 12 hours on a good day, but is best enjoyed with side trips to waterfalls and cave or log homes of the Tarahumara Indians who inhabit the rugged terrain and sell their crafts (finer than those found in Chihuahua's stores). It is actually preferable to follow the itinerary west to east, from Topolobamto to Chihuahua, so that the most extraordinary views aren't passed in darkness. Stops along the way include Los Mochis, San Blas, El Fuerte, Divisadero, and Creel. In Los Mochis, stay the night before the trip (and no longer) at the *Santa Anita, El Dorado,* or *Las Colinas Best Western* (see "Best en Route" in *Nogales to Mexico City,* DIRECTIONS for details on all three). Also see DIRECTIONS, *Juárez to Mexico City.*

SOURCES AND RESOURCES

TOURIST INFORMATION: If hotel travel desks cannot supply sufficient information about the city and surrounding areas, the staff at the State Tourism Office (Calle 13 and 1300 Libertad, 1st Floor; phone: 159879) is very helpful.

TELEPHONE: The area code for Chihuahua is 14. When calling from one city to another within Mexico, dial 91 before the area code.

CLIMATE AND CLOTHES: Chihuahua has a climate much like west Texas, plummeting to 10F or 20F in January and soaring into the 90s in May and June. Some snow may fall from December through February. The rainy season is July and August. This city is informal, and its population ranges from long-haired Indians to conservatively clad business executives; the choice of dress is optional.

GETTING AROUND: Bus – Chihuahua, like most Mexican cities, has plenty of public transportation. Several bus lines will take you from one side of town to the other for a minimal amount of money, and some of them run until midnight. Airport vans make the trip to and from town for about $3 (phone: 154589).

Taxis – Your hotel can always call a cab for you, but it is easy enough to hail one on the street. Fares are quite reasonable — less than $2 for most trips in the city.

Car Rentals – Among the leading car rental agencies are *Autorenta #1* (phone: 125100), *Avis* (phone: 141999), *Budget* (phone: 160909), *Gamma Fast* (phone: 155981), and *Alpri* (phone: 125145). All have offices at the airport.

Tours – Travel desks at the larger hotels (*Palacio del Sol, San Francisco Best Western,* and *Castel*) arrange city sightseeing, Copper Canyon rail trips, and visits to Mennonite communities.

SPECIAL EVENTS: Chihuahua's colorful *Fiesta de Santa Rita* is celebrated throughout town with music, dancing, fireworks, parades, food, and everything else that makes up a Mexican fiesta. It is held during the last 2 weeks in May. A huge cattle fair is held in October.

SHOPPING: Two large indoor markets on Calle Aldama provide some interesting browsing. With about 20 stalls each, they are open daily except at lunchtime; some sell Mennonite cheese, among other items. The *Museo de Arte Popular* (at Independencia and Reforma), and *Artesanías Mexicanas*

(across from the *Museum of the Revolution*), are good places to buy Mexican handicrafts; the latter also contains a rock shop with precious and semi-precious stones, along with a unique collection of fossilized stones that are not for sale. *Fotografía Ayala* has two reliable shops (at Doblado and Trece, and in the *Palacio del Sol*) for Kodak and Fuji film, processing, and a good range of cameras and other equipment.

 SPORTS: Chihuahua is not a big sports center, but there are a few options.
Baseball and basketball – Both sports are popular here. (Pitcher Fernando Valenzuela is from the state of Chihuahua). There is no regular season or schedule for either the professional or university games, but most are played in May or June. Professional games are played at the University of Chihuahua's sports center (Av. Universidad); it has a gymnasium, baseball stadium, swimming pool, and jai alai court. Amateur games are played at the *Estadio General M. Quevedo*.

Fishing – Freshwater angling is excellent at manmade lakes near Chihuahua. A favorite spot is Francisco I. Madero Dam at Ciudad Delicias, southeast of Chihuahua.

Hunting – The season runs approximately from September through February; the game is deer, turkey, quail, sandhill crane, duck, puma, and dove. To arrange an expedition, consult hotel travel desks. *Rancho La Estancia* (just north of Cuauhtémoc off Hwy. 28; phone: 122282 in Chihuahua) offers good logistics and lodging.

 NIGHTCLUBS AND NIGHTLIFE: The action after dark is primarily at the discos. The top choices are *La Mina* (in the *Victoria;* phone: 128893); *Medanos* (in the *Castel;* phone: 135445); *Robin Hood* (Av. Talavera; phone: 157283), and *La Puerta de Alcala* (Av. Revolución; phone: 158393). *Hostería 1900*'s video bar attracts a good crowd (phone: 161990). There is no real singles scene here, and unescorted women often have to contend with rude comments on the street.

BEST IN TOWN

 CHECKING IN: Chihuahua has a wide range of hotels. Visitors can expect to pay up to $90 for a double room with bath in a hotel we classify as expensive; about $40 in a moderate place; and $30 or less for inexpensive lodging. Most hotels listed below accept MasterCard and Visa; a few also accept American Express and Diners Club. All telephone numbers are in the 14 area code unless otherwise indicated. When calling from one city to another in Mexico, dial 91 before the area code.

Castel Sicomoro – Handsome and spacious, with 130 rooms, a pool shaped like the state of Chihuahua, the *Medanos* restaurant-bar-disco, a coffee shop, and a lively lobby bar. It is operated by Mexico's rapidly growing Castel chain. Three miles (5 km) from downtown. 411 Blvd. Ortiz Mena (phone: 135445; 800-448-6970 in the US; FAX: 131411). Expensive.

Palacio del Sol – This 17-story hotel has 190 large, comfortable, but dimly lit rooms, a restaurant, and an inviting piano bar in the lobby. 500 Independencia (phone: 166000; 800-852-4049 in the US; FAX: 159947). Expensive.

San Francisco Best Western – Cozy and centrally located, this 4-story spot features wet bars and US television programming in each of its 142 rooms. Its popular restaurant features Sunday brunch and buffet. 409 Calle Victoria (phone: 167770; 713-449-4900 in the US). Expensive.

Mirador – A comfortable, well-kept motel with 87 rooms and a large swimming pool, this place also features an inviting lobby, restaurant, cocktail bar, and free parking. A short drive from downtown. 1309 Av. Universidad (phone: 132205). Moderate.

Posada Tierra Blanca – It's a 3-level motel with 108 large rooms, a small swimming pool, a restaurant, coffee shop, cinema, and disco. On Niños Héroes at Camargo (phone: 150000). Moderate.

Victoria – The 125 rooms in this sprawling, 1940s dowager hotel need refurbishing, but the near-Olympic-size heated pool (the largest in the city) and the rose gardens are wonderful. It also has a restaurant and cocktail lounge. Near the restaurant district at Colón and Juárez (phone: 128893). Moderate.

El Campanario – It takes its name from the bell collection of the owner. A pretty place, only 2 stories high, with tiles galore and paintings from Spain, it has a restaurant, a bar, and TV sets in each room. Blvd. Díaz Ordaz and Pvda. de Libertad (phone: 154545). Inexpensive.

Parador de San Miguel – A small, colonial-style motel with 45 rooms, restaurant, and bar. 7901 Av. Tecnológico (phone: 170303). Inexpensive.

San Juan – Modest, but centrally located, and a find for penny pinchers. These 60 rooms, each with bath, are in the modern wing of a run-down colonial-style house. No credit cards accepted. 823 Calle Victoria (phone: 128492). Very inexpensive.

 EATING OUT: Chihuahua is renowned for its steaks, readily available from a variety of fine restaurants. Those who prefer other dishes won't be disappointed either. Service at restaurants is consistently attentive. Prices do not vary much, but a dinner for two at a place we classify as expensive will cost $30 to $40; under $20, moderate. Prices do not include drinks, wine, or tips. Most restaurants listed below accept MasterCard and Visa; a few also accept American Express and Diners Club. All telephone numbers are in the 14 area code unless otherwise indicated. When calling from one city to another within Mexico, dial 91 before the area code.

La Calesa – It's reckoned to be one of the best steak bars in Chihuahua. International dishes are also available, along with *puchero* (marrow soup with vegetables) and sea bass in garlic sauce. Open daily. Reservations advised. Across from the *Victoria* on Av. Juárez and Colón (phone: 128555). Expensive.

Salignac – A former candy and soda factory, this very inviting place serves international dishes with a French influence as well as good beef and seafood. The steaks with crayfish and the dishes prepared with the region's famous black bass are especially good choices. Live entertainment. Open daily. Reservations advised. 3309 Av. Juárez (phone: 158616). Expensive.

Club de los Parados – First-rate steaks are served in a rustic setting. Open daily. Reservations advised. 3901 Av. Juárez (phone: 153509). Expensive to moderate.

Los Parados de Tony Vega – The intimate colonial dining room with shuttered windows is a fine backdrop for great steaks. Check out the Hunters Salon upstairs. Run by the same folks who own *Club de los Parados*. Open daily. Reservations advised. 3316 Av. Juárez (phone: 151333). Expensive to moderate.

El Bigote Italiano – It's name means "The Italian Moustache." A cozy little place serving tasty pasta and pizza. Open daily. Reservations advised. Mirador and Periférico Ortiz Mena (phone: 168399). Moderate.

El Bigote Mexicano – The fare here is Mexican — everything from tacos to *cochinita pibil* (pork prepared in a special Yucatecan sauce). The skewered meats, chicken, and seafood are also good choices, and the service is very friendly. Open daily. Reservations advised. Next to *El Bigote Italiano* at Mirador and Periférico Ortiz Mena (phone: 155545). Moderate.

Chihuahua Charlie's – Another link in the ubiquitous Anderson's chain, it serves all the favorites including TBC salad (bacon, watercress, and mushrooms) and

Oysters 444, a sampling of oysters prepared in a variety of ways. Reservations advised. 3329 Juárez, a half block from the *Victoria* (phone: 157065). Moderate.

Hostería 1900 – The frontier decor includes skulls that would have caught Georgia O'Keeffe's eye, and intriguing photographs by Ignacio Guerrero. Try the wheat soup, *huitlacoche* (a corn fungus with a delicate mushroom taste) crêpes, or chicken Florentine. The video bar is open till 2 AM on Fridays and Saturdays. Restaurant open daily. Reservations advised. 903-A Independencia (phone: 161990). Moderate.

La Olla – Housed in an old brewery with a copper vat as its centerpiece, it specializes in beef dishes and unique atmosphere. Open daily. No reservations. 3331 Av. Juárez (phone: 123602). Moderate.

Los Vitrales – Named for the tiny, diamond-shaped panes surrounding its dining room, this lovely restaurant with piano bar features a variety of Oriental and other international dishes. Open daily. Reservations advised. Av. Juárez at the corner of Colón (phone: 150676). Moderate.

CUERNAVACA

(pronounced Kwer-nah-*vah*-kah)

Among the topics likely to be discussed when professional travelers congregate is which city in the world has the best climate. It might be one of those questions around which battle lines are drawn and ideological splits develop (ask two travel writers within earshot of one another to name the world's best beach, then sit back and watch the fur fly). There is an exception, however. For several centuries there has been one favorite with cognoscenti, from the Aztec kings and Hernán Cortés to hundreds of American and European expatriates who live there right now. That is Cuernavaca, with a name like poetry and a climate that is simply perfect. It is a weekend escape for middle class Mexico City residents and, like Paris, a place where good Americans go when they die — or just before that, if they are lucky.

Some 40 miles (64 km) south of Mexico City (about an hour's drive) on the road to Acapulco, Cuernavaca is Mexico's oldest resort and the capital of the state of Morelos. The Aztec named it Cuauhnáhuac, which the Spanish found unpronounceable when they arrived in 1521 and promptly changed to Cuernavaca (cow's horn). The city was 1 of 30 awarded to Cortés by the Spanish king, and he chose it as his retirement home; unfortunately, he died in Spain in 1547 before he could return to it.

Small wonder he yearned for Cuernavaca. At 5,000 feet, the city has spring-like weather throughout most of the year; when Mexico City (at 7,200 feet) is plunged in cold rain, the swimming pools of Cuernavaca glitter in the sun. Among its natural water sources are a series of thermally heated springs and mineral waters, traditionally soothing for rheumatism and other ailments of the joints and incredibly relaxing and restorative to the spirit, even if one's joints are in perfect condition. Even in the pre-Columbian period, the Aztec came to Cuauhnáhuac for mineral baths.

Despite its serene climate, Cuernavaca has been the scene of heavy political controversy since it was founded. The big sugar haciendas surrounding the city were first run by rich Spaniards, then, after 1810, by equally rich Mexicans, many of whom lived in Europe and left the management of their lands to overseers, who treated the Indian laborers like slaves.

The 1910 Revolution brought to prominence Emiliano Zapata, who grew up in the nearby town of Cuautla. Zapata harbored a deep hatred for both the resident and absentee landlords, and his battle cry — "Land and Liberty and Death to the Hacendados!" — reflected the deeply rooted frustrations of the peasants. Zapata's ragtag Army of the South sacked and devastated every hacienda in the region, burning crops and razing buildings to the ground. When President Francisco I. Madero didn't immediately divide the land in Morelos into small portions for Zapata's Indians after the Revolution, Zapata broke with him. He joined forces with the flamboyant bandit Pancho Villa in 1914, during the occupation of Mexico City. But Zapata was not an educated man and found himself uncomfortable in the sophisticated city, and he soon came home. Too impractical for the rest of the politicians, he was trapped by federal troops and shot in April 1919. Greatly beloved by his followers, Zapata was the one true idealist in the Revolution. He never sought a penny for himself, only for his people. A true folk hero, Zapata's memory is revered as almost sacred in Cuernavaca.

When you visit Cuernavaca, you will undoubtedly be impressed by its flowers before you get any sense of its politics or history. Geraniums reach to rooftops; fuchsia and red and coral bougainvillea grow wild. The bluish-lavender jacaranda and flaming poinciana tint the air with color. Stretching into the distance on the outskirts of town are fields of sugarcane, corn, beans, avocados, wheat, coffee, and peanuts. You'll also see groves of banana trees, mangoes, guavas, limes, and oranges. If you don't fall in love with Cuernavaca, you'll at least understand why so many people are fiercely attached to the place and why it generates such intense passion.

CUERNAVACA AT-A-GLANCE

SEEING THE CITY: The best views of Cuernavaca are from Route 95, as you enter the town from Mexico City, and from the hills called Lomas de Cuernavaca, just east of Route 95.

SPECIAL PLACES: Cuernavaca is a little too big for walking around, although it is only 4 short blocks between Palacio de Cortés (Cortés's Palace) and the Jardín Borda (Borda Gardens). There is a residential area south of the zocalo that is pleasant to drive around since the gardens are not set behind walls, as in most Mexican homes.

El Zocalo – Cuernavaca is unusual in that it has a double main plaza, or zocalo. One is Jardín Juárez (Garden of Juárez); the larger plaza is Jardín de los Héroes (Garden of Heroes). This is also one of the few towns where there is no church on the plaza. The government palace (state house) is here, though, and so are a number of sidewalk cafés. It's a favorite place for those who like to people watch and listen to lively band concerts (Thursdays, Saturdays, and Sundays). The mariachi bands that hang out around the plaza won't play without being paid. The zocalo is also frequented by vendors and poor people asking for coins.

Catedral de San Francisco (St. Francis Cathedral) – Founded by Cortés in 1529, this is one of the oldest churches in Mexico. It was originally part of a Franciscan monastery and during the colonial period housed missionaries en route to the Far East via Acapulco. The interior of the church was renovated in 1959. In the process of restoration, a mural depicting the sacrifice of a Mexican saint, San Felipe de Jesús, and his fellow missionaries was uncovered. In the rear of the cathedral compound, the Chapel of the Third Order has sculptures by Indian artists. The Mariachi Mass at 11 AM and 7 PM on Sundays is famous all over Mexico, so if you want to hear the musicians or Bishop Luis Reynoso Cervantes, make sure you get there early. At the corner of Hidalgo and Morelos.

Jardín Borda (Borda Gardens) – This was the playground of former Mexican rulers Maximilian and Carlota, who would thoroughly approve of the restoration job done on the magnificent old mansion and the grounds. José de la Borda, who arrived in Mexico in 1716 and amassed a huge fortune in mining, died in Cuernavaca in 1778, leaving his grand estate to his son Manuel. Manuel invested a considerable amount of his inheritance in landscaping the estate's extensive gardens. Art exhibits and concerts are scheduled frequently. Open daily. Admission charge. Across the street from the cathedral on Calle Morelos (phone: 140262).

Museo Cuauhnáhuac (originally Cortés's Palace) – Intended by Hernán Cortés to be a fortress, this rather forbidding pile of stones was used for many years to house the state government offices. Now renovated, it has been transformed into a state museum. The highlights of the collection are the Diego Rivera murals depicting the history of the state of Morelos from the conquest to the Revolution. There are good views of the city from the terrace and roof. As was customary during the 16th century, the Spaniards invariably chose to build their most important structures on top of existing Aztec constructions, and here you can see the Tlauican pyramid, which was buried until renovation efforts discovered it. Closed Mondays. Admission charge. On the southeast corner of the zocalo (phone: 128171).

Pyramid of Teopanzolco – The ruins of the pyramid — believed to date from the Aztec era — were discovered during the Revolution of 1910, when cannons mounted on a hillside shook loose the soil. Closed Mondays. Admission charge. Near the railroad station, southeast of the market on Guerrero.

Siqueiros Murals – Among the largest murals ever painted, these depict events from local history. David Alfaro Siqueiros is one of Mexico's three most famous artists — the other two are José Clemente Orozco and Diego Rivera. The work is characterized by intense, bright colors, bold forms, and a sympathetic portrayal of social problems. In the *Casino de la Selva Hotel,* 1001 Leandro Valle (phone: 124700).

Casa Municipal de la Plastica y la Cultura – The murals on the second floor depict Aztec rituals and scenes from the life of Maximilian and Carlota in Mexico. Among the most striking are the depiction of Maximilian and the beautiful Indian woman purported to be one of his love interests and that of Carlota pleading with Benito Juárez for Maximilian's life. Gallery exhibits change regularly. Open weekdays. In City Hall, on Morelos, in front of the cathedral (phone: 185748).

Salto de San Antón – A scenic waterfall cascades over a 100-foot-high ravine set in a pretty, landscaped area. At the top of the hill, you can buy local pottery. Be sure to bargain for the best price. About 1 mile (1.6 km) west of downtown.

Casa Museo Robert Brady (Robert Brady Museum and Home) – An expatriate American artist, Brady moved to Cuernavaca in 1961 and purchased La Casa de la Torre (the Tower House), originally part of a Franciscan convent built in the first half of the 16th century. Brady lived and worked in Cuernavaca until his death in 1986, amassing a collection of more than 1,300 Mexican and foreign works of art, pre-Columbian figures, Mexican colonial pieces, and fine examples of crafts from Mexico and many other parts of the world. The house's wildly colorful rooms and the unusual arrangement of its contents are exactly as Brady left them. Open Thursdays and Fridays from 10 AM to 2 PM and from 4 to 6 PM, and on Saturdays from 10 AM to 2 PM. Admission charge includes a guided tour, by appointment only. 4 Nezahualcoyotl (phone: 121136).

Xochicalco – About an hour from the center of town, this is a spectacular yet little-visited site with features that relate it to the Olmec, Maya, Zapotec, Toltec, and Xochicalco civilizations. Bas-relief designs are carved into the stone, and in one of the pyramids is a sunlit rooftop observatory used by Indian scientists to determine the date and time. Open daily. Admission charge. The best way to get there is to have your hotel provide a guide-driver.

Museo de la Herbolaria (Herb Museum) – Known as El Olvido, this was Maximilian's refuge from court etiquette, political intrigue, and (they say) his wife, Carlota. In addition to the herb gardens and a museum of "traditional" medicine, the *Society of Friends of the Ethnobotanical Gardens* also runs a small shop, where they sell arts and crafts and naturally grown products. Closed Mondays. No admission charge. 200 Matamoros (phone: 123108).

Zoofari – A wild-animal park with more than 100 species of birds and animals from all over the world. Part of the park must be visited by car since the animals roam free. There is also a restaurant, a handicrafts shop, a wide selection of pets for sale, rides on ponies and dwarf mules, and clean rest rooms. Open daily. About 35 miles (56 km) from Cuernavaca on the Carr. Federal to Taxco, just past Huajintlán.

Chapultepec Park – Cuernavaca's playground has had a complete face-lift, and is once again open to the public. Spring-fed canals wind through 500 acres of lush tropical gardens, and vestiges of a 16th-century aqueduct built by Cortés outline the hills. There is also a miniature train, an aviary, a lake where rowboats can be rented, children's games, and a planetarium. Closed Mondays. Admission charge. Plan de Ayala and the 95D interchange.

■**EXTRA SPECIAL:** About 35 miles (56 km) east of Cuernavaca, Oaxtepec is a vacation and convention center that was formerly the site of Montezuma's botanical gardens. In 1604, the Hospital of Santa Cruz was established here so that people could benefit from the curative waters. The hospital attracted people from as far away as Peru during its 200 years in operation. You can see the ruins of the hospital and the botanical gardens. There is also a recreation area with swimming pool, playgrounds, athletic fields, housing, and dining facilities. Two miles (3 km) away in Las Estacas — just off the road to Cuautla — there is a circular pool with a constant rolling, frothing, bubble of water at its center. It's wonderful to swim in. Take the Mexico City–Cuautla toll road (Carr. de Cuota) to the Yautepec cutoff and follow signs to Tlaltizapan. For information, call Tlaltizapan 31. A short distance south of Oaxtepec, at Cocoyoc, there's a sugar hacienda that has been turned into a fine resort hotel called *Hacienda Cocoyoc;* see *Checking In* for details.

If you're longing to get a look behind the high walls surrounding Cuernavaca's beautiful homes, the Guild and Las Damas de Morelos usually run house-and-garden tours every Thursday between *Christmas* and *Easter.* The tours start from the *Casino de la Selva* at 10 AM. Check the Cuernavaca page of the English-language newspaper, the *News,* for details. The cost, including transportation, is about $10.

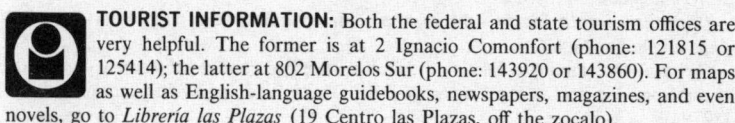

SOURCES AND RESOURCES

TOURIST INFORMATION: Both the federal and state tourism offices are very helpful. The former is at 2 Ignacio Comonfort (phone: 121815 or 125414); the latter at 802 Morelos Sur (phone: 143920 or 143860). For maps as well as English-language guidebooks, newspapers, magazines, and even novels, go to *Librería las Plazas* (19 Centro las Plazas, off the zocalo).

TELEPHONE: The area code for Cuernavaca is 73. When calling from one city to another within Mexico, dial 91 before the area code.

CLIMATE AND CLOTHES: Cuernavaca's climate is warm and dry, with an occasional cool, rainy day. It hardly ever gets colder than the 60s or warmer than the upper 70s and low 80s throughout the year. The rainy season is June through September. Dress is casual.

 GETTING AROUND: Taxi – Cabs are fairly inexpensive in Cuernavaca. You can pick one up at the zocalo and pay by the hour. Rates generally are about $10 an hour, but make sure you establish the price before stepping into the vehicle. It shouldn't cost more than $4 to travel from the zocalo to any hotel in Cuernavaca.

Car Rental – Many travelers drive to Cuernavaca from Mexico City or Acapulco. But if you haven't, you can rent a car from *Rente un Auto Monroy* (102 Av. López Mateos; phone: 143463); *Hertz* (300 Plan de Ayala; phone: 143800); or *Volkswagen Rent* (1304 Plan de Ayala; phone: 150008).

 SPECIAL EVENTS: Lively carnivals are held during the week before *Ash Wednesday* in the town of Tepoztlán and for a week beginning on *Ash Wednesday* in Yautepec, both about a half hour from Cuernavaca. The most unusual carnival in Mexico is the one that takes place in Tepoztlán, near the pyramid of Tepozteco. The Indians wear headdresses and perform folkloric dances. *Christmas posadas* are held in December, during which the Nativity is reenacted, but they aren't as elaborate or colorful as those held in Tepotzotlán, in the state of México. In April, a flower festival is held either at the Borda Gardens or in the main square of Cuernavaca.

 SHOPPING: Cuernavaca is not particularly noted for any indigenous crafts, although the residents do make cane furniture (usually unvarnished), straw hats, and huaraches. There is also a big local market that sells food, household items, and clothing. This is the best place for hunting down local arts and crafts. To find the market, use the zocalo as a starting point and walk 5 blocks north on Guerrero. When you come to the footbridge crossing a ravine, turn right and you'll be at the market. Although it's not a bargain hunter's paradise, there are artisans' stalls next to the *Museo Cuauhnáhuac*. There is an arcade with well-made crafts at the *Casino de la Selva* and an exclusive shopping center at Plaza los Arcos, 501 Plan de Ayala.

Aries-Casa de las Campanas – For leather goods and designer clothing. 2 Comonfort (no phone).

Bio-Art – An impressive selection of handicrafts, textiles, and decorative objects. Corner of Díaz Ordaz Blvd. and Alta Tensión (phone: 141458).

Carlota – Artwork by local artists, antiques, gifts, and wearable art. *Hotel Maximilian's,* 125 Galeana (phone: 122713).

Cerámica de Cuernavaca – Hand-painted dinnerware and objets d'art. 708 Plan de Ayala (phone: 156631).

Cerámica Santa María – More hand-painted dinnerware and objets d'art. 900 Zapata (phone: 130670).

Girasol – A stunning collection of Mexican-inspired clothes for women. Across the street from *Bio-Art,* at the corner of Díaz Ordaz Blvd. and Alta Tensión (phone: 182796).

Harms Joyeros – Unique jewelry and an exceptional collection of handicrafts, beautifully displayed. A few doors down from *Las Mañanitas,* 12 Ricardo Linares (phone: 124243).

Materials Coloniales – If you've admired the tiles in colonial inns throughout Mexico, you may buy some of your own at this shop. 2026 Av. Plan de Ayala (phone: 151270).

La Palomita Blanca – Marie Dowling, a very lovely and friendly lady, has antiques and art on consignment here. 6 Zempoala, in the Cuauhnahuac area (phone: 156308).

Rubén Torres – Chic sportswear for men and women. 813 Av. Morelos Sur (phone: 126595).

Telas Arte – Unique and original cotton fabrics. Across the street from *Bio-Art,* at the corner of Díaz Ordaz Blvd. and Alta Tensión (no phone).

 SPORTS: For a complete listing of sports activities, for both the spectator and the participant, visit the tourist office.

   Go-Carts – Races are held at the *Cuernavaca Track,* 715 Calle Domingo Diez (phone: 132377).

Golf – *Los Tabachines Club de Golf* (phone: 143999) is the site of the annual *Cuernavaca Golf Open Tournament* in February, and *San Gaspar* (phone: 194404) has a 280-yard practice tee and an 18-hole, par 72 course. *Los Tabachines* also has tennis courts and swimming pools. Guest privileges can be arranged through most Cuernavaca hotels. Other Cuernavaca golf clubs are *Club de Golf Santa Fe* (phone: 739-12011) on the Mexico-Acapulco toll road, near the Alpuyeca exit; *Club de Golf Cuernavaca* (1 Calle Plutarco Elias Calles; phone: 184927), the town's oldest and most beautiful course; and *Hacienda de Cocoyoc* (phone: 735-22000).

Swimming – When Mexico City residents want to go swimming, they head for Cuernavaca. Many of the public pools are jammed on weekends. Most hotels have pools, which are less crowded. Among the recreation areas with large swimming pools are *Isstehuixtla,* a famous resort operated by the Social Security Institute for Federal Employees (ISSTE) and open to the public, in La Fundición, 28 miles (45 km) south of Cuernavaca, which has 5 swimming pools; *Balneario Hacienda de Temixco* (phone: 127348), 3 miles (5 km) south of Cuernavaca in Temixco, with 15 swimming pools and 10 wading pools; *Agua Hedionda,* the most popular, in Cuautla; *Las Estacas; Oaxtepec;* and *Hacienda Cocoyoc* (phone: 735-22000).

Tennis – The *Villa Internacional de Tenis* (Lomas de Atzingo; phone: 173717) has 10 clay courts for members only. *Clarion Suites Racquet Club* (100 Francisco Villa; phone: 136122) has 9 courts for guests only. *Cuernavaca Track* (715 Calle Domingo Diez; phone: 132377) has 6 clay courts. *Tennis Palace* (903 Paseo del Conquistador; phone: 136500) has 5 courts. Consult your hotel about obtaining a visitor's card to private tennis clubs.

 NIGHTCLUBS AND NIGHTLIFE: After dark on weekends, Cuernavaca is a fairly lively place. *Barbazul* (phone: 131976), which means "Bluebeard," is one of the top discos, along with *Marjaba* (1000 Sonara; phone: 158004). Other favorites are *Ta'izz* (50 Bajada de Chapultepec; phone: 154060) and *Mambo* at the *Casino de la Selva* (phone: 124700). *Los Quetzales,* in the *Villa del Conquistador* (phone: 131055), has a piano bar as well as a restaurant, and *La Cueva* at the *Selva* (phone: 124700) has live music Fridays and Saturdays from 10 PM on.

BEST IN TOWN

 CHECKING IN: Most hotels in Cuernavaca are small, with large, beautiful gardens set behind high walls. Most have heated swimming pools, too. It's a good idea to make reservations at least a week in advance. Considering the high quality of accommodations, the prices are quite reasonable. Expect to pay $120 to $130 for a double room at places described as very expensive; $60 to $80 at the places listed as expensive; $50 in the moderate category; and $40 or less at the inexpensive inns. All telephone numbers are in the 73 area code unless otherwise indicated. When calling from one city to another within Mexico, dial 91 before the area code.

Casa Colonial – Ray Cote, who designed *Villa Montaña* in Morelia, has taken over an authentic colonial mansion in downtown Cuernavaca and filled its 13 rooms and 3 suites with fabulous antiques. There's a pool and dining room (for guests only). Rate includes three meals a day. No credit cards accepted. 135 Nezahualcoyotl (phone: 121683). Very expensive.

Clarion Suites Racquet Club – A posh playground for the Beautiful People. Those accustomed to the finer things in life can use the club's 9 tennis courts, swim in the pool, and dine well. Truly lovely. 100 Francisco Villa (phone: 136122; in the US, 800-221-2222; FAX: 175483). Very expensive.

Posada las Mañanitas – Several fireplaces and an elegant colonial decor distinguish this 4-room, 18-suite inn. It's also known for its exquisite gardens, which have peacocks, cranes, flamingos, and parrots in residence. Facilities include a heated swimming pool, cocktail lounge, and a fine dining room. No credit cards accepted. 107 Ricardo Linares (phone: 124646; FAX: 183672). Very expensive.

Villa Bejar – Antique cars transport guests and their luggage to the 25 deluxe suites, including 2 nuptial suites and a presidential suite, each with its own private garden. A lovely pool, tennis courts, boutiques, spacious gardens, impeccable service, and a good restaurant and bar with nightly entertainment make this place a favorite getaway for wealthy Mexicans. 2350 Domingo Diez (phone: 174811 or 175000; FAX: 174953). Very expensive.

Le Château René – The management of one of Cuernavaca's best restaurants (see *Eating Out*) also runs this colonial-style hotel with 12 suites, each of which is equipped with a color TV set and its own terrace overlooking a lovely garden and pool. 11 Calz. de los Reyes (phone: 172300 or 172350). Expensive.

Hacienda Cocoyoc – A restored 16th-century hacienda about 30 minutes from downtown Cuernavaca, it offers a 9-hole golf course, as well as access to an 18-hole course, not to mention horses, tennis, 2 large pools, and 5 restaurants. In addition to the 261 rooms, there are 28 deluxe rooms and 25 master suites, each with private pool. American Plan available. Popular for meetings and conventions. Cuautla Hwy. (phone: 735-62211; 5-550-6480 in Mexico City; FAX: 70488). Expensive.

Hacienda de Cortés – Built as a retirement home for the conqueror, this 420-year-old plantation now has 22 suites, plus lovely gardens, a pool, a Jacuzzi, and a good restaurant with live music. 90 Plaza Kennedy, Atlacomulco (phone: 158844). Expensive.

Hacienda Vista Hermosa – This 102-room hacienda-style place attracts tour groups and hordes of day-trippers on Sundays, but can be quite delightful mid-week. It has a pool, tennis court, squash, horseback riding, jogging track, disco, and restaurant. About 15 miles (24 km) south of Cuernavaca in Tequesquitengo (phone: 734-70492 in Tequesquitengo; 5-535-0107 in Mexico City; FAX: 70488). Expensive.

Hostería las Quintas – On spacious grounds, this dignified, colonial establishment has 15 rooms and 33 junior suites, some with terraces and some with fireplaces. There is a heated swimming pool, a restaurant, and a cocktail lounge. 107 Las Quintas (phone: 183949). Expensive.

Maximilian's – Twenty-nine of its 62 cozy suites have fireplaces, and all have a telephone and cable TV that picks up US channels. Facilities include a large garden, heated pool, piano bar (on weekends), beauty clinic, friendly service, and a fine restaurant specializing in international dishes. 125 Galeana, Colonia Acapantzingo (phone: 182010; FAX: 122152). Expensive.

Del Prado Cuernavaca – Rather large by Cuernavaca standards, it has 200 rooms, spacious garden, pool, 4 tennis courts, social activities for adults and children, restaurant, bar, and snack bar. 58 Nardo (phone: 174000; FAX: 174155). Expensive.

Posada Primavera – On a hill overlooking Cuernavaca, this property offers a heated swimming pool, color TV sets, restaurant, bar, and nightclub. 28 rooms and 8 suites. 57 Av. Paseo del Conquistador (phone: 138420). Moderate.

Posada San Angelo – A colonial inn with 17 rooms, it has a heated swimming pool, lovely gardens, TV sets in the rooms and satellite TV in the lobby, and a good dining room. 100 Cerrada de la Selva (phone: 141325). Moderate.

Villa Internacional de Tenis – There are 10 tennis courts for the 14 luxurious suites at this lovely resort. Spacious gardens, a large pool, satellite TV, and a restaurant are among the other amenities. Suite rate includes up to two adults and two children under 15. 702 Chalma (phone: 130829). Moderate.

Villa Vegetariana – It's a vegetarian health spa with 38 rooms, gym, aerobics classes, massage, sauna, squash, tennis, and a pool. Rate includes all meals, treatments, and use of all facilities. Mailing address: 114 Pino, Santa María Ahuacatitlán, Apdo. 1228 (phone: 131044). Moderate.

Vista Hermosa – This cozy inn, built around a charming patio, has a heated pool and wading pool, restaurant, and bar. Río Pánuco and Papaloapan (phone: 153049 or 152374). Moderate.

Casino de la Selva – Popular with families as well as a younger crowd, this 230-room resort hotel offers many amenities, including a cinema, bowling alley, swimming pools, disco, restaurant, and bar. 1001 Leandro Valle (phone: 124700; FAX: 121033). Moderate to inexpensive.

Posada Jacarandas – The 85 rooms in this inn are set in spacious, manicured gardens and most have porches; there is also a Love Nest suite built high up in a tree. Meals are served on an enclosed terrace overlooking the gardens, blooming with roses, bougainvilleas, mangoes, tulips, orchids, and, of course, jacaranda trees. Three tennis courts and swimming pools provide diversion. Rooms and dining facilities are separate for guests with and without children. 805 Cuauhtémoc (phone: 157777; FAX: 157888). Inexpensive.

Posada de Xochiquetzal – Americans run this 16-room colonial hotel, which has a lovely dining room with fireplace, a large garden, and a pool. 200 Calle Leyva (phone: 185767 or 120220). Inexpensive.

Villa del Conquistador – This 36-room hostelry has a spectacular view of Cuernavaca, as well as a heated pool, tennis, squash, miniature golf, 2 restaurants, and a bar with live entertainment. 134 Paseo del Conquistador (phone: 131055; 5-516-0483 in Mexico City; FAX: 5-516-0484). Inexpensive.

Quinta las Flores – All 25 rooms overlook a charming garden. There is also a terrace spacious enough to accommodate the hotel's pool and dining room. Meals are family-style, and breakfast is included in the price. 210 Tlaquepaque (phone: 141244). Very inexpensive.

 **EATING OUT:** Cuernavaca has interesting restaurants offering a wide variety of international dishes. *Huitlacoche* (a corn fungus with a delicate mushroom flavor) is popular and is prepared in a variety of ways. All the expensive hotels listed above have dining rooms rated among the best in town. Expect to pay up to $50 for a meal for two at one of the places we've listed as expensive; $25 to $30 in the moderate category; and about $20 or less at inexpensive spots. Prices don't include tips, wine, or drinks. Most restaurants accept MasterCard and Visa; a few also accept American Express and Diners Club. All telephone numbers are in the 73 area code unless otherwise indicated. When calling from one city to another within Mexico, dial 91 before the area code.

Casa del Campo – A lovely colonial home, it has been converted into one of Cuernavaca's most successful dining places. Tables are arranged on the delightful horseshoe-shaped balcony, and drinks are served in the garden. *Camarones amorosos* (shrimp baked in a white sauce and served in a puff pastry shell) and the *Princesa Verde* (almond cake filled with raspberry jam) are two major reasons for the growing popularity of this place. Open daily. Reservations advised. 101 Abasolo (phone: 182635 or 182689). Expensive.

Château du Lac – Set on the shores of Lake Tequesquitengo, about 33 miles (53 km) from Cuernavaca, this excellent French eatery is owned by Ghislaine and Phillip Mercier who are always on hand to preside over the kitchen and to see that everything runs smoothly. Open Fridays, Saturdays, and Sundays from 1 to 11 PM. Km 10 Curcuito Lake Tequesquitengo (phone: 734-70173). Expensive.

Ma Maison – French cooking techniques are blended with Mexican ingredients, creating such delicacies as filet of sea bass stuffed with *huitlacoche* and a pâté of smoked trout. Open daily. Reservations advised. 58 Francisco Villa (phone: 131435). Expensive.

Las Mañanitas – Perhaps the best restaurant in town, the international menu featured at this lovely spot is complemented by fine service and seating on the terrace and in the garden. Open daily. Reservations advised. No credit cards accepted. 107 Ricardo Linares (phone: 124646). Expensive.

Sumiya – The late heiress Barbara Hutton's former Japanese palace is now a restaurant. The menu is international, including tempura and sashimi, and the setting is magnificent. Open daily. Reservations advised. In Juitepec, 3 miles (5 km) past the CIVAC exit on the Acapulco highway (phone: 190622). Expensive.

Allegro – At the *Posada Xochiquetzal,* this place serves Northern Italian specialities. Diners may sit outdoors on a patio overlooking a garden. Open daily. Reservations advised. 200 Leyva (phone: 185767 or 120220). Moderate.

Le Château René – Housed in a venerable mansion, it offers French and Swiss dishes that are well prepared and thoughtfully served. Open daily. Reservations advised. 11 Calz. de los Reyes (phone: 172300). Moderate.

Hacienda de Cortés – Favored by Cuernavaca regulars, this place has an international menu, excellent service, and the romantic setting of a converted hacienda. Open daily. Reservations advised. 90 Plaza Kennedy, Atlacomulco (phone: 158844). Moderate.

Harry's Grill – A lively crowd gathers at this link in the ubiquitous Carlos Anderson chain of restaurants for barbecued chicken and ribs. Open daily. Reservations advised. 3 Gutenberg (phone: 127679). Moderate.

India Bonita – Operating for more than 40 years, this unassuming *fonda* (inn) has a reputation as one of the best restaurants in town for Mexican fare. Closed Mondays. No reservations. 6-B Morrow (phone: 121266). Moderate.

Maximilian's – Fine international and Mexican cooking are specialties here. Ask for the *huitlacoche* pâté, which is divine. American-style dishes are also available. Open daily. Reservations advised. 125 Galeana, Colonia Acapantzingo (phone: 123478). Moderate.

Las Quintas – Although the menu here is not especially creative, select dishes — especially the stuffed peppers and *huitlacoche* crêpes — are well prepared. Open daily. Reservations advised. *Hostería Las Quintas,* 107 Las Quintas (phone: 183949). Moderate.

Vienes – It's not fancy, but the food is excellent. Try the steak tartare and the lovely, soufflé-like Austrian dessert called *Salzburger nockerl.* Closed Tuesdays. Reservations advised. 4 Lerdo de Tejada, a block from the zocalo (phone: 184044). Moderate.

VIP's – A gringo-style eatery with a wide selection of American and Mexican dishes.

Good waffles. Open daily. No reservations. 9 Blvd. Juárez (phone: 128342). Moderate to inexpensive.

Palacio – Since a meal here can be 5 courses of delicious Spanish food, it's one of the best bargains in town. Open daily. Reservations unnecessary. 204 Morrow, next to *India Bonita* (phone: 120553). Inexpensive.

La Parroquia – This Mexican-sounding spot dishes up Middle Eastern meals. If you're addicted to souvlaki, shish kebab, and hummus, this place is for you. Other ethnic specialties served, too. Open daily. Reservations unnecessary. On the zocalo (phone: 185820). Inexpensive.

Los Pasteles del Vienés – Just a few steps away from — and owned by — *Vienes,* this is a nice place for pastries and European-style snacks. Open daily. Reservations unnecessary. Lerdo de Tejada and Comonfort (phone: 143404). Inexpensive.

Playa Dorada – Absolutely no atmosphere, but perfectly prepared fish and shellfish at reasonable prices. Open daily. Reservations unnecessary. 33 Morelos Sur (phone: 143633). Inexpensive.

■ **Note:** Along the Boulevard Plan de Ayala, one taco stand after another serves a very broad variety of traditional (and delicious) tacos, evenings after 7 PM.

ENSENADA

(pronounced En-say-*nah*-dah)

As a resort area, Ensenada may well be Southern California's best-kept Mexican secret. Few people outside Los Angeles and San Diego know the place well, but in fact it is the best beach and sea sport section of the northern Baja coast. With its emphasis on beach, sea, sun, and sport, it certainly provides a fitting complement to Tijuana's steadfast shopping-and-spectator-sport image. Ensenada is about 60 miles (96 km) south of the US–Mexico border at Tijuana, a short drive along the well-maintained scenic highway that connects the two cities.

Shipping is Ensenada's principal activity. The city is a big place, and, with more than 300,000 inhabitants, far larger than most visiting Americans realize. The tourist attractions are concentrated in an area along or near the waterfront and give Ensenada the appearance of a small, charming village when it is, in fact, a thriving port.

No tourist card is needed to visit Ensenada, nor is any automobile permit required for visits of 72 hours or less, or if you do not plan to venture farther into the interior. Drivers should buy Mexican car insurance before crossing the border, however. (For information on applicable US customs regulations and car insurance, see GETTING READY TO GO). There is also regular bus service to Ensenada from both San Diego and Tijuana.

Bahía Todos Santos (All Saints Bay) was named by Sebastian Vizcaino in 1602, and it became a harbor of some note, although for centuries the settlement on shore remained small. Ensenada was a trading town for the handful of ranchers in the area and a supply point for some of the missions. Then, in 1870, gold was discovered at nearby Real de Castillo.

The gold rush that followed gave enough substance to the town that it was made the territorial capital. From Ensenada, settlers ventured into the vast, empty lands of Baja California, but the shortage of water doomed most efforts to failure. When the mines played out in Ensenada and the capital was moved to Mexicali, the city went into decline.

Prohibition in the United States changed things. All Saints Bay turned into a safe harbor for rum runners (the 1975 film *Lucky Lady,* with Burt Reynolds, Liza Minnelli, and Gene Hackman, celebrated such adventures) and reckless film stars flew down in biplanes to drink and gamble at the old *Riviera Club.*

When drinking again became legal in the US and gambling illegal in Mexico, Ensenada might have withered once more, but its port facilities saved it. The Mexicali Valley, across the peninsula, had blossomed into a major cotton-growing area, and the cotton had to be exported. Ships put in at Ensenada to pick up the bales.

Wine production began here 2 centuries ago, and it continues to thrive today. In fact, 80% of the wine and brandy consumed in Mexico is produced in Ensenada's Mediterranean climate. (Mexico is one of the largest consumers of brandy in the world.) Fishing is another healthy industry here.

Multifaceted Ensenada caters to ever greater numbers of tourists, many of whom pass through on longer trips through Baja on Highway 1 or come down for a quick weekend getaway. However, as word gets out about its well-run hotels, excellent restaurants, quality shops and good bargains, lively nightlife, satisfying fishing, and appealing beaches, it is becoming more and more a popular destination on its own.

ENSENADA AT-A-GLANCE

SEEING THE CITY: For an overview of Ensenada, follow Calle 2 up Chapultepec Hill. There is an observation point marked "Mirador" from which the surprisingly large city may be seen. Another good view is from a boat in the harbor.

SPECIAL PLACES: Ensenada is a city full of nooks and crannies, some surprisingly large. Prime areas for strolling are Boulevard Costera and Avenidas López Mateos, Juárez, and Ruiz — streets loaded with shops carrying both Mexican and imported goods. The *malecón,* along the waterfront, is a pleasant promenade.

López Mateos Avenue – Officially Avenida Adolfo López Mateos, named after the man who was President of Mexico from 1958 to 1964, it is also known as Avenida Primera (First Avenue). This infinitely walkable street is where almost all of the hotels are located, as well as many restaurants and the better shops.

Harbor – The town lies at the north end of 10-mile-wide Todos Santos (All Saints) Bay. Several freighters usually lie at anchor here, and launches will take four or five people on tours around the bay for about $4 per person per hour.

Riviera del Pacífico (Pacific Riviera) – Built in the 1920s — it's said Al Capone was the owner — and managed by Jack Dempsey, this gambling casino brought in the jet setters before there were any jets. It is now a social, civic, and cultural center. Blvd. Lázaro Cárdenas and Av. Riviera.

Santo Tomás Winery – Baja California is famed in Mexico for its excellent wine, and this winery, founded by the Dominicans in 1888, is one of the major producers. On view are the storage casks and the thousands of bottles of sparkling white that must be turned by hand to make what the French would call champagne. Usually there are three tours daily at 11 AM, 1 PM, and 3PM, but it's a good idea to call ahead. Admission charge includes a sampling of wine and cheese. 666 Av. Miramar (phone: 82509).

La Bufadora (Blowhole) – A dramatic sea geyser where the ocean puts on a spectacular show, La Bufadora is at Punta Banda on the southern arm of the bay. The drive out takes about 30 minutes, passing Maneadero, which is an *ejido,* or communal farm. Be sure to wear comfortable shoes.

Isla Todos Santos (All Saints Island) – Some literary historians believe this was the inspiration for Robert Lewis Stevenson's *Treasure Island.* The author, along with his mother and niece, lived in Ensenada for a year. The island is visible from La Jolla beach and *La Cueva de los Tigres* restaurant. Tours and camping are part of the plans for its development.

■ **EXTRA SPECIAL:** Drive across the peninsula to San Felipe on the Gulf of California on Route 3. The 3-hour, 160-mile (256 km) trip across the desert is memorable, for this is one of the last wilderness areas left in North America; on Route 3 you will feel very much alone. San Felipe is a fishing village on Baja's eastern shore. Its tourist office is on Mar de Cortés Street, and there are several places to stop for lunch. If you decide to spend the night, try *Las Misiones* (phone: 657-71280; in the US, 800-336-5454) and *La Trucha Vagabunda,* San Felipe's oldest hotel, which has been remodeled elegantly (phone: 657-713333). You may want to take a different route for the return trip to California, via Mexicali or Tecate.

SOURCES AND RESOURCES

 TOURIST INFORMATION: The Chamber of Commerce (693 Av. López Mateos; phone: 82322) and the Convention & Visitors Bureau (Blvd. Costero and Teniente Azueta; phone: 82411) have friendly and helpful staffs; both offices are open long hours. The office of the state attorney for the protection of tourists is near *La Pinta* hotel (1350-13B Av. López Mateos; phone: 63718; FAX: 63686), and the tourist office (phone: 62222) is at the same address. The monthly *Baja Sun,* available in hotels, is full of information and discount coupons for merchandise and drinks in local establishments. Also take advantage of the Chamber of Commerce's booklet of discounts worth l0% to 25%. San Diego and Los Angeles newspapers are available at the *San Nicolas* hotel (López Mateos and Guadalupe) and *Bazar Móctezuma* (911 Av. López Mateos) early in the day.

 TELEPHONE: The area code for Ensenada is 667. When calling from one city to another within Mexico, dial 91 before the area code.

 CLIMATE AND CLOTHES: Just over 75 miles (120km) south of San Diego, Ensenada shares Southern California's climate. It can be cool in winter and rainy in January and February. Dress is casual, but somewhat more conservative than in the US.

 GETTING AROUND: The hotels, restaurants, and shops are mostly within walking distance of each other. Most visitors arrive in their own cars, and for those who don't, taxis are plentiful but expensive ($1.50 minimum trip, $15 to $20 round trip to Estero Beach). Car rental agencies include *Hertz* (phone: 83776), near the *Bahía* hotel; *Scorpio Rent a Car* (95 Alvarado, off Av. López Mateos; phone: 83275); and *Ensenada Rent-a-Car* is next door (phone: 83986). City buses are not helpful. *Viajes Guaycura* (1089 Av. López Mateos; phone: 83718), next to the *Best Western Cortés,* runs 3½-hour tours of the city and environs twice a week.

SPECIAL EVENTS: Something special seems to be going on in Ensenada all the time. The pre-*Lenten Carnaval,* or *Mardi Gras,* is one of the best west of New Orleans. In October and March, the *Fun Bicycle Ride* brings more than 9,000 participants from Tecate on the border. In late April or early May, the *Sailing Regatta,* several thousand yachts strong, sets off for Ensenada from Newport Beach. In June the *Baja 500* (mile) off-road race gets off to a screeching start in Ensenada. The *Fiesta Mexicana,* a high-spirited celebration complete with mariachis, traditional dancing, piñata parties, and contests from singing to tequila drinking, and the *Taco, Tamale, and Mole Fair* (also known as the *Antojitos Fair*), a food fair featuring myriad Mexican finger foods, make July a big party month. Those who don't get their fill can return in September for the *International Seafood Fair,* and again in October, when the *International Chili Cook-Off* takes place. In November, the *Baja 1,000* (mile) off-road race departs from Ensenada, and there is a large travel and handicrafts show. *Christmas* week is spiked with gaiety, with the partying going on through *New Year's Eve.*

SHOPPING: One of the most popular pastimes in Ensenada is buying things. Baja California is what Mexicans call a free zone (*zona franca*), and a great many items are imported untaxed. Many of the shops along Av. López Mateos sell handicrafts made in Mexico, including leather goods, pottery, baskets, textiles, resortwear, shoes and sandals, tiles and ceramics, and silver and gold jewelry. Though Tijuana has more of a reputation as a prime center for shopping and bargains, Ensenada has equally good prices and better quality and variety.

Artes Bitterlin – Filled to overflowing with large items for the home, from sculptures to paintings to furniture. 1000 Av. López Mateos (phone: 81733).

FONART – Choice crafts from all over the country. Next door to the tourist office at 1306 Av. López Mateos (phone: 61536).

Galería Anna – The outstanding crafts sold here include blankets, rugs, placemats, tablecloths, masks, furniture, and pottery. A showplace of a store. 122 Riveroll off Av. López Mateos (phone: 40704).

La Joya – Dark and off-putting, but a treasure trove of wrought iron home accessories and stained glass lamps waits inside. 725 Av. López Mateos (phone: 83191).

Joyas Jacqueline – Among the gold and silver jewelry here are especially nice earrings. 1077 Av. López Mateos (phone: 40816).

México Lindo – A saddle shop that attracts real cowhands. It has good buys in belts, leather bags, hats, and chaps. 679 Av. López Mateos (phone: 81391).

La Mina de Solomon – Redecorating a living room? Come here. The paintings and large mirrors are particularly nice. 1000 Av. López Mateos (phone: 81733).

La Piel – Stylish leather clothes for men and women. 720 López Mateos (phone: 81294).

El Solecito – Especially attractive metal ornaments and mirrors from Oaxaca. 124 Av. Blancarte off Av. López Mateos (phone: 82816).

Tianguis – Leather goods made from eel skin; huaraches, Mexican clothes, and a huge T-shirt collection. 744 Av. López Mateos (phone: 81155).

Xuchitl – A small shop filled with crafts and silver jewelry. Av. López Mateos and Alvarado (phone: 40976).

SPORTS: In Ensenada sports are all of the participation variety, with something for everyone.

Fishing – Yellowtail is what the fishermen go after, and both daily charters (from $200 to $1,000) and open-ticket vessels (about $30, including a license) vessels. *Gordo's Sports Fishing* (phone: 83515) and *Pacific Anglers* (phone: 40865) are reliable outfits. There's also good angling at Emilio López Zamora Dam, 3 miles (5 km) north of town on Av. Reforma; surf fishing is popular south of town.

Golf – *Bajamar,* 20 miles (32 km) north of Ensenada, has 18 holes and some of the finest facilities anywhere in the area (phone: 83838).

Horseback Riding – It's available for about $10 per hour at the *Mona Lisa* hotel and campground (no phone) and on the beach (at the end of Blvd. Costero).

Hunting – The quail season is from November to mid-January. The Ministry of Urban Development and Ecology (SEDUE; 1350-A Av. López Mateos; phone: 63120) arranges trips, and the tourism office will take reservations for the hunting ranch *Ejido Uruapan,* 26 miles (42 km) south of Ensenada. Hunters must bring their weapons with them, which involves some red tape but is worth the effort. Obtain a permit from a Mexican consulate and report the weapon at Customs (see GETTING READY TO GO).

Off-Track Betting – *Foreign Book* is the hot spot in town year round for placing bets on races being held at all the major US tracks, as well as on the horses and greyhounds at Tijuana's *Agua Caliente.* Straight bets, daily doubles, exactas, and more are on the agenda. It's behind the *FONART* store, at Av. López Mateos and Espinoza.

Surfing – Aficionados go 8 miles (13 km) north of Ensenada to San Miguel.

Swimming – The favorite beach is Estero, just south of the downtown area; go at low tide to avoid the undertow. Other possibilities are Playitas, La Jolla, Puerto Escondido, and El Faro.

Tennis – The *Baja Tennis Club* in Ensenada is a private club with 5 lighted courts (2 concrete, 3 lighted asphalt); reservations must be made through hotels. Also check the *Estero Beach* resort (phone: 66235) and *Bajamar* (phone: 83838).

Water Skiing – The best facilities are at the *Estero Beach* resort (phone: 66235), which faces a sheltered lagoon south of town. Guests from other hotels are welcome.

NIGHTCLUBS AND NIGHTLIFE: Fun after dark centers largely around the hotels, most of which have live entertainment or discotheques. Everybody either starts off the evening or ends it at *Hussong's* (phone: 83210), a cow-town saloon left over from the gold rush days, and still wild and woolly. There's a popular disco in the *San Nicolas* hotel (phone: 61901), and the *Bahía* (phone: 82103) has live music and dancing in the bar on weekends. Music videos are featured at *Upside Down* (phone: 83653), *Bananas* (phone: 82004), *El Bandido* (no phone), and *Papas & Beer* (phone: 70125), which attract a young crowd. The upstairs bar at *Smitty Gonzalez's* (phone: 40636) really comes alive after 9 PM. Sample different brands of tequila at the *Tequila Connection* (no phone). All are on or near Av. López Mateos.

BEST IN TOWN

CHECKING IN: During the summer and especially on weekends, Ensenada's hotels are very busy. Always make reservations and try to arrive early in the day. Hotel rates are reasonable. A double room listed here as expensive costs $85 to $100; a moderate room is $55 to $65; and an inexpensive one will run $50 or less. Prices tend to be lower December through February and Mondays through Thursdays. Most hotels listed below accept MasterCard and Visa; a few also accept American Express and Diners Club. All telephone numbers are in the 667 area code unless otherwise indicated. When calling from one city to another within Mexico, dial 91 before the area code.

Punta Morro – An elegant modern hotel overlooking the bay, it has 24 suites (21 have kitchens) with terraces and ocean views. All are equipped with refrigerators and cable TV, and there's a nice pool and Jacuzzi. One mile (1.6 km) north of Ensenada on Carr. 1 (phone: 44490 or 800-726-6426 in the US). Expensive.

Las Rosas Spa – The 31 attractive rooms all have balconies and ocean views. There is also a restaurant, piano bar, sauna, spa with Jacuzzi, and 2 pools that give the impression that they are almost in the sea. Two miles (3 km) north of Ensenada at Km 105.5 of the Ensenada Hwy. (phone: 44595 or 44310; FAX: 44595). Expensive.

San Nicolás Resort – Lovely, with 148 rooms decorated in colonial style, it has a view of the sea, a restaurant, 2 pools (1 is huge), bar, disco, security parking, and a complimentary margarita during check-in. They also sell foreign sports books. Av. López Mateos and Guadalupe (phone: 61901; FAX: 64930). Expensive.

Bahía – Built in 1953, centrally located, and casual, it has 62 rooms, cable TV, a pool, restaurant, 2 bars, music on weekends, parking, and a complimentary margarita during check-in. Av. López Mateos and Riveroll (phone: 82101, 82102, or 82103; FAX: 81455). Moderate.

Casa del Sol – Pretty and hospitable, this Best Western property has 43 rooms, a bar, restaurant, and a large pool. Av. Blancarte and Av. López Mateos (phone: 81570; FAX: 82025). Moderate.

El Cid – Built in the Mediterranean style, its 52 rooms are decorated with handicrafts from different towns in Mexico. There is also cable TV. There are 2 suites with Jacuzzis, plus a pool, restaurant, and live music in the bar. 993 Av. López Mateos (phone: 82401; FAX: 83671). Moderate.

Estero Beach – Perfect for sports enthusiasts, it has 106 rooms and features tennis, horseback riding, biking, sailing, water skiing, and fishing. On the beach 6 miles (10 km) south of town (phone: 66235; in the US, 800-762-2494; FAX: 66925). Moderate.

Misión Santa Isabel – A pretty place in the colonial style, it has 58 small rooms on only 2 floors, a small pool, a restaurant with tango shows on Thursdays and Fridays, and a bar with live music. Rooms must be paid for in advance. Blvd. Costero and Castillo (phone: 83616; FAX: 83345). Moderate.

La Pinta – Headquarters for a chain of hotels located at towns along the Transpeninsular Highway, it has 52 rooms, a small pool, a pretty restaurant, and a bar. Prices are considerably lower on weekdays. Half a mile (1 km) from downtown. Av. Los Bucaneros and Calle Floresta, off Av. López Mateos (phone: 62601). Moderate.

Travelodge – In a rustic setting, it has 50 rooms with wet bars, a suite with a Jacuzzi, remote-control TV sets, a cozy restaurant and bar, and a pool. Guests enjoy complimentary margaritas from 7 to 8 PM. Av. López Mateos and 130 Blancarte (phone: 81601; in the US, 800-545-6343; FAX: 40005). Moderate.

Villa Marina – In the heart of town, this 12-story hostelry has 130 rooms and 2 pools. Some rooms are equipped for the handicapped. Av. López Mateos and Blancarte (phone: 83321; FAX: 83321). Moderate.

Fiesta Inn – A mile (1.6 km) from downtown, it has 35 spacious rooms, 7 of which have kitchens. Daily, weekly, and monthly rates are available, but reserve 2 to 4 weeks ahead. 237 Sanguines (phone: 61361). Inexpensive.

Quintas Papagayo – Most of the suites and cottages here have kitchens and ocean views. There's a restaurant, pool, tennis courts, and private beach. One-half mile (1 km) north of Ensenada on the Tijuana-Ensenada Toll Road (phone: 44980; FAX: 44155). Inexpensive.

 EATING OUT: Ensenada has two of the best restaurants in Mexico (*El Rey Sol* and *La Cueva de los Tigres*), at which a visitor may sample the area's gastronomic specialties — quail, abalone, and Pacific lobster. Expect to pay up to $55 for a meal for two in an expensive restaurant; about $40 in a moderate one; and $25 and less in an inexpensive one. Prices don't include wine, tips, or drinks. Most restaurants listed below accept MasterCard and Visa; a few also accept American Express and Diners Club. Unless otherwise noted, all restaurants below are open daily. All telephone numbers are in the 667 area code unless otherwise indicated. When calling from one city to another within Mexico, dial 91 before the area code.

La Cueva de los Tigres – On the beach, 1½ miles (2 km) south of town by car (or a mile walking along the beach), the "Tigers' Cave" claims Ensenada's most delightful setting. Its abalone topped with shredded crab brings pilgrims from as far away as San Francisco and Seattle. Don't miss the sunset. Reservations advised. Av. Acapulco off Hwy. 1; watch for the sign (phone: 66450). Expensive.

El Rey Sol – Not to be missed, Baja California's great French restaurant has become an Ensenada legend. The quail in Madame Geffroy's own special sauce, *medallones de camarones Doña Pepita* (shrimp prepared with bacon and capers), and the fabulous desserts are the stuff of which dining dreams are made. The prix fixe menu includes numerous courses. Reservations advised. Av. López Mateos and Blancarte (phone: 81733). Expensive.

La Fonda – Worth the 19-mile (30-km) ride upbeach (or through the mountains) toward Tijuana, it's idyllically set above the Pacific on a flower-laden balcony. The Mexican food is a delight. In a pleasant hotel of the same name, it offers a ready excuse to stay and enjoy the ambience, food, and beach. Reservations advised. No credit cards accepted. Hwy. 1 (no phone). Moderate.

Hussong's El Pelicano & Oyster Bar – The fare includes abalone with crabmeat sauce, and a pretty mean chili con carne. Reservations advised. One mile (1.6 km) north of town at the *Quintas Papagayo Resort* (no phone). Moderate.

La Tortuga – Located in downtown Ensenada, popular selections here include breaded abalone, lobster burritos (tacos made with flour tortillas), and stuffed peppers — all served in a relaxed setting. Reservations advised. 800 Av. López Mateos (phone: 83075). Moderate.

Valentino's – Strawberry margaritas, homemade cheesecake, steaks, shrimp *Costa Azul* (stuffed with crab and rolled in bacon) are just some of the items on the extensive menu. Patio dining. Reservations advised. 915 Blvd. Costero (phone: 40022). Moderate.

Casamar – Seafood of all kinds is served here, and a soloist sings romantic ballads Wednesday through Saturday nights. Reservations advised. Across from the entrance to the harbor at 987 Blvd. Costero (phone: 40417). Moderate to inexpensive.

El Mesón de Don Fernando – A sidewalk café with 2 indoor dining rooms, it's a nice place for a breakfast of hotcakes or a break from shopping. Recorded music is played during the day, live jazz some nights. Reservations unnecessary. 914-5 Av. López Mateos (phone: 40155). Moderate to inexpensive.

China Land – More than 125 very well prepared Chinese dishes are featured here. Ragtime piano music provides a pleasant background. Closed Tuesdays. Reservations unnecessary. 1149 Riveroll, between 11th and 12th (phone: 86644). Inexpensive.

Haliotis – Fresh, delicious, and inexpensive seafood is the hallmark of this eatery. Closed Tuesdays. Reservations unnecessary. 179 Calle Delante (phone: 63720). Inexpensive.

GUADALAJARA

(pronounced Gwah-da-la-*ha*-ra)

Four major airlines fly into Guadalajara, making Mexico's second-largest city a top travel destination. Once proudly nicknamed the country's "biggest small town," Guadalajara is fast becoming sophisticated, cosmopolitan, and crowded. The city has benefited from all the best of Mexican history and culture. During the reign of the Spaniards, Guadalajara was an important center for commerce, and the city's great wealth was lavished on superb colonial architecture. Spain's power waned, but the beautiful buildings remain as a reminder of Guadalajara's past.

Guadalajara rests on a mile-high plain surrounded by rugged countryside 150 miles (240 km) due east of Puerto Vallarta, about 300 miles (480 km) west and slightly north of Mexico City. The relative isolation of the site fostered its characteristic sense of independence, self-reliance, and pride.

The Spanish influence is as strong in Guadalajara as in any city in the country. Following the Conquest, orders were given to open an outpost of the empire in the West. Settling it proved to be no small challenge. The Indians in the area were more difficult to subdue than the Aztec had been. Not until 1542, 20 years after Cortés seized what is now Mexico City, did Guadalajara get its start as a real city.

The charter sent from Spain instructed the builders to use the finest materials in constructing the city. Streets were to be wide, and ample space was to be set aside for parks. Along with government buildings, there was to be a church, monastery, hospital, and market, all near the central plaza.

During 3 centuries of colonial rule, those instructions served as a guide. Somewhat apart from the rest of the country, Guadalajara became "more Spanish than Spain." Its people came to be known as *tapatíos,* a name derived from the word for the tasseled cape favored by Spanish gentlemen. Even today residents of the state of Jalisco (of which Guadalajara is the capital) proudly refer to themselves as *tapatíos.*

Though Gudalajara largely escaped the century of turmoil that followed independence, it did have its moments. The city was one of the first to fall to Father Miguel Hidalgo in 1810, during the war against Spain, and it was there that a decree outlawing slavery was proclaimed, 50 years before Lincoln issued his Emancipation Proclamation. But by and large, Guadalajara kept to itself during the 19th century, clinging to the traditions its people still honor.

The city didn't really become an integral part of Mexico until the railroad reached it in the late 19th century. And the first railroad was so primitive and unreliable that its effect on the city was almost negligible. For decades the standard joke was that newlyweds taking the train to Mexico City for their honeymoon would have their first child before they got there. Nowadays, however, Guadalajara is at the hub of a network of railway lines, superhighways, and airline routes.

Despite its astounding growth, Guadalajara has managed to retain much of the gracious atmosphere of the past. It is a city of parks and fountains, of monuments and flower-lined boulevards. Many downtown streets have been closed to traffic and turned into pedestrian malls. Over the centuries, Guadalajara has been the center of one of Mexico's major agricultural areas; now it is rapidly industrializing. Modern skyscrapers rise above the city's traditional skyline, but Guadalajara has managed to modernize its industrial facilities without endangering its quality of life or altering the centuries-old city plan. The colonial center of the city is the Plaza Tapatía, which was laid out to show off historical Guadalajara at its best.

Guadalajara is famed for its talented craftsmen, for the artisans of the nearby village of Tlaquepaque, and for the tequila distilleries in the town called Tequila, about 35 miles (56 km) away. It is also the birthplace of José Clemente Orozco, one of this century's greatest artists, who did some of his best work here. He was one of the great muralists to come out of the Mexican Revolution (which began in 1910) and helped create a style of art that is world famous. For many people, seeing his two masterpieces on the walls of the *Cultural Center of the Americas* is reason enough to make a pilgrimage to Guadalajara.

Guadalajara is also one of Mexico's most delightful areas for tourists. It has a marvelous climate — eternal springtime, with a rainy season for 3 months during the summer. Over the past 20 years it has erected some of the most lavishly elegant hotels in Latin America. But most important, perhaps, it still has traces of the graciousness and gentility of old Mexico.

GUADALAJARA AT-A-GLANCE

SEEING THE CITY: The most superb views of the city are found from the rooftop lounges of the *Roma* and *Mendoza* hotels and from the hilltop perch of *El Tapatío.*

SPECIAL PLACES: With a clearly marked map you can easily get around Guadalajara on your own; compared with other Mexican cities, the traffic isn't heavy. However, if you want to really relax, hire an English-speaking guide for a 1-day tour. Many of the guides gather at the *Fénix* (160 Corona) at about 9 AM every day. After a short orientation tour, you will get a feel of the city and can go it on your own.

DOWNTOWN

Museo Arqueológico del Occidente de México (Archaeological Museum of Western Mexico) – Ancient Indian artifacts from the states of Colima, Jalisco, and Nayarit. Open 3:30 to 7 PM. Closed Sundays. No admission charge. On 16 de Septiembre, across the street from Parque Agua Azul, near the railroad station (no phone).

Instituto de la Artesanía Jalisciense (Handcraft Institute of Jalisco) – Display of contemporary handicrafts such as saddlery, furniture, blown glass, ceramics, pottery, textiles, tinwork, and woodcarving. There is a good exhibition of paintings on the second floor. All articles are for sale. Closed Sundays. No admission charge. Just north of the *Archaeological Museum* on Independencia in Parque Agua Azul. There is another showroom at 1221 Av. Alcalde (phone: 244518).

Museo Regional de Guadalajara (Regional Museum of Guadalajara) – This lovely museum is in a former seminary that dates from 1700. The exhibitions include the carriage used by Emperor Maximilian, excellent Spanish and Mexican paintings (11 by Murillo, among others), as well as archaeological exhibitions and regional arts and crafts. Open 9 AM to 3:30 PM. Closed Mondays. Admission charge. In the center of town at 60 Calle Liceo, 1 block north of the Palacio del Gobierno (phone: 149957).

Cultural Center of the Americas (formerly Cabañas Institute) – Built in 1803 as an orphanage, this magnificent structure is now a center for the arts. It houses two of Orozco's masterpieces, *Man of Fire* and *The Four Horsemen of the Apocalypse.* Plaza Tapatía (phone: 186003).

Cathedral – A strange hodgepodge of half a dozen architectural styles, including Gothic, Tuscan, Moorish, Mudejar, and Corinthian. It is appropriate that when an earthquake toppled the twin towers early in this century, they were rebuilt in yet another style — Byzantine. Construction was started in 1571 and the church was consecrated in 1618. The cathedral houses many art treasures that were donated by King Fernando VII of Spain in appreciation of the financial support the city gave Spain during the Napoleonic Wars. There are 11 different altars, all ornate (the one dedicated to Our Lady of Roses is superb). Don't miss the Murillo painting *The Assumption of the Virgin* in the sacristy. The two bell towers are over 200 feet tall. The cathedral is on the main plaza in the center of the city.

Teatro Degollado (Degollado Theater) – Guadalajara's major cultural center, a lavishly beautiful 19th-century building, decorated with rich reds, gold leaf, and crystal chandeliers, is the home of the *Guadalajara Symphony Orchestra,* the *Ballet Folklórico,* and other operatic and theatrical groups. The interior decoration includes a notable mural depicting Dante's *Divine Comedy.* Performances are held several times a week, with tickets starting at about $5. Just east of the cathedral on Plaza de la Liberación (phone: 131115).

Palacio del Gobierno (State House) – This historic structure, built in 1643, was the site of Hidalgo's landmark decree abolishing slavery in 1810. The building features dynamic murals by Orozco. Open daily. No admission charge. Southeast of the cathedral on Corona at Morelos (phone: 145414).

Iglesia de San Francisco de Asis (Church of St. Francis of Assisi) – Dating from the early years of the conquest, this historic church is particularly noted for its ornate façade. Next to San Francisco Park on Av. Corona, 6 blocks south of Av. Juárez.

Church of Our Lady of Aranzazu – Don't let the simple exterior fool you. Inside is one of the finest, most ornate altars in the city. Across the park from the Church of St. Francis of Assisi.

Church of Santa Mónica – A 250-year-old church with a lovely baroque façade. In the middle of a fascinating colonial neighborhood at the corner of Calle de Santa Mónica and San Felipe.

Plaza de Mariachis (Plaza of the Mariachis) – Sit at any of the sidewalk cafés and watch the strolling mariachis or, better yet, hire them to serenade you. Six blocks east of Av. Alcalde on Juárez, near the Mercado Libertad.

Mercado Libertad (Liberty Market) – Everything can be bought here — clothing, food, arts and crafts, even medicinal herbs. Housed in a huge modern building with over 1,000 stands, each of them privately owned. Be sure to bargain. Open daily. Covers four square blocks near the intersection of Juárez and Calzada Independencia.

Fábrica de Vidrio Soplado (Glass Factory) – Watch handmade glass being blown, then buy it here as inexpensively as anyplace. If you're going to be in the area long enough, the artisans will make up special orders in whatever color and design you want;

they ship anywhere, but we recommend carrying the fragile things home yourself. 232 Independencia, Tlaquepaque (phone: 397180).

Expo Guadalajara – An impressive complex that houses the city's fairs and expositions center, it's a showcase for national and foreign manufacturers. Two blocks from the *Plaza del Sol Shopping Center* at Av. López Mateos and Mariano Otero (phone: 475050).

Museo de Arte Huichol (Museum of Huichol Art) – The Huichol Indians are native to the states of Jalisco and Nayarit, and are one of the few groups that have been able to maintain their customs and traditions. The museum displays photographs of Huichol life, native costumes, replicas of their dwellings, and handicrafts (some for sale). Open daily from 9 AM to 1:30 PM and from 4 to 7:30 PM. No admission charge. 52 Eva Briseño, Zapopan (phone: 330141).

Parque Natural Huentitán (Huentitán Park) – Inaugurated in March 1988, the park features a planetarium, the *Severo Diaz Galindo Science and Techonology Center,* and a zoo that is not to be missed — with 1,500 animals, representing 230 species, in 27 special habitats. At the entrance are 17 columns, with a chimp by Sergio Bustamante (a Guadalajara native and world-famous sculptor and potter) perched atop each, and a huge vertical fountain with 1,200 fantastical animal faces, also designed by Bustamante. The zoo also has a 4-story aviary, ponds filled with black and white swans, a children's zoo, and an enormous snake house. A walk through the park takes about 2 hours. For those with less time (or energy), there are four mini-trains. Closed Mondays. Admission charge. At the end of Calz. Independencia Nte. and Flores Magón, about 10 miles (16 km) from Agua Azul Park (phone: 384307).

NEARBY

El Salto de Juanacatlán (Juanacatlán Falls) – One of the largest waterfalls in Mexico. Be sure to stop at the nearby village of Juanacatlán, where you can buy excellent woolens and textiles. It's 15 miles (24 km) southeast of the city on Rte. 44, then 8 miles (13 km) northeast on a paved road.

Tlaquepaque – (Pronounced *Tlah*-kay-pah-kay) Formerly a distinct village and now a sophisticated handicrafts center enveloped by Guadalajara, this place is famous for its pottery, almost all of it hand-painted. Visitors are welcome to watch the potters at work. There are also glass factories and artisans working in silver and copper, as well as Indian weavers working at handlooms. A month-long fiesta of handicrafts, food, drink, and folk dancing is usually held during June. The *Regional Ceramics Museum* (237 Independencia) is well worth a visit. The center is closed Mondays. No admission charge. About 5 miles (8 km) east of the city on Rte. 80 (phone: 355400).

Chapala – A town of about 40,000 on Lago de Chapala, Mexico's largest inland body of water (about 60 miles long and from 12 to 20 miles wide). The area has one of Mexico's largest retirement colonies of US citizens, complete with an American Legion post of several hundred members. A suburb, Chula Vista, is almost 100% US citizens. About 25 miles (40 km) southeast of Guadalajara on Rte. 44.

Ajijic – (Pronounced Ah-hee-*heek*) A picturesque village with a population mainly of writers and artists, this is a wonderful place for drinking, sitting, and generally lazing around. The village has some interesting little galleries and boutiques. About 3 miles (5 km) west of Chula Vista.

Jocotepec – This pretty little fishing village with very few foreign residents is famous for its white serapes, which you'll see for sale everywhere. (You can combine Juanacatlán Falls, Tlaquepaque, Chapala, Ajijic, and Jocotepec in a 1-day tour.)

Tequila – The town where tequila is chiefly made is about 35 miles (56 km) north of Guadalajara on Hwy. 15. Cuervo, Orendain, and Herradura are among the better-known distilleries. The town doesn't have much to offer otherwise, but the trip is a pretty one, and the fields of blue maguey (from which tequila is made) are memorable.

The *Sauza* distillery in Tequila arranges tours and offers cut-rate prices on their products. Call Aurora (phone: 20244). *Panoramex,* a reliable sightseeing outfit, runs tours to Tequila on Mondays, Wednesdays, and Fridays (phone: 105005 or 105057). The *Sauza* bottling plant has a "happy hour" from 10 AM to noon. Contact Jesús Orozco (phone: 479776 or 476674). The plant is in Guadalajara on 3273 Vallarta, in the direction of the *Camino Real* hotel.

Tonalá – About 6 miles (10 km) east of Tlaquepaque, it's small-town Mexico, with none of the sophistication of Tlaquepaque. A dark, sienna-colored pottery is the specialty. Thursdays and Sundays are market days. Don't miss the *National Ceramic Museum* (104 Constitución; phone: 840494). Closed Mondays. Admission charge.

■**EXTRA SPECIAL: Barranca de Oblatos (Oblatos Canyon)** – This 2,000-foot-deep gorge is lush with tropical vegetation and steaming hot springs spouting from the canyon walls. It's a steep climb, and, unfortunately, the cable car is for the exclusive use of the power and light company. It's 7 miles (11 km) northeast of the city via Calzada Independencia.

SOURCES AND RESOURCES

 TOURIST INFORMATION: The government tourist office (102 Morelos; phone: 148686) has maps, folders, and general information. They also have a Teletour hotline (phone: 582222) for up-to-date information. There is a Visitors and Convention Office (4095 Av. Vallarta; phone: 479481) and a US Consulate (175 Progreso; phone: 252700 or 252998).

 TELEPHONE: The area code for Guadalajara is 36. When calling from one city to another within Mexico, dial 91 before the area code.

 CLIMATE AND CLOTHES: Guadalajara is blessed with a delightful, moderate climate. The average daily maximum temperature is 73F in January, 85F in April, 79F in July, and 78F in October. Dress in Guadalajara tends to be slightly more conservative than in such tourist spots as Acapulco.

 GETTING AROUND: Bus – If you are adventurous and speak the language fairly well, you can take advantage of the dozens of buses crisscrossing the city. To get out to the Lake Chapala district, take the Cienega de Chapala bus, which leaves about every 45 minutes from the Central Camionera (bus terminal), between Calle Cinco de Febrero and Calle Los Angeles. *Panoramex* (phone: 105057) offers a variety of city tours as well as trips into the countryside (most notably, a trip to a tequila factory in the village of Tequila). Passengers are picked up at Parque San Francisco and at Parque Los Arcos, but the bus stops at hotels along the route on the way back. Information on current schedules is available in hotel lobbies.

Taxi – Taxis are the most convenient way to get around town. Fares are low. If you don't speak the language well, write your destination on a slip of paper and hand it to the driver, thus avoiding a misunderstanding or a possible argument.

Car Rental – Most of the major firms (*Avis, Budget, Hertz, National, Quick*), as well as many local companies, have offices in town and at the airport.

SPECIAL EVENTS: October is fiesta time in Guadalajara. The whole month is full of constant activity — sporting events, theatrical presentations, daily bullfights, ballet, folk dancing, and the *International Friendship Festival*. Countries from all over the world participate with exhibits and performances (somewhat like a world's fair), and almost daily homage is paid to each of the participating nations. It is exciting but very crowded, and reservations must be confirmed months in advance. There are paseos on Lafayette in the evenings and an old-fashioned *Serenata Tapatía* on Thursdays and Sundays at the Plaza de Armas from 6:30 to 9 PM. In a *serenata, charros* on horseback or in carriages ride around courting passing ladies — a colorful sight. October 12 is the date of the most important religious celebration in the area, when the Virgin of Zapopan is returned to her basilica after touring all the churches in Guadalajara. Year-round at the Plaza de Armas (Av. Dieciséis de Septiembre and Moreno, near the cathedral) the *Guadalajara Symphony Orchestra* gives concerts on Thursdays and Sundays (no promenading then). Every Sunday at noon, at Calle Dr. R. Michel and Calz. las Palmas, next to the Agua Azul Park, there's a *charreada,* in which the *charros* demonstrate their skill at calf wrestling, roping, and bull riding.

SHOPPING: Guadalajara has excellent shopping. Most stores in town don't bargain (you'll see signs stating *precios fijos,* which means "fixed prices"). Store hours are usually Mondays through Saturdays, 9:30 AM to 2 PM and 4 to 7 or 8 PM. Of particular interest are glass, pottery, serapes, and other handicrafts from the surrounding regions. Main shopping areas are on Avenida Juárez and Avenida Vallarta; also along Avenida Chapultepec and Avenida de las Américas. *Plaza del Sol* (Av. López Mateos and Mariano Otero), which claims to be Latin America's largest shopping center, has some 200 shops and is open daily. *Plaza México* (Av. México and Blvd. Homero) and *Plaza Patria* (Av. Avila Camacho) also offer a good variety of stores. At the *Mercado Libertad* (Liberty Market; on Calzada Independencia at Juárez) you can haggle for everything from clothes to medicinal herbs found in the more than 1,000 stands. The *Casa Fuerte* (224 Independencia; phone: 578499) is a group of shops selling native crafts from Chiapas, Oaxaca, Nayarit, and Jalisco. It also offers items from Guatemala and Peru, Irene Pulos designs for women, and unusual accessories. Many of the stores listed below are in Tlaquepaque, a handicrafts center. (For more information on Tlaquepaque, see *Special Places* above.)

La Aguila – Fashions by Josefa and tastefully chosen handicrafts. 120 Juárez, Tlaquepaque (phone: 357557).

Antigua de México – In an elegantly restored 17th-century villa and gardens. Unusual assortment of items for sale, ranging from objets d'art and antiques to gifts and made-to-order furniture. 255 Independencia, Tlaquepaque, and in the *Plaza Patria Shopping Center,* Guadalajara (phone: 353402).

Antigüedades Collignon – Arts and artifacts from the viceregal era and early years of independence. 123 Calle Bernardo de Balbuena (phone: 160437).

Bazar Hecht – A very pleasant place to shop for fine handicrafts and furniture. 158 Independencia, Tlaquepaque (phone: 352241).

Caoba – It carries an excellent selection of furniture typical of the area, as well as antiques, handicrafts, and ceramics. 156 Independencia, Tlaquepaque (phone: 359770).

Casa de las Artesanías de Jalisco (Jalisco Artisans' House) – At this trade school and exhibition hall, you can buy choice items from glass blowers, weavers, potters, jewelers. Fixed prices. Independencia at the entrance to Agua Azul Park (phone: 257537).

El Charro – This is the place to buy elegant Mexican cowboy wear, including boots fashioned from sharkskin and giant turtle. 132 Juárez (phone: 135795), 148 Juárez (phone: 147599), and *Plaza del Sol* (phone: 211969).

Galería los Kristian – Great handmade rugs, hand-painted fabrics, and beautiful clothes. 223 Juárez, Tlaquepaque (phone: 356034).

Irene Pulos – Fashions for women — caftans, jackets, dresses — trimmed with bright ribbons and appliqués. *Hyatt* (phone: 215985) and at *Casa Fuerte* in Tlaquepaque (no phone).

Ken Edwards de Tonalá – Beautifully crafted and colored stoneware in exclusive designs. 70 Madero, Tlaquepaque (phone: 352426).

El Palomar – Stoneware dishes are made on the premises at this highly recommended shop. Also outstanding jewelry, sculpture, and textiles, all in the finest taste. 1905 Blvd. Tlaquepaque (phone: 399896).

Sergio Bustamante – Wonderfully colorful sculptures of animals and birds in papier-mâché, copper, bronze, and tin — all from the master Mexican artist, who is a native of Gudalajara. 23 Independencia, Tlaquepaque (phone: 395519).

Tane – A branch of Mexico City's finest and most exclusive silver shop is in the *Hyatt* (phone: 227778).

El Zaguán – A wide selection of *equipales* (rustic furniture made of leather and wood) as well as crafts. 227 Independencia, Tlaquepaque (phone: 351683).

 SPORTS: Guadalajara is a cosmopolitan city with a wide range of spectator and participant sports ranging from bullfights to golf. Among the many attractions are the following:

Baseball – The season roughly parallels that in the US. Games are played at the *Technological Institute Stadium,* Revolución and Olímpico, and at the *Heliodoro Hernandez Loza Park* in Tlaquepaque.

Boxing – There are usually weekly matches at the *Arena Coliseo,* 67 Medrano.

Bullfighting – Bullfights are held on Sundays twice a month (twice a week during the October fiestas) at the *Plaza Nuevo Progreso,* north of the center of the city on Independencia. The season generally runs from September to May.

Charro Exhibitions – Mexican rodeos with *charro* cowboys performing take place Sundays next to Agua Azul Park, near the railroad station on Independencia.

Cockfights – Rooster battles are held at the *Palenque Agua Azul* during the *International Friendship Festival* in October.

Golf – *Guadalajara Country Club* (260 Mar Caribe; phone: 414045) has 18 holes, par 72. You have to be the guest of a member to play. *Club de Golf Atlas* (near the *El Tapatío* hotel; phone: 890085) is private, but playing privileges can be arranged. *Santa Anita Golf Club* (phone: 860386) is just a few minutes south of the city on Route 15. *San Isidro Golf Club* (phone: 332044) is a private course designed by Larry Hughes; it's in a scenic valley just north of the city on Route 54. Both *Santa Anita* and *San Isidro* are open to the public on weekdays. The *Chapala Country Club* (Vista del Lago, San Nicolas Ibarra, Jalisco; no phone), a 9-hole course that is open to non-members with golf club memberships in the US, has lessons.

Soccer – Check the paper or with your hotel for where and when; usually on Wednesday nights and Sunday afternoons at *Estadio Jalisco* (Jalisco Stadium) on Calzada Independencia and at the *Estadio 3 de Marzo.*

Tennis – The *Camino Real, El Tapatío, Fiesta Americana,* and the *Holiday Inn* have tennis courts. Often the larger hotels also can make arrangements for you to use the facilities at some of Guadalajara's best private tennis and swim clubs. Check at your hotel.

Trap and Skeet – *Club Cinegético Jalisciense* (Nogales Hwy.) Sundays at 11 AM.

NIGHTCLUBS AND NIGHTLIFE: In keeping with its small-town outlook, Guadalajara is not much of a stay-up-late kind of place. Indeed, its government has a rather puritanical view in this respect, and visitors who have been to Guadalajara before may find that favorite wee-hours haunts are now closed. Today, the hotels are where the action is. The *Caballo Negro* at the *Fiesta Americana* (phone: 253434), *La Fiesta* at the *Holiday Inn* (phone: 315566), *La Diligencia* nightclub at the *Camino Real* (phone: 478000), and *El Factory* at the *Aranzazu* (phone: 133232) have live music for dancing. The popular discos are *Romance Memories* at *El Tapatío* (phone: 356050), *Video Disco Genesis* at the *Carlton* (phone: 147272), and *Tucán* at the *Américas* (phone: 314415). There's live tropical music and dancing at *Coco Coco Dance Hall* at the *Fénix* (phone: 145714).

BEST IN TOWN

CHECKING IN: Expect to pay $100 to $150 for a double room in the hotels we've listed as expensive, $50 to $80 at those listed as moderate, and $40 or less at the inexpensive ones. Most hotels listed below accept MasterCard and Visa; several also accept American Express and Diners Club. All telephone numbers are in the 36 area code unless otherwise indicated. When calling from one city to another within Mexico, dial 91 before the area code.

Camino Real – A sprawling modern place with lovely gardens, 5 heated pools, a putting green, a lighted tennis court, a bar, and restaurant. About 4 miles (6 km) from the center of town on 5005 Av. Vallarta (phone: 478000; 800-228-3000 in the US; FAX: 476781). Expensive.

Fiesta Americana – One of the most striking modern, luxurious hotels in Mexico, this has become a center of social and recreational goings-on for visitors to Guadalajara. Guests may enjoy its many bars and restaurants as well as a large pool and tennis courts. 225 Aurelio Aceves (phone: 253434; 800-FIESTA-1; FAX: 303725). Expensive.

Holiday Inn – Although the heavy traffic makes getting here a chore, the grounds (near the magnificent *Plaza del Sol Shopping Center*) are beautiful. Most of the rooms have balconies or terraces, and the facilities include a heated pool, 4 tennis courts, a putting green, and a bar with entertainment. About 4½ miles (7 km) south of the city on Rte. 25, corner of Mariano Otero and López Mateos (phone: 315566; 800-HOLIDAY in the US; FAX: 319393). Expensive.

Hyatt Regency – One of Guadalajara's newer properties, it has a grand atrium within a crystal pyramid and boasts, among other features, the only hotel skating rink in Mexico. Occasionally the ballroom is turned into a nightclub offering top Mexican and international entertainers. At López Mateos and Móctezuma (phone: 227778; 800-233-1234 in the US; FAX: 229877). Expensive.

Quinta Real – A hacienda-style hostelry, it has 45 suites and 8 double rooms, all with fireplaces and remote-control satellite TV sets. Four of the suites have Jacuzzis (at no extra charge). There is a restaurant with an excellent Sunday buffet, lobby bar, lovely gardens, an outdoor Jacuzzi, and a pool. Near the Minerva traffic circle at 2727 Av. México (phone: 520000; 800-445-4565 in the US). Expensive.

El Tapatío – A luxury property surrounded by tropical gardens and quaint cobblestone walkways, on a hillside overlooking Guadalajara. The rooms are large and comfortable, all with either a balcony or terrace. Heated pool, jogging track, 10 tennis courts (4 lighted), sauna, riding, and bar. A spa includes a pool, a variety of exotic treatments, computerized nutritional analysis, as well as facials and several types of massages. 4 miles (6½ km) south of the city on 4275 Blvd. Aeropuerto, the highway to Chapala (phone: 356050; 800-888-4498 in the US; FAX: 356664). Expensive.

Carlton – In the heart of the city is this large, luxurious property with a heated pool, several restaurants, and bars with entertainment. Five blocks from the center of town at Av. Dieciséis de Septiembre and Niños Héroes (phone: 147272; 800-871-5278 in the US; FAX: 135539). Moderate.

Fénix Best Western – A downtown hotel, it has a deluxe wing in addition to a pleasant bar with entertainment, an accomplished restaurant, a nightclub, dance hall, and good service. Two blocks from the center of town at 160 Corona (phone: 145714). Moderate.

De Mendoza – Centrally located, this hotel has a heated pool, a fine restaurant, a rooftop lounge, and live dance music. Opposite *Teatro Degollado* at 16 Venustiano Carranza (phone: 134646; FAX: 137310). Moderate.

Plaza del Sol – There is a heated pool, restaurant, bar with entertainment and dancing, and secretarial service. About 4½ miles (7 km) south on Rte. 15, across the street from the *Plaza del Sol Shopping Center* (phone: 478765). Moderate.

Américas – Two heated pools and a cocktail lounge are among the comforts offered by this motor hotel, which has 21 suites with kitchenettes and 85 double rooms. There is also a video club, disco, and restaurant on the premises. Near the *Plaza del Sol Shopping Center* on Rte. 15 at 2400 López Mateos Sur (phone: 314415). Inexpensive.

Aranzazu – Business travelers favor this downtown property, which has some quite nice rooms and such facilities as a coffee shop, bar, nightclub, and restaurant. Av. Revolución, corner of Degollado (phone: 133232; 800-882-8215 in the US; FAX: 145045). Inexpensive.

Francés – The oldest hostelry in Guadalajara, it was designated a national monument following its renovation in 1981. Benito Juárez (Mexico's Abraham Lincoln), stayed here when he was president. Nearby are the *Regional Museum* and the *Degollado Theater*. The rooms are pleasant, and there is a restaurant, *Maxim's* bar with live music and dancing, and a lobby bar with piano music. 35 Maestranza (phone: 131190; FAX: 682169). Inexpensive.

Posada Guadalajara – This colonial-style hostelry, a favorite with repeat visitors to the city, has rooms built around a patio. Pool and restaurant. 1280 López Mateos (phone: 212022). Inexpensive.

EATING OUT: A number of excellent restaurants have opened in Guadalajara in recent years. Time was when the good burghers hurried home for both lunch and dinner, but now more and more of them dine out. Expect to pay up to $50 for two at the expensive places, about $30 at the moderate ones, and $20 at those we call inexpensive. Prices do not include drinks, wine, or tips. Most restaurants listed below accept MasterCard and Visa; several also accept American Express and Diners Club. Unless otherwise noted, all restaurants open daily. All telephone numbers are in the 36 area code unless otherwise indicated. When calling from one city to another within Mexico, dial 91 before the area code.

Aquellos Tiempos – The decor is very posh. At lunchtime, fine Mexican food is served, including *gusanos de maguey* (crisply fried cactus worms) to *quesadillas de huitlacoche* (tortillas filled with a delectable corn fungus) — as well as several less esoteric dishes. The dinner menu is more formal (and more expensive), with French specialties such as sea bass stuffed with shrimp and served with a ginger-flavored mango sauce. Reservations advised. In the *Camino Real Hotel* (phone: 478000). Expensive.

Arthur's – The decor is British and clubby, but the steaks are American cuts and quite good. Reservations advised. 507 Av. Chapultepec Sur at Mexicaltzingo (phone: 260167). Expensive.

Café Oui – Casual and pleasant, this place serves a large selection of interesting salads and a variety of coffees. The Oui salad, which combines cold meats and cheeses, is served with a bacon dressing. Closed Sundays. Reservations advised. *Plaza Vallarta Shopping Center* at Francisco de Quevedo and Av. Vallarta (phone: 300188). Expensive.

La Fuente – A very popular place in a chic part of town, offering a wide selection of international dishes and live piano music. Closed Sundays. Reservations advised. 1899 Plan de San Luis, in the Chapultepec Country section (phone: 247946). Expensive.

Place de la Concorde – A place to celebrate. It's romantic, formal, and elegant, with excellent food (including lots of flambéed dishes) and service. Closed Sundays. Reservations necessary. In the *Fiesta Americana Hotel* (phone: 253434). Expensive.

Quinta Real – Mexican and international fare is prepared and served to perfection in an exquisite, formal setting. Reservations necessary. *Quinta Real,* near the Minerva traffic circle at 2727 Av. México (phone: 520000). Expensive.

Restaurant with No Name – The sign on the door says "Restaurant, Art Gallery, and Music," and this indoor-outdoor spot serves some of the finest food in the area. Specialties include filet of beef in nut sauce, and mushrooms stuffed with three cheeses. The paintings are for sale. In the afternoons, a trio plays classical music; in the evenings, music is provided by a troubadour. Reservations advised. 80 Madero in Tlaquepaque (phone: 354520). Expensive.

Suehiro – A true Japanese restaurant, with a manager and staff imported from the Orient. Dishes are prepared at your table. Reservations advised. 1701 Av. de la Paz (phone: 260094). Expensive.

La Vianda – Set in a lovely garden, this intimate dining place specializes in French creole cooking. Reservations advised. 120 Chapalita at López Mateos (phone: 225926). Expensive.

Brazz Expo – Steaks and seafood are the specialties. Friendly, attentive service in cheery surroundings. A versatile trio plays from 3 to 6 PM, and violins are heard from 9 PM to midnight. At the *Fairs and Expositions Convention Center,* Mariano Otero and Las Rosas (phone: 475050 or 475090). Moderate.

El Che – This place serves Argentine food, including *churrascos* (grilled steaks). Reservations advised. 1798 Hidalgo (phone: 520325). Moderate.

Pierrot – Very French, with a small but select menu. The pâté and the filet of beef in green pepper sauce are good choices. The apple tart for dessert is a must. Closed Sundays. Reservations advised. No credit cards accepted. 173 Cervantes Saavedra (phone: 154588). Moderate.

Recco – Dine on Italian fare in an Italian villa, with Señor Luigi making certain that the pasta is prepared to perfection. Reservations advised. 1981 Libertad (phone: 250724). Moderate.

Río Viejo – Mexican and continental cuisine is well prepared here, and there's live music Thursdays through Saturdays. Reservations advised. 302 Av. de las Américas (phone: 165321). Moderate.

Riscal – Especially good paella is served here every day, in addition to a wide variety of other Spanish dishes. Reservations advised. 1751 López Cotilla (phone: 168677). Moderate to inexpensive.

La Chata – Mexican specialties, especially from Jalisco, in a Mexican setting. Reservations unnecessary. At four locations: López Mateos and Mariano Otero (phone: 321379); 2277 Francisco Zarco (phone: 169553); 250 Federación and Libertad (phone: 179514); and at the zoo (no phone). Inexpensive.

La Copa de Leche – A local favorite for years, it boasts something for every appetite: a coffee shop, a sidewalk café, and an elegant dining room. Reservations advised for dining room only. 414 Av. Juárez (phone: 141845). Inexpensive.

El Delfín Sonriente – The name translates as "the grinning dolphin," an appropriate moniker for a place that features good seafood, frogs' legs, seafood grill, and a few Japanese specialties. Reservations unnecessary. 2239 Av. Niños Héroes (phone: 160216). Inexpensive.

Las Margaritas – Vegetarian specialties of all kinds are served here. No reservations. No credit cards accepted. 1477 Av. López Cotilla (phone: 168906). Inexpensive.

Los Otates – The excellent Mexican food served here has made this eatery a favorite for more than 40 years. Reservations unnecessary. 28 Av. de las Américas (phone: 520481) and at 2455-2 Av. México (phone: 302855). Inexpensive.

Rose Café – Set in the oldest hotel in Guadalajara, it's under the management of Dayton Herzog and Felix Carrillo, owners of *The Restaurant with No Name,* in Tlaquepaque. The decor is eclectic and the atmosphere informal. The menu includes anything from a salad or hamburger to a cactus leaf stuffed with ham and cheese and baked in a spicy sauce. Reservations unnecessary. In the *Frances Hotel,* 25 Maestranza (phone: 131190). Inexpensive.

Sanborn's – A branch of Mexico City's restaurant-cum-drugstore in Guadalajara; good for lunch. No reservations. 1600 Av. Vallarta (phone: 213675). Inexpensive.

La Trattoria – This small place serves well-prepared, traditional Italian dishes. Reservations advised. 3051 Niños Héroes (phone: 221817). Inexpensive.

GUANAJUATO

(pronounced Gwah-nah-*hwah*-toe)

Thought by many to be Mexico's most beautiful city, Guanajuato, with a population of just under 100,000, is certainly its most European. Built into the mountainous terrain of the Sierra Madre at the bottom of a narrow canyon, the town was established in 1559 along the banks of the Río Guanajuato. This meandering river created a ground plan of winding maze-like streets, and the result is a hilly confusion occasionally opening up into small plazas and fading again into narrow alleys or steep stairways. Together with the Spanish and Moorish architecture imported by the founding families, Guanajuato looks as if it might have been transported directly from the hills of Andalucía.

Shortly after the original land grant was made to Rodrigo Vazques, a soldier who had taken part in the Spanish conquest of Mexico, silver was discovered in the surrounding mountainside. Guanajuato became a boom town, and as more and more veins were discovered, it soon became the richest city in Mexico. It has been estimated that by the turn of the 18th century, this isolated little town was producing more than a third of the world's silver. The Spanish mine owners, who quickly amassed vast fortunes, set about building opulent mansions both in the town of Guanajuato and over the mountains in what is now San Miguel de Allende. They also took it upon themselves to provide Guanajuato with a number of elegant and very well-endowed churches, such as La Valenciana, which was built by the Count of Valenciana next to his mine on the outskirts of town.

In 1732, the Jesuits added another luxury to the thriving city in the form of a university intended for the wealthy sons of the mining families. The Jesuits themselves were evicted soon after, but the institution has survived under one authority or another ever since. The result has been an emphasis on culture and learning that adds a European sensibility to the flavor of this small but hardly provincial city. There is a tradition in Guanajuato known as *estudiantinas* that clearly reflects this influence. Young male university students, dressed in colorful 16th-century costumes and carrying mandolins and guitars, play the part of roaming minstrels. They serenade señoritas throughout town and win as their reward some token of appreciation — a ribbon or flower — which is then proudly displayed on their jackets. This tradition is still practiced today, and the young students, dressed in britches and ruffled sleeves, wandering past colonial buildings, through narrow streets, and across tiny courtyards, make an enchanting picture. Guanajuato's large student population, some 50,000 strong, makes it a youthful, stylish place.

While many of the buildings are large and impressive structures, Guanajuato's streets are often little more than lanes or alleyways, narrow and cramped, and so steep that many must have stairs built into the sidewalks. These streets, lined with flowerpot-trimmed houses, bear quaint names such as the Tumbler, the Deer, the Little Birds, the Four Winds, Little Wells, the Five Gentlemen, the Backbone, the Monkey Jump, the Nosegay, the Blowpipe, and, most famous of all, the Kiss. This last is so named because one can supposedly lean from a balcony on one side of the street to someone on the balcony across the way and exchange a kiss.

Of all the buildings in Guanajuato, the largest and most forbidding is the Alhóndiga de Granaditas, which played an important role in the city's most exciting historical episode. It was here that the wealthy mine- and land-owning patriarchs fled during the 1810 invasion of the city by Miguel Hidalgo and his ragtag army of angry farmers and miners. The building had recently been completed as a warehouse for grain, but within minutes of the attack, it was transformed into a fortress that the city fathers considered secure from attack. With balls of fire flying from the parapets onto the attacking army below, the battle seemed decided in favor of the Spanish mine owners until a brave young miner, Juan Martínez, known by the nickname El Pípila, immortalized himself forever. The building was made entirely of stone, except for one large wooden door that had seemed impenetrable. In the face of gunfire and hurling flames, with a flagstone on his back to shield him, Martínez made his way to the great door and set it on fire. The building was opened and the revolutionaries poured in, killing their enemies and taking the city. They did not hold it for long, however, and soon after, Hidalgo, Allende, Aldama, and Jiménez — the four leaders of the revolt — were captured and executed in Chihuahua. Their heads were sent back to Guanajuato, where they were impaled on hooks at the corners of the granary, and so remained for the next 10 years. Happily, the heads are gone, but the hooks remain as grim reminders of the passions of the time.

Another reminder of earlier days is also one of Guanajuato's unique features, the subterranean highway system. Running the 2-mile length of the town, this channel was originally built as a drain to prevent flooding from the river. With the coming of the automobile, it was discovered that Guanajuato had such narrow streets that two cars traveling in opposite directions usually could not pass each other. The solution was a one-way system aboveground and a conversion of the subterranean waterway into a two-way rapidly moving thoroughfare from one end of town to the other. Lighted at night and surrounded by the foundations of ancient buildings, this sunken road provides an eerie ride unlike any other.

This adaptation of the waterway is one of the few concessions Guanajuato has made to modern living. Gas stations, bus stations, and such modern addenda are restricted to the edge of town and don't intrude on the pure Spanish architecture in the town's center. This purity will continue to be preserved, as the entire town has been declared a national monument, requiring that any restoration work or new building conform strictly to the old style.

GUANAJUATO AT-A-GLANCE

SEEING THE CITY: The scenic drive following the hills along the south side of Guanajuato offers several beautiful vantage points from which to see the town and surrounding area; the red, coral, gold, green, and blue façades of buildings made from the lovely *cantera* stone from the surrounding hills make Guanajuato look like a Cubist painting in pastel hues. The statue honoring El Pípila, Guanajuato's independence war hero, is the most outstanding stop along this route and offers magnificent views. Both Paseo de la Presa and the Irapuato Road lead to the drive. The statue can also be reached on foot from town by climbing a long set of steps, but we recommend this path only for those of hardy disposition and strong legs.

Lighthouse (El Faro) is another fine spot from which to see the city, and since it's more than 400 miles from the ocean, it is used for little else. The Presa-Estación bus will take you most of the way, leaving you with only a short walk uphill behind the dam to this lovely view. The road that leads to the Valenciana mine also offers some spectacular views.

 **SPECIAL PLACES:** Guanajuato is extremely hilly, and while the city is small enough to get around on foot, it is often easier and more relaxing to ride. There are also a few places of interest beyond the city limits. In all cases, public transportation is adequate.

Alhóndiga de Granaditas – Built by the Spanish as a grain warehouse and central to the revolutionary history of Guanajuato, this massive stone building has been converted into a regional museum of the Institute of Anthropology and History. Of particular interest are the murals by Chavez Morado in the stairwells and a chamber dedicated to the Heroes of Independence and lit by an eternal flame. There are exhibitions of local costumes and arts and crafts, photography exhibitions, and some especially lovely decor, including the lanterns on the walls of the large balconied patio. Closed Mondays. Admission charge. 28 de Septiembre (phone: 21112).

La Parroquia – This church with the coral and gold façade, also known as the Basilica of Our Lady of Guanajuato, dates from 1671. Here is housed the famous wooden image of the Virgin Mary, *La Virgen de Santa Fe de Guanajuato,* which was sent from Granada in 1557 as a gift from Felipe II of Spain. It is considered the oldest piece of Christian art in all Mexico. Three annual celebrations commemorate the virgin — her arrival, her status as patron saint, and the founding of the city itself. Seventeen chandeliers light the space inside. Plaza de la Paz.

San Diego – Noted for its beautiful and highly ornate doorway, this church is an outstanding example of churrigueresque art. First built in 1663, it was almost destroyed by flood waters in the late 18th century; though it was rebuilt, it is now on the worn side. Jardín de la Unión.

La Compañía – Many a camera has been trained at this lovely 17th-century church, with its pink stone baroque façade and cupola reminiscent of St. Peter's in Rome. Near the university, Lascurrain de Retana.

Jardín de la Unión (Garden of the Union) – Although Guanajuato does not really have one main square, or zocalo, as in other Mexican towns, this central plaza, known affectionately as El Pedazo de Queso because it's shaped like a wedge of cheese, is the most active one. Among its features are an old-fashioned bandstand, tiled pavements, sheltering *trueno* trees that form a canopy over the sidewalk, and ornate wrought-iron benches. On Tuesdays and Thursdays at 7 and 9 PM and Sundays at noon and 1:30 PM, concerts are performed here.

Teatro Juárez (Juárez Theater) – Standing as a testimony to the greatest of Guanajuato's mining booms, 1873–1903, this elaborate and ornate building is one of the town's special sights; the exterior is Doric, the foyer is French, and the interior is richly Moorish. Eight carved muses crown the edifice, gilt carvings and velvet fabrics adorn the interior, and graceful Art Nouveau railings line the various tiers and balconies throughout. All of it is a style introduced to Mexico in 1750 by brothers named Churriguera; the style became known as Mexican churrigueresque, and some of the best examples are found in Guanajuato, including the *Teatro Juárez.* The first performance here was of *Aïda,* on October 27, 1903. Still used for special events and open to the public, this theater welcomes all the great opera, theater, and dance companies of Europe. Closed Mondays. Admission charge. Jardín de la Unión (phone: 20183).

Diego Rivera Museum – This lovely building was the birthplace of Diego Rivera, one of Mexico's greatest muralists, and the place where he spent the first six years of his life. Furniture from the period, including the brass bed in which Rivera was born in 1886, fills the ground floor; on the second floor are 97 of the artist's works, including a large sketch for his mural in New York City's Rockefeller Center; and the third floor houses a gallery for changing exhibitions. Closed Mondays. Admission charge. 47 Calle Pocitos (phone: 21197).

Teatro Principal (Principal Theater) – Most of the cultural activity in Guanajuato takes place here; exhibitions of contemporary art and international films are always on the agenda. Calle Cantarranas, next to the university (no phone).

Mercado Hidalgo – This huge, vaulted, 2-story iron and glass building is the market, which is open daily and sells crafts, clothing, and just about everything you can imagine. Av. Juárez.

University of Guanajuato – One of the most important universities in Mexico is this descendant of the Jesuit school opened in 1732. Although it has changed hands several times, first with the expulsion of the Jesuits in 1767, later with the expropriation of church lands in 1857, and still later with Juárez's edict temporarily closing the school, the city of Guanajuato has had a functioning institute of higher learning almost continuously for about 250 years. It became a state university in 1945 and 10 years later opened its new building, a modern labyrinth of connecting patios and open hallways. The main wing of the structure is especially beautiful, with its glass roof and grand staircase. Courses are offered in both Spanish and English, and in the summer special programs are designed for American students in conjunction with several US colleges and universities. For the citizens of Guanajuato as well as for visitors, the university is a cultural focal point, offering symphony recitals, theater performances, a radio station, choir, library, and movie club. It also is the center of the famous *Entremeses* (students' comic plays). 5 Lascurrain de Retana.

Plazuela del Quixote (Quixote Plaza) – Tucked along the tour and bus routes, it sports the winsome statue of Don Quixote and Sancho Panza *a caballo* (on horseback). Beside the statue is the small, 450-seat *Cervantes Theater*.

Museo Iconográfico Cervantino – Works of art, including popular art (much of which could be considered kitsch), all inspired by Cervantes' *Don Quixote de la Mancha*. The entire collection was donated by Eulalio Ferrer, a Spanish expatriate who fought against Franco during the Spanish Civil War and now heads one of Mexico's most important advertising agencies. The museum was inaugurated by Felipe González, President of Spain, during the 1987 *Cervantino Festival*. Closed Mondays. No admission charge. San Francisco and Miguel Doblado (phone: 26721).

Valenciana – This suburb of Guanajuato is well worth a short bus trip or taxi ride because of its beautiful church and incredibly rich working silver mine. The church, La Iglesia de San Cayetano, known as La Valenciana, was built by Don Antonio de Obregón y Alcocer, the first Count of Valenciana and owner of the mine. Plans for the church were so grandiose that jealousies were aroused in Guanajuato. A compromise plan specified that only one of the towers would be completed so that the church would not be perfect. It is rumored that the church's patron had silver dust mixed into the cement that binds the stones of the foundation. True or not, he certainly spared no expense in decorating the church's interior. The ornate altars, heavily trimmed in gold leaf, are fine examples of Mexican chromatic art, and the pulpit came from China. In daily use since its completion in 1788, this church also hosts the annual celebrations honoring *La Purísima* (the Immaculate Conception) on December 8. Three miles (5 km) northwest on the Dolores Hidalgo Hwy., Rte. 110.

Valenciana Mine – One of the 17 silver mines still operating in Guanajuato, it is the largest and richest in Mexico. Until the early 19th century it was estimated that one third of the world's silver came from this one source, and today one can still see the miners at work bringing its incredible wealth out of the earth. Across from La Valenciana, 3 miles (5 km) northwest on the Dolores Hidalgo Hwy., Rte. 110, with spectacular views along the way.

Cerro del Cubilete – This 9,442-foot mountain peak is crowned with a monument of Christ the King (Cristo Rey) that is visible to travelers long before they reach Guanajuato. The statue is 82 feet high and marks what is said to be the geographical center of Mexico. The view of the *bajío* from here is magnificent, with agriculturally rich lands dotted by lakes and smaller mountain peaks visible in all directions. Ten miles (16 km) west of the city on Rte. 110.

Presa de la Olla (Olla Dam) and Parque de las Acacias (Acacia Park) – The dam, built in 1742 by the Marquis de Rayas, not only set up a reservoir to hold the city's water supply but also created a lake and surrounding park area for recreation. Boat rides are available, though the dirty water makes this rather unappealing, and food can be purchased in the restaurant or eaten at the picnic areas provided. There are also beautiful flower gardens and a large statue of Hidalgo, local revolutionary hero, right in the center. At the end of La Presa bus line, Calle de la Presa; pick up the bus underground by the stairway at Jardín de la Unión or in front of the *Mercado Hidalgo*.

Ex-Hacienda de San Gabriel de Barrera – This beautiful old Mexican hacienda, recently restored by the Mexican government, is furnished in colonial-period antiques and graced by several manicured gardens. Open daily. Admission charge. About 1½ miles (2 km) on the road to Marfil (phone: 20619).

Marfil – An abandoned mining area that reached its peak in the 17th and 18th centuries and was reduced to a ghost town when it was destroyed by a flood in 1905, it has recently undergone a revival. On the skeletal structures of the derelict haciendas, new homes were being built as we went to press, and a community, including several retired Americans, is springing up in this beautiful location. The Los Santos Dam here has peculiar stone statues of saints across its top. Two miles (3 km) south of Guanajuato on Rte. 110; local buses and taxis make the trip here very inexpensively.

■**EXTRA SPECIAL:** For some reason, possibly the dryness of the air, bodies left in the crypt of the Panteón (Pantheon) municipal cemetery in Guanajuato do not decompose; they mummify. They are on display in the *Mummy Museum* at the entrance to the cemetery, in glass cases lining the walls; one can almost reach out and touch the hollow-socketed bodies — with skin, tongues, hair, and beards intact — of about 50 men, women, and children. The vaults in which the dead are buried are rented out by the year, and by law every corpse must be left interred for 5 years, whether or not the payment has been met. If, however, at the end of that time a permanent resting place has not been purchased, the body is removed to a common grave (until recently, it was taken to an underground crypt inside the cemetery). It is a fascinating array, perhaps one to be avoided by anyone prone to nightmares. Take the Presa Panteon bus. Museum open daily. Admission charge.

SOURCES AND RESOURCES

TOURIST INFORMATION: The tourist office is helpful, but the map it supplies is as confusing as the winding, unmarked streets it tries to depict. Fortunately, the map is always accompanied by a detailed explanation of how to get where you want to go. Open weekdays from 8:30 AM to 7:30

PM and on weekends from 10 AM to 2 PM. At the corner of Av. Juárez and Cinco de Mayo (phone: 21574 or 20086).

Hotels are also a source of information, and usually can provide visitors with maps and suggestions. Next door to *Casa Valadez*, at Jardín de la Unión, a small shop sells a handy booklet, *Guide and Legends to Know Guanajuato*, that includes three walking tours; the broken English is actually charming.

TELEPHONE: The area code for Guanajuato is 473. When calling from one city to another within Mexico, dial 91 before the area code.

CLIMATE AND CLOTHES: There is a rainy season in late summer and early fall, but generally the temperature does not vary much from an average in the mid-60s. At 6,835 feet, this sheltered canyon setting gets neither too hot nor too cold, and clothing is consistently casual.

GETTING AROUND: Bus – In Guanajuato there are four bus lines of interest to tourists. One, named Presa Estación, follows the one-way system from one end of town to the other. It is a good way to get to know the lay of the land and get from one place to another. Another, Centro-Valenciana, goes from the *Alhóndiga de Granaditos* (a museum) up the hills, past the hotels bordering Dolores Hidalgo Highway, to the Valenciana mine. The third, Presa Panteon, is the one that takes you to the mummies, and the last, Cinco de Mayo Cata, follows the Scenic Highway to the Rayas mine (in which a Greek theater has been built), to the town of Mellado for a look at the Cata church, a striking example of Mexican baroque architecture dating from 1788.

Taxi – The aqua and white taxis are available for trips to specific destinations; they can also be rented by the hour for more general cruising and are always waiting at the bus station.

Car Rental – There are no car rental firms in Guanajuato. The alternatives are the *Quick* agency at the *Calzada* hotel (107 Calz. de los Héroes; phone: 471-64500) and *Hertz* (108 Calz. de los Héroes; phone: 471-66020), both in León (about an hour away).

Tours – Tours are a very practical, rewarding way to get to most of the places of interest. *Viajes Georama* (36 Av. Juárez; phone: 25102), a private company, operates several good and reasonably priced sightseeing excursions in and around Guanajuato. *Transportes Turísticos de Guanajuato* (2 Bajos de la Basílica; phone: 22134 or 22838) is a reliable place to hire a car and English-speaking guide.

SPECIAL EVENTS: Guanajuato celebrates several religious holidays as well as fiestas unique to the town. The religious festivals, which include regional dances, fireworks, and occasional parades, are May 21–31 for the *Virgin of Guanajuato;* June 15–24 for various saints, ending with *St. John's Day* and featuring a fair at Olla Dam (Presa de la Olla); July 31 for *St. Ignatius;* November 2 for the *Day of the Dead*, which begins on the last day of the week-long *Alfeñique Fair,* a festival of candy creations held in the Plaza de la Paz; December 8 for the *Virgin of the Immaculate Conception;* and, of course, December 12, the day of the *Virgin of Guadalupe.*

The secular events unique to Guanajuato are theatrical presentations. The *International Cervantes Festival,* which honors the author of *Don Quixote,* is a 2-week event in October, featuring some of the best performing artists from around the world. The town fills up for this famous festival, and you would do well to make hotel reservations several months in advance. The stages, some indoor and some out, include the *Teatro*

Juárez, Teatro Principal, Templo de la Compañía, Explanada de la Alhóndiga de Granaditas. Another unique theatrical event, performed outdoors at the Plazuela San Roque, is the *Entremeses,* or *Intermissions,* short comic pieces originally written to be performed between plays. Today they have come to make up entire evenings of splendid entertainment that are performed by university students in candlelit courtyards in period costumes. The mailing address for the *Cervantes Festival* is 304 Emerson, Piso 9, Col. Polanco, México, DF 11570.

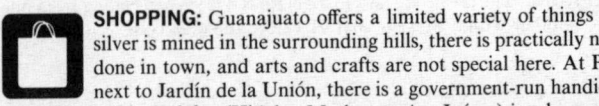 **SHOPPING:** Guanajuato offers a limited variety of things to buy. Though silver is mined in the surrounding hills, there is practically no silversmithing done in town, and arts and crafts are not special here. At Plaza del Agora, next to Jardín de la Unión, there is a government-run handicrafts shop. The central *Mercado Hidalgo* (Hidalgo Market on Av. Juárez) is a huge vaulted iron and glass building with elaborate grillwork. The ground floor is mostly Indian stalls selling fruits and vegetables. But upstairs are several stalls that offer shoppers a range of pottery, baskets, copper from nearby Santa Clara, and some clothing. The exquisite, and pricey, majolica pottery designed by Guanajuato's most famous contemporary craftsman, Gorky González, can be found in fine boutiques throughout Mexico, and is available at considerable savings from his studio on Calle Huerta de Montenegro (phone: 24326). Most shops in Guanajuato are closed between 2 and 5 PM.

Antiguedades Terra Cotta – Art and select antiques. 9 Jardín Unión (phone: 21998).

Artesanía San Francisco – Carefully chosen handicrafts from all over Mexico; mainly talavera-style ceramics and blown glass. 28 Sopeña (phone: 22268).

Capelo – Pottery from its workshop at 8 Cerro de la Cruz is offered for sale here at 57 Carcamanes (no phone).

Casa Blanca – Beautiful reproductions of antique jewelry. Calle Luis González Obregón (no phone).

Cerámica Telpatl – Handmade rustic pottery fired at high temperatures. *Plaza Mayor Shopping Center,* Plaza de la Paz (no phone).

El Cubilete – This sweets shop sells an interesting array of candies, including some shaped like mummies. 184 Av. Juárez (phone: 25934).

La Valencia – Prices are reasonable and the service is friendly at this shop chock-full of local crafts. Next to La Valencia church at 4 Mineral Valencia (phone: 22734).

 SPORTS: Sports are not a large part of Guanajuato's tourist attractions. The following activities, however, are available:

Swimming – There are pools at several of the major hotels, including *Real de Minas* (17 Najayote); *Castillo de Santa Cecilia* (1½ miles/2 km northeast of town on Rte. 110); and *Paseo de la Presa Best Western* (Carr. Panorámica).

Tennis – Courts are at the *Real de Minas, Paseo de la Presa Best Western,* and *San Gabriel de la Barrera* (see *Checking In* below).

 NIGHTCLUBS AND NIGHTLIFE: Guanajuato does not have a particularly vibrant nightlife. There are cocktail lounges in some of the larger hotels: *Castillo de Santa Cecilia* (Rte. 110); *Parador San Javier* (Rte. 110); *Real de Minas* (Rte. 110); *San Diego* (1 Jardín de la Unión); and *Hostería del Frayle* (3 Sopeña). On weekend evenings, local singing groups, *estudiantinas,* entertain at the bar in the *Real de Minas,* and there is live music at the *Paseo de la Presa Best Western* on Thursdays, Fridays, and Saturdays. The *estudiantinas* also perform occasionally at the *Posada Santa Fe.* The disco scene, too, is pretty well confined to weekends, with most of the action at *La Galería* in the *Parador San Javier* hotel, across from the *Castillo de Santa Cecilia; El Pequeño Juan* (on the Panoramic Hwy.); *La Calle* (on

Marfil el Alto) in the suburb of Marfil; and *Sanchos,* in a neighborhood known as Mineral de Cata.

BEST IN TOWN

CHECKING IN: While most of the hotels in Guanajuato are relatively new (post–World War II), the decor tends to be Spanish colonial. The larger, newer hotels are not downtown, so if being conveniently located is important, reserve early. The bus station provides a list of hotels, addresses, and price categories. Expect to pay about $50 for a double room in a hotel we classify as expensive; $25 to $35 in the moderate range; and less than $25 in the inexpensive ones. Most hotels listed below accept MasterCard and Visa; a few also accept American Express and Diners Club. All telephone numbers are in the 473 area code unless otherwise indicated. When calling from one city to another within Mexico, dial 91 before the area code.

Castillo de Santa Cecilia – A veritable walled, turreted medieval castle, it has a heated swimming pool, restaurants, and a nightclub with performances by the *Estudiantina de Guanajuato* on Fridays and Saturdays. Some of the 88 rooms have an excellent view of the city. Once inside its massive gate, you might be in a remote Alpine region. 1½ miles (2 km) northeast of town on Rte. 110 (phone: 20485; FAX: 20153). Expensive.

Museo Posada Santa Fe – This elegant, colonial-style, well-kept hotel has a popular outdoor café, a large collection of paintings by Manuel Leal (Guanajuato's first official chronicler) a piano bar, and occasional *estudiantina* performances on weekends. They offer a 15% discount for US senior citizens with identification. Jardín de la Unión (phone: 20084; FAX: 24653). Expensive.

Parador de San Javier – Set in the lovely grounds of a hacienda founded in 1670, this hotel has 117 units with baths (16 with fireplaces), a heated pool, cocktail lounge with live entertainment, a disco, a bullring, and rodeos. The original hacienda now serves as a lobby and reception area. 1½ miles (2 km) northeast of town on Rte. 110, at 92 Aldama (phone: 20626). Expensive.

Paseo de la Presa Best Western – A modern hostelry with a striking sea-green motif, its 60 rooms have commanding views; most have balconies. Facilities include a pool, tennis court, disco, and restaurant. Rate includes breakfast. Out of town a bit on the Panoramic Hwy. (phone: 23761; in the US, 800-528-1234; FAX: 23224). Expensive.

Real de Minas – This large (but quiet) hacienda-style property has a heated pool, tennis court, gameroom, cocktail lounge with nightly entertainment, and TV sets that get some US channels. Some of the 147 rooms have private balconies, others have fireplaces. Service is good. 17 Nejayote, at the entrance to town on Rte. 110 (phone: 21460 or 21508). Expensive.

San Gabriel de Barrera – On the grounds of a former hacienda with red flowerpots and tiles, is this comfortable, modern hotel, which has 139 intimate rooms, a pool, and tennis court. About a mile (1.6 km) from town on the Marfil Hwy., Ex-Hacienda San Gabriel de Barrera (phone: 23980; FAX: 27460). Expensive.

La Abadía – A small downtown inn, it has 43 spacious rooms, coffee shop, bar, and swimming pool. Four floors, but no elevator. Rate includes breakfast. 50 San Matías (phone: 22464; FAX: 22464). Moderate.

El Carruaje – Pleasant and comfortable, this place just outside town has a panoramic view, beautiful gardens, a swimming pool, and *El Asomadero* bar, where you sit in saddles as you sip your drinks. At Km 1 on the road to Dolores Hidalgo (phone: 22140). Moderate.

Embajadoras – Tucked away on a drive off a small park, this near-hideaway motel has a garden filled with trees, flowers, fountains, and parrots; it also has 27 rooms and a restaurant with atmosphere. Parque Embajadoras, en route to Olla Dam (phone: 20081). Moderate.

Del Frayle – Built in the 17th century as a coin factory, it has been converted to include 37 units, all with showers; there is also a dining room and a bar with a fireplace. Garage parking is 1 block away. Almost directly across from the *Juárez Theater*. 3 Sopeña (phone: 21179). Moderate.

Guanajuato – Offering a beautiful view of the town and the surrounding country-side, this motel has 50 units with showers, a pool, a restaurant, and bar. About 2 miles (3 km) northeast of town on Rte. 110 (phone: 20689). Moderate.

Hacienda de Cobos – In a former colonial silver and gold mill near the bus station, it has simple, comfortable rooms, a charming dining room under a white dome, a colorful lobby, its own little park, and ample privacy and tranquillity in the midst of the city. 3 Padre Hidalgo (phone: 20350). Moderate.

El Insurgente – Near the tourist office, it has all the facilities of a luxury hotel as well as parking. 226 Av. Juárez (phone: 22294). Moderate.

San Diego – It's the most central establishment in town, by the Jardín de la Unión. Originally a 17th-century convent, it now includes 55 rooms, a very popular bar with live music, and a restaurant, but the former inhabitants seem to lurk in the charming passageways. Garage parking is a block away. 1 Jardín de la Unión (phone: 21499). Moderate.

Socavon – A 10-minute walk from the heart of town, this colonial-style place decorated in earth tones has 37 large rooms, with equally large bathrooms, set around a courtyard; there's also a cheery restaurant-bar. 41A Alhóndiga (phone: 24885). Inexpensive.

Villa de la Plata – With 8 rooms and 28 condo-suites and villas (some available for rent), this spot also features a playground, indoor heated pool, tennis court, bar, coffee shop, restaurant, gameroom, and steam bath. At Km 3 on the road to Dolores Hidalgo (phone: 25200). Inexpensive.

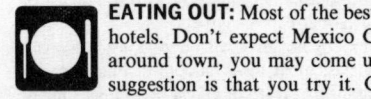 **EATING OUT:** Most of the best restaurants in Guanajuato are found in the hotels. Don't expect Mexico City–quality food, however. As you wander around town, you may come upon a clean café not mentioned below. Our suggestion is that you try it. Chances are you will get as good a meal as anywhere else, and you just might be lucky enough to hit a small jewel. There is not a wide price spectrum for dinner, and nothing that would be considered expensive compared to the major Mexican tourist towns, resorts, or large cities. Dinner for two at a restaurant we classify as moderate will run about $30; and inexpensive, under $10. Prices do not include drinks, wine, tips, or tax. All restaurants listed below accept MasterCard and Visa; a few also accept American Express. Unless otherwise noted, all restaurants listed below are open daily. All telephone numbers are in the 473 area code unless otherwise indicated. When calling from one city to another within Mexico, dial 91 before the area code.

La Antorcha – It offers a lovely view of the city and a good international menu. Specialties include mushrooms in garlic butter and *chicharrónes de pollo* (super-crisp chicken pieces). Reservations advised. Near the statue of El Pípila on Rte. 110 (phone: 22308). Moderate.

Guanajuato Grill – The owners of *La Antorcha* and *Casa Valadez* seem to be cornering the town's restaurant market. Here the setting is relaxed; the menu, international. The specialty of the house is *crepas de huitlacoche* (crêpes filled with a delightfully tasty corn fungus). Closed Mondays. Reservations advised. Downtown, at 4 Alonso (phone: 20287). Moderate.

El Patio – This started out as a tiny place with six tables that were constantly full because the food was so good. It now seats up to 120, and the food is still good — especially breakfast, where a tasty bowl of oatmeal awaits anyone tired of *huevos rancheros.* Reservations unnecessary. In the *El Insurgente,* 226 Av. Juárez (phone: 22294). Moderate.

Posada Sante Fe – An outdoor café in the hotel of the same name, right on the Jardín de la Unión. The cappuccino is great, but the cooking — Mexican and international — is uninspired. People come here mainly for the people watching. Reservations unnecessary. Jardín de la Unión (phone: 20084). Moderate.

Restaurant-Bar 4 Ranas – Good Mexican and international dishes, and a nice selection of domestic wines. Reservations unnecessary. 1 Jardín de la Unión (phone: 24257). Moderate.

La Tasca de los Santos – Better for drinking than dining, it is essentially a *taberna* with Spanish dishes. Reservations unnecessary. 28 Plaza de la Paz (phone: 22320). Moderate.

Venta Vieja – Quiet and romantic, it has only ll tables, laden with fresh flowers and set against large, curving windows. The fare is traditional Mexican. Closed Sundays. Reservations unnecessary. 1 Plaza San Javier (phone: 20626). Moderate.

Casa Valadez – Right across from the *Juárez Theater,* this simple eatery serves sandwiches and Mexican dishes. Grab a window seat. Reservations unnecessary. 3 Jardín de la Unión (phone: 21157). Inexpensive.

Las Embajadoras – A fine restaurant in the hotel of the same name. Don't pass up the dessert cart, with its flans, puddings, and pies. Reservations unnecessary. Corner of Paseo Mandero and Embajadoras (phone: 20081). Inexpensive.

La Manzana – Simplicity is the key here: Hamburgers and malts, plus tacos and beer. Look for the apple logo. Reservations unnecessary. 27 San Fernando (phone: 24353). Inexpensive.

Las Palomas – Foreigners gravitate here for Mexican dishes; the *liquados* (fruit drinks) are excellent. Reservations unnecessary. Behind the Basílica, at 19 Ayuntamiento (phone: 24936). Inexpensive.

El Retiro – A simple, popular café with a good *comida corrida* (lunchtime special); king-size tacos; *molletes* (sliced rolls topped with beans and cheese); and delicious cookies, including *campechanas,* puff pastry baked in different shapes and glazed with honey. Reservations unnecessary. No credit cards accepted. Just down the street from *Juárez Theater* at 12 Sopeña (phone: 20622). Inexpensive.

LAS BAHÍAS DE HUATULCO

(pronounced Wah-*tool*-ko)

Buoyed by the success of Cancún, Ixtapa-Zihuatanejo, Los Cabos, and Loreto, FONATUR has ventured into its newest resort development, the Bays of Huatulco, a project price-tagged at $200 million and expected to surpass Cancún in size and total visitors by its scheduled completion date in 2018.

Set on the Pacific coast in the state of Oaxaca, about 300 miles (480 km) southeast of Acapulco and 65 miles (104 km) east of Puerto Escondido, the Bays of Huatulco encompass 18 miles of cove-jagged coastline on nine lovely bays. Visually, Huatulco is absolutely stunning: Beach after beach is framed by white sands and the jagged gray-black peaks of the Sierra Madre del Sur, perfectly setting off the cerulean blue waters.

Known until recently to only the most adventurous travelers, tiny Huatulco was once apparently a pretty exciting place — until its decline around the end of the 16th century. It was an important Zapotec, and then Mixtec, settlement before the Spanish conquerors arrived, and by 1575 — because of its strategic location — it had become the most important port on the Pacific. That was the year that Sir Francis Drake attacked Huatulco; and 8 years later the infamous English navigator-pirate Thomas Cavendish, with three galleons and 120 men, also attacked the town. Furious at finding little of value in the homes of the humble villagers, Cavendish ordered his men to remove a wooden cross that stood on a nearby beach. But the sacred cross — the Santa Cruz de Huatulco — remained mysteriously untouched by their axes and saws. When even fire failed to destroy it, Cavendish had his men tie ropes from the cross to one of his vessels and tried to haul it out of the ground. This, too, failed. Many years later, church leaders decided to remove the cross "for safekeeping," and it was taken to the city of Oaxaca. There it was divided up among several churches and the bishop's family. A small part was set in silver and sent to the Vatican.

During the 19th century, Mexican president Vicente Guerrero was betrayed by traitors in Huatulco, and the town lapsed into anonymity until it was rediscovered by FONATUR.

At its formal inaugural (November 1988), Phase One of Huatulco, which encompasses 1,300 hotel rooms on Tangolunda and Santa Cruz bays, was nearly complete: The *Binniguenda* was open for business, and *Club Med* was already taking in a European crowd. Now the *Binniguenda* and *Club Med* have been joined by the *Sheraton* and *Royal Maeva*.

The Salina Cruz–Pochutla section of the coastal highway has been paved; a 9,000-foot runway normally accepts one flight a day from Oaxaca (two during the busy winter season); a small city, La Crucecita, has been built for the resort's employees and their families; electricity and water are running and phones are working; the zocalo has been landscaped; and Acapulco silver vendors and T-shirt sellers have set up their displays at Santa Cruz beach.

The region is gearing up for more major development over the next 30 years: Plans call for 4,270 hotel rooms by 1994, 8,870 rooms by the year 2000, and about 27,000 by 2018. Besides hotels, the overall plan includes the construction of villas, condominiums, and homes, and the local population is expected to exceed 300,000. All this means that the resort is currently being blasted and scraped from the jungle at the base of the Sierra Madre, and the nine relatively undeveloped, lovely bays are on their way to becoming major tourist attractions; folks who are used to coming to Huatulco for pure tranquillity may be disappointed in years to come.

At this point, Huatulco has a way to go before it becomes the sort of active traveler's destination like Cancún. Nightlife remains largely confined to the hotels, although there are a few seafood shacks on the beach in Santa Cruz Bay, and a couple of discos in town. Shopping is sorely limited. But the calm waters of the bays offer excellent swimming and snorkeling, the fishing is excellent, and there's plenty of sunshine. Oaxaca, with its Zapotec ruins and its wonderful *moles,* is only a half-hour flight away. Much like complementing a stay in Cancún or Cozumel with a few days in Mérida, a vacation that combines paradisiacal Huatulco and colonial Oaxaca provides the best of both worlds.

HUATULCO AT-A-GLANCE

SEEING THE CITY: If you're flying into Huatulco from Oaxaca, try to sit on the left-hand side of the aircraft. From that vantage point you will see the nine bays of Huatulco: one beach after another, the white sands and sparkling waters in marked contrast to the ominous Sierra Madre looming in the distance.

SPECIAL PLACES: The Chapel of Santa Cruz – A tiny open-air shack, a place out of the sun, where Huatulcans gather to worship — and to gossip. At Av. Benito Juarez, Santa Cruz, right across from the zocalo.

Zocalo – A spiffy plaza, it encompasses an outdoor theater, a handicrafts market, a kiosk dispensing tourist information, and a cultural center. At Av. Benito Juarez, Santa Cruz.

Conejos Bay – Reputedly named for the large population of rabbits that used to romp here, Conejos is still a picturesque place where sea turtles lay their eggs in the sand, pelicans stand sentry on the rocks, butterflies flit among the trees, and porpoises frolic in the sea. The beach is wide, and perfect for swimming, sunbathing, and shelling. Although this lovely beach is still relatively untouched by developers, three hotels were under construction here, as we went to press, including one scheduled to be run by Marriott. No opening dates had been set. Enjoy it while it lasts. Access is by boat only.

Bufadora – The water spouts like a whale at this natural geyser. Between Entrega and Organo bays; access by boat only.

SOURCES AND RESOURCES

 TOURIST INFORMATION: Information on accommodations, dining, and other activities is available from the tourist office (phone: 10326) across the street from the *Sheraton,* and from the FONATUR office (on Blvd. Chahue next to the Social Security Clinic; phone: 70030, 70262, or 70247). The local publication *Huatulco Espacio 2000,* available at most hotels, provides a good map and listings for visitors.

 TELEPHONE: The area code for Huatulco is 958. When calling from one city to another within Mexico, dial 91 before the area code.

 CLIMATE AND CLOTHES: Las Bahías de Huatulco is blessed with the climate that led one travel writer to dub Mexico's Pacific coast the Mexican Riviera. It lacks the humidity of Acapulco, year-round temperatures average 82F, and from October through June it never rains. As for clothes, anything goes, as long as it's lightweight. Don't forget to pack plenty of sunblock — you'll need it even when you're not intentionally taking the sun — and a pair of sunglasses.

 GETTING AROUND:
   Bus – Service between Las Bahías de Huatulco and Puerto Escondido is frequent, and there's even direct service to Acapulco.
   Taxi – It's better to take a van than a taxi to the hotels. *Transporte Terrestre's* vans meet the flights arriving in Huatulco daily, and hotels can arrange transportation to the airport by van for departing guests (phone: 40308). One-way fare between the airport and the hotels is about $6 per person, while the trip by private taxi costs about $15 per person. *Club Med* has vans that shuttle between the airport and the resort.
   Car Rental – *Budget* and *Dollar* cars can be rented at the airport. *Budget* also has offices at the *Posada Binneguenda* (phone: 40077) and the *Royal Maeva* (phone: 10000/48/64).
   Tours – *Viajes García Rendón* (phone: 70025 or 70125) operates excursions to Puerto Escondido for about $40; to Chacahua National Park, a 50-square-mile nature retreat, for about $70; and to Cipolite, a nudist beach, for $35. *Servicios Turísticos del Sur,* which operates out of the *Sheraton* (phone: 10055), offers an interesting tour to Tehuantepec, a town famous for having the only matriarchal society in the country and where many women still wear native costumes and are bedecked in gold.

 SHOPPING: Shopping is fairly limited to *Club Med*'s boutiques, the souvenir stands lining the zocalo, and a few entrepreneurial kids hawking black coral (it's forbidden to bring any into the US) and turquoise necklaces and earrings at the beach at Santa Cruz. FONATUR has opened a handicrafts *mercado* (market) at the zocalo, and a few shops also are cropping up in La Crucecita and at *Plaza Esmeralda,* the shopping center across from the *Sheraton.*

 SPORTS: Boating – The *Sociedad Cooperativa Turistica de Tangolunda* rents boats at the beach of Santa Cruz for about $25 an hour. A trip on their glass-bottomed boat costs about $60. If asked, drivers will offer some local lore. Huatulco's master plan includes a 100-boat marina and a cruise ship pier.

Camping and Hiking – There's a trailer park at Chahue Bay, and tent camping wherever suits your fancy. 39,000 acres will be retained as a wildlife preserve.

Fishing – These waters are superb for deep-sea fishing. You can charter a boat from the cooperative, but it's advisable to bring your own gear. *Club Med* takes members on excursions to its own fishing spot, La Pêche au Gros.

Golf – The 9-hole *Tangolunda* golf course (near the *Sheraton;* phone: 10059) is open to the public.

Sailing – *Club Med* has sailboats for unlimited use by members. Lessons are included in the price of accommodations. For non-guests *Club Med* also arranges for excursions on the *Stars and Stripes,* the highly disputed winner of the 1988 *America's Cup;* a one-hour sail, available Mondays through Saturdays, costs $70 per person.

Scuba and Snorkeling – The *García Rendón* travel agency in Huatulco (phone: 40025 and 40125) rents snorkeling equipment for $15 a day, and charges about $30 an hour for dive trips to Entrega, Organo, or Maguey. Snorkeling enthusiasts should head for Tangolunda Bay, where the great reef (just below the surface) is made up partly of giant cauliflower-shaped coral, and the friendly tropical fish spatter the underwater world with color. Visibility is good down to 20 feet. Another good coral reef is at Entrega Beach. You can rent snorkeling equipment and buy snacks on the beach. *Club Med* provides gear for its members.

Swimming and Sunning – The beaches outside *Club Med,* the *Sheraton,* and *Royal Maeva* are good for swimming, since all have calm waters. Maguey Bay is the only beach in the bay area with fine sand; you'll recognize it by the maguey plants jutting up out of the stone surrounding the beach. Maguey has four restaurants, one named *El Tiberon* (The Shark), but don't let that scare you. If you yearn for privacy, adjacent Organo Bay is quiet, but beware the undercurrent. There's good shelling and big waves at Conejos Bay, which is the next bay slated for development.

Tennis – *Club Med* has 8 courts; the *Sheraton* has 4; the *Royal Maeva* has 2.

Windsurfing – One of the many water sports available to members at *Club Med.*

NIGHTCLUBS AND NIGHTLIFE: Generally, nights in Huatulco are quiet, unless you're staying at the *Royal Maeva* or *Club Med,* where the *gentils organisateurs* (GOs) enthusiastically demonstrate the salsa, and a string of yellow beads buys *muchos* margaritas. At the *Sheraton,* mariachis serenade nightly. Otherwise, nightlife is limited to the *Magic Circus,* a disco about 2 blocks from the *Binneguenda* or *Club Tequila* in La Crucecita. For a quieter evening, take a walk on the beach or count the seemingly endless number of stars in the sky.

BEST IN TOWN

CHECKING IN/EATING OUT: Expect to pay up to $250 for a double room at a hotel listed here as expensive, about $120 at a moderate place, and about $60 at a place listed as inexpensive. Note that while considered expensive, *Club Med*'s rates include most activities, and both *Club Med* and *Royal Maeva*'s rates include all meals. Opportunities for eating out in Huatulco are very limited, but the dining rooms at *Club Med* and the *Sheraton* are open to the public and offer a tasty diversion from your own hotel's fare (see more details below). Hotels and their restaurants listed below accept MasterCard, Visa, American Express, and Diners Club. Restaurant reservations are unnecessary. All telephone numbers are in the 958 area code unless otherwise indicated. When calling from one city to another within Mexico, dial 91 before the area code.

Club Med Huatulco – The largest *Club Med* village in the Western Hemisphere, it has 500 rooms, each with a private terrace and hammock, set in casita clusters on 50 acres on Tangolunda Bay. The no-frills rooms can be divided by pulling the closets together to form a wall; marble bathrooms have two separate sink areas. The club offers a full range of water sports on 4 isolated coves, and there are 3 swimming pools and 12 tennis courts (6 lighted). Unfortunately, the hotel's four small beaches are only fair. Excursions are available to Oaxaca, Palenque, and Puerto Escondido. Besides the main cafeteria-style restaurant, there's an excellent Moroccan restaurant, a seafood place, a *churrasquería,* a fancy Italian restaurant, and a disco. Non-guests are welcome to a lunch or dinner buffet, which includes wine, beer, and soft drinks; access to the pool and other facilities during the day; and a show or entrance to the disco at night; the price is $30 per person, except Friday evenings ($40 per person) when there is a more elaborate meal and show. *Club Med* operates nonstop charter flights from New York, Chicago, Houston, and Los Angeles. Rate includes rooms, meals, and activities. Domicilio Conocido (phone: 40069 or 800-CLUB MED; FAX: 10101). Expensive.

Royal Maeva – Among the features are air conditioning in each of the 300 rooms, 2 restaurants, a coffee shop, bars and lounges, a pool, 2 tennis courts, gardens, and a playground for children. Four rooms are available for the handicapped. Rate includes 3 meals a day. Apdo. Postal 227 (phone: 10000/48/64; 800-GO-MAEVA in the US; FAX: 10220). Expensive.

Huatulco Sheraton – Set on a wide, crescent-shaped beach at the end of the bay, this contemporary Mexican-style resort is furnished throughout with Oaxacan crafts; the beaded, pastel Zapotec rugs loom large in the lobby. All 346 rooms have bay views, terraces, air conditioning, mini-bars, color TV sets and radios, safe deposit boxes, telephones, and 24-hour room service; 9 rooms are equipped for the handicapped. There are also two restaurants, a coffee shop, 2 bars, shops, a health club, and 4 tennis courts. Non-guests are welcome to the buffet dinner for $25 per person. Paseo de Tangolunda (phone: 10055; 800-325-3535 in the US; FAX: 10113). Moderate.

Posada Binniguenda – A colonial-style hostelry, Huatulco's first, set about 530 yards from Santa Cruz Bay. All 75 rooms have color TV sets and air conditioning. There's a lobby bar and a restaurant (for guests only). There's no beach, but a pool and gardens. 5 Blvd. Benito Juárez, Apdo. Postal 175, Santa Cruz (phone: 70077; FAX: 70284). Inexpensive.

IXTAPA AND ZIHUATANEJO

(pronounced Ees-*tah*-pa and Zee-whah-ta-*neh*-hoe)

Mexico's immensely long Pacific coast is blessed with port towns, fishing villages, and resort cities for every taste. From Kino Bay just west of Hermosillo to Acapulco, they dot the coast like convenient commas in a long sentence, and no one spot provides a stopping place exactly like any of the others. Among the newest of these resort areas are the twin towns of Ixtapa and Zihuatanejo, 150 miles (240 km) northwest of Acapulco. Though Ixtapa is only 3 miles (5 km) from Zihuatanejo, what is most exciting is how little alike they are; side by side, they provide alternate moods of Pacific Mexico.

They are a prime example of the Mexican government's program of resort development (Cancún is another) beginning in the 1960s. Zihuatanejo is a beautiful town that at one time could be reached only by a wandering old road or by private plane, and where a dozen oysters and a cold beer is still the standard breakfast. In its early stages of development some said Ixtapa was sired by a computer and incubated under the watchful eyes of urbanologists, sociologists, financial wizards, and tourist industry experts.

And therein lies a tale.

Back in the 1960s, some of the Harvard-trained whiz kids from Mexico's central bank hit on the idea that tourism, if it were increased, could help solve some of Mexico's economic problems. At the time, these fellows were looking for projects to reduce imports and increase exports, for decentralizing industry and increasing farm output, but every time they turned around, their figures showed that tourism was more rewarding.

The hospitality business directly generates a tremendous number of jobs, from customs inspectors and baggage handlers to taxi drivers, bellboys, room clerks, chambermaids, bartenders, and waiters. A number of jobs are also indirectly generated. These include the artisans who make handicrafts bought by tourists, store clerks who sell the handicrafts, and truck drivers who transport them across the country. Tourism even provides work for musicians who strum guitars to help *gringo* couples add a note of vacation romance.

Mexico's traditional resorts were pretty nearly saturated, and while some foreign vacationers came back year after year, most travelers wanted to try a new place. In the early 1960s, they didn't have too much choice.

What was needed were new resorts. While the first inclination was to develop already existing facilities, the central bankers had a better idea. They would build new resorts where there was nothing, thus helping to settle Mexico's largely empty coastal areas. They had to find places where tourists would want to go, but building a successful new resort involves all the risks of trying to come out with a popular new automobile or a hit movie. The bankers busied themselves investigating the sun spots around the country and fed their data into a computer.

High on the list (along with Cancún on the Caribbean) was Ixtapa. Virtually no one in Mexico had ever heard of Ixtapa, but it could usually be located by its proximity to Zihuatanejo, which itself was far from a household word during the 1960s, but which did have its devotees. Its bay is lovely, its beaches delightful, fishing off the coast outstanding, and the sun *always* shines. Ixtapa, just across the bay, contained 24 miles of beachfront lining seven picturesque coves.

FONATUR, the agency established to transform the central bank's dreams into reality, undertook a $50 million development program. A spiffy two-lane highway was put through from Acapulco; Zihuatanejo was given a sewage system, electrical and communications systems, and a general sprucing up, but its essential nature as a fishing village was untouched. Ixtapa, on the other hand, is something out of the 21st century. Shopping centers, a Robert Trent Jones, Jr. 18-hole golf course, luxurious hotels, manicured lawns — a sleek and elegant resort in high Mexican style.

Zihuatanejo's hotels are on the bay. Many of them are small, ranging from 13 to 50 rooms, and operate more like inns or what Europeans call *pensiones.*

The sea brings people to Ixtapa-Zihuatanejo, and activity centers around the water. Hotel guests usually are content to enjoy the stretch of sand on their doorstep, but those who enjoy exploring will find more than a dozen beaches in the area. There are boat trips to be taken and popular excursions to Ixtapa Island, a favorite snorkeling and scuba spot. Both light tackle and deep-sea fishing are available.

On shore, golfers will want to try the Robert Trent Jones, Jr. course at the *Ixtapa Golf Club.* The club also has floodlit tennis courts, as do several hotels. There are shops in Ixtapa at the hotels and at the shopping centers.

Zihuatanejo is an enjoyable place to poke around. The village is charming, with many nice shops, bars, and restaurants. Stroll along the Paseo del Pescador by the waterfront and browse along Calles Alvarez and Pedro Ascencio, where you'll find some excellent handicrafts shops. Fishing is still an important industry here, and by ten in the morning fishermen have already returned with their catch. Lobster, snapper, turtle, oysters, and clams top the local menus. After dark there are a couple of discos in town, but most of the nightlife is centered around the big hotels, which make a point of keeping visitors active, with beach parties and special programs throughout the week.

Ixtapa-Zihuatanejo's burgeoning popularity was slowed a tad when side effects of Mexico's 1985 earthquake shook, and slightly damaged, several hotels. But repairs were quickly completed, and despite the recent cutback of direct flights by both domestic and international airlines, Ixtapa-Zihuatanejo continues to gain recognition as a unique resort.

The resort's pace might well pick up even more within the next few years, however, since work has begun on a huge marina complex located on a cove northwest of the hotel zone in Ixtapa. The new development, Marina Ixtapa, will include a 400-slip marina, an 18-hole golf course, a shopping center, villas, at least two large hotels, condominiums, and other establishments catering to tourists — all of which FONATUR predicts will provide a considerable boost to the tourism business here. At the project's completion in the next year or so, still another Pacific Mexico move may emerge.

IXTAPA–ZIHUATANEJO AT-A-GLANCE

SEEING THE CITY: The drive in from the airport pretty much skips Zihuatanejo (unless that's where you're headed), but from the hills you get a nice view of Ixtapa. The best way to see them both is from the ocean, say, aboard a boat leaving the bay for Ixtapa Island. You can also admire the sweep of Ixtapa from the glass-enclosed elevator at *Stouffer Presidente* or Zihuatanejo's loveliest beach, La Ropa, and its fishing boats from the bar at the *Catalina-Sotavento*. During the winter season, the 36-foot catamaran *Tequila* takes up to 12 passengers on a cruise around the bay, with a stop for snorkeling at Isla Ixtapa. It leaves from Playa Quieta at 11 AM and returns at 2 PM (phone: 30007). The *Rainbow* (phone: 31066) offers a similar cruise that departs from the *Holiday Inn* at 10 AM and 3 PM; they also offer a sunset cruise.

SPECIAL PLACES: The two communities are about 3 miles (5 km) apart. Both have a number of interesting spots to visit and the countryside around is worth going out and enjoying.

Ixtapa – On a little inlet beyond hotel row, a new community called Marina Ixtapa is going up that will include a residential area, condominium vacation homes, and shopping centers with about 400 shops, boutiques, galleries, and so on. Construction had just begun at press time.

Ixtapa Golf Club – One of the nicest developments of its kind in Mexico, this Robert Trent Jones, Jr.-designed course offers natural water hazards from the former marshlands on which it sits. Open to the public, and worth a visit even if you don't want to play on its 18-hole course. The pro shop has a wide variety of athletic equipment, and the bar is a popular gathering place at sundown.

Zihuatanejo – The village is charming, with many nice shops, bars, and restaurants. Stroll along the Paseo del Pescador by the waterfront and browse along Calles Alvarez and Pedro Ascencio, where you will find some excellent handicrafts shops. Fishing is an important industry here, and by ten in the morning fishermen have already returned with their catch. Lobster, snapper, turtle, oysters, and clams top the local menus.

La Ropa – La Ropa means "clothes," and this beach is said to be so named because many years ago clothes, apparently the cargo of a wrecked ship, washed up here. This is the main beach for the Zihuatanejo hotels and is on the bay. Boats of all kinds are available here for sailing, water skiing, or just roaming about, and there are several good seafood restaurants.

Playa Quieta – The name means "quiet beach," but with the *Club Med* next door it's actually pretty lively. Sailing and windsurfing are popular activities, and boats leave from here for Ixtapa Island.

Las Gatas – Also a beach on the bay, but best reached by boat from Zihuatanejo (a little over a dollar round-trip), it was the royal watering place of the Tarasco kings before the conquistadors arrived. The conquerors found the Tarasco name a tongue-twister and came up with Las Gatas, which means "the cats." A great place to go for lunch and a swim or snorkel. Be sure to check when the last boat leaves.

Barra de Potosí – A small fishing village surrounded by grapefruit, coconut, papaya, mango, and tamarind orchards, it lies about 12½ miles (20 km) south of Ixtapa and extends to about 4½ miles (7 km) at the end of Playa Blanca, where the Potosí lagoon joins the Pacific. There are several palapa restaurants that serve *pescado a la talla* (whole fish charbroiled on spits). About 9½ miles (15 km) farther south is the town of Petatlan, where there's a small archaeological museum that houses artifacts uncovered at the La Chole archaeological site.

■**EXTRA SPECIAL:** Ixtapa Island, also known as Isla Grande, is a favorite place for a boat journey, and good for a day's — or half-day's — visit. The island is a wildlife preserve inhabited by deer, badgers, armadillos, rabbits, raccoons, and many species of birds. Two of the four near-deserted beaches are swimmable, the one where the boats dock, and a more isolated one you reach by following the trail by *La Princesa* restaurant and always bearing right. Snorkeling and diving are excellent, and you can rent hammocks on the beach for less than a dollar. Ten open-air seafood shanties with bar service, including the *Marlin* and the red brick *Isla Ixtapa,* run by the Solis family, serve up the day's catch.

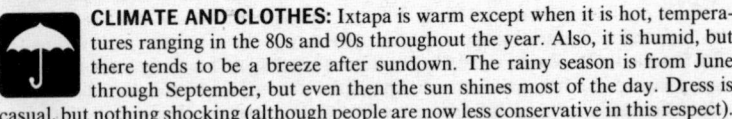

SOURCES AND RESOURCES

TOURIST INFORMATION: A helpful tourist office is located in the Municipal Palace in Zihuatanejo (phone: 42001 or 42355). The government tourist office is in Ixtapa, at *La Puerta Shopping Center* (phone: 31967). Hotel personnel are pretty well informed, too.

Local Coverage – *The News,* Mexico City's English-language newspaper, is available at most Ixtapa hotels and often features the area in its *Vistas* Sunday supplement. The newsstand at 23 Cuauhtémoc in Zihuatanejo carries a few American magazines, as well as *The News. Qué Hacer y a Donde Ir* (What to Do and Where to Go), a monthly, is available in English.

TELEPHONE: The area code for Ixtapa-Zihuatanejo is 753. When calling from one city to another within Mexico, dial 91 before the area code.

CLIMATE AND CLOTHES: Ixtapa is warm except when it is hot, temperatures ranging in the 80s and 90s throughout the year. Also, it is humid, but there tends to be a breeze after sundown. The rainy season is from June through September, but even then the sun shines most of the day. Dress is casual, but nothing shocking (although people are now less conservative in this respect).

GETTING AROUND: Bus – A bus runs from Ixtapa into Zihuatanejo about every half hour until 11 PM. Within Zihuatanejo, there is regular bus service from the hotel area downtown. Minibus service is available between Ixtapa and the airport (phone: 42785 and 42046); when two or more people are making the trip, however, it can be less expensive to take a taxi. When leaving, get to the airport early and reconfirm your return flight well in advance.

Taxis – Rates are standard, but you'd never know it from what some drivers ask; talk money in advance. The fare between Ixtapa and Zihuatanejo is about $3; to the airport, about $12; and from Zihuatanejo to La Ropa Beach, about $1.50.

Car Rental – *Avis* (phone: 42248), *Budget* (phone: 42189), *Dollar* (phone: 32025 at the *Dorado Pacífico;* 30333 at the *Krystal*), *National* (phone: 42618), and *Hertz* (phone: 42255) have airport locations and offices in Ixtapa hotels and in Zihuatanejo. On weekends and during the peak season reserve a vehicle in advance. Beware of very expensive rental prices, and if you have an accident, all *gringos* get blamed.

Cycles – Something that looks like a cross between a go-cart and a golf cart can be rented at *Ola Rent* in *La Puerta Shopping Center* across the street from the *Dorado Pacífico* hotel.

Tours – *Turismo Caleta* (phone: 30444), at locales number 6 and 12 of *La Puerta Shopping Center, Eturesa Travel* in *Ixpamar Mall* (phone: 31607 or 31667), and travel desks at Ixtapa hotels offer a number of programs, including trips into the back country and 1-day excursions to Acapulco and to Mexico City.

SHOPPING: There are about 400 shops in Ixtapa's seven shopping malls, and the shops in the *Camino Real* are fabulous for crafts, leather goods, beachwear, and silver. Calles Agustín Ramírez, Cinco de Mayo, Cuauhtémoc, Paseo del Pescador, and Pedro Ascencio in Zihuatanejo are good shopping streets. For rugs, hammocks, and crafts from Guerrero, Oaxaca, and Chiapas, visit *La Zapoteca* and *El Jumil,* both located at 9 Paseo del Pescador.

Chiquita Banana – Unusual handicrafts from all over Mexico. *Los Patios Shopping Center* (no phone).

Coco Cabaña – Absolutely tops for Mexican crafts. Same owners as *Coconuts* restaurant. Calle Vicente Guerrero (no phone).

Florence – Gold jewelry in pre-Hispanic designs from Oaxaca, original art, regional crafts, and hand-embroidered linen. *La Puerta Shopping Center* (no phone).

La Fuente – Hand-embroidered cotton clothing for women, including Suceso's casual clothing, Opus I, and Girasol designs, plus Donna Brown costume jewelry. *Los Patios Shoppping Center* (phone: 42131).

Galeria Maya – Folk art, leather goods, excellent crafts, and other unique items. Hermenejildo Galeana No. 5 (phone: 42047).

Luisa Conti – A sophisticated line of jewelry made with interesting combinations of materials in unique designs. Also carries an exclusive line of hand-knit sweaters. *Los Patios Shopping Center* (no phone).

Maria de Guadalajara – Easy-to-wear and easy-to-care-for crinkled cotton designs for women. *Los Patios Shopping Center* (no phone).

Polo Ralph Lauren – The well-known line of clothing for men and women, manufactured in Mexico and available for considerably less than in the US. *Plaza las Fuentes Shopping Center* (no phone).

Xochitl Bazar/Hyacinth – Art, handicrafts, and handmade dresses and jewelry — all in unique designs. *Plaza Bugambilias Shopping Center* (no phone).

SPORTS: Deep-Sea Fishing – Before Ixtapa was a gleam in anyone's eye, sportsmen came to Zihuatanejo to fish for marlin and sailfish. Large, fully equipped vessels will be found at the pier downtown. Arrange trips through the *Sociedad Cooperativa* (phone: 42056). Boats for 4 cost $180 for 7 hours.

Small Game Fishing – Another favorite sport in the area. Boats carry beer and soft drinks as well as tackle and bait. Arrangements can be made to put in at some isolated beach where the crew will cook the catch. Boats are available at the pier downtown.

Golf – The 18-hole *Ixtapa Golf Club,* designed by Robert Trent Jones, Sr., is both beautiful and challenging (see *Special Places*). It is open to anyone for a greens fee. There's a practice course behind *La Puerta Shopping Center.*

Horseback Riding – Riding is available at Playa Linda and Playa Quieta for about $5 an hour.

Parasailing – This is fun but risky: While wearing a parachute, you are pulled by a speedboat on the bay at Ixtapa. Accidents are rare, but they do happen. Available at the beaches of the *Stouffer Presidente, Holiday Inn, and Dorado Pacífico* hotels.

Roller Skating – *Roller Zihua* (on Prolongacíon H. Colegio Militar; phone: 44403) has a rink, skate rental, a skateboard ramp, video games, and go-carts.

Sailing – Catamarans and other boats are available with or without crew. Sailing and windsurfing may be done at La Quieta Beach, near *Club Med*.

Scuba and Snorkeling – Equipment and instruction are available at Las Gatas Beach from *Carlos' Scuba* (no phone) and in Zihuatanejo from *Zihuatanejo Scuba Center* (phone: 42147).

Swimming and Sunning – Though the surf seldom gets very rough at Ixtapa, once in a while the red flag goes up — beware of a dangerous undertow. The water always is calmer at La Quieta, La Ropa, and Las Gatas beaches. Don't count on lifeguards anywhere. A triathlon (swimming, bicycling, and running), held every year in early December, has become very popular.

Tennis – The *Ixtapa Golf Club* has lighted courts open to the public. *Camino Real, Club Med, Dorado Pacífico, Holiday Inn, Krystal, Stouffer Presidente, Sheraton Ixtapa,* and *Villa del Sol* all have their own tennis courts.

NIGHTCLUBS AND NIGHTLIFE: The action after dark centers around the hotels, especially those in Ixtapa, which attempt to see that guests don't get bored. The new *Euforia* disco, next to the *Lighthouse* restaurant (see *Eating Out*), is as popular as it is spectacular, and *Christine's* at the *Krystal* is an old favorite. Some of the Ixtapa hotels, such as the *Krystal* and *Sheraton Ixtapa* have bars or restaurants with live music and dancing; during the season reservations are recommended. A dance party held nightly on a platform raised over the beach at *Carlos 'n' Charlie's* always draws a big crowd. Mexican fiestas are held at the *Sheraton Ixtapa* and the *Villa del Sol* on Friday nights.

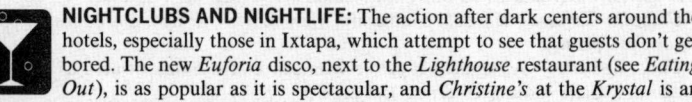

BEST IN TOWN

CHECKING IN: Ixtapa has elegant, luxury hotels, each with an English-speaking staff person and each exceptionally nice in its own way. Zihuatanejo's hostelries are older, mostly mom-and-pop operations, cozy and homey. The only trouble with the area is that it's likely to be either crowded or empty, depending upon when you visit. The best chance of striking a happy medium is during midweek, from December through March. On weekends or during other busy times, try to arrive before late afternoon. Expect to pay up to $200 per night for a double room at the very expensive hotels; $130 in the expensive category; $100, moderate; and $50, inexpensive. Rates are often 30% to 40% less during the summer. Most hotels listed below accept MasterCard and Visa; a few also accept American Express and Diners Club. All telephone numbers are in the 753 area code unless otherwise indicated. When calling from one city to another within Mexico, dial 91 before the area code.

Camino Real – Absolutely the best place to stay in Ixtapa, Westin Hotels' immense property is set cliffside on its own beach. Facilities include 428 rooms with hammock-slung balconies, 3 good restaurants, a lively lobby bar (though some find the lobby decor reminiscent of a "Moorish maximum security prison"), 4 tennis courts, 3 swimming pools, and some fine shops. Ixtapa (phone: 32121; 800-228-3000 in the US; FAX: 31091). Very expensive.

Club Méditerranée – One of the best-run resorts by this organization, it is a sumptuous 21-acre estate off by itself. Boats to Ixtapa Island; 12 tennis courts, golf nearby, all water sports, and even a computer workshop. Rates include all meals and most sports. Playa Quieta (phone: 30742; in the US, 800-CLUB MED; FAX: 30393). Very expensive.

Sheraton Ixtapa – One of Ixtapa's most luxurious properties, it has 358 rooms rimming an immense atrium, the fine *Casa Real* restaurant, and a lobby bar where mariachis play. There are 4 lighted tennis courts, too, and the pool is enormous. Across from *Ixtapa Golf Club* (phone: 31858). Very expensive.

Villa Ixtapa – Each of the three villas at this complex has 3 bedrooms, 3½ baths, a living room, terrace, air conditioning, fans, and maid service. The homes, with Spanish-Moorish influence, could use some renovation, but they are private and comfortable. Special services, such as private cooks and chauffeurs, are provided on request. The complex is set on a golf course. $300 per day ($400 in winter) for up to a maximum of 6 people. No credit cards accepted. 229-231 Paseo de las Golondrinas, Ixtapa (phone: 31619; 800-223-6510 in the US; FAX: 42758). Very expensive.

Villa del Sol – Right on the beach in Zihuatanejo and under the same management as the *Villa Ixtapa,* this delightful hostelry is just the right size with 22 pleasant rooms and 4 rather spectacular 2-bedroom suites — all air conditioned. The hotel is a spot that's hard to beat for self-sufficient beach lovers who enjoy just a little bit of sophistication with their casual, unstructured vacations. Facilities include a tennis court, lovely pools, water sports, and exceptional food (see *Eating Out*). Price in high season includes breakfast and dinner for two. Children under 14 are not accepted during the winter season. No credit cards accepted. La Ropa Beach, Zihuatanejo (phone: 42239; 800-223-6510 in the US; FAX: 42758). Very expensive.

Dorado Pacífico – One of Ixtapa's nicest accommodations, its 285 balconied rooms are pleasant and spacious, its restaurants and bars appealing. There's also a large pool with swim-up bar, 2 lighted tennis courts, and parasailing. Ixtapa (phone: 32025; FAX: 30126). Expensive.

Holiday Inn – It's not glamorous but it's extremely popular, with 230 pleasant rooms, lovely grounds, 2 restaurants, a coffee shop, two bars, pool, 2 tennis courts, and parasailing from the hotel's beach. The social program includes exercise classes. Ixtapa (phone: 31066; 800-HOLIDAY in the US; FAX: 31991). Expensive.

Krystal Ixtapa – The most exciting beachfront in Ixtapa. Besides 260 rooms, there is *Bogart's,* a *Casablanca*-style, continental restaurant, as well as *Rarotonga* (another restaurant), a cafeteria, tennis and racquetball courts (tennis classes available), and live music with dancing in the bar and at *Christine's* disco. The large pool has its own fountain, waterfall, and slide. Ixtapa (phone: 30333; 800-231-9860 in the US; FAX: 30216). Expensive.

Omni Ixtapa – Inaugurated in August 1989, it has 381 rooms, 13 junior suites, 12 master suites, and a presidential suite with a private pool. Facilities include a gymnasium, huge pool, restaurants, coffee shop, lobby bar, and *palapa* bar (phone: 30003; 800-233-2008 in the US; FAX: 31555). Expensive.

Stouffer Presidente – One of the first properties in Ixtapa and now, with its tower, one of the largest, it has 401 rooms. The balconies drip with greenery, and the facilities include restaurants, 2 bars, and 2 tennis courts. Ixtapa (phone: 30018; FAX: 32312). Expensive.

Catalina-Sotavento – Two old favorites, the *Catalina* and the *Sotavento* are now under the same management. This complex offers 121 spacious rooms on 8 terraced levels, plus hammocks strung on the balconies. The bar hangs high above La Ropa Beach and is a peaceful place to find oneself at dusk. The steep meandering steps here may be a problem for some. Service is good. Request a room with a view. Winter rates include breakfast and dinner. La Ropa beach, Zihuatanejo (phone: 42137; FAX: 42975). Moderate.

Fiesta Mexicana – A fine beachfront location with 58 rooms and a pool. The restaurant is poorly run. La Ropa Beach, Zihuatanejo (phone: 43776 or 43636; FAX: 43738). Moderate.

Irma – A favorite with frequent visitors, this pleasant 80-room hostelry has a bar, restaurant, beach club, and 2 small pools; daily deep-sea fishing tours can be arranged. La Madera Beach, Zihuatanejo (phone: 42025). Moderate.

Avila – It has a superb location on the beach; some of its 27 rooms are air conditioned. 8 Juan Alvarez, Zihuatanejo (phone: 42010). Inexpensive.

Las Uracas – Guests drive through a stone entryway into gardens filled with trees, plants, and pathways connecting 10 bungalows, each one unique, with a living room, bedroom, and kitchen, and named for a different bird. The name of the hotel itself translates as "the bluejays." Minimum 3-day stay. No credit cards accepted. La Ropa Beach, Zihuatanejo (phone: 42049). Inexpensive.

 EATING OUT: There are some excellent dining choices in Ixtapa and Zihuatanejo, with new places popping up every day. Listed as expensive are restaurants where dinner for two may cost $50; moderate, where the bill may reach $35; and inexpensive, $15 or less. Drinks and tips are extra. Most restaurants listed below accept MasterCard and Visa; a few also accept American Express and Diners Club. Unless otherwise noted, all restaurants are open daily. All telephone numbers are in the 753 area code unless otherwise indicated When calling from one city to another in Mexico, dial 91 before the area code.

Bay Club – Elegant continental dining indoors and a mesquite grill on the terrace. There's live jazz every evening during the high season. Open from 2 PM to 1 AM. Reservations advised. On the road to Playa la Ropa (phone: 44844). Expensive.

Coconuts – This elegant terrace place with hand-painted parasol lampshades is a favorite with the local café society for its good seafood, pâté, black bean soup, and salads.Closed September and October. Reservations advised. 1 Agustín Ramirez (phone: 42518). Expensive.

El Faro – Part of the *Club Pacifica* condominium complex, next to the funicular that connects the condos to the beach. Try the *medallones del chef* (three medallions of beef, each topped with a different sauce) or the "El Faro" (grilled fish served with an achiote-flavored sauce). Open for breakfast and dinner. Reservations advised. Ixtapa (phone: 31027, ext. 124). Expensive.

Lighthouse – A replica of a 19th-century lighthouse, it features an international menu especially created by chef Erick Du Bael and includes US prime meats, chicken, and seafood casseroles, and pasta. If you climb up the 54-foot tower and ring the bell, you get a drink on the house. Reservations advised. On Blvd. Ixtapa next to *Euforia* disco (phone: 31190). Expensive.

Villa Sakura – This modern, spacious Japanese place spans two levels and has a rock garden complete with a bridge and brook for wishing. The menu includes tempura, sashimi, yakitori, and seafood dishes. Open for lunch and dinner. Closed Wednesdays in the off-season. Reservations advised. *La Puerta Shopping Center* (phone: 30272). Expensive.

Villa de la Selva – What was once the home of Luis Echeverría, former President of Mexico, is now one of Ixtapa's most fashionable restaurants. It's wonderful for sunset cocktails and dinner, and special lighting after 7:30 PM makes a lovely view of the ocean possible even after sundown. Reservations advised. Beyond the *Camino Real Hotel*. Paseo de la Roca, Ixtapa (phone: 30362). Expensive.

Villa del Sol – The perfect place for a candlelit alfresco dinner, complete with strains of Beethoven wafting through the palms. Reservations necessary. No credit cards accepted. In the hotel of the same name, on Playa La Ropa (phone: 42239 or 44066). Expensive.

Da Baffone – An Italian eatery that serves fine pasta. Lunch and dinner only. Reservations unnecessary. *La Puerta Shopping Center* (phone: 31122). Moderate.

Benji Pio – Excellent Mexican and continental choices, steaks, and seafood. Open for lunch and dinner. Reservations unnecessary. *El Portal Shopping Center* in Ixtapa (no phone). Moderate.

Carlos 'n' Charlie's – It's part of the ribs 'n' beer chain, though more sophisticated than most. No reservations. Beachfront location next door to *Palmar-Ixtapa Hotel,* Ixtapa (phone: 30085). Moderate.

La Mesa del Capitán (The Captain's Table) – Steaks, lobster, and other seafood, topped off with Irish coffee, all prepared under the careful supervision of Luz Maria de la Garza. Open for lunch and dinner, and the place is usually packed. Reservations for large groups only. 18 Nicolás Bravo, Zihuatanejo (phone: 42027). Moderate.

O.K. Cantina & Oyster Bar – Fast becoming one of Ixtapa's most popular spots, this is the latest venture of one of the partners of the plush *Sumiya* restaurant in Cuernavaca and the *Villa de la Selva* in Ixtapa. The menu is international, and the decor is strikingly modern with accents of carved wood; the dining area surrounds a huge bar. A salsa group plays nightly. Open daily from 6 PM to 2 AM. Reservations advised. *Los Patios Shopping Center* (phone: 30973). Moderate.

El Sombrero – Even though the owner is an expatriate German, the emphasis here is on fine Mexican specialties, with meat, seafood, and some international dishes also on the menu. Open for dinner only. Closed Sundays. Reservations advised. *Los Patios Shopping Center* (phone: 30439). Moderate.

La Cabina del Capítan (The Captain's Cabin) – An English-style pub that specializes in hefty drinks and light lunches. It's become very popular, mainly because of the satellite dish and large-screen TV set, which make it possible to watch the big games live from the US. Opens at noon. Reservations unnecessary. Upstairs from *La Mesa del Capítan* at 18 Nicolás Bravo, Zihuatanejo (phone: 42027). Moderate to inexpensive.

Taboga – It's in a lovely Mexican-style home that was the first hotel in Zihuatanejo, now converted to an eatery. Shrimp Alberto baked with cheese and smothered in a mild chile sauce is a good choice. Closed Sundays. No reservations. Calle Juan N. Alvarez (phone: 42637). Moderate to inexpensive.

Las Brazas – Mexican food, well prepared and reasonably priced. No reservations. 13 Cuauhtémoc (phone: 42577). Inexpensive.

Kapi-Kofi – Popular for breakfast, this humble little coffee shop has become a downtown landmark. No reservations. No credit cards accepted. 12 Pedro Asencio, Zihuatanejo (no phone). Inexpensive.

100% Natural – A nice change of pace, this simple and wholesome spot offers fresh fruit drinks and salads, healthy breakfasts, sandwiches, and *tortas* (Mexican sandwiches made on a crusty roll with refried beans and avocado slices, plus a choice of tasty fillings). No reservations. Catalina González and Cuauhtémoc (no phone). Inexpensive.

LOS CABOS

(pronounced Loes *cah*-boes)

The *real* southern California lies a full thousand miles south of San Diego, at the tip of the Baja Peninsula. Known as Land's End, this neighborhood possesses all the remoteness and mystery that its name suggests, and the two towns there — together called Los Cabos, Cabo, or the Cape — combine with desert, rocks, and sea to create a compelling place to visit. But the greatest single lure of Los Cabos lies off the tip of Baja, in the form of commanding rock formations, not least of which is the graceful arch where the Sea of Cortés meets the Pacific Ocean. Without Land's End, Los Cabos would be just another pretty resort. Instead, it's much, much more.

San José del Cabo, the larger of the two towns, was founded in 1730 as a Jesuit mission on the banks of the San José River estuary by Padres Nicolás Tamaral and Visitador José Echeverría. It began with one cabin for the church and one for the missionaries, then moved to what is now called San José Viejo, and finally came to its present site.

This first small settlement caused some dismay among the Pericu Indians, a polygamous tribe whose members normally spent their time hunting, fishing, and gathering wild plants. While they were successful in killing off some of the Spanish intruders — as the tiles over the parish church door attest — diseases (particularly syphilis) brought by the newcomers were even more successful in killing off the Pericu. By 1750, 20 years after the founding of the mission, there were just a hundred Pericu left, and their number continued to dwindle.

Cabo San Lucas, often called simply Cabo, was discovered in 1537 by Francisco de Ulloa, Hernán Cortés's navigator. In time, it served as a regular port of call for the oceangoing *Nao de China* on its voyages between Manila and Acapulco. When the local pirates got wind of this schedule, word of profitable buccaneering potential spread quickly, and for a time the town was under siege. In 1587, the English pirate Thomas Cavendish captured the Philippine galleon *Santa Ana* off the Cabo coast and made off with many thousands of pesos worth of gold, silk, satin, damask, and wine.

Pablo Martínez called the area "eminently desolate and sad" in his *History of Lower California — The Only Complete and Reliable One,* published in 1960. Only the most adventurous souls, in rugged four-wheel-drive vehicles, used to venture down the unpopulated peninsula to Los Cabos, but times have changed. There are now direct and charter flights into the airport, which is only 15 minutes from San José del Cabo (45 minutes from Cabo San Lucas); cruise ships make a total of 160 calls a year.

Last year, more than 225,000 people visited Los Cabos, and about 95% of them arrived by air. That's more than four times the combined population of both towns (22,000 in San José, 15,000 in San Lucas). Another 165,000 visitors passed through on cruise ships. The Transpeninsular Highway, also known as Highway 1 — which opened in 1973, 10 years after the first resorts were built — is a wonderfully scenic and drivable two-lane paved road, though repetitive curves inhibit passing and keep speeds down. Traveling at night is not recommended, because there is no shoulder for pulling off.

Despite its accessibility, Los Cabos, 110 miles (175 km) southeast of La Paz, still feels delightfully removed from the rest of the world. After all, Baja California Sur (South) only attained statehood in 1974; the phone book for the entire state, including the yellow pages, is only about an inch thick.

San José del Cabo is the more developed of the two resort areas. It has a wide, landscaped boulevard, 9-hole golf course, and hotel strip, all creations of FONATUR, the national foundation for tourism development, currently in the throes of an extensive project to develop the whole 4,310-acre area, encompassing both towns. Increasingly, tourism is big business here. Within the next 10 years, the two towns may become one Cabo instead of Los Cabos. In between the two towns, yet another resort, the Cabo Real development, is springing up. Still under construction at press time, the development calls for a golf course (a projected 9 holes will be open by the end of this year), condominiums, and hotels, including the *Conrad* and the *Meliá Cabo Real,* which is now open.

Los Cabos already ranks fourth — after Cancún, Puerto Vallarta, and Acapulco — as Mexico's leading beach destination, and it could easily replace any one of them. The area gets a lot of sun, and in winter many northerners come to thaw out, as well as to view the great whales as they congregate in these waters during their December-to-March mating season.

Today the town of San José del Cabo, with its central plaza, low-lying houses, and dream-like quality, represents Old Mexico more than anywhere else in Baja. It feels forgotten by time, yet it is an important commercial, agricultural, and cattle-raising center. Here mangoes, avocados, oranges, plums, and guayabas grow in abundance. The San José River makes it a fertile, rather than a parched, area.

Modern Cabo San Lucas resembles a pint-size Ensenada, with plenty of shopping, watering holes, and Californians. FONATUR plans to improve the streets (there has already been some improvement), build a new 300-slip marina, and add several hotels (including the *Marina Fiesta* and the *Yenecami*) and a golf course. San Lucas has the hustle and bustle of youth, while San José, a trifle more sedate, attracts visitors who prefer to spend most of their time lolling by the pool or lingering over a good meal.

LOS CABOS AT-A-GLANCE

 SEEING THE CITY: The best view of San José del Cabo is from the terrace of the *Da Giorgio* restaurant, a 10-minute drive south of town on Highway 1. For a unique view of the church steeple, take a paddleboat or canoe along the first finger of the estuary. The *Finisterra* hotel affords a panoramic look at Cabo San Lucas, the Marina San Lucas, the market, and the Pacific. Drive a motorcycle or take a horseback tour up to Pedregal, the new crop of condos on the hill, where there are stunning views of the harbor. Keep driving (just follow the arrows) to a cluster of rocks and a spectacular view of the ocean, bluffs, and the old and new lighthouses. For a different perspective, take a sunset cruise on the trimaran *Trinidad* ($15) to bask in the mystery that is Land's End; the *Palmilla* travel agency (phone: 20540) can make arrangements. For an underwater view of Los Cabos, take a glass-bottom-boat ride that leaves from the dock next to the old ferry pier in San Lucas on the half hour from 9:30 AM to 2:30 PM.

 SPECIAL PLACES: Most of what there is to see and do here involves sheer natural beauty — beaches, desert, rocks, and bluffs. But there's more for those who want to explore.

SAN JOSÉ DEL CABO

Parish Church – This simple building, consecrated in 1940, was erected on the site of a far older church, built in 1734. The painted tiles above the door depict several scantily clad Indians pulling the just-murdered Father Tamaral through the desert by a rope. On Plaza Mijares.

Estuary – It's bigger than it looks, and is inhabited by 100 species of birds. Human beings can enjoy it via paddleboat or canoe for $6 per hour. Follow the first, and longest, finger of water as far as possible for a picturesque view of the church steeple in town. The San José River empties into the estuary, which in arid times has been known to disappear and then reappear when the rains come. Beside the *Stouffer Presidente Hotel.*

Barco Varedo – "Shipwreck" beach gets its name from the remains of a Japanese vessel found here. Transparent tide pools along the shore and rock formations (which make for good hiking and exploring) are the main attractions here. There are no restaurants or rental facilities. Turn into the road marked "Barco Varedo" at Km 9 of the Transpeninsular Hwy.

Municipal Palace – The 1730 inscription on the tower of this yellow colonial building reminds passersby of the founding of the town. The interior is now used for office space. Boulevard Mijares between Zaragoza and Manual Doblado.

Palmilla Beach – Next to the *Palmilla* hotel, it's the most convenient spot in San José for renting water sports equipment and fishing boats. There's a seafood restaurant here, as well as a motorcycle rental and taxi service. Swimming is allowed, but there are better places. Four miles (6 km) south of San José.

CABO SAN LUCAS

Land's End – The rugged, mysterious rock formations at the very tip of Baja are what makes this place so special, and they should not be missed. Sea lions and pelicans lounge in the sun on nearby rocks.

Playa del Amor (Lovers' Beach) – It faces both the Sea of Cortés and the Pacific, though locals cynically call its turbulent, unswimmable Pacific side "Divorce Beach." Campfires are permitted here, but there are no vendors or restaurants. Accessible by walking from the *Solmar* hotel in the direction of the arch, or by boat (about $16 round trip).

Médano Beach – A long strip of sand right in town, it borders the *Hacienda Beach* hotel and *Las Palmas* restaurant. It's the best beach for swimming and people watching. Lounge chairs, kayaks, jet skis, and big seagoing tricycles are availble for rent. Glass-bottom boats bound for Land's End (El Arco) also leave from here.

Santa María Beach – The most secluded beach in the area, and probably the best, it's good for swimming, snorkeling, diving, and collecting beach flora. The pebbles on the beach provide a fair massage for the feet and sizzle when the surf washes over them. It's beside the *Twin Dolphin* hotel. Park in the hotel parking lot, then walk to the left and down the hill; it will take about 10 minutes to get there. About 7½ miles (12 km) from San Lucas.

Chileno Beach – Small and clean, with crystal-clear water, it's great for swimming, snorkeling, and diving. *Cabo Acuadeportes* has an office here, at the *Cabo San Lucas* hotel (no phone at hotel; leave messages at its sister hotel, the *Hacienda Beach;* phone: 30664). Chileno Beach is 8 miles (13 km) from San Lucas.

Sandfalls – A special attraction for scuba divers, these unusual underwater cascades of sand — two of them, one deeper than the other — are near the arch at Land's End.

EXCURSIONS

Buena Vista – This pleasant beach is 45 miles (72 km) north of San José, on Bahía de Palmas. Comfortable *Rancho Buena Vista,* a fishing resort, is also here. Fishing boats are available.

La Rivera – An inviting stretch of sand and surf off the beaten path. There are small fishing boats for rent, but not much else. 7½ miles (12 km) off Hwy. 1, just south of Buena Vista.

Santiago – The zoo here is small but has a large variety of birds and animals: pheasants, parrots, goats, hawks, cockatiels, a lioness, a black bear, peacocks, toucans, raccoons, spotted skunks, coyotes, jaguar, gray foxes, even a couple of pigs and a badger in a cage with a Persian and a Siamese cat. Signs are in English and Spanish. All the animals are exceptionally tame, except the bobcats. There's no sign designating the zoo, only the letters DIF and a children's playground. Park right outside the fence covered with vibrant bougainvillea.

■**EXTRA SPECIAL:** Set aside a morning to explore southern Baja's rare, remote beauty; it's worth renting a car, if necessary. Drive along Highway 1 to Todos Santos, a quiet little town founded in 1734 by the Jesuits. One of the last missions established in southern Baja, the original settlement was destroyed by Indians a couple of years later. The drive, 50 scenic miles (80 km) — about an hour — is actually more impressive than the town. The road hugs the coast and flirts with the ocean, then swings away and passes occasional ranches with names like La Joya (the Jewel) and Las Piedritas (Little Rocks). Narrow dirt roads tease the driver into taking a closer look at secluded beaches. Butterflies drift effortlessly across the road, and it's often necessary to brake for the ubiquitous burro or incidental cow. Today, Todos Santos is a community based on agriculture and livestock, with inhabitants who can trace their ancestry back to a particular Dominican priest who, it's said, took fathering rather seriously. Stop for a bite at the *Santa Monica* restaurant on Degollado Street. The town still has dirt streets, as well as a little park and church, a hotel, and bed and breakfast accommodations.

Return to Los Cabos south along Highway 1. Diehard drivers may add another few hours to the itinerary by making a circuit on Highway 1. Head north via El Triunfo (where baskets are sometimes sold at the church), then south again, still on Highway 1, via the picturesque towns of San Antonio, Santiago (visit the zoo; see *Special Places*), and Miraflores (where leather belts, bags, and wallets are sold in the houses designated *taller* (pronounced tah-*yehr*); stop in at the big white house on the way into town. For a refreshing swim en route, stop at either Buena Vista or La Rivera beach.

SOURCES AND RESOURCES

TOURIST INFORMATION: The tourist office is in the Municipal Palace in San José del Cabo (phone: 20377), but it has limited information and a very erratic schedule. Hotel desks are much more helpful. The information booth (separate from the desk) in the lobby of the *Finisterra* in San Lucas is particularly useful to first-time visitors. Car-rental agencies can provide maps, as can FONATUR (phone: 20900), the national foundation for the development of tourism, with offices on Highway 1 just around the corner from the Hotel Zone in San José and at the Marina San Lucas beside the outdoor market in San Lucas.

For general reading on the history of the area, drop by the library on Plaza Mijares. There are some books in English, and reading them at a table under a lazily rotating ceiling fan is particularly relaxing. For news of home, pick up a copy of the *Los Angeles Times* at the *Hacienda Beach* hotel; it'll cost $3 — and that's not even the Sunday edition.

The post office, a palm-fronted edifice with a bell over the door, is on Plaza Mijares in San José. Also on the plaza is a stationery store that sells postcards, writing paper, envelopes, and film. The banks — Bancomer and Serfin in San José, and Banamex and Somex in San Lucas — are open weekdays from 9 AM to 1:30 PM. Their money-exchange service operates from 10:30 AM until noon, but despite the inconvenience, the rate of exchange is far more favorable at the banks than in the hotels. An even better exchange rate will be found at *casas de cambio* (currency exchanges), and the hours are usually longer than those in banks.

Aeroméxico (phone: 20198) has an office at the airport and in San José on Zaragoza Street. *Mexicana*'s office (phone: 20606) is at *Plaza los Cabos Shopping Center* in San José. *Alaska Airlines* (phone: 21015) and *Continental* (phone: 20959) are at the airport.

Local Coverage – Free local publications in English — *Los Cabos News, Baja Times, All About los Cabos, What to Do and Where to Go,* and the *Baja Traveller* — are good sources of current information about Los Cabos. They are all available at local newsstands, the tourist office, and at most hotels.

 TELEPHONE: A long-distance telephone office is on Doblado Street near the bus station in San José, or use the public phone booth on the plaza in Cabo San Lucas. Hours generally are from 8 AM to 8 PM. Payment for a long-distance call carries a 50% federal tax. Calls made from hotels receive a 35% to 56% additional charge, so it's wiser to call collect. The area code for Los Cabos is 684. When calling from one city to another within Mexico City, dial 91 before the area code.

 CLIMATE AND CLOTHES: There are 350 sunny days a year here, with an average temperature between 75F and 80F. August and September are the hottest months; the rains come in September and October. Winter temperatures dip to the mid to high 50s at night, so a sweater comes in handy. Residents say November through May is the best time to visit. Dress is casual, but not so much so that people wear shorts to a disco, and short shorts are normally inappropriate in downtown areas. Almost any day of the year is a beach day here. *Chusbascos,* or tropical storms, come through from August to early October and can cause cancellations of fishing trips for a day or two.

 GETTING AROUND:
Bus – The bus station in San José is little more than a storefront, but it's more than San Lucas has to offer. Buses make nine trips between the two towns daily, from 7 AM to 10 PM, for about 50¢. There are eight daily departures from San José to La Paz, with only a couple from San Lucas. Both the western (coast) route and the eastern (mountain) route are scenic; the one-way fare is about $3.

Taxi – Cabs are stationed in San José and San Lucas; a one-way ride between the two towns costs $18. From the airport to the *Calinda* hotel in San Lucas, for example, the fare is about $25; in vans, or *colectivos,* it's about $8 per person; from the hotel zone in San José, the fare is $2 into town. Cabs from San José to Palmilla are about $5 one-way. There's a large taxi stand on Plaza Mijares facing the church in San José and in front of the *Stouffer Presidente* hotel. In San Lucas, it's catch as catch can downtown.

Car Rental – For convenience and economy, a rented car is by far the best way to get around. *Dollar, Avis, Budget,* and *Hertz* are all available at the airport; *Budget* also has an office in the *Colli* hotel in San José and in the *Stouffer Presidente* in San Lucas; *Hertz,* at the *Finisterra* in Cabo San Lucas; *Dollar* (at Zaragoza and Guerrero Sts. in San José); and *Avis* (at Plaza de los Cabos, A-3). Expect to pay $60 a day for a Volkswagen, including insurance, tax, and unlimited mileage. Parking in Los Cabos is casual; anywhere's fine unless the curb is painted red.

Motorcycle – Cycle rentals are available from *Chubascos* (Marine Blvd. and Madero in San Lucas; phone: 30404) and from *Vagabundos Renta* (no phone) near the *Stouffer Presidente* in San José.

Tours – Most hotel lobbies have tour desks to help arrange for visitors staying in San José to visit San Lucas, and vice versa. It would be a shame not to make the trip, since the two are quite distinct entities, each charming in its own way. A tour by trimaran or minibus takes about 5 hours and costs $25 per person. A tour to San Lucas includes (or should) a boat trip to Land's End and Lovers' Beach. It's also possible to cruise between San José and San Lucas.

Boat – Glass-bottom boats depart from the beach in front of *El Galeón* restaurant in San Lucas on the half hour from 9:30 AM to 2:30 PM. The trimaran *Trinidad* departs four times a day from Marina San Lucas; the price is $7 for 1½ hours, $15 for the longer sunset cruise, which includes drinks; the *Palmilla* travel agency (phone: 20540) can make arrangements. Glass-bottom boats, which allow 2 hours of swimming at Lovers' Beach, depart from the dock next to the old ferry pier. For $16, *Cabo Acuadeportes* at the *Cabo San Lucas* hotel takes 1-4 passengers to Lovers' Beach with pick-up service at any agreed upon time (no phone at hotel; leave message at its sister hotel, *Hacienda Beach;* phone: 30664).

 SPECIAL EVENTS: Los Cabos is not big on special events, since almost everybody's gone to the beach. However, February heralds *Carnaval,* replete with cockfights and festivities. In October and November, the *International Black and Blue Marlin Fishing Tournament* is held at the *Hacienda Beach* resort. A wahoo tournament organized by *Venice Anglers* (PO Box 1022, Venice, CA 90294) is held at the end of November. San José's *Saint's Day* is in March, and San Lucas's is in October; both are accompanied by a celebration.

 SHOPPING: Visitors don't come to Los Cabos primarily to shop, but they rarely leave without doing some. There may not be an abundance of chic shops, but some are appealing. Popular items include resortwear, T-shirts, silver jewelry, and a limited assortment of crafts from all around the country. T-shirts that run $6 to $9 in town normally cost two to three times as much in hotel shops. No notable handicrafts are produced in Baja. The only indigenous product is *damiana,* an amber liquor made from a plant that grows wild on the peninsula; it is said by some to be an aphrodisiac. The plant is more often used to make tea. Both San José del Cabo and Cabo San Lucas are small enough that it's easy to wander around and see everything. Shops open at 10 AM and close from 1 to 4 PM, but they stay open as late as 8 PM. On Saturdays, most shops are open from 10 AM to 1 PM; most close on Sundays. Los Cabos has been a duty-free zone since the 1930s, but the shops primarily sell American appliances, which are of major interest only to Mexican consumers.

SAN JOSÉ DEL CABO

Here, the main streets for strolling, shopping, and sampling local fare are Zaragoza, running east; Doblado, which runs west; and Boulevard Mijares, running north and south.

Almacenes Goncanseco – Get a bottle of Guaycura-brand *damiana* liquor (worth buying for the pregnant-woman-shaped bottle alone), not to mention rum, whiskey, and Kahlúa at good prices. On Blvd. Mijares (no phone).

Baja Folkart – Baskets, mirrors, masks, and crafts. On Doblado near Mijares (no phone).

La Casa Vieja – A boutique with three rooms and a hallway filled with stylish clothing and jewelry for women, El Palomar stoneware by Ken Edwards, footwear for men and women, wood carvings, and woven rugs (don't overlook the sale rack in the back). 27 Mijares (no phone).

Curios Allen I – Everything from gold and silver jewelry to handicrafts and beachwear. On Zaragoza (no phone). *Curios Allen II* (phone: 20405) is up the street.

Curios Toño – Traditional Mexican clothing, rugs, pillows, toys, and some clothing for children. On Morelos (no phone).

El Dorado Gallery – Sculptures in ceramics, brass, and copper by Mario Gonzalez. 20 Blvd. Mijares (no phone).

Estero – Beach- and resortwear. On Blvd. Mijares and Zaragoza (no phone).

CABO SAN LUCAS

Cárdenas and Hidalgo are the major shopping streets in town, and neither the tiny shopping center, *Plaza Alamburu* (Marina Blvd.), nor the open-air market beside the marina should be overlooked. T-shirts, beachwear, crafts, pottery, and rugs are all popular items.

In *Plaza Alamburu,* visit *Local #4* for men's tropical shirts and *Bulnes Barrera* for fine ceramics. Merchandise and prices are about the same in most places, so comparison shopping is not really necessary. *Plaza Candidos,* a shopping center downtown, has several nice shops, including *La Bamba* for hand-painted clothes, *Caramba* for T-shirts, *Ellesse* for casual resortwear, and *El Portón del Angel* with an unusually good selection of handicrafts.

La Bugambilia – This is the place for shoes, handbags, and leather accessories. On the plaza by the cab stand (no phone).

La Cucaracha de Oro – Carries Irene Pulos designs, Guadalajara glassware, and Havana cigars. Blvd. Cárdenas (no phone).

Galería del Arco – Paintings, sculptures, and prints by contemporary Mexican artists. Across from Marina San Lucas at Cárdenas and Zaragoza (phone: 30551).

Joyería La Fortuna – Items from the Orient in jade, coral, lapis, malachite, ivory, and antique silver, from $4 to $700; also traditional *guayabera* shirts for men. At the *Cabo San Lucas Hotel* (no phone).

Mamma Eli's – Quality glassware from Guadalajara, silver jewelry, baskets, crafts, and traditional Mexican clothing. On the plaza (no phone).

Marisa Curios – A particularly good selection of T-shirts, from waist to knee length. On Blvd. Cárdenas (no phone).

Plaza Pancho – Fine silver jewelry at *Jocobo de Taxco Gallery,* and a gift shop selling paintings, crafts, and bags. At the *Hacienda Beach Hotel* (phone: 30122/3).

Poco Loco – A vast selection of T-shirts and other casual clothes for men and women. *Hacienda Mall* (no phone).

Ronnie's – Unique prints on T-shirts and fashionable cotton tops for men and women. On Hidalgo (no phone).

SPORTS AND FITNESS: Fishing and water sports are the reasons folks come to Baja, and it's often said that after 3 days here people grow fins. Water sports are more accessible in and around San Lucas, but it's also possible to drive an hour north of San José to Buena Vista and La Rivera beaches for good swimming. The best place to rent water sports equipment is *Cabo Acuadeportes* at the *Hacienda Beach* and *Cabo San Lucas* hotels in San Lucas (no phone at the *Cabo San Lucas;* leave message at its sister hotel, *Hacienda,* 30664).

Bicycling – *Chubasco* (on Marina Blvd.) 1 block from the *Giggling Marlin* in Cabo San Lucas, rents bikes, as does *Deportes Cabo Baja,* for about $10 a day.

Canoeing and Paddleboating – Both are available at the lagoon in San José for about $6 to $10 per hour. It's also possible to rent a canoe for the same price from *Cabo Acuadeportes* (they recommend taking it to Lovers' Beach for a look at Pelican Rock).

Diving – Dive sites in the area around Cabo San Lucas include Pelican Rock, Grand Sand Fall and Little Sand Fall (underwater cascades of sand near the Land's End rock formation), North Wall, South Wall, Shepherd's Rock, Sea Lion Colony, the Pinnacle, and the Shipwreck. A scuba course costs $85 per person; a one-dive package is $35, and two dives cost $60. *Cabo Acuadeportes,* at the *Hacienda Beach* and *Cabo San Lucas* hotels, rents equipment and underwater cameras (a camera with a roll of film and underwater housing costs $25 a day). Dive trips and equipment are also available from *Amigos del Mar* (on Blvd. Marina) across from the fishing pier. Diehards with a car head north from San José, past La Playita and Punta Gorda, to two shipwrecks; 6 AM is the best time to go; the trip takes about an hour.

Fishing – The Sea of Cortés, which has been called "the world's biggest fish trap," is famous for the large variety of fish in its waters; blue or striped marlin is the trophy most sought by the anglers. About 40,000 marlin are hauled out of "Marlin Alley" waters every year, and visitors are likely to witness this event repeatedly at Chileno and Palmilla beaches. The best season for large marlin, the black or blue, runs from November through January, though some big ones have been pulled in during the off-season. Sailfish are the main bounty in spring, with some swordfish. Striped marlin are abundant year round.

Fishing is equally popular in Cabos, San José, and San Lucas. *Pangas,* 22-foot outboard skiffs, carry a maximum of three people and are perfect for fishing for dorado, wahoo, and yellow fin. The famous Gordo (Fat) Bank, 7 to 10 miles off the coast of San José, is a particularly productive spot. The price of a 3-hour morning trip is about $75 for two to three people; a 28-foot boat for a maximum of four people costs $275 to $520 for 8 hours. The price depends on the size of the boat. Rather than renting a boat on your own, you can save money by asking to be teamed with other people who want to fish, or by buying a single ticket (about $40) for a spot on a boat. Check with *Deportes Baja Sports* (at Vicente Guerrero and Madero in Cabo San Lucas) or at the *Tourcabos* desk in the lobby of the *Stouffer Presidente,* at their main office (*Plaza los Cabos,* suite B-2) or *Amigos del Mar* at the entrance to the *Solmar* hotel. A 60-foot custom-made, air conditioned twin screw that bunks 10 is available at *Fleet Solmar* (phone: 30022 or 30410), or from *Tourcabos* for about $700 a day. In Cabo San Lucas, *pangas* are for rent at Palmilla Beach, which is recommended more for fishing than for swimming, and at *Cabo Acuadeportes,* on the beach by the *Hacienda Beach* and *Cabo San Lucas* hotels. They cost $75 for two people for 3 hours; $90 for up to four people. Hotels and some restaurants can supply box lunches for a day's outing; with advance notice, restaurants will often prepare the catch and serve it with rice and vegetables. Hotels may provide freezing service as well. Pack fish in a plastic, but *not* Styrofoam, chest for air transport home. Do-it-yourselfers in need of fishing tackle can check with *Baja Sports,* one-half block from the *Marina* hotel in San Lucas, or try *Cabo Acuadeportes.*

Golf – Nine holes of Los Cabos's golf course in San José del Cabo, *Campo del Golf Course* (phone: 20905), are open to the public, and another 9 were under construction at press time. Greens fee is $27; clubs can be rented for $12 and carts for $20. The course has a clubhouse and is in the Hotel Zone.

Horseback Riding – Horses are for hire, with a guide, from *Ramon's Horse Rentals,* in front of the *Cabo San Lucas* and *Hacienda Beach* hotels in San Lucas. Rates are $15 per hour. A 3-hour sunset tour *a caballo* that leads to the Faro Viejo, the old lighthouse that is now in disrepair, costs $30. Two men, Juan Angel and Jesus, also rent horses from 6 AM to 6 PM for $6 an hour in front of the *Stouffer Presidente;* the men are not employed by the hotel. No prior riding experience is necessary.

Hunting – The best hunting is found on the Pacific side, near Todos Santos. Dove, quail, and pheasant shoots can be arranged through the major hotels. Federico Aguilar, who may be reached through the *Palmilla* hotel (phone: 20582 or 20583), is an excellent guide who can help cut through some of the red tape involved in getting a license. For more information, see "Hunting" in *For the Body,* DIVERSIONS.

Parasailing – Most often found at Médano Beach, in front of the *Hacienda Beach* hotel. A 10-minute ride costs $20.

Sailing and Windsurfing – Minifish, sunfish, catamarans, and windsurfers are available for $12, $14, $17, and $12 per hour, respectively, from *Cabo Acuadeportes* at the *Hacienda Beach* and *Cabo San Lucas* hotels. Beach rafts go for $10 a day.

Snorkeling – Head for Chileno or Santa María beaches; Lovers' Beach is another possibility. Gear can be rented at Médano, Chileno, and Palmilla beaches. The brain coral and tropical fish, plus 60 to 70 feet of visibility, make Chileno Beach most popular; park by the fence and walk in (it's not far). Another favored spot lies between Km 9 and 10 on Highway 1, where there is a lot of beach camping; turn off on the only suggestion of a road. *Cabo Acuadeportes,* at the *Hacienda Beach* and *Cabo San Lucas* hotels, takes groups to Pelican Rock; $23 per person includes equipment, instruction, transportation, and a certified guide who conducts a tour of the bay.

Surfing – Head for Costa Azul, also known as Acapulcito, just below the lookout between San José and San Lucas. Another fertile spot is about 4 miles (6 km) north of La Playita. No signs point the way; just look for the break. *Deportes Baja Sports* (phone: 30732), rents boards for $10 a day.

Swimming – Charming Playa del Amor, also known by the inexact translation of its name, Lovers' Beach, is reached by boat from Marina San Lucas or from Médano Beach. The problem is that most waterborne rides don't leave their clients on the beach long enough. Pack your own drinks and snorkel gear. *Cabo Acuadeportes,* at the *Hacienda Beach* and *Cabo San Lucas* hotels in San Lucas, and *Deportes Baja Sports,* ½ block from the *Marina* hotel, rent beach chairs, air mattresses, and beach umbrellas. *Cabo Acuadeportes* also rents Boogie boards, view boards, coolers, and smashball rackets.

Visit Chileno Beach, with its clear, clean water, just south of the *Cabo San Lucas* hotel. Idyllic Santa María beach, more a secluded cove than anything else (see *Special Places*), is a 10-minute walk downhill from (and to the left of) the *Twin Dolphin.* Both beaches are about 6 miles (10 km) north of San Lucas. A couple of good, somewhat remote beaches are about an hour's drive north of San José: Buena Vista and La Rivera, which is just south of Buena Vista and 7 miles/12 km (but 20 minutes' driving time) after turning off Highway 1. Adventurers will find the beach most readily by skirting around the soccer field.

In this part of the world, many unmarked beaches pop into view unexpectedly. Enjoy their beauty, but remember that many are unsafe for swimming because of the dangerous undertow. A prime example is Buenos Aires Beach, an inviting sweep of sand between San José and San Lucas.

Tennis – The courts at the golf club are open to the public and cost $10 an hour during the day; $14 at night. In San José del Cabo, the *Palmilla, Posada Real* and *Stouffer Presidente* have tennis facilities, as do San Lucas's *Hacienda Beach, Meliá Cabo Real, Meliá Cabo San Lucas, Twin Dolphin,* and *Cabo San Lucas* hotels.

NIGHTCLUBS AND NIGHTLIFE: Start the evening at the *Whale Watcher's Bar* at the *Finisterra* hotel by taking in the sunset, dancing, and enjoying live entertainment (in San José near the Municipal Palace); *Bar Lovento* has live music every night except Mondays, at *Plaza los Cabos Shopping Center* in San José; impromptu dancing is encouraged. Then head down the boulevard to the *Cactus* video disco at the *Stouffer Presidente* hotel; the disco is open from 9:30 PM to 3 AM daily except Mondays, and the largest crowds turn out on Thursdays and Saturdays. The mosque-like *Nightime Lukas* at the *Plaza Marina* is Los Cabos's newest and most upscale disco. The *Cabo Wabo* has also become a very popular dance spot. Most hotels have theme evenings with buffet dinners. For instance, the *Palmilla* resort, near San José, has Mexican night on Fridays; and the *Solmar,* in San Lucas, has one on Saturdays. Mexican fiestas are held on Fridays at the *Stouffer Presidente* and on Sundays at the *Fiesta Inn.*

In Cabo San Lucas, have a drink at sunset at the *Solmar* hotel, or grab a table at the congenial terrace bar at the *Clarion Cabo San Lucas. The Giggling Marlin* (on Marina Blvd.) is the local watering hole and after-hours haunt of surfers and swingers; when there's no one else around, the five video screens are themselves mesmerizing. Word has it that the *Oasis* disco is a little too rowdy for comfort. At *Las Palmas* (on Médano Beach) there's live music — *latina* and *americana* — for dancing and Mexican dances on Sundays, Tuesdays, and Fridays.

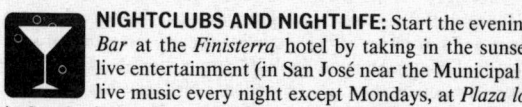

BEST IN TOWN

CHECKING IN: Each of the hotels we recommend in and between San José and San Lucas is distinctive, and all have extensive water sports facilities, tour desks, and air conditioning. Reserve 1 to 2 months ahead for rooms from November through May; for the *Christmas–New Year* vacation period, think in terms of 2 to 3 years ahead at the major resorts. Brisas del Mar, just south of San José in the Hotel Zone, and San Vicente Park, just north of San Lucas, are convenient for RV travelers. Los Barrilles Highway, between Km 9 and 10, has no hookups but is pristine and removed from everything except other enthusiastic campers. The resorts in Los Cabos, especially in San Lucas, cost more than those in other parts of the Baja Peninsula. Rates given here are for high season, November to May, and drop as much as 40% during the off-season. Expect to pay $200 to $300 per day for a double room at a place listed here as very expensive; up to $150, expensive; $80 to $100, moderate; and $50 or less, inexpensive. Most hotels listed below accept MasterCard and Visa; several also accept American Express and Diners Club. All telephone numbers are in the 684 area code unless otherwise indicated. When calling from one city to another within Mexico, dial 91 before the area code.

SAN JOSÉ DEL CABO

Palmilla – This Mexican Eden basks on a secluded bluff, and its 62 oversize rooms, 8 suites, two 5-bedroom villas, charming restaurant, and grounds impart the spirit of Old Mexico. There's a picturesque chapel (where marriages are performed), boutique, tennis, even croquet. Wake-up calls come with fresh orange juice, coffee, and croissants; rates include three meals a day (box lunches made on request). As we went to press, the hotel planned to add 200 rooms, a golf course, a marina, and 3 new restaurants. Three miles (5 km) south of San José on Hwy. 1 (phone: 20583; 800-637-CABO in the US). Very expensive.

Stouffer Presidente – The 250 rooms here, some with patios and others with balconies, overlook the gracefully landscaped grounds and the turbulent sea beyond (better not swim here). It serves as the sprawling social center for San José, with nonstop activities, including lobby and poolside games, horseback riding on the beach, paddleboat excursions on the adjacent lagoon, a bird sanctuary, and free tennis instruction. The *Cactus* video disco is open until 3 AM. Hotel Zone (phone: 20211; 800-HOTELS-1 in the US; FAX: 20232). Expensive to moderate.

Posada Real Best Western – A three-building complex with landscaped grounds, 150 comfortable rooms, swimming pool, tennis, volleyball, restaurant, and congenial (but noisy) lobby bar. Compared to the others in the neighborhood, the place is unassuming, but guests return again and again. Hotel Zone (phone: 20155; 800-528-1234 in the US; FAX: 20460). Moderate.

Colli – Think of it as offering bed and breakfast accommodations, but without the breakfast. For the budget-minded, it's right downtown, with 12 tidy rooms with private bath. Unfortunately, it's often full. Hidalgo between Zaragoza and Doblado (20725). Inexpensive.

CABO SAN LUCAS

El Rincón – Peter Wirth's property (his best known is *Casa de Sierra Nevada* in San Miguel de Allende) offers 2,500 acres on which to play, 6 secluded miles of beach, and (for now) a guesthouse with 6 suites. It's a California mission–style resort for up to 12 people. Complimentary airport pickup (for stays of a week or more), three meals a day, and picnics. About 20 miles/32 km (but an hour-and-20-minute ride) north of San José (phone: 465-20415 in San Miguel; no local phone). Very expensive.

Twin Dolphin – So private it doesn't even have a shingle out, this immaculate place offers desert decor; 63 rooms, suites, and cabanas; a pool; 2 tennis courts; a pretty dining room; a swimming pool; and picture-perfect Santa María Beach nearby. Its shop sells first class Mexican crafts, though at a high markup, as well as beachwear and traditional Mexican clothing. The air of exclusivity here is heady. Rate includes three meals daily. No credit cards accepted. 6½ miles (10 km) north of Cabo San Lucas (phone: 800-421-8925 in the US or 213-386-3940 in California; no local phone). Very expensive.

Cabo San Lucas – Built in 1959, this 2,500-acre resort is known locally as El Chileno. Along with attractive flowered patios, it has 75 rooms in 25 low-slung buildings as well as 2-, 3-, and 4-bedroom villas. It also has a pretty sea view, 5 pools, 2 tennis courts, dive shop, hunting club, fishing fleet, outstanding shops, and good food and service; no phones or TV sets. Credit cards are accepted for payment with 72 hours' notice. Hwy. 1, 6 miles (10 km) north of Cabo San Lucas (no local phone — call the sister hotel *Hacienda Beach;* phone: 30122/3; 800-SEE-CABO in the US). Expensive.

Clarion Cabo San Lucas – The only hotel in Los Cabos with a view of the Land's End rock formations, which can be easily admired from the poolside terrace or outdoor Jacuzzis. A congenial place, it has live music almost every night in season, with mariachis on Saturdays, and the recorded music of the likes of Lionel Richie and Willie Nelson in the bar. The 125 rooms are spacious, and service is attentive. Hwy. 1, about 3 miles (5 km) from Cabo San Lucas (phone: 30044; 800-228-5151 in the US; FAX: 30077). Expensive.

Conrad – The new property in the reliable chain was slated at press time to open by the end of the year with 241 rooms, 3 restaurants, and a fitness center (phone: 1-800-HILTONS). Expensive.

Meliá Cabo Real – A cobblestone drive leads to this glass and marble pyramid located on the Sea of Cortés. The first hotel to open in the new Cabo Real development in 1990, it has 299 rooms, 2 tennis courts, a huge pool, fitness center, 3 restaurants, bar, and disco. Arrangements can be made for fishing trips. Carr. Cabo San Lucas, Sector 5, Km 19.5 (phone: 30967; 800-336-3542 in the US; FAX: 31003). Expensive.

Meliá San Lucas – Situated over a wide strip of beach facing Land's End arch, this Meliá member, which opened in 1989, is decorated with white marble, modern wood furniture, and cool colors. The 187 rooms have private terraces and ocean views. Facilities include 2 pools, 2 tennis courts, a restaurant, coffee shop, and bar. Playa El Medano (phone: 31000; 800-336-3542 in the US; FAX: 30420). Expensive.

Fiesta Inn San José del Cabo – Five minutes from San José, this friendly place is set right on the beach. There are 151 rooms, a restaurant, and bar. Blvd. Malecón (phone: 20793; 800-FIESTA-1 in the US; FAX: 20480). Moderate.

Finisterra – Perched on a hilltop, it provides a sweeping view of the town, the marina, and the Pacific. It has 108 pretty colonial-style rooms with sitting area, two 2-bedroom cottages with kitchenettes, 2 tennis courts, 2 pools, a charming shop, and a helpful information booth in the lobby. Downtown San Lucas beside the marina (phone: 30000; in Alamitos, CA, 213-583-3393; 800-347-2252 in the US). Moderate.

Hacienda Beach – A secluded, 3-tiered property, with 113 comfortable rooms, including cabañas and suites, in seven buildings connected by palm thickets and stone walkways. Guests can enjoy a kidney-shape pool or the only swimming beach in downtown San Lucas, and the water sports center is tops. There are shops selling quality merchandise, a tennis court, and a good restaurant. On the beach (phone: 30122/3; FAX: 30606). Moderate.

Plaza Las Glorias – Located in the heart of town, this salmon, Mediterranean-style property forms part of the Marina San Lucas. It has 287 rooms, 2 restaurants and a snack bar, a lobby bar, pool, beach club, and disco. A variety of shops are on the first floor. Blvd. Marina (phone: 31220; 800-342-AMIGO in the US; FAX: 31235). Moderate.

Solmar – San Lucas's only oceanfront property. The water is too rough for swimming, but the view, especially at sunset, and the sound of waves as you drift off to sleep are mesmerizing. Although it's now somewhat run-down, this casual, low-key place, attracts a young crowd and is particularly popular with fishing enthusiasts; no phones or TV sets in the 70 rooms. On the beach, About a half-mile (1 km) from downtown San Lucas (phone: 30022; 800-344-3349 in the US; FAX: 30410). Moderate.

Mar de Cortéz – On a main shopping street in the heart of town, this congenial place has a large patio, 72 rooms, and a small pool. The rooms in the old section are smaller and cost about $10 less. Management is a little standoffish. Lázaro Cárdenas and Vicente Guerrero (phone/FAX: 30032). Inexpensive.

Marina – Small and conveniently located by — where else — the marina, it's worth a try if everything else is booked. It has 24 rooms, 7 nice suites, a tiny pool, a restaurant, and patio. Marina Blvd. (phone: 30030). Inexpensive.

 **EATING OUT:** Seafood dishes get top billing on most Baja menus, but it's possible to get good Mexican and continental cuisine as well. If it rains hard in San José, many restaurants close their doors until their patios dry out. If this happens, diners can still depend on *Andremar* (on Blvd. Mijares; see below). In Los Cabos, lunch is generally served from 1 to 3 PM and dinner from 7:30 to 10 PM. As a rule, hotel restaurants are best avoided. Of all the restaurants in Los Cabos, San José has the greatest number. Dinner for two, without drinks, wine, or tip,

can cost up to $50 in those places designated as expensive; $35, moderate; and $10, inexpensive. Most restaurants listed below accept MasterCard and Visa; a few accept American Express; none accept Diners Club. Unless otherwise noted, all restaurants below are open daily. All telephone numbers are in the 684 area code unless otherwise indicated. When calling from one city to another within Mexico, dial 91 before the area code.

SAN JOSÉ DEL CABO

Alfonso's – International nouvelle cuisine is served in the dining room and on the patio of a comfortable, colonial-style home. The prix fixe, six-course dinner offers a choice of three entrées. Dinner only. Reservations advised. Playa El Medano near the *Hacienda Beach Hotel* (phone: 30739). Expensive.

Añuití – An elegant steakhouse with a lovely lagoon-side location and a flair for prime cuts and seafood. There's terrace seating in winter and a cozy bar. Reservations advised from November through May. Hotel Zone (phone: 20103). Expensive.

Damiana – The ambience is pure Mexican, as is the food, in this restored, romantic 18th-century house. Specialties include charcoal-broiled lobster, shrimp, steaks, and abalone in garlic sauce. Try the *damiana* liquor to determine if it really is an aphrodisiac. Reservations advised. American Express accepted. Downtown on Plaza Mijares (phone: 20499). Expensive to moderate.

Andremar – A bohemian gathering place that's popular for breakfast. For other meals, it offers everything from *chiles rellenos* to lobster, not to mention a book exchange and music in the evenings. The owner speaks English. No reservations. American Express accepted. 34 Blvd. Mijares (phone: 20374). Moderate.

Da Giorgio – The most romantic spot in Los Cabos, it's Italian through and through, with a tile oven, where diners can watch food being prepared. Even if there's a wait, ask to dine on the terrace under the stars. Menu highlights include lasagna, ravioli, linguini, sea bass, and scampi. Added to these are *gelato* and fresh fruit pies. The bread is soft pizza crust; the salad bar, a dieter's delight. Open for lunch and dinner. Reservations advised. Hwy. 1 at Km 25, a 10-minute drive south from San José (no phone). Moderate.

La Playita – Known only to natives, this spot is where the anglers set out and, not surprisingly, it has the freshest fish — but the slowest service (bring a book). Nothing beats the grilled shrimp. No reservations. Pueblo La Playa; turn at the Pueblo La Playa sign on Blvd. Mijares at the entry to San José and drive 15 minutes (no phone). Moderate to inexpensive.

Swensen's Ice Cream Shop – Remember the days of the single scoop for 50¢? It still exists here. There are banana splits and sundaes, too. No reservations. Av. Hidalgo (no phone). Inexpensive.

CABO SAN LUCAS

Coconuts – Excellent chicken, meats, and seafood are served here in a tropical beach setting. Live music is featured nightly, except Mondays during the winter season. Open 8 AM to 10 PM. Dinner reservations advised. 1½ miles (2 km) northeast of San Lucas off Carr. 1 (phone: 30307). Expensive.

El Coral – A shanty-style *palapa* restaurant downtown. It's colorful and a good choice for a lunch of Mexican dishes or fish filet stuffed with seafood, the house specialty. No reservations. Av. Hidalgo and Blvd. Marina (phone: 30150). Expensive to moderate.

Candido's – Fine steaks and seafood are served in a lovely, intimate setting. Dinner only. Reservations advised. No credit cards accepted. One-half mile (1 km) east of San Lucas on Carr. 1 (phone: 30660). Moderate.

Cilantro's – Good food and lots of fun can be had at this spot specializing in mesquite-grilled seafood and Mexican dishes. Reservations advised. Playa El Medano (phone: 30744). Moderate.

El Faro Viejo – In spite of its location, this attractive open-air eatery is one of the best places in Los Cabos for steaks and seafood. No reservations. No credit cards accepted. At the trailer park of the same name (no phone). Moderate.

Las Palmas – *The* place to eat in Cabo San Lucas for good food, attentive service, and atmosphere. The menu touts shrimp, lobster, quail, and frogs' legs in season, topped off with a Kahlúa parfait or flan. Piña coladas come in double-decker glasses, and there's live dance music. Don't believe anyone who says the less expensive places are as good as this. Reservations advised. On Médano Beach (phone: 30447). Moderate.

Romeo & Julieta – Italian food — pasta, pizza, and exceptional veal with mushrooms are the specialties here. The bread and pasta are baked in an oven right in the middle of the patio. There's also a large antipasto bar. Open from 4 PM to midnight. Reservations advised. Blvd. Marina (phone: 30225). Moderate.

Señor Sushi – Sushi is the specialty here, but there are many other seafood dishes to choose from as well: sea bass stuffed with deviled shrimp, fajitas, and shrimp scampi. Reservations advised. Blvd. Marina across from *Plaza las Glorias* (phone: 31323). Moderate.

MANZANILLO

(pronounced Mahn-zahn-*ee*-yo)

Not too many years ago, Manzanillo, the small, slow-moving Pacific coast port town, was slated to become one of Mexico's foremost resorts, scheduled to play host to the cream of the international jet set. It all began in 1974, when the late Bolivian tin tycoon Antenor Patiño decided to build a fairy-tale resort just outside town. The result was *Las Hadas* — a magnificent, sprawling, whitewashed complex of villas and bungalows that vaguely resembled a Moorish village.

Unfortunately, in the succeeding years the management and ownership of the resort changed hands several times, and in the ensuing confusion, service and maintenance suffered. Almost a decade ago, however, the management of *Las Hadas* was taken over by the able Westin Hotels group, which also runs *Las Brisas* in Acapulco. A thorough renovation was undertaken, at a cost of $3 million — from fresh paint and plaster to new bedspreads, carpets, improved plumbing, and landscaping. The hotel is vastly improved, but Manzanillo has yet to blossom into a bustling resort center.

Manzanillo was settled early (1522) in the Spanish conquest effort — chosen for the natural harbor provided by its two large, wide, scallop-like bays. Cortés visited the place twice and directed early shipping expeditions from Manzanillo's beaches. (The port's name comes from the camomile, or *manzanillo,* tree, common in Colima state, that was found at the site where the first dock was built.) In November 1564, the expedition led by Miguel López Legazpi set sail from nearby Navidad harbor to conquer the Philippines for the Spanish crown. His ships were built by Indians and Spaniards on the beaches of Salahua, not far from where *Las Hadas* now sits.

These days, Manzanillo is the chief port for industrial activity in Guadalajara and Mexico's most important door to the Orient. The docks are downtown, and the railroad tracks to the wharves cut across the main street. Although most of the harbor is fenced off and heavily patrolled, it is possible to observe some fishing boat activity from a couple of harborfront restaurants.

If you take a morning flight from Mexico City to Manzanillo, about 40 minutes away, you'll fly to one side of the Volcán de Colima, one of Mexico's few active volcanoes. Steam and yellow fumes can sometimes be seen rising from the top, and its sides are covered with a fine, black volcanic sand. A river runs near the base, cutting its way through the Sierra Madre Occidental in a textbook example of the power of river erosion.

Your jet will slip over the coastal hill terrain and suddenly zoom out over the blue Pacific. On the right is a small airstrip that, from the plane, looks too small to land on. It isn't. The plane takes a wide clockwise sweep over the ocean and comes in from the north end of the runway on one of the few beachfront landing strips in Mexico. Breaking waves are to your right; coconut groves sway on your left.

The Manzanillo airport, like *Las Hadas,* opened in 1974; it was built at

Playa de Oro, on government land, with money donated by Señor Patiño. Passengers entering the airport building are greeted by a mural in brilliant colors depicting Mexican historical themes interpreted by local artist J. Chávez Carrillo. Colima Indian designs can be seen in mosaicwork on other walls of the terminal.

Since the airport is 27 miles (43 km) north of Manzanillo, visitors must rent a car, take a minibus, or hire a cab. The early morning jungle drive south on Highway 200, from the airport toward Manzanillo, affords fresh air, bright sun, and tropical greenery. Groves of coconut palms, avocados, and mangoes line the highway. First, the road crosses a wide tidal lagoon and you get an eyeful of hundreds of herons; then the harbor comes into view, and you see old ship hulks on the beach, cargo ships loading at the docks, navy patrol boats, and the Petróleos Mexicanos tank farm. In this coexistence of radiant beauty and homely industry one finds the paradox that is Manzanillo.

MANZANILLO AT-A-GLANCE

SEEING THE CITY: There isn't really any one best place from which to view Manzanillo. A large rock formation splits the city into two portions: the harborfront zone, encompassing the main square and public buildings; and the business district, to the south of the rock formation, entered by car on Calle Felipe Carrillo Puerto and on foot on Avenida México, an opposing one-way street.

SPECIAL PLACES: Manzanillo's downtown area is dusty and tired, and there are few compelling sights of interest.

Zocalo – Across the street from the waterfront is the zocalo, or main plaza, lined with old globe-shaped, cast-iron street lamps and decorated by two fountains that, when functional, spout water via recirculating pumps. Between the fountains is a gingerbread cast-iron bandstand with a brass weather vane on top; the bandstand dates from the Victorian era (Porfirian in Mexico) and has been rebuilt with a carved stone foundation and a plank floor. In the middle of the zocalo, busts of Father Hidalgo and Benito Juárez face each other across the lawn. The zocalo is the center of *Mardi Gras* activity, 2 days of parades and merriment before *Ash Wednesday.*

Crucero de la Atardecer – An agreeable way to spend a late afternoon watching the sunset is from one of the excursion boats that provide a 2-hour tour of the bay, daily at 5 PM. The boats leave from *Las Hadas* hotel (phone: 30000).

Playa Azul – One of Manzanillo's best beaches, it starts at *La Posada* hotel and curves northwest to the river at *Las Hadas.* Residents say the surf is calmest around *La Posada,* gets rougher toward the river, and then is calm again in the bay area protected by the Santiago peninsula. The sea is relatively calm all along the beach from December through May.

Playa las Hadas – If you are not a guest at *Las Hadas,* or at any of the residential complexes that are part of the development, it will be difficult to gain access to this lovely beach in its own private cove. On the beach there are small tents that look as though they came from the deserts of Morocco. Playa las Hadas is definitely for sunning, but not for hard-core swimming, since the beach is small and there's very little surf. Other beaches in the area have better waves.

Playa la Audiencia – This is the favorite beach of residents, set in a compact cove on the west side of Las Hadas Peninsula.

Playa Santiago – This beach starts at the *Playa de Santiago* hotel and continues around Santiago Bay to *Club Santiago*. It is one of the best beaches in the area and the largest close to town. Waves on the open bay can be rough, but the inlet in front of the *Playa de Santiago* is shallow, with small waves and no undertows. On this and other beaches, a man with a gourd on a string will sell you a sweet liquid called *tuba*, a slightly fermented beverage made locally from the sap of the coconut palm.

Playa Miramar – In the western extreme of Santiago Bay, about 7 miles (11 km) from Manzanillo, this is an excellent beach.

NEARBY ATTRACTIONS

Cuyutlán – About 30 miles (48 km) from Manzanillo is Cuyutlán, where the surf is similar to that of southern California beaches in the US. Legend has it that in April or May comes the "green roller," an immense wave of green water that continuously rolls in from the Pacific at heights of up to 30 feet and smashes on the white beach. The *ola verde*, as it is called, has to be seen to be believed, but there aren't many around who have seen it.

Colima – The state capital, founded in 1523, is reached by taking Highway 110 inland from Manzanillo; the trip takes about 2 hours. One of its attractions is the *Museo de las Culturas de Occidente* (Museum of Western Mexico Indian Cultures), with more than 3,000 archaeological pieces, housed in the *Casa de la Cultura* at Calz. Galván and Av. del Trabajo. Closed Mondays. The *Museo Nacional de la Danza, la Máscara, y el Arte Popular del Occidente* (National Museum of Western Dance, Masks, and Handicrafts) is in the *Fine Arts Institute* at 27 de Septiembre and Manuel Gallardo. Closed Mondays.

■ **EXTRA SPECIAL:** Thirty-eight miles (61 km) south on Highway 200 is Tecomán, the site of copra-processing plants. (Copra is coconut meat, from which coconut oil is extracted.) Farmers dry the copra at roadside; leftover coconut shells are piled high in yards of the processing plants and later burned. Also in Tecomán are lemon-oil–processing plants, for Colima is the world's largest producer of oil of lemon extract.

At Comala, about 5½ miles (9 km) northeast of Bolima, there's a crafts school and factory with colonial furniture, ironwork, art, tooled leather, and more.

Six miles (10 km) farther south, in Boca de Pascuales, fresh seafood is prepared to order. Guests sit under thatch roofs on straw-seated chairs that sink slowly into the sand.

SOURCES AND RESOURCES

TOURIST INFORMATION: The government tourist office is at 244 Av. Juárez, on the fourth floor (phone: 22090 or 22091). The staff will give you a map of Manzanillo and a list of sights in the capital of Colima.

Local Coverage – The local publication *Costa Azul* (Blue Coast), available free at hotels and the airport, offers fairly current information on what to see and do in Manzanillo.

TELEPHONE: The area code for Manzanillo is 333. When calling from one city to another within Mexico, dial 91 before the area code.

CLIMATE AND CLOTHES: The best time in Manzanillo is mid-November through May. From June through October it is warm and humid, but not uncomfortable with only a fan. September is usually the rainy season. Temperatures in Manzanillo average between 78F and 84F, with an average low of 70F. At the big resorts, dress is casual. Women may wear slacks, shorts, swimsuits, or less by day, and at night evening slacks, long skirts, or caftans. A shawl is advisable for coolish nights in December and January. Men can wear informal sports clothes and can forget about coats and ties, with the possible exception of the *Legazpi* restaurant at *Las Hadas,* where jackets (but not ties) are required.

 GETTING AROUND: Airport Transportation – Minibuses, whose fares are regulated, make the 27-mile (43 km) trip into town and cost about $3 per person. Airport taxis make the same trip for about $9.

Taxi – Cabs are abundant and are the best way to get into *Las Hadas* and *Club Maeva,* which have gate control. The local cabbies, known by sight and name, zip through. The fare from the airport to downtown is $12. If you are going farther, such as to Careyes and *Club Méditerranée,* the fare is about $40 per trip. Rental by the hour is a reasonable $10.

Car Rental – *Autorentas de México* (phone: 32580), *Avis* (phone: 30194), and *National* (phone: 30611) have offices in the airport.

Tours – *Hectur* travel agency (phone: 31701) arranges for excursions to Colima. It also handles horse rentals, fishing boat charters, reservations for sunset cruises, and ground transportation to and from the airport. *Bahía Gemelas* (phone: 31000), another travel agency, offers similar services, as well as excursions to Barra de Navidad, an unspoiled fishing village about an hour away.

 SPECIAL EVENTS: Manzanillo celebrates *Carnaval* for a week before *Ash Wednesday.* A queen is crowned, and there are dances, floats, parades, and general merrymaking. The *Fiestas de Mayo* are held on May 1–10, with dancing in the plaza and lots of food and drinks. (The celebration commemorating the incorporation of Manzanillo as a city is held on May 8.) The *International Sailfish Tournament* is held in November. From December 1 to 12, young children, especially girls, are dressed in native costumes and make pilgrimages to all the churches to pay homage to the Virgin of Guadalupe. They can be seen walking along roadsides.

 SHOPPING: While Manzanillo is not the best place to shop (Puerto Vallarta would be a better choice), there are a few notable places. Most stores are open from 10 AM to 2 PM and from 5 to 8 PM; closed Sundays.

Aries – Leather clothing of excellent quality and design for men and women. Shopping arcade, Puerto Las Hadas (no phone).

Boutique Maeva – Sportswear with the Maeva seagull, designed for the entire family. *Club Maeva* (phone: 30595).

Galeria de Arte – An art gallery selling Guadalajara artist Sergio Bustamante's fantastical creations in ceramics, papier-mâché, and copper. Plaza Albino, *Las Hadas Hotel* (phone: 30000).

Galeria Jaramar – Interesting fabrics, prints, folk art, rugs, and jewelry. Km 7.5 on the Manzanillo–Santiago Hwy; also at the Puerto Las Hadas shopping arcade (no phone).

Maria de Guadalajara – Easy-to-care-for and easy-to-wear 100% crinkly cotton clothing in earthy colors for women. Shopping arcade, Puerto Las Hadas (no phone).

Osteria Bugatti – A casual to dressy selection of chic resortwear for women. At the restaurant of the same name; see *Eating Out* below (phone: 32999).

Paco Silva – Creative designs in women's clothing by the talented local designer Silva. Next to *Galeria Jaramar,* over the Somex bank (no phone).

Tane – A branch of Mexico's most exclusive silver store specializing in sterling silver decorative items, serving pieces, flatware, and jewelry. Shopping arcade, Puerto Las Hadas (phone: 31861).

Tunanta – Beachwear, casual daytime clothes, and formal eveningwear for women. Next door to *Paco Silva* (no phone).

SPORTS: Fishing – Manzanillo is renowned as the sailfish capital of the world. The international tournament, held for 3 decades now, is an established event in November, and the national tournament takes place in February. Fishing trips can be arranged through the *Cooperativa de Prestadores de Servicios Turísticos de Manzanillo* (phone: 21071). *Flota Lori* has three fishing boats and is highly recommended (phone: 31323 or 20297).

Golf – The *Las Hadas* 18-hole golf course, designed by Roy and Pete Dye and set in a rolling palm plantation, is considered to be among the best in the tropics; open to non-guests. At *Club Santiago,* the 9-hole course designed by Larry Hughes is somewhat easier, but the first hole presents an exceptional challenge; open to non-members.

Horseback Riding – *Hectur* travel agency (phone: 31701) arranges for rides on the beach or in the mountains for about $15 an hour.

Sailing – The famed, biennial *San Diego–Manzanillo* boat race, (scheduled for February this year) runs 1,130 miles from California to the *Las Hadas* marina. It is followed by the biennial *Mexorc Circuit,* from Manzanillo to other ports on the Pacific coast; it will also be held this year. In alternate years, in February, Manzanillo co-hosts a regatta that begins in Marina del Rey, California.

Swimming – The beaches of Manzanillo (see *Special Places*) offer varied types of surf, from docile to dangerous. *Club Maeva* has one of the largest swimming pools in Latin America — three sections, with plantings, waterfalls, swim-up bars, and a rope-suspended plank bridge. In Boca de Apiza, about 25 miles (40 km) south, the calm, clear water is superb for swimming.

Tennis – *Club Maeva* has 12 courts, 6 of them lighted; *Club Santiago* has 6 courts; the *Sierra* has 4 lighted courts. *Club Las Hadas* has 10 lighted courts (8 hard surface and 2 clay), and is now one of the official sites of the *Royal Tennis Grand Prix;* the *Pirelli World Celebrity Tennis Classic* is held here in the fall.

NIGHTCLUBS AND NIGHTLIFE: The best night spots are *Baccho's* and the discos at *Las Hadas* and *Club Maeva.* Other good spots are *Oui* (at Km 9 on the Manzanillo–Santiago Hwy.) and *Solaris* (at Km 12.5). *Joy* is a little farther out, just before Miramar.

BEST IN TOWN

CHECKING IN: During the high season, expect to pay about $200 for a double room in a hotel listed as very expensive; around $100 in expensive; $40 to $75 in moderate; and less than $30 in an inexpensive one. Off-season, rates drop about 30% and ambience about 95%. All telephone numbers are in the 333 area code unless otherwise indicated. When calling from one city to another within Mexico, dial 91 before the area code.

Las Hadas – The management has been taken over by Westin Hotels, which has returned this large and impressive complex to the exclusive, world class resort it was designed to be — but never quite achieved until recently. Glamorized in the movie *10* and frequently featured on the television series "Lifestyles of the Rich and Famous," *Las Hadas* is a member of Leading Hotels of the World. The 220 whitewashed rooms, all with balconies, have been refurbished and renovated in a Moorish-Mediterranean-Mexican architectural mix that combines fantasy with considerable comfort. Facilities include an enormous free-form pool, a disco, several bars and fine restaurants, and use of the 10 tennis courts, 18-hole golf course, and 70-slip marina of *Club las Hadas*. The beach, set in a private cove, is fine for swimming and lovely for romantic moonlit walks. Dining at the hotel's restaurant, *Legazpi* (see *Eating Out*), is a must. On the Las Hadas Peninsula between Manzanillo and Santiago bays (phone: 30000 in Manzanillo; Westin reservations, 800-228-3000 in the US; FAX: 30430). Very expensive.

Club Méditerranée Playa Blanca – Daytime activities range from sailing and scuba diving to tennis, circus classes, and an intensive English horseback riding program; nighttime diversions include dancing and entertainment. Guest accommodations are in red brick bungalows. Good beach. Rate includes all meals and most activities. From December 15 to April 30 there's a 1-week minimum rate. Quite a distance from town. Costa de Careyes, Jalisco (phone: 20005; 5-203-3833 in Mexico City; 800-CLUB-MED in the US). Expensive.

Costa Careyes – A luxury resort about 1 hour from the Manzanillo airport, it has 90 rooms and 1-, 2-, and 3-bedroom villas (some with private pools). Facilities include 2 restaurants, tennis, fishing, horseback riding, and polo. No TV sets, clocks, or telephones. Costa de Careyes, Jalisco (phone: 70050; 800-878-4484 in the US). Expensive.

Sierra – The 351 rooms and suites all offer balconies and view of the beach and ocean. There are 4 lighted tennis courts, restaurants, bars, a pool, and a reproduction of a typical Mexican plaza. Playa la Audiencia (phone: 32000). Expensive.

Club Maeva – One- and 2-bedroom villas (some with kitchenettes) are available at this vacation village that seems to have everything — 12 tennis courts, a huge pool, horseback riding, water sports, a boutique, disco, and even a supermarket. There's a good social program, too. On Tuesdays, Thursdays, and Saturdays special theme nights, such as Brazilian Night and Hawaiian Night, are held. Two restaurants are on the property. Rates includes three meals and most activities. Santiago (phone: 30595; 800-GO-MAEVA in the US; FAX: 30395). Moderate.

Club Santiago Tenisol – This stately property offers both rooms and residential units (houses on or near the beach and condominiums near the beach with a central swimming pool) and features 6 tennis courts, water sports, and a 9-hole golf course. Check ahead on the availability of the residential units; some are rentals and some are for sale. Nine miles (14 km) from Manzanillo on Santiago Bay (phone: 30412/15; 303-371-5360 in the US; FAX: 30768). Moderate.

Playa de Santiago – Built in 1949, it was the first of the luxury establishments in Manzanillo, only now it's more reasonably priced. Its 100 units and the penthouse suite all have beachfront private balconies, a bay breeze, and ceiling fans. The hotel is kept remarkably clean. Facilities include a swimming pool, a so-so tennis court, miniature golf, restaurant, bar, shuffleboard, and a boat launching ramp. The beach, in a protected cove, is excellent. Covered parking for guests. On the west side of the Santiago Peninsula. Mailing address: Apdo. 90 (phone: 30270 or 30055; FAX: 30344). Moderate.

La Posada – A small pleasant place with its own beach, 23 rooms, pool, a coffee shop, and parking. On the beach at Playa Azul (phone: 31899). Moderate.

Colonial – With 38 rooms, some air conditioned, this is the only downtown hotel in Manzanillo that we would consider. Built in 1944 in Spanish colonial style with turned wooden window grilles, it has a cool open patio with an adjoining dining room. However, its bit of period charm and helpful staff cannot make up for the shabby rooms. 100 Av. México at the corner of Francisco González Bocanegra (phone: 21080, 21134, or 21230). Inexpensive.

Condotel Arco Iris – One- and 2-bedroom bungalows with bath and maid service. Swimming pool and an attractive garden. On the beach in Salahua. Mailing address: Apdo. 359 (phone: 30168). Inexpensive.

Parador Marbella – A real find for bargain hunters, this motel is on the beach and has a pool and restaurant. Km 9.5 on Manzanillo–Santiago Hwy., across the street from the Social Security hospital (phone: 31103). Inexpensive.

 **EATING OUT:** For dinner for two, expect to pay up to $50 in the restaurants listed as expensive; $30 in moderate; and $10 in inexpensive. Drinks and tips are extra. All restaurants below accept MasterCard and Visa; a few also accept American Express and Diners Club. Unless otherwise noted, all restaurants below are open daily. All telephone numbers are in the 333 area code unless otherwise indicated. When calling from one city to another within Mexico, dial 91 before the area code.

Hermosa Cove – A restaurant-bar, beautifully decorated in shades of blue with lots of seashells and plants. There's seating for cocktails outside and a dance floor inside. Beef and seafood are the specialties, and a television satellite dish brings customers in for all the big games from the US. Reservations advised. At the marina at Puerto Las Hadas (phone: 30888). Expensive.

Legazpi – This is as elegant as Manzanillo gets. Soft tones and candlelight complement the indoor and outdoor setting. The food, prepared with French cooking techniques and Mexican ingredients, is excellent, and service is nearly perfect. Jackets required. Closed Wednesdays and Fridays. Reservations advised. *Las Hadas Hotel* (phone: 30000). Expensive.

Margaritas – Mexican dishes, seafood, and a variety of flambéed specialties are served in the dining room or on the terrace. Reservations advised. Km 10.5 on the airport road (phone: 31414). Expensive.

Ostería Bugatti – At the crossroads where the road into Manzanillo forks to the left going in and the right fork goes to Las Brisas. Continental cooking is served here, with Italian dishes a specialty; good salads. Live music. Reservations advised (phone: 32999). Expensive.

L' Récif – Take a dip in the barside pool, enjoy a spectacular view, and savor the fine seafood prepared by the French chef who owns the place. During the winter, a champagne brunch is served on Sundays. Closed September 15–30. Reservations advised. At Vida del Mar (phone: 30624). Expensive.

El Vaquero – Charcoal-broiled steaks and chops are the specialty here. Beef is cut in the American manner and may even be ordered by the kilo (2.2 pounds!). Reservations advised. Las Brisas crossing, Manzanillo–Santiago Hwy. (phone: 31654). Expensive.

Oasis – On the beach in the heart of Club Santiago; the specialties here are seafood and Mexican dishes. There's a Mexican fiesta every Friday. Open for breakfast, lunch, and dinner. Reservations advised. Santiago Bay (phone: 30937). Expensive to moderate.

El Bigotes – Excellent seafood is served in a Mexican adobe-style eatery across the street from a banana plantation. Live music and relaxed atmosphere. Reservations advised. Cruce Las Brisas (phone: 23954). Moderate.

Carlos 'n' Charlie's – Part of the infamous chain, it calls itself "a sunny place for shady people." Dinner only. Closed Sundays. No reservations. Km 6.5 on the Manzanillo–Las Hadas Hwy. (phone: 31150) Moderate.

Chivis – Strictly gringo-style food, well prepared, and tasty homemade breads and pies. Open for breakfast, lunch, and dinner. Reservations advised. Km 8 on the Manzanillo–Santiago Hwy. (phone: 31212). Moderate.

Manolo's – Continental cooking, including seafood, steaks, and salad, in a tropical garden setting. Closed Sundays. Reservations advised. Three blocks from *Las Hadas*'s entrance on Salahua (phone: 30475). Moderate.

Willy's – Offering some of the best food outside *Las Hadas* hotel, this very popular beach spot serves red snapper, sea bass, lobster, shrimp, and various house specialties. Dinner only. Reservations advised. On Cruce Las Brisas, 2 blocks from Santiago (phone: 31794). Moderate to inexpensive.

Juanito's – Americans congregate here to watch the big sports games. Favorites from both sides of the border are served — fried chicken, ribs, burritos, tacos, and the like. No reservations. No credit cards accepted. Santiago–Manzanillo Hwy. (phone: 31388). Inexpensive.

Ly Chee – Small — about 10 tables — but with an excellent view of port activity. Standard menu of Cantonese food with some accent on fish dishes. Reservations unnecessary. In front of the building at 397 Calzada Niños Héroes (phone: 21103). Inexpensive.

100% Natural – Fresh fruit salads, fruit drinks, sandwiches, and hearty breakfasts are served in clean and pleasant surroundings. No reservations. Blvd. Costero (no phone). Inexpensive.

MAZATLÁN

(pronounced Mah-saht-*lahn*)

Just south of the Tropic of Cancer, in the state of Sinaloa, is one of the most popular resorts and active ports in all of Mexico. Mazatlán rests on a peninsula jutting out into the Pacific Ocean, with a natural bay and a sheltered harbor. The city is easily navigated on foot, with only one elevated area, the Cerro de Neveria (Icebox Mountain), which separates the rocky Pacific beaches to the south from the wide areas for swimming to the north. On the same latitude as the southern end of the Baja Peninsula as well as Honolulu, it has the same idyllic weather they do.

Mazatlán is striking with its long stretch of large beachfront hotels, seafood restaurants, nightclubs, and bright lights. Like the two other major west coast resort cities — Acapulco and Puerto Vallarta — its attractions are primarily sea-oriented. Yet Mazatlán is very different: It is much closer to the US-Mexico border, and although three direct international flights to Mazatlán are available (from Denver, Los Angeles, and San Francisco), a considerable part of its tourist trade arrives by car. It is less expensive; visitors are sportspeople — often fishermen and hunters — who tend to come for longer stays and watch their pennies more closely than the 1-week suntan-seeking pilgrims to Acapulco. And because it is so thoroughly imbued with the sports spirit — sports enthusiasts made Mazatlán the tourist destination it is today — it is exhaustively equipped for hunting and fishing expeditions. This is one of the few places where it is easy to hunt in Mexico. Guides and all the necessary equipment, including guns, are available. (It is best, by the way, to rent guns in Mexico; it is possible to import arms, but the red tape involved is staggering.) Deer and boar abound, and during the winter months, the duck and dove shooting is magnificent.

But fishing is what Mazatlán is mostly about. The port is at the mouth of the Sea of Cortés, also known as the Gulf of California, and it is one of the world's great fishtraps. The marlin bite from November to May; sailfish, from May to November. Equally challenging is light tackle fishing, to be tried along the inland lagoons. The trophies may not be quite as impressive as giant billfish, but, if anything, the little fighters require more skill to land them.

The name Mazatlán, from the Nahuatl Indian word meaning "place of the deer," refers to the large herds that once migrated along this beautiful coast. While there is still an abundance of game in the surrounding countryside, the pattern of migration has changed, with animals avoiding the immediate Mazatlán area and its flourishing tourist and fishing trades.

Once the home of the Chibcha Indians, Mazatlán also served Pacific coast pirates who, according to legend, buried their treasures in the coves and inlets up and down the coast near the city. A few Spaniards settled here in the early 1600s, but the town was not incorporated until 1806 and had no municipal government until 1837. It was really a group of enterprising Germans who developed Mazatlán's port so they could import agricultural equipment. By the end of the 19th century, Mazatlán was involved in international trade with countries as far away as the Orient.

Today the city supports Mexico's largest shrimp fleet. Tons of shrimp are frozen here every day and shipped off to the US, Mexico's major customer. Cruise ships and freighters are usually moored at the docks, and ferry boats run daily across the Sea of Cortés to La Paz, Baja's largest southern city.

Mazatlán has many beautiful white beaches with water that rarely gets warmer than 75F in summer; sometimes during winter, though, the water can get quite cold. Mazatlán is not as sophisticated as Acapulco, and far less crowded, and perhaps precisely for these reasons it is fast becoming a favorite spot among seasoned travelers seeking rest and recreation in the sun. With a population of only 380,000, Mazatlán draws some half-million tourists a year. This resort city now offers a wide range of facilities, ranging from trailer parks to luxury hotels, and in recent years has also developed a lively nightlife. Visitors not too tired from an active day in the sun may want to head uptown, along a beach called Los Sábalos, where they will find many of the city's trendiest restaurants and late-night clubs.

MAZATLÁN AT-A-GLANCE

SEEING THE CITY: The traditional way to see the lovely ocean views of Mazatlán is to take a *pulmonía,* a taxi that looks something like a golf cart with open sides. The alternative is to take a leisurely stroll — or to both walk and ride. Late afternoon is a particularly good time to go. The air has cooled off and the sunsets are frequently spectacular. And the best stop for a panoramic view of Mazatlán and the surrounding waters is El Faro, the massive lighthouse at the end of Centenario Drive. Actually on Cerro de Crestón, once separated from the mainland and now connected by landfill, this strip of land and its crowning lighthouse mark the entrance to the busy harbor. The lighthouse is the second highest in the world, standing more than 500 feet above high water, with a light that is visible for more than 30 miles out to sea and a view that is magnificent. To one side lies the Pacific, the beaches, and hotel row. On the other side is the harbor. Here are the fishing boats that provide shrimp for a hungry world, freighters from around the globe, and the oceangoing ferry that makes overnight trips to La Paz in Baja California.

From either outside or inside *Valentino's* disco (at Punta El Camarón in the Valentino complex), with its lofty window wall, it is mesmerizing to gaze out at the sea crashing against the rocks below and the boomeranging beaches of Mazatlán beyond.

SPECIAL PLACES: Mazatlán is a resort town, a beach and fishing paradise, an orgy of sunshine and seafood; but that doesn't mean that all one does here is eat, swim, and fish. From the busy harbor and beaches, the bustle around the zocalo, or the toing-and-froing along the *malecón,* Mazatlán offers plenty of entertainment. But beaches are the first priority.

Las Gaviotas Beach – A 15-minute drive from the center of town, it's a pleasant place to swim.

Olas Altas Beach – The name means "high waves," which says it all. It's a popular spot for surfing, but the tide can be tricky and there are no lifeguards. Olas Altas is popular with the younger set and is a good place to enjoy those magnificent sunsets.

Playa Norte – Not quite as exclusive as Sábalo or Las Gaviotas, but for many, more fun. Lockers are for rent here, as are beach chairs and umbrellas. Mariachis play at the little restaurants that dot the beach and provide nice spots for lunch.

Sábalo Beach – Way out toward the *Holiday Inn, Camino Real,* and beyond, Sábalo is Mazatlán's sheltered, quiet, and quite fashionable beach. One need not be a guest at the hotels to use the beaches; in Mexico there are no private beaches.

El Mirador – This lookout point on Olas Altas Beach, along the *malecón* on the Pacific side of Mazatlán, is used as a high dive by the young daredevils of the town. Almost any afternoon or evening when the tide is in, you can see young men jump from the top of this rock into the shallow, fast waters below. Contributions are collected before the dive is made — just in case. Paseo Claussen and Olas Altas.

Angela Peralta Theater – Named for the Mexican diva who died in Mazatlán, this theater once functioned as the city's opera house, and now hosts pop concerts, plays, and a variety of other performances. It is set in the historic section of Old Mazatlán, which dates back some 200 years, and was declared an historical monument in 1990 by the President of Mexico. The area around the zocalo here has been beautifully restored. Theater open weekdays. No admission charge. 76 Sixto Osuna (phone: 853503).

Anthropology Museum – The small museum contains a collection of pre-Hispanic artifacts and exhibits of contemporary art. Closed Mondays. Admission charge. Olas Altas.

Aquarium – Filled with fish and kids, it has 250 species (of fish) on display. There is a small sea museum, an auditorium where documentary films are shown, and a small botanic garden outside. Don't miss the turtles, Morena eels, or sharks. Open daily from 10 AM to 6 PM. Admission charge. 111 Av. de los Deportes, just off Av. del Mar (phone: 817815).

La Gruta de Cerro del Crestón – Beneath the craggy peak on which the lighthouse stands, separating the ocean from the harbor, is a small cave. Revealed only at low tide, it is said that pirates used this secret hollow to store their stolen treasure. Approaching the cave is dangerous, but it is fun to note in passing, especially for children and adults with active imaginations.

Malecón (Sea Wall) – Starting at the Olas Altas, north of El Mirador, this wall marks the beginning of the swimming beaches of Mazatlán. At this southernmost point are several of the better shops, restaurants, and some of the older and more popular hotels. From here it stretches north past Paseo Claussen, a rocky beach good for shell collecting but not for swimming; on to Playa Norte (North Beach), a local favorite (with lockers, showers, and beach umbrellas for rent); and ending at Avenida del Mar beach, a wide strip of sand bordered by newer hotels. Farther north, beyond the wall, are Las Gaviotas Beach, Sábalo Camanónes, and Sábalo Cerritos, the city's three most beautiful and luxurious beaches, each wide, white, and lined with palms.

Fishermen's Monument – A Mazatlán landmark on the ocean side of the *malecón,* it marks the beginning of hotel row. This statue of fisherman and mermaid is vaguely erotic, somewhat sexist, and, unfortunately, poorly maintained.

■**EXTRA SPECIAL:** Several islands in the bay off Mazatlán's harbor make lovely day excursions. Palmito de la Virgen is a bird watcher's paradise and is accessible by boat, which makes the trip daily; your hotel or the tourist office will provide the current hours and rates. Seashell collectors and snorkel fans can take an amphibious boat to Isla de los Venados (Deer Island) for an afternoon. One, the *Tiburón* (Shark), leaves from the *El Cid* beach; another, the *Super Pato* (Super Duck), leaves from the *Las Flores* beach. Both cost about $7 per person, round trip. And for those who have had enough "resort living" and are looking for something out of the ordinary, there is a jungle trip to San Blas in the state of Nayarit that includes a river ride in a dugout canoe, a swim, a visit to Padre Kino's mission, and a short tour of the town of San Blas. Be certain to take a good supply of insect repellant if you go. (For more information on San Blas, see "San Blas" in *Nogales to Mexico City,* DIRECTIONS.) A trip to Isla de la Piedra (Stone Island) is also worthwhile. A good part of the island is being turned into a tourist complex, which will eventually have golf and tennis clubs, hotels, villas, and condominiums, but for now the island remains relatively quiet — a haven for those seeking some privacy. Boats leave Mazatlán from near the freighter docks. Check with your hotel travel desk or the municipal tourist office (phone: 832545) for more information.

About 40 miles (64 km) from Mazatlán, over a spectacular road, is Copala, a truly authentic and historically rich Mexican pueblo. A mining town that boomed during the late 1800s and early 1900s, it now has only 600 inhabitants (among them several Americans). Of particular interest are the Iglesia de San José, which was completed in 1785, and the Trewartha House, a home built by a mining family from Cornwall, England. *Daniel's* restaurant serves excellent Mexican food and an unbelievably delicious banana-coconut cream pie, all accompanied by Mexican tunes sung by Don Juan. There's even a hotel — the *Posada San José* with bungalows and a good restaurant. José Jiménez, who runs the *Copala* travel agency in Mazatlán (2313 Belisario Dominguez; phone: 828326), is a native of Copala and a descendant of the Trewartha family. He organizes visits to the village, as well as Spanish and art courses. His English is perfect, and his love and enthusiasm for his hometown make the trip particularly enjoyable. He is also very reliable for fishing and hunting trips, and provides all other travel and real-estate services. For more details, see "Copala" in *Reynosa to Mazatlán,* DIRECTIONS.

SOURCES AND RESOURCES

TOURIST INFORMATION: The municipal tourist office (100 Rodolfo T. Loaiza, Suite 2; phone: 832545) and the office of the Public Ministry for Tourism Affairs (same address), may be particularly helpful in finding accommodations when all the hotels seem to be full. The *Mazatlán Guide* — published by the Chamber of Commerce and available for free at the airport and tourist office — contains a comprehensive list of activities and an excellent map of the city. A very helpful map is also published by the *Arts and Crafts Center;* it's complimentary from most hotel travel desks. There is a US Consulate (120 Circunvalación, corner of Carranza; phone: 852205).

Local Coverage – The *News,* Mexico's only English-language newspaper, is sold throughout Mazatlán. Many hotels provide complimentary copies of *About Mazatlán* and *Welcome to Mazatlán,* magazines that provide useful information about the goings-on and the going out in the area. *Información Turística de Mazatlán,* a bilingual publication of the chamber of commerce, is also helpful. The *Los Angeles Times,* which is flown in daily and is usually available after noon, is also available in Mazatlán.

TELEPHONE: The area code for Mazatlan is 69. When calling from one city to another within Mexico, dial 91 before the area code.

CLIMATE AND CLOTHES: Mazatlán is blessed with an idyllic climate. Its mild and sunny winters make it attractive to escapees from the north. The temperature is usually in the 70s, with an all-time low of 52F. The water is close to air temperature. And there is little or no rain. The summers are slightly hotter and have a tendency to get humid. But even then the highs are in the 90s and the water somewhere in the 70s. Expect rain from June to October, briefly in the afternoon, or at night; it is never much of an inconvenience. The town is a sportsman's resort, and the dress and general tone is extremely casual. About the only things you're sure to need are a bathing suit, hat, and sunglasses.

GETTING AROUND: Bus – Several bus lines run throughout Mazatlán. They are easily found on all the major streets, and the destination of each bus is clearly marked on its front. Service is good along Camarón Sábalo and Avenida del Mar, a single street that runs along the shore and where most of the hotels are located.

Taxi – There are two kinds of "taxis" in Mazatlán. The first can be called from the hotel at which you're staying or hailed on the streets; cab fare to or from the airport should run about $10. The second is called a *pulmonía* and looks like a golf cart (each has its special name — "El Fugitivo," for example); it offers a breezy ride — perfect for this hot place — for up to 3 people for about $2, and the driver may bargain a little. Minibus transportation from the airport is available for about $6 per passenger (phone: 815554).

Car Rentals – Rentals are very easily arranged through a hotel, at the airport, or at the downtown offices of the various agencies. *Avis* (phone: 821487) and *Budget* (phone: 832000) are at the international airport and in town. *Hertz* also has an office at the airport and one in town at the *Don Pelayo* (1111 Av. del Mar; phone: 834955). *National,* too, has a desk at the airport and one in town (phone: 834077). *Rent Me!* (between the *Quijote* and *Caravelle* hotels; phone: 846433) has replicas of old-fashioned cars available for $10 an hour. Reservations are advised at all agencies.

Mopeds – An excellent way to get around, they're available from *Maria's Mopeds* (1666 Camarón Sabalo and Río Ibis); rent in the morning to be sure of getting one.

Ferry – Large ferries, called *trasbordadores,* make the trip between Mazatlán and La Paz, Baja California, and will even transport your car. Cabins with sleeping accommodations cost from $45 to $55 but they are hard to come by, so reservations should be made well in advance. The ferry leaves the main pier daily at 5 PM (phone: 815808 or 826268).

Amphibian – There is regular amphibian service to Isla de los Venados (Deer Island) from the beach in front of *El Cid* resort. The *Tiburón* (Shark) departs at 10 AM, noon, and 2 PM. The last boat back from the island is at 4 PM (phone: 833333). The *Super Pato* (*Super Duck*) leaves from Las Playas Beach every 2 hours from 9 AM to 5 PM. Both cost about $7 round trip.

Fiesta Cruise – This 3-hour tour of the harbor and bay is a lovely way to spend a morning. The boat leaves from El Faro around 11 AM and gets you back to your hotel in time for a siesta after a hard morning's tour. There are usually English-speaking guides on board to point out various places of interest along the way, including the fishing harbor, lighthouse, the pirate caves of Cerro de Crestón, and a seal rock (the seals arrive in November and leave in May). Often there is musical entertainment and a short stop off one of the small islands dotting the bay. Tickets, scheduling, and departure locations can be obtained from most hotel travel desks, or contact the tourism office (phone: 832545) for more information.

SPECIAL EVENTS: Mazatlán celebrates every year with a big *Carnaval* that lasts a week, from Wednesday to *Shrove Tuesday,* the Tuesday before *Ash Wednesday.* It has been taking place since 1898 and is now one of the biggest in Mexico. A queen is selected and crowned, a poetry prize awarded, and there is a rodeo, *Mardi Gras,* and a lot of music and dancing. If you are planning to attend, make hotel reservations at least 6 months in advance; prices often double during *Carnaval.*

To open the fishing season, October 15, the Bishop of Mazatlán leads a procession to the harbor to bless the fleet. This ties in with the *Independence Day* celebrations that night and the next day.

The *Feast of the Immaculate Conception* is December 8, the most important religious fiesta in Mazatlán. A statue of the Virgin Mary is paraded through town and there is a huge display of fireworks in the evening. A grand time is had by all.

SHOPPING: There's a lot to buy in Mazatlán, and new stores are opening all the time. Note that the port and the surrounding state of Sinaloa are not known for much in the way of regional handicrafts, but the shops do have an ample selection of goods from the rest of Mexico. Expect to pay more than you would in the local area where the handicrafts were made, but less than in the US. Early afternoon is a pleasant time to head off on a store crawl.

Aca Joe – A center for T-shirts and part of the chain of sportswear boutiques found all over Mexico. Av. Camarón Sábalo and Gaviotas (no phone).

La Carreta – The finest of Mexico's crafts — brass and tin, paper flowers, clay pots, candles, furniture, and rugs. At *El Cid* (phone: 833333) and *Costa de Oro* (phone: 835344).

Casa Pacífica – Exclusive jewelry and gifts, along with paintings and other works of art. 335 Av. Camarón Sábalo (phone: 835065).

Casa Roberto – *Regalos* are gifts, and Roberto has tasteful ones, from rugs to accessories for home decorating to original artwork. At the shopping center at the *Playa Mazatlán* (phone: 838320).

Designers' Bazaar – Clothes by the Vercellinos, Señor and Señora, along with jewelry, leather, handicrafts, paintings. Shop around before coming here; prices on some items here can be considerably higher than at other places. 217 Rodolfo T. Loaiza and Av. Sábalo Gaviotas (phone: 836039).

Galerías Indio – The merchandise here comes from all over Mexico and includes silver and handicrafts. 32 Av. del Mar Norte (no phone).

Mazatlán Art Gallery – Good for browsing and buying. Across the street from *Sea Shell City* at *Plaza Tres Islas* (phone: 846312).

Mazatlán Arts and Crafts Center – A cooperative of 28 shops with some craftspeople working on the premises. Wood carvings, metal sculptures, and paper flowers are among the items tempting buyers. 417 Rodolfo T. Loaiza (phone: 825055).

Mercado del Rey – This small shopping center is open daily and sells mostly clothing and some leather goods. Across from the *Aristos* (no phone).

Mr. Indio – Gold and silver jewelry is the specialty here. Across the street from the *Playa Mazatlán* on 311 Rodolfo T. Loaiza (no phone). At their other location at 206 Angel Flores Poniente, artisans may be seen at work in their shops (phone: 813753).

Plaza las Palmas – Linked by balconied walkways, the stylish shops here sell items for both men and women, especially beachwear. There's also *Fellini's Pub* and a do-it-yourself or drop-it-off laundry. Playa de las Gaviotas (no phone).

Sea Shell City – Two floors of seashells and souvenirs. Gawdy and grand; fun for kids. Don't miss the shell mosaics upstairs. 407 Rodolfo T. Loaiza (no phone).

Sucesos – Casual clothing and unusual accessories for women. At the *El Cid* (phone: 833333).

Tane – A branch of Mexico's most prestigious and costly silver shop, it carries jewelry, flatware, and decorative items. *Camino Real* (phone: 831301).

The Tequila Tree – Crafts, women's clothes — including María de Guadalajara casuals — and wonderful items for kids; there's also a men's shop with very nice sandals and beachwear. No tequila. 1000 Av. Camarón Sábalo (no phone).

SPORTS: Baseball – Mazatlán has a team in the Mexican Pacific Coast League, where Fernando Valenzuela and many other big leaguers got their start. The season runs from October to January and the stadium is but a 5-minute taxi ride from most hotels.

Boating – Motorboats, sailboats, banana boats, water skiing, and parasailing are available all along the northern beaches. For parasailing, you wear a parachute and are pulled by a speedboat. The speed and wind lift you into the air; for about 6 minutes, you soar like a kite. If you're lucky, when the boat stops, you float down gently into the surf below. Also known as kite sailing, it is something for the adventurous spirit who swims well and is not afraid of heights.

Bullfighting – From *Christmas Day* to *Easter Sunday,* bullfights are held every Sunday at the *Plaza de Toros Monumental* on Calzada Rafael Buelna or at *El Toreo* on Calzada Camarón Sábalo.

Fishing – There are 10 fishing fleets in operation, with more than 75 cruisers for 2 to 6 passengers, and while November to May is the most popular time, fishing is good all year. Marlins are most plentiful, with sailfish close behind, and often both of these weigh in at over 100 pounds. Mazatlán is considered the best billfishing port on the Pacific coast, and there is also plenty of black, blue, and striped marlin, sea bass, tuna, bonito, red snapper, and many others. Most of the better fishing fleets come equipped with refrigerators, ship-to-shore radios, tackle, and bait; arrangements can be made to charter a boat through any hotel or through a travel agent before you arrive. If you are coming in the winter, it is wise to reserve a boat at the same time you make your hotel reservation. *Mike's Sportfishing* (phone: 812824) at the Marina Flota Faro is quite reliable. They charge from $180 to $200 for up to 8 passengers or $45 per person on their *Safari* boat. *Bill Heimpel's Star Fleet* (phone: 822665) is also very reliable.

Small game fishing also is excellent in Mazatlán, both in the lagoons and casting into the surf. Gilberto Aviles has good guides (phone: 813640).

Golf – There is an 18-hole course at *El Cid* resort (5½ miles/9 km northwest on Sábalo Beach Rd.) and a 9-hole course at *Club Campestre de Mazatlán* (at International Rd.)

Horseback Riding – Mazatlán's horses may be rented at the *Rancho Guadalupe, Gaviotas,* or next door to the *Tres Islas* restaurant.

Hunting – Several varieties of duck are plentiful during the winter months, with a season from about November to March. There is also an abundance of pheasant, quail, and dove; in the nearby mountains in the north and east are wild boar, deer, rabbit, and several kinds of wildcat. Of the latter, ocelot and jaguar are on the endangered species list, but everything else is fair game. Trips that include a guide, guns, licenses, and transportation can be arranged through all hotels. Gilberto Aviles's brother, Roberto, can make all the arrangements (phone: 813728 or 816060).

Rodeos – The *Lienzo Charro* in the Juárez section of town is where rodeos (known as *charreadas*) are held year round.

Skeet Shooting – Mazatlán has its own skeet club where markspersons can test their skills. Visitors are welcome. Hotel travel desks can make all arrangements.

Skin Diving – The diving is good at Isla de los Venados, Isla Dos Hermanos, and Isla los Cardones. Venados is best for beginners; Hermanos is only for the experienced. *Aquasport,* on the mainland, offers trips, including equipment and guides, for about $45 for certified divers, $55 for others (phone: 833333).

Swimming, Snorkling, and Surfing – The various beaches extending north from the center of town for 10 to 12 miles are all open to the public for swimming and snorkling. The best time for skin diving is from November through June, and the favorite spots are Cerritos, Connor's Point, and Deer Island. Surfing is king in Mazatlán, and most of it is done off Lupe's Point (next to the Playa las Brujas) or north of the *Camino Real* (recommended only for experts; the waves are very rough).

Tennis – *El Cid* resort has 17 clay courts (6 lighted) that can be rented by the hour. The *Costa de Oro* has 3 courts; the *Los Sábalos,* 2 courts; the *Club Reforma,* next to the *Plaza de Toros Monumental,* has 8 courts; the *Camino Real,* 2 courts; *Las Gaviotas Racquet Club,* 7 courts; and *Tequila Charlie's,* 2 courts.

Tobogganing – Youngsters will especially enjoy the giant toboggan, *Mazagua* (on Calz. los Cerritos). Open daily from 10 AM to 6 PM. Admission is about $15.

NIGHTCLUBS AND NIGHTLIFE: The disco scene is very big in Mazatlán, and the leading hotels all have their own spots. The discos take reservations, and during the winter it's wise to call ahead. *Valentino's* (phone: 836212), which clings to a bluff above the sea, at Punta El Camarón (in the Valentino complex), draws big crowds. Other possibilities include dancing at the *Chiquita Banana* restaurant in the *Camino Real* (phone: 831111); *Caracol Tango Palace* at *El Cid* (phone: 833333); *Fandangos* in *Las Palmas Shopping Center* (phone: 836761); and *Frankie O's* (Av. del Mar; phone: 825800). *Bora Bora,* a *palapa* bar on the beach at the Valentino complex, has disco dancing from noon until 4 AM. *Aleluya's Republic* (phone: 832040), a combined steakhouse and disco, has an all-day Happy Hour and a pit for dancing. *La Guitarra* disco (phone: 827000) at the *Hacienda* has live music Wednesdays through Sundays. Great fun and a fine place to meet people are at the Mexican fiestas at the *Playa Mazatlán* (phone: 834444) on Tuesdays and Saturdays; the *Plaza Maya,* where the show includes a performance by the *Flying Indians of Papantla;* or at the *Fiesta Piñata* (phone: 830666) at the *Oceano Palace* Tuesdays and Fridays.

BEST IN TOWN

CHECKING IN: Two main areas of Mazatlán have accommodations. One is in town, near the center of the city and along the Olas Altas, a street bordering the more southerly beaches. The other is farther north, along the beaches that have been developed since Mazatlán's growth as a resort. Older and less expensive hotels are more likely to be in the first location, while the newer, more luxurious ones are along North Beach (Playa Norte), Las Gaviotas (Gull) Beach, and Sábalo (Shad) Beach to the north. There are, of course, exceptions. All listed hotels have air conditioning, baths, and telephones. Expect to pay $115 for a double room in most of the hotels we classify as expensive; $50 to $85 in moderate places; under $40 in the inexpensive range; and $25 or less in very inexpensive. Rates may drop as much as 40% in the summer. All hotels accept MasterCard and Visa; several also accept American Express and Diners Club. All telephone numbers are in the 69 area code unless otherwise indicated. When calling from one city to another within Mexico, dial 91 before the area code.

Camino Real – The best-situated luxury property in town, with a commanding location by the sea, it has 170 units, a heated pool, beach, tennis, masseuse, and social program. Dancing is featured in *Chiquita Banana* (just a few yards from the shoreline) nightly, and there's live music and dancing in the *Lobby Bar.* About 7½ miles (12 km) northwest on Sábalo Beach Rd. (phone: 831111; 800-223-1818; FAX: 840311). Expensive.

El Cid – This impressive 800-acre property, originally with 600 rooms and suites in the *Granada Country Club* and the *Castilla Beach* hotels, has more recently added the 25-story *El Moro* hotel, which includes 400 suites (studio, junior, executive, and presidential); 2 penthouses on the 25th floor; 1 floor with a modern health spa; 72 shops, boutiques, and galleries; and a heliport on the roof. Facilities shared by the three hotels include 11 restaurants and lounges, a disco, an 18-hole golf course, lighted tennis courts, 5 swimming pools, squash and racquetball courts, a gym, and a jogging path. The resort's *Aquasport Center* offers scuba diving, snorkeling, windsailing, water skiing, and Hobie-Cat sailing and surfing. Arrangements can be made for fishing, horseback riding, and skeet shooting. About 5½ miles (9 km) north of downtown on Sábalo Beach Rd. (phone: 833333; 800-525-1925 in the US; in Colorado, 303-320-6771; in California, 800-446-1069; FAX: 841311); or write to *El Cid,* 5475 Leetsdale, Denver, CO 80224. Expensive.

Pueblo Bonito – A low-rise condo/hotel forming a horseshoe around a pretty garden and large pool, it has 133 junior, luxury, and executive suites. A fine Italian restaurant, coffee shop, good beach, and several bars complete the facilities. One block from the *Camino Real* at 2121 Av. Camarón Sábalo Nte. (phone: 843700; 800-262-4500 in the US; FAX: 841723). Expensive.

Los Sábalos – On the beach, with 185 beautifully decorated rooms and a sparkling white façade with bright yellow flowers on each balcony. Health club, tennis courts, a restaurant, and wet bars in the rooms. If you love wicker furniture and fresh flowers, this is for you. 100 Rodolfo T. Loaiza (phone: 835333; 800-528-8760 in the US). Expensive.

El Aquamarina – Another well-managed Best Western property, this one has air conditioning and cable TV; some rooms have balconies. The beach is across the street. 110 Av. del Mar (phone: 817080; FAX: 824624). Moderate.

Costa de Oro – Well situated on Sábalo Beach, with 40 rooms and two 2-bedroom suites. Some of the rooms have kitchenettes, some have balconies. Three pools and 3 lighted tennis courts. Av. Camarón Sábalo (phone: 835344 or 835366; 213-462-4348 in the US; FAX: 844209). Moderate.

Hacienda Mazatlán – Each of the 95 rooms here has a balcony, beach view, and large bathroom. There is also a heated pool, sauna, dining room, cocktail lounge, and a nightclub. Guests have access to the tennis facilities of the *Reforma* club. Parking. Near town, 1½ miles (2 km) northwest on Av. del Mar (phone: 827000; FAX: 843477). Moderate.

Holiday Inn Mazatlán – Not chic but comfortable, with 204 units, a nice pool and grounds, sailboat rentals, parasail rides, 2 restaurants, and a Mexican fiesta on Thursdays. About 5½ miles (9 km) northwest on Sábalo Beach Rd. (phone: 832222; 800-HOLIDAY in the US; FAX: 841287). Moderate.

Océano Palace – Can a discotheque be turned into a hotel? Perhaps a free-wheeling one, where the disco ambience still prevails. Designed for the young, it has 200 rooms, 2 pools, a restaurant, and a bar with live music nightly. Complimentary tennis passes. *Fiesta Piñata* on Tuesdays and Fridays. About 7 miles (11 km) northwest on Av. Camarón Sábalo (phone: 830666; FAX: 839666). Moderate.

Playa Mazatlán – All the Americans in Mazatlán seem to gravitate here, if not to the hotel, then to its terrace bar. This vast complex has 435 rooms, a heated pool, whirlpool bath, social program, fishing, boating, water skiing, skin diving, nightly outdoor dancing, and a dining room. Borders on the frenetic at times. 4½ miles (7 km) northwest on Las Gaviotas Beach (phone: 834444). Moderate.

Riviera Mazatlán – With one section located on the beach and another across the street, the property has 244 rooms and suites, plus tennis courts, a restaurant, bar, and gym. A Mexican fiesta is held on Wednesday nights. 51 Av. Camarón Sábalo (phone: 834822; FAX: 844532). Moderate.

Suites las Flores – This beachside high-rise has 108 apartments with kitchens, perfect for an extended stay; it also has 21 standard rooms. Casual atmosphere, popular bar, lively beachfront, access to tennis courts, pool, bar, restaurant. Las Gaviotas Beach in front of Los Venados Island (phone: 835100; in the US, 800-421-0787; in California, 800-252-0327). Moderate.

Suites las Palmas – Located 2 blocks from the beach, this property has 178 rooms and 12 suites in a cluster of 6 attractive 3-story buildings. There's a restaurant, lobby bar with live music, and a pool. 305 Av. Camarón Sábalo (phone: 834366; FAX: 843477). Moderate.

Los Arcos – A 20-unit beach motel in the shadow of *Suites las Flores,* it has no dining room, but the 1- and 2-bedroom suites have kitchenettes. It is pleasant and often full. Las Gaviotas Beach (phone: 835066). Inexpensive.

De Cima – One of Mazatlán's first beach hotels — and still popular — with 150 rooms, a good piano bar, and a restaurant. Av. del Mar near downtown (phone: 827855; FAX: 827311). Inexpensive.

Posada Don Pelayo – Although it's not on the beach, it's still a popular place. Some of the rooms have balconies, refrigerators, and/or kitchenettes. There's a pool and tennis court, and *Chico's* beach club is across the street. 1111 Av. del Mar (phone: 831888; FAX: 840799). Inexpensive.

Puesta del Sol – Fifty rooms and 16 bungalows with kitchenettes. There is a restaurant and a bar. Camarón Sábalo (phone: 835522; FAX: 843381). Inexpensive.

Solamar Inn – It resembles an ancient villa, set across the street from the beach; 38 spacious rooms with kitchen, sitting room, and pool. 1942 Bd. del Sábalo (phone: 836666). Inexpensive.

San Diego – An unprepossessing and cordial motel, it has 37 rooms and will appeal to those who want to economize on lodging and splurge on seafood. Rocking chairs on the porch provide a friendly welcome. No credit cards accepted. Across from *Valentino's* disco on Av. del Mar (phone: 835703). Very inexpensive.

Sands – Across the street from the beach, this low-key place has 84 comfortable rooms equipped with television sets and refrigerators, a pool, and *La Rana Sonriente* restaurant. Av. del Mar (phone: 820000; FAX: 851025). Very inexpensive.

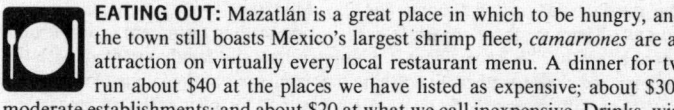

EATING OUT: Mazatlán is a great place in which to be hungry, and since the town still boasts Mexico's largest shrimp fleet, *camarrones* are a major attraction on virtually every local restaurant menu. A dinner for two will run about $40 at the places we have listed as expensive; about $30 at the moderate establishments; and about $20 at what we call inexpensive. Drinks, wine, and tips are extra. Most restaurants accept MasterCard and Visa; several also accept American Express and Diners Club. Unless otherwise noted, all restaurants are open daily. All telephone numbers are in the 69 area code unless otherwise indicated. When calling from one city to another within Mexico, dial 91 before the area code.

Angelo's – A very pretty place decorated in pastels, it specializes in fine Italian and international dishes. Dinner only. Reservations advised. At *Pueblo Bonito,* 2121 Av. Camarón Sábalo Nte. (phone: 843700). Expensive.

Casa Loma – Unique and secluded, this spot features excellent international cuisine and impeccable service. Closed in the summer. Reservations necessary. No credit cards accepted. 104 Av. Gaviotas (phone: 835398). Expensive.

Casa de Tony – Traditional Mexican dishes, seafood, and steaks are served in a 150-year-old Mazatlán home, with a fireplace and a romantic patio. Closed Sundays. Reservations advised. 111 Mariano Escobedo Pte. (phone: 851262). Expensive.

El Marinero – Stop here for a fresh seafood lunch or, in the evening, for dinner and a mariachi serenade. Dinner is often cooked on a charcoal brazier right at guests' tables. It's a popular place quite near the harbor and pleasantly decorated. The waiters are friendly and offer good advice on what to eat and what to see. Reservations advised. 530 Cinco de Mayo Norte (phone: 817682). Expensive.

Miyiko – Set in a Japanese garden with a small stream, this spot offers excellent Japanese fare. Reservations advised. 70 Av. del Mar (phone: 816590). Expensive.

Señor Pepper – One of Mazatlán's most elegant spots, it offers candlelit dinners, live music, and dancing. Lobster and steaks cooked over a mesquite grill are the specialty. Dinner only. Reservations necessary. Across the street from the *Camino Real,* Calz. Camarón Sábalo (phone: 840120). Expensive.

Sheik – The spectacular setting makes up for the mediocre food and service. There are three large, lavish levels with a waterfall, tropical fish, stained glass windows of desert scenes, domed skylights, and marble floors. The menu offers international fare. Dinner only. Reservations advised. Valentino complex (phone: 844478). Expensive.

Casa de Bruno – At this sidewalk café and indoor restaurant, meals are prepared right at your table under Bruno's supervision. Reservations advised. Av. Camarón Sábalo (phone: 836241). Expensive to moderate.

Señor Frog's – This bar and grill was Anderson's second venture (his group is now all over Mexico, and even in the US). Noisy and a bit crazy, which is the Anderson touch, it's open from noon to midnight. At night there's music and dancing. Reservatins advised. Av. del Mar (phone: 851110 or 821925). Expensive to moderate.

Tequila Charley's – It looks like a Bavarian beer garden, the atmosphere is relaxed, and the food — make-your-own tacos, grilled meats, and seafood dishes — is not bad. A good place to make new friends. Reservations advised. At the *Arts and Crafts Center* (phone: 832031). Expensive to moderate.

Anifanti – It's hard to miss a place like this, where an airplane sticks out over the front door. The interior is more subdued, and the Italian food is very tasty. Try the lamb au jus. 550 Av. Camarón Sábalo (phone: 842000). Moderate.

El Jardin – Set in the *Plaza Gaviotas* hotel, this eatery serves shrimp, fish, hamburgers, and salad in a traditional Mexican setting. Reservations unnecessary. Across from the *Playa Mazatlán* (phone: 834322). Moderate.

Mamucas – There are those who say this is the best seafood restaurant in all Mexico, although few tourists know about it. Unpretentious and family-oriented, with the tables pushed close together. Everything that comes out of the kitchen looks great, but the specialty is *parrillada de mariscos* (seafood for two, grilled in an earthen pot). No reservations. Downtown at 404 Poniente, 2 blocks from Paseo Claussen (phone: 813490). Moderate.

El Parador Español – Spanish, not Mexican, cooking is the specialty here. Reservations advised. Av. Camarón Sábalo, next to *El Cid* resort (phone: 830767). Moderate.

El Patio – The rustic decor includes a bale of hay and a collection of oversize wooden spoons hanging from the ceiling. A good place to start the evening with a coco loco, piña colada, or other cocktail, followed by some seafood. Reservations advised. 30 Av. del Mar (phone: 817301). Moderate.

El Shrimp Bucket – Something of a national shrine, this is where Carlos Anderson (Mexico's best-known restaurateur) got his start. It's a trifle more sedate than some of his other places. There's dancing to a marimba band on the patio and romantic music and dancing indoors. Reservations advised. In *La Siesta Hotel,* on Olas Altas (phone: 816350 or 828019). Moderate.

Tres Islas – Right on the beach, this seafood restaurant has a fabulous view of the three islands. Try the excellent *parrillada* — a selection of different seafood, grilled over glowing coals. Reservations advised. Calz. Camarón Sábalo, 1½ blocks from the *Holiday Inn* (phone: 835932). Moderate.

La Cueva – A large, family-style restaurant where the grilled fish is the hands-down favorite. Open for breakfast, lunch, and dinner. Reservations advised. 2002 Av. del Mar (phone: 827802). Inexpensive.

Doney's – Good Mexican food is served here at bargain prices. Open for breakfast, lunch, and dinner. No reservations. 610 Mariano Escobedo (phone: 812651). Inexpensive.

Jungle Juice – A natural foods restaurant and juice bar, serving yogurt and fruit smoothies, fresh carrot juice, whole-grain pancakes, hefty sandwiches, even box lunches with a day's notice. No reservations. Corner of Laguna and Las Garzas, near the *Tequila Tree* (no phone). Inexpensive.

Lario's – Another good choice for Mexican food, they serve an excellent seafood chowder. No reservations. Near *Tequila Charlie's* at 413 Rodolfo T. Loaiza (phone: 841767). Inexpensive.

Pekin – Here you'll find the best Chinese food in town. Reservations advised. Near the cathedral at 4 Benito Juárez Norte (phone: 813330). Inexpensive.

Shangri-la – When a craving for Oriental dishes strikes, this is the place to go. Reservations advised. Av. Rodolfo T. Loaiza near the *Playa Mazatlán* (phone: 836746). Inexpensive.

MÉRIDA

(pronounced *May*-ree-dah)

The capital of the state of Yucatán and, with 700,000 people, the only city of significant size on the peninsula (the entire state has only 1.4 million people), Mérida was founded on January 6, 1542, by Spanish nobleman Don Francisco Montejo. On June 10, 1542, 250 Spaniards fought off between 40,000 and 60,000 Maya Indians who attempted to lay siege to the 6-month-old city. This battle marked the end of the Maya era and the beginning of a land ownership system in which large tracts of land were owned by the Spanish and worked by Indians who toiled virtually as slaves. It wasn't until the 1930s that a more equitable system of distribution gave the Indians of the Yucatán a fairer stake in the land their families had lived on for centuries.

Until the middle of this century, the Yucatán Peninsula was so cut off from the rest of Mexico that it was easier to get there from Cuba, the US, or even Europe. It is east of the highlands, and the flat, steamy, tropical jungle peninsula covers about 1,000 square miles of parallelogram-shaped land jutting northeast from the Mexican mainland into the Gulf of Mexico. Nowadays, it's possible to drive the 1,000 miles (1,600 km) between Mexico City and Mérida in about 3 days.

Formerly known as the Paris of the West, the White City, and the City of Windmills, Mérida has outgrown all of its old sobriquets. It was called Paris of the West during the heyday of sisal production, when people were getting rich and importing many luxury products from Europe, particularly France. With the development of synthetic products, this era dissolved. It was known as the White City because residents used to wear white and the streets were spotlessly clean. Today, the streets are still pretty clean by Mexico City standards, but all colors are worn. And the windmills that used to pump water from the subterranean rivers have disappeared in favor of more efficient pumps.

Mérida is an excellent stopover for travelers en route to the Maya ruins of Chichén Itzá, Uxmal, Sayil, and Kabah, which are among the most remarkable testimonies to a historic civilization anywhere on the American continent — or in the world, for that matter. The Maya were heir to the Olmec culture, the first Mesoamerican civilization. The Olmec mysteriously appeared around 1200 BC. Known for their ability to move giant 10-ton stones over long distances by water, they built giant temples, were sculptors of great facility — carving giant basalt heads as well as intricate jade miniatures — and had a written language. Before they disappeared as mysteriously as they had emerged around the time of Jesus Christ, their civilization stretched from the Valley of Mexico in the north (surrounding what is today Mexico City) to the land that is now Guatemala and El Salvador.

The Maya culture spanned the centuries between the disappearance of the

Olmec and the coming of the Spanish, reaching its peak between AD 300 and 900. They are considered to have been the most advanced of the ancient Mexican civilizations, with a highly developed social structure, a vast knowledge of astronomy and mathematics, and a system of hieroglyphics. Their amazing accomplishments include the erection of immense, terraced pyramids and other places of worship, whose walls, portals, and stairways were embellished with frescoes and stone carvings. By the 8th century, the Maya controlled the entire Yucatán Peninsula.

Their culture flourished until the 10th century, when the Toltec, a militaristic branch of the Nahuatl Indians, seized control of the peninsula. The aggressive brutality of the Toltec was expressed in their art as well as their warfare. At Chichén Itzá there is dramatic evidence of this fierce stylistic influence in the sculptures with jaguar motifs, feathered serpents, birds of prey holding human hearts in their claws, and frescoes depicting human sacrifice. The invaders and inhabitants of the area around Mérida became more integrated between the 10th and 13th centuries, however, and a new culture emerged: the Maya-Toltec. The excavations of Chichén Itzá that began in 1923 have yielded a great deal of information on the merging of the two cultures. After 3 centuries of serving as the temple for the Maya-Toltec, Chichén Itzá was abandoned. Within the next hundred years, the Maya-Toltec civilization declined.

The Maya sites within driving distance of Mérida are certainly the reason why most travelers visit the city, but quite a number of others come with no thoughts of archaeology on their minds. Some of them are said to be marijuana smugglers. Others are hunters drawn to the area because of its duck, quail, deer, and wild boar. Indeed the area has become so popular that some sports enthusiasts make the city the headquarters of their annual or biannual outing.

Mérida's air conditioned international airport has flights to the US (via Mexico City, Cancún, and Cozumel) and Cuba, but Mérida is also something of a tourist destination in its own right. It has its share of interesting colonial buildings, with several good hotels, restaurants, and a few shops selling local handicrafts. And it has a distinctive-looking population. You will probably notice, if you look closely, that quite a few residents have broad faces with high cheekbones, and that their eyes are often almond-shaped and their noses somewhat hooked. They are also comparatively short. These are the descendants of the Maya, many of whom speak both Maya and Spanish, or sometimes hardly any Spanish at all — a haunting postscript to any tour of the ruins.

MÉRIDA AT-A-GLANCE

SEEING THE CITY: The best place to get a sense of the city, flat as a pancake and surrounded by jungle, is from the ground, along any of its main streets. An enjoyable way to sightsee is from a *calesa,* or horse-drawn buggy.

SPECIAL PLACES: Although most streets are numbered rather than named, except for a few main boulevards, it is easy to get confused in Mérida. It's helpful to remember that all east-west streets have odd numbers; north-south streets have even numbers. Once you've got that, it becomes much simpler. To get a feeling for the city, start at the main plaza, or zocalo, called Plaza de la Independencia. The most interesting sites, shops, hotels, and restaurants are within 3 blocks of the zocalo; you'll find walking pleasant and easy.

DOWNTOWN (CENTRO)

Plaza de la Independencia – As in all Mexican cities, the main plaza is the center of activity. This one has a wheel and spokes pattern and carefully tended hedges and is especially inviting toward sunset. If you sit on a bench and watch the people, you'll soon get a pretty good sense of Mérida's rhythm.

Casa Montejo – Now a bank, this lovely Spanish colonial home was built in 1549 as the residence for the Montejo family. It originally covered an entire block, and even though only a section remains, it is still impressive. The lovely, large rooms were built around two patios and furnished with imported European furniture. Most striking is the stone carving around the entrance door. It's the Montejo coat of arms flanked on each side by a Spanish conquistador with a foot on the head of a Maya Indian. The figures on top are Adelantado Montejo, his wife Beatriz, and daughter Catalina. Open Mondays through Fridays, 9 AM to 1:30 PM. On the south side of the plaza.

Cathedral – This rather majestic, twin-towered church, completed in 1598, was designed by Juan Miguel de Agüero, the architect who also created Morro Castle in Havana. Above the entrance is the royal coat of arms of Spain; inside, the Chapel of Christ of the Blisters, with a statue reputed to have been carved from the wood of a tree that burned all night but was found untouched the next morning. Open daily, 7 AM to noon and 4 to 8 PM. On the east side of the plaza.

Government Palace – Absolutely not to be missed. Walk into the courtyard and up the back stairs. All the murals lining the walls were painted by Carlos Pacheco, a leading *yucateco* artist. On the second floor of the building is the Hall of History, easily the most handsome room in all of Mérida. Open daily. No admission charge. On the north side of the plaza at the corner of Calles 60 and 61.

Franciscan Church of the Third Order – Frequently used for fashionable weddings, this is considered by many people to be the prettiest church in town. On the east side of Calle 60 at the corner of Calle 59.

La Ermita de Santa Isabel – This tiny church is notable for its gardens with Maya statuary. Built in 1742, it was originally outside the city's walls and used by travelers as a sanctuary in which they prayed for a safe journey. Nowadays, its small interior botanical garden is a wonderful place to relax. The gardens are open daily to 11 PM. Four blocks from the plaza between Calles 66 and 64.

University of Yucatán – Originally a Jesuit institution when it was founded as the Colegio de San Pedro in 1618, the university has expanded to include more than half a dozen separate faculties and several preparatory schools. Open daily. At Calles 57 and 60.

Parque Centenario – Popular with kids and adults, it has a zoo, pony rides, a small train for children, and lovely grounds.

Paseo Montejo – Wealthy 19th-century residents built splendid homes along this wide, tree-lined, imitation Parisian boulevard. An 8-block thoroughfare lined with small palaces, chalets, and extravagant monuments, this is one of the most amazing sights in Mexico. Make sure you stop at the Monument to the Flag, a giant — flagless — sculpture depicting Mexico's history from the pre-Columbian era to the 20th century.

Cantón Palace (Museum of Anthropology and History) – One of the finest provincial museums in Mexico, it beautifully depicts the lifestyle of the Maya, and a visit prior to touring the ruins helps bring Maya history into focus. The museum is housed in the Palacio Cantón, the largest and perhaps loveliest of the splendid mansions on the Paseo Montejo and formerly the official residence of Yucatán's governors. Closed Mondays. Admission charge. Entry is on Calle 43.

The Arches – Mérida was once a walled city with 13 Moorish gates, of which only 3 remain today. One is the Arch of St. John (Arco de San Juan), about 5 blocks south of the plaza on Calle 64 in San Juan Park, which has a statue of Rachel at the well near its central fountain. This arch leads to the hermitage, La Ermita de Santa Isabel. The Dragon Arch is near the Dragónes military regiment headquarters at Calles 50 and 61. The third, Bridge Arch, is at Calles 50 and 63.

Museo Nacional de Arte Popular – A bit of a hike from downtown, this small museum is worth it. On display are masks, pottery, clothing, and other examples of *yucateco* arts and crafts. Upstairs there is an excellent — though completely unorganized — collection of folk art from all over the country. There is also a shop on the first floor, with incredibly reasonable prices. Open Tuesdays through Saturdays from 8 AM to 8 PM and on Sundays from 9 AM to 2 PM. No admission charge. On Calle 59 between Calles 48 and 50.

ARCHAEOLOGICAL ZONES (ZONAS ARQUEOLÓGICAS)

Chichén Itzá – Some of the most dramatic ruins in all of Mexico, these cover 7 square miles. Plumed serpents, carved in stone, appear everywhere in this place whose name means "at the mouth of the well of the Itzá" (a Maya tribe). Especially wonderful is El Castillo (the Castle), which is scaled by a stairway of 91 steps on each of its 4 sides, plus the top platform, for a total of 365 steps, the number of days in the Maya calendar. Those who clamber to the top of this temple are rewarded with a glimpse of a jaguar throne with jade eyes and vestiges of red paint. An army of capless columns surrounds the Temple of the Warriors, at the top of which is found a sculpture of a reclining figure called a *chacmool;* it's speculated that this figure was used as an altar for sacrifices. Nearby is the immense ball court, the largest in Mesoamerica, where games lasted 10 to 15 days, the losers of which were killed; on the walls is a bas-relief depicting such a scene. Also interesting is the circular astronomical observatory whose windows align with certain stars at the equinox and solstice. There's a sound-and-light show with English narration nightly at 9 PM. Open daily. Admission charge. About 75 miles (120 km) east of Mérida on the Valladolid–Puerto Juárez Hwy.

Uxmal – Uxmal (pronounced Oosh-*mahl*) is not as large as Chichén Itzá, but it is equally fascinating. The buildings here are purely Maya in style, without Toltec influences, and are lavishly decorated with masks, cornices, and mosaics. Uxmal means "built three times," but a number of structures appear to have been rebuilt as many as five times. Among the most remarkable sites are the extremely steep and somewhat oval Pyramid of the Magician; the Nunnery Quadrangle, whose façade contains many carved rain god masks, serpents, and figures of warriors; the House of the Doves, so named for the dovecote design in the roof comb; and the huge, ornately carved, 320-foot-long Governor's Palace. Uxmal has a sound-and-light show with a recorded English narrative of its history nightly at 9 PM (in Spanish at 7 PM). Open daily. Admission charge. About 61 miles (98 km) south of Mérida on the Mérida–Campeche Hwy.

Dzibilchaltún (pronounced Zee-bee-chal-*toon*) – The archaeological site closest to Mérida and the place believed to have been inhabited longest by the Maya — from about AD 1500 until the arrival of the conquerors. The Temple of the Seven Dolls is especially interesting during the spring and autumn equinoxes, when the light is reflected through parts of this strange structure. There's a *cenote* (sinkhole) that can be used for a welcome dip. Open daily 8 AM to 5 PM. Admission charge. About 13½ miles (22 km) north of Mérida, just off the road to Progreso.

Kabah – This ceremonial center 12 miles (19 km) south of Uxmal was built in the same architectural style, though smaller. For the most part unrestored, Kabah is most notable for its Palace of the Masks, the façade of which is covered with innumerable carved masks of the rain god, Chac. Also found at Kabah is the great arch, the gateway to the ancient causeway linking this city with Uxmal. Open daily 8 AM to 5 PM. Admission charge.

Sayil and Labná – A paved road has replaced the old dirt lane that leads to these two ceremonial centers that previously could be reached only by jeep. Little of either site has been restored, but it is still possible to appreciate the fine sculpture and carving that decorate the façades of their palaces. Open daily 8 AM to 5 PM. Admission charge. Sayil is 20 miles (32 km) from Uxmal; Labná, 5 miles (8 km) farther.

OUTSIDE OF TOWN

Hacienda Yaxocopoil – Twenty miles (32 km) south of Mérida, this was once one of the most important henequen plantations in the Yucatán, covering more than 22,000 acres and maintaining 1,000 head of cattle. Though much smaller now, the plantation is still in operation, and visitors can watch henequen being processed. Part of the main house has been converted into a museum, open daily from 8 AM to sunset and to 1 PM on Sundays. Admission charge.

■**EXTRA SPECIAL:** The Balankanchén Caverns, only 5 miles (8 km) from the ruins at Chichén Itzá, lay sealed for 500 years. Their beauty is impressive, and entering them today gives one the feeling of stepping into sacred space; in fact, the local descendants of the Maya, who used to hold ceremonies here, thought carefully before opening the caves to the public. The passageways are narrow and steep, and even small children have to stoop sometimes; those prone to claustrophobia stand forewarned. At the end of the caves is a perfectly clear pool that gives the impression of peering into a canyon. Groups are limited to a minimum of 3 and a maximum of 15 (oxygen gets scarce fast). Tours, which last 45 minutes, are given by local guides from 9 AM to 4 PM daily, with a break from noon to 2 PM, or can be arranged through travel agencies in Mérida. Admission charge.

SOURCES AND RESOURCES

 **TOURIST INFORMATION:** As in most Mexican cities, the best source of information about Mérida is your hotel's travel desk or desk clerk, or the tourist information center in the *Peón Contreras Theater,* which is open daily, 8 AM to 8 PM (phone: 249290). There is a US Consulate (453 Paseo Montejo and the corner of Colón; phone: 255409 or 255011). Bands, marimbas, folk dancers, and the like perform daily in one of the parks or plazas. A city-sponsored program known as "Mérida on Sunday" schedules some kind of entertainment at all parks and plazas, including an antiques fair at Santa Lucia Park. Schedules for such events are posted on the bulletin board at *Casa de la Cultura* (Calle 63 between Calles 64 and 66).

The free local publication *Discover It Mérida* provides tips on what to see and do, information on local history and customs, and good maps of the downtown area. Surprisingly, another good city map is the placemat in the coffee shop of *Los Aluxes*

hotel (Calle 60 near Calle 51). Buy English-language publications at *Discolibros Holly-wood,* a block from the zocalo, at 496 Calle 60.

TELEPHONE: The area code for Mérida is 99. When calling from one city to another in Mexico, dial 91 before the area code.

CLIMATE AND CLOTHES: It is always hot in Mérida. Sometimes cooler winds occasionally blow from the north, during January and early February, but on a chilly day you'll need only a sweater. The weather is generally tropical. It rains a lot in summer, which increases the humidity. Dress is casual, though shorts are not typical attire. When visiting the ruins, be sure to wear slacks and sturdy shoes.

GETTING AROUND: Bus – Routes are marked on the front of the buses, which stop at every corner. Buses to the archaeological zones leave from the terminal at Calle 69 between Calles 68 and 70. First and second class service is available to Uxmal. The first class service, which is specifically for the light and sound show, leaves at 5:15 PM and returns when the last show is over. A deluxe bus makes the trip to Chichén Itza. It costs a bit more, but is well worth it. Departure is at 6:30 and 8:30 AM. Buses to the nearby port of Progreso leave from Calle 62 between Calles 65 and 67.

Taxi – Cabs can be rented by the hour or on a per-trip basis. Make sure you settle the price before starting. Generally, the fare for a ride within the city proper is no more than $5.

Car Rental – Mérida has numerous car-rental agencies, including *Avis* (phone: 237856), *Hertz* (phone: 238975 and 249333), *Budget* (phone: 272708), and *Volkswagen* (phone: 218128). All have offices at the airport.

Calesa – These quaint horse-drawn buggies can be hired to take you around town. Pick one up at the plaza. For about $10 an hour, you can take a ride to Paseo Montejo or Colonia México, a modern residential suburb. The ride from the plaza and back should take about an hour. Be sure to bargain with the driver before getting in.

Tours – There are some 3 dozen tour operators in Mérida, and they provide a good way to see the archaeological ruins and other sights; just book with one through your hotel travel desk.

SPECIAL EVENTS: During *Carnaval* — which usually begins at the end of February — parades, dancing, and musical events are held throughout the week. *Mardi Gras* starts on the Thursday preceding *Ash Wednesday* and consists of parades, costumes, dances, bullfights, cockfights, and a king and queen contest. A fiesta in honor of *Our Lady of Guadalupe* in the San Sebastian parish runs from December 12 through 14. There are free concerts and regional dance recitals at one of Mérida's many parks every weekday night. The tourist office or your hotel can provide details.

SHOPPING: The public market, or *mercado,* on the corner of Calles 56 and 67, is a good place to find local crafts. The García Rejón handicrafts market is at Calles 65 and 62. It's usually less expensive than anyplace else in town if you have the patience to bargain. Shops (and offices) usually open between 8 and 9 AM, close for lunch and a siesta from 1 to 4 PM (when the sun is at its strongest), then open again at 8 PM.The most popular native crafts are bags and placemats made of sisal, a hemp fiber. Yucatecan hammocks of various sizes, made of fine cotton thread, are a great buy; another is the *jipi,* a fine version of the Panama hat, made by hand near Mérida. The *guayabera,* a tailored men's shirt in solid colors with embroidered front, is a typical Yucatán product that you can buy in shops throughout Mérida. The average price for a good cotton shirt with long sleeves is less than $20. Most stores also stock a few articles made from tortoiseshell and, of course, there are replicas of the Maya idols. Stores usually have fixed prices, so you can't bargain as in the market. The main shopping streets are Calles 57 and 59 in the 10-block area between Calles 54 and 64.

Casa de las Artesanías – There is no bargaining at the government-run handicrafts store, but the prices are very reasonable. 503 Calle 63 between Calles 64 and 66.

Guayaberas Jack – Theme and variations on the traditional *guaybera* — short and long sleeves, white or pastels, embroidered or plain. The best are 100% cotton. 507 Calle 59 between Calles 60 and 62 (phone: 215988).

Marie-Soliel Boutique – Fernando Huertas sells a tasteful selection of crafts, as well as his French-inspired designs in cotton. 511 Calle 59, between Calles 62 and 60 (phone: 216035).

Palacio – More of Fernando Huertas's selection, as found at the *Marie-Soliel Boutique.* Calle 62 between Calles 59 and 61 (phone: 218550).

 SPORTS: Baseball – The baseball season runs from March through August. The *estadio de béisbol,* or baseball stadium, is in Kukulcán Park.

Bullfighting – Bullfights are held on Sundays throughout the year, but the big-name matadors usually perform only from January through March. The *Plaza de Toros Mérida* is on Paseo de la Reforma, a block from Av. Colón.

Golf – There is an 18-hole golf course at *Club de Golf La Ceiba* (phone: 247525), about 9 miles (14 km) north of Mérida on the Progreso Hwy.

Hunting and Fishing – Hunting for duck, quail, deer, and wild boar is excellent, but you should check with the Mexican consulate nearest your home for information on regulations for importing arms (see GETTING READY TO GO). Manuel Cano (147 Calle 33, Progreso; phone: 50727) arranges hunting and fishing trips. Victor Vales at *Maya Tours* (425-4 Calle 60; phone: 993-243022) has a hunting club and is also quite reliable. Inquire at your hotel or the tourist information center. Good angling can be found at Río Lagartos, famous for the pink flamingos that call it home. It's worth the 100-mile (160 km) drive from Mérida.

Swimming – Almost all the hotels have small swimming pools, and there are nice beaches and good water skiing 20 miles (32 km) north, at Progreso and Telchac Puerto.

Tennis – The *Holiday Inn* has 1 court (phone: 256877), *Club Campestre* (phone: 271700) has 16 clay and synthetic lighted courts, and there are several courts at *Club de Golf La Ceiba* (phone: 247525).

 NIGHTCLUBS AND NIGHTLIFE: After-dark action is on the quiet side in Mérida. The *Panamerica Calinda* (phone: 23911) has a Mexican fiesta Friday and Saturday evenings and regional dances other nights. *Los Tulipanes* (462 Calle 42; no phone) is where tour buses take the crowds to see native dancers, while the *Montejo Palace* (phone: 247644) has a rooftop supper club, and the *Misión Mérida* (phone: 239500) has a nightclub. *Pancho's* (phone: 230942) has live music and dancing Wednesdays through Saturdays. The *Trovedor Bohemio* (no phone) and *Peregrina Piano Bar* (no phone) by Santa Lucia Park both offer drinks and relaxed entertainment, including guitar music. *Kalia Rock House* (no phone), about 10 minutes from downtown, and *Excess* (no phone) are the current favorites. The *Holiday Inn's* nightclub (phone: 256877) is also a popular nightspot, as are the *Oasis, Charro* (no phones), *El Cocoon* at the *Panamerica Calinda* (phone: 23911), and *Bin Bon Bao* (no phone).

BEST IN TOWN

 CHECKING IN: Mérida offers a wide assortment of hotels, both in the downtown area and around the elegant Paseo Montejo. For a double room, expect to pay about $155 for those places we list as very expensive; $75 to $100 at an expensive hotel; $40 to $70 in moderate; and $35 or under in inexpensive. All hotels listed below accept MasterCard and Visa; some also accept American Express and Diners Club. All telephone numbers are in the 99 area code unless otherwise indicated. When calling from one city to another within Mexico, dial 91 before the area code.

MÉRIDA

Paraíso Maya – Set on a wide strip of beach at Progreso, this colonial-style hostelry was built to resemble a small Mexican village. There are restaurants, bars, a pool, and disco. The rate includes meals, drinks, and water sports. Km 32 Carr. Progreso-Telchac (phone: 281351 in Mérida; 800-331-9970 in the US; FAX: 232700). Very expensive.

Fiesta Inn Mérida – On the Gulf of Mexico, 22 miles (35 km) from Mérida, this hostelry has 88 rooms, beautiful gardens, 4 synthetic tennis courts, a restaurant, and satellite TV. Transportation to Mérida is complimentary. 91 Calle 19 (phone: 993-50300; 800-FIESTA-1 in the US; FAX: 993-50690). Expensive.

Holiday Inn – Built in the colonial manner, with old trees incorporated into the design. There are 213 rooms and suites, a tennis court, pool, nightclub, and a fine specialty restaurant. Air conditioned. Just off Paseo Montejo at Av. Colón and Calle 60 (phone: 256877; 800-HOLIDAY in the US; FAX: 257755). Expensive.

Sian Ka'an – A pleasant inn and beach club, it offers 22 rooms and suites, a restaurant, bar, and water sports. Carr. Chelem-Progreso, Ycalpetén, Progreso (phone: 993-51243). Expensive.

Los Aluxes – A modern hostelry, it rises white and impressively spotless between Paseo de Montejo and the zocalo. It has an outdoor pool and poolside bars, dining room, and a cheerful coffee shop whose placemats are the best city map available. 109 rooms. 444 Calle 60, between Calles 49 and 51 (phone: 242199; 800-782-8395 in the US; FAX: 233858). Moderate.

Casa del Balam – Only 2 blocks from the plaza, this neo-colonial establishment has 54 rooms, a swimming pool set in an attractive patio, a good dining room, and a bar. Air conditioned. At Calles 57 and 60 (phone: 248241; 800-624-8451 in the US; FAX: 245011). Moderate.

El Castellano – With 170 rooms, it's one of Mérida's largest and sleekest hotels, including a spacious, hacienda-style lobby. Amenities include shops, restaurant, bar, and swimming pool. Air conditioned. 513 Calle 57, between Calles 62 and 64 (phone: 230100; FAX: 263389). Moderate.

Misión Mérida – Entrance is through a beautiful 19th-century mansion. The 147 rooms are located in a modern tower, and have air conditioning and cable TV. There's a coffee shop, lobby bar, and restaurant. Three blocks from the zocalo at 491 Calle 60 (phone: 239500; 800-648-7818 in the US; FAX: 800-648-7818). Moderate.

Montejo Palace – Quiet, with 90 rooms, all with refrigerators and small balconies. In addition to a dining room and a good coffee shop, *Las Farolas,* there is a cocktail lounge. Air conditioned. 483C Paseo Montejo (phone: 247644; 800-221-6509 in the US; FAX: 280388). Moderate.

Panamerica Calinda Mérida – A Quality Hotels property with a lobby and reception area housed in a turn-of-the-century mansion, it has 110 modern, air conditioned rooms, color TV sets, a restaurant, and a bar. There is a Mexican fiesta Friday and Saturday nights; regional dances from the state of Yucatán are performed other nights. Downtown at Calle 59 between Calles 52 and 53 (phone: 239111; 800-228-5151 in the US; FAX: 248090). Moderate.

Autel 59 – A comfortable, modern property just a few blocks from the main plaza. Its 106 rooms are all air conditioned, and there's a restaurant and pool. 546 Calle 59 at Calle 68 (phone: 242100). Inexpensive.

Caribe – Once a convent, this small hacienda-like hotel now has 66 rooms, some with air conditioning, and a pool. 500 Rincón del Parque Hidalgo and Calle 60 (phone: 249022; FAX: 248733). Inexpensive.

Casa México – American Roger Lynn took an interesting 150-year-old Mérida home, complete with patios, sundecks, and balconies, and turned it into a bed and breakfast establishment, filled with antiques and crafts that reflect his love of the country. The 5 rooms have private baths, and there is a pool and Jacuzzi on the central patio. Mr. Lynn arranges for transportation from the airport. 485 Calle 68 between 57 and 59 (phone: 214032; 800-538-6802 in the US). Inexpensive.

Colón – An old-fashioned, air conditioned gem, a block from the zocalo, it has a pool, sauna, a pleasant restaurant, and breakfast buffet. Twelve of the 53 rooms have steam baths. 483 Calle 62 (phone: 234355; FAX: 244919). Inexpensive.

Del Gobernador – A tidy, tasteful spot, it offers a good restaurant, a bar with live music several times a week, and a very small pool. 535 Calle 59 at Calle 66 (phone: 237133; 800-458-6888 in the US; FAX: 281590). Inexpensive.

Gran – This replica of a turn-of-the-century French hotel has elaborate ceilings, columns, and large, old-fashioned rooms, some air conditioned. The 3-story building centers around a delightful patio. There is a good dining room. Cepeda Peraza Park (phone: 247622). Inexpensive.

Paseo de Montejo – A 5-story modern colonial-style establishment, it has 92 air conditioned rooms, color TV sets, restaurant, bar, and pool. 482 Paseo de Montejo (phone: 239033; FAX: 280388). Inexpensive.

Posada Toledo – Only some rooms are air conditioned, but it's set in a gorgeous old house that is furnished with antiques and has a magnificent garden in the patio. The owner speaks English. This is a delightful alternative to larger, more impersonal establishments. Three blocks from the plaza at 487 Calle 58 (phone: 232256). Inexpensive.

CHICHÉN ITZÁ

Hacienda Chichén – Just a century ago this was a hacienda; today it is a hotel with rooms available in individual bungalows. Facilities include ceiling fans, restaurant, bar, and a pool. Open from November through *Easter*. Chichén Itzá (phone: 985-62777; 248722 in Mérida; 800-824-8451 in the US). Expensive.

Mayaland – A fine, old-fashioned resort complex with ceiling fans in every room, a sweeping stairway, and a pool set amid tropical gardens. It could be the setting for a 1930s movie starring Sydney Greenstreet. Chichén Itzá (phone: 252122 in Mérida; 800-235-4079 in the US; FAX: 62777). Expensive.

Misión Inn Chichén Itzá – This modern hotel has 48 air conditioned rooms, bar, restaurant, pool, and lovely grounds. Pisté, about a mile (1.6 km) from Chichén Itzá (phone: 239500 in Mérida; FAX: 237665). Moderate.

Villa Arqueológica – One of the archaeological "inns" run by Club Med, only 5 minutes from the ruins. All rooms are air conditioned, and there is a pool, tennis, and a good French restaurant (phone: 62830; 5-203-3086 in Mexico City; FAX: 5-203-0621 in Mexico City). Moderate.

Pirámide Inn – So comfortable, it's hard to leave it to explore the ruins. Facilities include a pool, tennis courts, lush gardens, restaurant, bar, even a book exchange. The 47 air conditioned rooms are adequate. Chichén Itzá (phone: Pisté, Exchange No. 5). Inexpensive.

Dolores Alba – Absolutely lovely and a nice change of pace from hotel stays, this country house has only 18 rooms, each with a private terrace. There's also a cozy dining room, pool, and tropical grounds. You'll need a car to get about. Km 122, between Chichén Itzá and the Balankanchén Caves (phone: 213714; FAX: 283163 in Mérida). Very inexpensive.

UXMAL

Hacienda Uxmal – Elegant and charming, it has large, cool rooms, some air conditioned, that overlook lovely gardens. Restaurant, bar, shops, and 2 pools. Uxmal (phone: 232597; 252133 in Mérida; FAX: 247142). Expensive.

Misión Inn Uxmal – A modern, air conditioned place, with a restaurant and pool. Uxmal (phone: 247308; FAX: 247308). Moderate.

Villa Arqueológica – Right in front of the ruins, this air conditioned hostelry is equipped with the standard facilities of all Club Med *Villas Arqueológicas:* a good French restaurant, pool, and tennis (phone: 247053 in Uxmal; 5-203-3086 in Mexico City; FAX: 5-203-0681 in Mexico City). Inexpensive.

 EATING OUT: The Yucatán has a distinct cuisine. Very little chili is used in cooking, although it is served alongside the main dish as a sauce. Many meat and fish dishes are wrapped in banana leaves and then baked in outdoor ovens, a method that originated because of the hot climate. Pickled and charcoal-broiled meats are Yucatecan specialties, too. Try the *cochinita pibil* (pork baked in banana leaves); *papadzul* (hard-boiled eggs chopped into a filling for tortilla topped with a sauce of ground pumpkin seeds); *panuchos* (open-face tortilla topped with chicken and pickled onion); and *pollo pibil* (chicken baked with achiote sauce in banana leaves). The *Misión* hotels in Mérida, Uxmal, and Chichén Itzá all have fine dining rooms, as do the *Villas Arqueológicas,* the *Haciendas Chichén* and *Uxmal,* and the *Mayaland.* Expect to pay up to $40 for a meal for two in the restaurants we've listed as expensive; $25 at those places listed as moderate; and about $15 at inexpensive ones. Prices do not include drinks, wine, or tip. Reservations are advised at midday for all expensive places. In the evening, reservations are unnecessary unless otherwise noted. Most restaurants listed below accept MasterCard and Visa; some also accept American Express and Diners Club. Unless otherwise noted, all restaurants are open daily. All telephone numbers are in the 99 area code unless otherwise indicated. When calling from one city to another within Mexico, dial 91 before the area code.

Alberto's Continental Patio – Set in a lovely colonial mansion with outdoor and indoor dining areas, the Lebanese dishes here are first rate. There are also some continental and local specialties. The service is very friendly. 482 Calle 64 (phone: 212298). Expensive.

Amarantus – Decorated with light wood and rattan and lots of plants, this bright, spacious spot serving continental food is cheerful and friendly. There's a video bar with live music. 250 Paseo de Montejo (phone: 268752). Expensive.

Carlos 'n' Charlie's – A member of the Anderson group popular throughout Mexico, it features good salads and oysters, and winsome waiters. 447-A Prolongación Montejo (no phone). Expensive.

La Casona – Fifteen tile tables with caned chairs rim an interior courtyard with a lovely fountain; there's also an inside dining room, sporting unusual antique barber's chairs at the bar. Italian food, including homemade pasta, is the highlight, but the steaks and seafood rate, too. The restaurant's cellar stocks French and Mexican wines. Open for lunch and dinner. 434 Calle 60 at Calle 47 (phone: 238348). Expensive.

Château Valentín – Converted from one of Mérida's elegant 18th-century homes, this establishment serves well-prepared regional fare such as *pollo pibil* and *pzic venado,* as well as international dishes. 499-D Calle 58-A (phone: 255690). Expensive.

Le Gourmet – Once an elegant home, it specializes in French and creole cooking and is where the local gentry go to celebrate on big nights out. Closed Sundays. 109-A Av. Pérez Ponce (phone: 271970). Expensive.

Muelle 8 – Well-presented, fresh seafood is served in a wharf warehouse setting where you can almost taste the salty air. 142 Calle 21 (phone: 274976). Expensive.

Pancho's – In spite of its Mexican name, the owner is Canadian and the menu is continental, with lots of flambéed dishes prepared tableside. With its ancient photos and Victrola, it resembles an old antiques store. Kind of like *Carlos 'n' Charlie's,* Maya-style. Live music and dancing are featured Wednesdays through Saturdays. Dinner only. 509 Calle 59, between Calles 60 and 62 (phone: 230942). Expensive.

Picadilly's – An elegant English-style pub, but the atmosphere is casual (ties and jackets are not required) and the fine food is strictly *gringo:* barbecued ribs, onion rings, pasta, and grilled beef, with cherry cheesecake for dessert. Live music and dancing are featured in the evenings. 118 Av. Pérez Ponce (phone: 265391). Expensive.

El Pórtico del Peregrino – It consists of romantic courtyards and dining rooms in a chapel-like setting. The low-key atmosphere is enhanced by a menu that includes shrimp grilled in garlic, chicken liver shish kebab, baked eggplant casserole with chicken, delicious desserts, and homemade sangria. On Calle 57 between Calles 60 and 62 (phone: 216844). Expensive.

Yannig – Named after its inspired chef, this small, sophisticated spot set in a beautiful old home delivers well-prepared and appetizingly presented dishes, among them crêpes with a mild roquefort sauce, New Orleans-style chicken, and *popiette* (fish and mushrooms in a pastry shell). Open for lunch and dinner. 105 Av. Pérez Ponce (phone: 270339). Expensive.

Los Almendros – This is one of the best places to sample the finest in *cochinita pibil, panuchos, pollo pibil, papadzul,* and other Yucatecan delicacies. Service is slow, so be prepared to spend a long time. 493 Calle 50-A, between Calles 57 and 59, in front of the Plaza de Mejorada (phone: 212851). Moderate.

La Prosperidad – The local favorite, hands down, it serves Yucatecan dishes in a large, thatch-roofed dining room. A variety of appetizers accompanies each meal. Entertainment is live and lively, as is the ambience. Good fun. Calle 56, corner of Calle 53 (phone: 211898). Moderate.

Siqueff – An unassuming, cheerful place with hearty fare, its menu includes venison fillet (in season). The fruit drinks made with bottled water are quite good. There is also take-out service and, rare among restaurants here, a public phone. 553 Calle 59, corner of Calle 68 (phone: 249287). Moderate.

Dulcería y Sorbetería Colón – A well-known, well-loved ice cream parlor. All the ice cream is made with fresh fruit (coconut is the most popular flavor), and you get a lot of it for a little money. No credit cards accepted. On the plaza and at Paseo Montejo between Calles 39 and 41 (phone: 213304). Inexpensive.

Jugos California – This Art Deco bar serves only juices, but what juices! Luscious tropical fruits line the walls, and all the drinks are made with honey. No credit cards accepted. Calles 62 and 63, on the plaza, and elsewhere around the city. (phone: 234142). Inexpensive.

Kon Tiki – If you're hungering for Chinese food, here's the local place to go. All the usual dishes, surprisingly well prepared. 194 Colón and Calle 14 (phone: 254409). Inexpensive.

Yaxbé – Almost identical to *Xaybé* in Chichén Itza (below), and run by the same owner, it's conveniently located at the edge of the ruins (no phone). Inexpensive.

CHICHÉN ITZÁ

Xaybe – A large, airy place with leather-strung chairs and a handsome wrought-iron mural, it offers attentive service and a fixed-price menu that includes good broiled pork chops and baked chicken. There are also buffets for large groups and a generous selection of mixed drinks. In the nearby town of Pisté (phone: 271233 in Mérida). Inexpensive.

MEXICO CITY

To describe Mexico City is to describe much of Mexico. It is the political, cultural, social, and economic center of the country, a city of about 18 million people — the largest city in the world — that is a magnet drawing Mexicans from all around the country at a rate of about 1,000 people a week. Everything that is Mexican originates or is represented here, and Mexicans call it simply Mexico, just as Americans refer to New York City as New York. In fact, the city gave its name to the country: After independence, the colonial designation New Spain was dropped. It is the one destination that virtually all visitors to Mexico share, the common terminus of the major north-south highways (see DIRECTIONS), and the best place from which to start tours of the Yucatán Peninsula, the jungles of Chiapas, and the southern reaches of Mexico's long Pacific coast, from Manzanillo to Acapulco.

Eighteen million inhabitants are in the Federal District (DF stands for *Distrito Federal;* the city is governed by the president through an appointed mayor, the chief of the Federal District) and another 4 million across the line in suburbs that are part of the state of Mexico. (A distressing result of Mexico City's expanding population, coupled with Mexico's general economic malaise, is a huge infusion of street vendors — selling everything from chewing gum to imported kitchen knives — jugglers, fire eaters, window washers, and beggars.)

Bigness is not something about which the *capitalinos* are very happy, but there it is. Lately, programs have been started to decentralize matters. No new industry is being allowed to come in, and for several years there was talk of moving some government agencies to the provinces, a step already taken by several large companies. After the September 1985 earthquake, it appeared that serious plans were being made to relocate several government ministries, including tourism, out of the Federal District. Although many thousands of people did leave the capital, moving huge bureaucracies proved to be much more difficult (and more expensive) than had been anticipated. The provinces simply did not have the infrastructure necessary to accommodate thousands of new residents, and the plans began and ended with the move of the Bureau of Federal Roads and Bridges to the *Casa de Piedra* hotel in Cuernavaca.

Tourists often can fly directly to Acapulco or Baja or the Yucatán without ever setting foot in the capital, but if you haven't seen Mexico City, you can't claim to have seen Mexico. The city is one of the oldest continuously inhabited areas in North America, and is at least a competitor for that title in the world. Some 20,000 years ago, small Indian villages were scattered across the Valley of Mexico (Valle de Anáhuac), a 570-square-mile plain in south-central Mexico, completely surrounded by mountains. The plain is more than 7,000 feet above sea level; the mountains that ring it rise another 3,000 feet.

Today, Mexico City covers about a tenth of the area of the valley, rising in the northwest along a series of hills that offers splendid views of the city below and the twin-capped volcanoes to the southeast, Popocatépetl and Ixtaccíhuatl, known affectionately as Popo and the White Lady. Each is more than 17,000 feet high, and among the saddest aspects of the overpopulation and overindustrialization of the district is the almost constant low-lying, yellowish smog that obscures the valley from the mountaintops, and vice versa.

The valley has changed radically since the first Indians settled here. At that time, the entire valley was a series of larger and smaller lakes dotted with islands and divided by masses of spongy land. The first villages were established around the lakes and islands, and the Indians developed a relatively secure, sophisticated agricultural life; the first corn ever cultivated by man was grown 100 miles east of the present city. Each island village was something of an independent state. In 1325 (1321 in some accounts), a branch of the Aztec, seeking a site for a permanent home, wandered into the valley and saw an eagle, perched on a cactus, in the act of devouring a snake. This they took as a sign from the gods and built their city on the spot, calling it Tenochtitlán. The eagle appeared in what is today Mexico City's zocalo, at the end of Madero. The Aztec built a temple here, and it was the site of the Halls of Montezuma (or Móctezuma, as the former Aztec chieftan is called in Mexico).

The Aztec were an aggressive and fierce tribe, and within 2 centuries they had conquered all the surrounding territory and were extracting taxes in the form of produce, slaves, and precious metal from tribes as far away as Acapulco, Veracruz, and Guatemala. When Hernán Cortés entered the city in 1519, he found a metropolis of 300,000 people built across several islands with subtly engineered bridges and sluices, wide avenues, great temples, marketplaces, and public buildings that rivaled any in Europe. Bernal Díaz, whose journals record Cortés's conquest, declared that Tenochtitlán was a city more impressive than Venice.

The Spanish ruled Mexico for 3 centuries, and during that time the foundation of modern Mexico City was built. In their zeal to destroy every trace of the Aztec, they tore down all of the public and religious monuments in the city and virtually leveled the rest of Tenochtitlán, often building churches and government buildings in the very spots where ancient temples had stood. They destroyed with great religious fervor, and built a European clone on what had been the most glorious city in the Western Hemisphere.

The city they built was spectacular in its own right and, because they pursued a policy of serious sanitation and drainage, a good deal more hygienic than the Aztec capital had been. Most of Mexico's important colonial landmarks are still standing. During Emperor Maximilian's short reign (1864–1867), the Paseo de la Reforma was laid out in a frank imitation of the Champs-Elysées in Paris. A walk down the Reforma, or from Lázaro Cárdenas to the zocalo along Madero, offers views of much of the city's Spanish and European heritage — from the ancient Church of San Francisco, built by Cortés with stones taken from the Aztec temple that stood on the site, to Iturbide Palace, the wonderfully preserved baroque mansion that was the home of Agustín de Iturbide, a Mexican emperor.

The zocalo is the very heart of the city — and of the country. Surrounded by the National Palace, the city halls (there are two of them, nearly identical, one dating from the 18th century and the other, a copy, completed in 1948), the Metropolitan Cathedral, and the National Pawnshop, the zocalo has seen revolutions, coronations — even Mexico's first bullfight.

Massive restoration has been carried out in what has been officially designated as the Historic Center of Mexico City. In a manner of speaking, it has become one great outdoor museum. Most of the buildings have been declared national monuments and have tiles telling something of their history. Paving blocks have replaced asphalt, and many streets are closed to automobile traffic. Turn-of-the-century electric globes now illuminate the neighborhood, and store merchants are toning down their more garish signs. Right next to the zocalo itself, archaeologists have uncovered the site of the Great Temple of the Aztec; this is one of the most exciting digs undertaken in Mexico in recent memory.

Over the years, the city simply spread out from the zocalo, Los Angeles style, but in the last couple of decades high-rises have begun poking their penthouses into the smoggy clouds. The old suburbs, such as Coyoacán and San Angel to the south, have retained their identity, but they are surrounded by neighborhoods that all too often are concrete slums.

This explosion has brought inevitable changes and inevitable problems. Until some 30 years ago, the siesta was as much a part of life in the capital as in villages in the most remote provinces. Workers would go home to eat a hearty midday meal and then nap before returning to work. Even from the center of the city, most people could be home within 15 minutes. Today, with the size of the city and the eternally congested traffic, most of a 2- or 3-hour lunch break would be devoured simply in getting home. At the same time, working hours have been staggered to ease traffic problems, and many government offices start as early as 8 AM, factories and some private offices at 7, banks at 9, and stores at 10; some executives come into their offices at 10 or 11. If you go to a restaurant for a very early dinner, it's likely that you will find people still dallying over their lunch.

Anyone flying into the Valley of Anáhuac today is struck by the thick haze of smog that floats above the city. Planes cross the high, beautiful barrier of the surrounding mountains only to descend through a thick layer of perpetual murk. Much of this comes from Mexico City's vehicular traffic, a snarling mess at best. There are over 2.5 million cars in use in the city — new, old, functioning, and only half functioning — pouring their noxious fumes into the thin air at 7,000 feet. There is rarely a time when the streets are really deserted in the metropolitan area. Traffic slacks off between 1 and 4 AM, but by 5 the buses are back on the streets and the tempo of traffic begins to increase again. In response to the severe pollution problem, the government has begun taking steps to improve Mexico City's air quality. Restrictions on driving have been imposed, and the government has considered stopping all industrial activity in the city if pollution levels become unbearable. In the spring of 1991, the government announced the closing of the city's largest government-run oil refinery. The cost of shutting down the plant was an estimated $500 million, but officials believe the closure is crucial to the health of Mexico City residents. The refinery will be rebuilt outside of the city, and the 430 acres on which it stood will be used for public parks. It will be some time before the air's improvement can be measured, but the government is on the right track, and touring the city can only prove to be more pleasant in coming years.

Considering its size, it's not surprising that Mexico City is an easy town in which to get lost. Walking can be confusing enough; driving is maddening. Streets change names as they cross from one neighborhood into another; neighborhoods are called *colonias,* and there are about 1,000 of them in 16 districts referred to as *delegaciones.* Only one avenue, Insurgentes, keeps the same name, as it runs the entire length of the city. To improve matters, a number of expressways have been built and the subway system is being expanded, tasks that involve much construction and numerous detours.

There are, as well, a great many curving and diagonal streets running obstacle courses around the city's many small squares, parks, and traffic circles. These make for three- and five-sided blocks, which add to the confusion. If you must drive, a required companion should be the *Guía Roji* map and street guide, which is available at any newsstand or bookshop and gives all the city streets and *colonias,* with routes, bus lanes, and subway and streetcar lines marked out. It costs about $5 and is well worth the price.

A far better transportation alternative is to take taxis during your stay in the city. Prices are reasonable compared to US fares, and if you don't speak Spanish, you can have your destination written on a piece of paper.

Mexico City residents may be demons behind the wheel of a car, but on foot they revert to type. They saunter, they stroll, they stop in the middle of the sidewalk to talk. No green space is left empty, no park bench totally unoccupied. Constant nibblers, they have turned the coffee break into a sidewalk-sitting art. It is a way of enjoying the city, of taking in the passing scene. And who can blame them? Mexico City is a place to be studied, a city that assails the senses with everything from the pervasive smell of flowers (the dividing lanes of major highways are filled with flowers that change with the seasons — dahlias and mums in fall, poinsettias at *Christmas,* azaleas in the spring) to the barking of street vendors and beggars, and the spectacle of the street markets "on wheels."

Markets are dear to the heart of every Mexican woman. Even with refrigeration, the great majority of Mexicans still buy produce daily. Marketing is a social event, especially for Mexico City maids, who can take an hour to buy two or three items while exchanging the daily gossip with other maids in the area. Deprive a maid of this daily outing and she will start looking for a new employer.

Ten years ago the largest of hundreds of markets was *La Merced,* a central produce market surrounded by warehouses, covering several blocks in the eastern part of the city along Calle General Anaya. In 1982, the warehouses were moved to the *Central de Abastos* produce market in the Ixtapalapa district. However, *La Merced* remains one of the city's most bustling commercial centers, a virtual street circus, as notable for its colorful characters — organ-grinders, tumblers, clowns, trained dogs — as for its more than 3,000 stalls offering a remarkable assortment of fruits and vegetables.

The city comes vibrantly alive on Sundays — it's one large carnival of activities. There is no better day to explore the city, and the best place to start is at the floating gardens of Xochimilco. When the Aztec empire began to expand across the vale, the small amount of farmland in the valley (which was mostly islands and lakes) disappeared. The ever-resourceful Aztec solved the problem by building dirt-covered rafts on which they planted their crops. The "floating islands" have long since taken root in the shallow waters, but Xochimilco continues to be an important producer of flowers and vegetables for Mexico City. You can ride a gondola through the canals or rent a boat on your own. Everywhere there are floating vendors hawking their wares (resist the temptation to buy a taco or fresh fruit either here or in any other Mexican market).

Sunday is also generally the day for bullfights. Tickets go on sale on Friday, but it is a better idea to let the travel desk at your hotel get them for you. They can obtain better seats and can also arrange transportation.

Sunday is also the day of the big sidewalk art fair at Parque Sullivan, where Paseo de la Reforma crosses Avenida Insurgentes. There's a wide variety of paintings — not by nationally known artists, to be sure, but often of high quality nevertheless. Best of all, the prices are right and the atmosphere is festive.

Don't miss the *Thieves' Market,* which spreads all over the street of Rayón on Sunday. It's adjacent to the *Lagunilla Market* (between Calles Allende and Chile, 8 or 9 blocks north of Calle Madero). There are genuine and (mostly) fake antiques, lots of old books (some of them in English), new power tools, antique keys, odds and ends of china, crystal bottle stoppers, cheap plastic toys, copper and brass articles, old clothes, new clothes, carpets, and furniture. Almost anything can be found here if you have the patience to look for it. It's also a great place to test your skill at bargaining. Never act interested in an item. If possible, hang back and see how much native buyers are paying for similar goods. Whatever the seller asks for an item, look pained and shake your head no. Then make an offer of about half or two-thirds the asking price. At first, visitors feel uneasy and uncomfortable about bargaining. In the markets, however, it is expected and accepted.

There are concerts and other types of live entertainment on Sundays at Alameda Park and at the most popular park of all, Chapultepec. Thousands of Mexican families spend Sunday afternoon there having picnic lunches or just strolling. Chapultepec's 2,100 acres include woods, playgrounds, lakes for boating, museums, a wonderful zoo, lavish botanical gardens, and a delightful amusement park. Started as the royal hunting grounds of the Aztec, it has been a place dedicated to enjoyment ever since. And it's at its best on Sunday afternoons.

The frantic nature of Mexico City's urban life was rudely interrupted in September 1985 by a massive earthquake (and subsequent aftershocks) that destroyed significant segments of the city. Most of its effects were quickly cleaned up, and repairs made, leaving no major evidence of the quake today. It's just another example of Mexico City's resilience in the face of some of the modern era's most vexing urban problems.

MEXICO CITY AT-A-GLANCE

SEEING THE CITY: The best all-encompassing view of the city is available from the observation deck of the 44-story Torre Latino Americana building on the southeast corner of Eje Central Lázaro Cárdenas and Calle Madero. One floor below is a restaurant and bar where you can relax and enjoy the view. The *Holiday Inn Crown Plaza*'s rooftop restaurant, the *Majestic*, offers a great view of the zocalo. The rooftop lounge of the *Seville Palace* also provides a spectacular view, as do the terraces and rooftop garden of Chapultepec Castle in Chapultepec Park.

SPECIAL PLACES: Mexico City's top tourist attractions are for the most part concentrated in several distinct areas, each of which could be explored in a day or so. Foremost is the historic area surrounding the zocalo; for shopping and nightclubbing, there's the Zona Rosa — the Pink Zone; for relaxation and beauty, there's Chapultepec Park, with the *Museo Nacional de Antropología* (National Museum of Anthropology) and other museums; north of the city are the pyramids; south are the strikingly beautiful National University and the floating gardens at Xochimilco.

ZOCALO

Formally Cube de la Constitución, the heart of the city, the zocalo, is the second-largest square in the world; only Red Square in Moscow is larger. It occupies what was once the ancient Aztec marketplace, and is also the site of the fabled Halls of Montezuma.

Palacio Nacional (National Palace) – Originally built as headquarters for Cortés from the rubble left from the destruction of Montezuma's palace, it later became the official residence of the Spanish viceroys. It was used by Emperor Maximilian during his short reign, and then by all the Presidents of Mexico. In addition to the presidential offices, it also houses the Finance Ministry, and the *Benito Juárez Museum* (closed Wednesdays and holidays; no admission charge). There are three patios, but only the center one, with its magnificent murals by Rivera, is open to the public. Over the center portal hangs the Liberty Bell, which was rung by Father Miguel Hidalgo in 1810 to rally his followers, the event that marked the beginning of the struggle for independence. Try to time your visit for late afternoon, when you will be able to see the changing of the guard. This is also the place to be for *El Grito* festivities, a national event commencing at 11 PM every September 15, when the president rings the Liberty Bell to signal the start of the celebration of Mexico's independence. The zocalo below is filled with celebrating Mexicans. The best way to see the ceremony is to take a table in the open-air *Terraza Colonial* restaurant atop the *Majestic* hotel or reserve a room facing the zocalo at the *Howard Johnson Gran Hotel.*

Catedral Metropolitana (Metropolitan Cathedral) – The cornerstone was laid in 1562, but it took 250 years to complete this imposing edifice. As a result, it reflects the most popular architectural styles of the 16th, 17th, and 18th centuries. Several of the 14 chapels are done in the wildly ornamental baroque style known as churrigueresque, a word derived from the name of the Spanish artisan José Churriguera. There are three altars besides the main one, plus a large choir stall, a sacristy, and a chapter room, all rich in art treasures. Next door, the façade of the chapel (*sagrario*) is considered the finest example of churrigueresque architecture in the city. North side of the zocalo.

Church of Santo Domingo – Set on a charming little plaza 3 blocks north of the zocalo, this beautiful church played a role in the Holy Inquisition. Professional letter writers work under the arches around the plaza typing out love notes and business letters for the illiterate. The church is on the north side of the Plaza de Santo Domingo.

Museo de las Culturas (Museum of Cultures) – In a historic building that was used as a mint during the colonial period, this museum has a widely varied collection of artifacts and art objects from Southeast Asia, ancient Greece, Africa, Oceania, Japan, Israel, Egypt, northern Europe, and all the Americas. Many of the rooms are closed to the public pending restoration, but nine rooms are open for viewing, and there is a delightful patio. Closed Mondays. No admission charge. North of the National Palace at 13 Calle Moneda (phone: 512-6452).

Monte de Piedad (National Pawnshop) – Literally translated, the name means Mountain of Pity. It was started in 1775 by the Count of Regla and offers low-interest loans on personal property. Of particular interest is the large corner room, which has jewelry, and a smaller room on the inside passageway, which has antiques. Closed Sundays. Across from the cathedral on the northeast corner of the zocalo (no phone).

Templo Mayor (Great Temple and Museum) – Accidentally unearthed in 1978 by the Mexican Power and Light Company, the Great Temple was once the holiest shrine of the Aztec Empire, depicting the legend of the god Huitzilopochtli, who avenged the death of his mother Coatlicue at the hands of his sister Coyolzauhqui on Coatepec ("hill of the serpents"). Artifacts found include an enormous sculpture representing Coyolzauhqui decapitated and dismembered, the Tizoc sacrificial stone, a sculptured seashell, and numerous weapons, masks, statues, and other artifacts that have been exhibited in museums around the world.

The *Museum of the Great Temple,* designed to house all these artifacts, stood half-completed for years and finally opened its doors in October 1987. To reproduce the concept of the temple itself, the museum is divided into two sections. The south wing is dedicated to Huitzilopochtli, the god of war, and provides background on how Tenochtitlán was settled, offering insights into the religious, political, and social structure of the Aztec, as well as the importance of war and sacrifice, tribute and commerce. The Hall of Monoliths contains impressive sculptures found during the excavations, including the *Guerreros Aguila* (Eagle Warriors). The north wing, dedicated to Tlaloc, the water god, contains a reproduction of part of the temple, a scale model of the sacred city, an exhibit of the fauna found in the offerings, and another on aspects of the people's daily lives. Finally, there is a room that tells the story of the conquest from the points of view of both the natives and Hernán Cortés. Guided tours in English are available by appointment (phone: 542-0606). Closed Mondays. One admission charge for both museums. Just off the zocalo.

Gran Hotel de la Ciudad de México – Set in Victorian splendor on the zocalo and Calle 16 de Septiembre, this building was constructed in 1899 to house Mexico City's first shopping center, *Centro Mercantil.* The façade belies the beauty of its Art Nouveau interior: a magnificent stained glass domed ceiling, a monumental wrought-iron French-style staircase, cage elevators, and singing birds in brass cages (no phone).

DOWNTOWN

Bellas Artes (Palace of Fine Arts) – The lavish, stunning opera house, famous for the striking Tiffany stained glass curtain, seats 3,500 people in opulent splendor. Construction was started in 1900 under the regime of Porfirio Díaz and was finished 34 years later at the then-staggering cost of $15 million. Built of Italian marble, the building is so heavy that it has sunk 15 feet into Mexico City's spongy subsoil. The lobbies of the balconies have murals by Rivera, Orozco, Tamayo, Siqueiros, and Gonzales Camarena. Most notable is a Rivera mural that's a replica of a controversial mural Rivera did for Rockefeller Center in New York. The mural, which, among other things, contained a portrait of Lenin, horrified the Rockefellers so much that they ordered it painted over. The striking building across the street at Calle Tacuba and Eje Central

Lazaro Cardenus is the main post office. The museum is closed Mondays and holidays. No admission charge. Corner of Av. Juárez and Eje Central Lázaro Cárdenas (phone: 585-4888).

National Art Museum – This magnificent building was constructed during Porfirio Díaz's administration to house the Ministry of Communications and Transport. It was then used as the National Archives and in 1983 was converted into a museum displaying art from the pre-Hispanic, colonial, and modern eras. Closed Mondays and holidays. Admission charge. 8 Tacuba, a few steps from Eje Central Lázaro Cárdenas (phone: 521-7320).

Casa de los Azulejos (House of Tiles) – This handsome house was built in 1596. The history of the place is fascinating. The son of one of the Counts of Valle de Orizaba was considered a ne'er-do-well by his father, who once chastised him with the remark "You will never have a house of tiles," that is, "You will never make good." The son set to work and became very wealthy. When he acquired this lovely house, he had every square inch of the façade covered with white and blue tiles. It's now occupied by *Sanborn's,* which has a restaurant, drugstore, and gift shop on the premises. Open daily from 7:30 AM to 11 PM. 4 Calle Madero (phone: 510-9613).

Church of San Francisco – The church was founded by Cortés and built with stones taken from the ruins of the Aztec temples. At one time the church was part of a vast Franciscan monastery, which was destroyed in the 1860s. A restoration project has returned the paintings on the ceiling to much of their former glory. Since being built, the building has gradually sunk in the city's soft earth. Open daily. On Calle Madero across from the House of Tiles.

Palacio de Iturbide (Iturbide Palace) – This beautiful 18th-century structure was the home of Agustín de Iturbide during his brief reign as Emperor of Mexico (1822–23). Later it became a hotel, then an office building. It has now been restored and is used by the Banco Nacional de México as a museum for temporary exhibits. Open daily, but closed between exhibits. No admission charge. 17 Calle Madero (phone: 521-8990).

Latin American Tower – No longer the tallest building in town (that title belongs to Pemex headquarters now), this is still the best place from which to view the city. The observation deck on the 44th floor is open from 10 AM until 11:30 PM; admission charge for observation deck. One floor below, the *Muralto* restaurant and cocktail lounge is open until 1 AM, with live music from 5 to 7 PM (phone: 521-7751/52). On a relatively smog-free day, it's a good place to watch the sunset. Calle Madero, corner of Eje Central Lázaro Cárdenas (phone: 585-4200).

Pino Suárez Subway Station – An ancient Aztec pyramid discovered during the construction of a subway line has been preserved in the middle of the ultramodern station. At Calle Pino Suárez.

Museo de la Ciudad de México (Museum of Mexico City) – This 16th-century mansion that was rebuilt in the 18th-century houses a display that illustrates the rich history of Mexico City from the time of the Aztec to the present. Closed Mondays. No admission charge. 30 Calle Pino Suárez, corner of Calle Republic of Salvador. It is across the street from the Church of Jesus of Nazareth, where Hernán Cortés was buried in 1519 (phone: 542-0487).

Banco Nacional de México (National Bank of Mexico) – You'll find the bank in a lovely 18th-century townhouse. Unfortunately, after the 1985 earthquake, which destroyed so many Banamex buildings, the area formerly housing a small museum was converted to office space, but this building is a gem and definitely worth a look. Open weekdays. Corner of Calles Isabel la Católica and Venustiano Carranza.

Plaza de Santo Domingo (Santo Domingo Plaza) – Surrounded by historical buildings, this is one of the oldest and most beautifully preserved plazas in the city. Public scribes, known as *evangelistas,* and small printing operations set up their "offices" under the arches. Facing the plaza, the Church of Santo Domingo is on the site of the first church founded by the Dominicans in New Spain. The building on the northeast corner of the plaza, now a nursing school, once served as the Palace of the Inquisition. Three blocks north of the zocalo at Venequela.

Iglesia de la Profesa (Church of the Nun) – Conservative opponents of Mexican independence plotted to import a monarch in this historic old church on Calle Madero, corner of Calle Isabel la Católica.

Hospital de Jesús (Jesus Hospital) – The oldest continuously functioning hospital in the Americas was founded by Cortés in 1527. Calles Salvador and Pino Suárez.

Alameda Central (Alameda Park) – The charm of this gracious colonial park belies the fact that it was once the "Burning Place," where victims of the Holy Inquisition were burned at the stake. The centerpiece of the park is the Juárez Hemicycle, a handsome marble monument constructed in 1919 to commemorate 100 years of independence. The park stretches along the north side of Av. Juárez between Eje Central Lázaro Cárdenas and Paseo de la Reforma.

Museo de la Alameda (Alameda Museum) – After the 1985 earthquake, a massive operation was launched to salvage a huge Diego Rivera mural from the lobby of the crumbling *Del Prado* hotel. The hotel is now gone, but the mural, entitled *Dream of a Sunday Afternoon in the Alameda,* was moved — in one piece — and a special pavilion was built around it. Rivera's work illustrates changes in the park through the centuries, as well as memories of his youth. Closed Mondays. No admission charge. On the western edge of Solidarity Plaza (Jardín de la Solidaridad), facing Av. Juárez (phone: 521-1016).

Franz Mayer Museum – The magnificently restored 16th-century Ex-Hospital de la Mujer (former Women's Hospital) is the home of one of the city's newest museums. Just behind Alameda Park on Plaza Santa Veracruz, it contains the awesome personal collection of Franz Mayer, a German-born Mexican financier. There are Dutch, Flemish, and Italian Renaissance paintings, but the bulk of the collection comprises Mexican, European, and Oriental applied arts (silver, ceramics, textiles, furniture, ivory — even a model of an 18th-century pharmacy) from the 16th to the 19th century. Closed Mondays. Admission charge. 45 Av. Hidalgo (phone: 518-2265).

Museo de San Carlos (San Carlos Museum) – The oldest museum of its kind in the Americas, it houses a superb collection of European paintings and sculptures, many of them donated by the King of Spain. Among its treasures are notable works by Peter Paul Rubens, Franz Hals, Tintoretto, Titian, and El Greco. Closed Tuesdays. Admission charge. At the corner of Calles Puente del Alvarado and Ramos Arizpe (phone: 535-4848).

Secretaría de Educación (Ministry of Education) – The walls and stairwells literally are covered with gloriously colorful murals painted by Diego Rivera and some of his disciples. The murals (close to 100 of them) depict the various regions of Mexico, the sciences, and many of Mexico's heroes — themes suggested by José Vasconcelos, one of Mexico's most famous philosphers and the former minister of education. Painted shortly after Rivera's return from studying in Europe, the murals reflect the influence of Picasso and Cézanne. Open Mondays through Fridays. No admission charge. At the corner of Argentina and Venezuela.

Museo de la Charrería (Charro Museum) – *Charro* means "gentleman rider," and in this colonial building there is a large collection of saddles, spurs, paintings, firearms, suits, and other trappings of this supremely Mexican pastime. Closed Saturdays and Sundays. No admission charge. 108 Calle Isabel la Católica (phone: 709-4793).

Pinacoteca Virreinal (Museum of Colonial Paintings) – Art of the 16th, 17th, and 18th centuries is displayed in what was once the Church of San Diego, built in 1591. Closed Mondays and holidays. No admission charge. 7 Calle Dr. Mora (phone: 510-2793).

ZONA ROSA

The lively part of the city, the Zona Rosa neighborhood extends south of the Reforma, bounded more or less by Insurgentes, Sevilla, and Chapultepec, and is filled with hotels, restaurants, chic boutiques, and cafés.

Museo de Cera (Wax Museum) – In a restored Victorian mansion. Technically not in the Zona Rosa, but close. Open daily. Admission charge. 6 Calle Londres (phone: 546-7670).

Mexican-American Cultural Institute – This is a good place to befriend Mexicans while attending art exhibits, lectures, films, and classes in English and Spanish. 113 Calle Hamburgo (phone: 511-4720).

CHAPULTEPEC PARK

Bosque de Chapultepec (Chapultepec Park) is the people's playground. This huge park is full of museums, restaurants, a large zoo (home to the surviving female of the original pair of "prolific" pandas — a gift to Mexico from the People's Republic of China — and her "babies," born in captivity), and a children's zoo, as well as playgrounds, miniature trains, a lake for boating, lovely fountains and walkways, plenty of picnic grounds, and a large amusement park with a frighteningly high roller coaster — all open Wednesdays through Sundays. Chapultepec has been a recreation center since it was used as the royal preserve of the ancient Aztec kings. One of the world's great parks, it is a definite must-see, especially on Sunday afternoons, when the place comes alive with activity.

Museo Nacional de Historia (National Museum of History) – Another must, this beautiful museum is housed in Chapultepec Castle overlooking the park, the site of much of the tragic story of Emperor Maximilian and Carlota; some of their elegantly furnished quarters are on view. It's a pretty steep climb up the cliffside (the elevator is no longer functioning), but many joggers run up the steps as part of their daily regimen. On the lower terrace, you can see the elegant royal coach used by Emperor Maximilian. The upper floor contains 3 centuries of ceramics, jewels, and art. The first floor above the ground level has salons containing collections pertaining to the history of Mexico from the conquest to the present. Among the art treasures are murals by Orozco, Siqueiros, and Juan O'Gorman. The exhibits are actually quite disappointing, but the castle itself and the view from its terraces make the climb worthwhile. Closed Mondays. Admission charge. Chapultepec Park (phone: 286-0700).

Museo Nacional de Antropología (National Museum of Anthropology) – This is one of the world's outstanding museums. Designed by one of Mexico's leading contemporary architects, Pedro Ramírez Vazquez, it was opened to the public in 1964. (Many important pieces housed here were stolen on *Christmas Eve* 1985, but they have since been recovered.) A tour through the exhibits provides a visitor with a general overview of the most important pre-Hispanic cultures in Mexico. The exhibition halls, which form a rectangle around a huge patio dominated by a gigantic umbrella-shaped fountain, are divided into anthropological displays representing the Mesoamerican, prehistoric, pre-classic, and Teotihuacan Mexica eras. Among the many treasures on view are the sun stone, more commonly known as the Aztec calendar stone; a fascinating reproduction of the Tlatelolco market; treasures from the Palenque tombs; and a reproduction of the Maya paintings at Bonampak (the originals, deep in the jungle, are not very easily viewed). The second floor is devoted to displays of how the Indians live in Mexico today. If possible, allow a full day (the restaurant on the premises is quite pleasant), or even better, 2 half days, to see the museum. Bilingual guides are available, and an excellent English language guidebook is sold in the museum shop. Closed Mondays. Admission charge. On the Reforma in Chapultepec Park (phone: 553-6266).

Museo de Arte Moderno (Museum of Modern Art) – Excellent permanent collection of Mexican masters, as well as rotating collections of current artists and visiting exhibitions. Closed Mondays and holidays. Admission charge. Chapultepec Park (phone: 553-6313).

Centro Cultural/Arte Contemporaneo (Cultural Center for Contemporary Art) – Funded by Fundación Cultural Televisa (Mexico's private television monopoly), this 4-story atrium houses the foundation's exciting collection of 20th-century art (paintings, sculpture, graphics, and decorative), a photographic collection selected by Mexico's grand master Manuel Alvarez Bravo, and a rich collection of pre-Hispanic art. Temporary exhibits are also on display. Closed Mondays. Admission charge. Next door to the *Stouffer Presidente* at Av. Campos Elíseos and Calle Jorge Eliot (phone: 250-2327).

Tamayo Museum – This museum houses the personal collection of Rufino Tamayo, one of the country's greatest contemporary painters, plus works by more than 165 other modern artists. Closed Mondays and holidays. Admission charge. The building lies between the *Modern Art* and the *Anthropology* museums on Paseo de la Reforma in Chapultepec Park (phone: 286-5889).

Galería de Historia–"La Lucha del Pueblo Mexicano por su Libertad" (Gallery of History–"The Mexican People's Fight for Liberty") – Great moments in Mexico's struggle for liberty are depicted in 3-dimensional displays with light and sound in this snail-shaped building, commonly known as the Museo del Caracol. Closed Mondays. No admission charge. At the entrance to Chapultepec Park (phone: 553-6285).

SOUTH OF THE CITY

Ciudad Universitaria (National University) – The university claims to be the oldest institution of higher learning in the Western Hemisphere — although you'd never guess it when you see its dynamic, daring contemporary architecture. The buildings are notable for their vivid exterior murals, including ones by Rivera (the Stadium) and Siqueiros (the Rectory); most famous of all is the 10-story wraparound mosaic by Juan O'Gorman covering the façade of the library. In the southern part of the city on both sides of Av. Insurgentes Sur.

Xochimilco – These are Mexico City's marvelous floating gardens. As you drive into the canal area, you inevitably will be accosted by self-styled guides. Ignore them and go directly to the main docks (Embarcadero Nuevo Nativitas) on Calle Mercado. Here you can rent a flower-bedecked boat (*trajinera*) and have a Mexican-style gondolier pole you around the floating gardens, which are actually pre-Hispanic manmade islands called *chinampas*. You're sure to enjoy the flower vendors and the floating mariachi bands. Xochimilco is great fun on Sundays and somewhat quieter and less charming on weekdays. Open daily. Official government rates for boats are posted at dockside. Calzada Tlalpan to the traffic circle at the *Azteca Stadium;* follow the signs to the left.

A recent addition to Xochimilco is the *Dolores Olmedo Foundation Museum.* Dolores "Lola" Olmedo, longtime friend and patron of Diego Rivera, has turned her magnificent private home, a splendidly restored 16th-century monastery, into a museum which displays a fine collection of works by Rivera, as well as a smaller collection of pieces by one of his wives, Frida Kahlo. The museum also houses Mexican folk art and pre-Columbian pieces. Closed Mondays. Admission charge. 5843 Av. México (phone: 676-1166).

In the nearby town of Santa Cruz Acalpixcan, street vendors sell locally produced colorful seed candies. A candy fair is held in June, but the candy "factories" (residents' homes) may be visited at any time and can be reached by car or *trajinera.* Also in the town is the *Museo Arqueológico de Xochimilco* (Xochimilco Archaeological Museum), which houses more than 2,300 pieces from the Teotihuac and Aztec cultures. Closed Mondays. No admission charge. On the Xochimilco–Tulyehualco Hwy. at the corner of Calle Tenochtitlán (no phone).

Siqueiros Cultural Polyforum – Many forums for many arts, but mural painting predominates. The paintings are monumental, the final work of the great, if controversial, David Alfaro Siqueiros. Also on the grounds are theaters for dance and drama, a concert hall, and a crafts shop, offering a fine selection of pieces from all over Mexico. Towering above it all is the World Trade Center, which has been under construction for years; 2 floors were in use at press time, but the completion date had not been set. The Polyforum is open daily. Admission charge to see the mural. Av. Insurgentes Sur and Calle Filadelfia (no phone).

Reino Aventura – Mexico's first theme park is quite attractive, with its French, Swiss, Polynesian, American, and Mexican villages. This south-of-the-border *Disneyland* is where you can see Mexican families out for a day of fun. Open Thursdays through Sundays. On the southern edge of the city, Carr. Picacho a Ajusco, Km. 1.5 (no phone).

Carmen Convent – Combine this with your trip to the *Bazar Sábado* and the *Casa del Risco* since they are only a few blocks away. Wander around the picturesque convent at your leisure but don't miss the crypt in the basement, which has well-preserved mummies dressed in the clothes of their era. Open daily. No admission charge. 4 Av. de la Revolución on the Carmen Plaza.

Museo de Frida Kahlo (Frida Kahlo Museum) – This is the interesting home and studio of the next to last wife of Diego Rivera, a famous artist herself. Many of her works are displayed here, along with mementos of her marriage. Closed Mondays and holidays. No admission charge. 247 Calle Londres, Coyoacán (no phone).

Museo de las Intervenciones (Museum of Foreign Interventions) – The largely military museum is in the former Convent of Churubusco, which was built in 1768. It was here that General Anaya surrendered to General Winfield Scott on August 20, 1847, during the Mexican-American War. The simple coach used by Benito Juárez is on display. The adjoining Church of St. Mary of the Angels is worth a brief visit. Closed Mondays. Admission charge. 20 Calle de Agosto, Coyoacán (no phone).

Alvar and Carmen T. de Carrillo Gil Museum – On permanent display here is an outstanding collection of works by the famous Mexican muralists Orozco and Rivera. There are also temporary exhibitions of contemporary artists. Closed Mondays and holidays. No admission charge. 1608 Av. Revolución, San Angel (phone: 604-0981).

Cuicuilco – This archaeological site is noted for its unusual circular pyramid. Astronomically oriented, the site is considered the earliest urban center in the valley of Mexico. Additional pyramids were discovered in 1967 during the construction of the nearby Olympic Village. No admission charge. On Av. Insurgentes Sur, east of the Olympic Village.

Anahuacalli – This marvelous museum was designed by Rivera to house his vast collection (some 60,000 pieces) of pre-Columbian sculpture and pottery. Upstairs is a replica of his studio with artwork ranging from his first sketch (a drawing of a train done when he was 3 years old) to a canvas he was working on at the time of his death. Closed Mondays and holidays. No admission charge. 150 Calle del Museo (phone: 677-2984).

Museo Estudio Diego Rivera (Diego Rivera Studio Museum) – The home and studio of one of Mexico's most famous painters and muralists has been turned into a museum filled with the objects with which he lived. The restoration work was modeled on one of Rivera's own paintings, *The Painter's Studio,* which is on view here. The 2-story structure — designed by his friend Juan O'Gorman, an architect and fellow artist — seems uncomfortably snug for a person of Rivera's girth, but the fact is that he lived here happily for many years. Closed Mondays. No admission charge. A block from the *San Angel Inn* restaurant, at Av. Altavista and Calle Diego Rivera (phone: 548-3032).

Leon Trotsky Museum – The Russian revolutionary's last home has been converted into a museum filled with his furnishings and memorabilia. One of the more unique exhibits is a collection of photographs of Trotsky with other famous figures of the 1930s. (As you walk through the house watch your head, since the doorways are unusually low.) Perhaps more interesting than the museum itself is the story behind the house. Forced into exile from the USSR in 1929, Trotsky eventually came to Mexico, upon the suggestion of the famous Mexican muralist Diego Rivera. Trotsky took up residence in a house owned by Rivera's wife, Frida Kahlo, with whom he had an affair. His friendship with Rivera subsequently ended, and Trotsky was forced to find other living quarters. This house, with its high walls and towers, seemed the perfect refuge from Stalinists who continued to pursue him. It was here that David Siquieros, another Mexican muralist, and a group of his followers, made an unsuccessful attempt on Trotsky's life. More successful was Ramón Mercader, a Spanish Stalinist who in 1940 assassinated Trotsky while he was at work at his desk. The museum is closed Mondays. Admission charge. In Coyoacán at Calles Viena and Morelos (no phone).

Nezahualcoyotl Hall – An acoustically outstanding concert hall, it is ranked among the world's greatest. Even if you don't attend a concert, its striking architecture makes it worth a visit. On Av. Insurgentes Sur, past the National University.

Museo Nacional de Culturas Populares (National Museum of Folk Cultures) – Fascinating temporary hands-on exhibitions concentrate on one of Mexico's folk cultures or occupational areas. Exhibits are strictly low budget but very imaginative. Closed Mondays and holidays. No admission charge. 289 Calle Hidalgo, Coyoacán (phone: 554-8848).

NORTH OF THE CITY

Basílica de la Virgen de Guadalupe (Shrine of the Virgin of Guadalupe) – Catholics consider this place one of the most holy in the Americas. Catholic heads of state, such as Charles de Gaulle and John F. Kennedy, traditionally paid homage here during visits to Mexico, and Pope John Paul II said mass at the shrine in 1979. On this spot in 1531 the Virgin Mary appeared before an Indian farmer and asked him to see to it that a church be built in her honor. The bishop did not believe the farmer's story and drove him away. The Virgin appeared to the Indian again and directed him to a barren, stony place where she said he would find roses growing. He wrapped the roses in his cloak and brought them to the bishop. When he unwrapped the roses, he discovered the image of the Virgin imprinted on the cloak. The cloak, unfaded by time and conceded by art experts as something they cannot otherwise explain, is exhibited on the main altar of the shrine that commemorates the miracle. The apparition marked a great upturn in the conversion rate of the Indians, and the Virgin of Guadalupe quickly became the patron saint of all Mexico. There are actually two basilicas: The old shrine, where the cloak had been on display for about 250 years, was closed to the public because it had been badly damaged over the years by earthquakes and was sinking into the spongy subsoil. Later it was converted into a museum of religious art. The new basilica, designed by Pedro Ramirez Vazquez (who also designed the *Museum of Anthropology*), was inaugurated in 1976 and stands right next to the old shrine. There is never a time when the shrine is not thronged with pilgrims, but it is especially crowded in December. The shrine is north of the city via Av. Insurgentes Nte. (phone: 577-6088).

Pirámides de Teotihuacán (Pyramids of Teotihuacán) – The pyramids were built sometime between AD 400 and 800. They served as the religious center of a large city that was abandoned long before the Aztec came to the valley. No one knows why they left, but it is surmised that they went south and were eventually incorporated into the Maya. The largest pyramid is the Pyramid of the Sun — 216 feet high with a base covering 750 square feet. In tunneling through the pyramid to see if there were any treasures buried inside, archaeologists discovered a series of pyramids built on top of one another. The Indians marked time in 52-year cycles, and it is assumed that every 52 years a new pyramid was built over the older one. A short distance away is the smaller Pyramid of the Moon. A thoroughfare known as the Avenue of the Dead runs from the Pyramid of the Moon past the Pyramid of the Sun to the Temple of Quetzal-cóatl. The avenue is lined on both sides with smaller temples and shrines for a distance of a mile and a half. There's an immense walled-in arena that was presumably used for games and religious spectacles. At one end is the main temple, which has magnificently preserved carvings of Quetzalcóatl (the plumed serpent) and Tlaloc (the rain god). The archaeological site is open daily from 9 AM to 5 PM (the on-site museum is closed Mondays, and the whole site is closed on religious holidays). Admission charge plus a parking fee. The pyramids are 31 miles (50 km) northeast of Mexico City. Take Av. Insurgentes Nte., which connects with the toll road to Teotihuacán. There is also regular bus service from the Central de Autobúses del Norte, Av. Cien Metros in Mexico City (phone: 595-60188).

Plaza de las Tres Culturas (Plaza of the Three Cultures) – The site of the final defeat of the Aztec. Until the 1985 earthquake, the plaza had the remains of a pre-Columbian pyramid, a Spanish colonial church, and the tall modern Foreign Ministry building — three cultures standing side by side. Of the three, the Foreign Ministry building was the only structure to suffer serious damage from the quake, but now has been completely rebuilt. In the middle of the Tlaltelolco housing development, much of which was destroyed by the 1985 earthquake.

Tenayuca – This excellently preserved, stepped pyramid rests on a base 223 by 250 feet. Started by the Toltec, it was taken over by the Aztec in the 15th century and is considered one of the finest surviving examples of Aztec architecture. On the northwest outskirts of Mexico City via Calzada Vallejo.

Acolman – Construction of this imposing monastery-fortress started in 1538. Medieval in appearance, the façade has stone carvings of the Augustinian shield and the figures of St. Peter, St. Paul, and the Virgin Mary, as well as of Indians with baskets on their heads. Now a national monument, the site has been partially restored to depict how monks lived during the colonial era. Closed Mondays. Admission charge. On the road going out of Av. Insurgentes Norte, which connects with the toll road to the pyramids (no phone).

Museo Nacional del Virreinato – Founded by the Jesuits in 1584 as a school for natives, it was later used as a college for parish priests, although the structure was not completed until the second half of the 18th century. Today, it is a museum containing some of the most outstanding works of Mexican religious art. The beautiful novitiate's chapel in the monastery section is just a prelude to the extraordinary churrigueresque altarpieces in the church next door (accessible by a staircase at the rear). High up on the left of the altar are gratings that enabled the sick to hear the mass being celebrated below. Above the altar is a painting of the Virgin of Guadalupe by Miguel Cabrera, one of the most famous artists of that period. The Chapel of Nuestra Señora de Loreto, near the church's main entrance, contains a house representing the home of the Virgin Mary in Nazareth. Behind it is a vaulted ceiling so ornate that a mirror has been placed below it to allow the public to appreciate all of its intricacy. There is a very pleasant restaurant in one of the patios, and there are several others around the town's main plaza. Closed Mondays. Admission charge. About 40 minutes from the Petroleum Monument in Mexico City via the toll road to Querétaro, in Tepozotlán, state of Mexico (phone: 876-0245).

SOURCES AND RESOURCES

 TOURIST INFORMATION: The best general source of information is the tourist ministry's hotline; from the US, dial 5-250-0123/0493/0151/8601 (collect calls accepted) for answers in English (or Spanish, French, or German) to almost any travel question. The tourist ministry (172 Presidente Mazarik in Polanco) can be quite helpful both in answering ordinary questions or in dealing with serious problems. The government of the Federal District has a central tourism office in the Zona Rosa (at the corner of Calles Amberes and Londres; phone: 525-9380 through 87). The consular section at the US Embassy (305 Reforma; phone: 5-211-0042) will help only in cases of dire emergency, and such help will be limited.

Local Coverage – The *News,* Mexico City's English-language daily, keeps visitors informed about world events, what's at the movies, what's on TV, and a great deal more. The *Daily Bulletin* and the *Gazer,* available free in hotel lobbies, list restaurants, nightly entertainment, and other data of note. The *International Herald Tribune, USA Today, The New York Times, Los Angeles Times,* and the *Miami Herald* are available at most large hotels and at newsstands.

 TELEPHONE: The area code for Mexico City is 5. When calling from one city to another within Mexico, dial 91 before the area code. For additional information on dialing directly from the US, see "Mail, Telephone, and Electricity" in *On the Road,* GETTING READY TO GO.

 CLIMATE AND CLOTHES: The capital has a temperate climate with an average year-round temperature of 60F. From October until May, days are dry and sunny. Expect afternoon rains between June and September. Carry a light jacket or wrap at night. Dress casually during the day and more formally for the evening. (Men are often required to wear jackets and ties at the more expensive restaurants.)

 GETTING AROUND: Bus – Buses and minibuses run along the main avenues and arteries known as *ejes viales.* They tend to become impossibly crowded during rush hours, but at other times service is fair to good. *One word of warning:* Pickpockets are frequent passengers.

Metro – Mexico's subway is clean, fast, and efficient. The cars have rubber tires and are extremely quiet. Classical music is piped in over the sound system in the stations. It is also incredibly inexpensive at 300 pesos (about 10¢) per ride. The actual cost per passenger of operating the metro is considerably more than the fare charged, but the government is subsidizing it to keep fares affordable. Some 2 million people ride the Metro daily, and it has done much to relieve some of the traffic congestion. It is possible to ride the entire system on one ticket, but note that luggage is not allowed.

The subway was supposed to open in time for the *1968 Olympics,* but it took longer to build than originally planned. When workers started digging, they found they were burrowing through the remains of ancient Tenochtitlán, and hundreds of tons of artifacts were removed. Most things were taken to various museums, but a shrine to Ehecatl, god of the wind, was left in place in the Pino Suárez station (one can safely say that this is the only subway station with a pyramid in it). The stations are interestingly decorated and have numerous shops and restaurants. You can get quite a slice of Mexico in a single subway ride, but keep a good grip on your purse or wallet.

Taxi – First the good news: Whatever the fare, a trip by taxi in Mexico City probably will cost less than it would at home. How much less depends. There are several types of taxis in Mexico City; they charge different rates, and drivers are always asking the authorities for the right to charge more.

At larger hotels, there is usually a taxi stand in front with perhaps two types of vehicles. The larger and more comfortable are unmarked, distinguishable only by the color of their license plates, and are driven by bilingual guides. A guide with no client at the moment will work as a hackie. By Mexican standards, his fee will be high, but the mere fact that you can speak to him in English may make it worthwhile.

There will also be white and red-orange or white and maroon cars at the hotels. The colors indicate that these are *sitio* cabs; that is, they work from a cab stand and supposedly cannot cruise for passengers. They, too, charge higher rates, but the extra tariff often is worth the price, especially when less expensive cabs are unavailable. The *sitio* cabs often don't bother with their meters, so it is a good idea to ask the price before getting in. Many of the drivers at hotel stands understand at least some English.

White and yellow taxis have meters and are supposed to cruise for passengers. There are thousands of these taxis, but they always seem to be full. They charge less than the fare of a *sitio* cab, but because of frequent rate increases and unwieldy numbers, the meters measure distance and time in numbers (starting at 1) rather than pesos. A chart providing the rates for the meter reading should be posted. The driver will usually look at the number on the meter, whip out a rate sheet, and quote a price. (If there has been a recent official increase in rates, the driver may charge the amount stipulated on the newest rate sheet).

VW vans — with a horizontal stripe around them and marked with a triangle — called *peseros* (once upon a time they charged only a peso) operate like buses, cramming in as many people as will fit and following set routes. Tourists are fond of taking the *peseros* that run along Reforma, but be careful. Some of these go to the zocalo; others don't. Even if you don't speak the language, you can ask: "Zocalo?" If the cab drives off without you, he's not going there. Again, hold onto your belongings.

Tourists frequently believe that they have been overcharged, and perhaps they have been. They aren't alone. Residents get overcharged, too. It's well to remember that hacking isn't much fun in Mexico City and not very profitable; drivers rarely own their own cabs. If you do want to argue over charges, take down the cab's number and call 250-0123, the tourist ministry hotline. They will tell you where to go to file a formal complaint.

Car Rentals – All the major rental agencies are here with branches all over town. Cars can be picked up at the airport or at any number of locations around the city. The following agencies, among others, can be contacted at the Airport: *Budget* (phone: 784-3011), *Hertz* (phone: 762-8372), and *Avis* (phone: 762-3688). A good local firm that is considerably less expensive than the larger international franchises, and quite reliable, is *Romano Rent a Car* (195 Thiers, Colonia Anzures; phone: 545-5722 or 250-0055).

Bear in mind that Mexico City's pollution controls, a welcome and necessary restriction, affect resident and visiting drivers alike. Laws prohibit drivers from using their cars on certain days, depending on their automobile's license plate number. Do not drive on Mondays if your license plate ends with 5 or 6; on Tuesdays if it ends with 7 or 8; on Wednesdays, with 3 or 4; on Thursdays, with 1 or 2; and on Fridays, with 9 or 0. The fine for driving on a prohibited day is about $115.

Tours – The central tourism office can provide information on a variety of tours offered throughout the city. Before leaving for Mexico, you may want to purchase the audiocassette "Mexico City On Your Own." The recorded tour, which describes over 30 sights in the historic downtown section, is available for $9.95 through *Vivid Walking Tours* (800-233-3792 in the US).

SPECIAL EVENTS: The biggest events of the year include *Independence Day* on September 15–16, the *Anniversary of the 1910 Revolution* on November 20, and the feast day of the *Virgin of Guadalupe* on December 12. There are numerous celebrations around *Christmas* through the *Day of the Three Kings* on January 6. The *Festival of Mexico's Historic Center,* with ballets and concerts performed in the cathedral and in churches and museums in the downtown area, is held for 2 weeks in March. There is an admission charge for some of the events; others are free.

One of the highlights of the *Independence Day* celebration is an elaborate fireworks display in the zocalo on September 15 at 11 PM that's best viewed from the terrace of the *Majestic* or on TV, since the crowd in the plaza can get pretty rough. The following morning there is a parade from the zocalo to the Monument to Independence, in front of the *María Isabel–Sheraton* hotel. The huge parade starts at 11 AM and lasts until about 2 PM. *All Saints'* and *All Souls' Day* are celebrated with special enthusiasm on November 1 and 2 in the town of Mixquic. The *Anniversary of the Revolution of 1910,* on November 20, is a national holiday marked with huge celebrations and a parade that follows a route similar to that of the *Independence Day* parade. The feast day of the *Virgin of Guadalupe,* the patron saint of Mexico, is the most important religious holiday in Mexico (December 12). The entire *Easter* season is marked by numerous celebrations, ranging from solemn religious processions to wild fiestas. There are so many fiestas — including the one on March 19 that's celebrated by anyone named José — that it's almost inconceivable you won't run into at least one during your trip.

SHOPPING: If you like to shop, Mexico City is your kind of place. Native crafts and regional specialties from all over Mexico are available in the capital. The best, most concentrated shopping area is the Zona Rosa, a 12-square-block area bounded by Reforma on the east, Niza on the east, Chapultepec on the south, and Florencia on the west. The neighborhood is chock-full of boutiques, jewelry stores, leather goods shops, antiques stores, and art galleries, as well as dozens of great little restaurants and coffee shops. Day or night, the Zona Rosa is fun to explore. It is always busy — you can run into a traffic jam even at 2 AM, between shows at the nightclubs.

The Polanco area is fast catching up to the Zona Rosa. With three of Mexico City's major hotels (*Nikko, Stouffer Presidente,* and *Camino Real*), literally hundreds of shops and restaurants have sprung up, turning what was once an elegant residential area into a hubbub of activity.

There are hundreds of equally good shops spread out along the length of Avenida Insurgentes, in the San Angel and Coyoacán areas, as well as along Avenida Juárez and in the old downtown area.

The major department store chains are *Liverpool* (1310 Av. Insurgentes Sur and 425 Av. Mariano Escobedo); *Suburbia* (203 Av. Horacio, 180 Calle Sonora, and 1235 Av. Insurgentes Sur); and *Palacio de Hierro* (the corner of Calle Durango and Calle Salamanca), noted for the fashions of Nina Ricci, Pierre Cardin, and Oscar de la Renta, among others, at prices considerably lower than in the US. *Domit,* which carries fine shoes and leather accessories for men, has several locations (44 Calle Genova in the Zona Rosa; Calle Dolores and Av. Juárez downtown; and 360 Av. Presidente Mazarik in Polanco). *Zapico* and *High Life* offer stylish designs for men and women in a number of shops around the city. All these chains have branches in the posh and pricey shopping mall *Perisur,* on the southern edge of the city near where the Periferico Expressway meets Avenida Insurgentes. Department stores generally are open from 10 AM to 7 PM Mondays, Tuesdays, Thursdays, and Fridays and from 10 AM to 8 PM Wednesdays and Saturdays. FONART, a government bureau dedicated to keeping Mexican crafts in Mexico, lends money to artisans, gives them technical assistance, and helps them distribute their wares nationally and internationally. The quality of the merchandise is impressive. These crafts may be found at various locations (691 Av. Patriotismo; 89 Av. Juárez; 1630 Av. Insurgentes Sur; 136 Calle Londres in the Zona Rosa; 17 Av. de la Paz in San Angel; and the *Ciudad Satélite Shopping Mall*).

Following is a list of stores and markets, by area, to get you started. As you get around, you will find hundreds more on your own.

DOWNTOWN

Avalos Glass Factory – Glass blowers can be seen at work in the mornings. Goblets, serving pieces, and entire sets of dishes are for sale. Beware: They are very fragile, so it's best to buy a few more than you think you need. Two blocks from *La Merced,* 5 Calle Carretones (phone: 523-5311).

Bazar del Centro – A cluster of tasteful shops selling jewelry, Taxco silver, stoneware, and art are set around a lovely patio in a historical building that dates from the late 17th century. Visitors are invited for a complimentary drink at the bar, *La Cueva de Emiliano,* where a group of musicians plays in the afternoons. 30 Isabel la Católica (phone: 521-1923).

Dulcería Celaya – A candy freak's dream or a dieter's nightmare, this charming little shop carries colorful and very sweet sweets from all over the country. 39 Av. Cinco de Mayo (phone: 521-1787).

De la Fuente Bustillo – Exclusive gold jewelry and antiques. 28 Calle Madero (phone: 518-7272) and 276 Paseo de la Reforma (phone: 525-7272).

Galería Reforma – This collection of handicrafts, including furniture, jewelry, ceramics, clothing, and brass and copper items, is probably the largest in Mexico. Open daily. 575 Paseo de la Reforma Norte and Calle Gonzalo Bocanegra (phone: 525-7272).

Mercado Abelardo Rodríguez (Abelardo Rodríguez Market) – In an interesting area filled with lovely Spanish colonial buildings, the market is especially interesting at *Christmas,* when there's a great selection of piñatas, nativity scenes, and toys. Open daily. On Calle Venezuela between Calles Carmen and Argentina (no phone).

Mercado de la Ciudadela (Ciudadela Handicrafts Market) – Almost 200 craftsmen exhibit their works at this condominium project of 1-story buildings. You can usually see some craftsmen hard at work. Each stall has its own hours, but most are open every day. Balderas between Ayuntamiento and Donde (no phone).

Mercado de Curiosidades (Curiosities Market) – Craftsmen and merchants from all over the country display popular arts and crafts in this modern building, also known as *Mercado de San Juan.* A spiral ramp links all the floors. Open daily. Ayuntamiento between Calles Dolores and Luis Moya (no phone).

Mercado la Lagunilla (Lagunilla Market) – The poor Mexican's department store sells food, clothing, and household goods. The best time to visit is on Sunday, when it sprawls out into nearby Calle Rayón and becomes the weekly *Thieves' Market.* It has everything from used eyeglasses and false teeth to estate jewelry and antiques. Open daily. Eight blocks north of Calle Madero on Calle Allende (no phone).

Mercado Sonora (Sonora Market) – Part of the huge *Mercado Merced,* this smaller market offers a wide variety of herbs for cooking and medicinal use, as well as poultry and other foods. There's a huge toy market here at *Christmas.* South of *Mercado Merced* at Fray Servando Teresa de Mier and San Nicolás (no phone).

Museo de Arte Popular (Museum of Popular Arts) – This government-run shop has an exceptionally good selection of textiles and pottery as well as a huge crafts map of Mexico in the front room. Open daily. 44 Av. Juárez (phone: 521-6679).

Platería Alameda – Formerly in the Zona Rosa under the name of its proprietor, Moishe Rosenberg, this popular shop carries jewelry and decorative objects designed in 18K gold and sterling. 58 Av. Juárez (phone: 518-6829).

Sanborn's – A retail chain that also boasts good informal restaurants, it sells silver, crafts, and gift items at locations all over the city, most notably at the *House of Tiles* at 4 Calle Madero. Also at 45 Paseo de la Reforma, 333 Paseo de la Reforma, and 70 Calle Hamburgo (no phone).

Victor's – Rare lacquerware, quality ceramics, and traditional Indian jewelry. Open Mondays through Fridays from 12:30 to 7 PM. 8 and 10 Madero, Room 305 (phone: 512-1263).

ZONA ROSA

Aca Joe's – T-shirts and beachwear. Several locations include 19 Calle Amberes in the Zona Rosa, and 310 and 318 Av. Presidente Mazarik in Polanco (phone: 207-5682).

Antil – Good leather in a variety of styles and prices. 22 Calle Florencia (no phone).

Aries – One of Mexico's finest stores for leather goods, including suede ready-to-wear goods, luggage, handbags, and so on. 14 Calle Florencia (phone: 533-2509) and in the *Stouffer Presidente Hotel,* opposite the National Auditorium at 110 Paseo de la Reforma (phone: 533-2509).

Arte Popular en Miniatura – A tiny shop filled with tiny things, from dollhouse furniture and lead soldiers to miniature nativity scenes. 130 Calle Hamburgo (phone: 511-7454).

Cartier – It's the real thing now, with the Mexican *Cartier* and the French *Cartier* finally having joined forces. 9 Calle Amberes (phone: 207-6109).

Los Castillo – The originator of the method of melding silver, copper, and brass. Considered by many to be Taxco's top silversmith. 41 Calle Amberes (phone: 511-6198).

Curryer – The best chocolate shop in Mexico is across the Paseo de la Reforma at 77 Calle Guadalquivir (phone: 525-3800).

Flamma – Fantastic array of candles in a beautiful townhouse. Calle Hamburgo at the corner of Calle Florencia (phone: 514-4787).

Galería Arvil – Artworks by established older artists and promising newcomers. Closed Sundays. 9 Cerrada de Hamburgo, between Calles Florencia and Estocolmo (phone: 514-5255).

Galería Hachisuzume – "Hachisuzume" means hummingbird in Japanese, but the merchandise here is strictly Mexican. The attractive shop is packed with fine contemporary Mexican handicrafts, from ironwood figures carved by the Seri Indians to intricately embroidered costumes from Oaxaca and Chiapas. *María Isabel–Sheraton Hotel* (phone: 207-3933, ext. 3932).

Ginatai – Excellent leather suits, boots, and purses. 46 Calle Niza (phone: 514-1353).

Girasol – Wonderful shop famous for its superb handloomed fabrics and its delightful hand-embroidered gowns and skirts. Three locations: 39 Calle Génova, *Perisur Mall,* and in Polanco at Calle Francisco Petrarea and Av. Horacio (phone: 533-3723).

Gucci – No relation to the world-famous Italian name. Nevertheless, it has fine shoes, gloves, and handbags. 136 Calle Hamburgo (phone: 511-8018).

Insurgentes – A neighborhood market where, along with artistically arranged stalls piled with meats and produce, there is a wide selection of handicrafts, embroidered clothing, and silver. Prices are quite good, but there is always room for negotiating. Entrance is on 154 Londres or 167 Liverpool.

Misrachi Gallery – Paintings, sculptures, lithographs, and prints by such top Mexican artists as Tamayo, Cuevas, and Siqueiros. Closed Sundays. 20 Calle Génova (phone: 533-4551).

Mullers – Just about everything that can possibly be made from Puebla onyx. Open daily. 52 Calle Florencia, corner of Londres (phone: 511-0143).

Sullivan Park Art Show (Jardín de Arte) – The place to find Mexico's aspiring artists before they become famous. Sundays only. Sullivan Park, where the Paseo de la Reforma and Av. Insurgentes cross.

Tamacani – Handwoven wool rugs with original and unusual designs. 51 Calle Varsovia (phone: 533-5155).

Tane – A treasure trove of superb silver and gold, ranging from museum-quality reproductions of antique pieces to bold new designs by young Mexican silversmiths. The main store is at 70 Calle Amberes (phone: 525-1522); there are branches in Polanco at the *Nikko* and the *Stouffer Presidente*, and in the southern part of town in *Perisur Mall* and the *San Angel Inn*.

POLANCO

Las Artesanías y La Dulcería – It's actually two small shops adjacent to one another on a small patio. One is filled with typical Mexican candies; the other, with select and unusual crafts. In the heart of Polanco's shopping center, 29 Oscar Wilde (phone: 254-2557).

Artesanías Michoacán – Not to be missed, this boutique of beautifully displayed handicrafts is run by the government of the state of Michoacán. In addition to an impressive collection of lacquerware and copper items, there are lace and other textiles, prints, and an interesting selection of crafts books. 199 Av. Campos Elíseos (phone: 203-1503).

Basil – A tiny antiques shop a few steps from the *Stouffer Presidente*, it specializes in French furniture and porcelains, with a good selection of Art Nouveau and Art Deco pieces. 215-C Av. Campos Elíseos (no phone).

Benetton – Smart, casual Italian sportswear in a wide range of colors and patterns. 219 Av. Homero (no phone).

Concepto Visual – A select collection of modern designs in stoneware, jewelry, and prints, as well as choice pottery and metalwork from Michoacán and Oaxaca. 315 Calle Torcuato Tasso (phone: 250-8102).

Estela Shapiro Gallery – Works by internationally known Mexican artists, as well as young aspirants. 72 Calle Victor Hugo, Colonia Anzures (phone: 525-0123).

Feders – Great hand-blown glass and Tiffany-style lamps. Two locations: the factory at 67 Lago Moritz, Colonia Anahuac (5 minutes from Polanco) and in the *Bazar Sábado*, Plaza San Jacinto, San Ángel (phone: 250-3732).

Pladi – Beautifully designed jewelry and jewelry/sculpture, as well as some prints and accessories. Calle La Martine between Avs. Newton and Horacio (no phone).

Populartes – With many unique items, it's probably the most exceptional collection of Mexican handicrafts in the city. 103 Campos Elíseos (phone: 254-2236).

Lo Que el Viento Se Llevó – "What the wind blew away" is an outstanding collection of Mexican colonial furniture and decorative objects. Around the corner from the *Camino Real* at 56 Calle Victor Hugo (phone: 672-5192).

ENVIRONS

Bazar Sábado (Saturday Bazaar) – Over 100 top craftsmen display their creations in a 17th-century mansion. The work is top-quality, much of it unique and available no place else in Mexico. There's a wonderful restaurant in the patio where visitors can soak up the atmosphere. The art show (in front) and the sidewalk vendors add to the festive, joyous bustle of the place. Saturdays only. 11 Plaza San Jacinto in San Ángel (phone: 572-7517).

Dupuis – An impeccable selection of furniture, icons, and gifts. 180-B Av. de las Fuentes in Pedregal and 240 Paseo de las Palmas in Lomas de Chapultepec (phone: 271-3386).

Galería Kahlo-Coronel – This gallery has earned a reputation for variety, freshness, and originality in its art and photographic exhibitions. 17 Calle Carmen, 2nd Fl., Colonia Ermita Chimalistac (phone: 548-2279).

Tapetes de Temoaya – Oriental-style hand-loomed wool rugs, incorporating Mexican motifs and colors. 2375 Av. Insurgentes Sur in San Angel (phone: 548-8175).

 SPORTS: Mexico is very sports conscious, and physical fitness is stressed on television and radio, as well as in the schools.

Auto Racing – Speedsters head for the *Autódromo Hermanos Rodríguez,* where the *Grand Prix Formula I* race is held in May. Near the airport.

Baseball – The season runs from April to August. Mexico City has two home teams, the *Red Devils* and the *Tigers.* Weeknight games are generally held at 7 PM and Sunday games at 11 AM at the *Parque Seguro Social* (Social Security Park), Av. Cuauhtémoc and Obrero Mundial.

Boxing and Wrestling – Both of these events are held regularly at the *Arena Coliseo.* The atmosphere is very rough: Don't be surprised if a live cigarette butt lands in your lap or a firecracker explodes over your head. Downtown at 77 Beru (phone: 526-1687).

Bullfighting – Held Sundays in the renovated *Plaza México,* starting promptly at 4 PM. Tickets can be purchased at the stadium where about half a dozen different box offices sell tickets for different sections of the plaza. If you don't know what you're doing, you're likely to wind up with a bad seat in the blazing sun. It's best to ask the travel desk at your hotel to get the tickets for you. *Plaza México* is at 6 Ege (phone: 563-3959/3961).

Golf – The city has no public golf courses, but there are five excellent private country clubs. Some of the major hotels can arrange temporary memberships for guests, but usually on weekdays only. Exchange visiting privileges are available for members of US country clubs. The clubs are *Bellavista* in Ciudad Satélite; *Hacienda* in Tlalnepantla; *México* (Av. San Buenaventura in Tlalpan); *Chapultepec* (Calle Conscripto near the racetrack), and *Vallescondido* (Av. Club de Golf in Atizapan.) If you don't mind a drive, the *Acozac Club* (Km 29.8 on the old Puebla Hwy.) and the *Cactus Golf Club* (20 miles/32 km north of the city on the Pachuca Hwy.) are open to the public.

Horse Racing – The *Hipódromo de las Américas* (phone: 557-4999/4888) is a beautiful track. It is open all year except for 2 weeks in December/January. Races are run on Tuesdays, Thursdays, and Fridays at 3 PM and Saturdays and Sundays at 2:30 PM. Admission is about 25¢ or complimentary with purchase of a program for less than $1. You can eat at the *Gay Dalton Club* on the second tier, the *Nuevo Laredo Turf Club,* the *Derby,* the *Handicap,* or the *Palermo.* Some of the more exclusive hotels can make arrangements if you would like to visit the elegant *Jockey Club* on the top level. There's no off-track betting in Mexico.

Jai Alai – After being closed for 3 years because of a workers' strike, the *Frontón México,* famous for its jai alai games, recently reopened. Betting goes on throughout the game, but unless you're familiar with the complicated wagering system, you're better off just being an interested spectator. There are three games nightly, Tuesdays through Sundays, beginning at 7:30 PM. Admission charge is $7. 17 Plaza de la República, at the northwest corner of the plaza (no phone).

Polo – Matches are held occasionally on Sunday mornings at *Campo Marte* in Chapultepec Park.

Soccer – Called *fútbol,* this is the most popular sport in Mexico. The season runs through the summer and fall. Games are played in the huge *Azteca Stadium* (3465 Calz. de Tlalpan; phone: 677-7198) usually held on Fridays at 8:45 PM, Saturdays at 5 PM, and Sundays at noon. Make arrangements through your hotel for tickets.

Swimming – If your hotel does not have a pool, the manager can usually make arrangements for you to use the pool at a nearby hotel, or can set up guest privileges at a private sports club.

Tennis – *Club de Tenis Reyes* (34 Calle José María Tornel; phone: 277-2690 or 515-6004) in the San Miguel Chapultepec district has 4 indoor courts, or your hotel can make arrangements with the private golf clubs, which have courts and generally accept visitors on weekdays.

NIGHTCLUBS AND NIGHTLIFE: Mexico City has a lively nightlife and interesting cultural events. Foremost among them is the wonderful *Ballet Folklórico.* The troupe is known around the world for its brilliantly staged and costumed dance presentations. If you haven't seen it before (or even if you have), an evening at the *Folklórico* is 2 hours of joy. The *Folklórico's* home is the *Bellas Artes.* Performances are on Wednesdays at 9 PM and on Sundays at 9:30 AM and 9 PM. *Bellas Artes* also presents excellent concerts, symphonies, classical ballets, and operas. On Plaza Central Alameda.

Often concerts or other performances that appear at the *Bellas Artes* later move to the *National Auditorium,* in Chapultepec Park, where the facilities are less elegant but the prices are far cheaper. The *Ollin Yoliztli* and *Nezahuacóyotl* concert halls (both near the *Perisur Shopping Center*) and *Teatro de la Ciudad de México* (36 Donceles), just a few blocks from *Bellas Artes,* also offer excellent concerts by local and international orchestras and concert artists. The *Mexico City News* carries a complete listing of cultural events in Mexico City in a column, "What's On in Mexico Today."

Plan to spend an evening at the Garibaldi Plaza, where you can sit and watch the people while the mariachi bands play. The plaza is just a few blocks off Reforma Norte. Among the well-known bars on the plaza are *Guadalajara de Noche* and *Tenampa,* and there's an excellent Mexican fiesta at *Plaza Santa Cecilia.* For terrific mariachi music in more elegant surroundings, try the *Jorongo Bar* in the *María Isabel–Sheraton.* The beautiful, intimate, brass and glass lobby bar in the *Maria Isabel–Sheraton* is a lovely place for a quiet drink. *Club 25,* the rooftop bar at the *Holiday Inn Crowne Plaza,* is also a good place to enjoy an early evening drink and a nice view. The music and people watching are best at the lobby bars of the *Nikko* and *Stouffer Presidente;* for music and dancing with a view try *Torre de Oro* on the 22nd floor of the *Seville Palace. Yesterday's* at the *Aristos* is a popular nightclub. The clubs with the best floor shows include the *Premier* (190 Av. San Jerónimo), *Maquiavelo* in the *Krystal Zona Rosa, Feelings* at the *Century, Can Can, Señorial,* and *Marakesh* in the Zona Rosa. The top discos are *Danzateria Zoo* (1333 Av. Insurgentes Sur), *Magic Circus* (3 Calle Rodolfo Gaona), *Cero-Cero* at the *Camino Real, Disco Club* at *Stouffer Presidente* in the *Galería Plaza, Zazzy* at the *Nikko,* and *News* (225 Av. San Jerónimo). *Lipstick* at the *Aristos* has good rock groups and the best popcorn in town. Other old favorites include *El Patio* (9 Calle Atenas), *El Hijo del Cuervo* (17 Jardín Centenario in Coyoacan), and *Capri* (77 Av. Juárez). Salsa is king at *Antillano's* (Calle Francisco Pimental in Colonia San Rafael), and there's a great belly dancer at *Adonis* (424 Av. Homero), a Lebanese restaurant-nightclub. There's an all-male strip show (for women only) at *Chippendale* (1231 Av. Insurgentes Sur). Mexico has come a long way.

BEST IN TOWN

CHECKING IN: Mexico City offers hotels to suit every taste and budget, but be sure to confirm your reservation. At times, every place in town is full. Expect to pay about $120 and up for a double at very expensive hotels, $90 to $110 at an expensive one, $50 to $80 at moderate, and $35 or less at inexpensive. All telephone numbers are in the 5 area code unless otherwise indicated. When calling from one city to another within Mexico, dial 91 before the area code.

Camino Real – A Mexico City landmark whose bold architecture brings to mind an Aztec temple. The posh accommodations run by the Westin chain include beautiful gardens, 3 heated pools, tennis courts, 3 bars with entertainment, a discotheque, the *Azulejos* and *Foquet* restaurants (see *Eating Out*), and a coffee shop. 700 Av. Mariano Escobedo (phone: 203-2121; 800-228-3000 in the US; FAX: 250-6897). Very expensive.

Clarion – Small and attractive, this Calinda Quality property has 67 tastefully furnished suites, all with Jacuzzis and/or saunas. There is live music in the bar, an Italian restaurant, and parking. 373 Paseo de la Reforma (phone: 207-9075 or 208-4428; 800-228-5151 in the US; FAX: 207-2719). Very expensive.

María Isabel–Sheraton – Large and luxurious, with a wide range of facilities — a restaurant and a coffee shop, an impressive brass and glass lobby bar, 2 other bars with entertainment, and a solarium and a heated rooftop pool. All rooms have refrigerators. 325 Paseo de la Reforma (phone: 207-3933; 800-325-3535 in the US; FAX: 207-0684). Very expensive.

Nikko México – Overlooking Chapultepec Park and next door to the *Stouffer Presidente,* this 38-floor "grand" hotel boasts 750 stylish rooms, including 2 sumptuous presidential suites, 7 executive suites, 9 junior suites, and 2 Japanese suites, all equipped with an ultramodern security system. Among the many amenities are *Les Célébrités,* for French cuisine, *Benkay,* a traditional teppanyaki grill direct from Tokyo, a cafeteria, a disco, 3 tennis courts and a practice court, and an athletic club with an indoor swimming pool. 204 Av. Campos Elíseos (phone: 203-4020; 800-NIKKO-US in the US; FAX: 255-5586). Very expensive.

Galería Plaza – Westin Hotels' second Mexico City property (built after Westin's *Camino Real*) has 434 rooms, most with traditional Mexican decor, and 2 executive floors. The emphasis here is on good food and drink at the hotel's *Ile de France* restaurant (see *Eating Out*). There is also a disco, lobby bar, and coffee shop. Guests have access to the tennis courts and health club at the *Camino Real.* In the Zona Rosa, 195 Calle Hamburgo at Varsovia (phone: 211-0014; 800-228-3000 in the US; FAX: 207-5867). Expensive.

Holiday Inn Crowne Plaza – The facilities of this large property hotel include 3 dining rooms, 2 executive floors, bars, and nightclubs. An excellent place for nightlife. 80 Paseo de la Reforma (phone: 705-1515; 800-HOLIDAY in the US). Expensive.

Imperial – A member of Grupo Hoteles Unidos, a Spanish hotel chain, this historic turn-of-the-century landmark — with its gilt cupola — has 65 air conditioned units — including 5 master and 5 junior suites — comfortably furnished and equipped with color TV sets (5 satellite channels), direct-dial phones, radio-alarm clocks, robes, hair dryers, and safes. There is also a restaurant, coffee shop, lobby bar with live music in the evenings, and parking. 64 Paseo de la Reforma (phone: 566-4879; FAX: 535-2730). Expensive.

Krystal Zona Rosa – Excellently run and centrally located, it has good facilities, including a heated pool, 2 restaurants, a lobby bar with live music, and a popular nightclub. 155 Calle Liverpool (phone: 211-0092; 800-231-9860 in the US; FAX: 511-3490). Expensive.

Marco Polo – A small establishment offering personal service on the Zona Rosa's chicest street, it has 60 tastefully furnished, comfortable rooms, and 4 penthouse suites — each with a spectacular view of the Angel and Reforma from its Jacuzzi. Also valet parking, color cable television, direct-dial long-distance telephone, and a small restaurant-bar. Bilingual secretarial service is available. 27 Calle Amberes (phone: 207-1893; FAX: 533-3727). Expensive.

Stouffer Presidente – On the edge of Chapultepec Park, this popular hostelry is within easy walking distance of the *National Anthropology Museum* and the park's many other facilities. Its 5-story lobby is designed in the shape of an Aztec pyramid, with restaurants, including a branch of *Maxim's* of Paris (see *Eating Out),* and shops on each level. The lobby bar, with live classical music and jazz, is a congenial place to meet people. With 750 rooms. 218 Av. Campos Elíseos (phone: 250-7700; FAX: 250-8830). Expensive.

Century – An elegant Zona Rosa hotel, it has marble Roman bathtubs, a restaurant, a heated pool, nightclub, and strolling violinists at the *Regine* restaurant. Calle Liverpool at Amberes (phone: 584-7111). Expensive to moderate.

Aristos – This active place in the center of the Zona Rosa features a gym and discotheque, as well as a sauna to help take the kinks out the following morning. There are 2 dining rooms, a cocktail lounge, and a nightclub. 276 Paseo de la Reforma (phone: 211-0112; 800-5-ARISTO in the US). Moderate.

Calinda Geneve – A popular old favorite that was taken over by Calinda Quality Hotels, spruced up and made more comfortable. Its *El Jardín* restaurant serves Teutonic snacks to the accompaniment of live music. 130 Calle Londres (phone: 211-0071; 800-228-5151 in the US; FAX: 208-7422). Moderate.

De Cortés – Best Western's small, simple, and evocative hostelry is conveniently located across the street from Alameda Park. Rooms on the ground floor and balcony of this historic property circle an open-air inner courtyard filled with trees and a small fountain, where the hotel restaurant serves drinks and meals. Rooms away from the street are quietest. 85 Av. Hidalgo (phone: 518-2181/82/83/84/85; 800-528-1234 in the US; FAX: 518-3466). Moderate.

Howard Johnson Gran Hotel – Formerly the *Gran Hotel de la Ciudad de México,* this really is a "grand" hotel — sophisticated, charming, and gracious, downtown on the corner of the zocalo, an area of the city that's interesting during the day but rather dull at night. Even if you're not staying here, take a peek in to see the cage elevators and magnificent Tiffany-glass ceiling of the lobby. 82 Calle Dieciséis de Septiembre (phone: 510-4040; 800-654-2000 in the US; FAX: 512-2081). Moderate.

Seville Palace – At a superb location right on the Reforma, there are 414 rooms, a restaurant, a coffee shop, a covered rooftop pool, a health club with a Jacuzzi, disco, and a terraced rooftop lounge with a spectacular view of the city. 105 Paseo de la Reforma (phone: 566-8877; FAX: 535-3842). Moderate.

Bristol – Very reasonably priced and pleasant, it's in an interesting neighborhood not far from the Zona Rosa and Paseo de la Reforma, with a restaurant and a bar. 17 Plaza Necaxa (phone: 533-6060; FAX: 533-6060). Inexpensive.

El Ejecutivo – Surprisingly comfortable and inexpensive, it has a restaurant and bar. 8 Calle Viena, just off Paseo de la Reforma (phone: 566-6422; FAX: 533-1027). Inexpensive.

Emporio – Conveniently located on the Reforma, midway between downtown and Chapultepec Park, this property has 150 air conditioned rooms, all with Jacuzzis and color TV sets offering several satellite channels. There's live music in the bar and a sushi bar. 124 Paseo de la Reforma (phone: 566-7766; FAX: 512-2081). Inexpensive.

María Cristina – Just a block from the Reforma, this Spanish-style inn has a piano bar and a lovely garden. 31 Calle Lerma (phone: 566-9688; FAX: 566-9194). Inexpensive.

Polanco – A real bargain and just a few blocks from the glamorous *Nikko,* it has 72 rooms and 6 junior suites, all on the small side but pleasant; color TV sets that pick up US channels, and a restaurant. 8 Calle Edgar Allan Poe (phone: 520-6040). Inexpensive.

Reforma – One of the first luxury establishments in Mexico City, it's a bit of a grande dame past its prime, but still pleasant. 109 Paseo de la Reforma and Calle Paris (phone: 546-9685 through 95; FAX: 546-4202). Inexpensive.

Ritz – A quiet Best Western in the downtown area that for years has been a favorite with wealthy Mexicans. All rooms have color TV sets, and there is also a solarium and restaurant-bar. 30 Av. Madero (phone: 518-1340; 800-528-1234 in the US; FAX: 518-3466). Inexpensive.

 EATING OUT: Mexico City is a sophisticated, cosmopolitan metropolis that abounds with restaurants of every ethnic stripe. Many of its hotels boast fine restaurants; among the most outstanding are *Fouquet* in the *Camino Real, Ile de France* in the *Galería Plaza,* and *Maxim's* in the *Stouffer Presidente.* The restaurants listed below are among the best in the city, but they are only a beginning. By all means explore on your own. If you don't like spicy food, tell the waiter that you want something that isn't too hot, or *picante* (pee-*kahn*-tay). If you want to try something new, order the *huitlacoche,* a corn fungus with a delicate mushroom flavor. Most of the restaurants listed here have English-speaking waiters. To play it safe, order bottled water, even in the finest restaurants. Remember that you'll have most restaurants pretty much to yourself if you go for lunch before 1:30 in the afternoon or for dinner before 9 PM. Our restaurant selections cost about $75 or more for dinner for two in the very expensive range; about $60 in the expensive range; about $45 in the moderate range; and seldom more than $25 in the inexpensive bracket. Prices do not include drinks, wine, or tips. Most restaurants accept MasterCard and Visa; a few also accept American Express and Diners Club. Unless otherwise noted, all restaurants are open daily. All telephone numbers are in the 5 area code unless otherwise indicated. When calling from one city to another within Mexico, dial 91 before the area code.

Fouquet – A branch of the famous eatery in Paris, it serves some of the finest French food in the city. Ties required. Open Mondays through Fridays from 2 to 4:30 PM and from 8 PM to 11:30 PM; dinner only on Saturdays; closed Sundays. Reservations necessary. In the *Camino Real Hotel,* 700 Av. Mariano Escobedo (phone: 203-2121). Very expensive.

Ile de France – For nearly impeccable service and fine French dishes prepared imaginatively (the menu changes four times a year), be sure to visit this lovely spot at the *Galería Plaza* hotel. Open Mondays through Fridays for lunch and dinner and on Saturdays for dinner only. Reservations advised. In the Zona Rosa, 195 Calle Hamburgo at Varsovia (phone: 211-0014). Very expensive.

Maxim's – A branch of *Maxim's* in Paris, the French food and atmosphere here are nearly as wonderful. Coat and tie suggested. Open Mondays through Fridays from 1:30 to 5 PM and from 8 PM to 12 AM; dinner only on Saturdays. Reservations necessary. At the *Stouffer Presidente,* 218 Av. Campos Elíseos (phone: 250-7700). Very expensive.

Sir Winston Churchill's – A restored Tudor mansion where the food and atmosphere are very British. Not surprising, then, to find roast beef with Yorkshire pudding the house specialty. Reservations advised. 67 Manuel Avila Camacho (phone: 520-0065). Very expensive.

Suntory – Japanese, with a lovely atmosphere created by its beautiful gardens. Reservations advised. 14 Torres Adalid, Colonia del Valle (phone: 536-943236), and 535 Calle Montes Urales and Paseo de la Reforma, Lomas (phone: 520-4496). Very expensive.

Antigua Hacienda de Tlalpan – Housed in a beautifully restored 18th-century hacienda set in 2 acres of gardens where peacocks roam freely, it specializes in fine Mexican and international cuisine. Reservations advised. 4619 Calzada de Tlalpan (phone: 573-9933). Expensive.

Azulejos – Set in cheerful and pleasant surroundings, this spot offers especially well prepared Mexican dishes. An excellent buffet is served on Sundays. Don't waste your calories on the disappointing desserts. Reservations advised. At the *Camino Real Hotel* (phone: 203-2121). Expensive.

Champs Elysées – A charming Parisian-style restaurant, overlooking the Reforma and serving authentic French cuisine. Specialities include the pâté and a wonderful bouillabaisse. Reservations advised. Calles Amberes and Reforma, in front of the US Embassy (phone: 514-6464). Expensive.

Cicero's – The crowd is fun and the food tasty at this New Orleans–style restored mansion in the heart of Zona Rosa. Carnivores will love the roast beef. Reservations advised. 195 Calle Londres (phone: 533-4276). Expensive.

Daruma – Many consider this to be the best Japanese restaurant in Mexico City. Reservations advised. 50 Calle Río Tiber (phone: 514-6023). Expensive.

Estoril – With a menu of excellent Mexican and continental dishes, the specialties here include fried parsley, mole, and *huitlacoche* crêpes. Reservations advised. Two locations: in the Zona Rosa at 75 Calle Genova (phone: 511-3421) and at 24 Calle Alejandro Dumas, Polanco (phone: 531-4896). Expensive.

Hacienda de los Morales – One of the most beautiful restaurants in Mexico City, housed in an impressive, meticulously restored hacienda dating from the 16th century. The atmosphere is wonderful and its international menu is excellent, but it is especially famous for its traditional Mexican dishes. Reservations advised. 525 Calle Vázquez de Mella (phone: 540-3225). Expensive.

Lago Chapultepec – Elegant, architecturally spectacular restaurant overlooking the lake in the new section of Chapultepec Park. Dressy, formal atmosphere, international fare. Bar and dancing. Reservations necessary. Chapultepec Park (phone: 515-9350). Expensive.

Mazurka – A wonderful Polish place, with a very European atmosphere and a fine kitchen. Pope John Paul II ate here during his visit to Mexico. A string quartet plays at dinner. Reservations advised. 150 Calle Nueva York (phone: 523-8811) and a new location in the Coyoacán section at 3 Calle Copilco (phone: 548-3065). Expensive.

Mesón del Cid – Delicious Spanish food, perhaps the best of its kind in Mexico, is served here. Suckling pig and spring lamb are among the best entrées. On Saturday nights a medieval dinner is served. Reservations essential on Saturday nights; advised other nights. 61 Calle Humboldt (phone: 521-1940). Expensive.

La Petite France – Filled with hanging plants, this lovely place is in the heart of the Polanco section. Filet of beef in a cream sauce flavored with *morilla* (a mild, flavorful mushroom) is a good choice. Reservations advised. 360 Av. Presidente Mazarik (phone: 250-4470). Expensive.

Prendes – Completely restored to its former splendor and an institution in Mexico's historical center since 1892, this landmark is frequented by artists and politicians. The faces of more than 100 celebrities — including ex-presidents, bullfighters, and even Walt Disney, are painted on murals here. Although the quality of food generally isn't what it used to be, the cream of corn and *huitlacoche,* suckling pig, and giant shrimp stuffed with cheese are among the best regarded selections. Reservations advised. 10-C Calle 16 de Septiembre (phone: 521-5404). Expensive.

San Angel Inn – Gorgeous restored hacienda with beamed ceilings, fireplaces, and beautiful gardens. In this historic old building Pancho Villa and General Zapata once signed a pact to stay out of one another's territory. We must confess that the food is mostly mediocre, but nobody seems to mind. Closed Sundays. Reservations advised. 50 Calle Diego Rivera, San Ángel (phone: 548-6746). Expensive.

King's Road – Elegant dining and excellent service. The prime ribs, salads, and pasta are superb. Reservations advised. 43 Av. Altavista, San Angel (phone: 660-1632). Expensive to moderate.

Anderson's – The warm, clubby atmosphere of this popular, festive, swinging place — one of a popular chain with branches in almost every major city and resort area in Mexico — makes it a hit with young people. Oysters 444 and the TBC salad are two of the favorites here. Reservations advised. 382 Paseo de la Reforma (phone: 528-7428). Moderate.

Arroyo – Sample the best of regional Mexican cooking — lamb steamed in maguey leaves; *huazoncles,* broccoli-like flowerettes strung along a slender stem stuffed with cheese and fried; *tlacoyos,* thick, doughy tortillas, also stuffed with cheese; crunchy *chicharrón,* fried pork rind; cactus (*nopales*) salad; and more. Reservations advised. In the district of Tlalpan, 4003 Av. Insurgentes Sur (phone: 573-4344). Moderate.

Bellinghausen – Delightful patio for midday dining. Exceptionally good fish dishes. Reservations advised. 95 Calle Londres, Zona Rosa (phone: 511-1056). Moderate.

La Bottiglia – The beautifully prepared Italian dishes and cozy, unpretentious atmosphere have made this spot one of the most popular in the Polanco area. Reservations necessary, especially at noon. In the *Polanco Hotel,* 8 Calle Edgar Allan Poe (phone: 520-2085). Moderate.

Capri – Nothing fancy, but very tasty Italian food served in a homey atmosphere. The fresh pasta is the special pride of Daniel Chioino, the proprietor, and there is a very respectable house wine. Reservations advised. 83 Calle Julio Verne (phone: 545-7856). Moderate.

La Cava – A spacious and beautifully decorated eatery specializing in Spanish, Mexican, and international dishes. Dining around the lovely patio is especially pleasant. *Huitlacoche* crêpes are one of the house specialties. Reservations advised. 2465 Av. Insurgentes Sur (phone: 548-8887). Moderate.

Chalet Suizo – Wonderful fondues and other Swiss and German specialties. Popular and crowded, but you rarely have to wait more than a few minutes. Reservations advised. 37 Calle Niza, Zona Rosa (phone: 511-7529). Moderate.

Delmonico's – Justly famous for its excellent food, with Mexican, American, and continental fare. Weekend brunches are works of art. Reservations advised. 87 Calle Londres, Zona Rosa (phone: 528-7530). Moderate.

Dos Puertas – It's large and lavish, with a garden setting, and serves fine continental and classic Mexican food. Popular with well-to-do Mexicans. Reservations advised. 102 Calle Pedro Luis Ogazón, San Angel (phone: 550-7489). Moderate.

Fonda del Recuerdo – A very popular, festive place that attracts a crowd that likes lots of loud, live Veracruz music (two groups are often playing at the same time). Try a *toritos,* a tequila-based drink that has the punch of nitroglycerin, and the *botana* (guacamole, fried pork rinds, roast pork, and so on, served in earthenware bowls). Open daily from 9 AM to midnight. Reservations advised. 39 Calle Bahía de las Palmas (phone: 531-9129). Moderate.

La Lanterna – Excellent Italian food is prepared here under the supervision of Ennio Petterino and his family. Stop counting your cholesterol long enough to sample the *filete a burro nero* (filet of beef in black butter). Closed Sundays. Reservations advised. 458 Paseo de la Reforma (phone: 207-8969). Moderate.

Loredo Hamburgo – Try its *carne asada* or *sábana* (large, very thin steaks that cover the entire plate). The seafood is also excellent. Reservations unnecessary. 29 Calle Hamburgo (phone: 566-3636). Moderate.

Mauna Loa – Extravagant Polynesian decor, with excellent Cantonese and international cooking. Stage show and music for dancing. Reservations advised. 240 Av. San Jerónimo, Pedregal (phone: 548-6884). Moderate.

Las Mercedes – Fine and fancy Mexican cooking. Try the lamb baked in maguey leaves or shrimp baked with cheese. Reservations advised. 113 Calle Darwin at Leibnitz (phone: 254-5000 or 254-8211). Moderate.

Mesón del Caballo Bayo – A beautiful restaurant in a restored and converted hacienda near the racetrack. This is the place for *barbacoa,* a dish made with lamb steamed in maguey leaves. Other Mexican specialties as well. The restaurant is very popular with the Beautiful People and is usually packed at midday and on weekends. Reservations advised. 360 Av. del Conscripto (phone: 589-8653). Moderate.

Mesón del Perro Andaluz – One of the Zona Rosa's most popular indoor/outdoor cafés for afternoon and evening people watching, sangria sipping, and appetizer munching. On the *pasaje,* a picturesque street closed to motor vehicles and lined with shops and other eateries. Reservations advised. 26 Calle Copenhague (phone: 533-5306). Moderate.

El Parador – To best enjoy the fine Spanish fare served in pleasant Iberian surroundings, visit this eatery in the evening when it's least crowded. Reservations advised. 17 Calle Niza (phone: 533-1840) and 198 Campos Elíseos (phone: 545-6465). Moderate.

Piccadilly Pub – This pub is nice for a change of pace, and it serves the best cherries jubilee in town. Reservations advised. 23 Calle Copenhague, Zona Rosa (phone: 514-1515). Moderate.

La Tablita – Hefty portions of good meats are prepared the Argentine way here. Reservations advised. Av. Presidente Mazarik and Torcuato Tasso in the Polanco area (phone: 250-2522). Moderate.

Café de Tacuba – Very old and traditionally Mexican, it's great for lunch. Specialties include many varieties of enchiladas. Make sure you try the house specialty, enchiladas Tacuba. Reservations unnecessary. 28 Calle Tacuba (phone: 512-8482) and 88 Newton (phone: 250-2633). Moderate to inexpensive.

El Caminero – Tacos filled with broiled meat and forged cheese are the specialty here. Order some *cebollitas* (grilled scallions) to accompany them. No reservations. No credit cards accepted. Behind the *María Isabel–Sheraton* on 138 Calle Río Lerma (phone: 514-5615). Inexpensive.

Clunny – The Aztec crêpes are sensational, as are the pizza and the chocolate mousse. Closed Mondays. No reservations, and be prepared to wait for a table. At two locations across the street from each other; Av. de la Paz and Av. Revolución in San Angel (phone: 548-9401). Inexpensive.

Fonda el Refugio – Authentic Mexican cooking. This wonderful little place in the heart of the Zona Rosa is very popular with local residents. The house specialty is *carne asada* (thin filet of beef broiled and served with beans, enchiladas, and guacamole). Closed Sundays. Reservations advised. 166 Calle Liverpool (phone: 528-5823). Inexpensive.

La Gondola – One of the best Italian eateries in the Zona Rosa, with many dishes prepared at the table. Reservations advised. 21 Calle Genova (phone: 514-0743). Inexpensive.

Hostería de Santo Domingo – In business at this downtown location for over 100 years, serving fine Mexican food. Colorful decor and excellent food. Lively music at noon. Closed Sunday nights. No reservations, but on weekends be prepared for a long wait unless you arrive before 2 PM. 72 Calle Belisario Domínguez (phone: 510-1434). Inexpensive.

Los Panchos – The best *tacos de carnitas* (tortillas filled with finely chopped roast pork) in town. For some reason, they always taste better eaten at the street stand than in the restaurant in back, but they are actually the same. No reservations. No credit cards accepted. 9 Calle Tolstoy (phone: 514-5025). Inexpensive.

Terraza Colonial – Great view of the zocalo and surrounding Colonial buildings. The Sunday brunch-buffet is a lot of fun. Reservations necessary for Sunday buffet only in the *Majestic Hotel,* 73 Av. Madero (phone: 521-8600). Inexpensive.

MONTERREY

(pronounced Moan-teh-*ray*)

Some residents claim that Monterrey — Mexico's third largest city (with a population of 3 million), the capital of the state of Nuevo León, and one of the country's major industrial centers — is just like an American city. Even rasher voices have gone so far as to call it the Pittsburgh of Mexico, not only because of the city's large steel mills but also because of the reputation of local industrialists for tightfisted business deals and hardheaded accounting.

Exactly how deeply this view of Monterrey and its residents is ingrained is evident in an old folk tale. Monterrey is beautifully situated in an 1,800-foot valley in the Sierra Madre, surrounded by the hulking 7,800-foot Cerro de la Mitra (Mitre Hill) to the west and the distinctive 5,700-foot Cerro de la Silla (Saddle Hill) to the east. Cerro de la Silla is known for its saddle-shaped crest, which according to legend was formed by a local citizen who lost a peso on the topmost ridge and kept digging frantically until he recovered it.

In fact, besides the common by-products of industrialization — such as noise and air pollution — there is almost no resemblance between Monterrey and any American city — including Pittsburgh. The foundation of Monterrey's contemporary ambience and reputation is thoroughly Mexican and profoundly Old World.

If Monterrey is similar to any other city, it is Mexico City, 600 miles (960 km) to the south. In Monterrey, as in the capital, tall, modern buildings are interspersed with colonial structures that line narrow streets. Fine old homes present simple and dignified façades and face inward to their flower-filled patios. Some are a few hundred years old and date from the city's origins.

Monterrey was a Spanish colonial outpost until 1596, when Don Diego de Montemayor named it Monterey (the second *r* was added later to avoid confusion with the California town) after the Count of Monterey, the Spanish viceroy. The early settlers were frequently attacked by Indians, but they survived and eventually prevailed. The town is a natural crossroads for anyone traveling north or south through eastern or central Mexico, and that put it in the way of just about every army that has marched in Mexico: Both the Spanish and the revolutionaries during the 1810 struggle for independence held the city at one time; a century later, when Pancho Villa began the 1910 revolution in the north, Monterrey's citizens were once again embroiled in battle. In 1847, during the Mexican-American War, Monterrey, like Mexico City and Veracruz, was invaded by the US and occupied by the forces of General Zachary Taylor, who stayed in the city until a peace treaty was signed. One of the most bitter battles of the war occurred on the hill crowned by Monterrey's Bishop's Palace, where Mexican forces held out for 2 days after the city surrendered.

In the long run, Monterrey's strategic location has been more of an advantage than a liability. If armies found it a convenient stopover, so have millions of travelers over the years. With excellent train service and the highway running direct from Laredo via Monterrey to Mexico City, practically everything and everybody on the way to Mexico from the US between the Atlantic Ocean and the Rocky Mountains follow this route. Some travelers fly directly to Mexico City, but for drivers Monterrey is an important stop. Visitors will find this a safe city, and one in which the US and its citizens are particularly welcome.

Monterrey did not develop into an industrial center until after 1888, when the Mexican government granted tax exemptions to new industries here. From then on it boomed, and today everything from steel, beer, cement, tiles, glass, and cigarettes to chemicals, textiles, and construction materials is manufactured here. John Deere, Chrysler, and General Electric all have factories in Monterrey.

But interest in Monterrey is not limited to the historian or the business-minded. It is also a big college town, with seven universities, among them Monterrey Technological Institute, the MIT of Mexico. The state University of Nuevo León and the private Monterrey University attract medical students from the US. The college crowd, along with most everyone else, strolls through the Grand Plaza in the evenings, until midnight in summer. Where young people are concerned, moreover, much of the "strolling" is done in cars in the popular Garza García section of town.

The city has a noticeably large collection of modern sculpture, much of it on the Grand Plaza. Among the most outstanding pieces are Rufino Tamayo's striking *Homage to the Sun* and Gabriel Ponsarelli's celebratory *The Children and Monument to Youth.* More controversial are Luis Barragán's orange *Beacon of Commerce,* with its piercing green laser, and the unwieldy *Fountain of Life* by Luis Sanguino. In Garza García is the prominent 100-foot-high pipeline sculpture, known locally as *Los Tubos* (The Tubes), by Xavier Melendez, which holds its ground most admirably.

If you want to get away from the city crowds, Monterrey's environs provide ample opportunity. Within 40 miles (64 km) of the city lie the García Caves, among the largest and most beautiful caverns in Mexico; Huasteca Canyon, a 1,000-foot gorge with striking rock formations; and La Boca Dam, a good place for swimming, water skiing, or boating.

MONTERREY AT-A-GLANCE

SEEING THE CITY: The Chepe Vera Hill, where the Bishop's Palace stands, commands a panoramic view of the city; on the west side of town, it's reached via Calle Padre Mier. Sunsets are lovely from atop Chipinque, the ridged plateau standing 12 miles (19 km) southwest of the city. Closer to home, the tower of Old City Hall at the northern end of the Grand Plaza and the second floor of New City Hall at the southern end both provide sweeping views of what lies in between.

 **SPECIAL PLACES:** The intersection of Juárez and Aramberri is the orientation point in Monterrey addresses. The numbers start at this intersection and ascend as you get farther away. Direction orientation also begins from here. Streets running north and south are designated *norte* (nte.) and *sur;* those going east and west, *oriente* (ote.) and *poniente* (pte.).

Grand Plaza – Also known as Marco Plaza, it's one of the largest town squares in the world. Abounding with fountains, flowers, walkways, modern sculpture, a theater, and an underground shopping mall, is also where the action is most evenings, with band concerts on weeknights in summer. The south end incorporates verdant Plaza Zaragoza, once the city's main square and site of City Hall, the cathedral, and the Beacon of Commerce tower. The stately building with the winding stair leading to the front entrance is the *Monterrey Casino,* a private social club. Bounded by Washington, Constitución, Zaragoza, and Dr. Coss.

Cathedral – Construction of this cathedral began in 1600 but was not completed until the mid-19th century. The richly carved baroque façade, the Catalonian bell tower, and the interior murals are notable. Zuazua and Ocampo.

Palacio del Gobierno (Government Palace) – Built in 1908, this decrepit but endearing red sandstone structure, with eight Corinthian columns in front, houses the offices of the governor and other state officials. Of interest inside is the pigeon-riddled colonial-style patio, the plaque commemorating the meeting between Franklin D. Roosevelt and Mexican President Manuel Avila Camacho, and the historical exhibition in the red reception room that includes the guns used by the firing squad to execute Emperor Maximilian. Open weekdays. No admission charge. Zaragoza and Cinco de Mayo.

Palacio Federal (Old City Hall) – Now occupied by the telegraph and postal services, this building at the northernmost end of the Grand Plaza features a beautiful 16th-century courtyard complete with wrought-iron lamps and tiled arches. From the upper floors you get an excellent view of this part of the metropolis. Sagrada Corazón (Sacred Heart Church) is next door. Open weekdays. No admission charge. Zaragoza and Washington.

Palacio Municipal (New City Hall) – The second floor and roof of this modern building offer fine views of the Grand Plaza; ask a guard for permission to look. The proud sculpture by Rufino Tamayo next to it, *Homage to the Sun,* is said to represent dawn. Zaragoza and Ocampo.

El Obispado (Bishop's Palace) – Built in 1788 as a retirement home for high-ranking clergymen and a museum since 1956, this palace, because of its strategic location, was turned into a fort during the Mexican-American War. The French also attacked this fort, and Pancho Villa occupied it for some time. The battle-scarred exterior tells the story; the small museum inside elaborates on it. Closed Mondays. Admission charge. On the west side of town atop Chepe Vera Hill, via Calle Padre Mier to Calle México — then take the next left (phone: 460404).

Purísima Church – The design, by Enrique de la Mora, draws architecture devotees from all over the world. Impressionistic bronze statues of the apostles adorn the façade of the cruciform shell and simple bell tower. The figure of the patron saint of Monterrey inside is said to have stopped the Santa Catarina River from flooding the city. 748 Hidalgo Poniente.

Sanctuary of Guadalupe – Another modern church, it looks like a giant tepee set against the Monterrey skyline. Statues of the Virgin of Guadalupe and Pope John Paul II flank it. The original church stands off to one side. Jalisco and Libertad, in Colonia Independencia.

Cuauhtémoc Brewery – Bohemia and Carta Blanca beers are produced here, in one of the largest breweries in Mexico. The original building now houses the *Museum of*

Monterrey (see below). The *Hall of Fame,* also on the brewery grounds, honors national and international baseball greats, as well as bullfighters, boxers, soccer stars, even cowboys. Tours of the brewery, given Tuesdays through Fridays, include free samples. Closed Mondays. No admission charge. Av. Universidad at Mora (phone: 336972).

Museo de Monterrey – A fine collection of contemporary Mexican art is displayed alongside huge wooden barrels and bronze and copper vats in what was the original Cuauhtémoc Brewery (see above). Among the artists represented here are Bartolomé Murillo, José Orozco, David Siqueiros, Diego Rivera, and Rufino Tamayo. Closed Mondays. No admission charge. 2202 Av. Universidad Nte. (phone: 741383).

Centro Cultural Alpha (Alfa Cultural Center) – A striking science museum that looks like a tin can set at an angle in the ground, it features hands-on exhibits that pique one's curiousity. The planetarium includes a giant-screen Omnimax theater. Open daily except Mondays from 3 to 9:30 PM. Complimentary transport to and from Alameda Park, at Villagrán and Washington. Admission charge. 1000 Av. Roberto Garza Sada (phone: 783466).

Casa de la Cultura (House of Culture) – For art and railroad lovers alike, it offers galleries with changing exhibitions of modern art, housed in a Tudor-style train station trimmed with beautiful woodwork. Open daily. No admission charge. 400 Colón Nte. and Carranza (phone: 742612).

ENVIRONS

Chipinque Mesa – A short drive up the pine-covered slopes of the Sierra Madre culminates in this ruffle-ridged, 5,000-foot plateau, surely a cousin to the New Jersey Palisades. It is also a resort area with summer homes, cabins for rent, a restaurant, and a modern motel (see *Best in Town*). The view of Monterrey from here is magnificent. 12 miles (19 km) southwest of Monterrey, off the highway to Saltillo.

Cola de Caballo (Horsetail Falls) – Within a 30-minute drive of Monterrey are the Horsetail Falls, a nice spot for picnicking that would be nicer minus the crowds and the litter they leave behind. Beside the main falls, there is a triple cascade known as the Three Graces. Walk the three-quarters of a mile to the base of the falls or hire a burro or horse. About 22 miles (35 km) south on Rte. 85 to the village of El Cercado, then 4 miles (6 km) west to the falls.

Huasteca Canyon – This 1,000-foot gorge with massive rock formations framing the stark ravines is great for an outing, particularly of a photographic nature. At noon the image of the Virgin of Guadalupe can be discerned in the rocks. Follow the highway to Saltillo beyond the turnoff to Chipinque to the village of Santa Catarina, then go 2 miles (3 km) south (left) on Huasteca. It can be hard to find, but signs leading to the canyon are posted along the way.

Saltillo – A 1½-hour drive west from Monterrey, Saltillo is a small town with much to offer. There is shopping at the *Mercado Juárez* (between Padre Flores and Allende) and *Platería Taxco* (428 Victoria; phone: 841-42726) for crafts items, and at the *El Saltillero* serape factory (569 Victoria) for custom blankets and ponchos; sophisticated dining at the lovely *El Tapanco* restaurant (phone: 841-44339), where *huitlacoche* crêpes are a specialty; and comfortable places to stay overnight — at the plush *Camino Real* (Hwy. 57 at Km 370; phone: 841-52525) or at the charming *Urdiñola* (211 Calle Victoria; phone: 841-40940).

■ **EXTRA SPECIAL:** The García Caves, among the largest and most beautiful in the country, are set high inside a mountain, one of only five such caves in the world. A cable car inches 915 feet to the entrance of the cavern, where 45-minute tours are conducted over well-lighted, meandering passageways that climb ever higher inside the mountain. The more than 20 rock formations are labeled in Spanish and

English. Open daily. Admission charge. 13 miles (21 km) on the highway to Saltillo and then 15 miles (24 km) north to Villa de García.

On your way to or from the falls, stop off at La Boca Dam, a large manmade lake popular for boating, water skiing, and windsurfing. It has been developed into a resort area known as Bahía Escondida, with a toboggan billed as the largest in Latin America, tennis, squash, a disco, and a 100-suite condo-hotel, with restaurant, bar, and convention facilities for up to 1,200 people. Unfortunately, the facilities are for members and hotel guests only (phone: 591000). The boat launch site is at El Cercado.

SOURCES AND RESOURCES

 TOURIST INFORMATION: The government tourist information office is on the 4th floor of the Kalos Building (at Constitución and Zaragoza; phone: 401080). It offers information and brochures. *Osetur* (phone: 436616) runs two tours on Wednesdays, Fridays, Saturdays, and one tour on Sunday mornings to such places as Grand Plaza, Kristaluxus, Chipinque, García Caverns, and other sites for about $4. Pick up a useful *Guía Roji* map of the city at *Sanborn's* (just inside the 464 Morelos entrance). For up-to-the-minute information in English on entertainment and special events in Monterrey, call *Infotur* (at Matamoros and Zaragoza; phone: 450870; or Laredo Hwy. next to the airport; phone: 457681); their offices are open Tuesdays through Sundays from 10 AM to 5 PM. *Spot Light* magazine, with highlights of timely goings-on, is available in most hotels; the free *Guía Monterrey* is published monthly. The US Consulate (411 Constitución Pte.; phone: 452120) has maintained an office in Monterrey since 1892.

 TELEPHONE: The area code for Monterrey is 83. When calling from one city to another within Mexico, dial 91 before the area code.

 CLIMATE AND CLOTHES: Temperatures over 80F are common from April through October, but all the larger hotels have air conditioning. In winter, cold snaps necessitate a light topcoat, but generally the days are sunny and warm. Only at night do you need a wrap. Though it rains in August and September, Monterrey doesn't have a pronounced rainy season. Generally, visitors to the city dress casually.

 GETTING AROUND: Taxi – Prices for the 12-mile (19-km) trip to and from the airport in yellow and white cabs are fixed, about $6 one way; other prices are not. A short ride in the downtown area costs about $2; from downtown to Colonia del Valle, $5; ask before getting in. Tips are additional. Taxis cruise, and they are available at *sitios* (taxi stands) opposite the *Ambassador* hotel on Hidalgo, as well as at the corner of Padre Mier and Escobedo. For pick-up service to the airport, contact (in Spanish) *Autotransportes Aeropuerto* (117 Corona Nte.; phone: 403840). They charge about $7 for one to three passengers.

Car Rental – All of the major US car rentals are available at the airport and the major hotels; among them are *Budget* (phone: 404101), *Dollar* (phone: 420503), *National* (phone: 447100), and *Avis* (phone: 422154). *Hertz* has two offices (at the airport and at 814 Garibaldi Sur; phone: 456136). Having a car in Monterrey is a boon, but it can be vexing because of heavy traffic, narrow streets, and few parking lots downtown.

 SPECIAL EVENTS: Mexican *Independence Day* is celebrated with special fervor in Monterrey, beginning with fireworks on the night of September 15 and followed by parades the next morning. On December 12, the *Day of Our Lady of Guadalupe* is celebrated with dances and parades that begin almost 2 weeks earlier; sick children dressed in white come to be healed.

 SHOPPING: Monterrey is not a great shopping town. Leatherwork is the only local craft, though if you are not traveling farther south, you will be able to pick up goods here from all over the country. *Centro Plaza Artesanal* (Juárez between Hidalgo and Ocampo) and *Mercado Indio* (Simón Bolívar and Calz. Madero) are filled with all sorts of Mexican crafts. *Artesanías de Nuevo León,* in a lovely old mansion (at Dr. Coss and Allende) has a more exclusive selection and good prices. Mexican crafts are sold also at the *Colón* (Colón and Constitución) and *Juárez* (Juárez and Aramberri) public markets. *Galerías Monterrey* (at Gonzalitos and P.A. Gonzalezone) one of Mexico's largest shopping centers, has more than 50 shops and restaurants. *Plaza Morelos* (Monterrey's Zona Rosa), the underground shopping center beneath the Grand Plaza, and *Plaza Dorada* (on Calle Hidalgo) are lined with shops and restaurants. The factories and the discounts they offer are what make shopping worthwhile in Monterrey. Most shops are closed in the middle of the day.

Carapán – The best place for crafts. Two blocks from the *Ancira Gran Hotel Intercontiental.* Hidalgo and Galeana (phone: 454422).

Cerámica Regiomontana – All sorts of tiles are available here, and portraits can even be styled in tiles. Tours may be arranged. At Km 335 of Blvd. Díaz Ordaz (phone: 360047).

Kristaluxus – Latin America's largest glass factory, its crystal store has markdowns of 30% to 50%. Factory tours weekdays, 9 AM to 1 PM and 2:30 to 6:30 PM; Saturdays, 9 AM to 1 PM. 400 José María Vigil, between Guerrero and Zuazua (phone: 514308).

Tane – A branch of Mexico's prestigious silver shop is at the *Galerías Monterrey* (phone: 336824).

 SPORTS: Baseball – The city's team, the *Sultans,* is a member of Mexico's professional Triple A League, and plays from March to August. Check with the tourist office or your hotel desk for the schedule.

Bullfights – Bullfights are held nearly every Sunday from May to December at the *Plaza Monumental* (Av. Universidad). Tickets are sold at the bullring (phone: 740505).

Charreadas – Mexican cowboys — some of them businessmen and professionals in real life — compete in rodeo exhibitions most weekends, usually on Sundays. The venue changes from week to week. Check with your hotel travel desk.

Cockfights – Popular at fairs and fiestas, and the betting runs high. Although legal, these bloody battles are not for everyone. The strong of heart and stomach can witness the spectacle daily (just as bloody, but no betting) at the *La Fe Palenque* restaurant (see *Eating Out*).

Golf – Monterrey has half a dozen private golf courses, though visitors usually can obtain temporary memberships through their hotel travel desk. The *Club de Golf Valle Alto* (7 miles/11 km south of Monterrey) has an 18-hole course, and many of the hotels can arrange for guests to play.

Hiking – Do as the local folks and climb up Chipinque. Follow Gómez Morín past the *Los Tubos* sculpture and proceed up the mountain to a toll booth and parking lot. From there, take a foot path straight up. The climb takes more than an hour.

Playing Fields – The government has converted the dry bed of the Santa Catarina River (dammed up in the 1970s) into a well-used 2-mile stretch of sports facilities — tracks, tennis courts, soccer fields, and baseball diamonds.

Water Sports – La Boca Dam is good for boating and water skiing (see *Extra Special,* above). There is a large swimming pool at the entrance to the García Caves.

 NIGHTCLUBS AND NIGHTLIFE: Popular discos include *Baccarat* (50 Grijalva; phone: 788648), *Sheresada* (*Granada Inn*), *AJA* (Calle Eduardo C. Livas; no phone), and *Scaramouche* (*Monterrey Crowne Plaza*). In the Colonia del Valle area, visit *Heaven* (108 Rio Orinoco; no phone) with its throbbing blue neon heart, *Privat* (304-4 Av. Roble; phone: 786972), or the *Disco Club S.S.* (105 Rio Orinoco; phone: 781818). A flamenco show is performed at *El Lugar de los Cantantes* (1006 Morelos Ote.; phone: 717154). Enjoy live jazz nightly at the *Pavilión Bar* of the *Ambassador* or in the elegant lobby bar of the *Ancira Gran Hotel Intercontinental* nightly, except Sundays. Latin American music is performed at *La Milpa de Valerio* in Colonia del Valle (200 Gómez Morín), and the *Monterrey Crowne Plaza* presents a variety of musical performers in the evenings.

BEST IN TOWN

 **CHECKING IN:** As the major automotive gateway from the eastern US, Monterrey has a fair variety of good accommodations. Most hotels have air conditioning, and many have pools. Expect to pay about $170 for a double room at a hotel listed as very expensive; about $125 to $165 at expensive; $50 to $100 in the moderate range; and about $50 or less at those listed as inexpensive. All hotels listed below accept MasterCard, Visa, American Express, and Diners Club. All telephone numbers are in the 83 area code unless otherwise indicated. When calling from one city to another within Mexico, dial 91 before the area code.

Fiesta Americana Monterrey – An ultramodern structure opened in late 1990, this property is located in Residencial San Agustín, one of Monterrey's most exclusive residential areas. It has 228 rooms and suites, a gym, tennis court, pool, restaurant, 24-hour coffee shop, and 2 bars. 300 Av. Vasconcelos Ote. (phone: 565622; 800-FIESTA-1; FAX: 356606). Very expensive.

Ambassador – Beautifully renovated, this 240-room establishment, now operated under the aegis of the Westin chain, has large, tastefully furnished rooms and a good dining room. Request an odd-numbered room for a mountain view. 310 Ocampo Ote. (phone: 422040; FAX: 451984). Expensive.

Antaris – Only for people with a car, it's comfortable, with striking black lacquer furniture, 44 small rooms with wet bars, and even a skating rink and movie theater nearby in the *Del Valle* mall. 400 Río Danubio Ote., Garza García (phone: 789966; FAX: 789966). Expensive.

Monterrey Crowne Plaza – This spacious but businesslike 15-story, 390-room hotel is part of the Holiday Inn chain. It has a restaurant, bar, tennis courts, pool, solarium, and aerobics classes. The daily breakfast buffet rates high, and the pricier Plaza Club floors are elegant. 300 Av. Constitución Ote. (phone: 449300 or 800-HOLIDAY; FAX: 443007). Expensive.

Ancira Gran Hotel Intercontinental – A Monterrey landmark for more than 75 years, this 300-room property retains its Old World charm. Amenities include a small pool, a restaurant, and a lobby bar with live music as well as a smaller bar that recalls a Toulouse Lautrec haunt. Its restaurant, especially the Sunday buffet, is popular. Plaza Hidalgo (phone: 451060; FAX: 445226). Moderate.

Clarion Hotel Monterrey – It has 197 air conditioned rooms, as well as a good dining room and bar with entertainment nightly. It's convenient and comfortable, though some rooms are a bit overdone. Morelos and Zaragoza (phone: 435120; 800-221-2222 in the US; FAX: 447378). Moderate.

Granada Inn – This hotel has 163 rooms, a pool, restaurant, a bar, and a popular disco. J. del Morral and Almazán (phone: 767383; FAX: 767384). Moderate.

Holiday Inn – Attractive grounds are a plus at this refurbished old motel; also a bar, nightclub, pool, and shops; 195 units. 6 miles (10 km) north on Rte. 85 at 101 Av. Universidad Nte. (phone: 762400; 800-HOLIDAY in the US). Moderate.

Río – It has 395 rooms, a pool, patio, cocktail lounge, and dining room. Padre Mier and Garibaldi, 7 blocks west of the Grand Plaza (phone: 449040; 800-421-0767 in the US; FAX: 451456). Moderate.

El Paso Autel – Not as centrally located as the larger hotels, this one nonetheless affords a pleasant stay. It's modern, with 64 rooms, a coffee shop, and a small pool. Near Old City Hall, at 130 Zaragoza Nte. (phone: 400690). Inexpensive.

Royal Courts – A modern colonial-style hostelry, with 75 rooms, a heated pool, restaurant, and satellite TV. Six miles (10 km) north of Monterrey at 314 Av. Universidad (phone/FAX: 762261/92). Inexpensive.

 EATING OUT: In addition to the good hotel dining rooms at the *Ambassador* and *Ancira Gran Hotel Intercontinental,* several of the restaurants in town specialize in *norteño*-style (northern-style) cooking, which means charcoal-broiled steaks, *cabrito* (kid), and thin tortillas made of wheat flour rather than cornmeal. The beef, which comes from Chihuahua and points west, is known for its tastiness. Good restaurants have sprung up south of the downtown area in the wealthy, international Garza García residential area. Expect to pay up to $50 for a full dinner for two at places in the expensive range; about $25 to $35 at the moderate places; and $20 or less at those listed as inexpensive. Prices do not include drinks, wine, or tips. Most restaurants accept MasterCard and Visa; a few also accept American Express and Diners Club. Unless otherwise noted, all restaurants are open daily. All telephone numbers are in the 83 area code unless otherwise indicated. When calling from one city to another within Mexico, dial 91 before the area code.

Gambrino's – *Filete Gambrino,* filet of beef stuffed with *huitlacoche* (a delectable corn fungus), is a delicious specialty offered at these elegantly decorated eateries. Reservations advised. At two locations: 265 Gómez Morín (phone: 789719) and in *Galerías Monterrey* (phone: 330752). Expensive.

Luisiana – The continental cooking is of high quality and the place itself is pretty posh — linen napkins, plush carpets, tuxedoed waiters, and soft piano music in the background. The soups and seafood are fine, and the wines reasonably priced. Reservations necessary. 530 Hidalgo Ote. (phone: 431561). Expensive.

El Mesón del Olivo – This Spanish eatery serves the usual Iberian fare, including suckling pig, tasty and well presented. On Fridays and Saturdays a *peña flamenca* is performed, complete with flamenco dancing, guitarists, and poetry recitals. Open for lunch and dinner. Reservations advised. 805 Juan I. Ramón Ote. and Dr. Coss (phone: 437474). Expensive.

Las Pampas – When it comes to ethnic food, Argentine fare is very popular in Mexico. *Churrasco* (grilled steak), *carnes asadas* (barbecued meats), and *empanadas* are specialties, in a fancy setting. Reservations advised. 2401 Garza Sada (phone: 582127). Expensive.

Le Pavillón – Very elegant. Decor, service, and food — Mexican and international dishes — can best be described as refined. Closed Sundays. Reservations necessary. In the *Ambassador Hotel* (phone: 422040). Expensive.

Résidence – An elegant, old-fashioned townhouse has been converted into an impressive international restaurant where the specialty is prime ribs. On Fridays, there is a *menú de degustación*, with samplings of seven dishes. It's a good place to view the movers and shakers of Monterrey society. Reservations necessary. 605 Degollado Sur at Matamoros (427230). Expensive.

El Tío – Another good choice for *cabrito* (kid), which is grilled over mesquite here. Reservations advised. Hidalgo and México (phone: 460291). Expensive.

Casa Grande – It offers mostly Mexican food and a view of Chipinque from its lamplit garden. Reservations advised. In Garza García, at 152 Vasconcelos Pte. (phone: 351165). Moderate.

La Fe Palenque – A *palenque*, in Mexico, is a place where cockfights are held, and that is exactly what accompanies the strictly Mexican fare in this huge establishment, which seats 400. Beware, however; this is not a spectacle for the faint of heart. Reservations unnecessary. 2525 Av. Morones Prieto Pte. (phone: 451347). Moderate.

Mesón del Gallo – Serving Mexican favorites and grilled US cuts of beef, this eatery with two bars features Latin American music and entertainers. There's also an art gallery and handicrafts store on the premises. Dinner only. Reservations advised. 943 Padre Mier Ote. (phone: 434630). Moderate.

El Molcas – Everything in this new establishment is strictly Mexican, including the waiters who wear regional costumes and the lively music performed daily and on Saturday and Sunday nights. The buffet is a real bargain, but there plenty of à la carte selections too. Reservations advised. At two locations: 2778 Av. Garza Sada Sur (phone: 580181) and next door to the new *Fiesta Americana* at 601 Monte Rocalloso (phone: 567521). Moderate.

Sanborn's – Quite popular for its American and Mexican dishes, including *molletes* (*bolillos*, or rolls, toasted with beans and cheese) and *carne asada* (grilled meat), this American-style restaurant charges reasonable prices. No reservations. 920 Escobedo Sur, a half-block north of Plaza Hidalgo (phone: 421441). Moderate to inexpensive.

El Pastor – This simple corner eatery with the *cabrito* (kid) roasting in the window was one of the first places to serve the local specialty and still does it best. You can order kid in several ways (*al pastor* means roasted) and have coffee and soft drinks, all for a modest price. No reservations. 1067 Madero Pte., 5 blocks west of Pino Suárez (phone: 740480). Inexpensive.

■ **Note:** For some of the best baked goods in town, stop in *Mary Lu — La Baguette*, open daily at two locations (250 Paseo La Victoria and 204 *Galerías Monterrey;* phone: 385593, 385592, or 382577).

MORELIA

(pronounced Moh-*reh*-lyah)

A stately, regal city, Morelia is among the gems in Mexico's colonial highlands. It's a wonderfully restful place and a happy choice as a base from which to explore the towns and villages of the lovely state of Michoacán, of which it is the capital. The city is about midway between Guadalajara and Mexico City — roughly a 6-hour drive from each — and sits on a plateau more than 6,000 feet high. It has a moderate climate and a leisurely, relaxing pace.

Antonio de Mendoza, Mexico's first viceroy, founded the city in 1541 and named it Valladolid after his home in Spain. It kept the name through 300 years of Spanish rule; after independence, the Mexicans renamed the town Morelia to honor a local hero of the War for Independence, José María Morelos.

The Tarasco Indians, who inhabited this area prior to the coming of the Spaniards, successfully resisted the Aztec, and those who remain have not allowed the modern world to encroach too much on their culture. A market still survives in nearby Pátzcuaro. The Tarasco also live on the nearby island of Janítzio in Lake Pátzcuaro. Although tourism is the main source of income on the island, the Indians living there generally go their own way — making pottery, wood carvings, and serapes and raising just enough food for themselves — much as they did in pre-Columbian times.

As in most Mexican towns, the main plaza in Morelia, shaded by trees and surrounded by colonnades, is the focal point of town life — the place to start sightseeing or just to sit and relax. As part of its Family Sundays program, the local government closes the downtown area to traffic, and concerts and cultural programs are held on the plaza. Don't be surprised if someone offers to sell you a guitar or violin. Both instruments are made entirely by hand in the surrounding villages. You might not have thought of buying a guitar to serenade someone back home, but if you like the idea, you'll probably get a good deal here.

This region is particularly famous for its folk art, due in large part to the efforts of Vasco de Quiroga, the first bishop of the state of Michoacán. Quiroga traveled around to the villages encouraging the artisans in their crafts and helping them to find markets for their work. He also established the College of San Nicolás, the oldest university in Latin America.

The best-known crafts of the region are pottery and wood carvings. Artisans make pottery in a great variety of styles — the different colors and painted designs usually indicate in which village the work was created. One popular pattern is a light beige background with brown line drawings of fish, animals, and people. You can buy a complete dinner set for reasonable prices; the only drawback is the fragility of the product — it doesn't always survive very well on the region's bumpy roads.

Another local craft is the elegant, slightly Oriental lacquerware that is produced in villages around Morelia. Though expensive, the lacquerwork is exquisite. You'll find trays, plates, and delicate boxes decorated by a process known as inlay: Tiny grooves are etched into the wood and filled with gold leaf to form a design, and the whole surface is lacquered to preserve the pattern. The best way to tell if an item has been inlaid is to lightly run your fingertips over the work. If it is perfectly smooth, it has only been painted; if it feels slightly bumpy, then it is legitimate lacquerwork.

MORELIA AT-A-GLANCE

SEEING THE CITY: You can get a good view of the city from the hills of Santa María, which overlook this 6,000-foot plateau. Follow Calle Galeana about 2 miles (3 km) off Rte. 15.

SPECIAL PLACES: Several points of interest are within walking distance of the main plaza, Plaza de los Mártires. You can reach the others by car or taxi.

Plaza de los Mártires (Plaza of the Martyrs) – Filled with fountains and flowers, it is the focal point of downtown socializing. People chat and read on its benches, lounge on its grass. Free band concerts take place here on Sundays at 7 PM.

Cathedral – Originally started in 1640 by Don Vasco de Quiroga, construction was completed only a century later. The building stands today as one of the best examples of the Plateresque style in Mexico, with its perfectly proportioned towers, rose stone façade, and colonial portal. On the east side of the Plaza de los Mártires.

Aqueduct – If you drive into Morelia from Mexico City, you will pass this remarkable engineering feat — an 18th-century masonry aqueduct 30 feet high with 253 arches. You'll know you're here when you see a large fountain with three striking, half-clad Tarasco women (though, a real Tarasco woman would never appear in public in such attire). While here, walk along the Calzada de Fray Antonio de San Miguel, shaded by trees hundreds of years old. Also stop in at the Sanctuary of Guadalupe. Inside you'll see Indian *retablos,* paintings that are done on wood or tin, depicting, in this case, the life of the Dieguinian monks who settled in Valladolid. The church is also of interest because of its natural and brightly colored clay ornamentation. Av. Tatavasco on Jardín Morelos.

Museo Casa Morelos (Museum of the Home of José María Morelos) – The home of the famed Mexican patriot José María Morelos after he came to prominence now houses a museum that contains many manuscripts and memorabilia, including the blindfold Morelos wore when he was executed. In the courtyard are two interesting carriages, one said to have carried the Holy Host on sick calls and the other — once the property of a town dandy — extravagantly furnished and decorated. (The birthplace of Morelos is nearby, at 113 Corregidora and García Obeso.) Open daily. No admission charge. 232 Calle Morelos Sur (phone: 32651).

Museo Michoacano (Michoacán Museum) – An impressive 18th-century palace houses the state museum, which has archaeological artifacts from the Michoacán region, an art gallery with Frederico Cantú's mural of the *Four Horsemen of the Apocalypse,* exhibitions of weapons, a puppet collection, and colonial furniture and paintings. Closed Mondays. No admission charge. On 305 Calle Allende and Abasolo, a few steps from the southwest corner of the main plaza (phone: 20407).

Colegio de San Nicolás (University of St. Nicholas) – Originally founded by Bishop Vasco de Quiroga in Pátzcuaro, the university was moved to its present site in 1580 and is now a high school. The murals on the walls of the patio are interesting. One block west of the plaza on Madero.

Museo de Arte Contemporaneo (Museum of Contemporary Art) – Housed in a very "unmodern" building, this lovely museum features 13 galleries of changing exhibitions. Closed Mondays. No admission charge. 18 Aqueducto and Cuauhtémoc Park (phone: 25404).

Museo de Arte Colonial (Museum of Colonial Art) – An interesting collection of Christ figures made from sugar and corn cane pulp, as well as several colonial paintings are on display in this 18th-century home that has been converted into a museum. Especially noteworthy is the Miguel Cabrera painting that hangs on the wall of the charming interior patio. Closed Mondays. No admission charge. 240 Calle Benito Juárez (phone: 39260).

Casa de la Cultura – One of the oldest and most impressive structures in Morelia, it was built in 1619 as a Carmelite monastery and is now part school, part museum. It contains an interesting *Mask Museum,* with examples from Chiapas, Jalisco, Oaxaca, Guanajuato, Veracruz, and other regions. There is also a small archaeology museum, as well as changing exhibitions of photography, painting, and sculpture. Open daily. No admission charge. Av. Morelos Nte. near Plaza de Carmen (phone: 31059).

Centro de Convenciones (Convention Center) – Besides conventions, this modern complex has a bookstore, a small handicrafts shop, the *Morelos Theater* — where classical and modern plays are performed and musical events take place — and the ultra-modern *Morelia Misión* (Av. Ventura Puente near Av. las Camelinas). There is also a lovely wooded area that shelters an orchid house, which is open daily, and a small planetarium, with shows at 7 PM on Fridays and Saturdays and 6:30 PM on Sundays. The orchids and "planets" can be found at Calzada Ventura Puente (phone: 46150).

Iglesia del Niño de la Salud (Church of the Christ of Health) – The image of the Christ Child here is said to have healing powers. Half a mile (1 km) beyond the state penitentiary on Rte. 15.

Museo del Estado de Michoacán (State Museum) – Once the home of Mexico's only native-born emperor, Agustín de Iturbide, this stately mansion is now a museum dedicated to the customs and traditions of Michoacán. One of the rooms contains Michoacán's first drugstore. Open daily. No admission charge. Guillermo Prieto 176 and Santiago Tapia (phone: 30629).

■**EXTRA SPECIAL:** A little more than an hour's drive southwest of Morelia lies Pátzcuaro, the heart of Tarasco country. Since the site is on a hillside beside a lake, comfortable shoes are suggested for walking the steep, cobblestone streets. The people are friendly, and they congregate in the streets and plazas at night. The beautiful basilica 2 blocks east of the plaza is famous for its Virgin of Health statue, made of cornstalks and glued together with a substance extracted from orchids. Many arts and crafts shops dot the village (especially around the main plaza and Calle Dr. Coss); the *Museo de Arte Popular y Arqueología* is worth a visit to get a general idea of the indigenous art. The best food in the area is served at the *Posada de Don Vasco,* a mile outside town. The café at the *Mansion Iturbide,* on lamplit Plaza Vasco de Quiroga, is a wonderful spot to sip cappuccino. Pátzcuaro is about 1½ miles (2 km) north of town on Calzada de las Américas.

At almost 7,000 feet, Lake Pátzcuaro is one of the highest lakes in the country. Local fishermen using butterfly-net fishing boats still navigate these waters. You can take a boat ride out to the island of Janítzio, where the Indians live pretty much the way they did centuries ago. A huge statue of Morelos crowns the island, and you can climb the staircase to the top for a spectacular view of the area. *Cabañas de Tzintzuntzan,* on the bank of Lake Pátzcuaro, has furnished cabañas with kitchenette and fireplace, as well as a pool and deck. The boat dock where you can catch a ferry or hire a private boat is outside Pátzcuaro, just off Route 120, less than a half mile (1 km) from the train station. An hour west of Pátzcuaro is Uruapan, where you can find the most beautiful lacquerware made in the area, see the extinct volcano Parícutin, and visit the Tzararacua waterfall. (For more detailed information on the area, see "Pátzcuaro" in *Nogales to Mexico City,* DIRECTIONS.

SOURCES AND RESOURCES

 TOURIST INFORMATION: Both the federal tourist office (303 Acueducto, Suite 4, across the street from Cuauhtémoc Park; phone: 20123 or 20522) and the local tourist office (79 Nigromante, near Av. Madero; phone: 32654) are excellent sources for information and maps of Morelia, Pátzcuaro, and Uruapan. The local office is worth visiting just to see the splendid colonial mansion that houses it.

 TELEPHONE: The area code for Morelia is 451. When calling from one city to another within Mexico, dial 91 before the area code.

 CLIMATE AND CLOTHES: Set on a 6,000-foot-high plateau, Morelia has a moderate climate with winter temperatures in the 60s and summer readings rarely exceeding 90F. Dress casually and for comfort, and in the summer carry an umbrella — that's the rainy season.

 GETTING AROUND: Bus – Local buses are a good way to see the city if you don't have a car, and they cost less than one cent per ride. The bus marked *Directo* travels to the *Plaza de las Américas Shopping Center,* the *Calinda Quality Inn Morelia,* and several good restaurants nearby, and the *Santa Maria* bus goes to the Santa María area, where *Villa Montaña* and several restaurants can be found, and it passes Juárez Park en route; both buses can be picked up downtown at the Melchor Ocampo Plaza on Santiago Tapía. Ask about other bus routes at the tourist office.

Taxi – Plentiful and inexpensive, cabs can be hired by the ride, hour, or day. If you can't get one at the main plaza, walk over to the bus station, at Calles Eduardo Ruiz and Valentín Farias, where there's always a string of them, or call 36100.

Car Rental – Rental agencies include *Budget* (at the *Misión;* phone: 50023); *Dollar* (676 Av. del Campestre across the street from the *Plaza de las Américas Shopping Center;* phone: 53050); and *Rent-a-Quick* (1454 Av. Camelinas; phone: 54466). All the major companies have booths at the airport.

 SPECIAL EVENTS: The *Day of the Dead* in early November is the biggest day of the year in Pátzcuaro and Janítzio. Candlelight processions visit the cemeteries to decorate the graves in an all-night celebration. If you are interested in attending, make your hotel reservations well in advance. The cathedral, with its extraordinary 19th-century organ, is the site of an international organ festival that takes place annually for about 10 days in May.

 SHOPPING: *Plaza de las Américas* – It's a modern, enclosed shopping center with men's and women's boutiques, an exceptionally good *Sanborn's,* a supermarket, a sporting goods store, and even a *Sears.* Av. del Campestre, across from the *Calinda Quality* hotel.

***Casa de las Artesanías* –** In the former Convent of San Francisco, it features handicrafts from all over Michoacán. It is more like a museum than a shop, save that the displays — pottery, copper kitchen utensils, guitars, and unique sweaters, vests, and dresses — are for sale; there is also a small crafts museum on the premises. The *Casa* is open daily. At Plaza Valladolid, Humboldt and Fray Juan de San Miguel (phone: 22486). *La Troje* is another branch on the grounds of the *Convention Center,* Av. Ventura Puente (phone: 46202, ext. 141).

***La Casona* –** Carries an extraordinary selection of crafts from all over the state. Av. Madero Ote. and Belisario Domínguez (phone: 30998).

***La Estrella Dorada* –** Everything is carefully wrapped and labeled in this fine, small candy store. Caramel lovers should definitely try the pancake-shaped *obleas,* made from goat's milk. 42-B Dr. Miguel Silva and Av. Madero Ote. (phone: 20477).

***Exportaciones Guare* –** Reproductions of colonial furniture, hand-lacquered in blooming colors. 421 Av. Héroes de Nacupétaro (phone: 25763).

***Fabrica Señal* –** Don Shoemaker's exceptionally beautiful hand-crafted colonial-style furniture and an extensive selection of quality folk art are for sale at his showroom. 134 Ramón López Velarde, in the Santa María del Guido area, behind the Villa Montaña (phone: 42438).

***Independence Market* –** Behind the Church of the Capuchins is an Indian market that carries Tarasco products, including natural cures for nerve, kidney, and liver ailments (no phone).

***Mercado de Dulces* –** A large market selling candies, including the area's specialty, *ate,* a very sweet candied fruit that comes in a variety of flavors. Directly behind the state tourist office on Calle Valentín Gómez Farias (no phone).

***La Troje* –** A branch of the *Casa de las Artesanías* (see above), it has lovely handicrafts. On the grounds of the *Convention Center* at Av. Ventura Puente (phone: 46202, ext. 141).

 SPORTS: *Club Campestre* (Av. del Campestre; phone: 41203), a private golf course, extends playing privileges to tourists; fishing is good at Lake Pátzcuaro; and there are tennis courts at the aqueduct. For those who prefer all their recreation in one place, the sports complex *Centro Deportivo Venustiano Carranza,* right where the aqueduct ends, has a pool, tennis courts, basketball, volleyball, and more. About 10 miles (16 km) from Morelia is *Balneario Cointzio,* a spa with thermal waters, 2 pools, lockers, and a snack bar. Open daily. Admission charge.

 NIGHTCLUBS AND NIGHTLIFE: The focus of social activity, from dining to dancing, has shifted from downtown Morelia to places along Avenida las Carmelinas. The *Calinda Quality* hotel has live music in its stylish lobby bar, and the *Bambalinas* (2225 Av. Lázaro Cárdenas; phone: 55354) attracts a lively crowd for rock and roll. The *Gyrovago* disco is also at *Plaza de las Américas Shopping Center* (no phone). Some of the bigger hotels, including *Morelia Misión* and *Virrey de Mendoza,* have cocktail lounges with entertainment, at least on the weekends.

BEST IN TOWN

CHECKING IN: Morelia has several good hotels, all the more reason to stop on the way between Guadalajara and Mexico City. Expect to pay about $155 for a double room in hotels listed here as very expensive, up to $60 in expensive, about $40 in moderate, and $25 or less in inexpensive ones. Prices may be lower in the summer. All telephone numbers are in the 451 area code unless otherwise indicated. When calling from one city to another within Mexico, dial 91 before the area code.

Villa Montaña – The ultimate in privacy and intimacy, this colonial villa–style hotel in the Santa María hills features 65 exquisitely decorated suites with fireplaces, set in a landscaped garden. There are many antique furnishings, two lovely sitting rooms, a restaurant (see *Eating Out*), TV sets, a pool, tennis court, and a game-room. Bringing children under 8 is discouraged during high season. Rate includes three meals daily. Mailing address: Apdo. 233, Calle Patzimba, c.p. 58090 (phone: 40231; FAX: 51423). Very expensive.

Calinda Comfort Morelia – Just 2 blocks from the pricier *Calinda Quality* (see below), this colonial-style hostelry opened in 1990. The 80 rooms are built around an interior patio with a pool. Guests may use (and sign for) the facilities at its sister hotel. 5000 Av. Camelinas (phone: 43398; 800-228-5151 in the US; FAX: 45476). Expensive.

Calinda Quality Inn Morelia – A beautiful, modern, 126-room hostelry, it has a tennis court, pool, Jacuzzi, pleasant restaurant, and spacious lobby bar with piano music every night but Monday. 3466 Av. de las Camelinas, in front of *Plaza de las Américas Shopping Center* (phone: 45969; 800-228-5151; FAX: 45476). Expensive

Catedral – At the zocalo, this colonial-style place has 44 comfortable, rustic rooms done in fall colors, with large bathrooms. Facilities include a cozy lobby, restaurant, and bar with live entertainment Wednesday, Thursday, Friday, and Saturday afternoons and evenings. 37 Ignacio Zaragoza (phone: 30783). Expensive.

Morelia Misión – Comfortable and modern — but somewhat sterile — it is set on the lovely grounds of the *Convention Center*. It offers a restaurant, coffee shop (incredibly slow service), a lobby bar with live music at night, TV sets, a pool, and 2 tennis courts. About 10 minutes from downtown at Av. Ventura Puente and Paseo de las Camelinas (phone: 50023; FAX: 50281). Expensive.

Posada de la Soledad – This converted monastery is the most authentically Mexican place to stay downtown. Most of the 60 rooms have wood-beam ceilings. Modern comforts, including a restaurant (see *Eating Out*) and bar have been added. There's a good lunch buffet on Saturdays. 90 Zaragoza (phone: 21888; FAX: 22111). Expensive.

Alameda – A sedate and rather sterile hotel in the heart of the city, with 116 rooms (36 in the newer section), restaurant, and bar. There are performances of the Dance of the Old Men on Fridays and Saturdays. Av. Madero, corner of G. Prieto (phone: 22023; FAX: 38727). Moderate.

Mansión de la Calle Real – Between the main plaza and the Aqueduct, this congenial place offers 66 cheery rooms and a lobby restaurant. 766 Av. Madero Ote. at Isidro Huarte (phone: 32856). Moderate.

Virrey de Mendoza – Originally built in 1565 (with a second floor added in 1744) as a private house, this colonial building on the main plaza provides old-fashioned comfort. It has a stone-arched patio, 54 rooms with soaring ceilings and antique furnishings, a good dining room (see *Eating Out*), and a piano bar. 16 Portal de Matamoros (phone: 20633). Moderate.

Casino – Right on the zocalo, it is clean and quiet. The 50 simple rooms have colonial furniture; the restaurant should be avoided. 229 Portal Hidalgo (phone: 31003). Inexpensive.

Mansión Acueducto – Those who prefer quaint to classy will love this house, said to have been built twice because the owner was such a stickler for detail. The stonework and some of the original furnishings, especially those in the dining room, are stunning. A portrait of the daughter who died young hangs eerily over the fireplace. There is a restaurant and pool, and clean but otherwise barely adequate rooms. 25 Acueducto, near Plaza Morelos and Cuauhtémoc Park (phone: 23301). Inexpensive.

Posada Vista Bella – A motor lodge in the Santa María hills, it has 16 apartments available monthly as well as 42 individual rooms, pool, and restaurant. 2 miles (3 km) off Rte. 15, down the street from *Villa Montaña* (phone/FAX: 40284). Inexpensive.

EATING OUT: The best food in Morelia is found at the more exclusive hotel dining rooms and at some of the new restaurants that have sprung up along Avenida las Camelinas. In almost all the restaurants listed here, however, from the elegant to the more modest, dinner is moderately priced, ranging from about $25 to $35 for two without drinks, with the exception of the ones listed as inexpensive, which run about $20 or less. Most restaurants accept MasterCard and Visa; a few also accept American Express and Diners Club. Unless otherwise noted, all restaurants are open daily. All telephone numbers are in the 451 area code unless otherwise indicated. When calling from one city to another within Mexico, dial 91 before the area code.

Grill Enrique – Fine Mexican food, charcoal-broiled meats, and a good wine list. Piano and organ music afternoons. Closed Sundays. Reservations unnecessary. 54 Hidalgo (phone: 22611). Moderate.

Inchátiro – A barn-like place decorated with Mexican crafts, it specializes in grilled meats, salads, and regional dishes. One of the favorites is the *pollo plaza,* grilled chicken served with enchiladas. Closed Mondays. Reservations unnecessary. 1643 Artilleros de '47 (phone: 51035). Moderate.

Monterrey – Surrounding an interior courtyard on the plaza, this place is the local choice for *cabrito* (kid), which is served from the grill here. Cornish hens and mixed grill are among the other good choices. The service is fast, the surroundings pleasant. Reservations unnecessary. 149 Portal Galeana (phone: 30867). Moderate.

Las Morelianas – This elegant establishment in a manor house has a sitting room with fireplace, a pool with adjacent bar, and a fountain dating from 1883. Specials include red snapper with shrimp, barbecued ribs, and *ensalada caranza,* with lettuce, shrimp, chicken, asparagus, and mushrooms. Reservations advised. 90 El Retajo (phone: 43750). Moderate.

Posada de la Soledad – In the hotel of the same name, it offers well-seasoned, home-style meals served in the rather austere dining room of this former monastery. The prix fixe luncheon menu is a real bargain. Reservations unnecessary. 90 Zaragoza (phone: 21888). Moderate.

La Posta del Gallo – A warm welcome, spotless surroundings, excellent grilled meats, generous drinks, and a huge salad bar, as well as efficient service are found here. Reservations unnecessary. 1035 Blvd. García de León (phone: 48935). Moderate.

Rancho Steak – It has an international menu; the shellfish and grilled steaks are particularly noteworthy. Reservations unnecessary. 514 Av. las Camelinas (phone: 47062). Moderate.

El Solar de Villagrán – This pretty place framed by gardens serves good Mexican food. There is music afternoons and evenings. Closed Mondays. Reservations unnecessary. 13 Av. Campestre and Rincón de las Comadres, near the *Calinda Quality Inn Morelia* (phone: 45647). Moderate.

Las Trojes de Gallo – The name refers to barns, but this looks more like a rustic Swiss chalet with pointed gables. It claims European dishes as its specialty, but recommends the grilled ribs, sausage, chicken, and other meats served with guacamole, cheese, onions, and beans. It also offers a good salad bar. There's organ music Tuesdays through Saturdays at 9 PM. Reservations unnecessary. 51 Calle Juan Sebastian Bach, off Av. las Camelinas; just follow the signs (phone: 47344). Moderate.

Villa Montaña – At the lovely hotel of the same name, this small dining room is striking, its black and white tablecloths ablaze with bright orange carnations and napkins. The fixed price menu, which is very limited, changes daily. Reservations necessary. Mailing address: Apdo. 233, Calle Patzimba, c.p. 58090 (phone: 40231). Moderate.

Virrey de Mendoza – The dining room of a pleasant, conveniently located hotel on the plaza, it offers good food and service, including breakfast, in authentic colonial surroundings. Reservations unnecessary. 16 Portal de Matamoros (phone: 20633). Moderate.

Sanborn's – One of Mexico's most popular chains. The food — Mexican and *gringo* — is well prepared, and the service is especially good. *Enchiladas suizas* (tortillas baked with chicken, cheese, and a spicy tomato sauce) and *jugo de 7 frutas* (a fresh fruit drink blended from seven fruits) are among the favorites. Reservations unnecessary. *Plaza de las Américas* (phone: 44233). Moderate to inexpensive.

La Cabaña de Vic – An attractive, greenery-filled place, it serves good Mexican food and steaks, including the *Vic especial* — a dish made of grilled beef and pork with bacon and mild chilies, topped with melted cheese. Closed Mondays. Reservations advised. 1535 Av. las Camelinas (phone: 40979). Inexpensive.

El Invernadero – Salads, crêpes (45 varieties), and skewered meats served in a rustic greenhouse. Closed Tuesdays. Reservations unnecessary. 412 Blvd. García de León (phone: 50258). Inexpensive.

La Tórtola – A cozy wood cabin where the tortillas are still made by hand. Piano and organ music daily. Closed Mondays. Reservations unnecessary. 477 Francisco Márquez (phone: 46033). Inexpensive.

Trattoria La Pasta Nostra – Surprisingly tasty homemade pasta and pizza. Reservations unnecessary. 2276 Lázaro Cárdenas (phone: 52810). Inexpensive.

OAXACA

(pronounced Wah-*hah*-kah)

High on the vast plateau of the Oaxaca Valley some 250 miles (400 km) south of Mexico City, Oaxaca is an Indian and colonial city surrounded, like all the valley, by the beautiful Sierra Madre del Sur. Outside the ring of the mountains are the jungles of Chiapas to the south, the Pacific Ocean 100 miles (160 km) to the west (Acapulco is almost due west of Oaxaca, if a world away), the Gulf of Mexico to the east.

But within the high, protective wall of the Sierra Madre is the plateau world — 5,000 to 6,000 feet above sea level in the city and rising to 9,000 feet in the surrounding mountains. The city is the capital of the state of Oaxaca; the city has a population of 400,000; the state, more than 3.7 million, almost all of whom are Indians. *Oaxaqueños,* as the natives are called, are mostly descendants of the Zapotec and Mixtec Indian tribes, whose tiny villages dot the valley and mountainside. At the Saturday market, you will hear their languages spoken more often than Spanish.

As part of their legacy, these two great cultures, which flourished in the area hundreds of years before Christ, have left the magnificent ruins at nearby Monte Albán, Mitla, and Yagul. All within a 25-mile radius of Oaxaca, these rich archaeological zones bear witness to an elaborate and highly religious civilization that was well versed in astronomy and had a system of writing that may be the oldest on this continent. In the late 15th century, however, they were conquered by the Aztec; when the Spanish arrived in 1521, they found the area under the hold of Montezuma's empire. Replacing the Aztec fort with their own stronghold, the Spanish named the site Antequera. But in 1529 a city was founded and the name changed to Oaxaca, which derives from an Indian word meaning "forest of gourd trees."

The city was spared some of the worst ravages of Spanish rule. There was no gold or silver to be mined, so Spain's interest in it was purely aesthetic. Cortés fell in love with the area, claimed much of the land for himself, and planned to build an estate fitting his title of Marqués del Valle de Oaxaca. The estate was never built (Cortés died in Spain in 1547), but his descendants kept the property until the 1910 revolution; the name lingers on in odd places — like the sign outside an old hotel or the label on a bottle of mescal.

Oaxaca is also famous for having produced two of Mexico's most important presidents, Benito Juárez and Porfirio Díaz. Juárez, often referred to as the Abraham Lincoln of Mexico, was a Zapotec Indian born in 1806 in Guelatao, a tiny village about 40 miles (64 km) from Oaxaca. He was totally uneducated and was working as a houseboy when he was taken under the wing of one of Oaxaca's most prominent citizens, who recognized his brilliance and had him trained for the clergy. He apparently didn't like any part of religious life, for in later years he almost totally destroyed the church in Mexico, taking away its property and its power. He left the seminary to study law, which he felt would serve him better to help his people. Extremely ambitious, he went into politics and rather quickly became governor of the state, Chief Justice of the Supreme Court of Mexico, and then president.

As President of Mexico, Juárez challenged the powers of the Catholic church, which at the time were formidable. Over the centuries, the wealthy had made a practice of leaving part of their property to the church when they died; by the mid-1850s the church was the largest landowner in Mexico. It also had a monopoly on education and handled such civil matters as marriages and the registration of births and deaths.

Juárez and the members of his Liberal party set about to change all that by permitting civil marriages, opening secular schools, and expropriating the property of the church. These moves were codified in the famous Reform Laws and, since many people opposed them, touched off a civil conflict, the Reform War. The conservatives brought over Maximilian to be emperor, wooed the French, who helped them, and almost chased Juárez out of Mexico. In the end, however, Juárez triumphed, French forces left the country, and the emperor was shot. All this took place about the same time as the Civil War in the US and profoundly affected Mexican history.

Porfirio Díaz, Oaxaca's other famed native son, emerged as a hero of the Reform War and went on to become President of Mexico a few years after Juárez died. Don Porfirio, however, was a different sort. Descended from the Mixtec Indians, Díaz got his start in the army, becoming a hero of the Reform War; he later fought in battles against the French. Although he and Juárez were contemporaries (Juárez died in office in 1872 and Díaz took power in 1876), they represented the interests of very different classes, and once in office Díaz became dictator of Mexico for 35 years. By encouraging foreign investment, he got the British to build railroads, the French to set up banks and establish commerce, and the Americans to invest in almost everything Mexican. Unfortunately for most people, few Mexicans profited directly from this outside commerical interest. The rich owned most of the land, and the poor worked on the land, in the mines, or in industry, and had little control over their lives. Labor was not allowed to organize, and there was no free press. He undid much of the good Juárez had accomplished (although the anticlerical laws remained in effect, as they still do), governing a rather feudalistic society until he was forced out by the Mexican Revolution in 1910.

Oaxaca is proud of Juárez, though its residents are very ambiguous about Díaz. While museums and monuments all over Oaxaca honor Juárez, only a few streets bear Díaz's name (the plaque has been removed from an obscure statue and never replaced).

As with most Mexican towns today, life begins in the main plaza, or zocalo, and Oaxaca's is especially lovely, with its grand old trees and delicate gazebo-shaped bandstand. The ideal places from which to view the lively comings and goings of the plaza are the sidewalk cafés under the Spanish colonnades around the square. Relax here with a drink or cup of coffee, sit back, and let the world come to you. And it will. In the evening, from around 8 to 10 PM, the tempo picks up, and whenever there is a big band concert, it seems the whole town turns up for the show.

OAXACA AT-A-GLANCE

SEEING THE CITY: Cerro del Fortín de Zaragoza, the hill north of Oaxaca that rises 350 feet above the city, offers the best panoramic view of the area. On its lower slope is the statue of native son Benito Juárez, the Zapotec Indian who became President of Mexico, and an open area from which to look out. Slightly farther up a short dirt road at the top of the hill is a pyramidal monument to the flag of Mexico. From both spots the view is magnificent: Rte. 190 about a mile (1.6 km) east of the Av. Madero turnoff; the hill directly south is Monte Albán, which is also a fine place from which to see the city and countryside. There, you will also find the magnificent ruins of an ancient Indian community and the present descendants walking with their goatherds down the hillside. Take García Vigil, cross the zocalo, and continue on Miguel Cabrera to the *periférico.* Cross the bridge and take the right fork.

SPECIAL PLACES: Oaxaca is an amazingly unspoiled city that has 16th-century architecture, 27 churches, two excellent museums, a colorful, active zocalo, a large outdoor Indian market, good shopping, and fascinating side trips to the archaeological ruins. There is always something to see, even if it is only from an outside café along the zocalo. When you get tired of sitting, there are wonderful places to move on to, and when you get tired of moving, there is always an equally wonderful place to sit. It is in many ways the quintessential Mexican city.

Plaza de Armas (Zocalo) – One of the gayest and liveliest squares in all of Mexico. There is a gazebo bandstand, numerous tree-shaded benches, outdoor cafés in all directions, hawkers, *evangelistas* (public letter writers), Indians, *Oaxaqueños,* tourists, students, old and young, rich and poor. Musical concerts are performed evenings and on Sunday afternoons, and wandering street musicians can often be heard at random hours. It is a marketplace, social gathering, and cultural event that should not, and really cannot, be missed.

Basílica de la Soledad (Basilica of Solitude) – This very old and weathered church is famous not for its structure but for the statue of La Virgen de la Soledad (Virgin of Solitude), who is the patron saint of Oaxaca and is considered to have great healing powers. The famous legend attached to her arrival in the city is represented on glass panels in the religious museum at the rear of the church. In the 17th century a pack train arrived in town with one more mule than the muleteer could account for. When the train got to the modern site of this church, the extra mule suddenly fell down and died. It was found to be carrying the incredible stone statue of the Virgin, and the people immediately decided to build a church to commemorate this miraculous event. The church was built in 1682. The statue is robed in a jewel-encrusted black velvet cloak, with a large pearl hanging on its forehead. It also has several changes of clothes for various religious occasions. Calle Independencia, on the Plaza de Baile (Plaza of the Dance).

Cathedral of Oaxaca – The cathedral was built in 1553, and its original lovely baroque façade remains intact in spite of various alterations. The clock, although several hundred years old and made with all wooden works, still keeps good time. It was a gift from the King of Spain to the city of Oaxaca. North side of the zocalo.

Church of Santo Domingo – Founded by the Dominican Fathers in 1570, this vast church is an exquisite example of baroque art and a favorite with the natives of Oaxaca. While the outside is certainly worth a close look, it is the interior that stands out as a truly exceptional work of art. Covered in gold scroll and polychrome reliefs set against a white background, with paved tile floors, massive gold chandeliers, and incorporating 11 chapels, including the lovely Chapel of the Virgin of Rosario (off to the right as you enter), this church is one of a kind and should not be missed. Gurrión and M. Alcalá.

Regional Museum of Oaxaca – Housed in the converted convent attached to the Church of Santo Domingo, this lovely museum is a series of rooms quietly arranged around an open courtyard. There are themes for each space, including regional arts and crafts, costumes, and archaeological artifacts. On the second floor, behind a heavily vaulted door, are the incredible, priceless jewels found at the excavation sites at Monte Albán in 1932. These objects date back to AD 500 and display considerable technical sophistication, with ornate filigree work, alabaster vessels, and jade and bone carvings of an earlier Indian culture, either Zapotec or Mixtec. Closed Mondays. Admission charge. Calle M. Alcalá (phone: 62991).

Rufino Tamayo Museum of Pre-Hispanic Art – Usually called the *Rufino Tamayo,* this museum traces the development of art in Mexico from 1250 BC to AD 1500. The 2,000 art objects that make up this collection were donated to the city by *Oaxaqueño* muralist and painter Rufino Tamayo and his wife, Olga. They are exhibited in a beautifully restored colonial mansion redesigned by Tamayo. Each gallery is arranged to represent a specific culture: Olmec, Totonac, Zapotec, Mixtec, Maya, Nayarit, and Teotihuacán. Closed Tuesdays. Admission charge (Sundays no charge). 503 Morelos (phone: 64750).

Fuente de las Siete Regiones (Fountain of the Seven Regions) – An impressive tribute to the natives of the region, it includes six statues of Indian women in regional garb and is topped by a figure of a male dancer from Teotitlán del Valle wearing a plumed headdress. Porfirio Díaz, past the *Misión de los Angeles Hotel.*

Tule Tree – Standing 4 miles (6 km) east of Oaxaca in Santa María del Tule, this huge ahuehuete cypress tree is estimated to be over 2,000 years old. Some 140 feet high, with roots buried more than 60 feet in the earth, the tree is traditional sentry for the town of Santa María and is larger than the church in front of which it stands. Tehuantepec Hwy. en route to Mitla.

Monte Albán – Once a Zapotec holy city of more than 40,000 people covering 25 square miles, this is now one of the most magnificent archaeological ruins in all Mexico. Monte Albán overlooks the Oaxacan valley from a flattened mountaintop 5½ miles (9 km) southwest of Oaxaca. The Zapotec leveled the area in about 600 BC. The buildings are carefully arranged on a perfect north-south axis, with the exception of one structure, thought to have been an observatory, which is more closely aligned with the stars than the poles. The oldest of the four temples is the Temple of the Dancers, so named because of the elaborate carved stone figures that once covered the building. They are naked and distorted in strange positions, and have since come to be thought of not as dancers but as patients in what might have been a hospital or school of medicine. Another major point of interest is the ball court, where a complicated game — part basketball, part soccer — was played by the young men of the community. The players' object was to navigate the ball with only their hips and elbows into a lowered area in the opponents' court. There is some speculation that the captain of the losing team was sacrificed, but this has never been confirmed. Sometime around 1,000 years ago, the Zapotec were conquered by the Mixtec, an enemy tribe. These new inhabitants never lived in Monte Albán but used it as a city of the dead, a massive cemetery of lavish tombs. More than 160 have been discovered, and in 1932 Tomb 7 yielded a treasure unequaled in this hemisphere. Inside there were more than 500 priceless Mixtec objects, including gold breastplates; jewelry made of jade, pearls, ivory, and gold; and fans, masks, and belt buckles of precious stones and metals. All are now on view at the *Regional Museum of Oaxaca.* Buses to Monte Albán leave Oaxaca from the *Mesón del Angel* (518 Calle

Mina). Schedules and place of departure can be checked at the tourist office; during the high season, it is best to arrive an hour early to get the bus you prefer, and try to get a seat on the right-hand side for the best views. The ruins are open daily until 5 PM (until 4 PM during the rainy season); most of the drive is straight up, tortuously slow, and splendidly scenic. Take García Vigil, cross the zocalo, and continue on Miguel Cabrera to the *periférico*. Cross the bridge and take the right fork.

Mitla – These ruins, 24 miles (38 km) southeast of Oaxaca, are another complex of ceremonial structures started by the Zapotec but taken over and heavily influenced by the Mixtec. The name, derived from an Aztec word, *mictlán,* means "place of the dead." The architecture here is totally different from that of any of the other ruins in the area. The walls of stone and mud are inlaid with small stones cut into geometric patterns, forming a mosaic that is Grecian in appearance. Unlike other ancient buildings in North America, there are no human figures or mythological events represented — only designs. Another unique feature of Mitla is the fact that it was still in use after the Spanish conquest of Mexico. A trip here can be nicely combined with a stop at the famous Tule tree mentioned above, and the *Frissell Museum of Zapotec Art,* just off the plaza in Mitla. This museum, which is also a regional research center of the University of the Americas, is in an 18th-century hacienda and houses a fine collection of Zapotec artifacts that are labeled in English and clearly trace the development of the Zapotec-Mixtec empires. It also houses the rustic *La Sorpresa* restaurant, which serves hearty country cooking and mescal cocktails. (The restaurant is open daily from 8 AM to 6 PM the museum is open daily from 9 AM to 6 PM.) Adjoining the ruins is a small handicrafts market. About a half mile (1 km) from the museum, the ruins can be reached by following the main, paved street, which is lined with small clothing shops. Second class buses leave every half hour from the terminal across from *Central de Abastos* (Central Market); pay the driver directly. The trip takes an hour each way. Rte. 190.

Yagul – About 19 miles (30 km) southeast of Oaxaca on the road to Mitla is yet another group of ruins. Not as elaborate as Monte Albán but set in a lovely spot on top of a hill, Yagul is certainly beautiful and interesting enough to make it worth the trip. This city is predominantly a fortress that's set slightly above a group of palaces and temples and includes a ball court and more than 30 uncovered underground tombs. Rte. 190.

■**EXTRA SPECIAL:** Puerto Escondido is a lovely, little-known hideaway on the Pacific coast which is about to be turned into Mexico's next major west coast resort. For the moment, however, it remains largely unspoiled. The highway that leads there is now paved, but the trip, through the Sierra Madre, takes 8 or 9 hours. As an alternative, *Aerovías Oaxaqueñas* (phone: 63833) has one daily flight that leaves at 10:30 AM. For details, see *Puerto Escondido,* THE CITIES.

SOURCES AND RESOURCES

TOURIST INFORMATION: There is a tourist office (Cinco de Mayo and Morelos; phone: 64828), and there are information booths at the airport, in front of the *Regional Museum of Oaxaca,* and at Monte Albán. The friendly and knowledgeable English-speaking staff can help plan your stay in the city, as well as any excursions you might want to make to nearby ruins such as Monte Albán, Mitla, and Yagul. The International Friendship Center (CENAI) at the Municipal Palace on the zocalo addresses visitors' problems and complaints.

TELEPHONE: The area code for Oxaca is 951. When calling from one city to another within Mexico, dial 91 before the area code.

CLIMATE AND CLOTHES: Geographically, Oaxaca is in the tropics, but its altitude keeps the temperature pleasant all year. Daytime is usually in the high 70s to mid-80s, cooling at night to the mid-60s. In the rainy season, morning and afternoon showers tend to cool the air, but the highs and lows remain much as they are the rest of the year. The one feature of a tropical location that the mountains cannot affect, however, is the rain; and Oaxaca has wet and dry seasons typical of the tropics. The wet season starts in May and lasts until October, with showers in the afternoons and occasional days of nonstop rain in July and August. Clearly the nicest time to visit Oaxaca is the dry season, which is between November and May. The city is very casual, so you needn't worry about what you wear except to make sure that you have a solid pair of walking shoes for exploring the ruins.

GETTING AROUND: Bus – Several bus lines cross Oaxaca, all with their destinations marked clearly on the front. They are inexpensive and run frequently. Buses also go to all of the major archaeological sites.

   Taxi – Oaxaca has about 700 taxis; they can be hired by the hour for more spontaneous sightseeing. Rates should be prearranged (phone: 51303 or 63611). Cabs are also always lined up at the plaza. *Transportación Terrestre Aeropuerto, S.A. de C.V.* (phone: 62438) operates a collective service to and from the airport for less than $2 per passenger.

   Car Rental – *Avis* (phone: 65030), *Budget* (phone: 60611), *Hertz* (phone: 65478), *Mini Rent* (phone: 54786), and other firms have stands at the airport or offices in downtown Oaxaca.

   Tours – There are several sightseeing agencies in Oaxaca, and almost every hotel can arrange guided tours to the archaeological sites as well as to colorful markets in nearby towns.

SPECIAL EVENTS: Oaxaca has managed to conserve its traditions and customs. Known for its colorful fiestas, the town often fills to capacity during a holiday. One of the most popular is *Lunes del Cerro* (Monday of the Hill), held in mid-July. Among the festivities are the *Guelaguetza*, a celebration dedicated to the god of rain and fertility, featuring music, magnificent costumes, and dances — including the famous *Danza de las Plumas* (Indian Feather Dance); the selection of the goddess Centeocihuatl (not for her beauty but for her knowledge of the customs and traditions of her region); and the *Bani Stui Gulal*, meaning "reenactment of the past," which tells the story of the Aztec and Spanish conquests and portrays the battle between the Zapotec and the Mixtec in which Donaji, the last Zapotec princess, was taken hostage and decapitated. The ceremonies are held on the Cerro del Fortín (on Rte. 190 about a mile/1.6 km east of the Av. Madero turnoff) and in the city; reservations are necessary for the main performances (book well in advance — no later than May; reservations can be arranged through US travel agents). On August 31, *oaxaqueños* spruce up their pets and livestock and take them to the Merced church to be blessed. October 12 marks the beginning of the 16-day *Stonecutting Festival* during which blocks of quarry stone are set up at key points around the city, and stone cutters from all over Mexico, as well as other countries, are invited to demonstrate their talents; other events, mainly cultural, are held simultaneously. As part of the celebration for the *Día de los Muertos* (Day of the Dead), a colorful altar contest is held in the zocalo on November 1 and 2. The fiesta for the *Virgen de la Soledad*, held at the Basílica de la Soledad, December 16–18, is the beginning of the *Christmas* celebrations. There are fireworks, regional dances, and a ceremony of lights reminiscent of the ancient winter solstice rites of the Indians. The highlight of the celebration is the *posada*, the procession from inn to inn that reenacts Joseph and Mary's quest for lodgings in Bethlehem; it is held in a different church every night from December 18 to 24. Finally, on December 23, *Noche de los Rábanos* (Night of the Radishes), the entire zocalo is set up with booths from one end to the other. Each has a display of large, imaginatively carved radishes in the shapes of animals, buildings, plants, and anything else conceivable. There also is a special dessert sold during this fiesta called *buñuelos*, thin, crisp pastries with syrup poured over the top. They are served on pottery plates, and it is the custom to smash these underfoot with a wish for the *New Year* as soon as the last drop of syrup has been licked off. On *Christmas Eve*, there are processions from the various churches of Oaxaca to the zocalo, with decorated floats, music, dancing, a colorful piñata contest, and the inevitable fireworks.

SHOPPING: There are a number of items that are unique to Oaxaca, and a number of places where they can be purchased. The famous dark green pottery of the nearby village of Atzompa is available at excellent prices in Oaxaca, as are the Miró and Picasso-inspired wall hangings from Teotitlán, and the black unglazed pottery of Coyotepec. Cotton and woolen shawls, blouses, bags, blankets, heavy serapes, and hammocks are all well made in this area, as are baskets and fine steel hunting knives and machetes with ornate hand-carved handles and engraved blades. Many pieces of jewelry on sale in Oaxaca are reproductions of pieces found at Monte Albán — including necklaces, earrings, and pendants of gold, jade, and seed pearls.

Saturday is the big market day in town, and merchants from all the neighboring communities come in, wearing their native costumes and speaking their various dialects of Zapotec, to sell their wares at the arts and crafts *tianguis* outside the *Central de Abastos*. All the different types of mole are available in the *Viente de Noviembre* market (at Viente de Noviembre and Aldama). Behind the market is a chocolate mill, *Mayordomo*, where Oaxacan chocolate can be specially blended to taste with almonds, sugar, and cinnamon. Considered one of the most colorful and interesting of all Mexican markets, it is worth a visit whether or not you are interested in buying. All the small towns around Oaxaca have their own market days as well, and a quick check with the tourist office should provide you with a list that could keep you busy for weeks. Another way to shop in Oaxaca is by sitting at a sidewalk café or on a bench by the zocalo. You don't have to move, and the vendors will come to you: men with serapes (blankets used as coats, beds, and rugs) over their arms; women with rebozos (woven shawls) carried on their heads; and young children offering everything from chicks to shoeshines or lottery tickets. For ambulatory shopping, Oaxaca has marvelous stores.

Alfarería Jiménez – Carries mostly pottery, brightly colored and handmade, including pitchers, plates, serving dishes, and vases. It's possible to watch the artisans at work here. 402 Zaragoza (phone: 62102).

Aripo – Ten rooms are filled with rugs, pottery, weavings, and ornaments, primarily from Oaxaca. You can watch craftspeople at work on wooden looms. 809 García Vigil (phone: 69211).

Artesanías Cocijo – Pottery, wood, tinware, and textiles. At several locations including 521 García Vigil (phone: 68081).

Casa Brena – This textile store and weavers' workshop has pottery as well. Walk to the rear — listening for the slapping of the looms — to see people spinning the yarn and dyeing the cloth. 700 Pino Suárez (phone: 50222).

Copil – An elegant shop with a wide selection of antique and contemporary masks. Talavera pottery from Puebla and crafts from all over Mexico also are available. 303 Av. Macedonio Alcalá (phone: 67302).

El Diamante – A selection of tinware, pottery, jewelry, and other local crafts. Behind the cathedral at 106-H García Vigil (phone: 63983).

FONART – Clothing, metal ornaments, and ceramics are the wares here. The selection and prices are quite good. In a red and white building at 116 M. Bravo (phone: 65764).

Joyeria y Artesanias – One of the few fine jewelry stores in town carrying silver pieces and precious and semi-precious gems. 226 M. Alcala (no phone).

Mercado de Artesanía – A clean market with well-displayed crafts, where weavers can be seen at work, it's open daily. Some items are 50% less than at other places, but bargaining is a must. Corner of J.P. García and Zaragoza (no phone).

El Oro de Montealbán – Reproductions of pre-Hispanic jewelry made on the premises. Plazuela Adolfo C. Gurrión (phone: 64523).

El Palacio de las Gemas – Regional gold jewelry with pearl and coral inlays as well as a large collection of semiprecious stones. Morelos and Alcalá (phone: 69596).

Productos Típicos de Oaxaca – Though unimpressive from the outside, this group of shops set around a sculpture garden is packed with quality pottery, textiles, handmade toys, and tin figures. They will ship items too big to carry. 602 Av. Belisario Dominguez (no phone).

Taller de Artes Plásticos Rufino Tamayo – The exhibition and sale of paintings, sculptures, and graphics produced by local artists in a workshop bearing the name of one of Oaxaca's most famous native sons. 306 Murguía (no phone).

Tianguis – A wide selection of native textiles, as well as other native handicrafts. Portal de Clavería, on the zocalo (phone: 69266).

Victor's – In a 17th-century monastery, it carries crafts as well as woven clothing. 111 Porfirio Díaz (phone: 61174).

Yalalag de Oaxaca – A tasteful selection of Indian and contemporary crafts, native clothing, and Josefa designs. 104 M. Alcalá (phone: 62108).

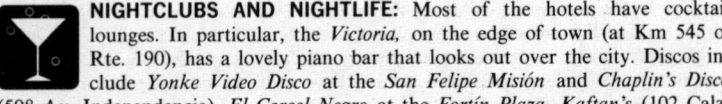

SPORTS: Charreadas – Mexican-style rodeos are held in the *Lienzo Charro*. There is no schedule, but events are always well posted around town.

     Swimming – The several pools in Oaxaca are at most of the large hotels and at the few resorts just outside town.

     Tennis – Both the *Misión de los Angeles* (phone: 51500) and the *Victoria* (phone: 52633) have tennis facilities.

NIGHTCLUBS AND NIGHTLIFE: Most of the hotels have cocktail lounges. In particular, the *Victoria,* on the edge of town (at Km 545 of Rte. 190), has a lovely piano bar that looks out over the city. Discos include *Yonke Video Disco* at the *San Felipe Misión* and *Chaplin's Disco* (508 Av. Independencia). *El Corcel Negro* at the *Fortín Plaza,* *Kaftan's* (102 Calz. Porfirio Díaz), and *Tanilaoo* (at the *Misión de los Angeles*) have live music for dancing. And, as expected, there is the nightlife on the zocalo, where music is heard from 7:30 to 8:30 PM nightly. People promenade, and lively socializing continues until 11 PM. *El Sol y La Luna* (Sun and Moon) restaurant and coffee house (105 Murguia) is a lively gathering place with music every night. At *Los Guajiros* (302 Alcalá) there's dining and dancing to salsa and Latin American jazz nightly from 8 PM to 1 AM. The *Monte Albán,* on the plaza, has a very fine nightly show of regional dances; it's free to guests. On Thursdays at 8 PM the *Misión de los Angeles* (105 Calz. Porfirio Díaz) features folkloric dancing.

BEST IN TOWN

 CHECKING IN: Expect to pay $90 to $125 for a double room in the expensive category; about $40 to $65 in a moderate hotel; and up to $35 in the inexpensive range. Most hotels accept MasterCard and Visa; a few also accept American Express and Diners Club. All telephone numbers are in the 951 area code unless otherwise indicated. When calling from one city to another within Mexico, dial 91 before the area code.

Stouffer Presidente – Beautifully restored, this unexpected jewel was formerly a convent, built in 1576. A monastic air still lingers in the form of breezy patios and small enclosed gardens. There is, however, now a reasonable complement of modern conveniences to the 91 rooms, including TV sets, a heated pool, dining room, and cocktail lounge. Stop by for a drink and look around even if you don't stay here. Jazz is played in the bar every night but Tuesdays from 9 to midnight. On Friday nights there is a buffet of traditional Oaxacan dishes and an excellent performance of regional dances. 300 Cinco de Mayo (phone: 60611; 800-472-2427 in the US; FAX: 60732). Expensive.

Fortín Plaza – Located on the Cerro del Fortín, this modern, 6-story hostelry affords a magnificent panoramic view of the city. Each of the 100 pleasant rooms has a TV set and a telephone, and there's a pool, bar, coffee shop, restaurant, and live music and dancing at *El Corcel Negro*. Av. Venus and Calz. Héroes de Chapultepec (phone: 57777; 800-826-6842 in the US; FAX: 51328). Moderate.

Hacienda la Noria – A 72-room hostelry, 13 blocks south of the zocalo, it has 2 swimming pools, a restaurant, and ample grounds. Periférico at 100 La Costa (phone: 67555; FAX: 65347). Moderate.

Margarita – About a mile (1.6 km) from downtown, this motel offers 60 units, a swimming pool, garden, dining room (see *Eating Out*), and cocktail lounge. 1254 Calz. Madero (phone: 64100; FAX: 61133). Moderate.

Misión de los Angeles – This pleasant place has 155 units, spacious gardens, a pool, 2 tennis courts, dining room (see *Eating Out*), a cocktail lounge with entertainment, the popular *Tanilaoo* with live music and dancing, a gameroom, and laundromat. It's a fine walk from here along Avenida Juárez to the Fountain of the Seven Regions. 102 Calzada Porfirio Díaz (phone: 51500; 800-221-6509 in the US; FAX: 51680). Moderate.

San Felipe Misión – This luxurious property boasts 156 large rooms — many with views of the city — a pool, restaurant, disco, and piano bar. A 10-minute trip out of town, but well worth it. San Felipe del Agua (phone: 50100; 800-648-7818 in the US; FAX: 50900). Moderate.

Victoria – Surrounded by terraced grounds and well-kept gardens, this sprawling, salmon-colored luxury complex is perched on a hill overlooking the city. Amenities include a very good dining room (see *Eating Out*), tennis court, heated pool, disco, and picture-perfect bougainvillea vines. Rooms, bungalows, and suites are available; ask for one with a view. At km 545 of Rte. 190 (phone: 52633; 800-448-8355 in the US; FAX: 52411). Moderate.

Calesa Real – Comfortable and pleasant, it has 77 units (8 with balconies), a small pool, dining room, and cocktail bar. 306 García Vigil (phone: 65544). Inexpensive.

California – Near the *Misión de Los Angeles*, this modern place has 32 rooms with balconies, good food, and friendly service. 822 Calz. Héroes de Chapultepec (phone: 53628). Inexpensive.

Marqués del Valle – Right on the plaza and in the middle of things, with 95 rooms.

The ground-floor restaurant serves a good breakfast, from bananas and cream to hotcakes. 1 Portal de Claveria (phone: 63295; FAX: 66294). Inexpensive.

Mesón del Rey – A nice little surprise of a hotel, only a block and a half from the zocalo, it offers 22 rooms, a cozy lobby, and cordial staff. No credit cards accepted. 212 Trujano (phone: 60033). Inexpensive.

Principal – Modest with only 17 rooms, it charms with geranium-filled clay pots on the balconies and skylights in the bathrooms on the top floor. The lobby has an excellent map of the town. No credit cards accepted. 208 Cinco de Mayo (phone: 62535). Inexpensive.

Señorial – With pool, roof garden, and cocktail bar open until 10 PM, this is one of the most conveniently located hostelries in Oaxaca. The one drawback is the thin walls between its 127 rooms. 6 Portal de las Flores (phone: 63933; FAX: 63668). Inexpensive.

Trebol – The entrance to this property, set amid some rather shabby shops, belies the sparkling cleanliness within. The 14 rooms are small but comfortable, built around a sunlit patio, and there is a restaurant and laundry service. No credit cards accepted. 201 Flores Magón (phone: 61256). Inexpensive.

EATING OUT: There are three specialties for which Oaxaca is known: mole sauce, tamales, and mescal. Mole is a spicy, multi-ingredient sauce made with chocolate, and served with chicken and pork that can be found throughout Mexico, but in Oaxaca it is made darker, thicker, and usually tastier because Oaxacan chocolate is very special. Local tamales are even more special. Moister than elsewhere in Mexico, flat and rectangular, they are wrapped in a banana leaf rather than the usual cornhusk. The most common fillings are chicken and mole sauce, and definitely should be sampled. Mescal, the local alcohol, is made from the maguey cactus (as is tequila), but with a different distilling process and altered taste. The bottle often contains a dead worm; aficionados eat bits of it while drinking the mescal, not unlike the way tequila drinkers lick salt. When eating in restaurants, expect slow service and a bill of around $40 for dinner for two in places we call expensive; about $25 in the moderate range; and under $15 in an inexpensive place. Prices do not include drinks, wine, or tips. Most restaurants accept MasterCard and Visa; a few also accept American Express and Diners Club. Unless otherwise noted, all restaurants are open daily. All telephone numbers are in the 951 area code unless otherwise indicated. When calling from one city to another within Mexico, dial 91 before the area code.

Del Vitral – It's a lovely mansion complete with European chandeliers and stained glass windows. Specialties include the traditional Oaxacan moles and such exotic regional specialties as *nido de grillo,* a basket of tortillas, fried grasshoppers, and guacamole. There's live music in the afternoons and evenings. Reservations advised. 201 Guerrero (phone: 63124). Expensive.

El Refectorio – The refectory of the original convent and the adjoining patio have been combined into a charming setting for continental and Oaxacan dishes. Fridays in the chapel there's a *quelaguetza,* at which an Oaxacan buffet is served. Reservations advised. At *Stouffer Presidente* (phone: 60611). Expensive.

El Tule – This hotel dining room serves excellent continental and Mexican food (chicken in mole sauce is a specialty) and offers a fascinating view of the city below (mist-shrouded in the morning; streetlight-sprinkled at night). Reservations advised. At the *Victoria Hotel,* Km 545 of Rte. 190 (phone: 52633). Expensive.

Ajos & Cebollas – Although the name of this popular restaurant and bar translates as "garlic and onions," these aren't the edible items for which it's known; chicken curry and veal parmesan are more likely choices. There are three separate dining areas whose ceilings grow increasingly low as you move from one to the next — part of the strange and appealing decor. The intimate bar boasts a peppery house cocktail made with mescal, and live music is provided by a trio. Reservations advised. 605 Av. Juárez, across from Paseo Juárez (phone: 63793). Moderate.

Antequera – Set in the *Misión de los Angeles* hotel, it features a pleasant dining room with music provided by local musicians. Dinner is finished by 10. Reservations advised. 102 Calz. Porfirio Díaz (phone: 51500). Moderate.

El Asador Vasco – Basque and Mexican dishes are the specialty here. Try the Oaxacan mole sauce — steamy, black, and marvelous on chicken — or the *cazuelas* — small casseroles of baked cheese, mushrooms, and shrimp in garlic. It's easy to order too much. Dining is elegant and the bar comfortable, but the waitresses can be dour. There's a show every night at 9 PM. Reservations advised. One flight up at Portal de Flores on the zocalo (phone: 69719). Moderate.

Mi Casita – Many consider this the best place to enjoy true Oaxacan cooking. The actual dishes are displayed here, so you can see what your food looks like before you order it. It is especially famous for *chapulines* (grasshoppers), but there are also more conventional local dishes such as enchiladas with chicken and spicy mole sauce. Try to get a table by the window (*Mi Casita* is 1 flight up). Closed Thursdays. Reservations advised. On the south side of the zocalo at 616 Hildalgo (phone: 69256). Moderate.

La Morsa – A large, open-air *palapa* serving excellent seafood and steaks with live music on Sunday afternoons. Reservations advised. 240 Calz. Porfirio Díaz (phone: 52213). Moderate.

El Sol y La Luna – This lively spot is a restaurant, coffeehouse, and gallery combined, with only 10 tables inside and another 5 on the terrace. It's worth the wait for an inside table to hear the music that begins at 9 PM every night. Pizza, salads, Italian dishes, and good chocolate-covered crêpes are on the menu. Open from 7 AM to midnight; closed Sundays. No reservations. 105 Murguía (phone: 62933). Moderate.

Catedral – A local favorite, it is nicknamed the "House of Filets," with no less than 11 tenderloin cuts from which to choose, as well as regional dishes, hamburgers, sandwiches, and a variety of soups. Guadalajara artist Miguel Angel España's paintings fill one of the pleasant dining rooms. Live entertainment at dinner. Reservations advised. A block from the zocalo, at the corner of García Vigil and Av. Morelos (phone: 63285). Moderate to inexpensive.

Alameda – The good food (mole and Oaxacan-style stuffed peppers), service, and decor (especially the indoor patio), as well as the reasonable prices, make this a very agreeable place to dine. Reservations unnecessary. Two blocks from the zocalo at 202 J. P. García (phone: 63446). Inexpensive.

El Biche Pobre – The hands-down favorite for local dishes (there are about seven types of mole) and Oaxaca's famous tamales. Closed Wednesdays. Reservations unnecessary. Mártires de Tacubaya and Abasolo (no phone). Inexpensive.

La Flor de Oaxaca – One block from the zocalo, this is where all the *oaxaqueños* come for breakfast, lunch, or dinner — or simply for a cup of hot chocolate. It's an especially good place to sample a typical Oaxacan breakfast. 311 Armenta (phone: 65522). Inexpensive.

Los Guajiros – An offshoot of *El Sol y La Luna* (see above), it serves the same type of food, but the real specialty here is the music: salsa and Latin American jazz. There's dining — salads and Italian dishes — and dancing from 9:30 PM to 1 AM. Closed Sundays. Reservations advised. 302 Alcalá (phone: 64762). Inexpensive.

La Sorpresa – The specialty in this 18th-century mansion is typical Oaxacan barbecue — marinated, tender, and pungent lamb and chicken. In Mitla, near the plaza (no phone). Inexpensive.

■**Note:** Many cafés line the zocalo; among the best are *El Jardín* and *Del Portal*.

PUEBLA

(pronounced *Pweh*-bla)

At one time, Puebla was the most Spanish city in Mexico. Unlike most of the colonial towns built on the ruins of old Indian cities and ceremonial centers in the century after the fall of the Aztec, Puebla was established on virgin territory about 80 miles (128 km) west of modern Mexico City. As a consequence, it was built from scratch, one of the first places in New Spain in which the burgeoning Spanish-Mexican culture could take root in its new soil and not strike the chalk and bones of the mighty Indian civilization that preceded it, and that it destroyed.

Puebla was founded in 1531 by the Spanish as a fortress town, midway between the defeated Aztec capital of Tenochtitlán and the east coast. According to legend, the bishop of nearby Tlaxcala dreamed of two angels laying out a perfect city on a beautiful expanse of land covered with flowers and trees and surrounded by tall volcanic peaks. The bishop set out in search of his vision and found the exact spot in a 7,000-foot-high valley surrounded by mountains, with 17,872-foot Popocatépetl (Smoking Mountain) and 17,454-foot Ixtaccíhuatl (White Lady) rising to the southeast.

This valley site was only a few miles east of Cholula, one of the greatest ceremonial centers of the Aztec civilization, the city of temples whose walls — according to the first Spanish accounts — were covered with the blood of sacrificial victims. It would have been customary for the new city to have been built over the rubble of this terrible place (Mexico City, after all, was built on top of Tenochtitlán), but this didn't happen. The bishop's dream is one explanation; a more logical one is that Cholula was so terrifying — and its Indian heritage so overpowering — that the early Spanish settlers preferred to start afresh in a spot with fewer Indian ghosts. Most of Cholula's temples were destroyed, and in their place were built dozens and dozens of churches.

The town was settled entirely by the Spanish, particularly by immigrants from Spain's Talavera region — famous for its tiles and pottery — who brought whole families to establish new lives. In this they were very different from the average Spaniard in New Spain, most of whom had come to the new country to make a fortune in gold, silver, slaves, or land and then hoped to skedaddle back to the mother country to enjoy the wealth. The *poblanos* (as residents are called) came to stay; their fortunes were the fortunes of the city and the country. But they were very Spanish, and Puebla was a strongly pro-Spanish city during Mexico's colonial period and consequently a stronghold of the Catholic church. *Poblanos* claim that a church was built for every day of the year in Puebla and its environs. Some 60 churches survive today, many with lovely tiled domes and façades. Catholicism is still a strong influence here; indeed, when Pope John Paul II visited Mexico early in 1979, he held a conference of Latin American bishops in Puebla.

Occupying a position between the Gulf of Mexico and Mexico City, Puebla witnessed the ebb and flow of various attacks and revolutions passing through it en route to the capital. Puebla's moment of greatest drama occurred on May 5, 1862, when a makeshift Mexican army under the command of General Ignacio Zaragoza repulsed the first French contingent sent to Mexico by Napoleon III after Mexico stopped paying indemnities to France. The victory itself was not nearly so important as what it symbolized — the halting of French intervention. Today, the *Fifth of May* is a national holiday. (The French were driven out of Mexico 5 years later, and Emperor Maximilian was executed in June 1867.) The battle was fought in the forts of Loreto and Guadalupe. Guadalupe is in ruins, but Loreto is now a military museum worth visiting for a history lesson, as well as for the fine view it commands of the Puebla valley and the volcanoes Popocatépetl and Ixtaccíhuatl. These imposing volcanoes have inspired many folk tales, the most famous of which claims that Popo was a warrior who went off to war and was mistakenly reported dead, whereupon Ixtaccíhuatl, his lover, sickened and died. Popo, returning home and finding her dead, stood watch over her body until death reunited them.

Puebla's strategic position has influenced its peacetime history as well. As the major city between Mexico City and Veracruz, travelers — including visiting dignitaries — traditionally stop in Puebla to rest and be feted by the *poblanos,* who are proud of their tiled city and their excellent cuisine, which is distinct from the cooking in other parts of the country. *Mole,* the unique light chocolate sauce, was first concocted in Puebla at the Convent of Santa Rosa by the nuns, who wanted to prepare a special dish for the saint's day of Bishop Manuel Fernández de Santa Cruz to thank him for building their convent. Their creation was a chili sauce mixed with spices, sesame seeds, chocolate, and ground almonds, served over turkey or chicken. *Mole* became an immediate success and is still one of Mexico's most famous sauces. Another original is *chiles en nogada,* which are always served during the independence celebrations in September. This dish was created for General Agustín de Iturbide, who stopped to spend his saint's day in August 1821 in Puebla; his friends honored him with stuffed green *chile poblano* topped with a white sauce of ground walnuts, cream cheese, and pomegranate seeds, representing the white, red, and green of the Mexican flag. Both dishes are quite complicated, but Puebla is the best place for them; you can sample *mole* anytime, while mid-August to mid-October is the time for *chiles en nogada.*

The patriotic color pattern recurs in the *china poblana* dress, a costume commonly associated with Mexican women that originated in Puebla. The costume consists of a white embroidered peasant blouse and a green and red skirt with the emblem of the Mexican flag worked on it in sequins. A Chinese girl first designed and wore the outfit; hence the name. She had been sold into slavery, but in Puebla some good Christian gentleman bought her and raised her as his daughter. To express her gratitude, she went about helping the poor in any way she could, dressing simply but with dignity, always in a cotton blouse and full embroidered skirt.

In recent years the city has taken on a more cosmopolitan air than at any time during its history, due in great part to an influx of foreign residents —

US students at the University of the Americas, German workers at the Volkswagen plant. (According to the 1990 government census, the current population is 1.2 million, although the office of the Secretary of Tourism calculates it at closer to 2.5 million.) Change started in the early 1970s with the arrival of the university, Mexico's only American-style college and an institution that continues to draw hundreds of American students every year. Just outside the city, Volkswagen runs Mexico's largest automobile plant (all cars sold in Mexico must be made in Mexico). The plant still makes the famous Beetles and several other models for the domestic market. The top brass at the plant are German and have brought a new cultural influence to Puebla. Puebla is a wonderful destination for first-time visitors to Mexico — a 2-hour drive from Mexico City, a uniquely Spanish-Mexican town with its own food, pottery, clothes, and jewelry — especially pieces made from local onyx, a stone resembling Carrera marble or alabaster.

PUEBLA AT-A-GLANCE

SEEING THE CITY: Fort Loreto stands outside town on a hill that has an excellent view of the city in the valley below and the surrounding mountains, including the two volcanic peaks, which both exceed 17,000 feet. Two miles northeast of the zocalo via Calzada de los Fuertes.

SPECIAL PLACES: Everything in Puebla starts at the main plaza, or zocalo. Many of the beautiful colonial buildings, old churches, and famous shops are concentrated nearby. Learn four words, and you'll be able to find almost anything in Puebla — *sur* means south; *norte* (nte.), north; *poniente* (pte.), west; and *oriente* (ote.), east. Streets north and east of the zocalo have even numbers, while streets on its south and west have odd ones. It helps if you have some sense of direction, but don't worry too much if you don't. The *poblanos* are used to people getting lost; if you just show them the address you are seeking, they'll point you in the right direction.

The Zocalo – This large plaza, the focal point of the city, is flanked on the east by the cathedral and on the other sides by the handsome portals of colonial buildings, shops, and souvenir stalls. Tall trees shade the area, and parterres of tropical flowers are laid out around fountains and a bandstand. Many of the park benches and nearby buildings are made of Puebla tile. In the center of town at Dieciséis de Septiembre, Av. Ayuntamiento 2 Sur, and Calle 3 Ote.

Cathedral of the Immaculate Conception – The construction of this twin-towered, tile-domed church started in 1575 but was not completed until 1649. The altar, designed by Tolsa and made of Puebla onyx and marble, is particularly fine; the wood carvings done by Pedro Muñoz on the doors and choir stalls are also notable; and the 14 highly embellished chapels contain valuable religious paintings. There are usually a couple of English-speaking guides who will explain the fine points for a modest tip. On the south side of the zocalo.

José Luis Bello y Gonzalez Museum – This is a fine exhibition of ornate furniture, paintings, ironwork, glassware, and gold and silver articles from the colonial period. Closed Mondays. Admission charge. At 302 Calle 3 Pte. (phone: 419475).

José Luis Bello y Zetina Museum – Not related to the similarly named museum above, this one houses a rich collection of furniture, ivories, sculpture, and crystal are housed here. Also on exhibit are a number of 16th- through 18th-century European and Mexican paintings — including a Goya drawing and a piece by Miguel Caberera. Closed Mondays. Admission charge. Next to the Santo Domingo church at 409 Calle Cinco de Mayo (phone: 414720).

Casa de Alfeñique (Regional Museum of Puebla) – This highly detailed façade combines florid ornamentation with elaborate tilework and looks something like the frosting on a cake (*alfeñique* means "almond cake"). Stepping inside the cake, you find historical exhibitions, colonial furnishings, and some archaeological artifacts. Closed Mondays. Admission charge. At Calles 4 Ote. and 6 Nte. (phone: 414296).

Church of Santo Domingo – This is the most lavishly decorated church in the city, famous for its extravagant Rosary Chapel and the carvings and sculptures that line every inch of wall, ceiling, and altar space and are all covered with gold leaf. The room glows with gold. The figure of the Virgen del Rosario is adorned with jewels. Open daily. No admission charge. On Av. Cinco de Mayo and Calle 4 Pte.

Santa Rosa – What was once the largest convent in Puebla has been restored by the government. Mole was first created in the beautifully tiled kitchen, and the elaborate arts and crafts throughout the building include a 6-foot earthenware candelabrum, handmade leather goods, and regional costumes. Closed Mondays. Admission charge. At 1203 Calle 3 Nte. (phone: 462271).

Museum of Religious Art (formerly the Convent of Santa Mónica) – In 1857 the Mexican government confiscated all church property and prohibited the operation of both monasteries and convents. The Convent of Santa Mónica, in Puebla, more or less went underground. With the help of secret staircases, unseen doors, and hidden passageways, it remained undiscovered until 1934. Today it is a museum, one of the more unusual in Mexico. Closed Mondays. Admission charge. It is quite close to Santa Rosa, at 103 Calle 18 Pte. and Av. Cinco de Mayo.

Palafox Library – An absolute must for bibliophiles, this library built in 1646 contains over 50,000 volumes and maps from the 17th and 18th centuries as well as the *Nuremberg Chronicle,* published in 1493 and illustrated with some 2,000 engravings. The spacious, high-ceilinged room with carved cedar bookshelves, red tile floors, and inlaid onyx reading tables creates an atmosphere of peace and a sense of the permanence of the written word. Closed Mondays. Admission charge. Located on the second floor of the *Casa de la Cultura* at 5 Calle 5 Ote.

Principal Theater – This restored theater is among the oldest in the Americas. Open only during concerts and scheduled events, but you can look inside in the mornings when the cleanup crew is working. At Calles 8 Ote. and 6 Nte. (phone: 416085).

Forts of Loreto and Guadalupe – Loreto, the site of the historic battle of the Fifth of May, 1862, is now a military museum commemorating the event. The prize of the collection is a photograph of Maximilian comforting the tearful priest who had come to give him last rites before execution. The forts form part of the Cinco de Mayo Civic Center complex, along with the *Museum of Natural History* (phone: 353419) and the *Planetarium* (phone: 352099), which has comfortable reclining seats and a 360° screen. Closed Mondays. Admission charge. Two miles (3 km) northeast of the zocalo (reached via the bus marked "Fuerte" or taxi).

Africam – This zoo cum park is Puebla's answer to the *Lion Country Safaris* in the US. About a half-hour ride from the center of town, the park encompasses 15,000 acres, within which live 3,000 animals of more than 250 species, including lions, elephants, giraffes, zebras, camels, tigers, llamas, and rhinoceroses, all roaming free. There is a restaurant, snack bar, restrooms, and a gift shop. You can drive your own car, or take one of the zebra-striped Africam buses that leave from the bus terminal at Boulevard Norte and Boulevard Tlaxcala three times a day, Monday through Friday, and four times a day on Saturdays, Sundays, and holidays. Open daily. Admission charge. Valsequillo Rd., 9 miles (14 km) from downtown (phone: 358713).

Cholula – Virtually a suburb of Puebla now, Cholula was once among the most important religious centers in Mexico, flourishing at the same time as Teotihuacán (the pyramids outside Mexico City). The area has not been excavated because it would involve tearing down much of the modern town at prohibitive cost and great inconvenience. Tepanapa, the main pyramid, is one of the largest in the world — 1,320 square feet at its base (Cheops in Egypt is only 756 square feet). In early September, native dances are staged on Tepanapa. Quetzalcóatl, the plumed serpent for whom the pyramid was built, is the same god honored at Teotihuacán. Five miles of lighted tunnels in Tepanapa have been opened and can be explored by the public daily, 10 AM to 5 PM. Five miles (8 km) northwest of Puebla along Rte. 190. Snub-nosed minibuses, known as *chatos,* leave Cholula every 15 minutes from Calles 11 Norte and 4 Poniente.

Six miles (10 km) south of Puebla in the town of Tonantzintla, be sure to visit the Iglesia de Santa Maria (Church of St. Mary), which has a wonderful cupola, and walls decorated with paintings of colorful baskets of fruits and flowers and images of Indian workers who built the church. A few miles farther south is one of the most beautiful churches in the state, the Iglesia de San Francisco Acotepec (Church of St. Francis of Acotepec), an ornate 18th-century structure that is covered in bright Talavera tiles.

A few miles farther along Route 190 is Huejotzingo, a small Mexican town where you can find a reasonably priced, bubbly apple cider known as *sidra.* During the fall, you will pass many roadside stands selling baskets of plums, apples, and other produce grown nearby. The Franciscan convent, which is on the main square, dates from 1570 and is one of the first in the Americas. It contains a magnificent altarpiece covered in gold leaf.

■**EXTRA SPECIAL:** Just 90 minutes southeast of Puebla is the spa town of Tehuacán — in Mexico, a name almost synonymous with "water." Like one of the German *bad* towns, Tehuacán is one of Mexico's classic spas, where for generations Mexico City residents came to take the waters. The town has seen better days, but it provides a glimpse of Mexican life visitors might not otherwise suspect or see, and it still has some interesting hotels. The *Spa Peñafiel* (phone: 20190), while run down, is fun and nostalgic. Tehuacán has another claim to fame: It is where corn (maize) was first cultivated. Here hunters became farmers, nomads settled down, and civilization in the New World was born.

SOURCES AND RESOURCES

 TOURIST INFORMATION: The state tourism office (3 Calle 5 Ote.; phone: 461285) is best for maps, brochures, and information; guides are also available. It is open 365 days a year.

 TELEPHONE: The area code for Puebla is 22. When calling from one city to another within Mexico, dial 91 before the area code.

 CLIMATE AND CLOTHES: Some 80 miles (128 km) east of Mexico City and also at a high altitude, Puebla's climate is similar to the capital's. Summers are relatively mild, and temperatures rarely exceed 90F and average in the 70s and 80s; winters are usually warm, in the 60s. There's plenty of sunshine, but carry an umbrella during the summer, which is the rainy season. Dress is generally casual.

GETTING AROUND: You can walk to almost all the places of interest since they are within a few blocks of the zocalo. However, there are taxi stands on the zocalo, and you can catch a bus here to the forts.

Car Rental – Agencies include *Maparent* (2015 Calle 25 Ote.; phone: 401366) and *Rente Ford Budget* (53 Calle I. Zaragoza; phone: 362028).

Tours – Hotel travel desks arrange sightseeing trips in town and excursions to the Cholula archaeological zone and Africam Park. Licensed guides can be found around the corner from the cathedral. They charge about $7 per hour but don't provide transportation.

SPECIAL EVENTS: Since May 5, 1862, when the Mexicans of Puebla defeated the French contingent, Puebla has been called *Puebla la Heroica,* and that date has been named a national holiday. On that day in Puebla, there are all kinds of celebrations and frivolity to commemorate the event. During the rest of the month the *Puebla Fair* is held, and frequently interesting cultural events are scheduled. Nearby, *Carnaval* (just before *Lent*) is spectacular in Huejotzingo, particularly the mock battles between Moors and Christians (check with the tourist office in Puebla for the exact dates). Fireworks mark the *Festival of St. Augustine* on August 28. On the last Sunday in September, the town of Atlixco stages a fiesta noted for its fine presentation of regional dances.

SHOPPING: Puebla is the place to look for objects made from onyx, Talavera tiles, and pottery. You will also see all kinds of fruit and quite a bit of *camote,* a candy made out of sweet potatoes and wrapped in white or pastel tissue paper. Best bets for tile and pottery are *Talavera de Puebla* (911 Calle 4 Pte.; phone: 421598); *Talavera de Santa Rosa* (3914 Calle 2 Sur; phone: 406455); and *Casa Rugerio* (111 Calle 18 Pte.; phone: 413843), where they still use techniques dating from the 16th century. Antiques, both originals and reproductions, are available at *Galería Chapis* (312 Calle 6 Sur; phone: 421155) and at many of the other shops along the same street. The work of Puebla artisans is featured in shops run by the state government at the *Santa Rosa Museum* in the tourism office and at the Chapel of the Third Order of the former Convent of San Francisco, on the corner of Blvd. Héroes de Cinco de Mayo and Calle 14 Ote.

Barrio de las Artistas – See local artists at work in their studios here painting portraits and scenes of Puebla. Calle 8 Nte. between Calles 4 and 6 Ote. (no phone).

El Parián – Right near the San Francisco church, this mall of handicrafts shops is a good place to bargain for onyx and other crafts (no phone).

Plaza Dorada – Puebla's elegant shopping center has some 140 shops. On Blvd. Héroes de Cinco de Mayo between Calles 31 and 43 Ote. (no phone).

Plaza de los Sapos – On Sundays it turns into a huge antiques market. Calle 7 Ote. near Calle 4 Sur (no phone).

SPORTS: Bullfights – Bullfighting is not especially popular in Puebla. There is a small bullring where events are held about six times a year and frequently during the *Puebla Fair.*

Golf – *Club de Golf,* at Prolongación 11 Sur, several miles past *Agua Azul,* is Puebla's 18-hole course, available to visitors who can prove membership in a US club. It also has a swimming pool, tennis courts, a restaurant, and a bar. A 9-hole course, pool, and 3 tennis courts are open to the public at *Club de Golf Las Fuentes,* near the *Mesón del Angel* at 510 Carr. Fábricas.

Soccer – The local teams, *Puebla* and *Los Angeles,* play at *Estadio Cuauhtémoc.*

Swimming – *Agua Azul* has a series of pools and artificial lakes. On weekends, as might be expected, it is crowded, but it's quite pleasant during midweek. Admission charge. Open daily. Prolongación 11 Sur (phone: 431330).

Tennis – Fifteen courts, a pool, and a squash court are open to the public at *Club Britania*. 3 Calle Santa Fé (phone: 490099).

NIGHTCLUBS AND NIGHTLIFE: Mariachis stand around in the Plaza de Santa Inés waiting to be hired, so don't expect to see them strolling through the crowds singing. The Plaza de los Sapos (Calle 7 Ote. near Calle 4 Sur) also draws the bands and strollers out at night. *Los Flamingos* has a cozy piano bar as well as a restaurant (1 Calle Teziutlán Norte). The top discos are *Carlos Cuches* (78 Calle Teziutlán Sur; phone: 487125); *Boom* (19 Av. Juárez; phone: 424675); *Karla* (2923 Av. Juárez; phone: 486306); and *Porthos* (Av. Recta a Cholula between Puebla and Cholula; phone: 486306). Some of the hotels have bars, and there are a few student discos near the University of Puebla and near the University of the Americas in Cholula. The most popular in Cholula are *Faces Rock Center* (no phone), *Paradise* (no phone), and *Keops* (no phone).

BEST IN TOWN

CHECKING IN: Puebla is not heavily tuned in to tourism, but there are several nice hotels. A double room for a night will cost up to $65 in a hotel listed as expensive; about $35 in the moderate range; and $25 or less in the inexpensive range. All hotels listed below accept MasterCard and Visa; a few also accept American Express and Diners Club. All telephone numbers are in the 22 area code unless otherwise indicated. When calling from one city to another within Mexico, dial 91 before the area code.

Gran Hotel de Alba – This large establishment on the western edge of the city has an attractive pool and garden but tends to be noisy, especially when families check in. Guests have access to the tennis facilities in the *Club Britania*. 141 Hermanos Serdán (phone: 486055; FAX: 487344). Expensive.

El Mesón del Angel – Situated at the edge of the city on nicely landscaped grounds, this 192-room luxury property offers rooms with showers, refrigerators, and terraces; some rooms have fine views of the volcanoes. Recreational facilities include 2 pools and a tennis court; there is also a bar and dining room (see *Eating Out*). 807 Hermanos Serdán (phone: 482100; FAX: 487935). Expensive.

Misión de Puebla – A modern high-rise in downtown Puebla, it has 225 rooms, pool, garden, restaurant, and three bars. 2522 Calle 5 Pte. (phone: 489600; FAX: 489733). Expensive.

Posada San Pedro – This colonial-style hostelry downtown has satellite TV, a restaurant, bar, and pool. 202 Calle 2 Ote. (phone: 465077). Expensive.

Villa Arqueológica – Run by Club Med at the Cholula archaeological zone, this hotel offers spartan comfort, tennis, a pool, and French cooking. 601 Calle 2 Pte., Cholula (phone: 471966; FAX: 471508). Expensive.

Aristos – One of Puebla's newest hotels, it's centrally located and has 120 rooms with color TV sets, a heated indoor pool, restaurant, and coffee shop. Av. Reforma and Calle 7 Sur (phone: 320655; FAX: 325982). Moderate.

Lastra – Pleasant and away from the center of town, it has 53 units a garden, pool, a good restaurant, and a bar. 2633 Calz. de los Fuertes, near Forts Loreto and Guadalupe (phone: 359755; FAX: 351501). Moderate.

Portal – A 98-unit, colonial-style hotel just off the zocalo, it has a restaurant and bar. 205 Maximino Avila Camacho (phone: 460211; FAX: 467511). Moderate.

Campestre Los Sauces – Another colonial-style resort, it has a pool, gardens, and a bar with entertainment. Midway between Puebla and Cholula; Mexico City Hwy. at Km 122 (phone: 471011; FAX: 471011). Moderate to inexpensive.

Palacio San Leonardo – Centrally located, this attractive hotel has a restaurant and bar; the rooms have TV sets. 211 Calle 2 Ote. (phone: 460555). Inexpensive.

Royalty Centro – This old, colonial-style hostelry on the zocalo is nothing fancy, but it's well maintained and offers adequate rooms, a restaurant, and bar. 8 Portal Hidalgo (phone: 424740). Inexpensive.

Señorial – Comfortably furnished, medium-size rooms with showers and phones, a restaurant, and Russian and Turkish baths. Calles 4 Nte. and 6 Ote. (phone: 46899; FAX: 468964). Inexpensive.

 EATING OUT: Puebla has several good places to eat. The area on Avenida Juárez known as the Zona Esmeralda has the newer stores and restaurants. Several of these places have a fairly sophisticated ambience, with the cuisine more international than Mexican. Expect to pay up to $45 for a full dinner for two, not including drinks, wine, or tips, in restaurants we list as expensive; about $35 at a moderate place; and $20, inexpensive. Most restaurants accept MasterCard and Visa; a few also accept American Express and Diners Club. Unless otherwise noted, all restaurants are open daily. All telephone numbers are in the 22 area code unless otherwise indicated. When calling from one city to another within Mexico, dial 91 before the area code.

Bodegas del Molino – Set in a remodeled 16th-century hacienda furnished with antiques, it serves fine Mexican and international food. Reservations advised. Molino de San José del Puente, at the edge of town in Puente de Mexico (phone: 490399). Expensive.

La Bola Roja – That Mexican delicacy known as *gusanos de maguey* (fried worms, or more precisely, cactus maggots) is served here, as well as less esoteric dishes such as *arroz à la poblana* (rice cooked with garlic, tomatoes, peas, and onions) and *mole poblano* (a rich sauce made of various types of chilies, chocolate, and almonds). Reservations unnecessary. Three locations: 1305 Calle 17 Sur (phone: 437500), in the *Plaza Dorada Shopping Center;* 3510 Av. Cinco de Mayo (phone: 407582); and in *Plaza Loreto* at 266 Calle I. Zaragoza (phone: 361422). Moderate.

El Caserio – Nicely appointed with a fireplace and attractive chandeliers, it serves international cuisine, including Italian, French, Spanish, and some Mexican specialties. Reservations unnecessary. 2105 Av. Juárez (phone: 418161). Moderate.

Charlie's China Poblano – One of Carlos Anderson's many restaurants throughout the country, this one has a strong following among both residents and tourists. The menu is varied, with international and Mexican specialties. Shrimp dishes are notable, as are the filet of beef *arriero* (prepared in banana leaves) and the famous spinach and mushroom house salad. Reservations unnecessary. 1918 Av. Juárez (phone: 463184). Moderate.

Hacienda de San Pedro – Still another member of the Carlos Anderson group, the specialty here is steaks, and the decor is strictly Mexican. Reservations unnecessary. At the *Plaza San Pedro Mall,* 2210 Héroes de 5 de Mayo (phone: 483011). Moderate.

J.M. McQuade – Puebla's most popular spot for *cabrito al pastor* (kid roasted in the ground). They also serve US-style steaks. Live music. Reservations advised. 3302 Calle 23 Pte. (phone: 498538). Moderate

Mesón del Vaquero Andaluz – Famous for *tapas* (typical Spanish appetizers), charcoal-broiled steaks, and the usual Iberian fare. Reservations unnecessary. 2504 Av. Juárez (phone: 490843). Moderate.

Sanborn's – This restaurant-cum-drugstore caters to homesick Americans by serving traditional American fare. Reservations unnecessary. Av. Cinco de Mayo and 6 Calle 2 Ote. (phone: 429416). Moderate.

El Tejado – At two locations, both are good steakhouses with excellent service. Reservations unnecessary. 2302 Dieciséis de Septiembre (phone: 401853); and at Blvd. Héroes de Cinco de Mayo between Calles 2 Sur and 16 de Septiembre (phone: 406027 or 404963). Moderate.

El Cortijo – Attractive bullfighting motifs and Spanish dishes such as paella, *fabada* (a bean, pork, and sausage stew), and snails make for pleasant dining. Reservations unnecessary. 506 Dieciséis de Septiembre (phone: 420503). Inexpensive.

Fonda de Santa Clara – This Mexican eatery serves good *mole* on chicken and enchiladas and has a full line of standard fare as well as some unusual drinks, including *chia,* a limeade-type drink, and *horchata,* which is made from ground cantaloupe seeds. Reservations unnecessary. Two locations: 307 Calle 3 Pte. (closed Mondays; phone: 422659) and 920 Calle 3 Pte. (closed Tuesdays; phone: 461919). Inexpensive.

Hostería del Virrey – A gathering place for local artists, it's is decorated with artwork for sale. House specialties include charcoal-broiled kid, mole, *chalupas,* and other regional dishes. Reservations advised. 1306 Calle 11 Sur (phone: 438439). Inexpensive.

El Vaquero Andaluz Bar and Grill – Steaks and Spanish dishes are the specialties. Reservations unnecessary. 3905 Calle 2 Sur (phone: 409579) and 2504 Juárez (phone: 490843). Inexpensive.

Vittorio's – Pasta and pizza are prepared in the Puebla manner in this café on the zocalo. Reservations unnecessary. 106 Portal Morelos (phone: 417900).Inexpensive.

PUERTO ESCONDIDO

(pronounced *Pwer*-toe Es-con-*dee*-doe)

Puerto Escondido — a town of 45,000 people on the Pacific coast in the state of Oaxaca — remains one of the lesser known, but one of the most beautiful, unspoiled, and unsophisticated, hideaways of southern Mexico. FONATUR, the government agency responsible for the development and improvement of Mexico's tourist sites, had very big plans for the area. Fortunately for lovers of unspoiled and unsophisticated hideaways, these plans seem to have been significantly scaled down in favor of a larger tourist development farther south, at the Bahías de Huatulco.

An airport opened in 1985, so Puerto Escondido can now be reached directly by jet from Mexico City. The town is no longer the lazy fishing village it was just a few years ago, but visitors can still find themselves a private spot on one of the long stretches of beach. Although Puerto Escondido boasts a handful of good hotels, and a few others were under construction as we went to press, it will probably be some time before rows of hotels line Zikatela Beach, as once was predicted.

About 95% of Puerto Escondido's population is of Indian descent, and most make their living from fishing or farming. With significant tourism just beginning to stir, it's still possible for a visitor to feel like an intruder here. Inhabitants aren't hostile or cold — it's just that they're gracious without being purposefully ingratiating, going about their lives as if no one with a foreign accent or camera had ever wandered into their midst. Service is inevitably slow (sometimes almost nonexistent), and there's little for visitors to do but enjoy the pristine, quiet beaches, snorkel over the fantastical coral reefs around the bay, and dine on fresh seafood in the town's handful of restaurants. Not yet — not nearly — the superstar resort, Puerto Escondido remains an unsophisticated hideaway; and its largely unpaved streets remain uncrowded, with cabs often cruising around empty, as though rehearsing for opening night.

PUERTO ESCONDIDO AT-A-GLANCE

 SEEING THE CITY: A lovely, sweeping view of Puerto Escondido and its beaches can be seen from the Carretera Costera, the Coastal Highway. A more immediate view is afforded by the *faro* (lighthouse), which can be reached by a 15-minute walk from the main street. Look for a sign that says Camino del Faro; it points the way to the red and white tower.

SPECIAL PLACES: Although Puerto Escondido is short on museums, historic houses, parks, or churches, it does have a handful of beautiful beaches, and because the resort is still relatively undiscovered, they tend to be blissfully uncrowded.

La Bajía (Main Bay) – This half-mile stretch of beach (onto which the town's hotels and restaurants face), is the center of most activities — fishing, swimming, and sunning. Boats also leave here regularly for nearby, popular Puerto Angelito Beach — not to be confused with the coast town Puerto Angel, 50 miles (80 km) away. The water at the Main Bay is so calm that locals refer to the western end of it as the "Bathtub" or "Kiddie.Cove," perhaps also due to its popularity with waders under 3 feet tall.

Playa Zikatela (Zikatela Beach) – A path around the Marinero (Fishermen's) Rocks at the east end of Main Bay leads to this 2-mile stretch of white sand and ruthless waves — considered by some to be one of the best surfing beaches in the world. From sunup to sundown, a dozen or so surfers match their skill against the waves while spectators watch enthralled from the beach. (All but the best swimmers should stick to the sand, however, since the undertow here is treacherous.) Joggers and walkers will also find this beach to their liking; an hour's stroll up and down the shore, followed by breakfast at the *Santa Fe,* is a fine way to start any day. At the far end of the beach is Zikatela Point, a haven for pelicans, seagulls, sandpipers, and other winged species, as well as for beach- and sunset-loving *Homo sapiens.*

ENVIRONS

Puerto Angelito – Protected from the waves by huge rock formations, the "Port of the Little Angel" offers tepid, tranquil water, two sandy beaches, and coral reefs attractive to snorkelers. There's easy access by boats that leave regularly from the Main Bay at Puerto Escondido; the fare is less than a dollar each way. Puerto Angelito can also be reached by car: Take the road to the airport, about 1½ miles (2 km) north of Puerto Escondido, and turn left at the sign for Puerto Angelito.

Playa Bacocho (Bacocho Beach) – This isolated, elongated bit of beach, with brilliant white sand, is the place to wallow in solitude and contemplate the open sea. (Don't swim here; the water's too rough.) The *Posada Real Best Western* hotel provides a stunning view of this beach, as well as a path to it.

Manialtepec Lagoon – Some 15 miles (24 km) west of Puerto Escondido and visible from the highway to Acapulco, this lagoon is brimming with tropical birds and surrounded by thick, luxuriant vegetation. Boats depart from *Alejandria* and *Hamacas* restaurants for a 1½-hour excursion across the lagoon to the ocean, which costs about $6 per person. The *García Rendón* travel agency (on Av. Pérez Gazga, in front of *La Michoacana* ice cream shop; phone: 20114) runs an 8-hour tour of the lagoon for about $30 per person, including lunch, boat ride, and ground transportation.

Puerto Angel – This small fishing community, about 50 miles (80 km) from Puerto Escondido, lacks the charm and ambience of its neighbor. The main attractions are Playa del Panteón (Cemetery Beach), which has a small graveyard with brightly painted tombstones perched above it (not morbid in the least), and Zipolite Beach, about 5 miles (8 km) out of town and one of the few nudist beaches in Mexico (beware of the undertow). The *Angel del Mar,* high on a hill above town, provides a fine view and adequate lodging. Taxis frequently make the 7-mile (11-km) run between Pochutla and Puerto Angel. It's less expensive to take the blue cabs *to* Puerto Angel, where they are based, and to *return* to Pochutla in the blue and beige cabs, for the same reason.

■ **EXTRA SPECIAL:** Parque Nacional Chacahua (Chacahua National Park) makes a wonderful day trip out of Puerto Escondido. This entrancing 50-square-mile retreat has fine sandy beaches and inviting inlets and coves, all populated by every kind of bird and fish known to the tropical Pacific. Three tiny fishing villages complete the serene landscape. The *García Rendón* travel agency charges about $30 per person for an 8-hour tour, including ground transportation and boat ride (phone: 20434, 20113, or 20458).

SOURCES AND RESOURCES

 TOURIST INFORMATION: The government tourist office (120 Av. Hidalgo, next to the bus terminal; phone: 20358 or 20175) has a friendly, helpful staff and offers a very good map as well as information on hotels and prices. It also can offer information on where to obtain a guide to Puerto Escondido called *Por La Costa,* available in English. Another useful source of information is *Aquario* (Av. Pérez Gazga), which sells a descriptive if somewhat dated guidebook to the area (in Spanish only), the English-language *Mexico City News,* and American magazines and paperbacks. Note: At press time, the Puerto Escondido Tourist Office was in the process of moving, and no new address was available; check with the government office (above) or your hotel desk for its new location and phone number.

 TELEPHONE: The area code for Puerto Escondido is 958. When calling from one city to another within Mexico, dial 91 before the area code.

 CLIMATE AND CLOTHES: Puerto Escondido enjoys a hot, dry climate. Average temperatures range between 73F and 91F, with the hottest days occurring in May, the coolest in January. Dress is casual; shorts and sandals usually suffice.

 GETTING AROUND: The town is small enough to be seen easily on foot, and almost anything one might want — hotels, restaurants, tourist office, bookstore — is within easy walking distance. To tour Puerto Escondido's beautiful environs, however, some form of motor transportation is necessary.

Bus – Rather homely to look at and short on legroom, they run frequently to Pochutla, where connections to Huatulco or Puerto Angel can be made. The bus station is just up the street from the power company in the center of town. *Flecha Roja* (at Juárez and Felipe) has service to Acapulco and Mexico City.

Taxi – Cab drivers are willing to drive anywhere, and it is possible to negotiate reasonable hourly rates. Cabs ride through the bus terminal area and also cruise along Avenida Pérez Gazga, the main street.

Car Rental – *Avis* (phone: 20151) and *Hertz* (phone: 20611) are both in town (on Av. Pérez Gazga). *Budget* is located in the *Posada Real Best Western* hotel (phone: 20312 or 20315).

Tours – *Transportadora Turística* and *Viajes García Rendón* — actually the same operation — on Pérez Gazga (phone: 20114) and at the *Posada Real Best Western* (phone: 20458) arrange all-day excursions by car, minibus, or bus (depending upon the number of passengers) to Bahías de Huatulco and Chacahua National Park, and half-day excursions to Puerto Angel, which include a visit to the Zipolite nudist beach. Cost is about $30 per person.

SPECIAL EVENTS: There's dancing every night during *Carnaval,* the week before *Lent,* as well as on *Independence Day,* September 15–16. The *Day of the Dead,* in early November, is a joyous occasion despite its name; the entire populace pauses to visit one another and to have picnics on the graves of their loved ones. Puerto Escondido's biggest bash begins on November 4. *November in Puerto Escondido* includes polo burro matches (polo — played here on donkeys and using brooms — is a sport that orginated in Puerto Vallarta), a fishing tournament, exhibitions of parachuting and ballooning, cultural events, and an *International Surfing Tournament,* in which surfers from Mexico, the US, and places as distant as Australia participate (a bikini contest, in which Miss Surf is chosen, is held on the day of the finals). *Christmas* celebrations take place between December 25 and January 6, the *Day of the Three Kings.*

SHOPPING: Shopping in Puerto Escondido is rather limited. There are only a few shops along Avenida Pérez Gazga, and items are sold at the *Posada Real* and the *Santa Fe* hotels. Most of the *artesanía* (handicrafts) for sale lack real distinction. On Saturday, the big market day, vendors stream in from surrounding communities to sell their wares at the Indian market, the *Mercado Antiguo Hidalgo* downtown.

SPORTS: Fishing – *Transportadora Turística* (phone: 20114 or 20458) has fishing boats for rent for about $20 per hour for 1 to 4 passengers, including rods and bait.

    Horseback Riding – Horses can be rented in Manialtepec, Barra de Colotepec, and in the town of Pluma Hidalgo from a man called Alejandro, "El Guapo" (the "handsome one"); inquire at the *Santa Fe* (phone: 20170). A typical half-day trip runs the gamut of Mexican scenery, from river crossings and thick jungle undergrowth to stark rock formations and hot springs. *Transportadora Turistica* (phone: 20114 or 20458) also arranges for horseback riding on the beach for about $15 an hour.

    Snorkeling and Diving – Tanks, masks, and flippers may be rented from *Transportadora Turística* (phone: 20114 or 20458). Dive trips are available for about $35 an hour, including one tank and equipment; snorkeling equipment is rented for about $10 per day. There's good snorkeling at Puerto Angelito, but the best diving areas are Puerto Angel (Vincente at the *Amigo del Mar* restaurant rents equipment; no phone) and Tangolunda Bay in Huatulco.

    Swimming and Surfing – Zikatela Beach attracts surfers from all over the world, but since the undertow is so strong, only the most skillful should attempt the waves. No surfboard rentals are available.

    Tennis – The *Fiesta Mexicana* hotel (phone: 20150) has 1 lighted artificial grass court open to the public.

NIGHTCLUBS AND NIGHTLIFE: Puerto Escondido has little nightlife; in fact, if this little fishing village had sidewalks, they would roll up very early. But for those who aren't satisfied counting stars, there's *Bacocho* (45 Tehuantepec), *Pauline* in the *Fiesta Mexicana,* *Macumba* (Av. Pérez Gazga), and even a show of female impersonators in *Discotheque Bahía,* also on the road to Pochutla. *La Cascada* (Av. Oaxaca; no phone) has dancing and a show featuring pop music. For music only, try the *Bar Las Máscaras* at the *Villa Sol.*

BEST IN TOWN

 CHECKING IN: For such a small town, Puerto Escondido has a fair number of hotels. Expect to pay about $80 for a double room in a hotel listed as expensive; $50 to $75, moderate; $25 or less, inexpensive. During the low season, summer through fall, rates are likely to drop about 25%. All telephone numbers are in the 958 area code unless otherwise indicated. When calling from one city to another within Mexico, dial 91 before the area code.

Posada Real Best Western – More typically resort-style than the others, this hotel isn't as quaint as some of the others in town, and guests must walk down a cliff to get to the beach, but the staff is delightfully friendly and helpful. There are 100 air conditioned rooms, *Cocos* restaurant (see *Eating Out*), 3 bars, 2 pools, tennis, live music nightly, and lovely grounds. Blvd. Benito Juárez (phone: 20133; 800-528-1234; FAX: 20192). Expensive.

Villa Sol – One of Puerto Escondido's newer places, it offers 72 rooms, 24 junior suites, and 12 two-bedroom master suites with refrigerators, along with free transportation to the beach, a pool, restaurant, and bar. Fracc. Bacocho (phone: 20382; FAX: 20451). Expensive to moderate.

Paraíso Escondido – This former hacienda has 20 rooms, all on the small side, but with whitewashed brick walls and tasteful furnishings, they're still tempting. The rooms upstairs have balconies with an ocean view; downstairs accommodations have porches and face the small pool. There's also a restaurant with bar service, *El Tecolote*. It's just a short walk to the beach. No credit cards accepted. 10 Calle Unión (phone: 20444). Moderate.

Santa Fe – The front door opens onto Main Bay, and the back door leads to Zikatela Beach. There are 40 air conditioned rooms, a small pool, and a fine dining area overlooking sand and surf. It contains authentic Mexican touches throughout: tiles from Puebla and Dolores Hidalgo, traditional ironwork and fabrics from Oaxaca, blown glass from Tlaquepaque, and furniture typical of Guadalajara and Puebla. Calle del Moro (phone: 20170; FAX: 20260). Moderate.

Loren – Simple, clean, and basic, it has 24 rooms with fans. 507 Av. Pérez Gazga (phone: 20057). Inexpensive.

El Mirador – Another one of Puerto Escondido's basic but pleasant places, it has 85 rooms, a restaurant, and parking. 113 Carr. Costera Pte. (phone: 20359 or 20398). Inexpensive.

Nayar – Two blocks uphill from the beach, there are 36 rooms, some with balconies, and the restaurant overlooks the town. No credit cards accepted. 407 Av. Pérez Gazga (phone: 20113). Inexpensive.

Las Palmas – It's simple, but clean and comfortable, with 40 rooms, a pleasant palm-filled courtyard, and a restaurant — an excellent place to start the day with a typical Mexican breakfast. Boats to Puerto Angelito can be rented right out front. Av. Pérez Gazga (phone: 20230). Inexpensive.

Rincón del Pacífico – A small place on the beach, with 26 rooms decorated cheerily in yellow and white, and 2 junior suites with air conditioning, TV sets, and refrigerators. It is well maintained, and the atmosphere is very pleasant. They also have a restaurant (see *Eating Out*). 900 Av. Pérez Gazga (phone: 20056). Inexpensive.

Villa Marinero – Situated close to the beach, each of the bungalows here is equipped with 2 bedrooms with fans, a small living room, and a kitchenette. Apdo. 16, Cerro el Marinero (phone: 20180). Inexpensive.

EATING OUT: Puerto Escondido is not known for elaborate dinners or polished service, but the seafood is almost always good. Expect to pay up to $35 for a meal for two in those listed as moderate, and less than $20 at an inexpensive spot. Prices do not include wine, tips, or tax. Most restaurants accept MasterCard and Visa; a few also accept American Express and Diners Club. Unless otherwise noted, all restaurants are open daily. Reservations are unnecessary at all places. All telephone numbers are in the 958 area code unless otherwise indicated. When calling from one city to another within Mexico, dial 91 before the area code.

Cocos – Seafood and a spectacular view. In the *Posada Real Hotel* (phone: 20394). Moderate.

Las Mariposas – Indoor or outdoor candlelight dining, an international menu, a guitarist, and a closing time of midnight (unusual in this sleepy town) are the draws here. Just up the hill from Av. Juárez (phone: 20197). Moderate.

La Palapa – Very attractive surroundings, good food, and friendly service. Across the street from the *Sardina Plata Beach* restaurant on Av. Pérez Gazga (no phone). Moderate.

Santa Fe – Those tired of *huevos rancheros* for breakfast might drop by this gracious restaurant for a vegetarian treat of homemade yogurt with granola or tofu hotcakes with fruit. The menu is basically vegetarian, but seafood — lobster, shrimp, squid, abalone, and oysters — is offered. In the *Santa Fe Hotel,* Playa Marinero (phone: 20170). Moderate.

Sardina Plata Beach – Well-prepared seafood and a magnificent view of the sea. There's also a swimming pool. 512 Av. Pérez Gazga (phone: 20328). Moderate.

Da Ugo Hostería del Viandante – At this little *palapa*-topped pizzeria, one of the most popular spots in town, there is sometimes a wait for a table. The menu includes a dozen varieties of pizza as well as lasagna, spaghetti, and enormous salads. Rock 'n' roll music sets an upbeat mood. Av. Pérez Gazga (no phone). Inexpensive.

Los Crotos – The service may be the slowest in town, but the prices and the food — *camarónes con frutas* (shrimp and fruit in a cream sauce) and *pescado con camarónes* (fish smothered in shrimp) — are worth the wait. On Av. Pérez Gazga next to the *García Rendón* travel agency (phone: 20025). Inexpensive.

La Perla – Simple and filled with plants. Seafood is the specialty. In town on Calle Tercera Pte. (phone: 20461). Inexpensive.

La Posada – Rustic, but serving good, basic Mexican food. Right next door to the *Macumba* disco (no phone). Inexpensive.

Rincón del Pacífico – In the hotel of the same name, with the same pleasant atmosphere and service. Seafood, naturally, and steaks. 900 Av. Pérez Gazga (phone: 20056). Inexpensive.

Siete Regiones – This huge place specializes in typical Oaxacan fare from, as the name implies, the seven regions of the state. There's no extra charge for the fine view. No credit cards accepted. On Pérez Gazga near *Los Crotos* (no phone). Inexpensive.

La Terraza – Seafood, as could be expected, as well as Mexican and international dishes and a lovely view. No credit cards accepted. In the *Nayar* (phone: 20133). Inexpensive.

PUERTO VALLARTA

(pronounced *Pwer*-toe Vah-*yar*-tah)

A developer's dream and a rustic's nightmare tell the Cinderella story of Puerto Vallarta. A small and remote fishing village until the early 1960s, it is today one of the fastest-growing seaside resorts in North America. Its resident population (which includes many foreigners) is approximately 250,-000, a figure that swells when tourists fill its 10,000-plus hotel rooms at the height of the season.

About 225 miles (360 km) from Guadalajara and an hour from the jungle, Puerto Vallarta, in the state of Jalisco, lies between the rugged, tropical Sierra Madre to the east and 25 miles of white sand beaches along the beautiful Banderas Bay (Bahía de Banderas) on the west. For US citizens suffering winter blues, it is an ideal spot for a summer vacation in December, with peak season from *Christmas* through the end of April.

Perched midway along Mexico's sickle-shaped Pacific coast, a bit below the point at which the Gulf of California empties into the Pacific Ocean, Puerto Vallarta is the perfect headquarters for deep-sea expeditions. Fishing and scuba diving are favorite recreations, and the marine population includes sailfish, marlin, bonito, tuna, squid, shark, and porpoise.

War and revolution, generals and statesmen count for little in Puerto Vallarta's past. Back in the 1950s, the guidebooks were touting Puerto Vallarta as one of Mexico's "Little Acapulcos," known and loved by a small group of discriminating travelers. There were then only a handful of small hotels, and getting to the town was something of a challenge. *Mexicana Airlines* flew DC-6s in three times a week from Guadalajara, and there were no highways — and no telephones — linking Puerto Vallarta to the rest of the country.

A number of Americans, however, were so enchanted with the place that they built their own homes along the hills that drop down to the Cuale River. The neighborhood came to be known as Gringo Gulch. (*Gringo,* by the way, is not necessarily an offensive term. Mexicans tend to give geographical nicknames to everyone; natives of Guadalajara are *tapatíos;* of Mexico City, *chilangos.* And what else can you call a gringo? Mexicans are North Americans, as are Canadians. There is a tongue-twisting term that translates as United-Statesian, but even that is vague, for Mexico, too, is officially designated as Estados Unidos Méxicanos, the United Mexican States.)

In the early 1960s, film director John Huston was searching for a locale to shoot *The Night of the Iguana,* and he found Puerto Vallarta. Richard Burton was one of the stars in the film and Elizabeth Taylor flew in to keep him company. They were not married, and at that time it was something of a scandal. Newsmen flocked in to report on the daily dallyings, and suddenly Puerto Vallarta was a dateline appearing regularly in newspapers all around the world.

The first person to cash in on the town's new fame was a foresighted Mexican with the unusual name of Suña Gershenson. Long before the movie people arrived, he had begun constructing the town's first luxury hotel, the *Posada Vallarta* (now the *Krystal Vallarta*). Others followed his lead: *Playa de Oro,* Westin Hotels' *Camino Real,* and then a *Holiday Inn.* The government pushed a highway through the mountains, and with it brought telephone lines (when the *Camino Real* opened, every room had a telephone, but about the only place a guest could call was room service). An international airport also was opened.

Yet Vallarta failed to grow the way many people expected. No one knew who owned the land. Originally, Puerto Vallarta was a fishing village that didn't even have a name until 1918. A mapmaker charged with carving the state of Jalisco into municipalities (which in Mexico are similar to counties) chose to name the area around Banderas Bay after one of the state's governors, Ignacio Luis Vallarta. A little later much of the land was declared to be *ejidos,* a Mexican legal concept that gives a family title to its homestead but prohibits the family from selling the land. A lot of property in Vallarta was sold by *ejido* members, but the titles were not valid. That led to chaos. During the early 1970s, the federal government expropriated everything (paying the original settlers), resold the property, and used the profits to put in water and drainage works, patch up the streets, and in general prepare the town for its future as a resort.

Puerto Vallarta's river, the Cuale, runs down from the mountains to the coast and divides the city into northern and southern sections. About two thirds of the city is on the northern side, near the older hotels and commercial district. The southern end is more residential and leads to some of the larger modern resorts built on the edge of town. There is a *malecón,* or sea wall, running north-south along the bay, and most of the town extends no farther than 5 or 6 blocks into the eastern hills. Near the docks and the airport is the Marina Vallarta, one of Puerto Vallarta's newest resort complexes with an 18-hole golf course and several hotels.

In the middle of the Cuale is a small rock island with a children's kindergarten. Here, too, is one of the few reminders of Puerto Vallarta's past — native women beating their laundry on the rocky shore, shaded by small palm lean-tos they have built as protection from the midday sun.

But this timeless scene is only a glimmer, for a visit to Puerto Vallarta is much more likely to produce visions of horseback riding on the beaches; parasails alighting on the calm waters of the bay; motorboats, sailboats, and cruise ships pulling into their moorings; sophisticated restaurants, luxury hotels, chic shops, and nightclubs.

Luxury hotels are on the beach, all of them a mile or two from town. Although all beaches in Mexico are federal property, those in front of the hotels are close to being private; few people are on them except hotel guests. In town are some of the older, less expensive hotels and the many shops, restaurants, and discos that contribute heavily to the resort's commerce.

There are any number of places to enjoy a sundowner, and the sunsets in Puerto Vallarta are spectacular. They're particularly impressive at the *Lobby Bar* in the *Camino Real,* the *El Set* in the *Conchas Chinas,* and the *Krystal*'s *Seven Columns Terrace* poolside.

The usual question people ask is: How does Puerto Vallarta compare to Acapulco? Currently Vallarta is a touch more sedate, though the population of construction cranes continues to grow. Acapulco swings, but most stands are for 1 night only. Vacationers arriving in Vallarta generally know with whom they'll be spending their time. When romance does bloom, there's a feeling it will last a while. The resort's most famous lovers, Burton and Taylor, did, after all, get married — twice.

Speaking of Acapulco is what almost everyone in Puerto Vallarta does. Around the bars and cocktail lounges, it must be Topic B: Will Puerto Vallarta become another Acapulco? The consensus is hopefully not, but probably so. More international airlines will be flying in, and new hotels are always opening. The din and dust of construction in Puerto Vallarta is currently exceeded only by the quantity of concrete currently being mixed in Cancún. The whole image of Puerto Vallarta as a sleepy little fishing village is, unfortunately, fast becoming outdated.

PUERTO VALLARTA AT-A-GLANCE

SEEING THE CITY: Hugged by lush mountains on one side and the 25-mile-long Bay of Banderas on the other, Puerto Vallarta is a perfect town for strolling. To get the lay of the land, we recommend that you follow the *malecón,* a promenade that runs parallel to the waterfront in the heart of the city, and then ascend any of the hills. From there you will get a panoramic view of the bay from above the red tile roofs of town.

SPECIAL PLACES: In theory, at least, the beaches are what lure people to Puerto Vallarta, so we'll look at them first. But beaches are only part of the scene in this most picturesque resort.

Las Amapas Beach – A small stretch of sand between Playa del Sol and the next beach down, Conchas Chinas, where visitors can see the cliffside mansions of the wealthy Mexicans and foreigners who have established homes in Puerto Vallarta.

Playa las Estacas – Even farther south, in a small inlet in front of the *Camino Real* resort, this beautiful beach is a lovely place to spend time. Fishing gear, motorboats, and water skis are available for rent at the hotel, on Rte. 200.

Playa de Oro – Less isolated than Conchas Chinas but still pleasant, this palm-fringed beach stretches from the airport to the *Krystal Vallarta.* Nearby is the marina, which has a 300-foot dock for cruise ships, a terminal building, and a yacht club with restaurant and bar.

Playa del Sol – Officially the beach is known as Playa del Sol (Sunny Beach), but its old name, Los Muertos (Dead Men's Beach), still clings. Supposedly it got the grim name from pirates many eons ago. Los Muertos tends to be grubby, but it's where the action is, one of the most populated bits of shore in Vallarta — with snack stands, cocktail bars, musical combos, young boys selling broiled fish on a stick, surfers, gigolos, and in the afternoon, dancing on the sand. Sailboats, speedboats, surfboards, and even horses are for rent.

Mismaloya – Seven miles (11 km) south of Puerto Vallarta, this is where *The Night of the Iguana* was filmed — which put the entire region on the tourist map. When John Huston arrived, the area was uninhabited jungle, but today there is a hotel, restaurant, bar, and a popular disco. Canoes can be rented and scuba diving arranged for exploring the lagoon above and below. Scuba divers must bring their own tanks. Hiking and hunting for sea turtles will keep the active landlubber busy; for others less ambitious, there is the beach and thatch-roofed open-air restaurant. VW vans bound for Mismaloya frequently leave from Calle Lázaro Cárdenas in front of *Daiquiri Dick's* restaurant; the fare is about 25¢. The fun way to get to Mismaloya is to rent a car — the Safari, VW's answer to the jeep, is a popular choice. Having a car for a day allows you plenty of time for exploring what is still largely a virgin stretch of coastline. Daily launch service is provided from Puerto Vallarta, and you'll find current schedules and rates at the desk of your hotel or at the tourist office.

South of Mismaloya, in Boca de Tomatlán, *pangas* (boats) depart for one of three beaches, including Playa las Animas — a popular spot for snorkeling and diving. The beaches also offer *palapa* restaurants, which serve grilled fish. Fare to each beach is $10 to $15, depending on the distance from Boca de Tomatlán.

Yelapa – One hour beyond Mismaloya by boat is a small fishing village with lovely beaches and tropical rustic surroundings. Yelapa, from the Indian word meaning "place of reunions," is an ideal refuge from civilization and has no telephone or television. It's great fun to eat at one of the open-air restaurants, then lie in the sun or rest in a hammock. *Lagunita* has fairly comfortable accommodations, including a few cabins for rent; since there are no phones, you must inquire about them once you arrive. The *Yacht Club* has disco dancing in the evenings. For the more energetic there is a hike to a beautiful waterfall and swimming hole, and at around 3 PM the boat makes the return trip with music, dance, and drink.

Sailboat Excursions – The *Sarape* (phone: 21003) departs every morning for Yelapa, spends 2½ hours in port, and returns around 4 PM, after which it makes a sundown dinner cruise, with snacks, free drinks (from the region), entertainment, and music and dancing. The trimaran *Cielito Lindo* (phone: 24646) provides daily day-long tours around the bay, with opportunities for snorkeling at La Manzanilla Beach, north of Vallarta. Another trimaran, the *Bora Bora* (phone: 23880), offers day-long cruises to Las Animas Beach; other boats make the trip to Quimixto Beach, where passengers can hike up to the waterfalls. Tickets and departure hours can be found at hotel travel desks or Playa del Sol Beach.

Children's Island – A nice place to stroll, it offers shops, restaurants, refreshments stands, and a small museum on a small island at the mouth of the Río Cuale, which divides Puerto Vallarta into northern and southern sections. At one end is a big restaurant where beer is available and mariachis play. Outside *Le Bistro* is a statue of the late film director John Huston.

El Salado Harbor – The maritime terminal, where the big cruise ships come in. At times it is possible to wangle an invitation for dinner aboard ship, a memorable experience.

Church of Guadalupe – With a crown atop its steeple, this 30-year-old church on the main plaza is Puerto Vallarta's most distinctive landmark. 370 Hidalgo.

The Cuale and Gringo Gulch – The Cuale, more of a stream than a river, cuts through Puerto Vallarta. Many of the lovely houses are occupied by foreigners (the former Burton-Taylor home always is pointed out, for example) in what is known as Gringo Gulch.

Malecón – The waterfront avenue looking out over Banderas Bay is Puerto Vallarta's most interesting street. There are several nice shops and restaurants, and it's a lovely place to stroll at sunset.

San Sebastián – Once a thriving mining town of 40,000, its population has dwindled to 1,000, and it is now a popular get-away-from-it-all place with hiking and horseback riding. Stay overnight in the charming 10-room hostelry *El Pabellón* (phone: 21649). About 20 miles east of Puerto Vallarta, the town can be reached by bus. For more information, call the tourist office (phone: 20242).

SOURCES AND RESOURCES

TOURIST INFORMATION: The Puerto Vallarta Tourist Office, staffed by English speakers, is downtown on Calle Juárez in the Municipal Palace (phone: 20242).

Local Coverage – *Vallarta Today* is an English-language daily with a good rundown of what's going on in town. The *News,* flown in daily from Mexico City, will keep you informed on international goings-on. Its Sunday travel section includes a page on Puerto Vallarta. Buy it at hotel newsstands.

TELEPHONE: The area code for Puerto Vallarta is 322. When calling from one city to another within Mexico, dial 91 before the area code.

CLIMATE AND CLOTHES: Puerto Vallarta's popularity is largely due to its splendid weather — clear, warm days and mild nights summer and winter, and a rainy season from late June to early October. If you are coming during the rains, bring a raincoat and heavy sweater. But for the winter season all you'll need are bathing suits and lightweight, comfortable sports clothes.

GETTING AROUND: Bus – There is a bus line running the length of the town, from the airport to Playa del Sol. It comes by frequently and is an easy, inexpensive way to get around.

Taxis – Cabs are plentiful in Puerto Vallarta and can be hailed in the street or called from a hotel. A list of fixed rates can be obtained at the tourist office.

Car Rentals – All the well-known names, and some not so well-known, are represented at the airport or will deliver a car to your hotel. A car comes in handy in Puerto Vallarta, with jeeps being the most popular. Reservations are a good idea, especially if you want automatic shift or air conditioning. In town call *Avis* (phone: 21112 or 21412), *Hertz* (phone: 20056 or 20024), *National* (phone: 21107), *Popo's* (phone: 22356), *Quick Transpocar* (phone: 24010), and *Dollar* (phone: 21700).

Mopeds – Rent A Scooter (phone: 25356), at the *Villa Vallarta Shopping Center,* rents mopeds for $40 a day.

Tours – Various agencies in town and hotel travel desks will arrange bay cruises, sightseeing in the backcountry, horseback excursions, and out-of-town plane trips to Mexico City and Guadalajara. *Big Al* (phone: 20102 or 20920) is a reputable agency offering a variety of tours in and around Puerto Vallarta. They also offer day cruises which take guests to several destinations, including Mismaloya beach. *Viva Tours* (phone: 24600 or 24646) arranges for horseback riding, hunting, and fishing trips.

SPECIAL EVENTS: A biennial regatta from Marina del Rey, California, takes place in February (it sails this year). Call the *Marina del Rey Yacht Club* (phone: 213-823-4664). During the entire month of May, the residents of Puerto Vallarta honor their city with a month-long festival. There are parades, a bullfight, soccer games, fireworks displays, dancing, and street music. It is very gay and feels more like Mexico than at any other time in Puerto Vallarta. The *International Fishing Tournament* takes place during the first week of November. Fishing fanatics come from all over, and even if you are not an enthusiast, it is still worth checking out this lively competition just for its color and high energy. The festivities for the *Virgin of Guadalupe* begin on November 28 and last until December 12, her feast day.

 SHOPPING: Browsing and buying are nearly as popular in Puerto Vallarta as swimming and sunning. The shops are almost all quite attractive and they tend to be small, with the owner doing the selling. The favorite buy is resortwear, and many a shop will whip up an exclusive design for a customer and have it ready the next day. Art can be as good a buy as clothing. At first glance, Vallarta doesn't appear to be a gallery-going town, but visitors soon find that indeed it is. Also available are items from all over Mexico, from Taxco silver to Oaxaca pottery. (Of course, if you're going on to Oaxaca, it would be better to buy your pottery there.) The municipal market, at Calle Matamoros and Augustín Rodriguez, near the bridge, bulges with local crafts and wares. *Bazar de Rocio* (217 Vallarta) is another crafts market ideal for browsing and buying. Cuale Island, on the river of the same name that divides Puerto Vallarta, is also a good place to shop. Several stalls sell local crafts and the *Katy Boutique* (across from *Franzi* restaurant) offers some of the most interestingly designed women's clothing in town. The following are among Puerto Vallarta's better shops:

Aca Joe – Known for T-shirts and tank tops telling the world where you've been, or where you wish you had been. Joe also carries pants, jackets, hats — what have you. 588 Paseo Díaz Ordaz, facing the bay (phone: 22454).

Alfarería Tlaquepaque – Native art and pottery from Guadalajara's famous crafts center as well as a complete selection of *equipales* (rustic chairs made of leather and wood). 1100 Av. México (no phone).

La Colección de Sergio Bustamante – Whimsical animal sculptures made by the highly imaginative artist from Guadalajara. 275 Juárez (phone: 21129).

Discover Rainbow – Wearable and unusual art, hand-painted clothing, textiles, cushions, frames, and other unique accent pieces. 107 Aldama in *Las Palomas* restaurant (phone: 23675).

Galería de Arte Huichol – Merchandise includes masks, yarn and bead "paintings," clothing, and accessories, all made by the Huichol Indians who are natives of the states of Jalisco and Nayarit. Also on display are works by José Benítez, a well-known contemporary Huichol artist. 164 Corona (no phone).

Galería Lepe – Manuel Lepe is a Vallarta institution, and his primitive paintings are virtually a symbol of the town. His work is something very special to take home. 237 Lázaro Cárdenas (phone: 21006).

Galería Pacífico – An excellent gallery that sells the works of some of Mexico and Latin America's finest artists, including Rufino Tamayo, Francisco Zuñiga, and Francisco Toledo. 519 Juárez (phone: 26768).

Galería Uno – A selection of painting and sculpture by some of Mexico's finest artists. The gallery itself is a showplace, an old-fashioned Puerto Vallarta home. 561 Morelos and at Plaza Malecón (phone: 20908).

Iguana de Oro – A very swank shop selling jewelry and gift items in copper and brass. The owners' taste is excellent. 302 Juárez (phone: 21413).

Irene Pulos – Striking fashions with a Mexican accent. 479 Juárez (phone: 26373).

Lety – Sandals originally were a Puerto Vallarta specialty; they still are here. A wide selection for the family; custom work is done as well. 472 Juárez and Plaza Malecón (phone: 21417).

Majolica – Distinctive Talavera pottery with its intricate patterns and brilliant colors. 191 Corona (phone: 24518).

Nelly – One of the best-known resortwear shops in the port, this is one spot that will whip up a custom order and have it ready the next day. *Fiesta Americana Hotel* (phone: 22010).

El Patio – Mexican antiques; items in wrought iron, ceramic, and wood; also some attractive woven bedspreads. 169 Corona at Morelos (phone: 22626).

Pladi – Attractive jewelry and objets d'art in silver, brass, and ceramics. *Plaza Vallarta Shopping Center* (phone: 24621).

Plateria Taxco – Nice selction of good-quality silver at reasonable prices. Stand number 49 in the *Río Cuale Market* (phone: 22173).

Plaza Malecón – A small shopping center where the boutiques offer a little of everything; quite inviting. There's also a good art gallery. Paseo Díaz Ordaz and Allende (no phone).

Ric – Carefully crafted silver jewelry with unusual designs from Taxco. Good quality at about half comparable stateside prices. 207 Juárez (phone: 20086) and at the *Villa Vallarta Shopping Center* (phone: 24598).

Rolling Stones – Leather boots and doodads in brass and onyx are the specialties. All are good buys. 525 Morelos (phone: 22658).

La Rosa de Cristal – A branch of the Tlaquepaque hand-blown glass factory, featuring goblets and dishes galore. 272 Insurgentes (phone: 21585).

Rubén Torres – Colorful, imaginatively designed casual sportswear. 592 Díaz Ordaz (phone: 24949).

Studio Zoo – This gallery offers an excellent selection of contemporary art. Francisco and Madero (phone: 22357).

Sucesos – Hand-painted fabrics, trendy designs, and unique jewelry. Three locations: 233 Libertad and Hidalgo (phone: 21002), *Plaza Malecón* (phone: 20558), and the *Villa Vallarta Shopping Center* (phone: 26251).

Tane – A branch of Mexico's most prestigious silversmith. On display are sterling silver serving pieces, art objects, tableware, and jewelry. Many pieces are combined with vermeil. *Camino Real Hotel* (phone: 30124).

Yolanda – Children's clothing is a specialty with Yolanda, but there is also an extensive selection of embroidered clothing for men and women. 415 Juárez (phone: 20558).

 SPORTS: Puerto Vallarta is one of Mexico's most luxurious beach resorts, with every kind of participatory water sport you might want and a few you probably never even considered. There are also a number of large hotels with facilities for the landbound sportsman, and miles of undeveloped surrounding countryside for the hunter, hiker, and horseback rider.

Baseball – During the season, a league team plays at the stadium every Sunday. Just north of the city on Rte. 200.

Boating – Canoes, sailboats, motorboats, and the accompanying water skis, scuba diving equipment, and snorkels can all be rented by the hour along the beaches, on the *malecón,* or at any of the major hotels.

Fishing – Bordered by rich fishing waters, Puerto Vallarta is an outstanding departure point for deep-sea expeditions. Catches include sailfish, marlin, bonito, tuna, red snapper, and shark, and the season extends throughout the year. Numerous charter companies have headquarters at the northern end of the *malecón,* and you can either arrange a rental yourself or have your hotel do it for you. Freshwater bass fishing at the Cajón de Peñadam can be arranged through *Rancho el Aguacate* (phone: 24754).

Golf – Up the coast beyond the airport, in a development called Nuevo Vallarta, is *Los Flamingos* (phone: 80034), with 18 challenging holes. There is also an 18-hole course at the Marina Vallarta complex (phone: 322-10073).

Horseback Riding – With beautiful trails surrounding the city and along the shore, riding is very popular in Puerto Vallarta. Horses can be rented by the day from several of the larger hotels: *Krystal Vallarta* (2 miles/3 km north, off Airport Rd.); *Holiday Inn* (2½ miles/4 km north on Airport Rd.); and *Playa de Oro* (3 miles/5 km north, just off Airport Rd.). They are also available by the hour on most of the major beaches. *Rancho El Charro* (near the *Plaza las Glorias Hotel;* no phone) also offers horseback riding. Trips sponsored by *Rancho Ojo de Agua* (located behind the Las Aralias section of town; phone: 22718, 22165, or 25244) follow trails through forests and fruit trees and into the mountains, and they include a swim in the Pitillal River. Mondays through Saturdays there are two guided, 3½-hour trips, at 10 AM and 3 PM, and one on Sunday mornings, for about $25 a person. *Rancho Ojo de Agua* also organizes a 5-day tour into the Sierra Madre; it includes a trip through the jungle and pine forests and a day exploring the archaeological site known as El Limbo. The 5-day, all-inclusive trip (with 1 night in Puerto Vallarta) costs $850. Never venture out on one of these trails without a guide.

Hunting – From October through April, hunting expeditions can be arranged for duck, quail, doves, deer, and wildcats, either in the country just outside Puerto Vallarta or at nearby Yelapa. Guides, transportation, and guns are all furnished, and arrangements can be made through your hotel.

Parasailing – As in all the major resort cities in Mexico, this sport is a big favorite on the beaches of Puerto Vallarta. Pulled by a speedboat and wearing an open parachute, the rider is lifted into the air like a kite. It is a magical feeling of flying, and ends — in theory — with a graceful descent. The *Krystal Vallarta* (2 miles/3 km north off Airport Rd.) and the *Holiday Inn* (almost next door on Airport Rd.), both have parasail facilities.

Scuba Diving and Snorkeling – *Chico's Dive Shop* (phone: 21895), next to *Carlos O'Brian's* restaurant on the *malecón* and at the *Fiesta Americana* (phone: 22010), offers daily outings. Depending on equipment and time, snorkeling ranges from $25 to $40, scuba from $46 to $75.

Soccer – This is the national sport, and when it is not baseball season, there is a Sunday afternoon game every week at the stadium, which is north of town on Rte. 200.

Tennis – Most of the large hotels have courts for guests, many illuminated for night games. The *John Newcombe Tennis Center* (phone: 24850), next to the *Plaza Vallarta* hotel, offers classes and clinics to anyone interested.

Windsurfing – Two-day courses are given on the beach in front of the *Holiday Inn;* reservations required (phone: 21700, ext. Travel Desk). Other schools are at the *Las Palmas, Fiesta Americana,* and *Krystal Vallarta* hotels.

NIGHTCLUBS AND NIGHTLIFE: Puerto Vallarta has a little of everything for fun after dark. There are the discos and the piano bars and organized beach parties. Start the evening on the *Sunset and Booze Cruise* which sails from 5:30 to 8 PM; the travel desk in most hotels can make arrangements. The *Krystal Vallarta* hotel hosts the *Fiesta Mexicana,* including mariachis, folkloric dancing, drinks, and an all-you-can-eat buffet on Tuesdays and Saturdays from December 20 through April 14 and on Saturdays only from April 15 through December 19 from 7 to 10 PM. The *Krystal* also hosts the *Fiesta Brava,* a mock bullfight in which the audience is invited to participate in a small bullring; this show also features a Mexican brass band, a lariat show on horseback, and a Spanish buffet on Thursdays from 7 to 10 PM. The cost for each of the *Krystal*'s shows is $30 a person. During the high season, the *Camino Real, Sheraton Buganvilias, Garza Blanca,* and *Plaza las Glorias* hotels also organize *Noches Mexicanas,* which usually include a buffet, entertainment, and dancing. They can be a lot of fun. Mariachis play in the lobby bar of the *Marriott,* and there's dancing nightly in their 1960s bar. *La Estancia* at the *Krystal Vallarta,* the lobby bar at the *Sheraton,* and the *Tiki Bar* at the *Playa de Oro* hotel have live music for dancing and, during the winter season, some kind of floor show. Jazz is played nightly at *Le Bistro* on Cuale Island. *Yesterday* (127 Púlpito) features dancing under the stars to live disco music; *Cactus Club* (399 Ignacio Vallarta; phone: 26037) has music for all ages; *El Panorama* (*Siesta* hotel) has a floor show; *Sundance* (at Lázaro Cárdenas) is popular and spacious; *Friday López* (at the *Fiesta Americana*) is lively and gaining popularity; and the *Krystal* hotel's *Christine,* which features a laser light show set to popular disco music, is another hot spot. The tourist information kiosk on Cuale Island often has free invitations to some of the discos; it's worth it to inquire. Those who simply crave a quiet spot for a drink should drop in at *Tequila,* upstairs at what used to be the *Oceano* hotel (on the *malecón*) or try *El Set* at *Conchas Chinas.*

BEST IN TOWN

CHECKING IN: The winter season is when Puerto Vallarta is at its best — and also when the hotels are jammed. New hotels are springing up all the time, however, including a good number in the Marina Vallarta complex; one of the development's newest properties will be the *Conrad* — slated to open later this year, with 280 rooms, including 15 suites (phone: 800-445-8667 in the US). The *Paraíso Radisson,* located in the Nuevo Vallarta development north of Puerto Vallarta, had also begun construction at press time. The hotel is due to open at the end of the year, with 300 rooms and suites, restaurants, bars, a pool, and tennis courts. Wherever you decide to stay, make a reservation, with confirmation from the hotel itself. Don't depend solely on a travel agent's voucher; request proof of confirmation. Be sure, by the way, to reconfirm your air reservation and get it marked on your ticket; a phone reservation may get lost. We've listed hotels charging $130 or more a day for two as expensive; $75 to $110 as moderate; and $65 or less as inexpensive. Rates are considerably lower from May through November. All telephone numbers are in the 322 area code unless otherwise indicated. When calling from one city to another within Mexico, dial 91 before the area code.

Camino Real – An elegant resort with lush grounds and a near-private beach, it offers 330 deluxe accommodations (250 rooms in the older 12-story tower and 80 rooms in the new tower). There are also beach facilities, tennis courts, swimming pools and a swim-up bar, spa, organized social programs for adults, and a playground for children. One and a half miles (2 km) south on Rte. 200, Playa las Estacas (phone: 30123; 800-228-3000 in the US; FAX: 30070). Expensive.

Fiesta Americana – A fine hotel with a gigantic, *palapa*-domed lobby and 291 luxurious rooms. Tennis, pool, beach, fine food, and a disco. On Los Tules Beach north of town (phone: 22010; 800-FIESTA-1 in the US; FAX: 22108). Expensive.

Garza Blanca – Perhaps the best place to stay in Puerto Vallarta for relative privacy, this place, nestled in a secluded cove, has 40 units, including split-level, 1-bedroom chalets with private pools perched on a cliffside; and beach-level suites. There is an unspoiled swimming beach across the road and a tennis court. Meals and drinks are served in an indoor dining room or on an open terrace. The cooking is simply acceptable, but the overall atmosphere first rate. 5 miles (8 km) south on Rte. 200

(phone: 21083 or 21023; 800-331-0908 in the US; 800-548-9121 in California). Expensive.

Hyatt Coral Grand Puerto Vallarta – A beachfront property surrounded by a beautiful garden complete with cascading waterfalls, it has 120 elegantly furnished suites, a tennis court, free-form pool, and restaurants. About 10 minutes south of downtown Vallarta at Km 8.5 Barra de Navidad Hwy. (phone: 25191; 800-233-1234 in the US; FAX: 22423). Expensive.

La Jolla de Mismaloya – A luxury property, it's located on a small bay in Mismaloya, about 7 miles (11 km) from downtown. The seafood restaurant of the same name, which is now part of the hotel, has been popular for several years, and a disco, *Iggy's*, has been operating since 1987. There are 450 suites in 5 buildings. Several swimming pools, tennis courts, bars, and a Jacuzzi were slated to be completed early this year. (phone: 21374; in the US, 800-322-2343). Expensive.

Marriott Puerto Vallarata – One of several hostelries that opened in 1990 in the Marina Vallarta development, it has 403 rooms, including 26 suites, all with private balconies. Facilities include 5 tennis courts, a health club, pool, several restaurants, and a disco. Marina Vallarta (phone: 10003; 800-228-9290 in the US; FAX: 10760). Expensive.

Meliá Puerto Vallarta – A new 9-story beachfront property in the Marina Vallarta complex, it's decorated in natural colors and vibrant pinks and blues. All 403 rooms have bay views. Facilities include tennis, a coffee shop, restaurants, and a lobby bar. Marina Vallarta (phone: 10200; 800-888-5515 in western US; 800-336-3542 in eastern US; FAX: 10715). Expensive.

Sheraton Buganvilias – Lavish, with greenery everywhere, it has 501 oceanfront rooms housed in 6 towers, and 3 buildings with 169 one- and two-bedroom suites. There are 4 tennis courts, a beach, a large pool, and several bars and restaurants. This is one of Vallarta's newer hotels. On the beach north of town (phone: 30404; 800-325-3535 in the US; FAX: 20500). Expensive.

Villas Quinta Real – An exquisite pink and white mansion set near the Marina Vallarta 18-hole golf course, this elegant hostelry has 50 suites and 25 one- and two-bedroom villas furnished with antiques and original works of art. 311 Pelicanos, Marina Vallarta (phone: 10800; 800-445-4565 in the US). Expensive.

Quinta María Cortéz – An eclectic "Mexaterranean" villa right on Concha Chinas Beach, with 1- and 2-bedroom suites, some of which have terraces and all of which come with kitchenettes and imaginative baths. Each is cluttered with antiques, interesting "junque," and original paintings. Fresh orange juice is delivered each morning and the housekeeper will prepare breakfast on request, but there are no telephones or TV sets — just the beach and a pool. No children under 5. Mailing address: Apdo. 356, c.p. 48390 (phone: 21317 or 21184). Expensive to moderate.

Fiesta Americana Plaza Vallarta – This impressive, 359-room, 79-suite hotel on the beach is perfect for tennis lovers. It has a *John Newcombe Tennis Center,* the first such tennis clinic in Mexico, with 8 courts. Playa las Glorias (phone: 24448 or 24360; 800-FIESTA-1 in the US; FAX: 25236). Moderate.

Holiday Inn – It has 229 rooms, 236 suites, 10 penthouses, and sports and beach facilities, although it's somewhat lacking in atmosphere. 2½ miles (4 km) north on Airport Rd. (phone: 21700 or 21600; 800-HOLIDAY; FAX: 25683). Moderate.

Krystal Vallarta – As much a secluded village as a hotel, this place was designed in a lovely classical Mexican fashion, complete with cobblestone walkways and gaslight lamps lighting the walkways at night. Having completed a 3-year-long, $20-million renovation at the end of 1989, the hotel now has 460 rooms, suites, and villas — all with air conditioning, satellite color TV, and mini-bars. The spacious lobby bar features live music. For swimmers there are 44 pools, including 38 private pools, 3 children's pools, and the impressive Seven Columns pool with fountains, waterfalls, and a swim-up bar. Other facilities include 2 clay tennis courts, beach *palapas* for all guests, 7 restaurants (see *Eating Out*), and *Christine's* disco. The hotel hosts the popular *Fiesta Mexicana* and *Fiesta Brava* (see *Nightclubs and Nightlife*). North of town, near the airport, Av. de las Garzas (phone: 21459, 21378, or 21041; 800-231-9860 in the US). Moderate.

Meza del Mar – Half of the 127 one- and 2-bedroom suites here face the sea. Not to worry, the other half face the mountains. Rate includes meals, regional drinks, and most activities. The staff is exceptionally friendly and helpful. 380 Amapac (phone: 24888; 800-876-3942 in the US; FAX: 22308). Moderate.

Plaza las Glorias – A pretty and comfortable place with an atrium lobby, 377 rooms and villas, 2 restaurants and bars, and 2 pools, around which there's a Mexican fiesta every Tuesday night. Playa las Glorias (phone: 22224; FAX: 26559). Moderate.

Conchas Chinas – With 40 pleasant suites, it also has a great beach, pool, and one of the town's best restaurants, *El Set* (see *Eating Out*). On Rte. 200, 1½ miles (2 km) south of town (phone: 20156; 800-424-4441 in the US; FAX: 20763). Inexpensive.

Fontana del Mar – A lovely place with 41 rooms (ask for one with a balcony facing the front), a vine-covered courtyard with fountain, and a rooftop pool where the sound of crickets accompanies a moonlight swim. Some of the rooms have kitchenettes, and the *Playa Los Arcos* restaurant is next door. Dieguez and Olas Altas (phone: 25030). Inexpensive.

Molino de Agua – At this rustic and romantic little hostelry right in town, there are 57 small rooms with river and ocean views and also terraces. The bar has live music in the evening during the winter; there are also 2 pools, a Jacuzzi, and a restaurant. Ignacio Vallarta, corner of Aquiles Serdán, at the river's edge (phone: 21907; 800-423-5512 in the US; FAX: 26056). Inexpensive.

Oro Verde – Centrally located and right on the beach, this Swiss-run establishment has 132 rooms and 28 suites, a restaurant, and a bar with live music. 111 Rodolfo Gómez (phone: 23050; 800-458-6888 in the US; FAX: 22431). Inexpensive.

Las Palmas – A spacious low-rise resort complex, its floors are linked by an interesting network of interior wooden bridges. Most of the 165 rooms and suites have balconies and beach views, and there is a restaurant and bar. Airport Rd. north of town (phone: 20650; FAX: 20543). Inexpensive.

Pelícanos – Located on a nice beach, its has 189 rooms, 16 bungalows and 3 pools. Km 2.5 on the Airport Rd. (phone: 22107; FAX: 21915). Inexpensive.

Playa de Oro – Immense, with 400 balconied units, it's also ideal for sports lovers: Besides the tennis courts, 2 pools, and beach facilities, there's skin diving, fishing gear, water skis, and horses available for hire. A Jacuzzi, 3 restaurants, and 5 bars complete the hedonistic setup. Three miles (5 km) north, just off Airport Rd. on Av. de la Garzas (phone: 26868; 800-882-8215 in the US; FAX: 20348). Inexpensive.

Posada Río Cuale – This brick and whitewashed inn has 25 rooms, a pool, a nice bar, and a popular, large, open dining room serviced by an accomplished kitchen (see *Eating Out*). Corner of Vallarta and Serdán (phone: 20450). Inexpensive.

Posada de Roger – Simple, charming, and appealing, it boasts 50 comfortable rooms (some are air conditioned); a delightful bar-restaurant, *El Tucán* (see *Eating Out*); and a pool. 237 Badillo (phone: 20836). Inexpensive.

 EATING OUT: In recent years, there has been an explosion of good restaurants in Puerto Vallarta. Every price range, type of food, and atmosphere are now available; service in most places is exceptionally friendly and good. While it's hard to have a bad meal here, it's also tough to happen on a great one. If you don't want to sit down in a restaurant, there are always the fried-fish salesmen up and down the beach or the prickly-pear vendors throughout town. (We don't recommend either, unless you've laid in a good supply of Lomotil.) Dinner for two in a restaurant we classify as expensive will cost about $50; moderate, $30 to $40; and inexpensive, under $25. Prices do not include wine, drinks, or tips, and are considerably lower off-season. Most restaurants accept MasterCard and Visa; a few also accept American Express and Diners Club. Unless otherwise noted, all restaurants are open daily. All telephone numbers are in the 322 area code unless otherwise indicated. When calling from one city to another within Mexico, dial 91 before the area code.

Alejandro's Café – Expertly prepared international and Mexican dishes and a relaxed atmosphere have made this a Vallarta favorite. Reservations advised. At *Meza del Mar Hotel* (phone: 24848). Expensive.

Le Bistro – Specialties include surf and turf, shish kebab, jumbo shrimp, and a variety of tasty crêpes. The handsome bar and recorded jazz make this a good place to relax after dinner. Closed Sundays, as well as Monday nights for the meeting of the expatriates' *International Friendship Club* (all invited). Reservations advised. Just off Insurgentes on Cuale Island (phone: 20283). Expensive.

Bogart's – Inspired by the film *Casablanca,* the menu features French continental fare in an exceptionally posh and romantic setting, with fountains and reflecting pools, stark white decor, semiprivate booths, velvet foot pillows for women guests, and piano music. The very friendly and attentive waiters dress in Moroccan attire, and the bar walls are decorated with Bogart memorabilia. Dinner only; seatings at 6 and 9 PM. Reservations advised. At the *Krystal Vallarta Hotel,* Av. de las Garzas (phone: 21459, 21378, or 21041). Expensive.

Café des Artistes – Elegant, intimate, and romantic, this new spot is owned and operated by the proprietors of *Le Bistro* (see above). Chef Thierry Blume prepares French nouvelle cuisine with a heavy Mexican accent, serving such dishes as shrimp in champagne and basil, or duck in *pipián* (a Yucatecan sauce made with pumpkin seeds, among other ingredients). Dinner only. Reservations necessary. Leona Vicario and Guadalupe Sánchez (phone: 23228). Expensive.

Kamakura – Guests enjoy dinner prepared at their tables at this lovely Japanese dining spot, which serves such specialties as sushi, teppanyaki, and sukiyaki. Dinner only, from 6 PM to midnight. Reservations advised. At the *Krystal Vallarta,* Av. de las Garzas (phone: 21459, 21378, 21041). Expensive.

Mogambo – Next door to *Il Mangiare* and under the same management. Specialties are prime ribs and lobster. Live jazz nightly. Reservations advised. 644 Díaz Ordaz (phone: 23476). Expensive.

Panorama – The view and international dishes here are both excellent, with dining available indoors or on a rooftop terrace. Many of the dishes are prepared right at the table. Try the *camarones gigantes al Panorama,* giant shrimp prepared with cheese and wine sauce. Reservations advised. On the 7th floor, atop the *La Siesta* hotel (phone: 21818). Expensive.

Señor Chico's – Surf and turf and a spectacular view from the hills of Conchas Chinas. Reservations advised. 377 Pulpito (phone: 23570). Expensive.

Chef Roger – The Swiss chef at this European-style bistro makes imaginative use of Mexican ingredients in an interesting selection of international dishes. Reservations advised. 267 Agustín Rodríguez (phone: 20604). Expensive to moderate.

Archie's Wok – A sampling of dishes from several Asian countries is prepared by Archie Alpenia, who was once the late film director John Huston's chef. Reservations advised. 130 Francisca Rodríguez (phone: 20411). Moderate.

Brazz – A large, airy eatery (part of a chain) behind the *Océano* hotel, it specializes in steaks — sirloin, rib-eye, T-bone, and tenderloin — and also serves Mexican dishes and seafood. The mariachis start to play at 9:30 PM. Reservations advised. Morelos and Galeana (phone: 20324). Moderate.

Carlos O'Brian's – Another member of the Carlos Anderson chain that's so popular with tourists all over Mexico, it serves lunch and dinner in a lively, upbeat atmosphere. There is a bar, a grill, and everything from ribs to "Chato Brian" for two. Closed on *Christmas* and *New Year's Day* only. No reservations. On the *malecón* (phone: 21444). Moderate.

La Cebolla Roja – Also called the *Red Onion,* it's a very popular place with lively Mexican decor. Dishes include barbecued ribs, Mexican platters, and chicken — fried, curried, or in *mole* sauce — and everything is prepared with care. The salad bar is good. Open for breakfast, lunch, and dinner. Reservations advised for large groups. No credit cards accepted. 822 Díaz Ordaz (phone: 21087). Moderate.

Chee Chee – Set on a cliffside amidst lush foilage and overlooking the Pacific Ocean, this open-air spot is currently an "in" place for good international cooking, especially seafood. There also are 2 swimming pools. Reservations advised for large groups. About 12 miles (19 km) up the road to Manzanillo (phone: 20920). Moderate.

Chez Elena – Established nearly 40 years ago, this spot offers dishes such as mixed *saté* (chicken and shellfish on a skewer with peanut sauce), chicken curry, and several Mexican favorites. There's live music and a great view of the town and bay. Reservations advised. *Los Cuatro Vientros Hotel* (phone: 20161). Moderate.

Chino's Paradise – At this popular thatch-roofed lunch spot south of town you can admire waterfalls and watch cliff divers as you eat. Reservations unnecessary. About 15 miles (24 km) south of Puerto Vallarta on Rte. 200 (phone: 22946). Moderate.

Daiquiri Dick's – Enjoy lunch and dinner on the terrace overlooking the beach. The handiwork of an expatriate Californian, both the decor and food are California *à la mexicana.* Reservations advised. 246 Olas Altas (phone: 20566). Moderate.

El Dorado – Perhaps the most popular spot in town for breakfast and lunch, it is a prime location for wave watching. Camaraderie abounds. Reservations advised. Amapas and Pulpito (phone: 21511). Moderate.

Franzi – This open-air garden café boasts the best setting on Cuale Island and serves good omelettes, quiche, and salad as well as Mexican dishes; the Sunday brunch is particularly good. Pâté comes with the bread and butter; classical music and river sounds provide a soothing background. Reservations advised. Cuale Island (no phone). Moderate.

Hard Rock Café – Another link in the fast-growing worldwide chain, this is one of Puerto Vallarta's most popular spots for eating, drinking, and dancing. Good rock music, large portions of well-prepared food, and efficient, friendly service are a constant here. Reservations unnecessary. 652 Díaz Ordaz (phone: 25532). Moderate.

Le Kliff – Perched on a cliff (surprise!), this multilevel, thatch-roofed restaurant provides a beautiful backdrop for first class food and friendly service. It's a good place for a very late lunch, when it's possible to dawdle long enough to savor the spectacular sunset for dessert. Reservations advised. About 10 miles (16 km) south of Puerto Vallarta (no phone). Moderate.

La Langosta – Lobster and shrimp are the best choices at this seafood place with piano bar entertainment. Reservations advised. Lázaro Cárdenas and Vallarta (phone: 20676). Moderate.

Il Mangiare – Italian food in the Mexican manner is served here. Lovely ocean view. Dinner only. Reservations advised. Díaz Ordaz, corner of Abasolo (phone: 22486). Moderate.

Moby Dick's – The menu at this eatery centers around seafood (what else) in simple, pleasant surroundings. Reservations advised. North end of the *malecón,* near the *Rosita* (phone: 20655). Moderate.

El Ostión Feliz – No view and no frills at this spot known in English as "The Happy Oyster," but the service is friendly and the seafood is luscious. Reservations advised for large groups. 177 Libertad (phone: 22508). Moderate.

Las Palomas – A variety of flags out front make it easy to spot this lively open-air place on the *malecón.* The fare, simple and satisfying, and the gentle breeze wafting thorough here are particularly welcome after an overdose of shopping and sightseeing. Reservations advised. Díaz Ordaz and Aldama (phone: 23675). Moderate.

Posada Río Cuale – A local favorite in the hotel of the same name, it has become so popular that the management decided to reduce the number of hotel rooms in order to enlarge the dining room. The setting is delightful. Lobster bisque, *huachinango* (Pacific red snapper), and pepper steaks are among the specialties. Reservations advised. Vallarta and Serdán (phone: 20450). Moderate.

El Set – On the cliffs overlooking the beaches, it is chock-full of *ambiente.* Fun at lunchtime, lovely at dinner, perfect for cocktails and "another lousy sunset in paradise." Reservations advised. On the southern highway, 1½ miles (2 km) from town (phone: 20302). Moderate.

Bing's – The pink and white façade marks the hottest spot for ice cream in town, with everything from *caramelo de menta* (peppermint stick) to *zarzamora* (blackberry). A *bola* is a scoop, and it's ample here. Waiting to get in at the end of the day is like lining up for the million-dollar lottery. Reservations unnecessary. No credit cards accepted. Just off the plaza (no phone). Inexpensive.

Mismaloya Beach – Open only for lunch, this is a seafood eatery by the ocean, not far from where *Night of the Iguana* was filmed. Reservations unnecessary. No credit cards accepted. Mismaloya Beach, south of town (no phone). Inexpensive.

Pietro's – A good choice for lunch (though also open for dinner), it has homemade pasta, pizza, and daily specials. The house wine, however, leaves something to be desired. Reservations advised. 245 Zaragoza and Hidalgo (phone: 23233). Inexpensive.

Pizza Nova – All kinds of pizza are served here. Closed Tuesdays. No reservations. 674 Díaz Ordaz (phone: 22204). Inexpensive.

Tucán – It's a quaint restaurant/bar in town with great appeal for singles. Reservations advised. In the *Posada de Roger Hotel,* 245 Badillo (phone: 20836). Inexpensive.

SAN MIGUEL DE ALLENDE

(pronounced Sahn Mee-*gehl* day Ah-*yen*-day)

Once the heartland of rebellion and the War of Independence, today San Miguel de Allende has become Mexico's most celebrated artists' colony. Founded in 1542 by a Franciscan friar, Juan de San Miguel, the village was settled by a group of Indians to whom he had taught European techniques of weaving and agriculture. The friar also marked off the streets, parceled out land, and established a tradition of artisanship and an artistic sensibility that survive to this day.

In the Bajío region of Mexico, San Miguel de Allende sits at an altitude of 6,000 feet, surrounded by rich farmland and the beautiful Sierra Madre. It was in these mountains, around the nearby town of Guanajuato, that silver was discovered early in the 18th century. The wealthy Spaniards who owned the mines soon began building elegant colonial palaces in San Miguel. The town was surrounded by vast estates, or haciendas, also controlled by wealthy Spaniards.

At that time, the town was still known as San Miguel el Grande — to distinguish it from the other communities in the area also named in honor of Saint Michael. As the name implies, San Miguel el Grande was the biggest of these and one of the more important towns in the wealthiest area (from mining and agriculture) in New Spain.

The Bajío region in those days seethed with rebellion. The Creoles — Spaniards born in the colony rather than in Spain itself — were very much second class subjects of the king, while the mestizos — of mixed Spanish and Indian ancestry — and the Indians were of even lower class. First the American and then the French Revolution sparked the notion that matters might be improved. When Napoleon invaded Spain and established his brother as king, a movement for immediate independence for Mexico was barely crushed by Spanish conservatives in the country. Colonists who could not bring themselves to rebel against the legitimate king had fewer qualms about taking up arms against a usurper.

The independence movement was born in nearby Querétaro, where the conspirators were discovered and captured. One, however, sent word to a kindred soul, Father Miguel Hidalgo, a parish priest in the town of Dolores. Late on the night of September 15, 1810, Father Hidalgo tolled the bells of his church and, having summoned his flock, cried that the hour of independence had come. He led his people, his insurgents, in an attack on Guanajuato, the largest city in the region. There they were joined by Ignacio Allende, late of a royalist regiment, and the Spanish garrison was defeated. A year later Hidalgo and Allende were captured by the royalists in Chihuahua and beheaded, but the movement that they had begun lived on. When Mexico achieved independence in 1821, it honored its heroes, naming the town of Dolores "Dolores Hidalgo" and changing San Miguel el Grande to "San Miguel de Allende."

A century later came the great upheaval that is known in Mexico as the Revolution. Among other things it resulted in the breaking up of the huge plantations. Many of the palatial manor houses were destroyed in the fighting and today stand only as ruins. Others have been restored as private residences, while several have been converted into hotels.

One became a school. In 1951, Nel and Enrique Fernandez (she's American, he was Mexican), founded the Instituto Allende in San Miguel as a place of study for would-be expatriate Americans who no longer could look forward to a junior year in Europe. At that time, the institute was thriving with an enrollment of former soldiers, who found the funds available to them under the GI Bill went further in San Miguel. Still run by Nel Fernandez (Enrique passed away), the institute continues as an intellectual center, attracting both young and old: college students picking up a few extra credits and pensioners taking courses ranging from sculpture to photography.

As a result, San Miguel de Allende has a large and rather notable American community. Gerald Greene (*Holocaust*) and Clifford Irving (*Death Freaks*) are among the writers frequently in residence. Almost any social gathering will include a painter or a concert artist and perhaps an actor or two. The conversation is intellectual, the food international.

San Miguel has one of Mexico's finest and most important art galleries, *Galería San Miguel;* a bilingual library; and three institutions of higher learning: the Academia Hispano Americana, which offers courses in Latin American studies, Spanish language, and literature; Centro Cultural Ignacio Ramírez, which principally features the study of the arts and is a branch of the famous Instituto de Bellas Artes in Mexico City; and the Instituto Allende, which teaches fine arts and offers recognized credits toward MAs and MFAs. There is also a branch of PEN, the worldwide organization of writers dedicated to the preservation of free speech.

The countryside around San Miguel de Allende is famous for health spas with hot springs. In the town itself, the beautiful Spanish buildings still stand, and the cobblestone streets from the colonial period are in good condition. Having been declared a national monument in 1926, San Miguel is protected from any new construction that is not in the colonial style. Today, 100,000 people live in the area.

The streets are narrow and steep, and while it is possible to drive around with very little competing traffic, walking (take a sturdy pair of shoes) is by far the most rewarding way to explore the city. The houses are built close to the street, with high, grilled windows looking out on passersby. There are beautiful hand-carved wood doors and stone coats of arms on many of the buildings. Weaving remains one of the most spectacular traditional crafts and is still done on the upright looms introduced by Friar Juan in the 16th century. Together with an abundance of hand embroidery, they make San Miguel an excellent place to buy distinctive cloth goods.

The center of town is the Plaza Allende, and all of the shopping, including the native market, is within easy walking distance of it. At the plaza you can also see an old and charming custom carried out by the teens and pre-teens of San Miguel. Every Sunday evening from 8 to 10 PM there is a promenade in which the young women walk in one direction and the young men in the other. In this way, they can admire and perhaps even meet one another. Hundreds of people congregate to watch, to stroll, or to socialize. It's a Mexican teenager's equivalent of cruising through a shopping mall.

SAN MIGUEL DE ALLENDE AT-A-GLANCE

SEEING THE CITY: San Miguel de Allende has two exceptional places from which to see the entire town and the surrounding countryside of lakes, farmlands, and mountains. Up a long flight of terraced stone steps behind and above the Instituto Allende and Benito Juárez Park is the Cerro del Chorro, the Hill of Springs. Named for the clear springs that surface here, the hill provides all of the drinking water for the city. There is a refreshment stand, and benches are provided for all who climb to see this magnificent view of the town and Laja River.

El Mirador, the Lookout, offers another magnificent panorama of the city and its environs. It is accessible by foot via Calle Real, an old cobblestone street, or by car via the Querétaro Road. It is across from the *Posada la Ermita* hotel; a visit here can be combined with a poolside drink.

There is a commanding view of the whole valley from the dining room of the *Hacienda de las Flores* hotel.

SPECIAL PLACES: San Miguel de Allende is a beautiful city with sights of historic interest at almost every turn. A walk around town with a camera is a rewarding venture you should not miss.

La Parroquia (Parish Church) – This unusual Gothic-spired church was built less than 100 years ago. The architect, Ceferino Gutiérrez, was a self-educated Indian who found his inspiration in the picture-postcard reproductions of European churches. Drawing blueprints in the dust as instructions for his workers, Gutiérrez constructed this amazing pink stone edifice, which dominates San Miguel's skyline. If you get lost in your wanderings, you need only glance up to find the central spire and the plaza below. Once inside, take time to look at the murals depicting the Indian heritage of the populace and to visit the crypt. Closed from 2 to 5 PM. South side of Plaza Allende.

Parque Benito Juárez (Benito Juárez Park) – Filled with fountains, flowers, and young lovers, this small park is located just below Cerro del Chorro on the outskirts of town. It dates from 1904 and has picnic tables, playground equipment, basketball courts, and a stream meandering through untamed woods. White lilies bloom here in spring. Between Calle de Tenerías and Puente de Animas.

Ignacio Allende's Home – The birthplace of Ignacio Allende is commemorated by a plaque hanging over the front door that reads: "Here was born the one who is famous." Allende, a military leader in Mexico's struggle for independence, worked with Miguel Hidalgo, the original revolutionary priest, to start the revolution in 1810. Only a year later both were captured and executed, but their memory endures. There are temporary art exhibits, mainly work done by the Otomí Indians. Closed Mondays. No admission charge. 1 Cuna de Allende, just off Plaza Allende (phone: 22499).

Palacio de los Condes de Canal (House of the Counts of Canal) – This imposing building constructed by a wealthy 18th-century mining family is a magnificent
example of the style of architecture built by the Spanish during the colonial era. It is
now used by the Banco Nacional de México, and can be seen during banking hours:
Monday through Friday from 9 AM to 1:30 PM. Northwest corner of Plaza Allende
facing Calle Canal (no phone).

Iglesia de San Francisco (Church of San Francisco) – Standing quietly on a
corner, this lovely old church offers itself to look through, a small park with benches
to relax on, and a weathered statue of Christopher Columbus to admire. On the *Day
of the Race*, known in the US as *Columbus Day*, a civic ceremony is held here, and
most of the town attends. Closed from 2 to 5 PM. Where Calle San Francisco and Calle
Juárez meet (no phone).

Instituto Allende – This old converted hacienda on the edge of town now houses
the school responsible for changing the population, economy, and way of life of San
Miguel. Throughout the year, courses are given in painting, sculpture, ceramics, photography, Spanish, and Mexican and Latin American literature; summer programs for
teachers and MA and MFA degrees are also offered. All classes are taught in English
and are well attended by American students. Even if you are only passing through or
are not interested in taking courses, this beautiful building and its grounds are worth
a visit. There is an exhibition room featuring the works of students and teachers, many
of which are for sale; and occasional performances can be seen in the school's theater.
20 Ancha de San Antonio (phone: 20190).

Centro Cultural Ignacio Ramírez – This center, which has been incorporated as
a branch of the Instituto de Bellas Artes of Mexico City, offers courses in music, art,
dance, weaving, ceramics, and metalwork. Once a convent, these buildings are now the
backdrop for various cultural events such as lectures, concerts, theater, and dance
recitals. There are two galleries with changing exhibits, murals, a café, a lovely patio,
and a bulletin board in English to keep residents and visitors alike posted on what's
happening around town. If the room housing the unfinished Siqueiros mural is closed,
ask permission to see it. The center is closed Saturday afternoons and Sundays. 75 Calle
Hernández Macías (phone: 20289).

House and Garden Tour – Every Sunday at noon, a small group leaves from the
library to tour some of the beautiful homes and gardens of San Miguel. It's a rare
opportunity for a look inside a Mexican house; refreshments and a talk are included.
Tickets are available in the library during regular opening hours and half an hour before
the tour leaves, as well as around the plaza. 25 Calle de los Insurgentes (phone: 20293).

Jardín de las Orquídeas (Orchid Garden) – Worth the strenuous uphill walk from
town along Calle Correo, it seems a truly secret garden — filled with thousands of
plants, including orchids, irises, cacti, and fruit trees, all entangled and among which
a stream flows. October and November are the months to see the most flowers. 38 Santo
Domingo.

Santuario de Atotonilco (Sanctuary of Atotonilco) – This 16th-century sanctuary, approximately 8 miles (13 km) north of San Miguel, is a religious center of some
renown. For centuries, Indians from all over Mexico have made pilgrimages to worship
here. Frescoes and sculptures provide a glimpse of Mexican popular art dating from
the 18th century; and from the 19th century comes a history lesson about revolutionary
fervor. It was here at the sanctuary that the Army of Independence, under the leadership of Allende and Hidalgo, made their first stop. They seized a banner of the Virgin
of Guadalupe, declared it their flag of liberation, and carried it into battle. It was the
choice of this popular religious figure that brought the Indians decisively into the
insurrection on the side of the rebels. Dolores Hidalgo Rd.

Teatro Angela Peralta – San Miguel's historic concert hall is considered one of the
most beautiful and acoustically perfect in all of Mexico (phone: 22544).

■**EXTRA SPECIAL:** Dolores Hidalgo, 24 miles (38 km) northwest of San Miguel de Allende, is known as "the cradle of independence." It was here on September 15, 1810, that the parish priest Miguel Hidalgo rang the church bell calling his parishioners together in the name of Mexican independence. It was this call to arms, known as the *Grito de Dolores,* or, more commonly, simply *El Grito,* that initiated the struggle for independence from Spain. There is a large monument at the entrance of town and a famous statue of Hidalgo in the main plaza, both commemorating this famous event. The town also has a museum in Hidalgo's home, which is now filled with memorabilia and artwork on the same theme. The town is best visited on a Sunday, when the local market offers its finest pottery, for which the town is also famous. Rte. 15, between San Miguel de Allende and Guanajuato.

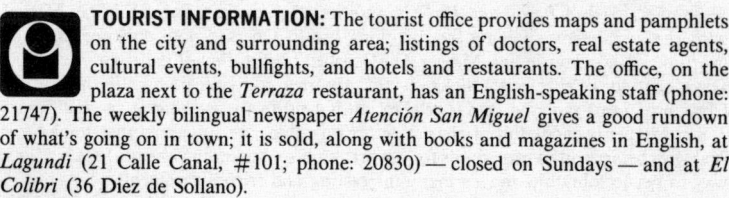

SOURCES AND RESOURCES

TOURIST INFORMATION: The tourist office provides maps and pamphlets on the city and surrounding area; listings of doctors, real estate agents, cultural events, bullfights, and hotels and restaurants. The office, on the plaza next to the *Terraza* restaurant, has an English-speaking staff (phone: 21747). The weekly bilingual newspaper *Atención San Miguel* gives a good rundown of what's going on in town; it is sold, along with books and magazines in English, at *Lagundi* (21 Calle Canal, #101; phone: 20830) — closed on Sundays — and at *El Colibri* (36 Diez de Sollano).

TELEPHONE: The area code for San Miguel de Allende is 465. When calling from one city to another within Mexico, dial 91 before the area code.

CLIMATE AND CLOTHES: The average monthly temperature in San Miguel de Allende ranges from 57F to 68F, with evenings slightly cooler than days. The rainy season is in late summer and early fall. If you visit between July and September, bring rainwear and bug repellent. The town is informal, and you will require nothing more than clothes in which you are comfortable and a stout pair of walking shoes.

GETTING AROUND: Buses – Three bus lines run through town. The bus terminal at Calzada de la Estación is pleasant, clean, and safe.
   Taxi – There are several taxi companies in San Miguel, each with a telephone number to call a cab directly to you. The town is so small, however, that almost anyplace inside the city limits can easily be reached on foot. Some taxi companies are: *Sitio Allende* (phone: 20192); *Sitio San Felipe* (phone: 20440); *Sitio San Francisco* (phone: 20290); and *Sitio Terminal* (phone: 21795).
   Car Rentals – A local firm, *Gama,* with offices on the plaza, has a small rental fleet (phone: 20815). The larger agencies are in the nearby towns of Celaya and Querétaro.
   Tours – The Centro de Crecimiento, a school for handicapped children, organizes "Saturday Sojourns" to interesting places outside of San Miguel. Past trips have included visits to working ranches, a monastery, a dairy, a cheese factory, old haciendas, and an equestrian center. The cost is about $10 per person, and the money goes toward the school's upkeep. A bus leaves the Centro de Crecimiento on Saturdays at 10:30

AM and returns around 1:30 PM. Tickets are available at the school (100 Hernández Macías; phone: 20318), *Casa Maxwell* (14 Canal), or *El Colibri* (30 Sollano).

SPECIAL EVENTS: Besides celebrating all the Mexican secular and religious holidays, San Miguel de Allende has a few of its own. The *Fiesta de San Miguel* (Feast of Saint Michael the Archangel) is an annual celebration of San Miguel's patron saint that begins on September 29 and usually lasts until October 4. It includes a fair with games, fireworks, a bullfight, plenty of sliced pineapple and other food, and much music and dancing. In June, thousands of local boys and girls dress up in crazy costumes to celebrate the *Fiesta de los Locos* to honor Saint Anthony of Padua. *Veintiuno de Enero* (January 21) celebrates the birth of San Miguel's secular patron, Ignacio Allende, independence hero. It consists mostly of civic ceremonies, a large parade through town, and the usual music and dancing on every square and street corner. Holy Week is celebrated with processions, altar displays in the windows of private homes, colorfully decorated churches, and a sunset procession on *Good Friday.* The *San Miguel Chamber Music Festival,* held in August, features internationally acclaimed groups from around the world. The national holidays, especially *Independence Day* (September 15 and 16 — the celebrations start at 11 PM on September 15) and *Revolution Day* (November 20), are quite special in San Miguel, with *charro* horsemen joining the marching bands. One sad note: Pickpockets work overtime on holidays in San Miguel. On October 12, the *Day of the Race* (Columbus Day), the city celebrates the discovery of America; a civic ceremony is held at the Church of San Francisco, and a celebration is held in the evening at the bullring.

San Miguel is chock-full of charitable organizations, and it seems that some event is always being held to raise funds for a worthy cause. Attending one of them is a good way to get to know the town's many interesting and friendly residents.

SHOPPING: Probably the most unusual thing to be bought in San Miguel is artwork. Shops lining Zacateros and its continuation, Ancha de San Antonio, feature paintings, sculpture, ceramics, textiles, tin, or wrought-iron objects.

Antigua Casa Canela – Handicrafts, textiles, antiques, and art are displayed in this museum-like setting, which includes replicas of a model colonial home, chapel, neighborhood store, and cantina. 20 Calle Umarán (phone: 21880).

Artesanías Chela – Tastefully fashioned tin and brass sconces, mirrors, and other decorative pieces. 6 Calle Correo (no phone).

La Calaca – A sugar shop filled with fantastical sugar sculptures used for offerings for the *Day of the Dead.* 93 Calle Mesones (no phone).

La Calandria – Tasteful collection of authentic antiques as well as reproductions. 5 Calle San Francisco (phone: 22945).

Casa Beckman – A wide collection of silver and jewelry, ranging from silver-plated decanters to fine, heavy ladles, salt and pepper shakers, even *Christmas* ornaments. 105 Calle Hernández Macías (phone: 21613).

Casa Canal – Locally designed colonial furniture is the highlight here, as well as Josefa's clothing designs, which combine embroidery and appliqué. Worth a visit for the building alone. 3 Calle Canal (phone: 20479).

Casa Maxwell – This place houses a vast collection of local crafts; shipping is possible. A block from the plaza, at 14 Calle Canal and Calle Umarán (phone: 20247).

David – David Salazar's jewelry store; he does marvelous work in silver and will take orders for special pieces. 53 Calle Zacateros (no phone).

Galería Atenea – Once a lovely home, now an attractive gallery filled with select crafts and contemporary paintings, sculpture, and photographs. 15 Calle Cuna de Allende (phone: 21284).

Galería San Miguel – San Miguel's most popular gallery, it has a good selection of paintings, water colors, and prints. On the main plaza; they also have a branch on Calle Umarán (phone: 20454).

Galería Sergio Bustamante – The fantastical sculptures of Bustamante, a native of Guadalajara, who is well-known worldwide. Calle Mesones (phone: 22647).

Itzcuinapan – An unusual selection of Huichol and Otomí Indian crafts, including carvings and textiles. 20 Calle Hidalgo (phone: 20594).

Josh Klingerman Gallery – Housed in what was once the stable of the Allende home, this gallery has an interesting selection of contemporary art. The proprietor, Josh Klingerman, is an expert on Mexican art and gives free lectures Tuesday afternoons. 6 Calle Umarán (phone: 20951).

Llamas – No less than six stores in San Miguel are called *Llamas* — it's a big family — and they each claim a particular specialty, yet all seem to carry a similar assortment of tin and brass goods, including beautiful lamps, chandeliers, mirrors, and picture frames. The oldest store is at Zacateros and Pila Seca (don't miss the upstairs); also visit the branches across from Instituto Allende and at 11 Calle Zacateros (no phone).

La Luciérnaga – This is the place to pick up some extra film or photo equipment, get film developed, or buy an original photograph. They also carry a selection of textiles. Closed Monday and Thursday afternoons. 1 Calle Aldama (phone: 21311).

Ono – Imaginative and educational toys, hand-painted textiles, archaeological reproductions, and unusual crafts. 2 Calle Codo and 38 Calle Mesones (no phone).

El Pegaso – A lovely shop and a hangout for the local American colony, with original clothing, jewelry, crafts, and a few tables to sit and sip coffee. A good information center. Across from the post office, at 6 Calle Corregidora (phone: 21351).

Zarco – For a wide selection of hand-painted plates, tiles, and tin and brass items. 24 Calle Sollano (phone: 20323).

SPORTS: San Miguel is well-equipped for such a small town.

Bullfights – The film *The Brave Bulls* was made here at the bullring on Calle Recreo. There is, however, no set season. Corridas are scheduled occasionally.

Golf – *Club de Golf Malanquín* (phone: 20516) has a good 9-hole course, no carts (but lots of caddies), an Olympic-size pool, and tennis courts.

Horseback Riding – Horses are available in Taboada, about 5 miles (8 km) north of San Miguel. Captain Santiago Canales runs a riding school, *Club Valle de Alcocer* (phone: 20350), about 2 miles (3 km) from town on the road to Querétaro. The staff at *Viajes San Migues* (phone: 22832) also can make arrangements.

Swimming – Many of the hotels have pools, and at *Hacienda Taboada* (5 miles/8 km north of town on Rte. 52) there is a large public pool with a playground and picnic area as well as a private pool.

Tennis – Courts are available at *La Unidad Deportiva* (in front of the *Misión Los Angeles* hotel; no phone). The *Rancho el Atascadero* (phone: 20206) and *Quinta Loreto* (phone: 20042) hotels also have tennis courts, and there are 3 courts at the *Club de Golf Malanquín* (phone: 20516).

NIGHTCLUBS AND NIGHTLIFE: San Miguel de Allende is rife with nightclubs, cantinas, and cocktail lounges with strong drink, good talk, and live music until the early hours of the morning. Official closing time is 1 AM, but this rule is often relaxed to accommodate the clientele. The following is a list of what can most legitimately be called nightclubs, though most of them serve dinner starting at 9 PM. The *Ring* (on Calle Hidalgo, a block off Plaza Allende; phone: 21998) is a popular discotheque with loud music. *Laberintos* disco (no phone) for the younger set, is also loud and has a cover charge; it's beside *Posada de la Aldea* and across from Instituto Allende. *Disque Disco* draws big crowds at the *Hacienda Taboada* (phone: 20850). Another lively place is *Mina de Rayas* (10 Calle Tinajitas; no phone). *La Fragua* (3 Calle Cuna de Allende; no phone) has a lovely patio and true Mexican flavor and occasionally features a variety show. *Mama Mia* (8 Calle Umarán; no phone) has live music, from Andean folk to jazz, in its patio nightly except Tuesdays; *La Princesa* (5 Calle Recreo; phone: 21403) is a favorite early evening spot for a drink and to listen to music. Aficionados of honky-tonk bars should not miss the *Cucaracha* (22 Zacateros; phone: 20196) with its jukebox and famous calendar shot of Marilyn Monroe. *Pancho and Lefty's* bar and dance hall (99 Calle Mesones; no phone) has live country music.

BEST IN TOWN

CHECKING IN: Considering San Miguel de Allende's modest size, there is a surprising number of good hotels, motels, and guesthouses from which to choose. The going rate for a double room with bath in a hotel we classify as very expensive ranges from $80 up to $130; expensive is $60 to $75; $30 to $45 in a moderate hotel; under $25, inexpensive. Some, however, include one to three meals a day. Most hotels accept MasterCard and Visa; a few also accept American Express and Diners Club. All telephone numbers are in the 465 area code unless otherwise indicated. When calling from one city to another within Mexico, dial 91 before the area code.

Casa de Sierra Nevada – Though very small, with only 18 suites, this is a lovely hostelry — actually 3 houses — centrally located and connected to a fine restaurant. In 1982 it became the first Latin American hotel to be admitted to the famous Relais & Châteaux hotel association. Suite 2 is decorated in peach, with a travertine marble bathroom and a large terrace overlooking the cathedral. Suite 7, with gray and yellow furnishings, is intimate and romantic. For senior guests, there is a ground-floor suite with a large carved fireplace. For extra privacy, an old mansion behind the owner's home has been remodeled as a VIP section, and includes 3 apartments with kitchenettes and a large pool. Four smaller, less expensive rooms are also available. Only American Express accepted. 35 Calle Hospicio (phone: 20415; 312-696-1323 in the US; FAX: 22337). Very expensive.

Hacienda Taboada – Family-oriented, this resort complex has 64 pleasant rooms, a large pool, a restaurant, poolside bar, tennis, and horseback riding. A nice touch is that the bathtub taps offer hot and cold thermal water for soothing soaks. Rate includes three meals. Six miles (10 km) north of town on Rte. 51, with free bus service into San Miguel (phone: 20850). Very expensive.

Villa Santa Mónica – San Miguel's prettiest hotel, this 18th-century mansion has only 8 rooms, no two alike, a restaurant that serves Mexican and international dishes, well-kept grounds, a massage room and sauna, and a small oval pool lined with floral tiles. Complimentary cocktails are served to guests with dinner reservations in the restaurant. All the suites have fireplaces and private patios. Breakfast is included. Across from Juárez Park, 22 Calle Baeza (phone: 20427 or 20451). Very expensive.

Aristos Parador San Miguel – Next to the Instituto Allende, this pleasant place has 56 rooms, a pool, and lovely garden setting. There's also a cocktail lounge and popular restaurant (see *Eating Out*). 2 Calle Cardo (phone: 20149 or 20392). Expensive.

Hacienda de las Flores – Another of San Miguel's lovely small hotels. There are 5 doubles and 6 junior suites, a fine restaurant with a panoramic view of the valley, TV sets, heat, electric blankets, interphones, purified water, a boutique, and a poolside bar where free films are shown. It is elegant without being imposing. The price includes two à la carte meals. No pets or credit cards. 16 Calle Hospicio (phone: 21808 or 21859). Expensive.

Mansión del Bosque – It's a meandering home away from home, a guesthouse with 24 rooms to let, and the rate includes breakfast and a family-style dinner of "international home cooking," from chop suey to borscht. There's a 1-month minimum in winter; summer sees a younger clientele. Non-guests must make dinner reservations. Modified American Plan from December 15 to April 15. 65 Calle Aldama (phone: 20277). Expensive.

Parador del Cortijo – This delightful spa, with just 19 rooms, has thermal waters, 2 pools, and a good restaurant. American Plan. Km 9 Carr. San Miguel–Dolores Hidalgo (phone: 21700). Expensive.

Rancho el Atascadero – This converted hacienda offers rooms with fireplaces, one of the few tennis courts in town, a sauna, a swimming pool, jai alai, a dining room with a good Sunday brunch, and extensive grounds that make you feel you're in the country. Hotel shuttlebus. A mile (1.6 km) east of town on the Querétaro Hwy. (phone: 20206 or 20337; FAX: 21541). Expensive.

Villa Jacaranda – An elegant mansion that offers intimate and quiet cordiality, fine food, 4 double rooms and 12 suites, a Jacuzzi, and parking. Videotapes of movies in English are shown. 53 Calle Aldama (phone: 21015). Expensive.

Real de Minas – It has 65 rooms with telephones, air conditioning, and satellite TV. There's also a large pool, lovely gardens, a restaurant, and disco/bar with live music on weekends. It is a 5-minute drive from downtown on Calle Ancha de San Antonio (phone: 21727). Expensive to moderate.

Casa de Lu Jo Inn – Perhaps Mexico's only authentic bed and breakfast establishment, it offers 7 luxurious rooms, each with its own patio and fireplace or heating. (*La Casita* is a wonderful choice.) Daily, weekly, monthly, even yearly rates are available. Breakfast, laundry service, afternoon tea, and short-term country club privileges are included. The owner is an art dealer and the place is crawling with original works, all for sale. 35 Calle Pila Seca (phone: 21564). Moderate.

Misión de los Angeles – Overlooking Allende Dam, it has 60 rooms with vaulted ceilings (some with king-size beds), a bar with a fireplace, a pretty restaurant, pool, and various sports facilities. A little over a mile (2 km) from town on Celaya Rd. (phone: 21026, 22047, or 22099; FAX: 22155). Moderate.

Posada de la Aldea – The rooms are a little worn, but the bathrooms all have tubs and interesting *azulejo* tilework; there's also a pool, a bar, and a small restaurant with a lovely view of the town at sunset. What looks like an old chapel is mere façade. Just across from the Instituto Allende, on Calle Ancha de San Antonio (phone: 21296). Moderate.

Posada Carmina – Best known locally for its restaurant (see *Eating Out*), this 10-room hotel often becomes a special stopping place for travelers, primarily because of Señora Carmina García, the consummate hostess, ever present and ever hospitable. Off the plaza, at 7 Calle Cuna de Allende (phone: 20458). Inexpensive.

Posada de las Monjas – A short hike from the plaza, this 65-room hotel has grown a little shabby yet remains pleasant, and rates are reasonable. The older rooms are somewhat smaller and less expensive than the newer ones. There's a large restaurant. 37 Calle Canal (phone: 20171). Inexpensive.

Posada de San Francisco – The 50 simple, functional rooms range from tiny and monastic to large and airy. Three have fireplaces, and all are furnished in spare colonial style. There are patios, a bar, and a small restaurant. No credit cards accepted. 2 Plaza Principal (phone: 21466). Inexpensive.

Quinta Loreto – Surrounded by gardens, it has 30 rooms in the older section, 8 rooms in a new wing, and a few apartments that are almost always rented. There's also a pool, a tennis court, and a good restaurant. One of San Miguel's bargains. 15 Loreto (phone: 20042). Inexpensive.

La Siesta – Each of its 28 motel rooms has a fireplace, and there's a palm tree–encircled pool, tennis court, and colorful restaurant-bar. Breakfast is included. About one-half mile (1 km) from downtown on the Celaya Rd. (phone: 20207). Inexpensive.

 EATING OUT: Many of San Miguel's finest restaurants are in hotels, and the cost of dinner doesn't vary much from place to place. Few are expensive when compared to eating places in Mexico's larger cities. Dinner for two will cost up to $45 in a restaurant listed as expensive, between $25 and $30 in moderate, and under $20 in inexpensive. Prices don't include wine, tips, or drinks. Most restaurants accept MasterCard and Visa; a few also accept American Express and Diners Club. Unless otherwise noted, all restaurants are open daily. All telephone numbers are in the 465 area code unless otherwise indicated. When calling from one city to another within Mexico, dial 91 before the area code.

La Casona – The service is gracious at this former home with a charming patio. From the kitchen come such continental favorites as cream of broccoli soup, shrimp Marseilles, veal scaloppine, cannelloni Rossini, and banana flambé. Reservations advised. 80 Calle Mesones (phone: 21062). Expensive.

Sierra Nevada – An excellent small restaurant that's connected to an equally excellent small hotel, its food is among the best in San Miguel. The menu includes homemade pasta and pastries, *escargots à la Provençal,* brochette of beef filet, beef tips in curry with chutney, and vanilla ice cream with homemade hot chocolate sauce. Coat and tie recommended. Reservations necessary for dinner. 35 Calle Hospicio (phone: 20415). Expensive.

Villa Jacaranda – Housed in a mansion with charming gardens and patios, this pretty place offers delightful ambience as well as a carefully prepared international menu. Champagne brunch is served on Sundays. Good wine list. Reservations advised. 53 Calle Aldama (phone: 21015). Expensive.

Hacienda de las Flores – Fine continental and local dishes, exquisitely served — and there's no extra charge for the magnificent view. Reservations advised. 16 Calle Hospicio (phone: 21808 or 21859). Expensive to moderate.

Hacienda Taboada – Try the buffet on Saturdays and Sundays; while there, you can also arrange for guest privileges at the pool. Reservations advised. Six miles (10 km) north on Rte. 51 (phone: 20850 or 20888). Expensive to moderate.

Aristos Parador San Miguel – The dining room of the hotel on the grounds of the Instituto Allende offers good, hearty fare. Reservations advised. 2 Calle Cardo (phone: 20149). Moderate.

La Bodega de Márquez – Set in an old 18th-century wine cellar with stone walls and dim lighting, it serves Chinese, Italian, Mexican, and American food. Closed Wednesdays. Reservations advised. No credit cards accepted. 34 Calle Correo (phone: 21481). Moderate.

Bruno – The owner Bruno, a Canadian of Italian parentage, supervises the preparation of the homemade pasta and bread, hot stuffed avocados, New Orleans trout, and tempting desserts. The food is good, the atmosphere fun. Open for lunch and dinner; closed Tuesdays. Reservations advised. 95 Calle Ancha de San Antonio (phone: 20629). Moderate.

Bugambilia – Mexican haute cuisine served in a lovely, 2-centuries-old home.

Among the specialties are *chicharrón guanajuatense* (fried pork rind, Guanajuato-style), cold avocado soup, and *chiles en nogada* (stuffed peppers in a nut-based cream sauce). Reservations advised. 42 Calle Hidalgo (phone: 20127). Moderate.

La Fragua – It feels like a country inn, with several dining rooms and terrace seating around an inner courtyard. The menu ranges from such dishes as chicken Parmesan and grilled beef to tortilla soup. The piano bar is in full swing from 6 to 8 PM; then a trio plays until closing time. Reservations advised. Off the plaza, at 3 Calle Cuna de Allende (phone: 21144). Moderate.

Pepe's Patio – A picture-book adobe patio with an international menu that includes "the best traditions of several countries" (including Mexico). Delicious cream soups, homemade bread, and shredded beef are among the specialties. Reservations advised. Enter through *Pancho and Lefty's*, 99 Calle Mesones (phone: 21958). Moderate.

La Dolce Vita – Pizza, pastries, coffee, and hand-cranked Italian ice cream. No reservations. 118 Plaza Colonial (no phone). Inexpensive.

Mama Mia – There are some cozy tables at this lively and popular beer hall, where a fine meal would be the cheesy pizza pie accompanied by the light or dark beer on tap. There's good music, too. Reservations unnecessary. 8 Calle Umarán, just off Plaza Allende (phone: 22063). Inexpensive.

Posada Carmina – Among residents of San Miguel, this is a favorite place for a quiet lunch under orange trees in a courtyard. They're also open for breakfast and dinner. Try the paella Valenciana, the Spanish-style tortilla, or the cheese and vegetable salad. Reservations advised. On 7 Calle Cuna de Allende (phone: 20458). Inexpensive.

Quinta Loreto – The large portions served at reasonable prices are perhaps the best bargain in town; stuffed pork chops are a tasty choice. Reservations unnecessary. 15 Calle Loreto (phone: 20042). Inexpensive.

La Terraza – In the old *Mercado Aldama*, dating from 1901, and on the plaza beside the tourist office, this watering hole is a pleasant place for a rest from sightseeing; however, the coffee's awful. No reservations. Plaza Allende (no phone). Inexpensive.

TAXCO

(pronounced *Tahs*-coe)

Nestled high in the folds of the Sierra Madre, 50 miles (80 km) south of Cuernavaca on the road from Mexico City to Acapulco, sits a treasure town full of silver. Aladdin with his magic lantern couldn't conjure up a more charming place: a village of silversmiths perched on a mountain. Halfway between Acapulco and Mexico City, Taxco is a natural overnight stop for drivers, and if you pamper yourself you'll plan to spend two nights.

Taxco slumbered away until 1930, untouched by modernization because of the lack of decent roads or highways. Even today, civilization's inroads have not seriously altered the classic, almost fairy-tale quality of this town of 200,000 people. Cobblestone streets still weave around the hills, over their tops, and along their gently curved sides. There is no such thing as a paved street in Taxco. White and pink stucco houses, with balconies filled with flowering plants, line the narrow thoroughfares. It is an artist's paradise, and if the Mexican government has its way, the town will remain that way: Taxco is one of several Mexican towns that have been declared national monuments.

Residents of the surrounding mountains live in whitewashed adobe houses capped with red tile roofs, the houses clinging to the sides of cobbled streets that twist their way to the main plaza, the zocalo. The 20th century is tolerated in Taxco, but not encouraged.

It seems that the ground floor of every other building in town contains a silver shop; there are more than 250 in all. There are textile and clothing stores and tin and curio shops, too, but in Taxco silver is king.

An American actually brought silversmithing to Taxco. William Spratling first came here around 1930, a tourist before there were tourists in Mexico, just after a new highway had opened up the long-isolated mining town. Don Guillermo, as he was known, found that the supposedly played-out mines were still producing enough to allow people to smelt silver in backyard furnaces; they were selling it by the pound to whomever they could. At the time, Spratling taught at Tulane University in New Orleans, but he decided to give up the academic life in favor of creating his own line of silverware in Taxco. He opened his shop on June 27, 1932.

The business prospered. Spratling took in local youths and taught them the trade. His designs integrated ancient Indian motifs into jewelry that was snapped up by buyers from Texas to New York. Many of his apprentices went on to open silver shops of their own, some good, others not so good.

All of these silver shops, combined with the charm of the town itself, helped make Taxco one of Mexico's first major travel destinations, and so it remains today. Many travelers come back year after year to spend their entire vacations in Taxco. In fact, the town has a small community of retired Americans — the ultimate test of a compatible climate and atmosphere.

There are those who grumble that Taxco has become too touristy, and truth to tell, there was a time in Taxco's recent past when it often appeared there were more foreigners than natives around the zocalo. Since the new toll road opened in 1989, though, you're likely to find just as many Mexican tourists as foreigners. The road connects Taxco with the Acapulco Highway and eliminates most of the treacherous curves that once had to be navigated en route from Cuernavaca. The toll road cuts driving time from Mexico City from 4 hours to about 2½ hours, making Taxco a convenient weekend retreat for Mexican families seeking an alternative to Cuernavaca. It is the rare visitor who regrets having made the trip. Taxco is Old Mexico as everyone expects it to be.

Before the area was discovered by the Spaniards in the early 1500s, its name was Tlachco, which means "place where the ball is played" in Nahuatl, an Indian language. Taxco is the Spanish adaptation of that name. Although remote, Taxco played a significant role in Mexico's history. Montezuma I conquered the region in 1455. Cortés, the Spanish conquerer, who took control of the country in 1521, had an intuitive sense about silver and gold — he seemed to have an invisible dowsing rod that enabled him to detect these metals even from a distance. Shortly after his conquest of Mexico City in 1521, Cortés sent two of his captains to Tlachco/Taxco to investigate its mineral resources. They struck silver, and in 1529 the Spanish moved into the area. The boom proved short-lived, however, and by 1581 only 47 miners were required to work Taxco's mines. When no new veins were discovered after the first mine opened in 1529, the city got a reputation as a played-out source. Its essentially Spanish nature, however, was confirmed; it remained firmly royalist — loyal to Spanish royalty — in the later wars of independence.

But early in the 18th century a wandering Frenchman, Joseph de la Borde (later changed to the more Mexican José de la Borda), undeterred by Taxco's reputation, struck a very rich vein of silver and started Taxco's Golden Age. A religious man (he had a daughter who became a nun and a son who became a priest), de la Borda built one of Mexico's most beautiful churches in Taxco, the Santa Prisca, in gratitude to God for his good fortune. He explained his generosity quite simply: "God gives to Borda, Borda gives to God." Apparently, he wasn't far wrong, because after his death in 1778 the silver boom died. Taxco was no longer of much interest to anyone. Politically, it certainly was inactive. The residents preferred quiet and relative solitude to the excitement that neighboring Cuernavaca generated. Taxco sided with the pro-Spanish royalists in the 1810 War of Independence and managed to repel an attack by revolutionaries in 1811. Soon after, however, the town was vanquished.

Even today, the town holds pretty much to its old ways. During *Holy Week,* at *Easter* time, parades are held daily. On *Good Friday,* Taxco residents reenact Christ's carrying of the cross. A man wears a crown of thorns, and penitents drag chains and go through rituals of mortification of the flesh. But apart from that touch of solemnity, Taxco residents like festivities. Almost every night, somebody shoots off fireworks to celebrate a wedding, a birth, a birthday, or a saint's day. It is a joyous place to visit.

TAXCO AT-A-GLANCE

SEEING THE CITY: A spectacular view of Taxco can be enjoyed while riding the aerial tramway to and from the *Fiesta Montetaxco* hotel — an experience no visitor should miss. The tram may be boarded near the main highway, Route 95 (called Av. J. F. Kennedy in town), by the arches near the northern entrance to town; the round-trip fare is about $3.50. The views from the hotel itself are breathtaking, as are those seen from the *Hotel de la Borda* (on Av. J. F. Kennedy), overlooking the town; *Rancho Taxco* (14 Soto la Marina); the restaurant *La Ventana de Taxco* in the *Hacienda del Solar* hotel (Km 89.5 on Rte. 95 south of town;) and the *Pagaduría del Rey* restaurant (Cerro de Bermeja). The Carretera Panorámica, or Panoramic Highway, delivers what its name promises; take the *combi* (little bus) from Santisima church.

SPECIAL PLACES: Most of Taxco's places of interest are within walking distance of each other. But in the process of getting from one to another, you'll come across lush patios filled with geraniums, cerise and orange bougainvillea, intricately carved doors, ornate ironwork, and cages of exotic singing birds. Nearly every street in Taxco is special.

Santa Prisca Church – The most important landmark in Taxco was built between 1751 and 1758 by Frenchman José de la Borda as an expression of thanks to God. The twin, 130-foot baroque towers and richly carved stone façade are impressive in their own right, but the blue tile dome and pink exterior walls of the church also account for this place's popularity with visiting photographers, both professional and amateur. Inside, there are 12 altars, gold altarpieces, and original paintings by artist Miguel Cabrera from the colonial era in the sacristy. On the zocalo.

Museo Guillermo Spratling (William Spratling Museum) – The American who gave so much to Taxco was a great collector of pre-Columbian artifacts, many of which are on display here. Downstairs is devoted to the life of New York–born Spratling and to silver mining. There are also fine exhibits on local history, photos of *Semana Santa* (Holy Week) festivities, and samples of silver ore. The 3-story museum was originally funded by Spratling himself before his death in 1967. Open Tuesdays through Saturdays. Admission charge. Behind Santa Prisca (no phone).

Casa Borda – This home was built by José de la Borda in 1759. Its front section is 2 stories high, but the back rises 5 stories. This is due to the slope of the land rather than eccentric architecture. Originally, José de la Borda lived in only half the house, and the other half was donated to the priests of the local church. Today it is the city hall and also houses a silver shop. Open daily. No admission charge. On the zocalo (no phone).

Casa Figueroa – Count Cadena, a friend of José de la Borda, built this house in 1767. It's also called the House of Tears, because the count, a local magistrate, made the Indians who could not pay their fines do the work on it. It became Casa Figueroa because Fidel Figueroa, a modern Mexican artist, restored the house in 1943 and used it as a studio and art gallery, which now exhibits his works. At press time the house was closed indefinitely for renovations; check first with your hotel desk or the tourist office (phone: 22279). If the house is open, take the tour to see the secret stashes, tunnels, and even a room where women hid during the 1910 revolution. On the western end of the zocalo (no phone).

Casa de las Artesanías Guerrerenses (Guerrero House of Crafts) – Known as Casa Humboldt, this house is notable for the fine details on the doors and windows, as well as its façade of bas-relief plaster. The overall style is Moorish. Originally built by Juan de Villanueva in the 18th century, it was renamed in honor of explorer and scientist Baron Alexander von Humboldt, who was a guest on the night of April 5, 1803, during the period of his extensive explorations in South America. Most of the house, unfortunately, is in need of renovation, save for its government-run store filled with interesting furniture, handicrafts, and dresses from the state of Guerrero. Open daily. No admission charge. 6 Calle Juan Ruiz Alarcón (no phone).

Convent of San Bernardino de Sena – Originally a Franciscan monastery founded in 1592, this building was destroyed by fire in 1805 but restored in 1823. It is considered a historic site because the Plan of Iguala was drawn up by Agustín de Iturbide here in 1821. Open daily. Plaza del Convento.

Instituto de Artes Plasticas (Modern Arts Institute) – These buildings are a fine example of modern architecture well integrated into a very natural setting. It's possible to visit the workshops here. No admission charge. Adjacent to the tram to the *Fiesta Montetaxco* hotel, on the grounds of the former *Hacienda del Chorrillo* (no phone).

Convention Center – Taxco's beautiful convention facility was built on the site of a 450-year-old hacienda near the stone aqueduct on the northern entrance to the city. The center has a large outdoor amphitheater and an auditorium (phone: 22279).

■**EXTRA SPECIAL:** The Caves of Cacahuamilpa (*Grutas,* or grottoes, is what everybody calls them since no one can pronounce Cacahuamilpa) are less than an hour's drive from Taxco. The astounding formations in this vast network of caves are aptly named: Sleeping Lady, The Hunchback, The Asparagus, The Snail, The Dawn, and The Champagne Bottle. They are well lit and have engineered walkways. Concerts occasionally are held in the caves — a real treat. Daily tours are given from 10 AM to 5 PM (phone: 21525).

SOURCES AND RESOURCES

TOURIST INFORMATION: Both the federal (phone: 21525) and state (phone: 22279) government tourist offices are helpful; both are in the *Convention Center,* across the street from the *Ex-Hacienda del Chorrillo.* There are information booths at both entrances to town. Young boys wearing white shirts and brown ties at Plaza Borda lead tours under the auspices of the tourist office and expect only a tip in return.

Casa Dominguez (3 Calle del Arco) sells American magazines as well as Mexico City's English-language newspaper, the *News.*

TELEPHONE: The area code for Taxco is 762. When calling from one city to another within Mexico, dial 91 before the area code.

CLIMATE AND CLOTHES: Taxco's temperature hovers near the 60s and 70s virtually year-round. The rainy season lasts roughly from June to October, but showers generally fall briefly only in the afternoon. Visitors to the town dress casually.

GETTING AROUND: Bus – Tiny, crowded *burritas,* as the small white buses are called, wend their way through the hilly streets along Avenida J. F. Kennedy from the zocalo to Route 95. You can pick one up anywhere along the route. *Burritas* run from early in the morning until about 9 PM.

Taxi – Cabs — dapper white Volkswagen Beetles with the front passenger seat removed — are readily available around town, and are reasonably priced.

Car Rental – There are no rental cars in Taxco; however, you can hire guides. Ask at your hotel or at the state tourism office.

 SPECIAL EVENTS: Nowhere in the world is there anything quite like Taxco's *Holy Week.* It begins on *Palm Sunday* with a procession. Daily parades follow, but by *Holy Thursday* it becomes a show that involves the whole town from noon until after midnight. The forecourt of the Santa Prisca church is transformed into the Garden of Gethsemane with guardian angels, Roman soldiers, and centurions. Then there is an enactment of the Washing of the Feet, the Last Supper, the betrayal of Jesus by Judas, and Jesus' imprisonment in Nicholas Temple. At 11 PM Pontius Pilate reads the sentence and washes his hands. While all this is going on, candlelit processions enter the town from surrounding villages. The crowds, many of them masked, black-gowned penitents bare to the waist, swell to 2,000 or 3,000. Some of the processioners carry heavy wooden crosses, others have their arms and backs laced with spikey branches of thorn, and you may see some carrying studded metal thongs with which they flagellate themselves. It is an incredible sight. On *Good Friday,* the Road to Calvary is reenacted. Christ, bearing his cross, passes through the zocalo around noon. The Crucifixion takes place at the Convent of San Bernardino (see *Special Places*). Christ is tied to the cross and taken down at 4 PM. The day ends at midnight with a Procession of Silence in which hooded men dressed in black flowing robes parade in total silence. Nothing is heard but the weird sound of shuffling feet. On Saturday morning, church bells ring out after 2 days of silence to mark the Ceremony of the Resurrection. On Sunday, there is a final procession at 5 PM. You must make hotel reservations for *Easter* months in advance.

The city's other major annual event is the *National Silver Fair,* which takes place the last week in November. All the silversmiths submit their best work for highly prized awards. A cultural festival held in mid-May, *Jornadas Alarconas,* honors one of Mexico's greatest dramatists, Juan Ruiz Alarcón; he lived in Taxco and wrote many of his important works here. Other holidays with parades and fireworks include: January 18, the *Fiesta of Santa Prisca;* February 2, *Fiesta de la Candelaria;* February 5, *Fiesta of the Patron Saint of the Silversmiths, Felipe de Jesús;* March 4, *Fiesta de Vera Cruz;* May 3, *Fiesta de la Santa Cruz;* September 24, *Fiesta de la Virgen de las Mercedes;* and, of course, *Corpus Christi Day* and pre-*Lent Carnaval Week.* On the Monday following the *Day of the Dead* (November 2), the whole town takes off for a picnic held in Huixteco (northwest of Taxco), where everyone eats *jumiles* (small insects very much like cockroaches, said to be delicious). It has become known as *Fiesta de los Jumiles.*

 SHOPPING: Silver is *the* thing in Taxco. Anything from a small, inexpensive ring to a complete silver service or tea set is available. There are silver shops all over town, but the heaviest concentration is around the main plaza and near the north entrance to town on Avenida J. F. Kennedy, near the *Posada de la Misión.* Taxco also mines amethyst, tourmaline, nephrite, garnet, topaz, and various kinds of agates and opals. At the public market, just off the zocalo, shawls, huaraches, straw products, leather goods, pottery, wood carvings, bark paintings, and seed, bean, and nutshell jewelry are sold. Silver is also available in the market, but it is advisable to buy it in reputable shops.

Andrés Mejía – A silver shop run by the eponymous Andrés, a very personable gentleman who is producing some of the most innovative and impressive work in town. 28 Av. J.F. Kennedy (phone: 23778).

Antonio Pineda – For beautiful pieces in enameled silver. 1 Plaza Borda (phone: 20658).

Casa Humboldt – A government-run store that carries handicrafts, including lacquerware from the town of Olinalá, and Tissot ceramics from all over the state of Guerrero. Open daily. 6 Calle Juan Ruiz Alarcón (no phone).

Los Castillo – The silversmiths who are renowned for their "wedding" of silver, copper, and bronze are now doing extraordinary work in ceramics and silver inlays. Ask to visit their workshop. 10 Plazuela Bernal (phone: 22935).

Elena de Ballesteros – A large, beautifully displayed selection of silver and gold jewelry. On the zocalo at 4 Calle Celso Muñoz (phone: 23767).

Gracias a Dios – Stunning Tachi Castillo jackets with appliqués of brightly colored ribbons. Also, a selection of regional crafts. 3 Bernal (phone: 20086).

Huarachería Los Angeles – Carries a wide variety of sandals and other comfortable shoes. Near the *Platería Rancho Alegre,* on Av. J. F. Kennedy (no phone).

Spratling – William Spratling's traditional designs made in silver from traditional molds. Km 17 Hwy. to Iguala (phone: 21878).

Virgilio – Exclusive designs in gold and precious stones. On Miguel Hidalgo in front of the San Nicolas church (no phone).

SPORTS: Taxco proper has no *Plaza de Toros* for bullfighting, although bullfights are often held at a small bullring about 3 miles (5 km) from the city (ask at the tourist office for specific details). There is no jai alai, and no soccer stadium, but there are facilities for some participant sports.

Golf – The *Fiesta Montetaxco* hotel (Rte. 95; phone: 21300), has a 9-hole golf course open to the public.

Horseback Riding – Mounts are available at the *Fiesta Montetaxco* (phone: 21300) and through the *Hacienda del Solar* (phone: 20322).

Swimming – The *Fiesta Montetaxco, Posada de la Misión, Hacienda del Solar, Posada las Palmas,* and *Loma Linda* hotels have swimming pools.

Tennis – The *Fiesta Montetaxco, Posada de la Misión,* and *Hacienda del Solar,* at Km 89.5 on Rte. 95 south of town, have tennis courts.

NIGHTCLUBS AND NIGHTLIFE: Discotheques have sprung up all over Taxco, among them *La Lechuza* (phone: 22565), the local favorite, and *El Jardín* (no phone; both on the zocalo); *Bougambilias* (below *Los Arcos* hotel at 7 Juan Ruiz Alarcón; phone: 21836); *El Corsario* (73 Benito Juárez; phone: 20201), with its 1,500 lights ; *Mazerata* (Av. J.F.Kennedy, just beyond the *Convention Center;* phone: 21516); *La Plazuela* (34 Av. J. F. Kennedy, near *Elena Ballesteros* jewelers; phone: 23976); and *Windows* disco-bar at the *Fiesta Montetaxco* (Rte. 95), which is the liveliest place in town. Mexican musicians often entertain at *Paco's Bar* and *Berta's. Paco's* is bigger and livelier, but *Berta's* is a landmark — it's named for the owner, whose fortune was made when she invented the drink of tequila, soda, lime, and honey that bears her name. *Berta's* place is on the zocalo, next to Santa Prisca church, and *Paco's* overlooks the lively street scene on the opposite side of the zocalo. For something a little out of the ordinary, buy a $15 ticket for Tony Reyes's show at the *Fiesta Montetaxco* (Rte. 95). Transportation, two drinks, a performance of the *Voladores de Papantla* (Flying Indians from Papantla), music, and dancing are included in the price. On Saturday nights, the *Fiesta Montetaxco* hotel hosts a Mexican

Fiesta with a show and lavish buffet of regional dishes, followed by an impressive fireworks display.

BEST IN TOWN

 CHECKING IN: Taxco is one of the major destinations on the Mexican tourist trail, so it's a good idea to make reservations well in advance, especially if you intend to visit during festival time. Expect to pay up to $70 for a double room in a hotel listed as expensive; $40 in moderate; and $25 or less in an inexpensive place. Most hotels accept MasterCard and Visa; a few also accept American Express and Diners Club. All telephone numbers are in the 762 area code unless otherwise indicated. When calling from one city to another within Mexico, dial 91 before the area code.

Fiesta Montetaxco – Set on a steep mountainside overlooking Taxco, with a welcome sign that reads *"Está Ud. en el cielo. Disfrútelo"* ("You're in heaven. Enjoy it"). There are 156 rooms and suites, each with a color TV set and air conditioning, and 32 villas (for four to six people) with kitchenettes. Its facilities and services include a cable car, a heated swimming pool, Swedish massage, steambaths, tennis, golf, horseback riding, a disco, and 2 restaurants (see *Eating Out*). On Saturdays and Sundays there are barbecues and fireworks. North of town, off Rte. 95 to the right on a fearsomely steep road; it's possible to take the cable car up from Rte. 95 (phone: 21300; FAX: 21428). Very expensive.

Hacienda del Solar – This resort complex sprawls across some 80 acres of property, but still feels like a country inn. Its 22 elegant bungalows are named after female friends and relatives of the owner; "Isabel" is especially appealing for its tiled bathroom with a garden and skylight. There is a pool and a tennis court. Breakfast is served on the terrace; try the excellent *Ventana de Taxco* Italian restaurant for dinner (see *Eating Out*). A Modified American Plan is also available. Two miles (3 km) out of town on Rte. 95 (phone: 20323). Expensive.

Posada de la Misión – Decorated in colonial style, this 150-room inn offers comfortable lodgings, TV sets, heated swimming pool, Jacuzzi, shops, an inviting poolside restaurant and bar, and a tennis court. The Juan O'Gorman mural alongside the pool is an attraction on its own. Electronic chimes housed in two lovely towers on the property toll the quarter hour and play "Taxco de Mis Amores" at midnight. Rooms and bathrooms are on the small side, except for numbers 39 and 27 and the newer section of 60 suites, which are exceptionally lovely but are more expensive. Price includes breakfast. 32 Cerro de la Misión, off Av. J. F. Kennedy, at the Mexico City entrance to the city (phone: 20063; FAX: 22198). Expensive.

Agua Escondida – It may lack the charm of many of the older establishments, but it's right on the zocalo and rates high with young people. It has a pool and Ping-Pong table, restaurant, and parking. The rooms in back are farther removed from the discos on the zocalo. Plaza Borda (phone: 20726). Moderate.

Santa Prisca – A favorite with repeat visitors, this old-fashioned downtown inn with two green courtyards and fountains has much charm and dignity. It has 40 comfortably furnished rooms, a bar, parking, and a lovely little restaurant, whose menu changes daily and includes homemade soups and other hearty fare for a low fixed price. Price includes breakfast. 1 Cena Obscuras (phone: 20080; FAX: 21106). Moderate.

Los Arcos – A small gem, it was a convent back in 1620; it has 25 rooms and 3 two-level suites perfect for 4 people, a nice restaurant, congenial bar, and on weekends the *Bougambilias* nightclub. Just a block from the zocalo at 12 Juan Ruiz Alarcón (phone: 21836). Inexpensive.

Loma Linda – A cheerful, small place offering modest accommodations, it has 65 rooms, restaurant, bar, pool, and parking (no large cars). 52 Av. J. F. Kennedy (phone: 20206; FAX: 25125). Inexpensive.

Posada de los Castillo – This small inn with only 15 rooms in the center of town is run by the famous silversmithing family. 3 Juan Ruiz Alarcón (phone: 21396). Inexpensive.

Posada las Palmas – Only 14 rooms and 10 bungalows, as well as a nice garden, pool, and parking. No credit cards accepted. Down the street from the post office at 1 Estacas (phone: 23177). Inexpensive.

EATING OUT: All the good hotels have restaurants of their own that serve adequate, if not outstanding, food. Expect to pay up to $50 for a meal for two at a spot listed in the expensive category; about $30 in moderate; and under $15 in inexpensive. Wine, tax, and tips are extra. All restaurants accept MasterCard and Visa; a few also accept American Express and Diners Club. Unless otherwise noted, all restaurants are open daily. All telephone numbers are in the 762 area code unless otherwise indicated. When calling from one city to another within Mexico, dial 91 before the area code.

La Pagaduría del Rey – Steaks, seafood, and Mexican fare are served in a colonial setting; the views are extraordinary. The menu is limited but varied. Reservations advised on weekends. Cerro de Bermeja (phone: 23467). Expensive.

Toni's – Excellent prime ribs and lobster, along with a sensational view, make this a popular spot. Reservations advised on weekends. At the *Fiesta Montetaxco* (phone: 21300). Expensive.

La Ventana de Taxco – There's a dramatic view of the city at night (the name means "window on Taxco") at this fine Italian eatery, which features guitar music nightly except Mondays during the high season. Reservations advised on weekends. *Hacienda del Solar*, Rte. 95, south of town (phone: 20587). Expensive.

Los Arcos – Pleasant surroundings, reasonable prices, and good Mexican and international dishes have made this restaurant very popular. Reservations unnecessary. *Los Arcos Hotel* (phone: 21836). Moderate.

Carrusel – A very popular place, it has pleasant service, good steaks, and generous portions. Reservations unnecessary. 8 Calle Cuauhtémoc (phone: 21655). Moderate.

Cielito Lindo – Considerable Mexican charm accompanies carefully prepared Mexican dishes and such American favorites as breaded veal cutlet or fried chicken, followed by lemon meringue pie. Reservations unnecessary. On the zocalo at 14 Plaza Borda (phone: 20603). Moderate.

D'Luis – Up the hill from the Santa Prisca church, this eatery offers a wonderful view of all the comings and goings in the main square. Try the *queso cilantro,* cheese that is breaded, fried, and covered with fried potato skins and a green sauce, then topped with cilantro and sesame seeds. Another favorite is the *filete guerrillero,* beef, onions, green chili, epazote (wormseed), ham, and cheese, all baked in foil. Reservations advised. 2 Palma (phone: 23392). Moderate.

La Hacienda – This 2-level eatery serves breakfast, lunch, and dinner. The Mexican platter reigns supreme here, enhanced by chilled mugs of beer. For dessert try crêpes filled with homemade jam. Reservations unnecessary. 4 Calle Guillermo Spratling and Plaza Borda (phone: 20663). Moderate.

Piccolo Mondo – Another pleasant spot at the *Fiesta Montetaxco,* this one specializes in *parrilladas* (a variety of meats grilled on a brazier at the table) and pizza baked in a brick wood-burning oven. Reservations unnecessary. Rte. 95 (phone: 21300). Moderate.

Sr. Costilla's – The name translates as "Mr. Chops," appropriate for an eatery serving good steaks and chops. The mood at this branch of the popular Carlos Anderson chain is lively and casual, with all sorts of baskets and hats hanging from the ceiling and additional seating in the balcony. Reservations unnecessary. Upstairs at 1 Plaza Borda (phone: 23215). Moderate.

La Taberna – A relatively new addition to Taxco's restaurant scene, it's run by the same family who owns the *Bora Bora* (see below). The menu here, which is more extensive, includes shrimp shish kebab, beef Stroganoff, crêpes, salads, and pasta. There are table games, and the TV set airs major sports events from the US. Reservations advised. 8 Benito Juárez (phone: 25226). Moderate.

Arnoldo – The menu offers the choice of straight Mexicana or roast chicken, chops, or hamburgers; the home fries on the side are great. Reservations unnecessary. Upstairs at 2 Plaza de los Gallos, across the zocalo from Santa Prisca church (phone: 21272). Inexpensive.

Bora Bora – No South Seas rhythms and swaying palms here. In spite of the name, the lure is good pizza and great people watching. Reservations unnecessary. Callejón de las Delicias (phone: 21721). Inexpensive.

TIJUANA

(pronounced Tee-*wah*-nah)

Bawdy, lusty Tijuana, once the sin city of the Western Hemisphere, has pretty well cleaned up its act. This most famous of Mexico's border towns now caters more often to the family trade. People go to shop, to bet on the jai alai games or the dog races or the horse races, or to see a bullfight. They go to enjoy an authentic Mexican meal, to send postcards, or simply because it is close, just 15 miles (24 km) south of San Diego. In any case, they go in droves. There were about 24 million border crossers at Tijuana last year (at least 2 million of whom actually spent the night), making it, as it has been for years, the foreign city most visited by American citizens.

Reformers had something to do with Tijuana's new image; after all, it is a major gateway into the country. Moreover, the city could no longer compete with San Diego's own growing supply of massage parlors, topless bars, and porno movie houses. The wicked spots of old Tijuana — the *Chicago Bar* and the *Molino Rojo,* for instance — are still there, but they don't do much in the way of tourist business. The crowd they get is local and rough. There are lots of store shingles, too, advertising marriages and divorces, but their worthless decrees have no legal value on either side of the border.

The real thing Tijuana offers is a travel experience. Here the Third World meets the First, and the contrast makes an impact that's hard to forget. There is the border fence itself, 10 feet high, topped with barbed wire, cut in places, sagging or knocked down in others, by hordes of would-be illegal immigrants trying, and usually succeeding, to get into the United States. Interestingly, many Mexicans are now moving to Tijuana from other parts of the country to take advantage of its employment opportunities and higher salaries. This is not a *mañana* kind of place; outside investors are placing their bets on the city, and progress is being made at breakneck speed. Tijuana has a sophisticated citizenry and a growing cultural life.

The city is prosperous, boasting the highest per capita income in Mexico. With a million residents, it is the sixth largest city in the country. The area immediately surrounding the border, which used to be a rather bleak landscape of shacks and ramshackle buildings, is rapidly being transformed into an impressive suburban neighborhood, known as Río Tijuana, linked by a maze of expressways. (Those who would otherwise be disappointed at Tijuana's newfound respectability will be happy to know that some dirt streets, wooden fences, and the feel of gritty Old Mexico still exist uphill from town.)

Downtown, Tijuana's main street, Avenida Revolución, has undergone some extensive face-lifting to become a pleasant shopping boulevard. The Baja California Peninsula is what the Mexicans call a free zone (*zona franca*), where many Mexican import and immigration restrictions don't apply. No tourist card or automobile permit, for instance, is needed to visit Tijuana (or any other border city). At the border checkpoint, visitors simply are waved through. (Anyone planning to stay more than 72 hours, or heading into Mexico's interior, will need a tourist card, however, and customs laws and duties do apply in most cases when returning to the US (see "Customs and Returning to the US" in *On the Road,* GETTING READY TO GO).

In many respects, Tijuana is one vast duty-free shop. The best buys are European fashions, perfumes, crystal, bone china, and to some extent, cameras and electronic goods — such as Japanese television sets, stereos, and microwave ovens. Liquor is another good buy. Savings on some items can be 60% or more, but serious buyers should arrive knowing what these items cost at home. When it comes to purchasing imports, forget about bargaining. Merchants can charge what they want, but the law says price stickers must be on all goods, and a storekeeper offering a discount may be fined.

Bargaining, on the other hand, is very much in order for anything made in Mexico. Tijuana has a wonderful selection of the best Mexican products. There is leather in its many forms, pottery, blown glass, wrought iron, baskets, tiles, cut crystal, resortwear, furniture, silver, gold, wood carvings, and textiles. There is also a lot of tourist junk.

Customs exemptions for US citizens have made shopping in Tijuana more popular than ever. First there is the General System of Preferences (GSP), which waives duty on almost everything made in developing countries. Mexico is a developing country, which means there is almost unlimited freedom in what locally crafted items can be brought back home untaxed (see "Customs and Returning to the US," in *On the Road,* GETTING READY TO GO). In addition, the duty-free limit is $400 on all other goods. That applies to the imports one buys in Tijuana, such as Swiss watches, Waterford crystal, and Paris fashions. All may be brought home in limited quantities untaxed. (And remember, duty on most merchandise exceeding the $400 duty-free exemption is usually very modest.) Big spenders, however, should check with US Customs before divesting themselves of their bankrolls.

For fun there are dog races 6 nights and 3 afternoons a week, horse races Saturday and Sunday afternoons, bullfights most Sunday afternoons from May through September, and jai alai every night but Thursday. Eating is a favorite pastime, and resolute diners from Los Angeles and San Diego frequently drive down to Tijuana just to visit a favorite restaurant.

The nighttime action these days centers around the discos, and there are many. A couple of places have good shows, and a few of the bars remaining downtown have strippers and people who wheedle a few drinks out of the customers. Love, too, is for sale, but it is no longer one of Tijuana's better buys.

A state attorney's office for the protection of tourists was established in 1978, a reassurance to Americans who in the past were afraid to visit Tijuana. They had heard too many horror stories about nights spent in jail, venal cops, and corrupt officials. The stories were only partly true. Brawling sailors and teenage drag racers were likely to end up in nasty scrapes and be worse off than if they were at home. There was little the US consulate could do. Now, assuming no one is murdered, the state attorney will come to their aid. Interestingly, the office reports that the vast majority of the complaints it handles come not from visitors who have run afoul of the law, but from the customers of auto body and upholstery shops and of dentists. Americans flock to Tijuana to get dents knocked out of their fenders or to buy inexpensive false teeth, and not all the clients are satisfied. The state attorney will look into these cases and usually can come up with a satisfactory solution.

Tijuana, to be sure, earned the reputation it is now trying so hard to live down. Historians say the city takes its name from an Indian word which, hispanicized, sounded like Tia Juana, or Aunt Jane. Myth has it that there was a real Aunt Jane, famous for her warm hospitality and good food, but the experts dismiss this as a picturesque tale. It is true that the village on the border blossomed into a city during Prohibition; it was one place Californians could go to get a legal drink.

During World War II, the crowds came for more than just drinks. The San Diego navy base swarmed with lonesome young men, and Tijuana was there waiting to satisfy every desire. It was literally "Sintown" until the sexual revolution more or less put it out of business.

In many respects, Tijuana, at the top of the arid, beautiful Baja Peninsula, existed for much of its life as a city without a country. The rest of Mexico ignored the place because it was too far away. Until the 1950s, no paved highway linked it to the rest of the country. Even the railroad is a relatively recent arrival. When it finally came, the huddled masses swept in and Tijuana mushroomed into the fastest-growing city in Mexico. The city never has been able to keep up with the demands of its population. Only in recent years has it even tried, and urban renewal projects have been launched to bring crucial services to the city's residents.

Most visitors come to the city for only a few hours, although there are some good hotels that make it a pleasant place to spend a night or two. The *Tijuana Trolley* zips to the border from downtown San Diego, picking up passengers along the way. Bus lines bring in throngs of people every day, and packages are available for travelers who want to go shopping or to the races, jai alai games, or the bullfights. Most people who come to Tijuana drive their own cars. However, US auto insurance policies are not valid in Mexico, so it is advisable to get Mexican car insurance. *Sanborn's Mexico Insurance Service* (P.O. Box 310, McAllen, Texas 78502; phone: 512-686-0711 or in Mexico City, 5-876-0515/0616) is one of the most reliable insurance companies and has agents all over Mexico. *Sanborn's* also provides its clients with a complimentary, detailed booklet of maps, restaurants, and tourist attractions. Insurance also is available through *Instant Mexican Auto Insurance* (phone: 619-428-3583), *Oscar Padilla Insurance* (phone: 619-428-4406), and *Asemex* at the tourist information center on the Mexican side of the *línea* (border). If you don't want to bring your car into Mexico, park just north of the international line, walk across the border, and then walk or take a taxi downtown. That avoids two problems: Parking spaces normally are in short supply in Tijuana, and while driving into Mexico is easy enough, it often takes an hour or more to cross back into California because of the long lines of cars. Despite these small inconveniences, Tijuana is more than worth going out of your way to visit and explore. Lots of folks are betting on it these days, and it looks like almost everyone is expected to win.

TIJUANA AT-A-GLANCE

SEEING THE CITY: From the hill leading to the *Casa de la Cultura* (House of Culture) in the Altamira district, Tijuana old and new can be seen crowding up to the border and extending to the sea — an unforgettable vista of Mexico meeting the US, of the Third World and the First World side by side.

SPECIAL PLACES: As one of the largest and fastest-growing cities in Mexico, Tijuana is striking and, to some, surprisingly modern. It pays to take the time to see as much of it as possible, especially the newer and rapidly growing Río Tijuana area.

Shopping District – The heart of the city has been made quite attractive, and the stores are tempting enough to lure scores of thousands across the border every week. Avenida Revolución is the main drag, and the shopping district extends along it from Calles 1 through 8. Certain shops, especially the large stores (see *Shopping*), are particularly outstanding, but many of them do not go in for quality goods or appealing displays.

Agua Caliente Boulevard – This is an extension of Avenida Revolución, farther south and dressed more elegantly. Some of the better hotels and good restaurants are along this street, as well as the racetrack and the country club.

Paseo de los Héroes (Héroes Boulevard) – A major thoroughfare that passes through the blossoming Río Tijuana section with its striking *Cultural Center.* It's especially notable for its statuary: a larger-than-life replica of the beloved Indian chief Cuauhtémoc; Abraham Lincoln holding a broken chain (a gift from former President Ronald Reagan to Mexico; its counterpart, a statue of Benito Juárez, given to the US by Mexico's former president, Miguel de la Madrid, resides in San Diego); and a modern sculpture in front of the *Cultural Center* that commemorates the making of the canal from the river.

Plaza Santa Cecelia – Gateway to the honky-tonk part of town, at the opposite end of Avenida Revolución from the *Jai Alai Palace,* this little pocket is where mariachis play in the evenings.

Centro Cultural(Cultural Center) – The ultramodern center houses a museum, a theater for dramatic presentations by writers such as Genet, Albee, and even Aristophanes, an Omnimax theater with a 23,680-square-foot dome for film projection (*People of the Sun,* an excellent travelogue on Mexico, is shown daily; admission is $5.50), a restaurant, and some good shops. Combined, they have the wherewithal to keep visitors enthralled for the better part of a day. Explanations for exhibits on the country's history and art are in English and Spanish; plays are only in Spanish. A few English-language books about Mexico and translations of Mexican authors are for sale. Paseo de los Héroes and Mina (phone: 841111).

"The Zone" – This is the red-light district, sometimes called the Zona Norte, or North Zone, but usually just known as "The Zone." The *Molino Rojo* and the other bars of yore are still there, sleazier than ever. Inflation has hit the ten-cents-a-dance joints; the women now charge a quarter and, like taxi drivers, carry change-makers around their waists. Start at the *Molino Rojo* if you must visit. Calle Coahuila near Av. de la Constitución.

Río Tijuana (Tijuana River) – A concrete channel has been laid across the Mexican side of the border to end the frequent floods of the past, and along its banks a new and attractive Tijuana is rising. Outstanding evidence includes the striking *Cultural Center,* the Government Center, where the Baja California State Tourism and Conventions Committee has its offices, and a large, modern shopping center, *Plaza Río Tijuana.*

Teniente Guerrero Park – Tijuana's main square is now rundown and in need of refurbishing. Templo San Francisco (Saint Francis Temple) fronts it. Between Calles 3 and 4 and Avs. Cinco de Mayo and Ortega.

Tijuana Beach – A pleasant seaside community called Las Playas de Tijuana. The locally famous bullring is here, as well as two *charro* rings, handicraft shops, and seafood restaurants. About 5 miles (8 km) from the border crossing.

The Border – The fence runs right along the Ensenada Highway, leading to the beach, where there is a small monument and flag marking the southwesternmost point of the continental US. The holes in the border fence are notable.

ENVIRONS

Tecate – The next border crossing, it is about a 40-minute drive east of Tijuana. Founded in 1831 and famed for its brewery, it is a typical Mexican farm town with an engaging plaza with roses, towering trees, and a bandstand. Visit the tourist office (305 Callejón Libertad) and have lunch at nearby *Passetto's* (phone: 41361), a pleasant Italian restaurant with good local wine. Buy some bread and rolls at *El Mejor Pan* (everybody does), and should you decide to shed a few pounds (and dollars), visit *Rancho la Puerta* (phone: 41005), a spa and fitness resort. On weekends it is often worthwhile to cross the border into the US at Tecate to avoid the long lines in Tijuana.

■**EXTRA SPECIAL:** Rosarito Beach, 18 miles (29 km) south of Tijuana, is the top choice of Tijuana residents for a day's getaway. It is a fast-growing resort where many Californians own condos. The area is also gaining a name for the quality home furnishings that are made and sold here. Several leading interior design shops are here; exemplary is *Interiores de México* (phone: 21651), beside the *Quinta del Mar* resort, where custom furniture can be ordered. For tiles, blown glass, carved wood, and *equipales* (attractive rustic wood and leather chairs), visit *Artesanías Hacienda* (182 Benito Juárez). The great little fish restaurants of Rosarito and Puerto Nuevo (known as "the lobster village") also deserve a visit. The modern *Quinta del Mar* resort (phone: 21301; 800-228-7003 in the US) has been remodeled, as has the landmark *Rosarito Beach* hotel (phone: 121126). Another alternative would be to venture 18 miles (29 km) south of Rosarito to the winsome cliffside *La Fonda* hotel (no phone), with its excellent Mexican terrace restaurant and fine beach below, or to the new resort hotel *New Port Baja* (Km 45 of the Tijuana-Ensenada Hwy.; phone: 661-41188; 800-678-7244; FAX: 661-41175). From Tijuana, follow the toll road south for fine beach views, the inland toll-free road for rural vistas.

SOURCES AND RESOURCES

TOURIST INFORMATION: The main *caseta de información turística* (tourist information booth) is at Puerta México (phone: 232885). Other booths are at the border crossing known as Mesa de Otai (no phone), as well as downtown (at Av. Revolución, between Calles 3 and 4; no phone). The Tourist Protection Office (108 Paseo de los Héroes, 2nd Floor; phone: 840537) handles complaints and helps visitors with a variety of problems. There also is a US Consulate in Tijuana (96 Tapachula; phone: 81740). For a map and discount coupons for local shops and night spots, pick up a free copy of the *San Diego–Tijuana Discount Guide*. The Tijuana Chamber of Commerce also offers a coupon booklet available at tourist information booths.

TELEPHONE: The area code for Tijuana is 66. When calling from one city to another within Mexico, dial 91 before the area code.

 CLIMATE AND CLOTHES: The climate in Tijuana is much like that in Southern California, although sometimes more overcast and humid. As might be expected, dress is extremely casual yet conservative. Going braless, shirtless, or shoeless invites unwelcome attention.

 GETTING AROUND: Bus – Travel by bus is inexpensive and convenient in Tijuana; the only problem is finding out where to pick up the bus you need. The easiest solution is to ask at the tourist information kiosk downtown on Avenida Revolución. For example, the green and cream buses that go to the racetrack are marked 5 y 10, Los Pinos, and La Presa. The terminal is on Avenida de la Constitución between Calles 5 and 6. Bus drivers accept US coins, and the cost of a ride is 25¢. *Mexicoach* buses and vans make numerous one-way trips daily from Avenida Madero and Calle 7 direct to the border for about $5.

Taxi – Rates are sometimes reasonable, sometimes not ($5 seems to be the going fare), and cabs are plentiful. You'll find them at the border (yellow jitneys charge $2 from the Mexican side of the border to downtown Tijuana), cruising along Revolución, and at stands by the *Jai Alai Palace* and at the hotels. Ask the fare at the outset and try to bargain if it seems too high. Brown and white, red and black, and blue and white jitneys (*colectivos*) pack in as many passengers as they can and run along the main boulevards; they charge a quarter per head.

Car Rental – *Alpri* (phone: 842268), *Avis* (phone: 832310), *Budget* (phone: 840253), and *Hertz* (phone: 832080) have offices at the airport or downtown, most along Boulevard Agua Caliente. Hertz also has an office in the *Palacio Azteca* hotel (phone: 861222). A car is handy if you plan to do any extensive exploring, but is not essential if you are staying downtown.

Tours – The *Tijuana Trolley* (phone: 859415) picks up passengers at the border and makes stops at Tijuana's major sights (the *Cultural Center,* racetrack, shopping centers, and more) for $12 a day; passengers can board the trolley as many times as they wish. *Greyhound* has transportation service into Tijuana where it stops at First and Av. Madero (phone: 619-239-9171 in San Diego). *Mexicoach/Five Star Tours* (phone: 619-232-5049 in San Diego; 856913 in Tijuana) operates daily express buses between San Diego and Tijuana.

 SPECIAL EVENTS: Tijuana is one big fiesta throughout the year, and at times the entire place looks more like a fairgrounds than a city. In August there is the *Gran Feria de las Californias* (Great Fair of the Californias), a show that lasts almost 3 weeks and is aimed at promoting exports, but with many carnival touches added. *Mexican Independence Day,* September 16, is a big bash that gets started the weekend before and attracts huge crowds.

SHOPPING: Reputable stores have replaced the honky-tonk joints that once lined Avenida Revolución. There's even a chrome and glass *Drug Store* (Av. Revolucíon), a replica of the one in Paris. European fashions, crystal, porcelain, perfumes, and Mexican handicrafts are now the stock in trade. The street hawkers, with their constant invitations to come in and browse, quickly get to be annoying, and the most pleasant shopping is often in the large ultramodern shopping centers. *Plaza Río Tijuana* is next door to the *Cultural Center. Pueblo Amigo,* a colonial-style "village" (on Paseo de los Héroes) is filled with shops, restaurants, and a disco. The newest and largest of the shopping centers is *Viva Tijuana,* which is about 220 yards from the border; many of the 200 or so shops were still vacant at press time. Fixed prices are set for all imports; dollars are used more than pesos. Stores generally are open from 10 AM until 7 PM; some are closed on Sundays.

Antón's – Fine Mexican jewelry, along with watches from Switzerland, Japan, and other places. Av. Revolución between Calles 3 and 4 (phone: 853585).

Arts and Crafts Center – Stalls filled with everything from jewels to junk. Calle 2 between Ocampo and Negrete (no phone).

Azteca – This jewelry store and perfumery sells pretty, but pricey, gold jewelry. 707 Av. Revolución (phone: 856828).

Casart – A wide selection of handicrafts from the state of Mexico, including the whimisical trees of life from the town of Metepec. In the *Cultural Center* near the museum (phone: 841111).

Castillo – Now a saddle shop, it carries some handbags and other leather articles. 2044 Díaz Mirón (phone: 852895).

Dorian's – A Mexican department store, it carries trendy clothing for women and men. 95-C Paseo de los Héroes, 1735 Calle 2, and at the *Plaza Rio Tijuana Shopping Center* (phone: 851888).

Dulce's Boutique – This tiny place is crammed with imported designer labels at attractive prices. 2219 J. Sarabia (phone: 848037).

Hand Art – Table and bed linen, blouses, and handkerchiefs from Europe and Asia. 735 Av. Revolución (phone: 852642).

La Herradura de Oro – A good place for *charro* (typically Mexican riding gear), western and English equestrian equipment, saddles, and clothes. 10001 Paseo de los Héroes and at the *Plaza Fiesta Shopping Center* (phone: 842252).

Lámparas y Vitrales – Tiffany-style lamps and stained glass windows produced in their own factory. They also carry blown glass items. 2269 Calle Juárez, and at the *Arts and Crafts Center* (phone: 855333).

Marco – The specialty here is heavy Mexican doors and fireplaces. The carved wood doors, some with leaded or stained glass insets, are lovely. 1422 Av. Revolución (phone: 853551).

Maxim – Imported clothing, porcelain, crystal, perfume, linen, and a selection of Mexican handicrafts. 604 Av. Revolución (phone: 881768).

Maya de México – Good selection of Mexican shirts for men. In *Caesar's* hotel, Av. Revolución and Calle 5 (phone: 851666).

Mizrachi – A landmark for shoppers seeking bargains in cameras, stereos, binoculars, clothing, and much more. Calle 7 between Av. Madero and Revolución, 2036 Galeana, and 10 Blvd. Agua Caliente (phone: 859186).

Del Museo – The prices are high in this jewelry store, but the designs, including works in gold and silver, are sophisticated and often unique. In the *Cultural Center* near the museum (phone: 841111).

Ralph Lauren's Polo Shop – Lauren's designs are priced below the going rate in the States. Calle 7 and Madero, behind the *Jai Alai Palace* (phone: 851389).

Renée – Cosmetics and designer clothes at good prices. 1004 Av. Revolución (phone: 855155).

Sara's – A department store with 3 floors of clothing and toilet articles from around the world. Av. Revolución and Calle 4, and the *Plaza Río Tijuana Shopping Center* (phone: 880049).

Tile Center – Hand-painted tiles, bathroom fixtures, and accessories. 4601-1 Blvd. Agua Caliente (phone: 862946).

Tolán – A quality selection of Mexican folk art and home furnishings, including the black pottery from Oaxaca. 1111 Av. Revolución (phone: 883637).

SPORTS: The great variety of sports facilities in Tijuana are a major attraction.

Beaches – Most popular is Rosarito (see *Extra Special*), about a half-hour's drive south on Route 1. Be warned that even in summer the water tends to be chilly.

Bullfights – The regular season runs from May through September, with *corridas* scheduled most Sunday afternoons at one of Tijuana's two bullrings. The best matadors appear at the *Plaza Monumental,* the bullring by the sea. The smaller *Toreo de Tijuana* gets the lesser fights. Tickets are available at the entrance to the Sonia Arcade beside *Caesar's* hotel and at the bullring gates.

Charreadas – Mexican rodeos are held occasionally on Sundays at several rings, including *Misión del Sol* and *Hacienda Arroyo* in Las Playas de Tijuana. The tourist information booths have details.

Dog Races – The greyhounds run for the money at *Hipódromo Agua Caliente,* with races on Saturdays and Sundays at 2 PM,, and 12 races nightly except Tuesdays. No admission charge. The track, one of Tijuana's top attractions, has several restaurants and bars on the premises. Blvd. Agua Caliente (phone: 817811).

Golf – The *Club Campestre* (Country Club) is a favorite with duffers and champions alike. The greens fee is $15 weekdays, $18 Saturdays and Sundays; golf carts may be rented. Both the club and the restaurant are open to the public. Reserve at least 1 week ahead, and ask about special packages. Blvd. Agua Caliente near the racetrack (phone: 863958).

Horse Races – On Saturdays and Sundays, there's always big excitement at the *Hipodromo Agua Caliente,* with l2 races daily during the winter months, 11 the rest of the year. Admission is charged only at the *Turf* and *Jockey* clubs. Blvd. Agua Caliente (phone: 817811).

Jai Alai – The *Tijuana Jai Alai Palace* is the best in Mexico; the game is exciting and fast (players propel balls at more than 160 miles per hour), dollar bets are welcome, and the language is English. It has a popular restaurant with a view of the goings-on. The action starts every night but Thursday at 8 PM. Admission charges are $2.50, $3, $4, or $5; most likely free if you show up after 11 PM. Avenida Revolución between Calles 7 and 8 (phone: 851612).

Off-Track Betting – Managed by the people who operate the *Hipódromo Agua Caliente,* it's called the *Foreign Book* and takes wagers on most races taking place at race tracks around the US. The place to bet is on Avenida Revolución, between Calles 3 and 4. There's a bar and grill on the premises to help pass the time while awaiting the results of the races. In Rosarito, the *Foreign Book,* a restaurant and bar, is at the *Quinta del Mar Shopping Center.*

Tennis – The *Fiesta Americana* hotel has 2 lighted courts.

NIGHTCLUBS AND NIGHTLIFE: Tijuana is at its best after dark, especially on nights when the dogs race and the jai alai matches are on. Most discotheques are open Thursday through Sunday nights, with *Baby Rock* (across from the *Lucerna* hotel) the hands-down favorite, attracting crowds of 1,000 a night on weekends (mostly Mexicans on Thursdays and Sundays, Americans on Fridays and Saturdays). *OH!* (50 Paseo de los Héroes in Río Tijuana) has a faithful following. Also popular are *Tequila Circus* (on 3rd and Revolución), *Baccarat* (*Fiesta Americana* hotel), *Excess* (at *Viva Tijuana*), *News* (at *Pueblo Amigo*), and the *London Club* (Blvd. Agua Caliente near the *Fiesta Americana*). The *Lucerna* hotel has a video bar and a small dance floor. Among several lively spots downtown on Avenida Revolución are *Club A* (at the corner of Calle 4); *Bol Corona* (520 Av. Revolución); *Tijuana Tilly's* (Calle 7); *Rio Rita* (744 Av. Revolución); *Viva Zapata,* (914 Av. Revolución between Calles 5 and 6, three flights up, with a nice view of the street); and *Casa Blanca*

(Calle 7 off Av. Revolución). *Güiri Güiri,* also downtown (148 Calle 7, off Av. Revolución) is a cantina featuring guitar and piano music. The old *Bol Corona,* a landmark for over 50 years, burned down a couple of years ago, but there's still a cantina in the *Convention Center* with music but no dancing.

BEST IN TOWN

 CHECKING IN: While most American tourists spend only a few hours in Tijuana, others prefer to stay the night, thus avoiding dreary rush-hour delays at the border and enjoying a night on the town more fully. There are several very good hotels here. Those listed as expensive charge up to $100 for a double room; moderate, about $50 to $75; and inexpensive, less than $45. All telephone numbers are in the 66 area code unless otherwise indicated. When calling from one city to another within Mexico, dial 91 before the area code.

Fiesta Americana – One of the newest — and the tallest — local hostelries, its 32-floor tower (flanked by a twin filled with condos, offices, and shops) dominates the Tijuana skyline. In addition to 422 comfortable peach-hued rooms, each with a king-size bed, there is a sophisticated lobby bar, 24-hour restaurant and room service, nightclub, disco, 2 lighted tennis courts, Jacuzzi, outdoor pool, gym, spa, and *Fiesta Book* where the races are shown live for off-track betting. 4500 Blvd. Agua Caliente (phone: 817000; 800-FIESTA-1 in the US; FAX: 817016) Expensive.

El Conquistador – This lovely, 2-story hotel in the colonial style has charming rooms, a pool, sauna, restaurant, and cocktail lounge. Service is haphazard, though. South of town, across the street from the *Fiesta Americana.* Blvd. Agua Caliente (phone: 817955; 800-326-0995 in the US; FAX: 861340). Moderate.

Country Club Best Western – A favorite with golfers and tennis enthusiasts because of its proximity to the local country club, it's casual and comfortable, with a pool and restaurant. The 100 rooms are on the small side, but there are 20 suites and 11 master suites that are considerably larger. 1 Tapachula (phone: 817203; FAX: 817066). Moderate.

Lucerna – A striking 6-story structure, with 168 rooms, 2 fine restaurants (see *Eating Out*), disco, bar, and a smashing pool. Reservations advised for weekends. Paseo de los Héroes at Abelardo L. Rodriguez (phone/FAX: 342000; 800-LUCERNA in the US). Moderate.

Paraíso Radisson – Formerly the *Baja Inn, Calinda,* and *El Presidente,* this pleasant chameleon has 200 rooms, a pool, Jacuzzi, restaurant, and bar. It's near the racetrack and overlooks the country club (guests have access to the golf facilities). 1 Blvd. Agua Caliente (phone: 817200; 800-333-3333 in the US; FAX: 863639). Moderate.

Hacienda del Río – Built to resemble a hacienda, it has 131 rooms, including 2 junior suites and 1 master suite. There is a restaurant, coffee shop, and pool. 1606 Blvd. Sanchez Taboada (phone: 848644; FAX: 848620). Moderate to inexpensive.

Palacio Azteca – Close to town, it's modern and nicely decorated, with 90 pretty rooms, a palm-shaded pool, 2 bars, and a restaurant. 213 Blvd. Cuauhtémoc Sur, off Blvd. Agua Caliente (phone: 818100). Moderate to inexpensive.

Caesar's – In the very heart of things, this 1930s landmark, now run-down, has 75 rooms, restaurant, bar, and shops. The plastic flowers in the rooms belie the historic significance. They claim Caesar salad was invented here. The old photos and toreador exhibit are interesting. Av. Revolución and Calle 5 (phone: 851666). Inexpensive.

Padre Kino – This clean, no-frills motel has a small pool and rock-bottom rates that leave plenty of money for jai alai. No credit cards accepted. 3 Blvd. Agua Caliente (phone: 864208). Inexpensive.

La Sierra – Not elegant but adequate, it has a pool, and bar. Near the *Palacio Azteca Hotel* on Av. Dieciséis de Septiembre (phone: 861601). Inexpensive.

EATING OUT: Tijuana claims its great contribution to gastronomy is the Caesar salad, said to have been prepared first at *Caesar's* hotel (but no longer at its best there). Beer and wine are two products of the region that are prized throughout Mexico. While there is a fair spectrum of ethnic cooking in Tijuana, by far the best are the Mexican specialties. People drive here from all over California to enjoy *carnitas* (cubes of roast pork) and Tecate beer. We consider any place charging $50 for dinner for two expensive; $30 to $40 moderate; and under $20 inexpensive. Drinks and tips are extra. Most restaurants accept MasterCard and Visa; a few also accept American Express and Diners Club. Unless otherwise noted, all restaurants are open daily. All telephone numbers are in the 66 area code unless otherwise indicated. When calling from one city to another within Mexico, dial 91 before the area code.

Alcázar del Río – Fine international and Spanish food and a long wine list draw Tijuana's wealthy to this place. *Solomilio* (sirloin steak) prepared with marrow and tarragon sauce is a favorite. Pianist Antonio Vásquez is on hand Fridays and Saturdays. Reservations advised. 56-4 Paseo de los Héroes (phone: 842672). Expensive.

Place de la Concorde – Swanky surroundings, delightful piano music, and inspired cooking are offered here. Try the boneless trout in lemon sauce and the Gran Marnier soufflé. Reservations advised. *Fiesta Americana* (phone: 817000). Expensive.

Rivoli – One of Tijuana's priciest dining establishments. The food and decor are strictly French. Specialties include filet of sole prepared in white wine. Closed Sundays. Reservations advised. In the *Lucerna Hotel,* Paseo de los Héroes at Rodriguez (phone: 841000). Expensive.

Boccaccio's – An old favorite, its specialties are international. Abalone is particularly good here, prepared in a garlic or oyster sauce, or in black butter. Reservations advised. 2500 Blvd. Agua Caliente across from the country club (phone: 861845). Moderate.

La Costa – Seafood is the specialty at this established Tijuana favorite; the *Siete Mares* (Seven Seas) soup is a meal in itself; the ambience is down-home. The fetching photos on the wall are of its celebrity-owner, Adrian Pedrin, also of *Pedrin* restaurant (see below), and his family. Reservations advised. Calle 7 between Revolución and Constitución (phone: 858494). Moderate.

La Fonda Roberto – Unusual regional specialties — beef tongue in sesame seed sauce, spicy shredded pork, two kinds of chicken *mole,* and beef in *chipotle* sauce — are the dishes to try here. Superb soups, too, plus good *crepas.* Reservations advised. In the *La Sierra Hotel,* 16 Av. Dieciséis de Septiembre (phone: 864687). Moderate.

Guadalajara Grill – The Maya dish *cochinita pibil* (stuffed roasted pig with a special blend of spices) is a specialty here, along with *ariero* (filet of beef prepared on a small hibachi with tomato, onions, and chilies), and strawberry margaritas. The interior is pure movie set. Reservations advised. 19 Diego Rivera and Paseo de los Héroes (phone: 842043). Moderate.

Pedrin's – Another favorite with locals and California day-trippers, this popular spot offers 67 seafood selections. Reservations advised. 1115 Av. Revolución (phone: 854062 or 854052). Moderate.

Reno's – Many call this the best in town. The menu is international, the decor plush. There's live entertainment in the evenings. Reservations advised. Calle 8 and Av. Revolución (phone: 859210). Moderate.

Tíajuana Tilly's – Reason enough to cross the border, it has an international menu, lively Mexican ambience, and good local drinks. Open daily; expect lines on weekends. Its offshoot, *Tilly's Fifth Avenue* (for snacks and drinks), is also open daily (Revolucíon and Fifth). Reservations advised. The original eatery is at the *Jai Alai Palace*, 701 Av. Revolución (phone: 857833). Moderate.

Turf Club – Linger over dinner here while watching the dogs race; the restaurant is open Wednesday through Sunday from 7 PM. No shorts or T-shirts allowed. Reservations advised. *Hipódromo Agua Caliente* (phone: 863948). Moderate.

Mr. Fish – A thatch hut that offers a surprisingly wide variety of seafood specialties. Try the *crepas* or the steamed or fried whole fish. Clam chowder and shrimp with mango are two of the other favorites. No reservations. 6000 Blvd. Agua Caliente, near the country club (phone: 863603). Moderate to inexpensive.

Birrieria Guanajuato – It's worth the trip up into the Tijuana hills just for the house specialties — *cabrito* (roast kid), *gorditas* (melted cheese wrapped in cornmeal), and *birria* (a spicy sauce). Open from 9 AM to 7 PM. No reservations. No credit cards accepted. 102 Av. Abraham González (phone: 377070). Inexpensive.

Bol Corona – The atmosphere is vintage Hemingway. The lure is the long hours it's open — 7 AM to 4 AM — and the crowds testify to the taste of the soups and 15 kinds of burritos. Reservations unnecessary. 520 Av. Revolución (phone: 857940). Inexpensive.

Carnitas Uruapan – The specialty here is carnitas (cubes of roast pork). Mariachis start playing at about 3 PM. *Reservations* advised. 550 Blvd. Díaz Ordaz (phone: 816181). Inexpensive.

Chiki Jai – Enjoy authentic Basque cuisine at this tiny, classic place (the name means "small party"). Reservations advised. No credit cards accepted. Next to the Jai Alai Palace at 1050 Av. Revolución and Calle 7 (phone: 854955). Inexpensive.

Guiseppi's – Good pizza is served at this casual spot with red and white checkered tablecloths and a mural of Venice. No reservations. No credit cards accepted. Several branches around town, including one on Blvd. Agua Caliente (no phone). Inexpensive.

La Leña – The decor is simple but attractive, the steaks and seafood excellent. Try puños ("fists"), made from marinated beef mixed with ham, pork, green onions, and cheese. The roast quail and chicken are both first-rate, and the *gaonera* (meat pounded thin and stuffed with beans, guacamole, or cheese) is a new taste treat. Reservations advised. Two locations: 4560 Blvd. Agua Caliente (phone: 862920) and 816 Av. Revolución (phone: 880908). Inexpensive.

Palacio Imperial – The best choice in town for Chinese food, it's easy to spot by the red and gold façade. Cheerful ambience and bar. Reservations unnecessary. Av. Revolución between Calles 8 and 9 (phone: 853560). Inexpensive.

VERACRUZ
(pronounced Veh-rah-*cruz*)

Veracruz is Mexico's oldest city, its largest port, and a thriving industrial center. Few of its 800,000 residents depend on tourism for their livelihood, and while that means it lacks some of the more sophisticated tourist facilities of dyed-in-the-wool resorts, the atmosphere is comparatively free of the insincere pandering associated with areas totally dependent on the tourist trade. What's more, it is a fascinating place to visit. The town and its people are the product of a blend of Spanish and Carib-Afro cultures, a combination present in no other city in Mexico. About a quarter of a million African slaves were imported to and through this port between 1540 and 1640, and many were put to work in the surrounding sugarcane and rice fields. The vast majority of the slaves eventually married mestizos (people of Spanish and Indian blood) or Spanish, and today it is rare to see a pure African.

The Carib-Afro influence in Veracruz is readily apparent — tangible in the architecture and audible in the music. The buildings are Spanish, of stucco or wood, with long overhanging balconies, but they are painted mellow Caribbean colors. A stroll through the city's neighborhoods creates a colorful impression — pale pink, ocher, salmon, and sky blue shade the tiny houses of clapboard and tiled roofs. Instead of the big brass sound of the mariachi bands characteristic of most Mexican music, local musicians play the marimba, an instrument similar to a xylophone, and strolling players carry harps and stringed instruments. The music they play — *huapangos* and *sones jarochos* (the music and dances typical of the people of Veracruz) — has softer tones than mariachi music, can be languid or very lively, and is often filled with jokes and double entendres.

Veracruz has a stormy history of invasion and attack by foreign powers intent on slicing Mexico into pieces like a pie. Considering this history, it is remarkable that the people are so tolerant of foreigners. The past seems to be forgotten or forgiven. Hernando Cortés landed in Villa Rica, about 20 miles north of Veracruz, in 1519, and burnt his boats to prevent fainthearted members of his crew from defecting. He planted a cross on shore and called the area La Villa Rica de la Vera Cruz (the Rich Village of the True Cross). Though the native population did not realize the significance of this event, their lives would be greatly changed in the name of this cross, as would civilizations throughout Mexico.

From Veracruz, Cortés set out on his march inland toward what is today Mexico City, conquering, colonizing, and plundering along the way in his mission to christianize the Indians. At the end of the Mexican War of Independence from Spain (1821), Spanish troops stationed in their last stronghold (the Castle of San Juan de Ulúa) severely bombarded the town, reducing it practically to dust. Seventeen years later, the French bombarded the town and castle. During the Mexican-American War in 1847, American troops landed in Veracruz, subdued the resistance they encountered, and marched on to

Mexico City. In 1860, the French entered the city again to prepare the way for Maximilian and Carlota; and then again, in 1914, the US bombarded the port.

The Spanish built the town you see today. The design features the ubiquitous main plaza (referred to as Plaza de Armas or Plaza de la Constitución), with a cathedral on one side, government buildings on another, and sidewalk cafés lining the remaining two sides. Here, more than in any other city in Mexico, the social life revolves around cafés. Drinking *café con leche* (a strong black coffee mixed with hot milk, poured carefully by the waiters to get just the right proportions), talking, playing dominoes, and watching people go by are the big activities.

You may find yourself gravitating to a café at least two or three times a day: in the morning for coffee, a roll, and a seat in the shade; in the afternoon for a cooling limeade, a beer, or a soda; in the evening after dinner for a final coffee. Street musicians stroll through the cafés in the evenings, and often there are band concerts in the plaza. The only slack hours are from two to four in the afternoons — lunch and siesta time. So join the rest of the population then and eat or sleep.

There is ample time during the rest of the day to shop, stroll, swim, and sun. The waterfront is a good place to walk around and watch the activity. Freighters from all over the world dock here. The shops along the waterfront sell the goods for which Veracruz is famous — fruit, seafood, coffee, and cigars. Shrimp, oysters, crabs, clams, red snapper, squid, and sea bass are served in waterfront restaurants just hours after they have been caught in the gulf. Oysters on the half shell make a great snack between meals, and are available everywhere — as are the plump, pink, fresh gulf shrimp. Local specialties include *caldo largo de camarones,* shrimp prepared in a rich spicy broth, and *huachinango à la Veracruzana,* red snapper in a tomato sauce seasoned with onion, capers, oregano, mild yellow peppers, and a touch of garlic.

The Veracruz climate is hot most of the time, even in midwinter, except when the occasional storm blows in from the north. The beaches on the east side of town provide pleasant relief from the heat. They are long and wide, free of undertows, and have long stretches of shallow water. There are no lifeguards on the beaches, however, so always be careful.

Veracruz is most exciting during *Carnaval,* the week before *Lent.* Like pre-*Lenten* celebrations throughout the rest of the Gulf and the Caribbean, the festivities are fervent and uninhibited; the prevailing philosophy seems to be that two can bamba well, but everybody can bamba better. The streets are filled with dancers, musicians, paraders in costume; the sky is filled with fireworks. The only prerequisite to having fun is a hotel reservation confirmed months in advance — and it is best to arrange this through a travel agent to be sure the reservation has been accepted and will be honored.

If you miss *Carnaval,* you haven't missed Veracruz. Fifty-one weeks out of the year it is a working seaport; the leavening in the labor is that fillip of Africa and the Caribbean so palpably a part of Veracruz life and so absent elsewhere in Mexico. It is as if in establishing itself here, perched on the very edge of the Caribbean with the whole somber continent before it, it could go no farther. So here it stays, and here you'll find it.

VERACRUZ AT-A-GLANCE

 SEEING THE CITY: Now that the Banco de Mexico tower is closed to the public, the best way to see the city and the harbor is from the glass-enclosed elevator at the *Emporio* hotel or the café at *Puerto Bello Centro,* both on the *malecón,* or from the terrace of the *Mocambo.* Another option is to take a boat ride on either *La Orca* or *Isla de Sacrificios* around the harbor; the boat excursions leave from the dock across the street from the *Emporio* and cost about $1.50. The hour-long trip takes passengers around Isla Verde (a flora and fauna preserve) and Isla Sacrificios, where the main lighthouse stands.

 **SPECIAL PLACES:** You can walk around the downtown area. Only 3 blocks northeast of the main plaza is another center of activity, the dock and *malecón,* with its shops and restaurants. The beaches and several other points of interest are accessible by taxi.

Plaza de la Constitución – The main plaza, attractively landscaped with tall palms, tropical flowers, and colored lights at night, is the social center of the city. Designed by the Spanish in the 16th century, it is said to be the oldest plaza in Mexico. During the day, people congregate here and at the surrounding sidewalk cafés. Vendors work the arcades, hawking everything from chewing gum to gaudy crucifixes made from painted shells. At night strolling musicians compete for attention, and there are band concerts Tuesday and Thursday evenings. In July and August and at *Christmas* and *Easter,* there are shows every day. The Municipal Palace with its arched portals flanks the plaza on the east side, and hotels line the north and west sides, where the parish church, La Parroquia, also stands on the site of an original church erected by the Spanish. Bordered by Independencia, Zamora, and Lerdo.

Museo Histórico de la Revolución Venustiano Carranza – Housed in a distinctive yellow and white building topped by a lighthouse, this museum pays homage to the life and times of native son Venustiano Carranza, a Mexican general who become president of the republic in 1915. Closed Mondays. Admission charge. Calles Serdán and Xicoténcatl at the *malecón.*

Villa del Mar, Hornos, Costa Verde, and Mocambo Beaches – The first three are some of the best beaches in town. Bigger and less crowded is Mocambo — the best of all — 4 miles (6 km) south on the beach highway. At all four, concessionaires rent chairs with umbrellas or canvas tops for a small fee. Itinerant peddlers plod along the strand selling a variety of items, some of them edible. To get here, catch the bus on Calle Serdán and Avenida Zaragoza downtown, or drive east along Boulevard Avila Camacho; the ride out provides views of the water on the left, some of Veracruz's finer neighborhoods on the right.

Malecón – This walkway along the harbor is a pleasant place for strolling. A few shops sell items made of tortoiseshell (which cannot be taken into the US), all sorts of shells that you can use for serving *coquilles* and other fish dishes, straw hats and baskets, embroidered blouses, shirts, and dresses. You can board some of the freighters moored here and you might be able to arrange to have a meal on board or buy wares such as cigars, fruits, seafood, and coffee from the purser. Three blocks northeast of the Plaza de la Constitución.

Castillo de San Juan de Ulúa – Now little more than a forbidding shell, this large island fortress is Veracruz's prime historical landmark and houses a small historical museum. Started in 1528 by the Spanish, the fort was built to defend the port but was later used as a prison for criminals and people with undesirable political leanings, some of whom were thrust into dungeon holes that were half-flooded at high tide; even Benito Juárez did time here, for a couple of weeks during the Revolution. Noted for its massive walls and ramparts, the *castillo* cost Charles V of Spain 40 million gold pesos. You can get to the fortress via the causeway that links the island to the city; the bus stops at the *malecón* and Avenida Landero y Cors. Closed Mondays. Admission charge. In the harbor on Gallega Reef.

Baluarte de Santiago – All that remains of the wall that once encircled Veracruz is this small fortress. Within is a museum displaying arms used long ago. Closed Mondays. Admission charge. Av. Gomez Farías and Calle Canal.

Boca del Río – This small fishing village, now considered a suburb of fast-growing Veracruz, has several modest, thatch-roofed restaurants that are popular with residents for freshly caught shrimp and other seafood. Some of the finest hotels in the area are found here. On CN-180, 7 miles (11 km) south of Veracruz.

Mandinga – Here you'll find a cluster of fishing shacks between two lagoons, one fished for shrimp, the other for oysters. Perch and bass are also good here. You can rent boats and fish or feast in one of several open-air restaurants that serve fresh shrimp, squid, oysters, and clams. At any time of day or night, you can also enjoy one of the local groups that play traditional Veracruz music. 4 miles (6 km) south of Boca del Río.

Escuela Naval Antón Lizardo (Mexican Naval Academy) – This modern academy faces the gulf and is surrounded by pine trees. A statue of Cadet Virgilio Uribe commemorates his death during the 1914 bombardment of Veracruz by American warships. Cadets serve as guides. Open daily. No admission charge. About 21 miles (34 km) south of Veracruz in the village of Antón Lizardo, via Rte. 48, and then Rte. 150 from Boca del Río.

Catemaco – This small fishing village has a lagoon and three lovely waterfalls; you can rent a boat here, and lodgings are available. 75 miles (120 km) south of Veracruz on Rte. 180.

> ■**EXTRA SPECIAL:** A day trip from Veracruz that's very worthwhile is a visit to the archaeological zone of Tajín. The ruins here are not as extensive as those in the Yucatán, but still quite impressive. The Pyramid of the Niches, on which traces of the original murals are still visible, is the highlight, and the 150-acre area includes six rebuilt temples, several pyramids, and a ball court. *ADO* buses, which leave from 1698 Díaz Mirón at 9 AM and 2:30 PM, offer a 4½-hour trip. For overnight trips, see "The Vanilla Route: Mexico to Tampico and Veracruz" in DIRECTIONS. The ruins are open daily. Admission charge. About 135 miles (216 km) northwest of Veracruz on Rte. 180.
>
> At Cempoala, also on Route 180 but only about 30 miles (48 km) north of Veracruz, are the well-conserved remains of the last capital of the Totonacan culture, the site of the first pact between the Spaniards and the natives. Worthy of note are the Throne of the Fat Cacique, the Fireplaces, and the Faces. Closed Mondays. Admission charge.
>
> Nearby is the town of La Antigua, which was the original site of La Villa Rica de la Veracruz where Cortés first planted a cross on the shore. The settlement was moved to "modern" Veracruz in 1600, but the remains of Cortés's house still stand on the main street, as does the Capilla del Santo Culto del Buen Viaje, believed to be the first Christian chapel in the western hemisphere.
>
> The *Museo de Antropologia de Xalapa* (Museum of Anthropology at Xalapa), one of the most beautiful archaeological museums in the world, is located in Xalapa, capital of the state and an easy 71½-mile (114-km) drive from Veracruz. *ADO* buses make the trip in about 2 hours and cost about $2 each way. The museum houses a vast collection, including several Olmec heads from the gulf cultures. After the museum, visit the historic *Ex-Hacienda El Lencero* museum

(Pancho Villa slept here), which has been restored to its former glory (9½ miles/15 km from downtown Xalapa, on the road to Veracruz). Both are closed Mondays. No admission charge.

SOURCES AND RESOURCES

TOURIST INFORMATION: The municipal tourist office (in the Municipal Palace on the zocalo; phone: 329842) is best for information, maps, and brochures.

TELEPHONE: The area code for Veracruz is 29. When calling from one city to another within Mexico, dial 91 before the area code.

CLIMATE AND CLOTHES: Veracruz is hot all year and humid in the summer during the rainy season. Starting in August and lasting through December is the season of the *nortes,* storms that blow down from the north bringing high winds and more rain. The best weather is from January through March. Dress is casual, although somewhat less so than at the Pacific coast resorts; for example, bathing suits are worn only on the beaches.

GETTING AROUND: Bus – Buses are no longer permitted to pass through the Plaza de Armas. The most scenic route is that designated Mocambo– Boca del Río. Two bus companies, *Autobuses de Oriente(ADO;* phone: 375744) and *Autobuses Unidos(AU;* phone: 372673), serve the city and the surrounding area.

Taxi – You can pick up a cab on the main plaza or have your hotel call one for you. The fare is reasonable, and sightseeing by cab is less expensive than taking a city tour. City tours are offered by *Ulúa Travel Agency* (432 Av. de los Insurgentes Veracruzanos; phone: 329079); and *Wagons Lits* (1076 Cinco de Mayo; phone: 323714).

Car Rental – *Avis, National, Budget,* and *Hertz* have agencies in town and at the airport. Keep in mind that most agencies charge about 32¢ a mile on top of the basic rental fee.

SPECIAL EVENTS: *Carnaval* is a full-scale blowout that is held for a week just before *Lent* to make the 40 days of abstention more tolerable. There's music, dancing, parades, fireworks, and all kinds of frivolity; to participate, make your hotel reservations a few months in advance.

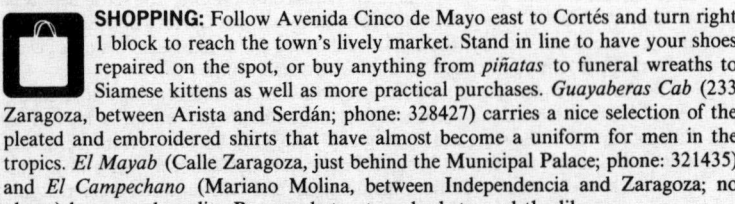

SHOPPING: Follow Avenida Cinco de Mayo east to Cortés and turn right 1 block to reach the town's lively market. Stand in line to have your shoes repaired on the spot, or buy anything from *piñatas* to funeral wreaths to Siamese kittens as well as more practical purchases. *Guayaberas Cab* (233 Zaragoza, between Arista and Serdán; phone: 328427) carries a nice selection of the pleated and embroidered shirts that have almost become a uniform for men in the tropics. *El Mayab* (Calle Zaragoza, just behind the Municipal Palace; phone: 321435) and *El Campechano* (Mariano Molina, between Independencia and Zaragoza; no phone) have good quality Panama hats, straw baskets, and the like.

SPORTS: If you want bullfighting and jai alai, visit the other parts of Mexico. The only spectator sport here is an occasional soccer game between amateur teams from different Mexican states. You can get information on when and where games are held from your hotel desk or the tourist office.

Fishing – For gulf fishing, rent boats and gear through the *Hostal de Cortés,* at the *malecón* and Xicoténcatl. You can go after perch, bass, shrimp, and clams at Mandinga, rent a boat at Catemaco, or do some river fishing at Boca del Río (see *Special Places*). An annual shad fishing tournament is held in April or May.

Golf – The 9-hole course at the *Club de Golf La Villa Rica* is open to the public. Km 1.5, on the road to Antón Lizardo.

Jogging – Join the locals for a run along the waterfront, from the *malecón* out to the beaches. Lots of folks do it, even at night.

Sailing – The *Amigos Regatta,* from Galveston to Veracruz, is held every 2 years. The next one will be this coming June.

Scuba Diving – There are five large reefs just off the coast of Veracruz: La Blanquilla, Anegadita de Adentro, Isla Verde, Pájaros, and an even larger area south of the city. *La Blanquilla* is Mexico's first national submarine park. *Tridente* (165-A Blvd. A. Camacho; phone: 327924) will arrange scuba diving trips. Ask at your hotel or the tourist office.

Swimming – Veracruz boasts several good beaches on the gulf: Villa del Mar, Hornos, Costa Verde, Mocambo, and Costa de Oro in Boca del Río (see *Special Places*).

Tennis – Most of the classier hotels have facilities, and 14 cement courts also are available at the *Las Palmas Racquet Club* in Mocambo (phone: 211970).

NIGHTCLUBS AND NIGHTLIFE: Some would say that Veracruz is at its very best after dark, starting with the street musicians who come out to entertain the crowds at the sidewalk cafés surrounding the Plaza de Armas. Favorite discos include *La Capilla* (*Prendes* hotel; phone: 310241), *Deus* (at Ruiz Cortines and Calle 22; phone: 372001), and *Climax* (Calz. Ruiz Cortines; no phone). *Moruchos* disco (*Emporio* hotel) is open Thursdays through Saturdays. Female impersonators perform at the *Hip Pop Potamus* in Costa Verde, and there's music, dancing, and a midnight show in the *Gaviota* bar of the *Veracruz* hotel (phone: 315134).

BEST IN TOWN

CHECKING IN: Veracruz has a fairly wide range of accommodations. Described here are several that could be rated as first class, some that are quite pleasant, and a few that are comfortable and will do since you won't be spending much time in your room anyway. Credit cards are accepted at all moderate and expensive restaurants and at all the hotels listed. Expect to pay about $60 per night for a double room in a hotel listed in the expensive range, about $40 to $50 in the moderate, and around $30 or less in the inexpensive range. All hotels accept MasterCard and Visa; those in the expensive category also accept American Express and Diners Club. All telephone numbers are in the 29 area code unless otherwise indicated. When calling from one city to another within Mexico, dial 91 before the area code.

Emporio – On the *malecón,* this comfortable hotel has 201 air conditioned rooms with large bathrooms (some suites have Jacuzzis), 1 indoor and 2 outdoor pools, a restaurant, a piano bar with a baby grand and wicker furniture, and a disco. 4 blocks east of the plaza at the *malecón* and Xicoténcatl (phone 320020 or 327520; FAX: 312261). Expensive.

Hostal de Cortés – Very attractive, with a mostly beige decor, it has 103 rooms and 5 suites, each with a color TV set and a fully stocked bar. There's also a pool, scuba, and fishing boat rentals. Across the street from the beach. Blvd. Avila Camacho, corner of De las Casas (phone: 320065; FAX: 315744). Expensive.

Mocambo – Set on the side of a hill overlooking Veracruz's best beach, the grande dame of local hotels has had an extensive face-lift. The 120 rooms are spacious, the grounds well kept, the room service excellent, and the terrace facing the ocean lovely. There is a good restaurant, a piano bar, a tennis court, a large outdoor swimming pool, 2 indoor pools, Jacuzzi, sauna, and satellite TV. 5 miles (8 km) south of town along the beach (phone: 371531 or 371660). Expensive.

Playa Paraíso – Small compared to the *Mocambo* and *Torremar* on either side of it, it's their equal in comfort and exclusivity, with sparkling white 3-story buildings, 41 villas and 34 suites, a restaurant, pool, and a fine beach. Boca del Río (phone: 378436; FAX: 378306). Expensive.

Torremar – The pride of Veracruz is this 176-room resort, formerly the *Hyatt,* a dark brown structure towering above Mocambo Beach which offers excellent service. A pool, a tennis court, and a fine restaurant are among the facilities. The cafeteria, however, is not recommended. 4300 Blvd. Ruiz Cortines, Boca del Río (phone: 352100; FAX: 210291). Expensive.

Puerto Bello Boulevard – Across the street from the beach, it has 110 spacious rooms, a delightful piano bar, a restaurant, coffee shops, and small pool. Don't confuse it with the less appealing *Puerto Bello* hotel on the *malecón.* 1263 Blvd. Avila Camacho (phone: 310011; FAX: 310867). Expensive to moderate.

Costa Sol – This beachfront place has 108 rooms as well as twenty 1- and 2-bedroom villas. There's a pool overlooking the beach, a pleasant dining room, and a lively bar. Rte. 180, corner of Ferrocarrill in Boca del Río (phone: 86002; FAX: 860364). Moderate.

Villa del Mar – Set on the beachfront a mile (1.6 km) from the plaza, it has 80 air conditioned rooms and 23 fan-cooled bungalows. Tennis, bar service, restaurant, and swing sets and garden in the back. Blvd. Avila Camacho (phone: 313366). Moderate.

Baluarte – An economical little place, with white balconies. It's across the street from the downtown fortress of the same name, and offers 73 rooms, restaurant, bar, air conditioning, and parking. The junior suites are larger and cost only a little more. 265 Calle Canal at Dieciséis de Septiembre (phone: 360844). Inexpensive.

Colonial – This well-maintained property right on the Plaza de Armas has 180 rooms (some with balconies), an indoor pool, a sidewalk café, and a large lobby. Some of the rooms are small; the junior suites are more expensive but also more spacious. The rooms overlooking the plaza are interesting but can be noisy; the crowds are out in full blast until midnight. 117 Miguel Lerdo (phone 320193). Inexpensive.

Prendes – Very popular and reasonably priced, right on the Plaza de Armas, with 34 air conditioned rooms, TV sets that get some US channels, a fine restaurant (see *Eating Out*), and a disco. Independencia and Lerdo (phone: 310241; FAX: 310366). Inexpensive.

Real del Mar – Offers 34 air conditioned rooms and a family atmosphere. 2707 Blvd. Avila Camacho (phone: 373634; FAX: 377078). Inexpensive.

EATING OUT: Veracruz's handful of notable restaurants serve fresh fish in an unpretentious atmosphere and at reasonable prices. *Nieve,* or ice cream, is excellent here, especially the stuff sold by vendors where Zamora dead-ends into Landera y Coss at the *malecón.* Try *mamey sandia,* in which the flavor of watermelon is even more intense than the fruit itself, *guanabana,* which is made from a tropical fruit, or the nutty *cacahuate.* For a full dinner, expect to pay about $35 for two people (excluding drinks, wine, or tips) at places listed here as expensive; $25 for moderate; $15 or less for inexpensive. Most restaurants accept MasterCard and Visa; some accept American Express. Reservations are unnecessary at all places. Unless otherwise noted, all restaurants are open daily. All telephone numbers are in the 29 area code unless otherwise indicated. When calling from one city to another within Mexico, dial 91 before the area code.

La Bamba – If you can't get enough seafood in this seafood town, here's another possibility. The house specialty is *cucaracha del mar* (don't ask what it means; just order it). On Camacho and Zapata, next to the yacht club (phone: 325355). Expensive.

El Gaucho – It's the best in town for steaks. Corner of Calle Colón and Bernal del Castillo (phone: 350411). Expensive.

Hostería Suiza – Excellent Central European cooking, including meat and cheese fondues. The chef once cooked for Maurice Chevalier, among other celebrities. Closed Mondays. Manuel Suárez between España and Estocolmo (phone: 379493). Expensive.

Prendes – The fresh seafood dishes and regional music here make this a local favorite. The *carne asada,* Mexican-style steaks prepared with sautéed vegetables, is also good. Opens around noon. Beneath the orange and white awnings of Plaza de Armas at Miguel Lerdo and Independencia (phone: 320153). Expensive.

Submarino Amarillo – The name translates as Yellow Submarine, but nautical phrasing notwithstanding, this is a steakhouse and, despite the unassuming decor, one of the best in Veracruz. Paseo del Malecón, corner of Rayón (phone: 361320). Expensive.

Garlic's – A very popular place, where the desserts are scrumptious but the seafood is only mediocre. Blvd. Avila Camacho (phone: 351034). Moderate.

Pardiño's Centro – The decor is basic, but the seafood here is exceptional, especially any dish served with *cangrejo* (crab). Portions are generous and the service is friendly. The terrace upstairs is not air conditioned, but it's a great place to watch the comings and goings on the *malecón.* Two locations: 146 Landero y Coss (phone: 314881) and 40 Guitiérrez Zamora in Boca del Río (phone: 860135). Moderate.

Winner's – Light, bright, and filled with plants, this spot specializes in grilled steaks, but fish and seafood are available, too. Midway to Mocambo at Bolívar and 23 de Noviembre (phone: 352517). Moderate.

La Parroquia – Like the proverbial Mexican bean, this place is always jumping. Stop in for a meal, a nightcap, or just a breather. The *media noches* ("midnights") — turkey, ham, and cheese sandwiches spiced with tomato sauce — are very good, as is the strong coffee. When diners tap their glasses, they aren't making a toast but hailing the waiter, bearing kettles of hot milk, to complete the *café con leche.* No credit cards accepted. On the Plaza de Armas (phone: 322584); another branch, less atmospheric, is on the *malecón* (phone: 321855). Moderate to inexpensive.

La Flecha – For a taste of classic *Veracruzana* cooking, lunch here on the delicious *róbalo* (sea bass) broiled and bathed in a lush sauce of tomatoes, garlic, green olives, chilies, capers, and sweet yellow peppers — or the *sopa de mariscos,* a fish stew brimming with the catch of the day. Closed Tuesdays. No credit cards accepted. Tlacotalpan, just south of Veracruz (phone: 288-42183). Inexpensive.

La Paella – Naturally, at this Spanish restaurant you'll want to try the paella — shellfish, chicken, and sausage served over rice. Open daily from 9 AM to 10 PM. On the plaza, at 138 Zamora (phone: 320322). Inexpensive.

Panaficadora Paris – Sweet rolls, cookies, even small whole wheat loaves line the shelves of this tempting bakery. Grab a tray and tongs, and dig in with the rest. No credit cards accepted. Av. Cinco de Mayo and Calle Mario Molina (phone: 321213). Inexpensive.

DIVERSIONS

DIVERSIONS

For the Experience

QUINTESSENTIAL MEXICO

Among other things, traveling south of the border doubtless has taught you that the real spirit of Mexico lies somewhere between the Maya and *mañana*. If you've tried on the requisite number of sombreros, admired the blossoms at Xochimilco, and haggled over a colorful serape, you've certainly scratched the surface. You may even have gone parasailing, mixed it up with a marlin, eaten an enchilada, and finally learned how to pronounce Zihautanejo. But, amigos, until you savor the places and pleasures listed below, you haven't experienced the true meaning of "Viva Mexico!"

WHALE WATCHING, Scammon's Lagoon, Guerrero Negro, B.C.S.: Every year the great gray whales journey 5,000 miles from the icy precincts of the Bering Sea to the warm, protected waters of Scammon's Lagoon, midway down the Baja Peninsula, where they mate, bear their young, and spend the winter, before returning north in the spring.

Wild creatures have always held a special fascination for man, yet few humans ever had the opportunity to observe them at leisure in their natural habitat. Fortunately, expedition organizers and conservation groups were able to convince the Mexican government that it was good business to cater to this fascination (and, at the same time, protect the animals), and this gave rise to another migration to Baja — by whale watchers.

Today, Scammon's Lagoon, and other protected areas stretching down to the southern tip of the Baja Peninsula, are designated wildlife refuges, and also serve as havens for sea lions, porpoises, and a wide variety of migrating shore and sea birds. With luck, it also may be possible to spot a humpback, fin, minke — and even a blue — whale from time to time. Calves swimming alongside their mothers are a common sight, and fortunate whale watchers may even catch a glimpse of one suckling the 50 gallons of milk each consumes every day.

Despite their tremendous size, whales seem genuinely friendly, hamming it up before an admiring public, as if they know their lives depend on it. Agile, graceful swimmers, they are able to propel their massive bodies up out of the water in a movement called "breaching," sending up huge sprays as they make their dramatic re-entry. Before setting out to sea again, the grays often give a flick of their flukes, as if waving good-bye.

The thrilling spectacle of these amazing creatures cavorting in the water can be seen from the last week in December through the first week in April from several spots along the shore, or from whale watching vessels that can be boarded in Guerrero Negro. Excursions are also available from Los Cabos. For information about naturalist-led tours to several whale watching sites, contact *Oceanic Society Expeditions,* Fort Mason Center, Building E, San Francisco, CA 94123 (phone: 415-441-1106).

BALLET FOLKLÓRICO DE MEXICO: In every Mexican town and village, music and dance express the soul of the people. Pre-Hispanic Mexican music, simple and almost hypnotic, was dominated by percussion and wind instruments, and was designed to accompany dances and religious rites; each of the many Indian cultures had its own dances and costumes. In spite of very forceful efforts by the conquistadores to stamp out all traces of indigenous cultures, music and dance survived, mainly because the Spanish clergy realized that these arts could be used as tools for recruiting the heathens into the church. The dances and music didn't really change; what changed was the name of the god to whom they were dedicated. Slowy, Spanish, French, and other European traditions found expression as part of this multicultural heritage. Even today, a church festival isn't considered complete without the performance of brilliantly clad folk dancers.

The credit for keeping the ancient dance alive goes to Mexico's *Ballet Folklórico*. Though they have their imitators, *this* troupe is the real thing. They perform Wednesday evenings at 9 PM and Sundays at 9:30 AM and 9 PM in the *Palace of Fine Arts* in Mexico City.

POPOCATÉPETL-IZTACCÍHUATL VOLCANOES, State of México: There was a time — not all that long ago — when the snow-covered peaks of these two volcanoes were a common, everyday sight in Mexico City. Now, on the few clear days of the year when they can be seen from the almost perpetually smog-blanketed capital, the awesome spectacle brings traffic to a halt on the busy *periférico*.

Popocatépetl ("Popo"), which rises to a height of 17,845 feet, last erupted in 1802. Iztaccíhuatl ("Izta"), only 550 feet shorter than its neighbor, also has been inactive for almost 2 centuries. Legend has it that the two volcanoes represent the love between an Aztec princess and a warrior. In exchange for the hand of his daughter, the king demanded that the warrior bring him the head of the most feared enemy of their people. But by the time the young swain returned with his prize, the princess had died of a broken heart. Grieving, he lay her body on a hill, knelt down, and remained in that position forever, watching over the eternal sleep of his beloved. The silhouette of Popo, whose full name means "smoking mountain," does resemble a kneeling man, and the outline of Izta, a sleeping woman.

From the town of Amecameca, a paved road leads to the Paso de Cortés and then to the Paso de Tlalmacas, the highest point on Popo accessible by car. It was at the Paso de Cortés that the Conquistadores crossed into Tenochtitlàn on their way from Veracruz on November 3, 1519, and where Cortés met with an envoy of Montezuma II — who tried to dissuade him from advancing on the Aztec capital. It was also from this place that the Spaniards first saw the valley of Anáhuac spread out before them, and Tenochtitlàn, which Bernal Díaz de Castillo described as seeming to float on the Lake of Texcoco, like a silver ship.

For an idea of what Cortés saw, take a look at the diorama of Tenochtitlàn in the *Templo Mayor Museum* in Mexico City before visiting Popo. To get to Popo from Mexico City, take Carretera 150 east 21 miles (33 km) toward Puebla, take the Chalco exit and continue 3½ miles (6 km) to the Amecameca-Chalco turnoff, and then follow Carretera 115 14 miles (22 km) to Amecameca.

CHICHÉN ITZÁ, Yucatán: When someone says that you haven't seen Mexico until you've been to the Yucatán, this is what it's all about. The most famous and complete of the ancient Maya cities, this site is a testament to their engineering genius. Here are temples, sacrificial wells, sacred ball courts, reclining idols, and the great El Castillo Pyramid. Stand and face El Castillo, which is topped by a temple to the feathered snake god, Quetzalcoatl; giant carved heads are at the base of the balustrade. The pyramid rises in a series of terraces, which cast shadows on the balustrade. Believe it or not, on the first day of spring and the first day of autumn, the undulating shadows form a serpent's body leading from the temple on top to the carved head on the bottom. It's worth planning your trip around the equinoxes!

DÍA DE LOS MUERTOS (DAY OF THE DEAD): Although Mexicans fear and respect death as much as any other peoples, they face it, defy it, mock it, and even toy with it more than most cultures. Never is this more apparent than on November 2, *All Souls' Day* — known in Mexico as the *Day of the Dead* — an eminently Mexican holiday perpetuating a tradition of death and rebirth.

By mid-October, bakeries and markets throughout Mexico are filled with sweets and toys created with death as their theme. Bake shops are piled high with *pan de muerto,* a coffee cake decorated with meringues fashioned into the shape of bones. Children, friends, and relatives are given colorful sugar skulls with their names inscribed on them; death figures shaped from marzipan are on sale at most sweets shops. Verses, called *calaveras,* containing witty allusions or epitaphs, are written about living friends, relatives, and public figures, and by the end of October, shop windows take on a macabre air, with shrouded marionettes, and other ghoulish-looking figurines heralding the holiday.

On the actual date, families gather in graveyards to picnic and spend the day with their departed, bringing along their loved ones' favorite foods and drink. Graves are decorated with bright orange *zempasuchil* (marigolds), the flower of the dead; *copal,* an incense that dates back to pre-Hispanic cultures, is burned. The celebration begins with prayers and chants for the dead, and usually ends with drinks to the health of the departed. Homes are decorated in much the same way, with tables filled with marigolds and objects of which the deceased was especially fond.

One of the most moving observances of this tradition is held on Janitzio Island in Lake Pátzcuaro. Here the ceremony begins on November 1, with the descendants of Tarasca Indians gathering on the lake at dawn for a ceremonial duck hunt. Using ancient Indian weapons, they paddle their canoes into a semicircle, trapping the ducks against the shore. At a signal from the leader of the hunt, the weapons are thrown. Shortly after midnight, the women make their way to the cemetery, laden with baskets of food — including traditional dishes of duck meat — incense, bouquets of *zempasuchil,* and thousands of candles, transforming the small graveyard behind the church of Janitzio Island into a glittering outdoor cathedral. As the women and children meditate at the gravesites and the church bells toll, the men begin the slow, steady, chants that they will continue through the night.

OAXACA, Oaxaca: If we had to choose just one place to represent the essence of Mexico, it would be the city of Oaxaca. Once the center of the Mixtec and Zapotec civilizations, the city is located in the southeastern part of the country, in a valley surrounded by the Sierra Madre del Sur.

Oaxaca itself is a colonial gem. The Church of Santo Domingo, founded by the Dominicans in 1570, is an exquisite example of baroque art, its interior walls covered with gold scrolls and polychrome reliefs set off by a white background. Sidewalk cafés under Spanish colonnades offer the perfect vantage point from which to view the lively to-ings and fro-ings of life around the Plaza de Armes. Oaxaca's *Benito Juarez Market* thrives and throbs year-round: the place where farmers, ranchers, and artisans come from neighboring towns and villages to display their wares. Covering several city blocks, the market is a mosaic of Indians in native dress; pyramids of beautifully displayed fruits and vegetables; an amazing variety of chocolate, chilies, beans, and moles; silvery black pottery from Coyotepec; filigree gold jewelry; fine wool serapes; pots and bowls and handicrafts; medicinal herbs; and even the mixings for magic love potions — with lots of advice thrown in free. And if you're lucky enough to be in Oaxaco during the *Christmas* season, be sure to join the festivities of the *Noche de los Rabanos* (Night of the Radishes): On December 23, the entire zocalo is set up with end-to-end booths, each one with a display of large, imaginatively carved radishes in the shapes of animals, buildings, plants, and just about anything else conceivable.

SANCTUARY OF THE MONARCH BUTTERFLY, Angangueo, Michoacán: Every year, hundreds of thousands of dazzling winged creatures, the monarch butterflies, make their annual migration from the cold climates of eastern Canada and the northern United States to certain areas in the states of Michoacán and México that were declared wildlife sanctuaries by the Mexican government in 1986. From December through March, monarchs blanket every inch of vegetation in a white-flecked, burnt-orange and black batik — one of the most visually stunning sights imaginable.

It's best to plan your visit for a weekday, when there are fewer crowds; try to get to the sanctuary by about 10 AM, because the monarchs wait for the warming rays of the sun to put on their spectacular show.

Reaching the butterflies is somewhat of a challenge. The sanctuary is located near the old mining town of Angangueo, midway between Mexico City and Morelia. We advise leaving your car in town and catching a ride on the back of one of the open-air trucks that make the dusty, hour-long trip up the eroded, unpaved road to the refuge. Overnight accommodations are available at the spa in San José Purúa, or in Zitàcuaro, which has a temperate climate, a few comfortable small hotels, but little else. *Turistoria* (114 Insurgentes Centro, Mexico, D.F.; phone: 5-592-8137 or 5-703-1544; FAX: 5-703-0391) offers several excursions to monarch sites each season. If you're planning an overnight stay, make reservations well in advance.

TEOTIHUACÁN, Mexico: Just 31 miles (50 km) northeast of Mexico City, it's possible to reach out, climb up, and touch history dating back to AD 400. This archaeological zone of pyramids, temples, and ancient ball courts covers more than 7 square miles, and once made up what was probably the first true city in central Mexico. Wandering around the Pyramid of the Sun (the largest one at the site) or the Pyramid of the Moon, conjures up visions of life that existed long before even the Aztec came to the valley. The spectacular Temple of Quetzalcoatl, the plumed serpent, puts you dead center in the midst of a mysterious ancient culture.

CHARREADA: Although there is evidence that horses once existed in the Americas, they had disappeared centuries before the arrival of the Spanish conquerors, who brought the first horses of Arabic origin to this continent. Though *charro* means "a man from the country" in Castillian Spanish, in Mexico it has come to denote a gentleman rider. Indeed, during the first decades of the colonial period, the use of horses was restricted to Europeans; Indians and *mestizos* could be put to death if caught riding. When more hands were neeeded to work the huge cattle ranches, however, the law was relaxed and the *criollos* and *mestizos* were allowed to ride. It's said that a true *charro* loves his horse at least as much as his wife — and probably respects it more.

Until *charrería* was formally organized in 1921 (it was declared a national sport in 1933), the sport was practiced spontaneously in cities and towns by groups of riders who wanted to improve and compare their skills. Today, most who participate in the events are professionals and businessmen who can afford to maintain their well-trained steeds and keep themselves outfitted in the costly costumes. The gala outfit, which has become a symbol of Mexico, consists of tight pants, a bolero jacket, and a wide-brimmed felt hat, all heavily adorned with silver. The saddle, bridle, and pistol are inlaid with silver, and sometimes gold.

Charreadas are especially popular in Jalisco and Mexico City, where they are practiced in rings called *lienzos* on Sunday mornings. The activities usually begin with an enthusiastic mariachi rendition of the "Zacatecas March," and the presentation of the competing teams. Riders then charge at full speed into the arena, bringing their mounts to an abrupt halt in the center of the ring. Other feats of horsemanship — lassoing, and the wrestling of steers and calves — are followed by the *paso de la muerte,* in which the rider leaps from his galloping mount onto the back of a wild horse. On special occasions, the exhibition includes a display of equestrian ballet called the *escaramuza.*

MARIACHI MUSIC: The melodies pervade all of Mexico. Groups of musicians roam the streets of cities large and small, serenading under the windows of apartment buildings and in the doorways of restaurants and shops. Students, carrying guitars and flutes on subways and buses, often play for their fellow passengers in hope of earning a few pesos on the way to and from school. Although every region of Mexico has its own special music, none is more associated with the country as a whole than mariachi (the word comes from the French for "marriage").

During Emperor Maximilian's reign, wealthy Guadalajara families, trying to imitate the customs of the court, hired musicians to entertain their guests. Today, mariachis — made up of at least one vocalist, a guitar, bass, violin, and a trumpet or two — are usually hired to serenade girlfriends or to play at special events (weddings, birthdays, anniversaries). Their vast repertoire consists of such sentimental love songs as "Si Estas Dormida," "Las Mañanitas" (the Mexican equivalent of "Happy Birthday," but sung for almost any special occasion), "Guadalajara," "La Bamba," or "Cucurrucucu Paloma." The traditional Mexican fiestas frequently held at large resort hotels normally include at least one group of mariachis, and any sizable town will have a few restaurants and bars where they provide the entertainment. Some of the best mariachis — dressed in their close-fitting pants, a pistol hanging from the belt, a bolero-type jacket decorated with silver, and a wide-brimmed hat — congregate on the Plaza de los Mariachis in Guadalajara and at Garibaldi Plaza in Mexico City.

DIVING IN COZUMEL: For those who can't resist crystal clear water and being near the second-longest reef in the world (Palancar Reef), this island just 12 miles off the Caribbean coast is the spot. Schools of tropical fish and a rainbow of coral deposits prove irresistible to diving enthusiasts — particularly from May through August. This is as good as the underwater world gets in this hemisphere.

COPPER CANYON, Chihuahua: The *Chihuahua-Pacífico Railway*, an extraordinary feat of engineering that travels 420 miles through 80 tunnels and over 30 bridges, was begun in 1903, but wasn't officially inaugurated until 1961. A trip along this route combines awesome natural beauty with a fascinating ethnological experience: The giant canyons of the Tarahumara mountain range are home to some 50,000 Tarahumara, the most primitive Indians still living in North America.

The approximately 12-hour trip from Chihuahua (on the Texas border) to Los Mochis (on the Pacific Ocean), or vice versa, can be made in a single day, with short stops along the way to enjoy the views. But it is best to leave enough time to spend a night or two in rustic comfort at one or more of the stops along the route. Starting from Chihuahua, the train winds its way west to Creel, an almost abandoned mining town where the few remaining inhabitants eke out a living today from timber from the Sierra Madre. From Creel, excursions go to Lake Arareco, the Cusárare Falls, and the now-abandoned Batopilas mine, situated in the depths of the canyon. Thirty-seven miles (59 km) beyond Creel the train arrives in Divisadero, where it stops just long enough for passengers to capture — personally and on film — the unforgettable views of the Copper Canyon and the deep gorges of the Tararecua, with its amazing variations of color. The final stop before the descent to Los Mochis, located in the heart of some of Mexico's richest farming country, is Bahuichivo, with overnight possibilities in Cerocahui (about a 40-minute bus ride away), at the very edge of the Urique Canyon.

MUSEUM OF ANTHROPOLOGY, Mexico City: Carved into a wall of Mexico City's *Museum of Anthropology* is the "Song of Huexotzingo," a lament composed by the Aztec after the Spanish conquest of Tenochtitlán.

> *Will I leave only this*
> *Like the flowers that wither?*
> *Will nothing last in my name*
> *Nothing of my fame here on earth?*
> *At least flowers! At least songs!*

The museum itself is a fitting answer to these poignant questions. Created by architect Pedro Ramirez Vazquez to house an unparalleled collection of archaeological treasures representing all the pre-Hispanic cultures of Mesoamerica, these magnificent buildings combine metals and concrete with marble, wood, stone, and open spaces, to capture the grandeur of an Aztec temple. The museum's core is a huge patio sheltered by an immense aluminum umbrella-like structure that is supported by a single column, covered in reliefs and sheathed by a cylinder of water. The surrounding galleries, which are interconnected but open onto the central patio, contain murals by some of Mexico's most renowned artists, and are a fitting showcase for the splendor of Mexico's past.

MOLE: To an uninformed gringo reading a Mexican menu, an entrée of turkey mole conjures up visions of a drumstick topped with hot fudge. Nothing could be further from reality. The word mole comes from the Nahuatl "mulli," which means sauce — and this one is made of more than 30 ingredients — only *one* of which is unsweetened chocolate. Most Mexican housewives pride themselves on preparing the sauce from scratch, a time-consuming recipe that involves at least four kinds of chilies (which have to be seeded, deveined, and roasted), sesame seeds, almonds, peanuts, raisins, prunes, plaintains, onions, garlic, coriander, anise, cinammon, and an infinitesimal amount of the aforementioned chocolate. Traditionally, it is served with chicken or turkey, as a filling for tamales, or as a sauce for enchiladas. If you are served mole in a Mexican household, you know you're an honored guest. If a private invitation isn't forthcoming, order it at the *Hacienda de los Morales*, 525 Calle Vazques de Mella, Mexico City.

DIEGO RIVERA MURALS IN THE NATIONAL PALACE, Mexico City: In their zeal to convert the indigenous population to Catholicism after their conquest of Mexico, the Spanish destroyed almost every manifestation of pre-Hispanic culture. During the 300 years after the conquest, the arts were dominated by Catholic Spain and later, in the 19th century, by France and England, although traces of Indian cultures managed to survive among the masses. But the Revolution of 1910 inspired a cultural revolution as well, and during that time, Mexican mural art was born.

Led by Diego Rivera, Mexican artists developed a unique style that was, in part, inspired by the country's folk art and its pre-Hispanic roots. They utilized this medium to illustrate the country's history of violence and social repression, as well as to expose its contemporary political and social problems. Only two kinds of people were shown: the good (the Indians and the workers) and the evil (the Spanish conquerors — especially Cortés — the church, and the rich and powerful). Rivera's brilliant murals, covering the walls of the stairway in the central patio of the National Palace, depict the history of Mexico from the pre-Hispanic era until 1929. Cauhtemoc is shown as an idealized youth; Cortés as a demented syphilitic. The mural on the north wall represents Rivera's vision of pre-Hispanic life. Those on the west wall show scenes from colonial life — slavery; the inquisition; the evangelizing of Catholic priests; the intervention of France and the United States; the dictatorship of Porfirio Díaz; Santa Anna; Reform; Independence; and, finally, the 1910 Revolution. A huge portrait of Karl Marx, Rivera's idol and hope for the future, dominates the south wall.

SUNSETS ON THE PACIFIC: Prime plaudits for the most spectacular sunset south of the border go to Playa del Amor (Lover's Beach) at Land's End on the tip of the Baja peninsula, where the Sea of Cortés meets the Pacific and seems to divide the sky into a rose gray on one side and a robin's egg blue on the other. Sundown at Pie de la Cuesta and Barra Vieja beaches in Acapulco, or from Conchas Chinas Beach in Puerto Vallarta, are also quite impressive. Just pick a spot, pull up a chair, sip from your margarita, and watch the sun set — you may feel that you've just had a glimpse of heaven.

Mexico's Best Resort Hotels

 Whether your idea of a resort is a place to bake elegantly under the tropical sun, with no greater exertion than raising your wrist to sip a tall, cool drink (remember that the now-famous "swim-up" bar was invented in Mexico, at Acapulco's *Villa Vera*), or whether you prefer a haven that inspires you to play tennis and golf in the morning, go boating or riding in the afternoon, and dance all night, Mexico has a spot that's absolutely perfect.

The major resort areas are Acapulco, Puerto Vallarta, Mazatlán, Ixtapa-Zihuatanejo, and Manzanillo on the Pacific coast; La Paz on Baja's Sea of Cortés coast; Cabo San Lucas at the tip of the Baja Peninsula; Cozumel, Cancún, and Isla Mujeres on the Caribbean; and Valle de Bravo and a few other inland spots near major Mexican lakes.

Prices vary significantly according to area of the country, location within the area (in town or on the beach), reputation, season, and meal plan, but first class Mexican resorts are almost always less expensive than their Caribbean or Hawaiian counterparts. Puerto Vallarta and Cancún usually offer (often require) that hotel guests agree to the Modified American Plan (MAP: That is, during the high season, breakfast and lunch or dinner are eaten at the hotel every day — or at least paid for). During the off-season, guests can usually choose between meal plans or rent rooms without any requirement to take meals at their hotel.

The peak season for most of the coastal resorts is from December 15 through April 15. Those who travel during the off-season (approximately April 15 to December 15) normally can save from 40% to 80% on accommodations. The temperature may be a bit hotter and the crowd a bit less chic, but there will be fewer people, and the lower rates may permit an increase in the level of hotel luxury and the length of stay.

BAJA PENINSULA

TWIN DOLPHIN, Cabo San Lucas: Has established itself as the classiest all-round (not just with the traditional Cabo fishing crowd) operation in the area. It is the pet project of American oil millionaire and ecologist (thus the "dolphin" theme) David Halliburton, who limited its size to 56 rooms and suites, all of which have an ocean view and private balcony. There is a big pool with a swim-up bar, a pretty (if not very good) beach, 2 lighted tennis courts, an 18-hole putting green (honest), and deep-sea fishing boats. Most of the hotel's food is imported from the US, and meals are just fine. Not a swinging place, but relaxing luxury in a fairly remote spot. About 20 miles (32 km) from the Cabo San Lucas airport, which has direct jet service from several US cities. Cabo San Lucas, Baja California Sur (no local phone; 213-386-3940 in California; 800-421-8925 elsewhere in the US; FAX: 684-30139).

CARIBBEAN COAST

CAMINO REAL, Cancún: A dramatic beachfront hotel with 381 air conditioned rooms and suites, all with Caribbean views, private lanais, and hammocks. There is a freshwater pool and a saltwater lagoon as well. There are tennis courts and all water sports. A big, beautiful place that's run by the Westin chain and clearly one of the best around. *Mailing address:* Apdo. 14, Zona Hotelera, Cancún, Quintana Roo 77500 (phone: 988-30100; Westin Hotels, 800-228-3000; Leading Hotels of the World, 800-223-6800; or 212-838-3110 in New York City).

STOUFFER PRESIDENTE COZUMEL: The larger of two islands off the tip of the Yucatán Peninsula, the Maya "Land of the Swallows" has many intriguing archaeological sites, beaches, and lagoons. This is one of the best hotels in the sophisticated, lively resort area, and has a pool, private beach, 2 bars, shops, tennis, and 246 rooms and 7 suites. On Costa Residencial, south of San Miguel, the only major town on the island, near the Chankanab Lagoon and Palancar Reef (both fine places to skin dive). Carr. Chankanab Km 6.5, Cozumel, Quintana Roo 77600 (phone: 987-20322; in the US, 800-HOTELS-1).

INLAND

EL TAPATÍO, Guadalajara: High on a hillside outside Guadalajara, Mexico's second-largest city, this may be the most complete resort hotel in inland Mexico. Its 207 rooms are spread over spacious grounds, and each contains a stocked refrigerator and has a private balcony. There is a big pool, fine tennis on 10 clay courts (the tennis package, with instruction, may be the best in Mexico), horseback riding (20 stables), and and a new spa offering a variety of treatments. Golf is played on a nearby course. *Mailing address:* 4275 Blvd. Aeropuerto, Apdo. 1-2953, Guadalajara, Jalisco 44100 (phone: 36-356050; in the US, 800-431-2822).

CAMINO REAL, Mexico City: A true resort hotel, even though it is in the middle of the most crowded city in the world. There are gardens, 3 pools, a spa and racquet club, and even rooftop tennis to go along with numerous restaurants (including a branch of *Fouquet's* of Paris), bars, and nightspots. Its 716 rooms have an impeccable location next to Chapultepec Park, a few blocks from the Paseo de la Reforma, the city's main avenue. A complete, self-contained gem. *Mailing address:* 700 Av. Mariano Escobedo, México, DF 11590 (phone: 5-203-2121; in New York City, 212-838-3110; Westin Hotels, 800-228-3000; or Leading Hotels of the World, 800-223-6800).

HACIENDA COCOYOC, Morelos: Built in 1520, this 314-room hacienda has been beautifully restored and furnished with Spanish colonial pieces. There's a 9-hole golf course and an enormous swimming pool, framed by a historic stone aqueduct and a waterfall. It's 48 miles (77 km) from the heart of Mexico City. *Mailing address:* Centro Comercial Relox-Local 44, 2374 Insurgentes Sur, México, DF 0100 (phone: 5-550-6480 or 5-555-06480; in Cocoyoc, 735-62211).

PACIFIC COAST

ACAPULCO PRINCESS, Acapulco: This comprehensive resort cost more than $40 million to build. The exterior of the main building resembles that of an Aztec pyramid; the interior looks like a movie set, complete with floral hangings and ample marble. Among the props are a championship golf course, air conditioned indoor tennis courts, outdoor tennis courts, 7 restaurants, a discotheque, a nightclub, 5 swimming pools, 1,100 rooms — even a bar under a waterfall. The traffic can get a bit hectic between lobby and lounge, but it's well run. On Revolcadero Beach, about 12 miles (19 km) out of town on the airport highway. *Mailing address:* Apdo. 1351, Acapulco, Guerrero 39300 (phone: 748-43100 or Princess Hotels, 800-223-1818).

LAS BRISAS, Acapulco: Just about the best resort address in Mexico for more than 3 decades, this pink hillside hideaway is among the most luxurious hotels anywhere. Three hundred semi-connected or solitary casitas and ten 4- to 6-bedroom villas climb up the 750 acres of *Las Brisas*'s posh mountainside. There are 250 pools (shared and private), 150 pink-and-white-striped jeeps available for rent, and 5 lighted tennis courts. Continuous jeep service brings guests down to the private seaside *La Concha Beach Club;* the view from the *Bella Vista* restaurant atop the mountain is among the most romantic in the world. The emphasis is on privacy and the recharging of human batteries. Continental breakfast is discreetly delivered each morning, there is fresh fruit every day, jeep-borne room service (some guests prefer never to leave their casitas), and fresh flowers floating in the pools. Possibly the planet's most perfect honeymoon address. *Mailing address:* Carr. Escénica, Apdo. 281, Acapulco, Guerrero 39868 (phone: 748-41580 or Westin Hotels, 800-228-3000).

PIERRE MARQUÉS, Acapulco: The brother resort of the *Princess,* this prince is the real royalty of the twosome. Originally built by J. Paul Getty, it is bordered by a palm-fringed golf course on one side and the Pacific on the other. It has gardens, terraces, lawns with bungalows, restaurants, bars, 3 swimming pools, water sports and fishing gear, tennis, golf, and shopping — and if that's not enough, there are the more frantic facilities at the adjacent *Princess,* too. Surprisingly elegant and discreet 344 rooms, junior suites, and villas. *Mailing address:* Apdo. 474, Acapulco, Guerrero 39300 (phone: 748-42000 or through Princess Hotels, 800-223-1818).

CAMINO REAL, Ixtapa: This modern, $63-million resort, in another area chosen by a computer with good taste, has a climate that rarely varies from 80F, acres of palm trees and tropical flowers, and 24 miles of beach. The 428-room hotel's decor was inspired by neighboring coconut plantations. An 18-hole Robert Trent Jones, Jr. golf course is minutes away, and 4 lighted tennis courts are near a complex of multilevel pools and waterfalls. Zihuatanejo, a fishing village with cobblestone streets and outdoor cafés, is 10 minutes away. *Mailing address:* Apdo. 97, Ixtapa, Guerrero 40880 (phone: 753-32121 or Westin Hotels, 800-228-3000).

LAS HADAS, Manzanillo: The creation of the late Antenor Patiño, once the Bolivian "Tin King," is a cross between a Moorish fantasy and a *Disneyland* set. The buildings originally cost more than $25 million. The 220 rooms include junior suites, suites, and master suites, all air conditioned. The beach is lovely, but for those who prefer fresh water, there is 1 huge pool and 2 smaller ones. Tennis courts, a fine golf course, and most water sports facilities are on the grounds. Westin management — it runs *Las Brisas* in Acapulco — has spent millions upgrading the physical facilities. About 20 minutes from Manzanillo and 30 minutes from the airport, on Rincón Las Hadas and Península de Santiago. *Mailing address:* Apdo. 158, Manzanillo, Colima 28200 (phone: 333-30000; 212-838-3110 in New York City; Westin Hotels, 800-228-3000; or Leading Hotels of the World, 800-223-6800).

CAMINO REAL, Mazatlán: Mazatlán is a special place for those who love the sea, and the *Camino Real* is a special place for those who love Mazatlán. On a small hill overlooking Sábalo Beach, the 170-room hotel has 2 restaurants, bars, beach club, shops, tennis, terraces, and class. The management has information on the best places to fish, on bullfights and *charreadas,* on where to rent boats to go to Maimero Lagoon or into the deeper parts of the Pacific for deep-sea fishing, on surfing, duck hunting, or anything else. A good time to visit is just before *Ash Wednesday,* which is *Carnaval* in Mazatlán — be sure to make reservations far in advance. Some 7½ miles (12 km) northwest of Mazatlán. *Mailing address:* Apdo. 538, Punta del Sábalo, Mazatlán, Sinaloa 82100 (phone: 698-31111 or Westin Hotels, 800-228-3000).

CAMINO REAL, Puerto Vallarta: Here is an attractive 337-room high-rise on its own private cove. Five top-floor suites each have a private pool. There's a fine beach, water sports, tennis, a health club, and a great Mexican fiesta weekly. Playa de las Estacas. *Mailing address:* Apdo. 95, Puerto Vallarta, Jalisco 48300 (phone: 322-30123; Westin Hotels, 800-228-3000).

GARZA BLANCA CLUB DE PLAYA, Puerto Vallarta: A secluded, exclusive beach enclave with 95 units, including split-level, 1-bedroom chalets with private pools perched on a cliffside, and beach-level suites. All have air conditioning, living room, and bedroom. There is tennis, golf (at *Los Flamingos* golf links), and water sports. Playa Palo María. *Mailing address:* Apdo. 58, Puerto Vallarta, Jalisco 48300 (phone: 322-21023/83).

KRYSTAL VALLARTA, Puerto Vallarta: Set in one of Mexico's most sophisticated resort areas, this quiet and secluded hacienda-style hostelry has reason to be more popular than ever since the completion of a 3-year, $20-million renovation in late 1989. There are now 460 rooms, suites, and villas, most with clay tile floors and whitewashed walls. All rooms have air conditioning, satellite color TV, and mini-bars. Other additions include a huge lobby bar with live Mexican music (and dancing if you wish), along with 44 pools (including 38 that are private), 3 children's pools, and the impressive Seven Columns pool with fountains, waterfalls, and a swim-up bar. Sunsets at the Seven Columns are truly special, particularly when followed by a romantic stroll along the hotel's gaslit cobblestone walkways. Two clay tennis courts, water skiing, scuba diving, horseback riding, and parasailing are available for sports enthusiasts. Each guest has a personal *palapa* (small thatch-roofed hut) on the beach. There are 7 restaurants (see "Eating Out" in *Puerto Vallarta,* THE CITIES) and *Christine's* disco, which draws an eager, young crowd. In the evening the hotel hosts the popular *Fiesta Mexicana* and *Fiesta Brava* (see "Nightclubs and Nightlife" in *Puerto Vallarta,* THE CITIES). On the beach, 2 miles (3 km) from town and 2 miles (3 km) from the airport. Av. de las Garzas, Puerto Vallarta, Jalisco 48300 (phone: 322-21459, 322-21378, or 322-21041).

Spa-Hopping Special

 Montezuma, the 16th-century Aztec emperor, was one of Mexico's earliest spa enthusiasts. In fact, three of the mineral baths that Montezuma visited — in Tehuacán, Ixtapán de la Sal, and Oaxtepec — are still in use today. A number of Mexican spas (*balnearios*) are true resorts, with swimming, tennis, horseback riding, and hiking available. Spas with these facilities are the most expensive. Others are mainly places to "take the waters," either outside in natural mineral springs or inside in spring-fed pools.

As more Americans discover the pleasures and benefits of mineral baths, the number of spas continues to grow. And Mexico's spa potential is formidable — there are more than 570 known warm-water mineral springs in the country.

Most mineral waters contain a mixture of sulfate of soda, sulfate of lime, carbonate of lime, sodium chloride, magnesium, and some sulfuric acid. This may not sound appetizing, and it certainly doesn't look appetizing (the mineral waters are usually a murky brown color), but for most people the waters are amazingly soothing.

Most of Mexico's spas are in the states of Aguascalientes (meaning hot waters), Guanajuato, Michoacán, Morelos, Puebla, Querétaro, San Luis Potosí, Jalisco, Sinaloa, and México.

BAJA CALIFORNIA

RANCHO LA PUERTA, Tecate: Some 52 miles (83 km) southeast of San Diego, this health and fitness resort has been operating for more than 50 years. The spa, on a 150-acre mountain site, has pools, tennis courts, gyms, a jogging track, hiking trails, and offers about 30 different exercise classes daily. It does not have mineral or thermal waters. Reservations should be made at least 6 months in advance, particularly for the popular spring, fall, and holiday periods. *Mailing address:* PO Box 2548, Escondido, CA 92025 (phone: 619-744-4222).

GUANAJUATO

SPA LA CALDERA, Abasolo: This resort on the Guadalajara–Mexico City route, 19 miles (30 km) from Irapuato, has 117 rooms (including a newer 80-room unit), a restaurant, bar, movies, gardens, outdoor thermal pools, 4 tennis courts, Jacuzzi, toboggan, and other sports facilities. Libramiento Carr. Abasolo Km 29, Abasolo, Guanajuato 36970 (phone: 469-30020).

BALNEARIO COMANJILLA, Comanjilla: About 18 miles (29 km) from León (235 miles/376 km northwest of Mexico City), this restful, pleasant spa has 3 outdoor pools, 124 rooms (each with its own thermal bath), horseback riding, restaurant, bar, movies, steam rooms, and a playground. The León Airport is an hour's flight from Mexico City, and transportation from the airport to the spa (15 minutes away) is complimentary. 45 Carr. Panamericana, Km 387. *Mailing address:* Apdo. 111, León, Guanajuato (phone: 471-20091).

BALNEARIO HACIENDA TABOADA, San Miguel de Allende: A lovely resort with swimming pools, thermal baths, horseback riding, tennis, and badminton, it's 6 miles (10 km) from town on Rte. 51, Carr. Dolores Hidalgo, Km 8. *Mailing address:* Apdo. 100, San Miguel de Allende, Guanajuato 37700; phone: 465-20888).

PARADOR DEL CORTIJO, San Miguel de Allende: Smaller and less costly than the *Balneario Hacienda Taboada* (see above), it's delightful with just 19 rooms, thermal waters, 2 pools, and a good restaurant. American Plan. Km 9 Carr. San Miguel-Dolores Hidalgo. *Mailing address:* Apdo. 585, San Miguel de Allende, Guanajuato 37700 (phone: 465-20850).

MÉXICO

IXTAPÁN, Ixtapán de la Sal: This longtime favorite hotel has thermal and freshwater pools, Roman baths, tennis, private pools, old-fashioned Swedish massage, a large beauty clinic and spa, movies, playground, horseback riding, a 9-hole golf course, and 250 junior and master suites and chalets. No credit cards, but the hotel does accept personal and traveler's checks. *Mailing address:* Ixtapán de la Sal, State of Mexico 51900 (phone: 724-30304); in the US, contact *E & M Associates* (phone: 800-223-9832; in New York State, 212-599-8280). *Balneario Nuevo Ixtapán,* public baths, belongs to the owner of the *Ixtapán* and offers thermal pools and a scenic train ride through beautiful gardens. Avoid weekends, when it is very crowded.

MICHOACÁN

BALNEARIO SAN JOSÉ PURÚA, San José Purúa-Zitácuaro: Probably the most famous spa resort in Mexico, it is located in the same area where the film *Treasure of Sierra Madre* was shot. The spa, which has 250 units set in a garden on the edge of a canyon, is almost bigger than the entire town of San José Purúa. Many of the rooms have their own private mineral baths. There are also 4 thermal-water pools, bowling, billiards, miniature golf, and restaurants. *For reservations:* 27 Colón and Paseo de la Reforma, México, DF. *Mailing address:* Apdo. 46, c.p. 61500, Zitácuaro, Michoacán. The hot springs, 4 miles (6 km) from town, may be reached via San José Purúa public transportation (phone: 725-31544 or 725-31455; when dialing from another city in Mexico, you must ask for operator assistance; in Mexico City, 5-510-4949).

MORELOS

OAXTEPEC VACATION CENTER, Oaxtepec: Once a favorite retreat of Montezuma, the site is now a Mexican Social Security Institute–sponsored spa, with accomodations for up to 2,300 people, swimming pools, playgrounds, athletic fields, and restaurants. It does not have mineral or thermal waters. It is 35 miles (56 km) east of Cuernavaca, near Cuautla, another mineral town. It's worth a visit, but never on Sundays or holidays, which is when most Mexicans arrive. *Mailing address:* Apdo. 153, Oaxtepec, Morelos 62738 (phone: 735-21960).

VEGETARIAN SPAS

Vegetarian resorts that combine thermal mineral springs, spa, and a diet center have become popular in Mexico. *Rancho Río Caliente,* at 5,100 feet in Río Caliente, an hour from Guadalajara, is run by Caroline Durston and has 3 pools fed by hot mineral springs, 1 cold-water pool, massages, facials, mud baths, scalp reflexology, yoga instruction, good food (much of it homegrown), and fireplaces in every room. In Guadalajara, call 36-157800; in the US, contact *Barbara Dane Associates* (480 California Terr., Pasadena, CA 91105; phone: 818-796-5577). The *Villa Vegetariana,* on the old Cuernavaca Highway in Morelos, emphasizes weight reduction and fasting cures. *Mailing address:* 114 Pino, Apdo. 1228, Sta. María Ahuacatitlán, Cuernavaca, Morelos 62508 (phone: 73-131044).

Evocative Small Hotels

The very best Mexican inns — usually called *posadas* — are a happy blend of Old World charm and New World plumbing. Not only do these small hostelries project the best of genuine Mexican ambience, but they fill a real need since most can be found on Mexico's great interior plateau, where the other pickings can be pretty slim when it comes to first class accommodations.

It is, therefore, fortunate that this area has a substantial number of colonial residences and public buildings. It is from this centuries-old reservoir that the best of the current crop of Mexican inns have emerged — although some are relatively new and have been constructed to imitate the Federal style of the colonial period or the traditional hacienda houses. The historic function of these structures explains why so many of them currently flourish in the center of their towns — occasionally right on or next to the town square — rather than being lost on some secluded country lane, as is the case with most comparable European inns.

Mexican inns also differ from their European counterparts in that they tend to depend more on location and romantic appeal than true elegance, service, or haute cuisine. That doesn't mean it's impossible to find a posada that rivals a fine *relais* — some are listed below — just that not every posada deserves three Michelin stars.

Many of these special inns can be found along the so-called Colonial Route, the mountainous corridor between Mexico City and Guadalajara. The inns on this trail (where altitudes range from approximately 5,000 to over 7,000 feet) require appropriate clothing; during the dry winter season it's desirable to carry clothes that protect you from the cool night air, for wood-burning fireplaces may provide the only heat in your bedroom at night. It's advisable to be prepared for the wet summer season as well.

Remember, too, that these inns may bear only passing relation to the modern conveniences of the many Mexican hotels that more regularly cater to masses of tourists. So if your taste runs to chrome-lined coffee shops and beauty salons, the inns that follow are not likely to make you feel very comfortable. And even under the most favorable circumstances, arranging accommodations at these inns requires a fair amount of advance planning, though the ultimate enjoyment is well worth the extra effort. Ideally, it's best to sample several of the places on our list, and hiring a driver (a relatively inexpensive undertaking in Mexico) is probably the best way to get from town to town.

We strongly suggest *not* driving yourself unless you are fluent in Spanish and undaunted by the often frightening Mexican driving attitudes. In most cases, the driving time will be no more than 3 or 4 hours between inns, and visiting several of these hostelries can produce a holiday adventure of a week or so that will immerse you in more of the real Mexico than you could find in several months spent in some beachside high-rise on either Mexican coast.

One last cautious suggestion: To be on the safe side, buy a large bottle of purified spring water in a supermarket before heading off on your journey. Many posadas do not provide bottled water in their rooms, and having your own potable is just a basic precaution to insure intestinal security.

HOTEL DE CORTÉS, Mexico City: Few would expect to find an inn as small, charming, tranquil — even romantic — as this in the center of one of the world's largest cities. But this jewel is right on Alameda Park, 1 block from the *Palace of Fine Arts* and 6 blocks from the city's main square. Perhaps even more surprising is that the 19-room, 8-suite hotel is housed in a baroque structure that was built in 1780 as an Augustine monastery and is now an official national monument. It has functioned as a hotel since 1943.

From the beginning, most of the guests have been drawn to the comfortable antiquity. Its rather somber exterior has a crumbling sculpture of St. Augustine as the sole relief on its fortress-like façade. But inside, beyond the registration desk, a spacious, plant-filled courtyard (with a small stone fountain at the center) opens grandly to set the tone of the place. This courtyard is surrounded by 2 stories of rooms with high ceilings and massive wood beams. They are simply but tastefully furnished, usually including fresh flowers. The walls, which are a full meter thick, effectively shelter guests from Mexico City's otherwise inescapable traffic noises.

Meals are served at umbrella-shaded tables set all around the courtyard, or, when the weather is uncooperative, inside a small, cheery dining room dominated by two huge paintings. Meals are a special treat and the kitchen has a reputation good enough to attract even fussy Mexico City businesspeople for lunch. The same exceptional cuisine is served by candlelight in the evening to the accompaniment of live music; Saturday evenings there is an elaborate fiesta. *Mailing address:* 85 Av. Hidalgo, México, DF 06030 (phone: 5-518-2181).

HOSTERÍA LAS QUINTAS, Cuernavaca: This cozy place provides a relaxed atmosphere amid the flower-filled city said to have been chosen by Hernán Cortés for his retirement. (He never made it, although his restored palace — now a museum — still stands in the city's main square.) There are 2 swimming pools, an excellent restaurant with bar service, beautiful gardens, and a lovely display of bonsai trees, for which it is well known.

The building was originally a private home but has been operating as a hotel since 1967; the suite section was added in about 1972. In addition to the hotel's 15 rooms, there are 33 suites, 11 with fireplaces, and all with private terraces overlooking a garden. It is wise to book well ahead for the busy winter months (December through *Easter*), when many Americans are in residence. *Mailing address:* 107 Av. Las Quintas, Cuernavaca, Morelos 62440 (phone: 73-183949).

LAS MAÑANITAS, Cuernavaca: Perhaps the most popular single inn in Mexico, hugely successful almost from the moment American Bob Krause opened its doors on November 19, 1955. His widow, Margot, now owns the inn; Ruben Cerda is the manager. In the winter, it's nearly impossible to get a room unless reservations have been made well in advance, and it may even be difficult to get a table for lunch or dinner, since *Las Mañanitas* ("'the little mornings") also happens to have the best restaurant in Cuernavaca. During high season, guests tend to stay for weeks, even months, and there are only 4 double rooms, 17 magnificent 1-bedroom suites, and 1 rather astonishing 2-bedroom suite to go around.

This inn was constructed slowly, with the original turn-of-the-century mansion as its center and units added carefully and selectively over the years. Each room is different, each finished with architectural elements salvaged from old houses in Puebla and furnished with real antiques and artful bogus pieces. Each room also has its own private patio or terrace, and suites in the older section also have individual fireplaces.

This hostelry can compete with the finest in Europe (it's a Relais & Châteaux member), a refined hideaway and true refuge. There is the fine kitchen, the impressive heritage, fine art (the garden is sprinkled with Francisco Zuñiga bronzes), live music, alfresco dining, alert service from a staff of more than 100 (at an inn that sleeps perhaps only 45 guests!), and an air of simple but genuine luxury. No credit cards accepted. *Mailing address:* 107 Ricardo Linares, Apdo. 1202, Cuernavaca, Morelos 62000 (phone: 73-124646).

CASA DE SIERRA NEVADA, San Miguel de Allende: In just a few years, a building that dates from 1735 and had previously been an archbishop's residence has become the best posada by far in historic San Miguel de Allende, and in 1982 it became the first Latin American hotel to be admitted to the prestigious Relais & Châteaux hotel group. This small artistic town, set about 6,000 feet above sea level, was one of Mexico's first colonial cities (1542) and a key center of the early-19th-century revolution for independence from Spain.

Now there are 14 suites and 4 rooms in the main building, and the rest are in 2 other structures across the street. Each room has its own individual decor and furnishings, but all are spacious, with high ceilings, and full of antiques. Most have at least 1 fireplace, some have 2 baths, and most have telephones.

The *Sierra Nevada*'s best feature is its dining room. The dining area itself is narrow and long, at once charming, homey, and a bit formal. The food is international without being fussy, and there are surprises like homemade pasta. Guests may use the tennis courts, swimming pool, and 9-hole golf course at the *Malanquin Country Club.* A boutique, *Primavera,* sells one-of-a-kind items chosen by Maria Celis, the owner's wife. A health and beauty clinic is also on the premises. No credit cards; personal checks accepted with prior arrangement. *Mailing address:* 35 Calle Hospicio, Apdo. 226, San Miguel de Allende, Guanajuato 37700 (phone: 465-20415; FAX: 465-22337).

MESÓN DE SANTA ROSA, Querétaro: Originally built as a hostel for visitors from the countryside, it later was turned into a market. It was the idea of former governor Rafael Camacho and Dr. Zavier Barbosa, a well-known San Miguel de Allende resident, to convert the structure to an all-suite hotel, a masterpiece of elegance and colonial restoration work. There are 20 units, an excellent restaurant, 3 patios, and a swimming pool. The hotel is on Querétaro's main plaza, which has been declared a national landmark and is closed to automobile traffic. Plaza de Armas, 17 Pasteur Sur, Querétaro, Querétaro 76000 (phone: 463-45781).

VILLA JACARANDA, San Miguel de Allende: An intimate, romantic inn on a quiet street 3 blocks from the main square, its 16 units (including 12 suites) are surrounded by gardens and furnished with products of local artisans. All have fireplaces, and most have private or semi-private patios and terraces. The bathrooms are done in hand-painted Mexican tiles. Rooms are equipped with cable TV showing US stations. There is a Roman Plunge and a Jacuzzi in the central patio, a cinema bar where the latest movies are shown, and an internationally acclaimed restaurant that is a favorite of San Miguel residents. 53 Calle Aldama, San Miguel de Allende, Guanajuato 37700 (phone: 465-21015 or 465-20811).

HACIENDA DE COBOS, Guanajuato: Guanajuato was once the richest city in Mexico, a center of vast wealth that issued from the surrounding silver and gold mines. It is said that at one time the mines of Guanajuato provided a third of the world's annual output of silver. So it isn't much of a surprise to learn that this hacienda is a former colonial silver and gold *hacienda de beneficio* (a mill where ore was crushed and washed) and an estate dating from 1765, which was rebuilt and converted into an inn in 1972.

The city is wedged in a mountainside — many of its main streets are actually subterranean — and consequently is cramped for space. It is a pleasure to find *de Cobos* shut off from the bustle outside by walls and gates. One enters the private compound from what is called "the most romantic street in America" (Padre Hidalgo), or through a gate and down a cobblestone drive leading from Guanajuato's main street (Av. Juárez). Either way, guests find a large, stone courtyard surrounded on all sides by walls and rooms. There are 40 rooms in all (5 suites, 6 double-bedded rooms, 29 standard rooms), all of which are rather plain, clean, and chilly (there are no fireplaces).

The interesting dining room, built against an original old wall of the estate with a high, domed ceiling, serves simple, good food. There are sitting rooms and television rooms in what were once the stables; bar service and comfortable lounging areas in the courtyard, which is highlighted by huge trees, the old well that once provided the water to wash the precious ore, and two giant millstones. Although not much English is spoken here, things are pleasant at *de Cobos,* and it's only 15 minutes from the city's central plaza. 3 Padre Hidalgo, Guanajuato, Guanajuato 36000 (phone: 473-20350).

VIRREY DE MENDOZA, Morelia: City records confirm that the ground floor of the inn, which faces the main square of Morelia, dates from sometime before 1565. Later, probably around 1744, a second floor was added, and then, in 1938, when the place was finally turned into a hotel, the third floor was constructed. In 1990, the inn was sold and renovated by its new owner.

The growth of the building has followed the original colonial plan — a large courtyard and two smaller patios surrounded by rooms on all sides. Broad staircases (and Morelia's first elevator) lead upstairs, past an authentic suit of armor and other intriguing objets d'art. The courtyard is now glassed over and contains the former dining room of Sr. de Mendoza, the first vice-regent sent from Spain.

The 55 rooms are squeaky clean and furnished extravagantly in colonial style, with very high ceilings and gleaming white tile baths. Four are magnificent suites, 2 of which face the historic Plaza of the Martyrs and are furnished with antiques (try hard to reserve one of them; they're not much more expensive than the far more ordinary double rooms). There's even a closed-circuit color television system showing recent films, mostly American with Spanish subtitles. 16 Portal de Matamoros, Morelia, Michoacán 58000 (phone: 451-20633).

VILLA MONTAÑA, Morelia: There are 65 rooms and suites at this posada, a few more than the arbitrary limit of 50 we originally set for an inn's inclusion here, but the *Montaña* is so appealing that we felt it would be a shame to ignore this tiny, private villa on the city's southern outskirts.

The place has been built in slow stages, with bits and pieces added continually since the 1958 opening, all radiating from the original hacienda estate building. There is a maze of levels, terraces, brick walks, sudden gardens, stone columns and carvings, and connected stuccoed cottages in several separate buildings. A small patio adjoins the dining room, which is in the original house (along with a piano bar with a fireplace), a patio bar, and a wonderful colonial sitting room with an unbeatable view of the city. The swimming pool and tennis court also have a wonderful view. All rooms have phones, and there is a television room.

Rooms range from fine to great. No two are alike, but all boast broad beams, furniture in authentic colonial style, and fireplaces (some suites have *three* fireplaces). Private patios abound. The food is well prepared, though the menu is very limited. The hotel levies a 10% service charge in lieu of tipping. Calle Galeana, in the Santa María area. *Mailing address:* Apdo. 233, Morelia, Michoacán 58000 (phone: 451-40231; FAX: 451-51423).

POSADA RÍO CUALE, Puerto Vallarta: It's rare to find a true inn in Mexico that's near the sea, but this one qualifies. *Río Cuale* is pleasant, quiet, friendly, and has nice rooms and good dining. English is spoken (95% of the guests come from the US or Canada), and there is a decent-size swimming pool and an eye-pleasing hacienda-like design. What's more, the location is perfect for seeing Puerto Vallarta — where most of the other decent hotels are far from the center of the village — since most of the good downtown restaurants, bars, discos, and shops are only a few steps away. Once in residence, you shouldn't need a taxi at all, *and* it's also only half a block from a very good beach.

As is the case with so many inns, this one has grown gradually since it first opened in 1968. There are now 25 well-furnished, clean rooms, all of which fetch the same price — despite no two being alike. There are 3 whimsical levels, lots of brick and whitewash, spiral staircases outside, and plenty of greenery. Downstairs (next to the pool) is a large, open, and justifiably respected dining room. The food is good — try the *huachinango* (Pacific red snapper). There is a good choice of wines and even espresso, and mariachis perform Thursday and Saturday nights. Very relaxed and nice and very unlike the high-rises most visitors stay in in Puerto Vallarta. 242 Aquiles Serdán. *Mailing address:* Apdo. 146, Puerto Vallarta, Jalisco 48300 (phone: 322-20450).

HACIENDA DEL SOLAR, Taxco: This 22-unit hotel, which includes individual or twin cottages, sprawls across a hilltop about 2 miles south of the center of town. The rooms, made of natural brick and white stucco, boast vaulted ceilings and arched doorways. All rooms are beautifully decorated with Mexican crafts, including the bathrooms, which are covered with hand-painted tiles. Terraces overlook the surrounding mountains, and huge open windows in the inn's restaurant, *La Ventana de Taxco*, provide spectacular views of the town. The food, international but featuring Italian specialities, is among the best in Mexico. A pool and tennis court are also on the grounds. *Mailing address:* Apdo. 96, Paraje el Solar, Taxco, Guerrero 40200 (phone: 762-20323).

VILLA DEL SOL, Zihuatanejo: "Zihuatanejo is for individualists," says German-born Helmut W. Leins, who owns and runs this place. "There are no fancy restaurants, no fancy places," he says. Maybe not, but some aficionados think this 26-suite inn is pretty special. Not luxurious exactly, but special. For one thing, it's set right on the best beach in this one-time sleepy fishing village 125 miles (200 km) north of Acapulco. It's interestingly designed, and built of native woods and other local materials around a small swimming pool and a large *palapa* (thatch-roofed shelter), which houses the bar and open-air dining area with a multi-story dining room next door (see "Eating Out" in *Ixtapa and Zihuatanejo*, THE CITIES). And the restaurants and discos of the big hotels at Ixtapa are just 7 miles (11 km) away.

The rooms are really suites, with sleeping lofts upstairs; four are 2-bedroom, air conditioned suites. The food is good and more international than Mexican. The music played under the *palapa* may be pop or classical. The *Villa del Sol* appeals most to those who appreciate a kind of refined informality, enjoy quiet conversation, and are able to unwind using their own resources, since there isn't much here besides the great beach and fine swimming. If you thrive on this sort of comfortable dropping out, this is about as good a place in which to enjoy it as you can find anywhere. No children under 14 during the winter season. *Mailing address:* Apdo. 84, Playa la Ropa, Zihuatanejo, Guerrero 40880 (phone: 753-42239; 800-223-6510 in the US; FAX: 753-42758).

Shopping at the Source

Almost any regional Mexican craft can be found in the shops of Mexico City's Zona Rosa, from handwoven serapes to Indian pottery and fine silver jewelry. But it's far more fun to buy them in the marketplace of their original provincial town, perhaps even from the artisan who made them. In many places, shoppers are expected to bargain for a purchase; to do this, a buyer really should know some basic Spanish, even if it's just a few numbers. (When absolutely necessary, however, body language will suffice.) There are several approaches to bargaining, depending on the place, the item you are after, and your personality. One way to shop is simply to look carefully, decide upon a fair price, and make a firm offer. Or you can offer half to two-thirds of the requested price and argue firmly from there.

Although bargaining is fun, very often the amount in question is so small that it is easier for most tourists to be generous. Bargaining is an art, and you should know when *not* to practice it, also. Don't bargain in shops that have the sign *"precios fijos"* (fixed prices), in government shops (often called *Artes Populares*), or in the shops of hotels.

Native crafts are usually less expensive in local markets than in shops. It is better to buy more expensive items — jewelry or gems — in reputable shops. And if someone offers to sell an archaeological relic from a Mexican ruin, turn him down flat. In most cases these "relics" are manufactured by the truckload, and if by some wild chance you are being offered a genuine artifact, the sale is illegal, and the item cannot be exported from Mexico without breaking the law.

Check carefully the quality of any merchandise you are considering buying. Goods are often presented as handcrafted that are patently machine-made — although if the price is right and the item attracts you, this is certainly no reason to refrain from buying it. But be sure you are paying what the item is worth.

Besides native crafts, Mexico does have occasional bargains on items produced outside the country. Many tourists flock to the Mexican border towns in order to buy duty-free items ranging from French perfume and Japanese and Chinese silks and laces to Irish linen tablecloths. *Warning:* Some expensive items carrying designer names are *not* the real thing, no matter what you're told — they are imitations made in Mexico and sold through a quirk in Mexican laws. Tijuana is the largest duty-free shopping zone in Mexico. Resort areas specialize in locally designed sportswear that is machine-made but of high quality and style.

Certain items are produced or crafted especially well in Mexico, though the areas in which they are found vary. Silver, pottery, woven goods, leatherwork, and copper and tin goods are all uniquely Mexican materials and are worked into enduring art by Mexican craftspeople. Well-made shoes are an excellent buy.

Silver has been plentiful in Mexico since before the Spanish conquest. Silver items should be marked *sterling* or *.925* so that you know that there are not less than 925 grams of pure silver for every 1,000 grams of weight. If you are told that the silver in the jewelry came from local mines, be skeptical. Nowadays, all silver from Mexican mines goes to the central Bank of Mexico, where it is melted into bars and then resold around the country to craftspeople.

Pottery is one of the major crafts of Mexico. There's a lot of it — some of high artistic value — and it's usually inexpensive, but don't buy it to cook in and don't store acidic foods in it, since lead compounds are often used in glazing. Each area of the country has its special designs and materials. Oaxaca pottery is satin black or with an unusual green glaze. You can choose as well from Tlaquepaque pottery, Puebla earthenware, or Mexico City's modern designs. Lacquerwork and ceramics are often of high quality, also. The lacquer is made from chía oil (a combination of wild sage and *aje,* the remains of plant lice). Dolomite and other minerals are added to this mixture to produce a lacquer as fine as that made from the sap of the Chinese tree. Lacquer trays usually have polished black backgrounds painted with flowers or gold lacquer.

Serapes, rebozos, blankets, and other woven articles, such as the beautiful bulky sweaters of Toluca, are usually great bargains. They should be handloomed from wool; examine the weave to make sure that other yarns weren't used.

You should examine leather goods, also, to make sure that they are pure rawhide, not leather glued to cardboard or plastic. Other native crafts that you will see are *huaraches* (braided sandals), *huipiles* (embroidered dresses), all sizes and shapes of baskets, hammocks, and *piñatas*.

Copper and tin goods can be found all over Mexico. Copper was once the most popular metal of the Mixtec and the Aztec Indians. Kettles, pots, pans, and pitchers are sold in markets as well as in the more expensive shops. Again, check for quality — some articles are actually made of iron sprayed with copper-toned paint.

Be wary of gems that are sold as bargains. Jade has not been found in Mexico since the Spanish conquest; turquoise, like all other stones, should only be bought in reputable stores; and gold is not much less expensive in Mexico than in the US. Mexico does, however, have high-quality amethysts and opals and some lovely onyx and black obsidian.

Mexico is the home of many working artists and craftspeople, some of whom combine new materials and design with the art of the past to produce original painting, sculpture, weaving, jewelry, and much more. In many ways, Mexico is the perfect place for an artist to live: Life moves slowly and is relatively inexpensive; also, the country's great natural beauty is inspiring. You can see the work of these artists in galleries and shops in towns and cities throughout the country. San Miguel de Allende has some of the best work. You are allowed to bring original works of art into the US duty-free under the Generalized System of Preferences (GSP) program. For complete details about customs regulations in the US, see *Customs and Returning to the US,* GETTING READY TO GO.

Below, we offer a survey of the best areas in which to shop in Mexico. See also the individual city reports in THE CITIES.

ACAPULCO: The best-known resort in Mexico has scores of shops selling beautiful resortwear, which is often locally designed and, therefore less expensive than in the United States. One of the best buys is the *guayabera,* the cotton, pleated-front, long-sleeve sport shirt (sometimes embroidered) worn everywhere from restaurants to beaches. There is excellent shopping in boutiques around the zocalo, and along the Costera Aleman, near the swanky high-rise hotels.

GUADALAJARA: *Mercado Libertad* (Liberty Market) is the central outdoor market in Guadalajara (Juárez and Calzada Independencia). More than 1,000 stands feature ceramics, serapes, rugs, embroidered blouses, rebozos, copper items, silver, and the goods of the Huichol Indians, especially "God's eyes" (yarn-covered crosses), yarn paintings of wool, and the belts and purses that Huichol men wear. The Plaza Tapatía, connecting major colonial buildings in the center of the city, is lined with shops. The restored suburb of Tlaquepaque is full of shops and studios.

JOCOTEPEC: Famed for its white wool serapes, this spot is on the shores of Lake Chapala, southwest of Guadalajara.

MAZATLÁN: This is a surprisingly fine shopping city. *Casa Roberto*'s shop in the *Playa Mazatlán* hotel is a wonder of Mexican handicrafts and clothing. *Designers' Bazaar* (217 Rodolfo T. Loaiza and Av. Sábalo Gaviotas) has superb original clothing. There are also several good jewelry boutiques and a busy market.

MÉRIDA: This center of business and shopping for the Yucatán has a good public market near Calles 56 and 67. The government-run *Casa de las Artesanías* (503 Calle 63 between Calles 64 and 66; no phone) sells regional crafts at reasonable prices. Mérida is the best place to buy hammocks (check the weave — the more threads, the better the hammock). It's also known for Panama hats, *huipiles* (the embroidered dresses mostly worn in Guatemala), *huaraches,* mosquito netting, *guayabera* shirts, silver, and gold filigree.

MEXICO CITY: You can find anything in Mexico City, but it may be more expensive than elsewhere in Mexico. If you don't plan to travel around the country, try the Sunday *Thieves Market* downtown (La Lagunilla); *La Merced* (Circunvalación, 1 block north of Fray Servando Teresa de Mier); *San Juan Crafts Market* (Calle Ayuntamiento between Dolores and Luis Moya); *El Bazar Sábado* (crafts on Saturdays only; at 11 Plaza San Jacinto, San Ángel); *Museo de Arte Popular* for a fine selection of textiles and crafts (44 Juárez); and the Zona Rosa (Pink Zone), with its hundreds of shops and boutiques for the latest fashions and Mexican mementos. Mexico City is best known for silver (try *Tane,* 70 Amberes; *Los Castillo,* 41 Amberes; and *Platería Ortega,* 18 Florencia, in the Zona Rosa); jewelry (*Cartier,* 9 Calle Amberes, and *De la Fuente Bustillo,* 28 Madero and 276 Reforma); handicrafts (all over town, especially the *La Ciudadela* handicrafts market on the Plaza Ciudadela and the *Insurgentes* market in the Zona Rosa; for exceptionally select handicraft items, *Victor's,* 8 and 10 Madero, and *Populartes,* 103 Campos Elíseos); leather (*Casa Aries,* 14 Florencia; several hotels; and *Antil,* 22 Florencia); glass (*Articulos Feders,* 67 Lago Muritz); colonial furniture (*Lo Que El Viento Se Llevó,* 56 Victor Hugo); antiques at the *Thieves Market* and the Lagunilla area, and at many fine stores downtown, in the Zona Rosa, and in San Angel. On Saturdays, an outdoor antiques bazaar is held from 10 AM to 6 PM in the *Plaza del Angel Shopping Center* in the Zona Rosa (Calle Londres between Calles Amberes and Florencia). There are also many fine art galleries in the Zona Rosa and in the Polanco district. FONART (a government program to develop craftsmanship) has several shops in Mexico City (691 Av. Patriotismo; 89 Av. Juárez; 136 Calle Londres; 37 Av. de la Paz in San Angel; 1630 Insurgentes Sur; and 10 Manuel E. Izaguirre in Ciudad

Satélite). *Perisur,* Latin America's largest shopping center, is on the southern outskirts of the city (where the Periférico Fwy. meets Av. Insurgentes); it has some of Mexico's most elegant merchandise.

MONTERREY: Known for its leather and hand-blown crystal. The *Colón* (Colón and Constitución) and the *Juárez* (Juárez and Aramberri) markets also have crafts. *Artesanías de Nuevo León,* a government-managed store, is in an old mansion (at 804 Allende and Dr. Coss). *Centro Plaza Artesanal* (on Av. Juárez between Hidalgo and Ocampo) and the *Morelos Shopping Center* (in the Zona Rosa) are goods place to shop for folk art. The *Gran Plaza Shopping Center* (under the zocalo) is full of boutiques and restaurants.

MORELIA: Tarasco Indians sell their wares at the *Independence Market.* Highest-quality products here include exquisite lacquerware, embroidered blouses, rebozos, and steel cutlery. The *Mercado de Dulces* (Gómez Farías) is a candy freak's dream. *Casa de las Artesanías* (Plaza Valladolid; phone: 451-22486) has folk art. For an extraordinary selection of crafts from all over the state, stop in *La Casona* (Av. Madero Ote. and Belisario Domínguez; phone: 451-30998).

OAXACA: Many people believe Oaxaca to be the crafts center of Mexico, probably because it's the central city for a number of original and talented Indian tribes in the state. Best buy is the pottery, which is the least expensive and best made in all of Mexico. Oaxaca has fine textiles, rebozos, serapes, and rugs. It is also known for silver, copper, tin, and gold filigree. Much of the gold filigree jewelry is modeled from the jewelry found in the Monte Albán tombs. The women of Oaxaca wear gold coin earrings, necklaces, and attractive handmade dresses. Two good shops in Oaxaca are *Casa Brena* (textile weavers, 700 Pino Suárez; phone: 951-50222), and *FONART* (116 Manuel M. Bravo; phone: 951-65764). Near Oaxaca are two small villages known for their fine handspun cotton, *huipiles,* rebozos, and jewelry: Mitla and Yalalag. *Aripo* (809 García Vigil; phone: 951-69211) also has textiles as well as pottery, baskets, and clothing with an Oaxacan influence. The traditional silvery black pottery from the town of San Bartolo Coyotepec is available at excellent prices in Oaxaca, as are the woven textiles, with designs inspired by Miró and Picasso, from Teotitlán.

PARACHO: Also in Michoacán, Paracho is the largest producer of handmade guitars in Mexico. Some fine examples of wood carving are here also.

PÁTZCUARO: Pátzcuaro means Place of Delights in Tarasco, and the name is appropriate. The Indian market is something you really shouldn't miss. Every Friday, Indians from the hill and lake villages stream into town with their wares. Pátzcuaro is best known for high-quality lacquerwork, serapes, embroidery, rugs, and ceramics. In town, visit the *Casa de las Artesanías Michoacán*; set in the House of the Eleven Patios, a convent from the colonial period, it displays local crafts, some for sale. Other towns around Lake Pátzcuaro are noted for their fine crafts: Erongaicuaro is a small Tarasco village that has some of the best cambric (*cambray*) handloomed fabrics and native embroidery. Tzintzuntzán also has fabrics, pottery, and furniture. Santa Clara del Cobre, about 20 minutes south of Pátzcuaro, is known for copper crafts, and each August the village has a colorful copper fiesta. To appreciate the importance of copper to the area, visit the *Museo de Cobre* (on the main street in Santa Clara del Cobre), which has a broad selection of pieces on exhibit and for sale.

PUEBLA: Puebla is called the City of Tiles for its Talavera tile-decorated buildings. Attractive ceramic objects can be found at *Centro Artesanal,* a crafts center sponsored by the state government (Héroes Cinco de Mayo and 14 Oriente), in *El Mercado Victoria* (Calle 3 Nte.), and at *Casa Rugerio* (111 Calle 18 Pte.; phone: 22-413843). Rebozos are imported from the nearby village of Izúcar de Matamoros. Other items produced in the Puebla area include hand-embroidered blouses, ponchos, and onyx carvings. *Vicki y Rafael* (Av. de las Américas, next door to Hosteria San Felipe; phone:

841-20235) features quality regional crafts: fine furniture, henequen rugs, handwoven cottons, and fancy embroidery. Majólica-style pottery — with a tin-enamel glaze — has been crafted here since the conquest.

PUERTO VALLARTA: Puerto Vallarta has fine local sportswear designers, whose creations are less expensive here than in the US. The best boutiques are concentrated in the cobblestone streets radiating from the small central square, and there are many more shops at the *Villa Vallarta* and *Marina Vallarta* shopping centers; the stores carry handicrafts from all over Mexico, but Tlaquepaque and Tonalá — towns renowned for their excellent craftspeople — are heavily represented. Good Mexican tequila is a smart buy here, too — most of it is made just over the mountains.

QUERÉTARO: Querétaro is mainly known for its fine gems, especially amethyst, opals, and topaz. Onyx is of high quality here, also. *Reminder:* Beware the street vendors; you should buy gems only at reputable shops. A reliable store is *El Rubi* (3 Av. Madero Pte., just off Plaza Principal, between Juárez and Allende; phone: 463-20984), which carries a wide assortment of fiery opals, as well as amethyst, topaz, agate, and alexandrite (sold set or loose). East of Querétaro is the Mezquital region, where the Indians produce hand-embroidered clothing.

SALTILLO: Saltillo is famous for its fine wool serapes. You can watch the process — spinning the wool, dying it in bright colors, and weaving it the old-fashioned way on a handloom — at *El Serape de Saltillo* (305 Hidalgo Sur; phone: 841-20187). Serapes also are sold at *El Saltillero* (217 Victoria). The central market also has stalls that sell other woven articles and rugs. For silver, stop in *Platería Taxco* (428 Victoria; phone: 841-28541). Nearby is the *Saltillo Silver Factory* (212 Victoria; phone: 841-42726), which offers tours and sells silver items. Better buys on Mexican goods, including silver, often are found closer to the border than at the source.

SAN MIGUEL DE ALLENDE: San Miguel is filled with art, both modern and traditional. Art galleries stock paintings, sculpture, weaving, pottery, and handcrafted jewelry; try *Galería San Miguel* (on the main plaza; phone: 465-20454), *Primavera* (at Casa Sierra Nevada; phone: 465-20415), *Josh Klingerman Gallery* (6 Umarán; phone: 465-20951), *Antigua Casa Canela* (20 Umarán; phone: 465-21880), *Ono* (38 Mesones; phone: 465-21314 and 2 Calle Codo; phone: 465-22932), and *Casa Maxwell* (14 Canal; phone: 465-20247 and 3 Umarán; no phone), but you should browse through as many shops as possible before making your purchases. San Miguel de Allende is also known for tin, serapes, rugs, rebozos, and embroidered articles.

TAXCO: Famous throughout Mexico for its silver crafts, Taxco had been one of the major silver-mining areas since the arrival of Cortés. The late William Spratling revived the art of silverwork by establishing the *Taller de las Delicias* workshop (phone: 762-21878). Since the early 1900s many workshops have been built, and silverwork is flourishing once again. There is a Sunday market, but silver, amethyst, garnet, topaz, opal, and brass should be purchased in a shop; try *Los Castillos* (10 Plaza Bernal in front of Casa Borda; phone: 762-22935) or *Elena Ballesteros* (4 Calle Celso Muñoz; phone: 762-23767).

TIJUANA: This bustling border town has become a duty-free haven for tourists on day trips from the US. Liquor, crystal, glass, Japanese and Chinese materials, and other foreign-produced items are fairly inexpensive here (again, watch out for fake Gucci products). Just walk down Avenida Revolución and you'll find the main shopping center.

TLAQUEPAQUE: On the outskirts of Guadalajara, Tlaquepaque is renowned for ceramics, pottery, glass, silver, copper, and lovely Indian weavings. The entire village is a shopping center, and a visit there is a highlight for many visitors.

TLAXCALA: East of Mexico City in central Mexico, Tlaxcala is one of the most famous wool-weaving areas in Mexico. Santa Ana, less than 2 miles (3 km) away, has shops with bolt textiles and serapes.

TOLUCA: Forty miles (64 km) west of Mexico City, this town has been famous for decades for its Friday Indian market — nowadays a mass of vehicles and visitors. The market, which is off Paseo Tollocan about a half mile (1 km) south of the city entrance, covers several blocks, and its stalls offer everything from imported appliances to live animals and crafts from all over Mexico. Woolens, especially sweaters, are a good buy. *Casart,* a handicrafts center run by the state of México and featuring indigenous crafts, has a branch in the *Zacongo Zoo. Centro de Artisanías Mexiquense* (Paseo Tollocan at Nezahualcóyotl) also sells pottery, serapes, rebozos, and wool and cotton garments made in nearby villages.

URUAPAN: Near Pátzcuaro in the state of Michoacán, Uruapan is famous for its lacquerware. This Tarasco town has a Sunday market, a good crafts museum (*La Guatapera* on the main street in Uruapan), and weaving.

URIANGATO: In Guanajuato state, this small village specializes in well-crafted rebozos and blankets.

Bullfights: The Kings of the Rings

 If you're truly interested in Mexican culture, you should experience at least one bullfight. The bullfight, a spectacle rather than a sport, dates from before the Christian era. Modern bullfighting originated on the Iberian Peninsula during the 12th century. (Cretans were known to have hand-wrestled bulls long before the Moors introduced bullfighting to Spain.) The Spanish brought bullfighting to Mexico just 8 years after the conquest, and the first official bullfight in the New World took place in 1529.

The history and meaning of the bullfight is described in *The Bullfight,* PERSPECTIVES, but it should be reiterated that you do not attend a fight with the idea of rooting for the bull as though it were the home team, because the bull never wins. Some people find the spectacle of an animal being killed before a cheering crowd thoroughly repugnant. If the idea offends you, don't go. Others consider the bullfight an art form, as much a part of Mexican culture as weaving, pottery work, or onyx sculpture. In any case, the bullfight is certainly a colorful event, especially at *Plaza México* in Mexico City — one of the best bullfighting rings in the world (1 block west of Insurgentes in the southern part of the city). Matadors, picadors on horseback, banderilleros, and helpers parade into the plaza accompanied by stirring *pasadoble* music.

In Mexico City, 12 *corridas* (bullfight programs) are held from November through January. *Novilleros,* young men who have not gone through the formal ceremony (the *alternativa*) of becoming full matadors do battle in the ring from April until June. The big names among current Mexican matadors are Miguel Espinoza ("'Armillita"), Manolo Martínez, Eloy Cabazos, Alejandro and David Silvetti, and Curro Rivera. If the matadors make graceful, artistic passes with their capes or muletas (the red kerchief), yell *"Olé!"* with the rest of the crowd. If they succeed and make a clean kill with a single sword thrust, wave your handkerchief — you may be rewarded by seeing the judge grant the matador one bull's ear, a pair of ears, or possibly a tail.

Bullfights are held in Mexico City each Sunday at 4 PM at *Plaza México,* and tickets cost anywhere from $2 to $15 at the ring. Your group will have tickets, or you can usually obtain tickets through the concierge at your hotel.

Guadalajara is the second major bullfight city in Mexico. The season lasts from September to January and resumes for the month of May at the *Plaza Nuevo Progreso* ring (on Col. Independencia near the soccer stadium). In *Cortijo La Venta* (725 Federación), you can watch bullfighting exhibitions in a small ring as you dine and drink.

The border towns of Tijuana and Ciudad Juárez have regularly scheduled bullfights that are supported predominantly by tourists from the US on day trips. Tijuana's bullring, *Plaza Monumental de Tijuana,* has a capacity of 23,000 people and is on the east side of town. *Corridas* are usually held on Sundays from May to September. Check the tourist office for the schedule. Ciudad Juárez has one bullring in operation: the *Plaza Monumental de Toros* (on Paseo Triunfo de la República about 3½ miles/6 km from downtown). Bullfights are held about six times a year, coinciding with long US weekends, mainly in spring and summer. Check the tourist office for the exact schedule.

Many smaller towns hold bullfights (or at least matches with aspiring bullfighters practicing on whatever bovine opponent is at hand), and local tourist offices can provide information. You can also visit farms where the bulls for Mexico City and Guadalajara rings are bred. Las Peñuelas, near Aguascalientes in north-central Mexico, is one of the best.

A Day at the Races

 A favorite day's diversion for Americans who live near the Mexican border in California or Texas is to visit Tijuana or Ciudad Juárez for the horse and dog races. The best horse races in central Mexico are held in Mexico City's *Hipódromo,* considered one of the best tracks in the country.

CIUDAD JUÁREZ: Several miles south of the Mexico-US border, Juárez's track offers greyhound racing at 8 PM, Wednesdays through Saturdays year-round. Horse racing is held on Sundays at 1:30 PM, May through September. Off-track betting is legal in Ciudad Juárez, and bets can be placed at the *Juárez Turf Club* (on Av. Juárez, 1 block south of the Del Norte Bridge).

MEXICO CITY: If you're an aficionado, Mexico City's *Hipódromo* (phone: 557-4100) is the place for horse racing. The *Hipódromo* is a beautiful track and is easy to reach from the city by car on Route 57 (exit at Legaria). *Peseros* (jitney cabs) to the *Hipódromo* leave from the terminal at the Chapultepec Metro station. Cab prices should be agreed upon beforehand; they shouldn't cost more than $5 from downtown.

If you like to sit with the elite, the more exclusive hotels can make arrangements for you at the posh *Jockey Club.* Below the *Jockey Club* on the second tier is the *Gay Dalton Club* (Gay Dalton was a famous stakes-winning horse in Mexico). Anyone can enter, so it really isn't a club, but you may have to slip the waiter a few dollars and spend some time at your table. Don't despair if you can't get into the *Gay Dalton;* there's also the *Nuevo Laredo Turf Club,* the *Derby,* the *Handicap,* and the *Palermo.*

Below the *Gay Dalton Club* is the grandstand where most of the locals sit. Admission to this section is free (except for the amount you may lose on your bets). The minimum bet is about 60¢. There are 11 races daily (6 exactas and 5 trifectas) and the "Pick 6:" picking the winners of 6 consecutive races (actually races 4 to 9). If you make a big killing, there are no US Internal Revenue Service men waiting to take your name and address, but a big bite is taken out of the winnings by the Mexican equivalent of the IRS.

Races are held Tuesdays, Thursdays, and Fridays at 3 PM, Saturdays and Sundays at 2:30 PM. Admission charge to the track.

TIJUANA: The *Hipódromo Agua Caliente,* 1½ miles (2 km) east of town, has a turf club, a clubhouse, and a grandstand that seats 15,000 persons. It's usually filled with a melting pot of natives and Californians who find the drive over the border an inexpensive vacation, for the entrance fee is nominal. Eleven races take place every Saturday and Sunday, except during the winter when there are 12. On the fourth through the ninth races there is a "Pick 6" pool. There is greyhound racing nightly (except Tuesdays) at 7:45 PM and Saturdays and Sundays at 2:45 PM year-round.

For The Body

Mexico's Amazing Beaches

 Unless it were to become an island floating freely between the US and Guatemala, it is hard to imagine how Mexico could be any better endowed with coastlines and beaches. Except for the borders with neighboring countries, it is entirely surrounded by warm, tropical waters: 5,500 miles of shoreline on the Pacific Ocean and the Sea of Cortés in the west, the Gulf of Mexico and the Caribbean Sea in the east. And by virtue of its spectacular geography — that spiny finger of the Baja Peninsula shooting 800 miles south into the Pacific — it actually has *two* coasts on both the Pacific Ocean and the Sea of Cortés. Mexico is a particularly favored haven for beach lovers, with as varied and vital a beach life as any strand east of Maui.

The west coast is a traditional sunning spot and boasts some of North America's most celebrated beach resorts, including Mazatlán, Ixtapa, Puerto Vallarta, and Acapulco. Wide, powder-white beaches, a tropical climate, warm waters, and spectacular sunsets (on this coast, the sun usually plunges into the sea with great drama, since most vistas look directly westward) attract thousands of tourists, beachcombers, and vacationing Mexicans all year round, year after year. But the Sea of Cortés–Pacific Ocean coast extends thousands of miles above and below this golden strip of resorts — past virgin beaches and lagoons, tiny fishing villages, and unexplored coves — from the start of the Sea of Cortés (south of Mexicali) at San Felipe to Puerto Madero (near the Guatemalan border).

The beaches on the Gulf of Mexico coast tend to be darker and less developed than those along the west coast. Mexico's Caribbean coast, however, has white, soft beaches and fine resorts at Isla Mujeres, Cancún, and Cozumel. The 1,400 miles of eastern shore are, however, susceptible to tropical storms and strong currents, and the beach season peaks from December through *Easter Week,* after which the rains and winds tend to increase. Though there is certainly a winter "season" on the west coast, it is social; physically, the beaches of the Pacific, from Mazatlán south, can be enjoyed all year.

Since all beaches in Mexico are open to the public, visitors can swim and use all the facilities, including those near luxurious hotels (though access to these resort strips may prove awkward or difficult). Beaches that are designated "public recreational areas" are maintained by the government and are much used by resident Mexicans. For those who prefer privacy and seclusion, there are hundreds of miles of undeveloped, largely untouched beaches along both coasts.

The beaches below are listed in general geographical order, north to south along each of Mexico's coasts. For more information on the individual towns and villages mentioned below, check the appropriate route in DIRECTIONS.

BAJA — THE PACIFIC COAST AND THE SEA OF CORTÉS

ENSENADA: A hard sand beach stretches for 10 miles south of Ensenada. It offers plenty of privacy and space for camping. Favorite beaches for horseback riding, as well as for bathing and sunning. (Note that the Pacific waters and air temperature are chilly here during the winter.)

PUNTA BANDA: This peninsula on Ensenada's Todos Santos Bay has 8 miles of beaches and coves. Cabins and campgrounds are open to the public.

VALLE DE SAN QUINTÍN: An agricultural town 120 miles (192 km) from Ensenada, San Quintín has beautiful beaches and pismo clams, which attract as many visitors as the sea. The beach in front of *La Pinta San Quintín* hotel (phone: 686-62601) is a lovely stretch of sand where clam diggers and horseback riders can be seen from dawn till dusk.

MALARRIMO: Off the dirt road from Bahía Tortugas, this west coast beach attracts beachcombers as well as people looking for seashells and driftwood — it has an abundant supply of both.

SANTA ROSALÍA: On the east coast of the Baja Peninsula, facing Guaymas across the Sea of Cortés, Santa Rosalía's beautiful beaches start south of town and get better all the way past Mulegé and into Bahía Concepción. Overnight accommodations are available at *El Morro* (Km 1 on Carr. Azul; phone: 685-20414). *La Terraza* (Carr. Norte; phone: 685-20578) has decent food.

LORETO: On the Sea of Cortés, north of La Paz, Loreto's beaches are shaded with date palms. Delicious seafood can be found at nearby restaurants. Loreto and its environs are being developed into a major resort area. The *Stouffer Presidente* hotel (Nopoló Point; phone: 683-30700) overlooks some of the area's finest beaches and offers a range of resort amenities.

PUERTO BALANDRO, ISLA CARMEN: In the Gulf of California, across from Loreto, this island port city is surrounded by wide, nearly empty, white-powder beaches and clear waters. Accessible by boat from Loreto.

LA PAZ: The charm and tropical weather of this capital on the Gulf of California coast lend themselves to a pleasant, easygoing beach life. Coromuel Beach, 3 miles (5 km) north of town, and Pichilingue Beach are both excellent for swimming.

SAN JOSÉ DEL CABO: This tranquil village, 23 miles (37 km) from the cape, has wonderful swimming beaches, although the waves and tides can become dangerous in places. The *Palmilla* (phone: 684-20582), a palatial resort hotel with a variety of recreational facilities, is right on San José del Cabo's beach.

CABO SAN LUCAS: Both a fishing and resort town, at the southern tip of the Baja Peninsula, it has beautiful beaches with campgrounds and deluxe seaside hotel accommodations. The best beach is protected by the calm bay and begins in front of the *Hacienda Beach* hotel and sweeps north. The beautiful quarter-mile-wide Pacific Ocean beach, opposite the *Finisterra* hotel, is treacherous because the currents of the Sea of Cortés and the Pacific crash together just offshore. There is a lovely sheltered beach along the Bahía Santa María, next to the *Twin Dolphin* hotel.

THE PACIFIC COAST

GUAYMAS: The beaches here are known more for shell collecting, clams, game fish, and skin diving than for sunbathing, but the swimming conditions are usually adequate. Guaymas's Playa Miramar on Bocachibampo Bay is average, but the beautiful beaches are 12 miles (19 km) north on San Carlos Bay, rivaling the shorelines of Cancún, Cozumel, and Puerto Vallarta. Both Playa San Francisco and Playa Algodónes have good swimming, snorkeling, windsurfing, fishing, and boating. Playa Algodónes is a white sand beach, and there is a *Club Med* here (phone: 622-60166).

MAZATLÁN: One of Mexico's most popular beach resorts, on a peninsula jutting into the sea, this beach lures sun lovers to its animated sandy shores and warm waters year-round. Playa Norte (North Beach), a slender strip of white sand extending for 6 miles (10 km) beyond Mazatlán's oceanfront boulevard, is the largest beach, catering primarily to the local population. It has restaurants where mariachi music is played at night, and *balnearios* where it's possible to rent a locker, shower, beach chair, or umbrella. Las Gaviotas and Playas Sábalo and Camanónes, on the west side of the peninsula farther from the center of town, are more often frequented by tourists and the surfing crowd. All three have restaurants, bars, and beachfront hotels. On the island beach of Venados (across from Las Gaviotas), visitors can enjoy torchlit evening beach parties and very calm, very clear waters. Piedra, another relaxing island beach off Mazatlán, offers long flat stretches of sand, clear blue-green waters, thatch-palm umbrellas, and delectable fish sticks sold by roving beach vendors. Unfortunately, the solitude of Piedra is becoming a thing of the past, since developers "discovered" the island and have earmarked several hundred acres for the site of a large tourist complex. The island's tranquility often is disrupted by the sound of steamrollers.

SAN BLAS: Not far down the coast from Mazatlán, in the state of Nayarit, is this unspoiled port city. Easy to reach, free from the tourist deluge, surrounded by lagoons, laced with coconut, papaya, banana, and mango trees, San Blas's beautiful white beaches begin 1 mile (1.6 km) south of town. They lack the charged, day-and-night-party atmosphere of Mazatlán's resort beaches, but they have all the requisite facilities — bathhouses, food stands, and a peaceful, relaxing atmosphere. Playa del Ray, on a peninsula opposite the port of San Blas, is a beautiful virgin beach reached by boat from the San Blas pier, near the Aduana (Customs) Building. Remote beaches such as Matanchén, south of San Blas, are good for camping and surfing.

PUERTO VALLARTA: One of Mexico's golden resorts, Puerto Vallarta has no dearth of luxurious hotels and restaurants, but its beaches (more than 50 are claimed) are the real attraction: Playa del Sol (also known as Playa los Muertos), just south of town, with full-scale commercial traffic, including beach vendors, snack bars, musical combos, and dancing pavilions; Las Palmas Beach, just north of town, quieter and less cluttered; Conchas Chinas (China Beach), south of town; and Las Estacas, a small inlet beach to the south of town.

MISMALOYA: This paradise of a beach is accessible by boat or car (7 miles/11 km south) from Puerto Vallarta. Situated at the base of towering, palm-studded cliffs, between clear green waters and thick clusters of tropical foliage, this beach was virtually unknown before John Huston used it as a central location for his movie *The Night of the Iguana.* Small craft (dugout canoes) with guides can be rented during the day to explore the nearby lagoon. There is a hotel, *La Joya de Mismaloya* (phone: 322-21374), which has a decent beach restaurant, *Mismaloya Beach,* serving good seafood and cold beer, a bar, and a popular disco.

South of Mismaloya, at Boca de Tomatlán, you can hire a *panga* (boat) to sail to one of three beaches, including Playa las Animas, a favorite snorkeling and diving spot. The beach also has many *palapa* restaurants serving grilled fish.

YELAPA: An hour down the coast by boat (the *Sarape,* with live music, lunch, and bar, costs $12 for the 7-hour trip). A popular day trip destination, Yelapa Beach has an open-air beach restaurant and a small hotel.

BARRA DE NAVIDAD: A small, isolated vacation village mainly used by Mexicans, it boasts a small bay and a good beach that is fine for swimming only when the breakers aren't too high.

COSTA CAREYES: "Turtle coast," a series of small coves north of Manzanillo, has a few superb beaches, such as those at *Club Med* and at the *Plaza Careyes* hotel.

MANZANILLO: Now a booming west coast resort catering to the wealthy (who usually stay at *Las Hadas* hotel), as well as to average tourists (who go to the less elegant hotels that are sprouting up), Manzanillo sits between Puerto Vallarta and Acapulco. In earlier days, it was quite isolated; today it is linked with Guadalajara by Route 80, and with other coastal spots by Route 200. There is also a jet airport. Most of the resorts are on the northern peninsula of the bay that Manzanillo overlooks. Local beaches include Playa Azul, one of Manzanillo's best beaches, between *La Posada* and *Las Hadas* hotels; Olas Altas on Santiago Bay; Playa de Oro beyond the peninsula; Cuyutlán, a resort hidden 30 miles (48 km) from town with modest beachside accommodations. Apiza, 25 miles (40 km) south, is good for swimming, but has no accommodations. Better yet is Los Pascuales, a few miles farther south from Manzanillo on Route 100, an idyllic resort at the mouth of the Río Armeria.

ZIHUATANEJO: It's a village hideaway, surrounded by mountains on the inner rim of a bay, with many lovely beaches. La Ropa, the longest and best for swimming, is one of the finest in Mexico. Las Gatas, on the tip of the peninsula and accessible only by boat, is flanked by palms, deep blue waters, and coral reefs. Barra de Potosí, a 4-mile stretch of beach 12½ miles (20 km) south of Ixtapa, is where the Potosí Lagoon meets the Pacific. Delicious grilled fish is served at all the beachside restaurants.

IXTAPA: This sophisticated luxury resort, next to Zihuatanejo, offers 24 miles of tropical beaches with good surf and breakers. Most hotels are built around the beach called Playa del Palmar.

ACAPULCO: Mexico's famous beach resort has more than 23 beaches of one size or another nestled at the base of the plunging rocks and surrounding cliffs. Playas Caleta and Caletilla (at the far end of Costera M. Alemán) are known as the traditional morning beaches, but despite efforts to revive "traditional Acapulco," Caleta has lost much of its popularity in recent years. Across from Caleta, on a secluded island that is accessible by a 10-minute boat ride, is La Roqueta Beach, very popular with families because the waters are calm and the sands white and beautiful. Afternoon beaches are Playa de Hornos and La Condesa, the latter most popular with *gringos;* sun and waves are best after 1 PM, but the real action is along the sandy strand, where the comings and goings can be epochal. Revolcadero Beach, 10 miles (16 km) southeast of town and beside which the *Acapulco Princess* and *Pierre Marqués* hotels have been built, is a beautiful — but often dangerous — ocean beach. About 14 miles (22 km) farther down the road is Barra Vieja, a strip of beach that separates the Tres Palos lagoon from the Pacific. This is the spot where *pescado a la talla* (fresh fish broiled on a spit) originated. Swimming in the ocean is out because of the surf and strong undertow, but the lagoon is safe for swimming and exploring by boat (available for rental); there are also horses for rent. Pie de la Cuesta, northwest of the city, has views of some of the most beautiful sunsets in the country, but suffers from the most dangerous undertows along this section of the coast. Watch, don't swim.

PUERTO ESCONDIDO, PUERTO ANGEL: In the state of Oaxaca, this area is becoming increasingly popular among lovers of natural beauty who don't expect luxury hotels or the activities available at larger resorts. The *Santa Fe* hotel (phone: 958-20170), on Zikatela Beach at Puerto Escondido, has 40 air conditioned rooms, all with an ocean view. Puerto Angel, more remote and primitive, is for the more adventurous.

BAHÍAS DE HUATULCO, OAXACA: Dozens of white, sunswept beaches, tucked into nine secluded bays, span a 10-mile stretch of Mexico's southern Pacific coast. This is the latest paradise discovered by FONATUR, the creators of Cancún and Ixtapa. Santa Cruz Huatulco, Cahué, and Tangolunda, the bays chosen for development during the first phase of the project, are joined by a coastal highway; the others can be reached by *panga* (boat), on foot, or by horse.

LA VENTOSA, SALINA CRUZ: Seven miles (11 km) south of the little town of Salina Cruz, near the border between the states of Oaxaca and Chiapas, is a beachcomber's paradise; principal accommodations are hammocks stretched out beneath thatch-roofed canopies. Not for the Acapulco-loving crowd, but a beautiful beach on the Pacific's Gulf of Tehuantepec.

ISTHMUS OF TEHUANTEPEC: Where Route 200 follows the Pacific coast to the Guatemala border, there are numerous side roads to almost unexplored, certainly uncrowded Pacific beaches. The sand is hot, the climate humid, and the accommodations rustic — but it's heaven for the sauna-and-steam-bath school of beach lovers.

THE GULF OF MEXICO

CHACHALACAS: Some 52 miles (83 km) north of Veracruz, this resort area offers a narrow, gray beach of dark volcanic sand, facing the open sea. Although the waters can be rough, swimming is safe near the shore, and surfing and fishing are good. Boats are for rent near the Jalcomulco River. Restaurants, baths, and showers are available.

TECOLUTLA: This enticing, palm-fringed beach in Papantla country, north of Veracruz, is one of the few good east coast beaches. The *Balnearic* (phone: 748-50901) and *Marsol* (phone: 748-50967) hotels offer simple but adequate rooms and meals. Although it shows signs of deterioration from its palmier resort days, it remains a quiet spot to enjoy warm water and a relaxed atmosphere.

VERACRUZ: Not noted for its beautiful beaches, it does have long stretches of dark sand skirted by shallow Gulf waters. Mocambo Beach, south of town, is a well-kept and lively area where visitors can hear marimba and guitar music and eat the *huachinango* (red snapper), the fish for which the city is famous.

ISLA DEL CARMEN (CARMEN ISLAND): One of the gulf's prime spots for beach lovers (and cruise ships), with exquisite white beaches lined with palm trees, villas, hotels, open-air bars, and dance pavilions. Bajamita, Playa Norte, and La Manigua are the best beaches.

THE CARIBBEAN COAST

ISLA MUJERES: Off Puerto Juárez, this small island has several white, uncrowded beaches; North Beach is the main one, covering the entire northern end of the island; the beach, on the Caribbean side, is good for sunbathing but dangerous for swimming. El Garrafón Beach, on the southern end of the island, is known for its crystal clear waters and skin diving. The journey from the mainland (usually Cancún) to El Garrafón by boat is an adventure in itself — crew members catch fresh fish en route while passengers view schools of astonishingly "tame" tropical fish and turtles. About midway on the island is a research center studying lobsters, shrimp, and giant turtles. Visitors can ride one of the turtles — if they can catch one.

CANCÚN: The Acapulco of the Caribbean, this computer-spawned resort city is among the most recent triumphs of Mexico's booming tourist trade. It is a 14-mile sandbar fringed with palms and gilded with plush hotels and a variety of recreational facilities. Primarily a spot for the sporty and socially oriented vacationer, many major hotels have beaches (although a good number of beaches are still narrower than they were before Hurricane Gilbert hit in 1988), and there are public beaches along Cancún Boulevard, such as Playa Tortuga and Chac-Mool. At the latter, there's a restaurant specializing in local seafood dishes. Dressing rooms and showers are available (open from 10 AM to 11 PM).

COZUMEL: Off the coast of Quintana Roo, 45 miles (72 km) south of Cancún, this island is edged by powder-white beaches, hidden coves, and azure-blue waters. The mainland side of the island has the more popular beaches, including San Francisco and San Juan. Beautiful, nearly deserted beaches can be found by following dirt paths on either side of the island. Chen Río Beach, on the southern end of the Caribbean side, is protected from unpredictable, turbulent Caribbean currents by a ledge of coral that juts into the sea. Punta Molas Beach, on the northern end of the island, is accessible by boat or jeep and offers a pleasant day's journey.

Scuba and Skin Diving:
Best Depths

 Some of the most noted skin- and scuba-diving spots in the world lie off Mexico's long coasts. On the Caribbean, the clear, warm lagoons of Cozumel, Cancún, and Isla Mujeres teem with tropical fish and incredible coral deposits of intricate formation and colorful hues. All major resort areas off the Pacific coast, including Baja California, offer ideal diving conditions.

Every major beach resort in the country rents equipment and offers instruction and organized diving tours. For those who haven't tried skin or scuba diving before, any of the spots listed below (in alphabetical order along each coast) would be a good place to begin.

BAJA — THE PACIFIC COAST AND THE SEA OF CORTÉS

Along the Baja's Pacific coast are innumerable beaches and lagoons that offer great scuba diving; these areas, however, primarily have no formal access trails. Divers on the good beaches around Ensenada, on the Pacific coast, find the water very cold in winter, and most wear rubber suits. Along the Pacific coast, especially in Baja Sur, there are few convenient places to get tanks filled.

The Sea of Cortés coast, however, offers better facilities. Tanks, regulators, fins, snorkels, and masks can be rented in La Paz, where pearl diving is the biggest attraction. Boats are available for about $65 per person per day, and *La Paz Skin Diving Service* (107-B Independencia, La Paz; phone: 682-21826) offers a diesel-propelled houseboat (it sleeps six) that can be rented for a 4-day cruise to the islands in the Gulf of California. *Baja Expeditions* (2625 Garnet Ave., San Diego, CA 92109; phone: 619-581-3311) operates weeklong scuba trips from La Paz from late June to November, at $1,245 per person.

PACIFIC COAST

ACAPULCO: Diving is extremely popular here, though the water in the bay is never as clear as that of the seas along less-developed sections of the Pacific coast or on the Caribbean. The best diving spot in Acapulco is off the shores of Roqueta Island, right in the bay opposite Caleta Beach. *Divers de México* (phone: 748-21397/98), *Aqua Mundo* (no phone), the *Hermanos Arnold* (phone: 748-20788) — all on Costera M. Alemán — and the larger hotels offer diving lessons, which start absolute beginners in a swimming pool. Lessons and equipment are also available at the entrance of Caleta Beach. There is fine snorkeling at *Las Brisas* hotel's private *La Concha* beach club (phone: 748-41580 or 800-228-3000).

GUAYMAS: The unspoiled waters, rocky coves, and resort facilities of this coastal town, on the eastern side of the Sea of Cortés, make Guaymas an ideal spot for diving. San Carlos Bay, 15 miles (24 km) south of town, is a particularly popular diving area, with a yacht club, marina, numerous rocky coves, and nearby islands. Small craft and a complete line of skin-diving equipment are available for rent at the *San Carlos Marina* (no phone). Bocochibampo Bay, just 2 miles (3 km) west of Guaymas, is another popular diving spot; the Playa de Cortés has shops with all kinds of diving equipment.

MANZANILLO: This old seaport, which has become increasingly popular as a resort area, offers skin and scuba diving along its beautiful white beaches. *Las Hadas,* a luxury resort complex, has a wide variety of equipment for rent (on Santiago Peninsula, write to *Las Hadas* (Apdo. 158, c.p. 28200; phone: 333-30000), as does the *Club Méditer-*

ranée (phone: 333-60230), *Playa Blanca* (phone: 5-203-3833 in Mexico City), 30 miles (48 km) northwest of Manzanillo on Playa Blanca.

MAZATLÁN: Although the diving here is not as good as in some other areas of Mexico, the waters afford a pleasant opportunity for underwater exploration, especially for beginners. The best places for diving are the beaches north of town, including Las Gaviotas, Camarón, Sábalo, and Escondido. Diving equipment is available.

PUERTO VALLARTA: This celebrated resort on the Pacific has good scuba diving, if divers go far enough out to where the waters are clear. Los Arcos, a wildlife refuge on a group of eroded rocks in the Bahía de Banderas, and Islas Marietas and Isla Venado — islands close to Puerto Vallarta — are all good diving spots. In town *Chico's Dive Shop* (next to *Carlos O'Brian's* restaurant on the *malecón*; phone: 322-21895; and at the *Fiesta Americana* hotel; phone: 322-22010) rents all equipment and offers guided skin-diving trips to Los Arcos by boat and with gear included. At Mismaloya Beach, south of Puerto Vallarta, it's easy to arrange for skin-diving guides and tours, but visiting divers must bring their own equipment.

ZIHUATANEJO-IXTAPA: A twin resort area, 150 miles (240 km) northwest of Acapulco, it's a skin and scuba diver's paradise. Zihuatanejo's shallow bay waters are perfect for skin diving, as are the 24 miles of palm-lined beaches and coves in Ixtapa. Las Gatas Beach, on the south side of the bay, has an offshore coral reef and warm waters, while Isla Grande, the uninhabited island a mile offshore, has powdery white beaches and clear waters. Los Moros de Potosí, rock formations several miles offshore, offer extraordinary underwater experiences for expert divers.

THE CARIBBEAN COAST

AKUMAL: A large barrier reef frames this 10-mile-long palm-fringed beach west of Cozumel and south of Cancún. The best diving spots are at *Club Akumal* and *Akumal Cancún* (both on the Tulum Hwy.), and the *Capitán Lafitte* hotel (at Punta Bete, about 6 miles/10 km past Playa del Carmen). The waters have 200-foot visibility and stay at about body temperature all year. At 80 to 100 feet, divers can observe magnificent coral gardens, fish, and remnants of 15th-century shipwrecks. The teaching staff of the *Club Akumal* offers excellent instruction, and the club rents all kinds of diving equipment. At Xel-Ha Lagoon, a wildlife refuge just south of Akumal, there is a deep, rock-surrounded inlet of crystal water where snorkelers can view an endless array of colorful fish (rental equipment available). Skin diving is not permitted.

CANCÚN: The island (which is linked to the mainland by a causeway) is perfectly situated for swimming and diving amid coral reefs, fish, turtles, and waters whose colors change from turquoise to indigo to emerald to tourmaline. Operators, such as *Aqua Tours* (phone: 988-30227), and all the larger hotels maintain boat centers with all equipment for rent and also provide skin- and scuba-diving tours, which run about $45 per person. Excellent diving instruction is also available. Items recovered from shipwrecks are on display at the *CEDAM Museum* (at Bajía de Mujeres and Blvd. Kukulcán). Xcaret inlet, surrounded by jungle and the site of caverns and Maya ruins, is outstanding for skin diving (rental equipment available).

COZUMEL: This island 12 miles off the Caribbean Coast is world-famous for its exquisitely clear water and its proximity to Palancar Reef, the second longest reef in the world, 200 feet below the surface of the water at some points. Diving is particularly good from May through August. Daily (except Sunday) trips to Palancar, which include organized diving tours, lunch, drinks, and a guide, leave *Aqua Safari* (near the pier at Av. Rafael Melgar between Calles 5 and 7; phone: 20101) every morning at 9:30 AM.

Chankanab Lagoon is another good spot — it swarms with reef fish. About one-quarter of a mile to the north and south of the lagoon, elkhorn coral and a variety of tropical fish are visible. Off the beach at *La Ceiba* hotel (phone: 987-20379) — probably the best equipped for divers — lies the hulk of the C-46 aircraft that was used for a crash in the movie *Cyclone*. Moonlight diving escapades through the fuselage of this wrecked plane, which settled amid clusters of coral, are a celebrated nocturnal event on the island.

Since currents are strong in Cozumel, don't dive without a guide. The tourist office (in the municipal palace on the main square) or any hotel desk can provide detailed information about scuba- and skin-diving lessons and equipment.

ISLA MUJERES: Small and remote, this island off Puerto Juárez, at the tip of the Yucatán Peninsula, has transparent waters, coral reefs, and lagoons that are renowned among skin divers around the world. Ferries leave for the island from Puerto Juárez (on the mainland, just north of Cancún) seven times daily (people and baggage only), and from Punta Sam, just north of Puerto Juárez, seven times daily (people, cars, campers, and so on). The *Cooperativa* (at Av. Rueda Medina; phone: 988-20274) rents boats and equipment, as does *Mexico Divers* next door (phone: 988-20131). Garrafón Beach, at the end of the 5-mile-long, half-mile-wide island, has crystal clear waters and lovely coral gardens teeming with brightly colored, seemingly tame fish.

Surfing Mexico's Pacific Coasts

 Although surfing is not a Mexican sport, American surfers claim that Mexico's Pacific coastline — with its abundance of reef breaks, point breaks, and river-mouth breaks — offers some of the best virgin surfing waters in the world. Despite the dangerous undertow in many areas, as well as a distinct lack of appreciation of surfers on the part of most Mexicans, dedicated American surfers readily travel up and down the Pacific coast to try waves at beaches big and little. Windsurfing also has become a popular sport at most major resorts.

There is some surfing on the Gulf of Mexico and Caribbean coasts, but waves along Mexico's east shore are erratic. Ideal conditions are found all year along the Pacific coasts, on the Baja from Ensenada to the tip of Baja Sur, and on the "mainland" from Mazatlán to Puerto Escondido.

A note of warning, however: There are few surfboards — and almost no rental facilities — in Mexico. The rentals that do exist (around Mazatlán, for instance) tend to be stocked mostly with boards that Americans in the area swear were stolen. Surfers who are familiar with the Mexican scene report that American boards are prime targets for theft, and advise newcomers to take particular care of their equipment.

Below, a quick survey of the best surfing spots now visited by American surfers. The listing is in geographical order, first covering the Baja Peninsula and then the long Pacific coast, starting at Mazatlán.

BAJA — THE PACIFIC COAST AND SEA OF CORTÉS

From Ensenada to the tip of Baja, there are hundreds of ideal surfing areas. Since many of them are near rugged terrain accessible only to four-wheel-drive vehicles, we mention only those that can be reached with relative ease.

HALFWAY HOUSE: Halfway between Tijuana and Ensenada, where the Baja's Route 1 skids along the Pacific coast, this spot, at the bottom of a 100-foot cliff, is a Baja favorite. Most surfers camp out or stay in Ensenada, spending the days on the waves or on the sand. Idyllic, anarchistic, hard-core, laid-back California surfer style reigns here.

ENSENADA: About 8 miles (13 km) north of Ensenada is San Miguel Village, an excellent spot for advanced surfing. An abundance of rocks and sea urchins, however, makes this a dangerous area for beginners. Mona Lisa is recommended for novices. Km 48, between Ensenada and Tijuana, is also good for surfing.

EL ROSARIO DE ARRIBA: Also known as Punta Baja, this area south of Ensenada has excellent, long, right-point waves in the summer only.

SANTA ROSALÍA: This friendly fishing village, with excellent waves for all surfers, is about 9 miles (14 km) off a dirt road from the Punta Prieta turnoff, 330 miles (528 km) south of Ensenada. The amiable, relaxing atmosphere of the village adds to the pleasure of good surfing. Accommodations are available at *El Morro* (phone: 685-20414), but many surfers prefer to camp out on the beach and enjoy the local supplies of fish.

THE PACIFIC COAST

MAZATLÁN: Many surfers agree that Mazatlán has some of the best surfing waters in North America. The beaches north of town, Las Gaviotas, Camarón, and Sábalo, attract the most surfers. Cañones Point, in front of the *Freeman* hotel, and Lupe's Point, 1½ miles (2 km) south of the *Playa Mazatlán,* are particularly good spots. The latter offers ideal waves for beginners. At the mouth of the harbor, just after entering Mazatlán, there is an excellent spot for advanced surfers.

SAN BLAS: Just south of San Blas, on the harbor of Matanchén Bay, there is a mile-long stretch of excellent right-point waves for beginners. Las Islitas beach, on the bay, is the best for surfing. Just north of the bay, about a half mile on foot, there is a well-known area for advanced surfers called Stoners Point. South of San Blas, in a small fishing village called Santa Cruz, thrives a small community of American surfers — most of whom came to enjoy the surfing and never left. Here the left-point waves are ideal. Playa del Rey, on a peninsula opposite the Port of San Blas, is best for windsurfing; it can be reached by boat from the pier near the Aduana (Customs) Building.

PUERTO VALLARTA: About 10 miles (16 km) north of the Puerto Vallarta airport, at the mouth of the Bay of Banderas, is Punta de Mita (Myth Point), a spot that first gained fame as a pirate port during the days of Spanish colonization. The waves are dangerous here, although there are quiet days when beginners can meet the challenge without unnecessary risk. There are no accommodations; most people camp on the beach or stay in Puerto Vallarta.

MANZANILLO: Some of the best virgin surfing beaches in the world are found along the dirt road that runs 20 to 30 miles (32 to 48 km) south of Manzanillo. There are also excellent waves of all types, good for all levels, off the beaches around town. Camping is common among the surfing crowd, which is never too large here.

PLAYA AZUL TO PETALCALCO BAY: Mexico's most dangerous waves, comparable to the largest waves in Hawaii, are found along this stretch of warm coastal water. Although Petalcalco Bay offers a spectacular vista point for ocean surfing, the area is also noted for robberies and unpleasant relations between natives and strangers. There are no accommodations, but the waves are definitely worth a day's journey for advanced surfers.

ZIHUATANEJO-IXTAPA: This resort area, 150 miles (240 km) north of Acapulco, offers 25 miles of white beach with rolling surf and pounding breakers. There are waves for all levels (except in the tranquil bay), but no boards.

ACAPULCO: Although the water is too calm for surfing at most beaches, and surfboard rentals are not available, the *Acapulco Princess* and *Copacabana* hotels have beaches with powerful waves; discretion is advised, as there is a fierce undertow and no lifeguards. Many surfers prefer the beaches just south of Acapulco.

PUERTO ESCONDIDO: This area, a growing tourist center on the Pacific coast, has some of Mexico's strongest surf. Good left-point waves for beginners can be found about 1½ miles (2 km) south of town, while excellent beach breakers for advanced surfers crash along the shore just south of town. There is excellent surfing on virgin beaches to the north and south of Puerto Escondido. These can be reached by four-wheel-drive vehicles (available for rent in town or at the airport) or by boat.

Sailing: Mexico Afloat

With Mexico's phenomenal coasts, it is not surprising that sailboat races and regattas are held throughout the year. Sailing is a sport Mexicans enjoy along the Gulf, Caribbean, and Pacific coasts, as well as on mountain lakes. Most resort hotels will rent small sailboats to guests, and windsurfing is becoming popular, especially at the *Club Med* enclaves and in Cancún and Cozumel. For exact dates of regattas and competitions, as well as general information, write to the *Mexican Sailing Federation,* 42 Córdoba at Puebla, México, DF (phone: 5-533-3412 or 5-533-4664).

ACAPULCO: One day every month, the bay of Acapulco is covered with sailboats participating in a regatta run by the *Acapulco Yacht Club.* Sailing in the calm bay waters of Acapulco is easy, while navigating the more turbulent Pacific waves and currents requires greater expertise and skill. Small sailboats, good for bay cruising, can be rented at any one of the many beaches in Acapulco, although beaching them can be tricky.

BAJA PENINSULA: While most water sports are easily accessible to tourists visiting the Baja, sailing is a more private affair, dominated by those wealthy enough to own their own boats. On the tip of the peninsula, however, in Cabo San Lucas, *Cabo Acuadeportes* (phone: 684-30117) and water sports concessions at a few of the luxury hotels rent sailboats.

CANCÚN: The calm, clear water of the Cancún lagoon offers pleasant sailing protected from Caribbean currents and wind. Boats can be rented at *Club Lagoon* (phone: 988-31111) or *Aqua-Quinn* (phone: 988-31883 or 988-30100).

COZUMEL: The two yacht basins on the mainland side of Cozumel, Caleta Marina and Puerto de Abrigo (a full-service marina), offer protection from tropical storms. They are the only protected harbors for sailboats along Mexico's Caribbean coast.

ENSENADA: The *Regatas Todos Santos* is held every August, and the annual *Newport–Ensenada Regatta* is held in April or early May.

ISLA MUJERES: In April or May, this tiny island welcomes the annual *Regata del Sol al Sol* boat race, which departs from St. Petersburg, Florida, and is followed by the *Amigos Regatta* around the island. The biennial *Regata del Golfo al Caribe Mexicana,* (next scheduled for 1993) starts in Galveston, Texas. Most participants come from Mexico or the US.

LAKE PÁTZCUARO: At 6,717 feet above sea level in the state of Michoacán, this freshwater lake is a popular sailing resort, with a regatta held every year. Rentals can be arranged at the lakeside dock in the town of Pátzcuaro; prices are controlled by the tourist department. Outings to nearby islands — especially Janitzio — are interesting. The hill at Janitzio is topped by a statue of the military leader Morelos; inside are murals and a circular stairway leading to the top where there's a good view.

LAKE TEQUESQUITENGO: This resort area south of Cuernavaca has a large lake of spring-fed water that's a favorite with Mexico City residents. Small boats are available for rent.

MANZANILLO: A large number of pleasure and racing boats are at anchor here year-round, and hundreds of people appear for the *San Diego–Manzanillo* and the *Marina del Rey* international races, held in late February or early March. Following the *Marina del Rey* race, a regatta known as the *Mexorc Circuit* is held from Manzanillo to other ports on the Pacific coast.

MAZATLÁN: The annual *Los Angeles–Mazatlán Race* ends here. Competitors meet at the *Mazatlán Yacht Club* (Cerro del Crestón), which, though private, makes drydock facilities available. Boat rentals are available up and down the beach, and can be arranged directly or through any of the hotels.

PUERTO VALLARTA: The biennial *Regata a la Costa Alegre,* which is held in odd-numbered years, usually in February, begins at Marina del Rey, California and ends here. Puerto Vallarta's beautiful coast, edged by miles of jungle, is perfect for accomplished sailors. Boat rentals are available at numerous operations along the *malecón,* on the major beaches (Playa del Sol, Playa del Oro, Playa Las Estacas), and through the hotels.

TAMPICO: The *Tampico Sailboat Club* organizes the *International Sailboat Tournament,* held annually during *Easter Week* at Playa Miramar. Boat rentals are available from the *Club de Yates Tampico* (3705-203 Av. Miguel Hidalgo; phone: 12-32585) and *Club de Regatas Corona* (at Laguna de Chairel; phone: 12-30788).

VALLE DE BRAVO, LAKE AVÁNDARO: Nestled in the woods and mountains 95 miles (152 km) west of Mexico City via Toluca, Lake Avándaro is known to many as Little Switzerland. It attracts sailing enthusiasts from Mexico City every weekend. Lakeshore hotels and boat shops can provide boat rental information.

ZIHUATANEJO: Windsurfers are available for rent on La Ropa Beach in front of the *Villa del Sol* hotel; small sailboats, in front of the *Catalina-Sotavento* hotel.

Tennis

 As with golf, the popularity of tennis is growing by leaps and bounds in Mexico. Almost all major resorts have tennis facilities, including the newer luxury accommodations in Cancún, on the Caribbean Coast, and Manzanillo, Ixtapa, and Puerto Vallarta on the Pacific Coast. Acapulco, however, remains the tennis capital, with almost perfect weather from October through June.

In addition to hotel courts, a growing number of tennis clubs — often part of golf clubs — have opened their courts to non-members for a fee. Below is a list of hotels and clubs around Mexico that are known to have good tennis facilities. For more information, write the *Mexican Federation of Tennis* (Federación Mexicana de Tenis), 953 Miguel Angel de Quevedo, Mexico City, DF 04330 (phone: 5-549-1618 or 5-514-1956).

ACAPULCO

ACAPULCO PRINCESS: With 2 of the most lavish air conditioned indoor tennis courts anywhere, it offers 11 courts (6 clay, 5 Laykold) overall. Reservations are necessary. Private lessons are available from local pros Tomas Flores and Juan Tellez or from one of the other instructors. The adjacent *Pierre Marqués,* run by the same management, has 5 courts of its own, and guests also have full access to the *Acapulco Princess* facilities. Airport Rd., 12 miles (19 km) south of Acapulco (phone: 748-43100).

ACAPULCO PLAZA: Here are 4 lighted, hard-surface courts atop a shopping center. 123 Costera Miguel Alemán (phone: 748-58050).

LAS BRISAS: With 309 rooms and a number of 4- to 6-bedroom houses, this resort overlooking Acapulco Bay is one of the best in the world. The 5 hard-surface courts, all lighted, a pro shop, and a tennis and backgammon club are all available to guests. Players must reserve playing time on the courts. 5255 Carr. Escénica, Acapulco (phone: 748-41580 or 800-228-3000).

HYATT CONTINENTAL ACAPULCO: Shares tennis facilities with the *Hyatt Regency* (below). *Mailing address:* Apdo. 214, c.p. 39580 Acapulco (phone: 748-40909).

HYATT REGENCY ACAPULCO: Five lighted hard-surface courts are available. There is also a good pro shop. Guests who purchase a tennis package can use the courts free of charge — don't forget to reserve playing time, though. 1 Costera Miguel Alemán, Acapulco (phone: 748-42888).

PIERRE MARQUÉS: There are 5 courts, plus the tennis facilities of its sister hotel, the *Acapulco Princess,* which is right next door. Rte. 200, 11 miles (18 km) south of downtown Acapulco (phone: 748-42000).

VILLA VERA: *The Villa Vera Racquet Club* has 3 lighted clay courts. 35 Lomas del Mar, Acapulco (phone: 748-40333).

PRIVATE SPORTS CLUBS: The best courts and the best players are usually found at the private clubs; you may also have some difficulty reserving a court, so ask your hotel to make arrangements for you. Acapulco's best include the *Tiffany Racquet Club* (phone: 748-47949) with 6 clay courts (2 lighted), next door to the *Villa Vera* and *Club de Golf* (phone: 748-40781), Costera Miguel Alemán and Av. de los Deportes (4 cement courts, 2 lighted).

BAJA CALIFORNIA PENINSULA

In La Paz: *Riviera del Sol Gran Baja* (phone: 682-23844 or 682-23900). In Tecate (near the California border): *Rancho la Puerta,* the health spa. In San Quintín (northern Baja): *La Pinta San Quintín.*

LORETO TENNIS CENTER: Loreto, where there are 10 lighted courts across the street from the *Stouffer Presidente* hotel, was launched as a major tennis center with the opening of the *Loreto Tennis Center.* Plans are for an eventual 24 courts, pool, pro shop, restaurant, and coffee shop.

LOS CABOS

CABO SAN LUCAS: 2 cement courts (phone: 30122/3, the sister hotel, *Hacienda Beach*; in Los Angeles, 213-205-0055; elsewhere in California, 800-282-4809; elsewhere in the US, 800-421-0777).

HACIENDA: 1 cement court (phone: 684-30122/23).

MELIÁ CABO REAL: 2 lighted artificial grass courts (phone: 684-30967).

MELIÁ CABO SAN LUCAS: 2 lighted artificial grass courts (phone: 684-31000).

PALMILLA: 2 hard-surface courts (phone: 684-20583).

STOUFFER PRESIDENTE: 2 lighted cement courts (phone: 684-20211).

TWIN DOLPHIN: 2 lighted hard-surface courts (no local phone; 800-421-8925 in the US).

POSADA REAL BEST WESTERN: 2 lighted cement courts (phone: 684-20155).

CANCÚN

ARISTOS: 2 cement courts (phone: 988-30011).

CAMINO REAL: 3 lighted artificial grass courts (phone: 988-30100).

CASA MAYA: 3 lighted asphalt courts (phone: 988-30555).

FIESTA AMERICANA: 2 indoor courts (phone: 988-31400).

FIESTA AMERICANA CONDESA: 5 lighted artificial grass courts (phone: 988-51000).

HYATT CANCÚN CARIBE: 3 lighted courts (phone: 988-30044).

KRYSTAL: 2 cement courts (phone: 988-31133).

MELIÁ CANCÚN: 3 lighted artificial grass courts (phone: 988-51114).
MELIÁ TURQUESA: 2 lighted artificial grass courts (phone: 988-32544).
POK-TA-POK GOLF COURSE: 2 lighted, synthetic courts (phone: 988-30871).
SHERATON: 6 lighted synthetic courts (phone: 988-31988).
STOUFFER PRESIDENTE: 2 lighted cement courts (phone: 988-20322).
VILLAS TACUL: 2 well-maintained hard-surface courts (phone: 988-30000).

COZUMEL

LA CEIBA: 1 cement court (phone: 987-20379 or 987-20844).
CLUB COZUMEL CARIBE (on San Juan Beach): 1 cement court (phone: 987-20100).
FIESTA AMERICANA SOL-CARIBE (on Paraíso Beach): 3 lighted cement courts (phone: 987-20700).
MELIÁ MAYAN COZUMEL: 2 synthetic courts (phone: 987-20072).
STOUFFER PRESIDENTE: 2 lighted cement courts (phone: 987-20322).
VILLABLANCA: 1 hard-surface court (phone: 987-20730).

CUERNAVACA

CLARION SUITES RACQUET CLUB: 9 clay courts (4 lighted) terraced into hillside gardens (phone: 73-130300).
CUERNAVACA TRACK: 6 clay courts (phone: 73-132377).
DEL PRADO CUERNAVACA: 4 lighted cement courts (phone: 73-174000).
VILLA INTERNACIONAL DE TENIS: 10 clay courts (phone: 73-130829).

GUADALAJARA

FIESTA AMERICANA:)2 lighted artificial grass tennis courts (phone: 36-253434).
CAMINO REAL: 1 lighted court (phone: 36-478000).
HOLIDAY INN: 4 lighted courts (phone: 36-315566).
EL TAPATÍO: Its tennis facilities are among the best in Mexico, with 10 red clay courts (4 lighted) as well as a pro shop, swimming pool, sauna, and health club. 4275 Aeropuerto Blvd. (phone: 36-356050).

Several golf clubs in and around Guadalajara make courts available to the public for a fee. A roundup: *Club de Golf Atlas* (Km 6 of Carr. Guadalajara-Chapala; phone: 36-890085); *San Isidro Golf Club* (Km 14.5 of Carr. Saltillo; phone: 36-332044); and *Guadalajara Country Club* (260 Mar Caribe; phone: 36-414045), which requires an invitation by a member or proof that you belong to another club.

GUAYMAS

CLUB MED: Features an intensive tennis program, with 29 synthetic-surface courts, 15 lighted (phone: 622-60230).
PLAYA DE CORTÉS GANDARA: 2 tennis courts. Bocochibampo Bay (phone: 622-20121, 622-20547, or 622-20135).
POSADA SAN CARLOS: Use of 13 lighted clay courts as well as the 18-hole golf course at the *San Carlos Country Club* (phone: at the hotel, 622-60015).

HUATULCO

CLUB MED: 12 synthetic-surface courts, 6 lighted (phone: 958-10033 or 800-CLUB-MED).
ROYAL MAEVA: 2 lighted, synthetic-surface courts (phone: 958-10000, 958-10048, 958-10064).
SHERATON: 4 lighted synthetic-surface courts (phone: 958-10055/60/80 or 800-325-3535).

IXTAPA

CAMINO REAL: 4 lighted Laykold courts (phone: 753-32025).

CLUB MED: 12 composition courts, 4 lighted (phone: 753-30944 or 800-CLUB-MED).

DORADO PACIFICO: 2 lighted cement courts (phone: 753-32025).

HOLIDAY INN: 2 lighted cement courts (phone: 753-31186 or 800-HOLIDAY).

IXTAPA GOLF CLUB – 5 lighted hard-surface courts (phone: 753-31858).

IXTAPA SHERATON: 4 lighted hard-surface courts (phone: 753-31858).

KRYSTAL: 2 lighted cement courts (phone: 753-30333).

STOUFFER PRESIDENTE: 2 lighted cement courts (phone: 753-30018).

VILLA DEL SOL: 1 lighted cement court, in Zihuatanejo (phone: 753-42239).

MANZANILLO

CLUB MAEVA: 12 clay courts, 6 lighted (phone: 333-30595; 800-GO-MAEVA in the US).

CLUB SANTIAGO: 6 clay courts, 2 lighted (phone: 333-30412/15 or in the US, 303-371-5360).

CLUB LAS HADAS: Built for jet setters and now settled in as Everyman's Posh, this fairy-tale place has 10 lighted courts (8 hard-surface and 2 clay) as well as golf. This is also one of the official sites of the *Royal Tennis Grand Prix;* the *Pirelli World Celebrity Tennis Classic* is held here in the fall. Pedro Rodríguez is the tennis pro (phone: in Manzanillo, 333-30000, or Westin hotels, 800-228-3000).

CLUB MED PLAYA BLANCA: 5 synthetic-surface courts, 4 lighted (phone: in Mexico City, 5-203-3833; 800-CLUB-MED in the US).

COSTA CAREYES: 2 cement courts (phone: 333-70050; 800-878-4484 in the US).

SIERRA: 4 lighted hard-surface courts (phone: 333-32000).

MAZATLÁN

CAMINO REAL: 2 cement courts atop a small bluff next to the surf (phone: 698-3111; 800-228-3000).

EL CID: 17 courts, 13 clay and 4 Laykold — 6 lighted (phone: 698-33333; in Colorado, 303-320-6771; in California, 800-446-1069; elsewhere in the US, 800-525-1925).

COSTA DE ORO: 3 cement courts (phone: 698-35344 or 698-35366; 213-462-4348 in the US).

HACIENDA MAZATLÁN: Hotel guests have access to the 8 cement courts at the *Reforma* sports club (phone: 698-27000).

REFORMA: 8 cement courts (phone: 698-33576).

LOS SÁBALOS: 2 lighted courts (phone: 698-35333).

MEXICO CITY

CAMINO REAL: 4 lighted Laykold tennis courts (phone: 5-203-2121).

CLUB DE TENIS REYES: 4 lighted, indoor, cement courts, open to the public from 7 AM to 10 PM. Lessons available. Reservations required. 34 Calle José María Tornel in the San Miguel Chapultepec area (phone: 5-277-2690 or 5-515-6004).

MARÍA ISABEL SHERATON: 2 lighted asphalt courts, a swimming pool, and a spa (phone: 5-207-3933).

NIKKO: 3 indoor Laykold courts and a practice court (phone: 5-203-4020).

PRIVATE SPORTS CLUBS: *Chapultepec Sports Club* (665 Mariano Escobedo; phone: 5-511-4848); *French Club* (75 Av. Francia; phone: 5-524-0424); *Israeli Sports Club* (620 Blvd. M. Avila Camacho; phone: 5-557-3000); *Italian Sports Club* (Gabriel Mancera, corner Eugenia); *Junior Sports Club* (3 Sindicalismo; phone: 5-227-7666); *Mexico City Country Club* (1978 Calz. de Tlalpan; phone: 5-549-3040); *Spain Club*

(2390 Av. Insurgentes Sur; phone: 5-518-3865); *Swiss Sports Club* (840 San Borja; phone: 5-559-3230).

LA PAZ

RIVIERA DEL SOL GRAN BAJA: 2 lighted hard-surface courts (phone: 682-23900 or -23844).

PUERTO VALLARTA

CAMINO REAL: 2 lighted composition courts (phone: 322-30123).

LOS FLAMINGOS GOLF CLUB: 4 lighted clay courts; play can be arranged through local hotels (phone: 322-80034).

JOHN NEWCOMBE TENNIS CENTER: 8 clay courts (6 lighted), with classes and clinics designed by *Wimbledon* champion John Newcombe. At the *Fiesta Americana Plaza Vallarta Hotel* (phone: 322-24448 or 322-24360).

KRYSTAL VALLARTA: 2 lighted clay tennis courts. Av. de las Garzas (phone: 322-21459, 322-21378, or 322-21041).

MEZA DEL MAR: 1 cement court (phone: 322-24888).

PLAYA DE ORO: 3 lighted cement tennis courts (phone: 322-26868).

SHERATON BUGANVILIAS: 5 lighted cement courts (phone: 322-23000).

LOS TULES: 2 cement and 3 asphalt courts, all lighted. Next to the *Fiesta Americana Puerto Vallarta Hotel* (phone: 322-22010).

Great Golfing

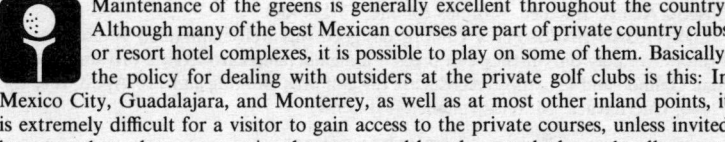

Maintenance of the greens is generally excellent throughout the country. Although many of the best Mexican courses are part of private country clubs or resort hotel complexes, it is possible to play on some of them. Basically, the policy for dealing with outsiders at the private golf clubs is this: In Mexico City, Guadalajara, and Monterrey, as well as at most other inland points, it is extremely difficult for a visitor to gain access to the private courses, unless invited by a member who accompanies the guest — although several places do allow non-members to play on weekdays. In resort areas such as Acapulco, Manzanillo, and Cancún, and inland points such as Avándaro, Querétaro, and Cuernavaca, access is generally easier. At any hotel that is connected with a golf course, or openly offers to secure greens privileges for its guests, few obstacles to entry are found. For more information on private clubs and tournaments, write to the *Mexican Golf Federation* (40-104 Cincinnati, Mexico City 03710; phone: 5-563-9194). *Best Golf Tours* (322 Forest Ave., Laguna Beach, CA; phone: 800-227-0212) offers golf packages to Guadalajara, Manzanillo, Cocoyoc, Mazatlán, Acapulco, Puerto Vallarta, and Ixtapa that include several rounds of golf on some of Mexico's best courses. Mexico's Secretary of Tourism publishes *Best's Golf Guide to Mexico*, which includes such details as course statistics, cart and caddy availability, and greens fees. The book is available for free from the Mexican Government Tourist Office (405 Park Avenue, 10th Floor, New York, New York 10022; phone: 212-755-7261 in New York, or 800-262-8900 throughout the US).

ACAPULCO

ACAPULCO PRINCESS: Ted Robinson designed this shortish, tight, 18-hole golf course, which features many water hazards. Lessons are available. Wayne Sisson is the golf director and Manuel Martinez is the resident pro. Non-guests can play here, and fees during the off-season are a bit lower than in the winter. On Rte. 200, 12 miles (19 km) south of Acapulco (phone: 748-43100).

PIERRE MARQUÉS: Now part of the *Acapulco Princess* family, this Percy Clifford 18-hole course, 11 miles (18 km) south of downtown Acapulco, is the longest and one of the best on Mexico's west coast, with challenging, well-maintained fairways. Reservations are accepted 2 days in advance, and the season runs from mid-December through mid-April. Wayne Sisson is also in charge here; José Dominiquez is the pro. Guests can enter most of its many tournaments. Playa de Revolcadero, just down the road from the *Acapulco Princess* (phone: 748-42000).

CANCÚN

POK-TA-POK: This 18-hole, Robert Trent Jones, Jr. course has a pro shop, bar, and restaurant, and faces the major hotels along Cancún's "hotel row" on Cancún Beach. The course was sold to a Japanese consortium by FONATUR. The pro is Felipe Galindo (phone: 988-30871).

CELAYA

CELAYENSE: The pro at this 18-hole course is Armando Barberi. At Km 264 of the Pan-American Hwy. (Carr. Panamericana), Celaya, Guanajuato (phone: 461-21475).

CUERNAVACA

SAN GASPAR: Designed by Joseph Finger, this layout is open to the public. Joaquín Cossio manages this 18-hole, par 72 course, where one of the main attractions is a 280-yard tee. Ernesto Salomon is the pro. There are also 8 tennis courts. Twenty minutes from Cuernavaca on the Federal Highway to Cuautla. 15 Av. Emiliano Zapata, Cliserio Alanís, Jiutepec, Morelos (phone: 73-194404).

LOS TABACHINES: Percy Clifford designed this well-maintained 18-hole course. Visitors can play only if they can present a membership card from a private US club. Juan Galindo and Fructuoso Acosta are the golf pros. *Mailing address:* Apdo. 168, c.p. 62440, Cuernavaca, Morelos (phone: 73-143999).

GUADALAJARA

ATLAS: Joseph Finger designed this 18-hole course, which is open to visitors on weekdays. The Guadalajara climate is perfect for golf every day of the year, but players should take care until they get accustomed to the 5,000-foot altitude. Sixto Torres and José Quezada are the pros. Km 6 of Carr. Guadalajara-Chapala (phone: 36-890085).

CHAPALA: A 9-hole course that is open to non-members with golf club memberships in the US. Lessons are available. Vista del Lago, San Nicolás Ibarra, Jalisco (no phone).

CHULA VISTA: This 9-hole course is open to non-members. 7 Paseo de Golf, Fraco. Chula Vista (no phone).

GUADALAJARA: An invitation from a member is necessary to play this 18-hole golf course. Manager: Carlos Gutierrez. Golf pro: Barry Willerson. 260 Mar Caribe (phone: 36-414045).

HACIENDA SAN ISIDRO: Larry Hughes designed this 18-hole course. The resident pro is Ruben de la Torre. Open to visitors. Km 14.5 of Carr. Saltillo (phone: 36-332044).

SANTA ANITA: Larry Hughes also designed this 18-holer. Visitors can play on weekdays. Manager: Juan Ramón Araiza. Pro: John Hosterman. Km 18.5 of Carr. Guadalajara-Morelia (phone: 36-860386, 860361, or 860321).

GUAYMAS

SAN CARLOS: Pete and Roy Dye designed this country club's 18-hole championship layout. *Mailing address:* Apdo. 472, c.p. 83010, Guaymas, Sonora (phone: 622-60339).

HERMOSILLO

HERMOSILLO: This 9-hole course was designed by Larry Hughes. There's an excellent restaurant on the premises. The club manager is Guillermo Robles, and the golf pro is David Pérez Acosta. Carr. International and Periférico Oriente (phone: 621-43095).

IXTAPA

CLUB DE GOLF IXTAPA: Formerly the *Palma Real*, this Robert Trent Jones, Sr. 18-hole golf course is part of a pleasant development in this popular resort area. It is managed by Manuel Domínguez; Eualalio Medina is the pro. The course is open to the public, and in the evening it serves as a gathering place for golfers and non-golfers alike. The pro shop sells a wide variety of sporting goods. There is also a bar and 5 lighted tennis courts. The club was recently sold by FONATUR to a Japanese consortium (phone: 753-31858).

LOS CABOS

LOS CABOS: A non-challenging, 9-hole course is open to the public. Dr. Estelio Arretos is the manager; José Serna is the pro. Clubs and cart rentals. Restaurant, bars. 1 Paseo Finisterra (phone: 684-20900).

MANZANILLO

EL PALMAR: Among the best in Mexico, this 18-hole course was designed by Pete and Roy Dye. Rafael Belmont is the pro. Not far from the *Las Hadas* hotel, on the Manzanillo–Puerto Vallarta Highway. Available to guests at *Las Hadas* resort (phone: 333-30000 or 800-228-3000).

SANTIAGO: This 18-hole Larry Hughes course, north of Manzanillo, has an exceptional first tee. The beautifully maintained course spreads over both sides of the highway in an idyllic seaside setting and is open to the public. Also 6 tennis courts. Ladizlao Alvarez is the manager (phone: 333-30413/14).

MAZATLÁN

EL CID: This 18-holer managed by Lucy Reina was designed by Larry Hughes. Tomas García is the pro. There also are tennis courts and a pool. Av. Camarón Sábalo (phone: 698-33333; in Colorado, 303-320-6771; in California, 800-446-1069; elsewhere in the US, 800-525-1925).

MÉRIDA

LA CEIBA: F. Mier y Terán designed this 18-hole course. The manager is Ramón Araiza; the pro, José Escalante. Km 14 of Carr. Mérida Progeso (phone: 99-240070).

MEXICALI

MEXICALI: This small club has an 18-hole course. The manager is Roger Vazquez; the pro, Efrén Huipa. Baja California is an area that has been gradually developing tourist facilities over the past decade, and golf is growing in popularity. The club also has a pool. Laguna Campestre (phone: 65-617130).

MEXICO CITY

ACOZAC: Two 18-hole Larry Hughes courses. At this large sports club, visiting players may use the facilities Tuesdays through Sundays. The manager is Gabriel Pando; pro, David Garcia. Km 29.8 of the Mexico–Puebla Federal Rd., Ixtapaluca, Mexico (phone: 5-972-0276).

CHAPULTEPEC: This 18-hole course is in a wealthy suburb at the end of Calle Conscripto, near the racetrack. Open only to members and their guests. Manager: Carlos Aridzmendi. Pro: Al Escalante. 425 Av. Conscripto Mexico City (phone: 5-584-1200).

MEXICO: The two courses here, a long 18-hole and a short 18-hole, were both designed by Percy Clifford. This large club also has tennis and a swimming pool. Jesús Morales is the golf pro, and Lewis Long is the manager. 64 Av. Glorieta Sur, San Buenaventura, México 2, DF 14620 (phone: 5-573-2000).

MEXICO CITY: A country club with an 18-hole course and a par 3 course; both were designed by George Brademus. Only a guest of a member may play. Tennis courts and a swimming pool on premises. Pro: Miguel Cruz. Manager: Rodolfo Loa. 1978 Calz. de Tlalpán, México, DF 04220 (phone: 5-549-3040, ext. 208).

MORELIA

Club Campestre: Francisco MacFarland is the club manager, and the pro is Angel Martínez. This 9-hole course was designed by Percy Clifford on what was the Hacienda el Molino. The fairways are somewhat narrow because of the trees. *Mailing address:* Apdo. 650, c.p. 58270 (phone: 451-46384).

NUEVO LAREDO

NUEVO LAREDO: This 18-hole, year-round course is managed by Ernesto González, and the pro is José Luis Pérez. The course is accessible from Laredo, Texas. Quince de Septiembre y Panuco (phone: 871-42334).

PUERTO AVENTURAS

PUERTO AVENTURAS GOLF CLUB: Part of the new Puerto Aventuras development about 6 miles (10 km) north of Akumal, this extraordinary course was designed to incorporate natural cenotes (sinkholes) and ancient Maya ruins into the playing field. (Nine holes were open at press time, and nine more were slated to be finished by early this year.) With so many spectacular sights from one hole to the next, it is almost impossible to keep your eye on the ball. It's a tough par 72 for men and 74 for women. The course has an unusually large number of sand traps; almost every green is surrounded by them. This long, winding course also has an exceptionally high share of doglegs and the roughs are literally jungles. Take a lot of extra balls. Electric carts and clubs can be rented from the pro shop, and the 19th hole is a favorite watering hole for golfers and yachtsmen alike. The manager is Edgar H. Giffenig and the pro is Desiderio Coot (phone: 987-22211 or 987-22233).

PUERTO VALLARTA

CLUB DE GOLF MARINA: At the Marina Vallarta complex, this 18-hole course is managed by Tim Tallman; Billy Sitton is the pro. Guests of the *Marriott, Quinta Real,* and *Sheraton* hotels have access to the links.(phone: 322-10171).

LOS FLAMINGOS: An 18-hole course, with full rental facilities and a clubhouse, open to the public. The course is a bit flat and unexciting, but not bad. Fidel Pérez is the pro; the manager is Héctor Almeida. In the Nueva Vallarta Complex (phone: 322-80034).

QUERÉTARO

JURICA (formerly the Hacienda Juriquilla): An 18-hole golf course where tournaments are held. The manager is Alberto de Icaza and the pro is Roberto Arena. The club also has tennis courts, swimming, and squash facilities. 6 miles (10 km) north of the city on Rte. 45, and 2 miles (3 km) west on Rte. 57 (phone: 463-80622).

QUERÉTARO: The 18-hole course was designed by Percy Clifford. To play, a visitor must be a member's guest or recommended by a local hotel. Golf lessons available. The manager is Manuel Contreras. The pro is Mario Moreno. There is also a swimming pool, tennis courts, and horseback riding. 223 Carr. Panamericana (phone: 463-62011).

SAN JUAN DEL RÍO

SAN GIL: An 18-hole course, next to *La Estancia de San Juan.* Guests of that hotel and of the *Antigua Hacienda de Galindo* can use the course. President: Alejandro García. Pro: Enrique Serna (phone: 467-21238).

TEHUACÁN

PEÑAFIEL: No credentials are needed to play at this 9-hole, year-round course. The president is Dr. Miguel Romero. At 356 Calle 7 Nte., Tehuacán, Puebla (no phone).

TIJUANA

TIJUANA: A challenging, well-maintained 18-hole course, where swimming and tennis are also available. The club president is Antonio Valladolid; the pro, Ernesto Pérez Acosta. Blvd. Agua Caliente (phone: 66-817851).

VALLE DE BRAVO/LAKE AVÁNDARO

AVÁNDARO: Percy Clifford designed this 18-hole course, at 6,000 feet, about 80 miles (128 km) west of Mexico City (phone: 726-20301). It is considered one of the finest courses in Mexico. Luis Labarca is the manager; Bernardo Terán is the pro. Accommodations are available nearby at the *Avándaro Club de Golf* motel, *Loto Azul* hotel, *Montiel* motel (phone: 726-20004), and *Los Arcos* hotel (726-20042).

VERACRUZ

MINATITLÁN SPORTS ASSOCIATION: A membership card from your US golf club is needed to play this 18-hole course. The manager is José Castellanos. Colonia Petrolera, Minatitlán, Veracruz (phone: 922-25100).

LA VILLA RICA: No credentials are needed at this 9-hole Percy Clifford course. Club president is Dr. Francisco Santiago; the pro, Lucio Melendez. Swimming and tennis are available as well. El Ponchal, 1351 Carr. Veracruz–Antón Lizardo, Veracruz.

Fishing Mexico's Rich Waters

Mexico's ocean coasts offer some of the best deep-sea fishing in the world, and American fishermen travel thousands of miles up and down the Baja, the Pacific coast, the eastern Gulf, and the Caribbean coasts for snook, bass, dorado, striped marlin, sailfish, red snapper, billfish, and shark. Many experienced anglers come to Mexico just for the numerous fishing competitions held in the major seaports each year. There is no problem bringing any kind of fishing gear into the country, and every major port has charter boats and fishing gear for hire (figure an average of $275 a day, gear and bait included). See individual city reports in THE CITIES for names and addresses. Even the smallest fishing village is likely to have at least one fishing boat that can be hired for a half day or a day.

Visiting anglers can readily obtain a Mexican fishing permit from the Secretaría de Pesca (269 Av. Alvaro Obregón, México, DF 06700), or from any one of its more than 140 offices throughout the country. Licenses are free for fishing from the shore. There is a charge of $7 to $20 a day for fishing from a small vessel. There are also weekly and monthly rates. Temporary permits are issued for boats and trailers entering Mexico. Anglers who bring a boat will be asked at the border to pay a small fee based on the weight of the vehicle, will be required to register the boat with the port captain, and must obtain a license (for a small fee), which is good for 1 year.

More information on fishing in Mexico, including guides, regulations, fishing seasons, and tournaments, can be obtained by writing to Dirección General de Administración de Pesca, 269 Av. Alvaro Obregón, Mexico City, Mexico 06700 (phone: 5-211-0063, ext. 350).

The fishing areas listed below are the best in Mexico.

THE BAJA PENINSULA

BAHÍA DE LOS ANGELES: Set on a magnificent bay 600 miles (960 km) north of La Paz, this harbor and famed fishing camp has spectacular sport fishing, particularly during the spring, when fish nearly clog the channel waters. Charter boats can be rented at the bahía de Los Angeles.

CABO SAN LUCAS: Referred to as Marlin Alley, the southern tip of the Baja Peninsula, where the Sea of Cortés empties into the Pacific, offers some of the best game fishing in the world. In addition to marlin and sailfish, there is an abundance of wahoo, mako shark, and smaller game fish year-round, and billfish in the spring. The *Cabo San Lucas* hotel, known as *El Chileno* (between San Lucas and San José del Cabo; no local phone; 800-SEE-CABO in the US), the *Twin Dolphin* (between San José and San Lucas; phone: 800-421-8925), and the *Finisterra* (at the tip of Cabo San Lucas; phone: 684-30000 or in Alamitos, CA, 213-583-3393) all have excellent facilities available through their fishing desks.

ENSENADA: Every May through November, this Pacific port, 70 miles (112 km) south of Tijuana, becomes the yellowtail capital of the world. Sea bass, barracuda, swordfish, bonito, albacore, and halibut are among the other inhabitants of the seas around Ensenada. Numerous charter boat services are found on the bay south of Avenida López Mateos. (For further information and monthly reports on fishing in Ensenada, write to the Ensenada Tourist Office, 1350 Av. López Mateos, Suite 13B, Ensenada, Baja California Norte.)

LORETO: The marlin and sailfish, which run from June through July, and September through November, are the main attraction of this fishing village 230 miles northwest of La Paz on Baja's Sea of Cortés coast. Mahi-mahi, rooster, and other fighting fish are also found here year-round, as well as Loreto clams. The *La Pinta* (phone: 683-30025) and the *Stouffer Presidente* (phone: 683-30700; 800-HOTELS-1 in the US) hotels arrange for fishing boats and equipment.

MULEGÉ: About 313 miles (500 km) northwest of La Paz, on the brackish estuary of the Río Rosalía, this village is the winter home of the black snook, a prized game fish that measures up to 6 feet and weighs up to 80 pounds. Clam digging and lobster diving are favorite sports at nearby Bahía Concepción. The *Serenidad* hotel (phone: 685-30111) has charter boats with all fishing gear, crew, and refreshments.

LA PAZ: The springtime run of marlin and the autumn run of sailfish are La Paz's biggest fishing attractions, with dorado, roosterfish, swordfish, yellowtail, cabrillas, tuna, sierras, and black sea bass available all year in the southern waters of the Sea of Cortés. The rates for motorboats and deep-sea charter cruisers with equipment are set by the captain of the port ($225 to $325 per day for charter boats). Boats with equipment are available at leading hotels, including *Los Arcos*, 498 Alvaro Obregón (phone: 682-23844).

SAN FELIPE: This sandy fishing village, 125 miles (200 km) south of Mexicali, is known for its sweet-tasting *totoaba,* a game fish about 5 feet long. Fishing folk can rent a boat or launch their own at the village pier.

THE PACIFIC COAST

ACAPULCO: The city's beaches are only slightly more crowded with people than its waters — sea, lagoon, and river — are crowded with fish. The Pacific is ripe territory all year for big game fish like marlin, tuna, sailfish, barracuda, bonito, and red snapper. The city's freshwater lagoons — Coyuca, Tres Palos, and Playa Encantada — and the Río Papagayo are good for carp, catfish, and mullet.

Plenty of equipment and lots of fishing boats are available for rent. Deluxe deep-sea charter boats, fully equipped for fishing, cost $220 to $500 per day, depending on the size of the boat and number of participants. The top price is for a fully equipped, air conditioned yacht, suitable for overnight or longer trips. Anglers can make arrangements through their hotel or can try bargaining with boat captains face to face — not an uncommon practice and one that can work to advantage, but make sure the price *includes* bait and beer. Most deep-sea boats are docked downtown at the *malecón.* For freshwater fishing, both the Coyuca Lagoon and Tres Palos Lagoon, about 16 miles (25 km) southeast of town, have boats with gear for rent.

An *International Billfish Tournament,* which usually brings catches averaging 90 pounds, is held in Acapulco in November or early December. The interclub tournament is in February.

HERMOSILLO: There is good bass fishing 90 miles (144 km) east of Hermosillo at Novillo Dam.

GUAYMAS: Near two bays 250 miles (400 km) south of Nogales, Guaymas is a genuine fisherman's paradise. Sport fishermen favor Guaymas for its abundant supply of marlin, sailfish, and other game fish. Marlin, sailfish, and dolphin season begins in early June and ends in October; yellowtail fishing lasts through the winter months.

Guaymas annually hosts the 4-day *International Game Fish Tournament* in July.

Although there are no longer any fishing boats for hire in Guaymas, hotels can easily arrange to have a vessel sent down from nearby San Carlos.

LOS MOCHIS/TOPOLOBAMPO: About 480 miles (768 km) south of the Arizona border, Topolobampo is the port for nearby Los Mochis and is well loved by big-game fishermen. From June through October, the Sea of Cortés at Topolobampo runs with marlin and sailfish. Pompano are available from November through April, and ladyfish, roosterfish, and yellowtail live in the waters year-round. Boats for up to 12 people can be rented for $300 per day through the *Santa Anita* hotel (corner of Leyva and Hidalgo; phone: 681-57046). There is good bass and perch fishing at nearby Lake Dominguez.

MANZANILLO: This ancient seaport, 220 miles (352 km) southwest of Guadalajara, offers good fishing all year and a sailfish tournament in November. Although mid-October to March is the big fishing season, when the large billfish run, dorado, sea bass, skipjack, and mackerel are available all year.

MAZATLÁN: Some of the most exciting game fishing in the world is done in the waters off Mazatlán. The striped marlin season lasts from January to May, black marlin from May to November, and sailfish all year. Offshore fishing is likely to bring in dorado, sea bass, yellowfin tuna, and bonito. Sport-fishing diesel cruisers — with tackle, bait, and experienced crews — rent according to size and type of equipment (ranging from $180 to $200 per day, or $45 per person on a safari boat). They are anchored at the central dock on the bay side of *Cerro del Crestón.* Motorboats for offshore fishing cost $20 to $40 per hour.

PUERTO VALLARTA: Abundant tuna, roosterfish, red snapper, snook, sea bass, grouper, sailfish, and marlin attract fishermen to this bustling resort area, where the lively *Deep-Sea Fishing Tournament* takes place the first week of November every year. Fishing buffs from around the world attend this event (first prize is a new car). During the peak season, from November through May, boats rent for about $160 to $340 per day. During the off-season, they are often available at a discount. *Cooperativa Progreso Turístico Vallarta,* a sportfishing cooperative (phone: 322-21202), offers deluxe cruisers with all equipment, including tackle and bait.

THE GULF OF MEXICO AND THE CARIBBEAN COAST

CANCÚN: This super-resort in the Caribbean is a haven for deep-sea and lagoon fishing. Sailfish and dolphin run from March through July; bluefin tuna in May; blue and white marlin in April and May; kingfish and wahoo from May through September. Boat rates are set by the *Boat and Yacht Association.* Deep-sea charters (for up to 6 people), including crew, tackle, and lunch, cost approximately $80 per day per person, or $280 to $440 per half-day, full boat charter; while small outboards cost about $30 an hour. For information, go to the *Chac-Mool* pier or the *Playa Blanca* hotel pier. *Aqua Tours* has a fleet of 30- and 36-foot boats (phone: 988-30400).

COZUMEL: The best fishing from this island off the Yucatán Peninsula occurs from March to July for sailfish, bonito, and dolphin, and from May to September for wahoo and kingfish. Marlin, barracuda, and red snapper can also be found in the Caribbean here. Fishing boats cost from $275 to $550 per day, including crew, tackle, and lunch, and hold up to 6 passengers. *Aquarius Travel* (2 Calle 3 Sur, next to the *Bajía* hotel) is a reliable place to charter a boat.

ISLA DEL CARMEN: This island on the Gulf of Mexico at the base of the Yucatán Peninsula has excellent deep-sea and lagoon fishing. The Laguna de Términos, an enormous sweetwater lake fed by streams, offers some of the best tarpon fishing in the world. Any hotel can make arrangements for deep-sea charters or lagoon outboards.

TAMPICO: This river port city, 375 miles (600 km) south of Matamoros (at the Brownsville, Texas, border crossing), is known to sportspeople around the world. Although the tarpon population was nearly eliminated by commercial fishing companies in recent years, the *International Tarpon Tournament* now takes place in Tampico every year in August, and there are other tournaments in February, April, May, and June. Snook and yellowtail thrive in the rivers and lagoons of Tampico, while sailfish, marlin, snook, mackerel, red snapper, bonito, pompano, and yellowtail fill the Gulf of Mexico seas. The *Club de Regatas Corona* (on Laguna de Chairel, at the far west end of town; phone: 12-137410 or 12-137650) and the *Club Internacional de Yates* (phone: 12-138110) will arrange boat rentals for the duration of the tournaments.

INLAND

The many lakes, rivers, lagoons, streams, and reservoirs of Mexico offer an enormous variety of fish, including black bass, catfish, trout, snook, and carp. Valle de Bravo, beyond Toluca, has excellent black bass; the Brockman Dam, in the state of Mexico at El Oro, has rainbow trout; Lake Chapala, 32 miles (51 km) southeast of Guadalajara, has a native species of catfish called *bagre,* a species of sunfish called *mojarra,* and a native whitefish called *blanco.* Lake Pátzcuaro, near Morelia, is famous for its white-fish. Laguna de Catemaco in southern Veracruz, also is renowned for whitefish. For expeditions on this freshwater lake, contact one of the fishing cooperatives.

Mexico on Horseback

 Along with the Catholic church, lust for gold, and a host of Spanish traditions that were to take root in Mexico and wreak various degrees of havoc for the next 3 centuries, Hernán Cortés reintroduced one thing to Mexico that proved to be an outright blessing: the horse. There were no horses in Mexico when Cortés arrived, although cave paintings discovered in northern Mexico indicate that a smaller species once existed, but apparently became extinct. Mexicans are enthusiastic and skilled horsepersons, and the tradition of horsemanship is a perfect marriage between the equestrian heritage of Spain and the workaday requirements of ranches and farms throughout Mexico's northwestern mountains and plains country.

Anyone driving from the US border to central Mexico (see DIRECTIONS) will cross Mexico's arid ranch and cattle country, where opportunities to ride are plentiful; most towns of any size have independent stables or hotels with riding facilities. But opportunities are just as rife along the eastern and western seacoasts. Beach riding is a favorite pastime, and horses can be rented in Acapulco on the beach near the *Acapulco Princess* and in Mazatlán at the *Rancho Guadalupe* (Av. de las Gaviotas) or next to the *Tres Islas* restaurant. There is riding in Puerto Vallarta, Cancún, on the Caribbean, and up and down the Baja Peninsula. Two *Club Med* resorts in Mexico, at Playa Blanca and Guaymas, offer horseback riding; the former has an intensive English riding program available at an additional cost.

Essentially, three kinds of horseback experiences can be enjoyed in Mexico. It is possible, throughout the country, simply to rent a horse by the hour for a leisurely ride around the countryside or for practice on the track of the renting stable. (Several places noted for good riding are listed below; there are literally dozens more.)

It's also possible to join expeditions on horseback into the Sierra Madre Oriental outside Chihuahua or into the jungles of the Yucatán Peninsula or the Indian forests of the state of Chiapas; some of the most beautiful sights in Mexico are reserved for those who get out of their cars and wander up mountains or into jungle valleys on horseback. Mexico is not a country tamed by highways; it has mountains, valleys, and beaches yet to be discovered even by the most enterprising visitor.

Finally, it's fun to spend a marvelous Sunday at a *charreada* and watch a fantastic display of traditional horsemanship and bravado.

STABLES

RANCHO LA ESTANCIA, Chihuahua: Situated 85 miles (136 km) from the city of Chihuahua, in the midst of a Mennonite colony at the entrance to the Sierra Madre Canyon. Horseback excursions to the canyon, as well as hunting and fishing, are offered. There is also a bar, restaurant, pool, sauna, and disco. *Mailing address:* Apdo. 986, 507 V. Carranza, Chihuahua, Chih. (phone: 14-122282).

EL MORILLO, Saltillo: In the state of Coahuila, this riding resort offers comfortable accommodations, a pool, and restaurant. Riding instruction and rental of horses are available at stables next door. Horses are unavailable during winter; rate is $25 per hour. *Mailing address:* Apdo. 304, Saltillo, Coahuila (phone: 841-26300).

JURICA, Querétaro: Horseback riding, along with golf (10 minutes away), tennis, squash, and volleyball, is featured at this restored hacienda, whose 180 rooms, including 12 rooms on an executive floor, are beautifully decorated in Mexican colonial style. Write to Km 229 México–Guanajuato–San Luis Potosí Hwy., Querétaro (phone: 463-80022).

EL MOLINO DE LA ALBORADA, San Cristóbal de las Casas: Chiapas is one of the least visited states in Mexico, but it's a tourist's paradise. El Molino, near the picturesque town of San Cristóbal de las Casas (in the Hueyzacatlan valley of Chiapas), is run by Fran Franklin. Recently renovated, it has a good restaurant and a panoramic view of San Cristóbal. The horseback riding is good, too. Write for reservations and information to Apdo. 50, c.p. 29200, San Cristóbal de las Casas, Chiapas (phone: 967-80935).

EXPEDITIONS ON HORSEBACK

If your idea of a riding vacation is to rough it, explore the magnificent Copper Canyon and environs (west of Chihuahua City) via horse or burro. Two lodges at the canyons rent horses: *Cabañas Divisadero Barrancas* (phone: 14-123362) and *Posadas Barrancas* (no phone). Less expensive accommodations and horse rentals are available at the *Nuevo* hotel (phone: 145-60022) and the *Copper Canyon Lodge* (phone: 14-128893), both in Creel, although this small railroad town is a bit beyond the canyons. An exceptional experience on horseback is sometimes accorded visitors to *Na Bolom House* (33 Av. Vicente Guerrero, in San Cristóbal de las Casas, Chiapas; phone: 967-81418). *Na Bolom* is run by Mrs. Gertrude Blom, the woman who, with her late husband, Franz Blom, is responsible for having saved the nearby Lacandon Indians from extinction. Her home is now a guesthouse, and several times a year (but not during the rainy season) she takes groups on horse tours of nearby Indian villages, where she is loved and revered. Such a ride is a once-in-a-lifetime experience. In Puerto Vallarta, *Rancho Ojo de Agua* (phone: 322-30607) offers 5-day horseback tours that include visits to an archaeological site, jungles, and pine forests. They also operate twice daily tours through back roads and villages.

CHARREADAS

For anyone more interested in observing than in participating, a chunk of Mexico's history and culture is available at the spectacle of a *charreada,* the Mexican original of which the popular western rodeo is a cousin. *Charreadas* are held throughout the year in most towns and villages in northwestern Mexico; they are informal affairs that only occur on Sunday mornings. The tradition is strongest in Guadalajara, and it's popular in Mexico City as well.

A day at the *charreada* includes a traditional roster: the *desfile,* the opening parade of the *charros* and *charras* (men and women riders); the *cabriolas,* an exhibition of fancy riding; *coleadas,* the pursuit and capture of a wild steer; and *manganas y peales,* a series of events featuring lasso roping of steers and wild horses. In the *paseo de la muerte,* the rider leaps from his horse to the back of a wild horse. The competition is interrupted frequently with exhibitions of folk dancing and equestrian ballet called the *escaramuza.*

There are over 300 *charro* clubs throughout Mexico, and most of the participants are amateurs — rich and poor, young and old. The *National Charro Museum* is in Mexico City at 108 Isabel la Católica.

Mountains and Mountain Climbing

For a country as well endowed with mountains as Mexico, there is disappointingly little general interest in mountain climbing among Mexicans. There are an increasing number of organized climbs on either the Sierra Madre Occidental or Sierra Madre Oriental, the two gigantic arms that sweep parallel to Mexico's eastern and western coasts. Mexico provides good climbs for experienced climbers, as well as organized parties with guides, equipment, and companions on three mountains relatively close to Mexico City, Ixtaccíhuatl, Popocaté-petl (known as the White Lady and Popo respectively, both visible from Mexico City), and Orizaba, in the state of Veracruz.

Depending upon snow conditions, ropes may not be needed, though it is advisable to carry at least one rope on any climbing expedition. Tents, ropes, and other major equipment are available in Mexico City and from guides at the mountains, but plan to bring your own personal equipment, such as a sleeping bag, boots, and a backpack. Never climb during the rainy season, March through September, when the weather greatly increases the hazard. Bring along crampons, despite their weight.

It's possible to arrange for guides through the *Club de Exploraciones de México*

(Exploration Club of Mexico). The club (146 Juan A. Mateos, Mexico City; phone: 5-578-5730) meets Wednesdays and Fridays, 8 to 10 PM. *Club Citlaltépetl de México* (9 Dr. Mora, Suite 25-C in Mexico City; phone: 5-512-2534), meets Fridays, 8 to 10 PM, and runs groups for experts (high mountain), beginners, and general tourists; Jorge Inzunza (phone: 5-523-4468, 6 to 9:30 PM) will help with reservations. *Gray Line Tours* (166 Calle Londres in Mexico City; phone: 5-533-1540), offers daily departures with professional mountain-climbing guides to the peaks of Orizaba and Popocatépetl. The company also rents all necessary equipment.

MEXICO'S MOUNTAINS — FOR THE CLIMBING

IXTACCÍHUATL (IXTA) AND POPOCATÉPETL (POPO): These two volcanic peaks, about an hour east of Mexico City, are challenging, but not dangerous for experienced climbers. Ixta, or White Lady, is the more difficult of the two and has two marked routes as well as a reputation for taking the lives of inexperienced climbers. Popo, or Smoking Mountain, is the more popular of the two, and has three marked trails. The climb up Popo via La Cruz takes about 8 or 9 hours and begins at the hut at Tlamacas, where gas, water, shelter, and baths are found. The climb up the eastern side is steeper, more difficult, and more direct.

Guides for the climbs up Ixta or Popo are available through the *Club de Exploraciones de México* (phone: 5-578-5730). *Club Citlaltépetl de México* (phone: 5-512-2534), or *Gray Line Tours* (phone: 5-533-1540). There are also guides and some equipment available in Amecameca, the Aztec town at the foot of the volcanoes.

ORIZABA: Mexico's highest mountain, and one of the world's highest, near the town of Orizaba in the state of Veracruz, Pico de Orizaba (also known as Citlaltépetl) reaches an elevation of 18,851 feet. It is covered with snow all year and is considered sacred by the Indians, who believe it contains the spirit of Quetzalcóatl. The first group to reach the Pico de Orizaba were American soldiers in 1848, part of General Winfield Scott's army. To make the climb beginning at Piedra Grande, take the road from Tlachichuca (Puebla) to La Blatchichieca. A jeep or four-wheel-drive truck will be needed here to travel the rough road to Piedra Grande. Some of the Orizaba trails are marked, but many of the markers are stripped away by storms as quickly as they are put up. Climbing experience is recommended, since some sections may require the use of ropes and crampons. It's best to avoid this mountain during the rainy season.

Camping and Hiking in Mexico's National Parks

In striking contrast with the US, organized camping and backpacking are not generally popular forms of recreation among native Mexicans. Yet, despite the relative lack of interest, trailer parks and national parks are an increasing concern of the government. This is due, in no small part, to the burgeoning tourist trade and greater mobility of Mexico's growing urban middle class. Also, the many free beaches and absence of laws prohibiting camping on public land open thousands of miles of secluded grounds to the adventurous camper. (*Beware:* There are *bandidos* who prey on unwary campers.)

Most camping in Mexico occurs outside national parks, and of all the regions of Mexico, the west coast of the mainland and the Baja Peninsula are by far the most popular for informal and trailer camping. Mexico's western Pacific coast offers beach after beach open to the public, and because of its popularity, has excellent trailer hookups. The Baja Peninsula is a far more informal affair and requires far more knowledge and competence. There are thousands of miles of off-trail, four-wheel-drive-only trails in the Baja, but only experienced campers should take off into the isolation of the Baja wilds.

Unless you camp along Mexico's main roads or at one of the many campgrounds (listed in "Camping and RVs, Hiking and biking" in *When and How to Go*, GETTING READY TO GO), or explore on your own, the national parks listed below offer the only areas in Mexico specifically set aside for camping and hiking. No permits or fees are required for camping, which is allowed anywhere within all park areas. Campers can obtain maps and trail information at the headquarters of each park or through the National Park Headquarters (20 Río Elba, México, DF 06500). Several parks have protected campsites with services. Some, such as Lagunas de Chacahua on the coast of Oaxaca, have fully equipped cabins.

THE BAJA PENINSULA

CONSTITUCIÓN DE 1857 NATIONAL PARK, La Rumorosa: Cradled in the Sierra de Juárez 90 miles (144 km) from Mexicali, this lovely forested area, with striking granite formations, towering ponderosa pines, and a large warmwater lagoon, is a secluded haven for hikers and campers. The park can be reached by taking the La Rumorosa turnoff 45 miles (72 km) west of Mexicali and traveling for 45 more miles (72 km) to the park.

SAN PEDRO MÁRTIR NATIONAL PARK, San Telmo: About 135 miles south of Ensenada, at an altitude of 9,000 feet, the breathtaking granite rock formations and majestic ponderosa pines of this park surrounded by contrasting rolling valleys and prairies make it a sensational spot for camping and hiking. The *National Observatory of Mexico* is at the peak of the park area, across from the north face of Picacho Diablo peak. Although camping near the observatory is not permitted, it is possible to enjoy the magnificent view of steep, forested cliffs dropping into eastern desert highlands. There are streams, forests, and trails throughout the park.

CENTRAL MEXICO

CUMBRES DE AJUSCO NATIONAL PARK, Mexico City: At an altitude of 12,800 feet, just south of Mexico City, this 2,000-acre meadowland has volcanic mountains covered with dense evergreen forests. It attracts lots of weekend picnickers and hikers from Mexico City.

DESIERTO DE LOS LEONES, Mexico City: The name of this park, 15 miles (24 km) west of Mexico City, is rather deceptive, for neither lions nor cacti live here. There are, however, tall pine trees, the remains of a 17th-century Carmelite monastery, and many good hiking trails. The spot is popular with the Mexico City weekend crowd, so for peace and quiet, visit during the week.

LAGUNAS DE ZEMPOALA, Morelos: Take the Tres Cumbres turnoff on the old (free) road to Cuernavaca to reach this 11,000-acre mountaintop park. Three lakes stocked with carp, bass, and trout, as well as many footpaths leading upward from the open meadow, attract fishermen and hikers from Mexico City all year. There is a small charge for parking and entry, but no charge for camping.

LA MARQUESA (MIGUEL HIDALGO Y COSTILLA NATIONAL PARK), Mexico City: Besides a government trout hatchery and an artificial lake, this 4,500-acre valley, surrounded by mountains, has many picnic sites near the highway, horseback riding, and good hiking. It is on the Mexico City–Toluca Highway (Rte. 15). Take the road marked Chalma near the entrance of the park to reach the Valle de Silencio (Valley of Silence), where there are lovely, quiet meadows and woodland areas for picnicking and relaxing.

SOUTHERN MEXICO

LAGUNAS DE MONTEBELLO NATIONAL PARK, Chiapas: Almost all the colors of the rainbow can be found in the more than 60 lagoons of this 13,000-square-mile area on the Mexico-Guatemala border. Besides exquisite lakes, there are lush woodland areas, a cave, the Río Comitán, and the Chinkultic Archaeological Zone, an ancient ceremonial site which has not been fully explored. Although there are no tourist facilities in the park, there are many lovely hiking trails.

Hunting

 Mexico is a hunter's paradise; game is plentiful from the hills of the Sierra Madre to the jungles of Yucatán. With the proper papers, hunters can go after wild turkey, most kinds of duck, geese, quail, wild boars, lynx, deer, grouse, doves, agoutis, peccaries, and armadillos. A special permit is required to hunt bighorn sheep, white-tailed Texas deer, and *bura* deer.

Different areas of the country have different types of game. Deer (*venados*) are most heavily concentrated in the northern border states — Sonora, Chihuahua, and Coahuila. The state of Tabasco also has deer, especially mule deer; Campeche and Yucatán have *temazate* — a small jungle deer. The northern border states are the best hunting grounds for quail (*codornices*) and doves (*palomas*). Ducks (*patos*) — especially teal, pintail, and mallard — geese (*gansos*), and wild turkeys are found mostly along the west coast, in central Mexico, and the Yucatán Peninsula. Bear are found in the states of Sonora and Chihuahua, and jaguar and wild boar in Nayarit, Campeche, Chiapas, Guerrero, Yucatán, and Quintana Roo. (*Important:* Check an updated list of endangered species before you decide what game to go after. Right now, jaguar and ocelot are on the endangered list. Your local zoo will be able to help.)

Hunting in Mexico is relatively easy once inside the country, but there is quite a bit of red tape involved in bringing guns into the country and taking game out. Plan a hunting trip well in advance, in order to obtain all the necessary papers.

Hunting seasons and bag limits vary according to the region and the abundance of game each year. For general information in English or Spanish, or for answers to specific questions, permit information, and the official hunting season calendar (*Calendario Cinegético*), write to the Subsecretaría de Ecología, Dirección General de Conservación Ecológica de los Recursos Naturales (20 Río Elba, 10th Floor, México, DF 06500; phone: 5-286-7051 or 5-286-9390). It will supply a current hunting season calendar and an application for hunting licenses or special permits for any game that require them. In order to obtain a special permit, state the game you are after and the season and the region in which you will be hunting. (*Note:* Because of the timing, you will probably have to write to the Hunting Bureau *twice:* once to obtain the calendar and list of game requiring special permits, and then again stating which animal you will be hunting, and when and where. It's realistic to start the process at least 3 months before arriving in Mexico.)

Every hunter in Mexico must be accompanied by a registered Mexican hunting guide, and each hunter must have a hunting license — a document completely separate from the special permit, which is required only for those going after particular species. But first you must obtain a permit to transport arms temporarily into Mexico. To get this permit, you must present — to the Mexican consulate nearest your American address — a valid passport, a letter from your sheriff or police department stating that you have no criminal record, fie passport photos, and a letter asking to temporarily take firearms into Mexico. The letter must state the brand name, caliber, and serial numbers of the arms you intend to take into the country. Hunters are allowed only one high-powered rifle of any caliber, or two shotguns of any gauge. Automatic weapons are prohibited. The Mexican consulate will issue a permit for firearms and a certificate of identity with a description of your weapons. The fee for this service is $43.70. To facilitate re-entry into the US, you should, before departure, register firearms and ammunition with US Customs. No more than three non-automatic firearms and 1,000 cartridges will be registered for one person.

There's more, however. Actual hunting licenses, good only in the state for which they are issued, can be obtained from the Dirección de Area de Flora y Fauna Silvestre (Wildlife Bureau), Dirección General de Conservación Ecológica de los Recursos Naturales (20 Río Elba, 8th Floor, México, DF 06500); or from the state delegations of the Ministry of Urban Development and Ecology (SEDUE). To obtain a license for hunting birds or small mammals, you must fill out and sign an application, show proof that you have hired a local hunting organizer (names and addresses are listed in the hunting calendar), pay the fee, and, most important, present your permit to transport arms temporarily into Mexico. "Special permits" are issued only through the Mexico City office of the Wildlife Bureau, and two passport-size photos again are required. Hunting licenses for birds or small animals cost about $22 per state. You will also be asked to register your weapons with the office of the commander of the local military garrison. Costs of licenses for other species vary. A license for hunting bighorn sheep, for example, costs about $4,800. Hunters must be accompanied by a licensed guide, and a medical certificate of good health is required in order to obtain the permit to hunt certain species, such as the black bear.

Once you've made it into the country, obtained your licenses and permits, tramped through the jungles, and bagged your game, your final task is to get your game out of the country and into the US. First, check bag limits with the Mexico hunting department *and* with US customs — they're different and they change. Game mammals and migratory game birds require a Mexican export permit or the permission of a Mexican game official. US law requires that a permit be issued from the Fish and Wildlife Service for wild game birds, wild fowl, or wild game animals. Animals may be protected by international law, by US law, or by both. The regulations covering them change periodically, so before going to Mexico, consult the Division of Law Enforcement (PO Box 3247, Arlington, VA 22203-3247) and the Office of Management Authority (PO Box 3507, Arlington, VA 22203-3507) — both part of the Fish and Wildlife Service, US Department of the Interior — about the specific laws and regulations involved in bringing game back into the US.

All of the above deals only with ground transportation. If you enter Mexico by air, and your license and permit are in order, you shouldn't have any trouble with Customs.

Some of this red tape can be avoided if you join a hunting expedition to Mexico from the US, or if you obtain a Mexican hunting guide (both are required in any case) before leaving the United States. You can do this through Mexico's Ministry of Tourism Branches (see: "Mexican Consulates and Tourist Offices in the US" in *Sources and Resources*, GETTING READY TO GO), or through local tourist offices listed in the individual city reports in THE CITIES.

Below is a survey of Mexico's best hunting spots, listed alphabetically by nearest large town or area, where guides are available through tourist offices or large hotels.

ACAPULCO: Duck hunting is excellent in the lagoons around Acapulco. Farther inland are wildcats, deer, wild pigs, and small game. The nearest office of the Ministry of Urban Development and Ecology is in the capital of the state of Guerrero, Chilpancingo (Dr. y General Gabriel Leyva and Ruffo Figueroa, Col. Buenavista, 39090 Chilpancingo, Guerrero). The wilder parts of the state of Guerrero are reputed still to have bandits lurking in the hills, so a guide probably is necessary, if just for peace of mind.

BAJA CALIFORNIA: Mexico's 800-mile peninsula of coast, desert, and mountains has good hunting near the available freshwater supplies, such as its inland oases and mountain streams. Californians regularly flock across the border for the annual autumn dove season. Mexicali Valley, just below the US border, has ducks, doves, quail, pheasant, and partridges. South of Ensenada, on the coast of northern Baja, is the San Pedro Mártir National Park, a rugged game preserve. The *Meling Ranch,* just outside Santelmo (*mailing address:* Apdo. 224, c.p. 22800, Ensenada, Baja California), organizes pack trips. *Mike's Sky Ranch* has a landing strip, pool, horses, restaurant-bar, and is about 22 miles (35 km) from San Matias. Reservations for *Mike's* can be made in Tijuana (phone: 66-845995). Baja California Sur is also known for good hunting, especially near La Paz, Buena Vista (for deer and mountain lions), Mulegé (for quail and ducks — especially during the winter), and El Major (for rabbit, doves, quail, and duck).

CAMPECHE: The gateway to the Yucatán, the state of Campeche is known for its large cats, especially ocelot and jaguar, both of which are currently protected.

GUAYMAS: Across from Baja California on the Pacific coast of Mexico, the Guaymas countryside offers some of the best white-winged-dove hunting in the country. Inquire at first class hotels about guides.

HERMOSILLO: About 175 miles (280 km) south of Nogales, Sonora's capital offers good duck, deer, coyote, and rabbit hunting in the immediate area.

KINO BAY: Some 65 miles (104 km) west of Hermosillo (on Rte. 15 between Nogales and Guaymas in the state of Sonora), Kino Bay is a favorite with campers who like to hunt. Quail, duck, and deer are plentiful here. Across the bay is Isla Tiburón (Shark Island), a game preserve established by the Department of Agriculture.

MANZANILLO: If you can bear to leave the beaches, there are grebe, jaguar, deer, peccaries, and migratory ducks in the area.

MAZATLÁN: A dream for hunters, Mazatlán has four species of duck, as well as quail, doves, and pheasant. The nearby hills offer deer, jaguar, mountain lion, coyote, rabbit, wild boar, and ocelot. Isla Palmito de la Virgen, between Laguna Caimanaro and the ocean, has great duck shooting, as do the surrounding marshes and fields. The area between Mazatlán and Durango is known for bear, deer, and big cats.

MÉRIDA: The largest city on the Yucatán Peninsula, Mérida is a hunting center. Hunting licenses can be obtained from the local bureau of Urban Development and Ecology (Desarrollo Urbano y Ecología; 70 Calle 27, 2nd Floor, Col. México Ote., Mérida, Yucatán 97137). Duck-hunting season runs from mid-December to mid-March, and the hunting is best on the north and west coasts (especially between Sisal and Celestúm). Bobwhites and quail can also be found in the flatlands near Mérida, and trips into the jungle for wild boar and a species of two-foot-tall jungle deer can be arranged.

LOS MOCHIS: Many different duck species can be found in the Pacific coastal state of Sinaloa, especially in the area between Guaymas and Mazatlán; pintail, teal, mallard, redhead, and bluebill are a few. There are also speckled geese and quail. Hunting season for birds is from late October through early March; for small mammals, from mid-August through late March. Nearby duck ponds and lagoons (with blinds) are just 25 to 40 minutes from Los Mochis. The surrounding mountains also hold wild pigs and deer.

NUEVO CASAS GRANDES: Near the Chihuahua-Sonora state line is a little-known but rich hunting area especially good for bear, deer, turkey, quail, and doves. The mountains (Sierra Madre Occidental) are breathtaking, but the high altitude may not be comfortable for everyone. Hunting season runs from late September to February for birds; from August through March for small mammals. Nuevo Casas Grandes can be reached either by road (123 miles/197 km off Route 10); by train; by bus; or by chartering a plane. The area is known not only for its hunting and camping, but also for its archaeological site, probably an outpost of the North American Southwest

Indian culture. It was later colonized by Mexican Indians who were influenced by the Toltec culture.

PUERTO VALLARTA: Though Puerto Vallarta is best known as a sun-filled beach resort, the mountains just outside town are a great place to hunt wild pig, mountain lion, ocelot, jaguar, and deer. In the winter and spring months, there are doves, duck, quail, pigeons, and wild turkey.

TAMPICO: Some 375 miles (600 km) south of Brownsville, Texas, Tampico is a leading port and refining center. It's also on the flyway of eastern migratory birds, and you can hunt deer, quail, turkey, and duck.

ZIHUATANEJO: About 150 miles (240 km) north of Acapulco on the Pacific coast, this town adjoins the resort of Ixtapa. You can hunt duck, geese, and pigeons in the lagoons outside Zihuatanejo.

For the Mind

Mexico's Magnificent Archaeological Heritage

 Astonishing ruins of ancient Indian civilizations have been found in the central, southern, and far eastern reaches of Mexico. Archaeological excavation and restoration have opened up the sites where these cultures flourished and have permitted visitors to take a close look at Mexico's extraordinary past. The following is a description of the architectural and cultural features of Mexico's major archaeological zones. For an invaluable overview of the civilizations and their monumental sculpture, a visit to the awesome *Museo Nacional de Antropología* (National Museum of Anthropology) in Mexico City is strongly recommended. For a full description of the historical background of the various civilizations, see *History,* PERSPECTIVES.

CENTRAL MEXICO

CHALCATZINGO, Morelos: To reach this site, it's necessary to hike for about 30 minutes from the village of the same name, but it is worth the trek. Dating from the Formative period (1600–500 BC), Chalcatzingo is noted for its Olmec bas-relief carvings, recently discovered stelae (upright stone slabs with inscriptions), and altar.

The site is up on a hill, with some reliefs at the base. Ascending, visitors find the imposing relief known as El Rey, portraying a king seated inside a highly stylized jaguar-earth-monster mouth. In Olmec culture, the jaguar cult was associated with fertility. This jaguar seems to signify agricultural fecundity: It's surrounded by rain clouds, and volutes symbolizing mist are issuing from its mouth.

On another slope, a variety of reliefs depict a procession, a scene with jaguars and humans, and a monster devouring a human. On the other side of the hill, the Flying Olmec relief portrays a person who is probably a ballplayer.

The altar shows the design of an earth-monster face associated with human sacrifice, which was a celebrated event and served as appeasement of the gods. In 600 BC, about when the altar was dedicated, several children and some 20 adults were sacrificed and buried in front of it.

Of the recently exposed stelae, one portrays a woman standing on a stylized earth-monster mouth, which is interesting because women are rarely represented in the monumental sculptures of this period, though they are depicted in small clay figurines. This may reflect the status of women in a society in which they rarely reached a level of high political or religious power.

To reach the village of Chalcatzingo from Cuautla, take Route 140 to Azúcar de Morelos, Puebla, until the Amayuca turnoff, then go south 1½ miles (2 km) and take the dirt road 8 miles (13 km) to Montefalco and Chalcatzingo.

CHOLULA, Puebla: Rising above the town of Cholula is the Tepanapa Pyramid; with a 40-acre span and 230-foot height, it's one of the largest structures in the New

World. On top of the Great Pyramid towers a Catholic church built by the Spaniards in 1549 — a stark, graphic symbol of Mexican history.

The town of Cholula is actually situated on the archaeological site built during the Formative period (1600–500 BC). The era witnessed the first of four constructions of the Great Pyramid as well as that of a small pyramid painted with polychrome murals of insects that can be seen by entering the tunnel excavated by archaeologists.

Cholula survived the disruption following the fall of Teotihuacán (see below) and shows influences from Teotihuacán in the use of the *talud-tablero* form and mural painting. Recently discovered murals depict life-size figures in a drinking ritual.

Cholula was conquered in AD 800 by an invading group of Indians and was liberated by the Toltec-Chichimec in AD 1292. During this period it was famous for crafts, including goldwork, turquoise mosaics, and lacquered, polychromed pottery so fine that the Aztec ruler Montezuma had some made to decorate his table.

It's about 9 miles (14 km) west of Puebla.

MEXICO CITY: In 1978, under the streets of central Mexico City, the discovery of an 8-ton Aztec monolith depicting the legend of the god Huitzilopochtli led to excavations around the zocalo, the city's main square. The foundations of the Templo Mayor (Aztec Great Temple), once the holiest shrine of the Aztec Empire, were uncovered here. Also unearthed were thousands of artifacts, including a Chac-Mool sacrificial stone, a sculptured seashell, the base of a temple ornamented with 240 stone skulls, and numerous masks, statues, and other artifacts, which have been exhibited in museums around the world and are now housed in a museum next to the site. Admission charge. Just off the zocalo (phone: 5-542-0606).

More recently, in 1988, the 12-ton Cuauhxicalli stone was unearthed from beneath the patio of the Archbishop's Palace (also near the zocalo). Human hearts were once sacrified on this stone as "food" for the Aztec gods. The stone is now housed in the *Museo Nacional de Antropología* (National Museum of Anthropology); see "Special Places" in *Mexico City,* THE CITIES. Closed Mondays. Admission charge. In Chapultepec Park (phone: 5-553-6266).

EL TAJÍN, Veracruz: This site was contemporaneous with Teotihuacán and was influenced by that powerful city. Though there are only a limited number of restored ruins, unexcavated sites extend for several hundred acres beyond. El Tajín survived the upheaval that occurred with the disappearance of Teotihuacán and the militarism of the following years. The site was destroyed by fire during the 13th century.

The Pyramid of the Niches is unique in its use of 365 niches in the *talud-tablero* architectural form. The typical Tajín style of architecture involves the use of scrolls and volutes; they are visible everywhere. Two of the area's seven ball courts have been reconstructed, one of which bears a bas-relief depicting the sacrifice of a player. The preponderance of yokes, *hachas,* and *palmas* — stone sculptures associated with the Indian ball game — has inspired theories that the ball game was invented in lowland Veracruz. The game was played with a rubber ball, so such theories are supported by the abundance of rubber trees in the area.

It is 8 miles (13 km) from the town of Papantla; take the road toward Espinal, turn right at El Chote, and drive one-half mile (1 km) past Tajín to the ruins.

TEOTIHUACÁN, Mexico: Just 31 miles (50 km) northeast of Mexico City, this archaeological zone comprises more than 7 square miles of remarkable pyramids, temples, and courts; its name means Place of the Gods. Teotihuacán was the capital of the Teotihuacán culture and was probably the first true city in central Mexico. Although inhabited from before the Christian era, the population exceeded 250,000 at its peak during the early classic period (AD 300–600), and the city controlled trade with distant regions of Mesoamerica. By AD 700, however, Teotihuacán had declined as a major power — for reasons not entirely clear — and its collapse was felt throughout Central America. The entire area entered a period of near anarchy, with roaming bands of Indian warriors making war on one another.

Along Teotihuacán's Avenue of the Dead, running north-south, is the Pyramid of the Sun, the tallest pyramid in the New World; the Pyramid of the Moon (at the north end of the avenue); and the Palace of the Butterflies (on the west side of the avenue), the residence of powerful priests.

The *ciudadela* compound at the southern end of the zone contains the most spectacular structure of Teotihuacán, the Temple of Quetzalcóatl, the plumed serpent, with its carvings of feathered serpent bodies; heads of gods including Tlaloc, the rain god; and marine shell motifs. There is an identical structure under the one that's exposed.

In all of these structures, notice the *talud-tablero* architectural form — rectangular spaces that are used for painting and sculptures and are supported by sloping walls with the remnants of frescoes preserved on them.

Most of the inhabitants of Teotihuacán lived in apartment compounds — clusters of rooms organized around patios that contained small altar-shrines. Tetitla, Zacuala, Xolalpán, and Tepantitla are apartment compounds, the largest of which (Tepantitla) contains 176 rooms, 21 patios, and 5 large courts. Brightly colored mural paintings using the religious symbolism of the early inhabitants are preserved in these areas.

The museum near the entrance booth has interesting displays of artifacts, as well as a comfortable restaurant. The archaeological zone is open daily from 9 AM to 5 PM; the on-site museum is closed on Mondays; the entire site is closed on religious holidays. Admission charge.

To reach Teotihuacán from Mexico City, proceed north along Av. Insurgentes and Route 85 to the toll plaza north of the city. At Venta de Carpio, follow the toll road east for some 30 miles (48 km). Numerous bus tours from Mexico City are also available.

TULA, Hidalgo: During the early post-classic period (AD 900–1200), the Toltec culture dominated most of north and central Mexico from its capital at Tula.

The legends of the Toltec were recorded by the Aztec; they relate the story of Ce Acatl Mixcoatl and his people, the Toltec-Chichimec, who settled in the Basin of Mexico and conquered surrounding peoples. Mixcoatl's son, Ce Acatl Topiltzin, moved the capital of the empire to Tula in AD 968. As a priest of the religious sect of Quetzalcóatl, he stimulated the expansion of the arts in Toltec culture and was a peaceful ruler. His major rivals were the followers of Tezcatlipoca, the God of the Smoking Mirror. In a struggle for power between these opposing sects, Topiltzin was forced to flee Tula. According to one legend, he set himself ablaze adorned in his quetzal feathers and rose into the sky as a beautiful bird to become the Morning Star. Another version has him journey out to sea eastward on a raft, vowing someday to return. He became associated with the god Quetzalcóatl, and his legend played a major role in the fall of the Aztec ruler Montezuma II (see *History,* PERSPECTIVES).

Under the rule of the followers of Tezcatlipoca, Tula's militaristic expansion reached its peak. However, drought caused the fall of Tula in 1156 and dispersed the Toltec.

The spacious central plaza of Tula is flanked by pyramids. Building B, north of the plaza, commemorates Quetzalcóatl as the Morning Star. The Burnt Palace, to the west of Building B, has colonnades and decorated benches around the walls. Two ball courts exist on the site, but only one has been excavated and reconstructed.

The stone sculptures of reclining figures holding receptacles on their stomachs are probably rain gods. Similar figures appear in the sculpture of the Tarasco and the Aztec.

Tula is 45 miles (72 km) north of Mexico City; follow the Pan-American Highway (Rte. 85) to the western turnoff at Actopán.

XOCHICALCO, Morelos: Constructed at the end of the classic period, Xochicalco, meaning "place of the house of flowers" in the Nahuatl language, is terraced from the top of the hill, the main ceremonial zone, down to the river. A series of walls and moats facilitated the site's defense. The mountain is riddled with caves, which were used for ceremonies.

The *talud-tablero*-style pyramid covered by bas-reliefs is the most interesting structure. Undulating feathered serpents and people with Maya features are depicted, but the tribal identity of the builders is unknown.

The Temple of the Stelae is south of the main pyramid. The palace where the rulers probably lived consists of many rooms, passages, courts, stairways, and baths. The ball court is similar to the one at Tula, though here the court has stone rings that served as goals.

It is 24 miles (38 km) southwest of Cuernavaca, reached via CN-95 (Carr. Nacional, or Federal Hwy., 95) to Alpuyeca, and then west for 5 miles (8 km) to the road marked to Xochicalco.

SOUTH MEXICO

MITLA, Oaxaca: This site, the name of which means Place of Rest, was an important religious center during the early post-classic period. Its five groups of buildings once housed the high priest and secondary priests of the Zapotec as well as the Zapotec king and his advisers. Beneath the buildings lie the catacombs that gave Mitla its name.

The architectural layout is that of rectangular patios surrounded by long, narrow rooms. The doorways and façade are covered with mosaics, some of which show the Mixtec influence in the form of step-and-fret motifs. A colonial church was constructed on one of the precincts of the site, graphically illustrating the superimposition of the Spanish culture on that of the Indians.

The site is 24 miles (38 km) southeast of Oaxaca.

MONTE ALBÁN, Oaxaca: This imposing site is on a mountaintop overlooking the city of Oaxaca. The site was first occupied from 300 BC to AD 300, destroyed, and rebuilt as it appears today.

Monte Albán was constructed around a large plaza. The hilltop bore a sophisticated network of dams and 2,000 terraces used by Zapotec Indians as foundations for dwellings. The *talud-tablero* architecture, similar to that at Teotihuacán, predominates at Monte Albán. At one time, the buildings were stuccoed and painted.

An I-shaped ball court lies in one corner of the main plaza. The ball game was a religious ceremony in which two teams competed to knock a rubber ball through the stone rings on either side of the court. The object was to keep the ball in motion using only the torso and head. When a team put the ball through a ring, it had the right to claim anything worn by the spectators, at which point the spectators usually fled. Like most Oaxacan ball courts, the stone rings are absent from Monte Albán. The two niches in the diagonal corners of the court probably served as shrines for the patron deities of the ball game.

The Temple of Danzantes has interesting bas-reliefs, including carved, numbered slabs on the façade that suggest the use of the Calendar Round, the calendric system based on a 52-year cycle. The Danzantes are the nude male figures and supposedly represent dead captives. The rubbery postures of the figures are interpreted as death poses, and the depiction of sexual organs in Mesoamerican art designates prisoners, because nudity was considered degrading. Some instances of sexual mutilation are represented in the reliefs.

Building J is an interesting arrowhead-shaped structure that harbors a series of internal chambers. The exterior of the building is set with carved slabs that relate a story of conquest; the inverted heads inscribed above the town names represent the defeat of the rulers.

Subterranean tombs, consisting of clusters of chambers decorated with frescoes, can be found throughout the site. The entrance of Tomb 104, at the northern end of the site, was blocked by a large slab of rock covered with hieroglyphs. Inside, pottery — including a magnificent gray urn representing Cocijo, the Oaxacan rain god — was found, along with a skeleton. Tomb 105 has a fresco depicting a procession of nine male deities and nine goddesses in a style similar to that of Teotihuacán. Tomb 7 yielded dazzling treasures, most of which are in Oaxaca's *Regional Museum.*

The site is 5½ miles (9 km) southwest of Oaxaca.

PALENQUE, Chiapas: Probably the most spectacular Maya site in all of Mexico. The ruins are set on a high plateau surrounded by lush mountain jungles where monkeys and wild birds still manage to survive and where dense vegetation abounds. Over this wild jungle, the pyramids establish a precision and order that stand in sharp contrast to their primordial surroundings. From the top of any of these elaborate structures, there's a sweeping view of the lowlands of Tabasco, an apparently limitless stretch of forest and savanna.

The ruins themselves are extremely significant. Similarities between the architecture at Palenque and that at places in the ancient Orient provide strong evidence to support theories of a direct ancestral link between Mexican and Asian cultures. The sacred tree or cross found on this continent only at Palenque, in the Temple of the Foliated Cross, has an almost exact counterpart in sculptured panels at Angkor Wat in Cambodia. Furthermore, the sculpted figures of divinities holding lotus flowers bear a strong resemblance to those found in Hindu-Buddhist temples in India.

In addition to viewing this impressive evidence, note the Temple of the Sun, which houses a tablet carved with a mask of the Jaguar Sun before crossed spears, and the Temple of the Cross, where the tablet is inscribed with branching trees topped by quetzal birds. The palace is a complex gallery of rooms organized around patios where exquisite reliefs portray prisoners in submission. The 4-story square tower probably served as an astronomical observatory or strategic lookout post. Underneath the palace, the stream that crosscuts the site is enclosed in a corbel-vaulted aqueduct. Upon excavation, the Temple of the Inscriptions revealed the funerary crypt of a ruler of Palenque. The walls of the chamber are decorated with stuccoed figures, and the crypt itself contained jewels and jade ornaments in addition to the remains. Inside all the temples, there is a vast assortment of Maya work and artifacts, including intricate reliefs, jade masks, earspools, necklaces, beads, rings, and pottery vessels.

Palenque is 89 miles (142 km) southeast of Villahermosa. Drive on Route 186 to Catazaja Junction, then south for 17 miles (27 km) on a paved road to the village.

THE YUCATÁN PENINSULA

CHICHÉN ITZÁ, Yucatán: This site is easily reached from Mérida or Cancún. Chichén Itzá was an insignificant Maya site until the Toltec conquered it, built their structures on top of existing Maya ones, and dominated the area until they abandoned it in AD 1224. (An evening sound-and-light show in English explains the site's history, though performances are frequently canceled because of power failures.)

The Toltec built structures in their own style, exemplified at Tula; good examples here are the Temple of the Warriors, the Group of a Thousand Columns, the Temple of Kukulcán, the Temple of the Chac-Mool, and the ball court.

The Toltec initiated rites of human sacrifice at Chichén Itzá. The *zompantli* (a platform on which human skulls were exhibited) is decorated with carved stone skulls, and the ball court displays carved relief figures depicting the traditional sacrificial deaths of the losing team. The bottom of the cenote, or natural well, nearby was littered with human skeletons and valuables; live victims were drowned here to appease the gods.

The Temple of Kukulcán displays a mixture of architectural features — Toltec warrior reliefs as well as Maya corbeled vaults. At the topmost altar, reached by an interior stairway, is a stone statue of a jaguar, painted red, with jade eyes and spots and white flint fangs still in place.

The Group of a Thousand Columns was probably the marketplace of the great center. Several acres in size, the area is completely surrounded by colonnades.

Sculptures of Toltec warriors are carved on the columns of the Temple of the Warriors. Chac-Mools, feathered serpents, and small Atlantean figures recall the style of Tula. Murals recount the story of battles between this tribe and surrounding groups.

In the Temple of the Chac-Mool, paintings on the benches show Toltec seated on jaguar thrones and Maya rulers on jaguar skin–covered stools.

The observatory is outside the Toltec compound. A spiral stairway leads to a small tower where openings in the structure were used to observe the equinoxes.

Chichén Itzá is 75 miles (120 km) east of Mérida on Route 180. (For more details, see "Chichén Itzá" in the *Yucatán Peninsula*, DIRECTIONS.)

UXMAL, Yucatán: This site, the name of which means "three times built," was the major site of the Maya classic period (AD 600–1000), and during this time it underwent several periods of transition. Uxmal, which was abandoned in the early post-classic period, when the neighboring Maya center, Chichén Itzá, fell to the Toltec, is generally considered the best example of fine, classic Maya architecture: The temples and other buildings are beautifully proportioned and designed. There is a sound-and-light show in English.

The two largest pyramids, the Temples of the Dwarf and Magician, contain intricate masks, panels, and mosaics. (Be aware that the steps of the Temple of the Magician make for a very steep climb.) The Governor's Palace, a majestic structure 322 feet long and 40 feet wide, is built on multiple levels with vaulted passages and lateral wings containing exquisite latticework and mosaics. The House of Turtles is a well-proportioned and simply adorned structure northeast of the Governor's Palace.

Uxmal is 48 miles (77 km) south of Mérida along Route 180.

THE CARIBBEAN COAST

TULUM, Quintana Roo: Perched on the edge of a cliff, this small, strange Maya site towers above sparkling white beaches on the Caribbean and is enclosed by a stone wall. This late post-classic city is often referred to as "decadent"; that is, it dates from the time of the waning of the Maya civilization. The architecture, although built by the Maya, lacks their refinement of style; it shows squarish Toltec influence and is crudely designed and constructed.

The principal structure is the Castillo, a pyramid topped by a small temple with simple columns marking the entrance. In the Temple of the Frescoes, murals and sculptured decorations are well preserved in bright colors.

Reached by day-long tours from Cancún, 75 miles (120 km) north, or boat trips from Cozumel; by car via Route 180 east to Puerto Juárez, then south, along Route 307.

COBÁ, Quintana Roo: This Maya city, not far from Tulum and Cancún, is slowly being reclaimed from the jungle. Already uncovered are a 130-foot pyramid, a 9-tiered castle, and remnants of a ball court. A *Club Med Villa Arqueológica* is at the site. On Rte. 307, 26 miles (41 km) from Tulum.

Mexico's Great Museums

Mexico has many fascinating museums that glorify its ancient and rich history, its strong artistic tradition, and its broad cultural diversity. The major museums are concentrated in Mexico City, but others scattered throughout the country have large displays of artifacts, paintings, murals, and relics dating back 10,000 years. The museums described below have the most extensive and interesting collections in Mexico; smaller city museums are listed in the individual city reports of THE CITIES.

WEST

INSTITUTO DE LA ARTESANÍA JALISCIENSE (HANDICRAFTS INSTITUTE OF JALISCO) Guadalajara: This combination shop-museum, run by the state, displays and sells (at fixed prices) a wide range of regional handicrafts, including saddlery, furniture, blown glass, ceramics, pottery, textiles, tinwork, and woodcarving. There is a good exhibition of paintings on the second floor. Located north of the *Archaeological Museum,* in Parque Agua Azul. (A showroom, at 122 Av. Alcalde, is closed Sundays.) No admission charge. Off Independencia in Parque Agua Azul (phone: 36-244518).

MUSEO REGIONAL DE GUADALAJARA (GUADALAJARA REGIONAL MUSEUM), Guadalajara: Displayed in the vine-covered patios of this 18th-century structure, which once served as a theological seminary, are outstanding Mexican and Spanish paintings, pre-Columbian relics, regional arts and crafts, portraits of dignitaries, and colonial period furniture. Open 9 AM to 3:30 PM; closed Mondays. Admission charge. One block north of the Governor's Palace at 60 Liceo, next to the cathedral (phone: 36-149957).

CENTRAL MEXICO

BELLAS ARTES (PALACE OF FINE ARTS), Mexico City: This marble structure, combining Maya, Mixtec, and Classic motifs, houses Mexico's best collection of works by Siqueiros, Orozco, Tamayo, Juan O'Gorman, and Rivera, as well as works of major contemporary international artists. The museum also offers performances by the *Ballet Folklórico* in a beautiful theater that contains a Tiffany glass curtain. Closed Mondays and holidays. Admission charge for special exhibits only. At the eastern end of Alameda Park (phone: 5-585-4888).

CENTRO CULTURAL/ARTE CONTEMPORÁNEO, Mexico City: The *Center for Contemporary Culture/Art* opened in October 1986 with funding from Fundación Cultural Televisa, Mexico's private television monopoly. The permanent exhibitions are from the foundation's exciting collection of 20th-century art and include painting, sculpture, graphics, and decorative art, both Mexican and international, a photographic collection selected by Mexico's grand master of photography, Manuel Alvarez Bravo, and a rich selection of pre-Hispanic art. There are temporary shows as well. Closed Mondays. Admission charge. Next door to the *Presidente Chapultepec* at Campos Elíseos and Jorge Eliot (phone: 5-250-2327).

DIEGO RIVERA MUSEUM (Anahuacalli), Mexico City: This striking Maya-style structure contains over 60,000 treasures from Mexico's ancient Indian cultures as well as some of Diego Rivera's masterful murals. Closed Mondays and holidays. No admission charge. On the outskirts of the city, 150 Calle Museo, off División del Norte.

DOLORES OLMEDO FOUNDATION MUSEUM, Mexico City: As a tribute to a great artist and her close friend, Dolores Olmedo converted her private home into a museum displaying a fine collection of works by Diego Rivera. Along with Rivera's paintings are pieces by his wife, Frida Kahlo, as well as Mexican folk art and pre-Columbian works. The museum was originally a 16th-century monastery. Closed Mondays. Admission charge. 5843 Av. México, in the Xochmilco area (phone: 5-676-1166).

FRANZ MAYER MUSEUM, Mexico City: The magnificently restored 16th-century Ex-Hospital de la Mujer (former Women's Hospital) houses one of Mexico City's newest museums. Just behind Alameda Park on Plaza Santa Veracruz, it contains the awesome personal collection of Franz Mayer, a German-born financier. There are Dutch, Flemish, and Italian Renaissance paintings, but the major portion of the collection consists of Mexican, European, and Oriental applied arts (silver, ceramics, textiles, furniture, ivories — even a model of an 18th-century pharmacy) dating from the 16th to the 19th century. There also is a library that contains 770 different editions of *Don Quixote*. Closed Mondays. Admission charge. 45 Av. Hidalgo (phone: 5-518-2265).

FRIDA KAHLO MUSEUM, Mexico City: Frida Kahlo, the accomplished artist who was married to Diego Rivera, lived in this colonial-style home with her husband. Besides the featured exhibits of her imaginative paintings, unique pieces of popular art and furniture are on display, and there is a lovely patio-garden where you can stroll and relax. Closed Mondays and holidays. No admission charge. In suburban Coyoacán, south of the city, at 247 Londres (phone: 5-554-5999).

JUÁREZ MUSEUM, Mexico City: The well-preserved home of Benito Juárez has displays of the former president's personal belongings, medals, clothes, encased letters, important papers, and silverware. Juárez's bedroom has clothes hanging in the closet, a dressing gown laid out on the bed, and everything arranged as it was when he was alive. Closed weekends and holidays. No admission charge. In the National Palace on the zocalo (no phone).

MUSEO ESTUDIO DIEGO RIVERA (MUSEUM STUDIO OF DIEGO RIVERA), Mexico City: The home and studio of one of Mexico's most famous painters and muralists has been turned into a museum filled with the objects and paintings with which he lived. The model for the restoration work was a Rivera painting, *The Painter's Studio,* which itself is on view. The 2-story structure was designed by his friend Juan O'Gorman, an architect and fellow painter. It may seem uncomfortably small for a person of Rivera's girth, but he lived here happily for 24 years. Closed Mondays. No admission charge. A block from the *San Angel Inn* restaurant at Av. Altavista and Calle Diego Rivera (phone: 5-548-3032).

MUSEO NACIONAL DEL VIRREINATO (NATIONAL MUSEUM OF THE VICE-REGENCY), Tepozotlán, State of Mexico: Founded by the Jesuits in 1584 as an Indian school and later used as a seminary, the building was not completed until the second half of the 18th century and today is a museum containing some of the most outstanding works of Mexican religious art. Among them are the beautiful novitiate's chapel, an extraordinary churrigueresque altar, a Miguel Cabrera painting of Mexico's patron saint, the Virgin of Guadalupe, and, in the Chapel of Nuestra Señora de Loreto, a house representing the Nazareth home of the Virgin Mary. A pleasant restaurant is in one of the patios, and several others are around the town's main plaza. Closed Mondays. Admission charge. About 45 minutes from Mexico City via the toll road to Querétaro (phone: 5-876-0245).

MUSEO DEL TEMPLO MAYOR (MUSEUM OF THE GREAT TEMPLE), Mexico City: A spectacular museum housing artifacts found during excavations of the Great Temple in the heart of Mexico City. In an attempt to reproduce the concept of the temple itself, the museum is divided into two sections. One is dedicated to Huit-zilopochtli and contains some of the most important monolithic sculptures found at the site, including the *Guerreros Aguila* (Eagle Warriors). The other section is dedicated to Tlaloc and includes a reproduction of part of the temple and a scale model of the sacred city. It also contains a room that presents versions of the conquest of Mexico as "told" by the Indians and by Hernán Cortés. Guided tours in English are available by appointment (phone: 5-542-1717). Closed Mondays. Admission charge. Just off the zocalo.

MUSEUM OF CULTURES, Mexico City: Once the national mint, this 18th-century structure has 15 rooms devoted to the subject of early cultures, including exhibits of arts and crafts from ancient Greece, southeast Asia, Africa, Japan, India, Israel, and northern Europe. Six of the rooms were under restoration, as we went to press, and could be closed indefinitely, since the museum's restoration funds are low. Closed Mondays and holidays. Admission charge. 13 Moneda (phone: 5-512-7452).

MUSEUM OF MEXICO CITY, Mexico City: Once the private mansion of the Count of Santiago, this striking building, with an intricately carved façade, now houses fine exhibits on all periods of the history of Mexico City, from ancient to contemporary. Included in the displays are graphic prints and maps depicting early Indian settlements and cities, as well as models of monuments, costumes, and furniture of past eras. One entire room off the courtyard is devoted to the history of transportation in Mexico City, while the second floor has wonderful photographs and portrayals of revolutionary leaders and of the current scene in Mexico City. The third floor is devoted to the works of Joquín Clausell, the Mexican Impressionist painter. Closed Mondays and holidays. Admission charge. 30 Pino Suárez (phone: 5-542-0487).

MUSEUM OF MODERN ART, Mexico City: This spectacular, circular, dark glass structure contains some of the most celebrated works of Velasco, Rivera, Orozco, Juan O'Gorman, Siqueiros, Tamayo, Covarrubias, and Icaza. Separated from the main building by a statue-filled garden is another gallery, which houses changing exhibits. Closed Mondays and holidays. Admission charge. Chapultepec Park (phone: 5-553-6313).

MUSEUM OF NATURAL HISTORY, Mexico City: A must for children and another of the capital's architectural wonders, this museum is composed of ten connected domed buildings surrounded by flowers and plants. Two of the buildings are dedicated to geology and astronomy, four to a progressive exhibit on the origins of life, and four to general biology. Displays include stuffed and preserved animals, simulated natural environments, and large maps illustrating such subjects as the mountains of Mexico and the origin of minerals in Mexico. Closed Mondays. Admission charge. No cameras are allowed. Chapultepec Park (no phone).

NATIONAL ART MUSEUM, Mexico City: In the historic Communications Palace, this museum displays paintings, sculpture, and graphics covering the history and development of Mexican art from its inception to the present. Closed Mondays and holidays. Admission charge. 8 Tacuba (phone: 5-521-7320).

NATIONAL MUSEUM OF ANTHROPOLOGY, Mexico City: Exhibitions here offer a glimpse of cultures that began their development 10,000 years ago. The museum, which is built around a sunny courtyard, is organized chronologically and geographically — walking through the rooms on the ground floor, visitors see displays on the evolution of man and the ancient Indian cultures of Mexico. Exhibits include every conceivable artifact and relic, from jewelry, musical instruments, stone carvings, pottery, lavish ornaments, tapestries, costumes, and footwear to medicinal herbs, gourds, feather and shell crafts, temple decor, burial offerings, gold and alabaster bowls, and figurines. On the second floor is a detailed exhibition of modern rural life in Mexico. Here also are the major familiar monumental pre-Conquest sculptures, such as the massive Aztec Calendar Stone. The museum has a cafeteria and restaurant, and guided tours are conducted in English. At press time part of the museum was closed indefinitely for renovations. Closed Mondays. Admission charge. Chapultepec Park (phone: 5-553-6266).

NATIONAL MUSEUM OF HISTORY, Mexico City: This 200-year-old castle commands a spectacular view of Mexico City and has displays of artifacts from the past 3 centuries. The castle has an interesting history of its own. Originally chosen as the site for Montezuma's country residence, the castle was used as a military academy and fortress during the Mexican-American War, and was converted into the residence of Emperor Maximilian and Empress Carlota in 1866. Since Maximilian's execution, it has served as a center for ceremonial events and as a museum. On display are the formal gardens designed by Carlota as well as the elegantly furnished quarters that she and the emperor occupied. Besides a collection of valuable jewels, Gobelin tapestries, furniture, ceramics, paintings, statues, and other historical relics, the castle has two rooms dedicated to the independence and the revolution of Mexico, with murals by Juan O'Gorman and Siqueiros.

The Gallery of History, in the circular structure west of the castle, contains a vast collection of items pertaining to the history of Mexico from the conquest to the present. The photographs and dioramas portraying the Mexican struggle against colonial rule and dictatorship are very moving. Closed Mondays. Admission charge. Grasshopper Hill, Chapultepec Park (phone: 5-286-0700).

PINACOTECA VIRREINAL (MUSEUM OF COLONIAL PAINTINGS), Mexico City: Art of the 16th, 17th, and 18th centuries is displayed in what was once the Church of San Diego, built in 1591. Closed Mondays and holidays. No admission charge. 7 Dr. Mora (no phone).

RUFINO TAMAYO MUSEUM, Mexico City: Opened in 1981, this striking, modern structure consists of two groups of exhibition salons linked by ramps and built around a central covered courtyard full of sculpture. Though named for artist Rufino Tamayo, the museum contains works by such artists as Picasso and Ernst, along with a few pieces by Tamayo. Closed Mondays. Admission charge. Chapultepec Park (no phone).

SAN CARLOS MUSEUM, Mexico City: This restored castle is Mexico's European art museum. Once inhabited by the Count of Buenavista, the building was a wedding gift from Maximilian to Marshal Bazaine, and subsequently served as a cigarette factory, school, national lottery, and post office. On display are works by El Greco, Titian, Van Dyck, Velázquez, Rembrandt, Brueghel, Rubens, Reynolds, Gainsborough, and Pissarro. Closed Tuesdays and holidays. No admission charge. 50 Calle Puente de Alvarado (phone: 5-535-4848).

SIQUEIROS CULTURAL POLYFORUM, Mexico City: The impact and incredible scope of this creation, which integrates various art forms, is a fitting tribute to Siqueiros, the prolific Mexican artist whose impassioned political and social conscience permeated his work. The actual structure of the Polyforum, which involved the work of over 30 artists from around the world, includes 12 exterior surfaces covered by mammoth sculpted figures and interior galleries housing a theater, murals, and arts and crafts exhibits. On the third level is *The March of Humanity,* a powerful mural depicting workers — and the Polyforum's pièce de résistance. Encompassing an area of 27,000 feet, the mural is composed of metals and acrylics on asbestos-cement panels over iron. Viewed from a revolving floor below, the mural manages to defy its stationary position by appearing to move on several planes simultaneously. Open daily. Admission charge. Insurgentes Sur and Filadelfia (phone: 5-536-4522).

MUSEO REGIONAL MICHOACANO (REGIONAL MUSEUM OF MICHOACÁN), Morelia: Archaeological artifacts from the Michoacán region as well as colonial weapons, furniture, and paintings are on display at this 18th-century palace. Cantú's mural *The Four Horsemen of the Apocalypse,* on the second floor, is the museum's most celebrated work. Closed Mondays. No admission charge. 305 Calle Allende at the corner of Abasola, a few steps from the southwest corner of the main plaza (phone: 451-20407).

CASA DE ALFEÑIQUE (REGIONAL MUSEUM OF PUEBLA), Puebla: Historical exhibits, colonial furnishings, and some archaeological artifacts are housed in this ornate structure. Closed Mondays. Admission charge. 416 Av. 4 Cuatro Ote. (phone: 22-414246).

JOSÉ LUIS BELLO Y GONZÁLEZ MUSEUM, Puebla: An excellent exhibit of artwork and items from the colonial period, including furniture, paintings, ironwork, glassware, and gold and silver articles, can be seen at this museum, which is open daily except Mondays. Admission charge. In downtown Puebla at 302 Av. 3 Pte. (phone: 22-419475).

JOSÉ LUIS BELLO Y ZETINA MUSEUM, Puebla: Although it is not a branch of the *Bello Museum,* it houses a similar collection. Closed Mondays. No admission charge. 409 Cinco de Mayo, next to the Santo Domingo church (phone: 22-414720).

SOUTHEAST

MUSEO REGIONAL DE OAXACA (REGIONAL MUSEUM OF OAXACA), Oaxaca: Of particular interest in this small but formidable museum is the large collection of silver, jade, turquoise, bone, and crystal jewelry found in a tomb at Monte Albán. Other exhibitions include a fascinating display of arts and crafts, costumes, and archaeological relics. Closed Mondays. Admission charge. Alcala St. next to the Santo Domingo church (phone: 951-62991).

TAMAYO MUSEUM OF PRE-HISPANIC ART, Oaxaca: The famous artist Rufino Tamayo and his wife, Olga, donated to their native city their collection of pre-Hispanic art and completely restored and decorated the 16th-century mansion that houses it. The five galleries within the museum contain displays of archaeological pieces from the Mixtec, Zapotec, and Totonac periods. The yard-patio has a huge fountain and beautifully landscaped gardens. Closed Tuesdays. Admission charge. Calle Morelos, 4 blocks from the zocalo (phone: 951-64950).

EAST

MUSEO DE MONTERREY, Monterrey: One of Mexico's finest museums of contemporary art, it houses works by Bartolomé Murillo, José Orozco, David Siqueiros, Diego Rivera, Rufino Tamayo, and others. The setting is also unique, as the collection is housed in the former Cuauhtémoc brewery, and many of the huge wooden barrels and bronze and copper vats remain among the exhibits. Closed Mondays. No admission charge. 2202 Av. Universidad Nte. (phone: 83-741383).

CARLOS PELLICER MUSEUM, Villahermosa: Carlos Pellicer was one of Mexico's greatest poets, and a native of the state of Tabasco. He directed this archaeology museum for 26 years, and is credited with amassing the outstanding collection of Olmec and Maya artifacts currently on display. Exceptional exhibits include a Pellicer drinking vessel, one of the finest examples of Maya art, which depicts a governor and his subjects; carved bricks used in the construction of Comalcalco, a Maya ceremonial center about 36 miles (58 km) northeast of Villahermosa; stelae; and colossal heads. Open daily. Admission charge. 511 Av. Carlos Pellicer (no phone).

LA VENTA, Villahermosa: In a jungle setting, this outdoor museum faithfully re-creates the original La Venta, an Olmec settlement built in a virtually inaccessible swampy area. The museum displays original altars, tombs, and sculpture, including massive heads weighing 20 to 30 tons. Open daily. Admission charge. Blvd. Grijalva, 2 miles (3 km) from the center of town (phone: 931-52228).

MUSEUM OF ARCHAEOLOGY, Xalapa (Jalapa): More than 3,000 pieces — representing the Olmec, Haustec, and Central Gulf cultures — are featured here. Among the most outstanding are several colossal Olmec heads dating from 1100 to 900 BC; delicate, charming *caras sonrientes* (smiling faces) from the Central Gulf region; and the *Sacerdote de las Limas,* a sacred priest holding the body of the Sun Child in his arms. The museum, designed by the New York architectural firm of Edward Durell Stone, is filled with bright interior patios, and is an absolute must for travelers interested in Mexico's past. Closed Mondays. Admission charge. Av. Xalapa and Primero de Mayo (phone: 281-30004).

DIRECTIONS

Introduction

The traditions of travel to and through Mexico have undergone a dramatic alteration in recent years, as more and more visitors to the lands south of the border have discovered that there's much more to Mexico than that which lies along the familiar Mexico City–Taxco–Acapulco Highway. Exploring a land so rich in archaeological treasures, dramatic history, spectacular scenery, and evocative accommodations has proved pure pleasure for those folks willing to do a bit of roaming on their own.

To tell the truth, our favorite parts of Mexico are those that attract the fewest typical tourists; our idea of wonderful traveling experiences doesn't include hand-to-hand combat for a chaise longue beside a crowded pool, or fending off vendors determined to wear visitors down by their constant hawking. And since Mexico is such a diverse destination, it isn't hard to create touring itineraries that offer the best and most authentic Mexican experience — and a minimum of anonymous high-rise hotels.

So what follows are the prime driving routes through Mexico, including the Baja's Transpeninsular Highway, the best routes to and from Mexico City, itineraries across the Yucatán Peninsula, and roads through the jungles of Oaxaca and Chiapas to the Guatemalan border. Each entry discusses the highlights of the route, including useful suggestions for shopping and dining; *Best En Route* lists suggested accommodations at the best available hotels and inns along the way. Simple one-page line maps introduce each itinerary and note the major reference points along the route.

We've made our route selections based on our opinions of the most memorable Mexican sites and sights, and it's certainly possible to string two or more of these itineraries together for more extensive roaming. For those with less time, following any single itinerary will help you to see the most notable points of interest (and the most attractive accommodations) in any given area.

Some words of advice about driving in Mexico: Although more and more of the roads included in the driving routes that follow are becoming four-lane, divided highways, it's still a good idea to give yourself plenty of travel time to reach your destination before dark. In fact, we earnestly advise you to limit your driving to daylight hours. In Mexico, many drivers do not turn on their headlights, and in the countryside, especially in the north-central states, animals roam freely on the roads. In addition, many highways do not have center lines, or the markers are worn and difficult to see in the dark. Many roads have no shoulder, and stalled vehicles frequently block traffic.

When entering a town, however small, you will often encounter a row of metal or concrete traffic studs set in the road to slow traffic. These obstacles are often, but not always, marked by the signs "Topes" or "Bordos." Be alert and slow down or you could easily ruin the front suspension system of your vehicle. Also keep in mind that on Mexico's highways the left-turn signal is often used to notify drivers that it's safe to pass, rather than to indicate a left turn. For more information, see "Touring by Car" in *When and How to Go*, GETTING READY TO GO..

Finally, as anywhere in the world, picking up strangers, camping on a lonely beach, or sleeping in a car in some isolated area can invite serious trouble. It takes only a little common sense, and some very basic planning, to make a driving tour of the Mexican countryside both a safe and an especially memorable travel adventure.

The Baja Peninsula

The Baja Peninsula stretches far longer than Italy and is twice as long as Florida. It drops from Mexico's border with southern California like a strong, slim root seeking anchorage in the Pacific Ocean — 750 miles of desert and semidesert separating the Pacific to the west from the Gulf of California (or Sea of Cortés) in the east, and facing the rest of Mexico across the gulf like an opposable thumb. Until 1973, its secrets were safe with the very few four-wheel-drive, off-the-road adventurers who were willing to risk the severity of the terrain — single-track sand lanes that shifted with the wind and often disappeared entirely with the coming of winter — for the exquisite pleasures of hunting, fishing, rock hunting, fossil collecting, bird watching, and surfing in one of the Western Hemisphere's purest natural environments.

Although isolation has been Baja's environmental blessing, it has also been a curse. Baja offered a grim existence for its inhabitants, as even the original Cochimi Indians have since become nearly extinct. It is estimated that some 40,000 Baja California Indians still roamed the peninsula when the European explorers arrived. This number diminished to about 5,000 by the 18th century, and today only a handful are believed to survive. One of the most famous of the many missionaries to explore and work in Baja, the German Father Johann Jakob Baegart, wrote of "poor shrubs, useless thorn bushes and bare rocks . . . piles of sand without water or wood." It has also been said that the Baja Peninsula has sunk and risen three times during its existence, and as evidence of this geological restlessness, shells can be found on mountaintops here.

For centuries, the Indians living here were ministered to by Jesuits lured to Baja in the 18th century by the prospect of new converts. The Jesuits built the first missions, around which villages developed, taught the Indians to farm, planted vineyards, olive trees, and date palms, and spread The Word. For years, the only means of access from one settlement to another was by foot along the shore or by boat. When the first primitive road — the Camino Real — was built down the peninsula, it was used primarily by *fayuqueros,* traffickers in goods smuggled into Mexico from the US, and carriers of news from one isolated village to the next.

In 1973, the Mexican government opened the Transpeninsular Highway, a 1,050-mile (1,680 km), two-lane strip of asphalt that effectively opened the full length of the Baja — from Tijuana to the southern tip at Cabo San Lucas — to more conventional tourism. Since then, millions of travelers have driven part or all of the road. To be sure, Baja still reserves its finest moments for the strong and brave who trek off the road, but for the rest of us, its pleasures are finally accessible.

Just what are those pleasures? With 800-mile-plus coasts along both the Pacific Ocean and the Sea of Cortés, Baja is a paradise for anglers, swimmers,

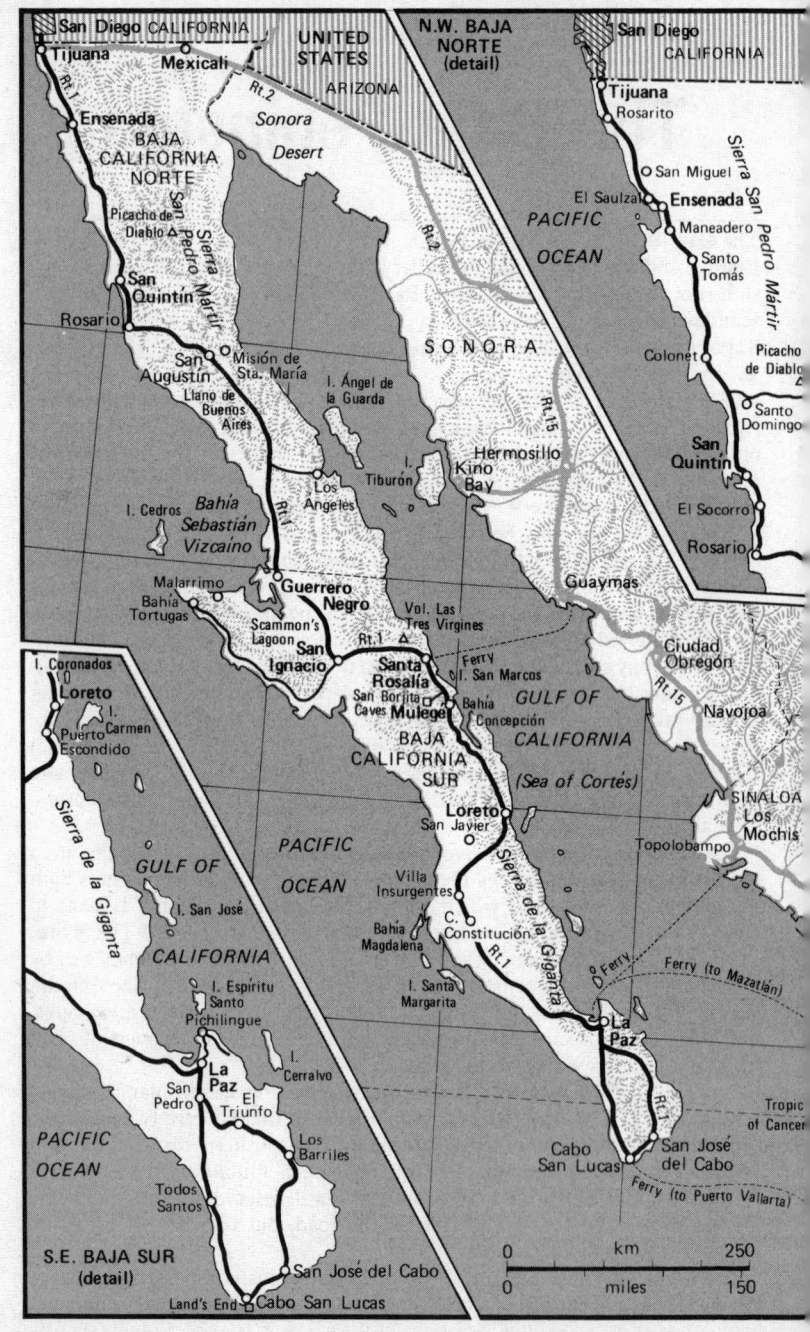

and surfers. Its beaches are laden with huge clams and oysters (there was a thriving pearl industry here until the beds were depleted by a still-undetermined disease during the early 1940s). The waters on the gulf side are emerald green, on the Pacific side deep blue; both support an incredible variety of big fish. At Scammon's Lagoon, on the west coast, California gray whales mate and calve every winter (see "Quintessential Mexico" in *For the Experience,* DIVERSIONS, and as the highway traverses Baja, crossing into the south, the dry landscape breaks into sudden, always surprising oases. The coasts are dotted with innumerable fishing villages and several excellent resort lodges devoted to fishing, swimming, and water sports of all sorts.

With the coming of the highway, this giant, sleeping peninsula began to awaken: Hotels and resorts appeared like mushrooms after a heavy rainfall, and travelers from the US began wandering down, slowly and cautiously, yet eager to explore this land of virgin beaches and unpolluted waters. Mexicans from the mainland, who before had regarded this remote corner as out of reach, began to cross the Sea of Cortés by ferry to visit and settle in this part of their country. The population grew, and several villages, developed for commerce and tourism, became cities overnight. Los Cabos, on the peninsula's southern tip, is fast becoming Mexico's newest mega-resort.

Baja California is divided into two states: Baja California Norte (North) and Baja California Sur (South). Baja California Norte comprises the area from the US border (including Tijuana and Mexicali) south to the 28th parallel (just about midway down the length of the peninsula), where Baja Sur begins and stretches to Cabo San Lucas, at the tip of the peninsula. Baja Norte has a population of 1.4 million; Baja Sur, only 282,000. The climate of the northern state is mild and dry during the summer, cool with a little rain during the winter, while southern Baja is warm and humid in summer, tepid and dry in winter. (Rain is an element that the people in Baja have learned not to expect.) Mexicali (pop. 750,000), the capital of Baja Norte, is an agricultural center in a fertile valley that is almost an extension of California's Imperial Valley. La Paz (pop. 150,000), on La Paz Bay in the Sea of Cortés, is the capital of Baja Sur. Its main activities are tourism, sport fishing, and commerce. Other major cities in Baja are Tijuana and Ensenada in the north, and, though not a vacation destination, Cuidad Constitución in the south.

Between and around these far-flung cities is Baja's almost untouched wilderness. At its widest point (the "elbow" just below the 28th parallel), the peninsula measures about 105 miles; at its narrowest point, near La Paz, the distance is only 28 miles (45 km) from the Sea of Cortés to the Pacific Ocean. Along the length of the peninsula run two major mountain chains, the Sierra San Pedro Mártir in Baja Norte and the Sierra de la Giganta in Baja Sur. The highest crest of these rises to more than 6,000 feet, but as in the lowlands surrounding them, the terrain is essentially semidesert. In a very few spots in Baja Sur, there is a climate and environment of total desert. But keep in mind that there is terrific trout fishing in many of the streams of the Sierra.

Both the Pacific and the Sea of Cortés are dotted with islands, of which the better known are Isla Cedros and Isla Santa Margarita in the Pacific, and Isla Carmen and Isla Espíritu Santo in the Gulf. Some of these are being exploited — Isla Carmen for its pure salt and San Marcos, also in the Gulf, for its plaster — while the others remain secluded settings of sun and sand.

The Transpeninsular Highway links Tijuana and Cabo San Lucas, passing through all the major Baja towns en route — Ensenada, San Quintín, Guerrero Negro, San Ignacio, Santa Rosalía, Mulegé, Loreto, and La Paz. From Tijuana to Ensenada, the highway is a divided toll road, but upon leaving Ensenada it narrows to a two-lane, two-way route that, although in good condition, is not recommended for night driving. The route is patrolled by an aid corps of the Mexican tourist department called the *Ángeles Verdes* (literally, Green Angels). These mobile mechanics travel in recognizable green trucks over 87% of Mexico's major highways and tourist routes. They speak English, can be picked up on CB radios, go out of their way to be helpful and friendly, and are a most welcome sight for anyone stranded on the road with a flat tire. Their service is free of charge; you only pay for parts needed for the repair. Good accommodations and some elaborate resorts can be found in and between cities all along the way. Just remember to drive carefully, in full daylight, and to fill up at every gas station along the way. Then you're bound to enjoy an exciting adventure.

At hotels listed along this route as very expensive, expect to pay $115 to $135 for a double room; $80 to $110 at expensive places; $40 to $75, moderate; and $35 or less, inexpensive.

TIJUANA: For a detailed report on the city, its hotels, and restaurants, see *Tijuana,* THE CITIES. With about 20 million border crossings a year, Tijuana has the highest transient population of any border town in the world. Only a handful of the Americans entering Mexico at Tijuana actually continue any distance down the Baja Peninsula; the town itself is their objective, as it is a duty-free port and an excellent spot for shopping of all sorts, dining, bullfights, and gambling on jai alai, dog racing, and horse racing.

En Route from Tijuana – The journey into Baja begins on the scenic toll road that follows the Pacific coast (or the pastoral toll-free road just east of it) for 70 miles (112 km) to Ensenada. Small resorts, other tourist facilities, and beaches mark the way. The ocean water is cold here, and surfers normally wear wet suits. Rosarito Beach is a popular resort where many families from Mexicali and California, fleeing the intense city heat, come to spend the summer months. A delightful spot to stay is the *Rosarito Beach* hotel (Km 27 Tijuana-Ensenada Hwy.; phone: 706-612-1106), or try the *Quinta del Mar* resort complex (35 miles/56 km miles from San Diego, CA on the Tijuana-Ensenada Hwy; phone: 661-21106). There are particularly good seafood restaurants, too. Thirty miles (48 km) south is the Cantiles exit, well worth a small detour, for it leads to Puerto Nuevo, a small fishing village with several restaurants that serve fresh lobster *à la Puerto Nuevo* (with Mexican refried beans, rice, flour tortillas, and hot sauce), a dish found at many points along the route. These places in Puerto Nuevo look alike, though the one facing the road that bears the sophisticated name of *Newport* is most likely to catch your eye. Sunday is busy here; most places are closed Mondays.

Back from Puerto Nuevo onto the Transpeninsular Highway, the road follows the coastline closely in this stretch, with Pacific breakers lapping its rocky base. On clear days, when there is no fog, the view is magnificent, and the ocean's deep blue is framed by snatches of brown cliffs and green landscape as the road twists and turns along the coast road. There's an excellent Mexican restaurant in *La Fonda* hotel, on a cliff above the ocean, just 19 miles (30 km) north of Ensenada.

The highway now crosses Río San Miguel, one of the largest streams in Baja. Nearby, San Miguel Village has a popular resort with a restaurant and camping areas, tennis courts, horses, and a beautiful beach with good surfing. Shortly after passing El Sauzal, a fishing village built around a huge cannery, Ensenada comes into view. This view inspired the late Mexican journalist Fernando Jordán to write: "Ensenada is the only city on the Pacific coast of Baja California which did not fear the ocean, for it deliberately turned its back to the land and spends its life facing its ocean window and running down the mountain to the beach."

ENSENADA: For a detailed report on the city, its hotels, and restaurants, see *Ensenada,* THE CITIES. On the north end of the 10-mile-wide All Saints Bay (Bahía Todos Santos), this town smells strongly of salt and fish — appropriate for a town that depends on the ocean for its survival. In addition to commercial fishing, sport fishing is excellent here, as is seafood dining. About 200 miles (320 km) southwest of Ensenada lies Isla Guadalupe, with its large colony of sea elephants (manatees), a species that was once close to extinction.

En Route from Ensenada – The road continues through Maneadero, a large agricultural valley where chilies, melons, beans, and corn are grown. The highway narrows and turns down into the broad valley of Santo Tomás, an old agricultural community that has suffered in recent years from lack of water. In the town of Santo Tomás are the adobe ruins of an 18th-century Dominican mission.

Five miles (8 km) past Colonet, a tiny farming town with an excellent bakery, the highway crosses Meling Road, which leads to the *Meling Ranch,* a cattle ranch and comfortable lodge with a swimming pool. From here you can rent horses and guides and ride to the Sierra San Pedro Mártir, the highest mountains in Baja, and Picacho del Diablo (Devil's Peak) at 10,100 feet. La Grulla is a lovely spot in the fir-pine forest, a valley strewn with ponds and streams where trout abound. Reservations at the ranch can be made by writing to Aida Meling Barré, Apdo. Postal 1326, Ensenada, B.C., México (no phone).

Back on the main road, a few miles past Camalú, a branch road leads to Santo Domingo, where the adobe walls of the second mission founded by the Dominicans (1775) are still standing. It was once the best preserved of the Dominican missions, but treasure hunters have laid waste to it in recent years.

VALLE DE SAN QUINTÍN: Most of the people in this agricultural town of about 20,000 live in nearby ranches, but there is a strip with stores that cater to the people who come here to enjoy the beaches, fishing, and clamming.

In 1883, Valle de San Quintín was part of a concession granted to Huller & Company, an American agricultural firm. The Americans soon discovered there was too little water for profitable farming and wanted to get rid of the property; they sold it to an English firm whose interest was aroused after an unusually heavy rainy season had garlanded the valley in green. It became evident soon after the purchase, however, that the English had been snookered. Deciding to unload the property themselves, they created an elaborate hoax, digging water wells and irrigation channels, and spreading the word about the fine prospects of their project. They even constructed a flour mill and put it to work milling imported grain. The deceit never bore fruit, however, because before any buyers could be found, the Mexican government annulled the concession that had been granted the company, and the English left, leaving behind only an English cemetery — still there, on the southern shore of the bay.

In 1931, the government decided to do something with these lands, which had returned to their normal, desolate state soon after the departure of the English. Five hundred families were sent to settle and farm here. This turned out to be something of a disaster, and the settlers found themselves stranded in the desert without food, water, or the means to obtain necessities. All but 11 of the original 500 families left. But 11 was a lucky number because one of this group discovered water running just

98 feet below ground, and soon after, the valley became even more fertile than the English had ever dreamed it could be.

Today, San Quintín is remarkably fertile, with potatoes, tomatoes, carrots, chilies, and grain growing as abundantly as the number of new settlers who come from north and south.

The beach at *La Pinta San Quintín* hotel is long and very beautiful, perfect for clamming. Visitors can also rent horses here and ride off into the spectacular sunsets.

En Route from San Quintín – The highway parallels the ocean, and many side roads lead to the beach. But beware of sand traps that have snagged hundreds of innocent vacationers who tried to drive too close to the beach and had to be pulled out by tractors. El Socorro beach has excellent clamming and good camping.

In Rosario, a small farming village, a café owned by Señora Espinosa serves good meals, and the señora provides information about the history of the area. Rosario is the site of the Dominicans' first mission in 1774; its remains can still be seen.

South of Rosario, there are two species of vegetation unique to the Baja desert. The cardon cactus is a giant plant that can reach a height of 60 feet and bears edible fruit that ripens in the summer. The cirio has a tall trunk covered with short, spiny branches, and clusters of red or yellow flowers on top.

Past San Agustín, the highway begins crossing the Llano de Buenos Aires, a sandy desert with a landscape of gigantic boulders and cardon and cirio plants. The *La Pinta Cataviña* hotel (phone: 667-62601), which appears in what seems to be the middle of nowhere, is a Mexican colonial-style facility with air conditioned rooms, a restaurant, bar, and a pool.

Eleven miles (17 km) away lies the site of Misión de Santa María, the last mission founded in Baja by the Jesuits (1767). A small road leads to the ruins. An old legend claims that the Jesuits founded another mission named Santa Isabel, where they hid a huge treasure of gold, silver, and pearls when they learned they were about to be expelled from the peninsula. For years, adventurers have been searching for the "lost mission" without success, so keep your eyes open.

Some 64 miles (102 km) farther south, a branch of the Transpeninsular Highway shoots off to the left to make the crossing to the Sea of Cortés coast of the peninsula. (The main highway continues along the Pacific side of the peninsula until it reaches a point south of Guerrero Negro and Scammon's Lagoon.) The branch leads to Bahía de los Ángeles, a harbor right across from the Isla Ángel de la Guarda in the Sea of Cortés. The bay offers shelter to vessels of all sizes, and a small fishing village, Los Ángeles, graces its shore. Cabin lodgings are provided by Señor and Señora Díaz, who also serve fine meals, including a special stew said to contain coyote meat. Caguama turtles abound in this area, and the fishing season lasts from April to September.

From the Bahía de los Ángeles turnoff, the main highway continues south across a plain thick with desert plants. The boundary between Baja Norte and Baja Sur, the 28th parallel, which is marked by a stylized eagle monument, is reached within an hour's driving time.

GUERRERO NEGRO: This important town has a promising future, for it claims the largest salt flats in the world, as well as oil and natural gas deposits. But progress could become a problem. When a French company wanted to install oil drilling platforms just offshore, conservationists objected that they would hamper the mating habits of migrating whales and, therefore, endanger their very existence. So the local government voted down the company's proposal. Then there are people: The town attracts increasingly large numbers of whale watchers every year to visit the nearby lagoons, where the California gray whales come annually (from November to early spring) to mate and calve.

Scammon's Lagoon, a shelter for large numbers of migrating gray whales, is one of the most interesting spots in Baja. The lagoon is in Bahía Sebastián Vizcaíno, and is reached via a 17-mile (27 km) dirt road 8 miles (12 km) south of the eagle monument. The road is fairly well marked and passes the salt flats. The whales can usually be seen in Scammon's Lagoon from the last week of December to the first week of April.

Besides Scammon's Lagoon, the whales take refuge in the adjoining Guerrero Negro Lagoon and nearby San Ignacio Lagoon. The whales begin their migration from Arctic waters in October and travel thousands of miles with only their instincts to guide them. This area has been designated as a wildlife refuge, and special permission is required to take a boat into Scammon's Lagoon during the whale season. Though whales are not violent, they are huge and naturally protective during mating and calving season, so you may feel safer watching them from the shore or elect to hire a small plane in Guerrero Negro to fly overhead. For information about naturalist-led tours to several whale watching sites, contact *Oceanic Society Expeditions,* Fort Mason Center, Building E, San Francisco, CA 94123 (phone: 415-441-1106).

En Route from Guerrero Negro – Here the Transpeninsular Highway turns inland and southeastward, crossing the desert mainland to the Sea of Cortés coast, some 130 miles (208 km) away. Midway along the hot, weary route is San Ignacio, a place of respite.

SAN IGNACIO: After driving from Guerrero Negro through some 80 miles (128 km) of sun-baked desert, it's difficult not to feel that this oasis town, shaded by date palms, provides welcome relief. Like many other towns in Baja Sur, San Ignacio started out as a Jesuit mission, established in 1728 by Dominican Padre Piccolo. The mission at the heart of town is very well preserved, and it faces a little plaza shaded by a lush canopy of Indian laurels. Don't be surprised to find prices are higher here than in surrounding towns.

The main crop of the area is dates, introduced by the Jesuits during the 1700s, though other fruit trees also grow here. The dates are harvested in October and then set out to dry all around the town. Though San Ignacio is inland, midway between the Pacific Ocean and the Sea of Cortés, many of the men from San Ignacio are fishermen. During fishing season, they set up camps on the Pacific coast and catch cabrillas, bass, lobsters, and abalones. A dirt road at the southern end of town leads to Turtle Bay (Bahía Tortugas), the largest fishing establishment on the west coast. Sport fishing is good here from May to September, and rustic accommodations are available. Farther along this road lies Malarrimo Beach, an ideal place for beachcombing, where shells and driftwood wash ashore from as far away as Alaska, Japan, and the China Sea; swimmers, beware the strong undertow.

San Ignacio provides two possibilities for lodging: *La Pinta San Ignacio* hotel just outside of town and the tiny *La Posada* motel (see *Best en Route* for both), which is run by Oscar Fischer, who also leads tours to the mysterious painted caves in the area; his hotel rates are low; his tour prices, too high ($70 for 4 hours). The caves are almost impossible to find on one's own, but consummate explorers can find one by driving 22 miles (35 km) to the tiny goat raising community of San Francisco (pop. 300), asking directions of someone there, and backtracking slightly.

En Route from San Ignacio – The highway passes the volcano of Las Tres Virgenes (The Three Virgins), believed to be the most recently active volcano in the area and, according to local lore, used at one time as a natural lighthouse by colonial-era seafarers. The ground surrounding the volcano is covered with hardened lava, which forces the vegetation to struggle for survival. The Sea of Cortés comes into view just before arriving in Santa Rosalía.

SEA OF CORTÉS: This sea, also known as the Gulf of California and the Vermilion Sea, is bounded by the Mexican mainland on the east, the Baja Peninsula on the west, and Baja and the state of Sonora to the north. It originates at the mouth of the Colorado

River, 50 miles (80 km) south of the US-Mexico border, and ends at the peninsula's tip, where it merges with the Pacific Ocean. Its formation was a result of the San Andreas Fault, which caused a large chunk of the west side of Mexico to separate from the mainland, creating a new peninsula linked to the mainland on the north and open to the Pacific Ocean on the south. When the volcanic peaks of the mountainous Baja Peninsula split off and slid into the crevasse, their tops projected above the water's surface, creating the many islands that stand off the eastern coast.

The Sea of Cortés reaches great depths and harbors more than 650 species of fish because its warm and calm waters provide an abundant supply of food and ideal conditions for spawning. Naturally, it is a paradise for fishing enthusiasts, but it also attracts many others who come to swim in its clear, warm waters, collect shells on its beaches, water ski on its mirror-smooth surface, or go scuba diving.

The surrounding land is rich hunting country for doves, quail, and duck; deer, jaguars, and mountain lions are found farther inland. Many resorts have sprung up in the area for the ever-increasing numbers of travelers who make their way here.

SANTA ROSALÍA: This town is unique on the Baja Peninsula: It resembles an Old West town with quaint wooden buildings, and its tiny church was designed by Gustave Eiffel. When you learn something of its history, you find out why. Santa Rosalía (pop. 14,000) was founded in 1855 by a rancher named Rosas, from the nearby village of Santa Agueda, who discovered rich copper deposits in the area. Two years later, El Boleo, a French mining company, obtained the concession for extracting the metal. The town was divided into three sections: Mesa Francia, where the French executives lived in stately homes overlooking the port; Mesa México, center of the local government offices; and La Playa, where the mine workers lived in miserable conditions. After 70 years, the quality of the ore dropped, and by 1953 El Boleo had ceased its operations entirely, though the ore was not altogether played out. Today, the economic vacuum has been filled by boat building, for which the fishing industry along the coast creates a constant demand. Santa Rosalía is also the Baja terminus of the Guaymas ferry, which provides constant traffic and inconstant service. The town also has an airstrip, and small planes make the trip back and forth to Guaymas, where there is a *Club Med,* for about $50 one way. The flight takes half an hour, as opposed to 8 hours by ferry.

One of the directors of El Boleo once visited a world exposition in Brussels, where he bought a church designed by Gustave Eiffel (of Eiffel Tower fame) — a galvanized structure that was transported section by section from Europe to Santa Rosalía. This charming structure, the Misión de Santa Rosalía, stands in the center of town, quite beloved by the local populace. Catholic services are still held here.

Stroll along Calle Obregón, the town's main street, past the bakery and shops, to get the feel of this friendly place. For overnight accommodations, try *El Morro,* south of town. *La Terraza,* a mile (1.6 km) north of Santa Rosalía, is a good choice for breakfast or a seafood meal. The beaches to the north and south of town are beautiful. For a stunning view of the surrounding area, drive or take a taxi up the hill capped with the dish antenna; from here you can see the Three Virgins and Reforma peaks and Isla Tortuga (Turtle Island), better known for snakes than turtles.

En Route from Santa Rosalía – Several miles south of town, a side road leads to the caves of San Borjita, site of the oldest cave paintings found in Baja. Although the road to the entrance is only about 1 mile (1.6 km) long, it is in very poor condition and takes over 2 hours to negotiate. The entrance to the caves faces west, so it is best to visit in the afternoon, when plenty of sunlight pours in. The main themes of the paintings are war and hunting, and life-size works depict humans, lions, deer, fish, and rabbits. Reds, blacks, whites, and yellows predominate, and the colors are still very bright.

MULEGÉ: Pronounced Moo-lay-*hay,* this lush green town is home to about 3,500 people, and lies at the mouth of Río Santa Rosalía, better known as the Mulegé River.

An oasis springing up in the midst of barren country, it is a place where groves of date palms and semitropical fruit trees grow densely. *Mulegé* is an Indian word meaning "wide river, white water." The environs look like John Wayne territory and, indeed, "Duke" was fond of visiting here.

The Misión de Santa Rosalía, founded by Jesuit Juan de Ugarte in 1705, is across the river. Below the mission is a stone dam, a small lake, and roads running the 2 miles (3 km) to the Sea of Cortés. Above town stands an interesting old prison; the view is worth the climb. Cemetery buffs will enjoy the one here (corpses are interred within 24 hours, as there is no embalming).

Good bathing beaches are found near the *Serenidad* hotel and in front of El Sombrerito, the tall hill on the north side of the river mouth; it gets its name from the lighthouse on top, which resembles a sombrero. Mulegé is gaining a reputation for scuba diving; for more information, check at *Mulegé Divers* (on Calle Madero, the town's main street). *Punta Chivato* (12½ miles/20 km north of Mulegé, in front of San Marcos Island) offers excellent water sports.

Don Johnson, a US vice-consul, lives in Mulegé and can offer advice on everything from where to buy shells to how to find a boat that's strayed from its moorings. He also owns the *Serenidad* hotel (phone: 685-30111; see *Best en Route*). His wife, who is originally from the town, runs one of the gift shops, *Nancy's*, at the hotel.

Eat in town at the *Candil* and *Maranatha* (both on the main square) or go out to the *Serenidad* (Playa el Cachero) for a Saturday afternoon barbecue with a free margarita.

En Route from Mulegé – The highway plays hide-and-seek with immense Bahía Concepción for some 20 miles (32 km), passing Santispaquis, a beautiful cove in the bay, and El Coyote, so named because of a rock painting found in the area that shows a coyote in an attacking position. The most beautiful beach on the bay is El Requesón, where a small island is connected to the mainland by a strip of stark white sand. This is a great place to get clams, when the fishermen come in around 5 PM. Camping sites are available in the bay area.

LORETO: In 1697, Jesuit Juan María de Salvatierra initiated the work of missionaries in the Californias by building a mission here — the "Mother of the Californias." In 1769, the Franciscans left Loreto and headed north toward Upper California. Loreto was the mission center and the headquarters of the civil government until 1829, when they were transferred to San Antonio, and a year later, to La Paz, where they remain today. The town, with some 12,000 people, is garlanded in the green of its vineyards, date palms, fig trees, and olive trees. A car is absolutely essential for getting around. Some 40,000 visitors come to the area every year, primarily to fish or play tennis. Hotels will pack and freeze the fish, and there is no problem flying back to the US with it.

FONATUR, the government tourism development agency, has begun a full-blown resort encompassing three separate areas and 25,300 acres: the existing village of Loreto; the Bay of Nopoló, a few miles south of town, which will be the site of luxury hotels (at present, the *Stouffer Presidente Loreto,* see *Best en Route,* stands alone), a golf course, and a marina; and the harbor at Puerto Escondido, 16 miles (26 km) south of Loreto in the shadow of Gorilla Mountain (not to be confused with the Pacific resort in the state of Oaxaca). At press time, construction was under way in Puerto Escondido on three new hotels — the *Sierra Intercontinental*, the *Costa Serena*, and the *Paraíso Radisson*. The *Stouffer Presidente Loreto* hotel is set in what must be one of Mexico's most spectacular locations, Nopoló Point, where rust-colored mountains plummet headlong into a turquoise sea. Across the street from the hotel, the *Loreto Tennis Center* (phone: 683-30408) offers year-round clinics. Next door to the *Stouffer Presidente Loreto* is a beach club with a waterfront restaurant, Loreto's first. On the beach adjacent to the hotel, *Fantasia Divers* operates a water sports center offering scuba, snorkeling, windsurfing, water skiing, sailing, and instruction.

The original Misión de Nuestra Señora de Loreto, in the heart of town, was severely damaged by earthquakes and has been almost completely rebuilt. One of its bells dates from 1743, but the tower is newer (donated by a priest in 1957, after he won a lottery) and has a modern clock. The peaceful mission has thick walls, with windows laced with carved wood bars.

The *Museo de las Misiónes Californias,* next door to the mission church, was organized by personnel from Mexico City's *Museum of Anthropology and History;* it offers exhibits of artifacts and manuscripts related to the old mission days.

Northeast of Loreto, Isla Coronado has a variety of sites worth visiting, including a large colony of sea lions, the San Javier mission, an oasis known as Primer Agua, and Bah.

Bahía Concepión (an almost virgin beach): Arrangements for boat excursions to Isla Coronado can be made at the *Stouffer Presidente Loreto* (phone: 683-30700) and *La Pinta* (phone: 683-30025) hotels in Loreto. Next to Isla Coronado, at Isla Carmen, more than 100,000 tons of salt are extracted annually from a salt mine. It's possible to go snorkeling or scuba diving off the islands, as well as at Puerto Escondido, and there's wonderful swimming at Nopoló Point.

En Route from Loreto – South of the Loreto junction, a dirt road painstakingly crosses the mountains toward San Javier, site of the best preserved of the many Jesuit missions in Baja; unfortunately, the 20-mile (32 km) trip takes 2½ hours. The mission was originally founded in Rancho Viejo in 1699 and was moved to its present site by Padre Juan Ugarte. The architectural style is Moorish, and you'll see remarkable stonework, a gilded high altar brought from Mexico City, and a statue of St. Francis. The first wheat fields and the vineyards in the peninsula were planted in the mission garden, where two stone reservoirs built by the Jesuits are still in use.

Farther southwest, the highway climbs dramatically across the Sierra de la Giganta and swings toward the Pacific side of the peninsula. From here to La Paz is a 2½-hour trip on a flat, nondescript stretch. The highway leads to Villa Insurgentes, a rich agricultural center for wheat and cotton. The town is developing as an industrial and cattle raising center. A side road leads to fishing villages strewn along the Pacific coast — Domingo, Comondu, and La Purísima, where abalone and lobster abound.

Ciudad Constitución lies in the fertile Santo Domingo Valley and is the second-largest city in Baja Sur, with a population of 40,000. It is the largest cotton-ginning center and produces grain.

The nearby Bahía Magdalena is the largest bay in Baja. Isla Santa Margarita, one of three in the bay, is a major shelter for sea lions, and up to 3,000 gather here at one time. At this point, the highway turns southeastward again, to La Paz and the east coast of the peninsula.

LA PAZ: The capital of Baja Sur (pop. 150,000) is on a deep inlet in La Paz Bay on the Sea of Cortés. The city overlooks the bay and is protected from the open waters of the Cortés by a long sandbar called El Mogote. La Paz lies only 51 miles north of the Tropic of Cancer and has a sunny and mild climate nearly all year.

La Paz used to be renowned for pearl fishing. For over 400 years, beautiful black and pink pearls were discovered here, the most extraordinary of which adorn various European crown jewels. The pearls are almost nonexistent now, but the deep-sea fishing is reputedly among the finest in the world, with equally fine hunting available in the mountains nearby. La Paz also draws large numbers of tourists with its variety of water activities and good beaches.

Hernán Cortés landed in La Paz in 1535 and named it Bahía de la Santa Cruz (Bay of the Holy Cross). The land was then inhabited by a group of Indians, the Guaicuru. They were friendly to the European invaders, and for this reason, another Spaniard,

Sebastián Vizcaíno, changed the area's name to La Paz (peace) when he arrived in 1596. Other Spanish expeditions and groups of pearl hunters came here, but it wasn't until the Jesuits arrived in 1720 and founded the mission of Nuestra Señora de la Paz that the town really began to develop.

In 1830, La Paz became the capital of Baja Sur, at that time a territory (it was not proclaimed a state until 1974). A comment of the late Mexican journalist Fernando Jordán gives some understanding of the nature of the city and its inhabitants: "Every city has a name; but here we have a name that has a city. La Paz, a name that in the beginning was the symbol of a possession without violence, was gradually converted into a trait of character for its inhabitants. Thus, it is not called La Paz because its people are peaceful; they are quiet and gentle because their town has been named La Paz."

La Paz still has a tranquil ambience and is set amid Indian laurel trees and coconut and date palms. Its very helpful tourist office is on the water, at Obregón and Dieciséis de Septiembre. Though new hotels and shopping areas have been built, the city retains a provincial atmosphere and maintains its old colonial structures. The Sea of Cortés can be seen from every point in town, and at sunset — a blazing spectacle of red and yellow — its waters appear red; thus the moniker Vermilion Sea.

The *malecón* is a great place for strolling. The *paceños* (as the locals are known) go there to meet friends, enjoy the sunset, and exchange news as the *coromuel,* the evening breeze, cools the town. Above the *malecón* on a hill is the main plaza, along one side of which stands an old Catholic church (1861) that's now the cathedral. The Government Palace, a striking modern structure, is nearby (on Av. Isabel la Católica). A modern youth hostel can be found at Calles Cinco de Febrero and Forjadores de Baja California Sur (also known as Carretera al Sur).

Fishing probably draws more people to this area than anything else. Anglers catch marlins, sailfish, swordfish, roosterfish, yellowtail, mahi-mahi, cabrillas, tuna, and sierras in the bay. The best season for deep-sea fishing is March to September. Marlins are caught from March through July and sailfish from June to October. Rental of fishing gear and boat charters can be arranged through any of La Paz's leading hotels (see *Best en Route*). Boats rent for $200 to $300 a day for 3 to 5 passengers. The more expensive of these have sleeping facilities and can stay out for 2 days. *Pangas* rent for $100 a day for 3 passengers. A 38-foot boat that sleeps 4 comfortably can be rented from *La Paz Skin Diving* (phone: 682-21826).

La Paz is ideal for other water sports, especially scuba, jet skiing, and water skiing. The area around El Mogote is good for scuba; you can rent gear at the *Riviera del Sol* and *Los Arcos* hotels. The kiosk across from *Los Arcos,* on Obregón, has information about equipment rental and yacht cruises as well as fishing and bike rentals. Joggers will find company along the promenade beginning at the arched Mill Bridge just north of town, but golfers will be sorry to learn that there is no golf course nearby.

Coromuel, 3 miles (5 km) from downtown and the beach closest to the city, has a sandy swimming area, a little dock for diving, a water slide, refreshment stand, and music on weekends. It is only half a mile from the *Riviera del Sol Gran Baja* hotel, and you can walk there via the beach by maneuvering some rocks along the way. Perhaps the most popular family beach is Pichilingue, which has a couple of open-air restaurants; get there by driving north on the road past the *Riviera del Sol Gran Baja.* This road also leads to Balandra (12 miles [20 km] from La Paz), Coyote, and Tecolote beaches, none of which has bathhouses. Balandra is excellent for snorkeling. Coyote and Tecolote are a little more remote and face the open sea.

Visitors can cruise the bay, as well as the islands and beaches in the immediate vicinity. Several excursions, including a sunset cruise, are available on the glass-bottom boat *Reina Calafia* (phone: 682-25837). Arrangements can be made through one of the many travel agencies along Obregón (the *Calafia* office is at 220 Obregón) and at the major hotels. Espíritu Santo Island, with its emerald coves and brick-red rocks, is also a worthwhile excursion; cruises can be arranged through *La Paz Skin Diving* (phone: 682-21826). From La Paz it's also possible to explore the Sea of Cortés on adventurous kayaking trips offered by San Diego-based *Baja Expeditions* (phone: 800-843-6967 in the US). Taxis, readily available, can be hired (for a pretty peso) for the day to take vacationers to local beaches. If you plan to drive, be warned that the road to the beaches takes its toll on automobile suspensions.

One of the city's greatest attractions is shopping, the best of which is done along Dieciséis de Septiembre and just off it, on Calles Cinco de Mayo, Madero, and Revolución. Imports from all over the world are for sale at duty-free prices (the Mexican government exempted the entire peninsula from import taxes in a so-far successful effort to speed up the region's economic and tourist development). Among the fine stores in town are *La Perla de la Paz* (the largest and oldest department store on the peninsula), *El Trébol,* and *Mary's Imports. El Delfín* and *La Paloma* carry all types of handcrafted items. Quality wool blankets, clothing, and other items are available at *México Lindo* (on Alvaro Obregón, just off Lerdo de Tejada). *The House of Arts and Crafts* (on the *malecón*'s Plaza Cuauhtémoc) has an impressive display of local crafts such as shell-framed mirrors, macrame articles, woven baskets, and shell jewelry. The store is sponsored by the state government. The *Francisco Madero Market* (at Revolución and Santos Degollado) is clean and interesting for local color. *El Tiburón Negro* (on Jalisco) sells jewelry and decorative items carved from black coral. Stores accept credit cards; most are closed from 1 to 3 PM.

A fine museum, *Agora de la Paz,* built in 1981, has an extensive exhibition on the cave paintings of Baja. These mysterious primitive representations of humans and animals, painted in red and black as high as 40 feet above the floor of some 160 caves, still have no logical explanation. The museum (no admission charge) is at Cinco de Mayo and Altamirano. The old government palace, on the main plaza opposite the cathedral, has exhibitions on the history of the region, with explanations in English and Spanish. The City Hall (Calle 15 de Septiembre) has a lovely inner courtyard decorated with handsome historical murals.

Several restaurants in town serve fresh seafood and meats. The top choice for lobster is *Bismark II* (at Degollado and Altamirano); *Samalú* (near the *Riviera del Sol Gran Baja* hotel) is also very good. *La Pazlapa* (at the beginning of the *malecón*) is a thatch-roofed seafood house very popular among *paceños*, particularly the younger crowd. Specialties include fresh abalone steaks and caguama soup. *El Moro* (about 1 mile/1.6 km out on the road to Pichilingue) is another good choice. The *Riviera del Sol Gran Baja* hotel (Calle Rangel) has an outstanding restaurant that sometimes features live music. The *Oakey* disco (on the *malecón*) is popular with locals and visitors alike.

En Route from La Paz – Here, as the peninsula narrows to its southern tip, at Cabo San Lucas 118 miles (190 km) away, resorts on both the Pacific and the Sea of Cortés coasts are equally accessible. San Pedro is a small ranching community with semitropical vegetation. South of town a junction provides the opportunity to travel to San José del Cabo via the Pacific or to take an inland route, 20 minutes longer but actually more scenic. Following the Pacific route leads to Todos Santos, a farming village 1 mile (1.6 km) from the ocean that's popular with surf bathers and families escaping the summer heat of La Paz.

El Triunfo was once an important mining town rich in gold and silver, but today is practically a ghost town. Its few inhabitants struggle for survival by making crafts from palm fiber and selling them at roadside stands.

San Bartolo offers the hot and weary traveler a freshwater spring shaded by banana and palm trees. The townspeople prepare jams and jellies from the fruit they grow and sell them at roadside stands.

Los Barriles is a small fishing village with several nice resorts, each with its own fishing fleet and airstrip: *Playa Hermosa* (no phone), *Palmas de Cortés* (no local phone; 818-887-7001 in California), and *Punta Pescadero* (phone: 682-50377), which is the most deluxe and has a private beach.

Just south on the highway, *Rancho Buena Vista* (no local phone; 818-303-1517 in California; 800-258-8200 in other parts of the US) is a fine resort with its own fishing fleet, thermal waters, beach and pool, lighted airstrip, horses, hunting, and diving. Doves, quail, rabbits, and mountain lions are hunted in the area. *Punta Colorada* (no local phone; 818-703-1002 in the US), a few miles beyond, has a private beach and fishing fleet.

SAN JOSÉ DEL CABO: For a detailed report on the city, its hotels, and restaurants, see *Los Cabos,* THE CITIES. Once surely the Lake Wobegon of Mexico, this is the small town that time almost forgot. Yet FONATUR, the government's tourism development agency, has begun an extensive project that could easily achieve the popularity of Cancún within the next few years. The 4,310-acre area encompasses San José del Cabo and Cabo San Lucas, 23 miles (37 km) to the south, and is known as Los Cabos (The Capes).

San José del Cabo is the most important commercial center on the peninsula's southern tip as well as an agricultural and cattle raising community. Mango, avocado, and orange trees are abundant. The town's House of Culture has a museum and a library, and the old church next to the plaza stands on the site previously occupied by its mission (residents don't appreciate visitors wearing shorts inside). The small municipal office building, with its clock tower, was built in 1730. The Paseo Mijares, with its stone arches and white cottages full of flowers, is a lovely place to stroll.

Shop at *La Casa Vieja* (27 Blvd. Mijares) for quality clothing and summer shoes for men and women; prices are high. A few of the downtown stores rent bikes. For the feel and taste of Old Mexico, visit *Damiana Mesón* restaurant (on Plaza Mijares); try the combination plate and the house margarita. *Añuití* (beside the *Stouffer Presidente* hotel) is a popular American-style steak and seafood house. *Da Giorgio,* an Italian restaurant just south of San José, serves pizza along with lasagna and spaghetti; open for lunch and dinner.

Sun and sea lovers swim and snorkel at Bahía Santa María, by the *Twin Dolphin* hotel; they also snorkel at Palmilla Beach. Surfers go to Acapulcito, a mile (1.6 km) south of San José, and to the sight of a shipwreck, 12 miles north; some attempt to surf in front of the *Stouffer Presidente,* but the waves are bone-breakers. Beside the *Stouffer Presidente* and just 100 feet from the Sea of Cortés lies a lagoon brimming with wildlife. Canoes and paddleboats can be rented here; rent horses in front of the hotel. Hunting and surf fishing are excellent in the surrounding area.

The *Stouffer Presidente* hotel (phone: 684-20211) is the real social center of San José del Cabo, with seemingly nonstop activities that include games with prizes, Mexico Night with mariachis on Saturdays, a disco, and special events during holidays. Also along the *zona hotelera,* or "hotel row," the strip being developed by FONATUR, is the *Posada Real* hotel (phone: 684-20155). If you prefer a larger selection of hotels and livelier nightlife, you'll be happier in Cabo San Lucas, half an hour down the road. In between the two lies the exclusive *Palmilla* hotel (phone: 684-20583). In downtown San José, there is only one possibility for lodging, the small but neat *Colli* (on Hidalgo between Zaragoza and Doblado; phone: 684-20725), but it's less a hotel and more a bed and breakfast — minus the breakfast.

From San José del Cabo, the highway follows the coast, which is spotted with beaches.

CABO SAN LUCAS: For a detailed report on the city, its hotels, and restaurants, see *Los Cabos,* THE CITIES. The deluxe resorts are the main attraction here, and though they're higher priced than most other places on the peninsula, they're good for a bit of indulgence at the end of a long trip. Many more hotels are being built as the town is developing into a major tourism center. Americans live in the large homes in the residential area above the town.

Take a boat ride to the famous arch known as Land's End, where the Sea of Cortés and the Pacific waters merge in a swirling spectacle, and spend the day at Lovers' Beach (take a box lunch). A boat drops you off in the morning and picks you up later in the day for about $16. Sunset cruises to Land's End also are available on the trimaran *Trinidad* for about $15. (Your hotel desk can make arrangements for either trip.) Sea lions live happily on the surrounding rocks. Divers shouldn't miss the sand falls discovered by Jacques Cousteau.

Crafts sold in San Lucas run the gamut from embroidered blouses to pottery to huaraches. Shop for them along the town's main street, Lázaro Cárdenas, and at the outdoor market by the marina. More sophisticated clothing, swimwear, jewelry, and gift items are available in the shops across from the dock, on Marina Boulevard, as well as in the shops at the *Hacienda Beach* and *Finisterra* hotels.

San José provides more variety for eating out than Cabo San Lucas. In Cabo San Lucas, the garden restaurant *El Galeón* (on the *malécon,* opposite the marina) has lobster and steaks; lively *El Coral* (Av. Hidalgo and Blvd. Marina) serves good seafood and grilled dishes; lobster is the top choice at the somewhat removed, seaside *Las Palmas* (on Médano Beach). San José offers *Añuiti* (Hotel Zone; phone: 684-20103) and *Damiana* (Plaza Mijares) for steaks; for seafood, *Terraza del Mar* and *La Playita* (Puebla La Playa; turn at the *Puebla La Playa* sign on Blvd. Mijares at the entry to San José and drive 15 minutes); *Andremar* for Mexican food; and for Italian food, the romantic *Da Giorgio* (Hwy. 1 at Km 25, 10-minute drive south from San José). The local watering hole, *El Marlin Sonriente* (The Giggling Marlin; on Marina Blvd.) also serves breakfast from 6 AM, prepares meats over mesquite, and will make up box lunches.

Cabo San Lucas may have less than half the inhabitants of San José del Cabo, but it has many more hotels, a number of which are undergoing expansion. Among the best are the *Hacienda Beach* (phone: 684-30122/23), the *Twin Dolphin* (no local phone; in California, 213-386-3940; elsewhere in the US, 800-421-8925), the *Cabo San Lucas* hotel (no local phone; 213-852-0824 in Los Angeles; 800-282-4809 elsewhere in California; 800-421-0777 elsewhere in the US), the *Plaza Las Glorias* (phone: 684-31220), and the *Melia Cabo Real* (phone: 684-30967; 800-336-3542 in the US). For more information on hotels in Cabo San Lucas, see "Checking In" in *Los Cabos,* THE CITIES.

The Faro Viejo is an old lighthouse that stands on the huge Friars, giant rock formations at the very tip of the peninsula, right where the land and water meet.

BEST EN ROUTE

ROSARITO BEACH

Rosarito Beach – A 1920s-vintage, hacienda-style property overlooking the ocean, it's Baja's oldest hotel and a longtime favorite of such celebrities as Orson Welles and Lana Turner. Refurbished over the years, it's as charming now as it was when it first opened. Between Tijuana and Ensenada, Km 27 of the Tijuana-Ensenada Hwy. (phone: 706-612-1106). Moderate.

PUERTO NUEVO

Newport Baja – In town, overlooking the beach, it has a swimming pool, 2 tennis courts, and a restaurant. Carr. Tijuana-Ensenada, Km 45 Puerto Nuevo (phone: 661-41166; 800-678-7244 in the US). Moderate.

VALLE DE SAN QUINTÍN

La Pinta San Quintín – Attractive Mexican colonial structure offering 60 rooms with ocean view, air conditioning, restaurant, bar, tennis, beach, horseback riding, clamming, and fishing. In town (phone: 686-62601 in Ensenada; 800-262-2656 in the US). Moderate.

GUERRERO NEGRO

La Pinta Guerrero Negro – With 28 rooms, a restaurant, and bar, this place also arranges whale watching excursions and trips to the salt mines. On the Tijuana-Ensenada Hwy., facing the eagle monument (phone: 685-62601; 800-262-2656 in the US). Moderate.

SAN IGNACIO

La Pinta San Ignacio – Lovely patio, 28 comfortable rooms, a restaurant, bar, small pool, and volleyball. Reservations advised. Just south of town (phone: 667-62601 in Ensenada; 800-262-2656 in the US). Moderate.

La Posada – A clean, basic motel with 6 rooms. Check here for information about visiting the area's painted caves. 22 Av. Carranza (no phone). Inexpensive.

SANTA ROSALÍA

El Morro – Just outside town, a motel with 20 rooms, restaurant, bar, and pool in a tropical setting. 1 mile (1.6 km) south of town (phone: 685-20414). Moderate.

MULEGÉ

Serenidad – A beachfront place that offers fishing, a restaurant, pool, bar, scuba gear rental, an airstrip, 50 air conditioned rooms, and 35 trailer hookups. Every Saturday night, owner Don Johnson throws a pork barbecue; Wednesday is Mexican fiesta night. 2 miles (3 km) from town on Playa el Cacheno. Mailing address: Apdo. 9, c.p. 23980 (phone: 685-30111). Moderate.

Vista Hermosa – Formerly the *Mulegé*, in a lovely location overlooking the river and bay beyond it, there are 18 cozy rooms, restaurant, poolside cookouts, water skiing, diving, snorkeling, an airstrip, and live music on Sunday nights. 3 miles (2 km) from town on Camino al Puerto (phone: 685-30222). Moderate.

LORETO

Stouffer Presidente Loreto – Idyllically placed on Nopoló Beach, it has 250 terraced rooms, 2 shallow pools, sailing, snorkeling, tennis, water skiing, a restaurant, popular bar, and the *Disco Duna*. On the beach, 25 minutes from downtown (phone: 683-30700 or 800-HOTELS-1). Very expensive to expensive.

Oasis – The perennial favorite of fishing diehards, it has 35 air conditioned rooms, restaurant, bar, pool, and tennis court. Two blocks from downtown, on Baja California (phone: 683-30112). Moderate.

La Pinta Loreto – A modern, comfortable hotel with 48 large rooms, a small pool, game room, and shuffleboard. It has the best beach right in town. The restaurant is known for its Mexican food. On the beach, 6 blocks from the plaza (phone: 683-30025; 800-262-2656 in the US). Moderate.

Tripuí Trailer Park – Outstanding in its genre, it offers 116 traditional hookups, a restaurant, large pool, and laundromat. Perfect for fishing enthusiasts. At Puerto Escondido (phone: 683-30413). Inexpensive.

LA PAZ

La Concha – This 3-story beachfront hotel has 107 rooms, a large pool, outstanding restaurant, and 2 bars. Playa Caimancito at Km 5, on the road to Pichilingue (phone: 682-26544). Expensive to moderate.

Los Arcos – An attractive colonial-style structure with 130 balconied rooms (and 52 thatch-roofed cabañas next door at *Cabañas de los Arcos*), air conditioning, a restaurant, coffee shop, 2 pools, sauna and massage, and fishing facilities. There's also a wonderful bar here that was a favorite hangout of John Wayne and Humphrey Bogart. Rooms in back are quietest. Right on the bay, at 498 Obregón (phone: 682-22744). Moderate.

La Posada de la Paz – Spanish colonial style, cool and peaceful, lovely tiled baths, small pool, 25 rooms including cottages with kitchens, restaurant, and bar. Same management as *La Misión* on El Mogote island. Near the *Riviera del Sol Gran Baja* at Nueva Reforma and Playa Sur (phone: 682-24011). Moderate.

Riviera del Sol Gran Baja – An 11-story structure (the tallest in the state) with 250 air conditioned rooms and 22 junior suites, all with an ocean view. It has a beach, 2 restaurants, 2 bars, a disco with live music, convention facilities, car rental, shops, 2 lighted tennis courts, a lobby bar, a large outdoor pool, and a variety of facilities for fishing and water sports. Calle Rangel (phone: 682-23900 or 682-23844). Moderate.

Aquario's – With a staff that's eager to please, it's 3 blocks from the center of town, and has a pool, restaurant, and low prices. 1665 Ramírez (phone: 682-29540). Inexpensive.

The West Coast: Nogales to Mexico City

The 1,450-mile (2,320-km) route from Nogales (Nogales, Arizona, on the US side of the border; Nogales, Sonora, on the Mexican) to Mexico City provides one of the most fascinating Mexican journeys available to a driver. If the objective is to reach Mexico City as quickly as possible, the trip can be made in just under 4 days of intense driving; to do so, however, would be to miss an unparalleled opportunity to explore the longest stretch of Mexico's Gulf of California and Pacific coast accessible by car and to pass unheeding an astounding diversity of landscape, climate, and culture.

This western route wanders for 1,000 miles (1,600 km), most of it parallel to the Gulf of California coast. The route begins inland at Nogales and leads 225 miles (360 km) southwest to Guayamas where the long coastal stretch of the trip begins. Eventually, at Tepic, the route leads inland again for the 400-mile-plus (640-km) trip to Mexico City. In the course of this epic journey it crosses the dry, naked desert hills of the state of Sonora, drops south through the subtropics of Sinaloa into the very real tropics of Nayarit (passing as it goes the very best — and many of the least known and yet to be discovered — resorts and fishing spots on the western coast) and at last turns east to cross the Sierra Madre Occidental through the lake districts of Jalisco and Michoacán into the state of Mexico and the Federal District of Mexico City. It could well be called the "route of options," for the traveler driving this road can find in the same day the adobe huts of Mexico's northwestern countrypeople and the beautiful mansions of the rich. Driving its full length, you'll see a tiny island community called Mexcaltitlán — known as the Venice of Mexico — where only a handful of people live; where during the rainy season the water level rises and fills the streets; where men still hollow out canoes from giant trees; where you couldn't make a phone call if you had to. On the same route, you can choose between the chic discos of Mazatlán and the undeveloped simplicity of Kino Bay, where it's tough to find a postcard for friends. You'll encounter incredibly plush resorts on the Gulf of California, the best sport fishing and hunting in the country, and at the end of the road, Mexico City.

From Nogales to Guaymas and from Ciudad Obregón to Navojoa, the route follows a divided four-lane highway. Farther south, from Los Mochis, a toll road leads to Culiacán, and more stretches of divided highway lead to Guadalajara. From here, the road is a narrow, two-lane highway along which you might see as many cows, horses, burros, goats, dogs, old men, and children as you will fellow drivers. From Toluca you'll reach the toll road leading to Mexico City. We strongly discourage you from driving at night,

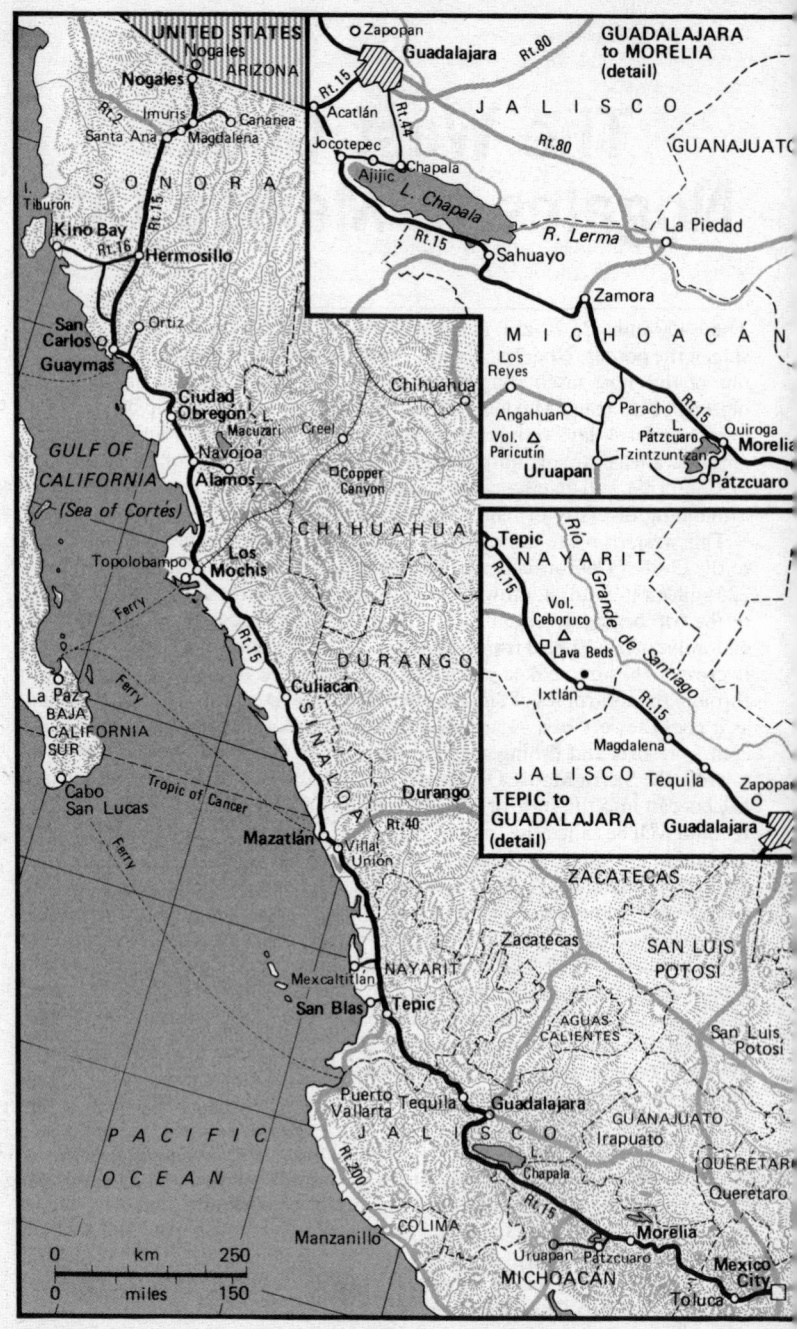

especially on the undivided, two-lane roads, most of which do not have shoulders.

A sign reading *Puente Angosto* or *Un Solo Carril* indicates a narrow bridge ahead. Usually there's room for only one vehicle to cross at a time. The rule is that the first driver to flash his car lights on and off has the right of way.

Other signs you might see include *Cruce de Caminos* (crossroads); *No Hay Paso* (road closed); *No Dar Vuelta a la Derecha* (no right turn); *No Dar Vuelta a la Izquierda* (no left turn); *Poblado Proximo* (nearby town); *Camino Sinuoso* (curving road); *Curva Peligrosa* (dangerous curve); *Hombres Trabajando* (men at work); *Conserve su Derecha* (keep to the right); *Desviación* (detour); *Bajada Frene con Motor* (hill: brake with motor); *Escuela* (school).

For the trip to Mexico City, you need two complete sets of clothes: jeans, swimsuits, and light casual clothing for the warmer, northern country and seaside resorts; heavier, more formal wear for chilly Mexico City nights.

If you have any trouble or need help or information, your best bet is the nearest Mexican Government Tourist Office. The following is a list of these offices in the order in which you will encounter them on your journey down Route 15 from Nogales to the capital:

Nogales, Sonora: Edificio Puerta México (phone: 631-26446)
Magdalena, Sonora: Presidencia Municipal (phone: 632-21377)
Hermosillo, Sonora: Edifico Pitik, 100 Blvd. Eusebio Kino (phone: 621-46304)
Guaymas, Sonora: 437 Serdán (phone: 622-22932)
Ciudad Obregón, Sonora: Presidencia Municipal (phone: 641-52525)
Navojoa, Sonora: Presidencia Municipal (phone: 642-20130)
Los Mochis, Sinaloa: Allende and Cuauhtémoc (phone: 681-50405)
Culiacán, Sinaloa: Palacio de Gobierno (phone: 67-140610)
Mazatlán, Sinaloa: 1300 Paseo Olas Altas, 2nd Floor (phone: 69-851220/1/2)
Durango, Durango: 408 Hidalgo Sur (phone: 181-11107 or 181-12139)
Tepic, Nayarit: 253A Av. México Sur, 1st Floor (phone: 321-30993 or 321-37644)
Puerto Vallarta, Jalisco: Edificio Parian del Puente, Local 13, Libertad and Miramar (phone: 322-20242 or 322-20243)
Guadalajara, Jalisco: 102 Morelos (phone: 36-140123 or 36-131196)
Pátzcuaro, Michoacán: 9 Portal Hidalgo (phone: 454-21888)
Morelia, Michoacán: 79 Nigromante (phone: 451-25244/23710/29816)
Toluca: 101 Lerdo Pte. (phone: 72-141342/133014/130296)
Mexico City: 54 Calle Amberes, corner of Londres (phone: 5-525-9380 through 86)

At hotels along this route categorized as expensive, expect to pay $75 or more for a double room; at moderate places, $45 to $70; at inexpensive, $40 or less.

NOGALES: A fence along the international boundary separates the twin cities of Nogales, Arizona, and Nogales, Sonora. The United States and Mexican governments maintain their own customs facilities for tourists crossing the border, both of which are open 24 hours a day. In the Mexican immigration office just beyond the border, officials issue tourist cards or validate the one you already have (see *Traveling by Car,* GETTING READY TO GO). Then go to customs (*aduana*) to obtain a vehicle permit. A money exchange on the premises is open daily from 9 AM to 8 PM. Little of interest will keep you dallying in Nogales, a trading center for ranching, dairying, and irrigated farming. Head out of town on the one-way street and onto Route 15. About 15 miles (24 km) down the road, you'll arrive at a customs check, where your baggage may be examined.

En Route from Nogales – Hermosillo, the first major stop along the way, is 175 miles (280 km) along Route 15, about a 4-hour trip. Leaving Nogales, the highway passes through a series of narrow valleys before emerging on the rim of a cultivated plain watered by the Río de los Alisos and Río Magdalena. At Imuris, a paved road branches off 53 miles (85 km) northeast to the copper mines of Cananea. Ore mined here is shipped by train to smelters in Bisbee and Douglas, Arizona.

Just south of Imuris is a small town named Magdalena, where the bones of the renowned Padre Kino were discovered in 1966. This Spanish Jesuit priest, the "Conquistador of the Desert," came to Mexico in 1687 and remained for the rest of his life. He established 25 missions and converted seven Indian tribes (the Apache, Yuma, Seri, Maricopa, Papago, Pima, and Cocopa) and proved that Baja California was not an island. He died in Magdalena in 1711, and his remains are on display in a mausoleum.

At Santa Ana, an agricultural community 11 miles (18 km) south of Magdalena, is the junction with Route 2, a good, two-lane highway connecting Route 15 with Mexicali and Tijuana in Baja.

HERMOSILLO: The capital of the state of Sonora is not really a bustling tourist town. Most American tourists stop for lunch and move on, but the town does have some of the best motels and restaurants (see *Best en Route*) you'll find on this route as well as a few interesting sights. The mild, dry winters have made it a popular winter resort.

The town was named after José María González Hermosillo, a revolutionary leader in the war of Mexican independence. A four-lane road with two auxiliary streets sweeps through the center of town. Palm and orange trees line the median strip. Many of the city's early colonial buildings are still standing and offer an excellent introduction to Spanish colonial architecture, but in recent years a number of modern buildings have gone up, including those at the University of Sonora. For exhibits of pre-Columbian artifacts, visit the *Museo de la Universidad de Sonora* (Museum of the University of Sonora; on Blvds. Rosales and Luis Encinas).

The *Rodríguez Museum and Library,* the Rodíguez Dam and Lake, and Rodríguez Boulevard, which leads into town, are all named for former President Abelardo Rodríguez, a native of Sonora who served from 1932 to 1934 and promoted industry in this area. The dam, which impounds the waters of the Río Sonora, is one of the largest earthfill dams in Mexico and has played an integral part in converting this desert region into a substantial agricultural producer.

Points of interest in Hermosillo include the Plaza Zaragoza in the center of town and the fine cathedral there, and Madero Park, a favorite promenade and sports center in the southeast section of the city, with areas for baseball, tennis, handball. Also worth seeing are the new *Museo Costumbrista,* a museum converted from an old prison, and Cerro de la Campana, the scenic Hill of the Bell.

Deer, coyote, rabbit, and duck hunting is good in the immediate area. The Novillo Dam, 90 miles (144 km) east of town, is noted for its bass fishing. The *Foto y Deportes Moreno* sporting goods shop carries the best selection of hunting equipment in the city (phone: 621-31313).

Eating establishments in Hermosillo serve everything from tacos, steaks, spaghetti, and pizza to Chinese fare. The *Pitic Valle Grande Coffee Shop and Dining Room,* in the motel on the main highway toward the north end of town, serves good American food from breakfast through midnight snacks, but it is a bit expensive. *Merendero la Huerta* (136 Calle 11 Ote.) has a no-frills atmosphere and serves some of the best seafood in town at reasonable prices. The place is air conditioned, and some English is spoken. *Jo Wah* (South Hwy. 15 at Rosales St.) is a clean Chinese restaurant with moderately priced fare. *Los 20's Pizzería* (Rodríguez at Calle Durango) specializes in pizza — three sizes and 20 varieties, including "New York style" (with thick crust), even though owner Victor Martínez is from Los Angeles; the air conditioned restaurant also has sandwiches, spaghetti, and cold draft beer. *Miyako* (Carr. Bahía Kino at Km 4) is a Japanese restaurant established by a local businessman who brought chefs from

Japan and created a convincing atmosphere with Japanese gardens and seating on the floor, Japanese-style. On the road to Kino Bay, it is expensive. *Villa Fiesta* (33 Yañez) is a traditional Mexican restaurant with excellent food.

En Route from Hermosillo – You have the option of going 84 miles (134 km) south to Guaymas or 69 miles (110 km) west to Kino Bay, both on the Gulf of California coast. Named after the Jesuit priest mentioned earlier, Kino Bay is a unique spot along Mexico's west coast. If you enjoy comfortable seclusion and the absence of push-button anything, it's an attractive stop. In Hermosillo, leave Route 15 at Transversal just before the university and join Rte. 16 west. This good two-lane road takes you right to the Sea of Cortés.

KINO BAY: There are actually two bays on the gulf, Old Kino and New Kino. New Kino, with immaculate beaches and excellent fishing, is fast giving Guaymas a run for its money as Sonora's most popular beach resort. Fine beach houses and motel accommodations are on this short strip of beach. Offshore are a number of islands, the largest of which is Tiburón, or Shark Island, a wildlife refuge. The *Club de Yates Bahía Kino* (Kino Bay Yacht Club) operates a sightseeing boat to Tiburón Island; departure times vary.

The paved road leads directly into town, with the beach on the west side. This main road ends in a dirt road that wanders away from the beach to a Seri Indian camp about a quarter of a mile down the road. The Seri are descendants of the tribe originally converted to Christianity by Padre Kino. Seri women often can be seen weaving heart-shaped baskets called *coritas*, while men fish or carve ironwood animals, such as roadrunners, quail, and chickens. The work is priced according to its intricacy, size, and color. Some of the ironwood figurines are so fine they are considered collectors' items.

Beyond the camp, the road winds along the jagged coastline where groups of fishermen stand outside their shacks and huddle around open fires chasing away the early-morning chills. Every day, they venture out in boats with outboard motors to net mackerel, which they sell locally and in Mexico City. Beyond the tiny fishing villages, the beach is great for secluded sunbathing.

Sport fishing is not commercialized here as it is in Mazatlán or Acapulco. Most people come to Kino Bay with their own boats, rent space at one of the local trailer camps, and launch their own excursions.

En Route from Kino Bay – You're just a kiss away from Guaymas and its neighbor San Carlos. From Hermosillo, continue on Route 15 south over dry range country for the 84-mile (134-km) trip to Guaymas. From Kino Bay, get back on Route 16 east. About 35 miles (56 km) out of Kino Bay, take the right fork (marked Guaymas); this shortcut takes you 56 miles (90 km) to Route 15 south, right into Guaymas. Guaymas is just 13 miles (21 km) southeast of San Carlos, and both of them offer easy access to the sea.

GUAYMAS: Backed by high mountains, Guaymas is one of Mexico's finest seaports and a developed fishing village with an interesting history. Spanish explorers landed here as early as 1535, but the area was not settled until the 18th century, after it had become a mission base under Fathers Salvatierra and Kino. The settlement was opened as a general trading post in 1841 and served as a Spanish-Mexican free port, a prized outlet for Sonora's rich mineral resources.

Guaymas was attacked by US naval forces in 1847 and occupied until 1848. In 1854 it was the scene of battle once again when the French buccaneer Count Gastón Raouset de Bourbon and some 400 pirates attempted to seize the city. Bourbon was captured and executed by General Yañez, defender of the port. Eleven years later, the French, under Maximilian, took the port. During the US Civil War, supplies destined for troops in Arizona were shipped in through Guaymas from San Francisco and then transported overland.

Guaymas today is actually two communities. The city section, with its 18th-century

Church of San Francisco, its shrimp docks, freighters, and tankers in the harbor, is divided by a mountainous peninsula from the resort areas along Bocachibampo Bay and San Carlos Bay. Most of the inhabitants of the city are active in the shrimp and oyster trade, a large industry engaged principally in shipping to the United States. For the tourist, the principal interest is sport fishing.

The Sea of Cortés teems with fish all year. Between June and September the sailfish, marlin, and dolphin run heavily. From October to April, yellowtail, red snapper, bass, white fish, and sea perch run. There is fine shore fishing, with plentiful totoaba, corbina, sierra mackerel, roosterfish, and rockfish. Arrangements for fishing trips can easily be made through the San Carlos Marina (see below).

The *Fiesta de la Pesca* (Fishing Festival) and *International Game Fish Tournament* are held every July.

In the surrounding area, duck and dove hunting is excellent. There are several stables in San Carlos that rent horses for rides through the country. Farms in the area produce wheat, safflower, and corn, and products from them are sold locally. Sesame seeds, chick-peas, and cotton are grown and exported.

Guaymas is also noted for its abundance and variety of seashells. Each year conchologists visit the area during the period of lowest tide (November to March) to gather specimens. *La Casona* (3 Calle 24) has a large collection of shells and shell jewelry for gatherers of a different ilk. Clamming is another popular activity. The best clam areas are the lagoons near Puerto San Carlos and the Estero del Soldado, both northwest of Bocachibampo Bay. For Guaymas oysters, you must go to the lagoons south of Empalme. (Drive south past Cruz de Piedra and just before Peón, turn right to Las Guásimas.) At low tide, the oyster pickings are terrific.

If you aren't interested in bagging your own dinner but would like seafood plus a little entertainment, *Del Río* (Calle 9 and Av. Serdán) is one of Guaymas's better-known, moderately priced restaurants. Steaks are also a specialty here, and shows start at 9 PM. *El Paradise* (20 A. L. Rodríguez) is a small but clean place offering sand lobster, shrimp (the house specialty), and frogs' legs; it also has a branch in San Carlos. For steaks and lobster and colonial decor, try *Del Mar* (Calle 17 and Av. Serdán).

Besides the Cathedral of San Fernando, other attractions in Guaymas include the Plaza of the Three Presidents, a monument to the fisherman, a municipal palace, and the façade of the municipal jail. All are within walking distance of each other.

Club Med, 17 miles (27 km) away at Algodónes Beach, has outstanding tennis clinics, overnight horseback trips, and river rafting. It is built in the shadow of Goat's Teats Mountain.

SAN CARLOS: Some 13 miles (21 km) northwest of Guaymas, this town is officially named Nuevo Guaymas. It provides easy access to the sea and offers more tourist facilities than its neighbor in a more resort-like atmosphere — plush motor inns, condominiums, and sleek sport fishing boats. San Carlos is famous for its accessibility to deep-sea fishing.

The *Marina San Carlos* (phone: 622-60230) is the best base of operations for fishing. *Lanchas Deportivas de Sonora* (phone: 622-60011 or 622-60565) has 11 boats, from 30 to 42 feet long. The works — 8 hours at sea, a guide and a boat hand, bait, ice, and tackle — cost $20 to $30 per person. A 27-foot glass-bottom boat leaves from the marina every day for 2-hour cruises of the bay area, and there is a sunset cruise for $11 per person, including unlimited margaritas.

Gary's Place (phone: 622-60049) outfits scuba divers with everything from wet suits to weights. They also rent small fishing boats, about $30 for a 4-hour trip, not including equipment.

Continue on the rugged, poorly paved road past the marina for about 4 miles (6 km) to Los Algodónes Beach, a secluded area that was the location for part of the filming of *Catch-22* and *Lucky Lady.*

Probably the best place to eat in San Carlos is the hotel dining room of *Posada San Carlos* (Carr. Bahía San Carlos), which serves seafood; *L'Club* (at the *Country Club*; phone: 622-60399) is also an excellent choice. *La Terraza* (no phone), about 1 mile (1.6 km) from the *Teta Kawi Trailer Park* and overlooking San Carlos Bay, serves international food and seafood at moderate prices. *La Roca* (no phone), across the street from *Teta Kawi,* also serves good seafood.

En Route from Guaymas/San Carlos – Route 15 passes through several agricultural and industrial towns before reaching Mazatlán, almost 500 miles (800 km) down the road. The highway is the same two-lane blacktop along the entire route, with the exception of some short stretches of the Ciudad Obregón and Los Mochis bypasses, four and six lanes respectively.

Thirteen miles (21 km) from Guaymas, a side road on the left leads to Ortiz. A mile (1.6 km) down this road is the old NASA Space Capsule Tracking Station, which the US has since turned over to the Mexican government.

At the village of Cruz de Piedra (Cross of Stone), 16 miles (26 km) out of Guaymas, begins a Yaqui Indian reservation that extends southeastward to the Río Yaqui. The Mexican government set aside this tract for the fierce Yaqui after an uprising in 1928. The next stop of major interest is Ciudad Obregón about 78 miles (125 km) south of Guaymas; along the way notice how the brown cacti and scrub brush blossom into lush vegetation — this is the result of huge irrigation projects for the cultivation of cotton, corn, and sugarcane.

CIUDAD OBREGÓN: The city is in the center of the bountiful Yaqui Valley, where wheat, cotton, rice, corn, alfalfa, flax, and sesame grow. Founded in 1928, Ciudad Obregón is a flat, open city with wide streets and no colonial atmosphere at all. Its contemporary buildings and the concentric rings of storage elevators and granaries that circle the city spread out across the surrounding Mexican countryside.

Ciudad Obregón is a good base for hunters after deer, wild turkeys, and bears in the Sierra Madre foothills 50 miles (80 km) to the east. Between November and March, there's some of the best duck hunting in Mexico.

The town also has a few notable restaurants. *Mr. Steak* (near *Norotel Cajeme Valle Grande*) has a western atmosphere and lunch and dinners for a modest price. *El Cortijo* (Calle 5 de Febrero, 2 blocks west of Hwy. 15) specializes in *cabrito* (kid) and paella.

NAVOJOA: About 44 miles (70 km) south of Ciudad Obregón, in the center of a vast agricultural area devoted to cotton, Navojoa is an old Maya Indian center and a burgeoning new agricultural one. Navojoa is the largest center of the Mayo (not Maya) Indians. They are known for their *danza de venado* (deer dance) and the *matachines* (masquerade and coyote dance) performed during the festivities of *Easter Week* and also in late June. Macuzari Dam, on nearby Río Mayo, is part of a federal program to irrigate three rivers in Sonora and northern Sinaloa.

Navojoa also has two excellent moderate hostels (*El Rancho* and *Alameda Trailer Park*), and it is a good place to leave Route 15 long enough to visit the beautifully maintained antique city of Alamos, 33 miles (53 km) to the east on Route 19.

ALAMOS: This onetime prosperous mining town and capital of the area is now a national monument and authentic relic of Mexico's past grandeur. Alamos is one of the earliest Spanish settlements in this part of Mexico and one of the very few to have escaped modernization. Though the town is equipped with electricity, telephones, good hotels, and an airstrip, the newest building is more than 100 years old. Federal decree prohibits construction of new buildings or alteration of the town's colonial atmosphere.

Exploitation of the gold and silver deposits led to a population of 30,000 by 1781. Large homes, many in the Moorish style, were built by the wealthy governors and mine owners. Embellished by wealthy Spanish with lavish tastes, Alamos became one of Mexico's colonial jewels.

The history of the old mines is an endless source of interesting tales. The Doña María

Mine (Huacal District) was at one time owned by a Spanish widow, Doña María de Rodríguez, who accumulated an immense hoard of ingots. Planning to retire to Spain, she reportedly loaded the treasure onto the backs of 40 mules, fortified her cache with a small army of retainers, and traveled to Mexico City, where, according to the old chronicles, she did not sleep soundly until she had entrusted her fortune to the hands of the Spanish viceroy for safekeeping. Very soon thereafter, Doña María suddenly and mysteriously disappeared.

By the beginning of this century, however, Alamos was a fading star. A combination of exhausted mineral resources, successive Indian attacks, drought, famine, and the 1910 revolution left Alamos a ghost town. After World War II, a group of American artists and retirees, drawn by the invigorating climate and warm winters, reclaimed the ancient manor homes and restored them. The flow of Americans has not stopped, and more and more people are settling in Alamos and restoring its buildings and homes. These structures are among the town's biggest attractions.

The most famous of the restored homes in Alamos is the *Casa de los Tesoros,* a half-block-square, 1-story building with an inner courtyard in the center of town, a block and a half from the plaza. The building is now a hotel (see *Best en Route*). The Plaza de Armas is surrounded on three sides by arched *portales* and fine buildings and at one end by the church of La Señora de la Concepción, built in 1784 on the site of the old mission, which was burned by Indians.

The colonial cemetery is interesting for a look at its above-ground vaults and wrought-iron crosses. At La Uvulama, a cluster of thatch huts known as a pottery village, female potters buy and sell clay bowls. La Aduana is a nearby ghost town that was built around the great smelter works where Alamos silver was once cast into ingots. An important Maya Indian festival is held here each November 20.

Another big, if bizarre, attraction of Alamos is that it is the home of the Mexican jumping bean. Powered by a hyperactive larva, the beans are picked from wild plants that grow in the hills nearby. Some Alamos natives earn fairly comfortable livings by catering to the largely American market for these frisky little creatures, known in Alamos as *brincadores.*

The hills around Alamos are a treat for duck, blue pigeon, white-wing dove, and quail hunters. And halfway between Navojoa and Alamos is the road heading 10 miles (16 km) north to Macuzari Dam and Lake, where the bass fishing is excellent.

Sightseeing tours are inexpensive in Alamos. Self-employed guides hang around the main plaza every day, and each will hop in your car and give you a 2-hour tour of the town for about $4 per person. At the jail on top of Guadalupe Hill in the middle of town, you can buy a horsehair bolero tie made by the prisoners. The *Museo Costumbrista de Alamos* (Museum of Alamos Customs; at Calle Victoria and Cárdenas) is open Wednesdays through Sundays, and is well worth a visit.

Both *La Mansión de la Condesa* (2 Calle Obregon) and *Casa de los Tesoros* (phone: 642-80010) have excellent restaurants, and *Polo's* (phone: 642-80002), on the plaza, serves charcoal-broiled steaks, chicken, and short orders in a no-frills atmosphere.

En Route from Navojoa/Alamos – The countryside here is peppered with *éjidos,* parcels of land loaned to peasants by the government. The plots are marked with white and black lettered signs. The *éjidos* are central to the Mexican way of life and explain many of the problems that cripple Mexico's agricultural system and burden her economy. For years, land ownership has been this country's most emotionally charged political issue. Almost 400 years ago, Philip II promised to give land to every Mexican peasant, and every Mexican hero since has repeated the pledge. In 1910, that unfulfilled promise helped spark the country's 7-year revolution. The *éjidos* program is the government's effort to fulfill its long-term pledge: Farmers may use the land but do not own it. At one time the *éjiditarios* were at the mercy of the *latifundistas* (large landowners), who illegally maintained large tracts of land through political connections and bribes, in spite of Mexican laws that limit the amount of land a man could own. In recent years the Mexican government has worked hard to the reform the system, distributing the land more evenly. While the peasants have more land today, the *éjidos* program is under attack because the land is being worked inefficiently. The rickety shacks, the antiquated oxen-and-plow farming techniques, and the fact that these *éjiditarios* barely eke out enough to feed their own families all testify to the problems the system still faces.

LOS MOCHIS: A new system of irrigation has transformed Los Mochis into a boom town. The 250,000 farmers in Los Mochis (the name means "the turtles") grow more sugarcane than in any town on Mexico's west coast and also bring in significant crops of rice, cotton, and winter vegetables.

Los Mochis was just a small group of huts in 1903 when Benjamin Johnston arrived from the United States and started to grow sugarcane. He later built a sugar mill, which became one of the biggest in Mexico. Johnston laid out the streets, constructed a huge mansion, and watched Los Mochis mature.

Acres of marigolds are grown here, and the city is literally wrapped in the beautiful flowers. They are actually a cash crop. Their petals contain a natural dye, which, when added to chicken feed, enhances the deep yellow of egg yolks.

Los Mochis is the major coastal terminal of the *Chihuahua-Pacífico Railway,* though technically the line ends in Topolobampo, 10 miles (16 km) to the south. Upon its completion and connection with American railroads, Topolobampo became the closest Pacific railhead for cargo destined for and arriving from New York.

While Los Mochis proper has few attractions, it provides easy access to some interesting places. You can take advantage of one of the most scenic train rides anywhere while passing through the area. The *Chihuahua-Pacífico Railway* leaves Los Mochis daily for points east. The diesel-powered engine pulls air conditioned (or heated) cars, usually with a lounge and dining car. This is by far the most scenic way to cut cross-country to Chihuahua and the central highway. The ride passes Copper Canyon, a series of huge, deep gorges that rival the US Grand Canyon in beauty and is four times its size. Visitors can stay at a number of comfortable, rustic lodges along the route to do more exploring in the land of the cave-dwelling Tarahumara Indians (see *Copper Canyon,* JUAREZ TO MEXICO CITY).

If train rides don't beckon, you can take the southwest branch of Rte. 32 to Topolobampo, only 10 miles (16 km) from Los Mochis. Topolobampo is a small fishing village known for its shrimp fleet and abundant sport fish — with skipjacks, yellowtail, sierra mackerel, and roosterfish. Sailfish and marlins run heavily from July to November. The town has good beaches and duck hunting as well. Nearby Las Animas Islands are a breeding place for sea lions and are great for offshore sunbathing and spearfishing. A ferry that links Topolobampo with La Paz, Baja California, makes the journey twice a week. You can charter a fishing boat for up to 12 people at the *Santa Anita* hotel in Los Mochis for about $300 a day.

The best food in Los Mochis is available at the hotels, particularly the *El Dorado* and *Santa Anita* (see *Best en Route*). Also try *El Farallon* (495 Obregón, around the corner from the *Santa Anita* hotel); with nautical decor, the place serves seafood only.

CULIACÁN: The name of the capital of the state of Sinaloa derives from the Nahuatl Colhuacán, or place where the god Coltzin is revered. The city was built on an ancient Indian settlement and is a busy mining and agricultural center.

The surrounding region, between the foothills of the Sierra Madre and the Pacific, abounds in cotton, peanuts, and some of the world's finest tomatoes.

Culiacán is a progressive city where modern buildings stand beside well-preserved colonial structures. On the zocalo on Plaza Obregón, a lovely old cathedral faces the park near some of the most avant-garde architecture in the country.

On the outskirts of Culiacán there are two thermal swimming spots: Carrizalejo Hot Springs and Ymala Hot Springs, 12 miles (19 km) beyond Carrizalejo on the right bank of the Río Ramazula. Two seaside resorts popular with Culiacán residents are Altata Beach (42 miles/67 km west, at Boca del Río) for surfing and fishing, and El Dorado (43 miles/69 km south).

En Route from Culiacán – The next major stop along the route is Mazatlán (for a detailed report on the city, its hotels and restaurants, see *Mazatlán,* THE CITIES). Beyond that resort town the highway crosses rolling country, and the vegetation begins the change from semiarid to tropical. Just a few miles north of Mazatlán, the road crosses the Tropic of Cancer; a sign marks the point of the crossing. To the east rises the Sierra Madre Occidental. At this point you can take an interesting side trip to Durango. Route 40 cuts inland from a junction 1 mile (1.6 km) south of Villa Unión (15 miles — 24 km — south of Mazatlán) to lead across the mountains to Durango (For a detailed description of Durango, see *Reynosa to Mazatlán,* DIRECTIONS.) This link between the Pacific and the central highways takes you through spectacular mountain country.

Along the 183-mile (293-km) stretch between Mazatlán and Tepic, you have the opportunity to make worthwhile side trips to the island of Mexcaltitlán and the village of San Blas.

MEXCALTITLÁN: Four miles (6 km) beyond the Río Chilapa crossing (136 miles — 218 km — south of Mazatlán), a bumpy dirt road leads from the highway to this island village. Turn right down the road; take a right at the second orange water tower; then take the first left to the village for a total of 20 miles (32 km) or an hour's drive. The road passes through tobacco and cornfields, and farther along swamps line both sides of the road. You may see one or two villagers from Mexcaltitlán standing in the hip-deep water fishing.

When the causeway ends, you'll see the island and realize (if you haven't already) that you're on to something unique. The tiny island resembles a *National Geographic* foldout in three dimensions, complete with dugout canoes and naked children playing on the shore. (In fact, *National Geographic* did an interesting photo essay and article on Mexcaltitlán back in 1968.)

Though few if any tourists come through Mexcaltitlán, there's always someone to take visitors for a canoe ride around the island. One guide has been using the same boat for over 25 years. The island's fewer than 3,000 residents either fish or farm tobacco and corn. On shore you can stroll to a stately church with a cracked bell tower.

En Route from Mexcaltitlán – Return to Route 15 and travel 24 miles (38 km) south to the San Blas turnoff, where you pick up Route 54 for another 24 miles (38 km) to San Blas itself. The drive takes 3 to 4 hours.

SAN BLAS: This tropical seaside village could have been taken right out of a Hemingway novel or a Bogart movie. In fact, San Blas is better known as the place where Longfellow wrote his last poem, "The Bells of San Blas," in 1882.

Part of the fun of San Blas is getting there. The paved road drops rapidly from an altitude of 1,000 feet to sea level, passing vibrant vegetation and large coquito palms that form a living green canyon. As you near the sea, there are estuaries and dark mangrove swamps, the exposed roots of the trees crusted with oysters. Coconuts, papayas, bananas, and mangoes grow everywhere.

This quiet, peaceful town has about 25,000 inhabitants. Adobe and thatch houses line the sandy streets. Though San Blas offers no real competition to heavily visited resorts like Mazatlán and Acapulco, those who like it are fanatic about it, enjoying the easygoing utopian life of the natives.

High on a rise of ground behind the village is Old San Blas, the stark, stone ruins of a fortress and ancient mission church built by the Spanish. There was once a waterfront here from which Coronado launched many of his colonizing expeditions. Across from the port on a spit of land stands the San Blas lighthouse, built on the Cerro

(Hill) de Vigía in the 18th century. In the old days, the Spanish developed San Blas as one of their major shipbuilding centers. Many of the ships that sailed in the Philippine trade were constructed here.

Along with San Blas's undeniably positive assets — mystique, history, great deep-sea fishing, and a casual pace — come two equally undeniable liabilities — grade B accommodations and *jejénes* (pronounced hay-hay-nays), tiny gnats that prosper and grow during the summer months. Insect repellent is the only relief; bring a lot.

The semi-restored ruins are the best vantage point from which to get an idea of the whole area. Most hotels will arrange for guides.

San Blas is great for deep-sea fishing. Antonio Aguayo is a member of the *Unión de Lancheros Pesca Deportiva* (Sport Fishermen's Union) and operates fishing trips for tourists. You can reach him at the *Moto Marina* (phone: 321-50364) or by asking the desk clerks at the *Las Brisas* hotel to find him. For $80, Antonio takes you deep-sea fishing from 7 AM until 2 PM for sailfish, marlins, and dolphins, or closer to shore for mackerel, yellowtail, and bonitos. The price includes bait, tackle, and ice. Two people are allowed to fish at once, though another two may be on the boat. The boats are 26-foot fiberglass and equipped with auxiliary motors. Abraham (pronounced *A*-bram) Murillo has a larger boat on which five can fish for $130 per day (phone: 321-50362).

Jungle boat trips have also become popular with San Blas visitors. A 3- to 4-hour trip departs from Estéro San Cristobal (St. Christopher Estuary) at the bridge at the mouth of Río La Tovara on Highway 15 toward Tepic; it goes down the river for a short way, and then up the La Tovara tributary to La Tovara Springs, where the water is crystal clear. A shorter 1½-hour trip departs further up La Tovara at El Embarcadero on the road to the village of Matanchén, southeast of town. You can swim and get refreshment at La Tovara. The *Unión de Lancheros,* in front of the Presidencia Municipal Building, rents boats for these trips. Any hotel in San Blas can advise on arrangements or contact the San Blas Tourist Information Center (Presidencia Municipal; phone: 321-50005).

Good meals are served at *Las Brisas* (on Paredes) and *Misión* (on Cuauhtémoc) hotels. *La Familia* (18 Batellón; phone: 321-50298) is a Mexican restaurant set in a colonial home. *Tony's,* also known as *La Isla,* (Calle Paredes Sur) serves excellent steaks and seafood.

TEPIC: At the foot of the extinct Sangangüey Volcano, this town is the capital of Nayarit, one of the smaller and lesser-known states in Mexico. The city, an interesting mixture of Mexico's past and present, dates from the 16th century but has developed slowly because of its isolation.

The town's historical claim to fame came in 1542, when Hernán Cortés occupied the Indian village that then stood on the site. A Spanish king gave it the title "Noble and Loyal City" in 1711, but Tepic didn't really get moving until 1912, when the first locomotive whistled through.

Points of interest include the old cathedral, which was completed around 1750 and is noted for its two fine Gothic towers, and the Church of the Holy Cross, founded in 1744 and once part of a Franciscan convent of the same name. The *Museo Regional de Nayarit* (91 Av. México Nte.) has exhibits of Meso-American pottery and jewelry.

At the stores bordering the main plaza, you can pick up beads and other items made by the Huichol and Cora Indians, the most colorful of all Mexican natives. On Sundays they come into Tepic to sell their crafts. If you're lucky, you may see a beautiful and mysterious ritual when, several times a year, they come into Nayarit to make offerings to the sea.

You can take an excursion to El Salto, a beautiful waterfall, and to Playa Miramar on the Pacific, both west of the city. Other attractive spots are Ingenio de Jala Falls, which flows only in the rainy season, and Laguna Santa María, a volcanic crater lake about 20 miles (32 km) southeast of Tepic.

There are several decent places to eat in the area. *Roberto's,* also called *Internacional* (at Militar and Insurgentes), serves good food at modest prices. *The Beachcomber* (at Insurgentes and Durango, east of the *Cora* motel, near Loma Park) serves seafood specialties, as does *Maryskos El Farallon* (on Hwy. 15, across from Loma Park).

En Route from Tepic – Here the road turns inland, first to Guadalajara and then on to Mexico City. However, if you are loath to leave the Pacific coast just yet, you can follow Route 200 south and, from Tepic, west to the beautiful resort town of Puerto Vallarta (for a detailed report on the city, its restaurants and hotels, see *Puerto Vallarta,* THE CITIES) and travel even farther south to Manzanillo. The total trip is about 275 miles (440 km). Route 15 leaves Tepic in the opposite direction — inland over the Sierra Madre to Guadalajara, 140 miles (224 km) east of Tepic on a roller-coaster road that whips from side to side for most of the journey. Forty miles (64 km) down this roller coaster, the famous lava beds of Ceboruco are stacked along both sides of the road — a gray moonscape typical of volcanic formations that is impossible to miss. Seventeen miles (27 km) beyond the lava beds, the road passes the Ixtlán archaeological ruins, most of which have yet to be uncovered. Less than 100 miles (160 km) out of Tepic (about 36 miles — 58 km — beyond the Ixtlán ruins) is the small village of Magdalena, tucked away in the Sierra Madre and famous for the quality of its opals. Two small shops side by side on the west side of the plaza sell these gems as well as beautiful carved black obsidian objects. The next major town is Tequila.

TEQUILA: This is the town that gave its name to Mexico's world-famous liquor. There are 24 tequila distilleries here, including Mexico's two largest family producers of the beverage, the Sauza family and the Cuervo family.

The town was founded in 1530 by a Spanish captain, Cristóbal de Onate. Tequila was first distilled here in 1600; since 1875 the Sauza family has been operating La Perseverancia, the oldest and largest tequila distillery in Mexico. The Cuervo family has been operating La Rojena since 1888, which makes it the second oldest firm. The word tequila means "the rock that cuts," and the drink was named after the town, which is surrounded by hills of sharp obsidian rock. Tequila is made from the juice of the heart of the spiny maguey cactus, the ones that grow in profusion in this part of the country; you've seen them constantly along the last 50 miles of road. The heart is cooked and the juice drawn from the pulp, fermented, distilled, and bottled.

For a tour of the Sauza distillery, free drinks, and tequila at discount prices, call Aurora at the distillery (phone: 374-20244). Visitors are also welcome at La Rojena distillery (no phone). If you'd like a guide through either distillery and around town, stop in at *Mario's* restaurant (on Hwy. 15, close to Calle Morelos just before crossing the bridge over Arroyo de Atizocoa on the way to Tepic). Mario Sanchez, who is well-regarded at both distilleries, is often available for half-hour or hour-long tours. (For more information on the Sauza bottling plant in Guadalajara, see "Special Places" in *Guadalajara,* THE CITIES.)

Tequila is a nice place to visit, but the hotels are strictly for an emergency situation. Don't plan to stay overnight. You can easily tour Tequila on your own: Simply walk around the town or hire one of the dozens of nervy little kids who will swamp your car when you drive into town.

En Route from Tequila – About 20 miles (32 km) from Tequila is the little town of Zapopan, site of the Virgin of Zapopan Shrine, considered the second holiest place in Mexico (after the shrine to the Virgin of Guadalupe in the capital). Pope John Paul II made a pilgrimage to the Zapopan Shrine during his visit to Mexico in January 1979. About 30 miles (48 km) beyond Tequila is the junction of Route 15 and the belt route around Guadalajara. Route 15 leads straight into town; travelers pushing on to Morelia and Mexico City should take the belt loop. (For detailed information on Guadalajara, see the individual city report in THE CITIES.) The journey from Guadalajara and Morelia is the next to last on the road to Mexico City and is one of the most beautiful and interesting along the entire route. Take the highway straight 5 miles (8 km) past Guadalajara to Minerva Circle and onto Route 44 south; this leads some 32 miles (51 km) to the town of Chapala, on the northwest side of Lake Chapala, Mexico's largest lake, and within a stone's throw from several other lakeside villages. These villages have become popular summer resorts for Mexicans and retirement spots for Americans.

CHAPALA: Lake Chapala, on which the town is located, once alarmed authorities because of its loss of water, but the level has been restored and fishing is fairly good. The Chapala whitefish resemble Lake Superior whitefish and are served throughout Mexico.

Chapala itself is primarily a resort town of about 40,000. The Chapala Society Information and Library Center, in the middle of town, is run by the Americans and Canadians who live in the area and is a handy place for free information on everything from fishing to home rentals. A few miles to the west is the Chula Vista subdivision, where many American and Canadian residents have built homes.

For dining, try *Cazadores Chapala* near the lake, next to the church on the main street. It has been converted from an old mansion and specializes in charcoal-broiled steaks — expensive but excellent; other specialties are chicken in banana leaves and cheese fondue. A good steakhouse is *La Viuda* (The Widow) on Highway 94 to Ajijic.

AJIJIC: Just west of Chapala, down Highway 94 along the lake, is Ajijic. Once noted for its bohemians, would-be writers, and would-be artists, in recent years the town has acquired some real talent, with a number of reclusive Mexican and American writers, artists, and photographers settling here. There are several interesting shops and galleries in town.

At *Telares Ajijic* (1 Av. 16 de Septiembre) Indian women weave fabrics into native costumes and contemporary fashions. Across the street is *Posada Ajijic* (4 Av. 16 de Septiembre), the town's social center with a restaurant and bar; it also offers views of spectacular sunsets over the Lake Chapala. *El Mesón de Ajijic* (16 Av. Hidalgo) is a flower-filled courtyard restaurant featuring such dishes as *pollo al vino blanco* (chicken in white wine), barbecued spareribs and pork chops, crêpes Suzette, and bananas Foster.

JOCOTEPEC: Some 10 miles (16 km) west of Ajijic is this unspoiled fishing village and refuge for writers and artists. The village is also noted for its fine serapes. In January, the locals hold a lovely fiesta, including bullfights and cockfights, and regional dances held on the shores of the lake.

En Route to Morelia – The road passes through increasingly beautiful mountain terrain, scores of small villages that suggest Colorado mining towns 100 years ago, and Pátzcuaro, one village in particular that is worth a stop. From Chapala, take Route 44 to the junction of Route 15. Follow Route 15 to Quiroga; Pátzcuaro is about 40 miles (64 km) south. (See also *The Bajío,* DIRECTIONS, for more information on Pátzcuaro.)

PÁTZCUARO: This town is an eclectic combination of Mexico's past and present, its good and bad, its mysterious and mundane. Pátzcuaro has always been of interest to Mexican history buffs because it was central to the careers of two diametrically opposed characters in Mexico's colonial past. The first was Nuño de Guzmán, the vicious conquistador who plundered the area for gold. He burned alive the local Tarasco Indian chief when that man couldn't or wouldn't tell him where Indian gold was hidden. Eventually his crimes against the Indians became so extreme that the Spanish were forced to arrest him. In his place they sent Don Vasco de Quiroga, a former judge from Mexico City who had become a priest. As bishop of the state of Michoacán, he helped the Tarasco Indians by introducing new crops and establishing schools and hospitals. He died at the age of 95, and in these parts he is considered a saint for his good works.

The immutable, stoical Tarasco Indians survived de Guzmán and their descendants live today, though many of them exist in dire poverty. The men usually have little to say, but the town itself and the surrounding area speak of the valiant efforts by the missionary Vasco de Quiroga, who lent his name to Quiroga, a small town on Route 15 north of Pátzcuaro. In his efforts to reconstruct the life of the Tarasco Indians, Vasco de Quiroga also taught the inhabitants of each of the surrounding towns a trade. Quiroga is known for its colorful masks; Santa Clara for its fine copperwork; Uruapan for its lacquerware; and Paracho for its guitars and masks. The *Best Western Posada de Don Vasco* in Pátzcuaro is also named for the bishop and is the finest hotel in the immediate area (see *Best en Route*).

Hidden high in the mountains of the state of Michoacán, Pátzcuaro is veiled from the outside world by a curtain of tall pine trees. To the north is Lake Pátzcuaro, noted as one of Mexico's highest lakes and also for its fishermen, who dip their delicate butterfly nets in quest of whitefish. These fishermen are excellent subjects for photographs and have become the Pátzcuaro trademark.

Pátzcuaro was founded in 1540, and in contrast to other colonial villages that have been swept up in the wave of modernization, the town retains its ancient atmosphere. It consists largely of 1-story adobe or plaster-over-brick buildings with red tile roofs. The streets are dusty cobblestones traveled by horse and auto alike.

Plaza Vasco de Quiroga, Pátzcuaro's central square, is a private little world surrounded by high buildings and treetops that lend it an air of isolation. Grass covers the plaza, and a statue of Vasco de Quiroga stands in its center. Only a passing car shatters the illusion of antiquity preserved here.

In the language of the Tarasco Indians, the name Pátzcuaro means "place of delights," which may be related to the fact that there were once as many as 250 species of hummingbirds in the area. The town was noted for a now-lost art. The Indians would arrange the bird's colorful feathers on copper plates, forming pictures of exceptional beauty. These plates were often sent back to Europe by early colonists.

Centro Regional de Educación Fundamental para America Latina (CREFAL), a UN training school for Latin American teachers and one of the earliest and largest projects of UNESCO, was undertaken in Pátzcuaro. The school's main building was once the mansion of former President Lázaro Cárdenas (1934–40), who donated it to the UN.

Friday is the big market day, when Indians from surrounding villages come to sell their wares in the market square. On Fridays, the square teems with buyers, sellers, and browsers; town shops carry henequen rugs, lacquered trays, serapes, Indian masks, and wooden boxes every day.

Pátzcuaro's lacquered trays are quite famous; the lacquer is supposedly made from the crushed bodies of purple insects, which provide the deep, rich finish and durability. The masks are especially interesting, as each design is supposed to have a special significance in relation to the Indian dances in which it is used. Mask collecting is a growing hobby among Mexicans and foreigners alike, but the quality, originality, and variety has declined significantly over the years.

On the east side of the downtown area is the Basílica of Our Lady of Health, the city's patron, built between 1546 and 1554. Don Vasco de Quiroga directed his Indian followers in the construction of the corn pith and orchid honey statue. In December, a fiesta honors Our Lady of Health with folk dances and crafts exhibitions.

The College of Saint Nicolás, south from the basílica on Arciga, was founded by Don Vasco in 1540 and houses the *Museum of Popular Arts and Archaeology,* which has exhibits of carvings, pottery, weaving, and archaeological artifacts.

The Cathedral of Michoacán, near the college at the corner of Cuesta de Portugal, was built by Don Vasco and opened in 1546. Today it serves as the temple of the Jesuits.

The House of Eleven Patios, a block south of the cathedral, is the former monastery of Saint Catherine, founded by Dominican nuns in 1747. The building is now a center for local artisans, and you can watch them work.

The Mansion of the Counts of Menocal, on the east side of the main plaza, was built in 1653 and is now called the House of the Giant because of the huge warrior sculptured on one of the pillars.

The public library has a mural depicting the history of the surrounding area by one of Mexico's leading artists, Juan O'Gorman. The building is the former temple of Saint Augustine and was built by Fray Alonso de la Veracruz and Fray Francisco de Villafuerte in 1580.

The *Dance of the Viejitos* (Old Men), one of the best and most widely known native dances of Mexico, is presented at the *Best Western Posada de Don Vasco* on Wednesday and Saturday nights at 9 PM. The dancers wear wooden masks that depict smiling old men to show that, at least in Mexico, old age is not a time of listless despair, but rather a season to enjoy the fruits of life.

The area surrounding Pátzcuaro has several interesting attractions. The lake is dotted with seven islands, and Janítzio should be the first stop on your list. You can drive down to the dock yourself and arrange a boat ride out to the island or just a ride on the lake. The trip to Janítzio takes about 30 minutes each way and costs about $10 for a boatload of 4 passengers, with a 1-hour stopover. Or you can get a ride out on a launch that holds up to 80 people and usually costs less than $1 each way. On the way, you'll probably pass fishermen with their nets who will be more than happy to pose for a few pictures — for a tip.

The fishing village of Janítzio is huddled near the shoreline and above it on the island's crest towers the statue of José María Morelos, famous revolutionary general and hero. Morelos was a native of this state (the city of Morelia was named after him), a country priest, a schoolteacher, and a leader for Mexican independence in the fight against Spanish colonists. The statue was begun in 1933 and is actually hollow. Those in good physical shape can tackle the taxing 135-foot climb to the top, past more than 50 murals depicting Morelos's life. The top of the statue affords a magnificent view of the lake and exhibits the death mask of Morelos. In the village, you can buy some clever little models of fishing gear made and sold by the villagers.

If you are lucky enough to visit on *All Saints'* and *All Souls' Day* (November 1 and 2), you can witness the yearly all-night vigil in the village cemetery in honor of the dead. During this *Day of the Dead Celebration,* families hold picnics by candlelight by the graves of their loved ones.

In Pátzcuaro, try to stop at one of the restaurants at the dock, where they serve tiny whitefish that are deep fried, wrapped in a tortilla, and sprinkled with lime juice and hot sauce. They are excellent with cold beer. Several of the hotels in the area have good restaurants, including the *Posada de Don Vasco* (Av. las Américas), *Mesón del Cortijo* (Av. Obregon), *Posada de la Basílica* (6 Calle R. Ciga), and *Posada San Rafael* (Plaza Don Vasco de Quiroga). Also good are *El Patio* (Plaza Don Vasco de Quiroga), which serves whitefish, and *Fonda del Sol,* (Av. de las Américas), which specializes in the regional food of Pátzcuaro.

Several other nearby towns are interesting to visit; though they have overnight facilities, they are close enough to Pátzcuaro to allow a comfortable all-day excursion and an early return to Pátzcuaro's better accommodations. The largest of these is Uruapan, 40 miles (64 km) west of Pátzcuaro. (You may have already passed through here en route to Pátzcuaro.) Uruapan is known primarily for its proximity to the famous Paricutín Volcano, which first erupted in 1943 and for the next 10 years spewed boulders and lava across surrounding terrain. Drive to the village of Angahuan, about an hour northwest of Uruapan, and hire a donkey to take you on the 15-minute ride to one of the most startling sites in Mexico. Paracutín's lava flow buried a small village of 1,000 people under 40 feet of molten rock. The only building that withstood the wave of red-hot rocks was the church, whose steeples can still be seen jutting some 70 feet above the lava. Also worth seeing is Parque Barranca del Cupatitzio, a national park with a beautiful tropical garden.

Today Uruapan is famous for its lacquered goods. The *Mercado de Artesanías,* near the entrance to the national park, carries handpainted lacquered trays, dishes, jewelry boxes, and plaques, all at reasonable prices. Good buys can also be found on embroidered blouses and dresses, pottery, and copper. On the high side of the main plaza are an ancient church and government palace, which have been converted into a regional crafts museum whose annual competitions attract the finest work in the state. Museum employees will either sell you the items on display or provide the names and addresses of the craftsmen so you can buy directly from them. Also worth seeing is the *Mercado de Antojitos Típicos,* a market filled with typical foods of the region, at Constitución and Corregidora. In July, native dances and parades are held to honor St. Mary Magdalen.

Just north of Uruapan is Paracho, the city of guitars. Though you can buy a guitar in just about any of the villages near Pátzcuaro, you can almost pick them off the trees in Paracho. Look around, then bargain with dealers, because prices are flexible.

At Tzintzuntzan, 8 miles (13 km) north of Pátzcuaro on Route 120, there's an interesting market specializing in pottery and other Tarasco Indian arts and crafts. The remains of some small pyramids are within walking distance.

Quiroga, on Route 15 at the junction of Route 120, also has a fine selection of lacquerware. And at Erongaríquaro, a pretty town of 2,500 on the west side of Pátzcuaro Lake, the villagers weave cambric fabrics on handlooms and barter at market. The rocky road leading there makes the journey from Pátzcuaro hard but satisfying.

En Route from Pátzcuaro – The next major stop is Morelia, about 34 miles (54 km) east via Route 15 or 120. (For detailed information on Morelia, see the individual city report in THE CITIES.) Between Morelia and Mexico City lie Morelos National Park, Mirador de Mil Cumbres (View of a Thousand Peaks), and Bonsecheve National Park, plus 154 miles (246 km) of hairpin turns along steep mountains that take about 4 hours to negotiate.

If you travel between late December and early April, your next stop should be Zitácuaro (during the rest of the year, drive on to Toluca). There is no reason to stop in Zitácuaro except to see the spectacle of the monarch butterflies. Beginning in mid-December, hundreds of thousands of them migrate from Canada and the northern US to certain areas in the states of México and Michoacán. The beautiful creatures literally cover every inch of rock and vegetation in areas that the Mexican Government has set aside as refuges. In order to see the butterflies at their best, it is wise to stay overnight in one of the hotels of the area — *Balneario San José Purua, Rancho San Cayetano,* or the tiny *Las Azaleas* — are good choices (see *Best en Route*). Weekdays, when the crowds are smaller, are the best times for a visit. Besides, it's almost impossible to get hotel reservations on weekends when the monarchs are in town. The next morning, put on comfortable shoes, a long-sleeve shirt and long pants and, after breakfast, drive to the nearby town of Angangueo, where you can leave your car and board an open truck for the rough, 45-minute drive to the fields where the butterflies are found — an unforgettable sight. The next stop is Toluca.

TOLUCA: This town is the capital of the state of México, a busy commercial center, and well worth a visit, especially on Fridays. The city of Toluca is considerably higher than Mexico City in elevation and is generally a bit cooler. The Friday market here is quite popular, one of the largest in the country, and is held on the outskirts of town on the peripheral highway. Toluca produces sausage, liqueurs, dried meats, wines, dairy products, native needlecraft, pottery, and baskets.

The Cosmovitral and Botanical Gardens are just off the main square in a turn-of-the-century Art Nouveau structure that was once the main market. Inside, 48 spectacular stained glass windows depict man's relationship to the universe. The *Zacongo Zoo,* in a former hacienda a few miles from the city, is also a pleasant place to spend a few hours.

Nevado de Toluca, an extinct volcano, towers above the city. Its peak (15,036 ft) is snowcapped most of the year and frequently is obscured by clouds. In the crater are the Lakes of the Sun and the Moon; rainbow trout fishing is especially good in the Lake of the Sun.

MEXICO CITY: From Toluca you actually descend through the mountains that surround Mexico City to enter the Valley of Mexico. If you approach after sunset, Mexico City looks like a gigantic bowl of sparkling lights in a dark sea. If you make the descent while there is still light, the bowl is filled with what looks like mushroom soup, a gray mass of a city too large and still too far away for its individual components to be distinguishable. The city seems flat. Built on the soft soil of what was once a lake, the buildings are, of necessity, relatively low, so that they don't sink into the earth. If it hasn't rained recently, the "soup" will be steaming with the smog retained by the surrounding mountains.

You'll enter on the Paseo de la Reforma, Mexico City's main east-west artery, and pass through Las Lomas, or the Heights, where you can see some of the city's most exclusive mansions.

Stay on the Reforma past the large monument with the golden angel on top. At the next monument turn right into the Zona Rosa, (the Pink Zone), where the comfortable hotels, shops, and restaurants make this area the home of the tourist in Mexico City. For a complete description on the points of interest, hotels, and restaurants in Mexico City, see *Mexico City,* THE CITIES.

BEST EN ROUTE

HERMOSILLO

Holiday Inn – All 218 rooms and suites have wet bars, satellite TV, and air conditioning. There's also a pool, restaurant, coffee shop, and tennis court. 369 Blvd. Kino (phone: 621-51112). Expensive.

Bugambilia – This older motel has 109 units, 82 of which are in its newer section. The older section consists of bungalows in neatly landscaped grounds. Pool, heat, air conditioning, cable TV sets showing US programs, and a restaurant. 712 Blvd. Padre Kino (phone: 621-45050). Expensive to moderate.

Hermosillo Comfort Inn – A high-rise that has 115 rooms with air conditioning and heating. Pool, restaurant, bar, and cafeteria. In midtown at Rosales and Morelia (phone: 621-52621 or 621-72396). Expensive to moderate.

Pitic Valle Grande – One of the newest and largest in the area, this 144-unit, 2-story colonial-style motor hotel has central air conditioning, TV sets, pool, lobby bar, restaurant, and coffee shop. Blvd. Kino and Ramón Corral (phone: 621-44570). Expensive to moderate.

San Alberto – Contemporary ambience along with a pool, restaurant, bar, cafeteria, disco; 175 units. Calles Rosales and Serdán (phone: 621-21800). Moderate.

Kino – Situated downtown, it has 114 rooms, a restaurant, heated pool, hot tub, and sauna. 151 Pino Suarez Sur (phone: 621-24599 or 621-24442). Moderate.

Gándara – You can stay in a newer air conditioned, hotel-type section or an older section that has been completely remodeled, with bungalows and larger rooms (2 double beds) at slightly higher rates. 154 units with air conditioning and heating. Pool, coffee shop, cocktail lounge, restaurant, lobby bar, cable TV. 1000 Blvd. Padre Kino (phone: 621-44414 or 621-44241). Inexpensive.

Kino Trailer Park – This place has modern facilities and good connections to the highway. Just outside town on Rte. 15 (phone: 621-53197). Inexpensive.

KINO BAY

Kino Bay – This clean, comfortable, 18-unit, 2-story, air conditioned motel is on the north side of New Kino. The small restaurant in front of the motel is noted for its good shrimp. Also on the premises are a trailer park and 2 furnished bungalows, with boat launching facilities nearby (phone: 624-41492 or 624-41732). Moderate.

Islandia Marina – Here are 100 trailer hookups and 8 rustic cabins on the beach with kitchens and private baths. There is a boat ramp. In Old Kino (phone: 624-20080 or 624-20220). Moderate to inexpensive.

Posada del Mar – The 48 air conditioned hotel units have ocean views; a colonial-style restaurant. Right across from the beach in New Kino (phone: 624-44194 or 624-44193 in Hermosillo). Moderate to inexpensive.

Posada Santa Gemma – In addition to 14 air conditioned bungalow units with bedrooms, kitchens, and satellite TV, this motel also has a trailer court with hookups on the grounds. On the beach in New Kino (phone: 624-20026 or 624-20001). Moderate to inexpensive.

GUAYMAS

Club Med Guaymas – An outstanding property that resembles an adobe village, with 2 beaches (one on a lagoon), 30 tennis courts (15 lighted), 3 outdoor Jacuzzis, 2 saunas, a gym, 2 restaurants, a pool, and all water sports. Deep-sea fishing, rafting trips down the Yaqui River, and overnight horseback riding excursions are available for an extra charge. Closed November through March. 17 miles (27 km) from Guaymas (phone: 622-60166; in the US, 800-CLUB-MED, but in New York State, 212-750-1687). Expensive.

Fiesta San Carlos – It has 33 air conditioned units, a restaurant, bar, and pool. On the beach. At Km 8 of the Nuevo Guaymas Rd. *Mailing address:* Apdo. 828, c.p. 85400 (phone: 622-60229). Moderate.

Flamingos – A white, 55-unit motel with restaurant, bar, and pool. All rooms have air conditioning, and some have kitchenettes. 2 miles (3 km) north of town on the main road. *Mailing address:* Apdo. 118, c.p. 85020 (phone: 622-20960). Moderate.

Armida – Air conditioning in 125 moderately priced units, 39 suites, pool, lobby bar, video disco, French restaurant, steakhouse, cafeteria, and TV sets. Arrangements can be made for tennis, skin diving, fishing, and water skiing. In town, at Carr. Internacional Norte (phone: 622-23050). Inexpensive.

Playa de Cortés Gandara – Built by the Southern Pacific Railroad Company when it operated the *Nogales–Guaymas–Mexico City* line, this old hotel features an excellent dining room, pool, dancing, fishing, and 2 tennis courts; 120 air conditioned units. 4 miles (6 km) north of town on the Bacochibampo Bay. *Mailing address:* Apdo. 66, c.p. 85450 (phone: 622-20121 or 622-20135). Inexpensive.

Las Playitas – Primarily a trailer park with 120 spaces and all connections, it also has 30 rooms and 7 bungalows with kitchenettes. Excellent restaurant, bar, pool, dock, and boat ramp. For reservations, write Apdo. 327, Guaymas. On the bay at Km 6 of the road to the Varadero Nacional (National Shipyard; phone: 622-22727 or 622-22753). Inexpensive.

SAN CARLOS

Club Med Sonora Bay – Twenty miles (32 km) south of San Carlos, this "club" member is a 300-room resort known for its tennis facilities — 30 courts. There also is a beach and restaurant. Playa los Algodones (phone: 622-60070; 800-CLUB-MED in the US). Expensive

Totonaca – With 140 full trailer hookups, laundry, restaurant and bar, coffee shop, gardens, and showers, there are also some rooms and apartments. Across the road from the beach, 5½ miles (9 km) west of Hwy. 1 (phone: 622-60481 or 622-60323). Moderate.

Posada San Carlos – The hotel offers 136 modern, well-furnished units with good facilities — 2 pools, tennis court, access to 18-hole golf course, boat ramp, fishing, skin diving, a western-style saloon with live music, and dining rooms specializing in seafood with live entertainment. *Mailing address:* Apdo. 200, c.p. 85506, Guaymas, Sonora.; 13 miles (21 km) north of San Carlos (phone: 622-60015 or 622-60122). Moderate to inexpensive.

Solimar – One of San Carlos's newer spots, it has 83 condominiums, 135 rooms, 3 pools, 2 Jacuzzis, restaurant, bar, satellite TV, and access to the 18-hole golf course and 13 tennis courts at the *San Carlos Country Club* next door. *Mailing address:* Apdo. 510, c.p. 85506, Guaymas, Sonora (phone: 622-60007 or 622-60231). Moderate to inexpensive.

Creston – A clean, comfortable hostelry with 24 large rooms, each with 2 double beds. Pool, parking. At Km 15 of Guaymas–San Carlos Hwy. (phone: 622-60020). Inexpensive.

Fiesta – Modern motel units with balconies overlooking the bay. Pool, dining room. 5 miles (8 km) west of Rte. 15 junction, in San Carlos (phone: 622-60229). Inexpensive.

Shangri-la – The big layout includes 327 trailer spaces, plus beachfront efficiency apartments and a few motel rooms. All connections and a good restaurant. Near the bay (phone: 622-60235 or 622-60238). Inexpensive.

Tecalai – This modern setup has 200 hookups, pool, snack bar, and a congenial staff. Across from the *Fiesta Motel* (phone: 622-60190). Inexpensive.

Teta Kawi – Space for 132 trailers, all connections, Jacuzzi, some cable TV hookups. Across from the beach (phone: 622-60220). Inexpensive.

CIUDAD OBREGÓN

Costa de Oro – Moderately priced, this motor inn has 122 units, with TV sets, air conditioning, restaurant, bar, disco, and pool. M. Alemán and Allende (phone: 641-41775 or 641-48200). Moderate.

Norotel Cajeme Valle Grande – This inn has 89 air conditioned units, pool, dining room, color TV sets, and a bar with live entertainment. M. Alemán and Cajeme (phone: 641-41300 or 641-48369). Moderate.

Norotel Nainari Obregón – The same chain as the *Cajame* runs this inn with 135 air conditioned rooms, a restaurant, pool, and color satellite TV. M. Alemán and Tetabiate (phone: 641-40940). Moderate.

NAVOJOA

El Rancho – An excellent choice, it has 65 air conditioned units, satellite TV, disco, a restaurant, bar, and coffee shop. They arrange fishing and hunting trips. Km. 1788 Carr. Internacional Norte (phone: 642-20310 or 642-20004). Moderate.

Del Río – A 60-unit, air conditioned motel with a pool, tennis, and restaurant. Off Alameda (phone: 642-25601 or 642-25402). Moderate.

ALAMOS

Casa de los Tesoros – The "Treasure House" is a fine 14-unit Mexican inn — a colonial relic with many period furnishings, excellent food, pool, nightly music. Reservations essential: Apdo. 12, c.p. 85760, Alamos, Sonora. In town, a block and a half from the plaza at 10 Obregón (phone: 642-80010). Expensive to moderate.

Acosta Ranch – There are 6 hotel rooms and 25 trailer spaces; it offers camping and guide service for hunting, fishing, and bird watching. Meals served in the owner's home (with 24-hour notice). A half mile (1 km) beyond Alamos (phone: 642-80246). Inexpensive.

El Caracol – With spaces for 40 trailers, an excellent restaurant, and horses to rent. 10 miles (16 km) west of Alamos (no phone). Inexpensive.

Dolisa – Within walking distance of the town center, this is an air conditioned, 8-unit motel with fireplaces in each room. On Hwy. 15 into town (phone: 642-80131). Inexpensive.

La Mansion de la Condesa Magdalena – In a 300-year-old mansion originally built for a wealthy mine owner, there are 19 charming rooms, a Jacuzzi, exercise room, and a cozy restaurant. 2 Obregón (phone: 642-80221). Inexpensive.

LOS MOCHIS

Plaza Inn – A recently remodeled 38-unit motel with a pool. There's a cafeteria next door. Corner of Leyva and Cardenas (phone: 681-20075 or 681-20284). Moderate.

Santa Anita – A total of 133 rooms, with a bar and dining room specializing in fish dishes. Fishing, hunting, and canyon trips can be arranged here. Gabriel Leyva and Hidalgo, downtown (phone: 681-57046; in Mexico City, 5-510-3398). Moderate.

Las Colinas – Here are 120 comfortable rooms, 3 tennis courts, color TV sets, basketball, volleyball, toboggan, heated pools and wading pools, coffee shop, nightclub, and a restaurant. Just south of the Rte. 15 interchange (phone: 681-20101, 681-20117; or Best Western Hotels, 800-528-1234 in the US). Moderate to inexpensive.

El Dorado – There are 93 rooms with cable TV, restaurant, bar, pool, and parking. Gabriel Leyva and H. Valdez (phone: 681-51111 or 681-51546). Inexpensive.

Los Mochis Copper Canyon – Offers 100 RV spaces with complete hookups, 12 complete bathrooms, laundry facilities, and fishing. Half a mile (1 km) after the Hwy. 15 overpass going toward Navajoa (phone: 681-26817). Inexpensive.

Posada Real – There are 35 air conditioned motel units and a pool. Calles Leyva and Buelna (phone: 681-22179 681-22363). Inexpensive.

Suites Florida – This 66-unit hotel has a coffee shop and a nightclub. Leyva and Ramírez. (phone: 681-21200). Inexpensive.

CULIACÁN

Los Tres Ríos – Probably the best in town, it's a combination motor inn with 70 bungalow-type units and 100-space trailer park with all connections. A good international restaurant, a pool, 2 bars, and nightclub. Km 1423 of the Carr. Internacional and Républica de Brazil (phone: 67-154040, 67-154140, 67-154440, or 67-154540). Moderate.

Ejecutivo – It has 218 rooms and 11 suites, air conditioning, restaurant, bar, nightclub, pool, tennis, solarium, and satellite TV. Madero and Obregón (phone: 67-139300 or 67-139310). Inexpensive.

Del Valle – Pleasant modern decor and 42 air conditioned units with TV sets; restaurant. 180 Blvd. Solano Ote. (phone: 67-139120, 67-139020, 67-139080, or 67-139170). Inexpensive.

SAN BLAS

Las Brisas – One of the better establishments in town, offering 42 units (some air conditioned) restaurant, bar, and pool. Paredes (phone: 321-50112 or 321-50480). Moderate.

Los Caminos – A remodeled 51-room, 2-story hostelry with restaurant, bar, pool, and night security. South end of Solano Blvd. (phone: 67-153300, 67-153310, 67-1534700, or 67-153490). Inexpensive.

Los Cocos – With 100 trailer spaces and all connections. Bar. San Blas (phone: 321-50055). Inexpensive.

Marino Inn – These motel rooms are air conditioned, and there is a pool, disco, good restaurant, and bar. Av. Heróica Batallón de San Blas (phone: 321-50340 or 321-91321). Inexpensive.

Playa Amor – A 40-unit RV facility on the beach. Hookups, showers, toilets, hot water, security wall and a guard. Take the San Blas turnoff to the Santa Cruz–Aticama exit on the outskirts of San Blas; then 13 miles (21 km) to Santa Cruz (no phone). Inexpensive.

Suites San Blas – It has 23 suites with kitchenettes, plus a pool, playground, and parking. Aticama and Palmas; *Mailing address:* Apdo. 12, c.p. 63740 (phone: 321-50047 or 321-50505). Inexpensive.

TEPIC

Corita – Features 35 units, pool, restaurant, disco, and bar. 310 Av. Insurgentes Pte. (phone: 321-20477). Moderate to inexpensive.

Fray Junípero Serra – An 85-unit hotel with restaurant, TV sets, and bar. Across from the main plaza at 23 Lerdo Pte. (phone: 321-22525, 321-22290, or 321-22175). Moderate to inexpensive.

KOA – Offers 61 spaces with water and electrical connections (34 have drainage), showers, recreation room, and moderate rates. Just 3 miles (5 km) south of town on Rte. 15, then a half mile (1 km) down a paved road (phone: 321-33113). Moderate to inexpensive.

Génova – All 65 units are moderately priced. Restaurant, some rooms with TV sets, and parking. On Hwy. 51 North at 51 Zaragoza Pte. (phone: 321-21604). Inexpensive.

La Loma – This motel has 50 air conditioned rooms, restaurant, bar, and pool facing a lovely park. 301 Paseo de la Loma (phone: 321-32052, 321-32057, or 321-32947). Inexpensive.

San Jorge – A 3-story, downtown hostelry with 39 rooms, restaurant, and parking. No air conditioning. 124 Lerdo (phone: 321-21324). Inexpensive.

Sierra de Alica – A colonial-style hotel, it has 60 units — some with air conditioning, all with TV sets — a restaurant, nightclub, and parking. Near main plaza, downtown (phone: 321-20322, 321-20324, or 321-20325). Inexpensive.

Villa las Rosas – This 31-unit, moderately priced hotel has a restaurant and fans, but no air conditioning. 100 Av. Insurgentes Pte., opposite Loma Park (phone: 321-31800, 321-31857, or 321-31058). Inexpensive.

AJIJIC

Real de Chapala – Colonial-style inn with 80 spacious suites, some offering a view of the lake. There's tennis, access to golf at the *Chapala Country Club,* a barbecue on Saturdays, and a Mexican fiesta on Sundays (phone: 376-52468 or 376-52519). Moderate.

La Nueva Posada de Ajijic – Twenty-two colonial-style suites (6 with fireplaces), pool, gardens, restaurant, and bar. 9 Calle Donato Guerra (phone: 376-53395). Inexpensive.

Posada de las Calandrias – A total of 29 units, including 10 efficiency apartments, set in a lovely garden. Three blocks from the main square (phone: 376-52819). Inexpensive.

SAN JUAN COSALA

Amueblados Condominio Cosala – All 33 moderately priced apartments have kitchenettes and private pools. 440 Av. de la Paz (phone: 376-30323). Inexpensive.

Balneario San Juan Cosala – A moderately priced, 33-unit, 2-story motel on the lake. On the road into town, about 5 miles (8 km) before reaching Jocotepec (phone: 376-30302). Inexpensive.

JOCOTEPEC

Posada del Pescador – Features 21 moderately priced units, cafeteria, and pool. Just outside town on Chapala Hwy (no phone). Inexpensive.

PÁTZCUARO

Best Western Posada de Don Vasco – The best place in town, this colonial-style hotel has excellent food, a good bar, tennis court, playground, bowling, and a pool. The *Dance of the Old Men* is performed here on Wednesday and Saturday nights at 9 PM. 450 Calz. de las Américas (phone: 454-20227 or 454-20262). Inexpensive.

Chalamú – A neat and unpretentious motel, it has 10 units with fireplaces and 4 suites with kitchenettes, overlooking a large garden. At Km 20 of Carr. Quiroga-Pátzcuaro. *Mailing address:* Apdo. 137, c.p. 61600 (phone: 454-20948). Inexpensive.

Mansion Iturbe – Charming 14-room hostelry in a restored 17th-century mansion. Restaurant and souvenir shop. 59 Portal Morelos, off Plaza Vasco de Quiroga (phone: 454-20368). Inexpensive.

Mesón del Cortijo – Restored hacienda with 14 units in colonial decor, complete with fireplaces; decent food. On Obregón (phone: 454-21295 or 454-21037). Inexpensive.

Mesón del Gallo – An extremely well maintained colonial-style inn offering small but comfortable rooms, a restaurant, and pool. 20 Dr. Coss (phone: 454-21474). Inexpensive.

Misión de San Manuel – Near the main plaza, an old townhouse has been converted into a 42-unit colonial-style hotel and restaurant. Plain but cozy. 12 Portal Aldama (phone: 454-21313). Inexpensive.

Posada de la Basílica – Small colonial inn with modest prices and a good restaurant. At the south end of town at 6 Arciga (phone: 454-21108). Inexpensive.

Posada San Rafael – Colonial inn setting with 104 units and a decent restaurant. On the main plaza (phone: 454-20770 or 454-20779). Inexpensive.

El Pozo – Twenty lakefront trailer spaces, all connections, and low rates. One of the nicest in the country. On the north end of town on Rte. 120 (phone: 454-20937). Inexpensive.

URUAPAN

Cabañas Tzintzuntzán – Basic, but well maintained, cabins with fireplaces, kitchenettes, and outdoor grills. Each cabin accommodates up to 5 people. Its location on the edge of the lake makes it a perfect place for viewing *Day of the Dead* activities. Km. 6 Carr. Quiroga-Pátzcuaro (phone: 454-31003 for reservations). Inexpensive.

Mansión de Cupatitzio – Lovely, colonial-style hotel with 53 rooms, 3 junior suites, color satellite TV, restaurant, bar, handicrafts shop. About 2 miles (3 km) from town next to the national park at the source of the Cupatitzio River (phone: 452-32100, 452-32090, or 452-32070). Inexpensive.

Paraíso Uruapan – Attractive colonial-style hotel in a lovely garden setting, with dining room, bar, pool, and parking. At the east end of town on the road to Pátzcuaro (phone: 452-38478, 452-38511, or 452-30333). Inexpensive.

Pie de la Sierra – Fine motel accommodations in Spanish colonial decor with fireplaces in each room, a children's playground, heated pool, restaurant, and bar. For reservations: Apdo. 153, c.p. 60000, Uruapan, Michoacán (phone: 452-21510). Inexpensive.

Plaza Uruapan – Here is a hotel with 124 rooms, color TV sets, a bar, restaurant, coffee shop, and disco. 64 Ocámpo (phone: 452-33700, 452-33813, or 452-30333). Inexpensive.

El Tarasco – A 55-unit hotel, 2 blocks from the main plaza, it has a pool, restaurant, bar, and TV sets. 2 Calle Independencia (phone: 452-41500 or 452-21680). Inexpensive.

ZITÁCUARO

Balneario San Jose Purua – Many of the 250 units have private mineral baths. Set in a garden on the edge of a canyon, there are 4 thermal water pools, bowling, billiards, miniature golf, and restaurants (phone: 725-31544; when calling long distance you must go through the operator; in Mexico City 5-510-4949). Expensive to moderate.

Las Azaleas – Tiny, 4-room hotel with a remarkably good restaurant set in an orchard. At Km 103.5 of Route 15 (phone: 5-651-3022 in Mexico City; no local phone). Inexpensive.

Rancho San Cayetano – The accommodations are as fine as the food. Reservations necessary on weekends, especially from late December to early April. Apartado 23 (phone: 725-31926). Inexpensive.

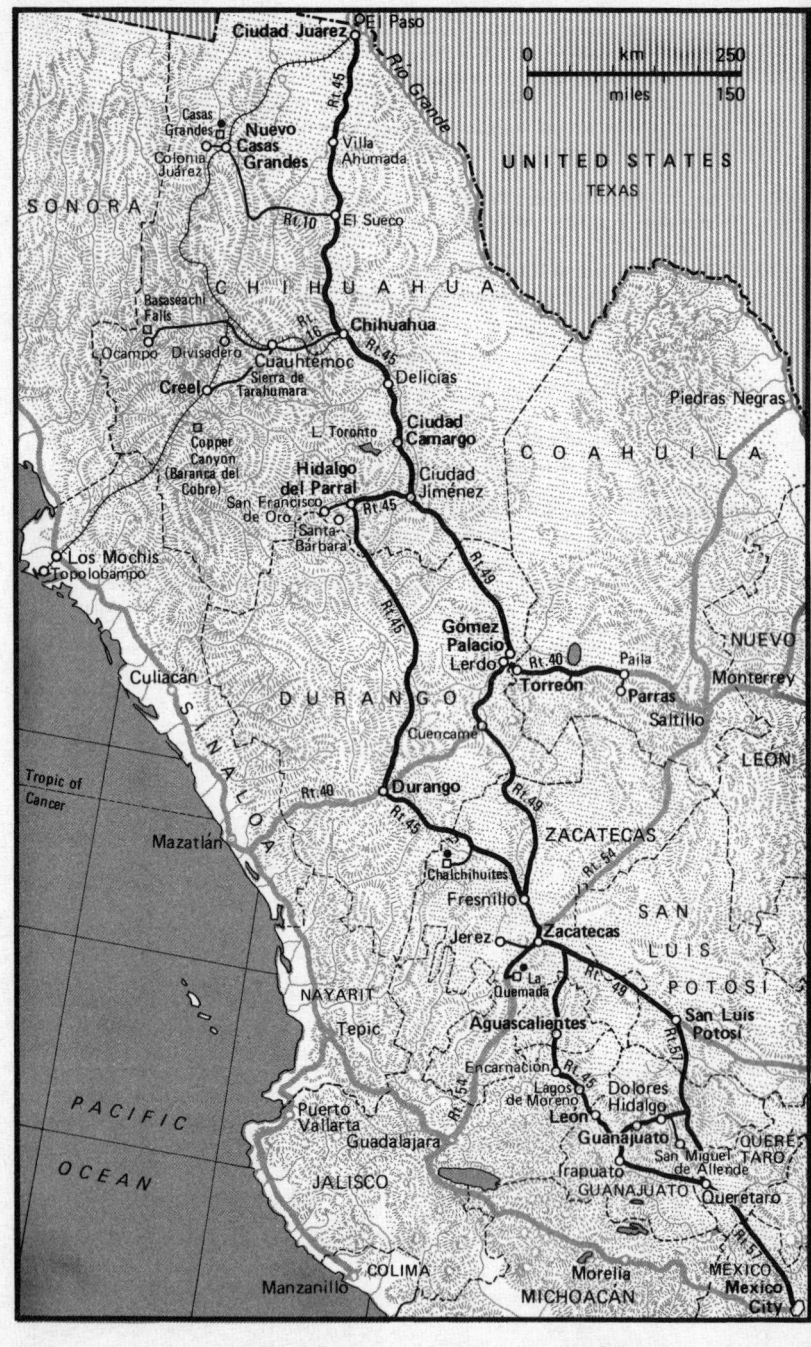

Juárez to Mexico City

The 1,200-mile (1,920-km) route from Ciudad Juárez (across the border from El Paso, Texas) to Mexico City is not the most popular entry route into Mexico. The cities along the way, especially in the northwest, are not as large or exciting as those along more easterly routes; the distances to be covered are mammoth, and the road leads through desert that is harsh (if beautiful) and skirts the jagged eastern edge of the Sierra Madre Occidental. But it is the route that burrows straight through the center of the country, a landscape offering magnificent mountain and desert sunsets, long-abandoned archaeological ruins, and, in the Bajío region near Mexico City, the country's most beautiful colonial cities.

In the course of this journey you cross a gently sloping tableland that rises from an altitude of 3,000 feet in the north to more than 7,000 feet in the Valley of Mexico, wherein the nation's capital lies. Much of the north is desert, although some of the land is irrigated and can support a cotton crop. Farther west are mountain areas and wildlife reserves filled with bears, sheep, deer, pumas, wolves, quail, and geese.

North-central Mexico has never been primarily an agricultural area; the land is too harsh without irrigation. This may be one of the reasons why the Indian cultures never prospered as they did in the south. In fact, only two major Indian tribes continue to live here: the Yaqui and the Tarahumara. The region has less of an Indian tradition than other areas of the country, perhaps because, as a border region, its cultural ties are closer to those of the US. Also, the Indian culture was largely destroyed by the ruthless exploitation by the Spanish, who were attracted to this area by its fabulous mineral wealth.

You can see the remnants of the glory and the tragedy of that world as you pass the ghost towns, abandoned silver mines, and ornate churches that the wealth from gold and silver mines supported. As you drive on Route 45 from Ciudad Juárez to Chihuahua to Durango, the deserts, the plateaus, the mountains, and canyons of the Sierra Madre resemble a set for an old-fashioned cowboy-and-Indian western. And in fact, westerns are still filmed here, especially around Durango.

North-central Mexico has had an adventurous past: a past filled with bandits, Apache and Comanche raids, Mexican Revolution battles and assassinations, Spanish conquests, and ruthless fights for gold and silver. It was here that Miguel Hidalgo y Costilla, the father of Mexican independence, was killed in 1811. Hidalgo had suffered defeats in central Mexico. As he returned with his ragged army from a desperate effort to reach the US for help, a lieutenant betrayed him to the Bishop of Monterrey. Hidalgo was captured at Acatita de Baján on March 21 and tried by the Inquisition; he recanted, but was defrocked, executed, and finally beheaded in Chihuahua. His severed head hung for 10 years on a fortress wall in Guanajuato. In the Palacio del

Gobierno (Governor's Palace; on Calle Aldama, between Guerrero and Carranza), fiery murals depict the dramatic story.

Later in the 19th century, the region became the center of the Mexican government when President Benito Juárez moved his armies to Chihuahua to organize the battle to defeat Emperor Maximilian. The emperor was terribly weakened when Napoleon III pulled the French troops out of Mexico just before the Franco-Prussian War. Maximilian was captured by Juárez at Querétaro and executed on June 19, 1867.

This is also the land where the revolutionary-bandit Pancho Villa helped Francisco Madero spark the Revolution of 1910 and the overthrow of the dictatorship of Porfirio Díaz.

Some of the most dramatic sights in Mexico can be seen here: the canyon country in the Sierra Tarahumara (and the breathtaking train ride from Chihuahua to Los Mochis across the mountains); Basaseachi Falls in the Sierra Madre; the ruins of Casas Grandes (the Toltec-inspired archaeological area south of Ciudad Juárez); and La Quemada, the abandoned fortress near Zacatecas that is believed to have been part of the Teotihuacán culture in the 4th, 5th, and 6th centuries.

Farther south, as you approach the fertile Bajío region (see *The Bajío*, DIRECTIONS), you'll discover some of the most attractive colonial cities in Mexico — Guanajuato, San Miguel de Allende, and Querétaro.

The north, however, is where the journey begins. From Ciudad Juárez to Mexico City the drive leads you through the states of Chihuahua, western Coahuila, Durango, Zacatecas, Nuevo León, San Luis Potosí, Guanajuato, and Querétaro.

It's an easy ride into Mexico from El Paso, Texas. You can take one of four bridges from El Paso: the Good Neighbor Bridge (Stanton St.) or the Del Norte Bridge (Av. Juárez), both of which enter downtown Juárez; the Bridge of the Americas, which enters the suburb of San Lorenzo, east of the city; or the new eight-lane Zaragoza Bridge, off Loop 375, which passes through the south side of town. The Zaragoza replaces the old two-lane steel bridge built in 1942; the original bridge was a wooden one built in 1929 to accommodate folks seeking alcoholic refreshment across the border during Prohibition. All bridges charge a toll. US Customs is open 24 hours, as are Mexican Customs and immigration offices.

In recent years much of the road leading from Ciudad Juárez to Mexico City has been expanded to four lanes — at least as far as Chihuahua — and the goverment is continuing to improve the roads beyond Chihuahua.

CIUDAD JUÁREZ: The fifth-largest city in Mexico (pop. 1.7 million) has a much lower rate of unemployment and poverty than other cities of its size. Originally known as Paso del Norte, one of the stops on the old Santa Fe Trail, it is still an interesting blend of Mexican and Texan, with a redolent dash of the Old West that has never dissipated.

In the 1880s, Juárez was linked with its sister city, El Paso, by mule-pulled trolley cars. By 1902 this colorful means of transportation between the two countries gave way to electric trolleys. Today, those who don't drive themselves make the journey in drab buses, but at least the trip across the border is fairly painless.

Because it is a border town, Juárez has the requisite racy nightlife, but it has never been quite as honky-tonk as some of the other border cities. There's quite a lot to see and do in town — there are wide boulevards and tree-filled parks, imposing statues of Benito Juárez and Abraham Lincoln, a Spanish mission that has been active since 1659, two bullrings, a convention center, a good market, and a museum. Bizarrely, among the most popular stops for 1-day visitors are the dental clinics that have proliferated in town. US citizens find bargain rates for dental work in Mexico, and some combine a root canal with a vacation in the sun.

If you've come to Mexico for its sights, however, Juárez is filled with places to visit. The Mission of Our Lady of Guadalupe, commemorating Mexico's patron saint, was built in 1659 by Father Francisco García. The town that grew around the church was called Nuestra Señora de Guadalupe del Paso del Norte. It was changed in 1888 to Ciudad Juárez in honor of Benito Juárez, the Zapotec Indian leader who became the President of Mexico.

Mexican goods from all over the country are exhibited at the *Centro Artesanías* (Arts and Crafts Center) in the *Centro Comercial Pronaf* (off Lincoln and Dieciséis de Septiembre). This complex also has a collection of picturesque shops selling a variety of Mexican wares. Nearby, the *Museo de Arte e Historia* (Museum of Art and History) has archaeology and art exhibitions; admission charge.

You can visit the headquarters of Juárez's government (16 de Septiembre between Mariscal and V. Carranza). When Maximilian's army occupied Mexico City from 1865 to 1866, President Juárez established his government in this building. There is a monument to Juárez on Calle Vicente Guerrero, nearby.

Bullfights are held at the *Paseo Triunfo de la República* (Plaza Monumental de Toros) about 6 Sundays a year, spring through fall, usually coinciding with long US holiday weekends. The *Galgodromo* is the site of greyhound racing. The dogs race at 8:30 PM every night except Mondays and Tuesdays.

There are also a number of excellent restaurants in Juárez. *Casa del Sol* in the *Arts and Crafts Center* serves international fare at reasonable prices; black bass is a specialty. If this is the first meal you have in Mexico, it might be wise to pamper an unaccustomed stomach at one of the more expensive places. The *O.K. Corral* (735 Av. de las Américas Nte.) has good Mexican and international dishes, and *Sanborn's* (Paseo Triunfo de la República and López Mateos) is always a safe choice. *Corona* (Av. Dieciséis de Septiembre) tones down *picante* (spicy) Mexican dishes for tourist palates. If you are nostalgic for good Chinese food, try the *Shangri-La* (133 Av. de las Américas Nte., 3 miles/5 km south of the Bridge of the Americas), which is open from noon to 1 AM.

En Route from Juárez – Don't forget to fill up your gas tank at one of the Pemex gas stations; it is 100 miles (160 km) to the next one at Villa Ahumada on the Juárez-Chihuahua road. As you leave Juárez, you pass an immigration and customs checkpoint just south of the city. From Juárez you have a choice of routes. Route 45 will take you directly into Chihuahua, capital of the state, in 4 or 5 hours. However, you can leave it at El Sueco (some 150 miles/240 km south of Juárez) and take a side trip to Nuevo Casas Grandes and the ruins at Paquimé.

CASAS GRANDES: This archaeological area is about 4 miles (7 km) from Nuevo Casas Grandes. Turn right off Route 45 at El Sueco and follow Route 10 to Nuevo Casas Grandes, about 123 miles (196 km) away. You can also take the train (*Ferrocarril Noroeste de México*) from Juárez.

The ruins resemble those of the pueblo dwellers of Arizona and New Mexico. Excavations have unearthed pyramids, a ball court, and small potsherds that resemble Toltec objects. The town was probably established by Indians of the North American Southwest. Mexican Indians moved into the area later, about AD 1300.

Nuevo Casas Grandes is highland country filled with forests and clear streams. Once you reach Colonia Juárez, a remote village southwest of Nuevo Casas Grandes, the roads get rough and you'll need a guide to take you over the trails. (Contact the *Piñon* hotel; phone: 169-40655.) Fishing season is from May to mid-October, and the best streams for fishing are the San Juan de Dios, Tres Ríos, Gavilán, Paraíso, Largo, and the Cañada del Oro.

CHIHUAHUA: For a detailed report on Chihuahua, its hotels and restaurants, see *Chihuahua,* THE CITIES. Figuratively and literally, this is a town built on silver. The mines are responsible for Chihuahua's growth — its buildings were constructed to exhibit the wealth they bestowed, and its population (mostly Indians and the priests who came to convert the Indians) grew to serve them in one capacity or another. There is a rumor that some of the walls of Chihuahua's oldest buildings contain silver ore. This has never been proven, although it does make an attractively allegorical legend. In any event, the builders did their job well, even if the buildings are not of silver. The broad boulevards and congenial squares of the city are a welcome contrast after the long journey through the desolate plateau from Ciudad Juárez.

Some of Mexico's most spectacular scenery is just west of Chihuahua — the massive canyons and trenches in the Sierra Madre known as the Barrancas de la Tarahumara (Tarahumara Canyons), better known as the fabled Barranca del Cobre (Copper Canyon). This area contains 1,000-foot-high Basaseachi Falls and some of the best hiking in all Mexico.

En Route to Copper Canyon – You can reach the Sierra de Tarahumara and canyon country in three ways: by road via Cuauhtémoc and Creel; by rail on the *Chihuahua-Pacífico Railway;* or by air from Chihuahua to Creel. The road journey can take as long as a day, depending upon the state of your car, since the mountain roads are rough. Take Route 16 to Cuauhtémoc, a city of about 145,000 people 67 miles (108 km) west of Chihuahua. Cuauhtémoc is the home of a Mennonite community of 55,000 people. (The Mennonites, who fled from Prussia, the Ukraine, and other parts of Europe, have maintained their religious customs and native languages in Mexico; they make and sell excellent cheese.) From Cuauhtémoc, take the mountain road to Creel, a small town on the *Chihuahua-Pacífico Railway* line and about 20 miles (32 km) from the canyons along a twisting mountain road. In the heart of Tarahumara country, Creel is an excellent jump-off point for numerous half-day or longer excursions into the canyons. Divisadero, reachable from Creel by train, offers the best vantage point for seeing the canyons and the Tarahumara Indians at work at their exceptional baskets.

The *Chihuahua-Pacífico Railway,* quite rightly called the "world's most scenic railroad," provides the best way to see the Copper Canyon. It was long argued that building a railroad through the Sierra Madre Occidental couldn't be done, and it almost wasn't. Albert K. Owen, a US citizen who founded a utopian colony in Los Mochis in 1872, thought that a route from the southwestern US to Topolobampo on the Pacific coast would reduce overland freight shipping distances and costs. Finally, in 1953, Mexico agreed to attempt the project. Eight years later the exceptional engineering plan became a reality. The most difficult section of the railway was the 161-mile gap crossing Tarahumara Indian territory to the Copper Canyon and through the mountains. In order to construct this route, 86 tunnels (one a full mile long) and 39 bridges had to be built.

The *Chihuahua-Pacífico* Copper Canyon train leaves from the Chihuahua-Pacífico train station in Chihuahua (Méndez and Calle 24) at 6 AM, arriving in Los Mochis at 6 PM. — or you can take it from Cuidad Juárez and spend the night in Chihuahua. The 12-hour trip includes stops at Creel and Divisadero. The return trip leaves the Los Mochis train station at 7 AM and arrives in Chihuahua at 7 PM. The train has a first class car serving steaks, grilled chicken, fish, and other fine dishes. A box lunch is provided in other cars. The trip has become very popular, so it is advisable to make reservations well in advance (phone: 800-228-

3225 in the US). Travelers should be advised that this 400-mile (640 km) trip is best made from west to east, Los Mochis to Chihuahua, to avoid passing through the most spectacular scenery after dark. To reach Chihuahua, the *Rapido de la Frontera* train also leaves from Ciudad Juárez daily at 6 PM, arriving in Chihuahua at 10 PM. For more information on both trains, contact the Commercial Passenger Department, National Railways of Mexico (Buenavista Grand Central Station, Mexico D.F. 06385). For train fare and schedule information call 5-547-6593/1097/1084.

Sanborn Viva Tours (P.O. Drawer 519, McAllen, TX 78502; phone: 512-682-9872; or 1007 Main St., Bastrop, TX 78228; phone: 512-523-1400 or 800-531-5440) offers two Copper Canyon tours, El Pronto (6-day/5-night) and Copper Canyon/Mazatlán (9-day/8-night). In addition, small aircraft fly to the canyon country from Chihuahua; for more information, check at your hotel or the tourist office in Chihuahua.

SIERRA TARAHUMARA (Tarahumara Mountains): You should explore at least one part of the vast Sierra Madre range to get some idea of the size of the whole. A 2-night stay in Creel is an excellent way to become familiar with some of the canyons, waterfalls, and caves inhabited by the Tarahumara Indians. Stay in the rustic but removed *Copper Canyon Lodge* or the less expensive but central *Parador de la Montaña*. The next stop along the train route should be Divasadero, where there is nothing but an Indian market and the *Cabañas Divisadero Barrancas* hotel (see *Best en Route*), perched dramatically on the edge of the canyon. Make a final stop in the mission village of Cerocahui (the train stop is Bahuichivo); stay at the *Misión* and explore the beautiful Urique Canyon. (For more information on hotels, see *Best en Route.*) At each stop, hotel management will arrange your trips — by van, horseback, or foot — into the canyons. By all means camp in the canyons if it's to your liking. The bases of the canyons are almost tropical, with bamboos, oranges, and orchids in abundance. In fact, many of the Tarahumara Indians "go south" for the winter simply by walking from the top of the canyons to the base.

The Tarahumara, holdovers of the Stone Age of some 30,000 years ago, are the largest and least-known tribe in northern Mexico. People who keep to themselves, they have managed to avoid both extermination and modernization. Some 40,000 of them live in the Sierra de Tarahumara region, in caves or log cabins, and they can be identified by their long jet-black hair tied with a headband. The men often wear little more than a loincloth. Traditionally, the Tarahumara are excellent runners and hunt deer by chasing them for days until the animals drop from exhaustion. As do a number of other tribes in Mexico, the Tarahumara hold peyote sacred. Although the Indians are Christians, the peyote plants occupy a space on their altars next to the crucifix. Outsiders may find it easy to think of these Indians as a collective curiosity, yet they, like most of us, are people simply trying to survive.

On your way back to Chihuahua, explore Basaseachi Falls, if you didn't go there on a tour. You can reach the falls by heading northeast from Creel to Cuauhtémoc (also a stop on the railway line from Chihuahua). From Cuauhtémoc follow a mountain road to the town of Ocampo. A steep path through a forest leads to the site where the Basaseachi River drops a sheer 1,000 feet into the Candameña Canyon — the sight is worth the journey.

En Route from Chihuahua – Route 45 south from Chihuahua is quite good for the next 150 miles (240 km) to Camargo. About halfway you pass Delicias, a modern industrial town that is a good stop for a stretch but little else.

CAMARGO: This lively town of 65,000 people, originally called Santa Rosalía, was founded in 1740 and almost destroyed by Apache attacks in 1797. The new settlement grew quickly, and today the city is a busy industrial center, with meat-packing plants, textile mills, and other industries. The *Fiesta de Santa Rosalía* is celebrated in Camargo from September 4 to 12. A number of hot springs are all within 7 miles (11 km) of town: Ojo de Jabalí, Ojo Caliente, and Ojo Salado — all known for their curative powers. Ojo Caliente is generally considered the best of the lot. And about 18 miles (29 km) southwest of Camargo is the La Boquilla Dam and its adjoining lake, Lake Toronto, so named because it was first stocked with black bass from the Toronto area. Spring is the best time for fishing (the lake is closed for fishing in July and August), and you'll find bluegills, perch, and catfish in addition to black bass. Nearby, the *Club de Esquís* rents small boats and launches.

En Route from Camargo – About 45 miles (72 km) south of Camargo on Route 45 is Ciudad Jiménez, an agricultural center. It's a nice rest stop. At Jiménez, the route divides. Route 49 passes through the towns of Gómez Palacio, Lerdo, and Torreón, and Route 45 passes through Hidalgo del Parral and Durango.

GÓMEZ PALACIO: Founded in 1886, Gómez Palacio was named after an early governor of the state of Durango. The well-irrigated area around the city seems like an oasis in the desert; cotton keeps the city bustling. Gómez Palacio is one of the government's three "La Laguna" cities — objects of an ambitious land reclamation project. It is most interesting for the irrigation projects that surround it. Northwest of Gómez Palacio, at Ojuelo, is a 990-foot-high pedestrian bridge that is suspended 330 feet across a vast canyon. (Take Carretera 49 northwest for 26 miles/42 km to Bermejillo; turn left on Mexico 30 and proceed 12½ miles/20 km; turn left again on a dirt road and proceed 4½ miles/7 km.) Nearby is a Mapimí, bejeweled with quartz, geodes, and other glistening minerals. To reach Mapimí from Ojuelo, return to Mexico 30 and continue 2½ miles (4 km) to Mapimí. Further information can be obtained from the tourist office (250 Blvd. Miguel Alemán Ote.; phone: 17-144434).

LERDO: Lerdo is also an agricultural center. It's 1½ miles (3 km) from Gómez Palacio, just within the borders of the state of Durango. Just southwest of Lerdo, Raymundo National Park has good fishing and other water sports.

TORREÓN: Torreón is another "La Laguna" city. Cotton is one of Mexico's major exports, and here it was a familiar crop for the Indians long before the Spanish arrived. According to Toltec legend, Quetzalcóatl, the god of agriculture, could grow cotton in different colors. Weaving was a highly respected craft among the pre-Hispanic Indian cultures. The *Isauro Martinez* theater (at Matamoros and Galeano) is considered to be one of the most beautiful in Mexico. Pre-Hispanic artifacts are on display at the *Museo Regional de la Laguna* (Laguna Regional Museum; at Juárez and Carranza).

Torreón has some good and inexpensive places to eat. For seafood, try the *Apolo Palacio* (259 Valdez Carillo Sur, on the main plaza). It's a modern restaurant and also serves international cuisine. *La Mojada* (Blvd. Independencia and Donato Guerra) has good meats, especially roast kid, as does *Rodeos* (Colón and Ocampo). The *Aténas* (239 Acuña Sur) offers Greek-Arabian cuisine.

Some spectacular sites are within easy driving distance of Torreón. The Bilbao dunes (take Route 40 east 25 miles/40 km and turn right at the *Ejido Hermosa*) and the Zona del Silencio (Zone of Silence) are abundant with giant turtles, fossils, and aerolites, as well as brilliantly colored cacti (about 87 miles/140 km northeast on Rte. 49).

The small, isolated town of Parras (Parras de la Fuente), southeast of Torreón, is also worth a detour. In the state of Coahuila, Parras is midway between Torreón and Saltillo, off Route 40. Parras, founded in 1598, was originally called Santa María de las Parras. It is the birthplace of Francisco Madero, father of the Revolution of 1910. Nowadays it is best known for its wine industry, specifically the winery of San Lorenzo, which has been producing some of Mexico's best wines since 1626. It is a lovely, uncommercialized town.

HIDALGO DEL PARRAL: This old mining town (pop. 79,000) about 200 miles (320 km) south of Chihuahua on Route 45 was the capital of the state of Chihuahua 300 years ago. The mining boom hit Parral during the 1600s, and about 7,000 Indians worked the two major mines, Cerro de la Cruz and La Negrita. Napoleon's troops occupied Parral during Emperor Maximilian's reign.

Pancho Villa was assassinated in Parral; his house, now the Francisco Villa library, is the major tourist attraction in town. At the corner of Calle Juárez and Calle M. Herrera, in front of the Escuela Mexico high school.

The Palacio Municipal, on the central plaza, has pleasant gardens and a plaza. La Iglesia de la Virgen del Rayo (Church of the Virgin of the Thunderbolt) is definitely worth a visit. Built between 1690 and 1710, the church is a source of special pride to the Indians of the area. An Indian miner financed much of the church; he arrived each week with a gold ingot to pay the workmen. When the church was completed, the Spanish governor demanded to know where the Indian had found this gold. He refused to answer and was tortured to death, and the location of his mine is still a mystery.

There is a more modern church in town: Iglesia de Nuestra Señora de Fatima (Church of Our Lady of Fatima). Pieces of gold, silver, manganese, zinc, copper, and antimony from mines in the area are embedded in its foundation.

The Palacio de Pedro Alvarado is an amazingly ornate building that was constructed by a poor miner who struck it rich in La Palmilla silver mine. He became famous when he offered to pay Mexico's national debt.

En Route from Parral – Two mining towns about 24 miles (38 km) west of Parral, San Francisco del Oro and Santa Bárbara, were founded in 1547, when the Spanish struck gold. In 1580 Santa Bárbara became the seat of government for the Spanish territory of Nueva Vizcaya, which then included the present areas of Chihuahua, Sonora, Coahuila, Texas, New Mexico, Arizona, and California.

DURANGO: (For a detailed description of Durango, its restaurants and hotels, see *Reynosa to Mazatlán,* DIRECTIONS.) Durango has one special claim on modern travelers: It has been the scene of dozens of westerns. Even John Wayne hunted bandits in the desolate hills outside Durango, and many of the sets are still standing. However, Durango's movie industry has had a lot of competition from Cuernavaca in recent years and has suffered a sharp decline. Permission to visit can be obtained from the Turismo y Cinematografía office, at 408 Calle Hidalgo Sur (phone: 181-11107).

There's still good hunting west and northwest of the city (mostly bears, deer, and wildcats) and in the backcountry, which is accessible by train as far as Tepehuanes. From there, hunters follow the trails into Tepehuan Indian country.

The city itself was built from mining money. In fact, one of the largest iron deposits in the world is just north of Durango, El Cerro del Mercado (Market Hill). Gold and silver were discovered during the 1500s in the nearby Sierra Madre, and local Indians worked the mines for the Spanish. One outcome of the wealth of the mines is the massive, Tuscan-style Cathedral of Durango that faces the main square of town. Built between 1695 and 1750, the cathedral reflects a number of different decorative periods.

For dining, *La Galeria* in the *Casablanca* hotel (see *Best en Route*) serves Mexican food at reasonable prices. *Cafe Neveria* (907 Av. Veinte de Noviembre) serves Mexican and German fare.

Durango is on the coast-to-coast highway from Matamoros to Mazatlán, and it is a good place to pick up the spectacular cross-country road to the west coast.

En Route from Durango – Route 45 rejoins Route 49 near Fresnillo (pop. 35,500), a small colonial town where you might want to stop for a rest on your way to Zacatecas, about 40 miles (64 km) to the south.

ZACATECAS: Named from the Aztec words *zacatl,* grass or hay, and *tlan,* place, the city was originally the home of the Zacateco Indians. You enter the city along a winding road past picturesque houses sprawled across a mountain called Cerro de la Bufa (a *bufa* is a Spanish wineskin). Steep cobblestone streets give the city a medieval look.

The Spanish, who first arrived in the region in 1529, found Zacatecas inhabited by various tribes of Indians. It was declared property of the Spanish Crown in 1546. In 1554 the first mining expedition was launched, and Zacatecas, like most cities in the area, became a profitable silver mining center. The King of Spain, who received a royal 20% of the profit from its mines, renamed it "The Very Noble and Loyal City of Our Lady of Zacatecas" in 1588. Between the 16th and 18th centuries the mines poured out more than a billion dollars worth of silver, and some of those mines are still being worked. Guided tours in English are available through the tunnels of the Eden mine which stretch out below the city.

Zacatecas itself has some beautiful colonial architecture. The cathedral, completed in 1752, is on the south side of the main plaza. Its construction was financed by a tax on the city mines. In colonial times the cathedral was a shining example of the amazing wealth of the Spanish mining towns.

The Church of Santo Domingo (a block west of the plaza) is a good example of Spanish baroque style. The Palacio del Gobierno (Municipal Palace) and the *Calderón Theater* are both examples of colonial Spanish buildings. Not to be missed is the *Pedro Coronel Museum*. Coronel, a native Zacatecan, left his extensive private collection to his home state. Housed in what was formerly a Jesuit school, the first floor is devoted entirely to pieces from Mexico's pre-Columbian period. Greco-Roman, Oriental, and contemporary art collections are displayed on the second floor, where there are also two rooms devoted to Goya and Piranesi and another to works from Mexico's colonial period, including two magnificent figures of Christ done by Zacatecans. Coronel's mausoleum is also on the premises. Closed Thursdays. Admission charge. Near the main square on the Plaza Santo Domingo.

Zacateas, in fact, has produced some of Mexico's finest artists. Another museum not to be missed is the *Museo Francisco*. And *Goitia*, which houses works of Goitia, Julio Ruellas, Pedro and Rafael Coronel, José Kuri, and Manuel Felguerez, is another fine museum. Closed Mondays. No admission charge. Parque General Enrique Estrada.

Southeast of the city is the former Guadalupe Convent which now houses an important collection of colonial art. Don't miss the Napoles Chapel, with its gilded stucco walls and extraordinary cupola.

For a good view of the city, visit the chapel of La Capilla de los Remedios on the summit of El Cerro de la Bufa, on the northeast edge of town. A cable car makes the trip between Cerro del Grillo and Cerro de la Bufa. The chapel, also known as El Patrocinio, contains an image of the Virgin that, according to the Indians, has magical powers. The *Mercado González Ortega,* once the central market, has been turned into a shopping center. *La Guija* (in the *Mercado*) serves steaks and international fare, and *Hostería de la Moneda* (501 Dr. Hierro) is a good place to sample local specialties. *La Cuija* serves steaks and international food in the old market complex downtown. Another good spot is *El Caballo Loco* (Hwy. 45, east of town), a steakhouse serving *cabrito* (kid) and other Mexican dishes. There is a very helpful tourist office (at Av. Hidalgo and Callejón de Santero; phone: 492-26683 or 492-28467).

In addition to a number of attractive places to see in Zacatecas, you can visit the ruins of the pre-Hispanic city of La Quemada (Chicomoztoc), 30 miles (48 km) southwest of the city. Also, just south of Zacatecas, in Guadalupe, is the Convent of Nuestra Señora de Guadalupe, considered one of Mexico's most important monuments. Now a national museum, the convent has valuable paintings from the colonial period, a library of rare books, and lovely chapels. Getting to the La Quemada–Chicomoztoc ruins is fairly easy. Take Route 54 toward Guadalajara. About 28 miles (45 km) from Zacatecas there is a turnoff on the left, and the ruins are about 2 miles (3 km) from the main highway along this road. La Quemada is fairly well preserved, probably because of the dry air of the region. Divided into three sections — the temple, the palace, and the citadel — the ruins are spread over a large area. It is believed that the roots of this civilization were in Teotihuacán culture from the 4th to the 6th century AD.

About 100 miles (160 km) beyond the La Quemada ruins on the same road from Zacatecas are the ruins of El Teul and Las Ventanas. Since the road is bad and the ruins are in a very primitive state, it is a good idea to hire a guide. You would also do better with a guide at the ruins of the fortress-like city, Chalchihuites. To the northwest of La Quemada, near the Zacatecas-Durango state line and south of the railway town Suchil, these ruins have characteristics similar to those of La Quemada.

JEREZ DE GARCÍA SALINAS: This colonial town of 80,000 is about 30 miles (48 km) west of Zacatecas in the midst of the best cattle raising country in Mexico. It's known for its 10-day rose festival, which begins *Easter Sunday,* and for the old and very romantic *Hinojosa Theater.* García Salinas, who was born here, was Latin America's first advocate of free compulsory education.

En Route from Zacatecas – From Zacatecas you can take Route 49 to Querétaro via San Luis Potosí or you can continue on Route 45 toward Querétaro through Aguascalientes, with a side trip to Guanajuato and San Miguel de Allende.

SAN LUIS POTOSÍ: (For a detailed description of San Luis Potosí, see *Nuevo Laredo to Mexico City,* DIRECTIONS.) The Spanish named the city Potosí after the fabulously wealthy mines in Bolivia (*potosí* is a Quechua Indian word meaning "richness") in 1538, when they found the Chichimec Indian town of Tangamaga, which had been inhabited for 3 centuries. Silver was discovered in the nearby town of San Pedro, but the mineral springs in San Luis made it a better place to settle. Religion — in the form of Franciscans, Jesuits, and Carmelites — followed commerce and was responsible for the architectural treasures that give San Luis its character.

Benito Juárez made San Luis his base in the fight against European intervention during the Mexican revolution. He condemned Maximilian to death from the Palacio de Gobierno (on the Plaza de Armas).

San Luis Potosí is a picturesque and prosperous town with some lovely colonial buildings. The beautifully proportioned cathedral, on the central plaza (Plaza de Armas, also known as Jardín Hidalgo), was built between 1670 and 1730 on the site of two earlier churches. Inside the cathedral you'll find a medley of styles: Byzantine, Doric, Gothic, and many combinations thereof.

The Church of Nuestra Señora del Carmen is ornate even when judged by the elaborate standards of the baroque style. A block east of the plaza, the church is probably the most interesting of the city's colonial buildings. The country's best mask museum, *Museo Nacional de la Mascara,* is at 2 Vilerías (phone: 481-23025).

San Luis Potosí's market is about 10 blocks from the central plaza; just walk down Calle Hidalgo — it's 3 blocks past the flower market. Baskets, rebozos, and straw furniture are available at good prices. The tourist office is at 130 Manuel José Ohón, 2nd Floor (phone: 481-42994 or 481-23143).

If you decide to take the alternate route from Zacatecas (Rte. 45), you'll reach the city of Aguascalientes, about 77 miles (123 km) to the south.

AGUASCALIENTES: Named for the thermal springs found in the area, Aguascalientes is also known for the extensive system of tunnels beneath it. For this reason, the city is sometimes called La Ciudad Perforada ("'the perforated city"). The tunnels are clearly manmade, but no one knows by whom; Indian histories shed no light.

In 1522, Cortés ordered Pedro de Alvarado into the western territories near Aguascalientes. His troops were badly mauled by the Indians, and for a number of years the city was deserted except for a small group of Chichimec Indians. The discovery of rich silver mines at Tepezala infused life into the area. First the Indians, then the mines, then the Jesuits, then rapid growth: It is the same pattern of development found in almost all of the silver cities of north-central Mexico.

One of the most famous festivals in all of Mexico is Aguascalientes's *San Marcos Fair,* from about April 20 to May 10. Bullfights, fireworks, rodeos, and craft exhibits make the city come alive. Most of the activities take place in the Jardín de San Marcos, just one of the many pleasant parks in Aguascalientes.

A stroll in the parks is one of the best ways to begin a tour of this city; fine weather is almost guaranteed. In the center of town is the Palacio de Gobierno, on the Plaza Principal, known for its fine historical mural by the Chilean painter Oswaldo Barra. The palace used to be the feudal castle of the Marqués de Guadalupe. Also of interest are the Palacio Municipal (City Hall), the Church of San Marcos, the Church of San Antonio, and the *Morelos Theater. El Museo de la Ciudad* (the City Museum) is on 505 Calle de Zaragoza .

Through local hotels, a visit can be arranged to Las Peñuelas, a bull breeding hacienda near the city. You can also visit nearby wineries by asking your hotel to arrange it. The *Grape Festival* is hosted in Aguascalientes in August or September.

Aguascalientes is also known for fine hand-embroidered and crocheted articles and for the nearby hot springs. San Nicolás de la Cantera, Ojo Caliente, and Colombo are all within a short ride. Here, you can submerge yourself in a mixture of sulfate of soda, sulfate of lime, carbonate of lime, chloride of sodium, magnesia, and sulfuric acid. It's supposed to make you feel like a new person.

For a good binge before you get healthy, try the restaurant at the *Francia* (on the main plaza) or the *Rincón Gaucho* (110 Arturo Pani). *Caballo Loco* (310 V. Carranza), has good service and moderately priced food. *Aguas 'n' Charlie's* (902 José Ma. Chavez) and *La Vendimia* (Arturo J. Pani) also are good choices.

En Route from Aguascalientes – You may want to stop off at the town of Encarnación de Díaz, 16 miles (26 km) south of town on Route 45. In the zocalo you'll see the *Niña,* the *Pinta,* and the *Santa María* — all sculpted from the trees in the park. About 35 miles (56 km) south you'll pass the pleasant little colonial town of Lagos de Moreno in the state of Jalisco. It's a decent place to stop for a break. If you can hold out for 25 miles (40 km), you'll be in León.

LEÓN: On June 18, 1888, a huge wall of water from the Río Gómez crushed León, destroying 2,230 houses, killing more than 200 persons, and leaving 20,000 homeless. El Puente del Coecillo, a huge dike nearly a mile long and 10 feet thick, was constructed to prevent another disaster.

Today León is a large and important commercial center with a number of parks, colonial buildings, and a busy market. The city is also the shoe manufacturing capital of Mexico and a major production center of leathergoods. Artisans here do fine leatherwork, such as boots and saddles.

If you don't really care for shoe shopping, you might want to spend your time visiting the Templo Expiatorio. Construction workers are still attempting to finish the church, which was begun more than 50 years ago. The catacombs beneath the church are well worth a visit — as you'll see a series of chapels, statues, altars, paintings, all underground.

Also worth a visit are the Palacio Municipal (City Hall) and the cathedral, both on the main plaza. The beautifully proportioned cathedral was built by the Jesuits in 1746 and dedicated to Nuestra Señora de la Luz (Our Lady of Light).

On *San Sebastian Day,* January 20, a fair and folk dancing is held.

Good restaurants include *El Molinito* (111 Hidalgo), *Los Venados* (511 Blvd. López Mateos), and *La Casa Grande,* (in the *Convention Center*).

En Route from León – You can reach the Mexico City toll road in León or you can head toward Guanajuato, about 30 miles (48 km) southeast, which really shouldn't be missed. Take Route 45 as far as Silao, then turn onto Route 110. From here it's about 16 miles (26 km) of twisting through the hills to the city.

GUANAJUATO: (For a detailed description of the city, its hotels and restaurants, see *Guanajuato,* THE CITIES.) From your first glimpse of Guanajuato nestled in a ravine between mountains, you'll find the city delightful. Since much of Mexico's history can be traced in her colonial architecture, Guanajuato is more than a pleasant place to visit; it's a museum.

The streets are steep and narrow, and the city is small — a town made for walking. Its churches, statues, theaters, even its cemeteries can be explored on foot. Guanajuato is not built around a central plaza, as are most of Mexico's cities. At first it may seem to be a hopelessly confusing place, probably because the subterranean highway that runs through the town has no clear exit markings.

Three miles (5 km) west of Guanajuato on Route 115 are the ruins of Marfil.

MARFIL: Once a wealthy suburb of Guanajuato, Marfil was founded in 1554 and reached its peak in the 18th and 19th centuries, when 20,000 people lived here. It was named for Pedro Marfil, a rich miner and landowner. Other wealthy people in Guanajuato built their homes in Marfil, but the mansions were almost totally destroyed in the flood of 1905. Today, artists are attempting to imaginatively renovate the old homes.

En Route from Guanajuato and Marfil – About 10 miles (16 km) west of Guanajuato is the Cerro del Cubilete, thought to be the geographic center of Mexico. A statue of Christ the King stands atop the 9,440-foot peak. The bronze statue is 75 feet high and weighs 200 tons. Pilgrims from all over Mexico flock to the monument and climb the interior stairway to a chapel near the figure's heart.

From Guanajuato you can either return to Route 45 and continue to Mexico City via Irapuato; or you can take Route 110 north from Guanajuato to Dolores Hidalgo, then Route 51 to San Miguel de Allende, and then the toll road at Querétaro to Mexico City. Via the direct route, Guanajuato is about 300 miles (480 km) from Mexico City; if you take the toll road (marked *cuota*), the journey will take from 4 to 5 hours. You'll pass through Irapuato, the Strawberry Capital of Mexico — stop and try them out at one of the roadside stands. The alternate route through Dolores Hidalgo and San Miguel will add about 100 miles (160 km) to your trip, but it's worth it.

DOLORES HIDALGO: (For a detailed description of the city, see *The Bajío,* DIRECTIONS.) Don Miguel Hidalgo y Costilla made this town famous when he proclaimed Mexico's independence here on September 16, 1810. It is a tradition that each Mexican president send a personal representative to the town during the annual reenactment of the Grito de Dolores, the battle cry that sparked an insurrection against the Spanish colonists. The president himself proclaims the *grito* from the main balcony of the National Palace, on the north side of the Mexico City zocalo.

You can visit the *Casa de Don Miguel Hidalgo* (1 Morelos at the corner of Hidalgo). Originally the home of Hidalgo, it is now a museum. The Parroquia de Dolores Hidalgo, the parish church, is on the Plaza de Independencia. Across from the church is a statue of Hidalgo said to stand on the site of a bullring in which the priest fought. The Sunday market in Dolores Hidalgo is noted for its fine pottery and copperware. Also, there is an Indian fair on January 1 and an *Independence Day Fair* on September 15 and 16.

SAN MIGUEL DE ALLENDE: (For a detailed description of the city, its hotels and restaurants, see *San Miguel de Allende,* THE CITIES.) San Miguel was a quiet, pleasant little town 50 years ago; then the art and language schools were founded and the town blossomed. More than just the place where independence leader Ignacio Allende was born and the site of a somewhat bizarre parish church, San Miguel became an international artists' colony.

No other town in Mexico is quite like it — it is sophisticated, yet quaint and picturesque; while it is historically one of the most Mexican of the country's cities, Americans and Canadians have had a major influence in the town. The major occupation in San

Miguel seems to be enjoying life. Exploring the lovely homes and shops, sitting out in the sun, and finding some delightful restaurants are some of the ways in which this goal can be achieved.

Some of the sights you may want to visit include the Parroquia, the church built by Ceferino Gutiérrez and modeled on a Gothic cathedral, the Palacio Conde de Canal (the Palace of the Counts of Canal), the Instituto Allende, Las Monjas, the Centro Cultural Ignacio Ramírez, the Church of la Salud, the Oratorio de San Felipe Neri, and the Church of San Francisco.

San Miguel also has terrific shops where you can buy silver, textiles, embroidery, needlework, papier-mâché, wall hangings, copper, brass, tin, straw weavings, and paintings.

A new development in the San Miguel area is water sports. The Ignacio Allende Dam is 5 miles (8 km) south of town, and a lake was formed by Río Laja. This provides a new element in the Bajío vocabulary: the motorboat.

QUERÉTARO: For a detailed description of the city, see *The Bajío*. Probably the most historic city in Mexico, Querétaro is more spread out than its sister cities, Guanajuato and San Miguel de Allende. This city's historical importance is not based on architecture, although there are some magnificent buildings. It's based on its people.

One of the most famous of Querétaro's residents was Josefa Ortiz, known as "La Corregidora." In 1810, she warned the rebels that the Spanish planned to capture them. These fighters, including Allende and Hidalgo, escaped and started the campaign that would eventually bring freedom to Mexico.

Querétaro was the place to which Emperor Maximilian fled in 1867 shortly before he was betrayed, court-martialed, and executed. His place of execution is commemorated with a small chapel, a shrine to the man who became the pawn of Napoleon and to those opposed to Benito Juárez.

In 1917, Querétaro was chosen as the place in which to write Mexico's new constitution after the overthrow of dictator Porfirio Díaz.

Querétaro continues to be an important Mexican city, best known as a commercial center and the site of some fine colonial architecture.

En Route from Querétaro – The toll road to Mexico City is good, but take care — mist and clouds reduce visibility, and the moisture makes the road surface dangerous. If you follow Route 57 into the center of Mexico City you will eventually reach the Paseo de la Reforma at Chapultepec Park.

BEST EN ROUTE

CIUDAD JUÁREZ

Plaza Continental – Here are 64 air conditioned units, bar service, a restaurant, parking, and a barbershop. At 112 Lerdo Sur (phone: 16-150084). Expensive to moderate.

Del Prado – If you want to spend a night in luxury before starting on your pilgrimage, this is the place to do it. It has 150 rooms and suites, air conditioning and numerous extras, including TV sets, bar, cocktail lounges, pool, shops, valet, laundry service, and — best of all — good service. The dining room is open from 7:30 AM to 11 PM. Credit cards accepted. In the *Centro Comercial Pronaf*, 1½ miles (2 km) south of the Córdoba Bridge (phone: 16-130047). Expensive to moderate.

Calinda Juárez Quality Inn – Pleasant and moderately priced, it has 103 rooms, a pool, and restaurant. About 2 miles (3 km) south of the Bridge of the Americas, at 3515 Av. Hermanos Escobar (phone: 16-163421). Moderate.

Colonial Las Fuentes – Its 250 colonial-style motel units are arranged around a beautiful garden and courtyard. Air conditioning, 3 pools, a 24-hour *Denny's* restaurant, and even a stockbroker. 1355 Av. de las Américas (phone: 16-135050). Moderate.

Plaza Juárez – This luxury motel has 178 air conditioned units, a swimming pool, a coffee shop, and a dining room open from 7 AM to 11 PM. On Av. Abraham Lincoln and Coyoacán in the *Centro Comercial Pronaf,* about 1 mile (1.6 km) south of the Córdoba Bridge (phone: 16-131310 or 16-132078). Moderate.

Sylvia's – This hotel offers 91 rooms with air conditioning, a pool, gardens, bar service, a barbershop, dining room (open 7 AM to midnight), and free parking. Dieciséis de Septiembre and Venezuela (phone: 16-150562). Moderate.

NUEVO CASAS GRANDES

La Hacienda – Highly recommended motel with 63 air conditioned units, pool, tennis court, restaurant, and bar. On 2603 Av. Benito Juárez (phone: 169-41048). Moderate.

Piñon – These 42 air conditioned motel units have central heating; there is a pool, a fair dining room, and a museum with a collection of Casas Grandes artifacts. Guides are available for visits to the ruins. On 605 Av. Benito Juárez (phone: 169-40655, 169-40847 or 169-40166). Inexpensive.

SIERRA TARAHUMARA

Cabañas Divisadero Barrancas – At the very edge of the Divisadero canyon, 2 hours from Creel. All of its rustic but comfortably furnished rooms have spectacular views as well as fireplaces. Meals are included in the price of a room, and the dining room is completely surrounded by clouds in the mornings. Excursions to the Tarahumara caves and settlements on foot and horseback are arranged. For reservations, 1216 Calle 7A, in Chihuahua (phone: 14-123362 in Chihuahua). Expensive.

Misión – In the midst of paradise, this small, comfortable hostelry offers 30 rooms, trips to nearby waterfalls, the startling Urique Canyon, the mission Church of San Francisco, and the defunct Urique mine. Get off at Bahuichivo on the *Chihuahua-Pacífico Railway,* and a hotel bus will take you to the hotel, 75 minutes away in Cerocahui. Make reservations through the *Santa Anita* hotel in Los Mochis (phone: 681-57046; 14-165950 in Chihuahua). Expensive.

La Mansion Tarahumara – One of the newest hotels on the route, in the town of Areponapuchic, with 15 cabins, electrical lights, hot water, and a restaurant and bar. Posada Barrancas stop on the *Chihuahua-Pacífico Railway* (phone: 14-162672 in Chihuahua). Expensive to moderate.

Parador de la Montaña – A colonial-style motel with tile floors and trim, 35 rooms, small restaurant with ho-hum service (Full American Plan available), and more than half a dozen delightful tours into the canyons. Room maintenance could be better, but the location in Creel is practical (phone: 145-60075; in Chihuahua, 14-122062 or 14-155408). Expensive to moderate.

Posada Barrancas del Cobre – Offers 35 rooms, panoramic view of the Copper Canyon, tours of the canyons and Tarahumara caves, and horseback trips. Posada Barrancas station on the *Chihuahua-Pacífico Railway.* Make reservations through the *Santa Anita* hotel in Los Mochis (phone: 681-57046; 14-165950 in Chihuahua). Expensive to moderate.

Copper Canyon Lodge – Twenty-nine primitive log and adobe rooms. No heat and occasional hot water. Good family-style meals. In Creel (phone: 14-128893 in Chihuahua). Moderate to inexpensive.

CIUDAD CAMARGO

Florido, Jiménez – A comfortable motel with air conditioning, heat, pool, bar service, and a decent café. Av. Juárez and Veinte de Noviembre, in nearby Jiménez (phone: 146-20186 or 146-20400). Inexpensive.

Los Nogales – One of the better establishments in town, with 39 heated and air conditioned units, a restaurant, parking, TV sets, and pool. 404 Av. Juárez (phone: 146-21247). Inexpensive.

Santa Rosalía – There are 33 heated and air conditioned rooms, showers, and free parking. Centrally located at Calle Abasolo and Benito Juárez (phone: 146-20214 or 146-20170). Inexpensive.

GÓMEZ PALACIO

Posada del Río – A total of 84 air conditioned rooms, with color satellite television, pool, cafeteria, restaurant, bar, parking. Av. Francisco Madero and Juárez (phone: 17-143399). Inexpensive.

La Siesta – Not the *Ritz*, but an inexpensive, comfortable motel with 29 heated rooms, restaurant, bar, parking, and pool. Av. Francisco Madero and Centenario (phone: 17-140291). Inexpensive.

LERDO

Villa Jardín – This fine motel has 120 air conditioned rooms, a pool, tennis court, playground, disco, satellite television, and lovely gardens. Blvd. Miguel Alemán and Carr. Mexico-Durango, 5 minutes from downtown (phone: 17-147025). Moderate to inexpensive.

TORREÓN

Palacio Real – An older hotel remodeled in the 1970s with 140 rooms and suites, cable TV with US programming, restaurant, bar, and access to facilities at the *La Rosita Country Club*. 1280 Av. Morelos Pte. (phone: 17-160000). Moderate .

Paraíso del Desierto – A hotel with 164 rooms, restaurant, cafeteria, pool, garage, and TV sets with US programs. Blvd. Independencia and Jiménez (phone: 17-161122). Moderate.

Del Prado Torreón – Modern, 8-story building with 140 rooms and 6 suites, air conditioning, and color TV sets. There's also a pool, sauna, restaurant, coffee shop, and bar. Paseo de la Rosita and Diagonal de las Fuentes (phone: 17-174040). Moderate.

El Paso – Newer motel with 53 air conditioned units, bar. 400 Saltillo at Carranza (phone: 17-137364 or 17-137079). Moderate to inexpensive.

Posada del Rey – Downtown spot with 40 air conditioned units, TV sets, and a restaurant. 333 Valdez Carrillo Sur (phone: 17-168004 or 17-160015). Moderate to inexpensive.

Río Nazas – A 157-room, 9-story high-rise hotel with air conditioning, free garage, bar service, dining room, and coffee shop. Downtown at Av. Morelos and Treviño (phone: 17-161212). Moderate to inexpensive.

Paraíso del Camino – Pleasant and clean with 47 rooms, cable television, pool and 7 trailer spaces with full hookups. Juárez and Reforma (phone: 17-139930). Inexpensive.

HIDALGO DEL PARRAL

Adriana – Features 62 clean, comfortable motel rooms with a restaurant. 2 Colegio (phone: 152-22570). Inexpensive.

El Camino Real – Convenient motel for a stopover. It has a restaurant (next door), rooms with fans, and pool. One mile (1.6 km) south of the city on Av. Independencia (phone: 152-22050). Inexpensive.

San José – Its 55 air conditioned units are inexpensive. 5 Santiago Mendez (phone: 152-22453). Inexpensive.

DURANGO

Los Arcos – Here are 56 units, a restaurant, and a bar. 2204 H. Colegio Militar Ote. (phone: 181-81239 or 181-87777). Inexpensive.

Campo Mexico Courts – The best place to stay in town and moderately priced. Set in a lovely garden, with old rooms and new rooms equally pleasant. Heat, bar, satellite TV, and dining room open from 7 AM to midnight. Pets accepted. Far east on Av. 20 de Noviembre Ote. (phone: 181-87744 or 181-15560). Inexpensive.

Casablanca – Some of the 46 rooms are suites. Every indoor area is air conditioned, and there's a restaurant and bar on the premises. 811 Av. Veinte de Noviembre Pte. (phone: 181-13599). Inexpensive.

El Gobernador – Set in lovely gardens, this hotel has 100 rooms, restaurant, bar, cafeteria, pool, and TV sets. 257 Av. Veinte de Noviembre Ote. (phone: 181-10480 through 92). Inexpensive.

Plaza Cathedral – Set in a colonial building more than 400 years old with 40 large rooms (some with refrigerators) and a restaurant. Beside the Cathedral of Durango. 103 Av. Constitución Sur (phone: 181-14866). Inexpensive.

ZACATECAS

Paraíso Radisson – The façade of this building has been declared a colonial monument. Inside, its 115 air conditioned rooms surround an interior patio. Restaurant. Av. Hidalgo, on the main square (phone: 492-26183 or 492-26187; worldwide reservations, 800-333-3333). Expensive.

Quinta Real – Beautifully designed to blend in with the 200-year-old aqueduct and the old bullring next door, this hotel has 49 rooms (including a 3-bedroom presidential suite), fine restaurant, and bar. 434 Av. Rayón and González Ortega (phone: 492-29104 through 07; 800-227-0212 in California; 800-445-4565 elsewhere in the US). Expensive.

Gallery Best Western – A modern hotel with 134 rooms, TV sets, restaurant, bar, nightclub, pool, and squash. Blvd. López Mateos and Callejón del Barro (phone: 492-23311). Moderate.

Aristos Zacatecas – Highly recommended hotel with 102 units, restaurant, coffee shop with an impressive view of the city, nightclub, and pool. Loma de la Soledad (phone: 492-21788). Inexpensive.

Del Bosque – You can get a great view of the city from this motel. The restaurant is open from 8 AM to 10:30 PM, and only MasterCard is accepted. 60 rooms available; moderately priced. On Cerro de las Peñitas (phone: 492-20745 or 492-21034). Inexpensive.

Del Fresno, Fresnillo – An extremely clean, sun-filled, and moderately priced hotel with 55 rooms, restaurant, parking, and TV sets. 411 Av. Hidalgo (phone: 473-21126 or 473-21120). Inexpensive.

Posada de los Condes – 58 colonial-style and moderately priced units downtown. Restaurant and bar. 18 Juárez (phone: 492-21412 or 492-21093). Inexpensive.

Zacatecas Courts – A pleasant, 64-unit motel with heat and showers. At the southern edge of town on the highway, 602 Av. López Velarde (phone: 492-20328). Inexpensive.

AGUASCALIENTES

Las Trojes – Perhaps the best place in town, with 160 rooms (some in a newer wing), air conditioning, telephones, color TV sets, restaurants, bars, disco, tennis courts, and pool. Blvds. Norte and Campestre (phone: 491-40468). Expensive.

Francia – This palatial, imposing hotel has 80 units and a good restaurant and bar. In the lobby there's a huge print of Aguascalientes a century ago. Av. Madero and Plaza Principal (phone: 491-56080). Moderate to inexpensive.

La Cascada – There are 78 units, TV sets, restaurant, bar, and pool. 501 Blvd. José Ma. Chavez (phone: 491-61411). Inexpensive.

Colonial – A rambling colonial-style hotel with 39 medium-priced units and pleasant staff. Centrally located at 552 Cinco de Mayo (phone: 491-53577). Inexpensive.

Medrano – A motel with 85 air conditioned rooms, restaurant, bar, nightclub, and pool. 904 Blvd. José Ma. Chavez (phone: 491-55500). Inexpensive.

La Vid – Modern, with 68 units, restaurant, bar, disco, and pool. 1305 Blvd. José Ma. Chavez (phone: 491-60150). Inexpensive.

LEÓN

León – A pleasant 89-room older hotel. The remodeled rooms, which are fairly expensive, have TV sets, and there is a restaurant. Just off the zocalo on 113 Madero (phone: 47-141050). Expensive to moderate.

Real de Minas – Colonial-style inn with 175 comfortable rooms, restaurant, heated pool, and a lobby bar featuring live music at night. Blvd. López Mateos (phone: 47-143677). Moderate.

Balneario Comanjilla – In addition to its 124 units, guests can enjoy horseback riding, a tennis court, thermal waters, steam baths, projection room, 3 pools, restaurant, bar, and free parking. At Km 387 of Carr. Panaméricana No. 45, about 18½ miles (30 km) from León (phone: 47-120091). Moderate to inexpensive.

La Estancia – Classy motel with 162 units, air conditioning, TV sets, restaurants, bar, pool, Jacuzzi. 1311 Blvd. López Mateos Ote. (phone: 47-163939). Inexpensive.

Nuevo Laredo to Mexico City

The border crossing from Laredo, Texas, to Nuevo Laredo, Mexico, is one of the entry points into Mexico most used by American drivers. Called the Constitutional Highway, the 740-mile (1,184-km) road that leads from Nuevo Laredo to Mexico City follows three major routes — Route 85 from the border to Monterrey; Route 40 from Monterrey to Saltillo; and Route 57 south from Saltillo to Mexico City. Beginning at Mexico's northeastern border with Texas along the Río Grande, this route takes drivers through some of Mexico's major mining, industrial, and agricultural regions, as well as to the most interesting towns in Mexico's northwest — Monterrey, Saltillo, and San Luis Potosí.

The geography of the journey is rather starkly divided between the arid deserts of the north and the rich farmlands of the central highland area, which leads into Mexico City. The change occurs as the road leaves the plains below Texas and enters the Sierra Madre Oriental, the range whose spiny cliffs, canyons, winding roads, peaks, and valleys you actually travel twice in the course of the journey. After crossing a 250-mile (400-km) stretch of nearly empty desert plateau, the road continues past the hills of Mexico's richest mining regions to the Bajío and the fertile farmlands of the central highlands district, where trees, mineral springs, rivers, farms, and maguey fields dominate the landscape.

Besides visits to large and interesting cities, this route offers opportunities for adventure and off-the-road exploration. By burro, jeep, turn-of-the-century railroad coach, or car, you will be able to journey to a ghost town, hidden caves, an abandoned mining tunnel, natural health spas, and the major archaeological zone of Tula.

In the high altitudes of the Sierra Madre, the highlands and peaks are mild and dry all year. It can become chilly at night, but seldom cold. The desert and northernmost regions along this route tend to be very hot and dry, with few breezes. All along the route March through October are the warmest months, while November through February are the coolest; you might need a sweater at lower altitudes and a light coat at higher ones in cooler months. Two of the larger cities you will visit, Saltillo and San Luis Potosí, are noted for their ideal weather conditions and offer opportunities for tennis, swimming, and golf all year. At off-the-road spots along the more southerly portion of the route, where mineral springs flow, you can look forward to spending an afternoon relaxing and losing your travel fatigue.

At hotels we classify along this route as expensive, expect to pay $70 to $90 for a double room; $40 to $65 at moderate places; and less than $40, inexpensive.

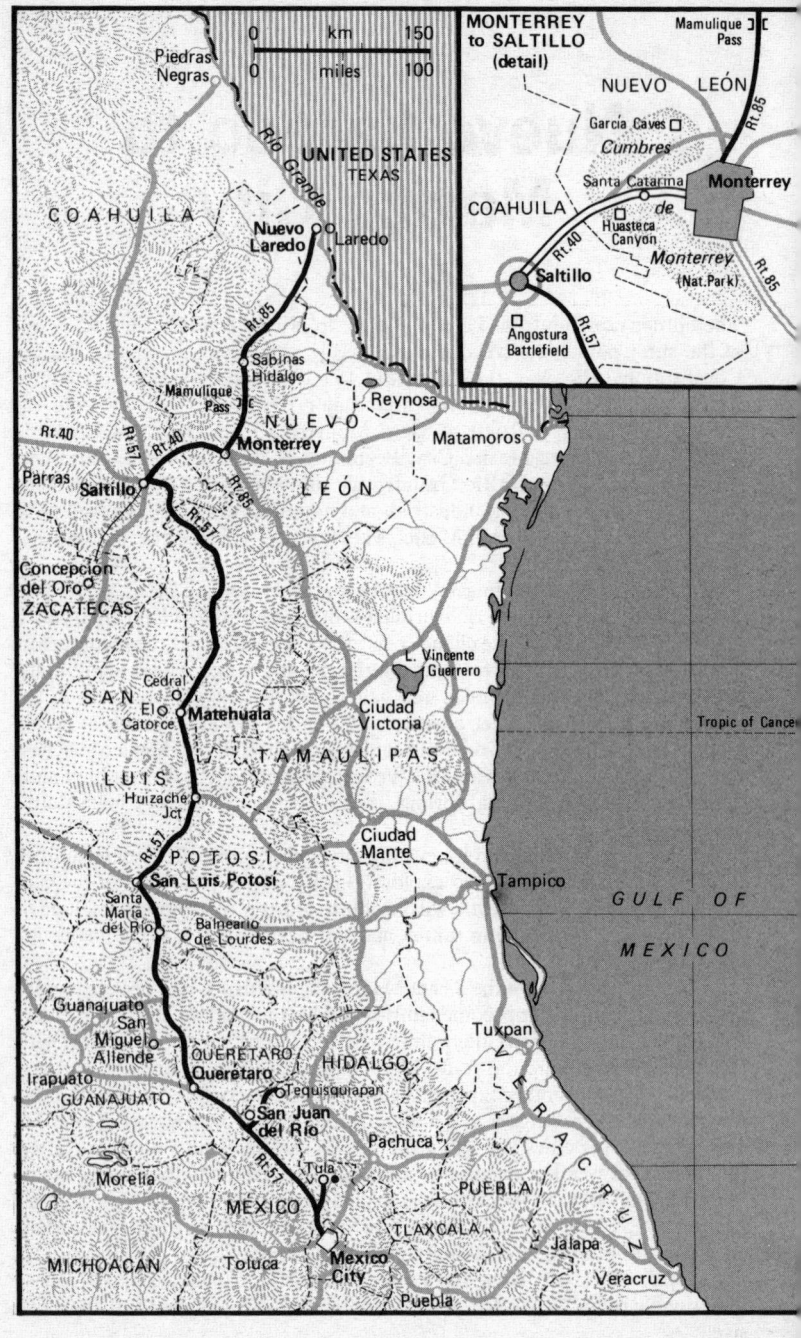

MONTERREY to SALTILLO (detail)

Mamulique Pass

NUEVO LEÓN

García Caves

Cumbres

Santa Catarina

Rt.85

Monterrey

COAHUILA

Huasteca Canyon

Saltillo

Monterrey (Nat.Park)

Rt.40

Rt.85

Angostura Battlefield

Rt.57

km   150
0
miles   100
0

Piedras Negras

Río Grande

UNITED STATES
TEXAS

COAHUILA

Nuevo Laredo   Laredo

Rt.85

Sabinas Hidalgo

Mamulique Pass

Reynosa

NUEVO

Rt.40

Monterrey

LEÓN

Matamoros

Parras

Rt.51   Saltillo

Rt.85

Rt.57

Concepción del Oro

ZACATECAS

Cedral

SAN   El
Catorce

Matehuala

L. Vincente Guerrero

Ciudad Victoria

Tropic of Cancer

LUIS

Huizache Jct

Rt.57

TAMAULIPAS

POTOSI

Ciudad Mante

San Luis Potosí

Santa María del Río

Balneario de Lourdes

Tampico

GULF OF

MEXICO

Guanajuato
San Miguel Allende

QUERETARO

Querétaro

Tequisquiapan

Tuxpan

VERACRUZ

Irapuato

GUANAJUATO

San Juan del Río

HIDALGO

Pachuca

Morelia

Rt.51

Tula

MEXICO

PUEBLA

MICHOACÁN

Toluca

Mexico City

TLAXCALA

Jalapa

Veracruz

Puebla

En Route from Laredo, Texas – Although the Texan streets of Laredo are known to many through the famous folk song, the Mexican city of Nuevo Laredo is known to few. Connected by an international bridge, these two cities might be considered twins of different nationalities. Together they constitute one of the principal ports of entry into Mexico. Nuevo Laredo is certainly the livelier of the two, and it is here that the southern journey to Mexico City really begins after you pay a toll in Laredo ($1 per car) and go through customs and immigration procedures after crossing the international bridge.

NUEVO LAREDO: Besides the thousands of tourists who visit Nuevo Laredo each year, a stable population of 350,000 inhabits this 400-year-old city in the state of Tamaulipas on the flat plains of Mexico's northeastern frontier. Although industry is growing here, tourism continues to provide major fuel for the town's economy. Like most border towns, Nuevo Laredo offers no shortage of hotels, motels, restaurants, shopping areas, and nightlife. If your visit happens to coincide with a major US holiday weekend, you might even catch a bullfight; however, since there are no set schedules, it's difficult to plan for one.

If you want to stay near the action in the center of town, there are several hotels with good service, clean facilities, and moderate prices. Otherwise, the motels on the Nuevo Laredo–Monterrey Highway leading out of town offer quieter surroundings but more facilities, such as swimming pools, good restaurants, and spacious grounds (see *Best en Route*).

Although there are numerous shops throughout the downtown area that sell crafts and goods typical of several Mexican regions, southbound travelers will have the opportunity to buy the same items along the route in their indigenous areas. The *Maclovio Herrera Handicrafts Market* (at Guerrero and Belden) fills a square block and sells products from all over the country. Lunch or snacks may be had at the pleasant umbrella-shaded restaurant-bar in the patio. Here, as in other markets and shops in Mexico, it's wise to buy something you like even though you may be going to the area of origin, for you may not be able to find the exact piece again. Before starting the long journey south, you might have a meal at the *Cadillac* bar (Ocampo and Belden), a border institution since 1926; although the service and food aren't quite up to the old standard, the seafood and *cabrito* (kid) specialties are good, and prices are moderate. *Mexico Típico* (on Guerrero) offers dining inside or out, with wandering Mexican musicians. For American dishes (steaks and a salad bar) stop in the *Winery Pub and Grill* (308 Matamoros). Or try the fine food and house beer at *Victoria 3020* (3020 Victoria). As you leave town, follow Avenida Guerrero to Route 85 to Monterrey (about a 2½-hour drive), and you will pass a monument to Benito Juárez, one of the country's most beloved presidents.

En Route from Nuevo Laredo – Sixteen miles (26 km) out of town is the only customs and immigration checkpoint on the route between Laredo and Mexico City. Official procedures include a look at your tourist card and the inside of your car trunk. Customs officials are quick and usually friendly, and the whole process is quite simple.

Sabinas Hidalgo is a small town 25 miles (40 km) into the foothills of the Sierra Madre Oriental, 78 miles (125 km) from Nuevo Laredo. Since it is the only town on Route 85 between Laredo and Monterrey (125 miles — 200 km — farther south), you might want to take advantage of its filling stations, stores, and restaurants. The *Ancira* restaurant, which is right on Route 85, has adequate, simple food.

Mamulique Pass is a vista point in the Sierra Madre peaks and a good place to stop, rest, and catch a glimpse of surrounding cliffs and distant valleys before making the descent to Monterrey. The pass is marked on the road. Before entering Monterrey you'll see a large turnoff sign to Route 40 and Saltillo. Don't take this unless you want to bypass Monterrey and go straight to Saltillo, the city on the route after Monterrey. Stay on Route 85 for Monterrey.

MONTERREY: (For a detailed report on the city, its hotels and restaurants, see *Monterrey,* THE CITIES.) In a valley surrounded by Sierra Madre peaks and slopes, the Colossus of the North is Mexico's main industrial center and third largest city. Some 3 million people live in this sprawling metropolis, which sits at an altitude of 1,767 feet. Everything from steel, beer, cement, and glass to cigarettes, building materials, and textiles is manufactured here.

En Route from Monterrey – Take Avenida de la Constitución out of the city to Route 40. (Follow the signs to Saltillo, which direct you to Route 40, along Río Santa Catarina.) By turning left at the sign to Santa Catarina on Monterrey's outskirts and following a paved road for 2 miles (3 km), you will reach the breathtaking Huasteca Canyon, site of a 1,000-foot gorge with towering walls and unusual rock formations caused by the erosion of the area's soft stone. The paved road ends at a tidy fenced-in picnic area and children's playground (admission charge is about 70¢), and a stony, unpaved road leads into the canyon. This is a desolate place, but a police car usually is stationed at the entrance for security.

About 13 miles (21 km) beyond Monterrey on Route 40 is the turnoff for Villa de García and the García Caves, the most spectacular caverns in North America. You should not miss them. Discovered a century ago, the García Caves have 17 different chambers and natural pools, magnificent stalactite and stalagmite formations, and spectacular natural stairways. (Be sure to wear sensible shoes — climbing around requires some agility.) The caves are open daily, except December 12, from 9 AM to 4 PM. Admission charge is about $4 for adults, $2 for children. Just outside Villa de García, a cable car (about $4 for adults, $2 for children) travels up 2,460 feet, providing terrific panoramic views; you can also rent a burro to make the trip.

SALTILLO: This capital of the state of Coahuila, at an altitude of 5,245 feet in the Sierra Madre Oriental, has a population of 650,000. The modern city is a major industrial center, with manufacturing plants producing pottery, silverware, engine parts, and large textile mills that are the major source of serapes. The city has two universities that attract students from around the world. Because of its mild, sunny, dry climate — which draws refreshing breezes from the surrounding mountain slopes — Saltillo has become a recreational center of the northeast. Its golf courses and tennis courts are open all year, while swimming facilities remain full during the warmest season, from March through October. Saltillo has two tourist offices, one at the *Convention Center* (phone: 841-54444 or 841-54504; FAX: 841-54564) and the other downtown (at Calle Francisco Coss and Manuel Acuña; phone: 841-54050). Both offices provide information on accommodations, activities, and facilities in Saltillo as well as brochures and maps. Each office also has an English-speaking officer on hand to aid tourists.

Saltillo was founded in 1575 when Captain Alberto del Canto selected this pleasant spot as a teaching center for the semibarbaric Indians of the north. By importing "civilized" Tlascala Indians from the central highlands, Captain Urdiñola hoped to influence the less manageable northern plains Indians. Under his leadership the northeast underwent its initial stages of colonial development and Saltillo became a colonial center.

During the 18th and 19th centuries, Saltillo served as a staging area for northern expansion as well as the capital of an enormous area extending across Texas to Colorado.

Although modernization has destroyed much of the original architecture and flavor of Saltillo, several examples of its early colonial life remain. They can be found mostly in the southwest section of town, on Avenida Allende, by the central square, Plaza de

Armas. The Cathedral of Santiago, which took more than 50 years to build (1746–1801), overlooks the Plaza de Armas and is considered one of the finest examples of churrigueresque architecture in North America (churrigueresque is an ornate Spanish style of building decoration that flourished in the 18th century). The main tower offers a panoramic view of Saltillo. Across from the cathedral, also overlooking Plaza de Armas, is the capitol. It was here that Governor Venustiano Carranza recruited an army to fight the assassin of Mexico's first revolutionary president, Francisco Madero. The building has more historical than visual interest.

Other parks and historical sites to visit in Saltillo are the Alameda and the Fortress of Carlota. The Alameda, situated west of Plaza de Armas (off Victoria and Ramos Arizpe), is a quiet, pleasant spot that contains the Pond of the Republic, which is built in the shape of Mexico, and the equestrian statue of General Ignacio Zaragoza. The Fortress of Carlota, in the old section of town not far from the Plaza de Armas, was dedicated to Maximilian's wife, Carlota, who fled to France to seek Napoleon III's aid against the Mexican anticolonialist, independence forces.

Plaza Acuña, in the center of town between Aldama and Carranza, lacks historical interest but is the city's busiest square and the place to go to get a sense of daily life in Saltillo. Other plazas seem positively formal when compared to the beehive comings and goings in Plaza Acuña, where street vendors sell a variety of goods, senior citizens gather in cabals, and late lunch crowds tarry over coffee. Don't be tempted by the street-stand tacos; they are fine for Mexican stomachs but usually play havoc with systems not yet acclimated to local foods.

Saltillo is a center for a wide variety of reasonably priced, well-made handicrafts and curios. The colorful serapes for which Saltillo is noted can be found in many stores and small shops, as can silver goods, pottery, grotesque tin masks, furniture, and leather goods. At the *Mercado Juárez,* the central marketplace (between Padre Flores and Allende), you can find Mexican curios and embroidered blouses at reasonable prices. But the marketplace does not offer the best selection of other local handicrafts. Calle Victoria, the main street, and nearby side streets have the largest concentration of interesting local products: for silver goods, such as tea sets and jewelry, the *Platería Taxco* (428 Victoria) and *Moeller* (212 Victoria) offer a good variety; for leather, *La Azteca* (159 Acuña North) has a wide selection of purses, billfolds, saddles, and belts, while *Zapatería Victoria* (642 Allende Nte.) has good boots; for handcrafted Mexican colonial-style furniture, *Muebles Coloniales el Arte* (1036 Zarco Ote.) has a reasonably priced, varied, high-quality stock. *Artesanías del DIF* (Blvd. Francisco Coss and Acuña) carries every kind of handicraft from paper flowers and wrought-iron chandeliers to sculptured candles and copper, brass, alabaster, and glass items. You can watch the entire process of serape and rug making from the carding of the wool to the final weaving (done on hand looms) at *El Sarape de Saltillo* (305 Hidalgo Sur). *El Saltillero* (217 Victoria) also sells serapes.

Three foods to taste while in Saltillo are *dulces de leche,* a kind of milk candy that is boiled; *pan de pulque,* a deliciously sweet bread that is made with pulque; mescal, the alcoholic drink made from the maguey cactus; and *huitlacoche,* made from an inky wheat fungus and quite a delicacy. The bakery *La Reina Panadería* (at Allende and Alvarez) is the best place to sample the sweet bread; *Dulces Caseros* (Acuña and Ramos) offers an excellent array of *dulces de leche. El Tapanco* (225 Allende Sur; phone: 841-44339) is the best restaurant overall, and the loveliest, in the area. The setting is a converted 17th-century home, and the food is Mexican and international; order the *huitlacoche* crêpes if they are available.

Saltillo houses not only a university (Universidad Autónoma del Noroeste, Blvd. E. Reyna and Américas Unidas) and a technological institute (Instituto Tecnológico de Saltillo, 2400 Blvd. V. Carranza), but also three schools where foreigners come to learn Spanish. They are Instituto México-Norteamericano de Relaciones Culturales, (Pres.

Cárdenas and Purcell), Instituto de Filología Hispánica (844 Pérez Treviño Pte.), and Instituto de Idiomas Franco-Mexicano (591 Juárez Ote.).

The festival season in Saltillo is late summer and early fall. The biggest event, *Festival of the Cristo de la Capilla,* takes place on August 6. According to legend, this festival was inspired by an unattended donkey that wandered into town on August 6, 1608, carrying a box so heavy it finally collapsed under the load. Curious townspeople pried open the box to find inside an image of Christ. As soon as the box had been breached, the unconscious donkey disappeared. A chapel was built on the site of the miracle, and the annual *Festival of the Cristo de la Capilla* celebrates the event with fireworks, bullfights, and *La Malinche,* the Huastec dance in which participants wear carved wooden masks signifying betrayal between blood brothers. La Malinche was a Gulf Coast Indian princess who fell in love with Hernan Cortés and betrayed her own people by helping him conquer the Aztec empire. To this day, *malinchista* is a derogatory term for someone who prefers foreign goods and culture over his own.

Other festivals are the *Water Festival,* normally held during the first week of September, and the *Festival and Wine Fair,* October 4, in nearby Parras.

Two side trips from Saltillo warrant special mention and a high recommendation. The *Zacatecas and Coahuila Railroad* leaves Saltillo daily for the gold- and silver-mining town of Concepción del Oro. The journey follows narrow mountain ridges in coaches that were built in 1895 and are still heated by wood-burning stoves; for railroad buffs it could be a high point of the entire route. The round trip covers 164 miles (262 km) and constitutes a day's excursion. Consult the tourist office or any local hotel for schedules and ticket information.

Just outside Saltillo is the La Angostura Battlefield, the site of a major battle between US and Mexican forces during the Mexican-American War. In February 1847, US General Zachary Taylor confronted General Santa Anna and the Mexican forces on the La Angostura, also known as the Buena Vista Battlefield. Santa Anna's army greatly outnumbered Taylor's. After capturing most of Taylor's strongholds in two days, Santa Anna inexplicably withdrew, leaving the field to the US forces. Historians say the battle left 694 Mexicans dead while the US lost 267.

Although Saltillo is not well supplied with good restaurants that are independent of its fine selection of hotels (see *Best en Route*), exceptions are the aforementioned *El Tapanco*, *La Canasta* (2485 V. Carranza and Michoacán), and *El Principal* (702 Allende Nte. and the Monterrey Hwy.).

En Route from Saltillo – Heading east on Route 57, you begin a gradual ascent for 9 miles (14 km) through rugged mountain terrain before reaching the rim of a broad semi-arid plateau that continues until you make the descent into real desert. The desert road, which you will follow before and after the next stop at Matehuala, has its own particular blend of native charm and high risk; although it looks deserted and void of life, except for ubiquitous cactus plants, there are desert dwellers who stray into the road, unseen and unexpected. Those with four legs tend to show little or no interest in the oncoming traffic, while those with two legs (usually young boys carrying boxes) are likely to wave you down and try to sell you an iguana or *tuna,* the fruit of the prickly pear cactus tree. It is best to keep an eye out for these unexpected visitors along these long, flat, seemingly abandoned stretches of desert road.

MATEHUALA: The only town along the 250 miles (400 km) between Saltillo and San Luis Potosí, and the third-largest city in the state of San Luis Potosí, Matehuala is usually a welcome sight and stop on the journey southward. It has some good eateries and a pleasant zocalo, and is a convenient departure point for interesting side trips. In the restaurant of *Las Palmas* (on Rte. 57) you can find a superb version of the regional dish *enchiladas potosinas,* a cheese-filled soft tortilla generously topped with peas, carrots, and chorizo. *San Angel* (301 Altamiradas; phone: 488-20536) and *Santa Fe*

(709 Morelos) have international menus, and *Fontella* (618 Morelos) is good for steaks. All are downtown.

Some 31 miles (50 km) west of Matehuala, across difficult mountain terrain, is the authentic ghost town of Real de Catorce, listed on some maps as El Catorce. The first silver and gold mines were begun in this area in 1773; by the beginning of the 19th century, Real de Catorce's gold and silver veins had become Mexico's third most productive mines. Once an active mining town with a population of 40,000, Catorce now has only about 800 people. Although no longer a boom town, Catorce still offers adventure to the desert traveler. The word *catorce* means "fourteen," and in this case it refers to the 14 bandits, known as the *Frito Bandidos* from the José Frito Gang, who once plagued Catorce. Most signs of banditry have disappeared, yet some of the hazards of past mining days remain. The entrance to Catorce, for instance, is a 2-mile-long abandoned mining tunnel. Don't drive your own car. The trip by taxi costs $5. Once you pass through the tunnel and enter the town of Catorce, La Purísima Concepción church and the abandoned government mint are among the most interesting of the many empty colonial structures that teemed with fortune seekers and speculators during the late 18th century.

Another interesting trip from Matehuala is to the Cedral Marble Quarry, 12 miles (19 km) northwest of town. Visitors can watch marble being cut and sculpted or shop among the slabs and beautifully carved statues of marble for sale.

En Route from Matehuala – As soon as you turn into the main southbound highway, you are likely to see native women and children selling the fauna of the surrounding desert — roadrunners, desert rats, snakes, and sometimes even baby coyotes. Fourteen miles (22 km) out of town, an obelisk marks the spot where the road crosses the Tropic of Cancer.

The La Paz Silver and Gold Mine, just 10 miles (16 km) southwest of Matehuala, off Route 57, has operated since 1864. Signs to the mine are posted on Route 57 after you leave Matehuala. As a functioning mine, La Paz is well worth a visit on your way to San Luis Potosí.

The plateau road from Matehuala to San Luis Potosí along Route 57 remains curveless and deserted until the Huizache junction, where the plateau terrain begins to roll and rise.

SAN LUIS POTOSÍ: This bustling city with a population of some 800,000 (some sources say up to 1 million) is the capital of the state of San Luis Potosí and one of Mexico's most picturesque mining towns. The abundance of colonial architecture, narrow streets, flower-filled boulevards, and attractive parks reflects the city's 400-year history. At an altitude of 5,158 feet, San Luis Potosí not only boasts a mild, invigorating climate and Old World atmosphere, but also serves as a mining and industrial center where lead, zinc, silver, and steel are processed and flour, beer, and leather are produced.

Named after Louis, "the saintly monarch" of France, and *potosí,* the Quechua Indian word for "extremely wealthy" (originating from the rich Potosí mines of Bolivia), this town became San Luis Potosí after it was founded by Fray Magdalena and Captain Caldera in 1592. Its history, however, began much earlier than the 16th century; Chicunec Indians, a semi-nomadic tribe, inhabited this site (which they called Tanga-maga) for 3 centuries before the Spanish arrived. Although the bulk of gold and silver, which brought the Spanish flocking to the area, was in a town called San Pedro, 25 miles (40 km) south of San Luis Potosí, the mineral springs of the latter made it a better place to build a settlement and central mining town. Much of the spectacular colonial architecture still remaining in San Luis Potosí is the result of the zealousness of missionaries who expended their energies protecting the city and the Indians from the speculators who rushed here during boom mining days only to leave when the mines played out.

In 1863, when Benito Juárez led the fight against further French colonization, and in 1867, when he pronounced the death sentence on Maximilian and his two generals, San Luis Potosí functioned as the capital of northeast Mexico, which included Texas at the time. Old records kept here are still consulted by Texans who want to authenticate claims, deeds, and land titles that are in dispute.

It was in San Luis Potosí, while being held prisoner by president and dictator Porfirio Díaz, that Francisco I. Madero drafted the famous Plan de San Luis Potosí, calling for a revolt against the dictatorship. The first article of the plan denounced as void all national elections under the Díaz regime. On November 27, 1910, one week after the date designated in the plan, the Mexican Revolution erupted. Though the insurrection would last until 1917, Díaz was overthrown in 1911.

The main plaza of San Luis Potosí, called the Plaza de Armas (or Jardín Hidalgo), is on Calle Hidalgo. The plaza provides a garden for surrounding historical and ecclesiastical structures and a central point for exploring town; Calle Hidalgo offers an open, pleasant walking area with smooth tiled streets where pedestrians can meander and shop, unimpeded by traffic.

Overlooking Plaza de Armas are two of the city's landmarks, the Government Palace (Palacio de Gobierno), dating from 1770, and the Catedral de la Virgen, built from 1690 to 1737. Each of these structures has undergone change, restoration, and repair since its construction, but each retains some aspects of the original structure and decor. The lower floors and façade of the palace remain from the 18th-century building, as does one of the bell towers of the cathedral (which seems to have developed, over its years of renovation, into a potpourri of architectural styles, including baroque, Byzantine, Doric, and Gothic). Inside the palace you will find the ornate Hall of Mirrors and the Gallery of Mexican Heroes, which are two of the city's noted attractions. The prominent structure that can be seen on the north side of the cathedral, also facing Plaza de Armas, was built by the count of Monterrey, and was once a lavish palace. Since 1921, however, it has functioned as San Luis Potosí's Palacio Municipal (City Hall).

By walking 3 blocks east of Jardín Hidalgo to Plazuela del Carmen, you can visit the unusual Church of Our Lady of Carmen, which was built in churrigueresque style in 1764. The unique façade of this church is adorned with shells, columns, and a dome of blue, yellow, green, and white tiles. The interior, which was designed by the noted 18th-century architect Eduardo Tresguerras, contains an intricately carved pulpit and paintings by Vallejo. One block past this church is the *Teatro de la Paz,* where folkloric ballets, concerts, and operas are performed and Fernando Leal murals are exhibited. Across the street from the theater is one of Mexico's most fascinating museums, the *National Mask Museum* (2 Vilerias), which contains about 1,500 masks from pre-Hispanic to modern times. They show the influence of the social, religious, and political conquest of Mexico; the blending of the native and Spanish cultures; and the influence of the Catholic religion (closed Mondays; no admission charge). Just east of Plazuela del Carmen is the city's largest park, Alameda Park. Well shaded with trees and far enough from the busy center of town to provide a peaceful retreat, this park is a fine place to picnic, stroll, and relax. Just past the southwest corner of Alameda Park, along Avenida Universidad, is the *Fermín Rivera Bullring.* If you don't catch a bullfight, you might settle for a visit to the photographic exhibit in the museum next door to the Plaza España, where a variety of bullfighting memorabilia and exhibits are open to the public. Across from the northwest corner of Alameda Park, where Othon and Azteca intersect, stands the city's railroad station, where Fernando Leal's magnificent frescoes depicting the history of transportation in Mexico cover the walls.

Three blocks south and 1 block west of Plaza de Armas, along Calle Aldama, is the Plaza de San Francisco, which was once a vast Franciscan monastery. On the south side of the plaza is the Church of San Francisco, with its lovely blue and white tile dome on the exterior and a substantial display of ancient paintings on the interior. On the west side of the plaza, in striking contrast to the 18th-century cathedral, stands the *Museo Regional de Arte Popular* (Regional Museum of Popular Art; 6 Jardín Guerrero; phone: 481-275210). Set in a completely renovated turn-of-the-century mansion, the collections cover the full spectrum of local crafts from ceramics, inlaid wood, and papier-mâché sculpture to rebozos, pottery, and other artifacts. Open Tuesdays through Saturdays from 10 AM to 3:45 PM and from 6 to 8 PM; Sundays, 10 AM to 4:45 PM; Mondays, 1 to 5 PM. Admission charge.

Shopping is particularly pleasant in San Luis Potosí along the tiled Calle Hidalgo. If you follow the tiled street north from Plaza de Armas, you will pass many of the smaller, fine shops of the city that sell the famous silk rebozos made in the nearby village of Santa María de Oro. You will also pass the flower market, housed in the renovated structure of the city's old marketplace. Eventually, by walking north along Calle Hidalgo, you will reach the central marketplace, an enormous building containing a vast array of local crafts, foods, and other delights of all kinds. Among the special attractions are the local culinary treat called *queso de tuna,* a sweet paste made from the prickly pear cactus fruit, baskets, straw furniture, pottery, leather goods, and a variety of sweet-tasting fruits and vegetables.

Eating is a special pleasure in San Luis Potosí. *La Virreyna* (830 Carranza; phone: 481-23750), one of Mexico's best restaurants, is set in an elegantly converted Maximilian mansion and has excellent regional dishes and an international menu as well. Open noon to midnight daily. For both local and international fare, try *La Lonja* restaurant and bar (Madero and Aldama; phone: 481-28119). *La Gran Via* (560 Carranza; phone: 481-22899) serves first-rate international food in a formal setting.

For tourist information, city maps, and general information, call or visit the tourist office at 130 Manuel José Othon (phone: 481-42994 or 481-23143).

En Route from San Luis Potosí – About 45 miles (72 km) south of San Luis, just before a tiny chapel and cemetery on the left-hand side, is the Santo Domingo ranch, where fighting bulls are bred. The Labastida family will usually allow anyone who expresses an interest in bullfighting to wander around the old hacienda, but the bulls are kept far away and out of sight, in the belief they will not perform well in the arena if they become too accustomed to humans.

Proceeding south on Route 57, you'll find that the terrain begins to change. You'll pass through fertile farmlands and see stone fences, red tile roofs, and church towers in the small towns dotting the valley landscape. Santa María del Río is a small village where most of the rebozos seen and sold in San Luis Potosí are produced. In a lavishly forested valley 30 miles (48 km) south of San Luis Potosí, on Route 57, it is a charming, peaceful spot to visit and watch the women at their work. Ten miles (16 km) southeast of Santa María del Río is *Balneario de Lourdes,* a thermal spa and hotel in the lush green country through which the Río Santa María flows. It can be reached by following a dirt road for 7 miles (11 km) from the *Balneario de Lourdes* turnoff on Route 57 (a few miles south of Santa María del Río). Here you can enjoy the cold river water of Río Santa María and the warm, relaxing mineral water of the village's natural springs at the *Balneario y Manantailes de Lourdes* (phone: 481-23132 or 481-36313), a spare but impeccably clean hotel that matches the healthy, invigorating atmosphere of its surroundings. Besides the unheated pools, this inexpensive spot has a dining room, tennis courts, horses, a game room, a cordial staff, and free parking; it's on the main road — you can't miss it in this town.

Some 62 miles (99 km) south of San Luis Potosí is a junction where Route 57 meets Route 110. Here you enter the Bajío country, a part of Mexico that is rich in ancient, colonial, and revolutionary history. At this junction you can take roads west leading to Hidalgo and Guanajuato or, farther down Route 57, you can take the turnoff for San Miguel Allende. All of the Bajío country, including these three cities, is covered in *The Bajío* section of DIRECTIONS. Just before reaching Querétaro, Route 57 enters a junction with Route 45 (called Querétaro Corner). Here Route 57 becomes a four-lane toll road that continues until Mexico City.

QUERÉTARO: The capital of the state of Querétaro, with a population of over 1,000,000 and at an elevation of 5,700 feet, is an ancient and fascinating city of tree-filled plazas, splendid mansions, busy marketplaces, and colonial architecture. Although it is a growing industrial center with plants manufacturing everything from sewing machines, cars, and tractors to corn flakes and fertilizer, its historic landmarks and traditional charm remain intact.

Before the Spanish arrived in the 16th century, Querétaro was an outpost used by the Aztec tribes as protection against the marauding tribes to the north. In 1531, the Spanish conquered the city and the Chichimec and Otomi Indians who lived in the area. Under the governorship of Don Fernando, agriculture expanded, mining began, and the city became a colonial center. Besides being the home of the famous Creole rebel La Corregidora (Doña Josefa, whose portrait appeared on the now-long-forgotten Mexican copper 5-centavo coin), it is the place where Maximilian and his two generals were executed, the notorious Treaty of Guadalupe Hidalgo was signed, and the current constitution of Mexico was written.

Among the several sites of interest in Querétaro are the lovely Plaza Obregón (the central plaza), the Cathedral of San Francisco, the Church of Santa Rosa, the Plaza de la Independencia, and the Cerro de las Campanas (Hill of Bells), where Maximilian was executed. The semiprecious opals, which are mined in the surrounding town, are another of Querétaro's attractions. Opal jewelry and artifacts are sold throughout Querétaro by street vendors, in small stores, and in lapidary shops, where they are set into jewelry. Opals are likely to find you in Querétaro before you go looking for them. You are advised to be wary of street vendors, who offer an assortment of semiprecious stones that might or might not be the real thing. For more information on Querétaro, see *The Bajío* route in DIRECTIONS.

En Route from Querétaro – Returning to the toll highway, Route 57, you will begin climbing and winding through a stretch of maguey fields known as La Cuesta China, the Chinese Slope. Beyond them lies San Juan del Río, a small town of special interest for its crafts, wine, and cheese.

SAN JUAN DEL RÍO: This town, with a population of 125,000 and an elevation of 6,500 feet, is just off Route 57, 31 miles (50 km) from Querétaro. It is one of the weaving centers of Mexico, where wicker (willowreed) goods of all kinds and shapes are sold at the *portales* along the road. Opals and other semiprecious stones are also sold here, as are nondescript and worthless stones that can readily fool the unknowing buyer. Once again, as in Querétaro, be very cautious about buying gems.

TEQUISQUIAPÁN: A peaceful Otomí village of cobblestone streets and 1-story adobe houses is on Route 120, 12 miles (19 km) north of San Juan del Río. As one of Mexico's most noted natural health spas, it appeals to harried city dwellers, tired travelers, and health-seekers. Besides natural mineral springs and a peaceful atmosphere, Tequisquiapán offers horseback riding, fishing, and hunting.

TULA: One of Mexico's major archaeological zones, Tula is 14 miles (22 km) off Route 57 at the Tepeji del Río interchange, 45 miles (72 km) north of Mexico City. You will see road signs at the interchange for Tula, which once served as the capital city of the Toltec. The 15-foot tall Atlantes, basalt figures towering atop Pyramid B, are outstanding. The site is open daily from 9:30 AM to 4 PM. Admission charge includes parking and entrance to the museum.

En Route from Tula – Return to Route 57 and head south for the final 50 miles (80 km) to Mexico City.

BEST EN ROUTE

NUEVO LAREDO

El Río – A motel with spacious grounds, excellent facilities and service, 152 large units, 2 swimming pools, a bar, and an excellent dining room. Most credit cards accepted. 3 miles (5 km) south of the international bridge on the Nuevo Laredo–Monterrey Hwy. 15 (phone: 871-43666). Moderate.

Hacienda – Another motor hotel with 74 units, swimming pool, and a restaurant-bar. Just 4 miles (6 km) south of the international bridge, on the Nuevo Laredo–Monterrey Hwy. 15 (phone: 871-44666). Moderate to inexpensive.

Reforma – In the center of town, this established hotel has 38 air conditioned rooms and 10 junior suites with, showers, TV sets, phones, bar service, and a dining room with mediocre food. 822 Av. Guerrero (phone: 871-26250). Moderate to inexpensive.

Don Antonio – Thirty-eight air conditioned units in a simple, clean setting. 2435 Gonzales (phone: 871-21140). Inexpensive.

SALTILLO

Camino Real Saltillo – One of the finest hotels in northern Mexico, with acres of landscaped gardens, colonial decor, heated pool, 2 tennis courts, putting green, playground, restaurant, coffee shop, cocktail lounge with live music, a disco, cable TV with US programs, and 116 rooms. All credit cards accepted. 3½ miles (6 km) southeast of Saltillo on Rte. 57 (phone: 841-52525). Expensive.

Eurotel Plaza Best Western – One of Saltillo's newer hotels, offering 102 rooms, heated pool, restaurant, cafeteria, cable TV with US programs, and pleasant service. 4100 Canadá and Venustiano Carranza (phone: 841-51000 or 841-51120). Expensive.

San Jorge – This modern, 120-room downtown hotel has a restaurant, bar, indoor pool, cable TV, and parking. 240 Manuel Acuña Nte. (phone: 841-22222). Expensive to moderate.

Torre los Magueyes – Its 190 rooms are distributed between an older colonial-style section and a modern 12-story structure. There are 2 tennis courts, a restaurant-bar, coffee shop, pool, disco, and cable TV. Km. 869 Carr. 57 (phone: 841-53333). Moderate.

Huizache – Pleasant, older, long-established hotel with 62 rooms, Cablevision showing US programs, heated pool, wading pool, restaurant, and bar. Major credit cards accepted. 1746 Blvd. V. Carranza, on Rte. 57 coming into town (phone: 841-61000 or 841-62662). Inexpensive.

Plaza Urdiñola – A downtown hostelry with definite charm, a striking entry, and hand-decorated walls. Prices are low. 211 Calle Victoria (phone: 841-40940). Inexpensive.

Rancho El Morillo – A small establishment offering 14 units, restaurant, bar, heated pool, tennis, and horseback riding at a neighboring ranch. 2 miles (3 km) west of Saltillo (phone: 841-26300). Inexpensive.

MATEHUALA

El Dorado – Here is a 42-room motel with spacious gardens, restaurant, and a small playground. Km. 615 Carr. 57 (phone: 488-20174). Moderate.

Oasis – A simple motel with lots of trees and grass, 38 units, pool, good restaurant, phones, showers, bar service, and free parking. Pets are allowed. It also has 5 trailer spaces, with the use of motel facilities. On Rte. 57 (phone: 488-20742). Moderate.

Hacienda – A 16-unit motel with a pool and beautiful grounds. The adjoining disco will not keep guests awake because it is nearly always empty. At the northern entrance to Matehuala (phone: 488-20065). Inexpensive.

Las Palmas – Not elegant, but a clean and tastefully decorated motel with good service; 89 rooms, a big pool, nice grounds, miniature golf course, a couple of bowling alleys, and an excellent restaurant. The property also has 28 trailer spaces with all connections, a bathhouse, and the use of hotel facilities. Km 617 on Rte. 57. (phone: 488-20002). Inexpensive.

SAN LUIS POTOSÍ

Hostal del Quijote – All 211 air conditioned rooms have TV sets, restaurant, nightclub, pool, tennis. Southeast at Km 420 of the Mexico–Piedras Negras Hwy. 57 (phone: 481-81312 or 481-81411). Expensive.

Cactus – Spacious motel with well-tended grounds, 110 rooms with air conditioning, heating, some rooms with refrigerators, service bars, steam bath, saunas, dining room, cocktail lounge with entertainment, disco, convention facilities, swimming pool, satellite television, playground, and a trailer park with full services. Pets are accepted. Just south of Juárez Circle on Rte. 57 (phone: 481-21871 or 481-21872). Expensive to moderate.

Panorama – Excellent 10-story downtown hotel with 127 rooms nicely furnished (some with private balconies), 6 suites, TV sets (with some US channels), swimming and wading pools, phones, showers, a rooftop restaurant, a cocktail lounge with panoramic view of the city, and a ground-level coffee shop. 315 Carranza, 3 blocks west of the Plaza de Armas (phone: 481-21777). Expensive to moderate.

Real de Minas – A colonial-style hostelry, it has air conditioning, TV sets, restaurant, bar, and lovely gardens. Just off the Juárez Circle (phone: 481-82736 or 481-82676). Expensive to moderate.

Real Plaza – Modern and centrally located hotel with 138 air conditioned units, a restaurant, coffee shop, and disco. 890 Carranza (phone: 481-46969). Expensive to moderate.

María Cristina – Its 71 units are equipped with fans, and the hotel has a restaurant-bar and a pool. 110 Juan Sarabia (phone: 481-29408). Inexpensive.

María Dolores – One of San Luis's newest hotels, with 213 rooms, 2 pools, a garden, restaurant, coffee shop, disco, lobby bar, and playground. Next to the *Cactus* at Km 1 on Carr. San Luis Potosí–Mexico off Rte. 57 (phone: 481-25109 or 481-25116). Inexpensive.

Sands – A motel with colonial decor, pleasant grounds with gardens and swimming pool, 50 spacious rooms, TV sets, cocktail service, and a nice restaurant. Most credit cards accepted. Across from the *Cactus* (phone: 481-82533). Inexpensive.

Tuna – Well-kept motel with landscaped grounds, 50 units, pool, playground, restaurant. 200 Dr. Manuel Nava (phone: 481-31207). Inexpensive.

The Bajío

About 150 miles (240 km) northwest of Mexico City, the Bajío country begins. Although set in the Sierra Madre highlands at an elevation of between 6,000 and 7,000 feet, the Bajío is not quite as high as Mexico City, so getting used to the altitude is easier. The area is known geologically as the Central Volcanic Highlands, but the Bajío region is commonly called the Historic Lowlands precisely because of its height in relation to the capital.

This part of Mexico was an agricultural center as early as 3,500 years ago. Because of the rich soil, people were able to grow corn, beans, chili peppers, and squash. The earth also yielded clay, which the first inhabitants molded into pottery and shelters. In the 11th century the Chichimec Indians invaded from the north, and the Aztec arrived about 100 years later. But the Bajío really came into its own after the 16th-century Spanish conquest. It was here that the first colonial cities were built, and as a result the Bajío contains an abundance of colonial and other historic monuments. The main battles of the Mexican War of Independence were fought in Querétaro and Guanajuato, the two states that make up most of this rugged area, and Guanajuato is known as the Cradle of Independence. Here, revolutionary leader Captain Ignacio Allende allied himself with Father Miguel Hidalgo y Costilla in the movement against Spain in 1810. Both men fought courageously to liberate Mexico, but they were captured and decapitated in 1811. The Spanish hung their heads on public display in Guanajuato. However, after independence was won in 1821, in honor of their heroism, their places of birth were renamed San Miguel de Allende and Dolores Hidalgo, and they are now two of the most famous cities in the Bajío. In 1867, Mexico's Austrian ruler Maximilian was executed on Bajío soil, in Querétaro.

As in pre-colonial and colonial times, this is still one of the richest farming regions in the entire country. Visitors get fresh strawberries and asparagus in December as well as in August. In fact, farmers regularly harvest two and three crops of strawberries, asparagus, tomatoes, sorghum, corn, wheat, and other important produce in the course of a year. The Bajío is also rich in minerals, especially silver, which made it a center of Spanish colonial activity. Today, it is a center of heavy manufacturing, petrochemical processing, and petroleum refining plants. In addition to strengthening Mexico's domestic economy, these industries produce enough surplus for exports, which, in turn, bring much-needed foreign exchange into the country.

Though by no means as popular with American tourists as Mexico City or the better-known coastal resorts, the Bajío region is well equipped to handle visitors. Of greatest interest are its splendid colonial towns, but it has outdoor sports facilities, comfortable accommodations, vineyards, and craft pavilions. The weather is cool, dry, and moderate all year, with days tending to be

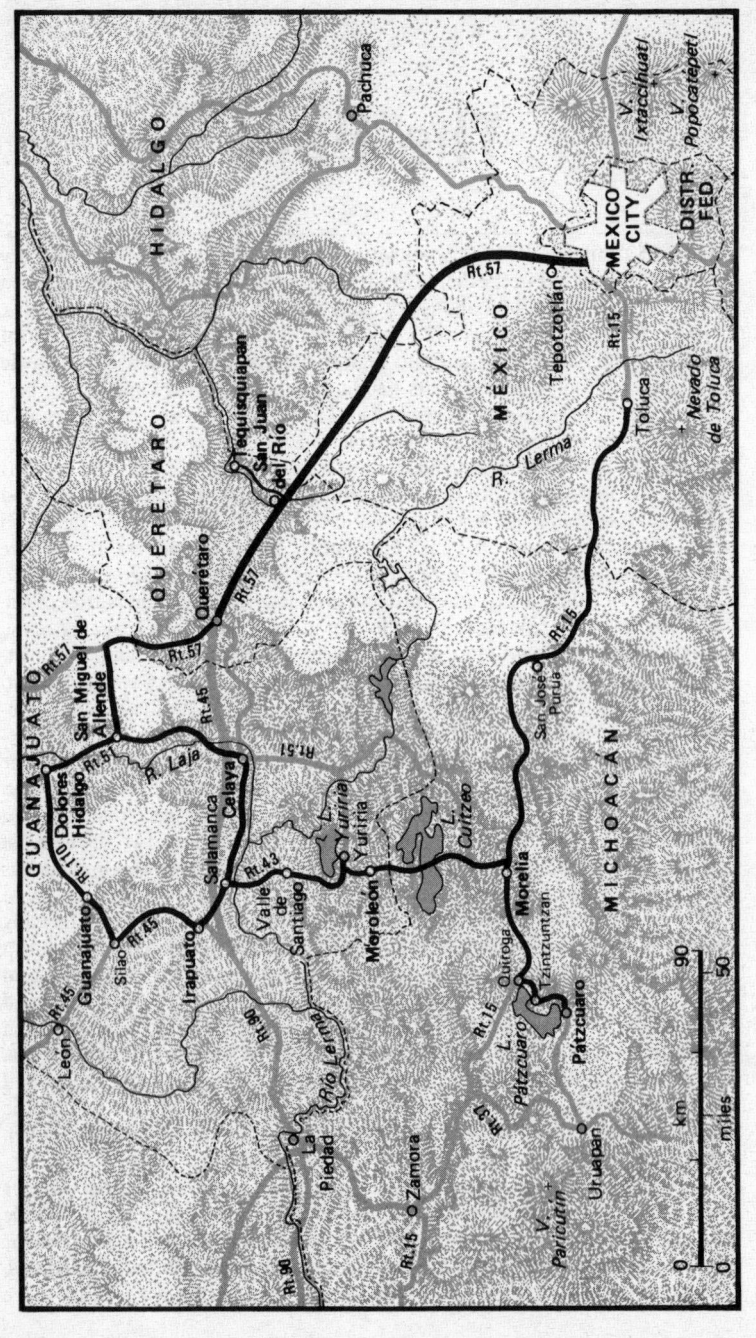

sunny. Temperatures drop at night, so bring warm sweaters. Otherwise you needn't worry about what to wear in this informal part of the world.

We suggest you tour this part of the country via a circular route from Mexico City, beginning with Route 57, stopping at San Juan del Río, Tequisquiapán, Querétaro (the junction of several major highways), then taking Route 51 to San Miguel de Allende and Dolores Hidalgo, Route 110 to Guanajuato and Celaya, traveling west on Route 45 to Salamanca, then south on Route 43 to Morelia, returning to Mexico City on Route 15, stopping in Toluca. Because each of the larger cities takes more than 1 day to cover, this circuit requires a bit more than 5 days, if you want to do it justice. And we suggest that you do take the time, especially as this is one part of Mexico that is still relatively undiscovered. You can enjoy yourself, absorb the history and tradition, and get a sense of what Mexico was like before 20th-century North American architecture planted itself on the horizon.

At hotels along this route we categorize as expensive, expect to pay $65 or more for a double room; $30 to $60 at moderate places; and less than $30, inexpensive.

En Route from Mexico City – From the Fuente de Petróleos monument at Plaza Comermex in Mexico City, where the Paseo de la Reforma crosses the beltway called the Periférico, it is 23½ miles (38 km) on Route 57 to the turnoff for Tepotzotlán. Make sure that you do not go through the toll gate to Tepotzotlán. The turnoff comes before the toll booths and takes you on an overpass. About a half mile (1 km) west of the overpass going toward Tepotzotlán, the road becomes Avenida Insurgentes.

BALNEARIO SAN PEDRO TEPOTZOTLÁN: Before you get into town, this recreational park offers a choice of natural springwater baths or traditional swimming pools. Parking is available for campers and trailers, but there are no full hookups. Other facilities include handball, volleyball, and tetherball.

TEPOTZOTLÁN: This town of 23,000 people is at a comfortable altitude of 5,528 feet. Continue west on Avenida Insurgentes — Tepotzotlán is actually only about 1 mile (1.6 km) from Route 57. The *Museo Nacional del Virreinato* (Viceregal Period National Museum; on Av. Insurgentes), one of the most important historic museums in the country, is in a former Jesuit seminary built partly in the late 17th century and completed in 1762. The National Institute of Anthropology and History, which runs the museum, has edited an excellent guidebook in English explaining its collection. The book, available at the museum, is highly recommended. The museum contains an astounding collection of relics, artifacts, paintings, statuary, silver and gold objects, and vestments owned and used by the Catholic church in Spanish colonial Mexico. The items include alleged pieces of bone from St. Peter and St. Paul (circular bone slices displayed in an ornate silver reliquary), an Italian silver chalice with coral inlays, and some of the most opulent gold leaf retablos in Mexico. There is also a major collection of religious paintings. Possibly the most ingenious feature, the Chamber of the Virgin, which was built in the early 1700s, has a cupola or dome in which a frieze above the altar can be seen by means of a tilted mirror. This enables you to see the carved sun, moon, and stars as well as an assortment of beaming cherubim. In the central portion of the chamber, which can best be seen from the front of the partition, the Virgin Mary appears in the lantern, surrounded by the apostles in the scene from the Pentecost, with the Holy Spirit presiding from the upper portion. You have to study the entire composition for several minutes in order to find the figures and relate them to the whole of the chamber. Tepotzotlán may well be the capital of the bizarre churrigueresque style of architecture, with almost every inch of several buildings gilded, flourished, curlicued, and topped with statues of beaming cherubs.

Hostería del Convento de Tepotzotlán (1 Plaza Virreinal; phone: 5-876-0243) is a lovely restaurant that serves Mexican food with lots of *mole* sauce, to the accompaniment of a group of lively musicians. Sit at a small table inside or outside the portals, sip a mug of beer, and eat *huerepos* (small, dried, salted fish) or *huitlacoche* crêpes (the Mexican delicacy of black corn fungus). Service is slow, but that doesn't matter on a lazy afternoon. A *Christmas* pageant held nightly from December 16 to 24 comes complete with mariachis, spiked punch, Mexican food, piñatas, and fireworks.

En Route from Tepotzotlán – It is 76 miles (121 km) from Tepotzotlán to the turnoff for San Juan del Río on Route 57 on the toll road.

SAN JUAN DEL RÍO: A town of 125,000 people at an altitude of 6,500 feet, this is a good place to purchase a wide range of handicrafts and choose from extensive selections of semiprecious stones. Most of the better handicrafts shops are in the colonnades along the main street. The nearby Trinidad opal mines supply the stonecutting, polishing, and jewelry-making industries here, in nearby Tequisquiapán, and in Querétaro. Although this is the center of the Mexican gem industry, not all the stones sold are domestic. Many come from Brazil, Colombia, and the US and are cut and polished locally. You should purchase expensive items only in well-established shops, since items sold by street peddlers and small stands often turn out to be bogus. Aquamarines sold in street stands are rarely of the same quality as those in the more reliable establishments. *Lapidaria Gabriel Guerrero M.* (4 Calle Juárez Pte.) is one of the largest lapidary shops, specializing in opals, turquoise, amethyst, and topaz. Items range from finely set rings, bracelets, necklaces, and earrings to loose cut and polished stones and geodes. Wicker and reed-grass (called *carrizo*) basketry competes with semiprecious stones for the title of leading merchandise in San Juan del Río and Tequisquiapán. We recommend Tequisquiapán for *carrizo,* although San Juan del Río has nearly identical wares. Prices tend to be high in both towns, but the basketry and weaving are finer in Tequisquiapán.

Wines are another important regional product. The vineyards of San Juan del Río are the most southern in Mexico and produce some quite passable red and white table wines. Due to a Querétaro state law, wine tasting is forbidden in the wineries, but sometimes this is overlooked during the wine and cheese festivals held in Tequisquiapán during the last 10 days of May. Wines can be bought by the case, half case, or bottle in San Juan del Río at attractive savings over supermarket prices. The largest winery is Cavas de San Juan, less than a mile out of town on the road to Tequisquiapán, on the left. The owners, of Spanish descent, produce their wines by blending local grapes and grapes from the state of Aguascalientes. Tour their cellars, where thousands of bottles of wine are aging for three or four years each. The trade name of Cavas de San Juan is Hidalgo. Their cabernet sauvignon and pinot noir are especially good Mexican wines. Hidalgo also bottles a white semisweet wine called amabile. Closed Sundays. Also in San Juan del Río is La Madrileña, another large winery that specializes in port, vermouth, muscatel, sherry, brandy, rum, and liqueurs. You can pick up a bottle at the winery's showroom at Carretera Tequisquiapán; open daily. In 1977, a subsidiary of Martell de Mexico, called Sofimar, brought out a new red wine called Clos San José. It is passable but has a high acid content. Sofimar wineries also produce brandies. Sofimar is in Tequisquiapán.

En Route from San Juan del Río – About 11 miles (18 km) northeast is the town of Tequisquiapán, famous for its mineral hot springs and resorts (see *Best en Route*). From here to Querétaro, you'll find numerous stands along the road selling cheese, butter, cream, *cajeta* (a sweet made of goat's milk), candied fruit, and sausage. In fact, this part of the route is a well-loved wine and cheese circuit frequently driven by Mexico City residents on 1-day outings. The best of the cheeses are those produced by El Sauz, which has stands on both sides of the road. Their patagras, originally a Cuban cheese, is excellent. Other good choices are manchego, gouda, holandés (different from gouda), and asadero or tipo Oaxaca, used for baked dishes. Productos Walter, a dairy whose original owners came from Switzerland, also makes very good cheeses. It has a selection of approximately the same kinds of cheeses as El Sauz as well as butter and cream. There is hardly a more Mexican activity than sampling the wine and cheese along this portion of the Bajío route. Not to do so would be to miss one of its chief pleasures.

QUERÉTARO: A city of 960,000 people, Querétaro is one of the principal centers of Spanish colonial architecture in the Bajío region, and both literally and figuratively an important crossroads in Mexican history. Major events of almost every period since the Spanish conquest have occurred here. Querétaro was founded around 1446 by the Chichimec and Otomí Indian tribes. Spanish domination began in 1531 and their control was consolidated in 1538. Some of Mexico's best ecclesiastical architecture can be seen here. Father Junípero Serra studied in a convent here before setting out on his lifelong mission-founding career in the Sierra Gorda, north of the state of Querétaro. Father Serra's vocation culminated in the establishment of a string of elaborate missions along the California coast. The key characters in the independence conspiracy met here frequently. The Treaty of Guadalupe Hidalgo, in which Mexico lost more than half its national territory, was signed in Querétaro in 1848; Emperor Maximilian was executed on the nearby Hill of the Bells in 1867, and the present Mexican constitution was written and signed in Querétaro in 1917. Mexico's dominant political party, now called the Institutional Revolutionary Party (PRI), was founded in Querétaro in 1929 as the National Revolutionary Party (PNR).

Today the city has several thriving industries. Tractors, sewing machines, lift trucks, automobile transmissions, and food products are manufactured here. A local steel company makes oil drilling rigs. Automobiles produced in the US by Ford and Chrysler are equipped with standard transmission gearboxes manufactured in Querétaro. The company that manufactures these gearboxes is one of the largest exporters of manufactured products in Mexico. There is so much to see in Querétaro that 2 full days of even tightly scheduled activity would be insufficient.

The Jardín Obregón is the city's main square. In the Bajío, squares are sometimes called *jardínes,* or gardens, instead of plazas or zocalos. A large gingerbread wrought-iron bandstand in the middle of Jardín Obregón is the site of band concerts and folk music on Sunday evenings. There is also an ornate 19th-century fountain and water tank of cast iron produced by a foundry in Philadelphia. The fountain is dedicated to Hebe, the Greek goddess of youth. The Jardín Obregón is also a hangout for many vendors of opals and amethysts of generally low quality. Buyers beware. The Plaza de la Constitución is covered with the rose-colored *cantera* rock for which Querétaro is famous and has a large statue of Venustiano Carranza, who headed the triumphant Constitutionalists during the 1910 revolution. He later became a controversial president of Mexico. Bordering the plaza are posts bearing the names of Mexico's states and territories and the names of individual delegates to the constitutional convention.

Jardín de Santa Clara's Neptune Fountain is an imaginative piece of neo-classical architecture designed by Francisco Eduardo Tresguerras, one of Mexico's best-known architects. Constructed around the mythological figure of Neptune, god of the sea, the fountain was paid for by the city government in 1797. The Monument to the Corregidora shares the square (at Dieciséis de Septiembre and Corregidora) with the Friendship Tree. Dedicated on September 13, 1910, the monument is a bronze statue of the wife of the viceroy's lieutenant, who governed a division of New Spain while based in Querétaro during colonial times. Querétaro was then the third largest city in Mexico, superseded in size by Mexico City and Puebla. The statue contains a symbolic reproduction of the keyhole through which the Corregidora, a revolutionary, passed messages. The base of the statue is surrounded by large bronze eagles with spread wings atop a cannon barrel draped with Hidalgo's revolutionary banner. The Friendship Tree is actually two conifers (ponderosa pine or monkey puzzle) growing together, with a plaque between them stating: "Querétaro is the crossroads of all roads of the country and center of gravity of national history." The *Museo Regional de Querétaro* (Regional Museum of Querétaro; 3 Corregidora) incorporates the *Pío Mariano Museum.* Housed in the convent section of the San Francisco church, its exhibits cover the prehistoric, colonial, independence, imperial, revolution, and post-revolution periods of Mexican history. Not all the exhibitions are worth seeing, so you have to be selective. The collection of religious paintings, for example, is not as interesting as that at Tepotzotlán. However, the most interesting historical items include the keyhole and door latch of a household prison where Josefa Ortiz de Dominguez (La Corregidora) whispered instructions to a neighbor to get a horse and warn the Allende brothers and Father Hidalgo that their plot had been discovered. La Corregidora was under house arrest at the time. As a result of this information, the date of the revolution was pushed ahead by 3 months. Fighting began on September 15, 1810, instead of December of that year. In the same exhibit is the table on which the Treaty of Guadalupe Hidalgo was signed in Querétaro in 1848 by interim Mexican President Manuel de la Peña. Although Mexico's foreign relations minister and the US representative signed the treaty elsewhere, the exchange of government ratifications took place in Querétaro. A plaque near the table notes that Mexico turned over to the US the territory of Texas, the territory between the Nueces and Bravo (Río Grande) rivers belonging to the state of Tamaulipas, the territory of New Mexico, and the territory of Alta (Upper) California. As a result, Mexico lost 851,598 square miles of territory, and the US paid Mexico $15 million in compensation. In an adjoining room stands the desk at which sat the council of war that heard the case of Emperor Maximilian and signed his death sentence in the *Teatro de la República* in 1867. Also on display is the flatbed press that printed the first copies of the 1917 Political Constitution of the United States of Mexico, still in effect today. The tourist office (at Cinco de Mayo and Pasteur) offers free, 2-hour tours of historic Querétaro sites; they leave from the office daily except Sundays at 10:30 AM (phone: 463-40179).

The Church of Santa Rosa de Viterbo (Calle General Arteaga and Calle Ezequiel Montes) is one of the most exotic, if not downright bizarre, examples of church architecture in Mexico. Completed in 1752, the church has two enormous flying buttresses which help shore up the central structure, upon which an octagonal cupola is set. The lower half of the cupola is sculpted in stone, and the dome has patches of blue and white talavera tile. An intricate bell tower points magnificently toward the sky. The top of the tower is fashioned after an Oriental pagoda and contains the first multiple-face clock built in the Americas. The outermost extremities of the flying buttresses, which extend from the tower to the street, are flanked by ornately carved dragon faces. Inside, the Santa Rosa church contains enormous gold-leaf retablos and murals, some by Miguel Cabrera, and a pulpit with a giant crown of Oriental origin finished with silver and ivory inlay. A pipe organ and choir section, in the back portion of the nave at street level, are separated from the pews by wrought-iron bars. Across the street stands a group of municipal government buildings in the Plaza Ignacio Mariano de las Casas, named for the architect of the Santa Rosa church.

The Church of San Francisco dominates Jardín Obregón. Frequently mistaken for the city's cathedral, which it is not, the church was completed in 1545 and has undergone subsequent architectural modifications. The contiguous huge Franciscan convent, built between 1693 and 1698, houses the *Regional Museum of Querétaro,* described above. The building also served as a hospital and surgery ward during the siege of 1867, in which Maximilian was defeated; and soldiers were quartered here during the

1810–17 revolution. From the church steeple you can get a great view of *Christmas Eve* celebrations in which *fantoches* — huge papier-mâché dolls — are carried playfully around the Jardín, accompanied by music and fireworks. Preceding them is a much more solemn parade of floats depicting biblical scenes.

The Church of San Felipe Neri (Av. Madero at Ocampo) is a refreshing change from the ornate gold and silver resplendence of most Mexican cathedrals. Although the exterior consists of an ornate façade with six columns standing completely apart from the front wall, inside there is no gold leaf. A large dome allows lots of light to filter in. The small pipe organ in the choir loft is one of the best in the city. Construction on the cathedral began in 1755 and mass was first said here in 1763. It was completed in 1804 and was later restored.

The Church of Santa María de Guadalupe (at Dieciséis de Septiembre and Pasteur) is often ignored, but is well worth a visit for its organ music. Built around 1902, it is a tasteful example of a Mexican church devoted to the patron saint of the Americas. The huge organ in the choir loft has an elaborate set of pipes. Although some of the small organ pipes underneath the balcony of the choir loft don't work, the basic pipe organ works and reverberates magnificently throughout the building. The twin towers of the church are topped with wrought-iron crosses, and the upper portions of the towers are decorated with mosaic tiles in Mexico's national colors of red, white, and green.

Iglesia y Convento de la Cruz (Church and Convent of the Cross; at Plaza Venustiano Carranza) was built in the latter portion of the 17th century under the authorization of a bull issued by Pope Innocent XI on May 8, 1683. It became the center of operations for a Franciscan order, which immediately established its Colegio de Propaganda Fide (College of Faith Propaganda), the first such academy in the Americas. Father Junípero Serra and other friars left the college to establish missions in other parts of Mexico and California. Even in the late 17th century, the monastery was an important scientific and artistic center. Its library had more than 7,000 volumes, a record for that period of history. In addition to a fine collection of rare books, the Church and Convent of the Cross has artwork that includes a Christ Child from Naples and an ivory crucifix donated by a governor of the Philippines. One of the interior gardens is haunted by a puzzling myth. The tale goes that, unknown to the Franciscans, a monk slept in the convent one night and forgot his walking stick when he went on his way the next day. The stick took root and from it grew an unusual cactus whose thorns are in the shape of the cross.

The aqueduct (*acueducto*), which still carries water into Querétaro, is an example of Spanish colonial engineering that was completed in 1735, after nine years of work. The aqueduct, 93 feet high in some spots, was connected to a series of fountains in the city by 1738. Its 74 arches are dramatically lit at night. By driving on Calzada de los Arcos you can get a good view. Alternately, you can take the cutoff to San Luis Potosí under the arches. To the west of the city, the Cerro de las Campanas (Hill of the Bells) has a statue of Benito Juárez at the top and a chapel marking the site, farther down the slope, where Maximilian was executed. The statue was dedicated on May 15, 1967, the 100th anniversary of the triumph of the republic, when the Mexican general Mariano Escobedo laid siege to the city of Querétaro and conquered it. Maximilian surrendered at the Hill of the Bells that morning and was imprisoned in the Convento de la Cruz, where his cell is still furnished with his desk, sleeping cot, and chair. He was killed by a firing squad on June 19, 1867. An expiatory chapel financed by the last Emperor of Austria, Franz Josef, was built on the site in 1901. In front of the altar are the three truncated columns below which Maximilian and his two generals, Miguel Miramón and Tomás Mejía, stood facing their executioners. Both were faithful to their emperor to the end. The walls of the chapel are lined with photographs and paintings from the Maximilian era.

The *Plaza de Toros Santa María,* with a seating capacity of about 18,000, is one of the best bullrings in Mexico, second only to those of Mexico City and Tijuana. The main season is in November and December. Querétaro offers some of the best events, featuring top matadors from Mexico and Spain.

The name *Querétaro* is said to mean "rocky place"; in the early 20th century the area was famous for its production of opals. But the opal mines near Querétaro are becoming exhausted and the better stones are more scarce and expensive. For the best buy, consult the shopkeepers for prices and quality. Then ask the vendors, who sell crude, uncut opals, in Plaza Independencia or Jardín Obregón, who their suppliers are. Some of the best purchases can be made in the private homes of people who buy and sell gems. Don't be afraid to bargain. Perhaps the most common stone and the best buy now is the brown fire agate. When examining the gems for "fire," look at them under low light because opals or agates of high quality will reflect light in the dark.

In addition to *Parritacos* (59 Constituyentes), which has good meat and cheese dishes at reasonable prices, two other Querétaro restaurants are worth special mention:

La Fonda del Refugio (26 Corregidora) offers an international menu, including such expensive dishes as pepper steaks, chateaubriand for two, and *enchiladas con mole.* On warm days, tables are set on the plaza. You can also eat in the covered porch facing the plaza where the monument to the Corregidora stands.

Pizza la Rondine (38 Jardín Corregidora) is a small, cozy place with five tables inside and two outside on the plaza, all very clean. Pizza with Mexican red wine (mostly Hidalgo labels) is the specialty, although you can get pastrami sandwiches, too. The *Especial la Rondine,* with salami, parmesan cheese, mushrooms, and onion, comes in three sizes, as does the pizza *quattro stazioni,* with shrimp, mushrooms, ham, olives, and sausage. We recommend the Hidalgo cabernet sauvignon with any pizza. Other good Mexican wines are San Marcos, from Aguascalientes, and Santo Tomás San Emilión, from Ensenada, Baja California Norte. Open daily from 2 PM until midnight.

En Route from Querétaro – To continue counterclockwise through the Bajío, head north on Route 57 toward San Luis Potosí. You will pass the Hill of the Bells on the right, then the plants of Ralston Purina, Kellogg de México, Carnation de México, Singer Mexicana and then, on the left, the burgeoning Querétaro industrial park, with the plants of Transmisiónes y Equipos Mecánicos and Massey-Ferguson de México. About 28 miles (45 km) from Querétaro is a junction of Route 51 at which you turn left to San Miguel de Allende. The road passes a lake formed by a dam, goes through extensive cornfields, winds up into the hills, and crosses the state line into Guanajuato past a small fruit and vegetable canning plant. Then you suddenly drop down a winding, hillside, cobblestone street into San Miguel de Allende. Make sure your car's brakes are in good order.

SAN MIGUEL DE ALLENDE: For a complete description of the city, its restaurants and hotels, see *San Miguel de Allende,* THE CITIES. San Miguel de Allende has hot-mineral-springs resorts. The town itself has been declared a national monument by the Mexican government in an effort to retain its colonial flavor. The construction of modern buildings is forbidden, and any new structures must meet government requirements before work may begin. The Sanctuary of Atotonilco, built between 1740 and 1748, was the first stop of the disheveled Army of Independence, under the leadership of Father Hildalgo and Ignacio Allende, on its march to San Miguel. At the sanctuary Hidalgo seized the banner of the Virgin of Guadalupe, which his army carried into battle against the Spanish. The mystic quality of the Virgin helped attract Indian followers to the cause. The Sanctuary of Atotonilco is actually a complex of six connected chapels and a lofty assembly hall decorated with a great deal of gold leaf, silver, and flamboyant frescoes. The sanctuary also contains a large collection of early pagan-Christian Indian art. It is about 7½ miles (12 km) from San Miguel de Allende on the road to Dolores Hidalgo.

DOLORES HIDALGO: Some 25 miles (40 km) northwest of San Miguel de Allende on Route 51, this town of 75,000 people sits at an altitude of 6,240 feet. Here stands the parish church, built in 1712, where Father Miguel Hidalgo y Costilla rang the church bells to gather his flock so he could proclaim independence from Spain. They met at dawn on September 16, 1810, and after Hidalgo's proclamation, the makeshift army, armed mainly with sticks and farm tools, set out for San Miguel. This was the first phase of the independence movement that came to fruition in 1821. This is why Dolores Hidalgo is known as the Cuna de la Independencia Nacional (Cradle of National Independence). The bell that Hidalgo rang is said to be the one above the National Palace in Mexico City. Historians argue that it's only a replica, the original bell having been melted down for munitions during the 11-year war. Certainly the bell at the Dolores Hidalgo church is conceded to be a replica. Plaza Hidalgo has a statue of the parish priest holding the banner of the Virgin of Guadalupe as he leads his troops. In the southwest corner of the same plaza, an elderly man sells some of the best homemade ice cream in Mexico from an unpretentious cart. He has a variety of offbeat flavors, including mango and avocado. Try some. On Sundays, families drive over from San Miguel de Allende and Guanajuato just for this treat. Stores around the plaza and connecting side streets are jammed with ceramic goods made locally, generally of unimaginative design.

Casa de Don Miguel Hidalgo (1 Morelos, at the corner of Hidalgo) is a 10-room museum containing many of Father Hidalgo's personal effects, among them his eyeglasses, clothing, furniture, books, and papers. Patriotic paintings and independence-era mémorabilia fill the rooms and the surrounding two patios.

About 8 miles (13 km) south of town is Peñuelitas Dam. La Gruta, with thermal baths, is about 12½ miles (20 km) from town.

En Route from Dolores Hidalgo – Route 110 is a well-paved but tricky, twisting mountain road that can easily overheat a car's brakes. Don't try to break any speed records here.

GUANAJUATO: For a complete description of the city, its hotels and restaurants, see *Guanajuato,* THE CITIES. Almost from the moment of its founding, Guanajuato has produced silver from mines so rich that in the early 1700s they were the source of more than a third of the world's total silver supply. Today what is most notable about this beautiful city tucked into a canyon of the Sierra Madre is the legacy of buildings left from the Spanish colonial period. The most dramatic representative of the legacy is the Alhóndiga de Granaditas, the massive granary in which the Spanish mine owners and their families hid when the revolutionary army of 1810 arrived to capture the city. About 230 Spanish — including men, women, and children — were put to the sword or hanged when the granary fell to the revolutionaries, led by Allende and Hidalgo, securing their first major victory. The 1810 revolution, of course, failed in its immediate objective of independence (Spain maintained control of Mexico until 1821), and the two leaders were captured and killed in 1811. Their heads were transported to Guanajuato and hung on public display for the next 10 years, until the final War of Independence removed the Spanish for good.

En Route from Guanajuato – Route 45 goes through Irapuato, a town surrounded by extensive truck farms and one of the most important strawberry-producing areas in the country. In winter and summer, farmers and their children sell strawberries by the basketful from roadside stands at prices that usually can be bargained even lower. The annual *Strawberry Fair* usually begins March 15 and lasts a week. Activities include the crowning of the festival queen, fireworks, bullfights, and agricultural, industrial, and handicrafts expositions. Apart from strawberry fields forever, Irapuato has little to recommend it; if you wish to bypass the town, we suggest another route from Guanajuato, state highway Route 110. This runs southeast to Celaya and is generally considered of greater interest to travelers. From Celaya, you can take Route 45 to Salamanca, then Route 43 to Morelia. We also recommend making a side trip to Lake Pátzcuaro from Morelia and returning to Mexico City on the mountain highway from Morelia, with stops at San José Purúa and Toluca.

CELAYA: This city, with a population of 245,000 and an altitude of 5,930 feet, is considered one of the most important urban areas in the Bajío. It is known for its colorful street vendors, who offer fresh strawberries and jícama, a tasty white root similar to turnips that can be eaten raw. Mexicans eat jícama in slices, often sprinkled with bottled hot sauce. Street vendors also sell *cajeta,* a sweet, thick, brown syrup made of caramel and goat's milk. The word *cajeta* comes from the small, round boxes made of thin wood shingles in which the confection is jelled and packaged. Thanks to mass production, *cajeta* is now available in jars in supermarkets all over Mexico. It comes in cinnamon, wine, vanilla, and other flavors. Mexicans, who are known for their sweet tooth, spread *cajeta* on bread or dinner rolls or eat it by the spoonful. Sold with it is *rompope,* a yellow liqueur similar to eggnog or Tom-and-Jerry rum in the US. (The *rompope* made in Mexico generally has a low alcoholic content compared with that of rum.)

Templo de Carmen (Temple of Carmen; Madero and Obregón) is considered to be the masterpiece of Celaya's illustrious architect, sculptor, painter, poet, and engraver, Francisco Eduardo Tresguerras (1759–1833). Set on a slim rectangular lot, it has a single central tower, behind which is a long nave ending in a dome. The nave is topped by a balustrade. Viewed from the corner, the church is symmetrical, with a clean, neo-classic elegance unusual in Mexico. The present building was rebuilt in 1807 after a fire destroyed the original church in 1802.

The Church and Convent of San Francisco was originally built in the 17th century, then substantially rebuilt by Tresguerras. The master architect is buried here in a chapel he designed. The façade of the church has four Ionic columns and an entablature topped by a curved frontispiece, which is also rare in this part of the world. A 3-tiered bell tower stands to the left of the entrance, while the end of the nave is topped by an egg-shaped cupola.

The Jardín Principal, as in nearly all Bajío towns, has manicured trees. These have grown together to form a large overhead hedge. In the center of the square, the trees form a circle. In the early evening, hundreds of chattering birds return to roost in the trees overnight. Eight streets converge onto the square.

En Route from Celaya – It is best to return to the toll road west rather than to use the old road, which is invariably filled with slow trucks wending their way through cornfields and cow pastures. At Salamanca, the fields turn into petro-chemical plants serving the Pemex oil refinery, one of the largest in the country.

SALAMANCA: After the oil refinery, which is one of the largest in Latin America, the Convent and Church of San Agustín (Revolución and Andrés Delgado), also called San Juan, is the main sight in Salamanca. The convent was founded in 1615; the church wasn't completed until 1750. The balustrade of the presbytery and communion altar is similar to that of the Metropolitan Cathedral in Mexico City and is said to have been brought from Macao on the galleon *Manilla.* The style is Chinese, and it contains gold, silver, and bronze. The pulpit, filigreed with wood and ivory, is similar to one in La Valenciana church near Guanajuato and was also reportedly transported from Macao. The front is lined from top to bottom with paintings depicting the devil, paradise, the four races — European, Asiatic, African, and American — and the four elements — earth, wind, fire, and water.

En Route from Salamanca – Take Route 43 about 60 miles (100 km) south to Morelia. The road goes through Valle de Santiago.

VALLE DE SANTIAGO: Known as the "country of the seven fires" because of its once-active volcanoes, the area around Valle de Santiago has green farmlands alongside stark areas of rough volcanic rock. The contrast is phenomenal. Dormant craters have formed lakes good for swimming, rowing, canoeing, or fishing. Craters that have not filled with water can be explored on foot; you can hire a guide in Valle de Santiago. La Alberca is a lake in a dormant volcano that rises more than 8,000 feet from the valley floor. It is some 2,400 feet in diameter, and its deep inner pool changes colors according to the seasons of the year. The crater's sides have fissures of basalt rock, and its slopes are covered with different kinds of cactus. The Hoya de Rincón de Parangueo is popular with duck hunters because every season thousands of waterfowl visit during their annual migration south. In the forest area on the crater's slopes live badgers, coyotes, foxes, and wildcats. All these animals can be hunted in their respective seasons. Duck season runs from late October to mid-February, with a limit of five birds per day. Geese can be hunted from November to late January, with a limit of two per day. The Hoya de Rincón de Parangueo is 6 miles (10 km) west of Valle de Santiago on a dirt road, then almost 2 miles (3 km) on a turnoff. The Hoya de Parangueo should not be confused with the Rincón de Parangueo pit, which is a nearby crater lake of salt water that's good for swimming, rowing, and sailing. Along its slopes are two villages, one of which has neo-colonial houses. Take the road from Valle de Santiago to Huarapo, then turn left at Km 5.5, about 3½ miles (6 km) from town.

YURIRIA: Alongside the lake of the same name, the town has a fortress-like former Augustinian convent dating from around 1570, which is now a national monument. The structure's façade is said to be the most richly ornamented in the country and is often compared with the Convent of Acolmán, on the road to Teotihuacán near Mexico City. The Yuriria lake, with a dam built in 1548 by Fray Diego de Chavez, has swimming, fishing, rowing, and is the site of regattas.

    En Route from Yuriria – You pass through two small villages, Uriangato and Moroleón. Uriangato is famous for its rebozos (shawls), bedspreads, and woolen sweaters. Nearby Moroleón also has excellent woven goods. In making the trip from Morelia to Toluca, it is important to take the longer road, Route 51, to avoid the twisting mountain road (Rte. 15) through the Mil Cumbres. Take Madero Oriente out of Morelia to pick up Route 51. A 2-mile causeway crosses mirror-like Cuitzeo Lake, where fishermen can be seen in dugout canoes.

PÁTZCUARO: The town's name means, in the native Indian tongue, "place of delights"; some say it is because at one time more than 250 species of hummingbirds inhabited the area. Regardless, the town shouldn't be missed. The Tarasco, who founded Pátzcuaro in 1324, developed a rich artisan tradition that continues today, and you'll find beautifully made handicrafts here.

After the Conquest, Pátzcuaro was reestablished in 1540 by Vasco de Quiroga, first bishop of Michoacán and protector of the Tarasco, who brought humane treatment to them after governors like Nuño de Guzmán and Antonio de Mendoza had terrorized them with cruelty and abuses. "Tata" (Daddy) Vasco, as he became affectionately known to his Tarasco followers, set up schools, churches, and the beginnings of a craft industry, which still thrives today. Pátzcuaro consists of two sections: the lakefront, where you can eat fresh whitefish and trout at dockside restaurants; and the town proper, about 2½ miles (4 km) above the lake on a hill. The dockside area is called by two names: the Embarcadero and Muelle General. Proceeds from the minuscule dockside parking fee are used to pay for the clearing of water lilies and other plant growth from Lake Pátzcuaro. From early morning until about 6 PM, boat rides to Janitzio leave about every 30 minutes. If you are energetic, climb to the Morelos statue on top of Janitzio Island, then ascend the spiral staircase, the walls of which are lined with murals depicting the life of independence leader José María Morelos y Pavón. Lake Pátzcuaro fishermen no longer use traditional "butterfly" nets thrown from dugout canoes because better fishing techiques have been adopted, but along the boat route to Janitzio old fishermen will demonstrate for a small tip how the nets are made and how they are manipulated on the lake. Janitzio Island becomes especially colorful during the *Day of the Dead* celebration, which begins on the evening of November 1. Families stage an all-night candlelit vigil at the island's cemeteries, bringing food offerings for the spirits, who return once a year. Although the last boat from Janitzio usually leaves for the mainland around sundown, on this special night the boatmen ply the waters until the early hours of the morning. Check at the dock for the time of the last boat, or hire a private one that will wait for you. There are no hotels on the island. Bring very warm clothes because the temperature drops to near freezing after dark.

Back at the embarcadero (dock) in Pátzcuaro, we recommend that you concentrate on selecting a restaurant rather than on shopping in the proliferation of waterfront handicraft stands. Save your major purchases for the town of Pátzcuaro. Restaurants dockside and in town serve delicious trout and whitefish fried in garlic butter. Pátzcuaro whitefish, the leading local specialty, is famous throughout Mexico. Charales, small, silvery fish that are eaten dried and salted as snacks, like potato chips, run a close second. Inevitably, you'll be serenaded by mariachi groups. You can easily spend an hour here, eating fish and drinking cold beer while you watch the boats on their way to Janitzio. Outside restaurants on the dock, you'll be hounded by numerous little boys offering to be guides around the town. It's a good idea to hire one, for it saves time. To get an overview of the lake and the surrounding countryside, drive up the steep but safe cobblestone road about 2 miles (3 km) southwest of Pátzcuaro to Cerro del Estribo (Stirrup Peak), with its lookout point called Balcón de Tariácuri (Tariácuri's Balcony). On top, there is a pleasant picnic pavilion from which you can see the islands of Janitzio, Jarácuaro, Tecuén, Yunuén, and La Pacanda.

To get to the town of Pátzcuaro from the lake, drive uphill on Calzada de las Américas. The Plaza de San Agustín has neatly kept gardens and a quiet atmosphere. In the center stands a statue of Gertrudis Bocanegra, born of a Spanish father and a Tarasco mother in 1765. Known as the Heroine of Pátzcuaro, Gertrudis was a genuinely liberated woman. She and her husband and their 10-year-old son joined the independence cause in 1810. By 1811, they were helping in the attack on Morelia (then called Valladolid). When her husband and son were killed in combat, Gertrudis continued sending messages from Pátzcuaro to the independence forces; eventually she tried to join the battle herself. Commanders sent her back to Pátzcuaro to study the possibility of an attack and to seduce various royalists to get more information. When the Spanish discovered her purpose, she was tried and sentenced to death; she was executed by a firing squad on October 10, 1817, in the Plaza de San Agustín, where her statue stands. Facing the square is a public library named for her in which one of Juan O'Gorman's finest frescoes depicts the history of the area and the struggles of the Tarasco for land. On Wednesday and Saturday nights, the Los Viejitos dance is performed in the *Posada de Don Vasco* (on Calz. de las Américas). A Pátzcuaro tradition, it is a comical representation by local dancers of the foibles and eccentricities of old age.

The best place to buy handicrafts is the *Casa de los Once Patios* (House of Eleven Patios; half a block from the main plaza on Larín). Here, in the artisans' workshops, 24-karat gold leaf is applied to finely painted plates. You'll see Indian women weaving on the porches. Merchandise includes hammered copper from Santa Clara del Cobre (now called Villa Escalante), black clay pottery from Tzintzuntzan, wood carvings from various nearby towns, straw work, textiles, fine lacquerwork, and sets of furniture and woodwork. It takes several hours to browse through all the shops in the *Casa de los Once Patios.*

VALLE DE BRAVO: At Plan Cutzamala, turn right at the sign for Valle de Bravo/ Avándaro. Continue 20 miles (32 km) to this charming village of cobblestone streets and thatch-roofed houses set into the pine-covered hills surrounding Lake Avándaro, the large, manmade lake that forms part of the vast hydroelectrical system that furnishes electricity to the valley of Mexico.

"Valle," as it is known, is somewhat of an artists' colony and has become a favorite weekend retreat for well-to-do Mexican families. Sunday is market day, and the streets around the plaza become crowded with vendors from surrounding villages who come into town to sell produce and handicrafts, including a distinctive brown pottery, stoneware, and colorfully embroidered textiles. Hang gliding is also popular, and sailing and windsurfing are practiced in the lake. Sailboats and windsurfs are available for rent at some of the clubs around the lake.

Valle has some excellent restaurants: *La Taberna del Léon* (Carr. Panorámica; phone: 726-20573) serves nouvelle cuisine on Fridays, Saturdays, and Sundays only, and the *Vegetariano,* where everyone seems to congregate at one time or another; it's located in the patio of a lovely old home, one-half block from the plaza on Francisco González Bocanegra.

Avándaro, a smart suburb 7½ miles (12 km) west from Valle, receives many weekend visitors. There is an excellent 18-hole golf course and horses at the *Avándaro* motel (see *Best en Route*).

TOLUCA: At 8,712 feet, this city of 350,000 has many clean, quaint 1890s buildings as well as some from the colonial period. It is the capital of the state of México and has a lot of heavy industry. Healthy tax revenues paid by local manufacturing plants have been used for street cleaning and sanitation projects as well as for other public works programs. On Fridays, the great open-air Indian market spreads out around the modern, indoor market, drawing visitors from afar. The state of Mexico is as rich as the neighboring state of Michoacán in native handicrafts and artisan talent. The Friday Toluca market has a wide selection of regional handicrafts, including woolen blankets, *jorongos* or ponchos, thick woven sweaters, pottery from Metepec, colorfully painted furniture from Tenancingo, baskets, lathe-turned kitchen utensils, and more straw hats than you'll ever see — or need — in your life. The old marketplace, an Art Nouveau structure dating from 1909 just off the main plaza, has been turned into botanical gardens and decorated with a cosmovitral (48 spectacular stained glass windows depicting man's relationship to the universe). Closed Mondays. No admission charge. Don't miss the government showrooms called *CASART* (Center for Mexican Handicrafts; 700 Paseo Tollocan Ote.), which specialize in regional handicrafts. The selection includes stoneware pottery, furniture, copper, metalwork, jewelry, silver, woolens, and clay pottery. There are branches in Mexico City, Toluca, Cancún, Tijuana, Teotihuacán, and even the *Zacongo Zoo.* It is 35 miles (56 km) from Toluca to Mexico City on Route 15. In the center of town, a covered colonnade area called *Portal Veinte de Noviembre* has rows of turn-of-the-century iron, brass, and tin candy stands where all kinds of typical candies and local glacé fruits can be bought for pennies. The best restaurant, by far, is the *Real de Oro,* in the *Del Rey Inn* (just at the edge of town on the Mexico-Toluca Hwy.). *Hostería las Ramblas* (107-D Portal Veinte de Noviembre) serves good Mexican dishes inexpensively. The roast turkey in mole sauce is excellent, as are the smoked pork chops.

BEST EN ROUTE

SAN JUAN DEL RÍO

Antigua Hacienda Galindo – By far the most luxurious hotel in the region, this property, built around a remodeled 17th-century hacienda, has 163 units (18 with Jacuzzi and private terrace), 6 tennis courts (3 lighted), horseback riding, pool, and an 18-hole golf course nearby at San Gil. On the highway going into town off Hwy.

57. *Mailing address:* Apdo. 16, c.p. 76800, San Juan del Río (phone: 467-20050; in Mexico City, 5-533-3550 through 53). Expensive.

La Estancia de San Juan – A fine hotel in a 16th-century hacienda, with 108 rooms, 4 clay tennis courts, a large swimming pool, and an 18-hole golf course nearby. There is ample covered parking. About 5 miles (8 km) north of San Juan del Río at Km 172 of the Querétaro Hwy. *Mailing address:* Apdo. 16, c.p. 76800, San Juan del Río (phone: 467-20120 or 467-20155; in Mexico City, 5-514-5721). Inexpensive.

TEQUISQUIAPÁN

Balneario el Relox – Close to mineral hot springs, this 110-room resort has a restaurant with bar service, 4 open-air pools, and 10 covered family pools. 8 Morelos (phone: 467-30006 or 467-30066). Moderate.

Mari Delfi – This small gem is located right on the plaza. The rooms surround a delightful garden. There's a pool and a first class restaurant. On Juárez (phone: 467-30052). Moderate to inexpensive.

Las Cavas Tequisquiapán – The town's newest, this 3-story, colonial-style structure, has 88 rooms, a huge swimming pool, lush gardens, 4 tennis courts, a gameroom, movies, a putting green, volleyball, a restaurant, and a bar. About 1½ miles (2 km) out of town at 8 Calz. de la Media Luna (phone: 467-30804). Inexpensive.

Las Delicias – A well-kept hotel with 23 units, a fair restaurant, 3 spring-fed pools (2 covered), a wading pool, TV room, and lovely gardens. 1 Cinco de Mayo (phone: 467-30180 or 467-30017). Inexpensive.

La Plaza – There are 10 comfortable rooms, a spring-fed pool, satellite television, a restaurant, and a bar. 10 Juárez (phone: 467-30056). Inexpensive.

QUERÉTARO

Mesón de Santa Rosa – Here are 21 suites in a restored colonial hostel with a restaurant and bar. On the main plaza, 17 Plaza de Armas, Pasteur Sur (phone: 463-45781). Expensive.

Real de Minas – The 200 rooms have wall-to-wall carpeting, air conditioning, TV sets, piped-in music, and heating. Facilities include access to an 18-hole golf course, 6 tennis courts, swimming pool, billiards, piano bar, and private dining rooms. 124 Constituyentes Pte., next to the *Plaza de Toros Santa María* (phone: 463-60444). Expensive.

Azteca – A hotel with 44 rooms, plus 3 suites and 4 junior suites. The rooms, decorated in colonial style, are kept immaculately clean. Facilities include a restaurant, handicrafts shop, swimming pool, 2 tennis courts, and gasoline station. There are also 150 spaces for trailers, many with full hookups. About 9 miles (14 km) north of the city on Rte. 57. *Mailing address:* Apdo. 98-C, Querétaro (phone: 463-80076). Expensive to moderate.

Hacienda Jurica – The most elegant accommodations in the area, this country club resort was built around a former 17th-century hacienda. It has 180 rooms, 24 with computers. Facilities include a heated swimming pool, discotheque, restaurants, 2 lighted tennis and squash courts, horseback riding, and access to the *Club de Golf Jurica,* 10 minutes away. At Km 229 of Rte. 57, northwest of Querétaro. *Mailing address:* Apdo. 338, Querétaro (phone: 463-80022). Expensive to moderate.

Holiday Inn Querétaro – This hotel has 171 rooms, 1 master suite, and 3 junior suites. Facilities include air conditioning and heating, a restaurant, cafeteria, lobby bar, pool, TV sets that pick up US channels, miniature golf, and 2 tennis courts.

110 Av. Cinco de Febrero (phone: 463-60202; toll-free from Mexico City, 91-800-90123). Moderate.

Impala – One of the nicer downtown hotels, it features 102 units with TV sets, and restaurant. 1 Zaragoza at Colón (phone: 463-22570). Inexpensive.

DOLORES HIDALGO

Caudillo – This 32-room establishment has a restaurant and bar. 8 Querétaro (phone: 468-20198). Inexpensive.

Posada Cocomacan – In the middle of town, the 40 units here are rustic and clean. The inn has a restaurant. 4 Plaza del Grande Hidalgo (phone: 468-20018). Inexpensive.

IRAPUATO

Flamingo – A well-kept hotel with 65 units, including some junior and master suites, a swimming pool, and a cafeteria open from 7 to 11 AM and 7 to 11 PM. 72 Blvd. Díaz Ordaz (phone: 462-63666). Inexpensive.

Real de Minas – The 75 rooms and suites are comfortably furnished, and the hotel, which has a restaurant and bar, is 1 block north of the main square at 1 Portal Carillo Puerto (phone: 462-62380). Inexpensive.

CELAYA

Celaya Plaza – Its 144 rooms have air conditioning, telephones, and color TV sets. Hotel facilities include a coffee shop, restaurant, bar, disco, tennis court, and pool. Blvd. A. López Mateos Pte. and Carr. Panaméricana (phone: 461-32052). Moderate.

Isabel – This 80-room hotel is closer to the center of town than the *Mary* (below). There is a small charge for use of the garage, and a restaurant is on the premises. 207-C Hidalgo (phone: 461-22095). Inexpensive.

Mary – A good place for drivers, since the covered parking area is locked at night. There are 125 rooms with TV sets, and a good restaurant. It's popular with families traveling the Mexico City–Guadalajara route. On Blvd. Adolfo López Mateos and Zaragoza (phone: 461-20497 or 461-20450). Inexpensive.

MOROLEÓN

Posada Carreta – This 24-room hotel has a swimming pool, restaurant, and bar. At Km 1 of Rte. 43 to Morelia (phone: 466-71090). Moderate.

PÁTZCUARO

Best Western Posada de Don Vasco – The leading hotel in town, this is the site of the Wednesday- and Saturday-night Los Viejitos dance. Facilities include 104 hotel rooms, a 56-site trailer park with full hookups, restaurant, bar, tennis court, heated outdoor swimming pool, billiards, and bowling alley. 450 Calz. de las Américas. *Mailing address:* Apdo. 15, Pátzcuaro (phone: 454-20227). Moderate.

Loto Azul – There are 34 bungalows set in a lovely garden. Pool, restaurant, and 2 tennis courts. Av. Toluca (phone: 726-20796). Moderate.

Los Arcos – About 3 blocks up the hill from the plaza, its 25 rooms are built around an interior patio. Restaurant and pool. Calle Francisco Gonzalez Bocanegra (phone: 726-20042). Inexpensive.

Avándaro – Next to the golf course, this charming motel has 34 elegantly rustic cabins, a pool, restaurant, bar, horseback riding, and 2 tennis courts. Avándaro (phone: 726-20003). Inexpensive.

Cabañas de Tzintzuntán – Basic (but well-maintained) cabins with fireplaces, kitchenettes, and grills; each cabin accommodates up to 5 people. Its location at the edge of the lake makes it a perfect spot for viewing *Day of the Dead* activities. Km 6 Carr. Quiroga-Patzcuáro (phone: for reservations, 454-31003). Inexpensive.

Chalamú – Neat and unpretentious, this motel has 10 units with fireplaces and 4 suites with kitchenettes, overlooking a large garden. There are also 6 RV hookups. At Km 20 of Carr. Quiroga-Pátzcuaro. *Mailing address:* Apdo. 137 (phone: 454-20948). Inexpensive.

Mesón del Cortijo – In a remodeled hacienda, it has 14 rooms with fireplaces, Tarasco Indian decor, and handcrafted furniture. There is also a restaurant and a bar. Beyond the Tanganxhuan traffic circle on Av. Alvaro Obregón. *Mailing address:* Apdo. 402, Pátzcuaro (phone: 454-21295). Inexpensive.

Mesón del Gallo – The rooms are small but comfortable at this very well maintained, colonial-style inn with restaurant and pool. 20 Dr. Coss (phone: 454-21474). Inexpensive.

Misión de San Manuel – A colonial townhouse that's been converted into a plain but cozy 42-unit hotel with restaurant. 12 Portal Aldama (phone: 454-21313). Inexpensive.

Posada de la Basilica – Small colonial inn with modest prices and a good restaurant. At the south end of town. 6 Arciga (phone: 454-21108). Inexpensive.

Posada San Rafael – Another colonial inn, this one has 104 units and a good restaurant. On the main plaza (phone: 454-20770 through 79). Inexpensive.

El Pozo – Set on the shores of Lake Pátzcuaro, the immaculate trailer camp consists of 20 large spaces, and smaller areas set aside for tents. English is spoken. About 2 miles (3 km) east of Pátzcuaro on Rte. 120. *Mailing address:* Apdo. 142, c.p. 61600, Pátzcuaro (phone: 454-20937). Inexpensive.

TOLUCA

Castel Plaza las Fuentes – On the outskirts of the city, about 6 miles (10 km) from downtown, this hotel has 152 rooms, a restaurant, coffee shop, cable television, and heated indoor pool. On the Mexico-Toluca Hwy. (phone: 721-64666). Expensive to moderate.

Del Rey Inn – An excellent hotel with heated indoor pool, playground, outstanding restaurant, video bar, coffee shop, and sauna. Just at the edge of town on the Mexico-Toluca Hwy. (phone: 721-78591/79942/22122). Moderate.

The Vanilla Route: Mexico City to Tampico and Veracruz

One of the most interesting routes in Central Mexico, although one not frequently traveled by tourists, is a circuit from Mexico City through Pachuca, Tampico, Tuxpan, Papantla, and Veracruz. This route, which winds through a variety of terrains, has something for everyone — from mountainous pine country and lush orchid jungles to fine beaches.

From Mexico City the drive takes you to the capital of the state of Hidalgo, Pachuca, which is in the high pine country in the heart of the silver-mining area discovered by the Spanish. The drive continues across an eastern finger of the Sierra Madre, immortalized by B. Traven in *The Treasure of the Sierra Madre,* to Tampico, a colorful port city on the Gulf of Mexico. This turn-of-the-century oil boom town is no longer booming, but its old flavor still lingers; for hunting and fishing enthusiasts, the city and its environs offer game and both salt- and freshwater varieties of fish.

Leaving Tampico and traveling down the coast, you'll come to Tuxpan, a fishing town at the mouth of the Tuxpan River, another good place for angling, swimming, camping, or just relaxing on the fine, hard, sand beaches that stretch out along the gulf.

The route next goes inland a bit to Papantla, center of Mexico's vanilla industry. Papantla is nestled in a rich valley surrounded by lush vanilla orchid jungles, and nearby is El Tajín, the sacred city of the Totonac civilization, and its famous Pyramid of the Niches. Papantla is also the home of the *Los Valadores*, flying pole dancers, who perform their ancient ceremonial dance every Sunday (weather permitting) in the town square and at other times at the nearby ruins of El Tajín.

From Papantla, the route takes you back to the gulf and down to Veracruz along a beautiful stretch of coast road that wanders through picturesque villages and passes the nearby Zempoala (or Cempoala) ruins, part of another great Totonac city dating from the 14th and 15th centuries.

At hotels we classify as expensive along this route, expect to pay $85 to $100 for a double room; $50 to $80 at a moderate place; $25 to $45, inexpensive; and less than $25, very inexpensive.

En Route from Mexico City – Head northeast out of Mexico City on Avenida Insurgentes Norte and pass the Indios Verdes, two bronze Indians, now green with

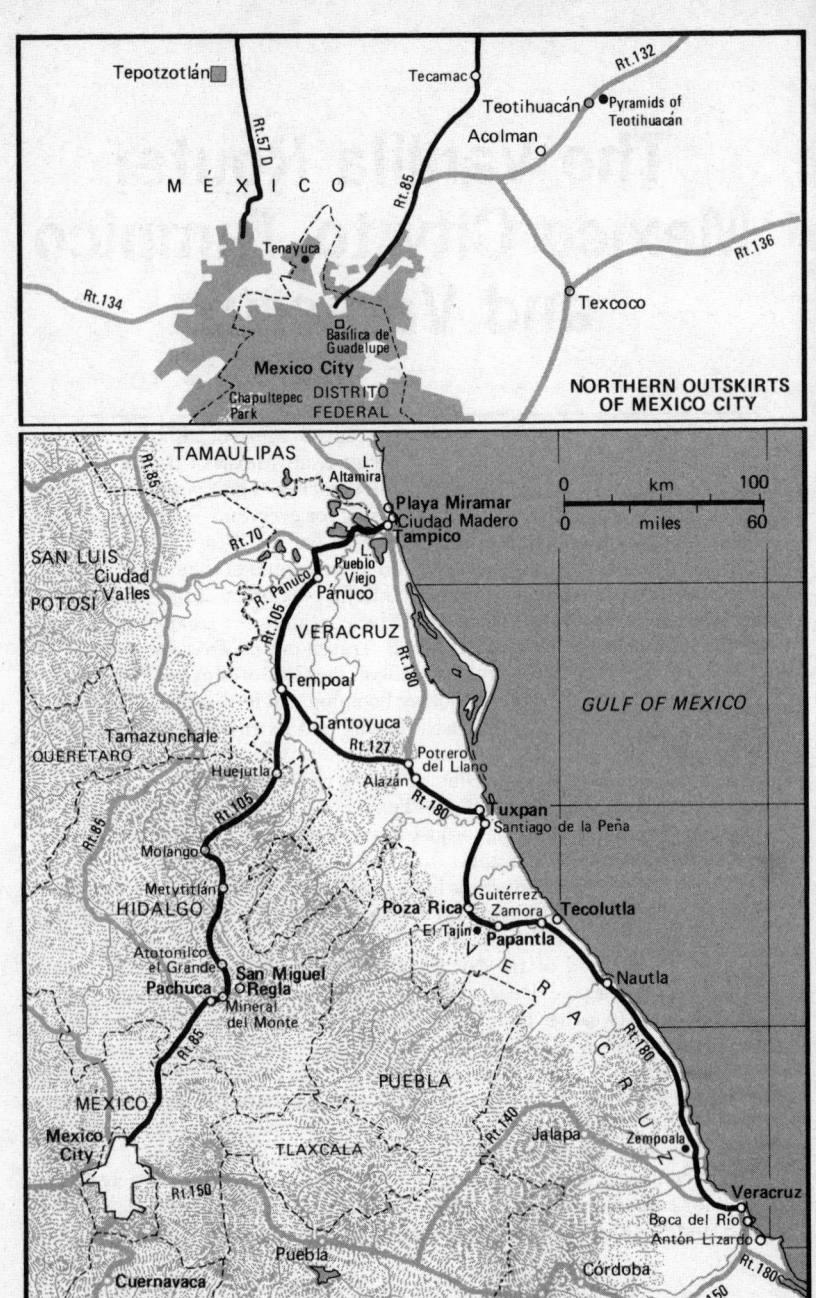

Tepotzotlán

Rt. 57 D

Rt. 132

Tecamac

Rt. 85

Teotihuacán

Pyramids of
Teotihuacán

Acolman

M É X I C O

Rt. 136

Tenayuca

Rt. 134

Texcoco

Basílica de
Guadelupe

Mexico City

Chapultepec
Park

DISTRITO
FEDERAL

NORTHERN OUTSKIRTS
OF MEXICO CITY

TAMAULIPAS

L. Altamira

Rt. 85

Rt. 70

Playa Miramar
Ciudad Madero
Tampico

SAN LUIS

Ciudad
Valles

Pueblo
Viejo

R. Pánuco

Pánuco

POTOSÍ

Rt. 105

VERACRUZ

GULF OF MEXICO

Rt. 180

Tempoal

km

miles

100

60

0

0

Tantoyuca

Rt. 127

Tamazunchale

QUERÉTARO

Huejutla

Potrero
del Llano

Alazán

Rt. 180

Tuxpan

Santiago de la Peña

Rt. 105

Rt. 85

Molango

Metytitlán

HIDALGO

Guitérrez
Zamora

Poza Rica

El Tajín

Tecolutla

Atotonilco
el Grande

San Miguel
Regla

Papantla

Pachuca

Mineral
del Monte

Nautla

V
E
R
A
C
R
U
Z

Rt. 85

Rt. 180

PUEBLA

MÉXICO

Rt. 140

Mexico
City

Jalapa

Zempoala

TLAXCALA

Rt. 150

Veracruz

Boca del Río

Cuernavaca

Antón Lizardo

MORELOS

Puebla

Córdoba

Rt. 180

Orizaba

Rt. 150

age, that stand sentry at the outskirts of the city. Drive over the hill toward the Pachuca toll highway. It is 14½ miles (23 km) from downtown Mexico City to the toll booth where Route 85 starts to Pachuca. After another 10 miles (16 km) you will come to the village of Tecamac on the right fork to Pachuca.

Tecamac has restaurants and tire service but no gas station. On the right-hand side of the road, at the foot of Calle Cinco de Mayo, is the Parroquia de Santa Cruz colonial parish church, with its plateresque three-portal archways at the entrance and on the north side of the churchyard.

Back on the highway, you will pass Tizayuca, which has two gas stations and a bank. The road continues north over a high desert plateau and is lined on either side with joshua trees, smaller than those of southern California's Mojave Desert, but something of a surprise here in the central mesa, so close to Mexico City.

PACHUCA: The capital of the state of Hidalgo, Pachuca (pop. 200,000) lies at an altitude of 8,000 feet. The road into town is lined with massive contemporary bronze statuary that depicts the silver-mining activity that first attracted the Spanish to this area. Pachuca was founded in 1524, on the site of an Otomi and Mexican village that was under the domination of the great Aztec center of Tenochtitlán at the time of the Spanish Conquest. Also on the road into town stands a gigantic statue of revolutionary leader Emiliano Zapata, as well as a Victorian gingerbread house, constructed for a British administrator of the mines. It is one of the few wooden houses you will see in the high valleys of Mexico, where lumber is at a premium and bricks are less expensive. The town still retains its reputation as a major silver producer, supplying approximately 10% to 15% of the world's silver output.

The Compañía Real del Monte y Pachuca, owned and operated by the federal government, controls the principal silver mine in Pachuca, which is honeycombed with 1,240 miles of tunnels through the mountains. Some of these tunnels emerge in vertical shafts at the town of Mineral del Monte, on a mountainside above Pachuca, where, in 1555, Bartolomé de Medina discovered the *patio* process of ore reduction by quicksilver amalgamation. This process greatly reduced the cost of separation and provided the technology that became the basis for massive silver production in the New World.

Inside Pachuca's contemporary Palacio de Gobierno (Government Palace), completed in 1974, is a large, three-paneled fresco presented to the United Nations General Assembly on December 12, 1974, by Luis Echeverría, who was at that time President of Mexico. The slightly surrealistic mural, completed by Pachuca artist Jesús Becerril, depicts the liberation of mankind to be realized by the signing of the Charter of Economic Rights and Duties of Nations. The artist gave some of the delegates the faces of people who actually attended the signing; others are drawn from history. Among the famous faces in the fresco are those of Archbishop Makarios, Pope Paul VI, Fidel Castro, Gerald Ford, Queen Elizabeth II, Indira Gandhi, and Ibn Saud. The mural brings together such diverse historical figures as Columbus, Emperor Cuauhtémoc, Sor Juana Inés de la Cruz, the heroes of Mexican independence, and Benito Juárez, restorer of the republic. Despite these surreal touches and combinations, the mural is essentially realistic, employing brilliant color and symmetry.

History buffs will enjoy the collection of photographs chronicling Mexico's history from the late 19th to the early 20th century that are displayed in the *Archivo Fotográfico Exclaustro, Colección Casasola* (Casasola Archives) in a converted 16th-century Franciscan convent. Closed Mondays. No admission charge.

In the large square between the Palacio de Gobierno and the small, neo-classical replica of the old *Bartolomé de Medina Theater* (now the *Teatro de la Ciudad*) stands a large bronze statue of Benito Juárez sculpted by Juan Leonardo Cordero and dedicated in March 1957. The *Regional History Museum,* in the former Escuela de Minas (Mining School) and former San Francisco convent, has several halls displaying Hidalgo folk arts and photographs.

About 10 miles (16 km) north of Pachuca is El Chico National Park, an *ejidatario*-owned camping spot of unequaled beauty. El Chico may well be the only forest in Mexico where the grass is mowed every week.

Food in Pachuca is ordinary but acceptable. Try *Noriega* (305 Matamoros), which offers a wide range of dishes and serves a particularly good breakfast.

En Route from Pachuca – Leaving Pachuca, head north from Plaza Independencia on Route 105 to Mineral del Monte, where you can see the elevator towers of the mine and one of the main entrances. About 13 miles (22 km) farther along the winding mountain road is the picturesque town of Huasca, and about another 4 miles (6 km) will bring you to San Miguel Regla. If you decide to spend the night in this lovely town you can stay at the *San Miguel Regla* hotel, situated in a pine grove next to the ruins of a colonial silver smelter. This smelter was responsible for the wealth of Pedro Romero de Terreros, founder of the Nacional Monte de Piedad, or National Pawnshop, in Mexico City.

At San Miguel Regla, Route 105 becomes a well-paved mountain road crossing the Sierra, passing through such small towns as Atotonilco el Grande, Metytitlán, and Molango, a mining company town at the site of one of the largest manganese ore deposits in the Western Hemisphere, which are operated by the Compañia Minera Autlán. The road forks at the town of Huejutla. Take a left on Route 105 to Pánuco and Tampico; it joins Route 127 about 32 miles (52 km) past Huejutla. Here you take a left to Tempoal and then proceed downhill to Pánuco and into Tampico. Along the way you'll see oil wells still operating in what were the very first oil fields of Mexico, vividly described by B. Traven in the opening chapters of *The Treasure of the Sierra Madre. A caveat:* Don't drive the Pachuca-Tampico stretch of Route 105 at night, when there are often heavy fogs or rain. It's a good idea to lay over at Pachuca or in San Miguel Regla instead.

TAMPICO: The largest city in the state of Tamaulipas, Tampico has a population of over 500,000. On the north bank near the mouth of Río Pánuco at an altitude of 33 feet, it is a busy Gulf of Mexico port and petroleum-refining center. The town enjoyed a boom at the turn of the century when oil was discovered in the region, but the international flavor of those days is largely gone. Nonetheless, there are remnants of its atmosphere, and for those willing to dig a bit beneath the somewhat commercial surface of life here, Tampico still offers a variety of things to do and see. A car, incidentally, is a great help for sightseeing.

Near Tampico are freshwater lagoons — Laguna del Chairel and Laguna del Carpintero are particularly good. Although deep-sea fishing and freshwater fishing in the lagoons are both recommended, fishing from the shore in the gulf is not, because of choppy and not-so-clean waters. Hunting is also popular here with available game including quail, turkey, duck, geese, white wing dove, rabbit, coyote, deer, wild boar, and mountain lion. Playa Miramar, northeast of the city, is an unusually long stretch of beach where one can sun or swim. You'll find golf courses nearby, too.

Tampico was founded in 1533 on the site of a Huastec settlement that was destroyed by the forces of Cortés in 1523. Fray Andrés de Olmos established a small mission church here a few years later, but it was shortly destroyed by the elements. In 1560 a Franciscan monastery was completed and the town became known as San Luis de Tampico. The oldest buildings in modern Tampico date from only the late 19th century, however. Earlier structures fell victim to the periodic hurricanes and flooding of Río Pánuco, which has been known to rise 15 feet or more above its normal level. Weather conditions in Tampico are erratic at best. Strong afternoon winds often blow off the river. The hot, humid season begins in April and reaches its height in July and August, with rains bringing some relief in September. During this period, it's advisable to check into an air conditioned hotel or go off to Miramar Beach.

The hurricane season begins in November and sometimes extends through December, January, and part of February. Characteristic of Gulf of Mexico ports, these strong, cold winds last anywhere from a day to a week.

Heavy rains, sometimes arriving as early as July and August, threaten the entire northeastern corner of Mexico with widespread flooding.

Most of the nighttime action and port atmosphere for which Tampico is famous occurs around the Plaza de la Libertad, a block from the waterfront. The plaza is bordered by Calles Madero, Rivera (sometimes Ribera on street signs), Juárez, and Aduana.

The *Bar and Saloon Palacio* (401 Ribera Ote.) faces the plaza and is the kind of place Tennessee Williams and Ernest Hemingway would have frequented (not, one hopes, on the same evening). In the corner of a sky blue turn-of-the-century hotel (now closed), the saloon features a dozen round, Formica-topped tables that seat eight people each. The coral-cushioned metal chairs are modern gauche, but the tables are large enough to set up an "office" and read several newspapers, if you happen to be in Tampico on business.

Women (as long as they're tourists) are occasionally allowed in the saloon if the owner has bribed local authorities, but there are tables and chairs on the wide porch facing on Calle Rivera, where a mixed group can get courteous service. There is even a women's restroom in the saloon, but it should be avoided unless it's absolutely necessary. In the mornings the swinging front doors are held open with jute strings so that people outside can observe the action inside the saloon without going in.

Tampico bars are the haunts of wandering vendors. Sitting with a glass of Superior light beer, you can watch an extraordinary parade pass by. The following roster is typical Tampico: a man selling ballpoint pens and Bic lighters; a short fellow from Veracruz in regional dress displaying embroidered kerchiefs made by Totonac women, and a wood carving of the eagle and serpent that appear on the Great Seal of the United States of Mexico; a boy selling lottery tickets for the Friday night drawing; a newsboy hawking *El Sol de Tampico* and *El Mundo;* a shoeshine boy; and a gold-toothed young man in the white pajama dress of the Totonac selling weird, scorpion-shaped figures fashioned from stalks of vanilla bean. In the afternoon and evening, things liven up. Habitués are often serenaded by a vocalist accompanied by wandering guitar, accordion, and saxophone players.

If you're in the mood for something non-alcoholic, *El Globito,* on the Plaza de Armas, is a stand-up place that offers root beer and the juice of fresh oranges, carrots, strawberries, or anything else that happens to be in season and can fit in a blender.

Walk south on Fray Andrés de Olmos past the *Inglaterra* hotel to Calle Rivera, where the street dips down toward the riverbank. This short section of the street, as steep as any in San Francisco, California, is lined with stands selling a wide range of shiny merchandise: flashlights and batteries, pocket mirrors, knives, imitation Zippo lighters, and a host of toiletries, cosmetics, and portable radios, many of them made in Hong Kong and Japan.

At Calle Pedro Méndez you will come upon the beginning of the public market, which sprawls across a full city block and spills into the adjacent streets. This is the place to choose from all manner of fresh produce, including the huge, beautiful avocados grown in Tamaulipas and northern Veracruz.

Tampico's market area still retains some of the flavor of older and better days. Venerable buildings with artificial balconies and cast-iron grillework line Calle Pedro Méndez, and this area, along with the closed hotels along the Plaza de la Libertad, gives Tampico some of the flavor of old New Orleans.

North of the market, beneath the portals of Calle Rivera, you will come upon the desks of the public scribes who, for a fee, help the illiterate and the poor write letters, fill out tax forms, or complete documents. These scribes are known as *evangelistas* and are as adept at composing a florid love letter as they are at executing a tax form.

Going east from the market past the long, Victorian customs house brings you to the railroad station, a fake mission-style monstrosity with blue, yellow, and green talavera tiles set in the lower inside walls. Handsome wrought-iron gates are on the passenger platforms, and steel signs above the arches announce trains to Monterrey, San Luis Potosí, and Magosal. An iron bell is still rung by hand to announce the departure of trains. The telegraph office in the station (for railroad use only) still uses ancient equipment; it's worth a look for antique buffs. There are reminders of the great flood of October 1955 on the walls of the waiting room and in the telegraph office, where the water left marks 8 feet high.

Tampico's port activity is run by the stevedores' union. Freight is hauled out of the long custom house on small dock trains with five cars. If you go down to the wharves (tourists are welcome here) you will find ships from the Soviet Union, Poland, and South America as well as Mexican freighters.

Tampico's main square is the Plaza de Armas, which is bordered by Calles Emiliano Carranza, Díaz Mirón, Colón, and Fray Andrés de Olmos. The plaza is a peaceful park shaded by slim palms, Oriental elms, and other trees and enlivened by squirrels, ravens, and pigeons, who frolic on the lawns and search the wide-bladed tropical grass for tasty tidbits. There is a bandstand in the center of the plaza called the Tampico Monumental Kiosk. This pink concrete curiosity of Moorish extraction (twisted candy cane columns on the inside and blue and yellow mosaic on the dome, which is supported by eight enormous and totally inappropriate flying buttresses) was dedicated in 1945. The kiosk is the focal point of carnivals, which are usually held in the first two weeks of February, and the plaza itself serves, as it does in most provincial towns, as Tampico's social center.

The Tampico cathedral was constructed in 1931 on the north side of the plaza, as is customary. It was built with funds donated by Edward L. Doheny and his wife. Doheny, the California oil tycoon who was linked with the Teapot Dome scandal of 1923–24, had extensive oil interests in the Tampico region until the expropriation of foreign holdings in 1938. The inside of the cathedral is essentially West Los Angeles Gothic. The center aisle of the terrazzo floor, built by a Monterrey contractor, carries a startling swastika motif. There is a working pipe organ in the choir loft, the high central dome sits on an octagonal base, and the walls are lined with rather pedestrian oil paintings depicting the Stations of the Cross.

The restaurants in the downtown area have some of the best and freshest seafood in Mexico. The crab (*jaiba*) is king. Indeed, *tampiqueños* are known throughout Mexico as *jaibas,* a reflection on their food, not their temperaments, for the people of Tampico are especially friendly to foreigners, particularly visitors from the United States, who, after all, have been in Tampico since oil was discovered at the turn of the century. Curiously, most longtime Tampico residents conclude agreements or business deals by announcing, "All right!"

Tampico's luxury restaurants are in the hotels and motels of the city and along Avenida Hidalgo near the Camino Real. Some of the best dining, however, and the most reasonable prices are to be found at the modestly decorated restaurants in the downtown area, where the emphasis is on food rather than ambience.

One of the best seafood houses in Tampico is the *Mariscos Diligencia,* in a high-ceilinged 19th-century building (at 415 Ribera Ote., on the corner of Calle César López de Lara, 2 blocks from Plaza de la Libertad). This restaurant, patronized by local families on Sundays, also specializes in inexpensive food. The front of the restaurant is kept cool by ventilator fans; if the weather is really hot you might opt for the rear section, which is air conditioned. Start with oysters on the half shell or raw crab and go on to a shellfish plate called *fuente de mariscos frescos,* or, if you've had enough seafood for the time being, try *carne a la Tampiqueña*, Tampico's famous spicy broiled beef dish. Other offerings are clams, oysters, crabmeat cocktail, marinated trout, hot bell peppers stuffed with crabmeat, and octopus in brine with rice. The best accompaniment for these dishes is beer — either a bottle of Superior or Bohemia or a can of Tecate, which natives drink straight from the can after sprinkling salt on the top and then squeezing lime juice over the salt. Try it — the resulting mélange of flavors is the perfect complement to seafood. They have a second restaurant, *Diligencias Norte* (on Av. Ayuntamiento). Another downtown restaurant, *Café y Nevería Elite* (211 Díaz Mirón Ote.), offers inexpensive specialties, including a *comida corrida* (mixed platter) at lunchtime, from noon to 4 PM. This is a good place for breakfast or dinner, too, and the menu, in English and Spanish, includes hotcakes and waffles with bacon, hamburgers with onion rings, grilled beef tenderloin tips, small T-bone steaks, haddock chops fried in garlic sauce, stuffed crabs, assorted seafood plates, and broiled meat Tampico-style. There is "American" coffee, espresso, and cappuccino as well as sherbets and ice cream. Local folk consider *Jardín Corona* (1915 Av. Miguel Hidalgo) to be the city's finest, serving seafood, steaks, and its own special *Tampiqueñia*, a spicy broiled beef dish.

While you're downtown, you might stop at *El Porvenir* for a drink and a look at the owner's collection of antique bottles. The owner also runs a family-style restaurant next door, at 1403 Hidalgo.

Tampico has a real museum, too. The *Museum of the Huastec Culture* is on the grounds of the Technological Institute of Ciudad Madero, where you can see its modest collection of pre-Columbian artifacts, culled from the area around Tampico, Soto la Marina, and other nearby regions of Huastec influence. Be sure to see the female figurine, articulated in bone, from the Pánuco III period (AD 200–700). Closed Sundays.

For collectors, downtown Tampico is the place to browse. *Bazar Numismático y Filatélico* (201 Fray Andrés de Olmos Nte.) is run by Abelardo Sánchez Sr. and Jr. and carries a rather limited selection of old clocks, telephones, ceramics, stamps, and coins as well as some bills issued by the Shanghai Bank of Communications in 1914 and 1935. If you're interested in chinoiserie, the *Chung King* (507 Emiliano Carranza Oriente, in the *Tampico*) has a good assortment of Chinese porcelain, as well as canned goods from Hong Kong, Taiwan, and the Chinese mainland.

When you've had enough sightseeing, there's still plenty to do in the area around Tampico. If the weather is hot, cool off at Playa Miramar, a beach only 10 minutes by car from Tampico. Drive east on Avenida Alvaro Obregón through Tampico's twin city, Ciudad Madero, and out past the Petróleos Mexicanos oil refinery, one of the country's three largest refineries. The left fork of the road approaching the beach leads north through a pine grove to a place called Pinar del Mar, where you can put up at the *Centro Recreativo,* a small seaside hotel little known to foreign tourists.

To get to the beach itself, take the right fork rather than the left one, which leads to the hotel. Here are several miles of sandy beach lapped by the placid surf of the Gulf of Mexico. The water is shallow and fine for swimming, miraculously unpolluted by the nearby Ciudad Madero refinery. Unfortunately, waste from the refinery has tainted the last section of Río Pánuco, but it is separated from the beach by a long jetty.

If you have a recreational vehicle, this is an ideal spot for camping. Separate toilet and shower facilities are available at intervals across the paved access road.

For hunting and fishing enthusiasts, Tampico's freshwater lagoons offer plentiful fish and game. The larger hotels will arrange trips for you, but it's best to consult the tourist office (101 Plaza de Armas at Olmos Sur Altos; phone: 12-122668 or 12-120007). Information about sport fishing (no license is required, except for a fishing vessel), can be obtained at the fisheries offices at 407 Carranza (phone: 12-122751) or 310 López Rayón and Avila Camacho (phone: 12-135737 or 12-133873). The best place to purchase ammunition is at Ciudad Reynosa, on the border across from Hidalgo and McAllen, Texas.

The different hunting seasons in the area around Tampico include: white-tailed deer, early December through early January (special permit required); duck, late October through mid-February; quail, late October through mid-February; coyotes, early December through January; white-wing doves, mid-August through mid-November; geese, late October through February; rabbits, mid-August through March. There are quail and deer in the Altamira Lagoon. There is good duck hunting in the Escondida, Jancal, and Pueblo Viejo lagoons. The Chila Lagoon is a good place for duck, coyotes, and deer.

Sadly, the game in Tampico's lagoons has been decimated over the years by petroleum exploitation, petrochemical and ore processing plants, and other industrial activity, but the area still holds considerable attraction for the sportsman. Many Texan enthusiasts make several trips a year. Local trip organizers and guides have the latest information on where to find the kind of game you are interested in, and hunters should be sure to get a copy of the free, pocket-size regulation manual, the *Calendario Cinegético,* published by the Dirección General de la Fauna Silvestre (the Mexican Bureau of Wildlife). Note that the regulations prohibit the use of motor vehicles (including boats with motors) for hunting any species of wildlife by land, air, or water, except in authorized cases.

For anglers, there is deep-sea fishing in the Gulf of Mexico for tarpon, white sea bass, sailfish, and mackerel, among others. Freshwater varieties — shad, porgies, catfish, and trout — can be taken on the Río Pánuco and in the surrounding lagoons. North of Tampico, at the mouth of the Río Soto la Marina, Italian investors are developing a sportsmen's resort area, where saltwater, river, and lagoon fishing offers white sea bass, trout, saurels (yellow jack), corbinas, and porgies.

En Route from Tampico – The next stop on this circuit is Tuxpan, 110 miles (177 km) south, and there are two possible routes from Tampico. One is Route 180, which runs close to the coast, but doesn't provide much in the way of scenery. More interesting is the trip covered by Route 105 and 127, which brought you into Tampico from Pachuca. The stretch from Tempoal (where you leave Rte. 105 for Rte. 127) is paved but has been beaten out of shape by the hundreds of oil trucks that pass through. The scenery is well worth the bumps; you will pass through the rich farm country of northern Veracruz state, past Tantoyuca, with its hillside houses, and on to Potrero del Llano (also called Alazán), where Route 127 joins Route 180. If you are driving on a winter's day, you will see farm girls at their roadside stands selling grapefruit and tangerines on strings as well as pineapples and honey at ridiculously low prices.

TUXPAN: Also spelled Tuxpam by traditionalists, this clean, pretty riverbank fishing town with a population of 120,000 and an altitude of 10 feet is a good place to fish, swim, or just enjoy the atmosphere of this lazy, romantic old port, now the home of a container service that makes five monthly sailings to Houston. The *embarcadero,* or dock, is on the main street as you enter town, on the north bank of Río Tuxpan.

On the other side of the river is a working class residential area called Santiago de la Peña. The local people pay a small charge to go back and forth across the river in small boats rather than make the long walk downriver to the bridge. The boats, some with outboard motors, will take up to eight people across the river and can also be hired for excursions.

Pre-*Lenten Carnaval* is a big event here, and at the end of June Mexicans and foreigners alike crowd into town for the annual tarpon-fishing tournament. Every August there is an agricultural and livestock exposition. About 7 miles (12 km) east of town is a long stretch of beautiful, hard sand beach, with shower and dressing rooms.

The inexpensive *Reforma* restaurant (in the hotel of the same name, at 25 Benito Juárez) has shrimp salad with mayonnaise made with two kinds of shrimps: small ones, taken from nearby lagoons, and the larger, deep-sea variety. The lagoon shrimps are exceptionally tasty. For a special treat try *hueva de lisa* (river fish roe), which is served in thick bars, sliced and fried in butter, then sprinkled with Mexican hot sauce. It's delicious but very salty. The restaurant also serves *hueva de lisa* in an omelette. *Villa Tamiahua* (134 Independencia), *Las Palmas* (Independencia, next to the bridge, and *Los Coquitos* (Carr. a la Playa) are also good choices for seafood. *Trendy Fisher's* (Calle Hernandez on the *malecón*) serves rich seafood casseroles, as well as meat and chicken dishes in an air conditioned dining room and on an outdoor patio.

En Route from Tuxpan – Head south on Route 180 for about 50 miles (80 km) to Papantla, and you'll pass through Poza Rica, a grimy oil-refining town with no visible attractions. If you must stop here overnight, the *Salinas* hotel is comfortable, and the *Poza Rica* hotel provides inexpensive rooms (see *Best en Route*).

PAPANTLA: Another 13 miles (21 km) will bring you to Papantla (pop. ca. 130,000; alt. 983 feet). Nestled in a rich mountain valley, the city spreads out on both sides of Route 180 and is surrounded by lush jungles fragrant with the aroma of the vanilla orchid. This is the center of Mexico's vanilla industry, and Papantla is now one of the world's largest producers of this important flavoring substance. The Totonac Indians, descendants of the great pre-Hispanic civilization, have become relatively wealthy because of the vanilla industry, and their cultural heritage has been maintained in ceremonies like the beautiful *voladores,* or flying pole dance. El Tajín, the sacred city of their ancestors, is nearby.

As you enter Papantla from the north you will see a gingerbread Gothic church, like something from a European fairy tale, perched on the side of the hill on your left. This twin-spired edifice, with its vaulted ceiling, is the Sanctuary of Christ the King, and boasts more than two dozen brilliant stained glass windows as well as tropical hardwood doors carved in high relief.

The flying pole dance is one of the most spectacular ceremonial displays in Mexico. Originally the dance was performed only on the weekends preceding *Corpus Christi Day,* a Catholic holiday that falls in May or June. Like so many other folkloric customs, the Christian holiday provided a convenient time to celebrate something more earthy — the annual vanilla harvest, on which the Totonac depended, and still depend, for their livelihood. The dance is now performed every Sunday (if the weather is good) at the ruins. In past times, the Totonac made a ritual of searching the jungle for a straight, tall tree, but in recent years technology has reared its head, and the pole is now made of steel — more durable, if less romantic. In *Treasury of Mexican Folkways,* Frances Toor describes this dance as "the most thrilling and beautiful of all." The four dancers, dressed in red, with headdresses of eagles or macaws, dance their way to the pole led by a musician playing a flute, a drum, or both. The dancers climb to their places on the frame at the top of the pole followed by the musician, who sits on a small drum platform.

After the musician has played a melody in homage to the East, West, North, and South, the dancers let their bodies fall backward, and the ropes with which they are bound begin to unwind, leaving them free to fly around the pole in circles, arms extended. They fly around the pole 13 times, to represent the 4 epochs of 13 years that made up the ancient Totonac life cycle of 52 years.

The ancestors of the present-day Totonac built the sacred city of El Tajín, about 5½ miles (9 km) southwest of Papantla on a mostly paved road.

The ruins here are believed to be from the height of the Totonac culture, around AD 800, although some archaeologists believe an earlier tribe built the site during the 5th or 6th century. The city is now divided into old and new sections. The old section is the site of the famous six-stepped Pyramid of the Niches, with its 365 niches marking each day of the year, and overhanging eaves. The ruins are only partially excavated, and the encroaching jungle adds to the charm and mystery of the site. Open daily from 9 AM to 5 PM.

Known for their beautiful clothing — both ceremonial garb and everyday wear — Totonac men wear long, full pants that tie at the ankle. These "pantaloons" are both picturesque and practical, for the jungle abounds in chiggers. When you visit El Tajín, you should take care to wear long pants with narrow cuffs or tie the bottoms, Totonac-style. If you stick to roads, paths, and fully cleared areas, you ought to be able to avoid these maddening little insects.

The Totonac are also known as Mexico's only polygamous tribe. The wealthier men keep up to five wives, and in some cases a young boy, to sate their sexual appetites. In addition, the Totonac Indians produce some of the most realistic ceremonial masks in the country. Covered with a thin coating of plaster and painted in lifelike tones, these masks are beautiful, especially when compared with mostly rough masks you'll find in Mexico City.

On either side of Route 180 in Papantla there are stores selling animal figures, baskets, and other aromatic and decorative items woven from the long pods of the vanilla bean. Packaged in cellophane and sold in tin boxes, these are often used as sachets in closets and bureau drawers. Also on sale are coffee liqueurs and a cream of vanilla liqueur.

En Route from Papantla – Head southeast to the turnoff to Guitérrez Zamora and Tecolutla, a distance of about 19 miles (30 km). The vanilla is processed in Guitérrez, and liqueurs are produced there. Route 180 now leads back to the coast through prosperous-looking citrus groves and banana and coconut plantations visible from the road. In Tecolutla, stay right on the beach at the *Balneario Tecolutla* or the *Flamingo* before traveling on to Veracruz (see *Best en Route*). From here to journey's end in Veracruz 135 miles (217 km) south, the highway runs right along the Gulf of Mexico, where sandbars create lagoons of shallow water and small, placid waves. Even in the winter (if it isn't norther season), the warm breeze that blows shoreward off the water often tempts people to roll up their trousers and wade, or even go for a moonlight swim. This beautiful stretch of coast is dotted with small hotels and motor courts. The busy season is *Easter Week,* the months of May, July, August, and December, and the mid-September *Independence Day* holiday. Most of these places are open all year.

About 29 miles (40 km) south of Palma Sola, on a turnoff to the right, are the Zempoala ruins, the remains of another great Totonac city that was built much later than El Tajín, in the 14th and 15th centuries. Here were pyramids and several temples, among them one that resembles the Temple of the Sun in the ancient Aztec city of Tenochtitlán. About 52 miles (84 km) south of Nautla, you will pass the controversial Laguna Verde nuclear power plant.

VERACRUZ: For a complete report on the city, its hotels and restaurants, see *Veracruz,* THE CITIES.

BEST EN ROUTE

PACHUCA

Calinda Pachuca – Pachuca's finest, this modern, 2-story hotel and country club is set in a beautiful garden and is yet undiscovered by tourists. Restaurant, bar, a thermal pool, tennis court, and a 9-hole golf course. Km 8.5 Carr. Mexico-Pachuca (phone: 771-39911). Expensive to moderate.

Emily – Bright 30-room hostelry with large rooms. Calle Hidalgo, facing Plaza Independencia (phone: 771-26517/18). Inexpensive to very inexpensive.

De los Baños – An older but well-kept hotel with the 62 rooms furnished in either traditional Spanish or a more modern style. 205 Matamoros (phone: 771-30700 or 771-30701). Very inexpensive.

SAN MIGUEL REGLA

Hacienda San Miguel Regla – Picturesquely situated in a pine grove next to the ruins of a colonial silver smelter, this rather exclusive hotel has 53 rooms and bungalows. There is hiking, horseback riding, and trout fishing right outside the entrance, and nearby are pools from the old refinery and a waterfall. Just outside town (phone: dial international operator and request operator 02 in the town of San Miguel Regla). Expensive.

TAMPICO

Camino Real Tampico – In downtown Tampico, this luxury hotel has 100 rooms surrounding a courtyard with a large L-shaped pool. *El Flamboyan* restaurant is Tampico's fanciest, and there's a bar and a cafeteria. Meeting rooms are available for between 15 and 300 persons. Parking is free and golf facilities are available at *Club Campestre Laguna del Chairel.* 2000 Av. Hidalgo (phone: 12-138811; 5-214768 or 5-103398 in Mexico City). Expensive.

Posada de Tampico – Formerly the *Holiday Inn Tampico,* this luxury hotel is 6 ½ miles (10 km) from downtown and 1 mile from Tampico Airport. There are 130 air conditioned, fully carpeted rooms with 2 double beds and a television set. There are also 4 junior suites and 1 presidential suite, and meeting rooms for up to 300 people. Other facilities include a swimming pool with *La Palapa* bar, *Salón Tamaulipeco,* a nightclub featuring dance music and international entertainment, *Laguna del Chairel* restaurant, and *El Jaguar* bar. The hotel will arrange hunting, fishing, golf, tennis. On Rte. 80 (an extension of Av. Hidalgo) to Ciudad Mante (phone: 12-280515). Expensive.

Inglaterra – A downtown hotel, it has 130 rooms and suites, all carpeted. The rooms have air conditioning with individual control, TV sets, and piped-in music. Other features are parking, a heliport atop the hotel, and a ballroom that has a 250-person capacity and offers the best view of the city. There is a good restaurant (which will pack a picnic lunch) and a lobby bar called *La Onda* (The Wave). 116 Salvador Díaz Mirón Ote., corner of Fray Andrés de Olmos (phone: 12-125678). Expensive to moderate.

Centro Recreativo – About 10 minutes by car from Tampico at Pinar del Mar, this small, seaside hotel, little known to foreign tourists, is owned and operated by Section One of the Petroleum Workers' Union of the Mexican Republic. Though a billboard at the turn-off carries a message about the socialist revolution, this hotel is run strictly on capitalist principles and caters primarily to the lower middle class. There are 16 rooms and 2 bungalows available to the general public. Foreign tourists are welcome. Basketball courts and baseball playing fields are nearby, and there is a freshwater swimming pool with showers. There is also a vegetarian spa offering weight-reduction programs, and the like, with homeopathic physicians in residence. The hotel's summer season runs from March through November; the winter season lasts from December through February. *Mailing address:* Apdo. Postal 10, c.p. 89600, Ciudad Madero, Tamaulipas (phone: Petroleum Workers' Union, 12-150302). Moderate.

Imperial – Not a luxury hotel, but decent accommodations. 94 units, some air conditioned. 101 Cesar López de Lara and Carranza (phone: 12-141363). Moderate.

Impala – Here is a modern, 83-unit hotel with air conditioning, restaurant-bar, TV sets with US channels, and parking. On 220 Salvador Díaz Miron Pte. (phone: 12-120990). Inexpensive.

TUXPAN

El Tajín – Near Tuxpan on the shores of the Pánuco River and 45 minutes from the Poza Rica airport, it has 163 air conditioned rooms, suites, and villas with color TV sets; restaurant and bar (phone: 783-42260). Moderate to inexpensive.

Plaza – There are 57 rooms, including 3 suites, 6 triples, and 3 "matrimonial" suites, in downtown Tuxpan. Facilities include air conditioning, color TV sets, and a small restaurant. 39 Av. Benito Juárez (phone: 783-40838 or 783-40738). Inexpensive.

Los Mangos – Offers 34 units (8 air conditioned, the rest with fans), as well as a restaurant, gardens, and pool. 100 Av. Independencia (phone: 783-40220). Very inexpensive.

Reforma – A traditional, turn-of-the-century hotel, most of its 98 rooms and suites are air conditioned. A restaurant adjoins the hotel. 25 Benito Juárez (phone: 783-40210 or 783-40625). Very inexpensive.

POZA RICA

Poza Rica – With 76 air conditioned rooms and a restaurant, this is a good choice downtown. Av. Dos Nte. and Av. Diez Ote. (phone: 782-20112). Very inexpensive.

Salinas – The best hotel downtown, it has 210 air conditioned rooms with TV sets, also a restaurant and pool. 1000 Blvd. Ruiz Cortines (phone: 782-30066). Very inexpensive.

PAPANTLA

El Tajín – Colorful 60-room hostelry perched on a hill. There is a restaurant and bar. 104 Calle Dr. José de Jesús Núñez y Domínguez (phone: 784-21062). Inexpensive to very inexpensive.

TECOLUTLA

Flamingo – A 64-unit hotel on the beach with a restaurant and a bar (phone: 784-50930). Moderate to inexpensive.

Totacapan – Modest, with small, clean, comfortable rooms. Just off the plaza at Calle Olivio and Calle 20 de Noviembre (phone: 784-21220). Moderate to inexpensive.

Balneario Tecolutla – A beach hotel with 72 rooms, restaurant, bar, billiards, and a freshwater swimming pool. At the end of the road turning off Rte. 180 to Guitérrez Zamora and Tecolutla (phone: 784-50901). Inexpensive to very inexpensive.

Marsol – On the beachfront, this white, 3-story property has spacious, fan-cooled rooms and sea views. Calle Aumas (phone: 784-50967). Very inexpensive.

The Yucatán Peninsula

The Yucatán Peninsula encompasses the three Mexican states — Yucatán, Campeche, and Quintana Roo — that jut into the Gulf of Mexico where it joins the Caribbean Sea, giving the peninsula coasts on both waters. Most famous for the magnificent Maya ruins at Chichén Itzá, the Yucatán also has a walled city that could have come right out of a late show pirate movie, outposts of an empire that novelist Graham Greene might have invented, and some of the most enchanting resorts in the entire Caribbean. The highways that loop the entire peninsula and eliminate the need to double back at any point make driving not only easy but a pleasure. Something new always lies ahead. The trip can be completed in 4 easy days of driving, seldom with more than 6 hours spent on the road in any one given day. But there's so much to see that for an in-depth look, even a week is not enough.

The three states on the peninsula in many ways comprise a country within a country. While the mainland is made up of hills, forests, and deserts originally settled by the Aztec, the peninsula consists of the flat jungles of the Maya. About the size of Arizona, the peninsula was isolated from the rest of Mexico for centuries. Mainland Mexicans may joke about the Yucatán as a "sister republic," but several times in the course of its history the peninsula has in fact almost become a separate state. During the 19th century especially, there were more than a few efforts at secession. When these failed, the Yucatecans responded by and large by simply ignoring the government of Mexico City, pretending as best they could that it didn't exist.

Expect to pay $110 and up for a double room in hotels we list along this route as very expensive; $75 to $105 at expensive places; $40 to $70, moderate; and $35 or less for inexpensive.

The Maya came from Central America to settle in the Yucatán about 500 BC, around the same time that the ancient Greek civilization was flourishing. The Maya, in fact, had more in common with the Greeks than just contemporaneity. Like the Greeks', theirs was a civilization more intellectual than political; and like the Greeks, they never managed to form any kind of unified national political organization. Each Maya city was a little kingdom unto itself. And for some reason as yet undiscovered, one after another the great cities of the Maya — really ceremonial centers — were abandoned. Though a number of theories have been put forward to try to explain this, no one really knows why. Just about the time the Normans were conquering England, in the 11th century, the Toltec conquered the Maya. The Toltec were from central Mexico and had a culture similar in many ways to that of the Aztec, who became the most successful and powerful tribe in pre-Spain Mexico.

Two large mysteries remain unexplained about the Maya before the Toltec invasion: why they moved from Central America into the Yucatán Peninsula in the first place, and why they periodically abandoned the magnificent cere-

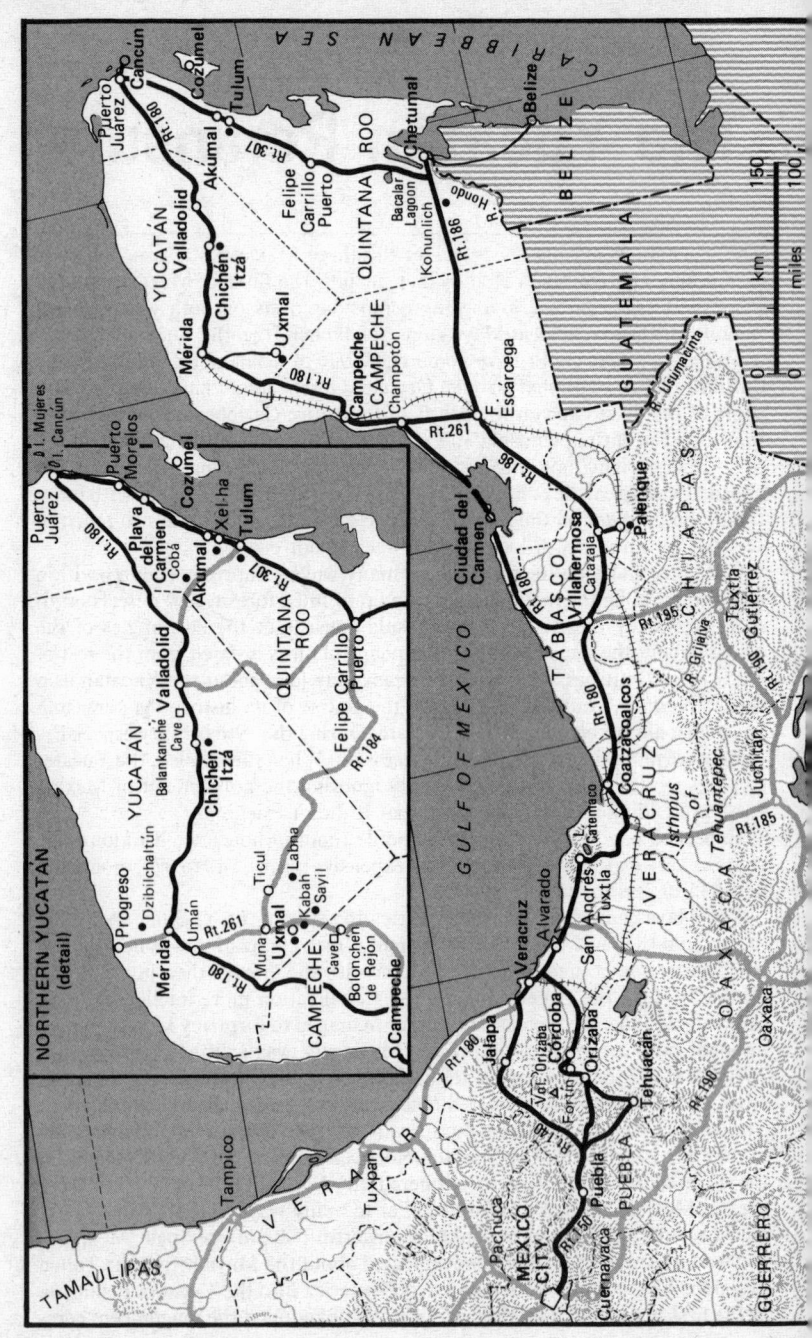

monial cities they built at various sites around the jungle peninsula. Some scientists speculate that the Maya of long ago, like their descendants, decimated the rain forests around the sites for the short-term gain of corn and bean crops. After about 3 years of cultivation, there is a large drop in corn production, so new forests are burned and cleared for agricultural production. Another theory holds that a prolonged drought could have prompted the Maya to move to the peninsula.

The true explanation as to why the Maya moved from Central America is most likely buried in the glyphs (pictographs etched into stone) found at Chichén Itzá and other ruins, but these have not been fully deciphered. It's thought that the long messages carved into the giant ruins contain information about the Maya god-kings' ancestors, their lives and deaths, rituals and relationships. The spoken language of the Maya, on the other hand, is very much alive. The chatter in any market in the Yucatán is more likely to be in Maya than in Spanish.

The Toltec invaded the Yucatán after they had been driven out of the central highlands near the Valley of Mexico, where the Aztec, that roaming and warlike group of Indians, eventually settled. The Toltec brought to the Yucatán the worship of the plumed serpent, Quetzalcóatl, whom the Maya called Kukulkán. The serpent was the symbol of a god whose other identities included those of a priest and a king. The founder of the Toltec capital, Tula, took Quetzalcóatl's name as his own and assumed the position of high priest to the god. According to legend, Quetzalcóatl populated the world by pouring his blood over the bones of people who had died from an earlier world; this myth of a god nurturing mankind with his own blood became the basis of ritual sacrifice, which the Toltec brought to the Yucatán.

Interestingly, the Maya absorbed the Toltec as much as the Toltec influenced Maya theology and building; many of the ruins show Toltec forms. Essentially the Toltec became latter-day Maya.

Although the Maya lands were occupied, the Maya could claim with some justification that they were never really conquered. The first Europeans to arrive were immediately chased away. The Yucatán was finally breached by Europeans in 1517 by Francisco Fernández de Córdoba. Juan de Grijalva renamed it New Spain in 1518. Hernán Cortés landed in 1519 and soon was greeted by Aztec emissaries from the north, who believed he was Quetzalcóatl. Cortés's march to the Aztec capital at Tenochtitlán started in Veracruz in 1519. Twenty years after the Halls of Montezuma had been sledged into rubble, Francisco de Montejo founded Mérida. The surrounding area never completely fell under Spanish domination, and Mexico's independence in 1821 did little to change things. The War of the Castes, in which remnants of the Maya battled outside domination, dragged on through most of the 19th century.

Eventually, economics did what force of arms could not. The production of henequen, a form of sisal used in making rope, changed the economic and social systems in the Yucatán. The United States and European nations needed rope for their ships. The Yucatán was a handy source of supply and the great henequen plantations began to thrive. A feudal system of land ownership developed and the Yucatán Indians became peons on great Spanish haciendas. The hacienda owners, for their part, discovered wealth beyond their avaricious dreams. Like the rich of many other lands, they turned toward Europe for cultural standards and status. They sent their children to schools on the Continent or, when they could not get to Paris themselves, settled for New Orleans. The owners of the haciendas were very similar to their counterparts in Peru, who allowed Indians to work the land while they partied in Paris rather than journey into the interior of their own country. The Yucatán *hacendados,* the landowners, ignored the rest of Mexico partly because, before the air age, it was difficult to reach and partly because, as far as the aristocracy was concerned, it was not worth the effort.

Only since the 1950s has a paved highway linked the Yucatán with the rest of the country. The rail service has always been painfully slow. Not that long ago the best route from Mexico City to Mérida was a pullman to Veracruz and a transfer to a coastal vessel bound for Progreso, the port 22 miles (35 km) away where taxis could be hired for the hour's drive to the state capital.

Today a highway system completely circles the peninsula, and driving is the best way to get a feeling for the entirety of this magnificent area — from the Gulf Coast to Mérida, from the government resort area of Cancún on the Caribbean to the inland routes passing Chichén Itzá and other major archaeological areas. In fact, the Yucatán Peninsula is the best area in Mexico for driving. The roads are good, the countryside flat, and destinations fairly close to each other.

Driving from Mexico City is not difficult, but the best bet is to fly to Mérida, the real starting place of a Yucatán journey, and rent a car there. (Rent in town, not at the airport.) Mérida is easily worth a day's visit (for a complete report, see *Mérida,* THE CITIES). It is a large enough city to have traffic jams and parking problems, so getting around by taxi is quicker and more pleasant than driving yourself. Arrange to have the rental car delivered the morning of your departure. Several international rental firms, as well as some from outside of Yucatán, have offices in Mérida. It's best to reserve a car in advance through a travel agent; and specify very clearly what kind of vehicle you require. Budget travelers can find VW Beetles and Nissans within their price range. For pure indulgence, try a big, air conditioned, automatic Ford, Dodge, or Chevrolet. These are the biggest autos available in Mexico, and they are constantly in demand, which is why advance reservations are so important. Without a reservation, an air conditioned, automatic car may not be available, which can make things sticky for drivers who never learned to shift gears. When you get right down to it, air conditioning, too, is more of a necessity than a luxury for most visitors. The Yucatán is hot all the time.

The Yucatán today is still vastly different from the rest of Mexico. The Yucatán accent is as distinct as a Southern drawl in the US. Henequen remains, to this day, the major crop and can be seen growing in expansive fields along the highways. Today, however, henequen has been replaced by stronger manmade fibers in the manufacturing of rope, and now is used primarily in making carpets. You can see this carpet making process at the huge Cordomex plant — 5 miles/18 km north of Mérida on Highway 261.

In the villages, people still speak Maya, live in white, oval, thatch huts called *chozas* and wear white garments — embroidered *huipiles* for the women, tailored *guayaberas* for the men. Almost nowhere else in Mexico are native costumes seen with such frequency as in the Yucatán. You'll see a good many Panama hats, which are made in Becal, a small village off Highway 180 between Mérida and Campeche. The hats are woven from *jipijapa*, dried and shredded palm leaves, and you can buy them from their makers who work in caves or cellars dug into the earth behind their homes. The town plaza has as its centerpiece a sculpture of three huge Panama hats leaning on each other. Besides maintaining their unique costumes, the inhabitants of the Yucatán have their own cuisine, too. Pork *pibil* is one of the favorite dishes. Yucatán beer, rare outside the immediate region, is prized throughout Mexico.

En Route from Mexico City – The route we recommend from Mexico City takes you to the town of Chetumal, where you embark upon the journey north along the Caribbean coast, then head west across the peninsula to Mérida. People who fly to Mérida can pick up the route looping north and east or south. (A description of the route from Mérida can be found later in this chapter.) The road along the Gulf of Mexico into the Yucatán Peninsula is almost as fascinating as the peninsular drive itself. This is a jungle route through coffee country, banana plantations, fishing villages, coastal boom towns, and a river port out of a novel. The small number of tourists who make this trek is an added attraction for those adventurers who do. From Mexico City to Chetumal, a distance of 881 miles (1,410 km), is a good 3-day drive. Chetumal is the first stop on the peninsula, but there will be two overnight stops, at Veracruz, 254 miles (406 km) from Mexico City, and Villahermosa, 286 miles (458 km) from Veracruz. Although you can make this drive in 3 days, you'll probably want to take more time, as there's a lot to see and do along the way. You'll have plenty of driving options, too. There is a choice of two roads (Route 150, which is a four-lane toll road, and a secondary back road) between Mexico City and Veracruz, and between Villahermosa and the Yucatán Peninsula (Route 186 or Route 180), a distance of about 350 miles (560 km). Returning on an alternate route, you can swing south at Coatzacoalcos on Route 185 to cross the isthmus in 4 hours, heading back up to Mexico City by way of Oaxaca — a trip totaling some 434 miles (694 km).

Plan carefully for this journey. Places to eat are scarce, as are places to spend the night. You can't count on pulling into a motel when you get weary of driving. You should know where you expect to arrive at the end of each day and about how long it will take to get there. As donkeys and cows are fond of turning highways into after-hours barnyards, driving at night should be avoided. The most difficult part of the first leg of the trip is choosing the route.

TLAXCALA: Until fairly recently, when some important pre-Hispanic murals were uncovered and the town was spruced up, the city of Tlaxcala was almost unknown. Today it is very much worth a slight detour on the way to Puebla. Take the Tlaxcala turnoff from the Puebla highway, and just before arriving in the town of Nativitas, about 12 miles (19 km) before Tlaxcala, you'll see an open-sided, stadium-like structure protecting the Cacaxtla archaeological zone. You will have to leave your car in the parking lot and walk about a quarter of a mile to the site. The small museum on the right describes the history of the area, which was settled by a group known as the Olmec-Xicalancas. The site is most noteworthy for its impressive and beautifully preserved frescoes, the largest of which depicts war in all its reality.

Continue on the road to Tlaxcala and once in town, follow Route 119 toward Puebla. After about 1½ miles (2 km), take a left and you will see the Ocotlán Sanctuary rising from the top of a hill. The sanctuary was built in the 17th and 18th centuries at the site of a miracle performed during a drought in the 16th century; the Virgin of Ocotlán is believed to have answered the prayers of an Indian by causing water to flow from the ground. The sanctuary is noteworthy for its 8-sided *Camerin de la Virgen* (Dressing room of the Virgin), with its white plaster façade, two red-tiled Poblano towers, and profusion of of baroque decorations covering walls and cupola. (The *Feast of the Virgin of Ocotlán* is usually celebrated at her sanctuary on May 15 with fireworks, music, and much food and drink.) Have lunch at one of the restaurants near Tlaxcala's main square, or at the *Misíon* hotel, next to the rushing waterfall, just outside of Tlaxcala in the town of Atlihuetzía. Return to Route 119 to connect with the toll road to Puebla.

PUEBLA: For a detailed report on the city, its hotels and restaurants, see *Puebla,* THE CITIES. About 79 miles (126 km) from Mexico City, Puebla is about a 2-hour drive from the capital. A toll road, Route 150, shoots eastward from Puebla to Córdoba, a distance of 160 miles (256 km), where it becomes an ordinary highway running the 60 miles (96 km) to Veracruz. The drive from Puebla to Veracruz takes about 4 hours, but with sightseeing it can be a full day. The alternate, turnpike route involves going to Córdoba and beyond via the back road through Tehuacán, 40 miles (64 km) from Córdoba.

TEHUACÁN: Tehuacán is Mexico's Vichy — where all the bottled water comes from. Ask for whiskey and soda in Mexico and you get whiskey and Tehuacán. It's also a spa town, reminiscent of the *bads* in Germany. Unfortunately its spas are not much in fashion anymore, and consequently Tehuacán is rather a sad little place. The hotels, however, are dignified dowagers surviving on their memories and their service (see *Best en Route*). The area has another claim to fame. It was here that corn was first cultivated some 10,000 years ago, which means that Tehuacán could be said to have spawned all the great civilizations of pre-Hispanic America. (Of course, no one so far has actually said that.) Visit the *Museo de la Valle de Tehuacan* (Museum of the Valley of Tehuacan) in the Convento del Carmen. The museum has agricultural exhibits pertinent to the cultivation of corn, and the convent has dazzling domes.

ORIZABA: If Tehuacán is where the water comes from, this town 25 miles (40 km) away is where beer is made. Mexico's brews are outstanding, and some of the very finest originate in Orizaba. The Móctezuma Brewery offers tours so you can see — and free samples so you can taste — how superior *cerveza* is made. A manufacturing town, Orizaba has a pleasant climate and marks the halfway point between the plateau and the coastal tropics. The volcano overlooking the town to the west, Orizaba (or Citlaltepetl), is the highest mountain in Mexico. It reaches a height of 18,851 feet. Orizaba's main plaza has in its center a giant evergreen surrounded by palms, symbolically reflecting the relation between the high country and the steamier lowlands.

A huge monolith (probably Mexican) in the local cemetery depicts a fish, a man, a rabbit, and two human feet that look as if they had been set in cement outside *Mann's Chinese Theater* in Hollywood. The Estanque de la Reina, in a canyon near the brewery, is filled with sensational vegetation — including trees covered with orchids. Both places are well worth a visit.

FORTÍN DE LAS FLORES (Fortress of the Flowers): This may be the most enchanting stop along the entire route. With the majestic Orizaba volcano towering in the distance, Fortín is a tropical village of gardenias, orchids, camellias, and azaleas. (A flower festival is usually held in April.) The *Fortín de las Flores* and *Posada Loma* (see *Best en Route*) are more pleasant places to stay overnight. Nearby are sugar, coffee, and citrus plantations.

CÓRDOBA: About 20 miles (32 km) east of Fortín de las Flores is Mexico's Yorktown, where independence from Spain was finally won in 1821. It's a lovely town of pink and blue buildings with supporting red tile roofs, mango-shaded streets, and an occasional squawking parrot or a peacock. We recommend spending the night in

Fortín, then driving to Córdoba in the morning for breakfast at the *Palacio,* on the plaza (see *Best en Route*).

Alternative Route from Puebla – You can also reach Veracruz from Puebla via Route 140 through Jalapa, a distance of 120 miles (192 km).

JALAPA ENRÍQUEZ: Residents prefer to spell their town's name "Xalapa," but no matter how it's spelled, it's pronounced "Hal-*a*- pa." Something of a tropical Guanajuato, Jalapa, like Fortín, is famous for its flowers. Jalapa is the capital of the state of Veracruz, and, in addition to a small government bureaucracy, it has a local university. Lately, it has started coming into its own as a provincial cultural center, with frequent ballet and modern dance recitals. Rain, or to be more specific, drizzle, is frequent, too. There are moments when the sun shines, but usually Jalapa is a lovely, misty greenhouse. The Jalapa route makes sense if you plan to drive straight through to Veracruz, and is a must if you are interested in archaeology for Jalapa now has one of Mexico's newest and most beautiful archaeology museums, the *Museum of Anthropology of Jalapa*, whose exhibits are mainly from the Toltec, Huastec, and Totonac civilizations. Designed by the New York firm of Edward Durell Stone, the museum displays nearly 3,000 items, including replicas of the famous massive Olmec heads from the La Venta archaeological site. Closed Mondays. Admission charge. The *Xalapa* hotel (Victoria and Bustamente) or *La Pérgola* (Loma del Estadio) are good choices for lunch.

El Lencero, located 9 miles (14 km) from downtown Jalapa, is a former hacienda that was once home to General Santa Anna. Beautifully restored, it is now open to the public Tuesdays through Sundays. No admission charge. Also not to be missed are the Clavijero Botanical Gardens, 2 miles (3 km) southwest on the old highway to Coatepec.

VERACRUZ: For a detailed report on the city, its hotels and restaurants, see *Veracruz,* THE CITIES. Whether you take Route 140 or Route 150, you should plan to spend at least 1 night in the port city of Veracruz where there is singing and dancing every night on the zocalo. If you have the time, spend a couple of nights in this unique town. Another option is to stroll around Veracruz in the evening, take in a bit more in the morning, then leave around noon, in time to arrive at Alvarado for a late lunch.

ALVARADO: Some 45 miles (72 km) from Veracruz on Route 180, Alvarado is famed throughout Mexico for its foul-mouthed citizens, who will neither offend nor delight you if you don't speak the language. More to the point, Alvarado is a leading fishing port.

CATEMACO LAGOON: From Alvarado, Route 180 leads 60 miles (96 km) to picturesque San Andrés Tuxtla, one of the prettiest towns on the gulf. Next door, Lake Catemaco is largely unvisited. Centuries ago, the lake was formed by the eruption of seven volcanoes. Trout, perch, and a small species called *pepesca* inhabit this 50-square-mile lake, from which the town of Catemaco derives a thriving fishing industry, and from where you can also take boat rides and water ski. The *Playa Azul* and *La Finca* on the lake and the *Berthangel* in town are the best hotels (see *Best en Route*). Try dining lakeside at *La Ola* (Paseo del Malecón), an open-air restaurant and bar set under a woven roof, where *mojarra* (sunfish) is caught fresh from the lake.

En Route from Lake Catemaco – Not far beyond the lake Route 185 splits off from Route 180 and runs south across the Isthmus of Tehuantepec. On your way back from Yucatán, you might want to try Route 185 as an alternative route to Mexico City and pass through Oaxaca. To get to Yucatán, however, follow Route 180 for 75 miles (120 km) to Coatzacoalcos.

COATZACOALCOS: This vibrant, booming port, fed by Mexico's Pemex oil monopoly, has no specific sights to see, but the lusty, raw, and exciting city is quite enough. It's a glimpse at the less romantic, tackier side of life in Mexico. The *zona de tolerancia,* or "tolerance zone," on the outskirts of the city features a slew of bars and discos where ladies of ill repute hustle for a share of the nation's oil money. If you're looking for atmosphere, eat at the *Valgrande* (Hidalgo and Morelos). The *Terranova* hotel (Carr. Coatzacoalcos) also serves an appealing lunch.

En Route from Coatzacoalcos – Cross the river from the state of Veracruz into the fabled Tabasco. Tabasco pretty much lives up to its reputation as a remote state of jungles and swamps where just yesterday only rivers were the highways. Today an excellent road cuts through about 80 miles (128 km) of the densest jungle between Coatzacoalcos and Villahermosa. It's an adventure just to pass through.

VILLAHERMOSA: Although never especially attractive, with the arrival of Pemex — the Mexican national petroleum company — Villahermosa has lost its remaining charm and dignity. The name Villahermosa ("'beautiful town'") belies its real character — the city's architecture is square and squat; its streets are lined with shabby stores and cafés; and its seedy hotels are swollen with oil-field workers. On the horizon are the ever-present orange flames created by burning off excess natural gas from the wellhead. Villahermosa is typical of the Pemex paradox: Government officials insist that the country as a whole benefits from oil revenues, but on an individual level, the Mexican suffers. The peasant's land is expropriated for drilling and the oil worker labors long hours for pay far below American standards.

Despite this dismal picture, Villahermosa does have a few special highlights that you shouldn't miss. One of the newest additions to Villahermosa is the spectacular Tabasco 2000 complex, which includes a shopping center with a department store (*Puerto de Liverpool*), art galleries, boutiques, and a *Woolworth's*; a planetarium; the 18-hole *Club de Golf*; and the *Holiday Inn Tabasco Plaza* (see *Best en Route*). Also worth visiting is the *Parque La Venta,* an outdoor archaeology museum with artifacts placed in the same type of setting in which they were found in the oil fields of La Venta (100 miles northwest), a former Olmec ceremonial site dating back more than 3,000 years. The park also has monkeys swinging in the trees, some animals roaming loose, and others caged. A path winds among the palms and vines, and around the various artifacts, including altars, stelae, and three ancient, giant sculptures of heads approximately 6 feet tall, displayed amidst natural jungle vegetation. The museum is off Paseo Tabasco and Boulevard Grijalva, 2 miles (3 km) from downtown, near La Laguna de Ilusiónes; guides are available.

The Olmec, thought by many experts to have established the earliest known civilization in Mexico, settled in the rain forest along the gulf coast around 1200 BC. They constructed plazas, ceremonial centers, and giant sculpted heads without bodies — the head was perceived as the most important part of the body. The ritual of cutting off someone's head evolved from the belief that this was the most effective way of stealing an enemy's power. Heads were considered good sacrifices to the gods. The Olmec were also fond of carving jaguars or babies with jaguars' heads. Although it is impossible at this time to determine the precise significance of this symbol, it is probably an image of esteem, as jaguars were the biggest felines on the continent.

The *Museo Regional de Antropologia* (1 block from the Grijalva River, downtown) is one of the best in all of Mexico, and justifiably so. Many of the ancient civilizations, including the Olmec, Maya, and Toltec, are represented. The full-scale reproductions of the murals at the jungle ruins of Bonampak depict a young warrior being presented to the Maya lords, as well as war dances, prayers for victory, and a battle. Bonampak is so remote it is almost impossible to visit, and authorities' fears that troops of tourists breathing on the ancient paintings might fade the colors make it unlikely that it will ever really be opened up. The paintings at this museum in Villahermosa are the next best thing to being in Bonampak.

If you come directly from Veracruz, whether or not you spend the preceding night at Lake Catemaco, you will probably arrive in Villahermosa late in the afternoon. We recommend checking in at one of the city's hotels, then hurrying off to the *Museo*

Regional de Antropologia. The next day, plan to get to *Parque La Venta* fairly early and then hit the road.

En Route from Villahermosa – Route 180 begins along the town's Blvd. Grijalva and continues northeast along the coast for about 110 miles (177 km), hopping over to Isla del Carmen and its town, Ciudad del Carmen.

CIUDAD DEL CARMEN: Carmen is quite a town, a shrimp port full of atmosphere and a haven for photographers. The island town was a pirate's lair for 160 years, beginning with a British privateer named McGregor, who in 1588 established it as a base from which he and his men attacked Spanish galleons carrying fabulous cargoes of gold and silver back to Spain. Many ships were sunk and it's believed their treasures still lie on the ocean floor.

Getting to Carmen can be a problem, however. Ferries connect either end of the island with the mainland. Normally, ferries run from 4 AM to midnight, leaving for the island at odd hours and from the island to the mainland at even hours and making the crossing in half an hour, but it can be very discouraging to pull up at the end of a long line and find there's no room aboard. More discouraging still is the bad weather, which causes cancellations in service. You can wait for hours or even a day. It doesn't happen often, but it does happen.

PALENQUE: About 90 miles (144 km) from Villahermosa on Route 186, the turnoff is about 70 miles (112 km) from Villahermosa, at the town of Catazaja. Of all the surviving Maya archaeological zones, none is more majestic than Palenque, in the state of Chiapas. Palenque is unique in that it is the only Maya ruin site buried in a rain forest and yet accessible by car. It remains lost from sight in the rain forest until a final hairpin turn. Then it stands against the jungle's deep green — the setting of a fable, except it's absolutely real.

First visited by Spanish explorers in 1750, these spectacular ruins have been a source of fascination ever since. Around 1840, the American explorer John L. Stephens hacked his way in to find "all that remained of a cultivated, polished people who passed through all the stages incident to the rise and fall of nations, who had reached their golden age, and perished unknown. The temples and pyramids of Palenque are the only memorials of their footsteps upon the earth." (For a more complete description of Stephens' experiences and impressions, you might read his book *Incidents of Travel in Yucatán.*)

Then the Mexico City–Mérida railway cut through the tropics close to Palenque, and it became possible to take a train to the ruins. It was a 13-hour trip each way, but still people came. It was, after all, more convenient than making the journey by mule. Nowadays, it's very easy to reach this impressive site. The undergrowth has been cleared away and many of the structures have been restored. Some purists object to the restoration, but most people find that the work has enhanced the beauty of the place.

In 1949, investigators probing the Temple of Inscriptions atop the largest of Palenque's pyramids found indications that there was something below. That would not have been unusual in and of itself, for pyramids have often been found built atop other pyramids. In this case, however, the hidden object seemed to be something different. Finding it took 4 years of careful digging. The pyramid contained a royal tomb, with the remains of a body tightly sealed in a stone coffin. Some archaeologists believe that it is the body of a Maya king, who is represented in many of the friezes found at the site. He was buried with a jade cube in his left hand, a jade ball in his right hand, and jade rings on his fingers. Artifacts from the tomb can be seen in the *Museo Nacional de Antropologia* (National Museum of Anthropology) in Mexico City. Guarding the chamber were the skeletal remains of servants who had been entombed with their master to accompany him on his journey to the next world. This is one of the few times a tomb has been found within a pyramid in Mexico. Although the pyramids of Egypt were mausoleums, those in Mexico were not. The Temple of Inscriptions at Palenque is an exception in this respect, and the entire process of entombment is quite similar to that practiced by the Egyptians. Yet it seems unlikely that there was any contact between the Maya and the ancient Middle Eastern civilization. The corpse was placed in the Palenque tomb about AD 620.

There are also apparent similarities between Palenque and the temple at Angkor Wat, and certain features that resemble lotus flower carvings in India. All that can be said for certain is that the ruins in Palenque today are remains of a great holy city that once spread over as many as 25 square miles. The small museum near the entrance to the ruins has a model that offers some idea of how the place once might have looked. "We have lived in the palaces of their kings," Stephens, the explorer, wrote. "We went up to their temples and fallen altars and wherever we moved we saw evidences of their taste, their skill . . . their wealth and their power." Stephens really did camp in the ruins for a while and found it an unpleasant experience — suffering ticks, gnats, and even worse jungle insects. Accommodations are somewhat better now; both the Viva and Misión chains have comfortable hotels there (see *Best en Route*).

En Route from Palenque –

If you're feeling up to an adventurous excursion after Palenque, head to Yaxchilan, a once-buried Maya site reached by taking an unmarked gravel and dirt road southwest out of Palenque to the settlement of Frontera Echeverria on the Usamacinto River bordering Guatemala. By car, it is a rigorous 5- to 6-hour drive, followed by a 2-hour open boat ride to the ruins. Tours are arranged by *Ruta de Usumacinta* (phone: 931-31915 in Villahermosa or 934-50091 in Palenque). To reach Yaxchilan in a less adventurous manner, contact *Sanborn Tours* (800-531-5440 in the US), which offers 1-day trips by plane to the site.

If you choose not to visit Yaxchilan from Palenque, return to the main highway, turn right, and head for the town called Francisco Escárcega, 115 miles (184 km) northeast. There you can head due north on Route 261 to Campeche or Mérida or continue east on Route 186 to Chetumal, heading north along the Caribbean coast on Route 307. If you fly to Mérida and rent a car, as we suggested earlier in this chapter, begin your drive from the capital by heading toward Francisco Escárcega via Campeche and Uxmal and then driving south on Route 261 toward the port city of Campeche. The entire 228-mile (365-km) trip shouldn't take more than 5 hours. That leaves time to poke around the Maya ruins at Uxmal (pronounced *Oosh*-mal), about 50 miles (80 km) from Mérida, and still get to Campeche by dusk.

Just beyond Mérida, take the left-hand fork at a town called Umán and keep going for about 30 miles (48 km) to Muna, where the road divides again. Bear right. These instructions may seem overly explicit, but Mexico is not the country in which to depend on road signs. Whenever there is any doubt, ask and ask again. Language is no barrier. If the response to "Uxmal?" is a shaking head or wagging finger, turn around. Although you can make it to Campeche the same day, you will probably want to spend the night at Uxmal if you have the time.

UXMAL: Apart from the obvious exotic appeal of spending the night at an inn adjacent to an abandoned Maya city, there is a sound-and-light show after dark. The script is a bit inane, although it does convey something of the feeling of the place, and the lighting is spectacular. Uxmal is noted for the marvelously intricate geometric designs worked into its structures. These can be seen and appreciated much better under artificial light than in the blazing sun.

Under any lighting conditions, Uxmal is a stunning place. With its towering, rounded pyramid and breathtaking nunnery, Uxmal was one of the sites to which the Maya returned again and again in the course of their civilization. The name means "thrice built," but apparently it was actually abandoned and rebuilt as many as five times. Why Uxmal was abandoned is not as hard to fathom as why it was built in the first place, or why it was rebuilt so many times. It has no water. The Yucatán is one vast limestone slab with rivers running underground. Here and there the rock has caved in, forming great natural wells of water called cenotes. These are prominent at other ruins, but there are none at Uxmal. The Maya carved their own giant reservoirs, but clearly there were years when the rains failed to come. Chac, the elephant-nosed rain god, was the most important god in the Maya pantheon, and sculptures of Chac are seen throughout Uxmal.

The Palace of the Governor at Uxmal is considered by many to be the most beautiful of all the Maya structures in Central America. Here, some 20,000 hand-cut stones have been set into acres of geometric friezes. The nunnery is the quadrangle where vestals allegedly spent a licentious final year of worldly pleasure before their sacrifice to appease Chac. Like many places in Indian ruins, the nunnery was named by early Spanish explorers who had little real idea of the purpose of various buildings. Never take names too literally.

Many of the ruins at Uxmal remain almost unexplored, and there is plenty to see. Archaeologists move slowly among the remote sections of the ruins, sifting through every spoonful of earth as it is removed. This is why Uxmal's large ball courts remain mostly wilderness. The House of the Old Woman and the Temple of the Phalli (a distinctly unerotic structure) still await further exploration. Guided tours through the ruins usually take about 4 hours. A lot of people like to come back after a tour and wander among the monuments on their own. Devotees of Maya culture usually journey to the ruins at Kabah, only 12 miles (19 km) from Uxmal, but visitors whose interests are more casual tend to be disappointed. The ruins at Kabah are mostly rubble. Most impressive are the Temple of the Masks, an entire building ornamented with long-snouted images of Chac, the rain god, and the Codz-Pop, a rare, spiraled pyramid.

From Uxmal, you can also visit Sayil and Labna, along the border separating the states of Yucatán and Campeche. Styles intermingle in this remote set of ruins. The Maya of Campeche built in what is called the Puuc, or hill, style; the Maya of Yucatán proper created the Chen, or well, forms. Both architectural styles are pure Maya, with no Toltec or any other outside influences. A paved road has replaced the rutted dirt one that leads to Sayil and Labna, thus making these ruins more accessible than in the past, when only the most devoted amateur archaeologists braved the trip. In the 1840s, explorer Stephens clambered around them and wrote of his experiences in *Incidents of Travel in Yucatán,* a fascinating book that has been reissued as a two-volume set (Dover; $4.95 per volume). The suffering endured by Stephens during his visit to the Uxmal area seems incredible, but if you get to Sayil and Labna, you might well come away convinced that little has changed. By the way, there have been no places to accommodate guests there for nearly 700 years, so you will have to head back to Uxmal, where there are extremely comfortable hotels in jungle settings (see *Best en Route*).

All the archaeological zones are administered by the National Institute of Anthropology and History of the Secretariat of Public Education. Uxmal and Kabah are open daily. Admission charge. For information, call the Tourist Department (phone: 99-249495) in Mérida. From Uxmal, Route 261 runs south 150 miles (241 km) to Campeche.

BOLONCHEN DE REJOÑ: This is a must for spelunkers. Even for amateurs, these stalactite-studded caverns 200 feet below the earth near the Campeche state line, about 100 miles (160 km) from Uxmal, are worth a look. Guides escort you through the subterranean passages.

CAMPECHE: One of Mexico's least visited and most picturesque port towns, Campeche has been walled and fortressed from the early days of the Spanish conquest. No one has ever bothered to promote tourism here, but with a couple of fine hotels and some unique monuments, Campeche certainly should be discovered. Its fortresses and walls make it a typical Caribbean city, but unique along Mexico's gulf coast.

Cortés first landed on Mexican soil at Campeche in 1517; in the years following, the city steadily increased in importance. The conquistadores discovered logwood, a rare and costly source of dye, growing in the nearby forests. By the mid-1550s, they were exporting the precious commodity to Europe and growing very rich. Though remote and isolated, Campeche rapidly grew into one of the most thriving cities of New Spain — and attracted the attention of Caribbean buccaneers. Rich as Campeche was, it was also defenseless. The city was first sacked by William Parck and his band of cutthroats in 1597. Thirty-five years later, in 1632, a pirate known as Diego el Mulato did it again. Then came Pegleg (yes, there really was a swashbuckler by that name) and a Dutch adventurer, Laurent de Graff, whom the locals dubbed Lorencillo. L'Olonois of France, who had a sweetheart in town, was another frequent visitor. This Frenchman earned a reputation as the most sadistic of buccaneers due to his habit of eating his victim's eyeballs! In 1685, when another buccaneer, Lewis Scott, sacked the place once again, the city decided to protect itself. The people began work on the wall and forts in 1686, a task that took 18 years to complete. Parts of the wall have since been removed, evidence of more peaceful times, but the two main gates and seven of the original eight fortresses remain. The wall and the gates offer endless possibilities to photographers and watercolorists, who may well never want to leave.

The former Fort of San Pedro is now a handicrafts market. The tourist office is in the former Fort of Santa Rosa (phone: 981-67364). This is where you can get a guide to show you around town. The rooftop of San Pedro is much as it was in days of old, its fighting deck heavy with now-ancient cannon. How these quaint guns managed to stop marauding men-of-war from taking everything in sight is not easy to understand, but clearly they did. The marksmen must have been remarkable. With a bit of persuasion and a few extra pesos, your guide will take you to the secret passageways beneath the fort. Now mostly sealed off with bricks, these tunnels once linked many houses in the city. Some of the passages were built in the Maya period and were simply expanded by the Spanish. These underground hiding places sheltered women and children when pirate ships came into view.

The *Casa del Teniente del Rey* (Lieutenant del Rey House) has been converted into the *Campeche Regional Museum* (on Calle 59), with an interesting collection of Maya objects, including a jade mask and a collection of jewelry discovered in the Colakmul tomb. Closed Mondays. Admission charge. *San Miguel,* the handsomest of all Campeche's fortresses, is now a museum displaying pirate arms and portraits of the worst scoundrels who harried the city. There is also a model of walled Campeche as it looked nearly 3 centuries ago. The guides are quite fond of telling horror stories about how San Miguel's moat was filled with quicklime instead of water, and how the water was stocked with crocodiles. They are somewhat vague about whether any malefactor ever earned his grisly reward by being tumbled into the moat. Open daily. Admission charge.

Church lovers, who will find pickings pretty slim along the Yucatán Peninsula, can score comparatively heavily in Campeche. The cathedral on the main plaza was completed in 1546 — only 6 years after Don Francisco de Montejoy-Léon ordered construction to begin on the same day he founded the city. The San Francisco monastery, just off the *malecón* (seafront esplanade), is nearly as old. Mass was first said here in 1546. About 20 years later, the grandson of Hernán Cortés was baptized here at a font still in use today.

Campeche has its modern side, too. The brightly colored Government Palace has been dubbed "the jukebox" by irreverent local citizens, and the modern Legislative Palace is known as "the flying saucer." In fact, these modern structures were rather carefully designed to fit in with Campeche's unique native architecture and have completely avoided the glass box look so prevalent in many high-rise sections of Mexican cities. Nonetheless they have offended the taste of the city's proud and conservative older guard. Other modern additions that have pleased residents more are the city's growing network of wide, handsome boulevards and the futuristic University City — rivaled only by the suburb of the same name in Mexico City.

Campeche is noted for its seafood, especially the shrimp it sells all over the world. Stone crab *(cangrejo moro),* pompano, and a black snapper (known as *esmedregal*) are local favorites. Campeche is also known for its intriguing seafood combinations. In addition to shrimp cocktails and oyster cocktails, there are *campechanos* in which both are served together. Light beer and dark beer are served half-and-half, too, on request. The restaurant in the *Baluartes* hotel, Campeche's most modern hotel (see *Best en Route*), serves good seafood and accepts major credit cards. The *Miramar* restaurant, in a junky waterfront setting across the street from the Government Palace, is less expensive, more crowded, but serves food that's at least as good as the *Baluarte*. Also in front of the government buildings you'll find three eateries in one — *Restaurant 303*, *Cafeteria Bamboo*, and *Bar La Escala* — for a relaxing meal.

En Route from Campeche (the Yucatán Loop) – The 260-mile (416-km) drive to Chetumal will probably take more than 6 hours and may run as long as 8 if you stop to see the ruins at Kohunlich. This is wild jungle country, and traveling through these parts is similar to roaming around the headwaters of the Amazon. Roads are relatively new in this part of Mexico, and amenities are sparse. It is a good idea to take along a box lunch and fill up whenever a gas station comes into view.

From Campeche, Route 180 takes you 41 miles (66 km) south to Champotón, the last stop on the Gulf of Mexico coast. Champotón is noteworthy because it was here the first Spanish blood was shed in Mexico. Francisco Fernández de Córdoba was mortally wounded while exploring the area in 1517. Route 261 leaves Route 180 at Champotón and continues due south to Escarcega. A little more than a collection of huts, Escarcega is where you pick up Route 186 to Chetumal. From here on, the jungle closes in, although the roadside vegetation is the typical low scrub.

Underscoring the remoteness of the region is the customs shed at the Quintana Roo state line. No one driving in has to stop, but vehicles leaving Quintana Roo are sometimes required to submit to a customs inspection. Quintana Roo is a zone beyond the reach of Mexico's protective tariffs. It got that way because, for many years, there was no way for Mexican goods to get into the area and no place for them to go once they were there. In order to stimulate an almost nonexistent economy, import taxes were eliminated. To some extent, this made the region a legal base for smugglers. Contraband is big business in this part of Mexico.

Quintana Roo (pronounced Kin-*tan*-a-*row*) is Mexico's newest state. Along with Baja California Sur, it was given full autonomy only in 1974. The state takes its name from Andrés Quintana Roo, a hero in Mexico's War of Independence. Originally it had been part of the state of Yucatán but was lopped off in reprisal for the Yucatec's rebellious ways. Until fairly recently, the Yucatec considered that no great loss. Once the former federal territory was granted statehood, however, Yucatán fomented a boundary dispute. Considering that the border runs through unexplored jungle, no one has taken Yucatán's challenge very seriously. Experts insist that much of the jungle contains the remains of lost Maya cities.

KOHUNLICH: This is one of them. It was discovered in 1967 when construction workers came upon the ruins while cutting a *trocha,* or path, for Route 186. It seems thieves had already spotted the place, because some artifacts said to come from here have turned up in New York. Dating from about AD 100, Kohunlich, like most Mayan cities, is believed to be a former ceremonial center or temple. Its pyramids were observatories from which the seasons were measured. In the tropics, where winter blends into spring with no robins to herald the change, spotting the equinox was a great problem and of vital importance to the Maya, for it told them when to plant their corn.

Probably only the priests, who lived in the temples and performed rites on top of the pyramids, knew how to measure the seasons. Kohunlich's Pyramid of the Masks might also have contained tombs, as did the Temple of Inscriptions at Palenque. As far as archaeologists know, these are the only two Maya pyramids that were used as burial places.

Four temples stand at Kohunlich, along with a plaza of large, stone, bas-relief plaques and the ever-present ball court, where the Maya played a game surprisingly similar to modern soccer or basketball. The idea was to get a hard rubber ball into the opposing team's goal, which was a small stone ring. Players were not allowed to use their hands to score. Considering the small circumference of the goal ring, this must have been quite difficult. The teams did their best, however, and according to legend, the winning captain celebrated his victory by lopping off his rival's head, symbolically fertilizing the ground with blood.

Kohunlich is by no means as well ordered as Uxmal. Archaeologists are still looking for clues about who the Maya really were. You may get a sense of ongoing exploration and feel you are actually in the midst of potentially important discoveries.

CHETUMAL: It's hard to imagine a more exotic introduction to Mexico's Caribbean coast. Though by no means as luxurious as the glamorous resorts farther north at Cancún, Chetumal is something like the setting of a delicious Grade B Hollywood thriller of the 1940s. It's balanced delicately on the Mexican border with Belize (formerly British Honduras) and the deep Bay of San José, on the Caribbean. Because Quintana Roo is a free port area in which Mexican import quotas don't apply, this odd little town is aglitter with shops selling Japanese electronic devices, Dutch cheeses, Czech crystal, Italian silks, and French perfumes. Mexicans usually have to pay 100% — or more — duty on goods from abroad, if the items are allowed into the country at all, so, for people from Mérida or Villahermosa, Chetumal is the next best thing to Hong Kong. Chetumal is also a staging point for hunting and fishing expeditions. One mile off shore is the small island of Tamalcab, home to the *tepezquintles,* small pigs that are a favorite with hunters and gourmets.

It will probably be late in the day when you arrive in Chetumal, which will give you enough time to stroll around town, have dinner, and get a good night's sleep (formal, numbered street addresses are rarely used in Chetumal; like many of the towns in the Yucatán, it is small and easy to negotiate, and shops, restaurants, and hotels simply don't use addresses). *La Cascada* at the *Continental* has a good selection of seafood and international dishes; if you like Arab food, try *Chez Farouk.* And *Sergio's Pizza* serves good grilled steaks as well as pizza.

From Chetumal Route 307 goes north to the resorts that spot Mexico's fabulous Caribbean coast. However, you might consider a day's diversion in Belize, just south of Chetumal, over the natural border provided by the Río Hondo.

BELIZE: Belize is in one of those obscure little corners of the world where practically nobody seems to have visited, but once a person has, the trip can supply cocktail party conversation for months. A good rest stop is *Cenote Azul* (off Hwy. 307 at Km 34), a thatch-roofed *palapa* serving breakfast and lunch.

Belize used to be known as British Honduras, England's last colony on the mainland of the Americas. English pirates, probably some of the same band that raided Campeche, settled Belize. They found shelter behind its protective reefs, and if they had any wounds to lick, this is where they licked them. From here they would sally forth to raid along the Spanish Main. Eventually, perhaps as they grew older, the buccaneers sought a less risky line of work. They found it in logging; harvesting the hardwoods of the Belize forests proved to be more profitable than pirating — as well as far safer.

The British colonists began importing black slaves to do the heavy work, and the Spanish, who controlled most of the general area at the time, looked with great disfavor on these English settlements. The Guatemalans were no happier, and, when they became independent, claimed the territory as their own. London really wanted nothing to do with the place, but yielded to the pleadings of its colonists, who begged for the protection of the British flag.

As early as 1961, the British government made it plain that Belize could cut its ties to the Mother Country anytime it wished, but because of the threat of takeover by neighboring Guatemala, it was not until Britain agreed to retain a small protective military presence in the country that independence was formally declared, in 1981.

Belize City, besides being hot and humid, has an interesting mixture of British colonial architecture and small-town ambience. With a population of 45,000, it is the only real city in the country. It is filled with old, mostly wooden buildings and ramshackle houses, the line broken only occasionally by Victorian government buildings.

The most colorful thing about the city is the street names: The Queen's Square uses animal names such as Antelope, Armadillo, and Seagull Streets; the Mesopotamia area has Middle Eastern names like Euphrates, Cairo, and Tigris; and the Caribbean Shores area relies on church figures for names.

The city's small business and shopping area is centered around the few blocks on either side of the Belize Swing Bridge. Here are Albert and Queen Streets, which make up the commercial district, and Regent Street, which houses most of the government buildings. At the northeast end of the bridge is the Paslow Building, an interesting bit of architecture which contains the post office. Across the street is the Belize Philatelic Bureau (91 Front St.), where stamps may be purchased by collectors. The Baron Bliss Institute, on Southern Foreshore, near the Swing Bridge, was dedicated to the multimillionaire who left several million dollars to Belize City in the 1920s; it contains carved stone monuments from the ancient Maya ceremonial center of Caracol, in the Maya Mountains.

Also located on the southern side of the Swing Bridge is Old Fort George, with its Memorial Park, and standing along Regent Street are some of the old slave quarters. Also on Regent, across from the *Mopan* hotel, is a bookstore which has a small selection of Belizean historical publications. St. John's cathedral is one of the oldest Anglican cathedrals in Central America, built in 1826.

You also can drop in on the studio of George Gabb, reputedly Belize's best carver, on the Northern Highway going out of town, just after the Texaco station. The workshop is open every day from 8 AM to 6:30 PM. The genial Gabb, widely known as a pork-barrel philosopher, will show you how he carves the native zirocote hardwood, which, when cut across the grain, reveals a brown and black "rose" on a white background. Most of his work is exported, and the 12-foot statue *To Be Born Again,* which he donated to the US for its bicentennial, is now at Lansing (Michigan) Community College.

The *Fort George* (phone: 501-77400), *Château Caribbean* (phone: 501-2813), and *Bellevue* (phone: 501-7051) are generally considered the best choices for lodging in Belize City. They provide the basic comforts — a clean bed, private bath, and air conditioning.

Crossing the border from Mexico to Belize is a fairly simple process, although sometimes it can take an hour or more if there are crowds. When you leave Mexico, you must relinquish your Mexican tourist card. If you plan to return to Mexico from Belize, stop at the Mexican Embassy in Belize City (20 N. Park St.; phone: 501-44301), to pick up another one. Otherwise, you may have to offer a *mordita* (bribe) to the Mexican border guards to get them to allow you to.

After completing the exit requirements on the Mexican side of the border, you must walk or drive across the bridge which spans the Rio Hondo. To enter Belize you must have a passport; the immigration office will stamp a visa in your passport. If you are driving your own car or a rental car, you must buy local insurance, available at a little shack at the edge of the customs house parking lot; the premium is $10 per day.

BACALAR LAGOON: After a morning in Belize, you can spend the afternoon back in Quintana Roo just lying around or swimming at this lagoon, about 25 miles (40 km) from downtown Chetumal. The lagoon is the place, the Maya said, where the rainbow is born. The turquoise waters reflect many colors. This is the best place for a special introduction to the Mexican Caribbean. The water is as clear as the air above it, ideal for snorkeling. There are a couple of hotels by the lagoon, the *Bacalar* and *Baluartes*. Both are good places for cocktails.

    En Route from Chetumal – Route 307 shoots north parallel to the coast to Felipe Carrillo Puerto, the town about 95 miles (153 km) north of Chetumal. There, several roads lead in different directions: to the coast; across the mainland to Mérida; and northwest, deeper into Quintana Roo.

FELIPE CARRILLO PUERTO: This town gets its name from a populist Yucatán governor of the 1920s who loved an American woman. The lady was Alma Reed, a reporter from San Francisco who could easily have been invented by a novelist. Long before the Chicanos were fighting against prejudice, Ms. Reed took up their cause. Her California paper allowed her to probe the murder conviction of a young Mexican, and her article convinced the authorities that the jury had made a mistake. The governor signed a pardon, and the Mexican government, pleased to have found a friend, invited the newswoman to tour the country as its guest. Those were rough and ready days, when the Mexican revolution had not been quite settled, and people were frequently finding themselves shot. Ms. Reed, undeterred, accepted the government's invitation and in the course of her journey visited Mérida. She interviewed Carrillo Puerto, then governor of the state of Yucatán. Apparently he was more impressed than she, because later he had a mariachi band drop by her hotel to serenade her, as Mexican swains are fond of doing. He went a step further and had a tune written especially for his lady, "Peregrina" (Pilgrim). It's still considered a classic among Mexican love songs. Alma Reed booked passage on a steamer for New York, where she planned to buy her wedding dress. While she was there, political fortunes turned in Mérida, and the other side grabbed the statehouse, took Carrillo Puerto prisoner, and executed him. For her part, Ms. Reed never married. She became a promoter of Mexican culture and archaeology. She died in 1966 and is buried in Mérida, very close to her beloved Felipe Carrillo Puerto. Aside from the tale of the man for whom it was named, the town of Felipe Carrillo Puerto has little to recommend it. To continue to the Caribbean coast, bear right at the highway junction.

SIAN KA'AN: Jungles, salt marshes, mangrove swamps, palm beaches, and coral reefs make up this 1.2-million-acre biosphere reserve that extends south of Tulum to Punto Herrero. It's a veritable paradise for bird lovers — and for biologists, who have also established crocodile and butterfly farms there. Two pricey hotels on the reserve, *Club de Pesca Boca Paila* and *Pez Maya,* are frequented by millionaire yachtsmen, who come for fishing and sunning. There are also a few modest bungalows. Guided tours are available (see "Sources and Resources" in *Cancún,* THE CITIES).

TULUM: Although small, the archaeological zone some 154 miles (248 km) north of Chetumal and 61 miles (98 km) north of Felipe Carrillo Puerto has some fine Maya buildings. In fact, this was one of the few cities that was still inhabited when the Spanish arrived. Juan de Grijalva described sighting it from his ship in 1518: "a city so large that Seville would not have seemed more considerable." Little of that metropolis remains, but what there is fascinates scholars. Tulum is the only Maya city known to have been encircled by a wall fortification. It is also one of the few Maya sites on the seacoast. Apparently, the site was founded hundreds of years before the Christian era began, yet it survived long after other Maya cities had been abandoned. To some, this would indicate that the wall and seafront location were a good idea. The formation the Spaniards called El Castillo (the Castle) is also known as the Temple of Kukulkán, the Maya name for the Aztec god Quetzacóatl. El Castillo is the zone's most curious structure; it does resemble a castle, and for all we know, may actually have been one. Walk carefully to the side facing the sea for a stunning view of white, sandy beaches at the bottom of 80-foot limestone cliffs. About 400 yards offshore is a "blue hole," the ocean equivalent of a cenote. The Temple of the Frescoes contains rare Maya paintings, but Tulum's most famous building is the Temple of the Descending God. Over the main door a carved deity can be seen descending head first. The conventional theory is that this may represent the rain god; an alternative theory is that it represents a descending spaceman. Other buildings of note are the Temple of the Initial Series and the Great Palace.

This area offers some natural, as well as manmade (however old) amenities. The beach just below the site is beautiful. The local waters can be fished year-round and hunting in the jungle is quite good. (Four major duck migrations rendezvous here each year; wilder game include boar, puma, deer, and crocodile.)

The area on the Quintana Roo mainland known as the Cancún-Tulum Corredor is peppered with a few delightful hotels and restaurants set at the edge of the sea. It's hard to predict how many more years of peace and tranquility remain here, since the Mexican government chose the area for another of its mega-tourist projects. *Puerto Aventuras*, a huge development of villas, condo-hotels, restaurants, tennis courts, a golf course, and marina is well underway near Akumal. For more details see "Excursions" in *Cancún and Cozumel*, THE CITIES.

About 30 miles (48 km) inland from Tulum, the city of Cobá, discovered in 1972, contains more than 6,500 Maya sites, most of which are uncharted. The highlight is a 150-foot-high pyramid surrounded by smaller ones. Along the coast, to the north of Tulum, there are hundreds of little sites. A NASA satellite survey using special infrared photography revealed a massive network of previously unknown irrigation canals that scientists say allowed the Maya to raise crops in a relatively waterless region.

XEL-HA: This lagoon — or series of lagoons — forms a natural aquarium filled with colorful tropical fish and turtles. Of interest is the bizarre phenomenon caused when the cold waters of an underground stream rise from the lagoon floor to form a 2-foot layer over the warmer water coming in from the Caribbean. Put on a diving mask, hold your breath, and watch the refraction between the two layers of water. It's no exaggeration to say that the Mexican Caribbean offers some of the best diving in the world. Xel-Ha is the place to start, especially if you haven't done it before. Resort facilities and diving equipment can be found at nearby Akumal.

AKUMAL: Next door to Xel-Ha, this began as the headquarters of a private club for the not-so-idle rich — the *Mexican Underwater Explorers' Club*. When the club was founded, its members flew down in private aircraft to put on wet suits and scuba tanks for expeditions to the sunken wrecks of Spanish galleons in the seas nearby. They also came upon submerged Maya ruins in places where the sea had swallowed up the land. Today Akumal is open to the public, and *Club Akumal Caribe* (see *Best en Route*) is a lovely hotel with grounds that contain cannons recovered from the ancient wrecks. If you would like some adventure right out of *The Deep,* minus the hazards, Akumal has an underwater museum where anchors and guns encrusted in coral lie among the rocks much the way they originally were found. The hotel is a great spot for lunch. Although Akumal stands by itself, it is also the beginning of a string of resorts along the coast.

PLAYA DEL CARMEN: This small beach community near Akumal is important for its dock and is becoming increasingly popular as a resort area. A ferry leaves from here for the island of Cozumel. The last departure is at 4 PM. The ferry does not take cars.

COZUMEL: For a detailed report on the island, its hotels, and restaurants, see *Cancún and Cozumel,* THE CITIES. Although now superseded by the more elegant Cancún, Cozumel is Mexico's original international Caribbean resort and is still very popular. There aren't too many Americans here; most of the visitors are Mexican and

European. In fact, throughout the Yucatán, less than half the tourists are *gringos.* You can fly to Cozumel directly from Houston, Miami, or Mexico City. There is also scheduled air service from Mérida and Cancún. Certainly, no one who has time will want to miss Cozumel. Perhaps the best bet would be to stop for the night at the *Molcas* hotel in Playa del Carmen, catch the 7:30 AM ferry to the island, and take the 6:30 PM ferry back. The crossing takes about 35 minutes.

For all of its popularity, and even in spite of the winter cruise ships that stop here and the crowds that visit from Cancún for a day, Cozumel still has much unspoiled territory. There are two roads on the island, one that bisects the land from east to west, and another that follows the shoreline around the southern half of the island. On the east side, the road is lonesome and runs along the beach on the wild, open sea where the surf crashes against black coral boulders. There are a couple of places that will sell wanderers seafood and a cold beer. For visitors interested in more activities and livelier crowds, stick to the other side of the island, in and near San Miguel; the island's only town, it divides into two parts: Hotel Row and downtown. As you would expect, hotel row has the bigger, more expensive establishments; downtown, the standard range of resort shops, restaurants, and motels.

CANCÚN: For a detailed report on the island, its hotels and restaurants, see *Cancún and Cozumel,* THE CITIES. One of Mexico's newer major resorts, Cancún is Mexico's great success story of the 1970s and '80s. Cancún is an island in the Caribbean about 50 miles north of Cozumel. Now Mexico's second-largest industry (after petroleum), a few years ago tourism was nothing more than a thriving weed. Eventually, the economists in the Central Bank woke to the fact that travelers were bringing a lot of money into Mexico. In response, they decided to clean up existing tourist favorites (like Acapulco) and develop new ones. They asked where Mexico's next resort area should be. The answer was Cancún.

With beautiful (if crowded) beaches, sailing, snorkeling, and water skiing, visitors to Cancún are seldom at a loss for something to do. For example, the sightseeing yacht *Fiesta Maya* sails around Nichupte Lagoon and passes through a jungle canal into the open Caribbean. The jungle swing gives passengers a chance to glimpse all kinds of wildlife, while the vessel's glass bottom allows views of the sea bottom. The 5-hour yacht cruise departs every morning at 10 AM and stops at Isla Mujeres for 2 hours. There are also sunset cruises from 4:30 to 7:30 PM, glass-bottom boat cruises, and trips to the wildlife preserve of Contoy, home of any number of species of birds; no people are allowed to live here.

Cancún even has a bullring. During the winter season, it often attracts the best matadors in Mexico. As a rule, only four bulls are killed instead of six. And as you might expect, nightlife in Cancún is the best in the Yucatán. At the *Convention Center,* there are regular performances of regional dances, for a change in pace from discos. Among the most popular nightspots are *Christine's, La Boom, Risky Business, Aquarius, Friday López,* and *Daphny's.* As for eating out: Try *Maxime* for French food in an elegant setting. *Hacienda el Mortero* serves excellent Mexican dishes. Continental cuisine, soft music, and candlelight by the sea are the specialty of *Chac-Mool* on Chac-Mool Beach. *La Habichuela, Carlos 'n' Charlie's* (part of the Carlos Anderson chain), and *El Pescador* in Cancún City are also very good.

ISLA MUJERES: Quintana Roo's other island resort is 6 miles north of Cancún. Almost everybody staying on Cancún takes a boat over for lunch and a swim. Car and passenger ferries leave for Isla Mujeres from the Punta Sam ferry dock (north of Puerto Juárez, approximately 5 miles north of Cancún), daily between 7 AM and 7 PM. Check at the dock for departure times, which can vary. The crossing takes 20 to 30 minutes and can be rough for even the strong-stomached.

Many people stay overnight on this very small island. The downtown section is a mere 5 blocks wide and 8 blocks long. Most of the streets are unpaved, and there are very few cars. Extremely informal, it's popular with younger people. Sweatshirts and jeans are about as elegant as anybody gets. Completely relaxed, it attracts an arty, intellectual crowd who stay on until money runs out.

The island's name in Spanish means "isle of women," but this is not intended to get male hopes up. Those first Spanish explorers found the place crammed with female idols. Apparently, the Maya chose the spot for fertility rites. Nowadays, the island is known mostly for its great swimming and snorkeling. Day trippers should be sure to get to El Garrafón (the Jug), another spectacular natural aquarium that's quite different from Xel-Ha's. Here, the fish are larger, although not so large as to be worrisome. You can swim through schools of thousands of them. At the turtle pen, you can ride sea turtles and, if you're up to it, wrestle a shark — a sand shark, that is, which has no teeth of any size. Treat yourself to a fresh seafood lunch at *Maria's Kan Kin* (5 miles/8 km south of town; phone: 988-20279), *Ciro's Lobster House* (11 Matomoros, in town; phone: 988-20102), or *Hacienda Gomar* (on the west side of the island on the road to El Garrafón; no phone).

En Route from Isla Mujeres – Ferries leave Isla Mujeres for Puerto Juárez on the Quintana Roo mainland frequently throughout the day. From Puerto Juárez, it is about 55 miles (88 km) west to Pueblo Nuevo, the border town on the Quintana Roo–Yucatán state line.

■ **Note:** The stretch of Highway 180 between the east coast and Mérida was in the path of Hurricane Gilbert that swept through the area in 1988, devastating Cozumel, Cancún, and Isla Mujeres. Though the area was decimated, the goverment has done much to restore, and even improve it. The area has been declared a nature preserve in which it is forbidden to hunt animals or cut down flora.

VALLADOLID: About 48 miles (77 km) west of Pueblo Nuevo on Rte. 180 is one of the Yucatán's largest cities. Valladolid doesn't have much to see. Its chief point of interest is a Franciscan monastery completed in 1560. The town was named for the city in Spain where Ferdinand and Isabel, the 15th-century Spanish monarchs, were married. The city also made the history books as the site of a bloody massacre during the War of the Castes, the 19th-century Maya uprising. At the rejection of the Catholic church by the new Mexican Republic, the long-converted and devout Maya, already distraught from other grievances, rose up against the wealthy landowners. The two sides slaughtered each other from 1847 to 1855, until the Mexican army claimed victory in 1901.

Just outside of town lies Balankanchén Cave. Discovered only in 1959, it was apparently abandoned 1,000 years ago and completely forgotten. It was a secret Maya temple, the House of the Sacred Jaguar. The throne, formed by a stalactite joined to a stalagmite, looks like a ceiba, the tree revered by the Maya. Little stalactites on the cavern ceiling are the leaves. The copal incense burners and hundreds of pots, bowls, and ceremonial artifacts in the chamber are believed to be exactly where the priests left them so many centuries ago. By a pool so still it scarcely seems to contain water at all stands an altar to the rain god, although there is some question as to whether it is the rain god Tlaloc, sacred to the Toltec, or Chac, of the Maya. It may well be, too, that the cavern was the secret temple of a persecuted religious group. The cave could have been abandoned when the persecutors caught up with their intended victims. There are guides to lead you through the interior, but exploring the place is rough going. The *Cenote Zaci* restaurant, beside a *cenote* (a natural well used by the Toltec for sacrifice), serves venison steaks, and the restaurant at the *Mesón del Marquez* (203 Calle 39; phone: 985-62073) offers both regional and international dishes.

CHICHÉN ITZÁ: Just a couple of miles beyond the caves on the road to Mérida is the most famous and complete of the ancient Maya cities. The archaeological zone is about 75 miles (120 km) from the capital of Yucatán on Route 180. It's about 25 miles (40 km) from Valladolid, just a couple of miles down the road from the caves.

The site of Chichén Itzá is most famous for its example of Maya engineering genius — the incredible optical illusion created by the great El Castillo Pyramid, also known as the Temple of Kukulkán, the Maya name for the Aztec god Quetzalcóatl. This structure is topped by a temple to the feathered snake god, Quetzalcóatl; at the base of the balustrade are giant carved heads of the deity. The pyramid rises in a series of terraces, which cast shadows on the balustrade. On the first day of spring and the first day of autumn (the vernal and autumnal equinoxes), the undulating shadows form a serpent's body leading from the temple on top to the carved head at the bottom. Even in this age of pocket calculators, the mathematics required to get those shadows to strike the right way on the right day boggles the mind. For years, nobody noticed. Then, a few years ago, a snapshot taken on March 21 revealed a shadow formation that was almost dismissed as a curious coincidence. Since then, it has been recognized as more than mere happenstance. Only on those two special days of the year does the shadow form an entire snake-like body.

The arithmetic that went into building the rest of El Castillo is impressive in itself. The stairways leading up the side of the pyramid each have 91 steps. Those, taken with the steps to the temple at the summit, add up to 365, the number of days in the year. The structure has 52 panels on its sides, which correspond to the number of years in a Maya century. There are a total of 18 terrace sections, representing the 18 months of the Maya year. The Toltec influence can be seen here, too. The giant, 16-foot statues of warriors and the huge serpent columns hark back to the time of the Toltec conquest, from the 10th through the 13th century. The Maya civilization spanned the years from 1000 BC to the Toltec invasion. A new architectural style, known as the Maya-Toltec, evolved after the conquest.

Part of Chichén Itzá, the "new" city, lies on one side of the highway, surrounding El Castillo (the Castle) Pyramid; the ball court (with acoustics so fine a voice scarcely louder than a whisper can be heard 500 feet away); the Temple of the Jaguars, dedicated to an order of warriors; the Temple of the Eagles and the Tigers; and the Thousand Columns, with pillars resembling plumed serpents that at one time, no doubt, supported a roof. Here and there are the Chac-Mools, reclining idols that, in spite of their name, are no relation to Chac, the rain god. Chac-Mools were the centerpiece on sacrificial altars. They held large bowls in which were placed the still-beating human hearts torn from living victims. Less gory is the sacrificial well, the large cenote lying a short walk from the other ruins. Its depths have been extensively explored, but archaeologists have only recovered a fraction of its contents. The bottom is a bramble of branches and twigs. Recently, divers have brought up the bones of the victims — men, women, and even children. Youngsters were considered most precious; hence, they were the greatest treasure that could be offered to the rain god.

The ruins of Old Chichén across the road are rather less impressive. There is another cenote, or sinkhole well, but it was used for more peaceful purposes, as a water supply. The original Maya, it would seem, were less than enthusiastic about sacrifices. The conquering Toltec were the ones who gloried in killing for their gods. A round observatory, El Caracol (The Snail), in Old Chichén gets its name from the spiral stairway within; its circular structure makes it a rarity among Maya buildings. Some of the observatory's features resemble the El Castillo Pyramid. The windows are aligned in such a way as to record the longest and shortest days of the year and are set to enable astronomical phenomena to be measured with precision.

Also in the group of ruins is the ossuary, or bone house, a 30-foot-high pyramid with stairways on each side and a miniature temple on top. The temple is in the same form as the El Castillo Pyramid. This building was used by the Toltec to bury people. Nearby are the Temple of the Sculptured Tablets, the nunnery (it wasn't really a nunnery, but the Spanish thought it looked like one because of all the tiny rooms), the abbey, the so-called church (another Spanish-bestowed misnomer), and the Akad-Dzib, a building of obscure writings and red handprints believed to have something to do with Kabul or Zamná, the god whose name meant "heavenly hand."

There is a smaller group of buildings in Old Chichén that are still overgrown with jungle vegetation. You have to walk along some rough trails to get to them. The structures in this part of Chichén Itzá include the Castillo of Old Chichén, the Temple of the Jaguar, the Temple of the Turtle, the Temple of the Sculptured Jambs, the Temples of the Lintels, and the Temple of the Hieroglyphic Jambs. The paths leading among the different temples are known as *sacbes,* or holy paths. People were led along the *sacbes* to the temples, where they were ultimately sacrificed. Anyone who can manage the time will want to spend the night at Chichén Itzá. Like Uxmal, it has a number of good hotels (see *Best en Route*).

En Route from Chichén Itzá – Continue about 75 miles (120 km) west on Route 180 to Mérida. From Mérida, you can take Route 180 south to Campeche to return to Mexico City. At Campeche take the gulf route, Route 180, or travel inland on Route 261 to Escárcega, picking up Route 186 west.

BEST EN ROUTE

For the most part, villages and towns in the Yucatán are simply too small and too informally arranged to require street addresses for hotels or restaurants. Most towns have only one or two streets. So, except where some confusion might result, addresses are not included in the listing below.

TLAXCALA

Misión Tlaxcala – Ten minutes from downtown, this pleasant, comfortable hotelry sits next to a rushing waterfall. In addition to having 120 rooms and suites, it has a heated pool, 3 tennis courts, satellite television, restaurant, and bar. Carr. Tlaxcala–Apizaco, Atlihuetzia (phone: 246-20178 or 246-24001). Moderate.

TEHUACÁN

México – The 86 units open onto a central patio. There's a rooftop garden with a Spanish fountain, movies, pool, parking, and a restaurant and coffee shop. 101 Independencia Pte. (phone: 238-20340, 238-20019, or 238-20067). Moderate.

ORIZABA

Trueba – This is a fair enough commercial hotel, clean and comfortable, but otherwise undistinguished, with a restaurant, bar, and TV sets. Arrangements can be made for tennis, golf, and swimming at the nearby club. Few tourists spend the night here. 6 Oriente and 11 Sur (phone: 272-42744). Inexpensive.

FORTÍN DE LAS FLORES

Fortín de las Flores – Here is a fine old-fashioned resort and inn noted for its extensive gardens. It also offers a pool, access to a tennis club, a video bar, restaurant, gameroom, and movies. The 1 suite has a fireplace (phone: 271-31031). Inexpensive.

Posada Loma – Like the *Fortín,* this great favorite is known for its tropical gardens. The rooms and bungalows have fireplaces and are nicely furnished. A botanical garden and pool are on the grounds. The personal service is courteous, friendly, and competent (phone: 271-30467). Inexpensive.

CÓRDOBA

Real Villa Florida – A modern, 3-story hotel with 82 pleasant rooms, gardens, restaurant-bar, and satellite television. 3002 Av. Primero (phone: 271-43333 or 271-26666). Moderate.

Palacio – Pleasant and provincial, this hotel has 74 units, restaurant, cafeteria, air conditioning, color TV sets, parking garage, and disco. Just a block from the main plaza of this pretty, relaxing, little city. Av. 3 at Calle 2 (phone: 271-22188). Inexpensive.

JALAPA ENRÍQUEZ

Xalapa – Jalapa's best, by far. A modern hotel with 199 rooms, all air conditioned, with satellite television, a restaurant, a coffee shop and a pool. Victoria and Bustamente (phone: 281-82222). Expensive.

CATEMACO LAGOON

Berthangel – Many of the 23 rooms have balconies and lovely views overlooking the plaza (phone: 294-30089). Moderate to inexpensive.

La Finca – All 36 rooms have balconies and a view of the lake. There's also a pool and a restaurant (phone: 294-30322). Moderate.

Playa Azul – On the shores of one of the most beautiful lagoons in the country, this hotel arranges boating, fishing, water skiing; 80 units, pool, and disco. Its restaurant serves local fish (phone: 294-30001 or 294-30042). Inexpensive.

COATZACOALCOS

Terranova – This outstanding modern hotel has 200 rooms, satellite television, bar, pool, tennis courts, beach club, disco, and heliport. The dining room serves exceptionally good food. Carr. Transístmica (phone: 921-45100 or 921-25046). Expensive.

Valgrande – The kind of decent, rather typical commercial hotel you would expect to find in a thriving seaport, this place is good, but unexceptional, with 60 air conditioned units, a restaurant, bar, and TV sets. Hidalgo and Morelos (phone: 921-21443, 921-21467, or 921-21387). Moderate.

VILLAHERMOSA

Cencali – Beside the lagoon, this hotel has 120 air conditioned rooms and suites, color TV sets, pool, and restaurant. Juárez and Paseo Tabasco (phone: 931-51999, 931-51997, or 931-51996). Moderate.

Holiday Inn Tabasco Plaza – The remodeled 11-story hotel has 271 rooms, 22 junior suites, a master suite and presidential suite, restaurant, bar, pool, air conditioning, satellite television, and access to the adjoining country club's 18-hole golf course and tennis courts. 1407 Paseo Tabasco, Tabasco 2000 (phone: 931-34407). Moderate.

Hyatt Villahermosa – With 205 rooms, 10 suites, 2 tennis courts, pool, restaurant, and bar. 106 Av. Juárez (phone: 931-51234, 931-51623, or 931-51624). Moderate.

Maya Tabasco – Fairly new and nice, this place has a swimming pool and 156 air conditioned units, including 3 suites and a penthouse. There is a fine dining room, satellite television, disco, coffee shop, and a *Hertz* agency. 907 Av. Ruíz Cortines (phone: 931-21111 or 931-24689). Moderate.

Villahermosa Viva – One of the biggest and newest hotels in town, with 256 air conditioned units. A bit out of the way, it is something of an urban resort hotel and has shops, restaurant, disco, nightclub, and a swimming pool. Av. Ruíz Cortines and 1201 Paseo Tabasco (phone: 931-50000). Moderate.

CIUDAD DEL CARMEN

Eurohotel – A 4-story, air conditioned hostelry with 50 rooms, a pool, lobby bar, disco, and boutique. Calle 22-A (phone: 938-23043 or 938-23060). Expensive to moderate.

Lli-Re – A large, commercial hotel a couple of blocks from the plaza, with 63 air conditioned rooms, a restaurant, and piano bar. 29 Calle 32 (phone: 938-20388 or 938-20588). Inexpensive.

PALENQUE

Misión Palenque – A 160-unit hotel with a restaurant, lobby-bar, tennis court, pool, and minibus service to the ruins (phone: 934-525-0393 through 99; or 800-90038 in Mexico). Expensive to moderate.

Chan Kah Cabañas – This place has 26 Maya-style cottages, a restaurant, and pool on the road leading to the ruins. *Mailing address:* Apdo. 26, c.p. 29960 (phone: 934-50318). Moderate.

Viva Palenque – This hotel has 59 units, including air conditioned suites and bungalows, a restaurant, bar, satellite television, extensive gardens, and river swimming. (phone: 934-50100). Moderate to inexpensive.

UXMAL

Villa Arqueológica – Run by Club Med, its rooms are simple to the point of being nearly spartan, but the simple French cuisine, bar, tennis, and nice swimming pool make up for the absence of fancy decor (phone: 99-247053; 5-203-3086 or 5-203-3833 in Mexico City). Very expensive to expensive.

Hacienda Uxmal – Here you'll find old-fashioned tropical luxury amid the ample gardens, a swimming pool, a fine dining room, and a good bar. It's operated by *Mayaland Tours* (phone: 99-247142 or 99-252133 in Mérida). Expensive.

Misión Inn Uxmal – A nicely managed establishment, it's run by the Howard Johnson's group in the US. Facilities include a pool, dining room, and bar (phone: 99-247308; 5-531-3424 in Mexico City). Expensive to moderate.

CAMPECHE

Baluartes – Here is a handsome, traditional hotel that is near the sea, with a swimming pool and restaurant; it is close to everything. 61 Av. Ruíz Cortines (phone: 981-63911). Expensive to moderate.

Ramada Inn – This is a fine hotel with a swimming pool, bar, disco, and restaurant. 51 Av. Ruíz Cortines (phone: 981-62233; 800-228-2828 in the US). Moderate.

Alhambra – Its 100 rooms are air conditioned, and there is a restaurant, coffee shop, disco, pool, and satellite television. 85 Av. Resurgimiento (phone: 981-66323 or 981-66352). Inexpensive.

López – Small and friendly, this hotel is known for its charming bar and restaurant. The air conditioned rooms are furnished quite comfortably. 189 Calle 12 (phone: 981-63344 or 981-62488). Inexpensive.

Siho Playa – If you want to stay around for more than 1 night, this small resort is perfect. With a tennis court, boat rental (about 3 miles — 5 km — from the hotel), swimming pool, and restaurant, the environment is very relaxing. At Km. 40 of the Carr. Campeche-Champotón (phone: 981-62989). Inexpensive.

BACALAR

Laguna – Overlooking the blue waters of the lake, this 3-story, white and turquoise inn has a pool, patio bar, and restaurant. 25 miles (40 km) north of Chetumal on Hwy. 307 (phone: 99-271304 in Mérida). Moderate.

CHETUMAL

Del Prado – Run by one of Mexico's largest hotel chains, with air conditioned rooms, a swimming pool, restaurant, and bar. This is the best in town by far. Héroes de Chapultepec (phone: 983-20544). Very expensive to expensive.

Continental Caribe – This first class hotel has air conditioned rooms, a swimming pool, bar, garage, movies, and a restaurant. 171 Av. Héroes (phone: 983-21100). Moderate.

Jacaranda – Clean and comfortable, this unforgettable bargain glows with outpost-of-empire atmosphere. 201 Alvaro Obregón (phone: 983-21455). Inexpensive.

Real Azteca – A pleasant hotel, with air conditioned units, parking, a restaurant, and a bar. 186 Belice (phone: 983-20666). Inexpensive.

COBÁ

Villa Arqueológica – The only hotel at the ruins in Cobá, it is set in an isolated jungle environment close to many unexplored ruins. You actually can get out of bed and hack your way through the jungle. Run by Club Med, it has tennis courts, a swimming pool, and a library on Mesoamerican archaeology (phone: in Mexico City, 5-203-3086 or 5-203-3833; 800-CLUB-MED in the US). Expensive to moderate.

AKUMAL

Club Akumal Caribe – Formerly a Shangri-la for the wealthy, this lovely place is now open to the general public. Near Tulum and Xel-Ha, it is also a fine spot for lunch (phone: in Cancún, 988-41975; in Cozumel, 987-21407; in the US, 800-351-1622). Expensive.

Akumal Cancún – Right on the beach, it has 81 air conditoned rooms with terraces, 11 two-bedroom suites with kitchenettes, a pool, 2 lighted tennis courts, all water sports, dive shop, disco, 2 restaurants, video bar and miniature golf (phone: 988-42272 or 988-42641). Moderate.

■**Note:** Set on the beautiful Chemuyil beach, a few miles down the road from Akumal, is a charming property (unnamed at press time) with 10 suites (including kitchenettes), a few rooms, and 12 double or family-size tents — with maid service, clean showers, and restrooms — for roughing it in style. There also are hammocks with screened *palapas*. Make reservations well in advance by writing to Don Lalo Roman Chemoir, Fideicomiso Xel Ha, Tulum, Q.R., Mexico (no phone).

PLAYA DEL CARMEN

Molcás – A small hotel on the beach with 36 air conditioned rooms, pool, restaurant, and bar. At the ferry landing (phone: in Mérida, 99-246099; in the US, 305-534-3716). Very expensive to expensive.

Maya-Bric – This 21-room hostelry has a pool and rooftop view. 4½ blocks north of the bus station (no phone). Inexpensive.

VALLADOLID

María de la Luz – Pleasantly modern, it's a nice little provincial hotel with a swimming pool, restaurant, and bar with live entertainment. 195 Calle 42 (phone: 985-62071). Inexpensive.

Mesón del Marquez – Heavy on atmosphere, this old-fashioned colonial inn is one of a dying breed, with 24 rooms and 2 suites, a restaurant-bar, and gardens. 203 Calle 39 (phone: 985-62073). Inexpensive.

CHICHÉN ITZÁ

Hacienda Chichén – Reasonably priced, comfortable but small motel with a restaurant, bar, and swimming pool on the highway outside town. Open November through *Easter Week* (phone: 99-62777 at *Mayaland* hotel for information and to leave messages; in Mérida, 99-252122/33). Expensive to moderate.

Mayaland – Overlooking the ruins, this luxury resort has large, old-fashioned rooms, a restaurant, cocktail terrace, swimming pool, and evening entertainment (phone: 99-62777; in Mérida, 99-252133). Expensive to moderate.

Misión Inn Chichén Itzá – A handsome motel with a swimming pool and its own zoo. Renovations have rendered it considerably more comfortable (phone: in Mérida, 99-239500; in Mexico City, 5-525-0393). Moderate.

Villa Arqueológica – This *Club Med* guesthouse attracts people who love Maya culture and modern comfort (phone: 985-62830; 800-528-3100 in the US). Moderate.

Piramide Inn Resort and RV Park – In nearby Piste, less than a mile from the ruins, this resort has a pool, tennis court, shuffleboard, and dining room with EP, AP, AND MAP rates. Guided tours to several nearby ruin sites are available. Reservations: P.O. Box 433, Mérida, Yucatán, Mexico or P.O. Box Piste, Yucatán, Mexico TE: Piste (no phone). Moderate to inexpensive.

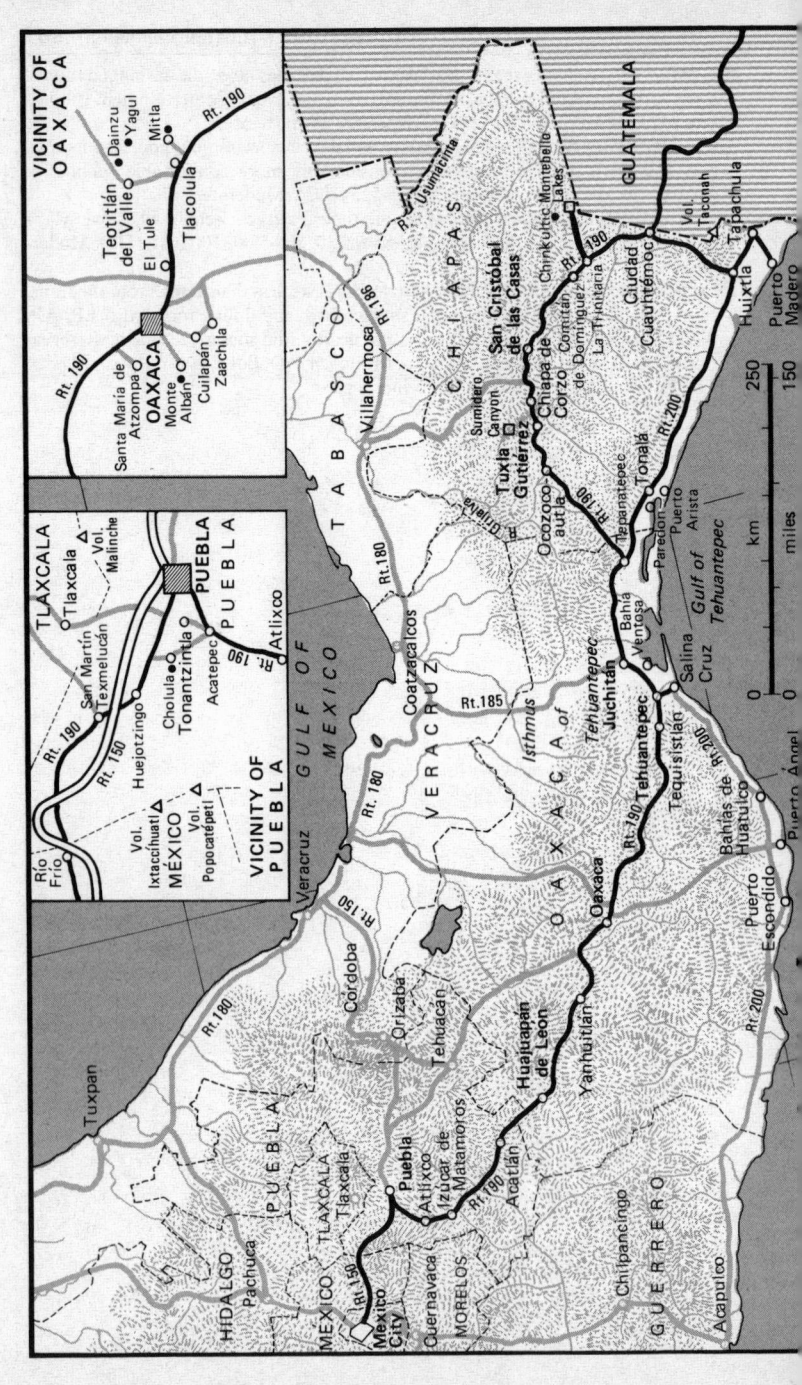

Mexico City to the Guatemala Border

If you want to lounge in the sun and be pampered by the luxury tourist trade, go to Acapulco, Mazatlán, or Puerto Vallarta. If you want cosmopolitan culture and sophisticated nightlife, Mexico City and Guadalajara have cultural facilities unmatched elsewhere in the country. And if it's colonial European charm and quiet, graceful living that you're seeking, Taxco, Guanajuato, and San Miguel de Allende are delights. But for Indian Mexico — hot and tropical, cold and mountainous, ancient, colorful, costumed, Indian-speaking Mexico — you must go south and east to the states of Puebla, Oaxaca, and Chiapas. And to get there, you must take the famous Pan-American Highway south.

The southern half of this road, from Mexico City to Guatemala, wanders through some of the most fascinating and rarely visited regions of Mexico. It is a route that offers the traveler an opportunity to explore 850 miles of almost every conceivable Mexican terrain and climate across three states, and a vast range of cultures, languages, and forms of social organization. But as colorful and educational as the journey may be, it is a trip for lovers of Mexico who are willing to deal with some of the hardships of travel in order to see what life is like outside the big cities and off the beaten track.

The Pan-American Highway, Route 190, takes you past towering, ice-capped volcanoes and up cactus-covered mountains to Oaxaca, the emerald city; down semitropical mountains to the beach at Salina Cruz; back up to Tuxtla Gutiérrez; and higher still, to the cool air of San Cristóbal de las Casas. From there it is down again into the lush tropical lands bordering Guatemala, the wild and exquisitely beautiful country of Los Lagos de Montebello.

The settlements through which you pass range from big cities to towns to tiny villages. The flora span everything from 20-foot-high cacti to wild tropical orchids. And the peoples and their cultures offer an astounding variety of human life.

From Mexico City, throughout the state of Puebla, you will witness the splendor of the Sierra Madre ranges. Ixtaccíhuatl and Popocatépetl volcanoes, as well as the lower slopes of the giant Orizaba peak, are all part of Rte. 190. But the barrancas and cascades for which the state is famous are found in the northern region, a vast mountainous area with few roads and isolated and primitive Indian villages — a great enticement for off-the-road travel, but not for any but four-wheel-drive vehicles.

Puebla is one of the largest and richest of Mexico's central states, with farming constituting the major industry. Wheat, corn, maguey, sugar, rice, and fruit are all raised in abundance, and miles of farm country surround every city and every road in the state.

The Pan-American Highway only cuts through a small portion of the western part of Puebla State. But along its route are several small Indian villages with 16th-century churches from the colonial era and Indian markets where various Indian dialects are spoken and textiles and ceramics of the area are sold. Texmelucán is known for its weaving, Acatlán and Izúcar for potters, and Puebla (the state capital) for pottery and polychrome tiles.

The state of Oaxaca is a wonderland of contrasts, from cool, forest-covered mountains and lush tropical valleys to a hot, humid coastline of beaches pounded by the Pacific surf. The contrasts are cultural as well as topographical, with ancient Indian ruins lying within sight of old Spanish colonial towns. Oaxaca, the fifth-largest state in the country, also boasts more ethnic groups than any other state except for Chiapas. Most of these maintain their original languages, customs, and dress, turning the villages and markets of Oaxaca into an amazing array of otherworldliness. Even geography aids the exotic atmosphere of the state. The rivers of Oaxaca often overflow their banks during the spring and summer rainy season, minor earthquakes occur frequently, and the state plays host to a diversified wildlife population. Though tapir, pumas, jaguars, ocelots, and margays have been severely reduced in numbers by the lumber, oil, and mining industries, they can still be found in some of the forests. Crocodiles, alligators, and boa constrictors thrive in the more humid areas in the south.

Two proud cultures dominate the many different ethnic groups in the state (including the Chinantec, Mazatec, Cuicatec, Chocho, Huave, Mije, Trique, and Amusgo) — the Mixtec and the Zapotec, whose civilizations reached great heights in architecture, sculpture, astronomy, and jewelry design long before the Europeans made their way to Mexico. In turns they built the impressive sacred cities of Monte Albán, Yagul, Dainzu, and Mitla.

The state of Oaxaca really represents three major geographical regions: the Valley of Oaxaca, the Isthmus of Tehuantepec, and the Pacific coast. The Pan-American Highway crosses the first two. The valley refers to the part closest to Mexico City and is the cultural, historical, and economic center of the state. The isthmus is where the west coast veers northeast and forms Mexico's narrow belt. The winds of this area are treacherous and the climate hot and humid, but a handful of interesting towns and beaches make it a fascinating part of the trip. The Pacific coast, lying south and southwest of Oaxaca City, is not easily accessible from the rest of the state. There is a modern highway from Acapulco that extends along the coast to the beautiful beaches of Puerto Angel and Puerto Escondido; from the Pan-American Highway this region is accessible, but not convenient driving.

One other section, the far northern part of the state, is almost entirely roadless and extremely mountainous. There is almost no tourist traffic, and other than cactus fanatics, people rarely go there.

Just below the isthmus, the Pan-American Highway crosses over into Mexico's southernmost state, Chiapas. This incredibly scenic land stretches from the hot, humid Pacific coastal area to fertile highlands, where the temperature varies from cool to downright cold. Clearly this state has the most fascinating folklore of any — a rich variety of peoples whose dress, customs, and language differ literally from one village to the next. Until 1950 these people and their land were inaccessible except by horseback. Even the

Spanish, who managed to occupy all the rest of this vast nation, made few inroads into the proud and treacherous country of Chiapas. To this day there are huge tracts of unexplored jungle and forest teeming with exotic vegetation and wild game. This is considered to be the finest hunting region in all of Mexico, but it is not for the weekend hunter and requires a most rigorous safari to match the drama, adventure, discomfort, and danger it offers. Also found in these unexplored and roadless jungles are the hundreds of known Maya ruins, most of which can only be reached by helicopter or on horseback. And beyond the registered sites, archaeologists estimate there are hundreds more yet to be discovered.

At hotels along this route categorized as expensive, expect to pay $50 to $70 for a double room; $25 to $45 at moderate places; and less than $25 at inexpensive.

En Route from Mexico City – Shortly after leaving the city via Calzada Ignacio Zaragoza or Ixtapalapa, you will have to choose between the toll road, Route 150, known as the Pan-American Highway, and the old free road, Route 190 Libre, which goes as far as Puebla. Your decision might well depend on how far you are planning to travel. A day trip to Puebla is probably more rewarding on the free road, Route 190 Libre; but if you are planning to continue on to Oaxaca, the toll road is faster and less tiring. There is some local color sacrificed on the toll road, but the trip ahead is long and sometimes grueling. Either choice will take you through picturesque pine-covered mountains and get you to the first major stop, Puebla, in a little less than 2 hours.

An early start out of Mexico City, about an hour before sunrise, will ensure your missing the early morning traffic jams for which Mexico City is infamous. (For specific restrictions on driving in Mexico City, see "Getting Around" in *Mexico City*, THE CITIES.) If the weather is good, it will also treat you to the spectacular sight of a sunrise reflecting off Popocatépetl and Ixtaccíhuatl, two of the four snow-capped volcanoes in this region. It is a vision that will set a charmed, almost magical tone to your whole trip, as you watch these great majestic pillars seem to come alive, emerging soft pink, red, and finally a fiery orange. Along the winding road to Puebla, you will see simple crosses erected on the highway's edge. They mark the places where people have lost their lives in serious accidents, and so are often a good indication of dangerous spots on the road. The memorials have been placed by relatives of the deceased and, in addition to their sentimental or religious significance, are public service reminders to drive carefully.

RÍO FRÍO (Cold River): This river, 40 miles (64 km) from Mexico City, marks the border between the states of Mexico and Puebla. It is also the halfway point between Mexico City and the city of Puebla. The spot is aptly named, for it is always cold, but there are facilities for picnicking, nature trails for hiking, icy water for hardy swimmers, and a restaurant for snacking. Eight miles (13 km) beyond Río Frío is the Continental Divide — 10,480 feet above sea level. No marker indicates the crossing, but for those who enjoy following the map and acting as navigator, it may be of interest.

SAN MARTÍN TEXMELUCÁN: 57 miles (91 km) east of Mexico City is the important weaving center of Texmelucán. At the weekly Indian market, the big attraction of this town, you'll find serapes and other woolen products of fine quality. However, if it isn't Tuesday, which is market day, there is not much to entice you out of your car. There is a 16th-century church and Monastery, as in all the towns of this area, but it is nothing special compared with many others along the route.

However, if you pass through in November, when the town is celebrating the fiesta of its patron saint, San Martín, it is worth stopping. Regional dancing, fireworks, music, and even a bullfight mark the festivities.

HUEJOTZINGO: This infamous bandit town, 25 miles (40 km) past the Río Frío, was the headquarters of guerrilla Agustín Lorenzo. *Carnaval* is celebrated during the 5 days before *Ash Wednesday,* and on *Shrove Tuesday,* Huejotzingo (pronounced Way-hote-*seen*-go) celebrates his capture with a colorful, fireworks-filled fiesta. Saturday is market day, and while it is a fascinating assortment of people, animals, colors, and sounds, some goods may be inferior and should be checked closely. Across the highway from the market is one of Mexico's oldest colonial monuments, the Church and Monastery of San Francisco de Huejotzingo. Begun in 1525, it is among the finest Gothic structures in the country and is well worth a visit.

CHOLULA: Ten miles (16 km) beyond Huejotzingo and only 5 miles (8 km) outside of Puebla, this town was once the Holy City of the Aztec Confederation. It is still noted for its enormous number of churches, the largest of which dominates the skyline and can be seen for miles around. It is Nuestra Señora de los Remedios and has a dome covered with glazed yellow, white, and green tiles. But even bigger and more impressive is the Tepanapa Pyramid upon which this church was built. Still mostly submerged under a hill, it has a few excavated tunnels that can be explored. This pyramid, thought to have been constructed by the Toltec, is almost twice the size of the great Cheops pyramid of Egypt, making it the largest yet found in the world. On the descent into Puebla, a first glimpse can be caught of Orizaba (Citlaltepetl) and Malinche, the other two large volcanic mountains of this region.

PUEBLA: (For a detailed report on the city, its hotels and restaurants, see *Puebla,* THE CITIES.) This major city, the first en route from Mexico City to Chiapas, lies 79 miles (126 km) southeast of Mexico's capital in a valley surrounded by volcanic mountains. As you enter town you will see the world's largest Volkswagen plant, from which Mexico exports Beetle parts to Germany. In fact, Puebla is a good city in which to think "car," because if there is the slightest hint that yours is not functioning at its best, this is the time to have it checked. The rest of the trip to Chiapas is over rugged, often isolated, mountain terrain, where the nearest repair facilities may be 20 miles (32 km) away and necessary parts are unlikely to be in stock.

If you left Mexico City at the early hour recommended and took the direct toll road instead of the more scenic, village route, you can get any car problems corrected as you breakfast in Puebla. Before leaving, stock up the car with lunch and snacks for the next segment of the journey to Oaxaca. Restaurants between Puebla and Oaxaca are few and cannot be depended on.

En Route from Puebla – It is approximately 8 hours of straight driving on the Pan-American Highway to Oaxaca, and all of it should be done in daylight. The total distance is 264 miles (422 km), much of which is on very windy roads through arid, semidesert land and an occasional fertile valley. At some points the dropoff at the side of the road is a good half mile. Beware of animals and people walking, standing, or sitting beside or actually in the road. And believe the speed limits. There are curves that should not be taken even 2 miles per hour faster than indicated. At this point on the route the distinction between 190-D and 190 Libre disappears. There is one highway, the Pan-American Highway (also called Route 190), all the way to Guatemala.

TONANTZINTLA (pronounced Toe-nan-*zint*-la): This small village off the beaten track is well worth the 20 minutes' detour from the highway. Take the Acatepec turnoff from Route 190, 8 miles (13 km) beyond Puebla, and continue 1 mile (1.6 km) northeast. The center of the village is dominated by the Church of Santa María Tonantzintla, which was built during the 16th century and has a misleadingly dull façade. Inside, the natives of this town, using their own funds and imaginations, have created one of the most breathtaking examples of popular art in Mexico. The intricately carved, vividly painted reliefs, embellished with gold leaf, flying cherubim, and dancing angels, are an exuberant expression of Indian artistry.

The village also boasts an ultramodern National Observatory equipped with a Schmidt camera that, with a 20-minute exposure, can reach a distance equal to 300 million light-years away. There are only two other cameras like it in the world, in Hamburg, Germany, and in Mount Palomar, California.

ATLIXCO: Back on Route 190 and 20 miles (32 km) from Puebla, a banner across the highway proclaims that drivers have just entered the best climate in Mexico. It is an announcement for the town of Atlixco (pronounced Aht-*leex*-coe), a thriving textile center surrounded by maize and wheat country. The ancient avocado (*aguacate*) trees that you see growing here provided the original stock for California's avocado industry. The central plaza of the town is very colorful and features a beautiful domed bandstand and bright tile benches. Fortunately, you can see everything of interest without a pause in your journey, since Route 190 goes through the center of town. Atlixco is an Aztec word meaning "on the surface of the water," so naturally the two major points of interest are Agua Verde Spa and Axocopan Spring. Also, if you pass through during the last weekend in September, look for a schedule of the big dance festival held in town. Performers come from miles around, and regional dancers fill the zocalo all weekend.

IZÚCAR DE MATAMOROS: This town, 42 miles (67 km) from Puebla, is announced by road signs all the way from the city and then abruptly stops being mentioned. Whatever happened to good old Izúcar? Well, the highway makes a neat, unannounced bypass, and the town itself is hidden a mile off the road and out of sight. If you have an extra 40 minutes or so, especially in October or on market day, Monday, it is worth a quick look-see. Izúcar is the source of the colorful ceremonial ceramics traditionally used for the *All Souls' Day* fiesta. These are the brightly glazed tree-of-life candelabra decorated with angels, skulls, and fruit. On *Corpus Christi* or *Santiago's Feast Day* (July 25) don't miss the presentations of the dance of the Moors and Christians. There is also a year-round resort, *Amatitlanes Spa*, which is 1 mile (1.6 km) from town and boasts a mineral spring and dry air, said to be good for the liver and kidneys.

ACATLÁN: About 54 miles (86 km) later, on Route 190, is the important pottery making town of Acatlán. Near the Oaxaca state border, the style of work produced here is more closely related to Oaxacan ceramics than that found in other parts of Puebla. A number of artists have their shops at the north edge of town, and although the dominant language is still Mixtecan, there should be no problem with bargaining. All the merchants speak Spanish and enough English to make dealing a stimulating but conquerable challenge. The effort is well worth it, as some of the gayest pottery in Mexico originates here. White clay, sculpted with curiously shaped animals, birds, and human figures, is built up into a pyramid or tree of life and decorated with bright colors. The figures are not entirely covered with paint; color is only used as a highlight on the white background. The result is unglazed, an example of Indian art that has remained unchanged in style or technique for many centuries.

Other potters of this town specialize in the black Coyotepec kitchenware typical of Oaxaca, but with a unique variation. Unlike the traditional Coyotepec pottery, which gets its rich metallic color from kiln-smudging and hand-burnishing, the Acatlán artists get the same effect by using a gloss-producing black slip (the runny clay used to finish pottery before firing). While these goods are available in other places, they are much cheaper and more fun to buy here at the source.

En Route from Acatlán – Roughly 21 miles (34 km) beyond the village, the road enters the state of Oaxaca. Keep in mind that most Mexican states have cities of the same name. On this trip there are three examples — Mexico, Puebla, and Oaxaca — so don't become confused if you see one sign saying "Welcome to Oaxaca" and the next saying "Oaxaca 120 kilometers."

HUAJUAPÁN DE LEÓN: This town marks the halfway point in the journey between

Puebla and Oaxaca. The main part of the town lies south of Route 190 in the Río Mixteco Valley. Huajuapán (pronounced Wah-hwah-*pahn*) was the birthplace of General Antonio de León, a hero of the Battle of Los Molinos during the US invasion of Mexico in 1847. A strong earthquake, the epicenter of which was near this town of 50,000 people, wiped out about 60% of the buildings in October 1980. Officials estimated that 40 people died in the Huajuapán de Léon area, but the town has been completely rebuilt.

Huajuapán is also in the mescal-producing region of Mexico, where it is not uncommon to see maguey plantations and farmers driving carts loaded with piles of cut maguey hearts. Mescal, a fermented alcoholic drink made from these hearts and bottled with each plant's own maguey worm, is similar to tequila and highly potent. The Mexicans have an expression *"Para todo mal mescal y para todo bien tambíen,"* which translated freely means, "Mescal makes the bad times good and the good times better."

Huajuapán de León is also known for its textiles, which are woven from palm leaves and sold at the Sunday market. The town holds its annual fairs May 19 and July 23, and if you are in the area, the dancing is well worth seeing. There are two decent hotels in town and a large resort complex nearby (see *Best en Route*).

YANHUITLÁN: The only thing of interest in this tiny hamlet looms up at you from miles away and grows to gigantic proportions as you get nearer. It's the former Dominican Convent of Yanhuitlán, built from about 1543 to 1568. This vast building with its carved and painted 100-foot ceilings now shelters dozens of chirping birds. There is a bas-relief behind one of the altars and several carved, wooden ornaments that are particularly interesting. Many of the church's decorations have been restored to their original splendor. When you have had your fill of manmade beauty, there is a tall, beautiful cypress tree to sit under on the patio adjoining the convent.

The convent is also infamous for an incident that took place here in 1642. The Holy Inquisition had taken exception to an Indian rite involving the use of hallucinogenic mushrooms, but the Indians ignored the edict that forbade the practice. The Inquisitors seized a number of Indian chiefs, tortured them until they confessed to being in league with the devil, and promptly burned them in the churchyard. The convent is open from 10 AM to 6 PM. Admission charge.

En Route from Yanhuitlán – From here the route to Oaxaca requires concentrated mountain driving and should not be attempted at night. Tiring even in daylight, the road becomes especially dangerous after dark.

SANTA MARÍA ATZOMPA: About 7 miles (11 km) before the city of Oaxaca, there is a turnoff from Route 190. If you are traveling with a list of all the people to whom you must bring gifts, this short side trip might do much to ease your mind. At the end of the road is the little town of Santa María Atzompa, where you will find a very unique and charming type of pottery. The object is a small horned animal with an unglazed, striated, or grooved body and a glazed green head. The animal is filled with water through a hole in its back, and chia seeds are planted in the surface grooves. Soon it is covered with a delicate, green, mosslike coat. It is particularly popular with children.

OAXACA: For a detailed report on the city, its restaurants and hotels, see *Oaxaca,* THE CITIES. This lovely, easygoing town closes early, and if you are planning to spend the night, you should probably find a hotel immediately upon arrival. Restaurants stop serving dinner earlier than in equivalent-size cities farther north, so plan accordingly to avoid going to bed still hungry. Daytime in Oaxaca is quite another story. Not for planning and scheduling, Oaxaca is a town made for lazing around, enjoying the zocalo, and watching the world go by. Just before you think you might take root here, you can make a number of side trips exciting enough to pull you away with only a minimal amount of effort. Monte Albán, only 6 miles (10 km) beyond the city limits, is one of Mexico's most spectacular archaeological sites. And on the road leading south out of the city are two little-known villages of some interest, Cuilapán and Zaachila. The archaeological site of Mitla, just 24 miles (38 km) southeast of Oaxaca, is also worth a visit (see *En Route from Tlacolula* below).

CUILAPÁN: This tiny Mixtec village, 9 miles (14 km) southwest of Oaxaca, is the site of another and very different kind of ruin. Here, in 1555, a group of Dominican friars began work on a massive monastery, but the project was never completed. Today it has deteriorated into an odd combination of functioning parts and crumbling ruins. The walls of the basilica (which is in use) hold the tombs of what was perhaps the last of the Zapotec and Mixtec royalty, the Mixtec Prince of Tilantongo and his wife Cosijopi, daughter of the King of Tehuantepec.

In its heyday, Cuilapán was the hub of the cochineal (red dye) industry, so important in the development of Mexico's traditional textiles. Long before the Spanish invasion, the Zapotec Indians used this dye, which is derived from the fried female cochineal mite. After they laid their eggs on the coccus cactus pads, the mites were gathered and dried for marketing. And it is from them that the rich and enduring scarlet dyes are obtained. During the colonial period, the Spanish crown had a monopoly on cochineal, and vast Oaxacan haciendas were built around the industry. The Spanish took their monopoly so seriously that anyone caught removing the cactus from Spanish territory was sentenced to death. Only the Spanish were allowed to export it, which they did, and scarlet soon became the rage in Europe. Even the resplendent red coats of the British army were dyed with cochineal.

In January 1979, Pope John Paul II made this stop one of the most emotional of his 8-day visit to Mexico. Hundreds of thousands of barefoot peasants trekked into the town to get a glimpse of the pontiff, who put on a native hat and picked up a little girl in a moving scene captured by a news photographer and sent around the world. Local officials welcomed the pope with a *guelaguetza,* a traditional ceremony in which natives don 3-foot fan-shaped hats decorated with streaming ribbons and dance to the haunting beat of a single drum.

ZAACHILA: Three miles (5 km) farther down the same road is this rustic, pastoral, and lovely village, the last capital of the Zapotec nation. There is an archaeological site on the edge of town that is only partially excavated. What has been unearthed so far in the way of clay figurines, gold plate, carved reliefs, and royal remains is quite fascinating, and much more is yet to be revealed.

En Route from Oaxaca – After you've made the half-day side trip to the two charming villages and spent as much time as you wish in Oaxaca itself, your way south continues on Route 190.

SANTA MARÍA EL TULE: On the highway, 6 miles (10 km) southeast of Oaxaca, is this little town with two claims to fame. The mangoes of Santa María el Tule are said to be among the most delicious in the world; and the town is also the home of Mexico's oldest living thing, "The Tule Tree." Towering above the churchyard in which it stands, it reaches 140 feet into the air, measures 160 feet around, and has a trunk 55 feet thick. Naturalists estimate that this grand cypress is about 3,000 years old. Close by stands another tree that would otherwise be impressively large. In a few hundred years, El Hijo, "the son of the monarch," may take over as the successor of a mighty tradition and serve as guardian of Santa María el Tule. Lively festivities are held in town on *Día de la Candelaria* (*Candlemas*), February 2, which features colorful dances, horse racing, water sports, and fireworks.

TEOTITLÁN DEL VALLE: Four miles (6 km) farther on Route 190 is the turnoff to Teotitlán del Valle. This pleasant village at the foot of the Sierra Madre is the center of Oaxaca's serape industry, and almost every home in town has a loom. The typical Teotitlán serape is all wool, usually of two panels, of light to medium weight, loosely woven, and decorated with stylized animal figures.

Nearby are the famous ruins of one of the finest of the Zapotec legacies, Dainzu, which has a symmetrical ground plan and a magnificent view of the surrounding valleys.

TLACOLULA: Back on the highway and about 10 miles (16 km) farther is the ancient town of Tlacolula. Dating from 1250, this Indian village has a wonderful Sunday market that you should visit if the timing is right. In town there is also a beautiful 16th-century church with a fine chapel.

En Route from Tlacolula – From Tlacolula, head south and stop off at the ruins of Mitla, at the end of a marked side road off Highway 190, about 24 miles (38 km) southeast of Oaxaca. Originally the home of the Zapotec and later the Mixtec, Mitla has puzzled archaeologists who have found no recorded representations of people, animals, or mythological symbols here. In the large Hall of the Monoliths, the designs are reminiscent of Greek fretwork. There's also a small museum of Mextec and Zapotec artifacts in the middle of town.

The road from Tlacolula begins its sinuous progress through rugged mountains with an occasional vista over the lush countryside. Curving, twisting, and winding back on itself, this road soars from peak to sweeping valley in rapid succession, rising, dipping, turning right and left, with every diabolical twist a road can make. It is no route for an inexperienced or timid driver, or for a passenger who suffers motion sickness. There are few places to pause for a breather. The driver's undivided attention is required at all times. And although the driving surface is excellent, there are the occasional surprise boulders offered up by the surrounding mountains. Again, believe the maximum speeds posted: The road is narrow, and it is a long way down.

After about 72 miles (115 km) the road begins to descend from 4,900 feet to 800 feet in a 39-mile (62-km) series of long, winding curves through magnificent scenery. Eventually the road levels out at the riverside town of Tequisistlán, which will, from this time on, occupy a warm place in your memory as the place the road stood still. From here you enter the tropical lowlands of the Tehuantepec Itsmo, with the town of the same name only 30 miles (48 km) down the road.

TEHUANTEPEC: This is one of two major cities on the isthmus, and it is the subject of a great controversy in the rest of Mexico. Here, in a country committed to machismo, a society exists in which women have social and cultural dominance. Women run the businesses, handle the commerce and trade, hold the purse strings, and run the banks, while the men are relegated to planting and harvesting the fields. The Tehuana are also said to be the most beautiful women in Mexico and appear even more majestic in their long, flowing skirts and stunningly embroidered jackets. Unfortunately, the town has little to recommend it other than this exceptional social structure. Sweltering under the tropical sun, with only one paved road, it is one of the least attractive towns along Route 190. But the sight of these women gliding gracefully along, balancing fully loaded baskets on their heads, is truly a pleasure. And at night they fill the zocalo, sitting around in the drowsy tropical air, swapping salty stories, and whistling at any attractive man passing by.

The daily costume of the Tehuana is rich and elaborate, gold embroidery on red cloth, but it is modest compared to their dress for special occasions. Fiestas call for satin or velvet skirts, sleeveless blouses, and starched ruffled petticoats of finely pleated white lace extending 7 or 8 inches below their hemlines. On their heads they sport magnificent *huipiles,* a term usually referring to loose-fitting blouses, but in this case meaning bonnets of white lace fashioned after a baby's baptismal dress, with two tiny sleeves uselessly hanging down over the ears. This particular form of headdress is said to have originated when a hapless sailor returned home from a long voyage without a gift for his wife. She promptly put him out of the house, telling him not to return empty-handed. He roamed all the way to Oaxaca, where in desperation he grabbed a package from a Spanish *doña* who was just leaving a local shop with a baptismal gown for her new baby. When the sailor returned home and his wife opened his offering, she didn't know what to make of it. The quick-thinking sailor, wishing to enjoy the comforts of home once again, told her the baptismal gown was a hat and the latest rage in Oaxaca. When she wore it out, it was so successful that all the women of the town followed suit, and soon its popularity moved it from style to tradition.

To complete the Tehuana costume there is the necklace of gold coins. Much like the gypsy women of Europe, these Indian queens carry the family exchequer on their person in the way of heavy gold chains, necklaces, and bracelets.

A final word about these women. They are known for their fiery tempers and are provoked by having their pictures taken or being approached by foreign men.

The town name, Tehuantepec, is the Nahuatl word meaning Jaguar Hill, referring to the hills around the town. According to legend, fierce jaguars once roamed this country until the local Indians appealed to a Huave sorcerer for aid. He, in turn, called upon a giant turtle to rise from the sea and drive the jaguars away. When the last jaguar was gone, the sorcerer transformed the turtle into a hill and ordered it to keep guard and see that none of the jaguars returned. If you climb the brush-covered path to the top of this mound, you, like the turtle, will get a spectacular view from Juchitán to the east to the great lagoon of Tehuantepec along the Pacific to the west. An annual regional arts and crafts fair is held in the town, usually beginning in late May.

En Route from Tehuantepec – If you are not planning to continue the trip into Chiapas, and if you are ready for a little ocean and beach life before returning north, there is a side trip from Tehuantepec that should more than satisfy you. Traveling 11 miles (18 km) south on Route 185 out of Tehuantepec, you will come to the once booming port town of Salina Cruz. Although today this harbor boasts very little of interest, an unpaved but good road leads east to Bahía Ventosa.

BAHÍA VENTOSA (Ventosa Bay): This beautiful 4-mile stretch of beach, only 20 minutes out of Salina Cruz, curves to form a small bay bordered by lush tropical vegetation. There are a number of thatch-roofed beach restaurants offering the local catch of seafood and generously providing hammocks for travel-weary visitors. If you decide to stay overnight, there are a few rooming houses (ask for the *Casa de Huéspedes* when you arrive); campers have taken over a coconut grove near the beach, although the facilities are primitive. The only road out of Bahía Ventosa is the one leading into it, and you will be retracing your steps all the way back to Tehuantepec. From here, the road into Chiapas is back on Route 190, east to Juchitán de Zaragoza.

JUCHITÁN DE ZARAGOZA: Only 16 miles (26 km) beyond Tehuantepec lies the busy isthmus town of Juchitán (pronounced Who-chee-*tahn*). Vying with its neighbor in weaving, pottery, gold jewelry, and poetry, this city has become the more important cultural and economic center for the Tehuana. The women of Juchitán, known as *Juchitecas,* are not thought to be as attractive as their sisters in Tehuantepec, but, like them, take pride in adorning themselves with colorful clothing and golden jewelry. The market and fiestas of Juchitán are cleaner and more elaborate than those of its rival, and at times in their history, these two cities have been known to struggle over everything from political allegiances to the length of hemlines and depth of necklines. Juchitán is the straw hat, basket, and weaving center of the isthmus, and handloomed and finely embroidered textiles can be found in shops near the zocalo. A festival featuring native dancing is usually held in the spring.

En Route from Juchitán – If you are tired or hungry, before continuing the 57-mile (91-km) journey to Tapanatepec, just west of the Oaxaca-Chiapas border, consider resting or eating in the Juchitán area. Just over the Rio Los Perros is the clean, air conditioned *Colon* restaurant. As you continue toward Tapanatepec, you'll come across a strip of road, near the junction of Routes 190 and 185, that warrants a word of caution. The wind is so fierce along this stretch of road that it has been known to blow the chrome from the sides of cars. It is sometimes an effort to stay on the right side of the highway, so slow down to avoid problems with oncoming vehicles.

At Tapanatepec the road through Chiapas to Guatemala divides, and drivers have the choice of two very distinct, very different routes. The longer trip, northward and inland along Route 190, offers a far better picture of Chiapas, one of Mexico's least-known and most exotic states. However, Route 200, the newer road, is faster and glides along the level Pacific coast. For anyone eager to reach Central America more quickly, or on the contrary, with enough time to dally along some of the country's most beautiful beaches (with a guarantee of privacy that is more secure than anywhere else on Mexico's sweeping Pacific coast), it can be delightful. Below, we discuss both routes, starting with the Pacific road, Route 200.

Note that no matter which road you take, the highways in Chiapas are in far worse repair than those in Oaxaca. Chiapas is a poor state, a situation made patently obvious when the middle-of-the-road white lines disappear from the highway and the pavement becomes rougher and harder.

CHIAPAS'S PACIFIC COAST — ROUTE 200

En Route from Tapanatepec – Route 200 crosses the Chiapas border east of Tapanatepec and then rolls along the Pacific coast for 198 miles (317 km) before crossing into Guatemala. While it parallels the coastline, it is several miles from the sea, and to find the best beaches and fishing villages you must leave it occasionally to drive south. The first town of any size across the Chiapas border is Arriaga. The next really interesting stop is Tonalá, which has roads to several marvelous sea spots.

TONALÁ AND PAREDON: Mostly a shipping point for shrimp and other ocean bounty, this is the turnoff point for Paredon and Puerto Arista, two of Chiapas's seaside resorts. Fifteen miles (24 km) southwest of Tonalá, Paredon is on a bay known deceptively as the Dead Sea, a fisherman's paradise. In addition to magnificent catches, the waters are perfect for swimming all year. A major attraction is the *cayuco* (dugout canoe) excursion along the 40-mile coastline of the bay, which can also be made by motorboat. There are facilities for camping and trailers, and there are also a couple of small hotels. The *Grajandra* (204 Av. Hidalgo) has a restaurant, bar, pool, and disco (phone: 966-30144).

Another road leading south from Tonalá goes to the virgin beaches of Puerto Arista, only 7 miles (11 km) from Tonalá. As yet untouched by commercial tourism, the only sign of man's encroachment is a few thatch-roofed restaurants, for which you will be grateful. To reconnect with Route 200 you must return to Tonalá. From there it is a fast, fairly flat stretch all the way to Tapachula, at the Guatemala border. The area through which the road travels is almost entirely undeveloped, and you'll see dense forests of rare woods and exotic orchids, plains of sugarcane, and stock farms.

TAPACHULA: Only 11 miles (18 km) from the Guatemala border, this city is the center for local coffee, cotton, cocoa, and banana plantations. Set at the foot of an extinct Tacaná volcano, Tapachula has a charming zocalo with neatly trimmed tropical trees, lively sidewalk cafés, and a choice of pleasant accommodations.

PUERTO MADERO: This beautiful Pacific resort is at the end of a 15-mile (24-km) paved road south of Tapachula. There are facilities for all sorts of water sports, and the beach is dotted with thatch-roofed restaurants serving freshly caught fish. You are likely to find yourself the only non-Mexican on this idyllic, unspoiled, and totally relaxing beach.

En Route from Tapachula – You are now at the edge of Mexico, ready to enter Guatemala. By backtracking to Huixtla, several miles west of Tapachula along Route 200, you can take a mostly dirt state road north and drive roughly parallel to Mexico's border with Guatemala to connect with Route 190 where it crosses the border. By driving west on Route 190 you can make a complete circle around the Chiapas countryside, served by the two highways. If at Tapanatepec, Oaxaca, you choose not to drive the coastal route, you have the inland road, Route 190. We recommend, however, that you avoid driving this stretch of Route 190 during the rainy season (November and December); just after Tehuantepec the road can become muddy and dangerous, especially in the mountains.

INLAND CHIAPAS — ROUTE 190

OCOZOCOAUTLA: This almost pure-blooded Zoque Indian town is only 50 miles (81 km) from the city of Tuxtla. The Zoque are a tall, stout people who farm and work as laborers. Of Maya descent, they speak the ancient Indian language of Zoque. The men of the village wear shirts and pants of a rough woven fabric called manta, and the women wear dresses cinched at the waist with blue fabric rolled into a belt. Above Ocozocoautla, a half-hour walk up the side of the mountain, is the tiny village of Ocuilpa. There artisans are at work making the beautifully decorated pots of this area, which have wavy black-and-white-lined designs around the rims.

TUXTLA GUTIÉRREZ: Standing on the left bank of Río Grande Chiapas 50 miles (80 km) east of Ocozocoautla is the capital city of the state, Tuxtla Gutiérrez. It replaced San Cristóbal de las Casas as the seat of government in 1892 and is now a prosperous, commercial distribution center for the surrounding coffee and tobacco plantations. Although there are some 40 hotels and motels in Tuxtla, they are booked to 95% capacity year-round, so it is advisable to make reservations in advance through a travel agent in Oaxaca (see *Best en Route*). Although the city is neither picturesque nor quaint, it is filled with tropical flowers and interesting sites, and it offers a good opportunity to rest up and regroup the senses. The Government Palace is a handsome building of Mexican and Spanish design fronted by a monument to the state's benefactor, Friar Bartolomé de las Casas, a Dominican missionary and bishop of Chiapas. In the town market and in shops near the central plaza one can find a large choice of inlaid wooden boxes, lacquered gourds, carved deer antlers, leather goods, native amber, and gold jewelry. The Zoque Indian women of the area are partial to gold filigree and wear necklaces of amber beads and small gold coins with gold filigree crosses. These rosary-like necklaces are heirlooms, and are much sought after by collectors.

Tuxtla also maintains a fabulous zoo and ecological park, the Zoológico Miguel Alvarez del Toro, where 110 species of animals native to the state — such as monkeys, jaguars, anteaters, ocelots, boars, snakes, and birds — roam free in lush vegetation. This collection is not only impressive, but has been written up in renowned scientific publications throughout the world.

Another place worth visiting is the *Museo Regional de Chiapas* (Chiapas Regional Museum), designed by Pedro Ramírez Vázquez — who created the *Anthropology Museum* in Mexico City — and devoted to pre-Hispanic treasures. Be sure to stop at the tourist office (950 Blvd. Dr. Belisario Domínguez). The staff speaks English and has done a remarkable job compiling tourist information for the entire state.

SUMIDERO CANYON: For an amazing side trip from Tuxtla, drive 15 miles (24 km) north of town to Tierra Colorada Hill. From a lookout point here, one can see the unique and spectacular natural formations of the Sumidero Canyon. This 26-mile-long, 6,000-foot-deep canyon was cut by the churning waters and once-treacherous rapids of the Río Grijalva, tamed after the construction of the Manuel Moreno ("Chicoaten") Dam.

It was in these waters that the fiercely independent Indians of Chiapas made their final stand against the invading Spaniards in the middle of the 16th century. Spanish troops pushed into Chiapas to subdue the united Indian tribes that had managed to resist them. Over a period of years the Indians were driven to El Sumidero, with their backs to the river. In the last prolonged battle, they held off the Spaniards for days with arrows and spears, until their food supplies ran out. Their numbers were dwindling, their weapons almost gone, and the Spanish called for their surrender. But the Indians refused and fought on with their remaining weapons, then with rocks, and finally with their bare hands. When they knew they could no longer hold off the enemy, rather than surrender and become slaves to the Spanish, they threw themselves into the ravine below. First the wounded, then the women and children, and finally the warriors made the leap, until some 1,000 Indians had committed suicide rather than submit to Spanish rule. The awed invaders, not wanting to be a party to the further genocide of such brave and freedom-loving people, withdrew their troops to Oaxaca, and the Indians of Chiapas were left to rule their own land.

Ruta de Usamacinta Tours (phone: 931-31915 or 931-34509 in Villahermosa; 934-50260 in Palenque) offers a 4-day tour of Chiapas, including a boat ride in the canyon.

Other excursions from Tuxtla include tours of coffee and tobacco plantations, which can be arranged through any hotel or the tourist office. Bonampak is the world-famous archaeological site hidden deep in the jungles of Chiapas and is particularly known for its amazingly detailed murals depicting the warrior rites of the First Maya Empire. The painted walls have been reproduced and can be seen at the *National Museum* in Mexico City as well as in the archaeological museum in Villahermosa, Tabasco. But remember, as you drive south through Chiapas, that in the jungles to the east are the remains of a once highly advanced and religious culture.

Bonampak is accessible from Palenque, but once the road ends, it's a muddy 5-mile hike into the jungle. (Be sure to wear protective clothing and use insect repellent.) You can reach Palenque via Route 186 from Villahermosa, Tabasco. (For detailed information, see *The Yucatán Peninsula,* DIRECTIONS.) The trip can also be made by road from Tuxtla, or by renting a small plane. *Sanborn Tours* offers a 1-day trip by light plane from San Cristóbal; reserve in advance (phone: 800-531-5440 in the US).

CHIAPA DE CORZO: This picturesque colonial village, built on a bluff overlooking the Río Chiapa, was founded on the site of an Indian settlement by conquistador Diego de Mazariegos in 1528. The zocalo is dominated by a strange and beautiful 16th-century fountain shaped like the crown of the King of Spain. This imposing octagonal structure (Moorish in style) is made of a Mozarabic brick. Reputed to be the finest example of Mozarabic architecture in the country, it is one of only two octagonal structures in Mexico.

Facing the plaza is the small *Museo Regional de la Laca* (Museum of Popular Arts and Crafts), devoted to exhibits of regional handicrafts. The specialty of the region is lacquered gourds called *jicaras,* and local potters specialize in green and black glazed ware.

Chiapa de Corzo is the site of an annual *Easter* carnival and the famed dance of the Parachicos, put on by hundreds of performers in brightly colored native dress and masks. On January 20, *San Sebatián Day* is also celebrated with a fair, folk dancing, and a reenactment of a traditional naval battle on the Grijalva River.

The Church and Convent of Santo Domingo (1 block off the plaza) is another 16th-century legacy to the city, this one Gothic. Hanging in its tower is a huge bell made of silver, gold, and copper. On the eastern edge of town is a Maya ruin that has pyramidal platforms and is worth looking at. Chiapa de Corzo is also the point of departure for river trips that go some distance into the El Sumidero Canyon. You can also take a boat downriver to Alcalá, and from there take a bus to the Indian village of San Bartolomé de los Llanos.

SAN BARTOLOMÉ DE LOS LLANOS: The attraction of this village is its inhabitants, who have one of the most unusual and attractive native costumes in all of Mexico. The women wear dark blue skirts embellished with brightly colored embroidery and lovely white lace blouses. The men wear white cotton jodhpur-like trousers, which are flared from the hip to the knee and narrow from there to the ankle. These pants are covered with tiny red embroidered figures, which also appear on the men's lacelike shirts. Both sexes wear their midriffs bare.

En Route from Chiapa – The 44-mile (71-km) drive east on Route 190 to San Cristóbal, the next major stop, is an amazing 5,000-foot climb through magnificent mountain scenery, with spectacular vistas at every turn. Watch out for local natives careening down the hillsides in tiny homemade wooden carts stuffed with the day's shopping or goods destined for the market. The carts have no brakes.

SAN CRISTÓBAL DE LAS CASAS: Set in the lovely valley of Hueyzacatlán, this town's colonial influence is immediately apparent, and it is easy to imagine that San Cristóbal is much as it was during the era of Spanish rule. The buildings are mostly 1-story stucco houses painted in pastel tones and topped with red tile roofs. And peering down from the two hills east and west of town are two churches, carefully and somewhat threateningly placed by the Spanish conquistadores. Indians of various tribes from the surrounding mountains fill the town and marketplace, each group wearing its own particular clothing and speaking its own language. The pace is slow, the weather warm under a morning sun but cold at night. San Cristóbal is a town strangely out of time.

In 1524, Captain Luis Marín and the famous soldier-historian Bernal Díaz del Castillo led their troops into this valley and discovered that the Chamula Indians had a stronghold on a nearby mountain. The Chamula fought bravely against the Spanish attack until their losses became too heavy. But although the Spaniards won this particular battle, 4 more years passed before they could secure the area and establish the town of San Cristóbal.

Once the Spaniards were firmly in control, the Spanish governor, Juan Enriqué de Guzmán, instituted repressive tactics to break the spirit of the Indians. When Bishop Bartolomé de las Casas arrived in this former capital of Chiapas in 1545 (then called Villaviciosa — "Vicious City"), conditions were at their worst. The bishop began to fight vigorously on behalf of the Indians. He spoke out against the political practices of the governor and wrote a detailed report to Madrid about the vile situation, earning himself the hatred of the conquistadores. His report was also widely circulated by the enemies of Spain in the rest of Europe. But it was some 20 years later, when the king issued "New Ordinances Governing Treatment of Indians in the New World," before the report had any effect. The new ruling recognized the Indians as humans. The natives previously were considered pagans without souls — in effect, animals. And even then, the proclamation went largely ignored. Nevertheless, de las Casas won a place in the hearts of the Indians, and thus the town is named in his honor.

Among the many places of interest in San Cristóbal is the cathedral (directly on the zocalo), notable for its baroque retablos, and magnificent gold-encrusted pulpit. Santo Domingo church, begun in 1547, stands about 6 blocks north of the plaza. The carvings on its baroque façade have weathered to a dusty pink, and its interior, approached through a laurel-shaded passageway, is covered with unusual retablos. Visitors are always drawn to the handsome façade on the Casa de Mazariegos, the palatial mansion of the city's founder; and to the town's Carmen church, with its Moorish Torre del Carmen, which has a street running through its base.

It is impossible to visit San Cristóbal and not see *Na Bolom Centro de Estudios Científicos* (Center of Scientific Studies; on 33 Av. Vicente Guerrero), part home, part library, part museum, run by Mrs. Gertrude Blom. The museum is open Tuesdays through Sundays, 4 to 5:30 PM. The library, which specializes in Chiapas and the Maya culture, is open Mondays, 2:30 to 6 PM, and Tuesdays through Saturdays, 9 AM to 1 PM.

Mrs. Blom's husband first came to Mexico from Denmark in 1919, and shortly thereafter began studying the Yucatán — at the time an area almost totally unexplored. He focused on the Lacandon, a group of Maya Indians who at that time lived totally isolated in the Chiapas jungle. He and his Swiss wife Gertrude, a writer, photographer, and linguist, were married in the early 1940s.

The couple ventured into the highlands and learned the local customs and languages of the inhabitants. The Bloms became an institution in this city and state, and are credited with having saved the once-dwindling Lacandon Indians from extinction. The Mexican government, in recognition of their work, bestowed on the Bloms the rare honor of Mexican citizenship. Pancho, as Mr. Blom was known, died in 1963, but Gertrude, who turns 90 this February, is still very much alive and active. Mrs. Blom now runs *Na Bolom,* dedicated to the ecology of Chiapas and the preservation of the Lacandon rain forest, and its small guesthouse, where kindred souls are warmly welcomed. Each guestroom is named for a different pueblo of the region and is decorated with textiles woven in that pueblo. Mrs. Blom is very selective about her clientele, but she does accept reservations (phone: 967-81418) and sometimes has room for drop-in guests for overnight stays or meals made with food from her organic gardens and orchard (see *Best en Route*). Mrs. Blom is still an expert horsewoman, and several times a year (but not during the rainy season) she leads parties of visitors on a tour of the Indian villages on horseback. This tour is an amazing experience up steep mountainsides into villages few outsiders have ever seen.

Anfitriones Turísticos de Chiapas (15 Cinco de Febrero; phone: 967-82550 or 967-82557), arranges charter flights from San Cristóbal to Bonampak, Palenque, and the Lacandon forest region. The company also arranges river trips, horseback rides, and bird watching.

A main attraction in San Cristóbal is people watching. With 28 ethnic groups, there are few other places on earth where you can see and hear so many distinctive peoples speaking their own languages, wearing native costumes, and following ancient traditions. The Indians, however, strongly dislike being stared at and definitely do not want to be photographed, so be discreet and considerate in observing them. The variations in clothing give clues to which Indian group an individual belongs.

For a fascinating overview of the area's attractions and regional clothing, contact Sergio Castro, an agricultural engineer who has worked with the Indians for almost 30 years. Along with his museum of regional dress (16 de Septiembre 32, San Cristóbal de las Casas, Chiapas; phone: 967-84289), he offers a slide show. Open evenings only; no admission charge, but a donation to help him continue his work is appreciated.

Chamula Indians – The women wear *huipiles* (shapeless blouses) and skirts of heavy black wool that are streaked with fine red and gray stripes. The only adornment on the *huipil* is two tassels of red wool or silk hanging down the front. The *huipil* is tucked into the wraparound skirt and belted by a red woolen sash with a large pleat in front. Heads are covered with a folded piece of the same material. The men wear white calf-length pants and shirts covered by black or white woolen tunics. The men of San Juan Chamula have white sleeves on their tunics; those from San Andrés Chamula, red sleeves; those from Santiago, brown sleeves; and those from Santa Marta and Magdalenas, blue sleeves. They all wear flat, handwoven straw hats held by bands tied under the chin. The Chamula seldom wear ribbons on their hats, except in combination with black tunics that indicate the wearer is or was an official of the village. Chamula Indians also wear goat horns tied around their waists; inside the horns they keep salt to use as a condiment and for barter.

Zinacantec Indians – These women wear *huipiles* of white homespun wool, often beautifully embroidered, that reach to their calves. The upper part is completely covered by diamond-shaped patterns that are formed by crisscrossing diagonals. The lower part and sleeves follow the same pattern but are embroidered in a smaller and more delicate stitch. The men wear short white or pale pink cotton tunics with very short pants intended to show off their well-formed, muscular legs. It is said that the males of the Zinacantec have the most beautiful legs in the world. They also sport handsome flat hats bedecked with gaily colored ribbons. Although an expert can tell a man's village by the decoration on his hat, the ribbons have a more obvious and important meaning. Married men wear their ribbons tied, while bachelors let their ribbons blow freely in the wind. A word of warning is in order regarding these hats. While they are an attractive purchase in the local markets, wait until you leave the area before wearing them. The Zinacantec resent strangers, especially women, wearing their finery.

Huisteco Indians – The women of this group wear short cotton *huipiles* embroidered lengthwise in very fine red lines. Across these lines diamond-shaped decorations are embroidered in orange, green, and magenta yarn. The *huipil* is worn with a dark blue wraparound skirt held up by a red-and-black-striped woolen waistband. The costume of the Huisteco men is one of the most interesting in the region. It consists of a wide piece of cotton material placed waist-level in the back and then crossed between the legs in numerous folds, diaper-fashion. The ends are brought up and fastened with a braided sash, the ends of which are left hanging to either side. The shirt, a sleeved *huipil* split up the sides, is worn tucked inside the pants. It is made from heavy cotton embroidered on the back of the shoulders with one line of simple geometric design in red or blue.

Their headdress is also unique. The Huisteco hat has a small, flat, straw crown with an upturned brim reminiscent of a dinner plate. It is worn at a rakish angle, slanted over the forehead and attached at the nape of the neck by a red ribbon. Under the hat, hanging from a strap and dangling down the back all the way to the waist, is a small flat bag. These colorfully embroidered pouches are used to support their folded blankets and to carry small items. It is interesting to note that women usually go barefoot, even on the most festive occasions, while the men are clad in huaraches, sandals made of interwoven leather straps with soles cut from automobile tires. In this region huaraches often have built-up heel guards that are a relic of Maya days.

There are many fascinating Indian villages in the mountains north of San Cristóbal. The two most accessible are San Juan Chamula and Zinacantán. Both are on unpaved roads about 8 miles (13 km) from the city. While both can be reached by car, they are wonderful trips to make on horseback. This form of transportation will make more adventurous, out-of-the-way trips possible. Horses can be rented in San Cristóbal for about $35 for a 5-hour trip. Try to attend Sunday services in San Juan Chamula's church. More pre-Hispanic than Christian, the services are conducted in Tzotzil, the native tongue. A permit must be obtained in advance at the Palacio Municipal for a small fee. Absolutely no photographs may be taken inside the church.

Within hiking distance of San Cristóbal are some barely explored Maya ruins that make a fascinating afternoon outing. And about 4 miles (7 km) south of town, just off Route 190 by way of a rough dry-weather trail, are the partially explored Grutas de Rancho Nuevo, an enticing series of caves for the experienced spelunker. (Largely unexplored, the caves can be entered only during the dry season.)

COMITÁN DE DOMÍNGUEZ: This small colonial community, built on the side of a mountain, marks the halfway point in the 110-mile (176-km) drive from San Cristóbal de las Casas to the Guatemalan border. Long before the Spanish settled here in the early 16th century, Comitán de Domínguez was the site of the most populated Maya-Quiche kingdom in southeast Chiapas. It was then called Bulumcanán, the Maya word meaning "new star." Today, this town is the chief entry port for products from Guatemala as well as the main marketing center for the Tzeltal Indians. Here you will find colonial houses perched atop huge rocks and connected by tortuous uphill-downhill streets, each with its own amazing view. The climate in Comitán is superb, and the whole area is teeming with some 500 varieties of orchids, which grow wild throughout town. A Moorish kiosk, in the form of a six-pointed star, stands in the center of the plaza surrounded by these tropical blossoms. The area also makes a sugarcane brandy, *comitecho* or *chicha.* It is a fiery spirit not to be taken lightly. The *Lagos de Montebello* (phone: 963-21092 or 963-21198) is a pleasant place to stay in town.

En Route from Comitán – Between Comitán and the border town of Ciudad Cuauhtémoc is the last stretch of Route 190 in Chiapas and Mexico. This is also the stretch of road that offers a unique side trip to Montebello Lakes, one of the most beautiful spots in Mexico.

LAGOS DE MONTEBELLO (Montebello Lakes): This chain of 59 magnificent lakes, set in forest and mountain country, is unquestionably one of the most beautiful and isolated places in Mexico. Although it's only a 40-minute drive from Comitán, once you get there you may feel as if time has collapsed and you are back in the age before man was important in the scheme of things. To get there, drive south from Comitán on Route 190 for 11 miles (18 km). Just before reaching La Trinitaria, turn east on the paved road that leads 27 miles (43 km) to Lago de Colores, one of the three more accessible lakes in the area. San José de Arco and Montebello, also known as Tziscao, are the other two.

Near the end of the road is the tiny village of San Rafael de Arco. Here you can hire a guide to accompany you through the forest to the natural bridge over the Río Comitán and just beyond to a cave into which the river seems to disappear.

Also a short walk from the highway is the Chinkultic archaeological zone, a large pre-Columbian ceremonial center that is worth the short hike.

In 1960 the Mexican government made the Montebello Lakes and the surrounding Lacandon Forest into a national park to preserve its beauty. The fishing in the lakes is reputed to be among the finest in Mexico. However, the only sleeping facility near the lake is very run-down, so it's better to return to Comitán for the night.

The forest and the vast unexplored lands to the east are the home of the Lacandon Indians. These people, totally isolated from the rest of the world, were near extinction when they were contacted and aided in the early 1920s by Franz Blom of San Cristóbal de las Casas. The Indians continue to live in isolation, following their own ancient lifestyle and religion and speaking a rarely heard dialect of Maya. But today, some of them have learned Spanish, and they are aware of, if not totally familiar with, the presence of other people beyond the forest. If you should happen to see a Lacandon Indian there is no chance you would confuse him or her with any other group. All members of the community wear their hair long, and the women, once they have reached puberty, adorn themselves with brightly colored bird feathers tied to the back of their hair. Men and women also dress alike, and wear loosely fitting white robes. The Lacandon are a shy and reticent people who have opted to continue their life of seclusion. They do not feel comfortable around strangers, nor do they like having their pictures taken. Any contact with them must be carried on in a spirit sensitive to their lives.

En Route from Lagos de Montebello – When you return to the Pan-American Highway from Lagos de Montebello, you will be about 44 miles (70 km) from the border crossing at Ciudad Cuauhtémoc. You should not, under any circumstances, attempt this section of road at night. The consideration is not only one of safety, but of pure pleasure, for if you do drive at night you will deprive yourself of seeing some of the most spectacular scenery in Mexico. It is so spectacular, in fact, that if there were absolutely nothing to see between Mexico City and this strip of road, the trip would still be more than worth it.

If you are planning to continue your trip into Guatemala, be prepared for the usual hassle at the border. US citizens will need a visa or tourist card to enter the country. Visas are free and can be obtained by showing a passport, birth certificate, or voter's registration card at any of the General Consulate offices in New York, New Orleans, Houston, Chicago, Los Angeles, San Francisco, Coral Gables (Florida), or Mexico City. Tourist cards can be purchased at the Guatemala border or, before crossing the border, from the Guatemalan Consulate (Av. 3A off Av. Centrale Ote.), open weekdays from 7 AM to 2 PM and on Saturdays from 7 AM to 12 PM. Obtaining a tourist card, however, is is likely to be time-consuming, confusing, and often more expensive than the actual $1 fee. Clearly it is better to plan ahead. If you are not continuing across the border, there is a highway that intersects with Route 190 at El Jocote, 3 miles (5 km) northwest of the border. From here it is a pleasant 130 miles (208 km) to the Pacific coast at Huixtla, and another 5 hours over the flat coastal road, Route 200, back up to Tapanatepec and the Pan-American Highway north.

BEST EN ROUTE

HUAJUAPÁN DE LEÓN

Casablanca – There's even a disco in this 36-room hotel. Other facilities include TV sets, a pool, restaurant, bar, and parking. 1 Amatista (phone: 953-20779 or 953-20979). Moderate.

Oaxaca – A modern vacation complex with 24 rooms, 2 suites, pools, a tennis court, toboggan, disco, restaurant, and movie theater. Km 6 Carr. Federal to Ituajuapan (phone: 953-20992; in Puebla, 22-482222). Moderate.

García Peral – Here are 33 rooms with telephone and TV sets, a restaurant, and parking. Colegio Militar (phone: 953-20777 or 953-20742). Inexpensive.

TEHUANTEPEC

Calli – The best accommodations between Oaxaca and Tuxtla Gutiérrez include 100 modest rooms with air conditioning and showers, a swimming pool, and dining room. Slightly more than a mile (1.6 km) past the turnoff to Tehuantepec, at Km 790 on the Cristóbal Colón Hwy. (phone: 971-50085 through 89 or 971-50113). Moderate.

JUCHITÁN DE ZARAGOZA

La Mansión – It has 38 air conditioned rooms and 5 suites. Restaurant, bar, parking. Prolongación 11 Av. Dieciséis de Septiembre (phone: 971-21055). Expensive to moderate.

TAPACHULA

Kamico – A 2-story, 92-room air conditioned motor inn with restaurant, bar, and pool. On Hwy. 200 on the east edge of town (phone: 962-62640). Expensive to moderate.

Loma Real – Another 2-story air conditioned motel, it has 85 units, a coffee shop, restaurant, bar, pool, and boutique. On a hilltop on Hwy. 200 north of town (phone: 962-61440). Expensive to moderate.

TUXTLA GUTIÉRREZ

Balun Canan – All 38 units have baths, and there is a restaurant. 944 Av. 14 Central Ote. (phone: 961-23050, 961-23103, or 961-23048). Moderate.

Bonampak – This modern, first class hotel with 112 units includes 26 bungalows, air conditioning, phones, showers, and baths. There is a swimming pool, fronton and tennis court, coffee shop, cocktail bar, video bar, and a dining room that is open from 7 AM to midnight. 180 Blvd. Belisario Domínguez (phone: 961-32050). Moderate.

Esponda – This 51-unit hotel has baths and fans in the rooms. 142 1A Calle Poniente (phone: 961-20080, 961-20731, or 961-20141). Moderate.

La Hacienda – Here are 42 air conditioned units, with a restaurant, satellite color TV, parking, and pool. Also 9 full hookups for trailers. 1197 Blvd. Belisario Domínguez (phone: 961-27986 or 961-27832). Moderate.

Humberto – Another large hotel, it has 112 units, all of which are air conditioned and have showers and TV sets. The dining room is open from 7 AM to midnight, and there is a cafeteria and garage. 180 Av. Central Pte. (phone: 961-22081/82/83). Moderate.

Posada de Rey – Comfortable but modest, with 45 air conditioned rooms and 3 suites, closed-circuit TV sets, and a rooftop restaurant. On the plaza at 310 Calle Primera (phone: 961-22871 or 961-22924). Inexpensive.

SAN CRISTÓBAL DE LAS CASAS

Bonampak – Offers 48 rooms and 1 suite, restaurant-bar, tennis court, and pool. There are also 21 spaces with complete hookups for trailers. At the entrance to town on 5 Av. México (phone: 967-81621). Moderate.

El Molina de la Alborada – Eleven comfortable rooms with fireplaces; good food and horseback riding. Apt. 50, 2 miles (3 km) southeast on Rte. 190 (phone: 967-80935). Moderate.

Palacio de Moctezuma – A 38-room hostelry with three lovely gardens, a restaurant, and bar. 16 Av. Juárez (phone: 967-805321 or 967-81181). Moderate.

Posada Diego de Mazariegos – A colonial-style, 80-unit hotel with TV sets and fireplaces in every room, a restaurant, bar, and video bar. 2 María Adelina Flores (phone: 967-81825, 967-80621, or 967-80513). Moderate.

Santa Clara – This delightful inn features a 31-room addition, as well as 22 older units, all with baths. There's also a pool, dining room, bar, cafeteria, handicrafts shop. Insurgentes and 1 Plaza Central (phone: 967-81140). Moderate.

Maya-Quetzal – About to undergo renovations as we went to press, this 50-room hotel has a restaurant and disco. Km 1171 Carr. Panamérica (phone: 967-81181). Moderate to inexpensive.

Español – A newly remodeled, peaceful hotel with 30 rooms, all with fireplaces. There's also a restaurant-bar. At Avs. 16 de Septiembre and Primero de Marzo (phone: 967-80045 or 967-80623). Inexpensive.

Na Bolom – Providing guests with a truly memorable stay, this hotel is run by the inimitable Gertrude Blom (see the Bolom Centro de Estudios Científicos — Center of Scientific Studies — under *San Cristóbal de las Casas* above). The rooms are comfortable, the food good, and the company of Mrs. Blom fascinating. 33 Av. Vicente Guerrero (phone: 967-81418). Inexpensive.

Villa Real – A renovated colonial building with clean, comfortable rooms and a restaurant. No frills, but it's efficient and economical, and the service is friendly. 8 Av. Benito Juárez (phone: 967-82930). Inexpensive.

Reynosa to Mazatlán

The 720-mile (1,152-km) drive along Route 40 from Reynosa to Mazatlán is the shortest route to the Pacific from the southern and eastern US. It offers a variety of interesting sites and spectacular terrain in a region of mines, major industries, large-scale agriculture, and cattle raising.

Beginning at the northeastern border of Mexico, along the Río Grande, this route rolls along flat plains before ascending, descending, and winding through the valleys, steep canyons, desert highlands, towering peaks, and the rugged rolling hills of Mexico's Sierre Madre Oriental and Sierra Madre Occidental to the Pacific Ocean. Besides passing through the states of Tamaulipas, Nuevo León, Coahuila, Durango, and Sinaloa, this route takes you to the major cities of Monterrey, Saltillo, Torreón, Durango, and Mazatlán, as well as to subterranean caverns, small, picturesque villages, mountain hideaways, locations used as movie sets, and dramatic mountains. The last 40-mile (64-km) stretch, reaching 9,000 feet in the Sierra Madre Occidental, is renowned for its beautiful scenery.

The climate along the route varies according to altitude and season. You can expect mild, dry weather with pleasant breezes at higher altitudes and warm, dry weather at lower altitudes. Although the warm season is March to October, the colder season is never too cold, although at night temperatures drop and you will need a jacket.

The history of the regions along this route is one of conquest and violence. During the 1800s Comanche and Apache Indians raided throughout the state of Coahuila, while the northeastern territories suffered numerous battles of the Mexican-American War. At the turn of the century Durango-born Pancho Villa and Coahuila-born Francisco Madero (whose homes you can visit en route) fought to overthrow dictator Porfirio Díaz.

The people of northern Mexico are known to be more American in their style of living and attitudes than are their compatriots farther south. The ancient Indian cultures and traditions, which are prevalent in the southern and central regions, are scarcely visible in this northern part of Mexico.

At hotels listed as expensive, expect to pay $60 to $70 for a double room; $30 to $55 at moderate places; and less than $30, inexpensive.

En Route from McAllen, Texas – The entry to Reynosa, Mexico, on Route 40 is made at the international bridge in McAllen, Texas. After paying a toll and going through customs and immigration (open 24 hours), you cross the bridge over the Río Grande and enter Reynosa.

REYNOSA: This northeastern border town serves as a junction for roads to Matamoros, Nuevo Laredo, and Monterrey. It has a population of more than 500,000 and stands at an altitude of 127 feet along the Río Grande. Founded by the Spanish in 1749,

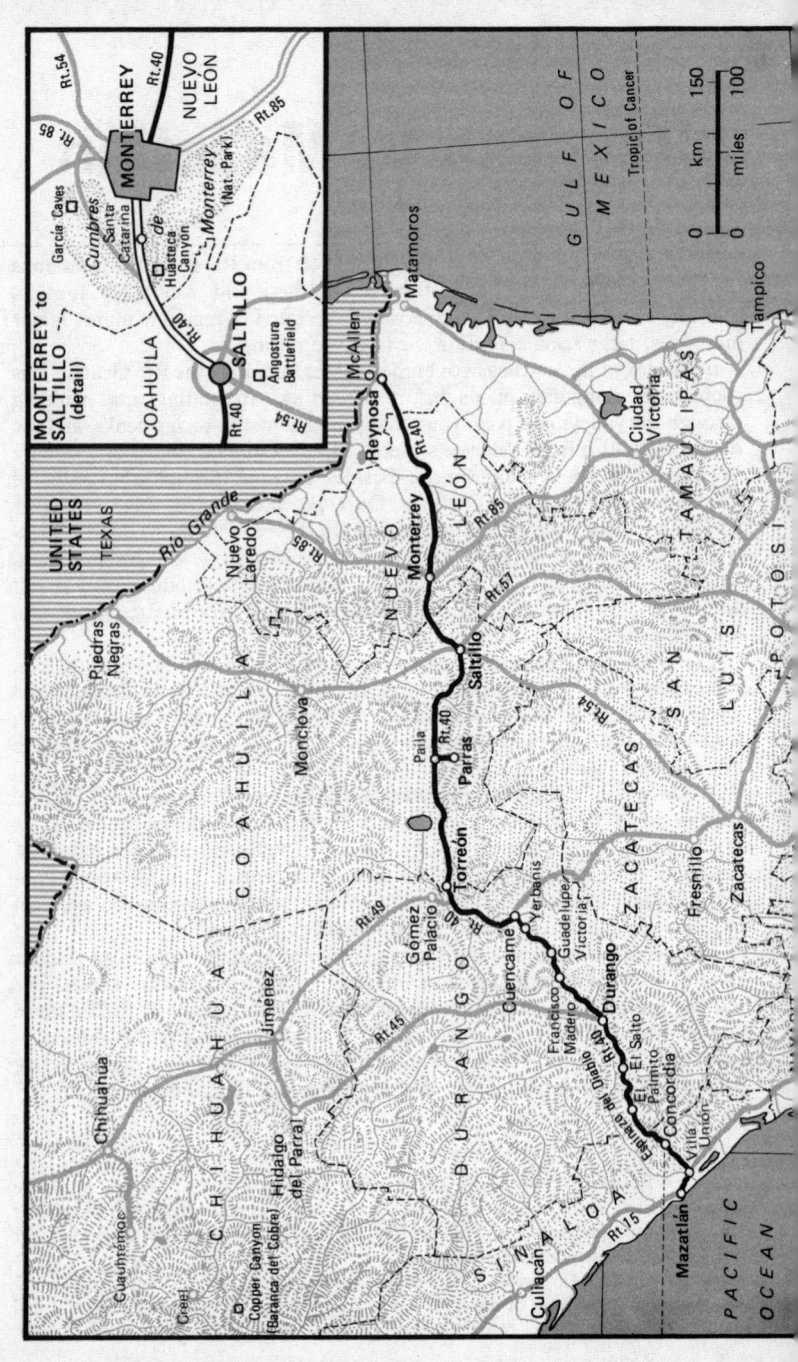

MONTERREY to SALTILLO (detail)

NUEVO LEÓN

Rt.54

Rt.40

Rt.85

Rt.85

MONTERREY

Cumbres de

García Caves

Santa Catarina

Monterrey (Nat. Park)

Huasteca Canyon

COAHUILA

Rt.40

SALTILLO

Angostura Battlefield

Rt.40

Rt.54

GULF OF MEXICO

Tropic of Cancer

km   0   150
miles 0   100

Matamoros

McAllen

Reynosa

Rt.40

NUEVO

LEÓN

Monterrey

Rt.85

Rt.57

Ciudad Victoria

TAMAULIPAS

Tampico

UNITED STATES

TEXAS

Río Grande

Nuevo Laredo

Rt.85

Piedras Negras

Monclova

COAHUILA

Saltillo

Rt.40

Paila

Parras

Rt.40

Rt.54

SAN

LUIS

POTOSÍ

Rt.49

Torreón

Gómez Palacio

Verbanis

ZACATECAS

Fresnillo

Zacatecas

Chihuahua

CHIHUAHUA

Jiménez

Rt.45

DURANGO

Cuencamé

Guadelupe Victoria

Rt.40

Cuauhtémoc

Creel

Copper Canyon (Barranca del Cobre)

Hidalgo del Parral

Francisco Madero

Espinazo del Diablo

Rt.40

Durango

El Salto

Palmito

Concordia

Villa Unión

SINALOA

Culiacán

Rt.15

Mazatlán

PACIFIC OCEAN

Reynosa hardly grew until oil deposits were discovered in 1940. After that it blossomed quickly into one of the urban centers of the state of Tamaulipas. Today, Reynosa is a thriving cattle raising, agricultural, clothes manufacturing, and commercial center. While it supports a steady flow of car, truck, and railroad traffic, it has all the trappings of a typical border town — plenty of hotels, commerce, and nightlife, but few unique, strikingly Mexican features. There are a few places worth seeing, however, such as the Cathedral of Reynosa (on Plaza Principal) — a colonial church, enhanced in recent years with such additions as a stained glass window.

On the way into town, coming from McAllen, after crossing the international bridge, you will see a large commercial area called the Zona Rosa where there are two restaurants of note — *Sam's Place* (Allende and Ocampo; phone: 131-20034) and *The US Bar* (105 Calz. Virreyes; no phone) — as well as some curio shops and several discos, including *Zodiak Le Club, Alaskan Club Disco* (1020 Ocampo Nte.; phone: 131-20481), and *Tréviños Bar*. Heading toward the downtown area, you will come to the main street, Calle Hidalgo, and the zocalo, or main square. Calle Hidalgo, a pedestrian mall swarming with shoppers and vendors, stretches from Plaza Principal to an open-air fruit and vegetable market. Besides hotels, mostly of the 1-night-stop variety, Reynosa has a bullring (*Plaza de Toros Reynosa*). Bullfights are usually held on Sundays, from August through November, but there is no regular schedule.

If you want to try *cabrito* (kid) prepared Mexican-style, stop in *El Pastor* (710 Juárez Ote.; phone: 131-24191), a place that specializes in Mexican fare. As you leave town on Route 40, headed for Monterrey, there is a motel called the *Virrey*. It has a good restaurant that serves international and Mexican dishes, as does the *San Carlos* hotel (970 Calle Hidalgo Nte.). Both places also are good for an overnight stop (see *Best en Route*).

En Route from Reynosa – Leaving Reynosa from downtown on Zaragoza, turn left onto Chapa, then right onto Calle Hidalgo to Route 40. Along the 140 miles (224 km) of paved road to Monterrey (about 3 hours of driving), you will pass some bumpy spots, possibly some stray livestock, one customs and immigration checkpoint (16 miles/26 km from Reynosa), several small towns, and some of the largest steel mills in North America. In Monterrey, turn left onto Zaragoza until you reach the downtown area and main plaza of Monterrey, also named Zaragoza.

MONTERREY: For a detailed description of the city, its hotels and restaurants, see *Monterrey,* THE CITIES. At 1,749 feet in a valley surrounded by Sierra Madre Oriental peaks, the Colossus of the North is Mexico's main industrial center and third largest city, with more than 3 million inhabitants. Although hardly a metropolis by US standards, Monterrey manufactures everything from steel, beer, cement, glass, and cigarettes to building materials and textiles. It is also a university town and the capital of the state of Nuevo León. Despite its development as a large, major, modern industrial city with tall new buildings, wide paved boulevards, and a lingering layer of smog, Monterrey is an old city with plenty of history.

En Route from Monterrey – Avenida de la Constitución (or General Pablo González Garza) will return you to Route 40, heading for Saltillo and Mazatlán. About 3 miles (5 km) from Monterrey on Route 40 (also called Avenida Gonzalitos), there is a turnoff to Chipinique Mesa, a resort that not only rests by a river surrounded with trees, but also has a pretty good restaurant with a magnificent view of Monterrey and its surrounding valley. Take the Chipinique Mesa turnoff and drive 14 miles (22 km) up an ascending road. About 10 miles (16 km) from Monterrey, Huasteca Canyon has a breathtaking 1,000-foot gorge and distinctive rock formations. Follow the signs after turning left at the Santa Catarina turnoff on Route 40. The pavement ends at a tidy, fenced-in picnic area and children's playground (admission is about 75¢), and a stony, unpaved road leads into the canyon. The area is rather desolate, but a police car usually is parked at the canyon's entrance for security.

García Caves (Grutas de García), 14 miles (22 km) from Monterrey, are a special, highly recommended side trip along Route 40 on the way to Saltillo. Discovered in 1834 by Father Antonio de Sobrevilla, these caves, with 17 different chambers, natural pools, and magnificent stalactite and stalagmite formations, are among the most dramatic in North America. (The caves are not easy to explore and visitors are advised to wear long slacks and flat shoes.) Take the Villa de García turnoff on Route 40 and follow a paved road to the town of Villa de García, where you can ride a cable car up 2,460 feet, providing good panoramic views (the ride costs about $4 for adults and $2 for children 12 years and under); burros also take visitors to the entrance of the caves. Open daily, except December 12, from 9 AM to 4 PM.

SALTILLO: For a more detailed description of the city, see *Nuevo Laredo to Mexico City*, DIRECTIONS. Besides being the capital of the state of Coahuila, the seat of two universities, and the main producer of the famous Mexican serape, Saltillo has factories that produce engine parts, rugs, pottery, and silver goods. Its eventful history has left its mark in the form of several interesting sites. Its mild to hot, dry climate makes it one of the recreational centers of northeastern Mexico. At 5,212 feet in the Sierra Madre Oriental, it has a population of close to 650,000.

Because of its history as a colonial city, a Mexican state capital, and a modern industrial center, Saltillo contains both old and new Mexico. Special places include the churrigueresque Cathedral of Santiago and the Palacio del Gobierno (both on the central square, Jardín Hidalgo, also called Plaza de Armas); the Fortress of Carlota (Fortín de Carlota, in the old section of town, near Plaza de Armas); Fuentes Atheneum, on the campus of the University of Coahuila on Venustiano Carranza, containing an art gallery with a collection of works by European and Mexican masters; and Alameda Park (Calles Carranza, Victoria, Aldama, and Ramos Arizpe). Well-made, reasonably priced leather, silver goods, and furniture can be found in shops around town. Two local culinary specialties, *pan de pulque* (sweet bread made with pulque, a cactus liquor) and *dulce de leche* (condensed milk candy) are sold at all local *panaderías* (bakeries) and candy counters. Saltillo's hotels are better than its restaurants, and you are likely to find the best food in the hotels. The *Camino Real* (Carr. 57) has an excellent restaurant featuring international and Mexican cuisine, as well as a disco and cocktail lounge. The *Huizache* (1746 Blvd. Caranza at Campeche) and *San Jorge* (240 Manuel Acuña) hotels also have good restaurants. The tourist offices in Saltillo would be glad to provide maps and information. There are two locations: *Centro de Convenciones* (Convention Center; at Blvd. Fundadores Km 6.5; phone: 841-54444 or 841-54504) and downtown (at Calle Francisco Coss and Manuel Acuña; phone: 841-54050). Both offices have bilingual staffs.

En Route from Saltillo – After passing the railroad tracks along Calle Carranza leaving Saltillo, return to Route 40 and head toward Torreón, 174 miles (278 km) away. The road winds through arid mountains before straightening out onto a semidesert highland terrain. Some 81 miles (130 km) from Saltillo you reach Paila, the junction for Parras. If you take the road to the left at the junction and drive 18 miles (29 km) past vineyards, groves of pecan trees, and a rustic mill, you will arrive in the town of Parras.

PARRAS: The lush country road leading to Parras provides an appropriately pleasant introduction to the town itself. Founded in 1598 and originally called Santa María de las Parras, Parras is the cradle of the North American wine industry and a major producer of denim. One of the oldest towns in northern Mexico, it was also the home of Francisco I. Madero, father of the Mexican Revolution. His home (Calle Almeda de Rosario) is open to the public. At the Casa Madera winery, you can tour the premises and taste samples of the local crop in a lovely vineyard setting. (A *Grape Fair* is held in the town during the summer.) A still-functioning ancient aqueduct adjacent to one of the Casa Madera winery buildings will be sure to catch your eye. The *Rincón del Motero* (see *Best en Route*), a resort hotel, has a swimming pool, a 9-hole golf course, horseback riding, and an excellent restaurant. The *Posada Santa María,* in the center of town, is another hotel with good food.

En Route from Parras – After leaving Parras on the same 18-mile (29-km) paved road, return to Route 40 and head west for Torreón (approximately 3 hours' driving time) along desert highlands.

TORREÓN: For a more complete description of Torreón, see *Juárez to Mexico City,* DIRECTIONS. At 3,700 feet, with a population of about 800,000, Torreón is Mexico's newest city. Before 1907, it constituted the largest of the Laguna cotton district tri-cities (with Gómez Palacio and Lerdo) and had a population of 4,000. After 1907, however, when the railroad came to town, Torreón became a major thoroughfare and commercial center in its own right, later serving as a key strategic point during the 1910 revolution. Residents of Torreón say that Pancho Villa and his roughriders were so delighted when they saw their first telephone in Torreón that they went from house to house making phone calls. Now Torreón is a modern, industrial city, and its grapes make it an agricultural leader as well.

En Route from Torreón – After leaving Torreón on Boulevard Miguel Alemán and returning to Route 40, you begin to move southwest to Durango (about a 4-hour drive). The first 18 miles (29 km) of this drive, along the Río Namas Valley road, are tricky and require cautious driving; besides the stray cattle who like this path, there are sharp curves and bits of worn, uneven pavement. After leaving the valley, the road climbs through high desert country where cactus and *topes* (small, tire-jarring bumps built into the road to slow down cars) abound. Since many of the *topes* are unmarked, it is best to exercise caution, particularly when nearing and passing the towns of Cuencamé, Yerbanis, Guadalupe Victoria, and Francisco I. Madero, on the way to Durango.

DURANGO: The capital of the state of Durango, with a population of nearly 400,000, Durango is a colonial city that for many years rated second only to Hollywood as the major movie-making location of the world. To date, more than 100 American, British, and Mexican films have been made here, including *A Man Called Horse, Five Card Stud, The Sons of Katie Elder*, and *Fat Man and Little Boy*. Besides the frontier movie sets on the outskirts of town, the vast, wild, rugged landscapes laced with canyons and plains that surround Durango make it a perfect setting for westerns. Today, fewer westerns are being made, and Durango has had a lot of competition from Cuernavaca for Hollywood's attention. More important than movie sets, however, is Durango's wealth of natural resources — as the Spanish discovered in 1563 when they arrived in search of precious metals. Gold, silver, lead, copper, and iron line the inside of Durango's hills. Cerro del Mercado (Market Hill), a hill of gigantic proportions and a proclaimed 65% to 70% iron content, is just a few miles north of the city. Surrounding ore mines have been producing tons of ore every day for centuries.

You can hear concerts (*serenatas*) performed by the *Durango State Band* on Sundays at the zocalo, Plaza de Armas, which is downtown at Veinte de Noviembre and Cinco de Febrero. Facing the plaza on the north side is the cathedral, a predominantly baroque structure that was under construction from 1695 to 1750. The last remaining cathedral of three that originally stood on this site, it contains noteworthy paintings and is said to be haunted by a lovesick Spanish maiden named Beatrice. Ghost watchers say that ever since the War of Independence (1810), when Beatrice died of a broken heart in the cathedral tower, her ghost has appeared in the tower on nights of the full moon. They recommend Avenida Constitución as the prime ghost viewing spot.

Palacio de Gobierno (Government Palace; Calle Cinco de Febrero between Calles

Bruno Martínez and Zaragoza) once served as the private residence of Spanish mining magnate Don José Zambrano. After Mexico declared its independence, however, the palace became the state capitol. The two murals facing the palace's main patio are among Durango's finest artistic displays. Next to the Palacio de Gobierno is the *Teatro Victoria,* which originally served as Don José Zambrano's private theater. In the Santuario de Guadalupe (Sanctuary of Guadalupe; off Esplanada Insurgentes in the northern, Guadalupe section of town), lie the remains of the priests who were executed near Durango in 1812 for participating in the fight for independence.

Durango's Guardiana Park (at the entrance to Route 40 east, toward Mazatlán) houses the Escuela de Artesanías (Arts and Crafts School), where handblown glass objects, ceramics, sculptures, and woven products can been seen. For purchases, go to *Los Tlacuilos* (Plaza de Armas). Other Mexican handicrafts, including Durango's own "scorpion under glass" ashtrays and other scorpion souvenirs (scorpions are Durango's trademark), are sold in the central marketplace, *Mercado Francisco Gómez Palacio* (Veinte de Noviembre and 5 de Febrero).

The outskirts of Durango offer a number of possible tours. Chupaderos, the most popular of the western movie sets — with saloon, hotel, bank, livery stable, mine, and public execution site — can be reached by following the signs and taking Route 45 north toward Hidalgo del Parral for 9 miles (14 km) before turning onto a dirt road for ¼ mile (0.4 km). Calle Howard, another movie set, is also on the road to Parral, about 5 miles (8 km) from Durango. On this route is San Juan del Río, which you must pass in order to reach Río Grande, the birthplace of Pancho Villa, 3 miles (5 km) away. One of the newest movie sets is at Alamos at Km 35 on the road to La Flor. Just about 22 miles (35 km) south of Durango, on Route 45, El Saltito Waterfall has amazing rock formations that western movie buffs might recognize. Two reservoirs near Durango offer opportunities for fishing, swimming, and water skiing — Peña del Águila, about 20 miles (32 km) north of town on an asphalt road, Route 39, that branches off from Route 45; and Guadalupe Victoria, 15 miles (24 km) south of Durango on an unnumbered asphalt road. The tourist and film office (408 Hidalgo Sur; phone: 181-11107 or 181-12139) will provide detailed information and maps to the reservoirs, and can help you make arrangements to watch a day of filming if a movie is being made during your visit.

Although none of the restaurants in Durango rates a rave review, there are several decent, adequate spots. *La Majada* (Calle Veinte de Noviembre, east end) is a popular restaurant that serves Mexican beef and goat at moderate prices. *La Bohemia* (Calles Veinte de Noviembre and Hidalgo) is a simple, clean restaurant offering typical Mexican and German fare, also at moderate prices. *Casablanca* restaurant (*Casablanca Hotel,* 811 Av. Veinte de Noviembre Pte.; see *Best en Route*) has passable international dishes at moderate prices. *La Venta* (Calles Veinte de Noviembre and Libertad), a plusher dining spot with a more elegant atmosphere, offers about the same fare as the *Casablanca* at higher prices. *Far West* (Calles Veinte de Noviembre and Independencia) is highly recommended for meat dishes. For an afternoon or evening coffee, try *Café y Arte Plaza Los Condes* (Cinco de Febrero Pte.), which serves a variety of blends to the accompaniment of live Mexican music.

En Route from Durango – Leaving Durango (no later than 10 AM to avoid late afternoon fog on the road ahead) on Veinte de Noviembre around Guardiana Park, you return to Route 40 and begin the final and most spectacular stretch of your journey to the Pacific. After climbing gradually and steadily through 40 miles (64 km) of semidesert covered with cactus and shrubs, you reach the beginning of the ascent of the Sierra Madre Occidental.

The last lap through the Sierra Madre Occidental is the most impressive part of the route to Mazatlán because of its extraordinary terrain and views. Although the road is in good condition, the turns and curves around canyons and steep cliffs require maximum concentration and a speed of no more than 45 mph. Since the road sustains a heavy flow of traffic, commercial and otherwise, you are likely to encounter many trucks along the way. Rather than becoming impatient and inviting trouble, wait for the truck driver ahead of you to blink his left taillight to signal you to pass. This is the acknowledged etiquette on Mexican roads outside of the cities, and it seems to work to everyone's benefit. El Salto, a lumber camp 63 miles (101 km) from Durango, is noted for good freshwater fishing (catfish and carp) and hunting (grizzly bears, red deer, mule deer, mountain quail, mountain lions, wild turkeys). Fine stands of pine and oak grow abundantly throughout the camp area, which lies at the end of a steep, sharply curved 2-mile (3-km) road. El Salto now has a small hotel, *Los Pinos,* with a coffee shop. Just before El Salto you'll see a restaurant, *El Bosque,* railroad tracks, and signs reading *Curva Peligrosa* (Dangerous Curve). The high ridge above you marks the Continental Divide. About 45 miles (72 km) down the road and at 7,000 feet in the Sierra Madre Occidental peaks, El Espinazo del Diablo (the Devil's Backbone) overlooks a steep 1,000-foot drop into deep canyons. The breathtaking view will tell you immediately where you are. After passing the Backbone, you enter El Palmito, 125 miles (200 km) from Durango, the spot where central time changes to mountain time and watches should be set back one hour. Ten miles (16 km) beyond El Palmito, *La Sombra de Paraíso* is a charming mountain restaurant beside a waterfall. Since there are few places along the road where you can pull over and stop, or take pictures, you might want to take the opportunity here. The descending road to Mazatlán winds through scenic hills covered with wildflowers and crosses a *vado* (place where the riverbed crosses the road) to Copala before reaching Concordia.

COPALA: On Route 40, about 140 miles (224 km) west of Durango, is this small, quiet town of cobblestone streets and picturesque buildings, inhabited by about 600 people. More than 400 years old, Copala was once a mining town, and in recent years the village has become a popular day-long excursion from surrounding cities. One of the town's main attractions is the 16th-century church, Iglesia de San José (Church of St. Joseph), set on a hill overlooking the surrounding countryside.

If you choose to stay overnight, the town's one and only hotel, the *Posada San José* (no phone), has charming, affordable bungalows, located on the square. The hotel also has billiards, as well as an upper verandah providing a romantic view of the Iglesia de San José and its beamed portico, seen through the lacy boughs of the bougainvillea vines. Downstairs, the *Copala Butter Company* restaurant serves enchiladas, quesadillas, and *chimichangas* prepared to please Yankee tastes. *Daniel's,* the only other eatery in the small village, is owned by a US expatriate who came to visit years ago and decided to stay. The restaurant serves good Mexican fare, followed by an incongruously New England dessert, banana-coconut cream pie.

Day-long tours from Mazatlán to Copala include enough time to walk along the town's cobblestone streets and visit the church and square. *Marlin Tours* (phone: 698-35301) and the *Copala* travel agency (2313 Belisario Domínguez; phone: 698-28326), both in Mazatlán, arrange trips. José Jiménez, who runs the *Copala* agency, is a native of Copala and can be especially helpful in organizing a trip to his hometown. For more details, see "Copala" in *Mazatlán,* THE CITIES.

CONCORDIA: From Copala, continue on Route 40 to Concordia. On the right side of Route 40 just beyond a restaurant and a furniture factory (on the left side of the road) this small village is filled with baroque architecture, handcrafted guitars, colonial furniture, wooden mugs, and dishes. A semi-paved hill beyond the restaurant leads to Concordia's tree-lined, sleepy zocalo, where an 18th-century colonial cathedral stands. It is the only baroque church in the state and has a pink stone portal and richly carved columns. At *Escuela de Artesanía de Concordia,* a few blocks away, handicrafts are sold (closed 2–4 PM).

En Route from Concordia – About 15 miles (24 km) past Concordia, at Villa Unión, Route 40 merges with Route 15, which becomes Avenida Gabriel Leyva, the street on which you enter Mazatlán. To reach the hotel district of town and the Pacific, turn right on Gutiérrez Najera and right again on Avenida del Mar to the ocean. For a detailed description of Mazatlán, its hotels and restaurants, see *Mazatlán,* THE CITIES.

BEST EN ROUTE

REYNOSA

Engrei – A 110-unit hotel with a restaurant, bar, pool, and air conditioning. On the road to Monterrey (phone: 892-31730). Moderate.

San Carlos – These 76 rooms are clean and simple, but each has a phone, shower, and TV set. There is bar service, an excellent restaurant, and parking. 970 Calle Hidalgo Nte. (phone: 892-21280). Moderate.

Virrey – Modern and popular with tourists, this 130-room hotel has spacious grounds with gardens, a swimming pool, a parking lot, and a good restaurant. On Hidalgo and Praxedis Balboa Pte. (phone: 892-31050). Moderate.

PARRAS

Rincón del Motero – Surrounded by ancient white ash groves, these resort accommodations offer 73 rooms, suites, and bungalows — old and new — with fans and showers; some have heat and air conditioning. Facilities include a 9-hole golf course, a swimming pool, a tennis court, horseback riding, extensive gardens, and an excellent restaurant. Write to: Apdo. 37, c.p. 27980, Parras, for reservations. At the north end of town (phone: 842-20540). Moderate.

DURANGO

El Gobernador – Durango's largest hotel has 100 air conditioned, comfortable rooms and some suites. Among the facilities are a restaurant (Durango's best), bar, and swimming pool. Hunting, fishing, and riding are nearby. 257 Av. Veinte de Noviembre Ote. (phone: 181-10480 through 92). Expensive.

Plaza Cathedral – In a building more than 400 years old, with 40 very large rooms (some with refrigerators) and a restaurant. 103 Av. Constitución Sur (phone: 181-14866). Moderate.

Los Arcos – There are 56 motel units, some of them suites, with restaurant, bar, gardens, and TV sets. 2204 H. Colegio Militar Ote. (phone: 181-87777 or 181-81239). Moderate to inexpensive.

Casablanca – Some of the 46 units are suites. Every indoor area is air conditioned. There is a restaurant and bar on the premises. 811 Av. Veinte de Noviembre Pte. (phone: 181-13599). Moderate to inexpensive.

Campo Mexico – The nicest place in town is set in a beautifully landscaped garden and has rooms in modern and colonial decor, a bar, satellite television, and a dining room. Pets are allowed. Av. Veinte de Noviembre Ote. (phone: 181-87744). Inexpensive.

Mexico City to Acapulco

One of the most traveled routes in all of Mexico is the road that leads south from Mexico City to the Pacific Ocean and links the capital with Acapulco. It is a trip that embraces three states, passes through the temperate city of Cuernavaca, and can be extended to include Taxco, the colonial showpiece of the state of Guerrero. There are also suggested stopovers at lakes, caves, archaeological ruins, and beautiful resort spas before you arrive in the most popular and populated of Mexico's seaside playgrounds. The several hours of mountain driving take you through dramatic scenery and highly varied topography. Though the 255-mile (408-km) trip can be made in 5 to 6 hours (traveling mostly on a two-lane toll road), we suggest more scenic alternatives, unless time is a problem. The first leg of the journey, from Mexico City to Cuernavaca, can be either a leisurely hour on the toll road, Route 95-D, or an almost equal amount of time spent driving the more dramatic mountain highway, Route 95. Taxco is 90 minutes on Route 95, and the longest part of the journey, from Taxco to Acapulco, takes approximately 4 hours, along rising and falling mountain roads with sweeping views and a spectacular descent into palm trees and coastline luxury.

Much of this country is Aztec in culture, with many Indians still speaking their original language, Nahuatl, rather than Spanish. While several of the resorts and hotels mentioned here cater mostly to Mexican tourists, they are more than happy to extend their hospitality to Americans and other foreign visitors. If your time is short and you want a rich mix of cities, villages, recreation areas, mountains, and ocean, this offers a fine driving route.

Expect to pay $80 to $110 for a double room in hotels categorized as expensive; $40 to $75 at moderate places.

En Route from Mexico City – If you have been staying in Mexico City for any length of time, you will already be familiar with Avenida Insurgentes, the busy shopping street that runs north and south through the city. If not, anyone can direct you there. Traveling south along it, you pass the National University of Mexico (which is worth a quick visit if you have missed it) and its stadium, where the *1968 Olympics* were held. About a mile (1.6 km) beyond the university on your right is the Olympic Village housing complex that was built for the visiting athletes and later turned into condominiums. Along this road, too, are various sculptures presented to Mexico by the participating nations. About 2 miles (3 km) farther at Tlalpan, is the fork where Route 95 (toll-free) and Route 95-D (toll road) split off, both going to Cuernavaca.

There are two other routes to the Tlalpan fork: the old Tlalpan freeway, just

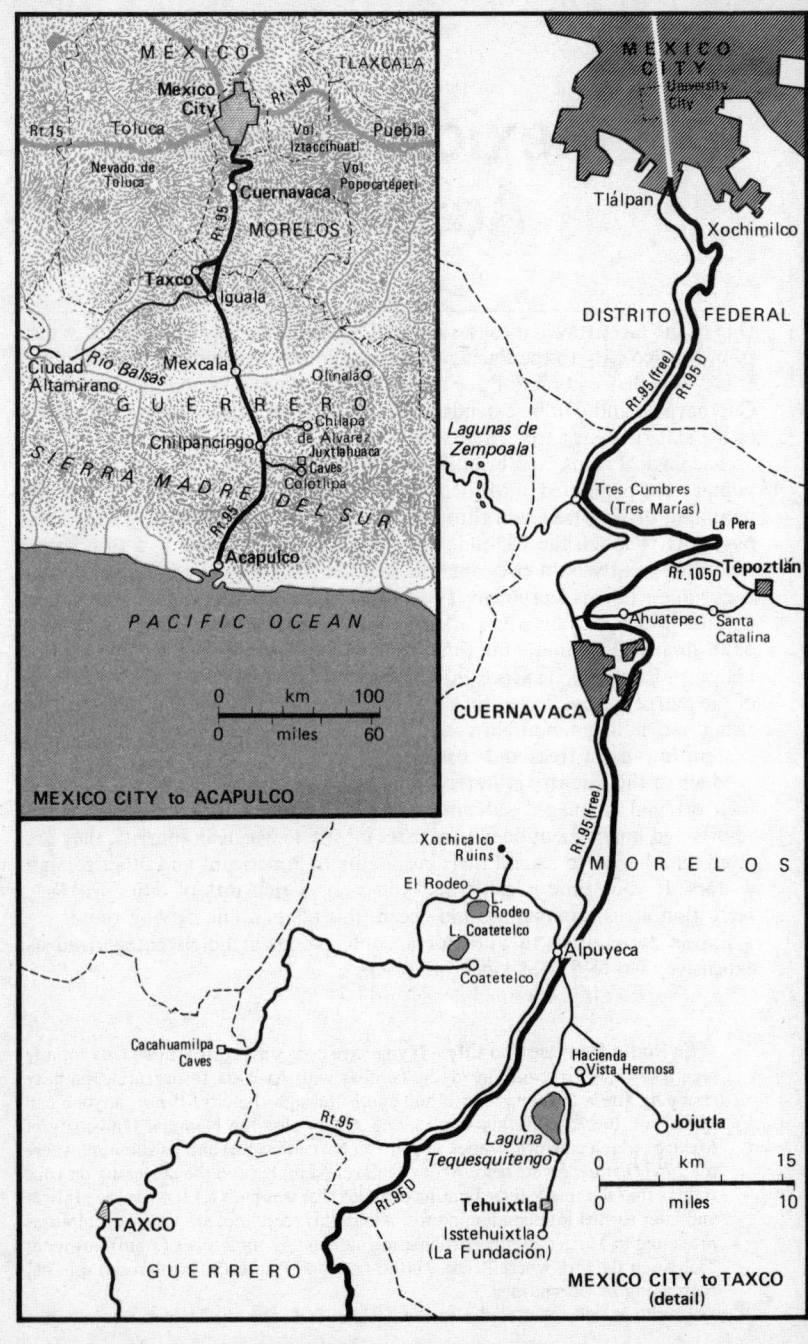

MEXICO CITY to ACAPULCO

MEXICO CITY to TAXCO
(detail)

south of the zocalo in downtown Mexico City; and west on Paseo de la Reforma, through Chapultepec Park, to the sign for Periférico Sur, the freeway entrance.

While both Route 95, the old mountain road, and Route 95-D, the newer four-lane toll road, will take you to Cuernavaca, very different side trips are possible from each. A group of mountain lakes is accessible from Route 95, and from Route 95-D, the village of Tepoztlán.

TEPOZTLÁN: On Route 95-D, you can catch the first glimpse of what is to come farther down the road. About 32 miles (51 km) south of the interchange is a lookout with an amazingly clear view of Popocatépetl and Ixtaccíhuatl, the snow-topped volcanoes that command the surrounding countryside and are visible from three states. After La Pera, a pear-shaped curve on the Cuernavaca highway, take the Cuautla turnoff, Route 115-D. Less than half an hour northeast of Cuernavaca, Tepoztlán (pronounced Teh-pos-*tlahn*) is a beautiful Indian village set among the mountains in a lush, green vale. The predominant language is Nahuatl, the customs are ancient, but it is a town prepared to deal with tourists quite happily.

A stately hotel, *Posada del Tepozteco,* overlooks the village and has a great view (see *Best en Route*). The marketplace is an outdoor area where once a week produce and household wares are spread out on the ground beneath cloth sunshades.

The streets in town are a picturesque network of steep and winding cobblestones, but the most unique and interesting sites in Tepoztlán are the temples and pyramid structures that stand on the mountain peak 1,200 feet above the town. The most famous, the Shrine of Tepozteco, was dedicated to Tepoztecatl, god of *pulque,* a popular alcoholic beverage fermented from the sap of the maguey plant, a member of the cactus family. There is a steep climb through the thin mountain air to the pyramid base of this shrine. A narrow stairway on the western side leads up to the inner shrine, where the walls are covered with bold-relief hieroglyphs. Though the trip up is strenuous, the view from the heights is awe inspiring.

An archaeological museum in one of the town's old convent buildings of the 16th century has an interesting collection of pre-Hispanic art and of objects that will give you a full sense of the lives of the people who worshiped at the shrine. Although Christianity did not take hold here as in larger, more colonialized areas, the Dominicans did attempt to convert the Indians and built the convent in 1559. The structure is huge, and for visitors who speak Spanish, there is a guided tour filled with tales of all the convent's incarnations, from the 16th-century destruction of native idols to early–20th-century revolutionary army barracks. Ask for *"el convento."*

At a fiesta on September 8, the whole town honors Tepoztecatl's connection with pulque by getting drunk. One other unusual festival is held annually on the 3 days before *Ash Wednesday,* when the men of the area dance the *brincos,* or jumps, an ancient Aztec movement performed in conquistador costumes, beards, wigs, and masks.

En Route from Tepoztlán – To continue to Cuernavaca, you need not retrace your steps to Route 95-D. There is a paved road that leads directly from Tepoztlán by way of Santa Catalina, Ahuatepec, to the capital of Morelos, Cuernavaca. There is an alternate route from Mexico City to be considered, too. Rather than the toll road, Route 95-D, there is an old mountain road, Route 95, which also leads directly from Mexico's capital to Cuernavaca. The mountain drive is fairly narrow, but the road is well maintained, and the views are one long series of knockouts. Passing through Tres Cumbres, also referred to as Tres Marías, a small lumber town that looks out over the valleys of Mexico and Cuernavaca, there is an interesting side trip to Lagunas de Zempoala. Veer west, leaving Route 95, and drive 8 miles (13 km) on a winding paved road.

LAGUNAS DE ZEMPOALA: Known to the Indians as Lakes of the Windy Place, these six small bodies of water are more than 9,000 feet above sea level. Each is very beautiful and kept well stocked with trout. Part of a national park, the lakes are set amidst pine woods and offer lovely picnic and camping areas. Weekends tend to get crowded, but weekdays are quiet, peaceful, and an idyllic contrast to the modern bustle of Mexico City, less than 2 hours away.

En Route from Lagunas de Zempoala – Unfortunately, there is no way from the lakes to Cuernavaca other then going back to Route 95 and south to the city.

CUERNAVACA: For a detailed report on the city, its hotels and restaurants, see *Cuernavaca,* THE CITIES. Entering from Route 95, Route 95-D, or the more southern road direct from Tepoztlán, you will find yourself in the northern section of the Morelos state capital. Blessed with a comfortable climate, it is an attractive and popular vacation and retirement center for people from the more rigorous climes to the north. There are several mineral baths in the area, and since Aztec times, people have been coming to Cuernavaca to take the waters. It is also a city with a dense political history. Emiliano Zapata, the famous revolutionary hero, was raised in the area from which he organized his troops. Vital, warm, and blooming all year with such plants as geraniums, fuchsias, bougainvilleas, jacarandas, and poincianas.

En Route from Cuernavaca – As the trip continues south from Cuernavaca, western and eastern alternatives are available. You can take Route 95-D straight through to Iguala, bypassing Taxco and any other side trips mentioned here. The other options are east to Vista Hermosa, Lago Tequesquitengo, and Tehuixtla; or west to Alpuyeca, the Ruinas de Xochicalco, and Grutas de Cacahuamilpa. Leave Route 95 or Route 95-D at the Alpuyeca interchange to go east or west. Taxco can be either included or bypassed on the eastern route, but is necessarily part of the western route on the way to Iguala.

HACIENDA VISTA HERMOSA: More than a luxury hotel, this is a resort spa created from the ruins of a colonial sugar mill. You can bring the whole family for swimming, tennis, bowling, horseback riding, or just sunning. There is open-air dining and a terrific Sunday brunch. Whether or not you are interested in staying overnight, it is a good place to spend an afternoon. It's about 5 miles (8 km) east of the Alpuyeca interchange on a well-paved road (see *Best en Route*). The former manager of the hotel, Alfonso Martínez, recently made an important archaeological find in a nearby town known as Pueblo Viejo.

LAGUNA TEQUESQUITENGO (Lake Tequesquitengo): About a mile (1.6 km) farther south, on the same paved road, and about 22 miles (35 km) southeast of Cuernavaca, this natural lake is an increasingly popular recreation spot with Mexico City's water enthusiasts. There are motorboats and water skis for rent, as well as swimming, fishing, tennis courts, restaurants, hotels, guesthouses, snack bars, and tourists from every part of Mexico. Weekends tend to get a little hectic, but weekdays are simply lively, with fewer people trying to be in the same spot at once. One strange feature of this lake is that the water level rises and falls drastically, and in the middle are the remains of an Indian village that once stood above ground. In 1820, the Indians were forced to move to the present location of Tequesquitengo (pronounced Tay-kays-kee-*ten*-go), but the shoreline continues to rise and fall.

En Route from Lake Tequesquitengo – A road surrounds the lake, and either branch will take you the 8 miles (13 km) south to Tehuixtla.

TEHUIXTLA: Less than a mile (1.6 km) south of the town of Tehuixtla is a bathing resort named La Fundación but better known simply as Isstehuixtla. (Run by the Social Security Institute for federal employees, the resort is open to the public.) There is an admission fee and a charge for locker rentals, but you can take advantage of the sulfur baths and swimming pools to your heart's content. There are five pools in all, but the main one is a very deep swimming hole filled with waters rising from the depths of the earth. A fast-flowing river runs through the property, with a suspension bridge connecting the two banks. Swinging wildly as you walk across and surrounded by tropical growth, the bridge is like an image from a childhood jungle movie. This exotic atmosphere is carried even further by the poolside waiters who serve you whole coconuts, chopping off the top to form a natural cup of cooling coconut milk. There are snack stands and a very pleasant restaurant with strictly Mexican food.

A short walk across the bridge takes you to another restaurant, pool, and bar, connected to the *Rivera* hotel (see *Best en Route*). It's not actually part of Tehuixtla, but a friendly exchange back and forth is taken for granted. No English is spoken in either place, but almost anything you might want can be pretty easily indicated with smiles, shrugs, and pointing. The people of Tehuixtla are friendly and helpful.

En Route from La Fundación – To get back to the highway to Acapulco, you must retrace your steps to Lake Tequesquitengo. Whichever side of the lake you come down, you can now go up the other, and, almost at the top, before reaching Vista Hermosa, you'll reach a road west that will take you to either Route 95 or Route 95-D. Here, your choice of highway is more critical than it has been so far, as Route 95 includes a diverting visit to Taxco, while Route 95-D is a direct four-lane drive to Iguala. But before evaluating the advantages of a side trip to Taxco, you might consider a western route from Cuernavaca. At Alpuyeca interchange, rather than traveling east to Vista Hermosa, take the road bearing north, then west.

ALPUYECA: In Alpuyeca, the town church has some wonderful Indian murals. While here, make sure you have enough water for the next part of your trip.

RUINAS XOCHICALCO (Xochicalco Ruins): About 5½ miles (9 km) farther west along this road, before you reach Laguna del Rodeo, you'll see a sign to the right for the mysterious ruins this area is known for. Pronounced Zo-chee-*cahl*-co, the Nahuatl word meaning "house of flowers," the mounds of this site cover 6 square miles and lie 24 miles (38 km) southwest of Cuernavaca. There is a ball court, a palace, a honeycombed network of underground caves, passageways, and one restored pyramid that sits on the top of a rocky hill. The walls of this pyramidal structure are elaborately carved with figures of serpents and human beings thought to represent the priests of the temple. While there are elements suggesting Toltec origins, other aspects indicate Maya or Zapotec influence. To investigate the ruins more fully, take a guide with you from Cuernavaca, but for most people a good strong flashlight should do the job.

GRUTAS DE CACAHUAMILPA (Caves of Cacahuamilpa): About 21 miles (34 km) farther along this road, near the Morelos-Guerrero state border, are the largest caverns in central Mexico, the Cacahuamilpa Caves (pronounced Cah-cah-wah-*meel*-pah). Discovered in 1835, the caves still have not been fully explored. At present they rival their northern neighbors at Carlsbad in size and in variety of formations, and it is believed that once fully explored, the caves also will prove to be bigger than Carlsbad's. Stalactites, stalagmites, arches, and boulders are lighted in the more central caves for easier exploration, and guided tours for groups or private parties re available daily, every half hour, from 10 AM to 5 PM; call a day in advance to request a tour in English. Weekends sometimes have fairly heavy traffic, with people coming and going on the buses from Mexico City and Cuernavaca, but the caves are large and fascinating. In addition to the tours, there is a sound-and-light show. For details, check with the tourist office in Taxco (phone: 762-21525).

En Route from Caves of Cacahuamilpa – Back on the main road, about a mile (1.6 km) farther west, are Laguna del Rodeo and its companion, Laguna de Coatetelco. There is swimming and fishing, and while El Rodeo is just a short walk off the road from the town of the same name, Coatetelco is farther and is only accessible by road from a completely different approach. Make a quick stop in the town of El Rodeo and inquire about the facilities at the two lakes. Just beyond these lakes, the road bears directly south across the state border into Guerrero, and in less than 3 miles (5 km), it joins Route 95 to Taxco.

TAXCO: For a detailed description of the city, its hotels and restaurants, see *Taxco*,

THE CITIES. If you have made no side trips, just straight driving, you would now be more than 2½ hours out of Mexico City. As it is, the western, eastern, or direct route joins Route 95 to Taxco, the silver capital of the world. Surrounded by high mountains and rich mines, this 18th-century colonial town is one of the jewels of Guerrero state. With steep, winding, cobblestone streets and lovely old Spanish architecture, this town is protected from modernization by its status as a national monument. No new buildings can be constructed in anything but the original style — the red tile roofs, white-washed walls, patios, and all the other artistic architectural features that distinguish Taxco. In addition to its beauty, Taxco is a city filled with artisans and designers who craft world-famous silver jewelry using silversmithing techniques and designs seen nowhere else on earth.

IGUALA: Iguala (pronounced Ee-*gwah*-lah), 22 miles (35 km) south of Taxco on Route 95 and halfway between Mexico City and Acapulco on Route 95-D, is the area's most important agricultural center. Set in a fertile valley, it is surrounded by beautiful mountains. Every Friday is market day, when Indians from the surrounding countryside pour into Iguala to sell their produce. Pineapples, cantaloupes, watermelons, and delicious peanuts fill the marketplace with luscious colors and smells. Baskets and pottery are also on sale, and, occasionally, the amethysts for which the state of Guerrero is famous. The zocalo of this town is filled with beautiful tamarind trees; and the town church standing nearby is quite lovely and worth a visit.

Iguala has a special place in Mexican history, because it was here that the flag of Mexico was created. In 1821, Agustín de Iturbide combined his troops with those of the rebel leader Vicente Guerrero, for whom the state is named; and in celebration he ordered Magdalena Ocampo to design and deliver a flag within 24 hours. She returned with the red, white, and green flag that is still in use today, and the main plaza, known as Plaza of the Flag (Plaza de la Bandera), commemorates this event with a vast monument. On it are inscribed the words, "Here the consummation of Mexico's independence from Spain was proclaimed on February 24, 1821." The act was known as the Plan of Iguala, which Iturbide composed. If you happen to pass through Iguala in December, look for the horse fair, which attracts traders from all over the country. Iguala is also the capital of the mask-making region of northern Guerrero state. Ordinary and recently carved masks can be purchased for as little as $10; antique masks, a rare few made of silver, can cost $500 and up.

MEXCALA: Farther south on Route 95, where the highway crosses the Río Balsas, this town offers an interesting diversion. Flat-bottom wooden rafts can be rented for exhilarating trips down the river. The trip can be extended as far as Ciudad Altamirano, where a second class bus will return you to Iguala, but information concerning the return trip should be checked out carefully in Mexcala before you leave town. We advise you to seek two collaborating reports, since Mexicans are likely to answer you whether they know the correct information or not, just to be polite.

CHILPANCINGO: After a 19-mile (30-km) drive through the dramatic canyon of Zopilote, with only an hour of travel left before reaching the final destination, Acapulco, you will come to Chilpancingo, the capital of the state of Guerrero. This town is another agricultural center, slightly smaller and quieter than Iguala, but with a university and a significant place in the history of Mexico. In this town the first Mexican Congress convened in 1813. The three brothers, Nicolás, Leonardo, and Victor Bravo, all revolutionary heroes, were born here. This tranquil mountain city has several points of interest, such as the state capitol on the main plaza, which has some excellent murals; La Asunción church; and the old cemetery.

CHILAPA DE ALVAREZ: From Chilpancingo there is a paved road stretching east. If you follow it for about 19 miles (30 km), then take a left a few miles beyond Ojitos de Agua onto a gravel road for 2 or 3 miles (3 to 5 km), you will come to Chilapa. This tiny but very interesting town is noted for the beautiful handloomed rebozos, or shawls, which are made here. It is also a takeoff point for a much more adventurous trek by horse to the mountain village of Olinalá, home of some of the most unique and elaborate lacquerware made in Mexico.

En Route from Chilapa de Alvarez – To continue south to Acapulco, you must retrace your steps back to Chilpancingo and reconnect with Route 95.

GRUTAS DE JUXTLAHAUCA(Caves of Juxtlahuaca; pronounced Whosh-tlah-wah-kah): After proceeding about 4 miles (6 km) south of Chilpancingo de los Bravos on Route 95, you will arrive at the small town of Petaquillas. From here there is a jeep road going east, rough but passable in the dry season, and a big adventure after a long drive any time of year. At Petaquillas and Chilpancingo you should consult with people about the conditions of this road. You can hire a guide at the tourist office in Chilpancingo. With consultations and escort in hand you can now continue the 30-mile (48-km) drive east to Colotlipa. This village is inhabited by people who can escort you farther, once you've gotten this far with a guide or on your own. From here it is a comfortable hike to the magnificent caverns of Juxtlahuaca. Among the largest in Mexico, these caverns contain Olmec cave paintings of humans and snakes estimated to be of the first millennium before Christ and therefore some of the oldest yet discovered in America. Footpaths connect the principal chambers, but the going is treacherous, with little illumination. In one cave is an underground lake. Old clothes, practical footwear, and anything waterproof will be appropriate because of the spray from subterranean waterfalls. These caves are very beautiful and exciting, but lest we have not yet made the point clear, let it be stressed again: Don't try it on your own. To reconnect with Route 95, turn around and go back exactly as you came.

ACAPULCO: For a detailed description of the city, its hotels and restaurants, see *Acapulco*, THE CITIES. Now you're back on the road for the last 80 mountainous miles (128 km) to Acapulco, rising and dipping until the first thrilling glimpse of the sea 5 miles (8 km) out of the city. From here, Route 95 leads directly onto Costera Miguel Alemán, the shoreline drive along Acapulco's bay. Suddenly you're in a world of coconut palm trees, high-rise hotels, sighing surf, and smooth golden beaches.

BEST EN ROUTE

TEPOZTLÁN

Posada del Tepozteco – Set on a hill overlooking the village of Tepoztlán, this lovely, old, recently remodeled colonial-style inn has 8 rooms and 5 suites. Facilities include 2 pools, extensive gardens, a fine dining room (try to get a window seat for an outstanding view of the surrounding valley and mountain peaks), and a bar. 3 Calle del Paraíso (phone: 739-50010 or 739-50323). Moderate.

Tepoztlán – Not much character but comfortable, offering 36 rooms, 2 suites with Jacuzzis, a restaurant-bar, and heated pool. On weekends the hotel fills up with families and gets quite noisy. At the entrance to town at 6 Calle de Industrias (phone: 739-50522 or 739-50503). Moderate.

JOJUTLA DE JUÁREZ

Hacienda Vista Hermosa – Built over 400 years ago, this grand estate was once a sugarcane mill. It is now an unusual and lovely resort offering swimming, tennis, bowling, and horseback riding. Meals are good all week but Sundays and holidays are particularly special, with a generous buffet that attracts people from as far as Cuernavaca. There is a bar and alfresco dining. Colonial-style furnishings fill the 100 available units. While there, you might ask to see Suite "500," which is rumored to have a swimming pool in the bathroom. 20 miles (32 km) southeast of Cuernavaca, off the Alpuyeca interchange (phone: 734-30300; in Mexico City, 5-535-0107). Moderate.

TEHUIXTLA

La Rivera – Adjacent to the famous bathing resort of Isstehuixtla, the rooms and cottages of this hotel are scattered over riverfront grounds. There is a restaurant, bar, and a swimming pool, and though everything here is strictly Mexican, foreign visitors are more than welcome. Off Route 95 and 95-D, southeast of the Alpuyeca interchange or the Vista Hermosa–Tequesquitengo cutoff, about 3 miles (5 km) south of Lake Tequesquitengo (phone: request assistance from operator #23 in Tehuixtla). Expensive to moderate.

Matamoros to Mexico City

American tourists frequently use this route on excursions south to Mexico City, but all too often they rush through the area without stopping to savor it. While the northeastern section of Mexico is hot and arid, its scenery is dramatic — cactus and mesquite give way to the Sierra Madre Oriental. Farther south, past the Tropic of Cancer, the countryside becomes lush and tropical; the road south from Ciudad Valles is especially beautiful.

The 625-mile (1,000-km) route from Matamoros to Mexico City starts across the desert land of northern Tamaulipas, which changes to irrigated farmland as you drive south toward Ciudad Victoria. Nearer Ciudad Mante, the terrain becomes semitropical. By the time you reach Tamazunchale you are well surrounded by jungle vegetation. As you cross into the state of Hidalgo, the terrain becomes mountainous, with breathtaking views. Pachuca, at 8,000 feet, is in the Sierra Madre Oriental range, and from here your drive to Mexico City will be through the mountains and valleys of central Mexico.

There is hardly a section of Mexico that has a past as turbulent as its northeast. The Indians fought ferociously against Spanish invaders, and the land is dotted with battle sites from the Mexican-American War of 1847–48. Today, the major Indian tribe living in Tamaulipas and San Luis Potosí states is the Huastec, distant cousins of the Maya, and you'll pass through villages in which their rich culture is kept alive.

The state of Tamaulipas is a popular spot for hunters and fishermen, especially in the vicinity of Ciudad Victoria and the manmade Lake Vicente Guerrero, northeast of the city. From Ciudad Victoria sportsmen travel to Soto la Marina and to La Pesca, on the Gulf of Mexico. Wildlife includes white-wing doves, armadillos, coyotes, wild turkeys, and white-tailed deer. See DIVERSIONS for further information on hunting regulations.

The route follows two major highways, Routes 101 and 85, through the states of Tamaulipas, San Luis Potosí, and small sections of Hidalgo and México. For the most part, road conditions are good, although fog in the Sierra Madre often presents a danger. Also, some of the mountain roads, especially the road from Tamazunchale to Pachuca in Hidalgo, have hairpin curves and, along some stretches, no center lines. Here, as in most areas of Mexico, the best insurance against an accident is a car in top condition and a well-rested, alert driver.

To enter Mexico at the easternmost crossing point in the US, you merely cross the bridge that spans the Río Grande at Brownsville, Texas. If you get a chance, walk rather than drive over the bridge. It can be quite a thrill to

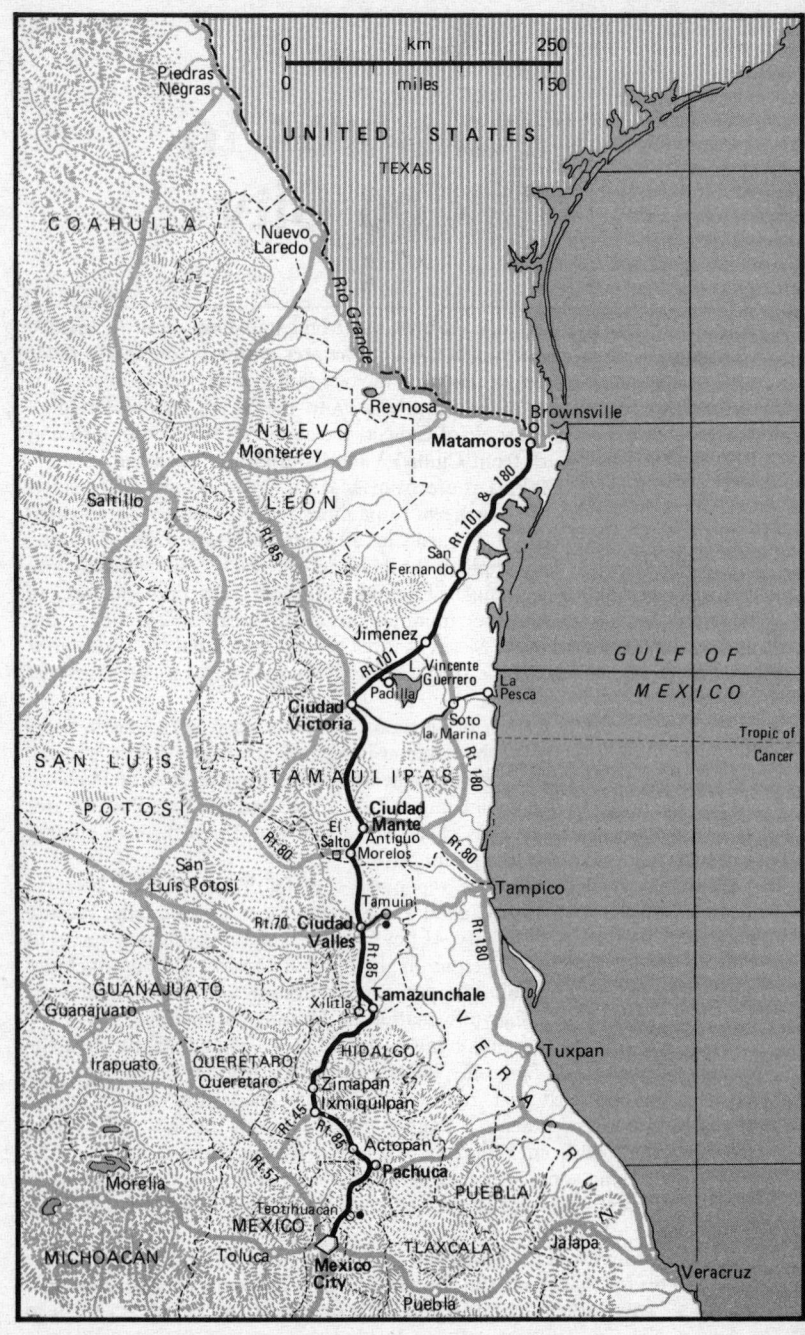

walk across what is perhaps one of the greatest natural boundaries of the world. The Matamoros border point is 32 miles (51 km) from the mouth of the Río Grande, where the river empties into the Gulf of Mexico, and more than 1,850 miles (2960 km) from the source of the river, in southwest Colorado.

You may enter Matamoros (or any other border town) for 72 hours without a tourist card. Many tourists take advantage of the opportunity to enter a different country so easily, especially to purchase duty-free items. However, if you are planning to go deeper into Mexico, you must have a tourist card and proper registration and Mexican insurance for your car. (For more information see "Traveling by Car" in *When and How to Go*, GETTING READY TO GO.)

Expect to pay $100 to $150 for a double room at a hotel listed as very expensive; $70 to $95 at an expensive place; $40 to $65, moderate; and less than $40, inexpensive. Bear in mind that a few of the expensive and moderate hotels include some or all meals in their rates.

MATAMOROS: Founded in 1765, this border town has a fascinating past. It was originally called Congregación del Refugio and in 1851 renamed H. (for "Heroic") Matamoros, after the priest Father Mariano Matamoros, who was executed for leading Mexican insurgents into battle against the Spanish during Mexico's Revolution of 1810–21. Between Apache and Comanche raids, early pirate raids, the Revolution of 1810, the Mexican-American War, and the US Civil War, Matamoros had its share of trouble. During the US Civil War, it was the only port not blockaded and open to the Confederacy, and it became a major supplier of contraband goods for the South. Bagdad, the settlement that grew up beside it during this period, developed into a wild, hard-shooting town of 20,000 people. Both Matamoros and Brownsville profited from the trade brought in by Bagdad — centered principally on its brothels. Today nothing remains of Bagdad but sand.

Matamoros, with a population of 500,000, is one of Mexico's 15 largest cities. The soil and the weather are perfect for cotton, and the town is a major supplier of cotton both in Mexico and abroad. An important center of industry (especially clothing, electronics, and chemical goods) together with Tampico and Veracruz, Matamoros forms part of the most important triangle of international commerce in Mexico.

Matamoros is also a pleasant way to accustom yourself to the Mexican lifestyle. The best place to start is in the zocalo, or town plaza (on Morelos and González between Fifth and Sixth). You may want to stop by at the *Café de Mexico* (González and Sixth) for breakfast — the food and the coffee are good and reasonably priced. Nearby is a parking lot that charges about 30¢ per hour.

Stroll across the street into the park, and you'll find a quaint bandstand reminiscent of bandstands of the early 1900s in the US. Flowers, trees, and statues line the paths; the statues are of Father Mariano Matamoros and Father Miguel Hidalgo. During the day the park is a haven for old men and their cronies, with an occasional working person or student darting in for refreshment at the several foodstands in the park. In the early evening, the plaza really comes alive. It's the time to see and be seen, in the old Spanish tradition. For the young, the major activities are promenading through the park and flirting. For the older dandies, it's the best time for a shoeshine before venturing off to the nearby nightclubs.

Shopping is a high priority for many tourists, and Matamoros has some good markets. The original market area was destroyed by fire in 1968 after more than 100 years of business. Two special stops are *Pasaje Juárez Market* (on Calle Bravo and Calle 9) and the *Mercado Juárez de Artesanías* (on Matamoros and Calle 10). *Mari's Curios* (Av. Alvaro Obregón) is also worth visiting. Together, these markets offer more than 200 shops and stalls, many of which feature jewelry, leather, and woven fabrics at bargain prices.

The Casa Mata Museum is in the old Fort Mata (Calle Cuba off Lauro Villar). This is the historical heart of Matamoros; the stone walls, cannon, and brick turrets have protected the city from numerous attacks. You can visit the fort from 9:30 AM to 5:30 PM every day except Tuesdays. The Mexican Tourist Office (on Puerta México; phone: 891-23630) has English-speaking employees who will provide maps and information.

Recommended restaurants are *Santa Fe* (71 Rosas), which has a cocktail lounge and free parking, and the *US Bar-Restaurant* (González and Quinta).

En Route from Matamoros – Route 101 south from Matamoros is not a particularly pleasant road; you pass the usual auto graveyards and dumps. About 6 miles (10 km) out of town is a turnoff to the Matamoros airport. From there on, it's a fairly clear road except for a large number of donkey carts, but be wary of animals wandering on the highway — horses, cows, sheep, goats, mules, donkeys, and burros all seem to be grazing untied on the sides of the road. This may present a hazard at night, and dogs are the main victims. If you're careful, you won't have problems.

You pass small farming communities, such as San Germán, about 20 miles (32 km) farther south. As you approach the 80-mile mark (134 km from Matamoros), the Sierra Madre Oriental foothills come into view. San Fernando, the nearest village, is a good place to break for a cold drink. If you continue on Route 101 you will eventually reach Ciudad Victoria, the capital of Tamaulipas. Two lesser-used roads turn off from the main highway here. The first left turn leads to the coast, and the second, about 6 miles (10 km) beyond, ends at a small airport. If you turn right, you'll hook up to a small road that links with Route 85 north to Monterrey.

Halfway between San Fernando and Jiménez is a turnoff that runs into Route 80 to Tampico (for more information on Tampico, see *The Vanilla Route,* DIRECTIONS). You might want to stop in Jiménez — it has a few small motels and a pleasant zocalo. From here it's only an hour's trip to the 90,000-acre, manmade Lake Vicente Guerrero.

LAKE VICENTE GUERRERO: When the lake was filled for the first time in 1970, some 600,000 black bass were imported to stock it. Climate and water conditions turned out to be exceptionally favorable — within a few years the bass were averaging more than 3 pounds. Fishing camps nearby boast photos of happy fishermen with catches topping 7 pounds. Although the supply has dimished somewhat, Lake Guerrero is particularly popular with fishermen because it becomes warm before most bass-stocked lakes farther north. As the water warms in the spring, the bass rise to the surface to spawn, and that's the time for the best catch.

Hunting is quite good, too, in the area around the lake — white-wing and mourning doves, pigeons, quail, wild turkey, deer, duck, and geese are abundant.

Near the lake is a signpost for the village of Viejo Padilla, where you might want to make a camera stop. Dam waters backed up some years ago, and you can still see a half-sunken church and a school. On Route 101, about 15 miles (24 km) past the lake, is Ciudad Victoria.

CIUDAD VICTORIA: A sportsmen's town and the capital of Tamaulipas, Ciudad Victoria was named in 1825 after Mexico's first president, Guadalupe Victoria (the original name when it was founded in 1750 was Villa de Santa María de Aguayo). Although it is a small city, it is a good place to stop before heading east toward Soto la Marina or La Pesca or heading south toward Mexico City.

Ciudad Victoria is not a tourist town, but there are a number of interesting places to see if you do decide to spend some time. The bullring, *Plaza de Toros,* is on the corner of Olivia Ramírez and Cinco de Mayo, and there is a large football stadium at Carrera Torres and Cinco de Mayo. Tamaulipas State College's grounds are open to visitors, and if you take a stroll between Hidalgo and Torres, you'll pass the school's museum and the *Juárez Theater.*

As in most Mexican cities, the city is filled with statues dedicated to practically everybody who contributed to Mexican history. The Monument to the Heroes of Independence is on the corner of Hidalgo and Teran; other monuments in Ciudad Victoria include the Juárez and Carranza Monument, the Monument to the Mothers, the Monument to Boy Heroes, and the Monument to the Martyrs of Chicago and Cananea.

There is a small art museum, the *Casa del Arte Tamaulipeco* (near the Palacio Federal on Calle Matamoros). Like most Mexican cities, Ciudad Victoria has a zocalo (central plaza), with a cathedral and a government palace. There is a helpful tourism office (16 Rosales; phone: 131-21057).

Good places to stay are the *Everest* hotel (on Plaza Hidalgo); the *Panorámico* motel (about one-half mile/1 km south on Rte. 85) which, as its name implies, offers a great view; and the completely renovated and rebuilt *San Antonio* hotel (1546 Blvd. Tamaulipas).

Ciudad Victoria is a good jumping-off place for trips; near the city are the waterfalls of Juan Capitán, Lauro Villar beach, and La Peñita, a great area for a picnic. For fishing and hunting enthusiasts, the road about 75 miles (120 km) east (Route 70) leads to Soto la Marina, a small village on the Soto la Marina River. The river is teeming with catfish and tarpon. In fact, 30- to 40-pound tarpon are not uncommon. Surf fishing at La Pesca, on the Gulf of Mexico coast, is popular. There is an airstrip at La Pesca and one about 25 miles (40 km) from Soto la Marina run by the *Club Noche Buena,* a fly-in fishing club.

En Route from Ciudad Victoria – The best way to continue to Mexico City is to head south on Route 85. Leaving Ciudad Victoria, you'll drive down Boulevard Juan Tijerina, with its lovely white- and pink-blossomed laurel trees. Off Route 85, approximately 60 miles (96 km) south of Ciudad Victoria, is a side road leading to Gómez Farias. If you have time, take this road to the dirt stretch heading to Rancho del Cielo National Park. Del Cielo, which means "heaven," is America's northernmost tropical cloud forest. At an altitude of 3,700 feet on the eastern slope of the Sierra Madre Oriental, it is operated as a biological field station by the Gorgas Society of Texas Southmost College in Brownsville, Texas. The park is home to a wide variety of animals, including 223 kinds of resident birds, 175 types of migratory birds, 21 types of amphibians, 60 species of reptiles, and 40 kinds of bats.

As you leave the park and travel along Route 85 toward Ciudad Mante, you will cross the Tropic of Cancer, which is marked by a small road sign, and soon the road begins to climb to a breathtaking view of the valley below. As you top the hills and descend 700 feet into Ciudad Mante, the vegetation becomes lush and semitropical. You are now entering the heartland of the Huastec nation.

According to the oldest chronicles, this area was originally inhabited by the Maya and the Olmec Indians. The Huastec, believed to be related to the Maya, built their capital city, Chila, on the shores of the Chairel Lagoon, where Tampico now stands. In about AD 1050, the Toltec moved into the region. It was a period of relative peace until the Aztec (under Montezuma Ilhuicamina) subjugated the Indians of the area in the mid-1400s. Even though the Aztec are long gone, their influence is still felt. Even the name of the state, Tamaulipas, is an Aztec (Nahuatl) word, meaning "place of high hills."

Aztec domination was powerful and sometimes cruel. An example is the story of King Ahuizotl of the Mexicatl (an Aztec tribe), who was obsessed with making his city beautiful. He captured natives from as far south as Costa Rica in order to complete a Grand Temple, dedicated to Huitzilopochtli, the Aztec war god. Finally, the town was destroyed by flood, fulfilling a prophecy made by a king of a nearby tribe that "the water would become thorny."

The Spanish arrived in 1516, 3 years before Cortés's historic encounter with the Aztec. Initial explorations were begun by the governor of Cuba, Diego Velásquez. Soon after this, Fernández de Córdoba initiated the first serious expedition along the Pánuco River and through the Huastec nation. Three subsequent expeditions were driven back by the Huastec. Today, the Huastec Indians live in peace, mostly in the states of Tamaulipas and San Luis Potosí. They have managed to keep much of their culture alive, especially their language, crafts, and dances.

CIUDAD MANTE: The center of Mexico's sugar region is surrounded by 40,000 acres of irrigated farmland. You can visit Mexico's largest sugar refinery here, open to the public from November through April.

En Route from Ciudad Mante – About 17 miles (27 km) south of Ciudad Mante on Route 85 is the small town of Antiguo Morelos. Turn west on Route 80 for a view of the famous waterfalls at El Salto. The falls are 8 miles (13 km) off the highway on a graded road. You will have to double back to Antiguo Morelos to pick up Route 85 on the way to Ciudad Valles and the state of San Luis Potosí.

CIUDAD VALLES: Originally named Villa Santiagos de los Valles de Oxitipa in 1533, this town is a popular stopping point on the way to Mexico City. At the crossroads of Route 70 (east to Tampico, west to San Luis Potosí) and Route 85 (north-south), Ciudad Valles was the first Spanish settlement in the state of San Luis Potosí. It has become something of a resort area because of the tourists passing through, and its hotels are pleasant. Two good restaurants in town are the *Valles Inn* (Km 36 of the Mexico-Laredo Blvd.), which serves international fare, and the *España* (442 Hidalgo), for regional and Spanish food. About 7 miles (11 km) south of town on Route 85 is the RV facility *El Bañito* (see *Best en Route*) which has a wonderful restaurant specializing in New York steaks (brought in frozen, daily from Monterrey), shrimp *en brochette*, and sandwiches — all served in a summer camp–style dining room; prices are moderate, and there's a decent wine list.

TAMUÍN: Just east of this village, which is on Route 70, on the banks of the Tamuín River, are the most important Huastec archaeological ruins yet discovered. They date from about the 10th century and have not been restored — all that's left are fragments of frescoes, altars (with notable Toltec influence), and platforms. It's hard to reach in the rainy season, from May until September, so plan accordingly.

En Route from Ciudad Valles – Start for Mexico City early in the morning, to avoid the late afternoon and early evening fog in the mountains. The drive to Tamazunchale is extremely beautiful; one of the most interesting villages in the area is the Huastec village of Xilitla. There is a paved road about 10 miles (16 km) off Route 85 before Tamazunchale (3 miles/5 km south of Hichihuayan). The road winds through banana, palm, and bamboo trees and dense jungle for 13 miles (21 km) until you reach Xilitla. The next major stop is Tamazunchale.

TAMAZUNCHALE: In the Huastec language, Tamazunchale means "place of the governor"; feminists might be pleased to learn that its most famous governor was a woman named Tomiya.

An ancient town deep in the Huastec hills, Tamazunchale was virtually isolated before Route 85 was finished in 1936. Then, the 67-mile (107-km) trip between Tamazunchale and Ciudad Valles took 2 days, and Mexico City was a week away by horseback.

Today, Tamazunchale is an attractive town with approximately 50,000 people, six banks, five schools, a hospital, and even a Lions Club (60 Morelos). Most of the natives, however, live in the valleys or on the steep (75° to 80°) slopes on which they cultivate coffee, oranges, bananas, and other fruits.

Tamazunchale is especially popular with bird watchers — more than 200 species have been sighted in the rain forests near town. Butterfly collectors will love the town; many shops feature mounted specimens.

In town, the principal attractions are a 16th-century church and the Sunday market — interesting because many Huastec Indians who live in the surrounding valleys come in for the day, a not-to-be-forgotten experience for anyone interested in Indian culture. Many jungle paths surround the town, leading into one valley or another, or across one hill to another, and if you are planning to spend any time in the area, they make fascinating exploring.

Check any local hotel to find out where you can see the unique flying pole dance of the Huastec (*danza del gavilán* — dance of the sparrow hawks), also called the *juego de volador*. It also takes place in the Huastec villages of four other Mexican states: Querétaro, Veracruz, Tamaulipas, and Hidalgo. The Huastec of San Luis Potosí have a specific ritual in preparing for the dance. The men of the village go together to find a suitable tree, usually over 100 feet high; they offer a prayer to Pulic-Minla, powerful god of trees, and then cut the tree. After they have stripped the tree, they dig a deep hole to hold it and then drop a live hen into the hole as a sacrifice and to provide food for the pole. Ropes are attached to the pole, and the dancers (fliers), adorned in war crests of feathers, tie ropes around themselves and "fly" down it. The dance is centuries old, and the accompanying music is hauntingly beautiful. *Easter Week* is celebrated with processions and the blessing of bread and grains, and "huehues," masked dancers, are chased through the streets.

En Route from Tamazunchale – Less than 10 miles (16 km) out of town on Route 85, you'll reach the Hidalgo state line. Hidalgo is the fourth smallest state in Mexico, covering a predominantly mountainous area that is dotted with small valleys. The 200-mile (320-km) drive from Tamazunchale to Pachuca, the capital of Hidalgo, winds and twists through the mountains. The road can be dangerous — there are long stretches with no center line and with hairpin curves. Beware of livestock grazing along the road and of occasional rock slides. As you drive through the mountains, you'll see Mexicans using machetes to clear the almost vertical slopes, and you'll also pass small villages with haunting names, such as Xhitha, Tetzu, and Jacalilla. This is a rugged and an ancient land. From Tamazunchale to Zimapán is about 100 miles (160 km).

ZIMAPÁN: Founded in 1522, Zimapán has old buildings, tree-lined streets, and a small plaza that looks as though it hasn't changed in centuries. And it hasn't. The town church, which dates from the 16th century, has a massive tower and a baroque entrance. It has a Moorish look about it — the arches and its red and white tiles are not typical of Mexico's churches. The Palacio Municipal is worth a visit, also.

IXMIQUILPÁN: This was one of the major cities of the Otomi Indians, and there is a colorful Monday Indian market with silver jewelry, ceramics, and woolen goods as specialties. An interesting town with colonial buildings, Ixmiquilpán has a lovely 16th-century church, Convento de San Miguel Arcangel, built by the order of St. Augustine. Some interesting polychromatic frescoes and older Indian murals can be viewed in the church. From here, it would be a shame not to make a side trip to one of the most beautiful, and undeveloped, sights in all Mexico — Las Grutas de Tolontongo (Tolontongo Caverns). Hot-spring caves (in this volcanic region, waters are heated deep within the earth) combine with an icy waterfall and lush tropical vegetation, where fruit can be picked from the trees. To reach Tolontongo, take the road to Cardonal and, before the town, turn off to the right onto an unpaved road in good condition; continue 45 miles (28 km) through a desert-like area. The last 13 winding miles (21 km) literally drop to the caverns. Make the trip only in a car that's in ace condition, and bring lunch.

En Route from Ixmiquilpán – Take Route 45 west to Route 57, which is a quick way to get to Mexico City, or continue south on Route 85 toward Pachuca.

ACTOPÁN: This Otomí Indian town (market day is Wednesday — a 400-year-old tradition) has an Augustinian convent, San Nicolás Tolentino, built in 1546 and distinguished by its lovely patio, frescoes, and Gothic cloisters. You can reach the ruins at Tula from here — they're about 35 miles (56 km) west on Route 126 (see *Mexico's Magnificent Archaeological Heritage,* DIVERSIONS; for more information on the city, see *The Vanilla Route,* DIRECTIONS).

PACHUCA: Pachuca, the state capital of Hidalgo, is 60 miles (97 km) north of Mexico City. Founded in 1534 by Spanish silver seekers, it is still an important mining center, and the most famous of its mines, Real del Monte, which is 6 miles (10 km) from town, still functions.

Generally, Pachuca is not a tourist town, but there are good accommodations and several places of interest to see, including the Casas Colorados (18th-century red-roofed houses built by the count of Regla) and La Caja, a strange, fortress-like building built in 1670 as a treasury for the royal tribute. The clock in the tower on the main square is a copy of Big Ben. Casa Rule, now the court house, was a turn-of-the-century mansion built by an Englishman, Francisco Rule, who made a killing in the mines. History buffs shouldn't miss the Casasola Archives, which house one of the most extensive and interesting photographic collections in Latin America.

North of Pachuca is a small, semi-isolated village, Atotonilco el Grande, with a beautiful 16th-century convent with colonial murals and galleries. Indian villages known for their beautiful weaving and jewelry dot the valleys of the area.

The mine, Real del Monte, was acquired by Romero de Terreros in 1739. By 1781 he had pulled more than 15 million pesos' worth of silver out of the mountain. Since labor was cheap and the peso went a long way (the peso was legal tender in the US until 1857 and had a one-to-one parity with the dollar until 1918), Terreros sent sizable sums to the King of Spain and was accordingly awarded the title of Conde de (Count of) Santa María de Regla.

En Route from Pachuca – The drive to Mexico City is a pleasant one, and the roads are relatively new. You are now heading into the Valley of Mexico, which rests about 7,500 feet above sea level and is surrounded by peaks rising 18,000 feet. You might want to stop at Teotihuacán on your way to Mexico City. Teotihuacán dates back several hundred years before the Toltec Indians first came into the area that is now Mexico City. Indeed, the Teotihuacán began building the famous Pyramid of the Sun, Pyramid of the Moon, and Temple of Quetzalcóatl as early as the period between 350 and 100 BC.

BEST EN ROUTE

MATAMOROS

Del Prado Matamoros – Here is a colonial-style building offering 122 rooms with air conditioning and cable television, as well as a restaurant, bar, and pool. 249 Alvaro Obregón (phone: 891-39440). Very expensive to expensive.

Minerva Paola – A downtown hotel with 30 rooms. All have air conditioning, heat, and color TV sets. There's also a restaurant, bar, and parking. Calle 11 and 125 Matamoros (phone: 891-63966 through 71). Moderate to inexpensive.

Ritz – This hostelry has 92 air conditioned rooms. Calle 7 and Matamoros (phone: 891-21190). Inexpensive.

LAKE VICENTE GUERRERO

Alta Vista – Rates include accommodations, hunting and fishing expeditions, three meals a day, field transportation, and game preparation. The main hotel has 11 rooms, each with 2 single beds and a bath; there are also 20 cabins, each with 5 beds, a shower, stove, and refrigerator. For reservations write: *International Hunting and Fishing,* PO Box 1511, Harlingen, TX 78551 (phone: 800-423-9965). Expensive.

Big Bass – As the name suggests, this place caters to the fishing fanatic. In addition to 18 air conditioned cabins, it offers boat rentals, restaurant service, and hunting, fishing, and boat permits. The rate includes three meals a day, a boating guide, soft drinks and beer on the boat, and cleaning and packing of fish. The owners are Hiram Villarreal Santos and Hector Aguilar of Monterrey. Bookings are handled by *Turismo Lago Guerrero,* 2103-12 Simón Bolívar, Colonia Mitras Centro, Monterrey, Nuevo León (phone: 83-464744 or 83-468066; in McAllen, TX, 512-687-8513). Expensive.

CIUDAD VICTORIA

San Antonio – Completely rebuilt, this place has 65 rooms, 1 suite, and a restaurant. 1546 Blvd. Tamaulipas (phone: 131-62616). Moderate.

Everest – Centrally located, with 100 air conditioned rooms, all equipped with color TV sets. A restaurant and coffee shop are on the premises. 126 Av. Colón (phone: 131-24050). Inexpensive.

Las Fuentes – This motel has 102 air conditioned rooms, satellite television, a pool, restaurant, and playground. Km 227 on the highway to Cuidad Mante (phone: 131-25342). Inexpensive.

Panorámico – A great view, 65 comfortable rooms, pool and restaurant. This motel is about one-half mile (1 km) south of Victoria on Rte. 85 (phone: 131-25506). Inexpensive.

Victoria – Set among banana, avocado, and papaya trees, there are 150 spaces for tents or trailers, with full hookups, cobblestone patios, laundry facilities, a grocery store, a souvenir shop, a stone barbecue pit, a swimming pool and golf course nearby, and a fountain in the shape of a Maya pyramid. Two miles (3 km) north of town on the Rte. 85 bypass, one-quarter mile east of the Rte. 101 intersection, and next to the San Carlos gas station (phone: 131-24824). Inexpensive.

Sierra Gorda – On the Plaza Hidalgo in the center of town, this pleasant hotel has 86 rooms and a good restaurant and bar. 990 Hidalgo Ote. (phone: 131-22280). Very inexpensive.

CIUDAD MANTE

Mante – The hotel has 60 air conditioned rooms with TV sets, a pool, a restaurant, bar, parking, and room for 5 trailers, 3 with utility connections. 500 Guerrero Pte. (phone: 123-20990, 123-20836, or 123-20942). Inexpensive.

Monterrey – Part hotel, part motel, with restaurant, bar, color TV sets, and parking. 503 Juárez Ote. (phone: 123-22712). Inexpensive.

CIUDAD VALLES

El Bañito – This trailer park on Route 85 in front of the *Covadunga Golf Club* has 53 hookups, thermal pools, and a restaurant (no phone). Inexpensive.

Posada Don Antonio – Downtown on Route 85, this hotel has comfortable rooms with air conditioning, color TV sets, a pool, and a restaurant (phone: 138-20066). Inexpensive.

Valles – It has 100 rooms, an Olympic-size pool, a children's playground, lovely gardens, 2 restaurants, a bar, and free parking; air conditioning and color TV sets are available in rooms in the newer section. There are also trailer facilities with hookups. At Km 36 of the Mexico-Laredo Blvd. (phone: 138-20050 or 138-20022). Inexpensive.

TAMAZUNCHALE

Mirador – Plain but clean, with ceiling fans and telephones in each of the 26 rooms. 61 Veinte de Noviembre (phone: 136-20004). Moderate.

INDEX

Index

BIRNBAUM TRAVEL GUIDES

Order by phone, toll-free: 1-800-331-3761

Name_____ Phone_____

Address_____

City_____ State_____ Zip_____

Discover the Birnbaum Difference
More Details and Discounts Than Any Other Travel Guide

Get the best advice on what to see and do and where to stay while benefiting from money-saving information from America's foremost travel experts.

Area and Country Guides 1992—$17.00 Each

☐ Canada

☐ Caribbean

☐ Eastern Europe

☐ Europe

☐ France

☐ Great Britain

☐ Hawaii

☐ Ireland

☐ Italy

☐ Mexico

☐ Portugal

☐ South America

☐ Spain

☐ United States

☐ Western Europe

New Warm Weather Destination Guides 1992—$10.00 Each

☐ Acapulco

☐ Bahamas
(including Turks
& Caicos)

☐ Bermuda

☐ Cancun/Cozumel/Isla
Mujeres (including Playa
Del Carmen)

☐ Ixtapa &
Zihuatanejo

New City Guides 1992—$10.00 Each

☐ Barcelona

☐ Boston

☐ Chicago

☐ Florence

☐ London

☐ Los Angeles

☐ Miami

☐ New York

☐ Paris

☐ Rome

☐ San Francisco

☐ Venice

Business Guides 1992—$10.00 Each

☐ Europe 1992 for the Business Traveler

☐ USA 1992 for the Business Traveler

Total for Birnbaum Travel Guides	$
For PA delivery, please include sales tax	
Add $4.00 for first Book S&H, $1.00 each additional book	
Total	$

☐ Check or Money order enclosed. Plase make payable to HarperCollins *Publishers*.

☐ Charge my credit card ☐ American Express   ☐ Visa   ☐ Mastercard

Card no._____ Exp. date_____

Signature_____

Send orders to:
HarperCollins *Publishers*, P.O. Box 588, Dunmore, PA 18512-0588